Need to know more about the constitutional law of the EU?

Hartley: *The Foundations of European Union Law*
provides a reliable and comprehensive introduction to the procedures and institutions of the EU.

'I find it an excellent book, extremely well written, clear and to the point. The style is pitched at just the right level, and there are frequent highlights of interesting points. In particular, the book embeds the law in a political context, which is essential on this topic'

Lorand Bartels, Senior Lecturer in Law, University of Cambridge

For more details and to ... EU law publishing visit
www. ... k/law

THE SUBSTANTIVE LAW OF THE EU

THE FOUR FREEDOMS

Fifth Edition

CATHERINE BARNARD

OXFORD
UNIVERSITY PRESS

OXFORD
UNIVERSITY PRESS

Great Clarendon Street, Oxford, OX2 6DP,
United Kingdom

Oxford University Press is a department of the University of Oxford.
It furthers the University's objective of excellence in research, scholarship,
and education by publishing worldwide. Oxford is a registered trade mark of
Oxford University Press in the UK and in certain other countries

Second edition 2007
Third edition 2010
Fourth edition 2013
Impression: 1

Public sector information reproduced under Open Government Licence v3.0
(http://www.nationalarchives.gov.uk/doc/open-government-licence/open-government-licence.htm)

Published in the United States of America by Oxford University Press
198 Madison Avenue, New York, NY 10016, United States of America

British Library Cataloguing in Publication Data
Data available

Library of Congress Control Number: 2016936822

ISBN 978-0-19-874995-0

Printed in Great Britain by
Bell & Bain Ltd., Glasgow

OUTLINE CONTENTS

DETAILED CONTENTS

PART I INTRODUCTION

PART II FREE MOVEMENT OF GOODS

NEW TO THIS EDITION

- The addition of further reading at the end of each chapter with an indication of coverage
- Restructuring of the material, especially in the section on persons, with a chapter on the free movement of workers and the self-employed, a chapter on free movement of services, and a separate chapter on the free movement of legal persons
- Coverage of the Intellectual Property Rights (IPR) case law in Chapter 6
- Detailed examination of the rapidly evolving case law on citizenship of the Union, including the controversial decision in *Dano* and its progeny

PREFACE

To entitle a book *The Substantive Law of the EU* inevitably offers a hostage to fortune. To do full justice to the sheer breadth of the subject requires several volumes, not just a single text. I am, therefore, more aware than most of the limitations imposed by producing a single volume. To keep the book within the bounds of the manageable, I have assumed that the reader has a basic knowledge of the institutional and constitutional structure of the EU. This allows this text to concentrate on an examination of the four freedoms, primarily in respect of the rules that regulate movement internally within the EU and, to a lesser extent, in respect of the rules that regulate movement from outside the EU. It is my hope that an understanding of the principles which underpin the four freedoms can be used as a guide to readers wishing to explore more closely specialist areas of EU substantive law. To assist with that process, I have used a number of free-standing case studies in the text, both to help illustrate the main points and to demonstrate how the general principles apply to more specialist areas.

When the first edition of the book was being written, the Constitutional Treaty was being negotiated. With the second edition, the French and Dutch 'no' votes had just put paid to the Constitutional Treaty. As the third edition was being put to bed, the Irish were persuaded to vote 'yes' to the Lisbon Treaty and, at the eleventh hour, the Czech President agreed to sign the text. The Treaty therefore came into force on 1 December 2009. The fourth edition was being written at a time when the economic crisis was still raging, when major constitutional change was on the cards to deliver full economic and monetary union for the Eurozone states. The fifth edition was being written as the UK Prime Minister, David Cameron, was renegotiating the terms of UK membership prior to a referendum on 23 June 2016. I have been able to incorporate some of the changes agreed by the Decision of the Heads of State or Government meeting within the European Council (the so-called 'New Settlement' deal) in this edition. However, just as the book was about to be printed the UK took the momentous decision to vote to leave the European Union. The consequences of this decision are only beginning to be explored. It will have major ramifications for the UK and for the rest of the EU for years to come.

For UK law students EU law remains and will remain important and relevant for three reasons. First, the UK is still a member of the EU and EU law continues to apply until withdrawal occurs. Second, the future relationship between the UK and the EU remains uncertain but many argue that the UK should have access to the single market which means benefiting from the four freedoms, the subject of this book. While the UK New Settlement deal will not now come into effect it might help to shape the UK's negotiations with the EU. So once again, a knowledge of the deal as well as the detailed content is important. Third, many UK law students will go on to work in law and accountancy firms as well as in business; they will need to know about EU law since the EU is the UK's largest trading partner.

So there is a strong case for studying—and enjoying EU law for UK and EU/EEA students alike.

At least this edition of the book has not witnessed a renumbering of the Treaty. I have used the Lisbon numbering throughout, even in respect of cases decided under the Rome or Amsterdam numbering. Occasionally I have used the Rome or Amsterdam numbering where I believe this helps to explain a particular decision of the Court or where the language of the old Treaty provision is significantly different to its Lisbon content. I have also decided to refer to the 'European Union' and 'Union law' throughout, except when talking historically where the distinction between EU, EC, and EEC was significant. I have not changed titles of books and articles which use the pre-Lisbon terms. Finally, I have used the abbreviation 'TEU' after Treaty numbers to identify provisions of the Treaty on European Union after Lisbon, and 'EU' to identify provisions of the Treaty on European Union before Lisbon. 'TFEU' is used to identify provisions of the Treaty on the Functioning of the European Union, 'EC' to indicate provisions of the European Community Treaty, and 'EEC' to identify provisions of the European Economic Community Treaty.

I owe debts of gratitude to many people who helped me complete the various editions of this book. I am particularly grateful to those who have read and commented on various chapters for the different editions—Albertina Albors-Llorens, Bill Asquith, Cathryn Costello, Marise Cremona, Alan Dashwood, Simon Deakin, Michael Dougan, Julian Ghosh, Rosa Greaves, Elspeth Guild, Hannes Hofmeister, Clive Lewis, Steve Peers, Catherine Seville, Jukka Snell, John Tiley, Helen Toner, Takis Tridimas, Joanne Scott, Eleanor Spaventa, Stephen Weatherill, John Usher, and Carsten Zatschler—as well as to the various anonymous referees provided by OUP and students who have written to me with suggestions. Their contributions have been invaluable, though, of course, any errors remain my own. Generations of students have helped shape my ideas, together with friends and colleagues in EU law both at Cambridge and elsewhere, and I am grateful to them all.

Matthew Cotton, Kate Salkild, and Penelope Woolf at OUP patiently saw the first edition through to completion; Melanie Jackson the second edition; Alex Clabburn, Jeremy Langworthy, Jonathon Price, and Anya Aghdam the third; Abbey Nelms, Sarah Stephenson, Marie Gill, and Gill Clack the fourth; and Emily Hoyland, Joy Ruskin-Tompkins, Philip Moore, and Sarah Stephenson the fifth. I owe them all deep gratitude, especially for their patience and forbearance. However, my most heartfelt thanks go to my patient and understanding family, especially to my men—large, larger, and medium—and my smaller woman, who is very much in charge.

Cambridge, January 2016

TABLE OF LEGISLATION

EU SECONDARY LEGISLATION

Regulations

TABLE OF CASES

Numerical

General Court Cases prefixed 'T' are tabled after the ECJ cases in each year.

EFTA Court

TABLE OF EQUIVALENCES[1]

TREATY ON EUROPEAN UNION

Old numbering of the Treaty on European Union	New numbering of the Treaty on European Union	Old numbering of the Treaty on European Union	New numbering of the Treaty on European Union
TITLE I	**TITLE I**		Article 11
Article 1	Article 1		Article 12
	Article 2	**TITLE III**	**TITLE III**
Article 2	Article 3	Article 9 (repealed)[8]	Article 13
Article 3 (repealed)[2]			Article 14[9]
	Article 4		Article 15[10]
	Article 5[3]		Article 16[11]
Article 4 (repealed)[4]			Article 17[12]
Article 5 (repealed)[5]			Article 18
Article 6	Article 6		Article 19[13]
Article 7	Article 7	**TITLE IV**	**TITLE IV**
	Article 8	Article 10 (repealed)[14]	Article 20[15]
TITLE II	**TITLE II**	*Articles 27a to 27e (replaced)*	
Article 8 (repealed)[6]	Article 9	*Articles 40 to 40b (replaced)*	
	Article 10[7]	*Articles 43 to 45 (replaced)*	

[1] Tables of equivalences as referred to in Article 5 of the Treaty of Lisbon. The original centre column, which set out the intermediate numbering as used in that Treaty, has been omitted.

[2] Replaced, in substance, by Article 7 of the Treaty on the Functioning of the European Union ("TFEU") and by Articles 13(1) and 21, paragraph 3, second subparagraph of the Treaty on European Union ("TEU").

[3] Replaces Article 5 of the Treaty establishing the European Community ("TEC").

[4] Replaced, in substance, by Article 15.

[5] Replaced, in substance, by Article 13, paragraph 2.

[6] Article 8 TEU, which was in force until the entry into force of the Treaty of Lisbon (hereinafter 'current'), amended the TEC. Those amendments are incorporated into the latter Treaty and Article 8 is repealed. Its number is used to insert a new provision.

[7] Paragraph 4 replaces, in substance, the first subparagraph of Article 191 TEC.

[8] The current Article 9 TEU amended the Treaty establishing the European Coal and Steel Community. This latter expired on 23 July 2002. Article 9 is repealed and the number thereof is used to insert another provision.

[9] – Paragraphs 1 and 2 replace, in substance, Article 189 TEC;
  – paragraphs 1 to 3 replace, in substance, paragraphs 1 to 3 of Article 190 TEC;
  – paragraph 1 replaces, in substance, the first subparagraph of Article 192 TEC;
  – paragraph 4 replaces, in substance, the first subparagraph of Article 197 TEC.

[10] Replaces, in substance, Article 4.

[11] – Paragraph 1 replaces, in substance, the first and second indents of Article 202 TEC;
  – paragraphs 2 and 9 replace, in substance, Article 203 TEC;
  – paragraphs 4 and 5 replace, in substance, paragraphs 2 and 4 of Article 205 TEC.

[12] – Paragraph 1 replaces, in substance, Article 211 TEC;
  – paragraphs 3 and 7 replace, in substance, Article 214 TEC.
  – paragraph 6 replaces, in substance, paragraphs 1, 3 and 4 of Article 217 TEC.

[13] – Replaces, in substance, Article 220 TEC.
  – the second subparagraph of paragraph 2 replaces, in substance, the first subparagraph of Article 221 TEC.

[14] The current Article 10 TEU amended the Treaty establishing the European Atomic Energy Community. Those amendments are incorporated into the Treaty of Lisbon. Article 10 is repealed and the number thereof is used to insert another provision.

[15] Also replaces Articles 11 and 11a TEC.

Old numbering of the Treaty on European Union	New numbering of the Treaty on European Union	Old numbering of the Treaty on European Union	New numbering of the Treaty on European Union
			Article 46
TITLE V	TITLE V		
	Chapter 1	TITLE VI (repealed)[17]	
	Article 21	Article 29 (replaced)[18]	
	Article 22	Article 30 (replaced)[19]	
	Chapter 2	Article 31 (replaced)[20]	
	Section 1	Article 32 (replaced)[21]	
	Article 23	Article 33 (replaced)[22]	
Article 11	Article 24	Article 34 (repealed)	
Article 12	Article 25	Article 35 (repealed)	
Article 13	Article 26	Article 36 (replaced)[23]	
	Article 27	Article 37 (repealed)	
Article 14	Article 28	Article 38 (repealed)	
Article 15	Article 29	Article 39 (repealed)	
Article 22 (moved)	Article 30	Article 40 (replaced)[24]	Article 20
Article 23 (moved)	Article 31	Article 40 A (replaced)[24]	Article 20
Article 16	Article 32	Article 40 B (replaced)[24]	Article 20
Article 17 (moved)	Article 42	Article 41 (repealed)	
Article 18	Article 33	Article 42 (repealed)	
Article 19	Article 34		
Article 20	Article 35	TITLE VII (replaced)[25]	TITLE IV
Article 21	Article 36	Article 43 (replaced)[25]	Article 20
Article 22 (moved)	Article 30	Article 43 A (replaced)[25]	Article 20
Article 23 (moved)	Article 31	Article 43 B (replaced)[25]	Article 20
Article 24	Article 37	Article 44 (replaced)[25]	Article 20
Article 25	Article 38	Article 44 A (replaced)[25]	Article 20
	Article 39	Article 45 (replaced)[25]	Article 20
Article 47 (moved)	Article 40	TITLE VIII	TITLE VI
Article 26 (repealed)		Article 46 (repealed)	
Article 27 (repealed)			Article 47
Article 27a (replaced)[16]	Article 20	Article 47 (replaced)	Article 40
Article 27b (replaced)[16]	Article 20	Article 48	Article 48
Article 27c (replaced)[16]	Article 20	Article 49	Article 49
Article 27d (replaced)[16]	Article 20		Article 50
Article 27e (replaced)[16]	Article 20		Article 51
Article 28	Article 41		Article 52
	Section 2	Article 50 (repealed)	
Article 17 (moved)	Article 42	Article 51	Article 53
	Article 43	Article 52	Article 54
	Article 44	Article 53	Article 55
	Article 45		

[16] The current Articles 27a to 27e, on enhanced cooperation, are also replaced by Articles 326 to 334 TFEU.

[17] The current provisions of Title VI of the TEU, on police and judicial cooperation in criminal matters, are replaced by the provisions of Chapters 1, 4 and 5 of Title IV of Part Three of the TFEU.

[18] Replaced by Article 67 TFEU.

[19] Replaced by Articles 87 and 88 TFEU.

[20] Replaced by Articles 82, 83 and 85 TFEU.

[21] Replaced by Article 89 TFEU.

[22] Replaced by Article 72 TFEU.

[23] Replaced by Article 71 TFEU.

[24] The current Articles 40 to 40 B TEU, on enhanced cooperation, are also replaced by Articles 326 to 334 TFEU.

[25] The current Articles 43 to 45 and Title VII of the TEU, on enhanced cooperation, are also replaced by Articles 326 to 334 TFEU.

TREATY ON THE FUNCTIONING OF THE EUROPEAN UNION

Old numbering of the Treaty establishing the European Community	New numbering of the Treaty on the Functioning of the European Union	Old numbering of the Treaty establishing the European Community	New numbering of the Treaty on the Functioning of the European Union
PART ONE	**PART ONE**	Article 18	Article 21
Article 1 (repealed)		Article 19	Article 22
	Article 1	Article 20	Article 23
Article 2 (repealed)[26]		Article 21	Article 24
		Article 22	Article 25
	Title I	**PART THREE**	**PART THREE**
	Article 2		**Title I**
	Article 3	*Article 14 (moved)*	Article 26
	Article 4	*Article 15 (moved)*	Article 27
	Article 5	**Title I**	**Title II**
	Article 6	Article 23	Article 28
	Title II	Article 24	Article 29
	Article 7	**Chapter 1**	**Chapter 1**
Article 3, paragraph 1 (repealed)[27]		Article 25	Article 30
Article 3, paragraph 2	Article 8	Article 26	Article 31
Article 4 (moved)	*Article 119*	Article 27	Article 32
Article 5 (replaced)[28]		*Part Three, Title X (moved)*	**Chapter 2**
	Article 9	*Article 135 (moved)*	Article 33
	Article 10	**Chapter 2**	**Chapter 3**
Article 6	Article 11	Article 28	Article 34
Article 153, paragraph 2 (moved)	Article 12	Article 29	Article 35
		Article 30	Article 36
	Article 13[29]	Article 31	Article 37
Article 7 (repealed)[30]		**Title II**	**Title III**
Article 8 (repealed)[31]		Article 32	Article 38
Article 9 (repealed)		Article 33	Article 39
Article 10 (repealed)[32]		Article 34	Article 40
Article 11 (replaced)[33]	*Articles 326 to 334*	Article 35	Article 41
Article 11a (replaced)[33]	*Articles 326 to 334*	Article 36	Article 42
Article 12 (repealed)	*Article 18*	Article 37	Article 43
Article 13 (moved)	*Article 19*	Article 38	Article 44
Article 14 (moved)	*Article 26*	**Title III**	**Title IV**
Article 15 (moved)	*Article 27*	**Chapter 1**	**Chapter 1**
Article 16	Article 14	Article 39	Article 45
Article 255 (moved)	Article 15	Article 40	Article 46
Article 286 (moved)	Article 16	Article 41	Article 47
	Article 17	Article 42	Article 48
PART TWO	**PART TWO**	**Chapter 2**	**Chapter 2**
Article 12 (moved)	Article 18	Article 43	Article 49
Article 13 (moved)	Article 19	Article 44	Article 50
Article 17	Article 20	Article 45	Article 51

[26] Replaced, in substance, by Article 3 TEU.
[27] Replaced, in substance, by Articles 3 to 6 TFEU.
[28] Replaced, in substance, by Article 5 TEU.
[29] Insertion of the operative part of the protocol on protection and welfare of animals.
[30] Replaced, in substance, by Article 13 TEU.
[31] Replaced, in substance, by Article 13 TEU and Article 282, paragraph 1, TFEU.
[32] Replaced, in substance, by Article 4, paragraph 3, TEU.
[33] Also replaced by Article 20 TEU.

Old numbering of the Treaty establishing the European Community	New numbering of the Treaty on the Functioning of the European Union
Article 46	Article 52
Article 47	Article 53
Article 48	Article 54
Article 294 (moved)	Article 55
Chapter 3	**Chapter 3**
Article 49	Article 56
Article 50	Article 57
Article 51	Article 58
Article 52	Article 59
Article 53	Article 60
Article 54	Article 61
Article 55	Article 62
Chapter 4	**Chapter 4**
Article 56	Article 63
Article 57	Article 64
Article 58	Article 65
Article 59	Article 66
Article 60 (moved)	*Article 75*
Title IV	**Title V**
	Chapter 1
Article 61	Article 67[34]
	Article 68
	Article 69
	Article 70
	Article 71[35]
Article 64, paragraph 1 (replaced)	Article 72[36]
	Article 73
Article 66 (replaced)	Article 74
Article 60 (moved)	Article 75
	Article 76
	Chapter 2
Article 62	Article 77
Article 63, points 1 et 2, and Article 64, paragraph 2[37]	Article 78
Article 63, points 3 and 4	Article 79
	Article 80
Article 64, paragraph 1 (replaced)	*Article 72*
	Chapter 3
Article 65	Article 81
Article 66 (replaced)	*Article 74*
Article 67 (repealed)	
Article 68 (repealed)	
Article 69 (repealed)	

Old numbering of the Treaty establishing the European Community	New numbering of the Treaty on the Functioning of the European Union
	Chapter 4
	Article 82[38]
	Article 83[38]
	Article 84
	Article 85[38]
	Article 86
	Chapter 5
	Article 87[39]
	Article 88[39]
	Article 89[40]
Title V	**Title VI**
Article 70	Article 90
Article 71	Article 91
Article 72	Article 92
Article 73	Article 93
Article 74	Article 94
Article 75	Article 95
Article 76	Article 96
Article 77	Article 97
Article 78	Article 98
Article 79	Article 99
Article 80	Article 100
Title VI	**Title VII**
Chapter 1	**Chapter 1**
Section 1	**Section 1**
Article 81	Article 101
Article 82	Article 102
Article 83	Article 103
Article 84	Article 104
Article 85	Article 105
Article 86	Article 106
Section 2	**Section 2**
Article 87	Article 107
Article 88	Article 108
Article 89	Article 109
Chapter 2	**Chapter 2**
Article 90	Article 110
Article 91	Article 111
Article 92	Article 112
Article 93	Article 113
Chapter 3	**Chapter 3**
Article 95 (moved)	Article 114
Article 94 (moved)	Article 115
Article 96	Article 116
Article 97	Article 117
	Article 118

[34] Also replaces the current Article 29 TEU.   [35] Also replaces the current Article 36 TEU.

[36] Also replaces the current Article 33 TEU.

[37] Points 1 and 2 of Article 63 EC are replaced by paragraphs 1 and 2 of Article 78 TFEU, and paragraph 2 of Article 64 is replaced by paragraph 3 of Article 78 TFEU.

[38] Replaces the current Article 31 TEU.   [39] Replaces the current Article 30 TEU.

[40] Replaces the current Article 32 TEU.

Old numbering of the Treaty establishing the European Community	New numbering of the Treaty on the Functioning of the European Union	Old numbering of the Treaty establishing the European Community	New numbering of the Treaty on the Functioning of the European Union
Title VII	Title VIII	*Article 123, paragraph 3 (moved)*	Article 141[42]
Article 4 (moved)	Article 119	*Article 117, paragraph 2, first five indents (moved)*	
Chapter 1	**Chapter 1**	*Article 124, paragraph 1 (moved)*	Article 142
Article 98	Article 120		
Article 99	Article 121	Article 119	Article 143
Article 100	Article 122	Article 120	Article 144
Article 101	Article 123	*Article 121, paragraph 1 (moved)*	*Article 140, paragraph 1*
Article 102	Article 124		
Article 103	Article 125	Article 121, paragraphs 2 to 4 (repealed)	
Article 104	Article 126	Article 122, paragraphs 1, 2, first sentence, 3, 4, 5 and 6 (repealed)	
Chapter 2	**Chapter 2**		
Article 105	Article 127	*Article 122, paragraph 2, second sentence (moved)*	*Article 140, paragraph 2, first subparagraph*
Article 106	Article 128	Article 123, paragraphs 1, 2 and 4 (repealed)	
Article 107	Article 129	*Article 123, paragraph 3 (moved)*	*Article 141, paragraph 1*
Article 108	Article 130		
Article 109	Article 131	*Article 123, paragraph 5 (moved)*	*Article 140, paragraph 3*
Article 110	Article 132		
Article 111, paragraphs 1 to 3 and 5 (moved)	*Article 219*	*Article 124, paragraph 1 (moved)*	*Article 142*
Article 111, paragraph 4 (moved)	*Article 138*	Article 124, paragraph 2 (repealed)	
	Article 133	*Title VIII*	Title IX
Chapter 3	**Chapter 3**	Article 125	Article 145
Article 112 (moved)	*Article 283*	Article 126	Article 146
Article 113 (moved)	*Article 284*	Article 127	Article 147
Article 114	Article 134	Article 128	Article 148
Article 115	Article 135	Article 129	Article 149
	Chapter 4	Article 130	Article 150
	Article 136	*Title IX (moved)*	*Part Five, Title II*
	Article 137	*Article 131 (moved)*	*Article 206*
Article 111, paragraph 4 (moved)	Article 138	Article 132 (repealed)	
Chapter 4	**Chapter 5**	*Article 133 (moved)*	*Article 207*
Article 116 (repealed)		Article 134 (repealed)	
	Article 139	*Title X (moved)*	*Part Three, Title II, Chapter 2*
Article 117, paragraphs 1, 2, sixth indent, and 3 to 9 (repealed)		*Article 135 (moved)*	*Article 33*
Article 117, paragraph 2, first five indents (moved)	*Article 141, paragraph 2*	*Title XI*	Title X
Article 121, paragraph 1 (moved)		Chapter 1 (repealed)	
Article 122, paragraph 2, second sentence (moved)	Article 140[41]	Article 136	Article 151
Article 123, paragraph 5 (moved)			Article 152
Article 118 (repealed)		Article 137	Article 153

[41] – Article 140, paragraph 1 takes over the wording of paragraph 1 of Article 121.
    – Article 140, paragraph 2 takes over the second sentence of paragraph 2 of Article 122.
    – Article 140, paragraph 3 takes over paragraph 5 of Article 123.
[42] – Article 141, paragraph 1 takes over paragraph 3 of Article 123.
    – Article 141, paragraph 2 takes over the first five indents of paragraph 2 of Article 117.

Old numbering of the Treaty establishing the European Community	New numbering of the Treaty on the Functioning of the European Union	Old numbering of the Treaty establishing the European Community	New numbering of the Treaty on the Functioning of the European Union
Article 138	Article 154		Article 189
Article 139	Article 155	Article 173	Article 190
Article 140	Article 156	*Title XIX*	*Title XX*
Article 141	Article 157	Article 174	Article 191
Article 142	Article 158	Article 175	Article 192
Article 143	Article 159	Article 176	Article 193
Article 144	Article 160		*Title XXI*
Article 145	Article 161		Article 194
Chapter 2	*Title XI*		*Title XXII*
Article 146	Article 162		Article 195
Article 147	Article 163		*Title XXIII*
Article 148	Article 164		Article 196
Chapter 3	*Title XII*		*Title XXIV*
Article 149	Article 165		Article 197
Article 150	Article 166		*Part Five, Title III, Chapter 1*
Title XII	*Title XIII*	*Title XX (moved)*	
Article 151	Article 167	*Article 177 (moved)*	*Article 208*
Title XIII	*Title XIV*	*Article 178 (repealed)*[43]	
Article 152	Article 168	*Article 179 (moved)*	*Article 209*
Title XIV	*Title XV*	*Article 180 (moved)*	*Article 210*
Article 153, paragraphs 1, 3, 4 and 5	Article 169	*Article 181 (moved)*	*Article 211*
Article 153, paragraph 2 (moved)	*Article 12*	*Title XXI (moved)*	*Part Five, Title III, Chapter 2*
Title XV	*Title XVI*	*Article 181a (moved)*	*Article 212*
Article 154	Article 170	PART FOUR	PART FOUR
Article 155	Article 171	Article 182	Article 198
Article 156	Article 172	Article 183	Article 199
Title XVI	*Title XVII*	Article 184	Article 200
Article 157	Article 173	Article 185	Article 201
Title XVII	*Title XVIII*	Article 186	Article 202
Article 158	Article 174	Article 187	Article 203
Article 159	Article 175	Article 188	Article 204
Article 160	Article 176		PART FIVE
Article 161	Article 177		Title I
Article 162	Article 178		Article 205
Title XVIII	*Title XIX*	*Part Three, Title IX (moved)*	Title II
Article 163	Article 179	*Article 131 (moved)*	Article 206
Article 164	Article 180	*Article 133 (moved)*	Article 207
Article 165	Article 181		Title III
Article 166	Article 182	*Part Three, Title XX (moved)*	Chapter 1
Article 167	Article 183	*Article 177 (moved)*	Article 208[44]
Article 168	Article 184	*Article 179 (moved)*	Article 209
Article 169	Article 185	*Article 180 (moved)*	Article 210
Article 170	Article 186	*Article 181 (moved)*	Article 211
Article 171	Article 187		
Article 172	Article 188		

[43] Replaced, in substance, by the second sentence of the second subparagraph of paragraph 1 of Article 208 TF[EU].

[44] The second sentence of the second subparagraph of paragraph 1 replaces, in substance, Article 178 TEC.

Old numbering of the Treaty establishing the European Community	New numbering of the Treaty on the Functioning of the European Union	Old numbering of the Treaty establishing the European Community	New numbering of the Treaty on the Functioning of the European Union
Part Three, Title XXI (moved)	Chapter 2	Article 197, first paragraph (repealed)[49]	
Article 181a (moved)	Article 212	Article 197, second, third and fourth paragraphs	Article 230
	Article 213		
	Chapter 3	Article 198	Article 231
	Article 214	Article 199	Article 232
	Title IV	Article 200	Article 233
Article 301 (replaced)	Article 215	Article 201	Article 234
	Title V		Section 2
	Article 216		Article 235
Article 310 (moved)	Article 217		Article 236
Article 300 (replaced)	Article 218	Section 2	Section 3
Article 111, paragraphs 1 to 3 and 5 (moved)	Article 219	Article 202 (repealed)[50]	
		Article 203 (repealed)[51]	
	Title VI	Article 204	Article 237
Articles 302 to 304 (replaced)	Article 220	Article 205, paragraphs 2 and 4 (repealed)[52]	
	Article 221	Article 205, paragraphs 1 and 3	Article 238
	Title VII	Article 206	Article 239
	Article 222	Article 207	Article 240
PART FIVE	PART SIX	Article 208	Article 241
Title I	Title I	Article 209	Article 242
Chapter 1	Chapter 1	Article 210	Article 243
Section 1	Section 1	Section 3	Section 4
Article 189 (repealed)[45]		Article 211 (repealed)[53]	
Article 190, paragraphs 1 to 3 (repealed)[46]			Article 244
Article 190, paragraphs 4 and 5	Article 223	Article 212 (moved)	*Article 249, paragraph 2*
Article 191, first paragraph (repealed)[47]		Article 213	Article 245
Article 191, second paragraph	Article 224	Article 214 (repealed)[54]	
		Article 215	Article 246
Article 192, first paragraph (repealed)[48]		Article 216	Article 247
Article 192, second paragraph	Article 225	Article 217, paragraphs 1, 3 and 4 (repealed)[55]	
Article 193	Article 226	Article 217, paragraph 2	Article 248
Article 194	Article 227	Article 218, paragraph 1 (repealed)[56]	
Article 195	Article 228	Article 218, paragraph 2	Article 249
Article 196	Article 229	Article 219	Article 250

[45] Replaced, in substance, by Article 14, paragraphs 1 and 2, TEU.
[46] Replaced, in substance, by Article 14, paragraphs 1 to 3, TEU.
[47] Replaced, in substance, by Article 11, paragraph 4, TEU.
[48] Replaced, in substance, by Article 14, paragraph 1, TEU.
[49] Replaced, in substance, by Article 14, paragraph 4, TEU.
[50] Replaced, in substance, by Article 16, paragraph 1, TEU and by Articles 290 and 291 TFEU.
[51] Replaced, in substance, by Article 16, paragraphs 2 and 9 TEU.
[52] Replaced, in substance, by Article 16, paragraphs 4 and 5 TEU.
[53] Replaced, in substance, by Article 17, paragraph 1 TEU.
[54] Replaced, in substance, by Article 17, paragraphs 3 and 7 TEU.
[55] Replaced, in substance, by Article 17, paragraph 6, TEU.
[56] Replaced, in substance, by Article 295 TFEU.

Old numbering of the Treaty establishing the European Community	New numbering of the Treaty on the Functioning of the European Union	Old numbering of the Treaty establishing the European Community	New numbering of the Treaty on the Functioning of the European Union
Section 4	Section 5	Chapter 2	Chapter 2
Article 220 (repealed)[57]			Section 1
Article 221, first paragraph (repealed)[58]		Article 249	Article 288
			Article 289
Article 221, second and third paragraphs	Article 251		Article 290[60]
			Article 291[60]
Article 222	Article 252		Article 292
Article 223	Article 253		Section 2
Article 224[59]	Article 254	Article 250	Article 293
	Article 255	Article 251	Article 294
Article 225	Article 256	Article 252 (repealed)	
Article 225a	Article 257		Article 295
Article 226	Article 258	Article 253	Article 296
Article 227	Article 259	Article 254	Article 297
Article 228	Article 260		Article 298
Article 229	Article 261	Article 255 (moved)	*Article 15*
Article 229a	Article 262	Article 256	Article 299
Article 230	Article 263		Chapter 3
Article 231	Article 264		Article 300
Article 232	Article 265	Chapter 3	Section 1
Article 233	Article 266	Article 257 (repealed)[61]	
Article 234	Article 267	Article 258, first, second and fourth paragraphs	Article 301
Article 235	Article 268	Article 258, third paragraph (repealed)[62]	
	Article 269	Article 259	Article 302
Article 236	Article 270	Article 260	Article 303
Article 237	Article 271	Article 261 (repealed)	
Article 238	Article 272	Article 262	Article 304
Article 239	Article 273	Chapter 4	Section 2
Article 240	Article 274	Article 263, first and fifth paragraphs (repealed)[63]	
	Article 275	Article 263, second to fourth paragraphs	Article 305
	Article 276	Article 264	Article 306
Article 241	Article 277	Article 265	Article 307
Article 242	Article 278	Chapter 5	Chapter 4
Article 243	Article 279	Article 266	Article 308
Article 244	Article 280	Article 267	Article 309
Article 245	Article 281	Title II	Title II
	Section 6	Article 268	Article 310
	Article 282		Chapter 1
Article 112 (moved)	Article 283	Article 269	Article 311
Article 113 (moved)	Article 284	Article 270 (repealed)[64]	
Section 5	Section 7		
Article 246	Article 285		
Article 247	Article 286		
Article 248	Article 287		

[57] Replaced, in substance, by Article 19 TEU.
[58] Replaced, in substance, by Article 19, paragraph 2, first subparagraph, of the TEU.
[59] The first sentence of the first subparagraph is replaced, in substance, by Article 19, paragraph 2, second subparagraph of the TEU.
[60] Replaces, in substance, the third indent of Article 202 TEC.
[61] Replaced, in substance, by Article 300, paragraph 2 of the TFEU.
[62] Replaced, in substance, by Article 300, paragraph 4 of the TFEU.
[63] Replaced, in substance, by Article 300, paragraphs 3 and 4, TFEU.
[64] Replaced, in substance, by Article 310, paragraph 4, TFEU.

Old numbering of the Treaty establishing the European Community	New numbering of the Treaty on the Functioning of the European Union	Old numbering of the Treaty establishing the European Community	New numbering of the Treaty on the Functioning of the European Union
	Chapter 2	Article 284	Article 337
	Article 312	Article 285	Article 338
	Chapter 3	Article 286 (replaced)	*Article 16*
Article 272, paragraph 1 (moved)	Article 313	Article 287	Article 339
Article 271 (moved)	*Article 316*	Article 288	Article 340
Article 272, paragraph 1 (moved)	*Article 313*	Article 289	Article 341
Article 272, paragraphs 2 to 10	Article 314	Article 290	Article 3
		Article 291	Article 343
Article 273	Article 315	Article 292	Article 344
Article 271 (moved)	Article 316	Article 293 (repealed)	
	Chapter 4	Article 294 (moved)	*Article 55*
Article 274	Article 317	Article 295	Article 345
Article 275	Article 318	Article 296	Article 346
Article 276	Article 319	Article 297	Article 347
	Chapter 5	Article 298	Article 348
Article 277	Article 320	Article 299, paragraph 1 (repealed)[67]	
Article 278	Article 321	Article 299, paragraph 2, second, third and fourth subparagraphs	Article 349
Article 279	Article 322		
	Article 323	Article 299, paragraph 2, first subparagraph, and paragraphs 3 to 6 (moved)	*Article 355*
	Article 324		
	Chapter 6		
Article 280	Article 325	Article 300 (replaced)	*Article 218*
	Title III	Article 301 (replaced)	*Article 215*
Articles 11 and 11a (replaced)	Article 326[65]	Article 302 (replaced)	*Article 220*
Articles 11 and 11a (replaced)	Article 327[65]	Article 303 (replaced)	*Article 220*
Articles 11 and 11a (replaced)	Article 328[65]	Article 304 (replaced)	*Article 220*
Articles 11 and 11a (replaced)	Article 329[65]	Article 305 (repealed)	
Articles 11 and 11a (replaced)	Article 330[65]	Article 306	Article 350
Articles 11 and 11a (replaced)	Article 331[65]	Article 307	Article 351
Articles 11 and 11a (replaced)	Article 332[65]	Article 308	Article 352
Articles 11 and 11a (replaced)	Article 333[65]		Article 353
Articles 11 and 11a (replaced)	Article 334[65]	Article 309	Article 354
		Article 310 (moved)	*Article 217*
PART SIX	**PART SEVEN**	Article 311 (repealed)[68]	
Article 281 (repealed)[66]		*Article 299, paragraph 2, first subparagraph, and paragraphs 3 to 6 (moved)*	Article 355
Article 282	Article 335	Article 312	Article 356
Article 283	Article 336	**Final Provisions**	
		Article 313	Article 357
			Article 358
		Article 314 (repealed)[69]	

[65] Also replaces the current Articles 27a to 27e, 40 to 40b, and 43 to 45 TEU.
[66] Replaced, in substance, by Article 47 TEU.
[67] Replaced, in substance by Article 52 TEU.
[68] Replaced, in substance by Article 51 TEU.
[69] Replaced, in substance by Article 55 TEU.

ABBREVIATIONS

ACT	Advance Corporation Tax
All ER	All England Law Reports
AFSJ	Area of freedom, security, and justice
AVMS	Audiovisual Media Services
BAA	British Airports Authority
BEPG	Broad economic policy guidelines
BVerfG	Bundesverfassungsgericht (German Federal Constitutional Court)
CCC	Customs Co-operation Council
CCM	Classic Community Method
CCP	Common Commercial Policy
CCT	Common Customs Tariff
CD	Customs Duties
CEEs	Charges having an equivalent effect to customs duties
CEN	Comité européen de normalisation
CENELEC	Comité européen de normalisation électronique
CFC	Controlled foreign company
Ch.	Reports from the Chancery Division of the English High Court of Justice
CLJ	*Cambridge Law Journal*
CLP	*Current Legal Problems*
CM	Common Market
CMLR	Common Market Law Reports
CMLRev.	*Common Market Law Review*
CN	Combined Nomenclature
CoOP	Country-of-origin principle
CPC	Community Patent Convention
CRD	Citizens' Rights Directive
CSA	Certain selling arrangements
CU	Customs Union
CUP	Cambridge University Press
CYELS	*Cambridge Yearbook of European Legal Studies*
Dec.	Decision
Dir.	Directive
DKr	Danish Kroner
DSU	Dispute Settlement Understanding (of the WTO)
EBLRev.	*European Business Law Review*
EC	European Communities
ECB	European Central Bank
ECHR	European Convention on Human Rights
ECtHR	European Court of Human Rights
ECLR	*European Competition Law Review*
ECR	European Court Reports

ECSC	European Coal and Steel Community (now defunct)
ECU	European Currency Unit
EEA	European Economic Area
EFSA Journal	*European Food Safety Authority Journal*
EFTA	European Free Trade Area
EFTA Ct Rep	European Free Trade Area Court Reports
EIPR	*European Intellectual Property Review*
EIRR	*European Industrial Relations Review*
EJIL	*European Journal of International Law*
ELJ	*European Law Journal*
ELRev.	*European Law Review*
EMI	European Monetary Institute
EMS	European Monetary System
EMU	Economic and Monetary Union
EP	European Parliament
EPL	*European Public Law*
ERM	Exchange Rate Mechanism
ERTA	European Road Transport Agreement
ESCB	European System of Central Banks
ESF	European Social Fund
ETA	The Basque terrorist organization
ETMR	European Trade Mark Reports
ETSI	European Telecommunications Standards Institute
EU	European Union
EuZW	*Europäische Zeitschrift für Wirtschaftsrecht*
EWC	European Works Council
EWCA Civ	The official individual numbering system for judgments delivered by the English Court of Appeal (Civil Division)
EWHC Admin	The official individual numbering system for judgments of the English High Court (Administrative Court)
FF	French Francs
FHR	fundamental human rights
Fordham Intl LJ	*Fordham International Law Journal*
FTA	Free Trade Area
FU	Full Union
GATS	General Agreement on Trade in Services
GATT	General Agreement on Tariffs and Trade
GDP	Gross domestic product
IGC	Inter-Governmental Conference
ICLQ	*International and Comparative Law Quarterly*
ILJ	*Industrial Law Journal*
IPRs	Intellectual Property Rights
IR	Irish Reports
JCMS	*Journal of Common Market Studies*
JEPP	*Journal of European Public Policy*
J.L. Econ. & Org.	*Journal of Law, Economics and Organization*
J. Law and Soc.	*Journal of Law and Society*

LIEI	*Legal Issues of European Integration*
LJIL	*Leiden Journal of International Law*
LQR	*Law Quarterly Review*
MCT	Mainstream Corporation Tax
MEEs	Measures of equivalent effect
MFN	Most Favoured Nation
MJ	*Maastricht Journal*
MLR	*Modern Law Review*
m.r.	Mandatory requirements
MU	Monetary Union
NAFTA	North American Free Trade Area
NLJ	*New Law Journal*
OJ	Official Journal of the EU
OJLS	*Oxford Journal of Legal Studies*
OMC	Open method of coordination
OUP	Oxford University Press
PIC	Prior informed consent
PL	*Public Law*
PU	Political Union
QB	Queen's Bench Division Reports
QMV	Qualified majority vote
QRs	Quantitative restrictions on trade
Reg.	Regulation
RIIA	Royal Institute of International Affairs
SE	Societas Europea
SEA	Single European Act
SGP	Stability and Growth Pact
TARIC	General Integrated Tariff of the European Communities
TCN	Third-country national
TFEU	Treaty on the Functioning of the European Union
TWF	Television without Frontiers
VAT	Value Added Tax
WCO	World Customs Organization
WHO	World Health Organization
WLR	Weekly Law Reports
WTO	World Trade Organization
YEEL	*Yearbook of European Environmental Law*
YEL	*Yearbook of European Law*

LIST OF TABLES AND FIGURES

PART I

INTRODUCTION

1

INTRODUCTION TO
THE ISSUES

A. INTRODUCTION

This book is about the free movement of goods, persons, services, and capital. It focuses principally on the rules interfering with movement from one Member State to another. To a lesser extent, it also examines the rules regulating those producers or people wishing to enter the European Union. The aim of this chapter is to place these rules in context. Why has the EU set about this policy of facilitating free movement? Who benefits, and who loses? What are the conditions necessary for free movement? And what is the ultimate objective of such policies? To begin with we start by examining the age-old question, why is free trade important? In the interests of maintaining the economic, political, and social integrity of the nation state, why not simply seal off national borders, keep out foreign goods, and protect national industries and national jobs?

B. THE IMPORTANCE OF FREE TRADE

1. INTRODUCTION

The benefits of free trade can be summarized briefly—free trade allows for specialization, specialization leads to comparative advantage, and comparative advantage leads
to economies of scale, which maximize consumer welfare and ensure the most efficient
use of worldwide resources. In his famous treatise on the *Wealth of Nations*, the classical economist Adam Smith noted, 'It is the maxim of every prudent master of a family,
never to attempt to make at home what it will cost him more to make than to buy ...
What is prudence in the conduct of every private family, can scarce be folly in that of
a great kingdom.'[1] Two hundred years later, the Leutwiler report,[2] prepared for GATT,
reflected similar sentiments: 'A farmer may know how to sew and a tailor may know
how to raise chickens—but each can produce more by concentrating on doing what each
can do most efficiently'. Since trade allows countries to concentrate on what they can do
best and, since no two countries are exactly alike in natural resources, climate, or workforce, those differences give each country a comparative advantage over the others in
the same products.[3] Trade translates the individual advantages for many countries into
maximum productivity for all.

2. THE THEORY OF COMPARATIVE ADVANTAGE

The theory of comparative advantage was developed by Ricardo in 1817,[4] using the
example of wine and cloth production in the UK and Portugal. Jackson explains the
operation of the model in the following terms.[5] In the UK it takes five hours of labour
to produce a yard of cloth and ten hours a gallon of wine; in Portugal it takes ten hours
of labour to produce a yard of cloth and six hours a gallon of wine. In these circumstances the UK has an *absolute* advantage in cloth production and Portugal has an
absolute advantage in wine production. In the absence of trade (the so-called 'autarky'
case), both countries will have to produce a mix of wine and cloth even though the
UK is better at producing cloth and Portugal better at producing wine. Assuming an
availability of 90 hours' labour then the total amount of wine and cloth produced in
the UK and Portugal is 13 yards of cloth and 14 gallons of wine. This is summarized
in table 1.1.

---

[1] A. Smith, *The Wealth of Nations* originally published in 1776, Bk IV, Ch. II cited in P. Kenen, *The
International Economy*, 4th edn (Cambridge: CUP, 2000), 9. Kenen himself says (at 20) that 'In a world of
competitive markets, trade will occur and will be beneficial whenever there are international differences in
relative costs of production.'

[2] The Leutwiler report of 1985 prepared for GATT, *Trade Policies for a Better Future: Proposals for action*
(Geneva: GATT, 1985), 23, cited in J. H. Jackson, *The World Trading System: Law and policy of international
economic relations*, 2nd edn (Cambridge, Mass.: MIT Press, 1997), 12.

[3] The Leutwiler report of 1985 prepared for GATT, n. 2, 12.

[4] D. Ricardo, *On the Principles of Political Economy and Taxation*, 3rd edn (London: John Murray, 1821),
Ch. 7 with the definitive version appearing in P. Sraffa (ed.), *The Works and Correspondence of David Ricardo*
(New York: CUP, 1953).

[5] This is taken from Jackson, n. 2, 15. A more detailed analysis can be found in Kenen, see n. 1, 47–61.

Table 1.1 Absolute advantage (autarky case)

	UK	Portugal	Total
Cloth	10 yds	3 yds	13 yds
	(10 × 5 hrs = 50 hrs)	(3 × 10 hrs = 30 hrs)	
Wine	4 gallons	10 gallons	14 gallons
	(4 × 10 hrs = 40 hrs)	(10 × 6 hrs = 60 hrs)	

However, if trade is opened up between the UK and Portugal (the so-called 'cosmopolitan case') and each state is allowed to specialize, then 18 yards of cloth and 15 gallons of wine can be produced, again assuming 90 hours of available labour (table 1.2).

Table 1.2 Absolute advantage (cosmopolitan case)

Absolute advantage (cosmopolitan case)	UK	Portugal	Total
Cloth	18 yds	0 yds	18 yds
	(18 × 5 hrs = 90 hrs)		
Wine	0 gallons	15 gallons	15 gallons
		(15 × 6 hrs = 90 hrs)	

From this we can see that specialization results in higher total productivity.

Even where one country has an absolute advantage in respect of *both* goods there is still an advantage in specialization. For example, if, in the UK, it takes five hours of labour to produce a yard of cloth and ten hours to produce a gallon of wine, while in Portugal it takes ten hours of labour to produce a yard of cloth and ten hours to produce a gallon of wine then, again assuming 90 hours of labour, table 1.3 shows production levels in the autarky case.

Table 1.3 Comparative advantage (autarky case)

	UK	Portugal	Total
Cloth	10 yds	5 yds	15 yds
	(10 × 5 hrs = 50 hrs)	(5 × 10 hrs = 50 hrs)	
Wine	4 gallons	4 gallons	8 gallons
	(4 × 10 hrs = 40 hrs)	(4 × 10 hrs = 40 hrs)	

If trade is opened up between the UK and Portugal then table 1.4 shows production levels in the cosmopolitan case.

Table 1.4 Comparative advantage (cosmopolitan case)

	UK	Portugal	Total
Cloth	18 yds	0 yds	18 yds
	(18 × 5 hrs = 90 hrs)		
Wine	0 gallons	9 gallons	9 gallons
		(9 × 10 hrs = 90 hrs)	

Even in the case of the UK having an absolute advantage in respect of both wine and cloth, there is an advantage for the two countries to trade if the *ratio* of production costs of the two products differs. Thus, in the second example, a gallon of wine in the UK costs two yards of cloth, whereas in Portugal it costs only one yard of cloth. It is therefore worthwhile for the UK to produce cloth and trade its excess for wine. Thus, as Jackson points out,[6] it is not the difference of absolute advantages but of comparative advantage that gives rise to gains from international trade.

These examples show that with specialization comes greater productivity and that ultimately free trade should lead to cheaper products for the British and Portuguese consumer and greater choice. If supply and demand can be brought into equilibrium, then *static* or *allocative* efficiency will be maximized (the wants or preferences of the various parties will have been satisfied to the greatest possible extent). Putting it another way, the welfare of consumers is maximized since they spend less of their finite resources on buying the goods they need. At a micro-level, employment is secure for workers making cloth in the UK and wine in Portugal, with the important social consequences that ensue from this security. It also means that employers should put in place good terms and conditions of employment in order to retain a skilled workforce who can meet the demand for their products. Thus, social benefits will arise as a consequence of free trade.[7] Indeed, going beyond Ricardo, specialization, competition, and access to larger markets should bring the incentive to invest in production facilities and thus greater economies of scale.

The economic benefits of operating in a wider market were spelled out in the Spaak report drawn up by the heads of delegation to the foreign affairs ministers prior to the signing of the Treaty of Rome. They noted that in such a market it would no longer be possible to continue with outdated modes of production which lead to high prices and low salaries. Instead of maintaining a static position, enterprises would be subject to a constant pressure to invest in order to develop production, improve quality, and modernize methods of exploitation. It would be necessary to progress to stand still.[8]

Free trade produces another consequence of great importance: the two nations, Portugal and the UK, are now dependent on each other for goods. The prosperity of the countries is enhanced, boosting the prospects for peace at home and also peace between the two trading nations: countries trading peacefully are less likely to go to war. This was Monnet's vision for the European Union.

---

[6] See n. 2, 16.

[7] This was recognized in Art. 151 TFEU, which provides that Member States believe that an improvement in working conditions 'will ensue not only from the functioning of the internal market ... but also ... from the approximation of provisions laid down by law, regulation or administrative action.'

[8] Author's translation of the Spaak report, Brussels, 21 Apr. 1956, Mae 120 f/56, 14.

3. THE PROBLEMS WITH THE BASIC MODEL

Ricardo's model is premised on a situation of perfect competition with no state intervention in the market. Economists make a number of assumptions about such markets:[9] buyers and sellers act rationally, are numerous, have full information about products on offer, can contract at little cost, have sufficient resources to transact, can enter and leave the market with little difficulty, and will carry out the obligations which they agree to perform. Under these assumptions market participants should continue to trade until no gains can be realized from further exchange. The distribution is *allocatively efficient*: assets are being employed in their most highly valued use.

Of course, the real world is not like this; the conditions of perfect competition do not exist in any market, not just transnational markets such as the EU's. For example, information failure, transaction costs, and the tendency of actors to shirk commitments are issues in all markets, albeit that the problems are exacerbated in the transnational context. However, there are certain problems which are associated with transnational markets which do not affect national markets in the same way. For example, national regulators tend to respond to local concerns, ignoring the external costs of their regulation, by generating trade barriers and granting inefficient subsidies. This can be seen in the following illustration.

In the process of achieving allocative efficiency, some, if not all, British wine makers go out of business, as do Portuguese cloth makers. This is the politically and socially difficult face of any free trade regime. In a democratic society, governments, needing to be re-elected, respond to public pressure about the actual or potential loss of domestic jobs caused by cheap imports. In the absence of any external restraining factor, they may put up trade barriers. So, under pressure from the Portuguese cloth industry, the Portuguese government might try to prevent the import of British cloth or at least limit the quantity of British cloth imported from the UK by issuing a limited number of import licences. These are quantitative restrictions on trade (QRs). Alternatively, the Portuguese government might lay down quality or other standards for the cloth sold in Portugal or it might allow Portuguese cloth producers to register a trade mark. Such steps are referred to as measures having an effect equivalent to quantitative restrictions (MEEs). These so-called non-tariff barriers (NTBs) may serve protectionist purposes (which would be condemned in a free trade regime) or they may further other, more legitimate, objectives such as consumer protection.

Any such action taken by the state might be reinforced by action taken by private parties: Portuguese cloth manufacturers might agree that they will supply cloth to wholesalers who agree to stock only Portuguese cloth. Such restrictions will inevitably reduce the gains from free trade.

The UK government might decide to retaliate by adopting fiscal measures designed to impede the import of Portuguese wine. It might impose customs duties (CDs) or other charges on the imported goods which have an equivalent effect to customs duties (CEEs). These tariff barriers would have the effect of making the Portuguese wine more expensive, as would taxing Portuguese wine at a higher rate than British wine or a rival product widely produced and consumed in the UK, such as beer. At the same time the Portuguese government might try to prop up its ailing domestic cloth industry by giving it large financial handouts (state aids) paid for by Portuguese taxpayers. It might also adopt a

---

[9] These are summarized by B. Cheffins, *Company Law: Theory, structure and operation* (Oxford: Clarendon Press, 1997), 6.

government purchasing policy based on the idea of buying national goods in preference to the cheaper imports. Once again, the taxpayer is footing the bill for a policy dictated not by economic efficiency but political necessity.

One way to remove such barriers is for the Portuguese and British governments to enter a bilateral agreement removing trade restrictions and requiring each Member State to recognize the goods produced by the other. If more states are involved, they might decide to set up a central institution to check that all participants are playing by the rules, a body whose decisions are binding on the national governments and take precedence over conflicting national laws. Ultimately, this body might begin to set the rules to deal with the problems of market failure which are specific to the transnational context. This then raises questions about the role of law in such an institutional arrangement and the legitimacy and accountability of the rule-making body. To maximize the benefits of free trade, such grouping needs to be global. The World Trade Organization (WTO) represents an important step in this direction. However, in the absence of global free trade, regional groupings (such as the EU) have formed which have tried to obtain the benefits of free trade from among a smaller number of states.[10] The classical thinking is that since worldwide free trade will maximize global welfare, so a smaller grouping must be the next best thing.[11] We turn now to consider what form these groupings might take.

C. THE DIFFERENT STAGES OF INTEGRATION

1. INTRODUCTION

Economists have developed a number of labels to describe different levels of intensity of market integration (see Box 1).[12] Each of these forms of integration can be introduced in its own right; they are not necessarily stages in a process which eventually leads to full union.[13]

Box 1: DIFFERENT STAGES OF INTEGRATION

- *Free Trade Area (FTA)*—Member States remove all impediments to free movement of goods among themselves but each state retains the autonomy to regulate its trading relations with non-Member States
- *Customs Union (CU)*—FTA + common external policy in respect of non-Member States (e.g., single customs tariff)
- *Common Market (CM)*—CU + free movement of persons, services, and capital
- *Monetary Union (MU)*—CM + single currency

[10] This is recognized by Art. XXIV:8 of GATT.
[11] This does not always occur if a customs union leads to trade diversion (replacement of cheaper imports from the outside world by more expensive imports from a partner): W. Molle, *The Economics of European Integration: Theory, practice and policy*, 5th edn (Aldershot: Dartmouth, 2006), 84.
[12] On the need to provide an economics analysis of issues of international trade, see R. Cass, 'Introduction: Economics and international law' in J. Bhandari and A. Sykes (eds.), *Economic Dimensions in International Law: Comparative and empirical perspectives* (Cambridge: CUP, 1997).
[13] A. El-Agraa, *The Economics of the European Community*, 4th edn (Hemel Hempstead: Harvester Wheatsheaf, 1994), 2.

- *Economic Union*—MU + single monetary and fiscal policy controlled by a central authority
- *Political Union (PU)*—Economic Union + central authority sets not only monetary and fiscal policies but is also responsible to a central parliament with the sovereignty of a nation's government. Such a parliament might also set foreign and security policies
- *Full Union (FU)*—the complete unification of the economies involved and a common policy on matters such as social security and income tax.

These stages are derived from B. Balassa, *The Theory of Economic Integration* (London: Allen and Unwin, 1961).

We shall now consider where the EU fits into these stages of integration.

2. FREE TRADE AREA AND CUSTOMS UNION

An FTA is characterized by a common internal policy (the free movement of goods between participating states) but different external policies (each state retains the competence to regulate trade with non-members). Loosely speaking, this describes the position in the European Free Trade Area (EFTA) and the North American Free Trade Area (NAFTA). The disadvantage of a free trade area is that goods coming from non-Member States will enter the area via the state with the most favourable trading regime (usually the one with the lowest tariffs) and then, taking advantage of the rules on free movement, benefit from the free circulation of its goods within the area.[14] A CU can overcome these problems. It is similar to an FTA internally but differs from an FTA externally because participating states have a common policy in respect of the non-members (e.g., a single customs tariff).

According to Article 28(1) TFEU, the EU comprises a CU where customs duties are prohibited between Member States and a common customs tariff (CCT) is adopted in respect of third countries. However, EU law has gone further than classical economic theory might expect by also prohibiting the use of non-tariff barriers, i.e. quantitative restrictions (QRs), which in welfare terms can be just as damaging to free trade without the revenue-producing benefits, and measures having equivalent effect (MEEs) (Articles 34–5 TFEU). The EU also prohibits anti-competitive behaviour by private actors which might attempt to resurrect barriers to trade which partition the market on national lines (Articles 101–2 TFEU), as well as state aids (Article 107 TFEU).

3. COMMON MARKET, SINGLE MARKET, AND BEYOND

3.1 The Common Market

An FTA and a CU focus on the free movement of *products*. A common market allows for free movement of *production* factors (workers and capital) as well as products. The idea is that the liberalization of factors of production allows for the optimum allocation of labour and capital. If production factors are missing from a place where production would be most economical, entrepreneurs in a common market can shift their capital from places of low return to states which have more potential.[15] Similarly, labour can move from areas of high unemployment to areas of high employment. Ultimately this should lead to the equalization of prices.

[14] This can be addressed in part through a system of certificates of origin. See further Molle, n. 11, 10.
[15] Molle, n. 11, 13.

This can be seen in the following example. Let's imagine that in Portugal labour is plentiful but capital is scarce and in the UK capital is plentiful but labour is scarce. Assuming that wine is relatively labour-intensive and cloth relatively capital-intensive, then wine will be cheaply produced in Portugal and cloth in the UK. In an FTA or CU, Portugal will export wine and the UK will export cloth. As we saw from table 1.2, Portugal will shift resources from the manufacture of cloth to wine while the UK will shift resources from the manufacture of wine to cloth. However, in a *common market* the goods *or* the factors of production can move. If the factors of production move then workers migrate from Portugal to the UK where they can earn more, and capital flows from the UK to Portugal. This will alter the relative scarcities of the two production factors in the UK and Portugal and thus equalize their prices.[16] This will reduce the cost differences between the two countries in the production of wine and cloth, thus removing the stimulus to trade in these goods.

This suggests that there is a relation of substitution between the movement of products and the movement of factors of production. Yet, as Molle points out, however interesting the results of substitution in theory, it is not very helpful for practical purposes, since its assumptions rarely hold good: markets are not characterized by perfect competition, factors are not perfectly mobile, and countries are differently endowed with natural resources. Thus, it is more likely that free movement of products and free movement of production factors are *complements*, not substitutes. As we shall see, free movement of goods is particularly important to the EU since in practice it is easier for goods to move to people than people to goods.

The creation of a common market lay at the heart of the European Community (now European Union) project. Article 2 EC (now repealed) said that the (then) Community had as its task the establishment of a common market (Art. 3(3) TEU continues to provide that 'The Union shall establish an internal market', which is defined in Art. 26 TFEU), and one of the activities of the Community listed in Article 3 EC (now repealed) was the creation of 'an internal market characterized by the abolition, as between Member States, of obstacles to the free movement of goods, persons, services and capital'.

The detail of these four freedoms are found in specific Articles of the Treaty: Articles 28–30, 110, and 34–5 TFEU on goods, Article 45 TFEU on workers, Article 49 TFEU on establishment, Articles 56–7 TFEU on services, and Article 63 TFEU on capital. These Articles are based on the principle of *negative* integration—removing barriers to trade. As the Court put it in *Gaston Schul*,[17] the aim of the provisions of the Treaties is to eliminate 'all obstacles to intra-[Union] trade in order to merge the national markets into a single market bringing about conditions as close as possible to those of a genuine [domestic][18] market'.

3.2 The Single Market

By the mid 1980s Euro-sclerosis had set in and the failure of the common market was plain for all to see. In 1985 Jacques Delors, the president of the European Commission, responded with his ambitious plan for the single market.[19] A White Paper, 'Completing

---

[16] Molle, n. 11, 169.

[17] Case 15/81 *Gaston Schul Douane Expediteur BV* v. *Inspecteur der Invoerrechten en Accijnzen, Roosendaal* [1982] ECR 1409, para. 33.

[18] The original quotation reads 'internal'. Earlier case law (e.g., Case 270/80 *Polydor* v. *Harlequin* [1982] ECR 329, para. 16) talks of 'domestic' market, and this term has been used for the sake of clarity.

[19] C. Grant, *Delors: Inside the house that Jacques built* (London: Nicholas Brealey Publishing, 1994), 66.

the Internal Market',[20] was drawn up under the direction of the British commissioner, Lord Cockfield, which focused on removing barriers which continued to prevent free movement.[21] It identified three principal obstacles to the completion of the single market:

- physical barriers to trade—e.g., intra-EU border stoppages, customs controls, and associated paperwork
- technical barriers to trade—e.g., meeting divergent national product standards adopted for health and safety reasons or for consumer and environmental protection, other technical regulations, conflicting business laws, entering nationally protected public procurement markets[22]
- fiscal barriers to trade—especially differing rates of VAT and excise duties.

The Cecchini Report on the Cost of Non-Europe[23] anticipated that the growth resulting from the single market would put between four and seven percentage points on the Union's domestic product and the creation of between two and five million new jobs.

The White Paper then identified 300 measures (the final count was actually 282) necessary to complete the single market. The Single European Act (SEA) 1986,[24] the first significant Treaty amendment after the Treaty of Rome, provided the necessary means to achieve these objectives. It introduced a new legal basis, Article 114 TFEU, which provided for qualified majority voting when enacting measures for the approximation of Member States' laws which have as 'their object the establishment and functioning of the internal market'. While the original EEC Treaty had also envisaged a role for *positive integration* (harmonization) the legal bases provided, notably Articles 115 and 352 TFEU, required unanimous voting in Council, and this hindered their utility as a means of adopting a large number of, often controversial, measures deemed necessary to complete the internal market. The introduction of Article 114 TFEU emphasized that the single market was essentially a lawmaking project. This raises the issue as to the type of (supranational) laws the EU requires. This question is considered in detail in Chapter 15.

The SEA also introduced Article 100b EEC, which required the Commission, together with each Member State, to draw up an inventory of national measures which fell under Article 100a EEC (now Article 114 TFEU) and which had not been harmonized. The Council could then decide whether the provisions in force in a Member State could be recognized as being equivalent to those in another Member State. This power was not used and Article 100b was abolished by the Amsterdam Treaty.

For presentation purposes, the SEA repackaged the four freedoms into the renamed 'internal' or 'single' market and, in Article 7a EEC (now Article 26 TFEU), set a new

---

[20] COM(85)310. See H. Schmitt von Sydow, 'The basic strategies of the Commission's White Paper' in R. Bieber et al., *1992 One European Market? A critical analysis of the Commission's internal market strategy* (Baden-Baden: Nomos Verlagsgesellschaft, 1988).

[21] Lord Cockfield, *The European Union: Creating the single market* (Chichester: Wiley Chancery, 1994), 39.

[22] P. Cecchini, *The European Challenge 1992: The benefits of a single market* (Aldershot: Wildwood House, 1988), 4. These problems persist: see the Commission's Internal Market Package (COM(2007) 35) discussed in Ch. 4.

[23] P. Cecchini, *The European Challenge 1992: The benefits of a single market* (Aldershot: Wildwood House, 1988), xvii–xviii.

[24] For critical comment on the SEA, see P. Pescatore, 'Some critical remarks on the Single European Act' (1987) 24 *CMLRev.* 9: 'the implementation of the Act [represents] … on the whole a major setback for the European Communities … It … [would be] better for our future together … if we were to abandon this ill-fated experiment.' For a more positive reaction, see D. Edwards, 'The impact of the Single Act on the Institutions' (1987) 24 *CMLRev.* 19.

deadline by which they were to be achieved: 31 December 1992.[25] While the deadline was psychologically and politically significant,[26] it had no legal effect.[27] The name change, from 'common' to 'single' or 'internal' market, also had little effect. At first glance, the term 'single market' appears narrower than 'common market' because the single market is defined by reference only to the four freedoms while the common market combines the four freedoms with flanking measures such as agriculture, competition, and social matters. In reality, the realization of the single market was, and is, dependent on further policy action in an ever-wider range of fields, including competition and social policy.[28] For this reason it is likely that the terms common, single, and internal market are largely synonymous.[29]

Although the deadline for the completion of the single market was 1992, in fact the single market is not yet complete. As the Commission puts it, creating a genuinely integrated market is not a finite task, but rather an ongoing process, requiring constant effort, vigilance, and updating. With technological and political developments, the environment in which the single market functions is changing all the time. Although many obstacles have been removed, others come to light and will continue to do so[30] and need to be addressed. For this reason the realization of the single market is an ongoing project, not a historical artefact, a point more recently confirmed by the UK's New Settlement deal of Febraury 2016:[31]

> The establishment of an internal market in which the free movement of goods, persons, services and capital is ensured is an essential objective of the Union. To secure this objective and to generate growth and jobs, the EU must enhance competitiveness.

3.3 Area of Freedom, Security, and Justice

The Amsterdam Treaty introduced a new concept, the area of freedom, security, and justice (AFSJ). Article 67(1) TFEU says:

> The Union shall constitute an area of freedom, security and justice with respect for fundamental rights and the different legal systems and traditions of the Member States.

---

[25] The deadline is merely noted in Case C–9/99 *Echirolles Distribution SA* v. *Association du Dauphiné* [2000] ECR I–8207. The deadline of 31 Dec. 1992 has been removed from Art. 26 TFEU. Article 26 TFEU remains significant for steering the interpretation of the four freedoms: Case C–102/09 *Camar* v. *Presidenza del Consiglio dei Ministri* [2010] ECR I–4045, para. 33.

[26] It represented the life span of two four-year Commissions. The original EC Customs Union was to be completed over three periods of four years. It was in fact completed in just over ten years in 1967.

[27] The declaration attached to the Article by the SEA said that the participants expressed their 'firm political will' to complete the internal market before 1 Jan. 1993 but that setting the date of 31 Dec. 1992 did not create 'an automatic legal effect'. See H. Schermers, 'The effect of the date 31 December 1992' (1991) 28 *CMLRev.* 275. See also A. Toth, 'The legal status of the declarations attached to the Single European Act' (1987) 24 *CMLRev.* 803. In Case C–378/97 *Criminal Proceedings against Wijsenbeek* [1999] ECR I–6207, para. 40, the Court observed that Art. 14 EC (now Art. 26 TFEU) could 'not be interpreted as meaning that, in the absence of measures adopted by the Council before 31 Dec. 1992 requiring the Member States to abolish controls of persons at the internal frontiers of the [Union], that obligation automatically arises from expiry of that period'.

[28] The terminology of 'single market' has in fact been used by the Court since the early 1960s: e.g., Case 32/65 *Italy* v. *Council and Commission* [1966] ECR 389, 405; Case 15/81 *Gaston Schul* [1982] ECR 1409, para. 33.

[29] K. Mortelmans, 'The Common Market, the internal market and the single market, what's in a market?' (1998) 35 *CMLRev.* 101, 107. See also Tesauro AG in Case C–300/89 *Commission* v. *Council (titanium dioxide)* [1991] ECR I–2867: 'the concept of the "internal market" [is based] on that of the "common market" '.

[30] COM(2007) 35, 6.

[31] European Council conclusions, 18–19 Febraury 2016, Section B Competitiveness.

The rest of the Article explains the meaning of the three terms. 'Freedom' means the absence of *internal* border controls for persons and a common policy—on asylum, immigration, and external border control—in respect of third-country nationals (TCNs). 'Security' is about measures to prevent and combat crime, racism, and xenophobia, coordination and cooperation between police and judicial authorities and other competent authorities, as well as mutual recognition of judgments in criminal matters. Finally, the 'justice' element concerns access to justice, in particular through the principle of mutual recognition of judicial and extrajudicial decisions in civil matters.

The introduction of the AFSJ shows how the EU has undergone a shift from 'merely' establishing an internal market to creating an area of freedom, security, and justice which complements and goes beyond the stages of economic integration defined in Box 1.[32] The elision between the two policy objectives of freedom and security can be seen in Article 3(2) TEU, which talks of the EU maintaining and developing 'an area of freedom, justice and security *without internal frontiers*'[33] in which 'the free movement of persons is ensured in conjunction with appropriate measures with respect to external border controls, asylum, immigration and the prevention and combating of crime'. The AFSJ is considered in more detail in Chapters 10 and 13.

4. ECONOMIC, MONETARY, AND POLITICAL UNION

The common market is at the heart of any economic, monetary, and political union. However, as Molle explains,[34] economic union also requires a high degree of coordination of economic policy, including macro-economic and monetary policies and possibly redistributive policies; while in a monetary union (MU) the currencies of the Member States are either linked through irrevocably fixed exchange rates and are fully convertible, or one common currency circulates in all Member States. Economic and monetary union combines the characteristics of economic union and monetary union and presupposes a high degree of coordination of macro-economic and budget policies. A political union (PU) goes further still, with integration extending beyond economics to include police, foreign policy, and security policy. Finally, the closest form of integration is full union (FU), which implies the 'complete unification' of the policies involved, and a common policy on such sensitive issues as social security and income tax. In these circumstances the situation of the union is virtually indistinguishable from that of a nation state.

The Maastricht Treaty provided the Union with the powers to achieve economic and monetary union. Chapter 1 of Title VIII TFEU concerns economic policy. It requires Member States to conduct their economic policies with a view to contributing to the achievement of the objectives of the Union[35] and in the context of the broad economic guidelines laid down annually by the Council.[36] Monetary policy is dealt with in Chapter 2 of Title VIII and applies to those countries which have satisfied the criteria for the single currency and have not opted out of the process. They are subject to the continuous duty of avoiding excessive government deficits[37] with the risk of being subject to a number of sanctions, including being fined. The economic crisis which started in 2008

---

[32] S. Iglesias Sánchez, 'Free movement of third country nationals in the European Union? Main features, deficiencies and challenges of the new mobility rights in the area of freedom, security and justice' (2009) 15 *ELJ* 791, 795.

[33] Emphasis added.   [34] Molle, n. 11, 17.   [35] Art. 120 TFEU.

[36] Art. 121 TFEU.   [37] Art. 126 TFEU.

has put a severe strain on the EMU and has cast serious doubt on the original Maastricht settlement. The crisis has shown that the EU has in fact a monetary union but not an economic union. The EU is only now trying to address this disequilibrium.

The Lisbon Treaty shows the extent to which the EU is moving towards political union with the introduction of a Union minister for foreign affairs[38] as well as a president of the European Council,[39] together with expanding powers over matters such as police and judicial cooperation, areas which are no longer confined to the intergovernmental processes of the third pillar.[40] For Eurozone Member States, much closer political union is now on the cards, with provision for EU control over national budgets and discussion of a further Treaty to deliver on further political union, a point recognised by the UK New Settlement deal:[41] 'In order to fulfil the Treaties' objective to establish an economic and monetary union whose currency is the euro, further deepening is needed.' For non-Eurozone countries, participation in such measures is voluntary but they must not 'create obstacles to facilitate such further deepening'.

D. UNDERSTANDING THE INTEGRATION PROCESS

Neo-functionalists argue that there is a spillover from one type of integration to another.[42] In other words, if states integrated one sector of their economies, usually an area of low controversy (e.g., harmonization of technical standards), technical pressures would push them to integrate other sectors which are increasingly controversial (e.g., monetary and political union). The following example illustrates this point.

Cutting Edge manufactures a successful range of lawnmowers in the UK. It wishes to break into new markets to sell more of its lawnmowers, with resulting benefits in terms of economies of scale. However, in order to sell on these new markets Cutting Edge needs to have both the right to export its goods from the UK without restriction and the right to import its lawnmowers into the new markets without fiscal or non-fiscal barriers to trade. It also needs to be able to promote and sell its lawnmowers in the host states without restriction. The provisions of the EU Treaties—especially Article 30 TFEU on customs duties, Article 110 TFEU on taxation, and Articles 34–5 TFEU on freedom to import and export—provide these rights.

Yet, removing barriers is not sufficient. Cutting Edge soon discovers that the levels of noise emission from lawnmowers permitted in France is lower than that in the UK. It is lower still in Germany. For Cutting Edge to sell on these markets, it has to redesign its lawnmowers for each market unless and until there is mutual recognition by each state of the standards prescribed by the other states or a single harmonized standard is enacted by the EU. In fact, the EU has now used its powers under Article 114 TFEU to enact a directive on 'the approximation of the laws of the Member States relating to the noise emission

[38] Art. 18 TEU. The formal title is High Representative of the Union for Foreign Affairs and Security Policy.
[39] Art. 15 TEU.   [40] See Chapters IV and V of Title V TFEU.
[41] European Council Conclusions, 18–19 February 2016, *Economic Governance*. See also the Five Presidents Report, *Completing Europe's Economic and Monetary Union*, June 2015.
[42] See the path-breaking work of E. Haas, *The Uniting of Europe: Political, social and economic forces 1950–1957* (Stanford, Calif.: Stanford University Press, 1958). Supplementing the technical logic of functional spillover, neo-functionalists added the idea of political spillover. This involved the build-up of political pressures by interest groups, trade unions, and other actors to encourage further integration, with the Commission acting as a catalyst for these pressures.

in the environment by equipment for use outdoors'.[43] However, Cutting Edge still needs a reliable and predictable application of these rules and an ability to enforce them in all Member States in which it wishes to trade.

Even with a harmonized standard, Cutting Edge is faced with the problem that currency fluctuations, often caused by governments using the exchange rate as a tool of economic policy, make it difficult for it to price its lawnmowers effectively. For Cutting Edge, a single currency and thus monetary union is the only solution. But for monetary union to work there needs to be centralized control of state expenditure. Thus monetary union creates strong pressure for economic union with economic and fiscal policy being regulated centrally for the whole area of the common market. As we have seen, for the Eurozone countries, economic and monetary union has become a reality. This in turn has created pressure for some form of political union to ensure political accountability of the economic actors.

The example of Cutting Edge shows how the process of integration involves a gradual reduction in the power of national governments and a commensurate increase in the ability of the centre—i.e., the EU's supranational[44] institutions (the Commission and the Parliament)—to deal with sensitive, politically charged issues. It is the logic which lies at the heart of the so-called 'Monnet method'. For Jean Monnet, (neo-)functionalism meant the creation of a supranational regime or organization—i.e., one with joint or pooled authority (the High Authority and subsequently the Commission)—initially with power over the production of coal and steel, and subsequently over other economic sectors, thereby creating 'the first concrete foundations of the European Federation which is indispensable to the maintenance of peace'.[45] His objective of creating a European federation was to be achieved by stealth, combining a mixture of *dirigisme* (removing existing tariff and non-tariff barriers) with market forces.[46]

Some commentators argue that the evolution of the EU from merely a coal and steel community to a major economic and monetary union in a period of less than 50 years, suggests that neo-functionalism is the best explanation for the integration process. However, others reject functionalism as an adequate explanation for what is actually occurring in the EU. For Moravcsik, in his theory of liberal intergovernmentalism,[47] the role of the European Council is central to understanding the integration process. He says that integration proceeds as far and as fast as the governments of the Member States allow. He argues that the Single European Act 1986 was the product of inter-state bargaining between the British, French, and German governments and that traditional tools of international statecraft, such as threats of exclusion and side payments, explained the final composition of the 1992 programme and the SEA 1986.[48]

[43] EP and Council Dir. 2000/14/EC ([2000] OJ L162/1).

[44] R. Keohane and S. Hoffmann, 'Conclusions: Community politics and institutional choice' in W. Wallace (ed.), *The Dynamics of European Integration* (London: RIIA, 1990), 280 note that 'supranationality refers to a process of decision-making in which the participants refrain from unconditionally vetoing proposals and instead seek to attain agreement by means of compromises upgrading common interests'.

[45] M. Holland, *European Community Integration* (London: Pinter Publishers, 1993), 7 and 8, citing J. Monnet, *Memoirs*, trans. R. Mayne (New York: Doubleday, 1978), 298. For a strong endorsement of this view, see the preamble to the ECSC Treaty 'to substitute for age-old rivalries the merging of their essential interests; to create by establishing an economic community, the basis for a broader and deeper community among people long divided by bloody conflicts'. See further W. Wallace, 'Introduction: The dynamics of European integration' in W. Wallace (ed.), *The Dynamics of European Integration* (London: RIIA, 1990).

[46] Holland, n. 45, 13.

[47] A. Moravcsik, 'Negotiating the Single European Act: National interests and conventional statecraft in the European Community' (1991) 45 *International Organisation* 19.

[48] Considered by A. Young and H. Wallace, 'The single market' in H. Wallace, W. Wallace, and M. Pollack (eds.), *Policy-Making in the European Union*, 5th edn (Oxford: OUP, 2005), 100.

Keohane and Hoffmann try to reconcile these approaches. In their reformulation of neo-functionalism they recognize that successful intergovernmental bargaining is a prerequisite to any form of spillover.[49] They note that, without a turnaround in French economic policy in 1983, and the decision of the British government to accept Treaty amendments to institutionalize deregulation, no consensus could have been reached on a programme to dismantle barriers in Europe.[50] Thus, spillover does not occur in a vacuum: it requires positive action on the part of the Member States.

These theories focus on the activities of states, but there is much more to the dynamic of European integration than states. Take, for example, the period leading up to the SEA 1986. While the involvement of the European Council was crucial in securing agreement on the objective of attaining the single market, in particular by resolving the issue of British budgetary contributions at the Fontainebleau summit in June 1984,[51] other institutions played a key role, especially the Commission. It was responsible for the Internal Market White Paper, which placed much emphasis on the principle of mutual recognition which had been developed by the Court.[52] Within the Commission certain key individuals played a decisive role, in particular Lord Cockfield and Jacques Delors.[53] This convergence of events and actors provides a clear demonstration that 'institutions matter'.[54] This lies at the heart of *new institutionalism*, which involves the study of formal and informal institutions, conventions, the norms and symbols embedded in them, policy instruments, and procedures.[55]

The emphasis so far on state actors risks overlooking the fact that private actors also play a key role. For example, in the period leading up to the SEA a coalition of business interests, especially the influential European Round Table of Industrialists (representatives from the largest European companies) strongly supported the renewed impetus to make the single market a reality.[56] Increasingly other actors, particularly those from civil society such as the social partners (management and labour), have been brought into the process of policy formation and implementation.[57] And, from the earliest days of the Union, individuals have been used to help make the common market a reality in their

---

[49] Keohane and Hoffmann, n. 44, 287.

[50] Keohane and Hoffmann, n. 44, 286.

[51] As early as Jun. 1981 the European Council expressed its concern about the undermining of the single market: Bull. EC 6/81. A specific Internal Market Council was created in Jan. 1983.

[52] See further P. Craig, 'The evolution of the single market' in C. Barnard and J. Scott (eds.), *The Law of the Single European Market: Unpacking the premises* (Oxford: Hart Publishing, 2002); and R. Dehousse, *The European Court of Justice* (Basingstoke: Macmillan, 1998), 86–8.

[53] 'Much of the success of the 1992 programme depended on our relationship. Delors left me to get on with it. I fathered it, launched it and drove it to the point of success': Lord Cockfield, quoted in C. Grant, *Delors: Inside the house that Jacques built* (London: Nicholas Brealey Publishing, 1994), 68. On the importance of Jacques Delors, see H. Drake, 'Political leadership and European integration: The case of Jacques Delors' (1995) 18 *Western European Politics* 140; and D. Dinan, *Ever Closer Union: An introduction to European integration*, 3rd edn (Basingstoke: Macmillan, 2005).

[54] K. Armstrong and S. Bulmer, *The Governance of the Single European Market* (Manchester: Manchester University Press, 1998).

[55] Armstrong and Bulmer, n. 54, 52.

[56] Armstrong and Bulmer, n. 54. For details on the influence of big business, in particular the European Round Table, see K. Middlemas, *Orchestrating Europe: The informal politics of European Union 1973–1995* (London: Fontana Press, 1995), 138–9.

[57] This is considered further in Ch. 10.

own states when the Court of Justice (quietly[58]) developed the fundamental principles of direct effect[59] and supremacy[60] of Union law.[61] In this way the Court has created an alliance between itself and individuals, thereby circumventing the Member States and the Union legislator. At the same time the Court of Justice has harnessed national courts into the process of enforcing EU law.

This brief description of actors and processes reflects the *multilevel* nature of the governance in the EU:[62] decision-making competencies are shared by actors at different levels rather than monopolized by governments. The multilevel governance model views political arenas as interconnected, with actors, both public and private, operating in both the national and supranational arenas creating transnational associations in the process.[63] In order to understand free movement, it is the multilevel governance model which perhaps has the most to tell us about policymaking and implementation in the EU. We return to this theme in the final chapter of this book. We turn now to consider the principles which underpin the four freedoms, principles which the Court has played a key role in developing.

E. THE PRINCIPLES UNDERPINNING THE COMMON MARKET

According to the integration theory, there are two approaches to attaining a common market: (1) the *decentralized* model, underpinned by the principles of non-discrimination, market access, and the concept of competitive federalism; and (2) the *centralized* model, which concerns harmonization. The choice between these two models says much about the respective power of the centre (the 'federal' government) and the states. We begin by examining the decentralized model.

1. THE DECENTRALIZED MODEL

The essence of the decentralized model is that states retain the freedom to regulate matters as diverse as product standards, qualifications to practise, and employment law so long as those national rules do not interfere with key principles of 'federal' law. In the early days of the EU, the key principle was non-discrimination. In more recent years the Court has developed the more intrusive 'market access' or 'restrictions' test to remove barriers to free movement. We shall now examine these two different approaches.

---

[58] E. Stein, 'Lawyers, judges and the making of a transnational constitution' (1981) 75 *American Journal of International Law* 1: 'Tucked away in the fairyland Duchy of Luxembourg and blessed, until recently, with benign neglect by the powers that be and the mass media', the Court of Justice has 'fashioned a constitutional framework for a federal-type structure in Europe'.

[59] Case 26/62 *NV Algemene Transport- en Expeditie Onderneming van Gend & Loos* v. *Netherlands Inland Revenue Administration* [1963] ECR 1.

[60] Case 6/64 *Flaminio Costa* v. *ENEL* [1964] ECR 585. See also Decl. 17 of the Lisbon Treaty concerning primacy.

[61] See generally J. Weiler, 'The transformation of Europe' (1981) 100 *Yale LJ* 2403.

[62] L. Hooghe and G. Marks, *Multi-Level Governance and European Integration* (Lanham, Md.: Rowman & Littlefield, 2001).

[63] Hooghe and Marks, n. 62, 3–4.

1.1 Non-Discrimination

The principle of non-discrimination on the grounds of nationality is the cornerstone of the four freedoms. It adopts a comparative approach, requiring out-of-state goods, persons, services, and capital to enjoy the same treatment as their in-state equivalents.[64] This model presupposes that domestic and imported goods, and national and migrant persons, services, and capital are similarly situated[65] and that they should be treated in the same way.[66] The advantage with the non-discrimination model is that it does not interfere with national regulatory autonomy. Member States remain free to regulate the way that goods are produced and services provided, on condition that their regulation applies equally to home and host state goods or persons. So, national rules which are genuinely non-discriminatory are lawful. However, if there is (unjustified) discrimination, Union law requires the discriminatory element of the national measure to be set aside, but the substance of the national rule remains intact. This can be seen in the following example.

Widgets are produced in the UK and Portugal. Each state regulates the standards governing the production of these goods. In Portugal, before widgets originating in the UK can be sold, they are required to satisfy higher standards than widgets produced in Portugal. Portugal is therefore directly discriminating against British goods. The application of the non-discrimination principle means that Portugal can continue to set quality standards for widgets but that the widgets produced in the UK must be subject to the same treatment as those produced in Portugal. So, Portugal has the choice of either requiring all of the UK's widgets to meet the same (lower) standards as those required of Portuguese widgets, or requiring all widgets produced in Portugal to be made to the same (higher) standards required by Portugal for British widgets. This example shows that the non-discrimination model says nothing about the level at which the standards should be set, merely that the imported and domestic goods must be treated in the same way. The result is that the diversity of national rules is preserved.[67]

However, this narrow approach to the principle of equal treatment may itself lead to discrimination, as the widgets example shows. Widgets produced in the UK have already been manufactured according to standards laid down by the UK. In order to be admitted to the Portuguese market they must also satisfy Portuguese standards. In practice, the effect of extending the principle of equal treatment to the British goods is to impose an additional burden on goods originating in the UK. One way of analysing this situation is to say that the Portuguese rule is in fact discriminatory: the discrimination arises because it involves treating identically goods which are actually differently situated. Another way of viewing this situation—and the one favoured by the Court of Justice[68]—is that Portugal's rule is indirectly discriminatory (or indistinctly applicable[69]): on the face of the measure the rule applies to both domestic and imported goods but in fact disadvantages the imported goods because of the double burden they must satisfy. Therefore, Portugal's rule is unlawful, even though equally applicable, unless Portugal can justify it by pointing to a

---

[64] See M. Poiares Maduro, *We the Court: The European Court of Justice and the European Economic Constitution* (Oxford: Hart Publishing, 1998).

[65] If the goods/persons are not similarly situated then different treatment is permitted: Case 15/83 *Denkavit Nederland BV v. Hoofdproduktschap voor Akkerbouwprodukten* [1984] ECR 2171.

[66] Cf. D. Wilsher, 'Does *Keck* discrimination make any sense? An assessment of the non-discrimination principle within the European single market' (2008) 33 *ELRev.* 3.

[67] N. Bernard, 'Discrimination and free movement in EC law' (1996) 45 *ICLQ* 82, 103.

[68] See Case 120/78 *Rewe Zentrale v. Bundesmonopolverwaltung für Branntwein ('Cassis de Dijon')* [1979] ECR 649 considered in detail in Ch. 4.

[69] This terminology is explored further in Ch. 7.

reason which should take precedence over the free movement of goods, such as the need to protect consumers or the environment.

1.2 Market Access

(a) Market access v. Discrimination tests

While the discrimination test has a number of advantages, there are drawbacks too. First, the model is premised on the fact that migrants and nationals are similarly situated when, by definition, they are not. Even if this intellectual hurdle can be surmounted, the choice of comparator is not always obvious and may be determinative of the outcome.[70] Secondly, the effect of the non-discrimination model is to allow barriers to movement to remain: it permits the host state to impose its own rules on imported goods/migrants provided those rules apply equally to domestic goods/persons. For this reason, some advocate that a broader, market access, test be applied. This provides that national rules preventing or hindering market access are unlawful, irrespective of whether they actually discriminate against imports or migrants. The market access approach therefore looks at the national rule solely from the perspective of the (usually out-of-state) claimants: does the national rule prevent or hinder their market access?

The Court of Justice increasingly favours the market access approach. For example, in *Gebhard*,[71] a case concerning national rules on the use of the title *avvocato* in Italy, the Court abandoned the language of discrimination and said that the national measures were 'liable to hinder or make less attractive the exercise of fundamental freedoms guaranteed by the Treaty'. Such rules breached Article 49 TFEU on freedom of establishment unless they could be justified. In *Commission v. Italy (trailers)*,[72] a goods case, the Court said that 'Any other measure which hinders access of products originating in other Member States to the market of a Member State' breaches Article 34 TFEU. In subsequent case law, particularly in the field of persons and capital, the Court has tended to simplify the terminology and increasingly the reference to market access is replaced by the question whether the measures create 'obstacles' to, or 'restrictions' on, free movement.[73]

While the discrimination and market access tests use different language, there is considerable overlap between the two models.[74] For example, quantitative restrictions for goods, refusal of entry/deportation of persons, and directly and indirectly discriminatory

[70] See, e.g., Case 270/83 *Commission* v. *France (tax credits)* [1986] ECR 273. France granted tax credits to shareholders receiving dividends from a company with a registered office in France but not to those with only a branch or agency in France (and a registered office in another Member State). The Court said that because Art. 49 TFEU expressly left traders free to choose the appropriate legal form in which to pursue their activities in another Member State, that freedom of choice could not be limited by discriminatory tax provisions (para. 22). The French rule therefore breached Art. 49 TFEU and could not be justified on the facts. Thus, in its application of the principle of non-discrimination, the Court required the French tax system to treat a branch or agency having no legal personality in the same way as a company registered in France. If, as Banks notes, the Court had selected the treatment of a branch or agency of a nationally based company as the appropriate comparator, the outcome might have been very different (K. Banks, 'The application of the fundamental freedoms to Member State tax measures: Guarding against protectionism or second-guessing national policy choices' (2008) 33 *ELRev.* 482, 488).

[71] Case C–55/94 *Gebhard* v. *Consiglio dell'Ordine degli Avvocati e Procuratori di Milano* [1995] ECR I–4165, para. 37, citing Case C–19/92 *Kraus* v. *Land Baden-Württemberg* [1993] ECR I–1663, para. 32; Case C–76/90 *Säger* v. *Dennemeyer & Co. Ltd* [1991] ECR I–4221, para. 12.

[72] Case C–110/05 *Commission* v. *Italy* [2009] ECR I–519, para. 50.

[73] Cf. J. Meulman and H. de Wael, 'A retreat from *Säger*? Servicing or fine-tuning the application of Article 49' (2006) 33 *LIEI* 207, 210–19.

[74] See, e.g., Case C–438/05 *International Transport Workers' Federation* v. *Viking Line* [2007] ECR I–10779, para. 74. In Case C–341/05 *Laval un Partneri Ltd* v. *Svenska Byggnadsarbetareförbundet* [2007]

measures, by definition, hinder market access.[75] However, the difference between these two models can be seen when dealing with non-discriminatory rules, as the facts of *Commission* v. *Greece (opticians)*[76] illustrate. Greek law prohibited qualified opticians from operating more than one optician's shop. Under a pure discrimination model, this rule would be *lawful*: both Greek opticians and out-of-state opticians are being treated equally (albeit equally badly). However, under the market access approach such a rule would be *unlawful* unless justified and this is the approach the Court adopted. It said this rule 'effectively amounts to a restriction on the freedom of establishment of natural persons within the meaning of Article [49 TFEU], notwithstanding the alleged absence of discrimination on grounds of nationality of the professionals concerned'.[77] This demonstrates the point already noted that while the discrimination approach focuses on a comparison between the treatment of the in-state and out-of-state person/trader, the market access test focuses solely on the perspective of the out-of-state traders or migrants: what stands in their way of getting onto the market? Market access, at least in the early days, was a way of challenging over-regulation by states, which makes cross-border trade difficult (just as it makes domestic trade difficult).[78] The question of nationality becomes irrelevant.

The advantage of the market access approach is that it goes a long way towards building a single market by removing any unjustified obstacles to trade. As Advocate General Jacobs noted in *Leclerc-Siplec*,[79] 'If an obstacle to trade exists it cannot cease to exist simply because an identical obstacle affects domestic trade.' The market access approach is based on the idea famously articulated in *Cassis de Dijon*[80] that goods lawfully produced in one Member State should presumptively have free and unrestricted access to the market in another Member State (the principle of equivalence or mutual recognition). This enables the trader to develop a pan-European strategy to expand the market for its goods, thereby creating greater economies of scale for the producer and greater choice and competition for the consumer. It is a win-win situation. Translating this to persons, those who are qualified to practise in one Member State should also, in principle, be free to practise in another Member State. Once again, this enables individuals to expand the market for their services or to move to a place where their skills are better rewarded/appreciated while offering greater choice to consumers in the receiving state.

ECR I–11767, para. 228 Mengozzi AG noted that it is often difficult to decide whether a set of rules adopted by private persons should be seen as indirect discrimination based on nationality, a restriction, a barrier or a deterrent to the freedom to provide services. See also S. Enchelmaier, 'The ECJ's recent case law on the free movement of goods: Movement in all sorts of directions' (2007) 26 YEL 115, 126–7.

[75] See, e.g., P. Van den Bossche, *The Law and Policy of the World Trade Organization: Text, cases and materials*, 2nd edn (Cambridge: CUP, 2008) who has one chapter entitled 'Principles of non-discrimination' and another entitled 'Rules on market access' which covers tariff barriers to trade (e.g., customs duties), non-tariff barriers (e.g., QRs, inspections, origin marking), and barriers to trade in services.

[76] Case C–140/03 *Commission* v. *Greece (opticians)* [2005] ECR I–3177.

[77] Para. 28. There is an argument that the Greek rule is indirectly discriminatory: there is a risk that it might operate to the particular detriment of out-of-state traders since they are more likely to want to establish a chain of opticians in Greece to justify the initial start-up costs. However, such arguments seem artificial (although this has not prevented the Court itself from relying on such artificiality: e.g., Case C–322/01 *Deutscher Apothekerverband eV* v. *0800 DocMorris NV* [2003] ECR I–14887, para. 74). A better analysis is that the rule should be regarded as non-discriminatory but that it still prevents or impedes market access.

[78] G. Davies, 'Services, citizenship and the country of origin principle', Mitchell Working Paper Series 2/2007, 3: as Davies puts it, 'There may be no identifiable inequality of effect, but there is a general suppression of economic activity.'

[79] Case C–412/93 *Leclerc-Siplec* v. *TF1 Publicité* [1995] ECR I–179.

[80] Case 120/78 *Rewe Zentrale* v. *Bundesmonopolverwaltung für Branntwein ('Cassis de Dijon')* [1979] ECR 649.

The disadvantage with the market access approach is that it is far more intrusive into national regulatory autonomy since Union law requires the national measure to be struck down, unless it can be justified, even though it may not discriminate against the non-national.[81] This has serious implications for national legislation adopted by democratically elected governments, not least because a case can be made that almost any national rule has some effect on inter-state movement, even if that was never the intention of the rule and the effect on inter-state trade is slight.[82] Take, for example, a national law on the minimum wage. This could be challenged under the restrictions model because it would prevent migrants from working for less than the minimum and this might discourage them from moving to that state in the hope of finding work (the rule would not be open to challenge under the non-discrimination approach provided the minimum wage rate was the same for all workers, domestic and migrant). There is some evidence that in recent cases the Court has recognized the risk that the market access model is too all encompassing and so it has experimented with different legal techniques to draw the line between those rules which should be caught by Union law and those which should be outside it. This is discussed in more detail in Chapters 5, 7, and 11 of this book.[83]

(b) The meaning of 'market access'

A further disadvantage with the market access test is the uncertainty which surrounds this 'inherently nebulous'[84] concept. Spaventa offers three possible interpretations.[85] The first, and narrowest, is that barriers to market access are those created by circumstances or legislation that make it 'more costly for new firms to enter an industry'.[86] There is some overlap between this approach and the discrimination model, especially if it is assumed, as the Court often does, that new market entrants come from out of state.[87] It is supported by *Commission* v. *Italy (motor insurance)*,[88] where the Court said that an obligation on an insurance company to provide third party insurance to cover any risks proposed to them and to moderate premium rates breached Articles 49 and 56 TFEU 'inasmuch as it involves changes and costs on such a scale that the obligation to contract renders access to the Italian market less attractive and, if they obtain access to that market, reduces the ability of the undertakings concerned to compete effectively, from the outset, against undertakings traditionally established in Italy'.[89]

The second, and much broader, approach to market access is that *any* regulation can be seen as a potential barrier to access, since *any* regulation imposes and implies compliance

---

[81] This question is discussed further in C. Barnard, 'Restricting restrictions: Lessons for the EU from the US?' (2009) 68 *CLJ* 575.

[82] Cf., e.g., Case C–353/06 *Grunkin-Paul* [2008] ECR I–7639, paras. 23, 24, and 29, where the Court talked of the 'serious inconvenience' caused by a discrepancy in surnames which created an obstacle to free movement of citizens under Art. 21(1) TFEU. In Case C–110/05 *Commission* v. *Italy (trailers)* [2009] ECR I–519 the Court referred to the '*considerable* influence' that a prohibition on the use of a product has on the behaviour of consumers.

[83] See the discussion of the *Keck* (Joined Cases C–267 and 268/91 [1993] ECR I–6097) line of case law in Ch. 5 and the *Viacom* (Case C–134/03 [2005] ECR I–1167) line of case law in Ch. 7 and Case C–518/06 *Commission* v. *Italy (motor insurance)* [2009] ECR I–3491 in Ch. 11.

[84] P. Oliver and S. Enchelmaier, 'Free movement of goods: Recent developments in the case law' (2007) 44 *CMLRev.* 649, 674.

[85] E. Spaventa, 'From *Gebhard* to *Carpenter*: Towards a (non-)economic European Constitution' (2004) 41 *CMLRev.* 743, 757–8.

[86] Citing F. E. Foldvary, *Dictionary of Free Market Economics* (Northampton: Edward Elgar Publishing Inc., 1998), 48.

[87] Case C–322/01 *DocMorris NV* [2003] ECR I–14887, para. 74.

[88] Case C–518/06 *Commission* v. *Italy (motor insurance)* [2009] ECR I–3491.   [89] Para. 70.

costs. This approach can be seen in the *Golden Share* case, *Commission v. UK (British Airports Authority (BAA))*.[90] BAA's articles of association prevented any person from acquiring BAA shares carrying the right to more than 15 per cent of the equity in BAA. The Court said that 'Rules which limit the acquisition of shareholdings … constitute a restriction on the free movement of capital.'[91] The Court added that although the restrictions were non-discriminatory 'they affect the position of a person acquiring a shareholding as such and are thus liable to *deter* investors from other Member States from making such investments and, consequently, affect access to the market'.[92] The answer to the question 'What is the deterrence?' is presumably the very existence of the rule: had the rule not existed there would have been no breach.

The third approach is what Spaventa describes as 'intuitive': rules which interfere with intra-Union trade should be subject to judicial scrutiny while rules considered neutral as regards intra-Union trade should not. The intuitive approach can be seen in *Laval*.[93] The case concerned a Latvian company which won a contract to refurbish a school in Sweden using its own Latvian workers. It faced ruinous industrial action by the Swedish trade unions when it refused to apply Swedish collectively agreed terms and conditions. Although this industrial action was permissible under Swedish law, Laval brought proceedings in the Swedish labour court, claiming that the industrial action was contrary to Article 56 TFEU. The Court said:

> the right of trade unions of a Member State to take collective action by which undertakings established in other Member States may be forced to sign the collective agreement for the building sector … is *liable to make it less attractive, or more difficult*, for such undertakings to carry out construction work in Sweden, and therefore constitutes a *restriction* on the freedom to provide services within the meaning of Article [56 TFEU].[94]

But how, precisely, did the collective action impose costs which made it 'more difficult' or 'less attractive' for Laval to operate in Sweden? Deakin suggests that one answer might be 'more difficult' in relation to the situation which would have prevailed had Latvian law and/or Latvian collective agreements applied.[95] If this is correct, it means that the effect of the restrictions analysis is to enable service providers to export their home country laws and have them applied extraterritorially. Another answer may be intuition: Laval was a Latvian company and it was having difficulty fulfilling a contract which it had legitimately won, largely due to its cheaper labour costs. The Swedish strike action therefore prevented it from doing the very thing that EU accession had promised to the new Member States, namely free access to the markets in services in other Member States; and that was enough to trigger Article 56 TFEU.

But if the effect of *Laval* is to allow challenges to host-state rules which differ from those which apply at home, this suggests that a mere difference between the rules of two states is sufficient to constitute a restriction on free movement, an understanding that the Court has rejected in the past.[96] Following *Laval* there is no reason why German tourists might

---

[90] Case C–98/01 *Commission v. UK* [2003] ECR I–4641.   [91] Para. 44.

[92] Para. 47, emphasis added. Cf. Case C–542/08 *Barth v. Bundesministerium für Wissenschaft und Forschung* [2010] ECR I–3189, para. 39.

[93] Case C–341/05 *Laval un Partneri Ltd v. Svenska Byggnadsarbetareförbundet* [2007] ECR I–11767.

[94] Para. 99, emphasis added.

[95] S. Deakin, 'Regulatory competition after *Laval*' (2007–8) 10 *CYELS* 581, 585–7.

[96] Case C–177/94 *Criminal Proceedings against Gianfranco Perfili, civil party: Lloyd's of London* [1996] ECR I–161, para. 17; Case C–384/93 *Alpine Investments BV v. Minister van Financiën* [1995] ECR I–1141, para. 27.

not argue that the requirement of having to drive on the left hinders their free movement since British rules are different to those in Germany. Here, the Court's 'intuition' might lead it to find that the rules are in fact neutral as regards intra-Union movement. This might explain why in *Burbaud*[97] the Court said that the requirement of passing an exam in order to take up a post in the public service could not 'in itself be regarded as an obstacle' to free movement.[98]

Despite the problems with the market access test, the Court continues to see it as the mainstay of its analysis, as demonstrated by two Grand Chamber decisions, *Commission v. Italy (trailers)*[99] and *Commission v. Italy (motor insurance)*.[100] In both these cases the Court endorsed the market access analysis and offered some guidance as to the meaning of the phrase. The *Trailers* case concerned an Italian prohibition on motorbikes towing trailers. The Court indicated that market access could be hindered by a rule which has '*considerable* influence on the behaviour of consumers, which, in its turn, affects the access of that product to the market of that Member State'.[101] Thus, (significant) reduction in demand is sufficient to satisfy the market access test. In the *Motor Insurance* case the Court also imposed a threshold. It said that the obligation of an insurance company to provide third party cover to every potential customer constituted a 'substantial' interference in the operators' freedom to contract,[102] and that the obligation was likely to lead, in terms of organization and investment to '*significant* additional costs for such undertakings'.[103]

For Snell, however, the notion of market access conceals rather than clarifies.[104] He argues that it covers a range of situations including discrimination against free movers or free movement,[105] substantial or direct obstacles to trade or free movement,[106] and substantial reductions in profitability.[107] He concludes: 'As the term lacks a clear content, the Court may use it freely either to approve or to condemn measures that it happens to like or dislike. Market access may simply provide a sophisticated-sounding garb that conceals decisions based on intuition.'[108]

(c) Market access v. Exercise

There is a further practical problem with the language of market *access*: it suggests that restrictions on initial access to the market (e.g., requiring individuals to have certain qualifications, linguistic skills, or a licence before they do a particular job) are more serious than restrictions imposed by the host state when migrants have actually got onto the market but are trying to exercise their freedoms (e.g., rules restricting tax and social

---

[97] Case C–285/01 *Burbaud v. Ministère de l'Emploi et de la Solidarité* [2003] ECR I–8219.

[98] Para. 96. To emphasize the point, the Court said that inasmuch as all new jobs are subject to a recruitment procedure, the requirement of passing a recruitment competition could not 'in itself be liable to dissuade candidates who have already sat a similar competition in another Member State from exercising their right to freedom of movement as workers' (para. 97).

[99] Case C–110/05 [2009] ECR I–519.   [100] Case C–518/06 [2009] ECR I–3491.

[101] Para. 56, emphasis added.   [102] Para. 66.   [103] Para. 68, emphasis added.

[104] J. Snell, 'The notion of market access: A concept or a slogan?' (2010) 47 *CMLRev.* 437.

[105] See, e.g., Poiares Maduro AG in Case C–446/03 *Marks & Spencer v. Halsey* [2005] ECR I–10837, para. 37, where he said national policies 'must not result in less favourable treatment being accorded to transnational situations than to purely national situations'.

[106] Case C–518/06 *Commission v. Italy (motor insurance)* [2009] ECR I–3491.

[107] Cf. Case C–518/06 *Commission v. Italy (motor insurance)* [2009] ECR I–3491 with Joined Cases C–544 and 545/03 *Mobistar SA v. Commune de Fleron* [2005] ECR I–7723.

[108] Some support for this view can be found in A. Rosas, '*Dassonville and Cassis de Dijon*' in M. Poiares Maduro and L. Azoulai (eds.), *The Past and Future of EU Law: The classics of EU Law revisited on the 50th anniversary of the Rome Treaty* (Oxford: Hart Publishing, 2009).

advantages).[109] Yet rules restricting exercise of a free movement right can have just as serious a consequence on free movement as the initial refusal of access.[110] This can be seen in *Steinhauser*,[111] where a German artist was permitted to work (access) but not to participate in a tendering process for the use of a boutique from which to sell his art works (exercise). The Court, rejecting the French argument that Article 49 TFEU applied only to conditions regulating *access*, said that 'The Treaty includes the right not only to take up activities as a self-employed person but also to pursue those activities in the broadest sense, including renting business premises.' The effect of this decision is now enshrined in the Services Directive 2006/123:[112] the directive applies to 'requirements which affect access to *or* the exercise of a service activity'.[113]

Given that it is often difficult to distinguish market access situations from those concerning exercise, the Court increasingly says that the national rules are 'restrictions' or 'obstacles' to free movement rather than hindering market access. We saw this in *Laval*, and can see it again in the *Motor Insurance* case, where the Court said 'the concept of restriction covers measures taken by a Member State which, although applicable without distinction, affect access to the market for undertakings from other Member States and thereby hinder intra-[Union] trade'.[114] In cases involving free movement of natural persons and citizens, the Court tends to abandon the (more commercial) market access language altogether, talking instead of how the national rule is liable to dissuade or deter an individual from exercising his right of free movement.[115]

(d) The convergence or unity thesis

One of the debates which has bedevilled the area of free movement is whether a single principle (e.g., non-discrimination or market access) should cover all four freedoms. The arguments in favour relate to the need for clarity, certainty, and consistency in interpretation,[116] particularly as an increasing number of cases raise issues affecting a number of freedoms (e.g., a restriction on advertising might engage both Article 34 TFEU on goods and Article 56 TFEU on services[117]).

---

[109] This is the view of Lenz AG in Case C–415/93 *Bosman* [1995] ECR I–4921, paras. 203 and 205. Cf. Alber AG in Case C–176/96 *Lehtonen* [2000] ECR I–2681, para. 48; and Fennelly AG's attempts in Case C–190/98 *Graf* [2000] ECR I–493 to reconcile the two.

[110] For a discussion on whether rules restricting market access and those restricting exercise of the freedoms are most serious, cf. Lenz AG in Case C–415/93 *Bosman* [1995] ECR I–4921, paras. 203 and 205 with Alber AG in Case C–176/96 *Lehtonen* [2000] ECR I–2681, para. 48.

[111] Case 197/84 *Steinhauser* v. *City of Biarritz* [1985] ECR 1819.   [112] [2006] OJ L376/26.

[113] 9th Recital, emphasis added. See also Art. 49(2) TFEU: 'Freedom of establishment shall include the right to *take up and pursue* activities as self-employed persons' (emphasis added).

[114] Para. 64.

[115] See, e.g., Case C–499/06 *Nerkowska* [2008] ECR I–3993: '31. With regard to the scope of Article [21(1) TFEU], the Court has already held that the opportunities offered by the Treaty in relation to freedom of movement cannot be fully effective if a national of a Member State can be deterred from availing himself of them by obstacles raised to his residence in the host Member State by legislation of his State of origin penalising the fact that he has used them ... 32. National legislation which places certain of the nationals of the Member State concerned at a disadvantage simply because they have exercised their freedom to move and to reside in another Member State is a restriction on the freedoms conferred by Article [21(1) TFEU] on every citizen of the Union.'

[116] A point recognized by Poiares Maduro AG in Joined Cases C–158 and 159/04 *Alfa Vita Vassilopoulos AE* [2006] ECR I–8135, para. 33.

[117] See, e.g., Joined Cases C–34–36/95 *Konsumentombudsmannen (KO)* v. *De Agostini (Svenska) Förlag AB and TV-Shop i Sverige AB* [1997] ECR I–3843.

On the other hand, there are significant differences between the freedoms, in particular those provisions relating to the movement of natural persons, where human rights have a more significant role to play than when, for example, free movement of goods are at stake. Further, there are differences between the freedoms in respect of which state has particular responsibility for regulation; in respect of free movement of goods and services, the principal regulator is the home state so any requirements imposed by the host state must take into account the controls already imposed by the home state. By contrast, in respect of free movement of workers and freedom of establishment, the principal regulator is the host state, which might suggest that there is more room for the host state to impose its requirements on the migrant.

The shift to the market access/restrictions test in respect of all the freedoms does suggest an increasing degree of convergence; the differences between the freedoms manifest themselves in respect of the crafting of the justifications, the role of fundamental human rights, and the Court's approach to proportionality. However, in concentrating on market access rather than discrimination as the basic test for establishing whether there is a breach of the Treaty, the Court has subtly altered the balance of power between the Union and the Member States. While a non-discrimination approach creates a space in which national regulators are free to act, untrammelled by Union law, the market access test has shifted the balance back in favour of the Union, giving the Court the power to scrutinize an ever-wider category of national measures for their compatibility with Union law.

1.3 Competitive Federalism

Both the non-discrimination and market access tests are premised on a *decentralized* model to market-building: Member States retain the freedom to regulate provided that they do not overstep the limits laid down by the Treaty (non-discrimination/market access). The effect of the EU rules on free movement of goods, persons, services, and capital is to place the different national systems into competition because those individuals or companies not satisfied with the political/legal/social environment in which they find themselves are free to move to another Member State which has a regime which suits them better. This freedom for individuals/capital to move has the effect of forcing the national systems to compete to produce the best rules to attract (or retain) valuable assets (capital and labour). This is known as competitive federalism or regulatory competition.[118]

For competitive federalism to function, two conditions need to be satisfied. First, the *federal* (central) authorities must lay down and enforce the rules giving goods, persons, and capital freedom to exit one Member State and enter another. Secondly, the *states* (the decentralized authorities) must remain free to regulate the production of goods and the qualifications of people according to their own standards so as to enable regulators to respond to the regulatory competition. The outcome of this process of regulatory competition should be to produce optimal, efficient, and innovative legislation (a race to the top) because state officials vie with one another to create increasingly attractive economic circumstances for their citizens, knowing that re-election depends upon their success.[119] Regulatory competition also promotes diversity and experimentation in the search for effective legal solutions by providing for comparative data to assist in regulatory reform. This reduces the risk of widespread adoption of flawed laws. This is the classic 'laboratory of democracy' theory,[120]

---

[118] This is based on Tiebout's famous 'pure theory' of fiscal federalism: C. Tiebout, 'A pure theory of local expenditure' (1956) 64(5) *Journal of Political Economy* 416.

[119] D. Tarullo, 'Federalism issues in the United States' in A. Castro, P. Méhaut, and J. Rubery (eds.), *International Integration and Labour Market Organisation* (London: Academic Press, 1992), 101.

[120] Tarullo, n. 119, 101.

which recognizes that competition is a dynamic process where trial and error is the best means of finding the optimal solution to complex problems.[121] Company law in the United States is often held up as an example of the success of regulatory competition. The American state of Delaware has been extremely successful in attracting companies to incorporate there,[122] and from this Delaware benefits from substantial incorporation fees. Some commentators attribute Delaware's success to its ability to offer the most suitable corporation laws,[123] which other states have tried to emulate by revising their acts along similar lines.

The model of competitive federalism, with an active role for state authorities (in shaping their laws to meet the demands of consumers) and a limited role for the central authorities (ensuring freedom of movement) influenced the thinking of the drafters of the Treaty of Rome. The original EEC Treaty owed much to the ordo-liberal school, which originated in Freiburg in the 1930s.[124] In simple terms, ordo-liberalists believed that the Constitution should protect economic freedoms (freedom of movement) from public (and private) intervention in the same way as it protects civil and political rights, and this would guarantee individual freedom.[125] Central to their idea was the concept of *Ordnungspolitik*, according to which individual government decisions should both flow from, and be constrained by, the principles embedded in an economic constitution.

However, some commentators say that the analogies between the EU Treaties and an economic constitution should not be pushed too far.[126] For example, Chalmers argues that ordo-liberalism assumes too rigid and too discrete a separation of the market from other policies.[127] Indeed, in the EU it is simply not possible to disentangle the four freedoms from social, consumer, health, and environmental policies. This is recognized in the TFEU itself, which provides express grounds for Member States to derogate from individual rights for reasons connected with wider public interests such as public health and public policy. These derogations have been supplemented by an ever-expanding range of public-interest or 'mandatory' requirements developed by the Court. Together they reflect a 'social market' tradition whereby state intervention in the operation of the markets is accepted and expected, not only to address market failures but also to secure social

---

[121] R. Van den Bergh, 'The subsidiarity principle in European Community law: Some insights from law and economics' (1994) 1 *Maastricht Journal of European and Comparative Law* 337, citing F. A. von Hayek, 'Competition as a discovery process' in his *New Studies in Philosophy, Politics, Economics and the History of Ideas* (Chicago, Ill.: University of Chicago Press, 1978), 149.

[122] Over 40 per cent of New York Stock Exchange-listed companies, and over 50 per cent of Fortune 500 companies, are incorporated in Delaware: D. Charny, 'Competition among jurisdictions in formulating corporate law rules: An American perspective on the "race to the bottom" in the European Communities' (1991) 32 *Harvard International Law Journal* 422, 428.

[123] See, e.g., Charny, n. 122, 431–2; R. Romano, 'Law as a product: Some pieces of the incorporation puzzle' (1985) 1 *J.L. Econ & Org.* 225, 257–8. Romano explains the advantages offered by Delaware: it offers comprehensive statutes and case law; the continuity in and small size of Delaware's Courts of Chancery provide an experienced judiciary specialized in corporate matters; Delaware's large population of corporations quickly generates legal controversies and thereby new precedents and rules; Delaware's reliance on incorporation fees binds Delaware to maintaining the stability and serviceability of its system.

[124] D. Chalmers, 'The single market: From prima donna to journeyman' in J. Shaw and G. More (eds.), *New Legal Dynamics of European Union* (Oxford: OUP, 1995), 56.

[125] D. Gerber, 'Constitutionalizing the economy: German neo-liberalism, competition law and the "New Europe"' (1994) 42 *American Journal of Comparative Law* 25, 45–6.

[126] N. Reich, 'The November Revolution of the Court of Justice: *Keck, Meng* and *Audi* revisited' (1994) 31 *CMLRev.* 459.

[127] Chalmers, n. 124, 66.

values which are seen as public goods in their own right. Some of these ideas are now reflected in Article 3(3) TEU, which identifies the establishment of a 'highly competitive social market economy' as one of the aims of the Union.[128]

These derogations and public-interest requirements do, however, themselves create considerable barriers to trade which can be addressed only through centralized regulation, and the Treaty envisaged this too, by providing the EU with powers to harmonize conflicting national laws (initially Article 100 EEC (now Article 115 TFEU) on the establishment and functioning of the common market and Article 235 EEC (now Article 352 TFEU), the residual legal basis).

2. THE CENTRALIZED MODEL

The need to have centralized standards is largely premised on market failure. If regulatory competition worked effectively Member States would compete against each other for the best laws. In these circumstances the host state would not need to invoke the public-health derogation or the consumer protection mandatory requirement because the goods/services produced in the home state would already be of a very high standard. Yet, in order to ensure successful regulatory competition, certain conditions must be satisfied:[129] there must be full mobility of people and resources at little or no cost; migrants must have full knowledge of each jurisdiction's revenue and expenditure patterns; and there must be a wide choice of destination jurisdictions to enable citizens to make meaningful decisions about migration. In reality these conditions are never met. For individuals the chances of exit are slim because they are unlikely to leave their own jurisdiction for linguistic, cultural, financial, or personal reasons; and capital (direct investment in business operations) is unlikely to leave unless a variety of factors (market proximity, transport costs, infrastructure levels, labour costs, and productivity levels) justify the move. Even if these conditions could be met, state legislation is often insufficiently responsive to the needs of its consumers. This creates the risk that the type of regulatory competition which emerges is undesirable.

The following example demonstrates this. The UK knows that in practice individuals are less mobile than capital and so it decides to gain a competitive advantage in the single market by reducing employment protection or environmental standards in order to remain attractive to capital.[130] While such a strategy might have short-term benefits (e.g., job creation or at least job retention) it undermines the longer-term interests of the citizenry as a whole (e.g., lower quality jobs and an inferior environment). Faced with such deregulation by the UK, Portugal—which risks losing capital and thus jobs to the UK—relaxes its own standards. The UK responds by lowering its standards still further and a race to the bottom ensues, with the UK and Portugal now competing on the basis of low standards.

Some commentators argue that this is the true explanation for what is actually happening in Delaware: its success in attracting incorporation is due to its victory not in a race to the top but in a race to the bottom. As Cary graphically puts it, Delaware, 'a pygmy among the 50 States prescribes, interprets, and indeed denigrates national corporate policy as an

---

[128] Note also the possible downgrading of the objective of ensuring that competition is not distorted by its removal from the list of objectives in Art. 3 TEU and its inclusion in Protocol No. 27.

[129] For the literature on the economics of federalism, see Tiebout, n. 118; F. Easterbrook, 'Antitrust and the economics of federalism' (1983) 26 *Journal of Law and Economics* 23, 34.

[130] This point was expressly recognized by Poiares Maduro AG in Case C–438/05 *Viking* [2007] ECR I–10779, para. 70.

incentive to encourage incorporation within its borders, thereby increasing its revenue'.[131] While there is much controversy about the likelihood of EU states engaging in a full-blown race to the bottom,[132] there is a perception that it may happen and that steps need to be taken by the central bodies to combat it. This is what Cary called for in the US—the enactment of a *Federal* Corporate Uniformity Act, allowing companies to incorporate in the jurisdiction of their own choosing but removing much of the incentive to organize in Delaware or its rival states.[133]

Centralization offers advantages in terms of economies of scale by establishing a single set of rules applying to a broad class of transactions. It also reduces the costs that stem from evasion, through forum shopping, externalization, and extraterritoriality.[134] On the other hand, it raises difficulties, both legal (e.g., does the central body have the power to act (competence); should it act (subsidiarity); and, if so, to what extent (proportionality)?) and practical (e.g., should the harmonized standard represent an arithmetical mean of existing national measures or the optimal solution?).[135] It also creates political problems: it does not leave room for national diversity (i.e., the result would be one centrally regulated standard, say, for an EU sausage, replacing hundreds of different regional varieties of sausage); it loses the benefits associated with local accountability; and it may lead to 'market freezing', reducing legislative innovation and experimentation. It also assumes a developed system of enforcement capable of preventing more complex forms of evasion. These issues are considered in detail in Chapter 15.

F. CONCLUSIONS

The driving force behind the European Union is, and has always been, the consolidation of a post-war system of inter-state cooperation and integration that would make pan-European armed conflict inconceivable. This has been promoted through a vigorous emphasis on free trade, with all the economic benefits this entails, albeit not to the exclusion of all other interests. As we have seen, the TFEU allows Member States to derogate from the rules of free trade where overriding national interests are at stake.[136] It also makes provision for structural funds to help those who are losers in the integration process, in particular the European regional development fund and the European social fund.[137] And as the EU's self-perception changed from a European *Economic* Community to a European Union, so its tasks and objectives have been broadened to take into account a wider range of policies which may complement, but may also obstruct, free trade. For example, Article 3 TEU identifies a number of tasks for the Union which were not found in the original Treaty of Rome including full employment and social progress, equality between men and women, environmental protection, and combating social exclusion and discrimination. The solidarity between citizens of the EU envisaged by these measures and the

[131] W. Cary, 'Federalism and corporate law: Reflections upon Delaware' (1974) 83 *Yale Law Journal* 663, 701.

[132] C. Barnard, 'Social dumping revisited: Lessons from Delaware' (2000) 25 *ELRev.* 57.

[133] Cary, n. 131, 701.

[134] J. Trachtman, 'International regulatory competition: Externalization and jurisdiction' (1993) 34 *Harvard International Law Journal* 47.

[135] A. Dashwood, 'Hastening slowly' in H. Wallace, W. Wallace, and C. Webb (eds.), *Policy Making in the European Community* (Chichester: Wiley, 1983), 178.

[136] See, e.g., Arts. 36, 45(3), and 52 TFEU considered in Chs. 6 and 12.

[137] Reg. 1083/2006 ([2006] OJ L210/25) laying down general provisions on the European Regional Development Fund, the European Social Fund, and the Cohesion Fund. See generally J. Scott, *Development Dilemmas in the European Community: Rethinking regional development policy* (Buckingham: Open University Press, 1995).

state/federal intervention they necessitate are a far cry from an ordo-liberal/neo-liberal agenda which underpinned the Treaty of Rome.

This change in orientation can be seen in the simple statement by the Court in *Deutsche Post*,[138] a case on Article 157 TFEU on equal pay. Originally, Article 157 TFEU was included in the EEC Treaty as a market-making measure. It was intended to stop French industry, which had to respect the principle of equal pay for men and women, from losing out to companies established in other states (such as Italy) where the principle of equal pay was not respected. This economic function of Article 157 TFEU was recognized by the Court in some of its earliest case law.[139] Yet by the time the Court decided *Deutsche Post* in 2000 the change in approach was clear. The Court said that 'the economic aim pursued by Article [157 TFEU]..., namely the elimination of distortions of competition between undertakings established in different Member States, is *secondary* to the social aim pursued by the same provision, which constitutes the expression of a fundamental human right'.[140] This is significant as it marks an important shift in emphasis—from a pure market-based, neo-liberal vision premised on deregulation, efficiency, and the assumption of formal equality between individuals—to one which recognizes the need to accommodate and indeed value a wider range of interests. This change is encapsulated by the reference introduced by the Lisbon Treaty in Article 3(3) TEU to a 'highly competitive *social market* economy' (emphasis added). This observation has already prompted Advocate General Cruz Villalón in *Santos Palhota* to suggest that the pre-Lisbon orthodoxy needs to be reconsidered.[141]

Since the 1970s the Court has tried to balance market rights with traditional civil, political, and social rights. This approach has now been legitimized by the adoption of the Charter of Fundamental Rights in 2000, now incorporated by reference into the Treaties.[142] This rights-based approach has increasingly shaped the contours of the Court's case law, particularly in the field of citizens' rights.[143] At a time when global movements are mobilizing forces against free trade, which they see as both wasteful to sustainable resources and producing inequality (where the rich—both people and regions—do better out of free trade than the poor),[144] the EU would find itself significantly out of step with its citizens if it did not recognize broader social and environmental interests.[145] While this book focuses on the four freedoms, it also considers how the free-trade imperative is counterbalanced by these broader interests. It begins by considering the free movement of goods. Chapter 2 provides an introduction to the different Treaty provisions on goods, and places them in the broader context of the WTO in which the EU must operate.

---

[138] Joined Cases C–270 and 271/97 *Deutsche Post* v. *Sievers* [2000] ECR I–929.

[139] Case 43/75 *Defrenne* v. *Sabena II* [1976] ECR 455.

[140] Para. 57, emphasis added. See also Case C–438/05 *Viking* [2007] ECR I–10779, para. 79: 'Since the [Union] has thus not only an economic but also a social purpose, the rights under the provisions of the Treaty on the free movement of goods, persons, services and capital must be balanced against the objective pursued by social policy.'

[141] Case C–515/08 [2010] ECR I–9133, paras. 51–53. See also the Monti Report, 'A new strategy for the simple market', 9 May 2010. See also C. Joerges and F. Rödi, 'The "Social Market Economy" as Europe's Social Model', EUI Workup Paper 2004/8.

[142] Art. 6(1) TEU.

[143] Case C–60/00 *Mary Carpenter* v. *Secretary of State for the Home Department* [2002] ECR I–6279; Case C–413/99 *Baumbast and R.* v. *Secretary of State for the Home Department* [2002] ECR I–7091. Cf. the case law considered in Ch. 10.

[144] See further, e.g., E. Bircham and J. Charlton (eds.), *Anti-Capitalism: A guide to the movement* (London: Bookmarks Publications, 2001); Friends of the Earth, 'What's wrong with world trade?', <http://www.foe.co.uk/resource/briefings/wrong_with_world_trade.pdf>. For a more academic account, see H. Daly and J. Cobb, *For the Common Good: Redirecting the economy toward community, the environment, and a sustainable future*, 2nd edn (Boston, Mass.: Beacon Press, 1994).

[145] Case C–271/08 *Commission* v. *Germany (occupational pensions)* [2010] ECR I–7091; Case C–368/10 *Commission* v. *The Netherlands (fair trade labels)* EU:C:2012:284.

FURTHER READING

Some theory

B. Balassa, *The Theory of Economic Integration* (London: Allen & Unwin, 1961).

R. Baldwin and C. Wylosz, *The Economics of European Integration*, 4th edn (Maidenhead: McGraw Hill, 2012).

A. El-Agraa, *The Economics of the European Community*, 4th edn (Hemel Hempstead: Harvester Wheatsheaf, 1994).

W. Molle, *The Economics of European Integration*, 5th edn (Aldershot: Dartmouth, 2006).

M. Pollack, 'Theorizing EU policy-making' in H. Wallace, M. Pollack, and A. Young (eds.), *Policy-Making in the European Union*, 6th edn (Oxford: OUP, 2010).

B. Rosamond, *Theories of European Integration* (Basingstoke: Palgrave, 2000).

The creation of the single market

P. Cecchini, *The European Challenge 1992* (Aldershot: Wildwood House, 1988), 4.

P. Craig, 'The evolution of the single market' in C. Barnard and J. Scott (eds.), *The Law of the Single European Market* (Oxford: Hart Publishing, 2002).

P. Craig, 'Integration, democracy and legitimacy' in P. Craig and G. de Búrca (eds.), *The Evolution of EU Law*, 2nd edn (Oxford: OUP, 2011).

J. De Zwann, 'The Single European Act: Conclusion of a unique document' (1986) 23 *CMLRev.* 747.

M. Egan, 'Single market' in E. Jones, A. Menon, and S. Weatherill (eds.), *The Oxford Handbook of the European Union* (Oxford: OUP, 2012).

M. Van Empel, 'The 1992 programme: Interaction between legislation and judiciary' [1992/2] *LIEI* 1.

A. Young, 'The single market: Deregulation, reregulation and integration' in H. Wallace, M. Pollack, and A. Young (eds.), *Policy-Making in the European Union*, 6th edn (Oxford: OUP, 2010).

Competitive federalism

C. Barnard and S. Deakin, 'Market access and regulatory competition' in C. Barnard and J. Scott (eds.), *The Legal Foundations of the Single Market: Unpacking the premises* (Oxford: Hart Publishing, 2002).

D. Fischel, 'The "race to the bottom" revisited: Reflections on recent developments in Delaware's corporation law' (1982) 77 *Northwestern University Law Review* 913.

J. Sun and J. Pelkmans, 'Regulatory competition in the single market' (1995) 33 *JCMS* 67.

The market access test

J. Snell, 'The notion of market access: A concept or a slogan?' (2010) 47 *CMLRev.* 437.

What sort of constitution does the EU have?

M. Streit and W. Mussler, 'The economic constitution of the European Community: From "Rome" to "Maastricht"' (1995) 1 *ELJ* 5.

PART II
FREE MOVEMENT
OF GOODS

2

INTRODUCTION TO THE FREE MOVEMENT OF GOODS

A. INTRODUCTION

For the European Commission, 'free movement of goods is one of the success stories of the European project'.[1] This chapter is intended to provide an overview of the rules on free movement of goods, looking at how the various provisions interrelate both within the EU and on the wider international scene.

The core of the rules on goods can be found in Article 28 TFEU:

> The Union shall comprise a *customs union* which shall cover all trade in goods and which shall involve the prohibition between Member States of customs duties on imports and exports and of all charges having equivalent effect, and the adoption of a common customs tariff in their relations with third countries.[2]

From this we can see that the free movement of goods has an internal and external dimension: goods originating *within* the EU enjoy the rights of free movement between the Member States, while goods originating *outside* the EU enjoy free movement only once they have paid the common customs tariff (CCT), if one is due.

---

[1] European Commission, *Free Movement of Goods: Guide to the application of Treaty provisions governing free movement of goods (Articles 28–30 EC [Articles 34–6 TFEU])* (the 'Commission guide'), SEC(2009) 673, 7.

[2] Emphasis added.

B. THE SCOPE OF THE PROVISIONS ON GOODS

For the Treaty provisions on goods to be engaged three conditions need to be satisfied:

(1) the product at issue must be considered a good

(2) it must be used in cross-border trade between Member States of the EU and EEA

(3) the person to whom the provision is being applied must be an addressee of the Treaty.

We shall examine these conditions in turn.

1. THE DEFINITION OF GOODS

Goods are defined as products which 'can be valued in money and which are capable, as such, of forming the subject of commercial transactions'.[3] As Advocate General Fennelly put it in *Jägerskiöld*,[4] goods 'possess tangible physical characteristics'. So the Court has found products as diverse as paintings and other works of art,[5] petroleum products,[6] animals,[7] coins which are no longer legal tender,[8] and waste (whether recyclable or not, even though it has no market value)[9] to constitute goods. More surprisingly, it has found electricity to be a good,[10] by reference to its treatment as goods in Union law and in the laws of the Member States as well as in the Union's tariff nomenclature. Goods can be imported either for commercial or personal use.[11]

Where goods are merely ancillary to the main activity, then other provisions of the TFEU will apply. Therefore, in *Schindler*[12] the Court said that the organization of lotteries did not constitute an activity relating to 'goods', even though lotteries necessarily involved the distribution of advertising material and tickets. Because the main activity was a service, the Treaty provisions on services (Articles 56 TFEU *et seq.*) applied instead.[13] In *Weigel*,[14] a case concerning a German couple moving to Austria for work, the Court found that the provisions of Article 45 TFEU on free movement of workers applied even

---

[3] Case 7/68 *Commission* v. *Italy (the art treasures case)* [1968] ECR 423, 428–9.

[4] Case C–97/98 *Jägerskiöld* v. *Gustafsson* [1999] ECR I–7319, para. 20.

[5] Case C–97/98 *Jägerskiöld* [1999] ECR I–7319, para. 20.

[6] Case 72/83 *Campus Oil Ltd* v. *Minister for Industry and Energy* [1984] ECR 2727, para. 17. As the Court explained, such goods could not be exempted from the Treaty just because of their importance for the life or the economy of a Member State.

[7] Case C–67/97 *Bluhme* [1998] ECR I–8033.

[8] Case 7/78 *Thompson* [1978] ECR 2247. Cf. donations in kind, which are not goods: Case C–318/07 *Persche* [2009] ECR I–359, para. 29.

[9] Case C–2/90 *Commission* v. *Belgium* [1992] ECR I–4431, para. 28; Case C–221/06 *Stadtgemeinde Frohnleiten* v. *Bundesminister für Land- und Forstwirtschaft, Umwelt und Wasserwirtschaft* [2007] ECR I–9643, paras. 36–8.

[10] Case C–393/92 *Almelo* v. *Energi bedriff Ijsselmij* [1994] ECR I–1477, para. 28; Case C–158/94 *Commission* v. *Italy (electricity)* [1997] ECR I–5789, para. 17.

[11] Case 218/87 *Schumacher* [1989] ECR 617.

[12] Case C–275/92 *Customs Excise* v. *Schindler* [1994] ECR I–1039. See also Case C–97/98 *Jägerskiöld* v. *Gustafsson* [1999] ECR I–7319: while fish are goods, fishing rights and angling permits derived from them did not constitute 'goods'; the services provisions applied instead. Cf. Case C–124/97 *Läärä* v. *Kihlakunnansyyttäjä* [1999] ECR I–6067, where the Court said that slot machines constituted goods.

[13] Case C–452/04 *Fidium Finanz* [2006] ECR I–9521, para. 32 made clear that, contrary to the apparent wording of Art. 57 TFEU which suggests that services are a residual category, Art. 57 TFEU does not establish any order of priority between free movement of services and the other freedoms.

[14] Case C–387/01 [2004] ECR I–4981.

though the couple were contesting the legality of the tax payable on registering their car in Austria. Where it is not possible to detect the 'main focal point of the national measure',[15] the Court will apply the goods provisions together with, say, the provisions on services.[16]

However, unlike the Treaty provisions on persons and services, the Court has not expressly required that the exchange of the goods needs to form part of an economic activity.[17] In this way, free movement of goods has more in common with free movement of capital: the Court assumes a movement of goods to be economic on condition that it is not 'provided for nothing'.[18]

2. THE TERRITORIAL ELEMENT

For any of the Treaty provisions on goods to apply there must be a cross-border element, i.e., there must be trade between Member States. The term 'Member States' covers the members of the EU,[19] together with the states of the EEA. The cross-border element is satisfied even when the goods are merely transiting the territory.[20] Generally, where there is no movement of goods between states then Union law does not apply.[21] This means that Member States can treat domestically produced goods less favourably than imports. This is known as the principle of reverse discrimination. As we shall see, goods with an EU origin, together with goods originally manufactured outside the EU which are in 'free circulation' in the EU, enjoy the right of free movement of goods.

3. ADDRESSEES OF THE TREATY PROVISIONS

According to the TFEU, the provisions on goods apply to the Member States. The phrase 'state' is broadly construed to include central and local government,[22] as well as other arms of government in whatever capacity they are acting (e.g., legislative, or executive).[23] In addition, as we shall see in Chapter 4, the Treaty provisions on goods have also been deemed to apply to professional regulatory bodies and private bodies supported by the state whether through finance or other forms of supervision.[24] The corollary of this is that the Treaty provisions on goods do not appear to apply to private parties acting in a purely private capacity. In other words, the goods provisions have vertical but not horizontal direct effect.[25]

---

[15] Commission guide, n. 1, 47.

[16] Joined Cases C–34–36/95 *Konsumentombudsmannen (KO)* v. *De Agostini (Svenska) Förlag AB and TV-Shop i Sverige AB* [1997] ECR I–3843, noted by J. Stuyck (1997) 34 *CMLRev.* 1445, 1465.

[17] O. Odudu, 'Economic activity as a limit to Community law' in C. Barnard and O. Odudu (eds.), *The Outer Limits of European Union Law* (Oxford: Hart Publishing, 2009), 238–9.

[18] See by analogy Case C–301/14 *Pfotenhilfe-Ungarn eV* v. *Ministerium für Energiewende* EU:C:2015:793, paras. 29–31.

[19] It also applies to European territories for whose external relations a Member State is responsible and to overseas territories dependent on or otherwise associated with a Member State. For full details see Annex B to the Commission guide, see n. 1.

[20] Case C–320/03 *Commission* v. *Austria* [2005] ECR I–9871, para. 65.

[21] Cf. the position under Art. 30 TFEU considered in Ch. 3.

[22] Joined Cases C–1 and 176/90 *Aragonesa de Publicidad Exterior SA* v. *Departmento de Sanidad y Seguridad Social de la Generalitat de Cataluña* [1991] ECR I–4151, para. 8. See also Case 45/87 *Commission* v. *Ireland (Dundalk Water)* [1988] ECR 4929.

[23] See, e.g., Case C–5/94 *R.* v. *MAFF, ex p. Hedley Lomas (Ireland) Ltd* [1996] ECR I–2553.

[24] See, e.g., Case 249/81 *Commission* v. *Ireland ('Buy Irish' campaign)* [1982] ECR 4005.

[25] Cf. the position in the field of free movement of persons, considered in Ch. 7.

In contrast to the dormant commerce clause in the US Constitution,[26] the nearest equivalent to the EU's free movement provisions, the Treaty provisions on goods also apply to the measures adopted by the Union institutions. However, given the broad margin of discretion left to the Union legislature, the standard set is higher: Union institutions will not be liable unless the measure is manifestly inappropriate to the objective pursued.[27]

Having established the meaning of the term goods, the aim of this chapter is to present an overview of the TFEU's rules relating to goods and briefly explain how the provisions interrelate.

C. THE INTERNAL DIMENSION: THE RULES ON FREE MOVEMENT OF GOODS

Goods originating in one EU Member State have the right to be exported from that state under Article 35 TFEU and the right to be imported into another Member State under Article 34 TFEU (see the dark arrow in the example in fig. 2.1). Articles 34–5 TFEU prohibit both quantitative restrictions (such as quotas) on imports and exports and measures having equivalent effect to quantitative restrictions (MEEs). These MEEs concern other barriers to trade, such as national rules on packaging and labelling.

Both Articles 34 and 35 TFEU are subject to the exhaustive list of derogations found in Article 36 TFEU. These derogations concern matters such as public policy, public security, and health, and can be invoked by the home or host state to justify a refusal to allow the import or export of particular goods. While cases where Member States prevent exports are rare, host states are willing to invoke Article 36 TFEU to try to keep imported goods out of their country, given that imports may well threaten the viability of national production. For this reason, the Court has adopted a narrow interpretation of the derogations listed in Article 36 TFEU. If the Court does recognize that there is a public interest at stake, it requires that any action taken by the Member State be proportionate.

Where a Member State successfully invokes one of the express derogations, it creates a barrier to inter-state trade which can be eliminated through Union harmonization. As we saw in Chapter 1, the power to harmonize is provided by a number of legal bases contained in the Treaty, most notably Articles 114–15 TFEU, and 352 TFEU. If the Union measure exhaustively harmonizes the field, Member States can no longer rely on the Article 36 TFEU derogations. If the measure only partly harmonizes the area, the national legislation in the unharmonized area is still subject to scrutiny under Articles 34–6 TFEU, as the jam and chocolate case study (4.1) demonstrates in Chapter 4.

While Articles 34–6 TFEU address 'non-fiscal' or 'non-tariff' barriers to trade, Articles 28–30 TFEU and Article 110 TFEU concern 'fiscal' or 'tariff' barriers to trade.[28]

---

[26] Art. 1, section 8, cl. 3 of the US Constitution provides: 'The Congress shall have Power ... to regulate Commerce with foreign Nations, and among the several States'. This 'Commerce Clause' gives the federal government the power to *legislate* in respect of commerce (very broadly defined). However, the Supreme Court has long read into the commerce clause the negative power (the so-called 'dormant' or 'negative' commerce clause) to restrict 'permissible state regulation of interstate commerce' (*Wyoming* v. *Oklahoma* 502 US 437, 454–5 (1992)).

[27] Joined Cases C–154 and 155/04 *Alliance for Natural Health* [2005] ECR I–6451, paras. 47 and 52.

[28] These Treaty provisions are mutually exclusive. As the Court said in Case 74/76 *Ianelli & Volpi SpA* v. *Ditta Paolo Meroni* [1977] ECR 557: 'However wide the field of application of Article [34 TFEU] may be, it nevertheless does not include obstacles to trade covered by other provisions of the Treaty ... Thus obstacles which are of a fiscal nature or have equivalent effect ... do not fall within the prohibition in Article [34 TFEU].' See also Joined Cases C–34–38/01 *Enirisorse SpA* v. *Ministero delle Finanze* [2003] ECR I–14243, para. 58.

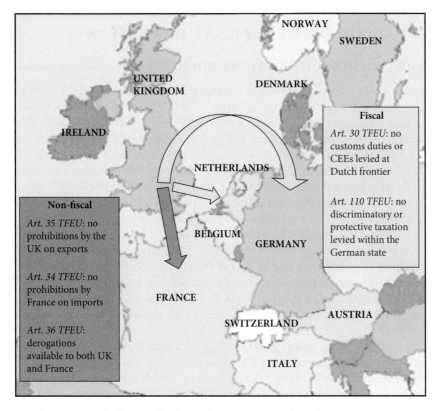

Fig. 2.1 Summary of the 'internal' rules on free movement of goods

Source: Map sourced and adapted from the European Commission. All text added by the author.

There is no equivalent to the express derogations found in Article 36 TFEU in respect of Articles 30 and 110 TFEU (see fiscal box in fig. 2.1). Article 30, which prohibits customs duties and CEEs, concerns charges which are levied at the *frontier* of the state. By contrast, Article 110 TFEU concerns charges which are levied *internally* within the state on imported, exported, and domestic products (see light arrows in fig. 2.1). While Article 30 TFEU contains an absolute prohibition on customs duties and CEEs, Article 110 TFEU prohibits only discriminatory or protectionist taxation.[29] In other words, Article 110 TFEU allows Member States to tax a product, provided the tax does not discriminate against foreign goods and is not protectionist of national production, whereas Article 30 TFEU prohibits the state from levying any charge whatsoever. For this reason Member States prefer their fiscal regime to be considered under Article 110 TFEU. Nevertheless, the combined effect of Articles 30 and 110 TFEU is to prevent host states from making imported goods more expensive than domestic goods by imposing an additional financial burden on the imports, thereby removing their competitive advantage.[30]

---

[29] Joined Cases C–441 and 442/98 *Kapniki Michaïlidis AE* v. *Idryma Kinonikon Asfaliseon (IKA)* [2000] ECR I–7145, para. 22.

[30] Case 252/86 *Bergandi* [1988] ECR 1343, para. 24.

D. THE EXTERNAL DIMENSION

1. THE COMMON COMMERCIAL POLICY

As Article 28 TFEU makes clear, a key component of the external dimension of the Customs Union (CU) is the Common Customs Tariff (CCT), which in turn forms part of the EU's Common Commercial Policy (CCP).[31] The CCT demonstrates an obvious distinction between the internal and external dimensions of EU trade policy. While Article 30 TFEU prohibits tariffs (customs duties) on goods crossing an internal frontier, tariffs are permitted at the EU's external frontier.[32] This distinction between the internal and external dimensions of the CU was emphasized in *Bouhelier*,[33] where the Court said that the characteristic feature of intra-Union relations was a complete liberalization of trade, as a result of the abolition of all obstacles to imports and exports, but that such provisions could not be transposed to relations with non-member countries. In a similar vein, the Court said in *EMI*[34] that the Treaty provisions on the CCP did not lay down any obligation on the part of the Member States to extend the binding principles governing the free movement of goods between Member States to trade with third countries. As the Court explained in *Polydor*,[35] this is because the aim of the EU Treaty is to create a single market. Agreements with third countries do not have the same objectives.

Once 'third country' goods (i.e., goods from a non-Member State) have legally entered the EU, after paying the CCT where necessary, the situation changes. The goods are described as being in 'free circulation', which means that they now benefit from the same rights as goods originating in the EU. However, the CCP is more than just the CCT. As Article 207(1) TFEU explains, it also covers 'the conclusion of tariff and trade agreements, and the commercial aspects of intellectual property ... the achievement of uniformity in measures of liberalization, export policy and measures to protect trade such as those to be taken in the event of dumping or subsidies'. Article 207(2) TFEU gives the European Parliament and Council power, acting by means of the ordinary legislative procedure, to adopt measures defining the framework for implementing the CCP. The Union has therefore adopted regulations concerning tariffs; most notably Council Regulation 2913/92[36] on the Common Customs Code, which was repealed and replaced by the Union Customs Code (UCC) in Regulation 952/2013.[37] It has also enacted measures concerning non-tariff barriers to external trade: Regulation 2015/479[38] and Regulation 2015/478[39] respectively concern freedom to export and import without quantitative restrictions. In addition, the Council has adopted defensive measures designed to protect Union

---

[31] Further details of the CCP can be found on the Online Resource Centre accompanying this book.

[32] Case 70/77 *Simmenthal SpA v. Amministrazione delle Finanze dello Stato* [1978] ECR 1453, para. 2.

[33] Case 225/78 *Procureur de la République de Besançon v. Bouhelier* [1979] ECR 3151, para. 6.

[34] Case 51/75 *EMI Records Ltd v. CBS United Kingdom Ltd* [1976] ECR 811, para. 17.

[35] Case 270/80 *Polydor Ltd and RSO Records Inc. v. Harlequin Records Shops Ltd and Simons Records Ltd* [1982] ECR 329, paras. 16–18.

[36] [1992] OJ L302/1 as amended.   [37] [2013] OJ L269/1.   [38] [2015] OJ L83/34.

[39] [2015] OJ L83/16. This regulation applies to states which are members of the World Trade Organization (WTO).

industry, in particular the regulations combating dumping by third-country importers[40] and subsidies by third-country governments.[41]

2. THE EFFECT OF THE WTO

While this book will focus primarily on the internal dimension to trade and, to a more limited extent, on the EU's external trade policy, it is important to see the EU's approach to trade rules against the broader international background, in particular the World Trade Organization (WTO), the successor to the General Agreement on Tariffs and Trade (GATT) 1947. The WTO was set up as a result of the Uruguay Round of trade negotiations (1986–94).[42] The WTO, itself established by a charter,[43] administers the Understanding on Rules and Procedures Governing the Settlement of Disputes (Annex 2) and the Trade Policy Review Mechanism (Annex 3). Its objective is to 'facilitate the implementation, administration and operation, and further the objectives' of the WTO Agreement and the Multilateral Trade Agreements.[44]

The Uruguay Round also led to the conclusion of a number of multilateral agreements (agreements between all the parties)[45] and plurilateral agreements (agreements between certain parties). For our purposes, the three most important multilateral agreements concern:

- trade in goods (GATT 1994, including GATT 1947) (Annex 1A)
- trade in services (GATS) (Annex 1B)
- Trade-Related Aspects of Intellectual Property Rights (TRIPS) (Annex 1C).

GATT 1947,[46] and now the WTO, have played a significant role in shaping the key trade provisions of the EU Treaty. For example, the national treatment clause in Article III (which prohibits discriminatory internal taxation and regulation) and Article XI (which prohibits quantitative restrictions on imports and exports)[47] are reflected in Articles 110, 34, and 35 TFEU, while Article VIII (on fees and formalities connected with importation and exportation) was incorporated into the notion of charges having equivalent effect under Article 30 TFEU. Much of the wording from Article XX on general exceptions was borrowed verbatim by the Article 36 TFEU derogations.[48] In addition, Article VI (which permits the imposition of anti-dumping and any countervailing duties)[49] and Article XIX

---

[40] Council Reg. 1225/2009 on protection against dumped imports from countries not members of the European [Union] ([2009] OJ L343/51).

[41] Council Reg. (EC) No. 597/2009 on protection against subsidised imports from countries not members of the European Union ([2009] OJ L188/93).

[42] The full text of these agreements can be found at <http://www.wto.org/english/docs_e/legal_e/final_e.htm> and World Trade Organization, *The Legal Texts: The results of the Uruguay Round of multilateral trade negotiations* (Cambridge: CUP, 1999).

[43] Properly known as the Agreement establishing the World Trade Organization, discussed in J. Jackson, *The World Trade Organization: Constitution and jurisprudence* (London: RIIA, 1998), Ch. 3.

[44] Art. III.1.   [45] Art. II.2.

[46] The EU has been represented in GATT since the Dillon Round of 1960–1. As a result of the Kennedy Round negotiations between 1964 and 1967, which achieved substantial cuts in tariff rates (the Protocol giving effect to these tariff cuts was ratified by Council Dec. 411/68 ([1968] OJ L305/2)), the Union was able to introduce the CCT 18 months early. With the CCT in place the Union has replaced the Member States in respect of the obligations imposed by GATT.

[47] See also Art. XI.

[48] Art. 345 TFEU on national security and trade in arms draws directly on Art. XXI of GATT.

[49] The details of this Article are fleshed out by the Agreement on Implementation of Art. VI (anti-dumping) and the Agreement on Subsidies and Countervailing Measures.

(on emergency action on imports of particular products) directly influenced the Union regimes on dumping, subsidies, and safeguards.[50]

The key provision of the GATT is the Most-Favoured Nation (MFN) clause contained in Article I.1. This provides that:

> any advantage, favour, privilege or immunity granted by any contracting party to any product originating in or destined for any other country shall be accorded immediately and unconditionally to the like product originating in or destined for the territories of all other contracting parties.

This provision, also known as the external non-discrimination principle, means that if, in the course of trade negotiations, State A agrees to reduce the tariff on widgets from 10 per cent to 5 per cent provided that State B removes the tariffs on gadgets altogether, then all other contracting states will gain the benefit of a 5 per cent tariff on widgets when imported into State A and a zero tariff on gadgets when imported into State B. However, in a Free Trade Area (FTA) and CU, where there are no tariffs between the states, the effect of the application of the MFN clause would be to apply this benefit to all other WTO members. This would not be the intention of the members of the FTA or CU. For this reason Article XXIV of GATT[51] contains an important exception to the MFN clause. It allows for the creation of CUs and FTAs to which the MFN principle does not apply, provided that certain conditions are satisfied. FTAs and CUs therefore achieve a high degree of trade liberalization between the parties at the expense of differential treatment of their trading partners.[52]

The rationale for the acceptance of such arrangements is based on the theory that the benefits of greater liberalization between some countries will outweigh the discriminatory effects of these preferential agreements on non-parties.[53] This reasoning was encapsulated in Article XXIV.4, which provides:

> The contracting parties recognise the desirability of increasing free trade by the development, through voluntary agreements, of closer integration between the economies of the countries parties to such agreements. They also recognise that the purpose of a customs union or of a free trade area should be to facilitate trade between the constituent territories and not to raise barriers to the trade of other contracting parties with such territories.

Although CUs derogate from the MFN clause, the Member States *and* the European Union continue to be bound by the provisions of the WTO. As the Court noted in *International Fruit*,[54] the *Member States* were committed to the GATT 1947 when they negotiated the Treaty of Rome[55] and the Union assumed the functions inherent in the tariff and trade policy on the expiry of the transitional period, by virtue of Article 207 TFEU. It continued

---

[50] This Article is fleshed out by the Agreement on Safeguards.

[51] See also the 'Understanding on the Interpretation of Art. XXIV of GATT 1994' agreed during the Uruguay Round.

[52] See *Turkey: Restriction on imports of textiles and clothing products* WT/DS34/AB/R, 22 Oct. 1999 (and the panel body report WT/DS34/R, 31 May 1999). See further M. Cremona, 'Rhetoric and reticence: EU external commercial policy in a multilateral context' (2001) 38 *CMLRev.* 359, 362.

[53] See *Turkey: Restriction on imports of textiles and clothing products* WT/DS34/AB/R, 22 Oct. 1999 (and the panel body report WT/DS34/R, 31 May 1999). See further Cremona, n. 52, 363.

[54] Joined Cases 21–24/72 *International Fruit Company NV v. Produktschap voor Groenten en Fruit* [1972] ECR 1219.

[55] See Art. 206 TFEU, which seeks the adherence of the Union to the same aims as those sought by the GATT, as well as the first para. of Art. 351 TFEU, which provides that the rights and obligations arising from agreements concluded before the entry into force of the Treaty are not affected by the provisions of the EU Treaty.

that, insofar as the Union has assumed the powers previously exercised by the Member States, the provisions of the WTO bind the Union.[56]

Such binding effect does not, however, extend to giving rights to individuals. As the Court said in *International Fruit*, Article XI of GATT (prohibiting quantitative restrictions) was not 'capable of conferring on citizens of the [Union] rights which they can invoke before the courts'.[57] In *Germany* v. *Council*[58] the Court went further. It said that GATT did not contain *any* provisions which could be invoked in a court, a view subsequently endorsed by *Portugal* v. *Council*[59] with respect to the WTO.

In *International Fruit* the Court tried to explain why it had ruled out direct effect of the GATT when it had found provisions of other international agreements to be directly effective.[60] It said that GATT was based on the principle of negotiations undertaken on the basis of 'reciprocal and mutually advantageous arrangements'.[61] For this reason GATT was characterized by great flexibility, particularly in respect of the provisions conferring on the contracting party the possibility of derogation, the measures to be taken in the case of exceptional difficulty, and the settlement of conflict.[62] In *Portugal* v. *Council* the Court added that because the most important commercial partners of the Union did not make the WTO Agreements enforceable in their own legal systems[63] it did not wish to tie the hands of the Union legislature or executive.[64]

Despite the case law on direct effect, the Court will review the legality of Union measures in the light of WTO rules in two situations: first, where the Union intended to implement a particular obligation assumed in the context of the WTO[65] and, secondly, where the Union measure refers expressly to the precise provisions of the WTO Agreements.[66]

---

[56] Para. 18.   [57] Para. 27.

[58] Case C–280/93 *Germany* v. *Council* [1994] ECR I–4973, para. 109.

[59] Case C–149/96 *Portugal* v. *Council* [1999] ECR I–8395, para. 47. Repeating its earlier case law, the Court said that 'the WTO agreements are not in principle among the rules in the light of which the Court is to review the legality of measures adopted by the [Union] institutions'. Cf. Tesauro AG in Case C–53/96 *Hermès International* v. *FHT Marketing Choice* [1998] ECR I–3603, paras. 22–37. For criticism of the Court's reasoning in *Portugal* v. *Council*, see S. Peers, 'Fundamental right or political whim? WTO law and the ECJ' in G. de Búrca and J. Scott (eds.), *The EU and the WTO: Legal and constitutional issues* (Oxford: Hart Publishing, 2001). See also the final recital in the preamble to Dec. 94/800 ([1994] OJ L336/1), according to which 'by its nature, the Agreement establishing the World Trade Organization, including the Annexes thereto, is not susceptible to being directly invoked in [Union] or Member State courts'. In Joined Cases C–300 and 392/98 *Parfums Christian Dior SA* v. *TUK Consultancy BV* [2000] ECR I–11307, para. 44, the Court said that the provisions of TRIPS did not create rights for individuals enforceable in the national court.

[60] See, e.g., Case 104/81 *Hauptzollamt Mainz* v. *C.A. Kupferberg & Cie KG* [1982] ECR 3641 (Portuguese Free Trade Agreement). Cf. Case 270/80 *Polydor Ltd and RSO Records Inc.* v. *Harlequin Record Shops Ltd and Simons Records Ltd* [1982] ECR 329.

[61] Para. 21, referring to the preamble to GATT. This was confirmed in Case 266/81 *Società Italiana per l'Oleodotto Transalpino (SIOT)* v. *Ministère italien des finances* [1983] ECR 731; Joined Cases 267–269/81 *Amministrazione delle Finanze dello Stato* v. *Società Petrolifera SpA (SPI) and SpA Michelin Italiana (SAMI)* [1983] ECR 801.

[62] Joined Cases 21–24/72 *International Fruit Company NV* [1972] ECR 1219, para. 21.

[63] Para. 43.

[64] Para. 46. J. Trachtmann, 'Bananas, direct effect and compliance' (1999) 10 *EJIL* 655.

[65] Case C–69/89 *Nakajima All Precision Co. Ltd* v. *Council* [1991] ECR I–2069.

[66] Case 70/87 *Federation de L'Industrie de l'Huilerie de la CEE (Fediol)* v. *Commission* [1989] ECR 1781. The Court has not ruled out the possibility of an action for damages under Arts. 268 and 340 TFEU for the Union's failure to respect WTO rules: Case C–93/02 P *Biret* v. *Council* [2003] ECR I–10497; Case T–19/01 *Chiquita Brands International* v. *Commission* [2005] ECR II–315; and Joined Cases C–120 and 121/06 P *Fabbrica italiana accumulatori motocarri Montecchio SpA and Fabbrica italiana accumulatori motocarri Montecchio Technologies LLC (FIAMM) and Giorgio Fedon & Figli SpA and Fedon America, Inc. (Fedon)* v. *Council and Commission* [2008] ECR I–6513.

The Court has also extended the doctrine of harmonious interpretation to the WTO, which means that it will take account of the WTO when interpreting Union legislation. Therefore, in *Germany* v. *Council*[67] the Court said that:

> the primacy of international agreements concluded by the [Union] over provisions of secondary [Union] legislation means that such provisions must, so far as possible, be interpreted in a manner that is consistent with those agreements.

E. CONCLUSIONS

This chapter has provided a brief introduction to the specific provisions of the Treaty on the free movement of goods. It has also given a taste of the broader international environment in which they operate. We shall now consider the specific EU rules, first by examining the provisions which prohibit fiscal barriers to trade (Articles 30 and 110 TFEU) in Chapter 3 and then those which concern non-fiscal barriers to trade (Articles 34–6 TFEU) in Chapters 4–6.

FURTHER READING

Economic activity

O. Odudu, 'Economic activity as a limit to Community law' in C. Barnard and O. Odudu (eds.), *The Outer Limits of European Union Law* (Oxford: Hart Publishing, 2009).

Introduction to the internal market

P. Oliver and W. H. Roth, 'The internal market and the Four Freedoms' (2004) 41 *CMLRev.* 407.

The role of GATT/WTO

E. Petersmann, 'Application of GATT by the Court of Justice of the European Communities' (1983) 20 *CMLRev.* 397.

F. Snyder, 'The gatekeepers: The European Courts and WTO law' (2003) 40 *CMLRev.* 313.

G. Zonnekeyn, 'The status of WTO law in the Community legal order: Some comments in the light of the Portuguese Textiles Case' (2000) 25 *ELRev.* 293.

---

[67] Case C–280/93 *Germany* v. *Council* [1994] ECR I–4973, paras. 110–11.

3

FISCAL MEASURES: CUSTOMS DUTIES AND INTERNAL TAXATION

A. INTRODUCTION

This chapter focuses on the Treaty provisions concerning fiscal rules, namely Articles 30 and 110 TFEU. As we saw in Chapter 2, these provisions are complementary but mutually exclusive. Article 30 TFEU contains an absolute prohibition and applies at the frontier (see fig. 2.1). Article 110 TFEU applies to discriminatory or protective charges levied internally within a state. We begin by considering Article 30 TFEU.

B. ARTICLE 30 TFEU: CUSTOMS DUTIES
AND CHARGES HAVING EQUIVALENT EFFECT

1. INTRODUCTION

In the early days of the Union, fiscal barriers to trade hampered the creation of a single market. However, with the completion of the internal market came the abolition of customs controls[1] and so opportunities for states to demand fees, duties, and other levies diminished. Nevertheless, Article 30 TFEU still retains some importance.[2]

It will be recalled that the definition of a customs union (CU) found in Article 28 TFEU contains both an internal and an external element. The internal dimension, the subject matter of this chapter, provides that the CU 'shall involve the prohibition between Member States of customs duties on imports and exports and of all charges having equivalent effect'. This must be read in conjunction with Article 30 TFEU. The original Treaty provision, Article 12 EEC, was drafted as a standstill clause:

> Member States shall refrain from introducing between themselves *any new customs duties* on imports or exports or any charges having equivalent effect, and from *increasing* those which they already apply in their trade with each other.[3]

Therefore, Article 12 EEC prohibited states from both introducing new duties[4] and increasing existing charges.[5] Article 12 EEC was at issue in *Van Gend en Loos*,[6] where customs duties on a product called ureaformaldehyde were increased from 5 per cent to 8 per cent. The Dutch government argued that this was due, not to an increase in the rate, but to a new classification of the product. Rejecting this argument, the Court said that it was of little importance how the increase in customs duties occurred: the fact was that customs duties on ureaformaldehyde were now higher than when the EEC Treaty came into force and so the charge contravened Article 12 EEC.[7]

The Amsterdam Treaty replaced the standstill clause in Article 12 EEC with an absolute prohibition, now found in Article 30 TFEU:

> Customs duties on imports and all charges having equivalent effect shall be prohibited between Member States. This prohibition shall also apply to customs duties of a fiscal nature.

---

[1] One of the key pillars of the single market is the abolition of all internal economic borders between Member States unless specific suspicion gives rise to individual control. Such controls cannot be systematic or concentrated on the border between states (COM(2001) 51, 6). The abolition of internal frontier controls has increased the importance of controls at the external borders. In the past such controls were largely physical. Today, the emphasis is on computerization, post-import and audit controls, and risk analysis which allows the selection of those consignments which constitute the greatest risk, while physical controls are often carried out at the trader's premises. Frontier controls are largely devoted to combating smuggling and fraud.

[2] See, e.g., Case C–163/90 *Administration des Douanes et Droits Indirectes* v. *Legros* [1992] ECR I–4625; Case C–363/93 *Lancry* v. *Direction Général des Douanes* [1994] ECR I–3957.

[3] Emphasis added.

[4] Joined Cases 90 and 91/63 *Commission* v. *Luxembourg and Belgium* [1964] ECR 625.

[5] Case 26/62 *Van Gend en Loos* [1963] ECR 1.   [6] Case 26/62 *Van Gend en Loos* [1963] ECR 1.

[7] Arts. 13 and 16 EEC provided for the abolition of *existing* customs duties and charges having equivalent effect and exports respectively. As a result of the Acceleration Dec. 66/532 ([1966] JO 2971), all customs duties were to be abolished by 1 Jul. 1968. Since these Treaty provisions are now of historical significance only, they were removed as part of the Amsterdam clean up and renumbering.

So Article 30 TFEU prohibits both customs duties (CDs) and charges having equivalent effect to a customs duty (CEEs). We shall examine these in turn.

2. CUSTOMS DUTIES

A customs duty is a charge, determined on the basis of a tariff, specifying the rate of duty to be paid by the importer to the host state. Customs duties are prohibited because they are protectionist: they make the imported good more expensive than the rival domestic product.[8] *Van Gend en Loos* (considered earlier) is one of the few cases where the Court has considered customs duties.

3. CHARGES HAVING EQUIVALENT EFFECT TO CUSTOMS DUTIES

3.1 Introduction

Article 30 TFEU also prohibits CEEs, thereby preventing Member States from circumventing the prohibition on customs duties by dressing up the charge as something else.[9] This was recognized in *Deutschmann*,[10] where the Court said that a charge, imposed on the issue of an import licence, which applied only to imported goods and not to similar domestic products had, 'by altering its price, the same effect upon the free movement of goods as a customs duty'.

The Court gave a fuller definition of CEEs in the *Statistical Levy* case.[11] It said:

Any pecuniary charge, however small and whatever its designation and mode of application, which is imposed unilaterally on domestic or foreign goods by reason of the fact that they cross a frontier ... constitutes a charge having equivalent effect ... even if it is not imposed for the benefit of the State, is not discriminatory or protective in effect and if the product on which the charge is imposed is not in competition with the domestic product.

We shall examine each aspect of the definition in turn.

3.2 'Any pecuniary charge, however small ...'

The reference to 'any pecuniary charge' reminds us that Articles 28 and 30 TFEU apply only to fiscal measures: non-fiscal rules relating to goods are likely to be covered by Articles 34–6 TFEU. The reference to 'however small' indicates there is no *de minimis* rule in Article 30 TFEU. As the Court said in the *Statistical Levy* case:[12]

The very low rate of the charge cannot change its character with regard to the principles of the Treaty which for the purpose of determining the legality of those charges, do not admit of the substitution of quantitative criteria for those based on the nature of the charge.

On the facts of the case, the Court found that a (very small) charge of 10 lire on each importer to cover the cost of collecting trade statistics breached Article 30 TFEU because it

---

[8] Case 7/68 *Commission v. Italy (the art treasures case)* [1968] ECR 423, 429.
[9] Joined Cases 2 and 3/62 *Commission v. Luxembourg and Belgium (the gingerbread case)* [1962] ECR 425, 432.
[10] Case 10/65 *Deutschmann v. Germany* [1965] ECR 469, 474.
[11] Case 24/68 *Commission v. Italy (statistical levy case)* [1969] ECR 193.
[12] Case 24/68 *Commission v. Italy* [1969] ECR 193, para. 14.

'hampers the interpenetration at which the Treaty aims and thus has an effect on the free circulation of goods equivalent to a customs duty'.[13]

3.3 '... whatever its designation and mode of application ...'

The reference to 'whatever its designation and mode of application' reinforces the point that, no matter how a Member State describes the charge, the Court is likely to consider it a CEE. So the Court has found a statistical levy to be a CEE,[14] as was a charge for health inspections on products from other Member States.[15] Similarly, a postal charge for the presentation of a parcel sent from another Member State for customs clearance was a CEE,[16] as was a tax on the export of a work of art to another Member State.[17] However, the Court has said that Value Added Tax (VAT) was not a CEE.[18]

3.4 '... imposed unilaterally on domestic or foreign goods by reason of the fact that they cross a frontier ...'

The reference to crossing a frontier emphasizes the distinction between Article 30 TFEU and Article 110 TFEU. While Article 110 TFEU applies to a charge borne by imported, exported, and domestic products *internally* within the Member State,[19] Article 30 TFEU applies to charges levied at the *frontier*.[20] It had been assumed that the reference to crossing a 'frontier' meant levies on goods crossing *national* frontiers (i.e., the frontier between State A and State B).[21] However, as the Court made clear in *Legros*,[22] Articles 28 and 30 TFEU also apply to charges levied on the crossing of a frontier *internal* to a particular Member State (i.e., from one part of State A to another). In *Legros* a charge (dock dues) was levied on all goods imported into Réunion, a French overseas territory, from Germany via Metropolitan France. All goods originating in Réunion were exempt from the dues; all other goods, including those from Metropolitan France and from other French overseas territories, had to pay the dues. The Court ruled:[23]

> A charge levied at a *regional* frontier by reason of the introduction of products into a region of a Member State constitutes an obstacle to the free movement of goods which is at least as serious as a charge levied at the national frontier by reason of the introduction of the products into the whole territory of a Member State.

---

[13] Case 24/68 *Commission* v. *Italy* [1969] ECR 193, para. 14

[14] Case 24/68 *Commission* v. *Italy* [1969] ECR 193, para. 14.

[15] E.g., Case 39/73 *Rewe-Zentralfinanz* v. *Direktor der Landwirtschaftskammer Westfalen-Lippe* [1973] ECR 1039; Case 314/82 *Commission* v. *Belgium* [1984] ECR 1543, para. 16. However, health inspection charges on goods coming from a non-Member State are permitted: Case 138/77 *Ludwig* v. *Freie und Hanseatische Stadt Hamburg* [1978] ECR 1645.

[16] Case 39/82 *Donner* v. *Netherlands* [1983] ECR 2305, para. 13.

[17] Case 7/68 *Commission* v. *Italy* [1968] ECR 423. The Commission argued that the tax was a CEE but the Court did not make a clear distinction between customs duties and CEEs. See also Case 18/71 *Eunomia* v. *Italy* [1971] ECR 811.

[18] Case 39/82 *Donner* v. *Netherlands State* [1983] ECR 2305.

[19] Joined Cases C–441 and 442/98 *Kapniki Michaïlidis AE* v. *Idryma Koinonikon Asfaliseon (IKA)* [2000] ECR I–7145, para. 22.

[20] This was emphasized in Joined Cases C–393/04 and C–41/05 *Air Liquide Industries Belgium SA* v. *Ville de Seraing* [2006] ECR I–5293, paras. 52–3.

[21] This understanding was strengthened by the fact that Art. 30 TFEU talks of the prohibition of customs duties and CEEs 'between Member States'.

[22] Case C–163/90 *Legros* [1992] ECR I–4625, paras. 16–18.   [23] Paras. 16–17, emphasis added.

It continued that 'the effect of such a regional levy on the unity of the [Union] customs territory is not altered by the fact that it is also charged on goods from the other parts of the territory of the Member State in question'. Therefore, the dock dues constituted a CEE, notwithstanding that the charge was also imposed on goods entering Réunion from another part of France. The Court said that this was not a situation of reverse discrimination[24] since it affected goods from other Member States as well as those from France.[25] In *Simitzi*[26] the Court said that the *Legros* principle applied equally to goods moving from one part of a Member State to another.[27] This led to the ruling in *Carbonati Apuani*[28] that a charge imposed on a specific good—marble—leaving Carrara, the town in Italy famous for the quarrying of marble, heading for other Member States as well as other parts of Italy, was a CEE.[29]

These rulings, while explicable in terms of ensuring the effectiveness of the provisions on customs duties and charges having equivalent effect, are controversial for two reasons. First, as Oliver and Enchelmaier point out,[30] these decisions were given without the benefit of any authority in support of the proposition. Secondly, they overlook the fact that Article 28(1) TFEU expressly states that the principle of free movement applies exclusively *between* the Member States. Undeterred, the Court in *Carbonati* buttressed its argument that Article 30 TFEU applied to intra-state free movement by reference to the fact that Article 28 TFEU had to be read with Article 26(2) TFEU, which defines the internal market as 'an area without internal frontiers in which the free movement of goods, persons, services and capital is ensured'.[31] It noted that Article 26(2) TFEU did not draw any distinction between inter-state frontiers and frontiers within a state. If this is the case, then, given that Article 26(2) TFEU applies to the other free movement provisions, the same reasoning should apply to Articles 45, 49, and 56 TFEU on free movement of persons and Article 63 TFEU on free movement of capital. However, the Court has steadfastly resisted such an extension.[32]

What constitutes a frontier has also been expanded in a more metaphorical sense. In *Viamar*[33] the Court found that a registration tax which had as its chargeable event the registration of motor vehicles in a Member State (Greece) and was thus internal taxation under Article 110 TFEU, ceased to be covered by Article 110 if it was collected and not refunded when vehicles were imported from other Member States which had never been registered in Greece. In this situation, said the Court, it was in reality collected solely by virtue of the crossing of the Greek frontier and so was a CEE.

---

[24] See further Ch. 4.

[25] See also Case C–363/93 *Lancry* [1994] ECR I–3957, para. 30, concerning the same dock dues, where the Court extended this ruling to goods which originated in France. See also Case C–37/96 *Sodiprem* v. *Direction Générale des Douanes* [1998] ECR I–2039.

[26] Joined Cases C–485 and 486/93 *Simitzi* v. *Dimos Kos* [1995] ECR I–2655.   [27] Para. 21.

[28] Case C–72/03 *Carbonati Apuani Srl* v. *Comune di Carrara* [2004] ECR I–8027. See also Case C–254/13 *Orgacom BVBA* v. *Vlaamse Landmaatschppij* EU:C:2014:2251, paras. 24–5 (levy on manure).

[29] See also Case C–293/02 *Jersey Produce Marketing Organisation* [2005] ECR I–9543.

[30] P. Oliver and S. Enchelmaier, 'Free movement of goods: Recent development in the case law' (2007) 44 *CMLRev.* 649, 652.

[31] Paras. 23–4.

[32] See, e.g., Case C–212/06 *Government of French Community and Walloon Government* v. *Flemish Government* [2008] ECR I–1683 discussed in Ch. 7.

[33] Case C–402/14 *Viamar* v. *Ellinki Dimosio* EU:C:2015:830.

3.5 '… even if it is not imposed for the benefit of the State, is not discriminatory
    or protective in effect and if the product on which the charge is imposed
    is not in competition with the domestic product.'

The absolute prohibition on CEEs applies even where the money is not used for a protectionist purpose. This can be seen in *Diamantarbeiders*,[34] where the charge of 0.33 per cent
of the value of imported diamonds was used to fund additional social benefits for workers
in the diamond industry. The Court said that customs duties were prohibited independently of any consideration of the purpose for which they were introduced and the destination of the revenue obtained.[35] Thus, under Article 30 TFEU the Court is concerned with
the *effect* of the charge—by imposing additional costs on the imported goods, the imports
become less competitive. No account is taken of either the potentially beneficial purpose
to which the charge is put[36] or the fact that the money is not used to benefit the national
treasury.[37] The Court believes that if a state wants to achieve welfare objectives, the revenue for this should come from a general system of taxation which is applied to all goods
(to which Article 110 TFEU may apply).

   Given that charges which do not have a protectionist effect are caught by Article 30
TFEU, *a fortiori,* charges which do have protectionist effect will also be caught by Article
30 TFEU. Therefore, in the *Gingerbread* case[38] the Court rejected as 'absurd' the Belgian
government's argument that the charge on the imported product was needed to 'equate
the price of the foreign product with the price of the Belgian product'.

4. REMEDIES

4.1 Direct Effect

Van Gend en Loos[39] established that Article 30 TFEU was (vertically) directly effective[40]
and so could be enforced in the national court. Given that, by their very nature, customs
duties are levied by the state, the question of horizontal direct effect does not arise in
respect of Article 30 TFEU. But what if private parties are responsible for collecting the
duties? In *Dubois* v. *Garanor Exploitation*[41] the Court said that Article 30 TFEU would
still apply. Garanor was the manager of an international road station where the customs
authorities had an office at which all customs formalities, normally completed at state
frontiers, could be carried out. Dubois had used the facilities but did not pay the transit
charge provided for in the contract between Garanor and Dubois. On the issue that the
charge was imposed not by the state but by a private individual, the Court ruled that a
Member State was still in breach of its obligations if it charged for the costs of inspections

---

   [34] Joined Cases 2 and 3/69 *Sociaal Fonds voor de Diamantarbeiders* [1969] ECR 211. See also Joined Cases
C–441 and 442/98 *Kapniki Michaïlidis AE* [2000] ECR I–7145, para. 17.
   [35] Joined Cases 2 and 3/69 *Diamantarbeiders* [1969] ECR 211, 222.
   [36] See also Case C–173/05 *Commission* v. *Italy (environmental protection tax on gas pipelines)* [2007] ECR
I–4917, para. 42: the fact that the tax was introduced with the 'sole aim' of protecting the environment in the
light of the requirements of the precautionary principle was irrelevant.
   [37] See also Case 7/68 *Commission* v. *Italy (the art treasures case)* [1968] ECR 423.
   [38] Joined Cases 2 and 3/62 *Commission* v. *Luxembourg and Belgium* [1962] ECR 425, 434.
   [39] Case 26/62 [1963] ECR 1.
   [40] See also Joined Cases 2 and 3/69 *Diamantarbeiders* [1969] ECR 211, 223.
   [41] Case C–16/94 *Edouard Dubois* v. *Garanor Exploitation SA* [1995] ECR I–2421. See also Case C–206/06
Essent Netwerk Noord BV v. *Aluminium Delfzijl BV* [2008] ECR I–5497, para. 45, where legislation implemented an agreement concluded by various economic operators. Arts. 30 and 110 TFEU in principle still
applied.

and administrative formalities carried out by customs offices. It made no difference whether the charge resulted from a unilateral measure adopted by the authorities or, as here, from a series of private contracts.

4.2 Repayment of Unlawful Charges

In *San Giorgio*[42] the Court ruled that a *restitutionary* claim was available to the trader who had paid a customs duty or a charge having equivalent effect contrary to Union law. The Court said that this was a consequence of, and an adjunct to, the rights conferred on individuals by the Union provisions prohibiting such charges. However, the Court said that there would be no restitutionary claim if it led to the trader being unjustly enriched (see point (1) on fig. 3.1), as a result of having passed on the cost to others.[43] As the Court explained in *Comateb*,[44] to repay the trader the amount of the charge already received from the purchaser would be tantamount to paying him twice over while in no way remedying the consequences for the purchaser of the illegality of the charge. The Court continued that it was for the national courts to determine whether the burden of the charge had been transferred in whole or in part by the trader to others and, if so, whether reimbursement to the trader would amount to unjust enrichment. If the burden of the charge had been passed on only in part, it was for the national authorities to repay the trader the amount which had not been passed on.[45] In *Lady & Kid*[46] the Court said that this was the only exception to the rule on restitution of unlawfully levied tax.

In *Comateb*[47] the Court developed its ruling in *San Giorgio* and said that if the charge had been passed on to third parties (e.g., the final consumer), they could obtain reimbursement from either the trader or the state. If reimbursement was obtained from the trader, the trader had in turn to be able to obtain reimbursement from the state (see point (2) on fig. 3.1). If, on the other hand, the third party could obtain repayment directly from the national authorities (see point (3) on fig. 3.1) the question of reimbursing the trader would not arise.

The likelihood of final consumers actually reclaiming the money is minimal. They are more likely to vote with their wallets and buy the rival (probably national) product which is not subject to these additional costs. For this reason, the Court added in *Comateb* that the trader could also have a claim for damages for loss of sales brought about by having to pass on the unlawfully levied charge.[48] If domestic law permitted the trader to plead such damage, the national court had to give effect to such a claim. If, on the other hand, national law did not provide such a remedy, then the state could still be liable for reparation of loss caused by the levying of charges not due, irrespective of whether those charges had been passed on,[49] in accordance with the principles laid down in *Brasserie du Pêcheur and Factortame III*.[50]

---

[42] Case 199/82 *San Giorgio* [1983] ECR 3595, para. 12.

[43] Case 199/82 *San Giorgio* [1983] ECR 3595, para. 13.

[44] Case C–192/95 *Comateb* [1997] ECR I–165.

[45] Case C–192/95 *Comateb* [1997] ECR I–165, para. 28. See also Case C–147/01 *Weber's Wine World Handels-GmbH* v. *Abgabenberufungskommission Wien* [2003] ECR I–11365, paras. 100–1. In Joined Cases C–441 and 442/98 *Kapniki Michaïlidis* [2000] ECR I–7145, para. 42 the Court ruled that Union law precluded any presumption or rule of evidence intended to shift to the trader the burden of proving that the charges unduly paid had not been passed on to other persons and preventing him from adducing evidence to refute any allegation that the charges have been passed on.

[46] Case C–398/09 *Lady & Kid A/S* v. *Skatteministeriet* [2011] ECR I-7375, para. 20.

[47] Case C–192/95 *Comateb* [1997] ECR I–165, para. 24.   [48] Para. 31.   [49] Para. 34.

[50] Joined Cases C–46 and 48/93 *Brasserie du Pêcheur and Factortame III* [1996] ECR I–1029.

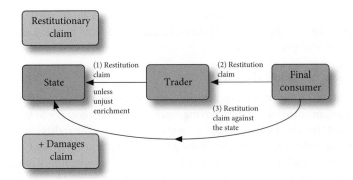

Fig. 3.1 The effect of *Comateb*

The principle of national procedural autonomy applies to the claims for restitution and damages with the result that national procedural rules govern the cause of action providing they are not less favourable than those relating to similar claims regarding national charges (the principle of non-discrimination) and are not framed so as to render virtually impossible the exercise of rights conferred by Union law (the principle of effectiveness).[51] National time limits will also apply to these claims, provided they are reasonable[52] and do not breach the principles of equivalence and effectiveness.[53]

5. 'PERMISSIBLE' CHARGES

As we have seen, since the TFEU provides no defence to a breach of Article 30 TFEU, the customs duty or CEE will not be allowed to stand, no matter how beneficial the purpose. The Court has firmly resisted attempts by Member States to invoke the Article 36 TFEU derogations and apply them by analogy to Article 30 TFEU.[54] Nevertheless, the Court has recognized that a charge can be lawful in the three circumstances listed in *Commission* v. *Germany*:[55]

> if it relates to a general system of internal dues applied systematically and in accordance with the same criteria to domestic products and imported products alike ..., if it constitutes payment for a service in fact rendered to the economic operator of a sum in proportion to the service ..., or again, subject to certain conditions, if it attaches to inspections carried out to fulfil obligations imposed by [Union] law.

These three situations are not judicially developed derogations to Article 30 TFEU; rather, they do not fall within the definition of a customs duty or a CEE at all and so escape the prohibition in Article 30 TFEU altogether.

---

[51] Case 199/82 *San Giorgio* [1983] ECR 3595, para. 12.

[52] Case C–231/96 *Edis* v. *Ministero delle Finanze* [1998] ECR I–4951. See also Case C–260/96 *Ministero delle Finanze* v. *Spac* [1998] ECR I–4997 and Joined Cases C–279, 280, and 281/96 *Ansaldo Energia* v. *Amministrazione delle Finanze dello Stato* [1998] ECR I–5025.

[53] See further Case C–62/00 *Marks & Spencer plc* v. *Commissioners of Customs and Excise* [2002] ECR I–6325; Joined Cases C–216 and 222/99 *Riccardo Prisco Srl* v. *Amministrazione delle Finanze dello Stato* [2002] ECR I–6761; Case C–255/00 *Grundig Italiana SpA* v. *Ministero delle Finanze* [2002] ECR I–8003.

[54] Case 7/68 *Commission* v. *Italy (the art treasures case)* [1968] ECR 423, 430, where the Court said that the derogations contained in Art. 36 TFEU applied 'clearly and solely' to Arts. 34–5 TFEU and could not be applied to Art. 30 TFEU.

[55] Case 18/87 *Commission* v. *Germany* [1988] ECR 5427, para. 6.

We shall consider each situation in turn.

5.1 Payments for Genuine Administrative Services Rendered to the Importer/Exporter

If the payment is consideration for a genuine service of direct benefit to the importer or exporter then it is not a CEE. As the Court put it in *Commission* v. *Belgium (warehousing)*,[56] Article 30 TFEU will not apply if the national court[57] considers that 'the charge in question is the consideration for a service actually rendered to the importer and is of an amount commensurate with that service'.[58] However, the Court is wary about abuse of this rule. For example, in *Commission* v. *Italy*[59] the Italian authorities charged traders for opening customs posts beyond the normal business hours worked by Italian civil servants. The Italian government argued that because this was a service to the traders the charge was legitimate. The Court disagreed, reasoning that because, under a Union directive, the customs posts should have been open at these hours anyway, the charge constituted a CEE.

The Court has emphasized that, for the charge to fall outside Article 30 TFEU, the services must confer a specific benefit on the individual importer/exporter.[60] Usually, however, the Court finds that this is not the case on the facts. So, when in the *Statistical Levy* case[61] the Italian government argued that the 10 lire levy constituted consideration for a service (because the information supplied afforded importers a better competitive position on the Italian market and exporters enjoyed a similar advantage abroad), the Court disagreed. It said that because the statistical information was beneficial to the public as a whole it should have been paid for by the public (through general taxation), and not by the individual importer/exporter. It added that because the connection between any competitive advantage gained by the importers and exporters and the collection of the statistics was so difficult to assess, the charge could not be regarded as the consideration for a specific benefit actually conferred.[62] In a similar vein, the Court ruled in *Bresciani*[63] that because compulsory veterinary health inspections on imported raw cowhides were imposed in the public interest they could not be regarded as a service rendered to the importer so as to justify the imposition of a pecuniary charge. Because the public as a whole benefited, the costs had to be met out of the public purse.

However, there are borderline situations. In the *Warehousing* case[64] Belgium charged for the use of a special warehouse within the state where customs formalities could be completed instead of at the frontier. The Commission argued that these storage charges contravened Articles 28 and 30 TFEU. Advocate General Mancini disagreed. He thought that the warehousing facilities constituted a specific benefit for the importer because the goods had customs clearance closer to their intended destination and the importer

---

[56] Case 132/82 *Commission* v. *Belgium (warehousing)* [1983] ECR 1649.

[57] Case 39/82 *Donner* [1983] ECR 2305, para. 12.

[58] See also Case 170/88 *Ford España* v. *Estado español* [1989] ECR 2305.

[59] Case 340/87 *Commission* v. *Italy* [1989] ECR 1483. See also Case C–209/89 *Commission* v. *Italy* [1991] ECR I–1575 and the follow up in Case C–125/94 *Aprile Srl* v. *Amministrazione delle Finanze dello Stato* [1995] ECR I–2919.

[60] Case 18/87 *Commission* v. *Germany* [1988] ECR 5427, para. 7.

[61] Case 24/68 *Commission* v. *Italy* [1960] ECR 193. See also Case C–389/00 *Commission* v. *Germany (waste shipment)* [2003] ECR I–2001.

[62] Para. 16.

[63] Case 87/75 *Bresciani* [1976] ECR 129. See also Case 63/74 *Cadsky SpA* v. *Istituto nazionale per il Commercio Estero* [1975] ECR 281, para. 8; Case 314/82 *Commission* v. *Belgium* [1984] ECR 1543, para. 12.

[64] Case 132/82 *Commission* v. *Belgium* [1983] ECR 1649.

did not have to pay commercial warehousing costs. However, the Court agreed with the Commission and found that when payment of storage charges was demanded solely in connection with the completion of customs formalities, it could not be regarded as the consideration for a service actually rendered to the importer.

5.2 Charges for Inspections Required by Union Law

According to *Commission* v. *Germany*,[65] costs for compliance with mandatory[66] inspections required by *Union* law[67] can be passed on to the importer. They do not constitute a CEE providing four conditions are satisfied:[68]

(1) they do not exceed the actual costs of the inspections in connection with which they are charged

(2) the inspections are obligatory and uniform for all the products concerned in the Union

(3) they are prescribed by Union law in the general interest of the Union

(4) they promote the free movement of goods, in particular by neutralizing obstacles which could arise from unilateral measures of inspection adopted in accordance with Article 36 TFEU.

Therefore, the German *Länder* were entitled to charge a fee to cover the costs of veterinary inspections on imported live animals carried out under a Union directive concerning the protection of animals during international transport.

By contrast, charges for inspections required by *national* law do constitute a CEE.[69] Therefore, the importer cannot be required to pay for the inspection even if the inspection itself (which is considered to be a measure having equivalent effect under Article 34 TFEU[70]) is justified under Article 36 TFEU.[71]

The explanation for this different treatment of charges levied in respect of inspections required by Union and national law lies in the fact that harmonization of inspection requirements by Union law removes an impediment to the free movement of goods that would otherwise arise as a result of a divergence between the national systems. As the Court noted in *IFG*,[72] if a public-health inspection is carried out in the state of origin, valid for the whole Union, this facilitates free movement of goods by reducing duplication of inspections at the frontier.[73]

5.3 Charges Falling within the Scope of Internal Taxation

If the charge 'relates to a general system of internal dues applied systematically and in accordance with the same criteria to domestic products and imported products alike' then the legality of the charge falls to be considered under Article 110 TFEU, and not

[65] Case 18/87 *Commission* v. *Germany* [1988] ECR 5427.
[66] This does not apply to inspections merely *permitted* by Union law: Case 314/82 *Commission* v. *Belgium* [1984] ECR 1543, para. 8.
[67] The same rule applies where the inspection, and thus the charge, is required by an international convention: Case 89/76 *Commission* v. *Netherlands* [1977] ECR 1355, para. 16, drawing parallels with the Union directive at issue in Case 46/76 *Bauhuis* [1977] ECR 5.
[68] Case 18/87 *Commission* v. *Germany* [1988] ECR 5427, para. 8.
[69] Case 46/76 *Bauhuis* [1977] ECR 5.   [70] See further Ch. 4.
[71] Case 46/76 *Bauhuis* [1977] ECR 5, para. 13; Case 251/78 *Denkavit Futtermittel* v. *Minister für Ernährung* [1979] ECR 3369, para. 31.
[72] Case 1/83 *IFG* v. *Freistaat Bayern* [1984] ECR 349, para. 9.
[73] Case 89/76 *Commission* v. *Netherlands* [1977] ECR 1355, para. 13.

Article 30 TFEU, because Articles 30 and 110 are mutually exclusive.[74] The relationship between Articles 30 and 110 will be explored more fully later. It is to Article 110 TFEU that we now turn.

C. ARTICLE 110 TFEU: INTERNAL TAXATION

1. INTRODUCTION

While Article 30 TFEU addresses fiscal barriers to trade levied at the *frontier*, Article 110 TFEU deals with fiscal rules which apply *internally* within a Member State.[75] Article 110 TFEU addresses two separate issues. Article 110(1) TFEU prohibits discriminatory taxation in respect of goods which are *similar*, such as one type of beer and another. It provides:

> No Member State shall impose, directly or indirectly, on the products of other Member States any internal taxation of any kind in excess of that imposed directly or indirectly on similar domestic products.

If the Court finds that the products are not similar, it then considers Article 110(2) TFEU, which concerns products *in competition* such as beer and (cheap) wine:

> Furthermore, no Member State shall impose on the products of other Member States any internal taxation of such a nature as to afford indirect protection to other products.

Together these provisions are intended to guarantee 'the complete neutrality of internal taxation as regards competition between domestic products and products imported from other Member States'[76] in order to ensure the free movement of goods between Member States in normal conditions of competition.[77]

Article 110 TFEU applies to *indirect* taxation (taxation on products[78]); it does not affect direct taxation (such as income tax on the producer), although any discrimination in respect of direct taxation may offend against other Treaty provisions, notably those on the free movement of persons.[79] We shall now turn to consider the detail of Article 110 TFEU, beginning with the basic rule that Member States are free to determine their own schemes of taxation.

---

[74] Joined Cases C–34–38/01 *Enirisorse SpA* v. *Ministero delle Finanze* [2003] ECR I–14243, para. 59.

[75] Despite its close relationship with the rules on customs duties, the provisions on internal taxation were placed in Part Three of the EEC Treaty on policies of the Community, while the provisions on customs duties were found in Part Two entitled 'Foundations of the Community'. This led some to suggest that the provisions on internal taxation were subsidiary to those on customs duties: see Case 193/85 *Cooperativa Co-Frutta Srl* v. *Amministrazaione delle Finanze dello Stato* [1987] ECR 2085. Post-Lisbon, both customs duties and internal taxation fall under Part Three entitled 'Union policies and internal actions'. However, Art. 110 TFEU falls under Title VII entitled 'Common rules on competition, taxation and approximation of laws' while Art. 30 TFEU falls under Title II entitled 'Free movement of goods'.

[76] Case 193/85 *Co-frutta* [1987] ECR 2085, para. 25.

[77] Case 252/86 *Bergandi* [1988] ECR 1343, para. 24.

[78] The importance of this point was stressed in Joined Cases C–393/04 and C–41/05 *Air Liquide Industries Belgium SA* v. *Ville de Seraing* [2006] ECR I–5293, para. 57, where the Court said that Art. 110 TFEU did not apply since the tax is not 'imposed specifically on exported or imported products or in such a way as to differentiate them, given that it applies to economic activities carried out by industrial, commercial, financial or agricultural undertakings and not to products as such'.

[79] See, e.g., Case C–204/90 *Bachmann* v. *Belgium* [1992] ECR I–249 considered further in Ch. 8.

2. MEMBER STATE AUTONOMY TO DETERMINE ITS OWN TAXATION POLICIES

Article 110 TFEU gives Member States considerable discretion to determine the content of their own taxation policy (which products to tax, on what basis, and at what level). This is known as the principle of fiscal autonomy or fiscal sovereignty. This (relative) freedom was emphasized in the *Johnnie Walker* case,[80] where the question was raised whether Denmark could tax whisky at a higher rate than fruit wine. The Court said that Union law did not restrict the freedom of each Member State to lay down tax arrangements which differentiated between certain products on the basis of objective criteria, such as the nature of the raw materials used or the production processes employed. It continued that such differentiation was legitimate under Union law 'if it pursues objectives of economic policy[81] which are themselves compatible with the requirements of the Treaty'.[82]

Thus any scheme of taxation which makes a distinction between products based on objective criteria (unrelated to origin) is compatible with Article 110 TFEU. Therefore, in *Bergandi*[83] the Court ruled that a French system of taxation which taxed 'bad' games machines (the use of which the French government wished to discourage) at a higher rate than other (less bad) games machines, was compatible with Article 110 TFEU. Similarly, the Court said in *Commission* v. *France*[84] that it was legitimate for France to tax natural sweet wines whose production in regions with poor soil and low rainfall was 'traditional and customary' more favourably than other liqueur wines, provided that such preferential treatment was extended to imported products. In much the same way the Court said in *Chemial Farmaceutici*[85] that the Italian government was free to tax denatured synthetic alcohol which had petroleum as its base at a higher rate than denatured alcohol obtained by fermentation. This pattern of taxation was intended to promote agriculture and to reserve petroleum for other 'more important uses'.[86]

These cases demonstrate that national taxation policy[87] is, by its very nature, discriminatory. It is a matter for an elected government to decide whether to tax product X (e.g., natural sweet wines grown in disadvantaged regions) at a lower rate than product Y (e.g., other liqueur wines). Provided that such discrimination or, to use a more neutral term, differentiation, is based on objective criteria[88] unrelated to the origin (nationality)[89] of the goods, the tax does not fall within the purview of Article 110 TFEU (stage 1 of the enquiry—fig. 3.2). This highlights a key difference between Article 110 TFEU and the other Treaty provisions discussed in this book: Article 110 TFEU is

---

[80] Case 243/84 *Johnnie Walker* [1986] ECR 875.

[81] In Case 252/86 *Bergandi* v. *Directeur Général des Impôts* [1988] ECR 1343, para. 29 the Court talked of 'legitimate economic or social purposes'.

[82] Para. 22. See also Case C–221/06 *Stadtgemeinde Frohnleiten* v. *Bundesminister für Land- und Forstwirtschaft, Umwelt und Wasserwirtschaft* [2007] ECR I–2613, para. 56.

[83] Case 252/86 *Bergandi* [1988] ECR 1343, para. 32.

[84] Case 196/85 *Commission* v. *France* [1987] ECR 1597, para. 7.

[85] Case 140/79 *Chemial Farmaceutici SpA* v. *DAF SpA* [1981] ECR 1. See also Case 46/80 *SpA Vinal* v. *SpA Orbat* [1981] ECR 77.

[86] Para. 13.

[87] Whether imposed by law or administrative practice: Case 17/81 *Pabst & Richarz* [1982] ECR 1331.

[88] For criticism, see M. Hedemann-Robinson, 'Indirect discrimination: Article 95(1) EC back to front and inside out' (1995) 1 *EPL* 439.

[89] In this chapter the terms will be used synonymously. 'Origin' is the more correct term but 'nationality' is the term used in respect of the other freedoms.

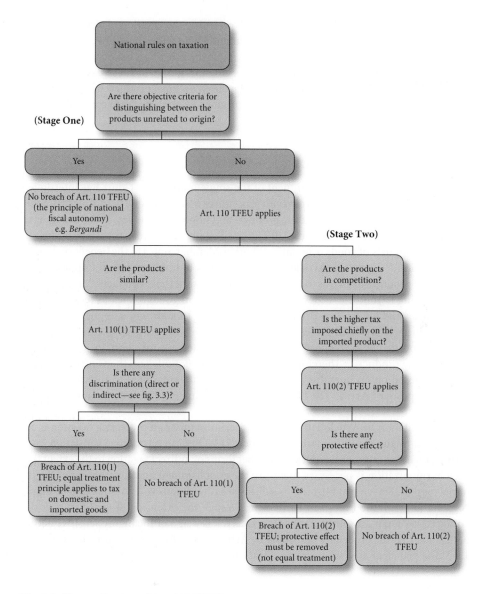

Fig. 3.2 The application of Art. 110 TFEU

essentially *permissive*: it allows Member States both to raise revenue by taxation and to determine the content of their own taxation policy. The other Treaty provisions are essentially *restrictive*: states cannot impose customs duties (Article 30 TFEU), prohibit imports or exports, etc. (Articles 34–5 TFEU).

If, however, the Court senses that the policy choices guiding the taxation decisions are underpinned by discrimination on the grounds of *origin*, it will apply Article 110 TFEU (stage 2 of the enquiry—fig. 3.2). Whether cases are dealt with at stage 1 or stage 2 of the enquiry seems to owe much to the Court's intuition. In *Bergandi, Commission* v. *France*, and *Chemial Farmaceutici* the Court clearly thought that the Member State's policy choices were legitimate and so found that the rules fell outside Article 110 TFEU (stage 1).

This can be contrasted with the line of cases concerning the taxation of alcoholic drinks where, for example, the UK taxed beer more leniently than wine;[90] and France taxed fruit-based spirits (cognac, calvados, and armagnac), of which it was a major producer, more favourably than grain-based spirits (whisky, rum, and gin).[91] In these cases the Court suspected that the national taxation schemes favoured national products to the detriment of similar or potentially equivalent products produced elsewhere, and so applied Article 110 TFEU (stage 2).

3. THE SCOPE OF ARTICLE 110 TFEU

Given its importance to the attainment of the single market, the Court has interpreted Article 110 TFEU widely 'so as to cover all procedures which, directly or indirectly, undermine the equal treatment of domestic products and imported products'.[92] For example, in *Bergandi* the Court said that Article 110 TFEU will apply 'whenever a fiscal levy is likely to discourage imports of goods originating in other Member States to the benefit of domestic production'.[93] Therefore, Article 110 TFEU applies to tax imposed on imported (and exported[94]) products as well as to tax imposed on the *use* of those products.[95] It also covers charges 'going beyond classic levies directly imposed on goods'[96] such as fees for health inspections[97] and for roadworthiness testing of cars.[98] In addition, it applies to a charge on a specific activity of an undertaking in connection with products (i.e., a necessary[99] service associated with the product) which is calculated according to, for example, the weight of the product.[100] Therefore, in *Stadtgemeinde Frohnleiten*, the Court ruled that a levy imposed on an operator of a waste disposal site amounted to internal taxation for the purposes of Article 110 TFEU because it was imposed indirectly on waste being deposited.[101]

The prohibition in Article 110 TFEU on discriminatory and protective taxation is accompanied by the power contained in Article 113 TFEU to harmonize legislation 'concerning turnover taxes, excise duties and other forms of indirect taxation to the extent that such harmonization is necessary to ensure the establishment and functioning of the internal market'. Such harmonization is subject to a unanimous vote in Council and simple consultation with the European Parliament. Despite the extension of qualified majority voting (QMV) to many other areas of the Treaty, it is a sign of the highly sensitive nature of taxation that the procedure laid down by Article 113 TFEU has not been changed since 1957. The principal area where harmonization has occurred is in respect of VAT[102] and

[90] Case 170/78 *Commission* v. *UK* [1980] ECR 417.
[91] Case 168/78 *Commission* v. *France* [1980] ECR 347.
[92] Case C–221/06 *Stadtgemeinde Frohnleiten* [2007] ECR I–2613, para. 40.   [93] Para. 25.
[94] Art. 110 TFEU does apply to tax on exports even though this is not expressly provided on its face: Case 142/77 *Staten Kontrol* v. *Larsen* [1978] ECR 1787. See also Art. 111 TFEU, which provides that where products are exported to the territory of any Member State, any repayment of internal taxation shall not exceed the internal taxation imposed on them directly or indirectly.
[95] Case 252/86 *Bergandi* [1988] ECR 1343, para. 27.
[96] Sharpston AG's Opinion in Case C–221/06 *Stadtgemeinde Frohnleiten* [2007] ECR I–2613, para. 32.
[97] Case 29/87 *Denkavit* v. *Danish Ministry of Agriculture* [1988] ECR 2965.
[98] Case 50/85 *Schloh* [1986] ECR 1855.
[99] Case C–206/06 *Essent Netwerk Noord BV* v. *Aluminium Delfzijl BV* [2008] ECR I–5497.
[100] Case C–221/06 *Stadtgemeinde Frohnleiten* [2007] ECR I–2613, para. 43.
[101] Case C–221/06 *Stadtgemeinde Frohnleiten* [2007] ECR I–2613, para. 47.
[102] Council Dir. 2006/112/EC ([2006] OJ L347/1) as amended.

excise duties on manufactured tobacco,[103] alcohol,[104] and mineral oils.[105] Together these measures form key components of the single market programme aimed at eliminating fiscal barriers to trade.

Article 110 TFEU applies independently of Article 113.[106] It is to the content of Article 110 TFEU that we now turn.

4. GOODS WHICH ARE SIMILAR (ARTICLE 110(1) TFEU)

4.1 Definition of 'Similar'

Article 110(1) TFEU prohibits the host Member State from imposing a higher tax on goods imported into the Member State than on similar domestic goods. The key question is whether goods are 'similar'. Over the years the Court has used two tests to determine similarity. At first it applied a formal test, examining whether the products in question normally come within the same fiscal, customs,[107] or statistical classification.[108] Subsequently, the Court adopted a broader test[109] which combined a factual comparison of the products with an economic analysis of their use. As the Court said in *Commission v. Denmark*:[110]

> it is necessary first to consider certain objective characteristics of both categories of beverages, such as their origin, the method of manufacture and their organoleptic properties, in particular taste and alcohol content, and secondly to consider whether or not both categories of beverages are capable of meeting the same need from the point of view of consumers.

Thus, the scope of Article 110(1) TFEU is determined not on the basis of the strictly identical nature of the products but on their similar and comparable use.[111]

Commission v. Denmark considered the question whether fruit wines and wines made from grapes were similar. The Court found that table wines, whether made from grapes or fruit, were manufactured from the same kind of basic product (agricultural produce) and by the same process (natural fermentation). Their organoleptic properties, in particular their taste and alcohol content, were also similar. Furthermore, both drinks met the same needs for both present and future consumers, as they could be consumed in the same way (to quench thirst, as refreshments, and at meal times), even though fruit wine had always been less popular with consumers than wine

---

[103] Council Dir. 2011/64/EU on the structure and rates of excise duty applied to manufactured tobacco ([2011] OJ L176/24).

[104] Council Dir. 92/83/EEC on the harmonisation of the structures of excise duties on alcohol and alcoholic beverages ([1992] OJ L316/21); Council Dir. 92/84/EEC on the approximation of the rates of duties on alcohol and alcoholic beverages ([1992] OJ L316/29).

[105] Council Dir. 2003/96/EC restructuring the Union framework for the taxation of energy products and electricity ([2003] OJ L283/51).

[106] Case 55/79 *Commission v. Ireland* [1980] ECR 481, para. 12. See the proposal for the financial Transactions Tax proposed under Art. 113 TFEU proposed under enhanced cooperation: COM(2013) 71.

[107] A more detailed discussion of customs classification is found on the Online Resource Centre.

[108] Case 27/67 *Fink-Frucht* [1968] ECR 223, 232; Case 45/75 *Rewe v. HZA Landau* [1976] ECR 181, para. 12.

[109] There are parallels here with the Court's approach to determining the relevant product market under Art. 102 TFEU on the abuse of a dominant position.

[110] Case 106/84 *Commission v. Denmark* [1986] ECR 833, para. 12, which was delivered on the same day as Case 243/84 *Johnnie Walker* [1986] ECR 875.

[111] Case 168/78 *Commission v. France* [1980] ECR 347, para. 5.

made from grapes.[112] For these reasons the Court considered the two products to be similar.[113]

The Court also adopted this broader approach in *Commission v. France (tobacco)*,[114] where it said that dark and light tobacco cigarettes were similar. It noted, first, that they were manufactured from different types of the same base product (tobacco), using comparable processes. Secondly, it said that their organoleptic characteristics, such as taste and smell, were similar, albeit that they contained different quantities of certain types of tobacco. Thirdly, it said they satisfied the same needs of consumers, given their similar properties. The fact that the average age of consumers of dark tobacco was higher than the average age of consumers of light tobacco did not affect this conclusion. Finally, it noted that the Union legislature treated both types of cigarettes in the same way and they fell in the same subheading of the Combined Nomenclature of the CCT.[115]

However, just because products contain the same raw ingredients does not always mean they will be similar. This can be seen in the *Johnnie Walker* case,[116] where the question was raised whether whisky and fruit liqueur wines were similar. Under Danish law, whisky (40 per cent proof and manufactured exclusively abroad) was taxed at a much higher rate than fruit liqueur wines (up to 20 per cent proof and manufactured almost exclusively in Denmark). The Court found that the two drinks were not similar since they exhibited 'manifestly different characteristics'.[117] It noted that fruit wine of the liqueur type was a fruit-based product obtained by natural fermentation, whereas Scotch whisky was a cereal-based product obtained by distillation. The alcohol content of the two drinks also differed significantly. The Court said that, for the products to be regarded as similar, the raw material had to be present in 'more or less equal proportions in both products'. It added that the fact that whisky could be diluted 'would not be sufficient to render Scotch whisky similar to fruit wine of the liqueur type, whose intrinsic characteristics are fundamentally different'.[118]

4.2 Types of Discrimination

If the goods are similar then the taxation applied to those goods must be the same.[119] In other words it must not discriminate against foreign goods on the grounds of their origin, either directly or indirectly.[120]

(a) Direct discrimination

Direct discrimination involves less favourable treatment of the imported product on the ground of its origin. It can come about in a number of ways. For example, direct

---

[112] See also Case 277/83 *Commission v. Italy* [1985] ECR 2049, where the Court said that marsala was similar to fruit liqueur wines.

[113] Para. 22. See also Case C–221/06 *Stadtgemeinde Frohnleiten* [2007] ECR I–2613, para. 60: domestic and imported waste deemed to be similar.

[114] Case C–302/00 *Commission v. France* [2002] ECR I–2055, paras. 24–8.

[115] The Combined Nomenclature is discussed on the Online Resource Centre.

[116] Case 243/84 *Johnnie Walker* [1986] ECR 875.   [117] Para. 12.

[118] It then looked at Art. 110(2) TFEU and found that, since whisky was taxed within the general framework of taxation of spirits, including many Danish-produced goods, the scheme also did not breach Art. 110(2) TFEU.

[119] Case 106/84 *Commission v. Denmark* [1986] ECR 833, para. 22. If there is no discrimination the tax is lawful: Joined Cases C–34–38/01 *Enirisorse SpA v. Ministero delle Finanze* [2003] ECR I–14243, para. 60; Case C–198/14 *Valev Visnapuu v. Kihlakunnansyyttäjä* EU:C:2015:751, paras. 60–5 (see fig. 3.3).

[120] These terms are interpreted broadly: Case 28/67 *Molkerei-Zentrale Westfalen v. Hauptzollamt Paderborn* [1968] ECR 143, 155.

discrimination may arise because only the imported product is subject to the tax. This was the situation in *Lütticke*,[121] where powdered milk from Luxembourg imported into Germany was subject to a tax not payable by the German product. Direct discrimination may also occur because the imported product is taxed at a different (usually higher) rate than the domestic product or the Member State uses different methods for calculating tax for the domestic and imported goods. Therefore, the Court found in *Haahr Petroleum*[122] that the national rule subjecting international transport to a tax 40 per cent higher than that imposed on domestic transport breached Article 110(1) TFEU,[123] as did the rule in *Bobie*,[124] where a Member State imposed a flat rate of tax on the domestic product but a graduated tax on the imported product. Likewise, in *Stadtgemeinde Frohnleiten*[125] a national law reserving the benefit of an exemption from internal taxation to certain domestic products only, breached Article 110(1) TFEU.

The conditions under which the tax is paid or tax relief granted may also lead to direct discrimination. For example, in *Commission v. Ireland*[126] Irish producers had longer to pay a tax than foreign producers. The Court said that although the benefit was small, 'the discrimination against products imported from other Member States is none the less obvious'.[127]

Since there are no express defences to Article 110 TFEU, any directly discriminatory tax breaches Article 110 TFEU and cannot be saved[128] (see fig. 3.3). This means that the Member State must remove the discriminatory element of the taxation policy and so equalize the tax.

Reverse discrimination is, however, permitted by the Treaty. It occurs where the national law treats *domestic* products less favourably than imported products. This can be seen in *Peureux*,[129] where French distillers were required by French law to pay a tax which was not payable by the distillers of equivalent imported alcohol. The Court said:

> Although Article [110 TFEU] prohibits any Member State from imposing internal taxation on products imported from other Member States in excess of that on national products, it does not prohibit the imposition on national products of internal taxation in excess of that on imported products.

The Court justified the continued existence of reverse discrimination on the ground that such disparities 'result from special features of national laws which have not been

---

[121] Case 57/65 *Lütticke v. Hauptzollamt Saarlouis* [1966] ECR 205.

[122] Case C–90/94 *Haahr Petroleum v. Åbenrå Havn* [1997] ECR I–4085. See also Joined Cases C–114 and 115/95 *Texaco A/S v. Middelfart Havn* [1997] ECR I–4263; Case C–242/95 *GT-Link A/S v. De Danske Statsbaner* [1997] ECR I–4449. See also Case C–47/88 *Commission v. Denmark* [1990] ECR I–4509.

[123] See also Joined Cases C–290 and 333/05 *Ákos Nádasdi v. Vám- és Pénzügyarség Észak-Alföldi Regionális Parancsnoksága and Ilona Németh v. Vám- és Pénzügyarség Dél-Alföldi Regionális Parancsnoksága* [2006] ECR I–10115: Hungarian law imposed a heavier tax burden on imported used vehicles than on similar used vehicles already registered in Hungary. In the Polish context, see Case C–313/05 *Brzezinski v. Dyrektor Izby Celnej w Warszawie* [2007] ECR I–513 and in the Dutch context, Case C–437/12 *X* EU:C:2013:857.

[124] Case 127/75 *Bobie v. Hauptzollamt Aachen-Nord* [1976] ECR 1079, para. 4; Case C–213/96 *Outokumpu Oy* [1998] ECR I–1777; Case C–101/00 *Tulliasiamies and Antti Siilin* [2002] ECR I–7487, para. 54.

[125] Case C–221/06 *Stadtgemeinde Frohnleiten* [2007] ECR I–2613, para. 52. Similarly, in Case 21/79 *Commission v. Italy* [1980] ECR 1 the Court found discrimination where Italy charged lower taxes on regenerated oil than ordinary oil but did not extend this benefit to imported regenerated oil. See also Case 277/83 *Commission v. Italy (marsala)* [1985] ECR 2049.

[126] Case 55/79 *Commission v. Ireland* [1980] ECR 481; Case C–68/96 *Grundig Italiana v. Ministero delle Finanze* [1998] ECR I–3775.

[127] Para. 9.   [128] Case C–302/00 *Commission v. France (tobacco)* [2002] ECR I–2055, para. 33.

[129] Case 86/78 *SA des Grandes Distilleries Peureux v. Directeur des Services Fiscaux de la Haute-Saône et du Territoire de Belfort* [1979] ECR 897, para. 32.

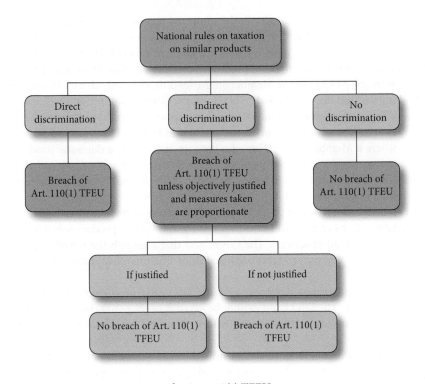

Fig. 3.3 Discriminatory taxation under Art. 110(1) TFEU

harmonized in spheres for which the Member States are responsible'.[130] Therefore, France was entitled to tax its own spirits at a higher rate than imported spirits.

(b) Indirect discrimination

(i) Establishing a prima facie case of discrimination

Direct discrimination is overt: it is clear on the face of the measure ('in law') that there is less favourable treatment of the imported goods. By contrast, a measure is indirectly discriminatory where on its face (in law) it makes no reference to the origin of the product, but in reality (in fact) it imposes a particular burden on the imported goods (sometimes referred to as disparate impact).

   Commission v. *France (tobacco)*[131] provides a good illustration of such discrimination. Dark-tobacco cigarettes were taxed more favourably under French law than light-tobacco cigarettes. The system was found to be indirectly discriminatory because, although the law made no reference to the origin of the product, in fact dark-tobacco cigarettes were almost exclusively domestically produced while light-tobacco cigarettes came from other Member States. The Court added that this finding was not affected by the fact that a small fraction of dark-tobacco cigarettes came from other Member States and a certain proportion of light-tobacco cigarettes were domestically produced. It concluded that '[i]t appears, therefore, that the system of taxation is designed in such a way as to benefit a typical domestic product and handicaps imported cigarettes to the same extent'.

---

[130] Case 86/78 *Peureux* [1979] ECR 897, para. 33.
[131] Case C–302/00 [2002] ECR I–2055, para. 30.

In *Humblot*[132] the Court found French car tax to be indirectly discriminatory. The French taxation system imposed a gradually increasing tax on all cars up to an engine size of 16 cv with a ceiling of 1,100 FF. A flat rate of tax (5,000 FF), known as the special tax, then applied to cars with an engine capacity of over 16 cv. The system was found to be indirectly discriminatory: on the face of the measure—in law—there was no discrimination, but in fact the special tax disadvantaged cars manufactured in other Member States because no cars with an engine capacity of over 16 cv were made in France. The Court noted that, in the absence of considerations relating to the amount of the special tax, consumers seeking comparable cars would naturally choose from among cars above and below the 16 cv rating. However, the French law affected their choice, especially because the special tax was payable for several years.[133] Therefore, the Court said that the special tax reduced competition faced by domestic cars, contrary to Article 110(1) TFEU.[134]

The Greek government operated a similar taxation scheme imposing a higher rate of tax on cars with an engine capacity in excess of 1,800cc. Greece produced cars only with an engine capacity of less than 1,600cc. However, in enforcement proceedings against Greece, *Commission* v. *Greece*,[135] the Court found that the Commission had failed to show that the Greek taxation system might have the effect of favouring the sales of Greek cars. Because no prima facie case of discrimination had been made out, there was no breach of Article 110 TFEU. This case demonstrates that where indirect discrimination is alleged under Article 110(1) TFEU, the Court requires the complainant, at least in the case of the Commission, to demonstrate *actual* (as opposed to potential[136]) disparate impact on the imported goods or actual benefit to the domestic producer.[137]

(ii) Objective justification

While a *directly* discriminatory tax breaches Article 110 TFEU, with no chance of being justified,[138] an *indirectly* discriminatory tax breaches Article 110 TFEU unless it can be objectively justified by the defendant Member State (see fig. 3.3). This means that where a prima facie case of discrimination is made out, the Member State can point to a national interest to justify its taxation policy. Provided that the national interest is (1) unconnected with the origin of the product, (2) pursues an objective recognized by the EU as legitimate, and (3) the steps taken to protect that interest are proportionate, then there is no

---

[132] Case 112/84 *Humblot* [1985] ECR 1367. See also Case C–402/09 *Tatu* v. *Statul român prin Ministerul Finanţelor şi Economiei* [2011] ECR I–2711, para. 37.

[133] Case 112/84 *Humblot* [1985] ECR 1367, para. 15.

[134] After *Humblot* France revised its tax system and replaced the 5,000 FF tax with nine more specific bands, depending on the power of the car. This system was challenged in Case 433/85 *Feldain* v. *Directeur des Services Fiscaux* [1987] ECR 3536 and also found to be indirectly discriminatory because the tax rate still increased significantly over 16 cv.

[135] Case 132/88 *Commission* v. *Greece* [1990] ECR I–1567.

[136] Cf. the case law on Arts. 34 and 45 TFEU: Joined Cases C–321–324/94 *Pistre* [1997] ECR I–2343; and Case C–237/94 *O'Flynn* v. *Adjudication Office* [1996] ECR I–2617, para. 19.

[137] See also Case 252/86 *Bergandi* [1988] ECR 1343; Case 196/85 *Commission* v. *France* [1987] ECR 1597; and Case 140/79 *Chemial Farmaceutici* [1981] ECR 1. The Court also demands this in the case of indirect *sex* discrimination under Art. 157 TFEU: Case C–167/97 *R.* v. *Secretary of State for Employment, ex p. Seymour-Smith and Perez* [1999] ECR I–623.

[138] Although cf. the possibility, gradually being introduced in Art. 34 TFEU whereby distinctly applicable measures can be objectively justified: Case C–54/05 *Commission* v. *Finland* [2007] ECR I–2473, where the Court allowed an import licence to be justified, at least in principle, by 'mandatory requirements' (the language used in Art. 34 TFEU to describe objective justifications) and again in Case C–297/05 *Commission* v. *Netherlands (roadworthiness testing of cars)* [2007] ECR I–7467, paras. 73–4, where the Court allowed roadworthiness tests of imported cars to be potentially justified by mandatory requirements.

breach of Article 110 TFEU.[139] One potential justification is environmental protection and this would have been the ground put forward by the Greek government in *Commission v. Greece*[140] had a prima facie case of indirect discrimination been established. The government said that '[i]n view of the poor infrastructure of the road network and the problems of pollution prevailing in Greece, tax legislation discouraging the purchase of large-engined cars was justified'.

Various commentators have suggested that other potential justifications have been recognized by the Court: the discouragement of certain types of games machines in *Bergandi*[141] (a type of consumer protection/public morality justification); regional development in the *Natural Sweet Wines* case;[142] and promoting agriculture and reserving petrol for other 'more important uses' in *Chemial Farmaceutici*[143] (a type of public-security justification). However, as we saw, these grounds were all successfully invoked by the Member States to justify tax arrangements which differentiated between certain products on the basis of objective criteria (stage 1 of the enquiry—see fig. 3.2). In none of the cases did the Court ever reach stage 2 of the enquiry, requiring it to consider the issue of discrimination and thus of justification in the strict sense of the term. However, in the light of the Court's jurisprudence in other fields, notably Article 34 TFEU on goods, and Articles 45, 49, and 56 TFEU on persons, it is safe to say that indirectly discriminatory taxation schemes breach Article 110 TFEU unless justified. Justifications based on environmental protection, regional development, and saving scarce resources are likely to be accepted by the Court,[144] provided that the steps taken are proportionate. However, given that a prima facie case of discrimination has been established, the level of scrutiny by the Court of the justification in stage 2 is likely to be more intense than at stage 1.

5. GOODS WHICH ARE IN COMPETITION (ARTICLE 110(2) TFEU)

If goods are deemed not to be sufficiently similar for the purposes of Article 110(1) TFEU, the Court will then examine whether they are in competition with each other under Article 110(2) TFEU,[145] even if only partially, indirectly, or potentially.[146] If so, the Court will consider whether the domestic goods benefit from some kind of 'indirect fiscal protectionism'. If this is the case, the prohibition in Article 110(2) TFEU applies (see fig. 3.2).

5.1 The Court's Approach to Article 110(2) TFEU

The Court has used a number of tests to determine whether goods are in competition. Sometimes it applies an economic test based on cross-elasticity of demand. With this test,

---

[139] Strictly speaking, the justifications are not defences because there are no express defences in respect of Art. 110 TFEU. If the national rule can be justified then there is no breach of Art. 110 (see fig. 3.2), so there is no need to look for defences, since the defences, if available, apply only if there is a breach of the Treaty provision.

[140] Case 132/88 *Commission v. Greece* [1990] ECR I–1567; considered at n. 135.

[141] Case 252/86 *Bergandi* [1988] ECR 1343, para. 32.

[142] Case 196/85 *Commission v. France* [1987] ECR 1597, para. 7.

[143] Case 140/79 *Chemial Farmaceutici* [1981] ECR 1, para. 8. See also Case 46/80 *Vinal* [1981] ECR 77.

[144] See the parallel cases on free movement of goods discussed in Ch. 6.

[145] Case 193/85 *Co-frutta* [1987] ECR 2085, para. 19 (the importation of bananas); Case 27/67 *Fink-Frucht* [1968] ECR 223, 232; see also Case 168/78 *Commission v. France* [1980] ECR 347, para. 12.

[146] Case 356/85 *Commission v. Belgium* [1987] ECR 3299, para. 7.

the Court considers whether, if the price of one product goes up, sales of another increase. If so, there is substitutability and cross-elasticity of demand and so the two products are in competition.

The Court also takes into account factors such as the manufacture and composition of the product, and consumer preference, both present and future. In this way the test is not so different from that to establish similarity under Article 110(1) TFEU. Ultimately the Court's approach is impressionistic: in view of its inherent characteristics, is a given tax mechanism *likely* to bring about the protective effect referred to by Article 110(2) TFEU?[147]

The British wine and beer case, *Commission* v. *UK*,[148] provides a good example of how the Court addresses the question whether two goods (beer and wine) are in competition. The Commission argued that British taxation policy contravened Article 110 TFEU because, if judged by equal volume, wine was subject to a tax burden approximately five times that imposed on beer.[149] The Commission said that the two drinks belonged to the same category of alcoholic beverages: both were the product of natural fermentation and both could be used for the same purposes, as thirst-quenching drinks or to accompany meals. It also argued—and the Court accepted[150]—that there was a competitive relationship between wine and beer, and therefore Article 110(2) TFEU applied: in the case of certain consumers the two drinks could actually be substituted for one another, and in the case of other consumers they might, at least potentially, be substituted.

In judging substitutability the Court emphasized that account needed to be taken of potential substitutes brought about by increased free trade:[151]

> For the purpose of measuring the possible degree of substitution, it is impossible to restrict oneself to consumer habits in a Member State or in a given region. In fact, those habits, which are essentially variable in time and space, cannot be considered to be a fixed rule; the tax policy of a Member State must not therefore crystallize given consumer habits so as to consolidate an advantage acquired by national industries concerned to comply with them.[152]

In other words, since tax is lower on beer than on wine, consumers can buy more beer for their money than wine. The taxation policy therefore reinforced the already advantageous position of beer on the market. In that respect it served to 'crystallize' consumer habits.

Despite its agreement with the Commission about substitutability, the Court also recognized the validity of the UK government's arguments that there were differences between wine and beer. For example, the alcohol content of wine is approximately four times that of beer, wine is appreciably more expensive than beer,[153] and wine and beer are produced according to different processes. Moreover, the Court recognized the

---

[147] Case 170/78 *Commission* v. *UK* [1980] ECR 417, para. 10.
[148] Case 170/78 *Commission* v. *UK* [1980] ECR 417.
[149] Case 170/78 *Commission* v. *UK* [1980] ECR 417, para. 17.
[150] Case 170/78 *Commission* v. *UK* [1980] ECR 417, para. 14.
[151] Case 170/78 *Commission* v. *UK* [1980] ECR 417, para. 6: 'it is necessary to consider not only the present state of the market but also the possibilities for development within the context of free movement of goods at the [Union] level and the further potential for the substitution of products for one another which may be revealed by intensification of trade, so as fully to develop the complementary features of the economies of the Member States in accordance with the objectives laid down by Article [3 TEU]'.
[152] Case 170/78 *Commission* v. *UK* [1980] ECR 417, para. 14.
[153] Case 170/78 *Commission* v. *UK* [1980] ECR 417, para. 13.

different circumstances in which the two drinks are consumed. As the UK government argued:[154]

> in accordance with long-established tradition in the United Kingdom, beer is a popular drink consumed preferably in public-houses or in connexion with work; domestic consumption and consumption with meals is negligible. In contrast, the consumption of wine is more unusual and special from the point of view of social custom.[155]

Although the Court thought that the British tax system showed a 'protective trend', when considered by reference to alcoholic strength rather than by volume (which the Court thought to be a more reliable measure[156]), it asked the parties to try to resolve the matter and report back.[157] Unable to reach an amicable settlement, the case returned to the Court three years later,[158] where it ruled that the decisive competitive relationship was between beer, 'a popular and widely consumed beverage', and the most accessible wines, namely the 'lightest and cheapest varieties'.[159]

Having considered that these goods were in competition, the Court then examined the question of protective effect. It said that the UK's tax system had the effect of subjecting imported wine to an additional tax burden of at least 100 per cent by reference to alcoholic strength and 400 per cent by reference to volume[160] so as to afford protection to domestic beer production, thereby suppressing any potentially competitive relationship. As the Court said, 'the effect of the United Kingdom tax system is to stamp wine with the hallmarks of a luxury product which, in view of the tax burden which it bears, can scarcely constitute in the eyes of the consumer a genuine alternative to the typical domestically produced beverage'.[161] The UK taxation scheme therefore breached Article 110(2) TFEU.

But what should the UK do about it? If the taxation scheme had been found to be discriminatory under Article 110(1) TFEU, equalized tax rates would have been the solution (see fig. 3.2). In *Beer and Wine*, however, the complaint concerned the protective effect of the scheme, and Article 110(2) TFEU merely required its removal (see fig. 3.2).[162] In fact, the Chancellor of the Exchequer lowered the tax on wine and raised it on beer. As Weatherill concluded, the increasing consumption of wine suggests that the Court might have been right and that the British public had been deterred from buying wine by high taxes.[163]

Nearly thirty years later, similar issues were litigated in *Commission* v. *Sweden*[164] but this time the Court found Sweden not to be in breach of Article 110 TFEU. As with *Beer and Wine*, the Commission thought that the difference in the tax treatment of beer and wine was liable to afford indirect protection to beer (mainly produced in Sweden) to the detriment of wine (mainly imported from other Member States). The Court adopted a three-stage approach.[165] First, it considered whether the goods were in competition with

---

[154] This proved to be a matter of some dispute in the subsequent case, Case 170/78 *Commission* v. *UK* [1983] ECR 2265, where the Court recognized that none of the criteria of comparison (volume, alcoholic strength, and the price of the products) was capable of yielding reliable results on its own (para. 18).

[155] Case 170/78 *Commission* v. *UK* [1980] ECR 417, para. 13.

[156] Case 170/78 *Commission* v. *UK* [1980] ECR 417, para. 19.

[157] Case 170/78 *Commission* v. *UK* [1980] ECR 417, para. 24.

[158] Case 170/78 *Commission* v. *UK* [1983] ECR 2265.

[159] Para. 12.   [160] Paras. 19–21.   [161] Para. 27.

[162] See A. Easson, 'The spirits, wine and beer judgments: A legal Mickey Finn?' (1980) 5 *ELRev.* 318 and 'Cheaper wine or dearer beer?' (1984) 9 *ELRev.* 57.

[163] S. Weatherill and P. Beaumont, *EU Law* (London: Penguin, 1999), 482.

[164] Case C–167/05 [2008] ECR I–2127.

[165] See also Case E–6/07 *HOB vín ehf* v. *Faxaflóahafnir* [2008] EFTA Ct Rep. 128, para. 52.

each other. It pointed out that wine and beer were, to a certain extent, 'capable of meeting identical needs, which meant that a certain measure of mutual substitutability must be acknowledged', and so the decisive competitive relationship between wine and beer had to be established by reference to those wines which were the most accessible to the public at large (i.e., 'the lightest and least expensive varieties').[166] So, the Court said that wines with an alcoholic strength of between 8.5% vol. and 15% vol. and a final selling price ranging between SEK 49 and SEK 70 shared a sufficient number of characteristics with 'strong' beer with an alcoholic strength equal to or higher than 3.5% vol. to represent an alternative choice for the consumer and thus to be in competition with strong beer. Secondly, the Court considered whether the higher tax rate applied chiefly to the imported product. It found that wine with an alcoholic strength of 12.5% vol. was subject to taxation per percentage of alcohol by volume approximately 20 per cent higher per litre than beer with which it was in competition.[167]

Thirdly, it considered the question of protective effect: was the higher tax on wine liable to influence the market in question by reducing the potential consumption of imported products so as to advantage competing domestic products?[168] It took into account the difference between the selling prices of the products per litre and the impact of that difference on the consumer's choice, as well as looking at changes in the consumption of those products.[169] The Court pointed out that the price difference between the two products was virtually the same before taxation as after it (a litre of wine of 12.5% vol. cost just over twice the price of a litre of beer).[170] So, the Court found that the Commission had not shown that the difference between the price of strong beer and the price of wine in competition with that beer was so great that the difference in the excise duty was likely to influence consumer behaviour.[171]

So why the difference in outcome? The Court's approach in the *Sweden* case demonstrates more rigour in respect of analysis of the market than had been seen in *Commission v. UK*. And because the burden of proof was on the Commission to show something close to actual protective effect,[172] the Commission had failed to make the case to the requisite legal standard and so the action was dismissed.

5.2 The Globalized Approach to Article 110 TFEU?

In some cases, particularly those in the 1980s, the Court did not distinguish clearly between whether the goods were similar under Article 110(1) TFEU or in competition under Article 110(2) TFEU. Instead, it adopted a globalized approach,[173] considering Article 110(1) TFEU and 110(2) TFEU together. From one perspective, this makes some sense: as the *Beer and Wine* case shows, the tests applied to both provisions do overlap. From another, it presents problems because the remedies under the two provisions are different. Nevertheless, the Court adopted the globalized approach in three 'spirits' cases: *Commission v. Denmark*,[174] where Danish tax law favoured acquavit over other competing spirits; *Commission v. Italy*,[175] where Italian tax law favoured grappa over rum;

---

[166] Case C–167/05 *Commission v. Sweden* [2008] ECR I–2127, para. 43.   [167] Para 50.

[168] Para 52.   [169] Para. 53.   [170] Para. 57.   [171] Para. 58.

[172] Cf. para. 60, where the Court said that 'it is impossible to require, in each case … that the protective effect of internal tax arrangements be shown statistically, but that it is sufficient for it to be shown that a given tax mechanism is likely, in view of its inherent characteristics, to bring about such an effect'.

[173] A. Easson, 'Fiscal discrimination: New perspectives on Article 95 of the EEC Treaty' (1981) 18 CMLRev. 521, 535.

[174] Case 171/78 *Commission v. Denmark* [1980] ECR 447.

[175] Case 169/78 *Commission v. Italy* [1980] ECR 385.

and *Commission* v. *France*,[176] where French law favoured cognac over whisky. The Court said that Article 110 TFEU 'taken as a whole, may apply without distinction to all the products concerned'.[177]

Subsequently, the Court has become more rigorous in distinguishing between Article 110(1) and (2) TFEU.[178] For example, in *Commission* v. *Italy (bananas)*[179] Italy taxed bananas[180] (largely from the French overseas territories) at a higher rate than other table fruit typically produced in Italy (such as apples, pears, peaches, and plums). The Court decided that bananas and other soft fruits were not similar under Article 110(1) TFEU because the organoleptic characteristics and the water content of the two categories of products differed.[181] The Court then looked at Article 110(2) TFEU and found that the goods were in competition.[182] It also found that the tax on bananas had a protective effect: the tax was equivalent to half the import price of the bananas; most domestic soft fruit was subject to no tax at all.

6. REMEDIES

As we have already seen, the nature of the remedy depends on whether the case is considered under Article 110(1) or 110(2) TFEU (see fig. 3.2). If the case falls within Article 110(1) TFEU then the discrimination must be eliminated by, depending on the circumstances, equalizing the taxes imposed on the domestic and imported goods or extending a benefit enjoyed by domestic goods to imported goods. Therefore, in *Hansen*[183] the Court said that where national tax law favoured spirits produced by small and collective farms, those advantages had to be extended to imported Union spirits which fulfilled the same conditions.[184] While *Hansen* suggests a levelling up of benefits (the imported goods obtain the benefit accorded to domestic goods) the principle of formal equality merely requires equality of treatment. This means that there is nothing to prevent a levelling down of benefit (domestic goods lose the benefit accorded to them, bringing their treatment into line with that of imported goods),[185] as well as a levelling up.

If the case falls within Article 110(2) TFEU the state must remove the protective effect from its taxation scheme. This does not necessarily mean equalizing the tax burden on the imported goods.[186] Therefore, as we saw in the *Wine and Beer* case,[187] the Court did not require the wine to be taxed at the same rate as beer, merely that the protection

---

[176] Case 168/78 *Commission* v. *France* [1980] ECR 347. See subsequently Case C–230/89 *Commission* v. *Greece* [1991] ECR I–1909 (Greek law taxed ouzo at a lower rate than whisky).

[177] Para. 13.   [178] See, e.g., Case 243/84 *Johnnie Walker* [1986] ECR 875.

[179] Case 184/85 *Commission* v. *Italy (bananas)* [1987] ECR 2013.

[180] Italy had only a negligible production of bananas in Sicily, which was ignored by the Court.

[181] It said: 'by way of example, the higher water content of pears and other fruit typically grown in Italy give them thirst-quenching properties which bananas do not possess. Moreover, the observation of the Italian government, which has not been challenged by the Commission, that the banana is regarded, at least on the Italian market, as a foodstuff which is particularly nutritious, of a high energy content and well-suited for infants must be accepted' (*Bananas*, para. 10).

[182] See also Case 193/85 *Co-frutta* [1987] ECR 2085, judgment delivered on the same day. Cf. Case 27/76 *United Brands* v. *Commission* [1978] ECR 207.

[183] Case 148/77 *H. Hansen jun. & O.C. Balle GmbH & Co.* v. *Hauptzollamt de Flensburg* [1978] ECR 1787, para. 20.

[184] See also Case 68/79 *Hans Just I/S* v. *Danish Ministry for Fiscal Affairs* [1980] ECR 501, para. 16.

[185] This is permitted in the field of sex equality: Case C–408/92 *Smith* v. *Avdel Systems* [1994] ECR I–4435.

[186] A. Easson, n. 173, 535.

[187] Case 170/78 *Commission* v. *UK* [1983] ECR 2265.

enjoyed by beer be removed so that the tax reflected the objective differences between the products.

The remedies considered so far are particularly relevant where the Commission brings enforcement proceedings against a Member State. By contrast, where individuals invoke Article 110 TFEU—which they can do because Article 110 TFEU is directly effective[188]— they may want the state to repay any tax unlawfully levied (see fig. 3.2). The availability of a restitutionary claim was confirmed by the Court in *Hans Just*,[189] where it said that Member States had to ensure the repayment of charges levied contrary to Article 110 TFEU, subject to the principle of national procedural autonomy and unjust enrichment.[190] Damages are also payable for loss of sales. National time limits will apply to these claims, provided they are not such as to make the claim less favourable than those governing similar domestic actions and do not render the exercise of the rights virtually impossible or excessively difficult.[191]

D. THE BOUNDARY BETWEEN ARTICLE 110 TFEU AND OTHER TREATY PROVISIONS

1. INTRODUCTION

According to the theory, Articles 110 and 30 TFEU are mutually exclusive[192] (as we have seen, Article 30 TFEU applies to charges levied at the frontier; Article 110 TFEU to charges levied within the Member State[193]), as are Articles 110 and 34 TFEU (Article 110 TFEU concerns fiscal measures; Article 34 non-fiscal (see fig. 2.1)). However, this division is not always so straightforward, as *Commission* v. *Denmark*[194] shows. Under Danish law the rate of duty applicable to private vehicles, calculated by reference to the value of the vehicle, was 105 per cent on the first DKr 20,000 and 180 per cent on the balance. The Court said that although Article 110 TFEU did not provide a basis for censuring the excessiveness of the level of taxation, charges of such a (high) level might impede the free movement of goods contrary to Article 34 TFEU. However, when, in *DBI*,[195] a professional association of car importers relied on this ruling to challenge the level of duty applied to cars imported into Denmark, the Court, having looked at the figures,[196] found that free movement of vehicles was not impeded.[197] Subsequently, in *Brzezinski*[198] the Court appeared to rule out entirely the application of Article 34 TFEU to fiscal situations when

---

[188] Art. 110(1): Case 57/65 *Lütticke GmbH* [1966] ECR I–205 and Case 28/67 *Molkerei-Zentrale Westfalen* [1968] ECR 143, 153; Art. 110(2): Case 27/67 *Fink-Frucht* [1968] ECR 223, 232.

[189] Case 68/79 *Hans Just I/S* [1980] ECR 501, para. 27.

[190] See the discussion of Case 199/82 *San Giorgio* [1983] ECR 3595 and Case C–192/95 *Comateb* [1997] ECR I–165 (fig. 3.1).

[191] Case C–90/94 *Haahr Petroleum* v. *Åbenrå Havn* [1997] ECR I–4085. The Court said a five-year limitation period was reasonable.

[192] Case 10/65 *Deutschmann* v. *Germany* [1965] ECR 469.

[193] Case C–313/05 *Brzezinski* v. *Dyrektor Izby Celnej w Warszawie* [2007] ECR I–513, paras. 22–3.

[194] Case C–47/88 *Commission* v. *Denmark* [1990] ECR I–4509, para. 10.

[195] Case C–383/01 *De Danske Bilimportører* v. *Skatteministeriet, Told- og Skattestyrelsen* [2003] ECR I–6065. DBI bought a new Audi for its director at a total price of just under DKr 500,000 which included just under DKr 300,000 in registration duty.

[196] During the period from 1985 to 2000 the total number of registered vehicles in Denmark rose from 1.5 million to 1.854 million and the number of new registrations varied between 78,000 and 169,000 per year.

[197] Para. 41.

[198] Case C–313/05 *Brzezinski* v. *Dyrektor Izby Celnej w Warszawie* [2007] ECR I–513, para. 50.

it said that 'obstacles of a fiscal nature or having an effect equivalent to customs duties, which are covered by Articles [28 TFEU], [30 TFEU] and [110 TFEU], do not fall within the prohibition laid down in Article [34 TFEU]'.

We now consider cases on the borderline between Articles 30 TFEU and 110 TFEU: the situation of a charge imposed on a product not produced in the Member State (the so-called exotic import); para-fiscal charges (those charges which apply to all goods but are then refunded in some form to the domestic producer); and other levies which appear to apply to all goods but are in fact targeted at the imported good.

2. THE 'EXOTIC' IMPORT

If there is no similar or competing domestic product (or a very low domestic production of the particular goods[199]) Member States are still free to tax the imported goods. As the Court said in *Co-frutta*,[200] any such charge does not constitute a CEE under Article 30 TFEU but internal taxation within the meaning of Article 110 TFEU, provided the tax fits within the general scheme of taxation applied systematically to categories of products in accordance with objective criteria irrespective of the origin of the products.[201] Therefore, an Italian tax on bananas, a fruit hardly grown in Italy, could be regarded as an integral part of a general system of internal dues within the meaning of Article 110 TFEU since it formed one of 19 consumer taxes of which three were charged on tropical products (coffee, cocoa, and bananas).[202]

This rule makes sense—if it were otherwise and Article 30 TFEU applied, Member States would not be able to tax products they did not produce themselves. However, even though the permissive regime under Article 110 TFEU applies, the Court will still consider the tax to ensure that it is neither discriminatory nor protective. In *Co-frutta*, decided the same day as *Commission v. Italy (bananas)*,[203] the Court found the tax on bananas to have protective effect.

3. PARA-FISCAL CHARGES

Para-fiscal charges wholly or partially offset the burden borne by domestic products but not imports. These may fall under Article 30 TFEU or 110 TFEU depending on the extent to which the charge is offset. As the Court explained in *Compagnie Commerciale*,[204] if the proceeds of the charge *fully* offset the burden borne by the domestic product when it is placed on the market, it has an effect equivalent to customs duties, contrary to Article 30

---

[199] Case 193/85 *Co-frutta* v. *Amministrazione delle Finanze dello Stato* [1987] ECR 2085, para. 11. See also Case C–313/05 *Brzezinski* v. *Dyrektor Izby Celnej w Warszawie* [2007] ECR I–513, paras. 22–3.

[200] Case 193/85 *Co-frutta* [1987] ECR 2085, para. 13. Case 27/67 *Fink-Frucht* [1968] ECR 223, 231. See also Case C–109/98 *CRT France International SA* v. *Directeur régional des impôts de Bourgogne* [1999] ECR I–2237, para. 21; Case 90/79 *Commission* v. *France* [1981] ECR 283, para. 14, where a levy of 3 per cent was charged on the sales of reprographic equipment and paid into the National Book Fund to subsidize the publication of quality works and to buy (French and foreign) books for libraries. French production of such equipment was extremely small. On the facts the Court found that this charge did fall within the scope of Art. 110 TFEU because it was levied in part to address the problems of breach of copyright.

[201] Para. 10.   [202] Para. 12.

[203] Case 184/85 [1987] ECR 2013 considered in the text related to n. 179.

[204] Joined Cases C–78–83/90 *Compagnie Commerciale de l'ouest* [1992] ECR I–1847, paras. 27–8. See also Case 105/76 *Interzuccheri SpA* v. *Società Rezzano e Cavassa* [1977] ECR 1029, para. 10, and Case C–72/92 *Scharbatke* v. *Germany* [1993] ECR I–5525, para. 10; Case C–17/91 *Lornoy en Zonen* v. *Belgian State* [1992] ECR I–6523; and Case C–347/95 *Fazenda Publica* v. *UCAL* [1997] ECR I–4911; Joined Cases C–149 and 150/91 *Sanders Adour* v. *Directeur des Services Fiscaux des Pyrenées-Atlantique* [1992] ECR I–3899.

TFEU. If, on the other hand, those advantages only *partly* offset the burden borne by domestic products, the charge is subject to Article 110 TFEU. However, in this case the charge will breach Article 110 TFEU and is prohibited to the extent that it discriminates against imported products (i.e., the extent to which it partially offsets the burden borne by the taxed domestic product). It is for the national court to determine whether the charge imposed on the domestic product is wholly or partly offset.[205]

The application of these rules can be seen in *Capolongo*[206] and in *Nygård*.[207] *Capolongo* concerned an Italian law which established a body called ENCC.[208] This body had the task of promoting the development of cellulose production in Italy, largely by providing subsidies to the national industry.[209] It was funded by a government charge on domestically produced and imported cellulose, paper, and cardboard. An importer of egg boxes from Germany argued that this charge contravened Article 30 TFEU; the Italian government said that since the charge applied to both domestic and imported goods it fell within Article 110 TFEU. The Court agreed with the importer. It said that a duty within the general system of internal taxation could constitute a CEE within the meaning of Article 30 TFEU when the charge was 'intended exclusively to support activities which specifically benefit the taxed domestic product'.[210]

While *Capolongo* concerned a national rule which *fully* offset the burden borne by domestic products, *Nygård* involved a charge which only *partly* offset that burden. The case concerned a levy charged by the Danish authorities on pigs produced in Denmark for slaughter for the domestic market and on those intended for live export to other Member States. However, 60 per cent of the revenue generated was used to subsidize activities relating to slaughtering and processing on the domestic market and the marketing of the domestic product, while only 40 per cent of the revenue was used to finance activities concerning primary production, which would benefit the production of pigs for export. The Court said that although the levy did not fall within Article 30 TFEU (because it was not a case of full offsetting), it could be considered discriminatory taxation prohibited by Article 110 TFEU to the extent that the advantages deriving from the use made of the revenue partially compensated for the charge imposed on pigs produced for slaughter in Denmark, thereby placing the production of pigs for export at a disadvantage.[211]

4. OTHER 'LEVIES'

As we saw, levies on goods crossing a frontier are usually considered to be CEEs under Article 30 TFEU and so are prohibited. Arguments, such as those raised in *Bresciani*[212] that domestic goods are subject to similar charges, are not usually enough to trigger Article 110 TFEU. Bresciani imported raw cowhides into Italy from France. These cowhides were subject to a health inspection for which a fee was charged to cover the costs of the examination and laboratory tests. Similar products of domestic origin were not

---

[205] If the money goes into the national exchequer and is used for the benefit of a particular national *industry*, this may be considered a state aid: Joined Cases C–78–83/90 *Compagnie Commerciale de l'ouest* [1992] ECR I–1847.

[206] Case 77/72 *Capolongo v. Azienda Agricole Maya* [1973] ECR 611, para. 13.

[207] Case C–234/99 *Niels Nygård v. Svineafgiftsfonden* [2002] ECR I–3657. See also Case C–517/04 *Visserijbedrijf D.J. Koonstr & Zn. Vof v. Productschap Vis* [2006] ECR I–5015.

[208] Ente Nazionale per la Cellulosa e per la Carta.

[209] See Roemer AG's Opinion in Case 77/72 *Capolongo v. Azienda Agricole Maya* [1973] ECR 611, 625.

[210] Para. 14.

[211] See also Case C–206/06 *Essent Netwerk Noord BV v. Aluminium Delfzijl BV* [2008] ECR I–5497, para. 57.

[212] Case 87/75 *Bresciani* [1976] ECR 129.

subject to the same duty, although when animals were slaughtered they were subject to a veterinary inspection to determine whether the meat was fit for human consumption, for which a charge was levied. The Court said this was irrelevant: the fact that the domestic production was subjected to a similar financial burden mattered little unless the charges on the domestic and imported goods were applied according to the same criteria and at the same stage of production.[213] If these conditions were satisfied, the charges would be considered as falling within a general system of taxation to which Article 110 TFEU would apply. This was the situation in *Denkavit*,[214] where the Court found that an annual levy charged in a like manner to importers and national producers of foodstuffs containing additives (intended to cover the costs incurred by the state in checking samples) was covered by Article 110 TFEU since it related to a general system of internal dues applied systematically and in accordance with the same criteria to domestic and imported products alike.[215] Furthermore, the charge was compatible with Article 110 TFEU since it did not discriminate against the imported goods in any way.

By contrast, in *Mikhailides*,[216] the Court found that a charge imposed on exported tobacco to compensate for a charge imposed on similar domestic products, but at a production stage prior to that at which the exported products were taxed, did not fall under Article 110 TFEU. Instead, the charge fell within Article 30 TFEU because it was not applied 'at the same rate, at the same marketing stage and on the basis of an identical chargeable event'.[217]

E. CONCLUSIONS

Article 110 TFEU serves as a valuable complement to Article 30 TFEU, while at the same time ensuring income to the national exchequer. However, as we saw in Chapter 1, the removal of fiscal barriers to trade is not sufficient in itself to realize free trade. Non-fiscal barriers can easily represent serious obstacles to trade. It is to this subject that we now turn.

FURTHER READING

Article 30 TFEU

R. Barents, 'Charges of equivalent effect to customs duties' (1978) 15 *CMLRev.* 415.

M. Dougan, 'Cutting your losses in the enforcement deficit' (1998) 1 *CYELS* 233.

P. Oliver and S. Enchelmaier, 'Free movement of goods: Recent development in the case law' (2007) 44 *CMLRev.* 649.

Article 110 TFEU

A. Easson, 'Fiscal discrimination: New perspectives on Article 95 of the EEC Treaty' (1981) 18 *CMLRev.* 521.

---

[213] Case 87/75 *Bresciani* [1976] ECR 129, para. 11.
[214] Case 29/87 *Denkavit* v. *Danish Ministry of Agriculture* [1988] ECR 2965.
[215] Para. 33.   [216] Joined Cases C–441 and 442/98 [2000] ECR I–7145.
[217] Para. 24. See also Case C–254/13 *Orgacom BVBA* v. *Vlaamse Landmaatschppij* EU:C:2014:2251, para. 31. Further, the Court ruled Art. 30 applied because the two levies were calculated at different levels.

4

NON-FISCAL MEASURES: QUANTITATIVE RESTRICTIONS AND MEASURES HAVING EQUIVALENT EFFECT

A. INTRODUCTION

In the last chapter we considered *fiscal* barriers to trade. Now we move on to examine *non-fiscal* barriers to trade. Such barriers—which can range from quotas to national measures prescribing the content and presentation of a product—can have a significant effect on intra-EU trade. Three Treaty provisions are relevant: Article 34 TFEU on *imports*, Article 35 TFEU on *exports*,[1] and Article 36 TFEU containing derogations (exceptions) from Articles 34–5 TFEU.

Article 34 TFEU provides: 'Quantitative restrictions on imports and all measures having equivalent effect shall be prohibited between Member States.' Article 35 TFEU is drafted in the same terms but concerns exports. Both provisions prohibit two types of national measure:

(1) quantitative restrictions on imports/exports (QRs) (in essence quotas or bans); and

(2) measures having an equivalent effect to a quantitative restriction (MEEs) (e.g., rules on licences, and, particularly in respect of Article 34 TFEU, regulations on the presentation of the product such as packaging).

Despite the similarity in drafting of Articles 34–5 TFEU, the case law on the two Treaty provisions diverged quite markedly between 1979 and 2008: while Article 34 TFEU prohibited both distinctly and indistinctly applicable MEEs (broadly equivalent to directly and indirectly discriminatory measures), Article 35 TFEU prohibited distinctly applicable MEEs only. This restricted reading of Article 35 TFEU was subject to much criticism and was finally reconsidered in *Gysbrechts*.[2] However, in *Commission v. Italy (trailers)*,[3] decided shortly after *Gysbrechts*, the Court extended the definition of MEEs under Article 34 TFEU to include, at paragraph 37, not only directly and indirectly discriminatory measures but also 'Any other measure which hinders access of products originating in other Member States to the market of a Member State'. There may be signs that the Court is moving in a similar direction in respect of Article 35 TFEU.

Given the overlap between Articles 34–5 TFEU both are considered in this chapter. The focus will, however, be on the case law under Article 34 TFEU, which is more extensive than that on Article 35 TFEU. There is a practical explanation for this difference: because Member States have an interest in encouraging exports, with the exception of economically sensitive exports such as essential raw materials (e.g., oil) and politically sensitive exports (e.g., cultural goods, weapons, and even wine), they are unlikely to create barriers to exports. By contrast, in respect of imports, Member States may be more willing to impose barriers to trade, especially when those imports threaten domestic production and thus domestic jobs.

This chapter will focus on the meaning of the terms 'quantitative restrictions' and 'measures having equivalent effect'. A new category of measure, 'certain selling arrangements' (CSAs), introduced by the Court of Justice in its (in)famous decision in *Keck*,[4] is considered in Chapter 5. The derogations and judicially developed justifications ('mandatory' or 'public interest' requirements) are considered in Chapter 6.

B. QUANTITATIVE RESTRICTIONS

In *Geddo*[5] the Court defined quantitative restrictions as 'measures which amount to a total or partial restraint of, according to the circumstances, imports, exports or goods

---

[1] Art. III-153 of the Constitutional Treaty merged these two Articles into one. This change did not survive into the Lisbon Treaty.

[2] Case C–205/07 *Gysbrechts and Santurel Inter BVBA* [2008] ECR I–9947.

[3] Case C–110/05 *Commission v. Italy* [2009] ECR I–519, para. 50.

[4] Joined Cases C–267 and 268/91 *Keck and Mithouard* [1993] ECR I–6097.

[5] Case 2/73 *Geddo v. Ente Nationale Risi* [1973] ECR 865, para. 7.

in transit'. Therefore, QRs include (non-tariff[6]) quotas limiting the quantity of goods coming into a state or leaving the state. So, in *Delhaize*[7] Spanish rules limiting the quantity of wine available for export in bulk to other Member States breached Article 35 TFEU. Other restrictions on imports and exports are also covered. This can be seen in *Rosengren*,[8] where Swedish rules prohibited private individuals from buying alcoholic drinks by mail order or over the Internet but allowed them to buy the drinks from the 'Systembolaget', the state-owned company with a monopoly over retail sales in wine, beer, and spirits in Sweden. Because the Systembolaget could refuse an order from a customer, the Court said the Swedish law constituted a QR.[9]

QRs also include a ban on imports or exports, which, as the Court noted in *Henn and Darby*,[10] is the most 'extreme form of prohibition'. This meant that the UK's ban on the import of pornographic material breached Article 34 TFEU. Often a Member State will concede that its ban breaches the Treaty. For example, in *Hedley Lomas*[11] the UK accepted that its refusal to issue an export licence for a quantity of live sheep intended for slaughter in a Spanish slaughterhouse was a QR contrary to Article 35 TFEU, as was a ban on the export of live calves in *CWF*.[12] In these cases the focus was instead on the Article 36 TFEU derogations, the only way a state can defend a quantitative restriction on trade (see fig. 4.1). The first sentence of Article 36 TFEU provides:

> The provisions of Articles 34 and 35 shall not preclude prohibitions or restrictions on imports, exports or goods in transit justified on grounds of public morality, public policy or public security; the protection of health and life of humans, animals or plants; the protection of national treasures possessing artistic, historic or archaeological value; or the protection of industrial and commercial property.

This is an exhaustive list of derogations which must be read in conjunction with the proviso in the second sentence of Article 36 TFEU. This says that '[s]uch prohibitions or restrictions shall not, however, constitute a means of arbitrary discrimination or a disguised restriction on trade between Member States'.

Thus, the Treaty allows national measures to take precedence over the free movement of goods where they serve important interests recognized by the Union as valuable (public policy, security, health, the protection of national treasures, and protection of industrial and commercial property), provided that the national measures are proportionate and do not constitute a means of arbitrary discrimination or a disguised restriction on trade between Member States. The detail of this provision is considered in Chapter 6.

C. MEASURES HAVING EQUIVALENT EFFECT

1. INTRODUCTION

Articles 34–5 TFEU prohibit not only QRs but also MEEs. In respect of national measures affecting imports, MEEs include rules on the shape, content, packaging, and

---

[6] Tariffs are covered by Art. 30 TFEU, discussed in Ch. 3.

[7] Case C–47/90 *Etablissements Delhaize Frères et Compagnie Le Lion SA v. Promalvin SA and AGE Bodegas Unidas SA* [1992] ECR I–3669. See also the follow-up in Case C–388/95 *Belgium* v. *Spain* [2000] ECR I–3123.

[8] Case C–170/04 *Rosengren* v. *Riksåklagaren* [2007] ECR I–4071. See also Case C–185/05 *Commission* v. *Sweden* [2007] ECR I–129. Cf. the case law on certain selling arrangements considered in Ch. 5.

[9] Para. 33.   [10] Case 34/79 *R. v. Henn and Darby* [1972] ECR 3795, paras. 12–13.

[11] Case C–5/94 *R. v. MAFF, ex p. Hedley Lomas (Ireland) Ltd* [1996] ECR I–2553, para. 12.

[12] Case C–1/96 *R. v. MAFF, ex p. Compassion in World Farming* [1998] ECR I–1251, para. 39.

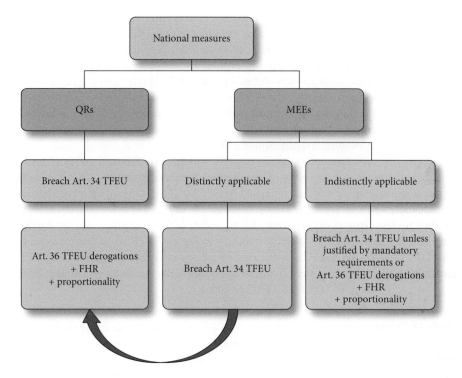

Fig. 4.1 QRs and MEEs: The traditional approach under Art. 34 TFEU

labelling of goods—all of which may hinder inter-state trade but which cannot be de-scribed as QRs.[13] In this section we examine the definition of MEEs and how the Court has developed a sophisticated case law around MEEs, distinguishing between distinctly and indistinctly applicable measures and, more recently, any other measure which hin-ders market access.

2. WHAT ARE MEASURES HAVING EQUIVALENT EFFECT?

2.1 The *Dassonville* Formula

The original definition of MEEs is found in the Court's decision in *Dassonville*:[14]

> All trading rules enacted by Member States which are capable of hindering, directly or indirectly, actually or potentially, intra-[Union] trade are to be considered as measures having an effect equivalent to quantitative restrictions.

In *Bouhelier*[15] the Court extended the *Dassonville* formula to Article 35 TFEU.[16]

The potential breadth of the *Dassonville* formula is striking. In principle, measures having only an *indirect, potential* effect on trade fall within the formula's scope and there-fore breach the Treaty. The decision thus provides individual traders with a vehicle to

---

[13] In Case 2/73 *Geddo v. Ente* [1973] ECR 865 the Court said 'whatever the description or technique employed, [MEEs] can also consist of encumbrances having the same effect' as QRs.

[14] Case 8/74 *Procureur du Roi v. Dassonville* [1974] ECR 837, para. 5.

[15] Case 53/76 *Procureur de la République de Besançon v. Les Sieurs Bouhelier* [1977] ECR 197; Case 68/76 *Commission v. France* [1977] ECR 515, paras. 15–16.

[16] Cf. Case C–412/97 *ED Srl v. Italo Fenocchio* [1999] ECR I–3845.

challenge any national rule which—even potentially and indirectly—stands in their way of participating on the market on whatever terms they choose. In other words, *Dassonville* supports a market access reading of Articles 34–5 TFEU, rather than a discrimination approach[17] and reinforces the view that the TFEU provides an economic constitution for the EU.[18]

Looked at in its historical context, *Dassonville* was an effective tool to cull the dead wood of centuries of accumulated legislation. However, taken to extremes, a broad reading of *Dassonville* might mean that Article 34 TFEU could be used to challenge national rules limiting Sunday trading or development in the green belt or age restrictions on who can buy alcohol. While such legislation does circumscribe general commercial freedom in various ways, the national rules are non-discriminatory, they serve a variety of social purposes, and their effects on *inter-state* trade are remote. For this reason the Court was eventually forced to curtail the broad sweep of the *Dassonville* formula when, in its judgment in *Keck*,[19] it recognized that non-discriminatory national measures restricting certain selling arrangements (CSAs) did not constitute MEEs and so fell outside the scope of Article 34 TFEU (see fig. 5.1). The details of this important case will be considered in Chapter 5. For now we shall examine the elements of the *Dassonville* formula.

2.2 'All Trading Rules'

According to *Dassonville*, Article 34 TFEU applies to 'all trading rules', which means that Article 34 TFEU concerns the marketing stage, and not the production stage, of the economic process. Therefore, in *Kramer*[20] the Court said that national rules limiting fishing in order to conserve fish stocks did not concern a trading rule and so did not constitute an MEE. In subsequent cases the Court has dropped the emphasis on the need to show a *trading* rule. For example, when defining MEEs in *Keck* the Court talked only of 'rules' that lay down requirements to be met by goods coming from other Member States.[21]

But even the reference to 'rules' is misleading. Article 34 TFEU itself refers to the more general term 'measures' and the Court has insisted that these measures need not be legally binding. Therefore, in *Commission* v. *Ireland ('Buy Irish' campaign)*[22] the Court said that a campaign sponsored by the Irish government encouraging its citizens to buy Irish goods amounted to the establishment of a 'national *practice* introduced by the Irish government and prosecuted with its assistance'.[23] It continued that, by influencing the conduct of traders and consumers in Ireland, the campaign's potential effect on imports was comparable to that resulting from government measures of a binding nature.[24]

Thus, *Buy Irish* shows that the term 'rules' includes practices and policies. *Commission* v. *France (postal franking machines)*[25] takes the definition one stage further. It says that 'rules' also include administrative regulations and actions[26] which show 'a certain degree

---

[17] Concepts discussed in Ch. 1. See also J. H. H. Weiler, 'The constitution of the common market place' in P. Craig and G. de Búrca (eds.), *The Evolution of EU Law* (Oxford: OUP, 1999), 351–64.

[18] See further Ch. 1.

[19] Joined Cases C–267 and 268/91 *Keck and Mithouard* [1993] ECR I–6097.

[20] Case 3/76 *Kramer* [1976] ECR 1279.   [21] Para. 15.

[22] Case 249/81 *Commission* v. *Ireland ('Buy Irish' campaign)* [1982] ECR 4005. See also Case 45/87 *Commission* v. *Ireland (Dundalk Water)* [1988] ECR 4929.

[23] Emphasis added.   [24] Paras. 27–8.

[25] Case 21/84 *Commission* v. *France (postal franking machines)* [1985] ECR 1355, para. 13. See also Joined Cases 266 and 267/87 *R. v. Royal Pharmaceutical Society of Great Britain, ex p. Association of Pharmaceutical Importers* [1989] ECR 1295, where a 'Code of Ethics and Guidance Notes' constituted 'measures'.

[26] See also the preamble to Dir. 70/50: 'Whereas for the purpose of Article [34 TFEU] et seq. "measures" means laws, regulations, administrative provisions, administrative practices and all instruments issuing

of consistency and generality'. Therefore, an administrative practice requiring prior approval to be given to postal franking machines, where approval was given to French machines but not those produced in the UK, breached Article 34 TFEU.[27]

2.3 'Enacted by Member States'

(a) 'Enacted'

The next element of the *Dassonville* formula, 'enacted by Member States', is also misleading. As Section 2.2 showed, the national measure does not need to be 'enacted' to fall within the scope of Article 34 TFEU: a consistent policy or practice will suffice. Further, the rules do not need to be 'enacted' by the central government of a Member State. Article 34 TFEU applies to measures adopted by the authorities of a federal state and other territorial authorities.[28] It also applies to bodies for whose acts the national government is responsible, as *Commission* v. *Ireland*[29] demonstrates. The 'Buy Irish' campaign was administered by the Irish Goods Council (IGC), a registered company. Nevertheless, the Court said that Article 34 TFEU still applied because the aims and broad outline of the campaign were set by the government, the management committee of the IGC was made up of ten people appointed by the Minister for Industry, and most of the funding for the council's activities came from the government.[30]

Not only does Article 34 TFEU (and Article 35 TFEU) apply to government or quasi-government bodies but it also applies to bodies which regulate the conduct of a particular profession or access to the particular market. For example, in *Ex p. API*[31] the Court ruled that Article 34 TFEU applied to the Royal Pharmaceutical Society of Great Britain, the professional body for pharmacy; and in *Fra.bo*[32] the Court said that Article 34 TFEU applied to a private law body (DVGW) which was in charge of authorising certificates concerning technical standardization where the national legislation considered the products certified by that body to be compliant with national law; without a certificate issued by DVGW the products could not be marketed.

Following *Viking*,[33] which is discussed in more detail in Chapter 7, Article 34 TFEU may also apply to bodies, such as trade unions, which have sufficient power to interfere with the free movement provisions.

from a public authority, including recommendations'. It adds that 'administrative practices' means 'any standard and regularly followed procedure of a public authority' and 'recommendations' means 'any instruments issuing from a public authority which, while not legally binding on the addressees thereof, cause them to pursue a certain conduct'.

[27] See also Case C–192/01 *Commission* v. *Denmark* [2003] ECR I–9693, para. 40; Case C–212/03 *Commission* v. *France (homeopathic medicines)* [2005] ECR I–4213, para. 17; Case C–88/07 *Commission* v. *Spain (medicinal herbs)* [2009] ECR I–13523, para. 54.

[28] Joined Cases C–1 and 176/90 *Aragonesa de Publicidad Exterior SA* v. *Departmento de Sanidad y Seguridad Social de la Generalitat de Cataluña* [1991] ECR I–4151, para. 8. See also Case 45/87 *Commission* v. *Ireland (Dundalk Water)* [1988] ECR 4929.

[29] Case 249/81 *Commission* v. *Ireland ('Buy Irish' campaign)* [1982] ECR 4005. See also Case 222/82 *Apple and Pear Development Council* v. *Lewis* [1983] ECR 4083, para. 17; and Case C–325/00 *Commission* v. *Germany (label of origin and quality)* [2002] ECR I–9977, paras. 19–20.

[30] M. Quinn and N. Macgowan, 'Could Article 30 impose obligations on individuals?' (1987) 12 *ELRev.* 163, 167 note that the Buy Irish Campaign was subsequently relaunched and exists through private sponsorship by means of a private company, Guaranteed Irish Ltd, set up with the intention of promoting Irish goods through the use of the 'Guaranteed Irish' symbol.

[31] Joined Cases 266 and 267/87 [1989] ECR 1295, paras. 14–15. See also Case C–292/92 *Hünermund* v. *Landesapothekerkammer Baden-Württemberg* [1993] ECR I–6787, para. 14.

[32] Case C–171/11 *Fra.bo SpA* v. *DVGW* EU:C:2012:453.

[33] Case C–438/05 [2007] ECR I–10779.

(b) Direct effect: Vertical and horizontal?

Commission v. *Ireland*, *API*, and *Fra.bo* support the view that Article 34 TFEU has *vertical* direct effect[34] and can be enforced against a broad category of state or quasi-state defendants or bodies acting in place of the state. This raises a further question: can or should Article 34 TFEU also have *horizontal* direct effect? This question has assumed a renewed importance since the decision in *Angonese*,[35] where the Court ruled that Article 45 TFEU on the free movement of workers has horizontal (as well as vertical) direct effect, at least in respect of a breach of the fundamental principle of non-discrimination.

From the perspective of ensuring the effectiveness of Article 34 TFEU, there are good policy reasons for giving Article 34 TFEU horizontal direct effect. If a large British supermarket chain were to refuse to stock French products on the ground that it objected to certain policies pursued by the French government, then the supermarket's decision would have a damaging effect on inter-state trade. On the other hand, Article 34 TFEU is addressed to the Member States[36] and not to private parties who should be able to contract freely, unconstrained by Article 34 TFEU. This was the view taken by the Court in *Sapod-Audic*,[37] where it said that a contractual obligation to affix the 'Green dot' recycling logo to packaging could not be regarded as a barrier to trade for the purposes of Article 34 TFEU 'since it was not imposed by a Member State but agreed between individuals'. *Sapod-Audic* thus suggests that Article 34 TFEU should not have horizontal direct effect.

Most commentators consider that, outside the field of intellectual property,[38] Article 34 TFEU (and Article 35 TFEU[39]) have only vertical direct effect and so do not apply to action between individuals. Their action is constrained by the (less demanding) regime of the competition rules (Articles 101–2 TFEU).[40] Article 101 TFEU applies only in the case of agreements between undertakings (so a unilateral decision by a supermarket is unlikely to be covered); Article 102 TFEU applies only if there is an abuse of a dominant position. Even the largest supermarket is unlikely to satisfy the criteria of dominance (40 per cent of market share). In these circumstances, our fictitious supermarket chain's conduct is likely to fall outside the scope of Union law.

That said, the state may have to take responsibility for the action of individuals either directly or indirectly. An example of direct responsibility can be seen in *A.G.M.-COS.MET*.[41] An expert advising the Finnish Ministry of Social Affairs and Health said in

---

[34] Case 74/76 *Ianelli & Volpi* v. *Meroni* [1977] ECR 557, para. 13; Case 83/78 *Pigs Marketing Board* v. *Redmond* [1978] ECR 2347, paras. 66–7.

[35] Case C–281/98 *Angonese* v. *Cassa di Risparmio di Bolzano* [2000] ECR I–4139.

[36] See also Case 7/68 *Commission* v. *Italy* [1968] ECR 428, 430: 'The subject of that chapter [the elimination of quantitative restrictions] is State intervention'; and Warner AG in Joined Cases 55 and 57/80 *Musik-Vertrieb Membran* v. *Gema* [1981] ECR 147, 175, talking of measures under Art. 34 TFEU, means 'a measure taken by a Member State; it does not mean a measure taken by a private person'. Cf. Arts. 157 and 45 TFEU, which are also addressed to Member States but nevertheless have been found to be binding on private individuals.

[37] Case C–159/00 *Sapod-Audic* v. *Eco-Emballages SA* [2002] ECR I–5031, para. 74.

[38] See further Ch. 6.

[39] Case 83/78 *Pigs Marketing Board* v. *Redmond* [1978] ECR 2347, para. 66, and Case C–47/90 *Delhaize* [1992] ECR I–3669, paras. 28–9.

[40] See Capotorti AG in Case 82/77 *Openbaar Ministerie of the Netherlands* v. *van Tiggele* [1978] ECR 25. This view is supported by Case 65/86 *Bayer AG* v. *Süllhöfer* [1988] ECR 5249 and Joined Cases 177 and 178/82 *Criminal Proceedings against Van de Haar* [1984] ECR 1797, para. 114, which suggest that Arts. 101 and 34 TFEU are mutually exclusive. Cf. Poiares Maduro AG in Case C–438/05 *Viking* [2007] ECR I–10779, paras. 31–56.

[41] Case C–470/03 *A.G.M.-COS.MET Srl* v. *Soumen valtio, Tarmo Lehtinen* [2007] ECR I–2749, para. 56. For criticism, see N. Reich, 'AGM-COS.MET or: Who is protected by EC safety regulation?' (2008) 33 *ELRev*. 85.

the press that vehicle lifts made by an Italian company, AGM, were not safe, even though they were certified as conforming to the relevant directive. This resulted in AGM losing sales in Finland. The Court said that if AGM could reasonably suppose that the statements were positions taken by the official with the authority of his office, they could be an obstacle to inter-state trade within the meaning of *Dassonville*.[42]

States may also take indirect responsibility for activities of individuals who have been disrupting the application of Article 34 TFEU, even though the activity of the individuals is not itself caught by Article 34 TFEU. This principle was established in *Commission v. France (Spanish strawberries)*.[43] For many years French farmers sabotaged imported agricultural produce while the French authorities simply stood back and turned a blind eye. Eventually, the Commission brought Article 258 TFEU enforcement proceedings against the French government 'for failing to take all necessary and proportionate measures'[44] to prevent the free movement of goods from being obstructed by the actions of private individuals. The Commission argued that the French government's failure to act contravened Article 34 TFEU read in conjunction with Article 4(3) TEU on the duty of loyal cooperation. The Court agreed, saying that Article 34 TFEU prohibited not only state action but also inaction:

> The fact that a Member State abstains from taking action or, as the case may be, fails to adopt adequate measures to prevent obstacles to the free movement of goods that are created, in particular, by actions by private individuals on its territory aimed at products originating in other Member States is just as likely to obstruct intra-[Union] trade as is a positive act.[45]

However, it seems that liability will arise only where the state has 'manifestly and persistently abstained from adopting appropriate and adequate measures' to put an end to individual action which jeopardizes free movement.[46] Less serious interference by individuals will not attract this sanction.[47]

2.4 'Directly or Indirectly, Actually or Potentially'

(a) 'Actually or potentially'

Given the problems associated with the first two limbs of the *Dassonville* formula ((1) all trading rules (2) enacted by Member States), it is not perhaps surprising that the Court has, in more recent decisions, increasingly referred to 'any *measure* capable of hindering, directly or indirectly, actually or potentially, intra-[Union] trade' as an 'obstacle' to free movement,[48]

---

[42] Case C–470/03 *A.G.M.-COS.MET Srl* [2007] ECR I–2749, paras. 56–7 and 60. The Court provided criteria for determining whether the statements were attributable to the state at para. 58.

[43] Case C–265/95 *Commission v. France (Spanish strawberries)* [1997] ECR I–6959. K. Muylle, 'Angry farmers and passive policemen: Private conduct and free movement of goods' (1998) 23 *ELRev.* 467, 469.

[44] See also para. 32 of the judgment.

[45] Paras. 30–1. See also Case C–309/02 *Radlberger Getränkegesellschaft mbH & Co.* v. *Land Baden-Württemberg* [2004] ECR I–11763, para. 80, where the state was liable under Art. 34 TFEU for its failure to ensure that private parties could effectively participate in a take-back system for beverage repackaging.

[46] Para. 65. See also Council Reg. (EC) No. 2679/98 on the functioning of the internal market in relation to the free movement of goods among the Member States ([1998] OJ L337/8), considered in Ch. 6.

[47] See Case C–112/00 *Schmidberger, Internationale Transporte und Planzüge* v. *Republic of Austria* [2003] ECR I–5659, considered in Ch. 6.

[48] See, e.g., Case C–470/03 *A.G.M.-COS.MET Srl* [2007] ECR I–2749, para. 60 and Case C–319/05 *Commission* v. *Germany (garlic capsule)* [2007] ECR I–9811, para. 80. Cf. Case C–143/06 *Ludwigs-Apotheke München Internationale Apotheke* v. *Juers Pharma Import-Export GmbH* [2007] ECR I–9623, para. 26, which talks more narrowly of 'all legislation'.

thereby dropping the first two limbs of *Dassonville*.[49] However, the third limb ('directly or indirectly, actually or potentially') remains good law. It is the most important element of the formula since it emphasizes the Court's concern with the *effect* of the measure, not the intention behind it. This can be seen from the facts of *Dassonville* itself.

Dassonville concerned a Belgian law requiring importers of Scotch whisky to hold a British certificate of authentication. This rule favoured those importing whisky directly from the UK over traders importing Scotch whisky into Belgium from other Member States where the whisky was already in free circulation. Such 'indirect' importers could obtain this certificate only with great difficulty. The Court did not analyse this problem in terms of discrimination; instead it merely said that the requirement to hold the certificate constituted an MEE. This effects-based approach to Article 34 TFEU stands in stark contrast to the narrower protectionist approach to the dormant commerce clause advocated by much of the US Supreme Court's jurisprudence.[50] Protectionist measures will, of course, be caught by Article 34 TFEU but so will a much wider range of measures, including those that are discriminatory and those that hinder market access.

While cases like *Dassonville* concern measures which have an actual effect on trade, the Court has recognized that it may be sufficient for the measure to have a potential effect to breach Article 34 TFEU. This can be seen in *Commission* v. *France (foie gras)*[51] concerning French rules on the composition of *foie gras*. Although very little *foie gras* was produced in other Member States,[52] the Court still found that because the French rule was 'capable of hindering, at least *potentially*, inter-state trade'[53] it breached Article 34 TFEU.

The *Foie Gras* case also demonstrates the point made explicitly elsewhere that originally no *de minimis* rule applied to Article 34 TFEU.[54] For this reason, the Court has said that national rules need apply only to part, and often a very small part, of the market to trigger the Article 34 TFEU prohibition. Therefore, in *Bluhme*[55] the Court said that Article 34

---

[49] Cf. Case C–244/06 *Dynamic Medien Vertriebs GmbH* v. *Avides Media AG* [2008] ECR I–505, para. 26 and Case C–110/05 *Commission* v. *Italy (trailers)* [2009] ECR I–519, para. 33, where the Court used the original *Dassonville* formula.

[50] D. Regan, 'The Supreme Court and state protectionism: Making sense of the dormant commerce clause' (1985) 84 *Mich. L. Rev.* 1091. Regan argues that the Supreme Court has rightly been exclusively concerned with preventing states from engaging in purposeful economic protectionism, which he defines to mean: (1) the statute was adopted for the purpose of improving the competitive position of local economic actors, just because they are local, vis-à-vis their foreign competitors; and (2) the statute is analogous in form to the traditional instruments of protectionism (the tariff, quota, or embargo).

[51] Case C–184/96 *Commission* v. *France (foie gras)* [1998] ECR I–6197, para. 17.

[52] Although cf. Case 118/86 *Openbaar Ministerie* v. *Nertsvoederfabriek Nederland BV* [1987] ECR 3883, para. 10: 'Since the rules described do not disclose any prohibition of imports, there is no need to consider Article [34 TFEU].'

[53] Emphasis added. See also Case C–325/00 *Commission* v. *Germany (label of origin)* [2002] ECR I–9977, para. 25. Cf. Art. 110 TFEU, where it seems that actual disparate impact must be shown: Case 132/88 *Commission* v. *Greece* [1990] ECR I–1567 and Case 252/86 *Bergandi* [1988] ECR 1343, considered further in Ch. 3.

[54] Joined Cases 177 and 178/82 *Van de Haar* [1984] ECR 1797, para. 13: 'If a national measure is capable of hindering imports it must be regarded as [an MEE], even though the hindrance is slight and even though it is possible for the imported product to be marketed in other ways'. See also Case C–126/91 *Schutzverband gegen Unwesen in der Wirtschaft ev* v. *Yves Rocher GmbH* [1993] ECR I–2361, para. 21, and Case C–67/97 *Criminal Proceedings against Bluhme* [1998] ECR I–8033, where Fennelly AG said 'the slight effect of the Decision, in volume terms, cannot in itself prevent the application of Article [34 TFEU]'. Cf. Case C–110/05 *Commission* v. *Italy (trailers)* [2009] ECR I–519, para. 56 (see Section F of this chapter), where the Court appeared to suggest the need for some form of threshold requirement. See also competition law where it is well established that Art. 101 TFEU is subject to a *de minimis* rule: Case 5/69 *Völk* v. *Vervaeke* [1969] ECR 295.

[55] Case C–67/97 *Bluhme* [1998] ECR I–8033. See also, e.g., Joined Cases C–277, 318 and 319/91 *Ligur Carni* v. *Unità Sanitaria Locale* [1993] ECR I–6621 (rule applied by a municipality to its slaughterhouse).

TFEU applied to a rule which affected the Danish island of Læsø, which covered only 0.3 per cent of Danish territory.

However, in cases which fall on the perimeter of free movement of goods, the Court has applied a remoteness test,[56] especially where the case does not concern a trading rule in the narrow sense of the term. This can be seen in *Krantz*[57] concerning a Dutch law allowing the collector of taxes to seize goods if purchasers failed to discharge their tax debts. The Court said the possibility that nationals of other Member States would hesitate to sell goods on instalment to purchasers in the Netherlands because such goods were liable to be seized by the collector of taxes was 'too uncertain and indirect' to warrant the conclusion that a national provision authorizing such seizure was liable to hinder trade between Member States,[58] and so Article 34 TFEU did not apply.[59]

(b) 'Directly or indirectly'

Dassonville also requires that the national measure must 'directly or indirectly' hinder intra-Union trade. Increasingly this was interpreted to mean that national rules which discriminated either directly or indirectly against imported goods were prohibited. The need to show some discrimination was also emphasized in *Keck* (considered in Chapter 5).

The Commission has always recognized that Article 34 TFEU prohibits discrimination. In Commission Directive 70/50[60] it distinguished between measures which discriminate directly against imports ('distinctly applicable measures') and measures that indirectly affect imports ('indistinctly applicable measures' or 'equally applicable measures').[61] This directive applied only during the Union's transitional period (now expired)[62] but continues to be an important source of information to help understand this terminology.[63] Up until the early 2000s the case law followed the distinction drawn by the Directive,[64] but more recent cases have paid less attention to whether the measure is discriminatory, focusing instead on the obstacle created by the rule to market access, thereby bringing the case law back to the original market access approach found in *Dassonville*. This shift was confirmed in *Commission* v. *Italy (trailers)*. It now seems that Article 34 TFEU prohibits not only distinctly and indistinctly applicable rules (Sections D and E) but also those that hinder market access (Section F). We shall now consider these categories in turn.

D. DISTINCTLY APPLICABLE MEASURES

1. INTRODUCTION

Distinctly applicable measures are loosely equivalent to directly discriminatory measures: the imported goods are treated less favourably than the domestic product when,

---

[56] See La Pergola AG in Case C–44/98 *BASF* [1999] ECR I–6269, para. 18.

[57] Case C–69/88 *Krantz* [1990] ECR I–583. This is considered further in Ch. 5.

[58] Para. 11. See also, e.g., Case C–93/92 *CMC Motorradcenter GmbH* v. *Pelin Baskiciogullari* [1993] ECR I–5009, para. 12; Case C–44/98 *BASF* v. *Präsident des Deutschen Patentamts* [1999] ECR I–6269, paras. 16 and 21.

[59] See also Case C–412/97 *ED Srl* v. *Italo Fenocchio* [1999] ECR I–3845 for an example under Art. 35 TFEU.

[60] [1970] OJ L13/29 ([1970] OJ Spec. Ed. 17).

[61] While this book will use the terms 'distinctly' and 'indistinctly applicable', it should be noted that there are many definitions and classifications of the measures. See, e.g., N. Bernard, 'Discrimination and free movement in EC law' (1996) 45 *ICLQ* 82 and C. Hilson, 'Discrimination in Community free movement law' (1999) 24 *ELRev.* 445.

[62] 1 Jan. 1970.   [63] See, e.g., Case 12/74 *Commission* v. *Germany* [1975] ECR 181, para. 14.

[64] See Van Gerven AG in Joined Cases C–401 and 402/92 *Criminal Proceedings against Tankstation 't Heukske vof and J.B.E. Boermans* [1994] ECR I–2199, para. 19.

in objective terms, they should be treated in the same way.[65] Putting it another way, the national measure has a different burden in law and in fact on the domestic and imported good. The need to show differential impact was emphasized by Article 2 of Directive 70/50:

> This Directive covers measures, other than those applicable equally to domestic or imported products, which hinder imports which could otherwise take place, including measures which make importation more difficult or costly than the disposal of domestic production.

In Section 2 we look at some common examples of distinctly applicable rules before going on to consider the defences available to the Member States (Section 3).

2. EXAMPLES OF DISTINCTLY APPLICABLE MEASURES

2.1 Imposing an Additional Requirement on the Imported/Exported Goods

Distinctly applicable measures include those which, as Article 2 of Directive 70/50 puts it, place conditions on imported products only, or demand higher standards of imports than of domestic products. Therefore, a requirement that imported, but not domestic, goods be inspected breaches Article 34 TFEU[66] due to the delays inherent in the inspection process[67] and the additional transport costs which the importer may incur.[68]

Other unlawful conditions relate to the requirement for the imported goods (but not the domestic goods) to have a licence[69] or other official approval,[70] such as a certificate of fitness.[71] Alternatively the condition may relate instead to the composition of the goods. So, in *Weinvertriebs*[72] the Court said that a German law specifying the minimum alcohol content for imported (but not domestic) vermouth breached Article 34 TFEU. The condition may also concern the circumstances under which the goods are promoted. Hence, a ban or other restriction on advertising foreign products, but not their domestic equivalents, would breach Article 34 TFEU.[73]

---

[65] The Court tends to use a variety of formulas to describe 'distinctly applicable' measures. It might say that the measure is 'discriminatory' or it might note, as in Case C–320/93 *Ortscheit* [1994] ECR I–5243, para. 9, that the national measure 'applies solely' to the foreign products.

[66] Case 251/78 *Firma Denkavit Futtermittel GmbH* v. *Minister für Ernährung* [1979] ECR 3369, para. 10; Case 50/85 *Schloh* v. *Auto contrôle technique SPRL* [1986] ECR 1855 (roadworthiness testing).

[67] Case 132/80 *United Foods* v. *Belgian State* [1981] ECR 995, para. 28 (24 hours' notice to be given in writing for health inspection of imported fish).

[68] Case 4/75 *Rewe-Zentralfinanz eGmbH* v. *Landwirtschaftskammer* [1975] ECR 843, para. 4 (phytosanitary inspections of imported apples to control the spread of the apple disease San José scale). For an example of such cases under Art. 35 TFEU, see Case C–293/02 *Jersey Produce Marketing Organisation Ltd* v. *States of Jersey* [2005] ECR I–9543, paras. 75–6 and Case C–12/02 *Grilli* [2003] ECR I–11585, para. 48.

[69] Even if the licence is granted automatically: Joined Cases 51–54/71 *International Fruit (No. 2)* [1971] ECR 1107, para. 9. See also Case 40/82 *Commission* v. *UK (turkeys)* [1984] ECR 2793, para. 24, and Case 124/81 *Commission* v. *UK (UHT milk)* [1983] ECR 203, para. 9. For an equivalent case concerning exports, see Case 53/76 *Procureur de la République* v. *Bouhelier* [1977] ECR 197, para. 11.

[70] Case 21/84 *Commission* v. *France (postal franking machines)* [1985] ECR 1355; Case C–434/04 *Ahokainen* [2006] ECR I–9171, para. 22 (prior authorization required for the import of undenatured ethyl alcohol of an alcoholic strength of more than 80 per cent).

[71] Case 251/78 *Firma Denkavit Futtermittel GmbH* [1979] ECR 3369, para. 11.

[72] Case 59/82 *Schutzverband gegen Unwesen in der Wirtschaft* v. *Weinvertriebs-GmbH* [1983] ECR 1217, paras. 7–8.

[73] Case 152/78 *Commission* v. *France* [1980] ECR 2299, para. 13 (alcohol); Case C–320/93 *Ortscheit* v. *Eurim-Pharm Arzneimittel* [1994] ECR I–5243, para. 9 (medicinal products).

2.2 Rules Limiting Channels of Distribution

A second group of situations considered to be distinctly applicable concerns national rules limiting channels of distribution. We have already seen in *Dassonville*[74] how a national rule requiring the production of a certificate of authenticity favoured direct importers over indirect importers and so breached Article 34 TFEU. This can also be seen in *De Peijper*,[75] where a parallel importer, who was not appointed to sell certain medicines directly on the Dutch market, bought them instead from a British whole-saler, and then imported them into the Netherlands. The parallel importer could not obtain the necessary authorization from the Dutch authorities because the appointed importer refused to give it access to the relevant documentation. The Court said that 'rules or practices which result in imports being channelled in such a way that only certain traders can effect these imports, whereas others are prevented from doing so' constituted an MEE.[76]

A number of Article 35 TFEU cases also concern national rules interfering with chan-nels of trade, particularly disposing of hazardous waste. For example, in *Inter-Huiles*[77] the Court said that national rules establishing a system for the collection and disposal of waste oils which prohibited export to a disposal or regenerating company in another Member State breached Article 35 TFEU. Similarly, in *FFAD*[78] the Court said that mu-nicipal rules which prevented even qualified intermediaries from participating in the collection of waste with a view to reselling it in other Member States breached Article 35 TFEU,[79] as did national rules requiring producers to deliver poultry offal to their local authority in *Nertsvoederfabriek*.[80]

2.3 National Rules Giving Preference to Domestic Goods

(a) 'Buy national' rules

A third group of distinctly applicable measures involves national rules which give pref-erence to, or an advantage for, domestic products. This can be seen in *Dundalk Water*[81] concerning a clause in a tender to supply pipes for drinking water which specified that the pipes had to be made according to an Irish standard by a firm approved by the Irish standards body as a supplier of pipes complying with the Irish standard. Only one (Irish) firm had been approved by the body. The authorities rejected a tender from an Irish/ Spanish consortium proposing to supply pipes manufactured according to an alternative international standard. The Court said that the terms of the tender discouraged those producing pipes to equivalent standards from tendering. This had 'the *effect* of restricting the supply of the pipes needed for the Dundalk scheme to Irish manufacturers alone'[82] and therefore breached Article 34 TFEU.

---

[74] Case 8/74 *Dassonville* [1974] ECR 837. See also Case 247/81 *Commission* v. *Germany* [1984] ECR 1111 (requirement to have a representative in the host state in which the goods were sold).

[75] Case 104/75 *De Peijper* [1976] ECR 613.   [76] Para. 13.

[77] Case 172/82 *Syndicat national des fabricants raffineurs d'huile de graissage* v. *Groupement d'intérêt économique 'Inter-Huiles'* [1983] ECR 555. See also Case 295/82 *Groupement d'intérêt économique 'Rhône-Alpes Huiles'* v. *Syndicat national des fabricants raffineurs d'huile de graissage* [1984] ECR 575.

[78] Case C–209/98 *Entreprenørforeningens Affalds/Miljøsektion (FFAD)* v. *Københavns Kommune* [2000] ECR I–3743.

[79] Para. 42.

[80] Case 118/86 *Openbaar Ministerie* v. *Nertsvoederfabriek Nederland BV* [1997] ECR 3883, para. 11.

[81] Case 45/87 *Commission* v. *Ireland* [1988] ECR 4929. See also Case C–67/97 *Bluhme* [1998] ECR I–8033.

[82] Para. 20, emphasis added. Cf. Case C–254/05 *Commission* v. *Belgium (automatic fire detection systems)* [2007] ECR I–4269, where the Court considered the requirement to apply a Belgian standard was 'applicable without distinction to all products' and could be justified by a mandatory requirement (para. 31).

'Buy national' campaigns are also considered distinctly applicable since, by their very nature, they are intended to encourage the purchase of national products in preference to imported products. Therefore, in *Commission* v. *Ireland ('Buy Irish' campaign)*[83] the Court condemned an Irish government-backed campaign designed to achieve 'the substitution of domestic products for imported products [which] was liable to affect the volume of trade between Member States'.[84] It reached this conclusion even though trade had actually fallen by 6 per cent over the three years of the campaign.

The *Buy Irish* case needs to be compared with *Apple and Pear Development Council ('buy British fruit')*,[85] where the Court said that a British government-supported development council could promote British fruit but was under a duty not to run advertising designed to discourage the purchase of products from other Member States, nor to disparage those products in the eyes of the consumers, nor to advise consumers to purchase domestic products solely by reason of their national origin. However, the Court did say that such a body could draw attention in its publicity to the specific qualities of fruit grown in the UK and could organize campaigns to promote the sale of certain varieties, mentioning their particular properties, even if those varieties were typical of national production.[86] This case law highlights the fine line between state-sponsored promotion of national goods generally, which is unlawful, and state-sponsored promotion of specific goods having distinctive qualities, which is permissible.

If 'buy national' campaigns are considered distinctly applicable, *a fortiori*, national rules requiring the purchase of certain quantities of the domestic product will be distinctly applicable. In *PreussenElektra*[87] the Court ruled that an obligation placed on electricity suppliers to purchase all of the renewable electricity produced in their region was an MEE since it limited the supplies those traders could obtain from producers in other Member States. The Court reached a similar conclusion in *Du Pont de Nemours*,[88] where Italian law reserved 30 per cent of public supply contracts to companies established in certain regions of Italy. In its defence, Italy argued that Italian regions not covered by the preferential system also suffered. The Court rejected the argument, saying that 'although not all the products of the Member State in question benefit by comparison with products from abroad, the fact remains that all the products benefiting by the preferential system are domestic products'. The measure therefore breached Article 34 TFEU.

(b) Origin marking rules

Origin marking cases are also considered distinctly applicable, as *Commission* v. *Ireland (Irish souvenirs)*[89] demonstrates. Irish law required that all imported (but not domestic)

---

[83] Case 249/81 *Commission* v. *Ireland* [1982] ECR 4005. See also Case C–255/03 *Commission* v. *Belgium (Walloon label of quality)* EU:C:2004:378.

[84] Para. 25.

[85] Case 222/82 *Apple and Pear Development Council* v. *Lewis* [1983] ECR 4083, para. 18.

[86] Case 222/82 *Apple and Pear Development Council* v. *Lewis* [1983] ECR 4083, para. 19. As a result of these two cases the Commission has offered 'Guidelines for the Member States' involvement in Promotion of Agricultural and Fisheries Products—Article [34] Aspects' ([1986] OJ C27/3). See also Reg. 3/2008 on information provision and promotion measures for agricultural products on the internal market and in third countries ([2008] OJ L3/1).

[87] Case C–379/98 *PreussenElektra AG* v. *Schleswag AG* [2001] ECR I–2099, para. 70. See also Case 72/83 *Campus Oil* [1984] ECR 2727, para. 16 and Case C–398/98 *Commission* v. *Greece* [2001] ECR I–7915, para. 26. These cases are considered in Ch. 6.

[88] Case C–21/88 *Du Pont de Nemours Italiana SpA* v. *Unità sanitaria locale No. 2 di Carrara* [1990] ECR I–889, para. 11. See also Case C–243/89 *Commission* v. *Denmark (Storebaelt)* [1993] ECR I–3353.

[89] Case 113/80 *Commission* v. *Ireland* [1981] ECR 1625. See also Case C–30/99 *Commission* v. *Ireland (hallmarking of precious metals)* [2001] ECR I–4619, para. 74.

jewellery depicting motifs suggesting that they were souvenirs of Ireland (e.g., an Irish character, wolfhound, or shamrock) had to bear an indication of the country of origin or the word 'foreign'. The Irish government justified its rule on the ground that the appeal of souvenirs lay in the fact that they were manufactured in the place where they were bought. The Court rejected these arguments, favouring instead the Commission's view that buyers did not need to know where a product came from unless the product implied a certain quality (which was not the case here). Rather dismissively, the Court said that since the souvenirs were of little commercial value, bought by tourists on the spot as 'pictorial reminders' of the place visited, they did not have to be manufactured in the country of origin.[90] Therefore, the Irish law *requiring* an indication of origin was a distinctly applicable MEE and breached Article 34 TFEU. However, the Court added that Article 34 TFEU did allow domestic manufacturers to *choose* whether to attach the mark of origin to their goods.[91] This might be to the manufacturers' commercial advantage for the very reasons given by the Irish government.

It might be thought that a rule concerning origin marking did serve the interests of consumers since, as the Court said in *GB-INNO-BM*,[92] the provision of information to the consumer is a fundamental right. However, in *Commission* v. *UK (origin marking)*,[93] a case concerning a British law that certain imported goods be marked with an indication of origin, the Court explained why this might not always be so. It said that the UK law breached Article 34 TFEU because the origin marking requirement enabled consumers to distinguish between domestic and imported products, allowing them to assert any prejudices they might have against the foreign product. In a single market an origin marking rule not only made the marketing of imported goods more difficult but it also had 'the effect of slowing down economic interpenetration in the [Union] by handicapping the sale of goods produced as the result of a division of labour between Member States'.[94]

As the Court suggested in the *Buy Irish* and *Origin Marking* cases, indications of provenance[95] and designations of origin[96] are lawful only where the product genuinely has distinguishing qualities and characteristics which are due to the fact that it originated in a specific geographic area.[97] This was confirmed in *Commission* v. *Germany (Weinbrand)*,[98] where the Court found that a German law reserving the well-known but generic names 'Sekt' and 'Weinbrand' to products originating in Germany or coming from countries where German was the official language breached Article 34 TFEU. The Court said that an area of origin defined on the basis of the national territory (Germany) or a linguistic criterion (German-speaking) could not constitute a geographic area capable of justifying an indication of origin[99] because the production of these drinks did not

---

[90] Case 113/80 *Commission* v. *Ireland* [1981] ECR 1625, para. 15.   [91] Para. 16.

[92] Case C–362/88 *GB-INNO-BM* v. *Confédération du commerce luxembourgeois* [1990] ECR I–667, para. 18.

[93] Case 207/83 *Commission* v. *UK* [1985] ECR 1202.   [94] Para. 17.

[95] Indications of provenance are intended to inform the consumer that the product bearing that indication comes from a particular place, region, or country: Case C–3/91 *Exportur* [1992] ECR I–5529, para. 11. Therefore, in Joined Cases C–321–324/94 *Pistre* [1997] ECR I–2343, para. 36, the description 'mountain' was not an indication of provenance. See further Ch. 6.

[96] Designations of origin guarantee not only the geographical provenance of the product but also that the goods have been manufactured according to quality requirements or manufacturing standards prescribed by an act of a public authority: Case C–3/91 *Exportur* [1992] ECR I–5529, para.11, citing the example of Case C–47/90 *Delhaize* [1992] ECR I–3669 (Rioja wine).

[97] Case 12/74 *Commission* v. *Germany* [1975] ECR 181, para. 7.

[98] Case 12/74 *Commission* v. *Germany* [1975] ECR 181, para. 7.

[99] Para. 8. In Case 286/86 *Ministère public* v. *Deserbais* [1988] ECR 4907, para. 9, the Court said that the designation 'Edam' was not an appellation of origin.

involve specific grapes or production methods. In other words, because the products did not have any qualities and characteristics rendering them typically German,[100] Germany could not reserve the generic names 'Sekt' and 'Weinbrand' to these national products.[101] Furthermore, the Court said that by reserving these names to domestic products, products from other Member States were compelled to employ names which were 'unknown or less esteemed by the consumer'.[102] As a result, the German legislation was 'calculated to favour the disposal of the domestic product on the German market to the detriment of the products from other Member States'.[103]

A common theme running through this line of case law is the Court's insistence on examining the effect of the measure.[104] If, in reality, the measure has a different burden in law and in fact on the imported goods it is considered to be distinctly applicable, no matter that the measure might be drafted in an indistinctly applicable (same burden in law, different burden in fact) manner. This can be seen most clearly in *Commission* v. *UK (origin marking)*,[105] where, in response to the UK's argument that the rule was actually indistinctly applicable, the Court said:[106]

> The requirements relating to the indication of origin of goods are applicable without distinction to domestic and imported products *only in form* because, by their very nature, they are intended to enable the consumer to distinguish between those two categories of products, which may thus prompt him to give his preference to national products.

3. DEFENDING DISTINCTLY APPLICABLE MEASURES

According to the orthodoxy, the significance for the defendant Member State of having its rule classified as a distinctly applicable measure is that it can justify it only by reference to one of the Article 36 TFEU derogations, not by the broader list of judicially developed 'mandatory' or 'public interest' or 'imperative' requirements which apply only to indistinctly applicable measures (see fig. 4.1).[107] However, there are signs that the Court is in the process of diluting, if not abandoning altogether, this well-established rule (see fig. 5.1). This change has come about in two ways.

First, in certain cases the Court has conveniently overlooked the fact that the rule was in fact directly discriminatory to enable the defending state to have recourse to the mandatory requirements. Perhaps the most blatant example of this is *Walloon Waste*,[108] which concerned a decree of the Walloon Regional Council prohibiting the storage or dumping in Wallonia of waste originating in another Member State or in a region of Belgium other than Wallonia. Most commentators consider this rule to be directly discriminatory[109] and

[100] Para. 10.
[101] Para. 16. In response to concerns that the Court's case law was having the effect of diminishing the quality of foodstuffs, the Commission adopted Reg. 2098/92 ([1992] OJ L208/1), which established a registration procedure for foodstuffs which have a link between their characteristics and geographical origins. This is considered further in Ch. 6.
[102] Para. 14.   [103] Para. 14.
[104] See esp. Case 45/87 *Commission* v. *Ireland (Dundalk Water)* [1988] ECR 4929.
[105] Case 207/83 *Commission* v. *UK* [1985] ECR 1202. For a similar approach see Case 177/83 *Kohl KG* v. *Ringelhan & Rennett SA and Ringelhan Einrichtungs GmbH* [1984] ECR 3651, para. 15.
[106] Para. 20, emphasis added.
[107] The Art. 36 TFEU derogations and the mandatory requirements are discussed in detail in Ch. 6.
[108] Case C-2/90 *Commission* v. *Belgium* [1992] ECR I-4431.
[109] The Commission argued this before the Court. See also, e.g., Bernard, n. 61, 93; N. Notaro, 'The new generation case law on trade and environment' (2000) 25 *ELRev.* 467, 478–9 and 482. However, this is a difficult area because Art. 191(2) TFEU recognizes that 'damage should as a priority be rectified at source'.

so it should have been justified only by one of the express derogations. Instead, the Court applied the 'imperative requirements of environmental protection'.[110]

Secondly, in more modern cases the Court does not expressly classify a measure as distinctly applicable, describing the rule instead simply as an MEE. For example, in *Commission v. Austria (roadworthiness of cars)*[111] the Court said that national rules making the registration of *imported* but not domestic used vehicles previously registered in other Member States contingent upon compliance with certain technical requirements constituted an MEE. However, the Court said the Austrian rule could be justified on the grounds of public health (an express derogation) or environmental protection (a mandatory requirement). As the Commission notes, this reflects a 'greening' of free movement of goods that has taken place in recent years, underlining the fact that certain grounds of justification may be viewed differently over time.[112]

But it is not just in cases concerning the environment where the Court is bending (ignoring?) its own rules. For example, in *Commission v. Finland*[113] the Court permitted a Finnish law requiring import licences for vehicles, traditionally a distinctly applicable measure, to be justified by the road-safety mandatory requirement.[114] Likewise, in *LIBRO*[115] the Court allowed a distinctly applicable book price-fixing scheme to be justified by the 'overriding requirement in the public interest', namely the 'protection of books as cultural objects'.[116]

Such cases have prompted some to call for the abolition of the distinction between the express derogations and mandatory requirements.[117] For example, in *PreussenElektra*[118] Advocate General Jacobs pointed to a number of decisions where the Court has 'relied on imperative requirements in cases in which it was at least doubtful whether the measure could be considered as applying without distinction'.[119] He called on the Court to clarify the situation, especially because 'it is desirable that even directly discriminatory measures can sometimes be justified on grounds of environmental protection'.[120] As cases such as *Commission v. Finland* and *LIBRO* show, the Court does seem to be moving in

---

[110] Case C–2/90 *Commission v. Belgium* [1992] ECR I–4431, para. 32.

[111] Case C–524/07 [2008] ECR I–187, paras. 54 and 55. For earlier examples, see Case C–67/97 *Bluhme* [1998] ECR I–8033, para. 19; Case C–120/95 *Decker v. Caisse de Maladie des Employés Privés* [1998] ECR I–1831.

[112] Commission, *Free Movement of Goods: Guide to the application of Treaty provisions governing free movement of goods*, SEC(2009) 673, 8.

[113] Case C–54/05 *Commission v. Finland* [2007] ECR I–2473.

[114] See also Case C–297/05 *Commission v. Netherlands (roadworthiness testing of cars)* [2007] ECR I–7467. The Court has finessed this change by merging the terminology: e.g., Case C–239/02 *Douwe Egberts NV v. Westrom Pharma* [2004] ECR I–7007, para. 55: 'Such a fetter may be justified only by one of the public interest grounds set out in Article [36 TFEU] ... or by one of the overriding requirements ensuring inter alia consumer protection.'

[115] Case C–531/07 *Fachverband der Buch- und Medienwirtschaft v. LIBRO Handelsgesellschaft mbH* [2009] ECR I–3717, para. 34.

[116] See, e.g., Case C–54/05 *Commission v. Finland* [2007] ECR I–2473, where the Court of Justice allowed an import licence to be justified, at least in principle, by mandatory requirements.

[117] See also Commission, *Free Movement of Goods: Guide to the application of Treaty provisions governing free movement of goods*, SEC(2009) 673, 42, which argues that the separation between the express derogations and the mandatory requirements is 'artificial and the Court is moving towards simplification and treating mandatory requirements in the same way as Article [36] TFEU justifications'.

[118] Case C–379/98 *PreussenElektra* [2001] ECR I–2099, para. 226. See also his comments in Case C–203/96 *Chemische Afvalstoffen Dusseldorp v. Minister van Milieubeheer* [1998] ECR I–4075 and in Case C–136/00 *Rolf Dieter Danner* [2002] ECR I–8147.

[119] Citing Case C–389/96 *Aher-Waggon v. Germany* [1998] ECR I–4473, considered in Ch. 6.

[120] Para. 226.

this direction, without expressly acknowledging what it is doing. However, it may well be that, as in *LIBRO*, the Court will be more likely to find the rule justified but disproportionate since it is directly discriminatory.[121] A more carefully tailored (indirectly or non-discriminatory) rule might survive proportionality review more easily.

4. DISCRIMINATION ARISING FROM TREATING NATIONAL AND IMPORTED GOODS ALIKE: PRICE FIXING

So far we have considered discrimination which arises from treating national and imported goods *differently*. This is referred to as formal discrimination. Sometimes discrimination can arise when national and imported goods are treated in the *same* way, where such equal treatment is not objectively justified. This is sometimes described as material discrimination. The price fixing cases—where the Member State sets either a maximum or minimum price for a particular good—provide examples of this. Fixing a maximum price may discriminate against imported goods because if the maximum price is set too low it does not take into account the transport costs borne by the importer. Fixing a minimum price may also discriminate against imported goods because it removes any competitive advantage they may have. These issues were considered in *van Tiggele*[122] and *Tasca*.[123]

In *Tasca* the Court said that although a *maximum* price applicable to both domestic and imported goods did not in itself constitute an MEE, it could have such an effect when it was fixed at a level such that the sale of the imported products became, if not impossible, then at least more difficult than for domestic products. The Court therefore said that a maximum price constituted an MEE if it was fixed at such a low level that dealers wishing to import the product into the Member States could do so only at a loss. In a similar vein, the Court ruled in *Danis*[124] that a national rule imposing a price freeze could also constitute an MEE where it prevented the increased prices of imported goods from being passed on to the consumer.

However, in *LIBRO*,[125] the Court appeared to change tack. It initially classified a maximum price fixing rule as a certain selling arrangement under *Keck*[126] and so therefore benefited from the presumption of legality. However, because the rule was directly discriminatory the Court ruled that it was in fact an MEE.

In *van Tiggele* the Court said that price control rules applicable to both domestic and imported goods did not in general constitute an MEE but could do so where, for example,[127] imports could be impeded when a national authority fixed prices or profit margins at such a level that imported products were placed at a disadvantage in relation

---

[121] Para. 35. Note the very brief discussion of the (dis)proportionality of the national rule.

[122] Case 82/77 *Openbaar Ministerie v. van Tiggele* [1978] ECR 25.

[123] Case 65/75 *Criminal Proceedings against Riccardo Tasca* [1976] ECR 291.

[124] Joined Cases 16–20/79 *Criminal Proceedings against Danis* [1979] ECR 3327, para. 7.

[125] Case C–531/07 *LIBRO Handelsgesellschaft mbH* [2009] ECR I–5317, paras. 20–2. See also Case C–63/94 *Belgapom* [1995] ECR I–2467, where the Court ruled that Art. 34 TFEU did not apply where a Member State prohibited any sale which yielded only a very low profit.

[126] See further Ch. 5.

[127] Para. 14. See also Case 231/83 *Cullet* [1985] ECR 305 and Case C–287/89 *Commission v. Belgium* [1991] ECR I–2233 on goods and Case C–442/02 *Caixa-Bank v. Ministère de l'Économie, des Finances and de l'industrie* [2004] ECR I–8961 (establishment); Joined Cases C–94 and 202/04 *Cipolla v. Fazari* [2006] ECR I–2049 (services) and Case C–565/08 *Commission v. Italy* [2011] ECR I–2101 (establishment and services). These cases suggest that the Court does regard price fixing cases as belonging to a distinct category, without ever saying so expressly.

to identical domestic products, either because they could not profitably be marketed in the conditions laid down or because the competitive advantage conferred by lower cost prices was cancelled out. The Court then identified two types of *minimum* sale prices which were legitimate: first, a national provision prohibiting the retail sale of products at prices below the purchase price paid by the retailer and, secondly, the fixing of a minimum profit margin at a specific amount, and not as a percentage of the cost price.

In *Scotch Whisky Association*[128] the Court took yet another approach. The case concerned the minimum price per unit (MPU) of alcoholic drinks (approximately €0.7) being proposed by the Scottish Parliament.[129] The Court said that the fact that the Scottish legislation 'prevented the lower cost price of imported products being reflected in the selling price to the consumer' and meant that that legislation was 'capable of hindering the access to the United Kingdom market of alcoholic drinks that are lawfully marketed in Member States other than the [UK]' and therefore constituted an MEE. In reaching this conclusion the Court cited, inter alia, paragraph 37 of *Trailers*[130] and *ANETT*,[131] both authorities for the third limb market access test (see fig. 4.2).[132] However, the main thrust of the case concerned the public health defence (which was made out but the Court indicated that the MPU was probably not proportionate).[133]

5. 'REVERSE DISCRIMINATION'

So far we have concentrated on the situation where the national rule has (overtly) discriminated against *imported* goods. We now turn to the (rarer) situation where the national rule discriminates against *domestic* goods. This is known as reverse discrimination. Because Article 34 TFEU does not apply to wholly internal situations,[134] reverse discrimination is compatible with Union law. Therefore, in *Mathot*[135] the Court said that a Belgian law, requiring butter produced in Belgium to have certain details listed on its packaging, without imposing the same requirement on butter produced in other Member States, did not breach Article 34 TFEU. As the Court explained in *Jongeneel Kaas*,[136] reverse discrimination is permitted because it encourages national rules which, while leaving imported products unaffected, have as 'their purpose to improve the quality of domestic production so as to make it more attractive to consumers'. In other words, although the

---

[128] Case C–333/14 *Scotch Whisky Association v. Lord Advocate and Advocate General for Scotland* EU:C:2015:845.

[129] The sale price was to be calculated according to the formula: MPU × S (strength of alcohol) × V (volume) × 100.

[130] Case C–110/05 *Commission v. Italy* EU:C:2009:66, para. 37.

[131] Case C–456/10 *ANETT* EU:C:2012:241, para. 35.

[132] This is considered further in Section F.

[133] For a full discussion of the potential application of *Keck* to this case, see the AG's Opinion, paras. 51–69.

[134] Art. 34: 'Quantitative restrictions on imports and all measures having equivalent effect shall be prohibited *between* Member States' (emphasis added). Cf. Case C–363/93 *Lancry v. Direction générale des Douanes* [1994] ECR I–3957, where the Court said that Art. 30 TFEU applied to duties levied on goods moving within the state (*in casu* from mainland France to French overseas territories) and P. Oliver, 'Some further reflections on the scope of Articles 28–30 (ex 30–36)' (1999) 36 *CMLRev.* 738, 787–8, and K. Mortelmans, 'The Common Market, the internal market and the single market, what's in a market?' (1998) 35 *CMLRev.* 101, 132–3.

[135] Case 98/86 *Criminal Proceedings against Mathot* [1987] ECR 809. See also Case 355/85 *Cognet* [1986] ECR 3241 (change in French law following ruling of Court in Case 229/83 *Leclerc v. Au Blé Vert* [1985] ECR 1, a ruling confirmed in Case C–9/99 *Échirolles Distribution SA v. Association du Dauphiné* [2000] ECR I–8207, para. 24). *Leclerc* makes clear that Art. 34 TFEU does not apply to a reimport situation (i.e., a domestic product leaves the Member State and then is reimported, where the sole purpose of the reimport is to circumvent domestic rules).

[136] Case 237/82 *Jongeneel Kaas BV v. State of the Netherlands* [1984] ECR 483, para. 20.

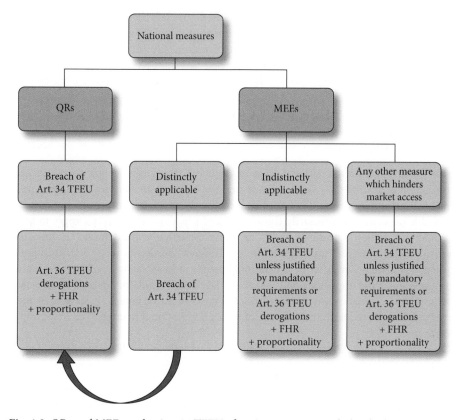

Fig. 4.2 QRs and MEEs under Art. 34 TFEU after *Commission* v. *Italy (trailers)*

national producers must bear additional costs as a result of their own government's action they may gain a competitive advantage in terms of quality.

The effect of decisions such as *Mathot* and *Jongeneel Kaas* is to prevent national traders faced with more onerous national laws from complaining that they suffer a competitive disadvantage in respect of goods produced by their foreign rivals and that only the standards of the lowest state should apply to them in the name of equal treatment.

Given the broad scope of the *Dassonville* formula it is in fact rare for a situation of reverse discrimination to arise because, as we have seen in the *Foie Gras* case,[137] it is relatively easy for a trader to argue that a national measure has at least a 'potential' effect on trade. *Pistre*[138] provides a further example. A French national was prosecuted for making unauthorized use of the word 'mountain' on a label. In his defence he said that the French law on the development and protection of mountain regions breached Article 34 TFEU. However, the French government argued that Union law did not apply since the case occurred on French territory, concerning French nationals marketing French products.[139] Advocate General Jacobs agreed and urged the Court to decline jurisdiction, but the Court insisted that Article 34 TFEU did apply. Citing the *Dassonville* formula, it said that while the application of a national measure having *no actual link* to the importation of goods did not fall within the ambit of Article 34 TFEU, 'Article [34 TFEU] cannot be considered inapplicable simply because all the facts of the specific case before the national

---

[137] Case C–184/96 *Commission* v. *France (foie gras)* [1998] ECR I–6197.
[138] Joined Cases C–321–324/94 *Pistre* [1997] ECR I–2343.   [139] Para. 41.

court are confined to a single Member State.'[140] The Court said that the measure facilitated the marketing of domestic goods to the detriment of imported goods,[141] and so created and maintained a difference of treatment between domestic and imported goods, 'hindering, at least *potentially*, intra-[Union] trade'.[142]

E. INDISTINCTLY APPLICABLE MEASURES

1. INTRODUCTION

So far we have considered national measures which are overtly discriminatory: the discrimination is clear on the face of the measure. We now turn to consider the more covert type of discrimination which is found in indistinctly applicable measures. Indistinctly applicable measures are primarily those rules and practices which in law apply to both national and domestic products but in fact have a particular burden on the imported goods (using the jargon: same burden in law, different burden in fact).[143] This different burden may arise because, while the national producer has to satisfy only one regulator (the home state), the imported goods have to satisfy a dual regulatory burden (home state and host state regulation), with the additional costs that this entails.[144] Such rules may have been introduced with the purpose of protecting national markets[145] or may simply have that effect.[146]

As early as 1970 the Commission identified indistinctly applicable measures as potential barriers to the free movement of goods. Article 3 of Directive 70/50 provides:

> This Directive also covers measures governing the marketing of products which deal, in particular, with shape, size, weight, composition, presentation, identification or putting up and which are equally applicable to domestic and imported products.[147]

Since then the Court has been assiduous in declaring unlawful indistinctly applicable measures—whether they constitute an absolute barrier or a mere hindrance to the import of the foreign goods[148]—unless they can be justified by the Member State in some way.

---

[140] Joined Cases C–321–324/94 *Pistre* [1997] ECR I–2343, para. 44.

[141] Para. 45. See also Case C–293/02 *Jersey Produce* [2005] ECR I–9543.

[142] Joined Cases C–321–324/94 *Pistre* [1997] ECR I–2343, para. 45, emphasis added. See also Joined Cases C–158 and 159/04 *Alfa Vita Vassilopoulos AE* [2006] ECR I–8135.

[143] Case C–14/02 *ATRAL SA* v. *Etat belge* [2003] ECR I–4431, para. 63. Sometimes this is described in terms of protective effect: see, e.g., Case 16/83 *Prantl* [1984] ECR 1299, para. 21. Generally, however, the Court does not consider the protective effect of national legislation in the case of either distinctly or indistinctly applicable measures. Cf. G. Marenco, 'Pour une interpretation traditionelle de la notion de mesure d'effet equivalent à une restriction quantitative' (1984) 20 *Cahiers de Droit Européen* 291, who argues that protective effect is the rationale behind Art. 34 TFEU; and the criticisms of this view in D. Chalmers, 'Repackaging the internal market: The ramifications of the *Keck* judgment' (1994) 19 *ELRev*. 385, 393–4. Clearly, measures which have as their purpose the regulation of trade in goods are caught by Art. 34 TFEU (Joined Cases C–267 and 268/91 *Keck* [1993] ECR I–6097, a contrario, para. 12).

[144] See, e.g., Case C–239/90 *Boscher* v. *SA British Motors Wright* [1991] ECR I–2023, para. 15.

[145] Case 788/79 *Gilli and Andres* [1980] ECR 2071, para. 10.

[146] Case 16/83 *Prantl* [1984] ECR 1299, para. 21.

[147] The Article continues: 'where the restrictive effect of such measures on the free movement of goods exceeds the effects intrinsic to trade rules. This is the case, in particular, where:—the restrictive effects on the free movement of goods are out of proportion to their purpose;—the same objective can be attained by other means which are less of a hindrance to trade.' As we shall see, the case law has tightened up the 'loose proportionality' aspect of this definition (W. H. Roth (1994) 31 *CMLRev*. 845, 850).

[148] Case 261/81 *Walter Rau* v. *De Smedt* [1982] ECR 3961, para. 13; Case C–448/98 *Criminal Proceedings against Jean-Pierre Guimont* [2000] ECR I–10663, para. 26.

'Product requirements'[149] are the classic example of indistinctly applicable measures, i.e., rules relating to designation, form, size, weight, composition, presentation, labelling, and packaging.[150] This list, found in paragraph 15 of *Keck*, is reminiscent of that contained in Article 3 of Directive 70/50. Measures concerning product requirements are assumed to affect inter-state trade, even where both parties to the case are nationals,[151] and this is often reflected in the language used by the Court. It replaces phrases such as discrimination and disparate impact on imported goods with a broad reference to the fact that the national rule 'hinders'[152] or creates an 'obstacle' to the free movement of goods (largely because of the dual regulatory burden).

In the past, the Court has considered other types of rules to be indistinctly applicable, including rules regulating advertising and sales promotion techniques.[153] These rules are now largely dealt with under the *Keck* 'certain selling arrangement' formula and the Unfair Commercial Practices Directive 2005/29, and are considered further in Chapter 5.

In addition, there was a group of cases concerning, for example, rules on authorizations and inspections, which could not be easily classified as either product requirements or certain selling arrangements but, for want of a better classification, tended to be lumped under the indistinctly applicable heading.[154] Since *Commission* v. *Italy (trailers)* it is likely that such non-product-related requirements, provided that they are not directly discriminatory, will be dealt with under the separate (and residual?) heading of 'Any other measure which hinders access of products originating in other Member States to the market of a Member State' (see fig. 4.2 and the discussion in Section F).

So it now seems that, following *Trailers*,[155] the indistinctly applicable category is reduced to covering product requirements only, to which the seminal decision of *Cassis de Dijon*[156] applies. In *Cassis* the Court had to balance two competing interests. On the one hand, it wanted to accommodate the interests of traders who resented the ability of host states to impose additional technical requirements on their goods each time they entered a new national market. Traders argued that if goods were lawfully produced according to the laws of one Member State, why could they not be sold on the markets of all other Member States?[157] On the other hand, the Court recognized the growing need for Member States to protect interests not identified in the exhaustive list of derogations found in Article 36 TFEU (such as environmental considerations and consumer protection). In *Cassis de Dijon* the Court managed to reconcile both interests.

---

[149] In Joined Cases C–401 and 402/92 *Boermans* [1994] ECR I–2199, para. 16, Van Gerven AG said: ' "product requirements" relate ... to the intrinsic or extrinsic characteristics of the product concerned'.

[150] Joined Cases C–267 and 268/91 *Keck* [1993] ECR I–6097, para. 15.

[151] Joined Cases C–158 and 159/04 *Alfa Vita Vassilopoulos AE* [2006] ECR I–8135.

[152] Case C–366/04 *Schwarz* v. *Bürgermeister der Landeshauptstadt Salzburg* [2006] ECR I–10139, para. 30; Joined Cases C–158 and 159/04 *Alfa Vita Vassilopoulos AE* [2006] ECR I–8135, para. 20.

[153] See, e.g., Case 382/87 *Buet* v. *Ministère public* [1989] ECR 1235; Joined Cases C–1 and 176/90 *Aragonesa* [1991] ECR I–4151.

[154] See, e.g., Case C–319/05 *Commission* v. *Germany (garlic capsule)* [2007] ECR I–9811, para. 81; Case C–88/07 *Commission* v. *Spain (medicinal herbs)* [2009] ECR I–1353.

[155] Case C–110/05 *Commission* v. *Italy* [2009] ECR I–519, para. 37.

[156] Case 120/78 *Rewe Zentrale* v. *Bundesmonopolverwaltung für Branntwein ('Cassis de Dijon')* [1979] ECR 649.

[157] Essentially this argument is derived from Art. IV of the US Constitution, the Full Faith and Credit clause, which provides 'Full Faith and Credit shall be given in each State to the public Acts, Records, and judicial Proceedings of every other State.'

2. *CASSIS DE DIJON*

2.1 Mandatory Requirements and the Principle of Mutual Recognition

Cassis de Dijon concerned a straightforward product requirement rule: the composition of fruit liqueurs. The German authorities refused to allow Cassis de Dijon, a blackcurrant fruit liqueur made in France, to be sold in Germany owing to its *insufficient* alcoholic strength. German law required fruit liqueurs to have a minimum alcohol content of 25 per cent, whereas the French cassis had an alcohol content of only 15–20 per cent. The Court said that '[i]n the absence of common rules [i.e., harmonization] it is for Member States to regulate all matters relating to the production and marketing of alcohol and alcoholic beverages on their own territory'.[158] The Court then laid down—what we now know to be—a general principle and an exception,[159] although at the time the focus was on the exception.[160] The Court said:

> Obstacles to movement in the [Union] resulting from disparities between the national laws relating to the marketing of the products in question must be accepted in so far as those provisions may be recognised as being necessary in order to satisfy *mandatory requirements* relating in particular to the effectiveness of fiscal supervision, the protection of public health, the fairness of commercial transactions and the defence of the consumer.[161]

To this the Court added in *Rau*:[162]

> It is also necessary for such rules to be proportionate to the aim in view. If a Member State has a choice between various measures to attain the same objective it should choose the means which least restricts the free movement of goods.

Thus, in the absence of harmonization legislation, host Member States can regulate product requirements and insist that national rules be applied to imported goods provided that the host state rules can be justified by showing one of the mandatory requirements (e.g., consumer protection) and that the steps taken are proportionate.

In *Cassis* the German government relied on two of the mandatory requirements: public health and the protection of the consumer against unfair commercial practices. It argued, first, that the minimum-alcohol-content rule prevented a proliferation of low-alcohol drinks on the national market since such drinks more readily induced tolerance towards alcohol than stronger drinks (!). Not surprisingly, the Court dismissed this argument. It said that German consumers could obtain a wide range of weaker alcoholic products and strongly alcoholic drinks were often consumed in a diluted form.

As far as the consumer protection/fair trading argument was concerned, the German government said that drinks with a lower alcohol content secured a competitive advantage over drinks with a higher alcohol content, since alcohol was the most expensive constituent of the product.[163] The Court rejected this too, saying that 'it is a simple matter to

---

[158] Case 120/78 *Cassis de Dijon* [1979] ECR 649, Para. 8.

[159] Commission Staff Working Document, *Free Movement of Goods—Guide to the application of Treaty provisions governing Free Movement of Goods (Articles 28–30 EC)*, SEC(2009) 673, 19.

[160] C. Barnard, 'The missing ingredient in *Cassis de Dijon*: An exercise in legal archaeology', forthcoming.

[161] Emphasis added.   [162] Case 261/81 *Rau* [1982] ECR 3961, para. 12.

[163] In Case 182/84 *Miro* [1985] ECR 3731 the Member State ran a similar argument that imported products could have a price advantage as a result of the application of national taxes and excise duties which were proportional to the alcohol content. The Court said this was irrelevant: such differences in taxes and excise duties were 'part of the objective conditions of competition of which every trader may freely take advantage, provided that purchasers are given information so that they can freely make their choice on the basis of the quality and price of the products'.

ensure that suitable information is conveyed to the purchaser by requiring the display of an indication of origin and of the alcohol content on the packaging of products'.[164] Therefore, the national rules constituted an obstacle to trade and breached Article 34 TFEU; labelling would have been an adequate response.

Having discussed and rejected the justifications put forward by the German government, the Court then laid down the general principle, almost as an afterthought:

> There is therefore no valid reason why, provided that they have been lawfully produced and marketed in one of the Member States, alcoholic beverages should not be introduced into any other Member State.[165]

This idea, subsequently called the presumption of *equivalence* or *mutual recognition*, is of great importance. It means that goods lawfully produced and marketed in one Member State (France) can, in principle, be sold in another Member State (Germany) without further restriction. Putting it another way, Germany must recognize French standards as equivalent to its own. However, this presumption can be rebutted by the host state (Germany)[166] demonstrating that its laws can be justified under one of the mandatory requirements,[167] and that the national rules are proportionate. In other words, as fig. 4.1 shows, owing to the presumption of equivalence, indistinctly applicable national measures which prevent goods lawfully produced in State A from being sold on the market in State B constitute a prima facie breach of Article 34 TFEU. However, if the host state (B's) rules can be justified by reference to one of the mandatory requirements (or by one of the Article 36 TFEU derogations) and the steps taken are proportionate, the national measure is lawful[168] with the result that the national interest takes precedence over the free movement of goods.[169]

2.2 The Implications of the Decision

The result of *Cassis* is to replace dual regulation of a product (by both the home and host states) with single regulation (home state)[170] which, under the principle of mutual

---

[164] Case 120/78 *Cassis de Dijon* [1979] ECR 649, para. 13.

[165] Para. 14.

[166] On the burden of proof, see the Mutual Recognition Reg. 764/2008 ([2008] OJ L218/21), considered further at n. 181.

[167] Case 120/78 *Cassis de Dijon* [1979] ECR 649, para. 8, sometimes referred to as the 'rule of reason' approach, which was first raised in Case 8/74 *Dassonville* [1974] ECR 837, para. 6: 'In the absence of a [Union] system guaranteeing for consumers the authenticity of a product's designation of origin, if a Member State takes measures to prevent unfair practices in this connexion, it is however subject to the condition that these measures should be reasonable and that the means of proof required should not act as a hindrance to trade between Member States and should, in consequence, be accessible to all [Union] nationals.' See also Case 33/74 *Van Binsbergen* [1974] ECR 1299, para. 12 for an equivalent case in the field of services.

[168] See, e.g., Joined Cases 60 and 61/84 *Cinéthèque SA v. Fédération nationale des cinémas français* [1985] ECR 2605, para. 24.

[169] Para. 14. It used to be thought that the mandatory requirements and Art. 36 TFEU derogations operated differently. If a national measure could be justified by a mandatory requirement then it did not breach Art. 34 TFEU. If the national measures could not be justified then there was a breach of Art. 34 TFEU and the Member State could in principle have recourse to the derogations in Art. 36 TFEU (see, e.g., Case 25/88 *Criminal Proceedings against Bouchara* [1989] ECR 1105, para. 11, and Case 298/87 *Smanor* [1988] ECR 4489, para. 15). However, the Court no longer seems to draw this distinction between mandatory requirements and Art. 36 TFEU derogations, often simply saying that the national measure can be justified under both Art. 36 TFEU and the mandatory requirements (see, e.g., Joined Cases C-34–36/95 *De Agostini* [1997] ECR I-3843, para. 45).

[170] N. Bernard, 'Flexibility in the European single market' in C. Barnard and J. Scott (eds.), *The Law of the Single European Market: Unpacking the premises* (Oxford: Hart Publishing, 2002).

recognition, the host state is required to respect. Thus, *Cassis* introduces the principle of home state control and, in so doing, gives extraterritorial effect to the laws and standards laid down by the home state. As we saw in Chapter 1, the result of the principle of mutual recognition is to put the different legal systems in competition with one another. Goods produced in France can be sold in Germany; the German consumers then have the choice between French goods and German goods, both produced according to different standards. This maintains a diversity of national rules.

However, since there is also freedom of establishment in the EU there is a risk that German business might move to France and set up there to produce fruit liqueurs according to the 'lower' French standards, which they can then sell onto the German market, relying on the principles in *Cassis*. This would have serious implications for German jobs. Alternatively, if capital does not move but the German consumers buy the cheaper French Cassis instead of the German fruit liqueur, this outcome will also be detrimental to German jobs. One response would be for the German producers to lobby their government for lower standards. If successful, this might prompt the French producers to request their government to lower standards still further, leading to a race to the bottom and a convergence (rather than a diversity) of standards at this low level. This problem was raised by the German government in *Cassis* itself:[171]

> to allow alcoholic products into free circulation wherever, as regards their alcohol content, they comply with the rules laid down in the country of production would have the effect of imposing as a common standard within the [Union] the lowest alcohol content permitted in any of the Member States, and even of rendering any requirements in this field inoperative since a lower limit of this nature is foreign to the rules of several Member States.

The mandatory requirements recognized by the Court in *Cassis* are intended to place a brake on any such race to the bottom. They allow for (residual) *host* state control where an important interest of the host state[172] is at issue. Therefore, if Germany could successfully invoke a mandatory requirement, this would require French products to comply with the higher German standards. However, as we shall see in Chapter 6, the Member States have experienced difficulties both in successfully invoking these mandatory requirements and in showing that the steps taken are proportionate. *Cassis* is therefore seen as a decision promoting the *Union* interest of market integration, but at the cost of potentially eroding diverse (high) national standards adopted by democratically elected national governments.[173] This may create a 'regulatory gap'—if the host state national law is struck down and not replaced by an equivalent Union law, the market is left unregulated (which may or may not be a good thing). However, if a Union law is enacted this will create a further brake on any race to the bottom.

While some have expressed concern about *Cassis*'s deregulatory potential, Weatherill warns against too much sentiment.[174] He argues that the development of European market integration confronts the dead wood of centuries of regulatory tradition in all the Member States. He says that '[t]he whole point of the exercise is regulatory renovation and a bonfire of red tape on the pyre of Article [34 TFEU]'. He continues that the Court is frequently asked to deal with the collision between, on the one hand, the making of a market

---

[171] Case 120/78 *Cassis de Dijon* [1979] ECR 649, para. 12.

[172] Or rather the host state's consumer whose interests are not represented in the home state.

[173] In practice, many legislatures will resist the pressure to lower standards because, while lower standards may suit one group of industrial interests, such a move might well be unpopular with the voting public as a whole. See further Ch. 15.

[174] S. Weatherill, 'Pre-emption, harmonisation and the distribution of competence' in Barnard and Scott, n. 170, 49.

for Europe and, on the other, national rules introduced for once sound reasons that lost their purpose generations ago, mixed together with other national rules cherished by national producers as a convenient means for insulating themselves from the threat of out-of-state competition.

The result of this collision in *Cassis de Dijon* was to favour market-making over the interests of German producers while benefiting both German consumers, who now have access to a wider choice of products, and traders from other Member States who can sell to a wider market. Furthermore, it is not always the case that consumers will exercise their choice and buy the cheaper, probably lower-standard good; they might go for quality instead. This can be seen in *3 Glocken*,[175] a case where Italy insisted that only pasta made from durum wheat could be sold in Italy and not pasta made from the cheaper common wheat. As the Court pointed out, trends in the export markets demonstrated that competition based on quality operated in favour of durum wheat,[176] with statistics supplied to the Court revealing a steady increase in the market share held by pasta products made exclusively from durum wheat. This suggests a race to the top in terms of quality and not to the bottom.

2.3 The Commission's Response to *Cassis*

The Commission was quick to realize the importance of *Cassis*.[177] It issued an interpretative communication on the judgment,[178] which recognized that the presumption of equivalence obviated the need for much harmonization legislation. Because each national standard was presumed to be equivalent, goods produced according to that national standard would have access to the market of all other Member States. Therefore, there was no longer a need for a directive prescribing the content of a 'Euro' fruit liqueur: harmonization would be confined to areas where Member States legitimately invoked a mandatory requirement or an Article 36 TFEU derogation. Outside those areas of harmonization, the principle of mutual recognition would apply and goods lawfully produced in one Member State would enjoy access to the market in another state, with the result that different regulatory traditions and different products would continue to coexist.

Nevertheless, despite the strong message sent out by the Court in *Cassis*, technical obstacles to the free movement of goods within the EU remained widespread and went unchallenged by traders. As Weiler put it, mutual recognition proved 'an intellectual breakthrough but a colossal market failure'.[179] The Commission therefore launched a 'Package on the internal market for goods' in February 2007[180] to reinvigorate the *Cassis* principles. For present purposes, the most important part of the package is Regulation

---

[175] Case 407/85 *3 Glocken GmbH* v. *USL Centro-Sud* [1988] ECR 4233, considered further in Case Study 6.1.

[176] Para. 27.

[177] K. Alter and S. Meunier-Aitsahalia, 'Judicial politics in the European Community: European integration and the pathbreaking *Cassis de Dijon* decision' (1994) 26 *Comparative Political Studies* 535. Cf. R. Barents, 'New developments in measures having equivalent effects' (1981) 18 *CMLRev.* 271: 'The *Cassis de Dijon* judgment, while constituting a continuation of the Court's policy outlined in the *Dassonville* case, is not quite so revolutionary as the Commission wishes to believe.'

[178] Commission, 'Communication from the Commission regarding the *Cassis de Dijon* judgment' ([1980] OJ C256/2), considered by L. Gormley, '*Cassis de Dijon* and the Communication from the Commission' (1981) 6 *ELRev.* 454. Various commentators suggested that the Communication went further than the Court's original judgment: see, e.g., M. Egan, *Constructing a European Market* (Oxford: OUP, 2001), 109.

[179] J. H. H. Weiler, 'Mutual recognition, functional equivalence and harmonization in the evolution of the European common market and the WTO' in F. Padoa Schioppa (ed.), *The Principle of Mutual Recognition in the European Integration Process* (Basingstoke, Palgrave Macmillan, 2005), 49.

[180] COM(2007) 35.

764/2008 laying down procedures relating to the application of certain national technical rules to products lawfully marketed in another Member State,[181] the so-called 'Mutual Recognition' Regulation. It has two elements. First, it lays down a procedure to be followed by national authorities wanting to ban a product or requiring the product to be modified. They must give the economic operator written notice of why they are taking this action and provide sufficient technical or scientific supporting evidence. The effect of this rule is to make clear that the burden of proof is on the host state as to why it is denying market access rather than on the trader as to why its goods should be admitted. This aspect of the Regulation is considered further in Chapter 6. The second element of the Regulation concerns the establishment of product contact points in each Member State which must provide information on the technical rules applicable. The provision of easily accessible information is an increasingly popular approach in Union legislation, as the discussion on the Services Directive 2006/123 in Chapter 11 demonstrates.

3. PRODUCT REQUIREMENT CASES

As *Keck* and *Commission* v. *Italy (trailers)* subsequently made clear, the principles in *Cassis de Dijon* apply to rules regulating products themselves, so-called 'product requirement' cases. While *Cassis de Dijon* itself concerned the composition of a product,[182] most of the product-requirement cases concern packaging and presentation. For example, in *Rau*[183] the Court said that a Belgian law requiring margarine to be marketed in cube-shaped packages, to avoid confusion with butter, was an indistinctly applicable MEE because it had the effect of requiring imported margarine to be repackaged before being sold on the Belgian market. A similar situation arose in *Prantl*,[184] where German law restricted the use of the traditional *Bocksbeutel* (a bulbous-shaped bottle with a long neck) to German producers of quality wine.[185] Italian wine, produced in a similar-shaped bottle, was excluded from the German market to prevent confusion. The Court noted that if Italian exporters wished to market their wine in Germany[186] they had to put their wine in bottles different from those traditionally used, which made the marketing of the imported wine more difficult or costly, and it also deprived Italian producers of the commercial advantages of using the bulbous-shaped bottle. The national rule was therefore an MEE which breached Article 34 TFEU.

Similar reasoning underpinned the Court's ruling in *Mars*.[187] Mars ran a promotional campaign, printing '+10%' on a flash on its sweet wrappers. Because the flash exceeded 10

---

[181] [2008] OJ L218/21. The three other measures resulting from the package are Reg. 765/2008 ([2008] OJ L218/30) setting out requirements for accreditation and market surveillance relating to the marketing of products, the so-called 'RAMS' Regulation; Dec. 768/2008/EC ([2008] OJ L218/82) on a common framework for the marketing of products; and an interpretative communication on procedures for the registration of motor vehicles originating in another Member State (2007/C 68/04). The RAMS Regulation and the decision are discussed further in Ch. 15.

[182] For other examples of cases concerning the composition of a product, see Case 407/85 *3 Glocken GmbH* [1988] ECR 4233 (durum wheat); Case 90/86 *Criminal Proceedings against Zoni* [1988] ECR 4285; Case 274/87 *Commission* v. *Germany (meat only meat products)* [1989] ECR 229; Case 94/82 *Criminal Proceedings against De Kikvorsh Groothandel-Import-Export BV* [1982] ECR 947 (maximum acidity in beer); Case 216/84 *Commission* v. *France (milk only milk powder)* [1988] ECR 793; Case 130/80 *Kelderman* [1981] ECR 527 (dry matter in bread); Case C–358/95 *Tommaso Morellato* v. *Unità sanitaria locale (USL) n. 11 di Pordenone* [1997] ECR I–1431 (national legislation prohibiting the marketing of bread with a moisture content exceeding 34 per cent or an ash content lower than 1.40 per cent or containing bran).

[183] Case 261/81 [1982] ECR 3961.   [184] Case 16/83 [1984] ECR 1299, para. 21.

[185] Para. 21.   [186] Para. 23.

[187] Case C–470/93 *Verein gegen Unwesen in Handel und Gewerbe Köln ev* v. *Mars GmbH* [1995] ECR I–1923.

per cent of the surface area of the bar, this contravened German rules on fair trade. The Court said that since the German rules compelled the importer to adjust the presentation of its products according to the place where they were to be marketed and consequently to incur additional packaging and advertising costs,[188] they breached Article 34 TFEU. *Mars* demonstrates the Court's determination to allow companies to adopt a Europe-wide marketing strategy.[189] Each time a host state, like Germany, insists on imposing its own rules the importer incurs an additional financial burden. Even if the costs are passed on to the consumer, the Court considers that the initial outlay of these costs acts as a disincentive to those traders contemplating marketing the products in the host state.[190]

So far, we have considered rules relating to composition, packaging, and presentation. Other requirements have concerned the (generic) designation of a product. So the Court has ruled that Member States cannot reserve a generic name for products that are manufactured out of specific raw ingredients or contain only a given proportion of raw ingredients. Therefore, in *Miro*[191] the Court said that a Dutch rule restricting the name 'jenever' to drinks containing at least 35 per cent alcohol, breached Article 34 TFEU because it excluded Belgian jenever which had been lawfully produced with an alcohol content of only 30 per cent. And in *Commission* v. *Italy*[192] the Court said that an Italian rule limiting the name chocolate to products made without vegetable fats and requiring chocolate with vegetable fats (primarily British and Irish chocolate) to be described as 'chocolate substitute' contravened Article 34 TFEU (see Case Study 4.1). Other labelling requirements, such as an age-limit label on videos and DVDs[193] or language requirements imposed on products sold to end users,[194] also constitute MEEs.

Finally, in *Alfa Vita*[195] the Court added rules relating to 'production conditions' to the list of situations where Article 34 TFEU applied. In that case anyone wishing to sell bread had to run a fully equipped bakery even where the bread was delivered half-cooked and needed only to be 'baked-off'. This was considered a barrier to imports breaching Article 34 TFEU.

Case Study 4.1: THE CASE OF JAM AND CHOCOLATE

One way of dealing with some of the problems about the use of names is through harmonization, identifying at Union level the permitted ingredients in a product before it can be called, say 'chocolate'. However, this is easier said than done, as the history of the directives on jam and chocolate show. The first, very basic problem relates to the definition of these products.

[188] Para. 13. See also Case C–315/92 *Verband Sozialer Wettbewerb ev* v. *Clinique Laboratories SNC* [1994] ECR I–317, para. 19.
[189] Case C–463/01 *Commission* v. *Germany (deposit and return)* [2004] ECR I–11705, para. 61.
[190] See, e.g., Case C–217/99 *Commission* v. *Belgium* [2000] ECR I–10251, para. 18.
[191] Case 182/84 *Criminal Proceedings against Miro BV* [1985] ECR 3731.
[192] Case C–14/00 *Commission* v. *Italy* [2003] ECR I–513, para. 77. See also Case C–12/00 *Commission* v. *Spain* [2003] ECR I–459, para. 81. Subsequently, the Court rejected an Italian rule which allowed the adjective 'pure' to be added to the sales name of chocolate products which do not contain vegetable fats other than cocoa butter. This contravened the 'Chocolate Directive', Council Dir. 2000/36: Case C–47/09 *Commission* v. *Italy* [2010] ECR I–12083.
[193] Case C–244/06 *Dynamic Medien Vertriebs GmbH* [2008] ECR I–505.
[194] Case C–366/98 *Geffroy and Casino France* [2000] ECR I–6579. See also Case C–369/89 *Piageme* v. *Peeters* [1991] ECR I–2971, which led to COM(93) 532 on the use of languages in the marketing of foodstuffs. See also Case 78/80 *Fietje* [1980] ECR 3839, para. 15.
[195] Joined Cases C–158 and 159/04 *Alfa Vita* [2006] ECR I–8135 and Case C–82/05 *Commission* v. *Greece (bake off products)* [2006] ECR I–93.

According to research, French consumers only countenance jams with pulp in them; the Dutch, on the other hand, like smooth, sugary jams.[196] The accession of the UK, Europe's largest jam consumer, to the EU in 1973 introduced a new difficulty: marmalade (which also happened to be the German word for jam).[197] Against this background it comes as little surprise that Directive 79/693/EEC[198] on 'the approximation of the laws of the Member States relating to fruit jams, jellies and marmalades and chestnut purée' (the Jam Directive), adopted under Articles 43 and 115 TFEU, took 14 years to negotiate. The accession of Portugal to the EU in 1986, with its fondness for carrot jam, saw carrots (and indeed tomatoes and sweet potatoes) designated as fruit for the purposes of the Directive.[199]

The definition of chocolate proved even stickier. In countries such as Belgium, chocolate is made using 100 per cent cocoa products. In the UK (and five other states) milk chocolate is made with a small proportion (up to 5 per cent) of vegetable fats. Both products are described as chocolate in the countries in which they are made. Directive 73/241,[200] adopted under, inter alia, Article 115 TFEU, approximated the laws of the Member States concerning the composition, manufacturing specifications, packaging, and labelling of cocoa and chocolate products in order to ensure their free movement.[201] Article 1 of the directive provided that 'cocoa and chocolate products' means 'the products intended for human consumption defined in Annex 1'. The Annex essentially laid down the minimum cocoa content for any product to be described as chocolate. Article 10(1) contained a free movement clause:[202] 'Member States shall adopt all the measures necessary to ensure that trade in the products referred to in Article 1 ... cannot be impeded by the application of national non-harmonised provisions.'

But where did these provisions leave British chocolate? The preamble to the directive recognized that the use of vegetable fats other than cocoa butter was permitted in certain Member States (especially the UK, Ireland, and Denmark) and 'extensive use is made of this facility'. It continued that economic and technical data were not sufficient to enable 'a decision relating to the possibilities and forms of any extension of the use of these fats in the [Union] as a whole [to] be taken at the present time'. However, Point 7(a) of the Annex prohibited the addition to chocolate of fats and fat preparations not derived exclusively from milk. Yet, this provision was 'without prejudice to Article 14(2)(a)', which provided that the directive 'shall not affect the provisions of national laws' at present 'authorizing or prohibiting the addition of vegetable fats other than cocoa butter to the products defined in Annex I'. The provisional nature of these rules was confirmed by the fact that Article 14(2)(a) required the Union to review the possibility of 'extending the use of these fats to the whole of the [Union]'.[203]

Given the complexity of these rules, it is not perhaps surprising that countries like Italy took the opportunity to protect their prized national chocolate from competition from abroad. Under Italian law chocolate originating in the UK, Ireland, and Denmark could be sold in Italy,

---

[196] Derived from *Wall Street Journal*, 2 Sept. 1989, cited in M. Egan, *Constructing a European Market* (Oxford: OUP, 2001), 74.

[197] According to the *Daily Telegraph*, an Austrian farmer was prosecuted for selling apricot jam under the name 'apricot marmalade': M. Leidig and A. Evans Pritchard, 'Farmer in marmalade rebellion', *Daily Telegraph*, 21 Oct. 2003, 17.

[198] [1979] OJ L205/5, now repealed and replaced by Council Dir. 2001/113/EC relating to fruit jams, jellies and marmalades and sweetened chestnut purée intended for human consumption ([2002] OJ L10/67).

[199] Annex III.A.I provides 'for the purposes of this Directive, tomatoes, the edible parts of rhubarb stalks, carrots, sweet potatoes, cucumbers, pumpkins, melons and water-melons are considered to be fruit'.

[200] [1973] OJ L228/23, now repealed by Council Dir. 2000/36 ([2000] OJ L197/19).

[201] 4th recital of the preamble.   [202] This term is considered in more detail in Ch. 15.

[203] Case C–14/00 *Commission* v. *Italy (chocolate)* [2003] ECR I–513, para. 54.

but only under the name 'chocolate substitute'. In *Commission* v. *Italy*[204] the Commission argued that this law contravened Directive 73/241 by preventing chocolate lawfully produced in the UK, in accordance with the requirements as to the minimum content of cocoa-based ingredients laid down by the directive (albeit with the addition of vegetable fats), from moving freely. The Commission also argued that the Italian law contravened Article 34 TFEU on the free movement of goods: the use of a pejorative term such as 'chocolate substitute' served to devalue the product in the minds of consumers. Italy, on the other hand, relying on Point 7(a) of the Annex, said that the free movement clause applied only to products which did not contain vegetable fats.

The Court said that Article 14(2)(a) made it clear that, as regards the use of vegetable fats, the directive did not 'seek to establish a fully harmonised system under which common rules completely replace existing national rules in the field, since it expressly authorises the Member States to lay down national rules which are different from the common rules which it provides for'.[205] Therefore, the free movement clause in Article 10 of the directive applied to goods which did not contain vegetable fats. However, under Article 14(2)(a) the directive allowed Member States to adopt national rules authorizing the addition of vegetable fats to cocoa and chocolate products manufactured within their territory. This meant that under the directive the UK, Ireland, and Denmark could authorize their own manufacturers to add vegetable fats to chocolate made there, but this chocolate could not benefit from the free movement clause. So it seemed that Italy had won.

However, the Court then turned to consider the effect of Article 34 TFEU. It said that Article 34 TFEU applied to obstacles to the marketing of products (British chocolate) whose manufacture was not the subject of comprehensive harmonization but which were manufactured in conformity with national rules explicitly permitted by the harmonizing directive (the addition of vegetable fats as permitted by Article 14(2)(a)).[206] Having recognised that Article 34 TFEU in principle applied to the case, the Court found that a rule prohibiting the use of the name 'chocolate' by (British) products might compel traders to adjust the presentation of their products according to the place where the goods were to be marketed and to incur additional packaging costs. It said the use of the name 'chocolate substitute' could adversely affect the consumer's perception of the chocolate in that 'it denotes substitute, and therefore inferior, product'.[207] The Italian law therefore breached Article 34 TFEU unless it could be justified by reference to one of the mandatory requirements and the steps taken were proportionate. The Court recognized that consumers needed to be properly informed about the products offered to them. It continued that where a product offered for sale under a particular name was so different in terms of its composition or production from the products generally understood as falling within that description in the Union, then the host state could require the importer to alter the description of the product. However, where the difference was of minor importance, appropriate labelling would suffice. On the facts, the Court found that the addition of vegetable fats to cocoa and chocolate products which satisfy the minimum contents required by the directive did not substantially alter the nature of those products, transforming them into different products.[208] Therefore, it said, the addition of a label of a 'neutral and objective statement' informing consumers of the presence of vegetable fats would suffice; the obligation to change the sales name was not necessary to satisfy the overriding interest of consumer protection.[209]

---

[204] See also Case C–12/00 *Commission* v. *Spain* [2003] ECR I–459.
[205] Para. 58.   [206] Paras. 67 and 70.
[207] See also Case C–166/03 *Commission* v. *France (gold)* [2004] ECR I–6535 (a French rule restricting the word 'gold' to products of a fineness of more than 750 parts per 1,000; products of a lower fineness could be called 'gold alloy' only. The rule breached Art. 34 TFEU because it had the effect of excluding products described as 'gold' in other states which had lower levels of fineness).
[208] Para. 87.   [209] Paras. 88–9.

> The result of this decision was that through the interpretation of Article 34 TFEU the Court
> almost achieved the free movement that the 1973 directive had failed to secure. The Court may
> well have been influenced by the fact that, by the time of its judgment, Directive 2000/36[210] had
> been adopted which had finally replaced Directive 73/241. Directive 2000/36 resolved the issue
> of whether chocolate containing vegetable fats could still be called chocolate.[211] The negoti-
> ations for this directive were protracted and acrimonious, with those states which did not allow
> the use of vegetable fats fighting to reserve the term 'chocolate' to products containing 100 per
> cent cocoa products. Some helpfully suggested that British chocolate might be called 'vegelate',
> 'vegette', or 'household chocolate' instead.[212] Directive 2000/36 inevitably contained a com-
> promise: the name chocolate could still be applied to products with no more than 5 per cent
> vegetable fat content. They would enjoy free movement provided that they were labelled with
> a 'clearly legible statement: contains vegetable fats in addition to cocoa butter'.[213] Thus 27 years
> after the first Chocolate Directive, which only partially harmonized the field, the Union now has
> its own exhaustive definition of chocolate.[214]

4. ARTICLE 35 TFEU AND INDISTINCTLY APPLICABLE MEASURES

So far we have concentrated on the application of Article 34 TFEU to indistinctly applicable measures and to product requirements in particular. As far as Article 35 TFEU
is concerned, the situation was—up until 2008—different. Previously, the rule had been
that only distinctly applicable measures were caught by Article 35 TFEU. This was made
clear in the *Groenveld*[215] case, which concerned a Dutch law prohibiting all manufacturers
of meat products from having horsemeat in stock, even though the sale of horsemeat was
not actually prohibited in the Netherlands. Since the presence of horsemeat is not easily
detectable in other meat products, the ban was designed to safeguard the export of meat
products to countries which prohibited the marketing of horseflesh. The Court said that
Article 35 TFEU concerned:

> national measures which have as their specific object or effect the restriction on the pat-
> terns of export and thereby the establishment of *a difference in treatment between the do-
> mestic trade of a Member State and its export trade* in such a way as to provide a particular
> advantage for national production or for the domestic market of the State in question at
> the expense of the production or of the trade of other Member States. [Emphasis added]

Because the rule in *Groenveld* was equally applicable (non-discriminatory) it did not
breach Article 35 TFEU. For the same reasons the Court found that the rule in *Oebel*[216]
did not breach Article 35 TFEU. The case concerned restrictions on night working in

---

[210] [2000] OJ L197/19. Parliament's report (A4–0310/97) provides an interesting taster to the chocolate
market.

[211] It also addressed the problem of 'milk chocolate': the UK and Ireland can sell in their own countries
a product labelled as 'milk chocolate' with higher milk and lower cocoa content than 'milk chocolate' made
and sold in the rest of the Union. If exported, it has to be described as 'family milk chocolate'. See 13th recital
and points 4 and 5 of Annex 1. See further E. Metx, 'Does Cadbury chocolate taste different in different
countries?', <http://www.bbc.co.uk/news/magazine-31924912>.

[212] 'EU cannot be serious!', *The Journal* (Newcastle, UK), 22 Jul. 2000, 1.

[213] Art. 2(2). See also the 5th to 7th recitals in the preamble.

[214] J. Walsh, 'Only the crumbliest, flakiest chocolate …', *Independent*, 17 Mar. 2000, 7.

[215] Case 15/79 *P. B. Groenveld BV* v. *Produktschap voor Vee en Vlees* [1979] ECR 3409.

[216] Case 155/80 [1981] ECR 1993, considered further in Ch. 6.

bakeries.[217] The Court said that since the national rules were part of 'economic and social policy which applied by virtue of objective criteria to all the undertakings in the particular industry ... without leading to any difference in treatment whatsoever on the ground of nationality',[218] there was no breach of Article 35 TFEU.

Various suggestions have been offered as to why the Court confined the prohibition of MEEs to distinctly applicable measures under Article 35 TFEU while developing a sophisticated framework for dealing with indistinctly applicable and non-discriminatory measures under Article 34 TFEU. One explanation is that export and import restrictions are fundamentally different. Import restrictions breach Article 34 TFEU because they subject the importer to a dual burden: importers have to satisfy the rules of State A (state of origin) *and* State B (host state). By contrast, exporters have to satisfy only one set of rules—the rules of the state of origin—which are applied equally to goods for the domestic and import market. Allowing exporters to challenge domestic regulation under Article 35 TFEU would essentially present them with a way of circumventing the wholly internal rule by allowing challenges to national rules which have no effect on inter-state trade. As Oliver and Enchelmaier point out, if Article 35 TFEU were to extend to all barriers to exports, regardless of discrimination or protective intent, it would cover a large number of restrictions on production, such as planning regulations for factories, which are far removed from inter-state trade, as well as catching measures properly the preserve of other freedoms such as Article 49 TFEU on freedom of establishment.[219]

Nevertheless, in *Gysbrechts*[220] the Court appeared to modify its approach in *Groenveld*. The case concerned a Belgian rule which prevented a supplier engaged in distance selling, often over the Internet, from requiring any payment in advance before the expiry of a seven-day cooling-off period. In practice this meant that suppliers could not require consumers to provide their credit card number, even though the supplier undertook not to use it until after the cooling-off period. The effect of this rule was (as the Belgian government itself admitted) to deprive the trader of an efficient tool to guard against non-payment.[221] The Court agreed, noting that the consequences of such a prohibition were generally more significant in cross-border sales made directly to consumers. This was due to the practical difficulty and commercial impracticality of bringing legal proceedings in another Member State against consumers who have received goods but not paid for them.[222] The Court concluded:

> Consequently, even if a prohibition such as that at issue in the main proceedings is applicable to all traders active in the national territory, its actual effect is none the less greater on goods leaving the market of the exporting Member State than on the marketing of goods in the domestic market of that Member State.[223]

The measure was therefore an MEE contrary to Article 35 TFEU.

---

[217] See also Joined Cases 141–143/81 *Criminal Proceedings against Gerrit Holdijk* [1982] ECR 1299, para. 11 (national rules laying down minimum standards for enclosures for fattening cows); Case 237/82 *Jongeneel Kaas BV* [1984] ECR 483, para. 22 (national rules laying down minimum standards of quality for domestic cheese production and rules on the compulsory use of stamps, marks, and inspection documents).

[218] Para. 16. See also Case C–80/92 *Commission* v. *Belgium* [1994] ECR I–1019, para. 24, which permits reverse discrimination (para. 25).

[219] P. Oliver and S. Enchelmaier, 'Free movement of goods: Recent developments in the case law' (2007) 44 *CMLRev.* 649, 686.

[220] Case C–205/07 [2008] ECR I–9947. See further, A. Dawes, 'A freedom reborn? The new yet unclear scope of Art. 29' (2009) 34 *ELRev.* 639.

[221] Para. 41.   [222] Para. 42.   [223] Para. 43.

A broad reading of this decision is that the Court has decided to bring its Article 35 TFEU case law fully into line with the Article 34 TFEU pre-*Commission v. Italy (trailers)* jurisprudence (see fig. 4.1), albeit with certain amendments to take into account the differences between rules on imports and those on exports. Certainly, this is what Advocate General Trstenjak had argued for in her opinion.[224]

A narrower reading of this decision, and one more consistent with the specific nature of Article 35 TFEU, is that the Grand Chamber was merely modifying its ruling in *Groenveld*: Article 35 TFEU is still very much concerned with discrimination, albeit discrimination not just in object but also in effect.[225] Even from this narrow perspective, the modification is significant because the third limb of the *Groenveld* formula ('to provide a particular advantage for national production') has, apparently, been dropped. Furthermore, the Court allowed Belgium to defend its law not only by reference to the Article 36 TFEU derogations but also, for the first time, the mandatory requirements. On the facts the Court found that the rule could be justified on the grounds of consumer protection[226] but that it was disproportionate to prohibit suppliers from requiring that consumers provide their credit card numbers (although it was proportionate to prohibit the supplier to require an actual advance or any payment from the consumer before the expiry of the withdrawal period).

F. THE MARKET ACCESS APPROACH

1. INTRODUCTION

In much of the case law considered so far, the Court has either explicitly or implicitly taken a three-stage approach: (1) it has identified a comparator domestic product; (2) it has determined whether the imported product is being treated less favourably than the domestic product either directly or indirectly (in other words, it has classified the host state measure as either distinctly or indistinctly applicable); and (3) it has considered whether, in the case of distinctly applicable measures, one of the Article 36 TFEU derogations exists, or whether, in the case of indistinctly applicable measures, a mandatory requirement or an Article 36 TFEU derogation applies (see fig. 4.1). However, in some more recent cases the Court has replaced this three-stage approach with two stages. Harking back to the *Dassonville* formula, it has (1) simply noted that the national measure 'impedes', 'hinders', or creates an 'obstacle' to inter-state trade, making little or no reference to the question of discrimination, and then (2) considered whether a mandatory requirement or an Article 36 TFEU derogation applies.

This two-stage approach can be seen in *Monsees*,[227] where the Court said that (1) Austrian rules laying down short maximum journey times and distances for the transport of animals for slaughter constituted an 'obstacle' to international transport and was therefore an MEE. It continued that (2) the rules could be justified on public-health grounds but were not proportionate. Likewise, the Court said in *Commission v. Austria*[228] that (1) by

---

[224] See esp. paras. 42–8.
[225] This is the view the Commission takes in its *Guidance*, SEC(2009) 673, 36: 'Article [35] catches trade barriers that have an actual and specific effect on exports and that create a difference in treatment between trade within a Member State and exports.'
[226] Paras. 47–9.
[227] Case C–350/97 *Monsees v. Unabhängiger Verwaltungssenat für Kärnten* [1999] ECR I–2921, para. 23.
[228] Case C–320/03 *Commission v. Austria* [2005] ECR I–7929, para. 67.

prohibiting heavy goods vehicles from being driven along a section of the A12 in the Austrian Tyrol (one of the main routes between southern Germany and northern Italy), Austrian law 'obstructs the free movement of goods' and therefore constituted an MEE. It added that (2) the rules could be justified on the grounds of environmental protection but were not proportionate.

This two-stage approach also assisted the Court in cases where the rules could not be easily classified as either a distinctly applicable measure or a product requirement. So, for example, it said that registration requirements were MEEs in *Commission* v. *France (reagents)*,[229] as were inspection requirements in *Celestini*,[230] and rules requiring prior approval for use of polyethylene pipes in *Commission* v. *Portugal*.[231] In *Commission* v. *Germany (garlic capsule)*[232] the Court said that the requirement for a marketing authorization as a medicinal product was an 'obstacle to intra-[Union] trade'; and in *Commission* v. *Netherlands* the Court said that a rule requiring cars to be subject to a roadworthiness-test regime was a 'restriction on the free movement of goods'.[233] These cases, in fact, presaged a more general shift towards a market access approach, confirmed by the Court in *Commission* v. *Italy (trailers)*.[234]

2. COMMISSION V. ITALY (TRAILERS)

The *Trailers* case concerned an Italian rule prohibiting motorcycles from pulling trailers. The case thus concerned a ban on *use* of a product. This situation had been the subject of much discussion: should the *Keck* case law be applied by analogy and so the Italian rule would benefit from the presumption of legality (as a number of Member States had argued in their submissions to the Court of Justice in *Trailers*[235] and as Advocate General Kokott had argued in *Mickelsson*[236]), or should the rule be considered an MEE (as Advocate General Bot had argued in *Trailers*)? The Court equivocated but concluded that the Italian rule was in fact an MEE.[237] It noted that while 'it was common ground' that the rule applied 'without regard to the origin of the trailers' (i.e., it was apparently non-discriminatory[238]) in fact the rule affected only imported goods[239] because Italian manufacturers did not manufacture trailers to be towed by motorcycles. The Court then identified in paragraph 37 three situations where a rule could be considered an MEE (see fig. 4.2):

(1) 'Measures adopted by a Member State the object or effect of which is to treat products coming from other Member States less favourably' (distinctly applicable measures)

---

[229] Case C–55/99 *Commission* v. *France (reagents)* [2000] ECR I–1149, para. 19, where the matter was conceded.

[230] Case C–105/94 *Celestini* v. *Saar-Sektkellerei Faber GmbH & Co. KG* [1997] ECR I–2971, para. 33.

[231] Case C–432/03 *Commission* v. *Portugal (polyethylene pipes)* [2005] ECR I–9665, para. 41. See also Case C–38/03 *Commission* v. *Belgium (wheelchairs)* ECLI:EU:C:2005:13, para. 19.

[232] Case C–319/05 *Commission* v. *Germany (garlic capsule)* [2007] ECR I–9811, para. 81. See also Case C–88/07 *Commission* v. *Spain (medicinal herbs)* [2009] ECR I–1353, para. 83.

[233] Case C–297/05 *Commission* v. *Netherlands (roadworthiness testing of cars)* [2007] ECR I–7467, para. 74.

[234] Case C–110/05 *Commission* v. *Italy* [2009] ECR I–519.   [235] Para. 22.

[236] Case C–142/05 *Åklagaren* v. *Mickelsson* [2009] ECR I–4273.

[237] A decision which had already been foreseen by Case C–265/06 *Commission* v. *Portugal* [2008] ECR I–2245, para. 36 concerning a ban on affixing of tinted film to the windscreen of cars. This confirms the earlier case, Case C–473/98 *Kemikalieinspketionen* v. *Toolex Alpha AB* [2000] ECR I–5681, where the Court said that the ban on the industrial *use* (not sale) of trichloroethylene, a substance with a known carcinogenic effect, constituted an MEE (para. 35).

[238] Para. 50.   [239] Para. 57.

(2) '[M]easures referred to in paragraph 35', namely for 'goods coming from other Member States where they are lawfully manufactured and marketed, rules that lay down requirements to be met by such goods ... even if those rules apply to all products alike' to which *Cassis de Dijon* applies (indistinctly applicable product requirements)

(3) 'Any other measure which hinders access of products originating in other Member States to the market of a Member State is also covered by that concept'.

It was the third limb that the Court relied on in the *Trailers* case itself. It said that 'a prohibition on the use of a product in the territory of a Member State has a considerable influence on the behaviour of consumers, which, in its turn, affects the access of that product to the market of that Member State'.[240] It continued that 'Consumers, knowing that they are not permitted to use their motorcycle with a trailer specially designed for it, have practically no interest in buying such a trailer.'[241] Thus, the Italian law prevented a demand from existing in the market at issue for such trailers and therefore hindered their importation.[242] The Court concluded that, to the extent that the effect of the Italian law was 'to hinder access to the Italian market for trailers which are specially designed for motorcycles and are lawfully produced and marketed in Member States other than the Italian Republic', it constituted an MEE under Article 34 TFEU unless it could be justified objectively[243] and was proportionate. On the facts the Italian law was found to be justified.

While *Trailers* concerned a total prohibition on use, *Mickelsson*[244] concerned merely a restriction on the use of a product, this time personal watercraft (such as jet skis) on waters other than general navigable waterways. The judgment closely followed the *Trailers* case, albeit that the language is somewhat more tentative, perhaps reflecting the fact that it is the result of an Article 267 TFEU reference rather than the enforcement proceedings in *Trailers*:

> Even if the national regulations at issue do not have the aim or effect of treating goods coming from other Member States less favourably, which is for the national court to ascertain, the restriction which they impose on the use of a product in the territory of a Member State may, depending on its scope, have a considerable influence on the behaviour of consumers, which may, in turn, affect the access of that product to the market of that Member State.[245]

The national rules therefore constituted an MEE contrary to Article 34 TFEU but could be justified on the grounds of environmental protection and public health. The question of proportionality was a matter for the national court.

3. THE IMPLICATIONS OF THE *TRAILERS* CASE

Trailers and *Mickelsson* send out a strong message that the market access test has returned to Article 34 TFEU. Subsequent case law would support this.[246] For example, in

---

[240] Case C–110/05 *Commission* v. *Italy* [2009] ECR I–519, para. 56.
[241] Citing Case C–265/06 *Commission* v. *Portugal* [2008] ECR I–2245, para. 33, see n. 237.
[242] Para. 57.
[243] Para. 58. See also Case C–142/09 *Lahousse* [2010] ECR I–11685, where the Court found a general prohibition on the sale or use of equipment designed to increase the power and/or speed of mopeds in breach of Art. 34 TFEU unless justified on the ground of road safety and the measure is proportionate.
[244] Case C–142/05 *Aklagaren* v. *Mickelsson, Roos* [2009] ECR I–4273. For the follow-up, see Case C–433/05 *Sandström* [2010] ECR I–2885.
[245] Para. 26.
[246] See, e.g., Case C–421/09 *Humanplasma GmbH* v. *Republik Osterreich* [2010] ECR I–12869, paras. 28–32, where the Court found that non-discriminatory rules on the marketing of blood constituted a 'hindrance

ANETT[247] a Spanish law prohibited tobacco retailers from directly importing tobacco from other Member States. Instead they had to buy their supplies from authorized whole-salers who might—or might not—have imported tobacco in stock. Applying paragraph 37 of *Trailers*, the Court said that the national legislation did not have the object or effect of treating tobacco coming from other Member States less favourably, nor did it concern the requirements that those products must meet.[248] However, the Court continued, 'it is still necessary to examine whether this legislation hinders the access of tobacco products coming from other Member States to the Spanish market'.[249] The Court then noted that, by prohibiting tobacco retailers from directly importing tobacco products from other Member States, the Spanish legislation forced them to procure their supplies from authorized wholesalers: 'Such a procurement method is likely to present various disadvantages which the retailers would not encounter if they carried out the importation themselves'.[250] The Court therefore concluded that 'All of these elements are capable of having a negative effect on the choice of products that the tobacco retailers include in their range of products and, ultimately, on the access of various products coming from other Member States to the Spanish market.'[251]

ANETT has thus clarified one point arising from *Trailers*: the market access approach seems to be a residual 'catch-all' category.[252] While the third limb of *Trailers* appears to have significant overlap with the other two (both distinctly and indistinctly applicable measures affect market access), in fact it is there to catch any other measure which cannot easily be classified as a distinctly applicable measure, a product requirement, or a certain selling arrangement.[253] Market access has therefore not, Triffid-like, subsumed the other tests.[254]

Many would applaud the reintroduction of the market access test to the field of free movement of goods. It certainly has received weighty support in the past. For example, Advocate General Jacobs in *Leclerc-Siplec*[255] argued that all undertakings which engage in a legitimate economic activity in a Member State should have unfettered access to the whole of the Union market, unless there was a valid reason why not. However, he recognized that a pure market access test risked encompassing potentially too much national regulation in its net. He therefore suggested a threshold criteria: where the measure is liable 'substantially to restrict access to the market'[256] then it should breach Article 34 TFEU and need to be justified. The Court may also have acknowledged the need for some sort of threshold in the *Trailers* case when it said that 'a prohibition on the use of a product … has a *considerable* influence on the behaviour of consumers, which, in its turn, affects the access

---

to intra-EU trade'. In Case C–443/10 *Bonnarde* v. *Agence de Services et de Paiement* EU:C:2011:641, para. 22 the *Trailers* market access test is expressly referred to but with no reference to the 'considerable' threshold (para. 30).

[247] Case C–456/10 *ANETT* v. *Administración del Estado* EU:C:2012:241.

[248] Para. 36.   [249] Para. 37.   [250] Para. 38.   [251] Para. 42.

[252] Cf. Case C–333/14 *Scotch Whisky Association* EU:C:2015:845, para. 32, where the Court went straight to the market access test; although in that case all the parties agreed that the measure did constitute an MEE and so classification was not in dispute.

[253] For a summary of potential situations which might fall under this third heading, see Case C–219/07 *Nationale Raad van Dierenkwekers en Liefhebbers VZW* v. *Belgische Staat* [2008] ECR I–4475, para. 22: 'Any legal provision of a Member State prohibiting goods which have not been previously authorised from being marketed, acquired, offered, put on display or sale, kept, prepared, transported, sold, disposed of for valuable consideration or free of charge, imported or used constitutes a measure having an effect equivalent to a quantitative restriction within the meaning of Article [34 TFEU]'.

[254] Although see the casual use of the term in Case C–423/13 *UAB Vilniaus energija* EU:C:2014:2186, para. 48 in the context of a possibly directly discriminatory measure.

[255] Case C–412/93 *Leclerc-Siplec* v. *TF1 Publicité SA* [1995] ECR I–179.

[256] Paras. 41 and 49. This is considered further in Ch. 5.

of that product to the market of that Member State'.[257] It is striking that the Court focuses on the effect of the rule on the demand side, i.e., on the consumers, not on the producer.[258]

However, the focus on market access raises questions as to how *Trailers* fits with the older case law which clearly states that no *de minimis* rule applies to Article 34 TFEU. One answer may be that in the case of distinctly applicable measures and product requirement cases (limbs 1 and 2 of *Trailers*), no *de minimis* rule applies. Only in respect of the rump of cases falling in the third limb of *Trailers* will there be some threshold criteria.

Yet, resorting to the market access approach engages the problems outlined in Chapter 1. What is the meaning of hindering market access and how can it be shown? It may be sufficient that 'an importer *might be dissuaded* from introducing or marketing the products in question in the Member State concerned'.[259] Generally, however, as the persons case law suggests, mere differences between national rules is not enough:[260] more will (usually) be required. It may be the Court will examine the evidence for *actual* interference with trade to demonstrate hindrance, as it did in *Commission* v. *Greece (computer games)*.[261] There the Court said that a Greek law prohibiting the installation and operation of electrical, electromechanical, and electronic games on all premises apart from casinos constituted an MEE, even though Greek law did not prohibit the import of the equipment, because in practice the importation of games machines stopped when the prohibition came into effect.[262] Or the Court might decide to apply a more competition-based test, as it did in *Commission* v. *Italy (lawyers' fees)*,[263] a case on Articles 49 and 56 TFEU, where the Court said that 'a restriction exists, in particular, if those lawyers are deprived of the opportunity of gaining access to the market of the host Member State under conditions of normal and effective competition'.

Alternatively, the Court might rely on the fact that the national rule generates additional costs, as it did in *Commission* v. *Italy (foodstuffs for sportsmen and women)*.[264] There the Court said that the prior-authorization regime for high-energy foods and the payment of administrative costs rendered 'the marketing of such foods more difficult and expensive' and so was an MEE contrary to Article 34 TFEU.[265] Likewise, in *Franzén*[266] the Court said that a Swedish rule permitting only holders of production licences or wholesale licences to import alcoholic drinks 'constituted an obstacle to the importation of alcoholic beverages from other Member States in that it imposes *additional costs* on such beverages'.[267] The rules therefore breached Article 34 TFEU and could not be saved under Article 36 TFEU since the licensing system was not proportionate.

However, the risk of relying simply on the fact that the national rules impose additional costs may not be enough. As Advocate General Poiares Maduro pointed out in

[257] Para. 56, emphasis added. See also Case C–142/05 *Mickelsson* [2009] ECR I–4273, para. 26 and Case C–28/09 *Commission* v. *Austria* [2011] ECR I–13525, para. 58.

[258] I. Lianos, 'In memoriam *Keck*: The reformation of the EU law on free movement of goods' CLES 5/2014, 11.

[259] Case C–385/10 *Elenca Srl* v. *Minister dell'Interno* EU:C:2012:634, para. 22, emphasis added.

[260] See, e.g., Case C–565/08 *Commission* v. *Italy (lawyers' fees)* [2011] ECR I–2101, para. 49: 'it must be borne in mind at the outset that rules of a Member State do not constitute a restriction within the meaning of the [FEU] Treaty solely by virtue of the fact that other Member States apply less strict, or more commercially favourable, rules to providers of similar services established in their territory'.

[261] Case C–65/05 *Commission* v. *Greece (computer games)* [2006] ECR I–10341, paras. 28–9.

[262] Para. 30.   [263] Case C–565/08 [2011] ECR I–2101, para. 51.

[264] Case C–270/02 *Commission* v. *Italy (foodstuffs for sportsmen and women)* [2004] ECR I–1559, para. 19.

[265] However, where the authorization requirement concerns the retailer or the distributor of the goods then it seems there may be no breach of Art. 34 TFEU: Case C–387/93 *Criminal Proceedings against Giorgio Domingo Banchero* [1995] ECR I–4663; Case C–189/95 *Criminal Proceedings against Franzén* [1997] ECR I–5909, para. 57; Case C–162/97 *Criminal Proceedings against Nilsson* [1998] ECR I–7477, para. 28.

[266] Case C–189/95 *Franzén* [1997] ECR I–5909.   [267] Para. 71, emphasis added.

Alfa Vita,[268] not every imposition of supplementary costs is wrongful. Some costs can arise from a mere divergence between the legislation of the state of production of the goods and the state where they are marketed. To be considered a restriction on trade, he said, 'the supplementary cost imposed must stem from the fact that the national rules did not take into account the particular situation of the imported products and, in particular, the fact that those products already had to comply with the rules of their State of origin'. In Advocate General Poiares Maduro's definition of a market access test,[269] a measure constitutes a 'barrier to access to a national market where it protects the acquired positions of certain economic operators on a national market or where it makes intra-[Union] trade more difficult than trade within the national market'. He then suggested that underpinning the market access approach is a discrimination test, based not on nationality or origin, but free movement: 'It seems to me that a consistent approach emerges from the Court's case-law … identifying *discrimination against the exercise of freedom of movement*' (emphasis added). If he is correct, then the difference between the market access approach and the discrimination analysis is not as much as would first appear.

The *Trailers* case raises as many questions as it answers. It does, however, make clear that the principles in *Cassis* remain strong: the Court objected to the fact that trailers specially designed for motorcycles which were 'legally produced and marketed' in other Member States could not, in practice, be sold in Italy.[270] *Trailers* also demonstrates an increasing convergence with the case law on the free movement of persons.[271] There are some signs, too, that the Court is also moving over to a market access approach to Article 35 TFEU. In *Fragkopoulos*[272] the Court found that a national law which required an exporter of grapes only to process and package grapes from that particular region of the state and not grapes from other parts of the state, was 'likely to hamper, at the very least potentially, intra-[Union] trade' and therefore constituted an MEE.[273]

G. LITIGATION AVOIDANCE: DIRECTIVE 2015/1535 ON THE PROVISION OF INFORMATION IN THE FIELD OF TECHNICAL STANDARDS AND REGULATIONS

So far, this chapter has focused on decisions by the Court that a Member State has breached or may have breached Article 34 TFEU. These rulings came about either from Article 258 TFEU enforcement proceedings brought by the Commission or Article 267 TFEU references from national courts which resulted from a challenge by a trader to the compatibility of a provision of national law with Article 34 TFEU. However, litigation is, by its very nature, uncoordinated and reactive: individual litigants raise a Union law challenge when its suits their interests. The Commission can be more coordinated in its approach under Article 258 TFEU but it lacks the resources to bring proceedings in respect of every breach of Union law, and the procedure itself is subject to political intervention. To overcome some of these problems, the Union adopted Information

---

[268] Joined Cases C–158 and 159/04 *Alfa Vita* [2006] ECR I–8135, para. 44.

[269] Paras. 45–6.   [270] Para. 54.

[271] See further Ch. 1 and A. Tryfonidou, 'Further steps on the road to convergence among the market freedoms' (2010) 35 *ELRev*. 36.

[272] Case C–161/09 *Kakavetsos-Fragkopoulos AE Epexergasias kai Emporias Stafidas v. Nomarchiaki Aftodioikisi Korinthias* [2011] ECR I–915.

[273] Para. 29.

Directive 2015/1535[274] (consolidating Directive 83/189 as amended and then Directive 98/34),[275] requiring Member States to notify the Commission of any draft technical regulations *before* they are adopted and before they create barriers to trade so that they can be checked for their compatibility with Union law.[276] In other words, as the Court put it in *Belgische Petroleum Unie*,[277] the directive is designed to protect, 'by means of preventive control, the free movement of goods, which is one of the foundations of the European Union'. At first glance this directive seems dry and technical, but it has assumed considerable significance in the light of the Court's rulings in *CIA*,[278] *Unilever*,[279] and *Sapod-Audic*.[280]

For our purposes, Information Directive 2015/1535 contains two important provisions: Article 5 on the obligation to notify and the standstill provision in Article 6.[281] Article 5(1) requires Member States to notify the Commission of any draft 'technical regulations' which is due to be adopted, together with a statement of why it is needed.[282] The definition of technical regulation is loosely equivalent to the sort of product requirements[283] listed by the Court in paragraph 15 of *Keck*.[284] Therefore, rules concerning the quality standards for flower bulbs;[285] prior approval for decoders for digitally broadcast television;[286] the compulsory marking or labelling of packaging;[287] the requirement that low prize games machines had to be located only in casinos or gaming arcades;[288] the

---

[274] [2015] OJ L241/1.

[275] For further information, see the TRIS (Technical Regulation Information System) website (<http://ec.europa.eu/growth/tools-databases/tris/en/>).

[276] L. Gormley, 'Some reflections on the internal market and free movement of goods' [1989/1] *LIEI* 9, 13.

[277] Case C–26/11 *Belgische Petroleum v. Belgische Staat* EU:C:2013:44, para. 49.

[278] Case C–194/94 *CIA Security International SA v. Signalson SA and Securitel SPRL* [1996] ECR I–2201.

[279] Case C–443/98 *Unilever Italia SpA v. Central Food SpA* [2000] ECR I–7535.

[280] Case C–159/00 [2002] ECR I–5031.

[281] In addition to this formal procedure, many Member States notify their draft regulations informally to the Commission. As a result of these discussions, Member States often modify the original drafts and the file is closed (Gormley, n. 276).

[282] Art. 1(f) defines 'technical regulation' as 'technical specifications and other requirements or rules on services, including the relevant administrative provisions, the observance of which is compulsory, de jure or de facto, in the case of marketing, provision of a service, establishment of a service operator or use in a Member State or a major part thereof, as well as laws, regulations or administrative provisions of Member States, except those provided for in Article 7, prohibiting the manufacture, importation, marketing or use of a product or prohibiting the provision or use of a service, or establishment as a service provider'. Art. 1(c) defines 'technical specification' as 'a specification contained in a document which lays down the characteristics required of a product such as levels of quality, performance, safety or dimensions, including the requirements applicable to the product as regards the name under which the product is sold, terminology, symbols, testing and test methods, packaging, marking or labelling and conformity assessment procedures'. For a discussion of the meaning of these terms, see Case C–159/00 *Sapod-Audic* [2002] ECR I–5031, paras. 26–30.

[283] Case C–267/03 *Lindberg* [2005] ECR I–3247, para. 60.

[284] The parallel between the definition of technical regulations and the Court's case law on Art. 34 TFEU is not exact. E.g., rules relating to language requirements are considered not to be technical regulations but they are measures having equivalent effect (Case C–33/97 *Colim NV v. Bigg's Continent Noord NV* [1999] ECR I–3175, para. 36). On other cases falling outside the definition, see Case C–37/99 *Roelof Donkersteeg* [2000] ECR I–10223; Case C–314/98 *Snellers Auto's BV v. Algemeen Directeur van de Dienst Wegverkeer* [2000] ECR I–863. Minor amendments do not need to be notified: Case C–433/05 *Sandström* [2010] ECR I–2885, para. 49 and Art. 5(1), para. 3 of Dir. 2015/1535.

[285] Case C–52/93 *Commission v. Netherlands* [1994] ECR I–3591.

[286] Case C–390/99 *Canal Satélite Digital SL v. Administracíon General del Estado* [2002] ECR I–607.

[287] Case C–159/00 *Sapod-Audic* [2002] ECR I–5031, para. 32. See also Case C–20/05 *Schwibbert* [2007] ECR I–9447, paras. 36–7 (affixing the distinctive sign 'SIAE' to products to inform consumers that the reproductions are legal).

[288] Joined Cases C–213, 214 and 217/11 *Fortuna v. Dyrektor Izby Celnej w Gdyni* EU:C:2012:495.

prohibition on the marketing of cotton buds which were not made from biodegradable materials;[289] and the composition, classification, packaging, and labelling of pesticides[290] all constituted technical regulations which had to be notified.

Not only do rules concerning the products themselves have to be notified but so do rules concerning their use. Therefore, in *Lindberg*[291] a Swedish prohibition on operators making certain types of gaming machines available to the players and thus to consumers also constituted a technical regulation and had to be notified. On the other hand, national measures restricting certain selling arrangements, considered by the Court in paragraph 16 of *Keck* to fall outside Article 34 TFEU,[292] do not constitute technical regulations[293] and so do not need to be notified. The requirement to notify does, however, apply only to goods; it does not apply to requirements imposed on economic operators/service providers.[294]

On receipt of the Member State's notification, the Commission must inform the other Member States, as well as the relevant Standing Committee, which can then make comments.[295] The Member State proposing the legislation must take these comments 'into account as far as possible in the subsequent preparation of the technical regulation'.[296]

Article 6 of Directive 2015/1535 contains the standstill clause. The notifying Member State must postpone the adoption of the draft technical regulation for three months, pending its consideration by the Commission and the other Member States.[297] The standstill period is six months if the Commission or another Member State delivers a 'detailed opinion' under Article 6(2) that the measure envisaged may create obstacles to the free movement of goods. The notifying Member State must respond to the Commission, explaining the action it proposes to take in the light of these opinions, and the Commission must then respond to this. Article 6(3) requires the notifying Member State to postpone the adoption of the draft technical regulation for 12 months if the Union announces its intention to adopt harmonization legislation, often based on the notified legislation.

So, Directive 2015/1535, with its procedural, as opposed to substantive, orientation is unusual in that it does not confer rights and obligations on individuals. Instead, it lays down a detailed procedure for a regulated dialogue between the Member State proposing the legislation, the Commission, and the other Member States.[298] This dialogue should result in the adoption of only those technical regulations which are compatible with EU law (although the Directive 2015/1535 procedure does not render the national

---

[289] Case C–303/04 *Lidl Italia* v. *Comune di Stradella* [2005] ECR I–7865.

[290] Case C–61/93 *Commission* v. *Netherlands* [1994] ECR I–3607. See also Case C–13/96 *Bic Benelux SA* v. *Belgian State* [1997] ECR I–1753.

[291] Case C–267/03 *Lindberg* [2005] ECR I–3247, para. 60. See also Case C–65/05 *Commission* v. *Greece (computer games)* [2006] ECR I–10341, para. 61.

[292] See further Ch. 5.

[293] Joined Cases C–418/93 etc. *Semeraro Casa Uno Srl* v. *Sindaco del Comune di Erbusco* [1996] ECR I–2975, para. 38.

[294] Case C–267/03 *Lindberg* [2005] ECR I–3247, para. 88. Cf. Art. 15(6) of the Services Dir. 2006/123 ([2006] OJ L376/36), considered further in Ch. 11.

[295] Art. 5(2).

[296] Art. 5(2). The final version of the text must be sent to the Commission: Art. 5(3).

[297] Art. 6(1), except in the case of urgency occasioned by 'serious and unforeseeable' circumstances: Art. 6(7). However, even in these circumstances the national rules remain subject to Art. 34 TFEU: Case C–55/99 *Commission* v. *France (medical reagents)* [2000] ECR I–11499. At the height of the BSE crisis the UK used the emergency procedure in 24 cases (Commission, 'Report on the Operation of Directive 98/34/EC [now 2015/1535] from 1995 to 1998', COM(2000) 429, 24).

[298] See Commission communication 86/C 245/05 ([1986] OJ C245/4) and Case C–194/94 *CIA* [1996] ECR I–2201, para. 40. See also R. Dehousse, '1992 and beyond: The institutional dimension of the internal market programme' [1989/1] *LIEI* 109, 115.

legislation immune from subsequent challenge by a trader on the grounds that the measure breaches Article 34 TFEU). Directive 2015/1535 therefore forms a key component in
the programme of helping to 'promote the smooth functioning of the internal market'[299]
and developing confidence between the national authorities.[300] However, the success of
Directive 2015/1535 depends entirely on the willingness of the Member States to notify
and comply with its provisions. In the early days of the operation of the directive the
Commission, concerned about the low level of Article 5 notifications, started a series of
enforcement proceedings against Member States for failing to notify.[301] The Court usually
condemned the Member State for failing to notify as well as condemning the substance
of the national regulations.[302] However, the Commission wanted the Court to go further
and argued in a Communication of 1986[303] that:

> when a Member State enacted a technical regulation falling within the scope of Directive
> [2015/1535] without notifying the draft to the Commission and respecting the standstill
> obligation, the regulation thus adopted is *unenforceable against third parties in the legal
> system of the Member State in question*. The Commission therefore considers that litigants
> have a right to expect national courts to refuse to enforce national technical regulations
> which have not been notified as required by [Union] law.[304]

At first, the Court was resistant to the Commission's approach but, in *CIA*,[305] it changed
its mind. The case concerned the failure by the Belgian government to notify its law on
security systems to the Commission under Article 5 of Directive 2015/1535 and its effect
on private litigation involving two rival companies, CIA Security and Signalson.

   CIA sold a prize-winning burglar alarm system, Andromède, which had not been approved in accordance with the (unnotified) Belgian law on security systems. Signalson,
a commercial rival of CIA's, took advantage of this and said in a marketing campaign
that the prize had been awarded on an improper basis and that the Andromède system
did not work.[306] CIA then brought proceedings against Signalson alleging unfair trading
practice, in particular libel. Signalson counterclaimed, seeking an order restraining CIA
Security from carrying on its business, on the ground that CIA was marketing an alarm
system which had not been approved. In response, CIA claimed that the Belgian rules requiring prior approval of alarm systems breached Article 34 TFEU and that, in any event,
the rules were invalid because they had not been communicated to the Commission
under Article 5 of Directive 2015/1535.

   The Court said that the Belgian rules constituted technical regulations within the
meaning of Directive 2015/1535 and so should have been notified under Article 5. Because
Articles 5–6 of Directive 2015/1535 laid down a precise obligation on Member States to
notify draft technical regulations to the Commission and because these Articles were
unconditional and sufficiently precise in terms of their content, they could be relied on by
individuals before national courts.[307]

   The Court then considered the legal consequences of Belgium's failure to notify.
Although a number of governments argued that since the directive concerned only relations between the Member States and the Commission it had no effect on relations
between private parties, the Court disagreed. Referring to the Commission's 1986

---

[299] Preamble to Dir. 2015/1535, para. 3.   [300] Case C–194/94 *CIA* [1996] ECR I–2201, para. 40.
[301] These continue to this day: Case C–65/05 *Commission v. Greece (computer games)* [2006] ECR I–10341,
para. 64.
[302] See, e.g., *Commission v. Germany* [1994] ECR I–2039.   [303] 86/C 245/05 ([1986] OJ C245/4).
[304] Emphasis added.   [305] Case C–194/94 *CIA* [1996] ECR I–2201.
[306] P. Slot (1996) 33 *CMLRev.* 1035, 1036–7.   [307] Para. 44.

Communication, to the directive's purpose of protecting free movement of goods, and to the elaborate procedure laid down by Articles 5–6, the Court said:

> The effectiveness of [Union] control will be that much greater if the Directive is interpreted as meaning that breach of the obligation to notify constitutes a *substantial procedural defect* such as to render the technical regulations in question inapplicable to individuals.[308]

Therefore, CIA could rely on Articles 5–6 against Signalson and raise the Belgian government's failure to notify as a defence to the counterclaim.

In *Unilever*,[309] the Court had the opportunity of clarifying its ruling in *CIA*. The case concerned a draft Italian law on olive oil labelling which had been notified to the Commission in May 1998 under Article 5 of Directive 2015/1535. Although the Commission informed the Italian authorities that it intended to legislate in this area, thereby triggering the additional nine-month standstill provision under Article 6, Italy nevertheless adopted the legislation in August 1998. In September 1998, on receipt of an order from Central Food, Unilever supplied Central Food with a quantity of olive oil. The next day, Central Food informed Unilever that, because the oil was not labelled in accordance with the contested Italian law, it would not pay for it. In response, Unilever argued that since the national law had been adopted in breach of the standstill clause in Article 6, the principle of non-enforceability laid down by *CIA* in respect of Article 5 applied equally to Article 6, and so it was not obliged to comply with the Italian labelling rules, and therefore Central Foods should pay what it owed.

Advocate General Jacobs disagreed with Unilever. He argued that the principle in *CIA* should not apply in this situation because it would have the effect of requiring traders to be experts, not only in their own contractual dealings but also in European Union law and, in particular, to know of the existence of Directive 2015/1535 and the judgment in *CIA*. They would also have to identify the technical regulation as such, and establish with certainty whether the Member State had complied with its obligations under Articles 5–6 of the directive. This last element, he noted, was particularly difficult, given the lack of publicity under the directive. He also thought that injustice could result: if a technical regulation was unenforceable in private proceedings an individual would lose a case in which such a regulation was at issue, not because of its own failure to comply with an obligation deriving from Union law, but because of a Member State's behaviour. This was all because of the need to ensure effective enforcement of Union law.[310]

The Court rejected these arguments and applied *CIA*.[311] It said that 'breach of the obligations of postponement of adoption set out in Article [6 of Directive 2015/1535] also constitutes a *substantial procedural defect* such as to render technical regulations inapplicable'.[312] The Court then said that the inapplicability of the Italian law could be invoked in civil proceedings between individuals concerning contractual rights and obligations. It could not see a distinction between *Unilever* and *CIA* in this respect: there was no reason to treat disputes between individuals relating to unfair competition, as in *CIA*, differently from disputes between individuals concerning contractual rights and obligations. Then, in *Sapod-Audic*[313] the Court considered the consequences of a finding by the national court that an unnotified national technical regulation was inapplicable. It said that it was for national law to determine the severity of the sanction to be applied in these

---

[308] Para. 48, emphasis added.   [309] Case C–443/98 [2000] ECR I–7535.
[310] Paras. 100–3.   [311] Para. 39.   [312] Para. 44, emphasis added.
[313] Case C–159/00 [2002] ECR I–5031, para. 53, noted by M. Dougan (2003) 40 *CMLRev.* 193.

cases but the sanction could include the nullity or unenforceability of a contract, subject
to the principles of non-discrimination and effectiveness.

The Court has, however, imposed some limits on the *CIA/Unilever* rule of the inapplicability of national legislation in the event of non-notification. In *Lemmens*[314] it
made clear that the *CIA* rule applies only to legislation which affects trade between
Member States. Lemmens was charged with driving a vehicle under the influence of alcohol. Under domestic law, the breathalyser used had to comply with certain standards
of quality, performance, and test methods. Lemmens argued that since the technical
regulations in which those standards were set out had not been properly notified to the
Commission under Directive 2015/1535, the results of the breathalyser test could not be
used against him.

The Court disagreed. It said that while failure to notify technical regulations rendered
the national regulations inapplicable inasmuch as they hindered the *marketing* of a product which was not in conformity with the regulations (*CIA*), it did not have the effect
of rendering unlawful any *use* of a product which was in conformity with unnotified
regulations.[315] It continued that the use of the breathalyser was not liable to create an
obstacle to trade which could have been avoided if the notification procedure had been
followed and therefore the directive did not preclude the use of the evidence.

Despite the limits imposed by *Lemmens*, the immediate practical effect of *CIA* on
national governments was dramatic. For example,[316] the Dutch government drew up a
list of 400 national regulations which should have been notified under the directive.[317] It
unilaterally withdrew 96 technical regulations and subsequently withdrew a further 77
following discussions with the Commission. It then formally notified 227 texts, of which
70 were not considered significant, but the rest contained provisions contrary to Union
law which needed to be rectified. This tale demonstrates the value of the Directive 2015/
1535 procedure: without it, 330 technical regulations would have formed part of Dutch
law and would have needed to have been addressed by Article 258 TFEU proceedings
or individual challenge. As with *Cassis de Dijon*, the old allies—the Commission and
the Court—worked together to ensure the effective application of Union law, with the
Court drawing on the Commission's 1986 Communication and with the Commission
proactively following up the Court's judgment.

H. CONCLUSIONS

Despite the apparent success of Directive 2015/1535, the Union has still introduced the
Mutual Recognition Regulation 764/2008 to deal with continuing problems of market
access for products.[318] The Regulation's *Cassis de Dijon* heritage is clearly expressed:

> Articles [34] and [36 TFEU] entail *inter alia* that Member States of destination cannot
> forbid the sale on their territories of products lawfully marketed in another Member State
> and which are not subject to [Union] harmonisation, unless the technical restrictions
> laid down by the Member State of destination are justified on the grounds described in
> Article [36 TFEU] … or on the basis of overriding requirements of general public im-
> portance recognised by the Court of Justice's case law, and that they are proportionate.[319]

---

[314] Case C–226/97 *Criminal Proceedings against Johannes Martinus Lemmens* [1998] ECR I–3711.
[315] Para. 35.   [316] COM(2000) 429, 35.
[317] For full details of the Dutch situation, see J. Jans, 'National legislative autonomy? The procedural
constraints of European law' [1998/1] *LIEI* 25.
[318] MEMO/07/54, 14 Feb. 2007, 3.   [319] COM(2007) 36, 2.

However, it would be a mistake to conclude that in *Cassis* the Court favoured free trade to the detriment of broader interests which are valued at national level. The development of mandatory requirements not only places a brake on any possible destructive regulatory competition (race to the bottom) but also recognizes that the European constitution is not merely economic but pluralistic, a constitution which embraces social and cultural values.[320] However, the broad scope of the *Dassonville* formula has forced the Court to recognize ever-more mandatory requirements to preserve a wide variety of national legislation. That said, in the majority of cases the Court either rejects the mandatory requirement put forward by the Member State on the facts or finds that the steps taken by the state to realize the objective are not proportionate. For these reasons, governments and commentators became increasingly concerned that the Court's interpretation of Article 34 TFEU was in fact leading to wide-scale destruction of national regulation, including rules which were non-discriminatory and which had little impact on cross-border trade. The Court eventually listened and in *Keck*, it carved out an area of national regulation, certain selling arrangements, and made it clear that Article 34 TFEU did not apply to it, even in principle. It is to the decision in *Keck* that Chapter 5 turns.

FURTHER READING

Introduction to the free movement of goods

Commission, *Free Movement of Goods: Guide to the application of Treaty provisions governing free movement of goods (Articles 28–30 EC)*, SEC(2009) 673.

P. OLIVER, 'Some further reflections on the scope of Articles 28–30 (ex 30–36)' (1999) 36 *CMLRev.* 738.

P. OLIVER and S. ENCHELMAIER, 'Free movement of goods: Recent developments in the case law' (2007) 44 *CMLRev.* 649.

P. OLIVER et al., *Oliver on Free Movement of Goods in the European Union*, 5th edn (Oxford: Hart Publishing, 2010).

M. POIARES MADURO, *We the Court: The European Court of Justice and the European Economic Constitution* (Oxford, Hart Publishing 1998).

J. SNELL, *Goods and Services in EC Law* (Oxford: OUP, 2002).

The question of horizontal direct effect

J. BAQUERO CRUZ, *Between Competition and Free Movement: The economic constitutional law of the European Community* (Oxford: Hart Publishing, 2002), Ch. 7.

M. QUINN and N. McGOWAN, 'Could Article 30 impose obligations on individuals?' (1987) 12 *ELRev.* 163.

S. VAN DEN BOGART, 'Horizontality' in C. Barnard and J. Scott (eds.), *The Law of the Single European Market: Unpacking the premises* (Oxford: Hart Publishing, 2002).

On the question of the market access v. discrimination approach

C. BARNARD, 'Restricting restrictions: Lessons for the EU from the US' (2009) 68 *CLJ* 563.

---

[320] M. Poiares Maduro, 'Striking the elusive balance between economic freedom and social rights in the EU' in P. Alston (ed.), *The EU and Human Rights* (Oxford: OUP, 1999).

M. Jansson and H. Kalimo, '*De Minimis* meets "market access": Transformations in the substance—and the syntax—of the EU free movement law? (2014) 51 *CMLRev.* 523.

P. Oliver, 'Of Trailers and Jet Skis: Is the case law on Article 34 TFEU hurtling in a new direction?' (2010) 33 *Fordham Intl. LJ* 1423.

E. Spaventa, 'Leaving *Keck* behind? The free movement of goods after the rulings in *Commission* v. *Italy* and *Mickelsson and Roos*' (2009) *ELRev.* 914.

Mandatory requirements

H. Unberath and A. Johnston, 'The double-headed approach of the ECJ concerning consumer protection' (2007) 44 *CMLRev.* 1237.

S. Weatherill, 'Who is the "average consumer"?' in S. Weatherill and U. Bernitz (eds.), *The Regulation of Unfair Commercial Practices under EC Directive 2005/29* (Oxford: Hart Publishing, 2007).

Mutual recognition

K. Alter and S. Meunier-Aitsahalia, 'Judicial politics in the European Community: European integration and the pathbreaking *Cassis de Dijon* decision' (1994) 26 *Comparative Political Studies* 535.

J. H. H. Weiler, 'Mutual recognition, functional equivalence and harmonization in the evolution of the European common market and the WTO' in F. Padoa Schioppa (ed.), *The Principle of Mutual Recognition in the European Integration Process* (Basingstoke: Palgrave Macmillan, 2005).

On the application of free movement of goods in the national systems

L. Gormley, 'Free movement of goods and preemption of state power' in A. Arnull, C. Barnard, M. Dougan, and E. Spaventa (eds.), *A Constitutional Order of States? Essays in honour of Alan Dashwood* (Oxford: Hart Publishing, 2011).

M. Jarvis, *The Application of EC Law by National Courts: The free movement of goods* (Oxford: OUP, 1998).

M. Poiares Maduro, 'Revisiting the free movement of goods in a comparative perspective' in A. Rosas, E. Levits, and Y. Bot (eds.), *The Court of Justice and the Construction of Europe: Analyses and perspectives on sixty years of case law* (The Hague: Asser Press, 2012).

UK government, 'Single market: free movement of goods report: review of the balance of competences', <https://www.gov.uk/government/consultations/single-market-free-movement-of-goods-report-review-of-the-balance-of-competences>.

Where does EU law stop?

E. Spaventa, 'The outer limits of the Treaty free movement provisions: Some reflections on the significance of *Keck*, remoteness and *Deliège*' in C. Barnard and O. Odudu (eds.), *The Outer Limits of European Union Law* (Oxford: Hart Publishing, 2009).

The wholly internal rule

A. Tryfonidou, 'The outer limits of Article 28 EC: Purely internal situations and the development of the Court's approach through the years' in C. Barnard and O. Odudu (eds.), *The Outer Limits of European Union Law* (Oxford: Hart Publishing, 2009).

Revisiting the old case law

J. HOJNIK, 'Free movement of goods in a labyrinth: Can *Buy Irish* survive the crises?' (2012) 49 *CMLRev.* 291.

M. POIARES MADURO and L. AZOULAI (eds.), *The Past and Future of EU Law: The classics of EU law revisited on the 50th anniversary of the Rome Treaty* (Oxford: Hart Publishing, 2010), section XI.

Free movement of goods and food

Commission, 'Green Paper on promotion measures and information provision for agricultural products: A reinforced value-added European strategy for promoting the tastes of Europe', COM(2011) 436.

C. MACMAOLAIN, 'Free movement of foodstuffs, quality requirements and consumer protection: Have the Court and the Commission both got it wrong?' (2001) 26 *ELRev.* 413.

5

ARTICLE 34 TFEU AND CERTAIN SELLING ARRANGEMENTS

A. INTRODUCTION

In Chapter 4 we considered the Article 34 TFEU prohibition on measures having equivalent effect to quantitative restrictions (MEEs). We saw that originally MEEs fell into two categories: distinctly applicable measures (different burden in law and in fact) and indistinctly applicable measures (same burden in law, different burden in fact). Following *Commission* v. *Italy (trailers)*,[1] the second category was confined to product requirements and a third category was added: measures hindering market access. While the original, two-tiered classification was sufficient to address the relatively straightforward situations arising in the early case law, it proved a rather blunt instrument for later, more complex cases. In particular, the Court struggled to decide how rules concerning the time, place, and manner of marketing

---

[1] Case C–110/05 [2009] ECR I–519.

products[2]—so-called 'market circumstances' rules—fitted within this framework. The Court's attempts to reconcile market circumstances rules with Articles 34 and 36 TFEU, the decision in *Keck*,[3] and the ramifications of this ruling, form the focus of this chapter. As we shall see, this chapter presents the story of a court struggling to locate the outer limits of EU law: how deep into the national system can and should EU law extend? Are there national rules—adopted by democratically elected national governments—which should be beyond the scrutiny of the Court of Justice? What legal techniques can be used to limit the reach of EU law?

These questions have troubled the Court—and commentators—not just in respect of free movement of goods but also persons, services, and capital. However, it is in the field of goods that they have been most fully articulated and it is for this reason that they are discussed in detail here.

B. MARKET CIRCUMSTANCES RULES AND ARTICLE 34 TFEU

1. WHAT ARE MARKET CIRCUMSTANCES RULES?

Mortelmans defines market circumstances rules as those concerning, '[w]ho (pharmacist, door-to-door salesman, employee) sells the product, and when (Sundays, at night), where (shop, door-to-door) and how (with a gift)' he goes about it.[4] Such rules differ from MEEs in three main ways. First, while market circumstances rules, like MEEs, restrict the volume of trade, unlike MEEs, they are neither *designed* to protect the home market[5] nor do they have the *effect* of protecting the home market. Secondly, while distinctly and indistinctly applicable MEEs are discriminatory in some way (e.g., same burden in law, different burden in fact), rules concerning market circumstances often affect the domestic producer and the importer in just the same way and so are non-discriminatory (same burden in law *and* same burden in fact).

A third difference relates to the regulatory burden. MEEs, particularly product requirements, are prohibited by Article 34 TFEU because of the double burden they entail: the disparities between the different national rules oblige the producer/importer to comply with both the home and host states' rules, thereby increasing costs.[6] By contrast, market circumstances rules generally affect the *retailer*, not the producer/importer. Retailers are at one stage removed from the importation process. Unlike producers/importers who often have to satisfy two sets of regulations (those of the home and host state), retailers have to satisfy only one set of rules (those of the home state). The reason why retailers complain about market circumstances rules is that these rules limit the commercial freedom of traders to sell under the most liberalized conditions,[7] i.e., they prevent traders

---

[2] See E. White, 'In search of the limits to Article 30 of the EEC Treaty' (1989) 26 *CMLRev.* 235, 259 and his submissions on behalf of the Commission in Case C–145/88 *Torfaen BC* v. *B & Q plc* [1989] ECR 3851.

[3] Joined Cases C–267 and 268/91 *Keck and Mithouard* [1993] ECR I–6097.

[4] K. Mortelmans, 'Article 30 of the EEC Treaty and legislation relating to market circumstances: Time to consider a new definition' (1991) 28 *CMLRev.* 115, 116.

[5] For an early recognition of this, see Slynn AG's approach in Joined Cases 60 and 61/84 *Cinéthèque SA* v. *Fédération nationale des cinémas français* [1985] ECR 2605.

[6] The Court emphasized this point in Case C–241/89 *SARRP* v. *Chambre syndicale des raffineurs et conditionneurs de sucre de France* [1990] ECR I–4695, para. 30.

[7] Van Gerven AG in Case C–145/88 *Torfaen* v. *B & Q plc* [1989] ECR 3851; Tesauro AG in Case C–292/92 *Hünermund* v. *Landesapothekerkammer Baden-Württemberg* [1993] ECR I–6787, para. 22; Van Gerven AG in Joined Cases C–401 and 402/92 *Boermans* [1994] ECR I–2199, para. 20.

from selling goods exactly when, where, and how they choose. In other words, traders complain about the very existence of market circumstances rules, not the fact that they differ from state to state.

Given the remoteness of market circumstances rules from inter-state trade and the fact that they generally affect the *retailers* and not the producers/importers, it might be thought that such rules should fall outside Article 34 TFEU altogether and, in the name of subsidiarity, the detail be left to the Member States, unhampered by Union law. However, the tentacles of the *Dassonville* formula, with its reference to measures which 'indirectly', 'potentially' hinder inter-state trade, are sufficiently all-embracing to bring national rules on market circumstances within the Article 34 TFEU prohibition.

This raises the fundamental question: what is the purpose of Article 34 TFEU? As Advocate General Tesauro succinctly put it in *Hünermund*,[8] is Article 34 TFEU intended:

(1) to liberalize inter-state trade, as governments would argue (in which case Article 34 TFEU should not apply to market circumstances rules) *or*

(2) to encourage the unhindered pursuit of commerce in the individual Member States, as some traders would argue (in which case Article 34 TFEU should apply to market circumstances rules)?

Putting it another way, is Article 34 TFEU there merely to mediate the relationship between market-liberalization on the one hand and national sovereignty on the other, the view supported by Advocate General Tesauro's first approach, or is its purpose to give all traders the right to trade and thus to challenge any state norms that stand in their way, the view supported by Advocate General Tesauro's second approach?

2. THE EARLY APPROACHES TO MARKET CIRCUMSTANCES RULES

For many years the Court struggled to fit market circumstance rules into its Article 34 TFEU case law.[9] It is possible to detect three different strands to the Court's early jurisprudence. The first reflected its methodology in *Cassis* (discussed in Chapter 4): market circumstances rules were MEEs and so breached Article 34 TFEU but were potentially justifiable.[10] This can be seen in *Oosthoek*,[11] where the Court said that a national law prohibiting the use of free gifts as an incentive to purchase a product—in this case encyclopaedias—could breach Article 34 TFEU because the producer might be required either to adopt an advertising or sales promotion scheme which differed from one Member State to another or to discontinue a scheme which it considered to be particularly effective.[12] In *Buet*[13] the Court said that its ruling in *Oosthoek* applied equally to rules depriving traders of a method of marketing whereby they realized almost all of their sales. Therefore, a national law prohibiting door-to-door selling of foreign-language teaching materials

---

[8] Case C–292/92 *Hünermund* [1993] ECR I–6787, para. 1.

[9] As Tesauro AG admitted in Case C–292/92 *Hünermund* [1993] ECR I–6787, para. 11: 'Case law which— why conceal it?—is certainly not amenable to systematic interpretation.'

[10] An approach supported by various academics: see, e.g., L. Gormley (1990) 27 *CMLRev.* 141, 149; A. Arnull, 'What shall we do on Sunday?' (1991) 16 *ELRev.* 112.

[11] Case 286/81 *Criminal Proceedings against Oosthoek's Uitgeversmaatschappij BV* [1982] ECR 4575.

[12] Para. 15. See also Case C–241/89 *SARRP* v. *Chambre syndicale des raffineurs et conditionneurs de sucre de France* [1990] ECR I–4695, para. 29 (national law prohibiting any statement in the advertising of artificial sweeteners alluding to the word sugar breached Art. 34 TFEU and could not be justified).

[13] Case 382/87 *Buet* v. *Ministère public* [1989] ECR 1235, para. 8.

constituted an indistinctly applicable MEE but could be justified on the grounds of consumer protection.

In respect of advertising, the Court ruled in *Yves Rocher*[14] that a prohibition on eye-catching advertising of price comparisons (showing the old price crossed out and the new one in red next to it) was an indistinctly applicable MEE, as was a law in *Aragonesa*[15] prohibiting the advertising of certain alcoholic drinks in public places. The Court also said that measures limiting the types of shops which could sell certain goods, such as the rule in *LPO*[16] granting opticians the exclusive right to distribute glasses, constituted an indistinctly applicable MEE, because it was capable of affecting the possibilities of marketing imported products insofar as they limited sales to certain channels. On the facts the rules could not be justified either by a mandatory requirement or an Article 36 TFEU derogation. As we shall see, the outcome in this line of cases beginning with *Oosthoek* will not be very different today post-*Keck*, albeit that the route to get there might be different.

The second approach adopted by the Court to market circumstances rules was to find that the national measure was not an MEE at all.[17] It therefore fell outside Article 34 TFEU, usually because it was not a 'trading rule' within the meaning of *Dassonville*, it was not discriminatory and it did not affect inter-state trade.[18] So in *Oebel*[19] the Court said that a German law forbidding night work in the bakery industry and transport and delivery before 5.45 a.m. did not breach Articles 34–5 TFEU[20] because the restriction applied to all producers, wherever they were established, and trade within the Union remained possible at all times. In *Blesgen*[21] the Court said that a national rule prohibiting the sale of drinks over 22 per cent proof for consumption on public premises did not breach Article 34 TFEU because it had 'no connection with the importation of the products and for that reason [was] not of such a nature as to impede trade between Member States'.[22]

The decision in *Krantz*[23] is perhaps the most important in this line of case law. The Court had to consider whether a Dutch law, allowing the collector of taxes to seize goods if purchasers failed to discharge their tax debts, contravened Article 34 TFEU. Having established that the national rule was non-discriminatory and did not seek to affect trade

---

[14] Case C–126/91 [1993] ECR I–2361. The case was brought by the extraordinarily named trade association, the Protective Association against Pernicious Economic Practices.

[15] Joined Cases C–1 and 176/90 *Aragonesa* [1991] ECR I–4151. See also Case C–362/88 *GB-INNO-BM* v. *Confédération du commerce luxembourgeois* [1990] ECR I–667.

[16] Case C–271/92 *Laboratoire de Prothèses and Groupement d'Opticiens Lunetiers Détaillants* [1993] ECR I–2899 (opticians' monopoly), para. 7. See also Case C–369/88 *Criminal Proceedings against Delattre* [1991] ECR I–1487, para. 51, and Case C–60/90 *Criminal Proceedings against Jean Monteil and Daniel Samanni* [1991] ECR I–1547 (pharmacists' monopoly), para. 38.

[17] A view supported by J. Steiner, 'Drawing the line: Uses and abuses of Article 30 EEC' (1992) 29 *CMLRev*. 749, 773.

[18] See also Joined Cases 60 and 61/84 *Cinéthèque* [1985] ECR 2605. According to a French law designed to encourage attendance at cinemas, videos of films could not be sold or hired within the first year of the film receiving its performance certificate. The legislation was non-discriminatory. Slynn AG said that because the national rules were not specifically directed at imports, did not discriminate against imports, and gave no protection to domestic producers, prima facie they did not breach Art. 34 TFEU, even if imports were restricted or reduced.

[19] Case 155/80 *Summary Proceedings against Sergius Oebel* [1981] ECR 1993.

[20] Para. 20.   [21] Case 75/81 *Blesgen* v. *Belgian State* [1982] ECR 1211.

[22] Para. 9. See also Case 148/85 *Direction générale des impôts et procureur de la République* v. *Marie-Louise Forest* [1986] ECR 3449, para. 19 (restriction on the quantity of wheat that could be milled has 'no effect on imports and is not likely to impede trade between Member States'); Case C–23/89 *Quietlynn* v. *Southend BC* [1990] ECR I–3059 (provisions prohibiting sale of sex articles from unlicensed sex shops have 'no connection with intra-[Union] trade' and so are not MEEs).

[23] Case C–69/88 *Krantz* [1990] ECR I–583.

with other Member States,[24] the Court found that Article 34 TFEU was not breached. It said the possibility that nationals of other Member States would hesitate to sell goods on instalment to purchasers in the Netherlands because such goods were liable to be seized by the collector of taxes was 'too uncertain and indirect' to warrant the conclusion that a national provision authorizing such seizure was liable to hinder trade between Member States.[25] In this case the Court appeared to be applying a test based on causation[26] and found that the national rule was too remote to affect inter-state trade so Article 34 TFEU did not apply. As we shall see in Chapter 7, the approach adopted in this line of case law has had an increasing influence in the field of free movement of persons.

The third and most controversial approach adopted by the Court to the market circumstances rules can be found in the confused decisions in the Sunday trading cases. As was common in many states, British law required most shops to be closed on Sunday. Responding to customer demands, some do-it-yourself (DIY) stores, which cater for home-decorating enthusiasts with leisure time at weekends, began trading on Sundays and were prosecuted under the Shops Act 1950. In their defence, they argued that the Shops Act breached Article 34 TFEU because goods could not be sold on Sunday, and those goods included goods made elsewhere in the EU.[27] The matter was first referred to the Court of Justice in *Torfaen*,[28] where the Court responded with one of its most opaque judgments. Without mentioning either *Dassonville* or *Cassis*, the Court said:

> It is therefore necessary in a case such as this to consider first of all whether rules such as those at issue pursue an aim which is justified with regard to [Union] law … Such rules reflect certain political and economic choices in so far as their purpose is to ensure that working and non-working hours are so arranged as to accord with national or regional socio-cultural characteristics.[29]

The Court then considered whether the effects of such national rules exceeded what was necessary to achieve its aim in view.

It was not clear whether *Torfaen* represented a mechanical application of the *Cassis* line of authority[30] or a new, two-stage test[31] based on establishing first whether the national measure pursued some objective consistent with Union law and then applying the 'superficial'[32] balancing act envisaged by Article 3 of Directive 70/50. Whatever *Torfaen* meant, it was left to the national courts to determine whether the restrictive effects of the Sunday trading ban exceeded its intrinsic beneficial effects. Because national courts reached different conclusions on the legality of the same piece of national legislation,[33] the Court of

[24] Case C–69/88 *Krantz* [1990] ECR I–583, para. 10. This is sometimes rephrased as 'its purpose is not to regulate trade in goods with other Member States': e.g., Case C–96/94 *Centro Servizi Spediporto Srl* v. *Spedizioni Marittima del Golfo Srl* [1995] ECR I–2883, para. 41.

[25] Para. 11. See also, e.g., Case C–93/92 *CMC Motorradcenter GmbH* v. *Pelin Baskiciogullari* [1993] ECR I–5009, para. 12; Case C–44/98 *BASF* v. *Präsident des Deutschen Patentamts* [1999] ECR I–6269, paras. 16 and 21.

[26] See La Pergola AG in Case C–44/98 *BASF* [1999] ECR I–6269, para. 18.

[27] The national court said that the ban on Sunday trading had the effect of reducing B & Q's total sales, that approximately 10 per cent of the goods sold by B & Q came from other Member States and that a corresponding reduction of imports from other Member States would therefore ensue: Case C–145/88 *Torfaen Borough Council* v. *B & Q plc* [1989] ECR 3851, para. 7.

[28] Case C–145/88 *Torfaen Borough Council* v. *B & Q plc* [1989] ECR 3851.

[29] Para. 13.   [30] See, e.g., L. Gormley (1990) 27 *CMLRev.* 141.

[31] C. Barnard, 'Sunday trading: A drama in five acts' (1994) 57 *MLR* 449.

[32] Tesauro AG in Case C–292/92 *Hünermund* [1993] ECR I–6787, para. 15.

[33] Cf. Northcote J in *B & Q* v. *Shrewsbury and Atcham BC* [1990] 3 CMLR 535 and Hoffmann J in *Stoke on Trent City Council* v. *B & Q* [1990] 3 CMLR 31 with Allen J in *Wellingborough BC* v. *Payless* [1990] 1 CMLR 773 and Mustill J in *Smiths-do-it-all* v. *Peterborough BC* [1990] 2 CMLR 577.

Justice took it upon itself to say in *Conforama and Marchandise*[34] that French rules prohibiting workers from working on Sunday (as opposed to the British rules requiring shops to be closed on Sunday) were not excessive and so were compatible with Article 34 TFEU. Subsequently, in *Stoke-on-Trent*[35] the Court ruled that Article 34 TFEU did not apply to legislation prohibiting retailers from opening their shops on Sunday[36] because the restrictive effects on trade were not excessive to the social aim pursued by the legislation.[37]

The Sunday trading episode revealed the inadequacy of the Court's analysis of measures relating to market circumstances but two commentators offered the Court a way forward. White proposed that a distinction should be drawn between, on the one hand, rules relating to *product requirements* (i.e., rules concerning the composition, characteristics, and presentation of products) to which Article 34 TFEU should apply, and, on the other, rules concerning *market circumstances* (i.e., rules concerning place, time, manner, authorized person), which should fall outside the scope of Article 34 TFEU, provided imported products enjoyed equal access to the market compared with national goods.[38] Mortelmans agreed with White's approach to product requirement rules but proposed a refinement of the market circumstances category.[39] He distinguished between:[40]

- rules 'with a territorial element' (i.e., rules relating to activities situated in a *fixed* or *static* location),[41] such as town and country planning legislation,[42] or a ban on selling certain alcoholic beverages, or Sunday trading rules[43]

- rules without a fixed location (sometimes referred to as *dynamic* rules), such as legislation prohibiting door-to-door selling (*Oosthoek*) and limiting the use of promotional gifts (*Buet*).

Mortelmans suggested that while static rules did not pose a real threat to the single market and so should fall outside Article 34 TFEU, dynamic rules did pose a threat to the single market and so should be caught by Article 34 TFEU.

The other point of influence for the Court was Advocate General Tesauro's Opinion in *Hünermund*.[44] The case concerned a German ban on pharmacists advertising parapharmaceutical products outside their pharmacies.[45] The Advocate General noted that this measure was applicable without distinction to domestic and imported goods and made neither access to the market nor marketing of imported products more difficult than for domestic products.[46] He recognized that the measure could (hypothetically) reduce imports, but only because it could (equally hypothetically) reduce sales. For these reasons he concluded that the national measure had to be regarded as falling outside the

---

[34] Joined Cases C–312 and 332/89 *U.D.S. CGT de l'Aisne* v. *Sidef Conforama; Criminal Proceedings against Marchandise* [1991] ECR I–1027.

[35] Case C–169/91 *Stoke-on-Trent and Norwich City Council* v. *B & Q plc* [1992] ECR I–6635.

[36] Para. 17.

[37] Para. 16. Meanwhile shoppers in the UK had grown so used to being able to shop on Sunday that the law was changed to allow this to happen: Sch. 1 to Sunday Trading Act 1994.

[38] E. White, 'In search of the limits to Article 30 of the EEC Treaty' (1989) 26 *CMLRev.* 235.

[39] See n. 4, 115.   [40] See n. 4, 116 and 130.

[41] Later (at 130) he talks of 'pub, shop, shopping centre, petrol station, bakery'.

[42] Case 20/87 *Ministère public* v. *André Gauchard* [1987] ECR 4879.

[43] Case C–145/88 *Torfaen* [1989] ECR 3851.

[44] Case C–292/92 [1993] ECR I–6787. This Opinion, rather than that of Van Gerven AG (the Advocate General in *Keck*), seems to have influenced the Court more in *Keck*.

[45] Pharmacists could advertise inside their shops but were not allowed to advertise in cinemas, on radio, or on television (Report for the hearing in Case C–292/92 *Hünermund* [1993] ECR I–6787, 6790).

[46] Para. 29.

field of application of Article 34 TFEU—it had 'nothing to do with trade, still less with the integration of the markets'.[47] This Opinion paved the way for the Court's decision in *Keck and Mithouard*.[48]

C. THE DECISION IN *KECK*

1. THE JUDGMENT

The facts of *Keck* were straightforward. Keck and Mithouard sold goods (Picon beer and Sati Rouge coffee) at a loss (i.e., at a price below that at which they had been purchased wholesale). Since such activity was prohibited by French law they were prosecuted. In their defence they argued that because the French law deprived them of a method of sales promotion it restricted the volume of sales of imported goods and so was incompatible with Article 34 TFEU. The Court disagreed. It began by noting that the purpose of the French law was not to regulate trade in goods,[49] even though such legislation could re-strict the volume of sales (including sales of products from other Member States).[50] It then indicated that it wanted to stop dissatisfied traders from using Article 34 TFEU to chal-lenge any restriction on their freedom to sell what they wanted, where they wanted, and when they wanted. It said that '[i]n view of the increasing tendency of traders' to invoke Article 34 TFEU as a means of 'challenging any rules whose effect is to limit their com-mercial freedom', even where such rules were not aimed at products from other Member States, it considered it 'necessary to re-examine and clarify its case law on this matter'.[51]

In this clarification the Court drew a distinction between 'product requirements' on the one hand, and 'certain selling arrangements' on the other. In respect of product require-ments, it reaffirmed in paragraph 15 that the principles in *Cassis* continued to apply:[52]

> It is established by case law beginning with *Cassis de Dijon* … that, in the absence of harmonisation of legislation, obstacles to the free movement of goods which are the con-sequence of applying, to goods coming from other Member States where they are lawfully manufactured and marketed, rules that lay down requirements to be met by such goods (such as those relating to designation, form, size, weight, composition, presentation, label-ling, packaging) constitute measures of equivalent effect prohibited by Article [34 TFEU]. This is so even if those rules apply without distinction to all products unless their applica-tion can be justified by a public-interest objective taking precedence over the free move-ment of goods.[53]

The examples in the brackets are an indicative list of product requirement situations to which *Cassis de Dijon* will apply.[54]

In paragraph 16 the Court turned its attention to 'certain selling arrangements'. It said that:

> contrary to what has previously been decided, the application to products from other Member States of national provisions restricting or prohibiting certain selling

---

[47] Case C–292/92 *Hünermund* [1993] ECR I–6787, para. 24.

[48] Joined Cases C–267 and 268/91 *Keck and Mithouard* [1993] ECR I–6097.

[49] Para. 12. By implication the outcome would be different if the legislation was designed to regulate trade: see Case C–158/94 *Commission* v. *Italy (electricity)* [1997] ECR I–5789, para. 31.

[50] Para. 13.   [51] Para. 14.

[52] The language of 'product requirements' is taken from Van Gerven AG's Opinion in Joined Cases C–401 and 402/92 *Boermans* [1994] ECR I–2199, para. 16.

[53] See Case C–12/00 *Commission* v. *Spain* [2003] ECR I–459, para. 76.   [54] See further Ch. 4.

arrangements is not such as to hinder directly or indirectly, actually or potentially, trade between Member States within the meaning of the *Dassonville* judgment ... provided those provisions apply to all affected traders operating within the national territory and provided that they affect in the same manner, in law and in fact, the marketing of domestic products and those from other Member States.

The Court continued in paragraph 17 that:

Where those conditions are fulfilled, the application of such rules to the sale of products from other Member States meeting the requirements laid down by that State is not by nature such as to *prevent* their [i.e., foreign goods'] access to the market or to *impede* access any more than it impedes the access of domestic products.[55]

Therefore, overturning previous, unspecified case law, the Court said that national provisions restricting or prohibiting 'certain selling arrangements' did not fall within the *Dassonville* formula and so, unlike QRs, distinctly applicable MEEs and product requirements, did *not* breach Article 34 TFEU where the two conditions set out in paragraph 16 were satisfied (the so-called paragraph 16 proviso), namely:

(1) the provisions apply to all affected traders operating in the territory

(2) the provisions are non-discriminatory (same burden in law and in fact).

In *DocMorris*[56] Advocate General Stix-Hackl described the two limbs of the proviso respectively as (1) the principle of universality and (2) the principle of neutrality. Generally, the Court has found the principle of universality satisfied and it was thought to be redundant.[57] However, in late 2015 the Court relied on it to explain why the Finnish rule fell outside the formula in *Keck*. In *Visnapuu*[58] the Court said that because the Finnish requirement to hold a retail sale licence in order to import alcohol into Finland and then sell it did not apply to Alko, the state-owned enterprise for the sale of alcohol in Finland,[59] the Finnish rule did not satisfy the requirement of universality in the first limb of *Keck*. The rule was therefore an MEE under Article 34 TFEU. The second condition—the principle of neutrality—is and remains important and is considered further below.

National rules satisfying the two paragraph 16 conditions do not breach Article 34 TFEU (see fig. 5.1) because, according to the Court, such rules do not prevent access to the market (first limb of paragraph 17) nor do they impede access for foreign goods more than they impede access for domestic products (second limb of paragraph 17). Thus, in *Keck,* the market access test is presented not as a condition of its own, but rather as a consequence of the fact that the paragraph 16 proviso is satisfied. As we shall see, in *Commission* v. *Italy (trailers)* the Court appears to have changed its mind on this point.

The bottom line in *Keck* is that national rules on certain selling arrangements do not breach Article 34 TFEU. This contrasts with the situation of national rules on product requirements which *do* breach Article 34 TFEU and so need justifying by the Member States to be lawful. The ruling in *Keck* is therefore significant because it confirms that

---

[55] Emphasis added.

[56] Case C–322/01 *Deutscher Apothekerverband eV* v. *0800 DocMorris NV* [2003] ECR I–14887, para. 59.

[57] P. Oliver and S. Enchelmaier, 'Free movement of goods: Recent developments in the case law' (2007) 44 *CMLRev.* 649, 681.

[58] Case C–198/14 *Valev Visnapuu* v. *Kihlakunnansyyttäjä* EU:C:2015:751, paras. 103–7.

[59] Further, the retail sale licence was available only to manufacturers of alcohol in Finland, thus excluding manufacturers in other Member States (para. 106).

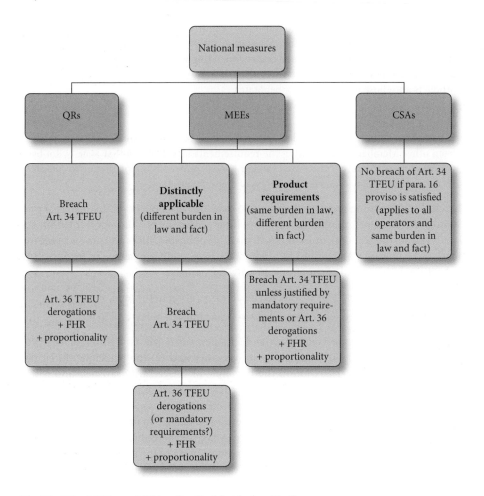

Fig. 5.1 QRs, MEEs, and CSAs after *Keck* but before *Trailers*

there are outer limits to Article 34 TFEU. The Court has carved out an area ('certain selling arrangements' (CSAs)) which is reserved for national regulators. The Court is not prepared to intervene unless there is evidence of discrimination. In so doing, it has recognized that some local regulatory choices do not damage the realization of economies of scale and wider consumer choice in an integrated market,[60] and so should not be subject to scrutiny under Articles 34 and 36 TFEU. Read together, paragraphs 16 and 17 of *Keck* provide the Court's answer to Advocate General Tesauro's question in *Hünermund*: Article 34 TFEU is intended 'merely' to liberalize *inter-state* trade rather than encouraging the unhindered pursuit of commerce in the Member States. And in reaching this conclusion the Court reintroduced the test of non-discrimination to Article 34 TFEU, apparently in preference to the alternative, wider test based on market access.

---

[60] S. Weatherill, 'After *Keck*: Some thoughts on how to clarify the clarification' (1996) 33 *CMLRev.* 885, 886–7, and 895.

2. ANALYSIS OF THE COURT'S APPROACH IN *KECK*

The decision in *Keck* received brickbats and bouquets in almost equal measure. The bouquets came largely from national governments delighted by the clear, bright line drawn by the Court which rendered some of their national regulation—at least that concerning certain selling arrangements—apparently immune from challenge under Article 34 TFEU.[61] The bouquets also came from those who welcomed both the reintroduction of the principle of non-discrimination to this area of law and the certainty which *Keck* appeared to offer after years of confusion generated by the Sunday trading case law. They applauded the clear division of regulatory competence endorsed by the Court: the *producing* state makes the initial choices about the level of regulation of product requirements, while the *importing* state makes the initial choice for its territory about the level of regulation of certain selling arrangements (sales, marketing, distribution, and consumption).

The brickbats came from those who, while broadly sympathetic to the Court's objectives in *Keck*, were critical of its realization. At the most basic level, they regretted that, in its 'clarification' of the earlier case law, the Court gave no indication of which cases it was overturning. They also complained that the distinction between product requirements and certain selling arrangements was by no means as clear as would first appear,[62] as the following example demonstrates. If national law requires the packaging of all power tools to bear a label indicating that power tools are dangerous, the labelling obligation is a product requirement and presumptively unlawful under *Cassis*. If, by contrast, national law merely requires retailers to place a sign containing the same message on the counter next to the power tools, that would be a certain selling arrangement and presumptively lawful under *Keck*.[63]

More fundamentally, commentators bemoaned the introduction of a new, formulistic classification, 'certain selling arrangements', which, unlike well-established legal concepts such as direct and indirect discrimination, had never before seen the legal light of day. We turn now to consider how the Court has interpreted the phrase.

3. WHAT ARE 'CERTAIN SELLING ARRANGEMENTS'?

The Court has found a number of market circumstances rules to constitute certain selling arrangements.[64] For example, it said that national rules limiting the time at which goods could be sold are certain selling arrangements. Therefore, in *Boermans*[65] the Court said that national rules requiring petrol stations to close at night did not breach Article 34 TFEU. Similarly, in *Punto Casa*,[66] *Semeraro Casa*,[67] and *Pelckmans*

---

[61] In subsequent cases governments have regularly argued that the national rules should be considered 'certain selling arrangements' even where the Court subsequently disagrees: e.g., Case C–368/95 *Familiapress* [1997] ECR I–3843, considered at n. 92; Joined Cases C–158 and 159/04 *Alfa Vita* [2006] ECR I–8135; Case C–244/06 *Dynamic Medien Vertriebs GmbH* [2008] ECR I–505.

[62] See, e.g., Case C–368/95 *Familiapress* [1997] ECR I–3843; Poiares Maduro AG in Joined Cases C–158 and 159/04 *Alfa Vita* [2006] ECR I–8135, paras. 31–3.

[63] See, e.g., Case C–159/00 *Sapod-Audic* [2002] ECR I–5031, para. 75 (the national rule did not require a mark or label to be applied to the product itself but imposed a general obligation to identify, at the point of sale, that the packaging was recyclable: this constituted a selling arrangement).

[64] Cf. May LJ in *The Countryside Alliance* v. *HM Attorney General* [2005] EWHC 1677 (Admin), para. 212: 'There is no magic in the label *certain selling arrangements*; that was merely a description of the measure in question in *Keck*'.

[65] Joined Cases C–401 and 402/92 [1994] ECR I–2199.

[66] Joined Case C–69 and 258/93 *Punto Casa SpA* v. *Sindaco del Commune di Capena* [1994] ECR I–2355.

[67] Joined Cases C–418/93 etc. *Semeraro Casa Uno Srl* [1996] ECR I–2975.

Turnhout NV[68] the Court found that Sunday trading rules were certain selling arrangements which did not breach Article 34 TFEU (and in so doing it laid to rest the ghost of *Torfaen*).

Other rules, directly affecting the retailers of goods, have also been considered certain selling arrangements. These include rules requiring retailers of particular goods to have actual premises in the locality (*Heimdienst*,[69] *DocMorris*,[70] *Commission* v. *Germany*[71]) and rules obliging retailers to be licensed (*Burmanjer*[72]). The Court has also said that national restrictions on the number or type of sales outlets constituted certain selling arrangements. Therefore, in *Commission* v. *Greece (infant milk)*[73] a Greek law requiring processed milk for infants be sold only in pharmacists' shops did not breach Article 34 TFEU, nor, in *Banchero*,[74] did Italian legislation reserving the retail sale of tobacco products to authorized distributors only.[75] In *A-Punkt*[76] the Court said that Austrian rules prohibiting selling in private homes (on the facts of the case, cheap silver jewellery) also constituted certain selling arrangements. Restrictions on pricing, too, can constitute certain selling arrangements, as the facts of *Keck* itself show (prohibition on resale at a loss). Similarly, a prohibition of sales yielding very low profit is a certain selling arrangement (*ITM*[77]), as is a rule fixing the retail price for books (*LIBRO*).[78]

In other cases the Court has said that restrictions on advertising constituted certain selling arrangements. So, in *Hünermund*[79] a German rule prohibiting pharmacies from advertising para-pharmaceutical products outside their premises did not breach Article 34 TFEU, nor did a French rule in *Leclerc-Siplec*[80] which prohibited the fuel-distribution sector from advertising on television. Perhaps most esoteric is the Austrian rule in *Karner*[81] prohibiting retailers from indicating to consumers that goods came from an insolvent estate when they no longer constituted part of that estate. This rule constituted a CSA and did not breach Article 34 TFEU. As we shall see, this line of case law on national rules restricting advertising and other forms of sales promotion techniques proved particularly problematic because, by now classifying the rules as selling arrangements, they benefited from the presumption of legality. This appeared to reverse pre-*Keck* decisions such as *Oosthoek*, *Buet*, and *Aragonesa* (considered at Section B, 2), where the Court found equivalent rules to constitute MEEs and were presumptively *un*lawful.

---

[68] Case C–483/12 *Pelckmans Turnhout NV* v. *Walter Van Gestel Balen* EU:C:2014:304, para. 24, which also makes clear that if the rule is classified as a certain selling arrangement (language not actually used by the Court) then EU law does not apply, and so the Charter does not apply.

[69] Case C–254/98 [2000] ECR I–151. Cf. Case C–323/93 *La Crespelle* [1994] ECR I–5077 rules on storage of semen treated as MEEs.

[70] Case C–322/01 *0800 DocMorris* [2003] ECR I–14887.

[71] Case C–141/07 *Commission* v. *Germany (pharmacies for hospitals)* [2008] ECR I–6935, para. 31.

[72] Case C–20/03 *Burmanjer, Van der Linden, De Jong* [2005] ECR I–4133.

[73] Case C–391/92 *Commission* v. *Greece* [1995] ECR I–1621.

[74] Case C–387/93 *Criminal Proceedings against Banchero* [1995] ECR I–4663; cf. Case C–189/95 *Criminal Proceedings against Franzén* [1997] ECR I–5909, para. 57.

[75] See also Case C–162/97 *Criminal Proceedings against Nilsson* [1998] ECR I–7477, para. 28

[76] Case C–441/04 *A-Punkt Schmuckhandels GmbH* v. *Schmidt* [2006] ECR I–2093, para. 17.

[77] Case C–63/94 *Groupement National des Négociants en Pommes de Terre de Belgique* v. *ITM Belgium SA and Vocarex SA* [1995] ECR I–2467.

[78] Case C–531/07 *LIBRO Handelsgesellschaft mbH* [2009] ECR I–3717, para. 20.

[79] Case C–292/92 *Hünermund* [1993] ECR I–6787.

[80] Case C–412/93 *Leclerc-Siplec* [1995] ECR I–179. The ruling in *Leclerc-Siplec* was confirmed in Case C–6/98 *ARD* v. *PRO Sieben Media* [1999] ECR I–7599, para. 46, where the Court said that since the restriction on advertising in this case (limitation on transmission time) is of a 'similar, but less extensive, kind, it also concerns certain selling arrangements' and the two conditions in para. 16 of *Keck* are 'clearly satisfied' (para. 48).

[81] Case C–71/02 *Herbert Karner Industrie-Auktionen GmbH* [2004] ECR I–3025.

In *Karner* the Court took the opportunity to summarize its case law on certain selling arrangements:[82]

> [P]rovisions concerning *inter alia* the place and times of sale of certain products and advertising of those products as well as certain marketing methods [are] provisions governing selling arrangements within the meaning of *Keck and Mithouard*.

This suggests that, despite the lack of clarity over the precise meaning of the phrase 'certain selling arrangements', the Court is prepared to interpret it to cover any rules relating to sales and marketing methods,[83] the word 'certain' seemingly redundant.[84]

However, the use of the phrase 'selling arrangements' raises a further problem in that it does not apparently catch national rules which the *Keck* formula might have been aimed at, such as non-discriminatory restrictions on planning and building in the green belt. There is a good argument that such rules should fall outside Article 34 TFEU (non-discriminatory rules not intended to affect inter-state trade) but linguistically it is difficult to argue that they concern 'selling arrangements'. How then should such situations be dealt with? Under *Keck* but shorn of the reference to certain selling arrangements (an approach which would seem to receive the support of Advocate General Kokott in *Mickelsson*[85])? Under the pre-*Keck* cases such as *Krantz* (that the effect on inter-state trade is too uncertain and indirect for Article 34 TFEU to apply)?[86] Or as an MEE which can be justified?[87]

Following *Commission* v. *Italy (trailers)*, the last approach might be the favoured one. In borderline cases which have already come before the Court, where there is uncertainty as to whether the rule is a certain selling arrangement or an MEE, the Court tends to classify it as an MEE. This can be seen in *Dynamic Medien*.[88] A German law on the protection of young people prohibited the sale by mail order of 'image storage media' (DVDs and video cassettes) unless they had been examined by the relevant authorities in Germany and given an age classification. Advocate General Mengozzi considered the German rules to be a CSA because he focused on ' "how" and "where" the products may be sold' and on 'the personality of the purchaser, that is to say, "to whom" the products may be sold'.[89] By contrast, the Court focused on the fact that in order to be sold by mail order, 'image storage media had to be subject to a national examination and classification procedure'

---

[82] Para. 38.

[83] Case C–244/06 *Dynamic Medien Vertriebs GmbH* [2008] ECR I–505, para. 30. See also Geelhoed AG in Case C–239/02 *Douwe Egberts NV* v. *Westrom Pharma NV* [2004] ECR I–7007, para. 72: 'the qualification of selling arrangement should be reserved for rules which govern the general conditions under which products are marketed, i.e. when, where and by whom, and which do not specifically concern commercialisation as such'.

[84] Cf. Tesauro AG in Case C–368/95 *Familiapress* [1997] ECR I–3843, para. 9.

[85] Case C–142/05 *Åklagaren* v. *Mickelsson* [2009] ECR I–4273. See the text relating to nn. 145–6.

[86] See by analogy Joined Cases C–418/93 etc. *Semeraro Casa Uno Srl* [1996] ECR I–2975, para. 32.

[87] Support for this view can be found in Case C–65/05 *Commission* v. *Greece (computer games)* [2006] ECR I–10341, paras. 28–9 (Greek law prohibited the installation and operation of electronic games on all premises apart from casinos. Even though Greek law did not prohibit the import of the equipment, merely the prohibition of installation, the measure constituted an MEE, because the importation of games machines stopped when the prohibition came into effect).

[88] Case C–244/06 *Dynamic Medien* [2008] ECR I–505. See also Case C–416/00 *Tommaso Morellato* v. *Comune di Padova* [2003] ECR I–9343; Joined Cases C–158 and 159/04 *Alfa Vita* [2006] ECR I–8135; and Case C–82/05 *Commission* v. *Greece (bake off products)* [2006] ECR I–93, where anyone wishing to sell bread had to run a fully equipped bakery even where the bread was delivered half-cooked. Because the rules related to 'production conditions', not product requirements or CSAs, Art. 34 TFEU applied.

[89] Para. 49.

regardless of whether those DVDs had already been classified in the state of export[90] and they had to be labelled. Because such rules made imports 'more difficult and more expensive' they constituted MEEs and so breached Article 34 TFEU[91] but could be justified on the grounds of protecting children.

The Court's conclusion in *Dynamic Medien* is unsurprising in the light of its earlier decision in *Familiapress*.[92] The case concerned an Austrian law prohibiting magazines containing prize competitions. This meant that the German magazine 'Laura', which contained prize competitions, could not be sold in Austria. In defending the legislation, the Austrian government argued that because the national law concerned a restriction on sales promotions, this constituted a selling arrangement within the meaning of *Keck* and so fell outside Article 34 TFEU. The Court disagreed, saying that:

> even though the relevant national legislation is directed against a method of sales promotion, in this case it bears on the *actual content of the products*, in so far as the competitions in question form an integral part of the magazine in which they appear.[93]

It continued that the legislation required traders established in other Member States to 'alter the contents of the periodical'.[94] As a result, the case did not concern a selling arrangement but a product requirement.[95] Similarly, in *Schwarz*,[96] the Court said an Austrian rule requiring chewing gum sold in vending machines to be packaged, while the same goods sold in Germany could be marketed without packaging, constituted an MEE because German producers had to package their goods, 'which makes their importation into [Austria] more expensive'.[97] In all three cases, the Court focused on the centre of gravity of the rule, namely to modify the product.[98] The national rule was therefore more akin to a product requirement to which *Cassis* applied, than a CSA to which *Keck* applied. These cases also suggest that in borderline cases the Court prefers considering the measure as an MEE rather than a CSA.

The meaning and scope of the phrase 'certain selling arrangement' was not the only problem thrown up by the *Keck* decision. *Keck* and its progeny also created uncertainty in respect of (1) discriminatory rules regulating sales, (2) rules preventing or (severely) restricting the *use* of goods, (3) rules preventing or (severely) restricting an *activity*, and (4) non-discriminatory selling arrangements preventing or restricting access to the market. We shall consider these situations in turn.

---

[90] Case C–244/06 *Dynamic Medien* [2008] ECR I–505, para. 33.   [91] Paras. 34–5.

[92] Case C–368/95 *Familiapress* [1997] ECR I–3689. The reasoning in this case may now be different following the Unfair Commercial Practices Dir. 2005/29, considered in Section E. This issue has been raised directly in Case C–540/08 *Mediaprint Zeitungs- und Zeitschriftenverlag GmbH & Co KG v. 'Österreich'-Zeitungsverlag GmbH* [2010] ECR I–10909.

[93] Para. 11, emphasis added. See also Case C–390/99 *Canal Satélite Digital SL v. Administracion General del Estado* [2002] ECR I–607, para. 30, 'the need in certain cases to *adapt the products* in question to the rules in force in the Member State in which they are marketed' prevented the requirements from being treated as selling arrangements within the meaning of para. 16 of *Keck*.

[94] Para. 12.   [95] See also Joined Cases C–158 and 159/04 *Alfa Vita* [2006] ECR I–8135, para. 19.

[96] Case C–366/04 *Schwarz v. Bürgermeister der Landeshauptstadt Salzburg* [2006] ECR I–10139.

[97] Para. 29.

[98] Case C–416/00 *Morellato* [2003] ECR I–9343, para. 28: 'the Court has never held that where national provisions, whilst regulating certain aspects of the sale of products, also require the products to be modified, these provisions are concerned with selling arrangements within the meaning of *Keck and Mithouard*.'

D. PROBLEM SITUATIONS

1. DISCRIMINATORY CERTAIN SELLING ARRANGEMENTS

1.1 The Nature of the Problem

In the cases immediately following *Keck* (e.g., *Hünermund* and *Leclerc-Siplec*), the Court failed to apply paragraph 16 of its own judgment in *Keck* properly. Rather, it unthinkingly equated a finding that a national measure constituted a certain selling arrangement with a ruling that there was no breach of Article 34 TFEU. This unthinking approach, while perhaps understandable on the policy ground of the Court's desire to remove certain types of rules altogether from the scope of Article 34 TFEU, was subject to much criticism. It is here that Mortelmans' distinction between 'fixed' and 'dynamic' rules (considered in Section B) becomes useful to help understand the nature of that criticism.

While the Court's approach in *Keck* was largely uncontroversial in respect of 'fixed' location situations, it was much criticized in respect of dynamic situations. In respect of *fixed* location situations—rules concerning the time and place in which goods are sold—there is little effect on inter-state trade because the rules apply to *retailers* rather than to the producers/importers of goods, i.e., the rules apply after the goods have gained access to the market in the host state.[99] For this reason, the Treaty provision on establishment (Article 49 TFEU) is more relevant than the provisions on goods,[100] and the principle of subsidiarity suggests that such matters should be left to the Member States, unconstrained by Article 34 TFEU. Commentators were therefore broadly content with the finding in cases involving limits on the time at which goods can be sold, such as *Boermans* and *Punto Casa*, that there was no breach of Article 34 TFEU. As Advocate General Tesauro put it in *Familiapress*:[101]

> [T]he only measures excluded from the scope of Article [34 TFEU] are those which are absolutely general in nature, which apply—needless to say—without distinction, which do not impede imports and which might lead to a (hypothetical) reduction in the volume of imports only as a consequence of an equally hypothetical reduction in the volume of sales.

However, as regards *dynamic* situations, controversy surrounded the automatic finding in *Hünermund, Leclerc-Siplec, Commission* v. *Greece, Banchero*, and even *Keck* itself that Article 34 TFEU did not apply. This is because the national rules at issue in these cases— restricting the sales outlets for particular goods[102] and restricting advertising and other forms of sales promotion, including resale at a loss[103]—were more closely linked to the activities of the actual producer/importer. This is because, as the pre-*Keck* cases demonstrated (e.g., *Oosthoek, Buet, Aragonea*, and *LPO*, considered in Section B), such rules do pose a particularly serious threat to market integration because they interfere with access to the market for new (usually imported) goods. New market entrants are reliant on sales promotion techniques, such as advertising, to promote their goods; rules prohibiting or restricting such sales promotion techniques may therefore particularly disadvantage out-of-state goods/traders.

---

[99] Stix-Hackl AG in Case C–322/01 *DocMorris* [2003] ECR I–14887, para. 77.

[100] Tesauro AG recognized this in Case C–292/92 *Hünermund* [1993] ECR I–6787, para. 27, citing Case 20/87 *Gauchard* [1987] ECR 4879. See also Joined Cases C–418/93 etc. *Semeraro Casa Uno Srl* [1996] ECR I–2975, para. 32.

[101] Case C–368/95 [1997] ECR I–3698, para. 10.

[102] As Jacobs AG pointed out in Case C–412/93 *Leclerc-Siplec* [1995] ECR I–179, paras. 38–9, severely restricting sales outlets can substantially restrict the access to the market of goods from other Member States.

[103] Van Gerven AG had argued in his Opinion in *Keck* that the French prohibition of resale at a loss could, in some cases, impede imported products' access to the French market more than that of domestic products: para. 5.

This suggests that not all rules concerning certain selling arrangements are non-discriminatory, as the Court assumed in *Hünermund* and the other early cases. They might at least be discriminatory in fact and so should breach Article 34 TFEU unless justified by Article 36 TFEU or one of the mandatory requirements. If the Court reached this conclusion in respect of dynamic rules it would bring the post-*Keck* case law back into line with its pre-*Keck* jurisprudence (*Oosthoek*, *Buet*, *Aragonesa*, and *LPO*). It could do this simply by applying the proviso in paragraph 16, instead of assuming, as it seems to have done in *Hünermund* and the other early cases, that once it had classified the measure as a certain selling arrangement, the proviso in paragraph 16 of *Keck* was automatically satisfied, leading to a finding of no breach of Article 34 TFEU.

Some of the Advocates General, in particular Advocate General Jacobs in *Leclerc-Siplec* and Advocate General Lenz in *Commission v. Greece*,[104] urged the Court to look at the effect of dynamic national rules on imported products to see whether they were discriminatory in fact. At first the Court was reluctant, but in *De Agostini*[105] it changed its mind.

1.2 *De Agostini* and Beyond

(a) *Discriminatory measures which prevent market access*

De Agostini concerned a Swedish ban on television advertising directed at children under 12 and a ban on misleading commercials for skin-care products and detergents. The Swedish consumer ombudsman brought proceedings against two traders for (1) advertising a magazine, *Everything You Need to Know about Dinosaurs*, targeted at children under 12 and (2) marketing a soap, Body De Lite, in breach of the rules on misleading adverts. Like *Leclerc-Siplec* the Court recognized that these restrictions constituted certain selling arrangements; unlike *Leclerc-Siplec*, the Court specifically addressed the proviso in paragraph 16 of *Keck*. It said that while the first condition of the paragraph 16 proviso (the measure applied to all traders operating within the national territory) was clearly fulfilled, the second condition (the measure affected all traders in the same manner in law and in fact) might not be. It said that an outright ban on a type of promotion for a product which is lawfully sold there might have 'a greater impact on products from other Member States'.[106] It continued that, while the efficacy of various types of promotion was a question of fact to be determined by the national court, 'in its observations De Agostini stated that television advertising was *the only effective form* of promotion enabling it to penetrate the Swedish market since it had no other advertising methods for reaching children and their parents'.[107]

These paragraphs contain a strong hint that the Court thought that the Swedish measure had the same burden in law but a different burden in fact; a point reinforced by its reference to the fact that television advertising was the only effective form of sales promotion available to De Agostini. The Court concluded that if an unequal burden in law or fact was found, then the national restriction would be caught by Article 34 TFEU as an MEE[108] and the burden would shift to the Member State to justify it under one of the mandatory requirements[109] or by an Article 36 TFEU derogation (see fig. 5.2).[110]

---

[104] See Joined Cases C–34–36/95 *Konsumentombudsmannen (KO) v. De Agostini (Svenska) Förlag AB* [1997] ECR I–3843, para. 42; Case C–391/92 *Commission v. Greece (infant milk)* [1995] ECR I–1621.

[105] Joined Cases C–34–36/95 *De Agostini (Svenska) Förlag AB* [1997] ECR I–3843, noted by J. Stuyck (1997) 34 *CMLRev.* 1445, 1465.

[106] Para. 42.   [107] Para. 43, emphasis added.

[108] Case C–322/01 *DocMorris* [2003] ECR I–14887, para. 68.

[109] Para. 45, although compare the apparently contradictory wording in para. 47. See also Case C–376/98 *Germany v. Parliament and Council (tobacco advertising)* [2001] ECR I–8419, para. 113: 'By imposing a wide-ranging prohibition on the advertising of tobacco products, the Directive would in the future generalise that restriction of forms of competition by limiting, in all the Member States, the means available for economic operators to enter or remain in the market.'

[110] Para. 45.

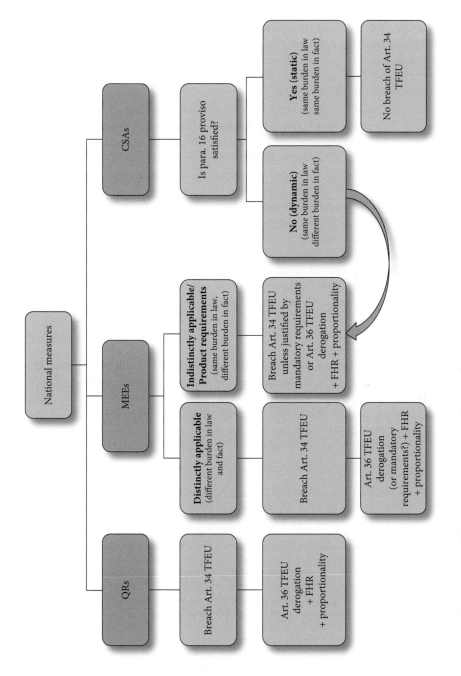

Fig. 5.2 QRs, MEEs, and discriminatory CSAs before *Trailers*

The decision in *De Agostini* is the outcome the Advocates General had predicted and sits more comfortably with the pre-*Keck* case law.[111] However, where *De Agostini* differs from the pre-*Keck* case law is that in *De Agostini* the Court took *Keck* as a starting point and decided that the measure constituted a certain selling arrangement. The measure therefore did not breach Article 34 TFEU *unless*, as the Court indicated in *De Agostini*, it was shown that the ban did not affect in the same manner—in fact or in law—the marketing of national products and products from other Member States.[112] In this situation there would be a breach of Article 34 TFEU which could be justified.

(b) Discriminatory measures which impede market access

Heimdienst[113] extended the ruling in *De Agostini* to any discriminatory selling arrangement which, while not actually *preventing* market access as in *De Agostini* itself, did nevertheless *hinder or impede* that access.[114] *Heimdienst* concerned an Austrian rule permitting bakers, butchers, and grocers to sell their produce door-to-door using a delivery van, but only if they also traded from a shop in that, or an adjacent, area.[115] Having classified the measure as a selling arrangement because 'it lays down the geographical areas in which each of the operators concerned may sell his goods by that method',[116] the Court then considered the *Keck* paragraph 16 proviso. It found that the legislation did not 'affect in the same manner the marketing of domestic products and that of products from other Member States'.[117] This was because the legislation obliged traders with a shop in another Member State to establish a shop in the locality (with the additional costs this entailed) before they could sell their goods door-to-door. Since traders established in other Member States suffered a disadvantage in comparison with local economic operators who already met the requirement of having a shop in the area, the Austrian rule breached Article 34 TFEU and needed to be justified. On the facts, the Court found the requirement to be disproportionate.[118]

Heimdienst paved the way for the Court's important decision in *DocMorris*.[119] DocMorris had a pharmacy in the Netherlands and also offered medicines for sale over the Internet. Both activities were licensed in the Netherlands. In Germany medicinal products could be sold but only in pharmacists' shops: sales by mail order were prohibited. The German pharmacists' association therefore tried to prevent DocMorris selling medicines to German consumers over the Internet. In paragraph 74 the Court

---

[111] See the post-*Keck* case, Case C–239/02 *Douwe Egberts* [2004] ECR I–7007, para. 52 concerning a national law prohibiting references to 'slimming' in adverts. In reaching the conclusion that the law breached Art. 34 TFEU the Court cited one of the pre-*Keck* advertising cases, C–241/89 *SARPP* [1990] ECR I–4695.

[112] See now the effect of the Unfair Commercial Practices Dir. 2005/29, considered in Section E. *A fortiori*, if the measure has a different burden in law as well as in fact then there will also be a breach of Art. 34 TFEU: Case C–320/93 *Ortscheit v. Eurim-Pharm Arzneimittel* [1994] ECR I–5243, para. 9, which concerned a distinctly applicable measure which fell within the scope of Art. 34 TFEU (citing *Keck*, para. 16).

[113] Case C–254/98 [2000] ECR I–151. For an earlier example of a pre-*Keck* case with similar facts, see Joined Cases 87 and 88/85 *Société coopérative des laboratoires de pharmacie Legia and Lousi Gyselinx v. Minister for Health* [1986] ECR 1707.

[114] See also Case C–141/07 *Commission v. Germany (pharmacies for hospitals)* [2008] ECR I–6935, paras. 35 and 37, where German law required external pharmacies wishing to supply medicinal products to a hospital to have a 'degree of geographical proximity between the pharmacy ... and the hospital for which those products are intended'. These rules constituted a discriminatory certain selling arrangement (paras. 31 and 35) and so breached Art. 34 TFEU (para. 43).

[115] Although note the unusual feature of the case in that the dispute concerned two Austrian traders.

[116] Para. 24.   [117] Para. 25.

[118] See further Ch. 6.   [119] Case C–322/01 *0800 DocMorris NV* [2003] ECR I–14887.

found that the prohibition of Internet sales was 'more of an obstacle to the pharmacies outside Germany than to those within it'. While German pharmacies also could not sell their products over the Internet, for them this was an 'extra or alternative method' of gaining access to the German market: they could still sell their products in their dispensaries. However, for pharmacies not established in Germany, the Court noted that 'the internet provides a more significant way to gain direct access to the German market'. It concluded that '[a] prohibition which has a greater impact on pharmacies established outside German territory could impede access to the market for products from other Member States more than it impedes access for domestic products'. Because the prohibition did not affect the sale of domestic medicines in the same way as it affected the sale of those coming from other Member States, the German rule breached Article 34 TFEU. While the breach could not be justified on public-health grounds in respect of non-prescription medicines,[120] it could be justified in respect of prescription medicines.

DocMorris is an important ruling from a practical and legal perspective. Viewed practically, it is a particularly significant decision for opening up the single market. New market entrants, however small, can now gain a foothold on markets in other states, via the Internet, without having to incur the significant costs of setting up their own distribution and retail networks in the host state.

From a legal perspective, the striking feature of the case is that, while couched in the language of discrimination, in fact the need to secure market access pervades the judgment,[121] as paragraph 74 (drawing on paragraph 17, rather than paragraph 16, of *Keck*) makes clear.[122] The Court is therefore more likely to find discrimination and thus a breach of Article 34 TFEU where the measure prevents or significantly impedes market access (*De Agostini, DocMorris*)[123] than where the impediment to market access is slight (*Hünermund, Leclerc-Siplec*).[124] This emphasis on market access is now reinforced by *Commission* v. *Italy (trailers)*[125] (considered in detail in Chapter 4).

Finally, *LIBRO*[126] considered the situation where the national rule was a distinctly applicable certain selling arrangement. In that case Austrian law prohibited importers of German language books from fixing a price lower than the retail price fixed or recommended by the publisher in the state of publication (Germany). Because the rule provided for less favourable treatment for imported goods the paragraph 16 proviso was not satisfied and so the rule was an MEE contrary to Article 34 TFEU.[127] On the facts, even though the rule was directly discriminatory, the Court said it could be justified not by Article 36 TFEU, since none of the derogations applied, but by the need to protect 'books as cultural objects', an overriding requirement in the public interest. However, the Court found that the rule was disproportionate.[128]

---

[120] See also Case C–497/03 *Commission* v. *Austria* EU:C:2004:685: ban on mail order sale of food supplements breached Art. 34 TFEU, with the Court citing *DocMorris* to support this finding.
[121] Staetmans (2002) 39 *CMLRev.* 1407, 1418. See also the influence of Stix-Hackl AG's Opinion: 'The decisive factor should therefore be whether or not a national measure significantly impedes access to the market' (para. 78).
[122] See also Case C–405/98 *Gourmet* [2001] ECR I–1795, paras. 21 and 24.
[123] This is particularly so given that these cases, viewed from a services perspective, would involve a breach of Art. 56 TFEU due to the fact that the prohibition creates a hindrance to the provision of cross-border services (see, e.g., Case C–405/98 *Gourmet* [2001] ECR I–1795) and Ch. 11.
[124] See discussion in paras. 71–2 of *DocMorris*.
[125] Case C–110/05 *Commission* v. *Italy* [2009] ECR I–519, considered at n. 152, para. 50.
[126] Case C–531/07 *LIBRO* [2009] ECR I–3717, para. 20.
[127] Paras. 20–2.   [128] Para. 35.

1.3 Presumptions and the Burden of Proof

The reasoning in *De Agostini*, *Heimdienst*, and *DocMorris* suggests that certain dis-criminatory selling arrangements breach Article 34 TFEU unless justified—in just the same way as indistinctly applicable MEEs (product requirements). This could be ex-pected because both discriminatory selling arrangements and indistinctly applicable MEEs concern rules which have the same burden in law and a different burden in fact (see fig. 5.2). If this is the case, does it really matter then whether the Court classifies the measure as a product requirement or a certain selling arrangement? The answer may be yes: there is a difference between the two approaches in respect of presumptions and the burden of proof.[129] If the measure is classified as a product requirement, it is presumed to impede market access (*Cassis*), no matter how small the impediment is or might be[130]—the per se illegal approach. If, on the other hand, the measure is classified as a certain selling arrangement then the presumption is that it does not hinder access to the market and so does not breach Article 34 TFEU—the per se legal approach.[131] In the case of a certain selling arrangement the trader will (usually[132]) need to work hard to rebut the presumption of legality, possibly by producing statistical or other evidence to prove disadvantage which might have to be *actual*[133] and probably *substantial* or at least not too remote.[134] This can be seen in *Burmanjer*,[135] where the Court said that even though insufficient information had been provided by the national court, the national rules prohibiting itinerant sales without a licence did not appear to affect the market-ing of products from other Member States more than products from the host state, and even if those rules did have such effect, 'it would be too insignificant and uncertain to be regarded as being such as to hinder or otherwise interfere with trade between Member States'.[136]

[129] See Van Gerven AG in Joined Cases C–401 and 402/92 *Boermans* [1994] ECR I–2199. See also Fennelly AG in Case C–190/98 *Graf* v. *Filzmozer Maschinenbau GmbH* [2000] ECR I–493, para. 19: 'It is legitimate for the Court to develop presumptions about the market effects of different broadly defined categories of rules, provided that, in concrete cases, the validity of the presumption may be tested against the underlying criterion of market access, rather than automatically being taken as being sufficient in itself to dispose of the case.'

[130] Joined Cases 177 and 178/82 *Van de Haahr* [1984] ECR 1797, confirmed by the Grand Chamber in Case C–463/01 *Commission* v. *Germany (deposit and return)* [2004] ECR I–11705, para. 62. See also Case C–67/97 *Bluhme* [1998] ECR I–8033.

[131] K. Armstrong, 'Regulating the free movement of goods' in J. Shaw and G. More (eds.), *Dynamics of European Integration* (Oxford: Clarendon Press, 1998), 482–3.

[132] Cf. Case C–322/01 *0800 DocMorris NV* [2003] ECR I–14887, where the Court glossed over all of these issues, although cf. para. 74: 'A prohibition which *has* a greater impact on pharmacies established outside German territory *could* impede access to the market for products from other Member States more than it im-pedes access for domestic products' (emphasis added). However, in Case C–441/04 *A-Punkt Schmuckhandels GmbH* v. *Schmidt* [2006] ECR I–2093, paras. 25–6 the Court again seems to require actual disparate impact as does the EFTA Court in Case E–16/10 *Philip Morris Norway* v. *The Norwegian State* [2011] EFTA Ct. Rep. 330, para. 50.

[133] See Case C–405/98 *Konsumentombudsmannen* v. *Gourmet International Products (GIP)* [2001] ECR I–1795, especially the AG's Opinion on the levels of evidence required to show actual disparate impact.

[134] If the national rule concerning a selling arrangement is genuinely non-discriminatory then it does not breach Art. 34 TFEU: Case C–71/02 *Karner* [2004] ECR I–3025.

[135] Case C–20/03 [2005] ECR I–4133.

[136] Para. 31. This does not appear in the dispositif. However, for a more recent confirmation of the *Burmanjer* line of authority, see Case E–16/10 *Philip Morris Norway* v. *The Norwegian State* [2011] EFTA Ct. Rep. 330, para. 50.

1.4 Conclusions

While in these cases of discriminatory certain selling arrangements the Court does now appear to be applying broadly common principles, in fact the Court's approach still contains a number of inconsistencies. Take the advertising cases as an example. It is clear that total bans on all advertising of alcohol and on television advertising, where that deprives the trader of the only effective form of sales promotion which would have enabled it to penetrate a national market (*De Agostini*), breach Article 34 TFEU. However, a limitation on where an advert can be placed (outside a pharmacists' shop in *Hünermund*), who can advertise (a ban on the distribution sector from advertising on television—*Leclerc*), and what they can say (*Karner*[137]) does not. Is it so easy to draw such a clear line? When do limits on the wording become so extensive that in practice the advert is banned?

A bigger inconsistency can be found in *Ker-Optika*,[138] where the Court (unwittingly?) appeared to reverse—or at least water down—its own presumption of legality of national rules on selling arrangements. Ker-Optika, a Hungarian company, was prohibited by the Hungarian authorities from selling contact lenses produced largely in other Member States on the Internet. While the Advocate General applied standard *Keck* analysis, informed by the decision in *DocMorris*, the Court apparently did something different. While still citing the key paragraphs from *Keck*, the Court said:[139]

> the application to products from other Member States of national provisions *restricting or prohibiting certain selling arrangements is such as to hinder* directly or indirectly, actually or potentially, trade between Member States for the purposes of the case-law flowing from *Dassonville, unless* those provisions apply to all relevant traders operating within the national territory and affect in the same manner, in law and in fact, the selling of domestic products and of those from other Member States.

The language in italics suggests that the Court is working on the presumption of the *illegality* of the certain selling arrangement rule; *Keck* of course suggested the presumptive *legality* of the national rule.

2. RULES PREVENTING OR (GREATLY) RESTRICTING THE USE OF GOODS

Discriminatory certain selling arrangements are not the only area of difficulty. There were other problem areas too: non-discriminatory restrictions on *use* (such as a prohibition on driving cross-country vehicles off-road in a forest or speed limits on motorways[140]) posed particular challenges for the Court.[141] Advocate General Kokott in *Mickelsson*[142] and Advocate General Bot in *Commission* v. *Italy (trailers)*[143] presented the Court of Justice with two starkly different alternatives as to how to tackle this situation.[144]

---

[137] Although cf. Case C–239/02 *Douwe Egberts* [2004] ECR I–7007, paras. 49 and 54 and Case C–470/93 *Mars* [1995] ECR I–1293, considered in Ch. 4.

[138] Case C–108/09 *Ker-Optika* [2010] ECR I–12213.   [139] Para. 51, emphasis added.

[140] Case C–142/05 *Åklagaren* v. *Mickelsson* [2009] ECR I–4273, Kokott AG's Opinion, para. 45.

[141] Cf. the earlier case, Case C–473/98 *Kemikalieinspektionen* v. *Toolex Alpha AB* [2000] ECR I–5681, para. 35, where the Court said that the ban on the industrial *use* of trichloroethylene, a substance with a known carcinogenic effect, constituted an MEE. The Court made no reference to the *Keck* line of case law.

[142] Case C–142/05 *Åklagaren* v. *Mickelsson* [2009] ECR I–4273.

[143] Case C–110/05 *Commission* v. *Italy (trailers)* [2009] ECR I–519.

[144] For a more detailed discussion, see T. Horsley, 'Anyone for *Keck*?' (2009) 46 *CMLRev.* 2001.

Advocate General Kokott favoured extending the *Keck* principle to restrictions on use[145] but with the caveat that if the national rule prevented or severely restricted access to the market Article 34 TFEU would nevertheless apply.[146] Advocate General Bot, on the other hand, proposed a narrow reading of *Keck*, a case he clearly did not like[147] but felt constrained by.[148] Adopting a strong integrationist perspective[149] and a deep-felt desire for convergence across the freedoms,[150] he urged the Court to apply a market access test: national legislation is likely to constitute an MEE if it 'hinders a product's access to the market, whatever the purpose of the measure'.[151]

His views appear to have won the day, at least for now. As we saw in Chapter 4, the Court said in *Commission* v. *Italy (trailers)*[152] that a non-discriminatory rule prohibiting the use of a product (trailers for motorcycles) has a 'considerable influence on the behaviour of consumers, which, in turn, affects the access of that product to the market of that state'.[153] It therefore constituted an MEE and so contravened Article 34 TFEU, unless justified.[154] And in reaching this conclusion the Court appears to have adopted a new category of measure (see fig. 5.3) which is neither a product requirement nor a certain selling arrangement: measures which hinder 'access of products originating in other Member States to the market of a Member State'.[155] As the facts of the *Trailers* case demonstrates, this new category certainly covers bans on use and so the Italian rule breached Article 34 TFEU but could be justified on grounds of road safety.

The Court relied extensively on this ruling in the follow-up case, *Mickelsson*,[156] concerning a restriction on the use of personal watercraft. The Court repeated the 'considerable influence on the behaviour of consumers' argument but then added, 'Consumers, knowing that the use permitted by such regulations is very limited, have only a limited interest in buying that product.'[157] It continued that where national regulations for the designation of navigable waters and waterways had 'the effect of preventing users of personal watercraft from using them for the specific and inherent purposes for which they were intended or of *greatly* restricting their use' such regulations had the effect of hindering the access to the domestic market for those goods and therefore constituted, save where there was a justification pursuant to Article 36 TFEU or overriding public interest requirements. Thus rules 'greatly' restricting use will, in principle, breach Article 34 TFEU.

Commission v. *Italy (trailers)* and *Mickelsson* (probably) do not reverse *Keck*[158] but suggest a narrow reading of the decision—that it should be confined to situations which concern arrangements for sale (*modalités de vente*) and should not be extended any further.

---

[145] Case C–110/05 *Commission* v. *Italy (trailers)* [2009] ECR I–519, paras. 55–6.

[146] Paras. 66–7.

[147] He thinks that a distinction between different categories of measures is not appropriate (para. 79); that the demarcation line is artificial and may be uncertain (para. 81); and that it has led to a differentiation between the goods regime and that for the other freedoms (para. 82).

[148] Para. 85. See also Poiares Maduro AG in C–158/04 *Alfa Vita* [2006] ECR I–8135, paras. 31–5.

[149] Para. 91.

[150] Para. 118. He also said that the access to the market test should not involve an appraisal of complex economic data (para. 116).

[151] Para. 136. Léger AG, who gave the first opinion in the case (5 Oct. 2006) assumed the rule was an MEE (para. 41) without any analysis. See also Case C–65/05 *Commission* v. *Greece (computer games)* [2006] ECR I–10341, paras. 41–2.

[152] Case C–110/05 *Commission* v. *Italy (trailers)* [2009] ECR I–519.   [153] Para. 56.

[154] Para. 58. The same approach would presumably be applied to restrictions on *possession*.

[155] Para. 37.   [156] Case C–142/05 *Åklagaren* v. *Mickelsson, Roos* [2009] ECR I–4273.

[157] Paras. 26–7.

[158] See Case C–531/07 *LIBRO* [2009] ECR I–3717, para. 20; a case decided after *Commission* v. *Italy (trailers)* but where the Court classified the rule as a certain selling arrangement.

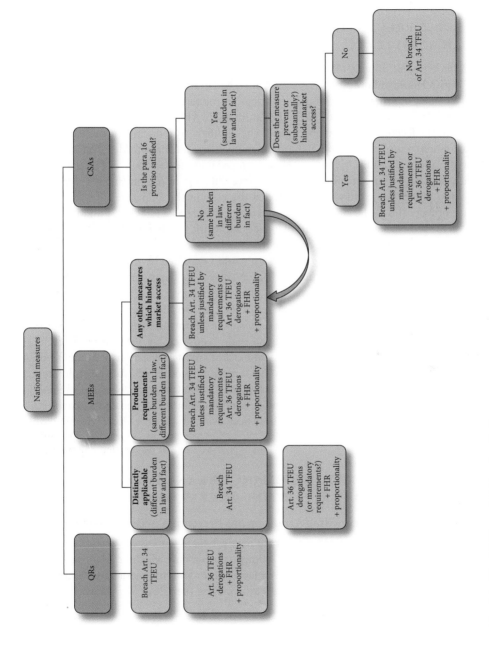

Fig. 5.3 QRs, MEEs, and CSAs after *Trailers*

Other types of measures will therefore not benefit from the *Keck* presumption of legality, and are likely to be considered rules hindering market access, and so will breach Article 34 TFEU, leaving Member States to justify their existence. If this analysis is correct then it means that the Court has now indirectly offered its solution to the next problem area: a ban on an activity.

3. RULES PREVENTING OR (SEVERELY) RESTRICTING AN ACTIVITY

In *R (on the application of the Countryside Alliance) v. Her Majesty's Attorney General*[159] the British House of Lords (now Supreme Court) had to consider whether a ban on an activity, namely hunting wild mammals with dogs, introduced in the controversial Hunting Act 2004, breached Article 34 TFEU. The Countryside Alliance argued that the Act had an indirect effect on the movement of goods (by significantly reducing the trade in horses and hounds coming from Ireland). Lord Bingham expressed his bewilderment as to how to apply Article 34 TFEU to the case. He recognized that the ban could not be characterized as a selling arrangement but, he said, 'I have difficulty in recognising it as a trading rule or a product rule either'. He supported the view of the Divisional Court and the Court of Appeal that the 2004 Act did not engage Article 34 TFEU but 'I find it hard to say, on the present state of the [Court of Justice] authorities ... that this conclusion is clear beyond the bounds of reasonable argument.'

Following *Commission v. Italy (trailers)*, it could be argued by the opponents of the Hunting Act that a non-discriminatory ban on an activity has a considerable influence on the behaviour of consumers (purchasers of horses and hounds), which, in turn, affects the access of those 'products' to the market in the UK. On the other hand, the facts of the *Countryside Alliance* case reveal the problems of (re)introducing the market access test to Article 34 TFEU: does the British law really 'considerably' affect market access? And if it does, it means the UK government must justify its legislation (presumably on the grounds of animal welfare, although this in itself is a contested assertion) and must show that its legislation is proportionate (as we shall see in Chapter 6, bans are often not deemed to be proportionate). If, on the other hand, the Court had decided to extend its approach in *Keck* these problems would have been avoided since the UK law would have been presumptively lawful.

4. NON-DISCRIMINATORY SELLING ARRANGEMENTS PREVENTING OR RESTRICTING ACCESS TO THE MARKET

4.1 Non-Discriminatory Selling Arrangements Preventing Access to the Market

Commission v. Italy (trailers) also appears to have provided the answer to another problem thrown up by *Keck*, namely certain selling arrangements which are genuinely *non-discriminatory* (same burden in law and in fact) but do *prevent* access by the imported goods to the market.[160] Examples include a total ban on the sale of a particular product

---

[159] *R (on the application of the Countryside Alliance) v. Her Majesty's Attorney General* [2007] UKHL 52.
[160] Although *quaere* whether it can be argued there is a ban on market access when there is no market to access due to the national ban on the existence of that market. Cf. Case C–110/05 *Commission v. Italy (trailers)* [2009] ECR I–519, para. 57, where the Court said that the Italian rule 'prevents a demand from existing in the market at issue for such trailers and therefore hinders their importation'.

such as cigarettes, pornography, alcohol, guns, or drugs.[161] According to the first limb of paragraph 17 in *Keck*, non-discriminatory selling arrangements do not breach Article 34 TFEU because they do not prevent access to the market. Yet, it is clear that a ban on the sale of a product does have serious implications for inter-state trade.[162] Following *Commission* v. *Italy (trailers)*, it would seem that the Court could now tackle this situation in one of two ways. First it could say that the ban on the sale of a product falls under the third limb of the definition of an MEE, i.e., 'Any other measure which hinders access of products originating in other Member States to the market of a Member State.' The rule would therefore breach Article 34 TFEU and would need to be justified.[163] The other possibility is that the rule is classified as a certain selling arrangement and, even though non-discriminatory, is subject to a market access test following *Commission* v. *Italy*. If this latter analysis is correct then *Commission* v. *Italy* has modified (corrected?) the first limb of paragraph 17 in *Keck* to include a market access test (see fig. 5.3). If market access is prevented or hindered then the rule breaches Article 34 TFEU and needs to be justified.

The more general introduction of a market access test has long been supported by Advocate General Jacobs. In *Leclerc-Siplec* he argued that all undertakings which engage in a legitimate economic activity in a Member State should have unfettered access to the whole of the Union market, unless there is a valid reason why not. His favoured test for determining whether non-discriminatory measures breach Article 34 TFEU is to ask whether the measure is liable 'substantially to restrict access to the market'?[164] He said that where a measure prohibits the sale of goods lawfully placed on the market in another Member State (as in *Cassis*), it is presumed to have a substantial impact on the market, since the goods are either denied access altogether or can gain access only after being modified in some way; the need to modify goods is itself a substantial barrier to market access.[165] On the other hand, he said, where a measure restricts certain selling arrangements, its impact will depend on whether it applies to some or all goods, the extent to which other selling arrangements remain available, and on whether the effect of the measure is 'direct or indirect, immediate or remote, or purely speculative and uncertain'. He continued that because the magnitude of the barrier to market access may vary enormously—from the insignificant to a quasi-prohibition—'a *de minimis* test could perform a useful function'.[166]

[161] There is an argument that bans on sales cannot be considered a 'selling arrangement'. However, para. 16 of *Keck* does talk of '*prohibitions* or restrictions' on selling arrangements and it therefore appears to envisage a 'ban' situation. See also, by analogy, Case C–210/03 R. v. *Secretary of State for Health, ex p. Swedish Match* [2004] ECR I–11893; Case C–434/02 *Arnold André GmbH & Co. KG* v. *Landrat des Kreises Herford* [2004] ECR I–11825, where the Court accepted that a measure banning the marketing of tobacco could be adopted under Art. 114 TFEU.

[162] See, by analogy, the services decision Case C–275/92 *Schindler* [1994] ECR I–1039. Some suggest that applying *Schindler* is unnecessary because the matter could be resolved by relying on Case 34/79 R. v. *Henn and Darby* [1972] ECR 3795, paras. 12–13, where the Court ruled that a ban on *imports* constituted a quantitative restriction (QR).

[163] Some support for that view can be found in Case C–142/09 *Lahousse* [2010] ECR I–11685, para. 46: 'the general prohibition on the *sale* or use of equipment … may impede the free movement of these goods'.

[164] Paras. 41 and 49. For academic support, see Weatherill, n. 60, 900; C. Barnard, 'Fitting the remaining pieces into the goods and services jigsaw?' (2001) 26 *ELRev*. 35. See also Mortelmans' discussion (n. 4, 128) of Van Gerven AG's implicit introduction of a *de minimis* rule in *Torfaen*. Cf. L. Gormley, 'Two years after *Keck*' [1996] *Fordham Intl. LJ* 866, 882–3; G. Davies, 'The Court's jurisprudence on free movement of goods: Pragmatic presumptions not philosophical principles' (2012) *EJCL/REDC* 217.

[165] Para. 44.

[166] Para. 45. See also Jacobs AG's Opinion in Case C–112/00 *Schmidberger* [2003] ECR I–5659. Cf. Weatherill, who objects to the term '*de minimis*' because it requires numerical quantification, see n. 60, 900).

4.2 Non-Discriminatory Selling Arrangements Restricting Access to the Market

Advocate General Jacobs' suggestion of the need for some sort of threshold requirement might have been picked up by the Court in *Commission* v. *Italy* when it referred to the fact that a prohibition on the use of a product has a '*considerable* influence on the behaviour of consumers, which, in its turn, affects the access of that product to the market of that Member State'. A threshold requirement would also help to address another problem area, namely non-discriminatory measures which merely hinder or make less attractive free movement of goods. This was the *Punto Casa/Boermans* situation. Rules prohibiting Sunday trading (*Punto Casa*) or restricting the opening hours of shops (*Boermans*) do hinder access to the market for imported (as well as domestic) goods. However, according to the second limb of paragraph 17 such rules do not breach Article 34 TFEU because access by foreign goods to the market is not impeded more than access of domestic products (i.e., there is no discrimination). As we have already seen, the Court's approach to these static rules is largely uncontroversial because they have so little effect on access to the market. However, if we were to take a more extreme version of the rule, the conclusions might be different. For example, if a national law required shops to be closed six days a week (e.g., Sunday to Friday) instead of just one day (Sunday), then instinctively it seems that because such a rule—albeit non-discriminatory—substantially impedes access to the market it should breach Article 34 TFEU (see fig. 5.3).

Commission v. *Italy (trailers)* supports this view,[167] as does the free movement of services case, *Alpine Investments*,[168] concerning a ban on cold-calling in the financial services industry. The Court, having noted that the measure was non-discriminatory, said that *Keck* did not apply because the national measure 'directly affects access to the markets in services in the other Member States and is thus capable of hindering intra-[Union] trade in services'.[169] The ban on cold-calling therefore breached Article 56 TFEU but could be justified. Extending this case law to goods, as Advocate General Jacobs suggests, would mean that non-discriminatory national measures which are liable to prohibit or otherwise (substantially) impede the free movement of goods should breach Article 34 TFEU unless justified.[170] By contrast, if the measure does not substantially impede market access, or using the tortious language employed in the goods case, *Krantz*, and the workers case, *Graf*,[171] if the effect of the national rule on free movement is 'too uncertain and indirect' (i.e., the causal link between the national rule and the impact on intra-EU trade is not established[172]), the Treaty will not be breached.

A test based on 'substantial' hindrance of market access has been subject to three criticisms: first, that it is a statistical test which the courts are ill-equipped to apply;[173] secondly, that it effectively reverses the well-established rule that the *de minimis*

---

[167] The Commission also takes this line in its submissions in Case E–16/10 *Philip Morris Norway* v. *The Norwegian State* [2011] EFTA Ct. Rep. 330.

[168] Case C–384/93 [1995] ECR I–1141. See also Case C–275/92 *Schindler* [1994] ECR I–1039.

[169] Para. 38. Robert Walker LJ in *R. (on the application of Professional Contractors Group Ltd)* v. *Inland Revenue Commissioners* [2001] EWCA Civ 1945 talked of 'indirect or debateable' (para. 69) and 'direct and demonstrable' (para. 74). Cf. also H. Toner, 'Non-discriminatory obstacles to the exercise of Treaty rights: Articles 39, 43, 49, and 18 EC' (2004) 23 *YEL* 275, 285–6 who argues that there are two possible thresholds: direct *or* significant. If the obstacle is direct then its effect needs only be perceptible; if the measure is significant or substantial then the obstacle does not need to be direct.

[170] The language is drawn from Case C–76/90 *Säger* v. *Dennemayer* [1991] ECR I–4221, para. 12.

[171] Case C–190/98 *Graf* [2000] ECR I–493, paras. 24–5.

[172] Case C–291/09 *Guarnieri & Cie* v. *Vandevelde Eddy VOF* [2011] ECR I–2685, para. 17.

[173] See, e.g., V. Hatzopoulos, 'Recent developments of the case law of the ECJ in the field of services' (2000) 37 *CMLRev.* 43.

principle does not apply to Article 34 TFEU;[174] and thirdly, that the language of market access itself is far from clear: does it merely refer to barriers to market entry which make it more costly for new firms to enter an industry or does it refer to any regulation which imposes and implies compliance costs.[175] It is for these reasons that some prefer a more legal test based on causation and remoteness. For example, Advocate General La Pergola said in *BASF*[176] that the aim of Article 34 TFEU is to verify whether a causal link exists between the national measure and the pattern of imports. The language used in *Krantz* and *Graf*, examining whether the effect on trade is 'too indirect and uncertain', supports the remoteness test. However, Weatherill has argued that the remoteness test could equally be recast as an application of the notion that internal market law does not affect measures that cause no direct or substantial hindrance of access to the market of a Member State.[177]

The Court has not addressed this issue directly, and in practice its approach seems to be rather intuitive. It does not engage in any sophisticated economic analysis of (substantial) hindrance of market access (see, e.g., in *DocMorris*) or any detailed legal analysis of remoteness (see, e.g., *Krantz*). If it senses that some rules have little to do with market integration then it finds that they do not breach the Treaty (e.g., *Punto Casa*, *Boermans*, and *Graf*). If, on the other hand, it considers that other rules do prevent or substantially hinder access to the market it will find that they do breach the Treaty and need to be justified (*Trailers*, *Alpine Investments*). In the interests of clarity and consistency, terminology based on 'substantial' hindrance of market access will be used throughout this book. It is supported by Advocate General Jacobs' Opinion in *Leclerc-Siplec* and it probably provides the best fit with the case law on persons, services, and capital. However, it will always be used subject to the caveats outlined here.

E. UNFAIR COMMERCIAL PRACTICES DIRECTIVE 2005/29

As we have seen, the interpretation of Article 34 TFEU given by the Court in *Trailers* has significantly reduced the areas of national law which benefit from the *Keck* presumption of legality. A further erosion to the *Keck* principle comes from a different quarter: the Unfair (business-to-consumer) Commercial Practices Directive 2005/29 (UCPD).[178] This directive marks a new stage in the evolution of consumer legislation because it adopts a maximum, not minimum, approach to harmonization.[179] The starting point of the directive is that commercial practices by traders are lawful. Therefore, any attempts by Member States to prohibit them contravene the directive. This was recognized by Advocate General Trstenjak in *VTB-VAB*:[180]

> the Directive presupposes that commercial practices are fair as long as the precisely defined legal conditions for a prohibition are not fulfilled. It thus follows an ... approach, in favour of the trader's entrepreneurial freedom, which accords essentially with the legal concept of '*in dubio pro libertate*'.

---

[174] Joined Cases 177 and 178/82 *van de Haar* [1984] ECR I–1797.
[175] See further Ch.1.   [176] Case C–44/98 *BASF* [1999] ECR I–6269, para. 18.
[177] See n. 60, 900.   [178] [2005] OJ L149/22.
[179] Although the 1985 Product Liability Dir. 85/374/EEC ([1985] OJ L210/29) also claimed to pursue total/maximum harmonization.
[180] Joined Cases C–261 and 299/07 *VTB-VAB NV* v. *Total Belgium NV* [2009] ECR I–2949, para. 81.

Article 2(d) UCPD defines unfair commercial practices broadly:[181]

> 'business-to-consumer commercial practices' (hereinafter also referred to as commercial practices) means any act, omission, course of conduct or representation, commercial communication *including advertising and marketing*, by a trader, directly connected with the *promotion, sale* or supply of a product to consumers.[182]

As the italicized phrases show, this definition overlaps with 'certain selling arrangements' as defined in the *Keck* case law.

The directive prohibits unfair commercial practices.[183] It sets out the rules as to when the commercial practices are unfair. These fall into three categories:

(1) an exhaustive list of 31 specific commercial practices, contained in the annex to the directive (Article 5(5))

(2) commercial practices which are misleading (by action or omission)[184] or aggressive[185] (Article 5(4))

(3) commercial practices which contravene the requirements of professional diligence and materially distort (or are likely to materially distort) the economic behaviour of the average consumer[186] (Article 5(2)).

Categories 2 and 3 are principles-based: they apply only if the effect of the trader's practice is likely to alter consumers' decisions in relation to trading practices; in other words, they always take account of the impact on the consumer and hence this impact needs to be assessed on a case-by-case basis.[187] By contrast the first type of commercial practice caught by the prohibition is not principles-based (i.e., no case-by-case assessment is necessary) and is always unfair.[188]

When assessing a national law banning a particular commercial practice (assuming that it falls within the scope of the directive[189] (see fig. 5.4)), the Court will first consider whether the commercial practice falls within one of the situations listed in the annex (category (1)). If so, the national law is compatible with the directive; the national prohibition does not depend on a further examination of, for example, its effects. If the annex does not apply, the Court will then examine whether the national authority has

---

[181] Art. 2(d), emphasis added. See also recital 7. Commercial practices include price reductions intended to induce consumers to buy products on an e-commerce website (Case C–288/10 *Wamo* EU:C:2011:443; Case C–13/15 *Cdiscount SA* EU:C:2015:560).

[182] Case C–391/12 *RLvS Verlagsgesellschaft mbH* v. *Stuttgarter Wochenblatt GmbH* EU:C:2013:669, para. 37: the practices must be commercial in nature, i.e., 'they must originate from traders, and they must be directly connected with the promotion, sale or supply of their products to consumers'.

[183] Art. 5(1).

[184] Arts. 6–7. On the definition of 'misleading', see Case C–281/12 *Trento Sviluppo* v. *Autorità Garante Adriatica della Concorrenza e del Mercato* EU:C:2013:859, para. 38: 'where that practice contains false information, or is likely to deceive the average consumer, and is likely to cause the consumer to take a transactional decision that he would not otherwise have taken'.

[185] Arts. 8–9.

[186] However, Art. 5(3) says 'Commercial practices which are likely to materially distort the economic behaviour only of a clearly identifiable group of consumers who are particularly vulnerable to the practice or the underlying product because of their mental or physical infirmity, age or credulity in a way which the trader could reasonably be expected to foresee, shall be assessed from the perspective of the average member of that group.'

[187] Recital 17 says that the list in Annex I is 'the only commercial practices which can be deemed to be unfair without a case-by-case assessment against the provisions of Articles 5 to 9'. See also Case C–206/11 *Köck* v. *Schutzverband gegen unlauteren Wettbewerb* EU:C:2013:14, para. 35.

[188] This is confirmed in Case C–428/11 *Purely Creative Ltd* v. *Office of Fair Trading* EU:C:2012:651, para. 45.

[189] See Art. 3.

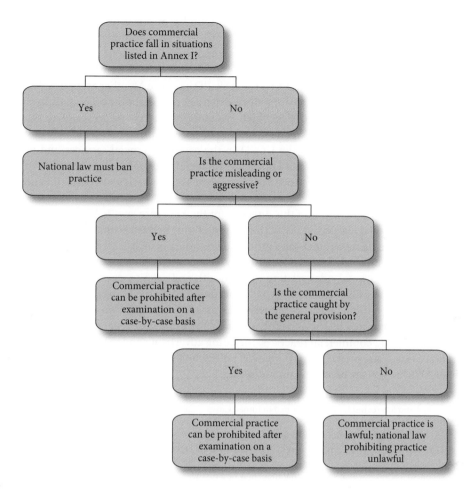

Fig. 5.4 Application of the UCPD

considered whether the commercial practice is misleading or aggressive within the mean-ing of Articles 6–9 (category (2)). If the practice is not misleading or aggressive,[190] the Court will finally check whether the national authority has considered whether the commercial practice contravenes the requirements of professional diligence and whether it materi-ally distorts the economic behaviour of the average consumer (category (3)).[191] Category 3 therefore acts as a safety net for practices which do not come under categories (1) and (2) and so is referred to as a general or residual clause.[192] If none of these three categories is satisfied, the national law prohibiting the commercial practice contravenes the UCPD.[193]

---

[190] If the practice is found to be misleading or aggressive it is not necessary also to determine that it is contrary to the requirements of professional diligence: Case C–435/11 *CHS Tour Services* EU:C:2013:634, para. 48.

[191] The directive relies on the assumption that, in relation to the trader, the 'consumer is in a weaker position, in that the consumer must be considered to be economically weaker and less experienced in legal matters than the other party to the contract': Case C–59/12 *BKK Mobil Oil* v. *Zentrale zur Bekämpfung un-lauteren Wettbewerbs eV* EU:C:2013:634, para. 35.

[192] See also Trstenjak AG's Opinion in Joined Cases C–261 and 299/07 *VTB-VAB NV* [2009] ECR I–2949, para. 79.

[193] See, e.g., Case C–206/11 *Köck* v. *Schutzverban gegen unlauteren Wettbewerb* EU:C:2013:14, where leg-islation providing for prior authorization of announcements of sales was found contrary to the UCPD.

In other words, because the UCPD is a maximum harmonization measure,[194] only in the three categories of situation already outlined can a commercial practice be prohibited.[195] Member States cannot go further and ban other practices, as they could under most of the earlier consumer protection directives which were minimum harmonization measures. However, Article 3(5) UCPD gave the Member States six years from June 2007[196] to continue to apply (pre-existing) national provisions within the field approximated by the directive which are more restrictive or prescriptive than the UCPD. Article 3(9) allows Member States to impose requirements which are more restrictive or prescriptive than the UCPD in the case of financial services and immovable property.[197] Where a state takes advantage of this possibility, its rules will be scrutinized by reference to the Treaty requirements, in particular Articles 34 and 56 TFEU.[198]

So what are the implications of this directive for the *Keck* case law?[199] As we have seen, under *Keck*, national legislation restricting or prohibiting certain selling arrangements, for example advertising or other sales promotion techniques such as free gifts and resale at a loss, is presumptively *lawful* under EU law. In areas falling outside the scope of the UCPD, such as 'national rules relating to the health and safety aspects of products',[200] Article 34 TFEU as interpreted by *Keck*, will continue to apply, including the presumption of legality of the national measure. However, for matters falling within the scope of the UCPD and not covered by the annex,[201] national laws drafted in general terms restricting or prohibiting commercial practices, including advertising and marketing and even resale at a loss,[202] are presumptively *unlawful* unless, following a case-by-case assessment under Articles 5–9, the practice is unfair (see fig. 5.5).[203]

---

[194] Art. 4 and 5th recital UCPD, confirmed in Joined Cases C–261 and 299/07 *VTB-VAB NV* [2009] ECR I–2949, para. 52.

[195] Art. 5(1) 'Unfair commercial practices shall be prohibited.'

[196] This six-year period was subject to review (Art. 18) but not extended (COM(2013) 139, 5. Art. 3(6) required Member States to notify the Commission of any national provisions applied on the basis of Art. 3(5).

[197] See also Recital 7, which suggests that there may be a further exception: that Member States be able to continue to ban commercial practices in their territory, in conformity with Union law, for reasons of taste and decency even where such practices do not limit consumers' freedom of choice.

[198] Case C–265/12 *Citroën Belux NV* v. *FvF* EU:C:2013:498 (a prohibition on a combined offer made to consumers, where at least one of the components of the offer is a financial service, may be compatible with Art. 56 TFEU).

[199] See further G. Anagnostaras, 'The Unfair Commercial Practices Directive in context: From legal disparity to legal complexity?' (2010) 47 *CMLRev.* 147, 152–61.

[200] Art. 3(3). See also Art. 3(9) on financial services and Art. 3(10) on the certification and indication of the standard of fineness of articles of precious metals. Recital 9 appears to go further: 'It is also without prejudice to [Union] and national rules on contract law, on intellectual property rights, on the health and safety aspects of products, on conditions of establishment and authorization regimes, including those rules which, in conformity with [Union] law, relate to gambling activities, and to [Union] competition rules and the national provisions implementing them. The Member States will thus be able to retain or introduce restrictions and prohibitions of commercial practices on grounds of the protection of the health and safety of consumers in their territory wherever the trader is based, for example in relation to alcohol, tobacco or pharmaceuticals. Financial services and immovable property, by reason of their complexity and inherent serious risks, necessitate detailed requirements, including positive obligations on traders.'

[201] Where, however, the national legislation has prohibited one of the practices listed in the annex (e.g., claiming to be a signatory to a code of conduct when the trader is not, or displaying a trust mark, quality mark, or equivalent without having obtained the necessary authorization), then the legislation would be compatible with the UCPD and thus, by implication, with the Treaty, without the need for going through the *Keck* analysis.

[202] Case C–343/12 *Euronics Belgium* v. *Kamera Express* EU:C:2013:154.

[203] Likewise, if a particular commercial practice is considered unfair after an assessment carried out under Arts. 5–9, the prohibition will be compatible with the directive and thus the Treaty.

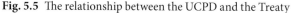

Fig. 5.5 The relationship between the UCPD and the Treaty

The effect of the directive is therefore essentially to restore the pre-*Keck* position, as laid down in cases such as *Oosthoek, Buet,* and *Aragonesa,* to national rules on commercial practices which fall within the scope of the directive. However, it is likely that now, following the UCPD, the litigation will focus not on Article 34 TFEU but on the directive. So if action is brought by the state against a trader for breaching a (national) rule prohibiting the use of promotional free gifts, the trader can invoke the UCPD (rather than Article 34 TFEU) in its defence.[204] As *VTB-VAB*[205] shows, by relying on the UCPD a trader can also

---

[204] Given the structure of the directive, in that it does not confer rights as such on the trader, it will be more difficult for the trader to use the provisions of the UCPD as a sword against the state to challenge national regulations which exceed what is permissible under the UCPD. Perhaps there might be some residual scope here for Art. 34 TFEU—as interpreted in *Keck*. See also Case C–253/00 *Antonio Muñoz y Cia SA v. Frumar Ltd* [2002] ECR I–7289, considered in Ch. 15.

[205] Joined Cases C–261 and 299/07 [2009] ECR I–2949. See also Case C–522/08 *Telekomunikacja Polska SA w Warszawie v. Prezes Urzędu Komunikacyjnej Elektronicznej* [2010] ECR I–2079, para. 33, on combined offers and Case C–540/08 *Mediaprint Zeitungs- und Zeitschriftenverlag GmbH v. Osterreich-Zeitungsverlag* [2010] ECR I–10909 (ban on making the offer of bonuses to customers subject to purchase of goods or services contrary to UCPD). For a further example, see Case C–304/08 *Zentrale zur Bekämpfung unlauteren Wettbewerbs eV v. Plus Warenhandelsgesellschaft mBH* [2010] ECR I–217 (UCPD precludes national legislation prohibiting in principle, without taking account of the specific circumstances of individual cases, commercial practices under which the participation of consumers in a prize competition or lottery is made conditional on the purchase of goods or use of services).

defend itself against any action brought by a private party (if this is possible in the national system).[206]

The significance of the change in presumptions introduced by the UCPD can be seen in *VTB-VAB*. Belgian law prohibited vendors from making combined offers to consumers. This meant that commercial practices such as offering a free breakdown service to consumers buying certain quantities of petrol, or a money-off voucher in a magazine for a discount in certain shops, contravened Belgian law. Under *Keck* such a law would have been presumptively lawful unless actually and substantially discriminatory. However, following the UCPD the approach was different. The Court noted that Article 2(d) gave 'a particularly wide definition to the concept of commercial practices', and that combined offers constituted commercial practices within the meaning of Article 2(d).[207] Because combined offers did not fall within the annex to the directive, the Belgian legislation was precluded by the UCPD insofar as it prohibited combined offers without any verification of their unfairness in the light of the principles-based, case-by-case criteria (categories (2) and (3)).[208] Having found the Belgian law to be in breach of the directive, the Court saw no need to consider the compatibility of the national rule with the Treaty.

F. CONCLUSIONS

The judgment in *Keck* represents a serious step towards establishing areas of national regulation where it is (and it is not) legitimate for Article 34 TFEU to intervene and, as the Court made clear in *Tobacco Advertising*,[209] over which the Union probably does not have the power to regulate under Article 114 TFEU.[210] Therefore, in the spirit of the subsidiarity principle, Member States retain their autonomy to regulate in areas which do not concern Union rules on free movement. However, in trying to delimit such an area, the Court reaffirmed the central place of the principle of non-discrimination in Article 34 TFEU. Yet, as we have seen, in its attempts to resolve the problem of dealing with market circumstances rules, the Court created further difficulties, particularly in respect of those rules which did not fit the category of certain selling arrangements and those rules which were non-discriminatory but did hinder market access. Inevitably, this led the Court back to (re)considering the market access approach and in so doing probably narrowed the scope of *Keck*. The UCPD seems to have narrowed *Keck* still further.

However, as we saw in Chapter 1, the problem with a market access test is that almost any national measure can have some effect on market access, albeit indirect and potential, leading to a finding of a breach of Article 34 TFEU. While such measures can be justified by Member States, this takes the courts (both European and national) into areas often involving sensitive choices of social policy, as the *Countryside Alliance* case shows. This is particularly true when it comes to assessing the proportionality of a particular measure. Generally, in the field of goods, the Court demands close scrutiny of the national measure. Yet, many national rules would not withstand close scrutiny, such as national rules imposing age restrictions on the purchase of cigarettes (why 18 and not 17?), alcohol, and guns.

---

[206] See by analogy Case C–194/94 *CIA* [1996] ECR I–2201 concerning the Technical Standards Dir. 98/34, discussed in Ch. 4, and the case law on triangular situations.

[207] Paras. 49–50.   [208] Para. 62.

[209] Case C–376/98 *Germany* v. *Parliament and Council* [2000] ECR I–8419, considered further in Ch. 15.

[210] Cf. G. Davies, 'Can selling arrangements be harmonised?' (2005) 30 *ELRev.* 371.

For these reasons, the Court has been reluctant to apply Article 34 TFEU to such cases. It now has a number of tools to achieve this: the *Keck* principle to deal with situations involving certain selling arrangements, the rule that the measure concerns a wholly internal situation, or arguments based on remoteness (that the effect of the measure on trade is too indirect and uncertain or not sufficiently substantial) to deal with other difficult cases. The Court is not always consistent or scientific in the application of these different tools, as it feels its way towards an appropriate solution to the problem of defining the outer limits of Article 34 TFEU. These problems are more obvious in the field of free movement of persons where the market access test has a longer history. We consider this issue in more detail in Chapter 7. First, however, we consider in the next chapter the derogations to the principle of free movement and the judicially developed mandatory requirements.

FURTHER READING

Potential solutions to the market circumstances problems

K. MORTELMANS, 'Article 30 of the EEC Treaty and legislation relating to market circumstances: Time to consider a new definition' (1991) 28 *CMLRev.* 115.

E. WHITE, 'In search of the limits to Article 30 of the EEC Treaty' (1989) 26 *CMLRev.* 235.

Sunday trading cases

P. DIAMOND, 'Dishonourable defence: The use of injunctions and the EEC Treaty—Case study of the Shops Act 1950' (1991) 54 *MLR* 72.

M. JARVIS, 'The Sunday trading episode: In defence of the Euro-defence' (1995) 44 *ICLQ* 451.

Comment on the judgments in *Keck* and beyond

C. BARNARD, 'What the *Keck*? Balancing the needs of the single market with state regulatory autonomy' [2012] *European Journal of Consumer Law* 201.

C. BARNARD, 'What the *Keck* are we doing?' [2014] *Revue trimestrielle de droit européen* 878.

L. GORMLEY, 'Reasoning renounced? The remarkable judgment in *Keck and Mithouard*' [1994] *EBLRev.* 63

L. GORMLEY, P. NIHOUL, and E. VAN NIEUWENHUYZE (eds.), 'What Standard after *Keck*? Free movement provisions and national rules affecting consumer usage or trade access' [2012] *European Journal of Consumer Law* special edition.

I. LIANOS, 'Shifting narratives in the European internal market: Efficient restrictions of trade and the nature of "economic" integration' (2010) 21 *EBLRev.* 705.

P. PECHO, 'Good-bye *Keck*? A comment on the remarkable judgment in *Commission* v. *Italy* Case C–110/05' (2009) 36 *LIEI* 257.

M. POIARES MADURO, '*Keck*: The end? Or just the end of the beginning?' [1994] *IJEL* 33.

L. PRETE, 'Of motorcycle trailers and personal watercrafts: The battle over *Keck*' (2008) 35 *LIEI* 133.

N. REICH, 'The November Revolution of the European Court of Justice: *Keck*, *Meng* and *Audi* revisited' (1994) 31 *CMLRev.* 459.

A. ROSAS, '*Dassonville* and *Cassis de Dijon*' in M. Poiares Maduro and L. Azoulai (eds.), *The Past and Future of EU Law: The classics of EU law revisited on the 50th anniversary of the Rome Treaty* (Oxford: Hart Publishing, 2010).

E. Spaventa, 'The outer limits of the Treaty free movement provisions: Some reflections on the significance of *Keck*, remoteness and *Deliège*' in C. Barnard and O. Odudu (eds.), *The Outer Limits of European Union Law* (Oxford: Hart Publishing, 2009).

S. Weatherill, 'After *Keck*: Some thoughts on how to clarify the clarification' (1996) 33 *CMLRev.* 885.

The Unfair Commercial Practices Directive

Commission, Communication on the application of the Unfair Commercial Practices Directive 2005/29, COM(2013) 138, updated by SWD(2016) 320.

G. Anagnostaras, 'The Unfair Commercial Practices Directive in context: From legal disparity to legal complexity?' (2010) 47 *CMLRev.* 147.

B. Keirsblick, *The New European Law of Unfair Commercial Practices and Competition Law* (Oxford: Hart Publishing, 2011).

J. Stuyck, 'The Court of Justice and the Unfair Commercial Practices Directive' (2015) 52 *CMLRev.* 721.

6

DEROGATIONS
AND JUSTIFICATIONS

A. INTRODUCTION

As we have seen, Article 36 TFEU provides an exhaustive list of derogations from the principle of free movement of goods. This list, drawn directly from Article XX of the

GATT reflected values deemed important in the 1950s. It has not, however, kept pace with the times, and social interests deemed valuable now, such as environmental and consumer protection, are not reflected in Article 36 TFEU. This has prompted the Court to develop an additional list of justifications—known as mandatory or public-interest requirements—which the Member States can invoke to justify the continued existence of their national rules. Traditionally, these mandatory requirements could be raised only where the measure was considered an indistinctly applicable MEE: they could not be used to justify distinctly applicable measures. Distinctly applicable measures could be saved only by the express Treaty derogations. However, as we saw in Chapter 4, the Court is increasingly recognizing that distinctly applicable measures can be saved by both the Article 36 TFEU derogations and the mandatory requirements. This is also the case with measures that interfere with market access following *Commission* v. *Italy (trailers)*. The distinction between the Article 36 TFEU derogations and the mandatory requirements is therefore becoming less significant. Nevertheless, the Court still considers Member States' arguments separately under each heading but then applies common principles. In particular, it requires Member States to demonstrate the proportionality of the steps they have taken to serve the public-interest objective and, where necessary, show that these steps are compatible with fundamental human rights and principles of good governance, including legal certainty. This chapter therefore examines the specific derogations under Article 36 TFEU, the mandatory requirements developed by the Court, and the application of the principles of proportionality and fundamental rights.

B. THE ARTICLE 36 TFEU DEROGATIONS

1. INTRODUCTION

The first sentence of Article 36 TFEU provides:

> The provisions of Articles 34 and 35 shall not preclude prohibitions or restrictions on imports, exports or goods in transit justified on grounds of public morality, public policy or public security; the protection of health and life of humans, animals or plants; the protection of national treasures possessing artistic, historic or archaeological value; or the protection of industrial and commercial property.

This is an exhaustive list of derogations which must be read in conjunction with the proviso in the second sentence of Article 36 TFEU. This says that '[s]uch prohibitions or restrictions shall not, however, constitute a means of arbitrary discrimination or a disguised restriction on trade between Member States'.

Thus, the Treaty allows national measures to take precedence over the free movement of goods where they serve important interests recognized by the Union as valuable (so-called 'public goods'), provided that the national measures are proportionate and do not constitute a means of arbitrary discrimination or a disguised restriction on trade between Member States. Eventually, restrictive national rules justified under Article 36 TFEU may be replaced by harmonized Union rules intended to protect the same interests at Union, rather than national, level.[1] In the absence of harmonization Member States remain free to invoke the derogations.

---

[1] These issues are considered in detail in Ch. 15.

The Court has imposed two constraints on the Member States' freedom to invoke the Article 36 TFEU derogations. First, since Article 36 TFEU constitutes a derogation from the basic rule of free movement of goods it has to be interpreted strictly. Therefore, in *Irish Souvenirs*[2] the Court said that the exceptions listed in Article 36 TFEU could not be extended to include cases other than those specifically laid down. This meant that the Irish government could not rely on consumer protection and fairness in commercial transactions as a defence to its (directly) discriminatory conduct. Secondly, the derogations cannot be used to serve economic objectives.[3] Therefore, in *Commission* v. *Italy*,[4] Italy could not justify its ban on the import of pig meat because of economic difficulties with its own pig industry.[5]

Subject to these constraints, Member States can invoke any one of the derogations laid down in Article 36 TFEU. The burden of proof is on the national authorities to 'demonstrate in each case that their rules are necessary to give effective protection to the interests referred to in Article [36 TFEU]'.[6] We shall consider the different derogations in turn.

2. PUBLIC MORALITY

Member States enjoy a margin of discretion to determine what constitutes public morality in their own country. This can be seen in *Henn and Darby*,[7] where the UK banned the import of obscene films and magazines from the Netherlands on the grounds of public morality. The Court upheld the UK's decision, noting that 'it is for each Member State to determine in accordance with its own scale of values and in the form selected by it the requirements of public morality in its territory'.[8] Therefore, in principle the UK could invoke the first sentence of Article 36 TFEU.

This decision can be contrasted with *Conegate*.[9] The UK prevented the import of sexy vacuum flasks and life-size inflatable dolls from Germany. Although the defendants argued that the dolls were to be used in window displays, their description as 'love-love dolls' and 'Miss World specials' suggested a different purpose.[10] This time the Court was more suspicious of the UK's justification based on public morality because the very same sort of goods could be manufactured in the UK. It said the fact that goods cause offence could not be regarded as sufficiently serious to justify restrictions on the free movement of goods where 'the Member State concerned does not adopt, with respect to the same goods manufactured or marketed within its territory, penal measures or other

---

[2] Case 113/80 *Commission* v. *Ireland* [1981] ECR 1625, para. 7.

[3] Case 95/81 *Commission* v. *Italy* [1982] ECR 2187, para. 27.

[4] Case 7/61 *Commission* v. *Italy* [1961] ECR 317, 329.

[5] See also Case C–324/93 *R.* v. *Secretary of State for the Home Department, ex p. Evans Medical Ltd (Generics (UK) Ltd intervening)* [1995] ECR I–563. In Case 238/82 *Duphar BV* v. *Netherlands* [1984] ECR 523, para. 23 the Court said Art. 36 TFEU could not justify a measure whose primary objective was budgetary (i.e., to reduce the costs of a sickness insurance scheme). Nor can the derogations be relied on to justify rules or practices which, albeit beneficial, contain restrictions explained primarily by a concern to lighten the administration's burden or reduce public expenditure: Case 104/75 *Adriaan de Peijper* [1976] ECR 613, para. 18.

[6] Case 227/82 *Criminal Proceedings against Leendert van Bennekom* [1983] ECR 3883, para. 40.

[7] Case 34/79 [1979] ECR 3795.   [8] Para. 16.

[9] Case 121/85 *Conegate* v. *HM Customs and Excise* [1986] ECR 1007.

[10] Counsel for the customs authorities told the magistrates that 'it is almost certain that the dolls were intended to be used as sex aids. I don't know about the sexy vacuum flasks': *The Guardian*, 22 Jan. 1986, cited in S. Weatherill and P. Beaumont, *EU Law*, 3rd edn (London: Penguin, 1999), 529.

serious and effective measures intended to prevent the distribution of such goods in its own territory'.[11] Therefore, the UK could not rely on the public-morality defence.

3. PUBLIC POLICY

3.1 Public Policy and the Import and Export of Goods

It is clear that the Union definition of public policy bears little resemblance to its broad common law equivalent. This derogation is narrowly construed and the Court has proved most resistant to all attempts to expand its scope. For example, in *Ringelhan*[12] the Court said, 'Whatever interpretation is to be given to the term "public policy" it cannot be extended so as to include considerations of consumer protection.'[13]

It is rare for the public-policy defence, as an independent free-standing defence,[14] to be successfully invoked in a goods case before the Court of Justice. *Thompson*,[15] however, is one such case. It concerned a British ban on exporting silver coins, even though they were no longer legal tender, to prevent them from being melted down or destroyed. Because it was also a criminal offence in the UK to melt down coins, the Court said that a ban on exports was justified on grounds of public policy because it stemmed from 'the need to protect the right to mint coinage which is traditionally regarded as involving the fundamental interests of the State'.[16]

This decision can be compared with *Commission v. Italy*.[17] Italian law required that, when making a payment in advance, importers had to provide security of 5 per cent of the value of the goods. Italy justified its requirement on the grounds of public policy, citing in particular 'the defence of its currency'.[18] The Court rejected this argument.

3.2 Public Policy and the Right to Protest

(a) The position under the Treaty

The public-policy derogation has increasingly been invoked by Member States in the context of public protests and the fear of civil unrest. The public-policy arguments take one of two forms. In one line of case law, the public-policy derogation has been invoked to justify the state allowing protesters to exercise their fundamental rights and, in so doing, interfere with free movement of goods. As we shall see in *Schmidberger*,[19] the Court has shown some sympathy with this argument.

In a second line of case law, the derogation has been invoked to prevent practices—usually by importers—which lead to civil unrest. Generally, the Court has not been sympathetic to such arguments, as *Cullet*[20] shows. When the Leclerc group started selling petrol at prices below those set by French law, a competitor brought proceedings against it

---

[11] Case 121/85 *Conegate* [1986] ECR 1007, para. 15.
[12] Case 177/83 *Kohl* v. *Ringelhan & Rennett SA* [1984] ECR 3651.   [13] Para. 19.
[14] In Case C–434/04 *Ahokainen* v. *Virallinen syyttäjä* [2006] ECR I–9171, para. 28 it was invoked in conjunction with the public-health defence when justifying Swedish measures used to control the consumption of alcohol.
[15] Case 7/78 *R.* v. *Thompson, Johnson and Woodiwiss* [1978] ECR 2247.   [16] Para. 34.
[17] Case 95/81 [1982] ECR 2187. See also Case 7/61 *Commission* v. *Italy* [1961] ECR 317, 329.
[18] Para. 26.
[19] Case C–112/00 *Eugen Schmidberger, Internationale Transporte und Planzüge* v. *Republic of Austria* [2003] ECR I–5659. See also Case C–36/02 *Omega Spielhallen* [2004] ECR I–9609, discussed in Ch. 12.
[20] Case 231/83 *Cullet* v. *Centre Leclerc Toulouse* [1985] ECR 305. Cf. Case 42/82 *Commission* v. *France (the 'wine war')* [1983] ECR 1013, where violent demonstrations occurred when French *vinicolteurs* protested at the import of wine from Italy. However, France did not consider it worthwhile to raise the public-order defence.

claiming that Leclerc's pricing policy was unlawful. The Court found that the French law setting minimum petrol prices breached Article 34 TFEU because it allowed the authorities to manipulate prices, which had the effect of preventing importers from entering the market.[21] The French government tried to justify the rule under Article 36 TFEU, by referring to 'the threat to public order and security represented by the violent reactions which would have to be anticipated on the part of retailers affected by unrestricted competition'.[22] However, because the French government had not shown that it was unable, using the means at its disposal, to deal with the threat to public order and security represented by the protesters,[23] the Court said that France could not rely on Article 36 TFEU.

Advocate General VerLoren Van Themaat adopted a different approach. He rejected the French government's arguments on principle. He said that there was no support for a wide interpretation of public policy to include civil unrest because private interest groups, rather than the Treaty and the Union institutions, would then determine the scope of Union freedoms. In such cases, he said that the concept of public policy requires effective action on the part of the authorities to deal with such disturbances.[24]

By turning the public-policy argument on its head, the Advocate General envisaged that public policy placed responsibility on the national authorities to deal with obstacles to free movement of goods created by interest groups. From a pure free movement perspective, he is right that interest groups objecting to the economic consequences of the single market should not be able to interfere with the operation of the single market, nor should Member States be able to use civil disobedience as a pretext for protecting national interests. But if the Advocate General's views are taken to their logical conclusion this would mean that the national government would be obliged to apply all means at its disposal (the entire police force, the army?) to ensure the free movement of goods. Where would this leave fundamental rights to protest and how does this relate to the principle of proportionality?

The Court provided partial answers to these questions in *Commission v. France (Spanish strawberries).*[25] The case arose out of a long history of violent attacks by French farmers directed against agricultural products from other Member States,[26] in particular Spanish strawberries and Belgian tomatoes.[27] Despite various tip-offs, the French police were either nowhere to be seen during these incidents or were present but did not intervene, even when they far out-numbered the perpetrators. Furthermore, the French authorities had prosecuted only a very small number of those involved, even though a number of the faces of the demonstrators had been caught on camera.[28] Eventually, the Commission brought enforcement proceedings against France, arguing that the failure by the French authorities to act breached Article 34 TFEU on the free movement of goods and Article 4(3) TEU on the duty of cooperation.

The Court agreed, ruling that Article 34 TFEU required the Member States 'not merely themselves to abstain from adopting measures or engaging in conduct liable to constitute an obstacle to trade but also, when read with Article [4(3) TEU] …, to take all necessary and appropriate measures to ensure that that fundamental freedom is respected on their territory'.[29] The Court then acknowledged that:[30]

the Member States, which retain exclusive competence as regards the maintenance of public order and the safeguarding of internal security, unquestionably enjoy a margin of

[21] Para. 20. [22] Para. 32. [23] Para. 33. [24] At 312.
[25] Case C–265/95 [1997] ECR I–6959. [26] Para. 2. [27] Paras. 4–6. [28] Paras. 48–50.
[29] Para. 32. More recently confirmed in Case C–573/12 *Ålands Vindkraft AB v. Energimyndigheten* EU:C:2014:2037, para. 74.
[30] Paras. 33–4.

discretion in determining what measures are most appropriate to eliminate barriers to the importation of products in a given situation.

It is therefore not for the Union institutions to act in place of the Member States and to prescribe for them the measures which they must adopt and effectively apply in order to safeguard the free movement of goods on their territories.

Taking due account of Member State discretion, the Court continued that it could only verify 'whether the Member State concerned has adopted appropriate measures for ensuring the free movement of goods'.[31]

This case shows that the Court's control is residual, and any sanction is available only in cases involving 'manifest and persistent failure'[32] by the state. This would suggest that a national authority does have the discretion to balance the competing interests of the free movement of goods, the fundamental rights of freedom of expression and to protest (not mentioned by the Court but a general principle of law),[33] and the cost of funding such operations. Lord Slynn took these considerations into account when applying the Article 36 TFEU derogation in the British case of *ITF*.[34] ITF exported live animals from the port of Shoreham in West Sussex, but these exports were met with much opposition from animal rights protesters.[35] Ultimately the Chief Constable of the Sussex Police told ITF that he would permit ITF only two sailings a week, due to the expense of the policing operation. ITF argued that this decision made its business uneconomic and contravened Article 34 TFEU.

In considering the public-policy defence raised by the Chief Constable, Lord Slynn gave a broad definition of public policy, broader than any articulated by the Court of Justice. He said that quantitative restrictions 'justified on grounds of public policy include not just situations where there is something inherently bad about the activity itself which justifies the restriction but also where the broader requirements of public policy, here the maintenance of public order,[36] justify steps being taken which so long as proportionate may have a restrictive effect'.[37] The House of Lords accepted that the Chief Constable of Sussex had carried out this exercise effectively and that the restrictions on free movement were proportionate.

The Court of Justice itself was forced to engage in such a balancing act in *Schmidberger*.[38] An environmental association, Transitforum Austria Tirol, organized a demonstration blocking a stretch of the Brenner Motorway (the A13, the major transit route for trade between Northern Europe and Italy) for 30 hours, to draw attention to the threat to the environment and public health posed by the constant increase in the movement of heavy goods vehicles on the motorway.[39] Schmidberger, a German

---

[31] Case C–265/95 *Commission* v. *France* [1997] ECR I–6959, para. 35.   [32] Para. 65.

[33] Cases C–23/93 *TV10* v. *Commissariaat voor de Media* [1994] ECR I–4795; C–260/89 *ERT* v. *DEP* [1991] ECR I–2925; and C–368/95 *Vereinigte Familiapress Zeitungsverlags- und vertriebs GmbH* v. *Heinrich Bauer Verlag* [1997] ECR I–3689, para. 24.

[34] *R.* v. *Chief Constable of Sussex, ex p. International Trader's Ferry Ltd (ITF)* [1999] 1 All ER 129, noted by C. Barnard and I. Hare (1997) 60 *MLR* 394 and (2000) 63 *MLR* 581.

[35] Unlike *Cullet*, *ITF* concerned largely peaceful and lawful protest, not by those objecting to the consequences of the single market, but by those concerned about animal rights.

[36] Reflecting the French 'ordre public'. See also Lenz AG's Opinion and para. 56 of the judgment in Case C–265/95 *Commission* v. *France* [1997] ECR I–6959 (noted M. Jarvis (1998) 35 *CMLRev.* 1371, 1381).

[37] *R.* v. *Chief Constable of Sussex* [1999] 1 All ER 129, 143j.

[38] Case C–112/00 *Schmidberger* [2003] ECR I–5659.

[39] This is a matter of serious concern for the Tyrolean authorities, which tried to ban all heavy goods vehicles over 7.5 tonnes carrying certain goods (e.g., logs, cork, stone, vehicles) from the A12 Inntal motorway (IP/03/984) but were stopped by the Court: Case C–320/03 R *Commission* v. *Austria I* [2003] ECR

transport company, sought damages for the losses it suffered because its lorries were not able to use the motorway.

Following *Commission* v. *France*, the Court said the state's failure to ban this demonstration breached Articles 34–5 TFEU, read together with Article 4(3) TEU.[40] However, the Austrian authorities justified their (in)action on the ground of the fundamental rights of the demonstrators to freedom of expression and freedom of assembly guaranteed by the ECHR and the national constitution, principles which the Court recognized formed an integral part of the general principles of EU law.[41] The Court continued that 'since both the [Union] and its Member States are required to respect fundamental rights, the protection of those rights is a legitimate interest which, in principle, justifies a restriction of the obligations imposed by [Union] law, even under a fundamental freedom guaranteed by the Treaty such as the free movement of goods'.[42] In other words, the Court, like the House of Lords, took the need to protect the fundamental rights as the reason for restricting freedom of movement; unlike the House of Lords the Court did not see fundamental rights as constituting the express public-policy derogation.[43] Instead, it saw fundamental rights as a free-standing public-interest (or 'mandatory') requirement.

However, since the two human rights at stake, described by the Court as 'fundamental pillars of a democratic society',[44] were not absolute, the Court recognized that their exercise could be restricted, provided that 'the restrictions in fact correspond to objectives of general interest and do not, taking account of the aim of the restrictions, constitute disproportionate and unacceptable interference, impairing the very substance of the rights guaranteed'.[45] The Court then engaged in a balancing act to determine whether a fair balance had been struck between the competing interests.[46]

It noted a number of factors which distinguished *Schmidberger* from *Commission* v. *France*: the demonstration took place following a request for authorization as required by national law and after the Austrian authorities had decided to allow it to go ahead;[47] the obstacle to free movement was limited (a single event, on a single route, lasting for 30 hours) by comparison with 'both the geographic scale and the intrinsic seriousness' of the disruption caused in the French case;[48] the demonstrators were motivated by a desire to express their opinion on a matter of public importance and not by a desire to restrict trade in goods of a particular type or from a particular source;[49] and various administrative and supporting measures had been taken by the Austrian authorities to limit the disruption to road traffic, including an extensive publicity campaign launched well in advance by the media and the motoring organizations, both in Austria and in neighbouring countries, as well as the designation of alternative routes.[50] The Court concluded that this isolated incident did not give rise to a general climate of insecurity such as to have a dissuasive effect on intra-Union trade flows as a whole, by contrast to the serious and repeated disruptions to public order at issue in *Commission* v. *France*.[51]

I–7929; and the judgment in Case C–320/03 *Commission* v. *Austria I* [2005] ECR I–9871. See, more recently, where the revised Austrian scheme was also found disproportionate: Case C–28/09 *Commission* v. *Austria II* [2011] ECR I–13525.

[40] Para. 64.   [41] Paras. 71–3.   [42] Para. 74.
[43] Cf. Case C–36/02 *Omega Spielhallen* [2004] ECR I–9609.   [44] Para. 79.
[45] Para. 80.   [46] Para. 81.   [47] Para. 84.   [48] Para. 85.
[49] Para. 86.   [50] Para. 87.   [51] Para. 88.

The Court also accepted the Austrian argument that all the alternative solutions (banning the protest altogether, limiting the location and duration of the protest) would have risked reactions which would have been difficult to control and would have been liable to cause much more serious disruption to intra-Union trade and public order, such as unauthorized demonstrations and confrontation between supporters and opponents of the group organizing the demonstration, or acts of violence on the part of the demonstrators who considered that the exercise of their fundamental rights had been infringed.[52] Therefore, the Court concluded that the fact that the Austrian authorities had not banned the demonstration was compatible with Articles 34–5 TFEU, read together with Article 4(3) TEU.[53]

(b) The Monti Regulation

Following the Court's ruling in *Commission* v. *France*, the Council adopted the so-called 'Monti I' Regulation 2679/98,[54] designed to set up an intervention mechanism to safeguard free trade in the single market. This provides that State A can complain to the Commission about obstacles to the free movement of goods which are attributable to State B—either through action or inaction[55]—where the obstacles lead to serious disruption of the free movement of goods, cause serious loss to the individuals affected, and require immediate action.[56] State B must then explain the action it has taken, or proposes to take, to address the problem. State B must also 'take all necessary and proportionate measures so that the free movement of goods is assured in the territory of the Member State in accordance with the Treaty'. It must also inform the Commission of the action which its authorities have taken or intend to take.[57]

However, all of this is subject to the fundamental rights recognized in Article 2. This provides that:

This Regulation may not be interpreted as affecting in any way the exercise of fundamental rights, as recognised in Member States, including the right or freedom to strike. These rights may also include the right or freedom to take other actions covered by the specific industrial relations systems in Member States.

No reference is made in this regulation to compensation for those affected by these serious obstacles to trade.[58] *Schmidberger* suggests that the Court will give Member States a wide margin of discretion when deciding what action to take in such cases and will usually not try to second-guess Member States' decisions.

---

[52] Case C–112/00 *Schmidberger* [2003] ECR I–5659, para. 92.   [53] Para. 94.

[54] [1998] OJ L337/8. See also the Resolution of the Council and of the Representatives of the Governments of the Member States meeting within the Council of 7 Dec. 1998 ([1998] OJ L337/10), which encourages the Court to adopt an expedited procedure in respect of cases arising under Reg. 2679/98. For further details see <http://ec.europa.eu/growth/single-market/barriers-to-trade/physical/index_en.htm>.

[55] 'Inaction' is defined in Art. 1(2) as covering the case when the competent authorities of a Member State, in the presence of an obstacle caused by actions taken by private individuals, fail to take all necessary and proportionate measures within their powers with a view to removing the obstacle and ensuring the free movement of goods in their territory.

[56] Art. 1(1).

[57] Art. 3. The use of this procedure, 'which is designed to bring as speedy an end as possible to obstacles to the free movement of goods between Member States', is not a precondition to bringing an Art. 258 TFEU action: Case C–320/03 *Commission* v. *Austria* [2005] ECR I–7929, para. 35. See also the ill-fated Monti II proposal discussed in Ch. 7, COM(2012) 130.

[58] See the Commission's Report on the application of Reg. 2679/98, COM(2001) 160.

4. PUBLIC SECURITY

In the past the Court has been more sympathetic to arguments based on public security than to those based on public policy, as *Campus Oil*[59] demonstrates. Ireland, a country which is totally dependent on imports for its supplies of petroleum products, required importers of these products to buy a certain proportion of their needs from a state-owned oil refinery at prices fixed by the Irish government based on the costs incurred by the refinery. Ireland justified this requirement on the basis of public security. The Court agreed. It recognized that because of the exceptional importance of petroleum products as an energy source in the modern economy, an interruption in supplies, with the resultant dangers for the country's existence, could seriously affect public security.[60] Given that Ireland's law served the purpose of public security, the fact that it also served objectives of an economic nature was not important. The Court said that 'the aim of ensuring a minimum supply of petroleum products at all times was to be regarded as transcending purely economic considerations'.[61]

Yet, in a highly interdependent world, a nation's ability to hold its own petrol supplies would not be enough to make it independent in a time of crisis. The Court recognized this in *Commission* v. *Greece*,[62] where it was more sceptical of the public-security arguments raised by the Greek government. Greece wanted to have minimum holdings of petroleum products on its territory.[63] Rather than storing petrol itself, it required petrol companies to hold minimum stocks of petrol at their own installations. This extremely onerous obligation was mitigated by the fact that these companies could transfer the storage obligation to refineries established in Greece, but only on condition that the marketing companies had bought a large quantity of petroleum products from those refineries in the previous calendar year. This grandfather clause had the effect of making the marketing of petroleum products from other Member States more difficult, since, if the marketing companies bought their products from foreign refineries, the marketing companies would not be able to benefit from transferring the storage obligation. For this reason the Court of Justice found that the national rule breached Article 34 TFEU.

The Greek government's defence was based on public security. It argued that the refineries' fundamental right to economic freedom would be excessively restricted if they were obliged to assume the marketing companies' obligation to store minimum stocks of petrol without benefiting from the marketing companies' obligation to purchase their supplies from the refinery in return. The Court rejected this defence, observing that these arguments were 'purely economic', which could never serve as a justification.[64]

However, the broad approach to public security seen in *Campus Oil* can also be detected in *Richardt*,[65] a case concerning strategically sensitive goods. Luxembourg law required a special transit licence for the import and export of goods of a strategic nature. Richardt imported a unit for the production of bubble memory circuits from the USA into France and then transported it into Luxembourg before exporting it to Russia. The unit

---

[59] Case 72/83 *Campus Oil* [1984] ECR 2727. See also the *Golden Share* cases, Case C–503/99 *Commission* v. *Belgium* [2002] ECR I–4809; Case C–483/99 *Commission* v. *France* [2002] ECR I–4781; Case C–463/00 *Commission* v. *Spain* [2003] ECR I–4581, considered in Ch. 14.

[60] Para. 34.   [61] Para. 35.   [62] Case C–398/98 *Commission* v. *Greece* [2001] ECR I–7915.

[63] This law was based on Dir. 68/414/EEC ([1968] OJ Spec. Ed. (II) 586), now Dir. 2006/67/EC ([2006] OJ L217/8).

[64] Para. 30.

[65] Case C–367/89 *Criminal Proceedings against Aimé Richardt and Les Accessoires Scientifique SNC* [1991] ECR I–4621. See also Case C–70/94 *Fritz Werner Industrie-Ausrüstungen GmbH* v. *Federal Republic of Germany* [1995] ECR I–3189 concerning dual use goods.

was seized on public-security grounds by the Luxembourg authorities because Richardt did not have a transit licence. The Court said that because the concept of public security covered both a state's internal and external security, the importation, exportation, and transit of strategic goods could affect the public security of a Member State.[66] For this reason, Luxembourg was entitled to make the transit of goods, described as strategic material, subject to special authorization[67] in order to verify the nature of the goods. However, the Court did add that seizure of goods which did not have this authorization might be considered disproportionate in a case where the return of goods to their state of origin would have sufficed.[68]

In addition to the specific public-security derogation found in Article 36 TFEU, the Treaty also contains some more general provisions in respect of public security. Article 346(1)(b) TFEU provides that Member States can take measures necessary for the protection of the essential interests of its security which are connected with the production of or trade in arms, munitions, and war material, although such measures cannot adversely affect the conditions of competition in the common market regarding products which are not intended for specifically military purposes.[69] Further, the Court has insisted that it is for a Member State seeking to take advantage of Article 346 TFEU to prove that it is necessary to have recourse to that derogation to protect its essential security interests.[70] Therefore, in *Commission* v. *Italy* the Court ruled that Italy could not rely on Article 346 TFEU to justify its refusal to apply customs duties on imports of military material coming from third countries on the ground that that military material would cost more. Finally, the Court has always maintained that, as a derogation, Article 346 TFEU is narrowly construed.[71] However, in the UK's New Settlement deal,[72] section C.5 provides:

> Article 4(2) of the Treaty on European Union confirms that national security remains the sole responsibility of each Member State. This does not constitute a derogation from Union law and should therefore not be interpreted restrictively. In exercising their powers, the Union institutions will fully respect the national security responsibility of the Member States.

Article 347 TFEU says that Member States must consult each other with a view to taking together the steps needed to prevent the functioning of the common market being affected by measures which a Member State may be called upon to take in the event of serious internal disturbances affecting the maintenance of law and order, in the event of war, serious international tension constituting a threat of war, or in order to carry out obligations it has accepted for the purpose of maintaining peace and international security.

If measures taken in the circumstances referred to in Articles 346–7 TFEU have the effect of distorting the conditions of competition in the common market, Article 348 TFEU provides that, together with the state concerned, the Commission must examine how these measures can be adjusted to the rules laid down in the Treaty. By way of

---

[66] Case C–367/89 *Richardt* [1991] ECR I–4621, para. 22.   [67] Para. 23.   [68] Para. 24.

[69] See also the Commission's Interpretative Communication on the application of Art. 296 of the Treaty (now Art. 346 TFEU) in the field of defence-related procurement, COM(2006) 779. Art. 346(1)(b) TFEU cannot be used to justify a derogating measure when purchasing material for civilian and possibly military use: Case C–615/10 *Insinööritoimisto InsTiimi Oy* v. *Puolustusvoimat* EU:C:2012:324, para. 39.

[70] Case C–239/06 *Commission* v. *Italy (duty-free imports of military equipment)* [2009] ECR I–11913, para. 50. See also Case C–414/97 *Commission* v. *Spain* [1999] ECR I–5585.

[71] Case C–239/06 *Commission* v. *Italy (duty-free imports of military equipment)* [2009] ECR I–11913, para. 47. See also the earlier cases in the field of sex discrimination: Case C–273/97 *Sirdar* [1999] ECR I–7403; Case C–285/98 *Kreil* [2000] ECR I–69; and Case C–186/01 *Dory* [2003] ECR I–2479.

[72] EU Council, 18–19 February 2016.

derogation from the procedure laid down in Articles 258–9 TFEU, the Commission or any Member State may bring the matter directly before the Court of Justice if they consider that another Member State is making improper use of the powers provided for in Articles 346–7 TFEU.

5. THE PROTECTION OF HEALTH AND LIFE OF HUMANS, ANIMALS, OR PLANTS

5.1 Human Health

(a) Level of scrutiny

The protection of health and life of humans, animals, or plants is the derogation most frequently invoked by the Member States and 'ranks foremost among the assets or interests protected by Article 36 TFEU'.[73] In the absence of harmonization,[74] the Court has ruled that each Member State has the right to determine the level of health protection desired for its citizens,[75] taking into account various factors such as the climate in the state,[76] the normal diet of the population, and its state of health.[77] However, while the Court recognizes that 'the health and life of humans rank foremost among the property interests protected by Article [36 TFEU]',[78] it is suspicious of attempts by Member States to use health protection as a means of affording a disguised restriction on trade. It therefore requires Member States not only to produce evidence that they have genuine health concerns,[79] which the Court will scrutinize carefully,[80] but also to demonstrate the existence of a seriously considered health policy.[81]

The intensity of this scrutiny can be seen in the *Beer Purity* case.[82] The German government banned the marketing of beer containing all additives (not just the additives for which there was concrete evidence of risks) on the grounds that Germans drank a lot of beer and the long-term effect of additives was not known. The Court said that the German rule could not be justified. Having examined the findings of international scientific research, the work of the Union's scientific committee for food, and the codex alimentarius of the United Nations and the World Health Organization (WHO), it found

---

[73] Case C–333/14 *Scotch Whisky Association* EU:C:2015:845, para. 35.

[74] See, e.g., Case 97/83 *Criminal Proceedings against Melkunie* [1984] ECR 2367, para. 18.

[75] Case 97/83 *Criminal Proceedings against Melkunie* [1984] ECR 2367, para. 18.

[76] Case 54/85 *Ministère public* v. *Mirepoix* [1986] ECR 1067, para. 15.

[77] Case 94/83 *Criminal Proceedings against Albert Heijn BV* [1984] ECR 3263, para. 16 (pesticides); cf. Case 178/84 *Commission* v. *Germany* [1987] ECR 1227, para. 48.

[78] See, e.g., Case C–320/93 *Lucien Ortscheit GmbH* v. *Eurim-Pharm Arzneimittel GmbH* [1994] ECR I–5243, para. 16; Case C–170/04 *Rosengren* v. *Riksåklagaren* [2007] ECR I–4071, para. 39.

[79] Case 90/86 *Criminal Proceedings against Zoni* [1988] ECR 4285 (because there was no evidence that pasta made from common wheat contained chemical additives or colourants, there was no need to exclude such pasta); Case 274/87 *Commission* v. *Germany* [1989] ECR 229 (because evidence that protein levels in Germany were more than adequate there was no need to restrict the import of a product with lower nutritional value to ensure a sufficient intake of protein); cf. Case 97/83 *Criminal Proceedings against Melkunie* [1984] ECR 2367 (because evidence that the risk of active coliform bacteria in milk could be a real source of danger to human health it was legitimate to impose a requirement seeking to exclude these bacteria); Case C–473/98 *Toolex Alpha AB* [2000] ECR I–5681 (there was 'hard' evidence that the carcinogenic effect of trichloroethylene upon the kidneys of a rat also occurs in humans).

[80] See, e.g., Case 118/86 *Openbaar Ministerie* v. *Nertsvoederfabriek Nederland BV* [1987] ECR 3883, para. 14.

[81] Case 40/82 *Commission* v. *UK (turkeys)* [1984] ECR 2793, para. 38. See also Case C–333/14 *Scotch Whisky Association* EU:C:2015:845, paras. 34–5.

[82] Case 178/84 *Commission* v. *Germany* [1987] ECR 1227.

that the additives did not present a risk to public health. It also noted that the German government's policy was inconsistent because Germany permitted the use of these same additives in other drinks.

A similar degree of close scrutiny of the public-health defence can be found in *DocMorris*.[83] German law prohibited sales of medicinal products by mail order (in this case over the Internet) with the result that in Germany prescription and non-prescription medicines could be sold only in pharmacists' shops. While the Court accepted that there were public-health grounds for restricting the provision of prescription medicines to pharmacies, this was not the case with non-prescription medicines. In the case of prescription medicines the Court said that given the risks attached to the use of these products, the need to be able to check the authenticity of doctors' prescriptions and to ensure that the medicine was handed over either to the customer directly or to another authorized person, Germany could justify a prohibition on mail-order sales. For good measure the Court added that given the real possibility of the labelling of a medicinal product bought in another Member State being in a language other than the buyer's, this might have more harmful consequences in the case of prescription medicines.[84]

Similar considerations did not apply in the case of non-prescription medicines. The Court noted the convenience of being able to place the order from the home or the office. It also recognized that, as regards incorrect use of the medicine, the risk could be reduced through an increase in the number of online interactive features which the customer had to use before being able to proceed to a purchase. As regards possible abuse, the Court said that it was not apparent that, for persons wishing to acquire non-prescription medicines unlawfully, purchase in a traditional pharmacy was more difficult than an Internet purchase.

In other cases the scrutiny is applied at the proportionality stage. For example, in *Humanplasma*[85] the Austrian authorities banned the import of blood unless the donations were made without any payment having been made, even in terms of covering costs. While the Court recognized that the Austrian law could be justified on the grounds of ensuring that blood and blood products marketed in Austria were of high quality and safe and that the approach encouraged voluntary and unpaid blood donations, it found that the rules were not proportionate. This was because since each donation had to be tested the requirement to make a blood donation without any costs was not necessary to ensure the quality and safety of the blood. In reaching this conclusion, the Court drew on the practice of various Member States which allow blood donors' costs to be introduced and the fact that under the relevant directive 'small tokens, refreshments and reimbursements of travel costs connected with the donation are compatible with voluntary, non-remunerated donation'.

(b) Scientific uncertainty and the precautionary principle

If the scientific evidence about the health risks of a particular product is uncertain then Member States can decide what degree of health protection they intend to assure, having regard to the requirements of the free movement of goods within the Union.[86] This can be seen in *Sandoz*,[87] where the Dutch authorities refused to grant authorization for the

---

[83] Case C–322/01 *0800 DocMorris NV* [2003] ECR I–14887. See further Ch. 5.   [84] Para. 119.
[85] Case C–421/09 [2010] ECR I–12869.
[86] Case 174/82 *Officier van Justitie* v. *Sandoz* [1983] ECR 2445, para. 16; Case 53/80 *Officier van Justitie* v. *Koninklijke Kaasfabriek Eyssen BV* [1981] ECR 409; Case C–121/00 *Criminal Proceedings against Walter Hahn* [2002] ECR I–9193, para. 45 (listeria).
[87] Case 174/82 [1983] ECR 2445.

importation of muesli bars with added vitamins from Germany (where they were lawfully sold). Given the uncertainties in scientific research about vitamins, albeit that vitamins are not harmful in themselves unless consumed in excess,[88] the Court said that the national rules were justified.

In *Commission v. Denmark*[89] the Court explained its approach in terms of the precautionary principle. It confirmed that, following a detailed assessment which reveals that scientific uncertainty persists as to the extent of the risk to human health,[90] Member States could rely on the precautionary principle to take protective measures,[91] without having to wait until the reality and seriousness of the risks were fully demonstrated.[92] These protective measures might be an authorization procedure based on a detailed assessment carried out on a case-by-case basis[93] or, in more extreme cases, a total ban. However, in *Mirepoix*[94] the Court required the Member State to review the prohibition and to allow, 'by means of a procedure that is easily accessible to traders', for exceptions to be made to the rules laid down where it appears that the use of the product is not dangerous to health.

(c) Healthcare services

The Court seems particularly sympathetic to public-health arguments when they are directly related to the functioning of the national healthcare system. For example, in *Evans Medical*[95] the British government refused to grant a licence to an importer of narcotic drugs on the ground that the imports might undermine the sole licensed manufacturer in the UK, jeopardizing the reliability of the supply of a particular drug in the UK. The Court said that such action could be justified on public-health grounds, provided there was no less restrictive way of achieving this objective and that the action was not being taken on economic grounds.

---

[88] Para. 17.   [89] Case C–192/01 *Commission* v. *Denmark* [2003] ECR I–9693, para. 47.

[90] 'Purely hypothetical considerations' are not sufficient to justify measures being taken on the grounds of the precautionary principle: Case C–236/01 *Monsanto Agricoltura* [2003] ECR I–8105.

[91] According to the Commission's Communication on the precautionary principle, COM(2000) 1, 9, the principle will be applied where 'scientific evidence is insufficient, inconclusive or uncertain and there are indications through preliminary objective scientific evaluation that there are reasonable grounds for concern that the potentially dangerous effects on the environment, human, animal or plant health may be inconsistent with the chosen level of protection'. See also Case C–157/96 *R.* v. *Ministry of Agriculture, Fisheries and Food (MAFF), ex p. NFU* [1998] ECR I–2211, para. 63, where the precautionary principle was first used by the Court, considered further in Ch. 15.

[92] Protective measures 'founded on mere suppositions which are not yet scientifically verified' cannot, however, justify Member State action: Case C–236/01 *Monsanto* [2003] ECR I–8105, para. 106. In Case T–13/99 *Pfizer Animal Health* v. *Council* [2002] ECR II–3305, when talking about the action that the *Union* could take on the ground of health protection, the General Court said 'under the precautionary principle the [Union] institutions are entitled, in the interests of human health to adopt, on the basis of as yet incomplete scientific knowledge, protective measures which may seriously harm legally protected positions' (para. 170) but the Union institution must examine carefully and impartially all the relevant aspects of the individual case (para. 171) basing any decision on 'scientific advice founded on the principles of excellence, transparency and independence' (para. 172).

[93] Case C–192/01 *Commission* v. *Denmark* [2003] ECR I–9693, para. 56. The Court will scrutinize any risk assessment carefully: Case C–319/05 *Commission* v. *Germany (garlic capsule)* [2007] ECR I–9811, paras. 91–5. The case law on vitamins has now been superseded by the Food Supplements Dir. 2002/46 ([2002] OJ L183/51) challenged in Joined Cases C–154 and 155/04 *Alliance for Natural Health* [2005] ECR I–6451, considered in Ch. 15.

[94] Case 54/85 *Ministère public* v. *Mirepoix* [1986] ECR 1067, paras. 16–17.

[95] Case C–324/93 [1995] ECR I–563. See also Case C–320/93 *Ortscheit* v. *Eurim-Pharm Arzneimittel GmbH* [1994] ECR I–5243; Joined Cases 266 and 267/87 *R.* v. *Royal Pharmaceutical Society of Great Britain, ex p. Association of Pharmaceutical Importers* [1989] ECR 1295.

In *Monteil*[96] the Court went even further and raised the public-health derogation to a presumption of legality. It said that a pharmacists' monopoly in France on retail sales of medicinal products could be 'presumed to constitute an appropriate way of protecting public health'. However, it did add that importers should be able to produce evidence to show that its products did not involve any serious danger to public health. More recently, in *Commission* v. *Germany (pharmacies for hospitals)*,[97] the Court said a German rule requiring pharmacies supplying medicinal products to hospitals to be situated close to that hospital was a proportionate public-health requirement: the rules were appropriate because they ensured a reliable supply of good quality health products to the hospital,[98] and they were necessary because they ensured that there was a pharmacist responsible for the supply of the medicines who could be available quickly.[99]

But there are limits to the Court's sympathy with the demands experienced by national health systems, as *Decker*[100] shows. Under Luxembourg law the authorities were required to give prior authorization before any medical product (in this case glasses) could be bought abroad while no such authorization was required if the goods were purchased in Luxembourg. The Court said the rule breached Article 34 TFEU and rejected Luxembourg's public-health arguments based on ensuring quality of treatment. It said that the Directives on Mutual Recognition of Diplomas[101] meant that an optician in another Member State had equivalent qualifications to those in Luxembourg and so was properly qualified; and the fact that the glasses were bought on a prescription from an ophthalmologist guaranteed the protection of public health.[102]

5.2 Animal Health

Article 36 TFEU protects not only human health but also animal health.[103] This was the justification raised by Denmark in *Bluhme*[104] to prohibit the import of any bee into the Danish island of Læsø except the Læsø brown bee. The Court said that measures to preserve an indigenous animal population with distinct characteristics contributed to the maintenance of biodiversity by ensuring the survival of the population of the Læsø brown bee. Because the prohibition on the import of other bees protected the life of the Læsø brown bee, the rules were justified under Article 36 TFEU.[105]

In the light of *Bluhme*, can it be said that the protection of health derogation includes environmental protection? This was of particular significance when the Court maintained a clear distinction in the scope of application between the express derogations and the broader, judicially developed, mandatory requirements which include environmental protection (see fig. 4.1). The case law is not clear on this point. *FFAD*[106] suggests that

---

[96] Case C–60/90 [1991] ECR I–1547, para. 43.
[97] Case C–141/07 *Commission* v. *Germany (pharmacies for hospitals)* [2008] ECR I–6935.
[98] Para. 49.   [99] Para. 56.
[100] Case C–120/95 *Decker* v. *Caisse de Maladie des Employés Privés* [1998] ECR I–1831.
[101] Considered further in Ch. 8.   [102] Paras. 42–4.
[103] Case C–323/93 *Société Civile Agricole du Centre d'Insémination de la Crespelle* v. *Coopérative d'Elevage et d'Insémination Artificielle du Département de la Mayenne* [1994] ECR I–5077; Case C–350/97 *Monsees* v. *Unabhängiger Verwaltungssenat für Kärnten* [1999] ECR I–2921.
[104] Case C–67/97 *Criminal Proceedings against Ditlev Bluhme* [1998] ECR I–8033, para. 19. See also Case C–510/99 *Tridon* [2001] ECR I–7777, para. 52.
[105] Para. 33.
[106] Case C–209/98 *FFAD* v. *Københavns Kommune* [2000] ECR I–3473, para. 48, although cf. the ambiguity in para. 49. See also Case C–203/96 *Chemische Afvalstoffen Dusseldorp BV* v. *Minister van Volkshuisvesting, Ruimtelijke Ordening en Milieubeheer* [1998] ECR I–4075, where the Court seems to suggest that the Art. 36 TFEU derogations and the mandatory requirement of environmental protection are different (para. 49).

environmental protection does not form part of the public-health derogation. The Court said that 'the protection of the environment cannot serve to justify any restriction on exports, particularly in the case of waste destined for recovery'. However, other cases point the opposite way. For example, in *Aher-Waggon*,[107] the Court said that a discriminatory German rule subjecting aircraft which had been registered in another Member State to stricter noise standards than those for equivalent domestic aircraft might be 'justified by considerations of public health *and* environmental protection'.[108]

PreussenElektra[109] also suggests that the public-health derogation might include environmental protection. The case concerned a national law requiring electricity supply undertakings to purchase all of the renewable electricity produced within their area of supply. The Court noted that the use of renewable energy sources for producing electricity was good for protecting the environment insofar as it contributed to the reduction in emissions of greenhouse gases. It then pointed to various Union documents which committed the EU to the greater use of renewable energy sources and added 'that policy is also designed to protect the health and life of humans, animals and plants'.[110] The Court also noted that Article 11 TFEU requires environmental protection to be integrated into the definition and implementation of other Union policies. Without explaining whether the ruling was based on Article 36 TFEU or the mandatory requirements, the Court concluded that 'in the current state of [Union] law' the national law was 'not incompatible with Article [34 TFEU]'. Although the reasoning is not clear, *PreussenElektra* may be authority for the fact that environmental protection is a mandatory requirement, which has long been established (and considered further in Section C, 4), or, more radically, that environmental protection can be read into the Article 36 TFEU public-health derogation.[111]

The latter reading might gain some support from *Commission v. Austria II*,[112] where the Court had to consider whether an Austrian rule prohibiting lorries over 7.5 tonnes carrying certain goods, which could be better carried by rail, from using a section of the A12 motorway could be justified. It said that 'it is apparent from Article [191 TFEU] that the protection of human health is one of the objectives of [Union] policy on the environment … Those objectives are closely linked, in particular in connection with the fight against air pollution, the purpose of which is to limit the dangers to health connected with the deterioration of the environment. The objective of protection of health is therefore already incorporated, in principle, in the objective of protection of the environment'.[113]

6. THE PROTECTION OF NATIONAL TREASURES POSSESSING ARTISTIC, HISTORIC, OR ARCHAEOLOGICAL VALUE

The Court has decided no case on the basis of the national treasures[114] derogation. The defence was, however, raised by the Italian government in *Commission v. Italy (art*

---

[107] Case C–389/96 *Aher-Waggon* v. *Germany* [1998] ECR I–4473, para. 19.

[108] Emphasis added. The Court also noted that the German measures were proportionate because Germany was a densely populated state which attached special importance to ensuring that its population was protected from excessive noise emissions (para. 19); and that limiting noise emissions from aircraft was the most effective and convenient means of combating the noise pollution they created (para. 21). See also Case C–142/05 *Mickelsson* [2009] ECR I–4273, para. 33.

[109] Case C–379/98 *PreussenElektra AG* v. *Schleswag AG* [2001] ECR I–2099.   [110] Para. 75.

[111] See also Case C–573/12 *Ålands vindkraft AB* v. *Energimyndigheten* EU:C:2014:2037, paras. 80–2.

[112] Case C–28/09 *Commission* v. *Austria II* [2011] ECR I–13525.   [113] Para. 122.

[114] Guidance as to the meaning of this term may be derived from Dir. 93/7/EEC on the return of cultural objects unlawfully removed from the territory of a Member State ([1993] OJ L74/74).

treasures).[115] The case concerned an Italian tax on exports of goods having an artistic, historic, archaeological, or ethnographic value. The Court found that since the tax was a charge having equivalent effect to a customs duty (CEE) under Article 30, and not an MEE, Article 36 TFEU did not apply.

The values recognized by this derogation were reinforced by the inclusion of the Title on Culture into the Treaty at Maastricht. Article 167(2) TFEU provides that 'Action by the Union shall be aimed at encouraging cooperation between the Member States' including 'conservation and safeguarding of cultural heritage of European significance'. Nevertheless, the existence of Article 167 TFEU did not persuade the Court in *LIBRO*[116] to extend the national treasures derogation to cover the 'protection of cultural diversity in general'.

More specifically, the objectives of Article 36 TFEU have been buttressed by the adoption of Directive 2014/60/EU on the return of cultural objects unlawfully removed from the territory of a Member State.[117] This directive, along with Regulation 116/2009 on the export of cultural goods from the EU,[118] is not a harmonization measure. Instead, Directive 2014/60 provides for cooperation between the states and a procedure for returning national treasures which have already left the territory of a Member State unlawfully. Regulation 116/2009, by contrast, goes further by setting up uniform preventive controls at the Union's external borders on the export of protected goods to third countries and requires the enforcement agencies to take account of the interests of other Member States.

7. THE PROTECTION OF INDUSTRIAL AND COMMERCIAL PROPERTY

7.1 Introduction

The derogation on the protection of industrial and commercial property covers patents, trade marks, copyright,[119] and other types of design rights. It also covers protection of geographical denominations, which are considered in Case Study 6.1. This derogation is intended to protect private, as opposed to the public, interests found in the other derogations.

Intellectual property rights (IPRs) present a particular challenge to the EU. On the one hand, they serve to encourage innovation. On the other, the specific nature of the property rights—their territoriality[120] and exclusivity[121]—which have traditionally been protected under national law means that their exercise can constitute a significant barrier to inter-state trade.[122] Although there has been harmonization of IP law, for example Directive 2015/2436 on the approximation of the laws of the Member States relating to

---

[115] Case 7/68 [1968] ECR 617.

[116] Case C–531/07 *LIBRO Handelsgesellschaft mbH* [2009] ECR I–3717, paras. 32–3.

[117] [2014] OJ L159/1.   [118] [2009] OJ L39/1.

[119] Copyright will not be discussed in this chapter. It has been the subject of significant harmonization: see W. R. Cornish, D. Llewelyn, and T. Aplin, *Intellectual Property: Patents, Copyright, Trade Marks and Allied Rights*, 8th edn (London: Sweet & Maxwell, 2013).

[120] Case C–9/93 *IHT Internationale Heiztechnik GmbH and Uwe Danzinger* v. *Ideal-Standard GmbH and Wabco Standard GmbH* [1994] ECR I–2789, para. 22.

[121] Patents are the obvious example: for a specific period (usually 20 years) only the patent holder can manufacture and market the patented product in the territory of the Member State that has granted the patent. During this period the rights conferred by the patent can be used even against an independent deviser. After that period, producers can manufacture products in accordance with the patent specification.

[122] Case 24/67 *Parke Davis* v. *Probel* [1968] ECR 55, 71.

trade marks,[123] the many national IPRs represent a serious challenge to the creation of the *single* market.

The Treaty provisions affecting IPRs appear difficult to reconcile. On the one hand, Article 345 TFEU says '[t]he Treaty shall in no way prejudice the rules in Member States governing the system of property ownership'. This is supported by the derogation in the first sentence of Article 36 TFEU concerning 'the protection of industrial and commercial property'. Both these provisions reinforce the maintenance of national IPRs. On the other hand, Article 34 TFEU provides for the free movement of goods. Because this is a fundamental freedom any derogation is narrowly construed.[124] The derogations in Article 36 TFEU are also subject to the caveat in the second sentence: derogations 'shall not constitute a means of arbitrary discrimination or a disguised restriction on trade between Member States' (this is considered further in Section 8). These provisions would point to the setting aside of national IPRs since, by invoking the IPR to keep imported goods out, the IPR holder's action would constitute a quantitative restriction on trade or a measure having equivalent effect.[125]

7.2 The General Principles: Existence and Exercise of IPRs, the Specific Subject Matter of IPRs, and the Doctrine of Exhaustion of Rights

The task has largely fallen to the Court to reconcile the different Treaty provisions with the IP laws of the Member States. The Court began this process in early competition cases, such as *Consten and Grundig*[126] and *Parke Davis*,[127] but soon extended the approach to free movement of goods in cases such as *Deutsche Grammophon*.[128] In these cases the Court distinguished between:

- the *existence* of an IPR (i.e., the conditions and procedures under which the IPR is granted in the Member State), a matter for national law, following Article 345 TFEU (and, to a lesser extent, the first sentence of Article 36 TFEU) and

- its *exercise*, a matter for EU law.

So what falls under the umbrella of existence? In *Deutsche Grammophon*,[129] the Court said:

> Article 36 only admits derogations from that freedom to the extent to which they are justified for the purpose of safeguarding rights which constitute the *specific subject-matter* of such property.

The specific subject matter of the IPR varies according to the type of intellectual property at issue but, in essence, it is the exclusive right of the IPR holder (or another undertaking with its consent) to the first marketing of the product. This gives the IPR holder the opportunity both to gain monopoly profits from putting a product on the market for the first

---

[123] [2015] OJ L336/1.   [124] Case 15/74 *Centrafarm v. Sterling Drug* [1974] ECR 1147, para. 8.

[125] Case 270/80 *Polydor Ltd and RSO Records Inc.* v. *Harlequin Record Shops Ltd and Simons Records Ltd* [1982] ECR 329, para. 7. In addition to the rules on free movement of goods, the Treaty provisions on competition may also affect the exercise of IPRs. In particular, Art. 101 TFEU prohibits anti-competitive behaviour (agreements between undertakings which prevent, restrict, or distort competition) and Art. 102 TFEU prohibits abuse of a dominant position.

[126] Joined Cases 56 and 58/64 *Consten and Grundig* [1966] ECR 299, 345.

[127] Case 24/67 [1968] ECR 55.

[128] Case 78/70 *Deutsche Grammophon* v. *Metro* [1971] ECR 487.

[129] Case 78/70 *Deutsche Grammophon* v. *Metro* [1971] ECR 487, para. 11, emphasis added.

time[130] and to take action against any infringement. In this respect, the first sentence of Article 36 TFEU prevails over both the second sentence of Article 36 TFEU and Article 34 TFEU. However, once the product has been put on the market anywhere in the European Economic Area (EEA),[131] the IPR holder is deemed to have *exhausted* its rights and so the principles of free movement prevail.

The application of these principles can be seen in the following example. XCo, the inventor of Wonderdrug, registers its patent in State A, where it manufactures and markets the drug. If XCo decides to manufacture and market the drug in State A only, then Union law does not apply and national IPR protection prevails (see fig. 6.1(a)). Using national patent law, XCo can prevent anyone else from manufacturing, marketing, or importing the drug.

However, if XCo decides to take advantage of the greater economies of scale offered by EEA-wide sales it would patent Wonderdrug in State B and manufacture and market the drug there itself or through a licensee, YCo. In the absence of EU law, XCo (or its licensees) would use the protection conferred by national patent law to ensure exclusivity in the production and marketing of the drug in each state. In other words, the holders of parallel patents, such as XCo and its licensees, would use their patents to prevent anyone else from selling Wonderdrug in those states, thereby ensuring a monopoly on the market with the resulting price benefits—and rewards—this entails. However, using the IPR in this way ensures absolute territorial protection for the patent holder, partitioning the market on national lines,[132] and insulating each national market from so-called 'parallel' imports from other Member States. Parallel importing occurs when PCo (a middleman) buys Wonderdrug from XCo in State A and imports it into State B, thereby undermining the patent holder's monopoly and introducing some price competition.

The Court of Justice is keen to encourage parallel importing and so the moment that XCo breaks onto the market of another state, EU law—and the doctrines of specific subject matter and exhaustion—applies. The application of EU law means that XCo continues to have the exclusive right to manufacture Wonderdrug and put it on the market for the first time in State A since this is an aspect of the *specific subject matter* of XCo's patent which is protected by EU law. However, once it has put the product on the market in State A, EU law applies, meaning that XCo has *exhausted* its rights in that batch of the drug in respect of the entire EEA. So, if PCo, a parallel importer, buys[133] Wonderdrug in State A where prices are low and parallel imports it into State B where the prices are high, YCo, which is marketing Wonderdrug in State B with XCo's consent, cannot invoke its patent to keep PCo's goods out of State B (see fig. 6.1(b)). The arrival of PCo's goods in State B introduces *intra*-brand competition which should reduce the price differences for the Wonderdrug product between States A and B, to the benefit of State B's consumers.[134] Ultimately this will result in the IPR holder setting the price in all countries at that charged by the IPR holder in the cheapest state. So, parallel importing has the effect of ironing out price differences across the EEA.

Although the example in fig. 6.1(b) is based on the fact that YCo is XCo's licensee, the position would be the same, as the Court pointed out in *HAG II*,[135] if XCo held the patent

---

[130] Case 187/80 *Merck v. Stephar (Merck I)* [1981] ECR 2063: 'That right of first placing a product on the market enables the inventor, by allowing him a monopoly in exploiting the product, to obtain the reward for his creative effort, without, however, guaranteeing that he will obtain such a reward in all circumstances.'

[131] I.e., EU and EEA (Norway, Iceland, and Liechtenstein) countries, as a result of the EEA Agreement.

[132] E.g., Case 19/84 *Pharmon v. Hoechst* [1985] ECR 2281, para. 23.

[133] PCo cannot manufacture the drug: Case C–316/95 *Generics BV v. Smith Kline & French Laboratories Ltd* [1997] ECR I–3929.

[134] Case 104/75 *Adriaan de Peijper, Managing Director of Centrafarm BV* [1976] ECR 613.

[135] Case C–10/89 *HAG II* [1990] ECR I–3711, para. 12.

in State B (as well as in State A) or if YCo was a separate person but 'legally or economically dependent' on XCo. In *Ideal-Standard*[136] the Court said that companies would be economically linked[137] where products were put into circulation by the same undertaking, by a licensee, by a parent company, by a subsidiary of the same group, or by an exclusive distributor.[138] At the heart of this case law lies consent: XCo has consented to YCo putting Wonderdrug on the market.

The corollary of this is that if there is no consent between the parties, then there will be no exhaustion of rights. If, for example, XCo holds the patent for Wonderdrug in State A and ZCo holds the patent for Wonderdrug in State C and there is no consent (i.e., no economic or legal links between the two companies—they are independent competitors in trade), then ZCo can continue to use the IP law of State C to keep PCo's goods imported from State A out of State C (see fig. 6.1(c)).[139]

A number of these problems would be resolved by the establishment of a unitary patent, i.e., a legal title granted by the European Patent Office (EPO) that would provide uniform protection across all EU countries on a one-stop-shop basis. There have long been plans for such a possibility—which would sit alongside national patents and a classical European patent taking effect in one or more European Patent Convention Contracting States which do not participate in the scheme, such as Switzerland, Turkey, Norway, and Iceland. However, disputes over the language regime led Spain and Italy (and later Croatia) to refuse to participate in the proposal, which went ahead on the basis of enhanced cooperation.[140] Italy subsequently decided to participate. The EU patent package will enter into force as soon as 13 states, including France, Germany, and the UK, have ratified it.[141]

So far we have focused on patents. Trade marks, such as Levis, Mercedes, and Fosters, function somewhat differently to patents. Trade marks are intended to protect the goodwill associated with the trademarked product and to inform the customer that the product is of a specific kind and not a copy (guarantee of origin). However, the Court has applied the principles of specific subject matter and exhaustion of rights to trade marks as well as to patents. So, for example, in *Centrafarm* v. *Winthrop*[142] the Court said that the specific subject matter of a trade mark is:

> the guarantee that the owner of the trade mark has the exclusive right to use that trade mark, for the purpose of putting products protected by the trade mark into circulation for the first time, *and* is therefore intended to protect him against competitors wishing to take advantage of the status and the reputation of the trade mark by selling products illegally bearing that trade mark.

On the facts of the case, the Sterling Winthrop group, subsidiaries of Sterling Drug, held the trade mark Negram in the UK and in the Netherlands. Centrafarm parallel imported the drug from the UK into the Netherlands, where the Dutch subsidiary of

---

[136] Case C–9/93 *IHT Internationale Heiztechnik GmbH and Uwe Danzinger* v. *Ideal-Standard GmbH and Wabco Standard GmbH* [1994] ECR I–2789.

[137] Para. 34.   [138] Para. 34.

[139] Case C–173/98 *Sebago Inc. and Ancienne Maison Dubois & Fils SA* v. *G-B Unic SA* [1999] ECR I–4103, paras. 19–20; Case C–10/89 *HAG II* [1990] ECR I–3711, para. 15.

[140] Reg. (EU) No. 1257/2012 of the European Parliament and of the Council implementing enhanced cooperation in the area of the creation of unitary patent protection ([2012] OJ L361/12); Council Reg. (EU) No. 1260/2012 implementing enhanced cooperation in the area of the creation of unitary patent protection with regard to the applicable translation arrangements ([2012] OJ L361/89).

[141] For details of the current position, see <http://www.epo.org/law-practice/unitary.html>.

[142] Case 16/74 *Centrafarm* v. *Winthrop* [1974] ECR 1183, para. 8, emphasis added.

(a) Exercise of Rights in one Member State only

XCo registers its patent for Wonderdrug in State
A only.

- Only XCo can manufacture and market
  Wonderdrug in State A
- XCo can use the patent to keep Wonderdrug
  manufactured in other Member States out
  of State A

**(b) Exercise of Rights in more than one
Member State: consent**

XCo registers its patent for Wonderdrug in State A and also consents to YCo, XCo's licensee,
putting the patented product on the market in State B.

- Exhaustion of rights:
  YCo cannot use
  its patent to keep
  Wonderdrug out
  of State B when
  imported from State A
  by a third party parallel
  importer, PCo.

**(c) Exercise of Rights in
more than one Member State: no consent**

XCo registers its patent for Wonderdrug in State A. ZCo has registered the patent for Wonderdrug
in State C. XCo has no economic or legal links with ZCo.

- No exhaustion of
  rights: ZCo can use
  its patent to keep
  goods out of State C
  when imported
  from the State A by
  PCo.

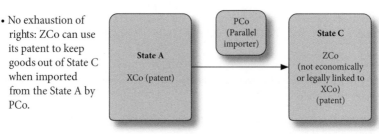

Fig. 6.1 The application of EU law to the exercise of a national patent

Sterling Drug invoked its trade mark to keep out the goods. The Court said that the exclusion of Centrafarm's products was not justified to guarantee the 'essence' of the exclusive right flowing from the trade mark.[143] Negram had been lawfully marketed in the UK with the consent of the trade mark holder, therefore the trade mark holder's rights had been exhausted.[144] This meant that the trade mark holder could not invoke national law to oppose the sale in that state (the Netherlands) of a product which had been marketed under the trade mark in another state (the UK) by the trade mark owner or with his consent.

The principles of specific subject matter and exhaustion of rights have been incorporated into Directive 2015/2436 on the approximation of the laws of the Member States relating to trade marks.[145] For this reason the Court said in *Bristol-Myers Squibb*[146] that 'the Directive must be interpreted in the light of the Treaty rules on the free movement of goods and in particular Article 36'. In particular, Article 10 of the directive concerns exclusive rights and the question of the specific subject matter of the trade mark; Article 15 concerns the doctrine of exhaustion of rights.

7.3 Quasi-IP Cases

The IPRs considered above are all examples of industrial and commercial property under Article 36 TFEU. However, as Cornish et al. put it,[147] at a certain moment IP shades off into surrounding forms of civil liability, which in the UK includes non-statutory liability for passing off and breach of confidence and, in continental thought, some aspects of unfair competition law.[148] In this area the Court tends to apply its *Cassis* line of case law,[149] considering the quasi-IP issues under the mandatory requirements of consumer protection or unfair commercial practice[150] rather than through the principles it has developed under Article 36 TFEU.

Sometimes the Court finds that the consumer protection justification is made out. For example, in *Beele*[151] the Court said that national case law prohibiting the precise imitation of someone else's product which was likely to cause confusion could protect consumers.[152] More usually, however, the Court finds no public-interest justification, as *Pall*[153] demonstrates. Dahlhausen marketed blood filters in Germany which it had imported from Italy. The Italian producer put the trade mark 'Miropore' on the filters and packaging. It also added the symbol ® indicating that 'Miropore' was a registered trade mark. Pall, a competitor, objected to this, arguing that the symbol constituted misleading advertising, contrary to German rules on unfair competition on the ground that 'Miropore' was not registered in Germany. The Court noted that a national rule enabling a trader to prevent

[143] Case 16/74 *Centrafarm* v. *Winthrop* [1974] ECR 1183, para. 11.
[144] As the Court said in Case C–10/89 *HAG II* [1990] ECR I–3711, para. 15, 'the determinant factor is the [presence or] absence of any consent on the part of the proprietor of the trade mark'.
[145] Repealing and replacing Dir. 2008/95, which in turn repealed and replaced Dir. 89/104. It is also possible to register an EU trade mark, which, like the unitary patent, enables undertakings 'by means of one procedural system [to] obtain [EU] trade marks to which uniform protection is given and which produce their effects throughout the entire area of the [EU]': Reg. 207/2009 ([2009] OJ L78/1).
[146] Joined Cases C–427, 429 and 436/93 [1996] ECR I–3457, para. 27.
[147] W. R. Cornish, D. Llewelyn, and T. Aplin, *Intellectual Property: Patents, Copyright, Trade Marks and Allied Rights*, 8th edn (London: Sweet & Maxwell, 2013), 749.
[148] See, e.g., the German Law against Unfair Competition in Case C–238/89 *Pall Corp.* v. *Dahlhausen & Co.* [1990] ECR I–4827.
[149] See further Ch. 4.   [150] See further Section C.
[151] Case 6/81 *IBV Industrie Diensten Groep* v. *J.A. Beele Handelmaatschappij* [1982] ECR 707.
[152] Para. 9. See also Case C–313/94 *Fratelli Graffione SNC* v. *Ditta Fransa* [1996] ECR I–6039.
[153] Case C–238/89 *Pall Corp.* v. *P.J. Dahlhausen & Co.* [1990] ECR I–4827.

the marketing of a product bearing the symbol ®, where the product had not been reg-istered in Germany, was an indistinctly applicable measure[154] which, like the other re-packaging case law,[155] forced Dahlhausen to change the presentation of its products.[156] The German rule therefore breached Article 34 TFEU. On the question of justification on the ground of consumer protection, the Court said that Pall had not established that the symbol ® was generally understood as indicating that the trade mark was registered in the country in which the goods were marketed. Even assuming that some consumers might have been misled, it said that such a risk could not justify such an obstacle to the free movement of goods, since consumers were more interested in the qualities of the product than in the place of the registration of the trade mark.[157]

8. THE SECOND SENTENCE OF ARTICLE 36 TFEU: ARBITRARY DISCRIMINATION AND A DISGUISED RESTRICTION ON TRADE

All measures for which an Article 36 TFEU derogation is claimed are justifiable only to the extent that they do not 'constitute a means of arbitrary discrimination or a disguised restriction on trade between Member States' under the second sentence of Article 36 TFEU. As we have seen, Article 36(2) TFEU played an important role in the balancing exercise in the IPR cases. It has also been considered in the context of cases involv-ing the other derogations, including public morality, which was at issue in *Henn and Darby*.[158] The case concerned the ban on the import of pornographic material, which the UK defended on the grounds of public morality. However, in the UK there was a discrepancy between the laws of the constituent parts of the UK on indecent or obscene articles. This, the defendants argued, breached the second sentence of Article 36 TFEU. The Court disagreed.[159] It noted that the function of the second sentence of Article 36 TFEU was to prevent restrictions on trade based on one of the Article 36 TFEU derogations from being diverted from their proper purpose and used in such a way as either to create discrimination in respect of goods originating in other Member States or indirectly to protect certain national products. This was not the case with the UK's prohibition. The Court said that since the British laws, taken as a whole, had as their purpose the prohibition of the manufacture and marketing of publications or articles of an indecent or obscene character, there was no breach of the second sentence of Article 36 TFEU.

The Court is particularly suspicious of the public-health defence being used as a disguised restriction on trade. At times this suspicion is justified, as the infamous *Turkeys* case[160] demonstrates. Shortly before Christmas 1981, the UK introduced a slaugh-ter policy to deal with flocks infected with Newcastle disease, a contagious disease affect-ing poultry. Previously the UK had used a vaccination policy, which the other Member States continued to use. At the same time, the UK introduced an import ban on poultry meat and eggs from all other Member States (except Denmark and Ireland) in order to protect animal health since, it said, in the absence of a vaccination policy the British flock would be susceptible to infection from imports.

---

[154] Case C–238/89 *Pall* [1990] ECR I–4827, para. 14.
[155] Case C–315/92 *Clinique* [1994] ECR I–317; Case C–368/95 *Familiapress* [1997] ECR I–3689. See further Ch. 4.
[156] See also Case 16/83 *Prantl* [1984] ECR 1299 on the use of the *Bocksbeutel*, considered in Ch. 4.
[157] Paras. 18–19.   [158] Case 34/79 [1979] ECR 3795.   [159] Para. 21.
[160] Case 40/82 *Commission* v. *UK* [1984] ECR 2793.

Despite these apparently strong health arguments, the Court noted that the circumstances surrounding the ban revealed a rather different picture. It found that there had been a dramatic increase in the number of turkeys imported into the UK, especially from France, and that British turkey producers had lobbied the British government to take action to protect the domestic industry.[161] This action was deliberately timed to prevent imports of turkeys from France for the 1981 Christmas season.[162] Given the lack of consultation with the EU institutions about the change of policy and, in the absence of detailed background scientific work, the Court concluded that the UK measures did not 'form part of a seriously considered health policy'.[163] Instead, it said that the British measures constituted a disguised restriction on imports,[164] since 'the real aim of the 1981 measures was to block, for commercial and economic reasons, imports of poultry products from other Member States, in particular from France'.[165] The Court also considered that the measures were disproportionate: there were less stringent methods for achieving the protection of animal health.[166] Subsequently the French turkey producers sued the British government for the losses they had suffered. Although the Court of Appeal struck out part of their claim,[167] they won £3.5 million in an out-of-court settlement.[168]

Generally, Member States must take equivalent action against their own producers to stand a chance of succeeding with a public-health defence. However, as the Court pointed out in *Rewe-Zentralfinanz*,[169] differential treatment is justifiable if there is a real risk affecting the import which is not present in the domestic product.[170] Therefore, the German authorities could conduct a phytosanitary inspection on imported apples to combat the apple disease, San José scale, where there was a real risk of the disease spreading to German apples in the absence of an inspection.[171] In these circumstances the inspection of imports, but not the domestic products, which were unaffected by the disease, was lawful: it was discriminatory but not arbitrary.

Not only must the second sentence of Article 36 TFEU be respected by the Member States but any measure taken by States must respect the general principles of law; in particular proportionality (considered in Section D) and fundamental human rights (considered in Section E). First, however, we shall examine the mandatory requirements.

C. THE 'MANDATORY' REQUIREMENTS

1. INTRODUCTION

As we have seen, in *Cassis de Dijon* the Court developed an open-ended list of (confusingly named) 'mandatory requirements' (the effectiveness of fiscal supervision, fairness of commercial transactions, protection of the consumer, and public health) to supplement

---

[161] Para. 22. [162] Paras. 23 and 37. [163] Para. 38. [164] Para. 40. [165] Para. 37.

[166] Para. 41. Cf. Case 74/82 *Commission* v. *Ireland* [1984] ECR 317 (there, licensing of poultry imports was in principle lawful).

[167] *Bourgoin* v. *MAFF* [1986] QB 716, in a case which, following Joined Cases C–46 and 48/93 *Brasserie du Pêcheur and Factortame (No. 3)* [1996] ECR I–1029, is probably no longer good law.

[168] HC Debs. vol. 102 col. 116 (WA) 22 Jul. 1986 cited in Weatherill and Beaumont, see n. 10, 538.

[169] Case 4/75 *Rewe-Zentralfinanz* [1975] ECR 843 (San José scale), para. 8. See also Case 42/82 *Commission* v. *France (wine)* [1983] ECR 1013, para. 56; Case 50/85 *Schloh* v. *Auto Contrôle Technique SPRL* [1986] ECR 1855, para. 15.

[170] Case 4/75 *Rewe-Zentralfinanz* [1995] ECR 843, para. 8.

[171] The Court added that effective measures also had to be taken to prevent the distribution of contaminated domestic products.

the Article 36 TFEU derogations. It did this to placate the Member States: its ruling on mutual recognition made significant inroads into states' competence to regulate products traded on their territory. The mandatory requirements were the states' compensation. Soon after *Cassis*,[172] the Court confirmed that mandatory requirements applied only to indistinctly applicable,[173] not distinctly applicable, measures[174] (see fig. 4.1), although, as we have seen, this rigid distinction is breaking down (see fig. 5.1).[175]

Mandatory requirements are now increasingly called 'imperative requirements'[176] or 'overriding requirements in the public interest'[177] or simply 'public interest requirements',[178] to dovetail with the Court's jurisprudence on the free movement of persons,[179] or objective justifications,[180] to reflect the language used both in the field of free movement of workers and indirectly discriminatory national taxes under Article 110 TFEU (see fig. 3.2). They are 'good' reasons put forward by the Member States to justify their conduct,[181] often based on Union policies identified in the Treaty, secondary legislation,[182] and international obligations[183] unrelated to the origin of the goods. As with the derogations under Article 36 TFEU, the mandatory requirements must also be accompanied by appropriate evidence showing that the rules genuinely serve the purposes for which they are intended:[184] mere assertion by the Member State is (usually) not sufficient.[185] Finally, as with the Article 36 TFEU derogations, mandatory requirements are available only in the absence of harmonization.[186]

---

[172] Case 788/79 *Criminal Proceedings against Gilli and Andres* [1980] ECR 2071, para. 6. See also Case 6/81 *Beele* [1982] ECR 707, para. 7; Case C–67/88 *Commission v. Italy* [1990] ECR I–4285, para. 4; Case 94/82 *De Kikvorsch* [1983] ECR 947, para. 6; Case 182/84 *Miro* [1985] ECR 3731, para. 10.

[173] See Joined Cases C–1 and 176/90 *Aragonesa* [1991] ECR I–4151, para. 13: 'whereas according to the Court's case law the question of imperative requirements … cannot arise unless the measure in question applies without distinction to both national and imported products'; and Case C–2/90 *Commission v. Belgium (Walloon waste)* [1992] ECR I–4431, para. 34: 'Imperative requirements can indeed be taken into account only in the case of measures which apply without distinction to both domestic and imported products.'

[174] Case 113/80 *Commission v. Ireland (Irish souvenirs)* [1981] ECR 1625, para. 11; Case 177/83 *Ringelhan* [1984] ECR 3651, para. 19; Case C–21/88 *Du Pont de Nemours* [1990] ECR I–889, para. 14; Cases C–321–4/94 *Pistre* [1997] ECR I–2343, para. 52.

[175] Case C–524/07 *Commission v. Austria (roadworthiness of cars)* [2008] ECR I–187, paras. 54–5.

[176] E.g., see Case 178/84 *Commission v. Germany* [1987] ECR 1227, para. 30, and Case C–239/90 *Boscher* [1991] ECR I–2023, paras. 17–18. As Weatherill and Beaumont point out, see n. 10, 575, the French term is *exigences impératives* and the Italian term is *esigenze imperative*. They note that neither 'mandatory' nor 'imperative' is entirely felicitous; the concept is closer to 'compelling' than 'compulsory'.

[177] Joined Cases C–267 and 268/91 *Keck and Mithouard* [1993] ECR I–6097, para. 15; Case C–368/95 *Familiapress* [1997] ECR I–3689, paras. 18 and 24; Joined Cases C–34–36/95 *De Agostini* [1997] ECR I–3843, paras. 45–6; Case C–3/99 *Cidrerie Ruwet SA v. Cidre Stassen SA and HP Mulmer Ltd* [2000] ECR I–8749, paras. 49–50.

[178] See, e.g., C–573/12 *Ålands vindkraft AB v. Energimyndigheten* EU:C:2014:2037, para. 76.

[179] See Ch. 12.   [180] Case C–573/12 *Ålands vindkraft AB* EU:C:2014:2037, para. 75.

[181] The burden of proof is on the Member State, which cannot rely on the justification in the abstract but must specifically demonstrate its genuineness: Case C–14/02 *ATRAL SA v. Etat belge* [2003] ECR I–4431, para. 67.

[182] See Joined Cases C–204–208/12 *Essent Belgium NV v. Vlaamse Gemeenschap* EU:C:2014:2192, para. 92.

[183] Case C–573/12 *Ålands vindkraft AB v. Energimyndigheten* EU:C:2014:2037, para. 79, which talks of the Kyoto Protocol to the United Nations Framework Convention on Climate Change, and with other EU and international greenhouse gas emission reduction commitments beyond the year 2012.

[184] Case C–254/05 *Commission v. Belgium (automatic fire detection systems)* [2007] ECR I–4269, para. 36.

[185] E.g., Case C–265/06 *Commission v. Portugal (tinted windows)* [2008] ECR I–2245, paras. 40–7.

[186] See Case 120/78 *Cassis de Dijon* [1979] ECR 649, para. 8; Case C–456/10 *ANETT* EU:C:2012:241, paras. 50–1.

2. EXAMPLES OF 'MANDATORY' OR 'PUBLIC INTEREST' REQUIREMENTS

In *Cassis* the Court recognized four mandatory requirements.[187] It has since recognized a range of other mandatory requirements, which can broadly be subdivided into the following (overlapping) categories:

- protection of public goods and values:
  - ▷ protection of the environment[188]
  - ▷ the protection of public health[189]
  - ▷ protection of cinema as a form of cultural expression[190]
  - ▷ protection of national or regional socio-cultural characteristics[191]
  - ▷ maintenance of press diversity;[192] and, in a similar vein, the protection of books as cultural objects[193]
  - ▷ protection of animal welfare[194]
  - ▷ the fairness of commercial transactions[195]

- protection of individuals:
  - ▷ defence of the consumer[196]
  - ▷ protection of working conditions[197]
  - ▷ protection of children[198]
  - ▷ road safety[199]

- protection of public order:
  - ▷ preventing the risk of seriously undermining the financial balance of the social security system[200]

---

[187] See Case 120/78 *Cassis de Dijon* [1979] ECR 649, para. 8; Case C–456/10 *ANETT* EU:C:2012:241, paras. 50–1.

[188] Case 302/86 *Commission v. Denmark* [1988] ECR 4607; Case C–389/96 *Aher-Waggon GmbH v. Germany* [1998] ECR I–4473; Case C–320/03 *Commission v. Austria I* [2005] ECR I–7929, para. 35.

[189] See, e.g., Case 178/84 *Commission v. Germany (beer purity laws)* [1987] ECR 1227; Case C–358/95 *Tommaso Morellato v. Unità sanitaria locale (USL), n. 11 di Pordenone* [1997] ECR I–1431; Joined Cases C–1 and 176/90 *Aragonesa* [1991] ECR I–4151, para. 13. The inclusion of this heading as a mandatory requirement, which repeats the derogation in Art. 36 TFEU, may have been a mistake: J. Mertens de Wilmars (1984–5) *Rechtskundig Weekblad*, No. 2 at 16, fn. 2.

[190] Case 60/84 *Cinéthèque v. Fédération Nationale des Cinémas Français* [1985] ECR 2605.

[191] Case 145/88 *Torfaen Borough Council v. B & Q plc* [1989] ECR 3851.

[192] Case C–368/95 *Familiapress* [1997] ECR I–3689.

[193] Case C–531/07 *LIBRO* [2009] ECR I–3717, para. 34.

[194] Case C–219/07 *Nationale Raad van Dierenkwekers en Liefhebbers VZW v. Belgische Staat* [2008] ECR I–4475, para. 27; see also Case 142/05 *Mickelsson* [2009] ECR I–4273, para. 30, discussed in n. 108.

[195] See also Case 58/80 *Dansk Supermarked A/S v. A/S Imerco* [1981] ECR 181.

[196] Case 120/78 *Cassis de Dijon* [1979] ECR 649. In more recent cases the Court merges the two headings and talks of 'fair trading and the protection of the consumer'. See, e.g., Case C–448/98 *Guimont* [2000] ECR I–10663, para. 30.

[197] Case 155/80 *Oebel* [1981] ECR 1993, para. 12 (prohibition on night working in the bakery industry).

[198] Case C–244/06 *Dynamic Medien Vertriebs GmbH* [2008] ECR I–505, para. 42.

[199] Case C–54/05 *Commission v. Finland* [2007] ECR I–2473, para. 40; Case C–265/06 *Commission v. Portugal (tinted film)* [2008] ECR I–2245, para. 36; Case C–110/05 *Commission v. Italy (trailers)* [2009] ECR I–519, para. 60.

[200] Case C–120/95 *Decker v. Caisse de Maladie des Employés Privés* [1998] ECR I–1831.

> ▷ protecting the effectiveness of fiscal supervision[201]
> ▷ protection of fundamental rights[202]
> ▷ preserving the maintenance of order in society[203]
> ▷ ensuring the fight against crime[204]
> ▷ preventing fraud.[205]

These fields of protected interests are broadly replicated in the context of free movement of persons and services considered in more detail in Chapter 12.

This (non-exhaustive) list of mandatory requirements demonstrates that the Court accepts most of the justifications put forward by the Member States, provided that the national policies do not pursue aims of a purely economic nature.[206] The list serves an important political role: it shows a recognition by the *EU* of non-commercial values important to the *Member States*, and a confirmation by the Court that the Treaty is not purely about creating an economic constitution. However, the problem facing the Court is that, each time it is called to adjudicate on any case where a mandatory requirement is invoked and the proportionality of the steps taken to achieve that objective are at issue, it has to rule on broad policy questions, thereby placing judges 'at the outer limits of their legitimate judicial role, where the judiciary risks substituting its assessment for that of the legislature'.[207]

We turn now to consider the mandatory requirements which have presented particular difficulties for the Court: consumer protection, environmental protection, and fundamental rights.

3. CONSUMER PROTECTION

The two mandatory requirements most commonly invoked by the Member States are public health and consumer protection. Public health reflects the more carefully worded derogation found in Article 36 TFEU and the Court invariably refers to Article 36 TFEU when justifications based on public health are raised. As far as consumer protection is concerned, the Court has in mind 'the presumed expectations of an average consumer who is reasonably well-informed and reasonably observant and circumspect'.[208] This individual also reads labels on products.[209] In other words,

---

[201] Case 823/79 *Criminal Proceedings against Carciati* [1980] ECR 2773, para. 9. In Case C–456/10 *ANETT* EU:C:2012:241, para. 50 the Court implicitly accepted, in principle, the need to ensure 'fiscal, customs and health control of tobacco products' as a justification.

[202] Case C–112/00 *Schmidberger* [2003] ECR I–5659, para. 82. See also Case C–36/02 *Omega Spielhallen* [2004] ECR I–9609.

[203] Case C–65/05 *Commission* v. *Greece (computer games)* [2006] ECR I–10341, paras. 32–4 referring to the services case law beginning with Case C–275/92 *Schindler* [1994] ECR I–1039, para. 58 considered further in Ch. 11.

[204] Case C–265/06 *Commission* v. *Portugal* [2008] ECR I–2245, para. 38.

[205] Case C–161/09 *Kakavetsos-Fragkopoulos* [2011] ECR I–915, para. 59.

[206] Case C–254/98 *Schutzverband gegen unlauteren Wettbewerb* v. *TK-Heimdienst Sass GmbH* [2000] ECR I–151, para. 33. This is considered further in Ch. 12.

[207] D. Wyatt and A. Dashwood, *European Union Law*, 5th edn (London: Sweet & Maxwell, 2006), 587.

[208] Case C–210/96 *Gut Springenheide GmbH* v. *Oberkreisdirektor des Kreises Steinfurt* [1998] ECR I–4657, para. 31. The Court added that it was not necessary to order an expert's report or commission a consumer research poll on whether the consumer was likely to be misled. See also Case C–358/01 *Commission* v. *Spain (bleach)* [2003] ECR I–13145; Case C–446/07 *Severi* v. *Regione Emilia-Romagna* [2009] ECR I–8041, para. 61.

[209] Case C–51/94 *Commission* v. *Germany* [1995] ECR I–3599, para. 34. H. von Heydebrand u.d. Lasa, 'Free movement of foodstuffs, consumer protection and food standards in the European Community: Has the Court of Justice got it wrong?' (1991) 16 *ELRev.* 391, 399, cites research suggesting that only 20 per cent of consumers read labels.

Union law does not permit national laws protecting the unobservant and unintelligent consumer,[210] when such laws stand in the way of market integration which is of benefit to the consumer body as a whole.[211] The Court has taken the view that, in general, the consumer is better served by having access to a wider choice of products,[212] some of which will be of better quality than others, than a narrower choice but with higher *national* standards of consumer protection. However, the Court has made this policy choice against a background of an increasing volume of *Union* level consumer legislation. The Court's approach can be seen in two references from Germany, *Clinique*[213] and *Mars*.[214]

In *Clinique* a German rule required that all 'Clinique' (cosmetic) products be sold under the name 'Linique' on the ground that the 'Clinique' name could mislead consumers into believing that the products had medicinal properties. Rejecting the consumer protection justification, the Court noted that the Clinique products were sold only in department stores, not in pharmacies, and they were presented as cosmetics and not as medicinal products. It concluded that the products were ordinarily marketed under the name Clinique in other countries where 'the use of that name apparently does not mislead consumers'.[215]

In *Mars* the German 'Association against Pernicious Trading Practices', which had complained about Mars's '+10%' promotion, argued that the campaign might conceal a price rise and that, since the '+10%' flash covered more than a tenth of the total surface area of the wrapping, consumers might be misled into thinking that they were receiving more than 10 per cent extra. The Court rejected both arguments. It said that Mars had not profited from the campaign by increasing its prices and that '[r]easonably circumspect consumers could be deemed to know that there was not necessarily a link between the size of publicity markings relating to an increase in a product's quantity and the size of that increase'.[216]

These cases show that, in defining a European approach to consumer protection, the Court rejected the German model based on the 'uninformed consumer' in favour of the model of the 'mature and prudent' consumer which dominates in other Member States.[217] In so doing, the Court adopted a 'majoritarian' approach, allowing the view of the majority of Member States to prevail over that of the (German) minority.[218] The Court is, however, prepared to relax its criteria for the average consumer in appropriate circumstances. For example, it has conceded that account can be taken of 'social, cultural

---

[210] S. Weatherill, 'Recent case law concerning the free movement of goods: Mapping the frontiers of market deregulation' (1999) 36 *CMLRev.* 51, 54. See also Art. 5(3) of the Unfair Commercial Practices Dir. 2005/29/EC ([2005] OJ L149/22), which makes special provision for 'consumers who are particularly vulnerable … because of their mental or physical infirmity'. This is considered further in Ch. 5.

[211] This is the view of the other Union institutions: see, e.g., Council Res. concerning the future orientation of the policy of the EEC for the protection and promotion of consumer interests ([1986] OJ C167/1); Commission Green Paper, 'European Union Consumer Protection', COM(2001) 531, 3: 'It is the cross-border movement of goods and services that allows consumers to search out bargains and innovative products and services and thus ensures that they optimise their consumption decisions.'

[212] Case C–456/10 *ANETT* EU:C:2012:241, para. 54: 'the removal of the prohibition at issue … is capable of benefiting consumers by allowing tobacco retailers to expand the range of products available'.

[213] Case C–315/92 *Verband Sozialer Wettbewerb ev* v. *Clinique Laboratories SNC* [1994] ECR I–317.

[214] Case C–470/93 *Verein gegen Unwesen in Handel und Gewerbe Köln* v. *Mars GmbH* [1995] ECR I–1923.

[215] Para. 21.   [216] Para. 24.

[217] H. Micklitz and S. Weatherill, *European Economic Law* (Aldershot: Ashgate, 1997), 271.

[218] M. Poiares Maduro, *We the Court: The European Court of Justice and the European Economic Constitution* (Oxford: Hart Publishing, 1998), Ch. 3.

or linguistic factors'[219] when assessing consumer protection. It has also upheld national laws designed to protect the below average consumer where, as in *Buet*,[220] the product is targeted at the 'particularly vulnerable consumer', such as those who are 'behind with their education and are seeking to catch up'.[221]

The case concerned a French law prohibiting doorstep selling of educational materials which, the Court said, while constituting an obstacle to the free movement of goods could be justified on the ground of consumer protection. It said that since teaching material was not a consumer product in daily use, an ill-considered purchase could cause the consumer harm other than mere financial loss because the purchase of unsuitable or low-quality material could 'compromise the consumer's chances of obtaining further training and thus consolidating his position on the labour market'.[222] In these circumstances the Court said a right to cancel the contract[223] was not sufficient and the Member State was permitted to retain its more protective national laws.[224]

If the Court considers that there is a sufficiently serious risk of consumers being misled,[225] owing to linguistic, cultural, and social differences, then the marketing of the product can be prohibited on the ground of consumer protection. Therefore, in *Graffione*[226] the Court said that a Member State was justified in prohibiting the sale of toilet paper and paper handkerchiefs under the trade mark Cotonelle if there was a sufficiently serious risk of consumers thinking that they contained cotton. Generally, however, the Court tends to be rather sceptical of the claims by states for consumer protection because it fears that such arguments are a simple disguise for protectionism. This can be seen in *GB-INNO*,[227] which concerned a Luxembourg rule prohibiting shops from advertising when their sales were due to take place and how long they would last. Because the effect of this rule was to deny consumers, particularly those in Belgium, access to certain kinds of information the Court said it could not be justified on the ground of consumer protection.[228] Thus the Luxembourg rule, which was intended to protect consumers, actually denied them a benefit and so contravened Union law.[229]

---

[219] Case C–220/98 *Estée Lauder Cosmetics GmbH & Co. OHG v. Lancaster Group GmbH* [2000] ECR I–117, para. 29.

[220] Case 382/87 *Buet* [1989] ECR 1235, para. 13. See also Case C–441/04 *A-Punkt Schmuckhandels GmbH v. Schmidt* [2006] ECR I–2093, para. 28, where the Court insisted that account be taken of the level of protection to be enjoyed by consumers in that case under what is now Dir. 2011/83 ([2011] OJ L304/64) on protecting the consumer in respect of contracts negotiated away from business premises.

[221] Conversely, if the consumer is 'specially informed' then lower standards of consumer protection are applied: Case C–239/90 *Boscher* v. *SA British Motors Wright* [1991] ECR I–2023, para. 20.

[222] Para. 14.

[223] As permitted by the Doorstep Selling Dir. 85/577 ([1985] OJ L372/31). This directive was a minimum harmonization measure. It has now been replaced by Dir. 2011/83 on consumer rights ([2011] OJ L304/64), which is largely full harmonization (recital 2).

[224] See also Case 286/81 *Oosthoek* [1982] ECR 4575, where the Court ruled that offering free gifts as a means of sales promotion could mislead consumers as to the real prices of certain products and distort the conditions on which genuine competition is based.

[225] There must be a high degree of consumer confusion: Case C–373/90 *Complaint against X* [1992] ECR I–131.

[226] Case C–313/94 *Fratelli Graffione SNC* v. *Ditta Fransa* [1996] ECR I–6039.

[227] Case C–362/88 *GB-INNO-BM* [1990] ECR I–667.

[228] Para. 19. This decision provided further stimulus for the need for a directive on comparative advertising to supplement the existing directive on misleading advertising, now EP and Council Dir. 2006/114 ([2006] OJ L376/21).

[229] On the essential role of advertising to provide users with information about the existence and availability of products, see Case C–320/93 *Ortscheit* [1994] ECR I–5243, para. 10.

4. ENVIRONMENTAL PROTECTION

Like consumer protection, environmental protection was not included in the Article 36 TFEU derogations and yet was one of the areas where an extension of the exceptions for the Member States was most needed to allow EU law to accommodate modern concerns. The first case to recognize environmental matters as a justification was *Commission* v. *Denmark (recyclable bottles)*,[230] concerning a Danish law requiring that all containers for beer and soft drinks had to be returnable. The Danish government justified the rule by reference to the protection of the environment, which the Court accepted. It found that while the deposit and return system was not disproportionate, the requirement that the containers be authorized by a national agency was disproportionate.

While *Commission* v. *Denmark* focused on reduction of waste, subsequent cases offered a broader interpretation of environmental protection. So, for example, in *Mickelsson*[231] the Court appeared to accept the Swedish government's argument that restricting the use of jet skis on inland waterways could be justified on the grounds of environmental protection, given that the use of personal watercraft had negative consequences for fauna, in particular where such craft were used for a lengthy period on a small area or driven at great speed.

More difficult for the Court have been cases considering national rules on the use of renewable energy sources for the production of electricity. We saw earlier the difficulties facing the Court in *PreussenElektra*.[232] The issue was considered again by the Grand Chamber in *Ålands vindkraft*[233] concerning the Swedish support scheme for the production of electricity from renewable sources (so-called green energy). Under this law, approved producers having an installation in Sweden were awarded electricity certificates (elcertificates) for each megawatt hour of green electricity produced.[234] These certificates could be traded on the open market. The demand for elcertificates stemmed from the fact that electricity suppliers and certain users were under an obligation to hold, and to surrender to the state on 1 April each year, a certain number (quota) of (Swedish) elcertificates corresponding to the proportion of the total quantity of electricity supplied or consumed during the preceding year. Failure to supply these certificates meant the suppliers and users had to pay a fee.

Ålands vindkraft, a Finnish wind farm, was refused any Swedish elcertificates on the grounds that only green electricity production installations located in Sweden could be approved for the award of elcertificates. Therefore, as a supplier, it had to buy those certificates on the basis of the electricity it imported, which the Court said impeded electricity imports. The Court also noted that the Swedish scheme allowed green energy producers to trade their elcertificates and the electricity they produce as part of a package which could lead to long-term relationships, which, again, had the potential to curb electricity imports from other Member States.[235]

---

[230] Case 302/86 *Commission* v. *Denmark* [1988] ECR 4607.

[231] Case 142/05 *Mickelsson* [2009] ECR I–4273, para. 30. For follow-up, see Case C–433/05 *Sandström* [2010] ECR I–2885.

[232] Case C–379/98 *PreussenElektra AG* [2001] ECR I–2099.

[233] Case C–573/12 *Ålands vindkraft AB* EU:C:2014:2037.

[234] For a similar judgment concerning green certificates and guarantees of origin, see Joined Cases C–204–208/12 *Essent Belgium* v. *Vlaamse Regulieringsinstantie voor de Elekticiteits- en Gasmarkt* EU:C:2014:2192.

[235] Paras. 70–3. The Court also suggested that the failure by Member States to adopt adequate measures to prevent barriers to the free movement of goods created through the actions of traders but made possible by specific national legislation was 'just as likely to obstruct intra-[Union] trade as is a positive act' (para. 74).

Thus, as with *PreussenElektra* (which concerned an earlier phase of the liberalization process), the Swedish scheme was directly discriminatory (albeit discrimination permitted by Article 3(3) of Directive 2009/28[236] on the promotion of the use of energy from renewable sources[237]). However, the Court merely said that the measures were MEEs which could be justified on the ground of promoting the use of renewable energy sources. The Court said that use of renewable energy sources for the production of electricity was 'useful for the protection of the environment inasmuch as it contributes to the reduction in greenhouse gas emissions, which are amongst the main causes of climate change that the European Union and its Member States have pledged to combat'.[238]

The Court then considered the question of proportionality. Given the difficulties of identifying green electricity at the consumption stage, any scheme to encourage the production of green electricity had to be focused on the production stage. Further, the EU directive had assigned to the Member States mandatory national targets to fulfil the EU's commitments entered into at international level and the directive had recognized the national and territorial nature of existing support schemes. Finally, given the costs of producing green electricity (especially when compared with the costs of producing electricity from non-green sources), green energy producers needed to be given certain guarantees about the future marketing of their electricity. For these reasons the Court found the certificate scheme proportionate. It also found the legislation as a whole to be proportionate provided the market for the certificate was genuine and the scheme more generally satisfied the requirement of legal certainty.[239] Thus EU law allowed a nationally based scheme to satisfy the requirements of international law.

5. FUNDAMENTAL RIGHTS

The other mandatory requirement which has raised difficulties for the Court is the protection of fundamental rights. As we saw in *Schmidberger*,[240] fundamental rights, particularly guaranteeing freedom of expression and freedom of assembly, were successfully raised by the Austrian government to justify its failure to ensure the free movement of goods during the environmentalists' protest. Austria also raised a species of fundamental rights argument to explain why, in *Familiapress*,[241] it prevented newspapers and magazines from offering prize competitions. Its justification was to preserve press diversity[242] by preventing large publishers from driving smaller publishers off the market owing to their ability to offer larger prizes. This is, in essence, an argument based on freedom of expression under Article 10 ECHR.

However, the potential scope of the fundamental rights justification is not unlimited, as *A.G.M-COS.MET*[243] demonstrates. This case concerned a Finnish expert expressing doubt about the safety of some imported Italian lifts, albeit that the lifts were certified as

---

[236] [2009] OJ L140/16.

[237] For this reason Bot AG had said that Art. 3(3) of the directive was invalid: EU:C:2014:37.

[238] Para. 78. See also Case C–379/98 *PreussenElektra* [2001] ECR I–2099, para. 73.

[239] Para. 125. See also Joined Cases C–204–208/12 *Essent Belgium* v. *Vlaamse Regulieringsinstantie voor de Elekticiteits- en Gasmarkt* EU:C:2014:2192 on how the levels of fine are to be set for those who do not fulfil their obligations.

[240] Case C–112/00 *Schmidberger* [2003] ECR I–5659; see text related to n. 38.

[241] Case C–368/95 *Familiapress* [1997] ECR I–3689.

[242] This was a particular problem in Austria, where the market share of the largest press group was 55 per cent, whereas in the UK it was 35 per cent, and in Germany 24 per cent.

[243] Case C–470/03 *A.G.M.-COS.MET Srl* v. *Soumen valtio, Tarmo Lehtinen* [2007] ECR I–2749, para. 72. This case is discussed further in Ch. 4.

conforming to the relevant directive. His remarks potentially breached Article 34 TFEU and the Finnish government relied on a human rights justification to escape liability. The Court rejected the justification:[244]

> Under Article 10(1) of the European Convention on Human Rights, everyone within the jurisdiction of the Member States is guaranteed the right to freedom of expression. That freedom is an essential foundation of any democratic society. Member States, however, cannot rely on their officials' freedom of expression to justify an obstacle and thereby evade their own liability under [Union] law.

Even where a Member State is successful in invoking an Article 36 TFEU derogation or a mandatory requirement it must also show that the measures are proportionate to the risk presented by the import. It is to the question of proportionality that we now turn.

D. PROPORTIONALITY

1. THE TEST

The principle of proportionality comprises essentially two tests: a test of suitability and a test of necessity. As Tridimas explains,[245] the first (suitability) refers to the relationship between the means and the end: the means employed by the test must be suitable (or adequate or appropriate) to attain the end (e.g., road safety). As the Court put it in *United Foods*,[246] there has to be a 'reasonable connexion' between the measures laid down by the authorities and the exercise of control. The second test (necessity) is one of weighing competing interests: the Court assesses the adverse consequences that the measure has on an interest worthy of legal protection and determines whether those consequences are justified in view of the importance of the objective pursued. Sometimes this second limb is viewed as having two distinct elements: whether there are other less restrictive means of producing the same result and, even if there are no less restrictive means, whether the measure, nevertheless, has an excessive effect on the applicant's interests.[247]

The burden of proof is on the national authorities to show that their rules satisfy the test of proportionality.[248] They must also show that they have pursued the stated objectives in a consistent and systematic manner,[249] by producing 'specific evidence substantiating [their] arguments'.[250] However, as the Court pointed out in *Commission* v. *Italy (trailers)*,[251] 'that burden of proof cannot be so extensive as to require the Member States to prove, positively, that no other conceivable measure could enable that objective to be

---

[244] Para. 72.

[245] T. Tridimas, 'Proportionality in Community law: Searching for the appropriate standard of scrutiny' in E. Ellis (ed.), *The Principle of Proportionality in the Laws of Europe* (Oxford: Hart Publishing, 1999), 68.

[246] Case 132/80 *NV United Foods and PVBA Aug. Van den Abeele* v. *Belgium* [1981] ECR 995, para. 28.

[247] For a variation on this theme, see Case C–170/04 *Rosengren* [2007] ECR I–4071, para. 50: 'they are necessary in order to achieve the declared objective, and that that objective could not be achieved by less extensive prohibitions or restrictions, or by prohibitions or restrictions having less effect on intra-[Union] trade'. See also Case C–141/07 *Commission* v. *Germany (pharmacies for hospitals)* [2008] ECR I–6935, para. 50.

[248] Case C–110/05 *Commission* v. *Italy* [2009] ECR I–519, para. 62.

[249] See, e.g., Case C–265/06 *Commission* v. *Portugal (tinted windows)* [2008] ECR I–2245, para. 43; Case C–500/06 *Corporación Dermostética* [2008] ECR I–5785, para. 39.

[250] Case C–333/14 *Scotch Whisky Association* EU:C:2015:845, para. 54.

[251] Case C–110/05 *Commission* v. *Italy* [2009] ECR I–519, para. 66. See also Case C–333/14 *Scotch Whisky Association* EU:C:2015:845, para. 55.

attained under the same conditions'. Further, the Court has emphasized the need to look at context: for example, how the restrictive domestic policy fits with other EU policies, including agricultural policy, and whether the domestic measure is subject to a sunset clause and/or a review clause.[252] The assessment of the proportionality of the national measure is not to be confined to examining only information, evidence, or other material available to the national legislature when it adopted that measure but on the basis of the information, evidence, or other material available to the national court on the date on which it gives its ruling.[253]

Thus, using the medium of proportionality, the court (usually the national court in preliminary references[254] but sometimes the Court of Justice[255]) performs a balancing exercise between the objectives pursued by the national measure and its adverse effects on free movement. There is some evidence that if the proportionality review is performed by the Court of Justice, it tends to find the national measure disproportionate. By contrast, if the review is conducted by the national court it tends to uphold the validity of the measure.

2. APPLYING THE PROPORTIONALITY TEST

The Court's approach to applying the proportionality principle can be seen in *Familiapress*.[256] It will be recalled that an Austrian rival sought to restrain sales of the magazine 'Laura' published in Germany on the ground that the magazine included prize competitions which contravened an Austrian law on unfair competition. The Court said that the rule breached Article 34 TFEU but could be justified on the grounds of press diversity (i.e., the need to protect small publishers who might be able to offer only smaller prizes from larger publishers able to offer larger prizes). It then left it to the national court to determine whether the national prohibition was 'proportionate to the aim of maintaining press diversity and whether that objective might not be attained by measures less restrictive of both intra-[Union] trade and freedom of expression'.[257] The Court then explained exactly how the national court should do this.

On the question of suitability, the Court said the national court had to commission a study to determine,[258] first, whether newspapers which offered the chance of winning a prize in competitions were actually in competition with those small press publishers who were considered unable to offer comparable prizes; and, secondly, whether the prospect of winning did constitute an incentive for potential consumers to purchase magazines and whether this was capable of bringing about a shift in demand. The Court continued that the national court also had to assess the extent to which, from the consumer's standpoint, the product concerned could be replaced by magazines which did not offer prizes. In making this assessment the national court had to take into account all the circumstances which might influence the decision to purchase, such as the presence of advertising on the front cover referring to the chance of winning a prize; the likelihood of winning; the value of the prize; or the extent to which winning depended on a test calling for a measure of ingenuity, skill, or knowledge.

[252] Case C–333/14 *Scotch Whisky Association* EU:C:2015:845, paras. 57–8.
[253] Case C–333/14 *Scotch Whisky Association* EU:C:2015:845, para. 65.
[254] See, e.g., Case 251/78 *Firma Denkavit Futtermittel GmbH* [1979] ECR 3369.
[255] See, e.g., Case C–189/95 *Criminal Proceedings against Harry Franzén* [1997] ECR I–5909, para. 76.
[256] Case C–368/95 *Familiapress* [1997] ECR I–3689. See also P. Oliver, 'A review of the case law of the Court of Justice on Articles 30 to 36 EEC in 1985' (1986) 23 *CMLRev.* 325, 348–50.
[257] Para. 27.   [258] Para. 30.

The Court then turned to the question of necessity (whether the Austrian legislature could have adopted measures less restrictive of free movement of goods than an outright prohibition on the distribution of newspapers). It said the national court had to consider whether national law could have required merely the removal of the page on which the prize competition appeared in copies intended for the Austrian market or the addition of a statement that readers in Austria did not qualify for the chance to win a prize.[259]

Familiapress demonstrates that the application of the tests of suitability and necessity enables courts to review not only the legality, but also to some extent the merit, of legislative and administrative measures.[260] As Tridimas says, for this reason proportionality is often perceived as a far-reaching ground of review.[261] This view is reinforced by *Campus Oil*,[262] where the Court said:

> Article 36 [TFEU], as an exception to a fundamental principle of the Treaty, must be interpreted in such a way that its scope is not extended any further than is necessary for the protection of the interests which it is intended to secure and the measures taken pursuant to that Article must not create obstacles to imports which are disproportionate to those objectives. Measures adopted on the basis of Article 36 TFEU can therefore be justified only if they are such as to serve the interest which that Article protects and if they do not restrict intra-Union trade more than is absolutely necessary.

The strict approach to proportionality can be seen in *Commission v. Portugal (tinted windows)*.[263] Portuguese law prohibited the fixing of tinted film on the inside of car windscreens. Portugal justified this rule on the grounds of the fight against crime and road safety: the absence of film enabled the 'passenger compartment of motor vehicles to be immediately inspected by means of simple observation from outside the vehicle' to check that individuals are not criminals and are wearing seat belts.[264] The Court said that the measure was appropriate but not necessary:[265] a visual inspection was only one means available to the competent authorities for making these checks. The Court added that the Portuguese case was 'further undermined' by the fact that it allowed the marketing of motor vehicles pre-fitted with tinted windows within the limits laid down by the relevant Directive 92/22.[266] The Court concluded that the ban had to be regarded as 'excessive and, therefore, disproportionate with respect to the objectives pursued'.[267]

The Court is also increasingly demanding about the evidence that is required to satisfy the necessity test. This can be seen in *Commission v. Poland (right-hand drive cars)*,[268] which concerned Polish legislation making it conditional that right-hand drive cars had

[259] Para. 32.
[260] Tridimas, n. 245, 68–9. See also, e.g., Case C–67/88 *Commission v. Italy* [1990] ECR I–4285 (requirement of adding colour-reactive sesame seed oil to edible vegetable oils to combat fraud not justified because there were no effective controls to see whether the sesame oil had been added).
[261] See further G. de Búrca, 'The principle of proportionality and its application in EC law' (1993) 13 *YEL* 105; G. Bermann, 'Proportionality and subsidiarity' in C. Barnard and J. Scott (eds.), *The Law of the Single European Market: Unpacking the premises* (Oxford: Hart Publishing, 2002).
[262] Case 72/83 [1984] ECR 2727, para. 37.
[263] Case C–265/06 *Commission v. Portugal* [2008] ECR I–2245. See also Case C–54/05 *Commission v. Finland (import licences for cars)* [2007] ECR I–2473, paras. 45–6; Case C–297/05 *Commission v. Netherlands (roadworthiness testing of imported cars)* [2007] ECR I–7467, paras. 78–9.
[264] Para. 40.   [265] Para. 41.
[266] Now repealed and replaced by Reg. (EC) No. 661/2009 ([2009] OJ L200/1). The Commission also pointed out that due to the wide range of tinted film available—from transparent film to film which is almost opaque—at least some film would permit the desired visual inspection of the interior of motor vehicles.
[267] Para. 47.   [268] Case C–639/11 *Commission v. Poland* EU:C:2014:173.

their steering wheel swapped to the left before they could be registered in Poland. The Polish government justified the requirement on the grounds of road safety but the Court found it disproportionate. It noted that the statistical data relied on by the Polish government did not 'prove to the requisite legal standard the relationship between the number of accidents put forward and the involvement of vehicles with the driver's seat situated on the right'.[269] It also looked at the position in other Member States and adopted a 'majoritarian' approach:[270] 'the legislation of 22 Member States, that is to say, the large majority of the Member States, either allows explicitly the registration of vehicles which have their steering equipment on the same side as the direction of the traffic, or tolerates such, even if, in some of those Member States, the state of the roads is similar to that in the Republic of Poland'.[271]

However, in areas of sensitivity the Court refers to the 'margin of discretion' left to the Member States when considering the question of necessity. This can be seen in *Dynamic Medien*[272] concerning the German authorities' insistence that they re-examine and classify imported DVDs aimed at young people (on the facts, Japanese 'Animes' cartoons) which had already been classified by the British Board of Film Classification, the relevant British authority. Because the protection of children was at stake the Court deferred to the discretion of the German authorities and gave only the most cursory examination of the proportionality principle.[273]

3. THE MEASURES THAT CAN BE TAKEN BY THE DEFENDANT STATE

3.1 Bans, Licences, and Authorizations

In deciding how to protect the interest invoked, the host state has a range of possible steps it can take from, at the one extreme, banning the product, to licensing or authorizing its use on the other. Generally the Court finds that a national rule *banning* the import of a product is disproportionate because less restrictive alternatives exist.[274] So in *Rosengren*[275] the Court said that the ban on imports of alcohol by anyone, irrespective of age, 'goes manifestly beyond what is necessary for the objective sought', namely to protect younger people against the harmful effects of alcohol consumption. However, there are exceptions: in *Toolex Alpha*[276] the Court found a Swedish ban on the import of trichloroethylene, a proven carcinogen, to be proportionate.

In some cases the Court will accept a more carefully tailored ban. So, in *Aragonesa*[277] the Court noted with approval that the ban on advertising of alcohol applied only to

---

[269] Case C–639/11 *Commission* v. *Poland* EU:C:2014:173, para. 62. See also Case C–61/12 *Commission* v. *Lithuania* EU:C:2014:172.

[270] See further M. Poiares Maduro, *We the Court* (Oxford, Hart Publishing, 1998), considered in Ch. 4.

[271] Para. 61.

[272] Case C–244/06 [2008] ECR I–505, para. 44; Case C–110/05 *Commission* v. *Italy (trailers)* [2009] ECR I–519, para. 65. See also Case C–284/95 *Safety Hi-Tech Srl* v. *S & T Srl* [1998] ECR I–4301, para. 66, where the Court simply said that a prohibition on the use and marketing of hydrochlorofluorocarbons (HCFCs) and halons to help protect the ozone layer could not be regarded as 'disproportionate to the aim pursued', without undertaking any of the analysis outlined in *Familiapress*.

[273] Paras. 47–8.

[274] See, e.g., Case 178/84 *Commission* v. *Germany* [1987] ECR 1227, para. 35; Case C–350/97 *Monsees* v. *Unabhängiger Verwaltungssenat für Kärnten* [1999] ECR I–2921. Case C–112/00 *Schmidberger* [2003] ECR I–5659, para. 89: 'an outright ban on the demonstration would have constituted unacceptable interference with the fundamental rights of the demonstrators to gather and express peacefully their opinion in public'.

[275] Case C–170/04 *Rosengren* [2007] ECR I–4071, para. 51.

[276] Case C–473/98 *Toolex Alpha AB* [2000] ECR I–5681.

[277] Joined Cases C–1 and 176/90 *Aragonesa de Publicidad Exterior SA* [1991] ECR I–4151, paras. 17–18.

strong drink and to adverts placed in specified public places frequented by motorists and young people, the principal groups intended to be protected; and in the *Loi Evin* cases[278] the Court approved an advertising ban which affected one medium only: television. By contrast, in *Gourmet*[279] the national court was left to decide whether a Swedish law prohibiting advertising of alcoholic drinks in periodicals in order to combat alcohol abuse could be achieved by less extensive restrictions. This called for an analysis of the circumstances of law and fact which characterized the Swedish situation, which, the Court of Justice said, the national court was better placed to assess.[280]

Generally, the Court prefers authorization (or equivalent) rules rather than bans. So, in *Schreiber*[281] the Court found that a system of prior authorization of biocidal products before they were placed on the market was proportionate. On the other hand, in *Franzén*[282] the Court said that a Swedish law requiring those selling alcohol to hold a licence, for which a high fee was charged, and to have sufficient storage capacity for that alcohol, was not proportionate to the public-health objective of reducing alcohol consumption. It said that this aim could have been attained by measures less restrictive of intra-Union trade.

Subsequently, in *Canal Satélite Digital*[283] the Court laid down four criteria for an authorization requirement to be justified and proportionate:

- it must be based on objective, non-discriminatory criteria known in advance
- it must not duplicate controls which have already been carried out
- any subsequent control would be too late to be genuinely effective
- it should not deter operators from pursuing their business plan due to its duration and disproportionate costs.

3.2 Minimum Pricing v. Taxation

In *Scotch Whisky*[284] the Court had to consider whether, by imposing a minimum price per unit of alcohol, the Scottish government's breach of Article 34 TFEU was justified and proportionate. The Court recognized that the measure could be justified on the grounds of public health: reducing in a targeted way both the consumption of alcohol by consumers whose consumption was hazardous or harmful, and also, generally, the population's consumption of alcohol.[285] The Court also thought the measure appropriate: 'it does not seem unreasonable to consider that a measure that sets a minimum selling price of alcoholic drinks, the very specific aim of which is to increase the price of cheap alcoholic drinks, is capable of reducing the consumption of alcohol, in general, and the hazardous or harmful consumption of alcohol, in particular, given that drinkers whose consumption can be so described purchase, to a great extent, cheap alcoholic drinks'.[286] Further, the Scottish government's policy was applied in a 'consistent and systematic manner': the

---

[278] Case C–262/02 *Commission v. France* [2004] ECR I–6569 and Case C–429/02 *Bacardi France SAS v. Télévision française 1 SA* [2004] ECR I–6613.

[279] Case C–405/98 *Gourmet International Products* [2001] ECR I–1795, para. 33. See also Case C–434/04 *Anders Ahokainen v. Virallinen syyttäjä* [2006] ECR I–9171, para. 37.

[280] See also Case E–4/04 *Pedicel v. Sosial- og helsdirektoratet* [2005] EFTA Ct. Rep. 1.

[281] Case C–443/02 *Schreiber* [2004] ECR I–7275.

[282] Case C–189/95 *Criminal Proceedings against Harry Franzén* [1997] ECR I–5909, para. 76.

[283] Case C–390/99 *Canal Satélite Digital* [2002] ECR I–607. See also the discussion in Section 5.

[284] Case C–333/14 *Scotch Whisky Association* EU:C:2015:845.

[285] Concerns about alcohol abuse had already been raised in Case C–198/14 *Valev Visnapuu v. Kihlakunnansyyttäjä* EU:C:2015:751, para. 115.

[286] Para. 36.

imposition of the minimum price per unit (MPU) was one of 40 measures whose object-ive was to reduce the consumption of alcohol by the Scottish population as a whole, irre-spective of where that consumption takes place or the nature of that consumption.

However, the Court thought the measures were more restrictive than necessary. It pre-ferred taxation: 'a fiscal measure which increases the taxation of alcoholic drinks is liable to be less restrictive of trade in those products within the European Union than a measure imposing an MPU' because the MPU significantly restricts the freedom of economic op-erators to determine their retail selling prices and, consequently, constitutes a serious ob-stacle to access to the UK market of alcohol lawfully marketed in other Member States.[287] However, the final decision on proportionality was left to the national court.

3.3 Labelling

Labelling is the Court's favoured solution to many proportionality problems connected with food. We can see this in *Rau*,[288] where the Court recognized that legislation designed to prevent butter and margarine from being confused was in principle justified, but said that the requirement to use only one specific type of packaging 'considerably exceed[ed] the requirements of the object in view'. It continued that consumers could be protected 'just as effectively by other measures, for example by rules on labelling, which hinder the free movement of goods less'.[289] This emphasis on the disclosure of information is in-tended to enable consumers to make an informed choice[290] rather than having that choice confined by government intervention.

The benefits of labelling were emphasized in the *Beer Purity*[291] case. According to the sixteenth-century German *Biersteuergesetz*, the name 'Bier' could be used for products brewed with malted barley, hops, yeast, and water only. The use of other products, such as maize and rice (often found in foreign beers), meant that the product could not be described as 'Bier'. The German government attempted to justify restricting the name 'Bier' on the ground of consumer protection: since Germans linked the word 'Bier' to products manufactured with only the ingredients listed in the *Biersteuergesetz* they might be misled if the name was applied to products containing other ingredients. The Court rejected these arguments and, referring back to its case law on Article 110 TFEU on tax-ation, said that the legislation of a Member State should not 'crystallize given consumer habits so as to consolidate an advantage acquired by national industries concerned to comply with them'.[292] It continued that consumers could be protected 'by means which do not prevent the importation of products which have been lawfully manufactured and marketed in other Member States and, in particular, by the compulsory affixing of suit-able labels giving the nature of the product sold'.[293] The Court noted that these labels could even be attached to the casks or the beer taps when beers were sold in draught.[294]

The *Biersteuergesetz* also banned the use of any additives in beer. The German govern-ment tried to justify this on the ground of public health: because of the amount of beer

---

[287] Case C–333/14 *Scotch Whisky Association* EU:C:2015:845, para. 46.
[288] Case 261/81 *Rau* [1982] ECR 3961, para. 12.
[289] See also para. 17. See also Case C–448/98 *Guimont* [2000] ECR I–10663, para. 33.
[290] See Council Res. of 5 Apr. 1993 on future action on the labelling of products in the interest of the consumer ([1993] OJ C110/1).
[291] Case 178/84 *Commission v. Germany* [1987] ECR 1227.
[292] Para. 32, referring to Case 170/78 *Commission v. UK (wine and beer)* [1980] ECR 417, considered in Ch. 3.
[293] See, more recently, Joined Cases C–158 and 159/04 *Alfa Vita Vassilopoulos AE* [2006] ECR I–8135, para. 25.
[294] Para. 36.

consumed by German drinkers (!), it was important to minimize the quantity of additives
ingested for reasons of general preventive health.[295] The Court rejected this argument
too, saying that the ban was disproportionate for two reasons: first, that additives were
allowed in other German soft drinks and, secondly, that the ban was not limited to those
additives where there was scientific evidence that they might cause harm.[296]

The *Biersteuergesetz* was eventually repealed: beers made in other Member States can
be sold without restriction in Germany, provided all ingredients other than water, malt,
hops, and yeast are clearly marked.[297] Subsequently, a French brewery sued the German
government for damages for the loss it had suffered as a result of having to discontinue
exports of beer to Germany since its beer did not comply with the *Biersteuergesetz*. In
Brasserie du Pêcheur[298] the Court established the principle of state liability for breach of
a Treaty provision. It said that in an area involving a wide discretion on the part of the
legislature, such as laying down rules on the quality of beer put on the market, Union
law conferred a right to reparation where three conditions were met: (1) the rule of law
infringed had to be intended to confer rights on individuals, (2) the breach had to be
sufficiently serious, and (3) there had to be a direct causal link between the breach of the
obligation resting on the state and the damage sustained by the injured parties.[299] The
Court suggested that the rules concerning the designation 'Bier' did constitute a serious
breach, since the incompatibility of such rules with Article 34 TFEU was 'manifest' in
the light of earlier decisions of the Court, in particular *Cassis de Dijon*. By contrast, in
respect of the German prohibition on additives, the Court said that since Union guidance
was significantly less clear, this aspect of the German law was unlikely to constitute a sufficiently serious breach. When the case returned to the German court it found that the
complainants were not entitled to damages, even as regards the provisions governing the
designation 'Bier', on the ground that there had been no direct causal connection between
Germany's sufficiently serious breach and the damage suffered.[300]

The *Beer Purity* case demonstrates how intrusive the Court's proportionality review
can be into the legislative choices made by the Member States. It also demonstrates the
Court's pragmatic approach to proportionality: the Court itself came up with a suggestion
for a more proportionate response to the problem of identifying the contents of beer (putting a label on the beer tap). Similarly, in *Heimdienst*[301] the Court suggested that, rather
than requiring grocers who sold their goods from a van to have a shop in the locality as
well, it would be more proportionate to require vans to have refrigeration equipment. In
this way the Member State could ensure the hygiene of goods supplied to outlying areas.

---

[295] Para. 48. See also Slynn AG's views that 'It seems to me disproportionate to seek to justify rules which
exclude the whole of society from beer other than nationally produced beer because some additives may
constitute a risk for a person who drinks in excess of 1,000 litres of beer a year or for an alcoholic already
suffering from cirrhosis of the liver. Accepting that such persons may need protection there are other ways
of achieving it, medical advice as to quantum and self-restraint to name only two.'

[296] See also Case 174/82 *Sandoz* [1983] ECR 2445.

[297] I. Murray, 'German beer law repealed', *The Times*, 2 Jun. 1990.

[298] Joined Cases C–46 and 48/93 *Brasserie du Pêcheur and Factortame III* [1996] ECR I–1029, developing the principle established in Joined Cases C–6 and 9/90 *Francovich and Bonifaci v. Italian Republic*
[1991] ECR I–5357. *Factortame III* is considered further in Ch. 11. See also Case C–445/06 *Danske Slagterier
v. Germany* [2009] ECR I–2119 (Danish association of slaughterhouse companies claiming compensation
from Germany for its import ban on meat from uncastrated pigs which produced a sexual odour).

[299] Para. 51.   [300] [1997] 1 CMLR 971.

[301] Case C–254/98 *TK-Heimdienst Sass GmbH* [2000] ECR I–151. In some cases the Court will adopt a
comparative approach seeing how other Member States have addressed a particular problem: Case C–126/91
Yves Rocher [1993] ECR I–2361, para. 18; cf. Case 286/81 *Oosthoek* [1982] ECR 4575, para. 20.

If labelling is the preferred solution, then national rules regulating the content and language of the label themselves raise issues under Article 34 TFEU because the label may have to be altered[302] depending on the country in which the good is sold. For this reason, the Court has prevented unnecessary changes to any label, as *Geffroy*[303] demonstrates. The case concerned the sale in France of Coca-Cola which had been bought in the UK and was labelled in English, contrary to French law requiring all labels to be in French. The importer argued that Coca-Cola was such a well-known product that consumers would not have been inconvenienced by the labelling in English, and the Court agreed. While recognizing that a Member State was entitled to impose language requirements concerning the labelling of foodstuffs, it said that national law could not require the use of a specific language for labelling of foodstuffs[304] without allowing for the use of another language easily understood by purchasers or ensuring that the purchaser was informed by some other means.

The Court's emphasis on labelling is not without its critics. For example, Von Heydebrand argues that the Court is wrong in thinking that consumers are adequately informed by labels.[305] He says that resources saved by forgoing harmonization are spent by national authorities determining whether the imported product is 'lawfully produced and marketed' in the Member State of origin.

Case Study 6.1: NAMING FOODS

One of the most vexed questions facing the Union legislature and the Court is the naming of foods. Each state jealously guards the product names it uses, often allowing them to be registered in the national system, and swears that the way the product is made in its country is the best.[306] The arrival of a product bearing the same or similar name on to its market, usually produced according to different rules, invariably threatens the quality and reputation of the domestic product. States therefore allowed national producers to invoke the national registration to keep these imported goods off the market. This inevitably had the effect of partitioning the market along national lines and undermined the aim of the single market.

The EU's response has been twofold. First, it has introduced so-called 'Euro-foods', designating what ingredients can be included in certain products before they can be given a particular name. We saw this with the chocolate and jam case study considered in Chapter 4. We also know how unpopular such moves tend to be. Secondly, the Union has recognized that the name of products typical of a particular region can actually be confined to products from that region. In the early days of the EU, this was largely done by the Court. However, the Court's approach

---

[302] See, e.g., Case 94/82 *De Kikvorsh* [1982] ECR 947, para. 10; Case C–217/99 *Commission v. Belgium* [2000] ECR I–10251, para. 17.

[303] Case C–366/98 *Geffroy and Casino France* [2000] ECR I–6579. See also Case C–369/89 *Piageme v. Peeters* [1991] ECR I–2971, which led to COM(93) 532 on the use of languages in the marketing of foodstuffs. See also Case 78/80 *Fietje* [1980] ECR 3839, para. 15.

[304] Art. 34 TFEU and Art. 14 of Dir. 79/112/EEC ([1979] OJ L33/1), now Art. 15 of Reg. 1169/2011 ([2011] OJ L304/18).

[305] von Heydebrand u.d Lasa, n. 209, 391.

[306] This patriotism is not confined to Member States: see Mancini AG's passionate opinion defending the need for pasta to be made only from durum wheat: Case 407/85 *3 Glocken GmbH v. USL Centro-Sud* [1988] ECR 4233, esp. para. 2. Particularly noteworthy is his lyrical argument that 'only pasta made with durum wheat does not become sticky during cooking and arrives on the plate as the Italians like it to be: "al dente" (and therefore, as André Gide put it in his journal, on 22 June 1942, "glissant des deux côtés de la fourchette")'.

has now been replaced by Union secondary legislation, originally adopted in 1992 but now found primarily in Regulation 1151/2012.[307] This regulation allows national products to be registered in an *EU* register, thereby replacing the former national systems.[308]

As far as the Court's approach to national registration is concerned, its case law in the early 1970s recognized names which were (1) a designation or origin and (2) an indication of provenance. Where a product possessed 'qualities and characteristics which are due to the fact that it originated in a specific geographical area',[309] the Court would allow the state to protect that name either as a consumer protection/fair trading mandatory requirement[310] or as an industrial or commercial property express derogation under Article 36 TFEU.[311] That protection could be extended to the territory of another Member State.[312] However, having recognized this protection as a matter of principle, on the facts the Court generally ruled that its criteria for designating origin or indicating provenance were not satisfied and so found that the use of the name breached Article 34 TFEU. This approach can be seen in *Commission* v. *Germany*.[313]

German legislation confined the name 'Sekt' and 'Weinbrand' to products originating in Germany or other German-speaking countries. The Court said that 'An area or origin which is defined on the basis either of the extent of national territory or a linguistic criterion cannot constitute a geographical area' capable of justifying an indication or origin, particularly as the products might be produced from grapes of 'indeterminate origin'.[314] Germany was therefore in breach of Article 34 TFEU. Likewise, Germany's insistence, in *Prantl*,[315] that only certain producers of domestic wine could use the traditional bulbous shape 'Bocksbeutel' bottle breached Article 34 TFEU because it kept Italian wine, also traditionally sold in similar shaped bottles, off the German market. The Court said that the consumer protection argument had to be fair to all sides.[316]

To help address some of the internal market problems created by a proliferation of names on national registers, the EU introduced an EU-wide register in 1992. This allowed three categories of names to be registered: PDOs (Protected Designation of Origin), PGIs (Protected Geographical Indication), and TSGs (Traditional Speciality Guaranteed). In March 2006 these registration systems were updated. The principal measure now is Regulation 1151/2012 on quality schemes for agricultural products and foodstuffs concerning PDOs and PGIs.[317]

---

[307] [2012] OJ L343/1.

[308] Case C–478/07 *Budějovický Budvar* v. *Rudolf Ammersin* [2009] ECR I–7721, para. 114: 'the aim of Regulation [1151/2012] is not to establish, alongside national rules which may continue to exist, an additional system of protection for qualified geographical indications … but to provide a uniform and exhaustive system of protection for such indications'.

[309] Case 12/74 *Commission* v. *Germany* ('*Sekt*') [1975] ECR 181, para. 7.

[310] Case 16/83 *Criminal Proceedings against Prantl* [1984] ECR 1299, para. 25.

[311] Case 16/83 *Criminal Proceedings against Prantl* [1984] ECR 1299, para. 34. Rules prohibiting false indications of origin are permissible: Case 207/83 *Commission* v. *UK* [1985] ECR 1201.

[312] Case C–3/91 *Exportur* [1992] ECR I–5529, para. 38.

[313] Case 12/74 *Commission* v. *Germany* ('*Sekt*') [1975] ECR 181.   [314] Para. 8.

[315] Case 16/83 *Prantl* [1984] ECR 1299.   [316] Case C–3/91 *Exportur* [1992] ECR I–5529, para. 32.

[317] Originally a separate regulation covered TSGs (Reg. 509/2006 ([2006] OJ L93/1) but these have now been brought under Reg. 1151/2012. 'Traditional speciality guaranteed' means a traditional agricultural product or foodstuff with a 'specific character', i.e., a characteristic or set of characteristics which distinguishes an agricultural product or a foodstuff clearly from other similar products or foodstuffs of the same category where the name has a proven usage on the Union market for a time period showing transmission between generations (i.e., at least 25 years) (Art. 2(1)). Examples of TSGs include *Pizza Napoletana* and *Mozzarella* (cheese) from Italy (although Mozzarella di Bufala Campana is a PDO) and *Lambic, Gueuze Lambic, Gueuze/Lambiek, and Geuze-Lambiek, Geuze* (beers) from Belgium. A TSG does not refer to the geographic origin but highlights traditional character, either in the composition or means of production.

As far as PDOs are concerned, Article 5(1) of Regulation 1151/2012 provides that 'Designation of origin' is the name which identifies a product originating in a specific place, region, or, in exceptional cases, a country whose *quality or characteristics* are *essentially or exclusively* due to a particular geographical environment with its inherent natural and human factors; and the production steps all take place in the defined geographical area. Examples of registered PDOs include Cornish clotted cream, Jersey Royal potatoes, Scottish salmon,[318] West Country farmhouse Cheddar, Camembert de Normandie, Roquefort, Tuscan extra virgin olive oil, Gorgonzola, and Parmigiano di Reggiano.[319]

Parma ham is also a PDO[320] and the Consortium for Parma Ham has worked hard to defend the integrity of its product. Prior to the introduction of the 1992 legislation, the Consortium unsuccessfully brought a claim for passing off in the English courts against Marks & Spencer (M&S), for marketing as 'genuine Parma ham' ham which had originated in Parma but had been sliced and packed in England.[321] However, the Consortium's hand was strengthened with the introduction of the 1992 Regulation when Parma Ham was registered as a PDO. The Consortium again brought proceedings in the UK, this time against the supermarket Asda, which, like M&S, sliced and packed Parma Ham in the UK. On a reference from the House of Lords,[322] the Court said that in principle the Consortium could rely on the Regulation to protect its PDO.[323] It said that while the requirement for the product to be sliced and packed in the region of production breached Article 35 TFEU, that breach could be justified on the grounds of protection of industrial and commercial property, namely the need to control the quality and authenticity of the product,[324] and that the slicing and packaging requirement was proportionate.[325] However, on the facts of the case the Consortium could not rely on the regulation against Asda because the particular regulation where the PDO was registered did not expressly state that slicing and packing had to be done in Parma[326] with the result that, in the name of legal certainty, the regulation could not be invoked against Asda.

As far as PGIs are concerned, Article 5(2) of Regulation 1151/2012 provides that 'Geographical indication' is a name which identifies a product originating in a specific place, region, or country whose *quality, reputation, or other characteristics* is *essentially attributable* to its geographical origin; and where at least one of the production steps (production, processing, or preparation) takes place in the defined geographical area. Registered PGIs include Melton Mowbray Pork Pie, Scottish beef, and Scottish lamb. Newcastle Brown Ale was one of the first products from the UK to be registered as a PGI.[327] However, when the Newcastle factory moved across the River Tyne to nearby Gateshead in 2004, it no longer satisfied the terms of the PGI, which required brewing to take place within the city limits of Newcastle upon Tyne. The owners of

---

[318] Note the lyrical description of the geographical area in the application for the PDO for Scottish salmon: 'The magical mix of climate, terrain, indigenous industries and the Scottish people's inherent love and respect for their surroundings has blended to create a unique environment. Pure coastal waters and sheltered lochs have sustained and nurtured each Scottish farmed salmon throughout its life cycle, while expert husbandry skills have ensured each salmon achieves and maintains prime condition.'

[319] For a full list see the DOOR website <http://ec.europa.eu/agriculture/quality/door/list.html>.

[320] Commission Reg. 1107/96 ([1996] OJ L148/1).

[321] *Consorzio del Prosciutto di Parma* v. *Marks & Spencer plc* [1991] RPC 351. N. Dawson, 'Case comment: The Parma ham case: Trade descriptions and passing off—shortcomings of English law?' [1991] *EIPR* 487.

[322] *Consorzio del Prosciutto di Parma* v. *Asda Stores Ltd* [2001] UKHL 7. S. Bennett and C. Thorne, 'Case comment: Parma ham labelling and repackaging' [2001] *EIPR* 592.

[323] See also Case C–161/09 *Kakavetsos-Fragkopoulos* [2011] ECR I–915, para. 54.

[324] Para. 76.   [325] Para. 79.

[326] Case C–108/2001 *Consorzio del Prosciutto di Parma* v. *Asda Stores Ltd* [2003] ECR I–5121.

[327] Commission Reg. 1107/96 ([1996] OJ L148/1).

the brewery, Scottish & Newcastle, therefore had to apply for their own PGI to be cancelled in order to allow beer from the Gateshead brewery to continue to be branded as Newcastle Brown Ale.[328]

Both PDOs and PGIs involve a clear link to a specific geographic region. As the Commission explains,[329] the main difference between the two is just how closely the product is linked to a specific geographical area. In general terms, a PDO product must derive its characteristics from the area (either from local raw materials, climate, soil quality, or other local factors) *and* it must be produced and processed in the locality. For PGIs it is sufficient that only one of the production stages takes place in the defined area. It is therefore much easier to satisfy the criteria for qualification as a PGI than a PDO yet the protection level against misuse is essentially the same.[330]

In order to initiate the registration process for a PDO or PGI, applicants—including applicants from third countries[331]—submit an application for registration to their own Member State[332] (or the Commission in the case of third-country applicants), specifying the name of the product for which they are seeking PDO or PGI status, providing a description of its organoleptic features, a definition of geographical area, evidence that the product originates in the defined area, and details of the link between the qualities of the product and its region of production. The Member State scrutinizes the application against the eligibility criteria, and if it considers that the eligibility criteria are met, it forwards the application to the Commission for a final decision. The Commission considers the application and, if it passes scrutiny, publishes the application in the Official Journal. Any person with a legitimate interest from any Member State other than the applicant's, may object within six months from publication. Thereafter the name is registered by Regulation. Registration commands a commercial advantage: the Commission estimates that registered products obtain a 30 per cent price premium over competing products.[333]

Once registered, the name is protected against direct or indirect commercial use by products not covered by the registration specification; any other false or misleading indication as to the provenance, origin, nature, or essential qualities of the product; and any other practice that is liable to mislead the public as to the true origin of the product.[334] Registration also protects against misuse, imitation, or evocation, even where the true origin of the product is indicated.[335]

The scope of the protection can be seen in the *Gorgonzola* case.[336] The Court said that the name 'Cambozola' was an evocation of the PDO 'Gorgonzola', even though the names were different, because both names were used to market a soft blue cheese, and both names had four syllables where the third and fourth syllables of both names were identical.[337]

Names which have become generic may not, however, be registered.[338] A generic name encompasses any product which, 'although relating to the place, region or country where the product was originally produced or marketed, [has] become the common name of the product in the Union'.[339] Examples of products whose names have become generic include Cheddar

[328] 2006/C 280/06.

[329] European Commission, 'European Policy for Quality Agricultural Products', <http://www.ec.europa.eu/agriculture/publi/fact/quality/2007_en.pdf>.

[330] C. MacMaoláin, 'Waiter there's a beetle in my soup. Yes Sir, that's E120: Disparities between actual individual behaviour and regulating food labelling for the average consumer in EU Law' (2008) 45 *CMLRev.* 1147, 1154.

[331] Therefore, Columbian coffee has a PGI registered in accordance with Reg. 510/2006.

[332] Arts. 4–7.   [333] European Commission, n 329, 12.

[334] Art. 13.   [335] Art. 13.   [336] Case C–87/1997 *Gorgonzola* [1999] ECR I–1301.

[337] Paras. 27–8. See also Case C–132/05 *Commission* v. *Germany* [2008] ECR I–957, para. 46, where the Court said there was a phonetic and visual similarity between the names 'Parmesan' and 'Parmeggiano Reggiano'.

[338] Art. 6(1) of Reg. 1151/2012.   [339] Art. 3(6) of Reg. 1151/2012.

cheese (although 'West Country Farmhouse Cheddar' is a PDO), Edam,[340] Dijon mustard, and Black Forest gateau.[341]

The name which has caused most difficulty in this respect is 'feta' cheese, a problem exacerbated by the fact that the name itself originated in Italy (*fetta* meaning slice), not Greece where the cheese is usually associated.[342] Greek feta is made from sheep's milk or a mixture of sheep and goats' milk by the traditional craft method of natural straining of the milk, without applying pressure. Feta production also commenced in the 1960s in Denmark, Germany, the Netherlands, and France, but this cheese is made from cow's milk, which is more economical, and by an industrial ultra-filtration process, which is cheaper than the traditional method of straining. In *Canadane*[343] Advocate General Colomer considered the question whether Greece could insist on Danish feta bearing the less than attractive label 'white cheese in brine made in Denmark from pasteurized cows' milk', a requirement which the Danish producer thought would make its feta harder to sell, contrary to Article 34 TFEU. The Advocate General found the name feta to be non-generic in Greece. In support, he referred to the defined status of feta cheese under Greek law, a Eurobarometer survey which demonstrated its geographical significance to Greek consumers and that Greece was the largest producer and consumer of feta in the EU. He therefore argued that the Greek rules were protected under Article 36 TFEU. The case was withdrawn before the Court ruled on the issue.

The Court did have to address the matter in *Denmark, Germany and France v. Commission*,[344] where the Northern European states successfully challenged registration of the name 'feta' as a PDO on the grounds that the Commission, when registering the name feta, took no account of the fact that the name had been used for a considerable time in Member States other than Greece. The Commission then sent Member States a questionnaire on how well the name feta was known among their consumers; its scientific committee unanimously concluded that the name feta was not generic and so the Commission re-registered feta as a PDO. Once again Denmark and Germany challenged the registration[345] but this time they were unsuccessful; the Commission had now identified various factors relating to the consumption of feta in the Member States to indicate that the name feta was not generic.[346]

Where the name has become generic (e.g., pasta, beer) but Member States continue to insist that its use be confined to products with certain ingredients or certain quantities of ingredients, the Court applies its traditional Article 34 TFEU case law, as it did in the *Beer Purity* case.[347] As we saw in *Beer Purity*, while recognizing that, in principle, the national rule might be justified on the grounds of consumer protection/fair trading, the Court usually finds the national measure disproportionate, insisting that clear labelling is more appropriate than prohibiting the sale altogether. Therefore, in *Deserbais*[348] the Court said that a French rule restricting the name 'Edam'

[340] Case 286/86 *Ministère public* v. *Deserbais* [1988] ECR 4907.
[341] The Commission attempted to draw up a list of products considered generic: COM(96) 38 final. Its proposal for a decision contained the following names as generic: Brie, Camembert, Cheddar, Edam, Emmentaler, and Gouda (but not feta). The decision was never adopted due to the absence of agreement by the Council.
[342] D. Gangjee, 'Say cheese! A sharper image of generic use through the lens of Feta' [2007] *EIPR* 172; C. MacMaoláin, 'Eligibility criteria for protected geographical food names' (2006) *ELRev.* 579; B. O'Connor and I. Kireeva, 'What's in a name? The Feta cheese saga' (2003) 9 *International Trade Law & Regulation* 110.
[343] Case C–317/95 *Canadane* [1997] ECR I–4681.
[344] Joined Cases C–289, 293 and 299/96 *Denmark, Germany and France* v. *Commission* [1999] ECR I–1541.
[345] Joined Cases C–465 and 466/02 *Germany and Denmark* v. *Commission* [2005] ECR I–9115.
[346] Para. 88.   [347] See n. 291.
[348] Case 286/86 [1988] ECR 4907; Case C–210/89 *Commission* v. *Italy* [1990] ECR I–3697 (Italian rule restricting the name 'cheese' to products with a minimum fat content). See also Case C–448/98 *Guimont* [2000] ECR I–10663: a French rule restricting the name 'Emmenthal' to cheeses with a hard, dry rind was

to cheese with a minimum fat content of 40 per cent breached Article 34 TFEU because it had the effect of excluding from the French market German cheese which had been lawfully produced with a fat content of only 34 per cent. The Court said that provided consumers had proper information, the German cheese could be sold in France. Similarly, in 3 Glocken[349] the Court said that an Italian ban on the sale of pasta products made from common wheat or a mixture of common wheat and durum wheat was an obstacle to the import of pasta products from other Member States made from these ingredients, contrary to Article 34 TFEU.[350] The 'compulsory affixing of suitable labels giving the nature of the product sold' was the proportionate response to Italian concerns about consumer protection.[351]

Where, however, the products are substantially different the Court may allow the national rules to stand. This was suggested in Smanor, [352] where French law reserved the name 'yoghurt' solely to fresh yoghurt; deep-frozen yoghurt could be sold but only under the name 'deep-frozen fermented milk'. The Court said that the French rules appear 'disproportionate in relation to the objective of consumer protection, when the characteristics of the deep-frozen products are not substantially different ... from fresh products, and when appropriate labelling ... would suffice to give consumers proper information'.[353] However, it was left to the national court to make the final decision whether the two products were sufficiently different to justify the difference in name.[354]

4. PROPORTIONALITY AND PUBLIC HEALTH

So far we have focused on the Court's general approach to proportionality. We turn now to consider the application of the proportionality principle in the specific context of public health, an area where, as the Beer Purity case shows, the Court fears that the derogation may be misused.[355] In some cases, the Court does uphold the host state's rule, as Schwarz[356] shows. Austrian law required chewing gum sold in vending machines to be packaged. The Court accepted the public health justification that 'in the past, non-packaged goods were impaired by moisture or insects, in particular ants, within vending machine containers'. The Court also accepted the argument that the requirement increased the safety of the chewing gum because 'consumers who buy non-packaged confectionery from vending machines must necessarily touch the goods and the delivery tray with their bare hands without having washed them beforehand'. It added that 'contamination of the delivery tray by pathogenic germs and their transmission onto the goods removed by the customer is by no means merely theoretical'.[357] The Austrian requirement therefore constituted an 'adequate and proportionate measure for the protection of public health'.[358]

---

an indistinctly applicable MEE, as was a French rule restricting the name 'cider' to 'alcoholic drinks made of apples' in Case C–366/98 Geffroy and Casino France [2000] ECR I–6579.

[349] Case 407/85 3 Glocken GmbH v. USL Centro-Sud [1988] ECR 4233.

[350] Para. 11.   [351] Para. 16.

[352] Case 298/87 Proceedings for compulsory reconstruction against Smanor SA [1988] ECR 4489.

[353] Para. 23.   [354] Para. 24.

[355] See also Case C–88/07 Commission v. Spain (medicinal herbs) [2009] ECR I–1353, para. 93, where the Court insisted on a 'detailed assessment, on a case by case basis, of the risk alleged by the Member States invoking Article [36 TFEU]'.

[356] Case C–366/04 Schwarz v. Bürgermeister der Landeshauptstadt Salzburg [2006] ECR I–10139, para. 34.

[357] Para. 35.

[358] Para. 36. Cf. Case C–270/02 Commission v. Italy (foodstuffs for sportsmen and women) [2004] ECR I–1559, para. 24, where the Court found that Italy had failed to produce any evidence to explain the link between the authorization procedure and public health and the proportionality of the regime.

In other cases the Court will intervene to declare the national measure contrary to EU law. The wine wars case, *Commission* v. *France*,[359] provides an example of this.[360] The early 1980s saw a large increase in imports of Italian table wine into France. This caused prices of wine to fall, prompting violent demonstrations by French wine growers. In response, the French authorities took a number of steps against the imported goods, which included subjecting every consignment of Italian wine to health inspections at the frontier. This whole process took weeks, sometimes months. By contrast, French wine was subject to only occasional checks. The Court considered the checks on Italian wine to constitute a 'disproportionate and discriminatory obstacle to imports'.[361] It said that, in the absence of any reasonable suspicion, the French authorities should have confined themselves to random checks.[362]

Commission v. *UK (UHT)*[363] provides a further example of this careful scrutiny of the proportionality of national measures justified on the grounds of public health. UHT milk could be imported into the UK only by a licence holder and could be marketed only by a licensed dealer who had packed the milk in a local dairy. The Court found that both measures breached Article 34 TFEU. The UK justified the import licence requirement on the ground that it needed to know the origin of milk in order to regulate the temperature of its heat treatment, which varied according to the disease status of the exporting country. The Court said that this objective could be achieved by less restrictive means, such as obtaining a declaration signed by the importer.

In respect of the dealers' licences, the UK argued that, owing to the disparities between the national laws on the production of UHT milk, this was the only effective means of protecting public health. Again the Court disagreed, saying that it would reject the public-health defence on the ground of proportionality if the same interests were already protected in the state of origin. It noted that UHT milk was made according to similar rules and using similar machines in all the Member States. It also recognized that UHT milk, by its very nature, could be kept for long periods, which obviated the need for control over the whole process. If it was concerned about protecting the health of humans, the Court said that the UK could ensure safeguards equivalent to those which it had prescribed for domestic production of UHT milk. However, the UK had to take into account certificates issued by the competent authorities of the exporting states. The Court said that these certificates would raise a presumption that the imported goods complied with the requirements of domestic health legislation, thereby enabling checks carried out on importation to be simplified.[364]

UHT shows how the principle of mutual recognition serves to limit the scope of the derogations by preventing the host state from replicating checks on imported products which have already been carried out by the state of origin. The Court says that such double checks either constitute a disguised restriction on trade[365] or are disproportionate.[366] In *Biologische Producten*[367] the Court reminded the Member States of their duty 'to assist

[359] Case 42/82 *Commission* v. *France (wine wars)* [1983] ECR 1013.

[360] See also Case C–420/01 *Commission* v. *Italy (energy drinks with caffeine)* [2003] ECR I–6445.

[361] Para. 61.   [362] Para. 57.

[363] Case 124/81 *Commission* v. *UK* [1983] ECR 203. See also Case C–170/04 *Rosengren* v. *Riksåklagaren* [2007] ECR I–4071, paras. 43–56.

[364] Para. 30.

[365] Case 272/80 *Frans-Nederlandse Maatschappij voor Biologische Producten* [1981] ECR 3277, para. 15.

[366] Case 132/80 *United Foods* [1981] ECR 995, para. 29; Case 188/84 *Commission* v. *France (woodworking machines)* [1986] ECR 419, para. 16.

[367] Case 272/80 [1981] ECR 3277. See also Case C–292/94 *Criminal Proceedings against Brandsma* [1996] ECR I–2159 and Case C–400/96 *Criminal Proceedings against Jean Harpegnies* [1998] ECR I–5121; Case C–212/03 *Commission* v. *France* [2005] ECR I–4213, paras. 42–3.

in bringing about a relaxation of the controls existing in intra-[Union] trade'.[368] It also said that while the host state was entitled to require the product to undergo a fresh examination, the authorities were not entitled to require unnecessary technical or chemical analyses or laboratory tests, where those analyses or tests had already been carried out in another Member State and the results were available to the host state authorities.[369] In *Commission* v. *Portugal* the Court went further and said that '[s]trict compliance' with the obligation to cooperate required 'an active approach' on the part of the authorities in the host state. The Member States also had to ensure that the competent approval bodies cooperated with each other to facilitate the procedures to be followed to obtain access to the national market of the host state.[370]

5. PROCEDURALIZATION OF PROPORTIONALITY

Cases such as *UHT* and *Biologische Producten* suggest an increasing emphasis on 'good governance' in the states' approach to the question of proportionality, a point emphasized in *Greenham and Abel*.[371] Greenham was prosecuted for selling meal replacement food supplements ('Juice Plus + vegetable mixture' and 'Juice Plus + fruit mixture') which had been imported from other Member States where they had been lawfully manufactured and/or marketed. The substance coenzyme Q10 had been added to these products, a nutrient whose addition was not authorized in France for human consumption (although authorized in a number of other Member States). The Court said that the French rules breached Article 34 TFEU but could be justified under Article 36 TFEU provided the following conditions were satisfied:

- The national rules had to make provision for a procedure enabling economic operators to have a nutrient included on the national list of authorized substances.
- The criteria for inclusion had to be based on objective and non-discriminatory criteria.[372]
- The procedure had to be readily accessible and completed within a reasonable time.
- If the application was turned down, this decision had to be open to challenge before the courts.[373]
- An application to obtain the inclusion of a nutrient on the national list of authorized substances could be refused by the competent national authorities only if such substance posed a genuine risk to public health following a detailed assessment of the risk to public health, using the most reliable scientific data available and the most recent results of international research.

---

[368] Para. 14.   [369] Para. 14.

[370] Case C–432/03 *Commission* v. *Portugal* [2005] ECR I–9665, para. 47. Cf. Case C–244/06 *Dynamic Medien* [2008] ECR I–505, where the Court did not take into account at the proportionality stage the fact that the British authorities had already classified the DVDs.

[371] Case C–95/01 *Greenham and Abel* [2004] ECR I–1333. See also Case C–24/00 *Commission* v. *France (nutrients)* [2004] ECR I–1277, noted in M. Jarvis (2004) 41 *CMLRev.* 1395. The Court is also applying similar principles to Member States wishing to derogate from the other fundamental freedoms, such as services, as the healthcare cases demonstrate (considered in Ch. 9). By contrast, it has in the past been less stringent in its application of the procedural aspects of the proportionality principle to acts of the *Union* institutions: see, e.g., Joined Cases C–154 and 155/04 *Alliance for Natural Health* [2005] ECR I–6451, considered in Ch. 15.

[372] This was added in Case C–219/07 *Nationale Raad van Dierenkwekers en Liefhebbers VZW* [2008] ECR I–4475, para. 34.

[373] *Greenham and Abel*, n. 371, para. 35. See also Case C–244/06 *Dynamic Medien* [2008] ECR I–505, para. 50; Case C–219/07 *Nationale Raad van Dierenkwekers en Liefhebbers VZW* [2008] ECR I–4475, paras. 33–7.

The state also had to show that the steps taken were proportionate.[374]

In other words, to satisfy the principle of proportionality there needed to be a procedure available for the applicant to obtain authorization for its product and this procedure had to comply with principles of good administration. In *Mickelsson*[375] the Court emphasized that the relevant national authorities also had to be proactive. The case concerned a Swedish rule limiting the use of jet skis to general navigable waterways and not inland waterways unless those inland waterways had been specifically designated by the relevant authorities. The Court said the rule was proportionate on environmental protection grounds, provided that those authorities had actually made use of the power conferred on them to designate inland waterways suitable for jet skis, and such measures had been adopted within a reasonable period after the entry into force of that law.[376]

The proceduralization of the requirements necessary to satisfy the proportionality test is also reflected in the Court's insistence that traders be given sufficient warning of changes in national regulation and adequate time to adapt. This can be seen in *Radlberger*[377] concerning the German deposit-and-return system. The Court accepted that the system, which had a discriminatory effect on importers,[378] could be justified on the grounds of environmental protection. It said that, while the measures were suitable for achieving that objective, they were disproportionate because of the manner in which they had been introduced: they did not afford the producers and distributors a transitional period sufficient to enable them to adapt to the requirements of the new system before the new system entered into force.[379]

The same argument about good governance influenced the Court in *Commission v. Austria (heavy lorries)*,[380] where it found that the Austrian ban on heavy lorries using the A12 in the Tyrol on environmental grounds was disproportionate: a transitional period of only two months for introducing the ban was 'clearly insufficient'.[381] The Court also said that the Austrian authorities were 'under a duty to examine carefully the possibility of using measures less restrictive of freedom of movement'[382] before adopting a measure 'so radical as a total traffic ban on a section of motorway constituting a vital route of communication between certain Member States'.[383] This decision is not surprising because, if the Court were to find otherwise, it would threaten the viability of the very principle underpinning the single market, namely specialization and comparative advantage. If Member States could simply block a major transit route then the benefits of geographical specialization in the production of goods would be lost if these goods could not be transported elsewhere in the Union.[384]

---

[374] Case C–219/07 *Nationale Raad van Dierenkwekers en Liefhebbers VZW* [2008] ECR I–4475, para. 36.

[375] Case C–142/05 *Aklagaren v. Mickelsson, Roos* [2009] ECR I–4273. See also Case C–433/05 *Sandström* [2010] ECR I–2885.

[376] Para. 39.

[377] Case C–309/02 *Radlberger Getränkegesellschaft mbH & Co. v. Land Baden-Württemberg* [2004] ECR I–11763, para. 70. See also Case C–463/01 *Commission v. Germany (deposit and return)* [2004] ECR I–11705, para. 67.

[378] Para. 68.

[379] Case C–463/01 *Commission v. Germany (deposit and return)* [2004] ECR I–11705, para. 79; Case C–309/02 *Radlberger* [2004] ECR I–11763, para. 81.

[380] Case C–320/03 *Commission v. Austria (heavy lorries)* [2005] ECR I–7929, para. 35.

[381] Para. 90.   [382] Para. 87.

[383] See n. 380. The authorities also should have ensured there was sufficient rail capacity to allow a transfer from road to rail before implementing such a measure (para. 88).

[384] See further C. Hilson, 'Going local? EU law, localism and climate change' (2008) 33 *ELRev.* 194, 209. He argues that the theory of comparative advantage assumes the absence of externalities. Given that the climate change costs imposed by trade-related transport are not currently paid by producers and consumers,

E. FUNDAMENTAL HUMAN RIGHTS

While proportionality has proved the most significant general principle of law limiting the Member States' right to take measures restrictive of free movement, the Court has also emphasized that fundamental human rights, including freedom of expression, the freedom to pursue a trade or profession, and the right to own property can limit a Member State's discretion (see fig. 4.1). Thus, fundamental rights can serve a twofold function in the jurisprudence on free movement of goods: (1) they can *constitute* a mandatory requirement, as in *Schmidberger*[385] (i.e., fundamental rights can be invoked defensively by a Member State to justify a restriction on trade); and (2) they can also be used to *limit* Member State action under a derogation or mandatory requirement.[386] It is this latter situation that we shall now consider.

In *Familiapress*[387] the Court said that, while a Member State can rely on overriding requirements to justify rules which may obstruct the exercise of free movement of goods, 'such justification must also be interpreted in the light of the general principles of law and in particular of fundamental rights', including freedom of expression.[388] The Court said that the Austrian prohibition on prize competitions in magazines, while justified on the grounds of the maintenance of the plurality of the press (in itself a human rights justification in the *Schmidberger* sense), could 'detract from freedom of expression'. However, most fundamental rights are not absolute and are subject to derogations, as the Court noted in *Familiapress*. It said that Article 10 of the European Convention did permit derogations for the purposes of maintaining press diversity, insofar as they are prescribed by law and are necessary in a democratic society.[389] The Court then said that it was for the national court to determine whether the national law was proportionate to the aim of maintaining press diversity and whether the objective could be attained by measures less restrictive of both intra-Union trade and freedom of expression.[390] In other words, as the Court said in *Metronome Musik*,[391] fundamental rights themselves may be restricted, provided that any restrictions 'correspond to objectives of the general interest pursued by the European Union and do not constitute in relation to the aim pursued a disproportionate and intolerable interference, impairing the very substance of the rights guaranteed'.

The introduction of the Charter of Fundamental Rights 2000—and now its incorporation (by reference) into the Treaty[392]—helps legitimize the Court's increasing reference to human rights and gives it a further steer as to what constitutes 'Union' fundamental rights.[393] Nevertheless, the balancing exercise is by no means straightforward. As the Court has said on a number of occasions, the economic freedom, free movement of goods, is deemed to be a fundamental right[394] in just the same way as more traditional civil and

there is almost certainly too much long-distance trade at present. This might (but not always in the case of, e.g., exotic produce grown out of season in greenhouses) favour local purchasing.

[385] Case C–112/00 [2003] ECR I–5659, considered at n. 38.
[386] Case C–260/89 *Elliniki Radiophonia Tiléorassi AE v. Dimotiki Etairia Pliroforissis and Sotirios Kouvelas* [1991] ECR I–2925, para. 45.
[387] Case C–368/95 [1997] ECR I–3689.   [388] Paras. 24–5.
[389] Para. 26, citing the judgment of the ECtHR of 24 Nov. 1993 in *Informationsverein Lentia v. Austria*, Series A, No. 276.
[390] Para. 27.
[391] Case C–200/96 *Metronome Musik GmbH v. Music Point Hokamp GmbH* [1998] ECR I–1953, para. 21.
[392] Art. 6(1) TEU.
[393] See Case C–244/06 *Dynamic Medien* [2008] ECR I–505, para. 41, where the Court expressly referred to the Charter to justify developing the new mandatory requirement, the protection of the child.
[394] See, e.g., Case C–265/95 *Commission v. France* [1997] ECR I–6959, para. 24; Case C–320/03 *Commission v. Austria* [2005] ECR I–7929, para. 63.

political fundamental rights. The hierarchy between the rights is therefore less obvious than in national systems.[395]

F. HARMONIZATION AND TRUST

A Member State can invoke the Article 36 TFEU derogations and the mandatory requirements[396] only in the absence of Union rules.[397] This can be seen in *Hedley Lomas*,[398] where the Court said 'recourse to Article 36 TFEU is no longer possible where [Union] Directives provide for harmonisation of measures necessary to achieve the specific objective which would be furthered by reliance upon this provision'.[399] The case concerned a refusal by the UK to issue licences for the export of live animals intended for slaughter in Spain, contrary to Article 35 TFEU, on the ground that the UK considered that Spanish slaughter houses did not respect the provisions of Directive 74/577/EEC[400] on stunning animals before slaughter. The UK justified its refusal on the ground of animal health under Article 36 TFEU. The Court rejected this defence because Directive 74/577 already occupied the field, which meant that the Member States lost the right to act in this area.

The principles laid down in *Hedley Lomas* were reiterated in *CWF*.[401] The case concerned the export of live calves for rearing in veal crates. Since there was a harmonization directive which exhaustively regulated certain minimum standards, the UK could not rely on the public-health defence to justify preventing the export of the calves to states with standards which complied only with the minima laid down by the directive but not the high standards provided by British law. But the case raised the question whether the UK could rely on the public-policy or public-morality derogations instead, based on the fact that a section of public opinion believed that the system put in place by the directive did not adequately protect animal health. The Court rejected this argument on the ground that the public-policy and public-morality arguments were not separate justifications but were rather part of the (impermissible) public-health arguments.[402] Consistently with *Cullet*, the Court argued that a Member State could not rely on the views or the behaviour of a section of national public opinion unilaterally to challenge a harmonizing measure adopted by the Union institutions.[403]

But what happens if one Member State suspects that another is not enforcing the harmonization directive? The answer from the Court in *Hedley Lomas* is simple: a Member State cannot unilaterally adopt, on its own authority, corrective or protective measures designed to address any breach by another Member State of rules of Union law.[404] The

---

[395] J. Coppel and A. O'Neill, 'The European Court of Justice: Taking rights seriously' (1992) 14 *Legal Studies* 227. For an example of this troubled relationship, see the discussion of Case C–438/05 *Viking* [2007] ECR I–10779 in Ch. 7.

[396] See Case 120/78 *Cassis de Dijon* [1979] ECR 649, para. 8.

[397] Cf. Case C–389/96 *Aher-Waggon* [1998] ECR I–4473; Case C–3/99 *Cidrerie Ruwet* v. *Stassen* [2000] ECR I–8749; Case 190/87 *Oberkreisdirektor* v. *Moorman* [1988] ECR 4689, para. 10.

[398] Case C–5/94 [1996] ECR I–2553.   [399] Para. 18.

[400] [1974] OJ L316/10, repealed and replaced by Council Dir. 93/119 ([1993] OJ L340/21).

[401] Case C–1/96 *R.* v. *MAFF, ex p. Compassion in World Farming* [1998] ECR I–1251.

[402] Para. 66. See also Case C–165/08 *Commission* v. *Poland (GMOs)* [2009] ECR I–6843, where the Court rejected ethical and religious reasons raised to explain Poland's failure to respect the directive.

[403] Para. 67. Case 231/83 *Cullet* [1985] ECR 305 is considered at n. 20.

[404] Para. 20. As a last resort Member States could start enforcement proceedings under Art. 259 TFEU or could ask the Commission to act under Art. 258 TFEU: Case C–11/95 *Commission* v. *Belgium* [1996] ECR I–4115, paras. 36–7.

Court added 'Member States must rely on trust in each other to carry out inspections on their respective territories.'[405] The importance of the concept of mutual trust has underpinned cases such as *Biologische Producten*[406] on double checks. But what happens if this trust has broken down?[407] The Union has tried to buttress the process of confidence-building in the field of customs and agriculture by passing Regulation 515/97[408] on mutual assistance between the administrative authorities of the Member States and cooperation between the Member States and the Commission to ensure the correct application of the law. However, as *Hedley Lomas* shows, considerable suspicion between different authorities still remains. Nevertheless, the Court means business: in *Hedley Lomas* it made clear that the UK would be liable in damages for state liability under *Factortame* principles[409] for refusing to issue the export licence in breach of Article 35 TFEU. And because this was an area in which the UK had no discretion, the breach was deemed sufficiently serious.[410]

G. THE MUTUAL RECOGNITION REGULATION 764/2008

Despite the talk of trust on which the principle of mutual recognition depends, Member States still invoke Article 36 TFEU or the mandatory requirements to prevent goods coming on to their market. This, of course, creates significant barriers to free movement of goods, especially when the host state assumes that it can do so as of right rather than as an exception. Harmonization (considered in Chapter 15) is one response to the problem, as *Hedley Lomas* and *CWF* show. However, in the absence of harmonization legislation, the Union institutions have introduced administrative procedures to supplement judicial recourse aimed at improving the transparency of national measures taken against imported products.[411]

The first of those measures was Decision 3052/95/EC establishing a procedure for the exchange of information on national measures derogating from the principle of free movement of goods.[412] This was a direct result of the inventory of national measures which had not been harmonized under Article 114 TFEU, drawn up by the Commission under the now defunct Article 100b EEC.[413] It was a catch-all measure[414] which applied in the absence of any more specific provisions, such as prior notification under the Information Directive 2015/1535[415] or the notification procedure laid down under the Product Safety

---

[405] Para. 19. In the context of external relations, see Case C–124/95 *R. v. HM Treasury and Bank of England, ex p. Centro-Com Srl* [1997] ECR I–81, para. 49.

[406] Case 272/80 [1981] ECR 3277, considered at n. 367 and Case 25/88 *Bouchara* [1989] ECR 1105, para. 18. See also Case 46/76 *Bauhuis* v. *Netherlands* [1977] ECR 5, para. 22 (inspections).

[407] This was the central preoccupation of the Sutherland report. See further Ch. 15.

[408] [1997] OJ L82/1.

[409] Joined Cases C–46 and 48/93 *Brasserie du Pêcheur and Factortame* [1996] ECR I–1029. See further Ch. 11.

[410] Paras. 28–9. See also Case C–445/06 *Danske Slagterier* v. *Bundesrepublik Deutschland* [2009] ECR I–2119 concerning a state liability claim brought by a Danish association of slaughterhouse companies against Germany alleging that Germany had breached various EU directives and the Treaty. The Court makes clear, inter alia, that a successful state liability claim is not dependent on a prior successful Art. 258 TFEU action, nor do Art. 258 TFEU proceedings suspend national limitation periods.

[411] Third preambular para. to Dec. 3052/95 ([1995] OJ L321/1). [412] [1995] OJ L321/1.

[413] Commission Communication, 'Management of the mutual recognition of national rules after 1992: Operation conclusions reached in the light of the inventory drawn up pursuant to Article 100b of the EC Treaty' ([1993] OJ C353/4). See further Ch. 1.

[414] COM(2000) 194, 2. [415] [2015] OJ L241/1.

Directive 2001/95 when a product is withdrawn.[416] Unlike the procedure under the Information Directive 2015/1535 (considered in Chapter 4), Decision 3052/95 required 'ex-post' notification to the Commission by a Member State which had taken measures[417] 'to prevent the free movement or placing on the market of a particular model or type of product lawfully produced or marketed in another Member State'. The Commission then informed the other Member States, which could, along with the Commission, request further information. The decision did not, however, allow the other Member States to make comments or to interfere with the rules of the notifying Member State.

Given the low-key nature of the Decision and the lack of any incentive to notify, it is perhaps not surprising that levels of notification were low (102 measures were notified between 1995 and 1998) with notification coming from just five countries.[418] Failure by a state to notify the Commission could lead the state to be condemned by the Court in Article 258 TFEU enforcement proceedings but again this was rare.[419] As a result, Decision 3052/95 was repealed and replaced by a strengthened procedure contained in Regulation 764/2008.[420] This so-called 'Mutual Recognition' Regulation was adopted as part of the Commission's 2007 'Package on Internal Market for Goods' (considered in Chapter 4). This Regulation replaces the process of notifying the Commission with a dialogue between the national authorities of the host state and the 'economic operator' (i.e., the manufacturer of the product, if established in the Union, or the person who has placed, or wishes to place, the product on the market[421]). This dialogue is triggered when the host state has taken or intends to take, on the basis of a technical rule,[422] a decision prohibiting the placing of a product on the market, requiring the product's modification or additional testing, or requiring the product to be withdrawn from the market (the so-called Article 2(1) decision).[423]

One of the key features of the Regulation is that it clearly places the burden on the Member State to explain—in writing—to the economic operator the technical rule on which the Article 2(1) decision is to be based and setting out technical or scientific evidence to the effect that:[424]

- the intended decision is justified on one of the grounds of public interest set out in Article 36 TFEU or by reference to other overriding reasons of public interest
- the intended decision is appropriate for the purpose of achieving the objective pursued and does not go beyond what is necessary in order to obtain that objective.

The regulation then lays down a time scale in which the economic operator must respond to defend its case. According to Article 6(2), if the host state persists with its decision it must notify the economic operator and the Commission, setting out why it is rejecting the arguments put forward by the economic operator and the technical or scientific evidence on which the decision is based, as well as identifying any remedies available under national law.[425] If the host state authority fails to follow the Article 6(2) procedure, 'the product shall be deemed to be lawfully marketed in that Member State'. The regulation

---

[416] [2002] OJ L11/4.

[417] Dec. 3052/95 defines 'measure' as any measure taken by a Member State, except for judicial decisions, which has the effect of restricting the free movement of goods lawfully produced or marketed in another Member State, regardless of its form or the authority from which it emanates: Joined Cases C–388 and 429/00 *Radiosistemi Srl v. Prefetto di Genova* [2002] ECR I–5845, paras. 67–73.

[418] Report from the Commission on the implementation of Dec. 3052/95/EC, COM(2000) 194 final.

[419] Case C–432/03 *Commission v. Portugal (polyethylene pipes)* [2005] ECR I–9665, para. 60; Case C–88/07 *Commission v. Spain (medicinal herbs)* [2009] ECR I–1353, para. 115.

[420] [2008] OJ L218/21.   [421] Art. 8.   [422] As defined in Art. 2(2).

[423] Art. 2(1).   [424] Art. 6(1).   [425] Art. 6(2).

also establishes 'product contact points' in each Member State, providing information about technical rules on products and explaining the implementation of the mutual recognition principle.

H. CONCLUSIONS

One of the strengths of the new procedure under the Mutual Recognition Regulation is that it takes as its starting point the position that goods lawfully marketed in one of the Member States should be capable of being sold in another. It is for the host Member State to explain why this is not the case. It therefore makes very clear that the derogations and mandatory requirements are the exception and not the rule. This will represent a significant change in perspective for a number of Member States.

FURTHER READING

Analysis of the derogations

C. BARNARD, 'Derogations, justifications and the Four Freedoms: Is state interest really protected?' in C. Barnard and O. Odudu (eds.), *The Outer Limits of European Union Law* (Oxford: Hart Publishing, 2009).

L. GORMLEY, 'Recent case law on the free movement of goods: Some hot potatoes' (1990) 27 *CMLRev.* 825.

P. KOUTRAKOS, 'The application of EC law to defence industries—Changing interpretation of Article 296 EC' in C. Barnard and O. Odudu (eds.), *The Outer Limits of European Union Law* (Oxford: Hart Publishing, 2009).

N. NIC SHUIBHNE, 'The free movement of goods and Article 28 EC: An evolving framework' (2002) 27 *ELRev.* 408, esp. 419ff.

P. OLIVER, 'A review of the case law of the Court of Justice on Articles 30 to 36 EEC in 1985' (1986) 23 *CMLRev.* 325.

J. SCOTT, 'Mandatory or imperative requirements in the EU and the WTO' in C. Barnard and J. Scott (eds.), *The Law of the Single European Market: Unpacking the premises* (Oxford: Hart Publishing, 2002).

E. SPAVENTA, 'On discrimination and the theory of mandatory requirements' (2001) 3 *CYELS* 457.

Specific derogations

A. BIONDI, 'The merchant, the thief and the citizen: The circulation of works of art within the EU' (1997) 34 *CMLRev.* 1173.

N. NIC SHUIBHNE and M. MASI, 'Proving public interest: The growing impact of evidence in free movement case law' (2013) 50 *CMLRev.* 965.

T. VAN RIJN, 'A review of the case law of the Court of Justice on Articles 30 to 36 EEC in 1986 and 1987' (1988) 25 *CMLRev.* 593.

Trust-enhancing principles

K. LENAERTS, '"In the Union we trust": Trust-enhancing principles of Community law' (2004) 41 *CMLRev.* 317.

G. Majone, 'The precautionary principle and its policy implications' (2002) 40 *JCMS* 89.

J. Scott and E. Vos, 'The juridification of uncertainty: Observations on the ambivalence of the precautionary principle within the EU and the WTO' in C. Joerges and R. Dehousse (eds.), *Good Governance in Europe's Integrated Market* (Oxford: OUP, 2002).

What the derogations and mandatory requirements are trying to achieve

B. De Witte, 'Non-market values in internal market legislation' in N. Nic Shuibhne (ed.), *Regulating the Internal Market* (Cheltenham: Edward Elgar, 2006).

M. Poiares Maduro, *We the Court: The European Court of Justice and the European Economic Constitution* (Oxford: Hart Publishing, 1998).

PART III

FREE MOVEMENT OF PERSONS AND SERVICES

7

THE FREE MOVEMENT
OF PERSONS:
KEY PRINCIPLES

A. INTRODUCTION

The right for people to move freely from one state to another is a distinguishing feature of a common market. Yet although Article 3(1)(c) EEC (now repealed) provided that the Community (as it then was) aspired to 'the abolition, as between Member States, of obstacles to freedom of movement for … persons',[1] the reality—at least for the first 40 years of the EU's existence—was rather different. The substantive provisions of the original Treaty of Rome did not in fact provide a general right of free movement for all people and companies: to qualify the individual or company had to be both a *national* of a Member State[2] (with nationality being a matter for national—not Union—law) *and* be engaged in an

---

[1] See also Case 118/75 *Watson and Belmann* [1978] ECR 1185, paras. 16–17.
[2] The same applies to companies: Case C–452/04 *Fidium Finanz AG v. Bundesanstalt für Finanzdienstleistungsaufsicht* [2006] ECR I–9521, para. 47.

economic activity as a worker (Articles 45–8 TFEU), a self-employed person/company/branch or agency (Articles 49–55 TFEU), or as a provider or receiver of services (Articles 56–62 TFEU). Those falling within the scope of these 'fundamental'[3] freedoms enjoyed—and continue to enjoy—the right to free movement subject to derogations on the grounds of public policy, public security, and public health, as well as a more tailored exception for employment in the public service.

Underpinning Articles 45, 49, and 56 TFEU is, at a minimum, the principle of non-discrimination on the ground of nationality (or seat in the case of corporations). Thus, the migrant has to enjoy the same treatment as nationals in a comparable situation. As we saw in Chapter 1, the principle of equal treatment gives Member States the autonomy to determine the substance of the rules applicable in their territory; Union law will not interfere with those rules provided that they do not discriminate directly or indirectly against EU migrants. However, in more recent case law the Court has moved beyond the discrimination model and, returning to the language of the original Article 3(1)(c) EEC, it has focused instead on removing 'obstacles' or 'restrictions' to free movement, including those which are non-discriminatory. While such an approach poses a greater threat to the Member States' legislative autonomy, it is an important step towards removing barriers to the creation of a single market where persons and services can, in principle, move freely.

B. THE EVOLUTION OF THE RIGHTS TO FREE MOVEMENT

The original idea behind Articles 45–62 TFEU was to ensure that the so-called 'factors of production' (workers, the self-employed, and service providers) could move from regions where jobs were hard to find to those areas needing extra workers. This was supposed to lead to an equalization in the price of labour across the EU and greater prosperity for all. Free movement of persons was also seen as something of a safety valve allowing individuals to move away from unemployment at home to employment abroad. In fact, in the early days of the EU few people took advantage of this opportunity to move. This was due to a variety of factors: social (workers did not want to move without their families), economic (the fear of losing entitlements to social benefits, especially pensions, if workers moved out of their home states), cultural (the familiarity and enjoyment of the way of life in their own states), and linguistic (individuals often lacked the necessary language skills).

By adopting secondary legislation in the late 1960s/early 1970s (legislation which has since been broadly construed by the Court), in particular Regulation 1612/68, now Regulation 492/11 on the free movement of workers,[4] the EU helped to remove some of these obstacles to free movement. But it was not until the enlargement of the EU in 2004 that significant movement of people occurred; and some Member States proved more popular destinations than others. As the UK's New Settlement Decision put it:[5]

> Different levels of remuneration among the Member States make some offers of employment more attractive than others, with consequential movements that are a direct result of the freedom of the market. However, the social security systems of the Member States, which Union law coordinates but does not harmonise, are diversely structured and this may in itself attract workers to certain Member States.

[3] See, e.g., Case 222/86 *Union nationale des entraineurs et cadres techniques professionnels du football (Unectef)* v. *Georges Heylens* [1987] ECR 4097, paras. 8 and 14 (Art. 45 TFEU).
[4] [2011] OJ L141/1   [5] European Council Conclusions, 18–19 Feb. 2016.

In 1990 the Union adopted three specific directives conferring a general right of movement and residence on the semi-economically active: the retired, students, and persons with independent means (PIMs). However, for this group the rights to move and reside in another Member State were subject to the requirement that the individual had sufficient resources and medical insurance,[6] limitations intended to stop benefit and healthcare tourism.[7] Nevertheless, these three directives demonstrated a gradual erosion of the link between *economic* activity and free movement and a shift in perception away from viewing migrants as merely factors of production to seeing them as individuals with rights which could be enforced against the host state. At Maastricht this change in perspective culminated in the recognition of the status of 'citizen of the Union' for every national of a Member State, with specific rights and duties attached (Articles 20–5 TFEU). In practice, the most important provision has been Article 21 TFEU, which has given citizens the right to move and reside freely in the Member States, subject to the limitations and conditions laid down in the Treaty and secondary legislation. The significance of the Treaty provisions on citizenship was emphasized in the leading case of *Grzelczyk*,[8] where the Court famously said:

> Union citizenship is destined to be the fundamental status of nationals of the Member States, enabling those who find themselves in the same situation to enjoy the same treatment in law irrespective of their nationality, subject to such exceptions as are expressly provided for.

Implicit in this language is the potentially transformative nature of the citizenship provisions, not only for the lives of the beneficiaries but also in terms of prompting the Court to reconsider fundamental tenets of its earlier jurisprudence.[9] This seemed to be the driving motivation behind the case law in the early 2000s. However, more recent case law has focused more squarely on the question of the limits of the rights of EU citizens. This is considered further in Chapters 10 and 12.

The consolidation of citizen's rights came with the adoption of European Parliament and Council Directive 2004/38 on the right of citizens of the Union and their family members to move and reside freely within the territory of the Member States (the Citizens' Rights Directive (CRD)).[10] This directive, repealing and replacing most of the previous secondary legislation adopted in the 1960s (but not Regulation 492/11 on free movement of workers) as well as the 1990 Residence Directives, has radically altered and improved the rights of migrant EU citizens and their families. It is discussed in detail in Chapter 10. For the present it is sufficient to note that the directive is premised on the idea that the longer individuals reside in the host state the more rights they enjoy. In particular, during the first three months of residence (Article 6(1) CRD) and after five years of residence

---

[6] Council Dirs. 90/364/EEC ([1990] OJ L180/26) on the rights of residence for persons of sufficient means (the 'Playboy' Directive), 90/365/EEC on the rights of residence for employees and self-employed persons who have ceased their occupational activity ([1990] OJ L180/28), and 90/366/EEC ([1990] OJ L180/30) on the rights of residence for students repealed and replaced by Dir. 93/96 ([1993] OJ L317/59). All three directives have been repealed and replaced by the Citizens Rights Dir. 2004/38 ([2004] OJ L158/77).

[7] That is, 'moving to a Member State with a more congenial social security environment': Case C–456/02 *Trojani* [2004] ECR I–7573, Geelhoed AG's Opinion, para. 13 (and para. 18).

[8] Case C–184/99 [2001] ECR I–6193, para. 31, echoing La Pergola AG in Case C–85/96 *Martínez Sala* [1998] ECR I–2691, para.18.

[9] See, e.g., Case C–138/02 *Collins* v. *Secretary of State for Work and Pensions* [2004] ECR I–2703, considered in Ch. 8 and Case C–50/06 *Commission* v. *The Netherlands (criminal convictions)* [2007] ECR I–4383, para. 32, considered in Ch. 12.

[10] [2004] OJ L158/77.

(Article 16 CRD) there is no need to show any economic activity at all. This illustrates the extent to which the link with economic activity has now been severed. This is a significant change in perspective, a change which serves to underline just how far the EU has moved from its common market origins. On the other hand, during the period three months to five years (Article 7 CRD) EU citizens must be engaged in economic activity or have sufficient resources or medical insurance to look after themselves and their families. A summary of the sources of legal rights for EU citizens exercising free movement can be found in fig. 7.1. It is not always clear when the Court will decide cases based on an interpretation of the Treaty provisions and when it will decide a case by reference to the secondary legislation; much turns on the nature of the questions referred by the national court. However, if a case concerns family rights or benefits, the Court will more often refer to the secondary legislation, especially the CRD.

The enactment of the CRD has also served to highlight an increasing divergence between the rights given to natural persons—through the introduction of Union citizenship, the CRD, and the sometimes generous application of fundamental human rights—and those given to legal persons. The rights of legal persons are considered in Chapter 11.

The free movement of persons has always been an area of greater sensitivity than the free movement of goods. People raise welfare and even security implications in a way that goods do not. This helps to explain why the original Treaty gave rights only to the economically active: they brought skills to the host state's economy and could support themselves financially. It also helps to explain why there is no equivalent to the Common Commercial Policy for people: fearing the pressure generated by an open border policy on national job markets and welfare systems, governments of the Member States refused to allow individuals holding the nationality of a non-Member State (known as 'third-country nationals' (TCNs)) who have entered the EU to benefit from the rights of free movement laid down in Articles 45–62 TFEU. However, the conclusion of the Schengen Agreement in 1985 marked a move—among at least some of the Member States—towards a common policy in respect of the immigration of TCNs, a subject which is outlined in Chapter 13.[11] Yet the principal focus of this book is on the specific rights to free movement enjoyed by nationals of the Member States of the EU. We start by examining the principles common to the Treaty provisions on persons, beginning with the most fundamental question: does EU law apply at all?

C. WHEN DO THE TREATY PROVISIONS ON FREE MOVEMENT APPLY?

In order for the rules on the free movement of persons to apply, the claimant must fall within the personal, material, and territorial scope of the Treaty provision; in addition, the claimant must be able to rely on the Treaty provision against the particular defendant. These questions are jurisdictional: if these four conditions are not satisfied, then Union law does not apply and the claimant will have recourse to national law only (if any).[12] We shall examine these conditions in turn.

[11] Further pressure was put on the EU to open its borders to TCNs with the conclusion of the General Agreement on Trade in Services (GATS).

[12] For a valiant—but ultimately unsuccessful—attempt by the defendant to argue that Union law does not apply to situations in addition to those outlined in this section, including matters involving fundamental rights, see Case C–438/05 *International Transport Workers' Federation* v. *Viking Line* [2007] ECR I–10779, paras. 38–55.

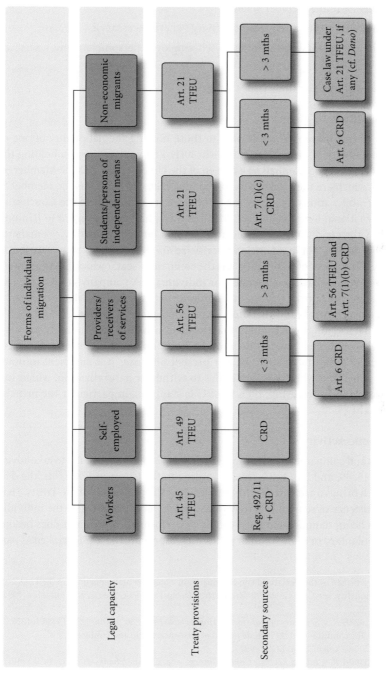

Fig. 7.1 Summary of sources of legal rights for EU citizens moving to another state

1. PERSONAL SCOPE

When considering the personal scope of Union law, there are three relevant elements:

- Is the individual a national of a Member State or, in the case of corporations, do they have their seat in a Member State?
- Are they engaged in an economic activity (where necessary)?
- Can they be classified as a worker, a self-employed person/company, a service provider, or a citizen?

This section will consider these issues in turn.

1.1 Nationality

The rights of free movement apply only to those holding the nationality of one of the Member States. This is made clear in Article 20(1) TFEU: 'Every person holding the nationality of a Member State shall be a citizen of the Union'. Thus, it is the Member States, not the EU, which are the gatekeepers to Union citizenship since it is the Member States which determine nationality.[13] This was confirmed in *Kaur*,[14] where the Court said that 'under international law, it is for each Member State, having due regard to [Union] law, to lay down the conditions for the acquisition and loss of nationality'.[15] Furthermore, one Member State is not in a position to criticize another Member State's attribution of nationality.[16] In respect of companies, it is the company's 'seat'[17] which has the same function for companies as nationality does for individuals. A company's seat is the state in which the company or firm, formed in accordance with the law of a Member State, has its registered office, central administration, or principal place of business.[18]

Although it had long been thought that the determination of nationality was a matter exclusively for national law, the decision in *Rottman*[19] cast doubt on this. This case is discussed in detail in Chapter 10. For present purposes it is sufficient to note that the Court ruled that where a state decides to withdraw naturalization, which in turn leads to loss of EU citizenship, then the EU law applies, in particular the principle of proportionality.[20]

1.2 Economic Activity

Individuals and companies need to be engaged in an 'economic activity' to take advantage of Articles 45, 49, and 56 TFEU. This, according to the Court in *Jundt*,[21] is 'the decisive factor' which brings an activity within the ambit of the provisions of the Treaty. In many cases the existence of economic activity is assumed, particularly where the individual or company is being remunerated for the activity performed. However, it does become an issue with voluntary or semi-voluntary activities, especially those undertaken as part of a

---

[13] This is confirmed by the Declaration on Nationality of a Member State appended to the TEU. For those with dual nationality, see Case C–369/90 *Micheletti* v. *Delagación del Gobierno en Cantabria* [1992] ECR I–4239, para. 10.

[14] Case C–192/99 *R.* v. *Secretary of State for the Home Department, ex p. Kaur* [2001] ECR I–1237.

[15] Para. 19. The conditions might include period of residence, birth, and family ties.

[16] Case C–200/02 *Chen* [2004] ECR I–9925.

[17] Case C–330/91 *R.* v. *Inland Revenue Commissioners, ex p. Commerzbank AG* [1993] ECR I–4017, para. 13. This issue is discussed further in Ch. 11.

[18] Case C–330/91 *Ex p. Commerzbank AG* [1993] ECR I–4017, para. 13. See also Case C–210/06 *Cartesio Oktató és Szolgáltató bt* [2008] ECR I–9641, para. 109.

[19] Case C–135/08 *Rottman* v. *Frestaat Bayern* [2010] ECR I–1449.   [20] Paras. 54–5.

[21] Case C–281/06 *Jundt* v. *Finanzamt Offenburg* [2007] ECR I–12231, para. 32.

rehabilitation programme.[22] In *Jundt* the Court emphasized that 'the activity must not be provided for nothing' for Article 56 TFEU to apply, albeit that there was no need for the service provider 'to be seeking to make a profit'.[23]

The position is different under Article 21(1) TFEU. There, non-economically active individuals can enjoy rights to free movement and residence in the host state, as the Court made clear in *Baumbast*:[24]

> the Treaty does not require that citizens of the Union pursue a professional or trade activity, whether as an employed or self-employed person, in order to enjoy the rights provided in Part Two of the [TFEU] on citizenship of the Union.

Therefore, in the case of citizens wishing to exercise their rights under Article 21(1) TFEU it is sufficient that they merely hold the nationality of one of the Member States; unlike individuals wishing to invoke Article 45, 49, or 56 TFEU, they need not be engaged in an economic activity. The detailed rules determining whether an individual is a worker, self-employed person, service provider or recipient, or citizen are set out in Chapters 8–11. For present purposes it is sufficient to note that the Court generally prefers to decide cases, where possible, under Article 45, 49, or 56 TFEU and the rights enjoyed by those who are economically active are greater than those who are not.

2. TERRITORIAL SCOPE

2.1 The Need for an Inter-State Element

Individuals must move from one Member State of the EU[25] (usually the home state) to another state (usually the host state) in order to fall within the material scope of Articles 45, 49, 56, and 21(1) TFEU.[26] This movement can take the form of individuals moving their residence to another Member State, usually for the purposes of employment,[27] or, in the case of frontier workers, having their residence in one state and working in another.[28] In the case of services, the provider or the recipient may not move but the service moves instead.[29] The requirement of an inter-state element is made explicit in Article 49 TFEU,

---

[22] Case 344/87 *Bettray v. Staatssecretaris van Justitie* [1989] ECR 1621, para. 17, considered further in Ch. 8.

[23] Case C–281/06 *Jundt* v. *Finanzamt Offenburg* [2007] ECR I–12231, para. 33.

[24] Case C–413/99 [2002] ECR I–7091, para. 83. See also the views of Jacobs AG in Case C–148/02 *Garcia Avello* [2003], para. 61 and Cosmas AG's even grander claims in Case C–378/97 *Wijsenbeek* [1999] ECR I–6207, para. 85: 'Article [21 TFEU] does not simply enshrine in constitutional terms the *acquis communautaire* as it existed when it was inserted into the Treaty and complement it by broadening the category of persons entitled to freedom of movement to include other classes of person not pursuing economic activities. Article [21 TFEU] also enshrines a right of a different kind, a true right of movement, stemming from the status as a citizen of the Union, which is not subsidiary in relation to European unification, whether economic or not.'

[25] The territorial scope of Union law is defined in Art. 355 TFEU to include all the states of the EU. Special provision is made for overseas territories. The free movement provisions also apply to the EEA states. For specific applications, see Case C–214/94 *Boukhalfa* v. *Germany* [1996] ECR I–2253 (EU law will apply to a national of a Member State (Belgium) who is permanently resident in a non-member country (Algeria) but employed by another Member State (Germany) in its embassy); Case 237/83 *Prodest* v. *Caisse Primaire d'Assurance Maladie de Paris* [1984] ECR 3153 (Union law may apply to professional activities pursued outside Union territory as long as the employment relationship retains a sufficiently close link with the Union).

[26] Case C–184/99 *Grzelczyk* [2001] ECR I–6193, para. 32.

[27] See, e.g., Case 53/81 *Levin* [1982] ECR 1035.

[28] This includes the situation where the individual resides in their home state and works in the host state (e.g., Case C–213/05 *Geven* v. *Land Nordrhein-Westfalen* [2007] ECR I–6347) or works in the home state but resides in another state (e.g., Case C–527/06 *Renneberg* v. *Staatssecretaris van Financiën* [2008] ECR I–7735).

[29] Case C–384/93 *Alpine Investments* [1995] ECR I–1141.

which refers to 'the freedom of establishment of nationals of a Member State in the territory of *another* Member State'.[30]

2.2 The Wholly Internal Situation

The corollary of the requirement of an inter-state element is that the free movement provisions cannot be applied to situations which are 'wholly internal to a Member State'.[31]
This can be seen in *Saunders*, where a British woman could not use Union law to challenge
an undertaking given to a criminal court in England that she return to Northern Ireland
and that she did not visit England or Wales for three years. As the Court said, Union law
does not apply to activities which have no factor linking them with any of the situations
governed by Union law[32] and which are confined in all aspects within a single Member
State.[33] This was also the situation in *Gauchard*,[34] where the manager of a French supermarket, who was prosecuted for extending his supermarket without permission, argued
that the French rules breached Union law. The Court disagreed, saying that Union law did
not apply because the company operating the supermarket was French and established
in France, and its manager was French and resided in France. Therefore, the case was
exclusively internal to a Member State. The Court seems to be firming up on this line.[35]

A purely hypothetical prospect of employment in another Member State is not sufficient to trigger the application of Union law. This can be seen in *Moser*,[36] where a German
national was denied access to a teacher training course in Germany because he was a
member of the Communist party. He argued that the refusal to admit him to the course
prevented him from applying for teaching posts in schools in other Member States and
was thus contrary to Union law. The Court said that this 'hypothetical' possibility did not
establish a sufficient connection with Union law to justify the application of Article 45
TFEU.[37] Similarly, in *Kremzow*[38] a retired Austrian judge, sentenced to life imprisonment
after having murdered another lawyer, could not invoke Union law to raise a question
of human rights. The Court said that while any deprivation of liberty could impede the
exercise of free movement, a purely hypothetical prospect of exercising the right of free
movement did not establish a sufficient connection with Union law.[39]

Conversely, Union law can be invoked by nationals against their own Member State
when they are exercising[40]—or have exercised[41]—their rights of free movement. This can

[30] Emphasis added.   [31] Case 175/78 *R. v. Saunders* [1979] ECR 1129, para. 11.
[32] Case 175/78 *R. v. Saunders* [1979] ECR 1129, para. 11.
[33] See, e.g., Case C–18/95 *Terhoeve v. Inspecteur van de Belastingdienst Particulieren* [1999] ECR I–345,
para. 26; Joined Cases C–64 and 65/96 *Land Nordrhein-Westfalen v. Kari Uecker and Vera Jacquet* [1997]
ECR I–3171, para. 16.
[34] Case 20/87 *Minstère public v. Gauchard* [1987] ECR 4879, para. 10. See also, e.g., Joined Cases C–330 and
331/90 *Ministerio Fiscal v. Lopez Brea* [1992] ECR I–323; Case 136/78 *Ministère public v. Auer (No. 1)* [1979] ECR
437; Joined Cases C–54 and 91/88 and C–14/89 *Criminal Proceedings against Niño* [1990] ECR I–3537.
[35] See, e.g., Case C–139/12 *Caixa d'Estalvis i Pensions de Barcelona v. Generalida de Cataluna*
EU:C:2014:174 (EU law did not apply because all aspects of the dispute were confined to a single state: the
dispute related to the acquisition of a significant shareholding in a property company, established in Spain,
by another company, also established in Spain, which was subject to tax on property acquired in Spain. See
also Joined Cases C–162 and 163/12 *Airport Shuttle Service v. Comune di Grottaferrata* EU:C:2014:74. In
Joined Cases C–419 and 420/12 *CronoService scarl v. Roma Capitale* EU:C:2014:81, para. 37 the Court said it
could not be presumed that the legislation would have any cross-border impact.
[36] Case 180/83 *Moser v. Land Baden-Württemberg* [1984] ECR 2539, para. 15.   [37] Para. 18.
[38] Case C–299/95 *Kremzow v. Republik Österreich* [1997] ECR I–2629.   [39] Para. 16.
[40] Case C–384/93 *Alpine Investments* [1995] ECR I–1141, paras. 15 and 20–2; Case C–60/00 *Carpenter*
[2002] ECR I–6279, para. 29.
[41] Case C–419/92 *Scholz* [1994] ECR I–505, para. 9.

be seen in *Surinder Singh*.[42] In 1982 Mr Surinder Singh, an Indian national, married a British citizen. From 1983 to 1985 they lived in Germany, where Mrs Singh was employed on a part-time basis. This meant that under Union law she was a worker who was entitled to be joined by her spouse.[43] In 1985 she returned to the UK to run a business. The question was whether Mrs Singh's husband could join her in the UK under Union law. If the situation was considered wholly internal then domestic law only would apply, with the result that Mr Singh was likely to be refused entry. If, however, the situation was not considered to be wholly internal then Union law would apply and Mr Singh could enter and remain in the UK as the spouse of an EU migrant.

The Court opted for the second approach.[44] It reasoned that a national like Mrs Singh might be deterred from exercising her Union law rights of free movement if, on returning to her state of origin (the UK), the conditions of entry or residence were not at least equivalent to those which she would enjoy on entering the territory of another state (e.g., France),[45] including the right to be accompanied by her spouse.[46] In this way *Singh* serves to confirm the earlier case of *Knoors*,[47] where the Court found that a Belgian-qualified Dutch plumber who had worked in Belgium was entitled to rely on his Union law rights to work in the Netherlands (his home state) using his Belgian qualifications. The Court said that his position was 'assimilated to that of another person enjoying their rights and liberties guaranteed by the Treaty'.[48]

2.3 Abuse and Fraud

Singh offers a glimpse of how Union law might be abused. What if the Singhs had gone to another Member State only for a short period? What if their marriage had been one of convenience? The Court dealt only briefly with these points. It said that Member States could prevent abuse of EU law where there was evasion of national legislation.[49] However, subsequent case law made clear that merely taking advantage of Union rights to free movement does not constitute abuse,[50] whatever the motive.[51]

In *O and B*[52] the Court provided some guidance as to how long an EU citizen had to live in another Member State before triggering EU-derived rights of residence for family members when they return to the home state. The Court said that the EU citizen's residence in the host state had to be 'sufficiently genuine so as to enable that citizen to create or strengthen family life in that state'.[53] Drawing on the different periods of residence laid down by the CRD, which applied by analogy to govern the situation of returning nationals, the Court said that EU citizens who migrated for three months did not intend to settle in the host state. So the refusal to confer on the TCN family members a derived right of residence, when the EU citizen returns to the

---

[42] Case C–370/90 *R. v. IAT and Surinder Singh, ex p. Secretary of State for the Home Department* [1992] ECR I–4265. See also Case C–18/95 *Terhoeve* [1999] ECR I–345. The decision in *Surinder Singh* may be qualified following the UK's New Settlement Decision (see further Ch. 10), cited later in this section.

[43] Under what are now Arts. 2 and 3(2) CRD, considered further in Ch. 10.   [44] Para. 21.

[45] Para. 19.   [46] Para. 21.

[47] Case 115/78 *Knoors v. Secretary of State for Economic Affairs* [1979] ECR 399. See also Case C–107/94 *Asscher* [1996] ECR I–3089.

[48] Para. 24.   [49] Case C–370/90 [1992] ECR I–4265, para. 24.

[50] Case C–212/97 *Centros* [1999] ECR I–1459, para. 27.

[51] Case C–109/01 *Secretary of State for the Home Department v. Akrich* [2003] ECR I–9607, paras. 55–7.

[52] Case C–456/12 *O and B v. Minister voor Immigratie, Integratie en Asiel* EU:C:2014:135, para. 61.

[53] Para. 51.

home state would 'not deter such a citizen from exercising his rights under Article 6'.[54] By contrast, those EU citizens residing in the host state for three months or more (under Articles 7 and 16 CRD) did establish genuine residence and so could return to the home state with their family members.[55]

The Court briefly addressed the question of abuse in *O and B*. It said that the scope of Union law could not be extended to cover abuses, and proof of abuse requires:

> first, a combination of objective circumstances in which despite formal observance of the conditions laid down by the European Union rules, the purpose of those rules has not been achieved, and secondly a subjective element consisting in the intention to obtain an advantage form the European Union rules by artificially creating the conditions laid down for obtaining it.[56]

However, the Court did not elaborate further, although in the past the Court has largely equated abuse with marriages of convenience.[57] Article 35 CRD also deals with abuse. It provides:

> Member States may adopt the necessary measures to refuse, terminate or withdraw any right conferred by this Directive in the case of abuse of rights or fraud, such as marriages of convenience. Any such measure shall be proportionate and subject to the procedural safeguards provided for in Articles 30 and 31.

In *R. (on the application of McCarthy)*[58] the Court said that Member States could not adopt a blanket rule (*in casu* requiring all TCN family members of an EU citizen to have an entry permit), even where the state considers itself to be faced with a high number of cases of abuse of right or fraud committed by TCNs, founded on considerations of general prevention. The Court required 'specific assessment of the conduct of the person concerned'.[59]

In its Communication on the CRD,[60] the Commission considers what constitutes both fraud and abuse of rights. It says *fraud* may be defined as 'deliberate deception or contrivance made to obtain the right of free movement and residence under the Directive.' It continues that in the context of the directive, fraud is likely to be limited to forgery of documents or false representation of a material fact concerning the conditions attached to the right of residence. Anybody convicted as a result can have their rights under the directive refused, terminated, or withdrawn.[61] In respect of *abuse*, the Commission says that abuse may be defined as an artificial conduct entered into solely with the purpose of obtaining the right of free movement and residence under Union law which, albeit formally observing of the conditions laid down by Union rules, does not comply with the purpose of those rules.[62] This is problematic as guidance for Member States because, as we have seen, the Court has long made clear that the motive for moving to another EU state is irrelevant.

---

[54] Case C–456/12 *O and B* EU:C:2014:135, para. 52.   [55] Paras. 54–6.

[56] Para. 58, citing Case C–110/99 *Emsland-Stärke* [2000] ECR I–11569.

[57] See Case C–127/08 *Metock v. Minister for Justice, Equality and Law Reform* [2008] ECR I–6241, para. 75, discussed in Ch. 10.

[58] Case C–202/13 *R. (on the application of McCarthy) v. Secretary of State for the Home Department* EU:C:2014:2450, para. 55.

[59] Para. 55.   [60] COM(2009) 313, 15.

[61] Citing Case C–285/95 *Kol* [1997] ECR I–3069, para. 29 and Case C–63/99 *Gloszczuk* [2001] ECR I–6369, para. 75.

[62] Citing Case C–110/99 *Emsland-Stärke* [2000] ECR I–11569, para. 52 and Case C–212/97 *Centros* [1999] ECR I–1459, para. 25.

Nevertheless, the tough line on abuse of EU law was reiterated in the UK New Settlement Decision:[63]

> In accordance with Union law, Member States are able to take action to prevent abuse of rights or fraud, such as the presentation of forged documents, and address cases of contracting or maintaining marriages of convenience with third country nationals for the purpose of making use of free movement as a route for regularising unlawful stay in a Member State or address cases of making use of free movement as a route for bypassing national immigration rules applying to third country nationals.

The Declaration adds that the Commission will *clarify* that Member States can address specific cases of abuse of free movement rights by Union citizens returning to their Member State of nationality with a non-EU family member 'where residence in the host Member State has not been sufficiently genuine to create or strengthen family life and had the purpose of evading the application of national immigration rules'.

2.4 Reverse Discrimination

Cases like *Saunders* and *Gauchard* demonstrate that nationals cannot invoke the free movement provisions against their own Member States if they have not exercised their rights of free movement in some way.[64] EU migrants (and nationals like Mrs Singh and Mr Knoors who have taken advantage of their Union law rights) may therefore enjoy more favourable treatment in the host state (since they enjoy the benefits of both EU law and national law) than non-migrant nationals who have not exercised their rights to free movement (they enjoy the benefits of national law only). This situation is referred to as 'reverse discrimination'.[65]

Why does Union law allow this apparently discriminatory treatment? The explanation for the rule is twofold. The first is jurisdictional. It acts as a divide between the application of EU law and the application of domestic law: EU law will apply where there is an inter-state dimension; domestic law will apply to facts wholly internal to the Member State. The second explanation is political and relates to what American scholars refer to as 'virtual representation':[66] migrants cannot necessarily gain access to the host state's political processes so Union law intervenes on their behalf to correct laws which discriminate against them. By contrast, nationals can and do enjoy access to the state's processes and so they can lobby to get the rules changed. This may be what the Court was referring to in *Uecker and Jacquet*[67] when it said 'Any discrimination which nationals of a Member State may suffer under the law of that State fall within the scope of that law and must therefore be dealt with within the framework of the internal legal system of that State.'[68]

---

[63] EU Council Conclusions, 18–19 Feb. 2016, Section D(c). See also the Declaration on issues related to the abuse of the right of free movement of persons which says 'The concept of marriage of convenience—which is not protected under Union law—also covers a marriage which is maintained for the purpose of enjoying a right of residence by a family member who is not a national of a Member State'.

[64] Although cf. Joined Cases C–321–324/94 *Pistre* [1997] ECR I–2343.

[65] 'Reverse discrimination arises when a national of a Member State is disadvantaged because he or she may not rely on a protective provision of Union law when a national of another Member State in otherwise identical circumstances may rely on that same provision' (D. Pickup, 'Reverse discrimination and freedom of movement for workers' (1986) 23 *CMLRev.* 135, 137).

[66] For a further discussion of the ideas underpinning 'virtual representation', see Ch. 1.

[67] Joined Cases C–64 and 65/96 [1997] ECR I–3171, para. 23. See also Case C–253/01 *Krüger* v. *Directie van de rechtspersoonlijkheid bezittende Dienst Wegsverkeer* [2004] ECR I–1191, para. 36.

[68] Para. 23.

However, while there are good legal and political reasons for the existence of the wholly internal rule, the Court has not always been consistent in its application and, in some cases, it has taken very little to trigger EU law: a 'potential' link with Union law may well be sufficient.[69] For example, in *Deliège*[70] the Court said that, in principle, Union law applied because there was 'a degree of extraneity, derived from the fact that an athlete participated in a competition in a Member State other than that in which he is established'. And in *Carpenter*[71] the Court said that Union law applied to (and prevented) the deportation from the UK of a Filipino woman married to a British man simply because her husband provided services to advertisers established in other Member States.[72] By implication, the presence of Mrs Carpenter in the UK, looking after Mr Carpenter's children from a previous marriage, enabled him to travel abroad to provide these services[73] and that was sufficient to provide a Union law element.

Cases such as these have led to calls that the wholly internal rule should be abolished or at least modified. The issue was considered by the Court in the *Walloon Government* case,[74] concerning a care insurance scheme for people with disabilities offered by the Flemish government. In order to benefit from the scheme, an individual had to be either resident in the Flemish-speaking region (or in the bilingual region of the capital, Brussels) or resident in another Member State (as a citizen of that Member State or a Belgian citizen who had made use of the free movement rights) but working in the Flemish-speaking region. By contrast, Belgian citizens living in the French-speaking region of Belgium but working in the Flemish-speaking region could not benefit from the scheme. This is a classic example of reverse discrimination (those living in the French region but working in the Flemish region were in a worse position than those living in other Member States and working in the Flemish region).

Advocate General Sharpston thought the time had come for a reconsideration of the wholly internal rule, at least in the circumstances of this case.[75] In part this was due to Article 26(2) TFEU, which provides that the internal market should be an 'area without internal frontiers'. This, she argued, following the case law on Article 30 TFEU,[76] applied to national *and* regional frontiers. She also argued that the citizenship provisions of the Treaty 'challenge the sustainability in its present form of the doctrine on purely internal situations',[77] especially in the context of this case, which comes 'as close to a classic cross-border situation as a supposedly internal situation can'.[78] The Court was not, however, prepared to follow its Advocate General. Reasserting the orthodoxy that '[Union] law clearly cannot be applied to such purely internal situations',[79] it added that the citizenship case law does not change this view because 'citizenship of the Union is not intended to extend the material scope of the Treaty to internal situations which have no link with

---

[69] See Case C–281/98 *Angonese* [2000] ECR I–4139.

[70] Joined Cases C–51/96 and C–191/97 [2000] ECR I–2549, para. 58. See also Case C–281/98 *Angonese* [2000] ECR I–4139, paras. 17–18.

[71] Case C–60/00 [2002] ECR I–6279.

[72] Case C–457/12 *S and G v. Minister voor Immigrtie, Integratie en Asiel* EU:C:2014:136, para. 40 extended this ruling to Art. 45 TFEU.

[73] See Mrs Carpenter's submissions to the Immigration Appeal Tribunal (para. 17).

[74] Case C–212/06 *Government of French Community and Walloon Government v. Flemish Government* [2008] ECR I–1683.

[75] She confessed to 'finding something deeply paradoxical about the proposition that, although the last 50 years have been spent abolishing barriers to freedom of movement *between* Member States, decentralised authorities of Member States may nevertheless reintroduce barriers through the back door by establishing them *within* Member States' (para. 116).

[76] Esp. Case C–72/03 *Carbonati* [2004] ECR I–8027, considered in Ch. 3.

[77] Para. 140.   [78] Para. 141.

[79] Para. 38, although cf. para. 40. The Court repeated this point in Case C–250/08 *Commission v. Belgium (immovable property)* [2012] ECR I–12341, para. 41.

[Union] law'.[80] For many states with devolved administrations which treat nationals from elsewhere in the state less favourably than residents and EU migrants (think about the fact that students resident in Scotland and EU students do not have to pay tuition fees to attend Scottish universities while English and Welsh students do[81]), the Court's decision came as a relief but the Advocate General's Opinion reveals the problems generated by the doctrine of reverse discrimination.[82]

D. THE SCOPE OF THE TREATY PROHIBITION

1. INTRODUCTION

Assuming Union law applies, the next question is what type of measure, conduct, or requirement is prohibited by the various provisions of the Treaty. In this section, we shall see that, at least in principle, refusal of entry/deportation, discriminatory measures, and non-discriminatory measures which impede market access (often referred to as 'restrictions' or obstacles' to free movement) are all prohibited by the various provisions of the Treaty. The analysis that follows is based on the 'unitary' thesis: that a common approach applies across all Treaty provisions on free movement of persons. This approach can be justified by the fact that, although Articles 45, 49, and 56 TFEU are 'mutually exclusive',[83] the Court said in *Royer*[84] that common principles apply to all three provisions both as regards the entry into, and residence in, the territory of the Member States and as regards the application of the prohibition of all discrimination on the grounds of nationality.[85]

However, there are differences between the provisions. When viewed from the perspective of the regulator, Article 49 TFEU on establishment has more in common with Article 45 TFEU on workers than with Article 56 TFEU on services. In the case of both Articles 45 and 49 TFEU the individual leaves State A to work in State B and it is the host state (State B) which has primary control over the individual's activities. By contrast, in respect of free movement of services, the service provider continues to be based in State A while providing services in State B. This time the principal regulator is the home state (State A). In this respect free movement of services has more in common with the free movement of goods:[86] both services and goods are primarily subject to home-state control with only residual host-state control. This suggests that a different regulatory approach is required for workers and establishment on the one hand, and goods and services on the other. In fact, as we shall see, the Court appears to be moving towards a convergence of approach under Articles 45, 49, 56, and now Article 21(1) TFEU on citizenship,[87] albeit

---

[80] Para. 39. See also Case C–127/08 *Metock* [2008] ECR I–6241, para. 77, considered further in Ch. 10.

[81] See further <http://www.saas.gov.uk/full_time/ug/eu/>.

[82] See also Sharpston AG's views in Case C–34/09 *Ruiz Zambrano* v. *ONEM* [2011] ECR I–1177, paras. 86–8, considered further in Ch. 10.

[83] Case C–55/94 *Gebhard* v. *Consiglio dell'Ordine degli Avvocati e Procuratori di Milano* [1995] ECR I–4165, para. 20, although cf. Case C–70/95 *Sodemare SA* v. *Regione Lombardia* [1997] ECR I–3395.

[84] Case 48/75 *Procureur du Roi* v. *Royer* [1976] ECR 497, para. 23.

[85] Case C–107/94 *Asscher* v. *Staatssecretaris van Financiën* [1996] ECR I–3089, para. 29 (concerning Arts. 45 and 49 TFEU).

[86] For an early example, see Case 155/73 *Giuseppe Sacchi* [1974] ECR 409, paras. 6–7 (transmission of a TV signal is a service but trade in sound recordings, films, and apparatus concerns goods).

[87] See, e.g., Case C–19/92 *Kraus* v. *Land Baden Württemberg* [1993] ECR I–1663, para. 32, where the Court said that 'national measures liable to hamper or to render less attractive the exercise … of *fundamental freedoms* guaranteed by the Treaty' breach the relevant Treaty provisions (emphasis added).

nuanced to reflect the different interests at stake. The common principles are outlined in this chapter; the differences are highlighted in Chapters 8–11.

2. REFUSAL OF EXIT AND ENTRY, AND THE STATE'S FREEDOM TO DEPORT

Refusal by the home state to allow a national to leave its territory,[88] refusal by a host state to allow an EU citizen to enter its territory,[89] and deportation of an EU citizen by a host state[90] are the most draconian steps a state can take against migrants. Because, under international law, states cannot deport their own nationals, deportation orders can be made against migrants only.[91] Such orders are the equivalent in the field of persons to quantitative restrictions for goods. They therefore breach the Treaty and can be saved only by reference to one of the express derogations—public policy, public security, and public health.[92] The state must show that the measure taken is proportionate[93] and, where appropriate, compatible with fundamental human rights (FHR)[94] (see fig. 7.2).

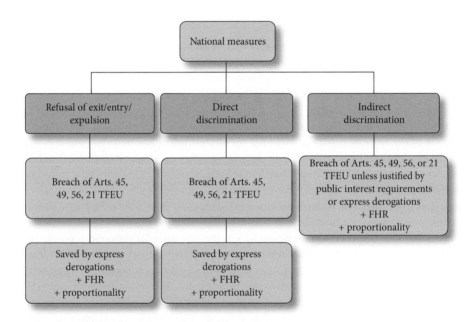

Fig. 7.2 Refusal of exit and entry, deportation, direct and indirect discrimination

---

[88] Case C–33/07 *Jipa* [2008] ECR I–5157; Case C–249/11 *Byankov v. Glaven sekretar na Ministerstvo na vatreshnite raboti* EU:C:2012:608, paras. 40–2.

[89] Case 41/74 *Van Duyn v. Home Office* [1974] ECR 1337, paras. 22–3.

[90] Case 30/77 *R. v. Bouchereau* [1977] ECR 1999; Case C–348/96 *Criminal Proceedings against Calfa* [1999] ECR I–11.

[91] Case C–348/96 *Calfa* [1999] ECR I–11, para. 20.

[92] Case 2/74 *Van Duyn* [1974] ECR 6311, paras. 22–3; Case C–114/97 *Commission v. Spain* [1998] ECR I–6717, para. 42.

[93] Case C–100/01 *Ministre de l'Intérieur v. Olazabal* [2002] ECR I–10981, para. 43; Case C–108/96 *Mac Quen v. Grandvision Belgium* [2001] ECR I–837, para. 31; Case C–3/88 *Commission v. Italy* [1989] ECR I–4035, para. 15.

[94] See Case C–260/89 *ERT v. DEP* [1991] ECR I–2925, para. 43.

3. DISCRIMINATION ON THE GROUNDS OF NATIONALITY

3.1 Introduction

Once an individual (or company) has been admitted to the *territory* of a Member State he or she cannot be discriminated against on the grounds of nationality in respect of access to, or exercise of, a particular trade or profession. The principle of non-discrimination on the ground of nationality has been central to the operation of the Treaty provisions on the free movement of persons. For example, Article 45(2) TFEU provides that freedom of movement of workers 'shall entail the abolition of any discrimination based on nationality between workers of the Member States'; Article 49(2) TFEU says freedom of establishment occurs 'under the conditions laid down for its own nationals by the law of the country where such establishment is effected'; and Article 57(2) TFEU provides that the person providing a service may temporarily pursue his activity in the host state 'under the same conditions as are imposed by that State on its own nationals'. These are specific manifestations of the more general principle found in Article 18 TFEU:

> Within the scope of application of the Treaty, and without prejudice to any special provisions contained therein, any discrimination on grounds of nationality shall be prohibited.[95]

In *Data-Delecta*[96] the Court said that the principle of non-discrimination required 'perfect equality of treatment in Member States of persons in a situation governed by [Union] law and nationals of the Member States in question'.[97] Therefore, the Court found that a Swedish law requiring a foreign national to lodge security for costs when no such security could be demanded from Swedish nationals contravened Article 18 TFEU.[98]

The consequence of the non-discrimination approach is that a migrant will enjoy equal treatment with nationals of the host state. This means that if a migrant from State A moves to State B which has lower social standards the migrant will enjoy only those lower standards. As the Court said in *Perfili*,[99] in prohibiting discrimination on the grounds of nationality, Articles 18, 49, and 56 TFEU were not concerned with disparities in treatment arising from differences between the laws in the Member States so long as the laws affected all persons subject to them in accordance with objective criteria and without regard to nationality. The Court will intervene only if the rule is discriminatory, and even then it will require only that the discrimination be removed without interfering with the substance of the rule.

The principle of equal treatment also forms the basis of the Citizens' Rights Directive 2004/38, albeit in a tailored form. As we have seen, the directive distinguishes between three groups of EU migrants: (1) those entering the host state for up to three months,

---

[95] In Case C–193/94 *Criminal Proceedings against Skanavi* [1996] ECR I–929 the Court said that Art. 18 TFEU applied independently only to situations governed by Union law in respect of which the Treaty laid down no specific prohibition on discrimination.

[96] Case C–43/95 *Data-Delecta* v. *MSL Dynamics* [1996] ECR I–4661. See also Case C–122/96 *Saldanha and MTS Securities Corporation* v. *Hiross Holding AG* [1998] ECR I–5325 and Case C–411/98 *Ferlini* v. *Centre hospitalier de Luxembourg* [2000] ECR I–8081.

[97] Joined Cases C–22 and 23/08 *Vatsouras* v. *Arbeitsgemeinschaft* [2009] ECR I–4585, para. 52 makes clear that Art. 18 TFEU does not apply to possible differences in treatment between nationals of Member States and *non*-Member States.

[98] Para. 22.

[99] Case C–177/94 *Criminal Proceedings against Gianfranco Perfili, civil party: Lloyd's of London* [1996] ECR I–161. See also Case C–387/01 *Weigel* v. *Finanzlandes direction für Vorarlberg* [2004] ECR I–4981.

(2) those resident for up to five years, and (3) those with permanent residence (usually because they have resided for more than five years in the host state) (see fig. 10.2). The first group—who do not need to be economically active—enjoy equal treatment with nationals in the host state but not in respect of social assistance or student benefits.

The second group comprises EU citizens who are engaged in gainful activity in the host state as a worker or a self-employed person (thereby bringing the worker and self-employed entitlements into close alignment); or they have sufficient medical and financial resources for themselves and their family members; or they are students with comprehensive sickness insurance and sufficient resources for themselves and their family members; or they are family members (including TCNs) accompanying or joining a Union citizen who satisfies one of the situations mentioned. All of these individuals enjoy the right to the same treatment as nationals of the host state, including in respect of social assistance. However, there is no right to equal treatment in respect of maintenance aid for studies, including vocational training, to individuals other than workers, self-employed persons, and members of their families.

The third group—those with permanent residence—do not need to show they are workers, self-employed, students, or adequately resourced. They enjoy equal treatment not only in respect of social assistance but also in respect of student maintenance in the form of grants or loans.

So what is meant by equal treatment? For lawyers, it translates into the principle of non-discrimination, i.e., no direct discrimination, unless justified by reference to one of the express derogations, and no indirect discrimination unless objectively justified. Thus the language of equal treatment may be misleading: Member States are, in fact, free to discriminate on the grounds of nationality if they have good reasons to do so. We shall now consider the meaning of the terms direct and indirect discrimination.

3.2 Direct Discrimination/Distinctly Applicable Measures

Direct (or overt) discrimination means different and usually less-favourable treatment on the grounds of nationality. Such measures (sometimes referred to as 'distinctly applicable') breach Articles 45, 49, 56, or 21 TFEU and/or Directive 2004/38. So in *Reyners*[100] a Belgian law permitting only nationals to become lawyers breached Article 49 TFEU.

According to the orthodoxy, distinctly applicable measures may be lawful but only if they are saved by one of the express derogations provided by the Treaty and, once again, the state must show that the measure taken is proportionate[101] and, where appropriate, compatible with fundamental human rights[102] (see fig. 7.2[103]). However, as with free movement of goods, there have been signs that the Court is contemplating a move towards allowing distinctly applicable measures to be justified not only by the express derogations but also by the judicially developed 'public-interest requirements',[104] although the case law is not consistent on this point.[105]

[100] Case 2/74 *Reyners* v. *Belgian State* [1974] ECR 631.
[101] Case C–100/01 *Olazabal* [2002] ECR I–10981, para. 43. As Davies notes, in practical terms nationality has become a legally redundant concept (G. Davies, '"Any place I hang my hat?" or: Residence is the new nationality' (2005) 11 *ELJ* 43, 55).
[102] See Case C–260/89 *ERT* v. *DEP* [1991] ECR I–2925, para. 43.
[103] See fig. 4.1 for the equivalent approach in respect of goods.
[104] See, e.g., Joined Cases C–338, 359 and 360/04 *Placanica* [2007] ECR I–1891.
[105] See, e.g., Case C–341/05 *Laval* [2007] ECR I–11767, paras. 116–17, where the Grand Chamber restated the orthodox position.

3.3 Indirect Discrimination/Indistinctly Applicable Measures

(a) Definition

The Treaty also prohibits indirect (or covert) discrimination. This involves the elimination of requirements which, while apparently nationality-neutral on their face (same burden in law), have a greater impact on nationals of other Member States (different burden in fact).[106] As the Court explained in *Sotgiu*,[107] the Treaty prohibits all covert forms of discrimination which, by the application of other criteria of differentiation, lead in fact to the same result as direct discrimination. The Court has found national rules imposing requirements concerning residence[108] and language[109] to be indirectly discriminatory: while nationals almost always satisfy the condition, migrants do not. Requirements as to holding particular qualifications[110] or licences[111] are also considered to be indirectly discriminatory, but in these cases the discrimination arises because the requirements create a double burden on migrants, who have to satisfy two sets of rules (those of the home and host states), while nationals need to satisfy only one set of rules (those of the home state). Sometimes these requirements are referred to as indistinctly applicable measures.[112] While this double-burden theory helps to explain the services case law where the service provider, like the manufacturer of the goods, is subject to two regulators (those of the home and host states),[113] it is less satisfactory in respect of workers and establishment where in practice only one regulator (the host state) controls the migrant.

Nevertheless, the Court appears to gloss over this problem and the conceptual difficulty that double-burden rules are indirectly discriminatory but indirectly discriminatory measures (e.g., those concerning language and residence requirements) do not necessarily impose a double burden, by giving a broad definition to the phrase indirect discrimination. This can be seen in *O'Flynn*[114] concerning a British rule making payment by the state to cover funeral costs conditional on the burial taking place in the UK. The Court said:[115]

> [C]onditions imposed by national law must be regarded as indirectly discriminatory where, although applicable irrespective of nationality, they affect essentially migrant workers ... or the great majority of those affected are migrant workers,[116] ... where they

---

[106] See, e.g., Case C–175/88 *Biehl* v. *Admininstration des Contributions* [1990] ECR I–1779, paras. 13–14; Case C–111/91 *Commission* v. *Luxembourg* [1993] ECR I–817, para. 9.

[107] Case 152/73 *Sotgiu* v. *Deutsche Bundespost* [1974] ECR 153.

[108] Case C–350/96 *Clean Car* [1998] ECR I–2521; Case C–388/01 *Commission* v. *Italy (museums)* [2003] ECR I–721, para. 14; Case C–20/12 *Giersch* v. *Etat du Grand-Duché de Luxembourg* EU:C:2013:411, para. 43.

[109] Case 379/87 *Groener* v. *Minister for Education* [1989] ECR 3967.

[110] Case C–340/89 *Vlassopoulou* v. *Ministerium für Justiz* [1991] ECR I–2357.

[111] Case 292/86 *Gullung* v. *Conseil de l'ordre des avocats* [1988] ECR 111.

[112] This reflects the Court's formulation of measures which are 'applicable without distinction to all'. See, e.g., Case 143/87 *Stanton* v. *INASTI* [1988] ECR 3877, para. 9.

[113] Cf. Case C–70/95 *Sodemare SA* [1997] ECR I–3395 and Case C–405/98 *Gourmet International Products AB (GIP)* [2001] ECR I–1795.

[114] Case C–237/94 *O'Flynn* v. *Adjudication Officer* [1996] ECR I–2617.

[115] Case C–237/94 *O'Flynn* [1996] ECR I–2617, paras. 18–19. In Case C–206/10 *Commission* v. *Germany (benefits for the blind)* EU:C:2011:283, para. 37, the Court offered a variation of the formula, 'a provision of national law must be regarded as indirectly discriminatory if it is intrinsically liable to affect migrant workers more than national workers and if there is a consequent risk that it will place the former at a particular disadvantage'. See also Case E–3/05 *EFTA Surveillance Authority* v. *Norway* [2006] EFTA Ct. Rep. 102, paras. 56–7 (regional residence requirement).

[116] In Case C–542/09 *Commission* v. *Netherlands (higher education)* EU:C:2012:346, para. 38 the Court said, 'it is immaterial whether, in some circumstances, the contested measure affects, as well as nationals of other Member States, nationals of the Member State in question who are unable to meet such a criterion. In order for a measure to be treated as being indirectly discriminatory, it is not necessary for it to have the effect

are indistinctly applicable but can be more easily satisfied by national workers than by migrant workers ... or where there is a risk that they may operate to the particular detriment of migrant workers.

The Court continued:

It is otherwise only if those provisions are justified by objective considerations independent of the nationality of the workers concerned, and if they are proportionate to the legitimate aim pursued by national law.

The Court found that the British rule constituted unjustified indirect discrimination (but did say that the UK could limit the allowance to a lump sum or reasonable amount fixed by reference to the normal cost of a burial in the UK).

From *O'Flynn* we can see that, unless objectively justified and proportionate to its aim (see fig. 7.2), the provision of national law must be regarded as indirectly discriminatory and contrary to Union law if it is *intrinsically liable* to affect migrant workers more than national workers and if there is a *risk* that it will place migrant workers at a particular disadvantage.[117] The Court added that it was not necessary to find that the measure did in practice affect a substantially higher proportion of migrant workers; it was sufficient that it was liable to have such an effect.[118] The broad formulation of indirect discrimination in *O'Flynn*, focusing on the *potential* effect on free movement, means that, as with the case law on goods following *Dassonville*,[119] more national rules are liable to be caught by the Treaty. Three consequences flow from this: first, there is a risk that the rule that Union law does not apply to wholly internal situations is eroded; secondly, that the distinction between the market access approach considered in Chapter 1 and the discrimination approach is more apparent than real; and thirdly, the broader the scope of measures caught under the heading of indirect discrimination, the greater the need for Member States to justify the continued existence of their national rules.

(b) Justifications

In recognition of the need for Member States to be able to justify their rules on grounds other than the narrowly defined express derogations, the Court has allowed Member States to justify their indirectly discriminatory national rules by reference to 'objective justifications' (the language used in *O'Flynn* in the context of free movement of workers) or justifications in the 'public' or 'general interest' or 'imperative requirements' (the language more commonly used in the field of establishment and services).[120] These various terms appear synonymous[121] and are the equivalent of the 'mandatory

---

of placing all the nationals of the Member State in question at an advantage or of placing at a disadvantage only nationals of other Member States, but not nationals of the State in question'.

[117] Case C–237/94 *O'Flynn* [1996] ECR I–2617, para. 20. The fact that nationals may also be affected by the rule does not prevent the rule from being indirectly discriminatory, provided that the majority of those affected are non-nationals: Case C–281/98 *Angonese* [2000] ECR I–4139, para. 41.

[118] Para. 21. Cf. the position in respect of Art. 110 TFEU on internal taxation, where actual disparate impact must be shown: Case 132/88 *Commission* v. *Greece* [1990] ECR I–1567, considered in Ch. 3.

[119] Case 8/74 *Dassonville* [1974] ECR 837.

[120] Case C–76/90 *Säger* v. *Dennemeyer & Co. Ltd* [1991] ECR I–4221, para. 15; Case C–55/94 *Gebhard* [1996] ECR I–4165, para. 37.

[121] This view is supported by the workers case, Case C–195/98 *Österreicher Gewerkschaftsbund* v. *Republik Österreich* [2000] ECR I–10497, para. 45, where the Court reported that the Austrian government contends that the restrictions on free movement are 'justified by *overriding reasons of public interest* and are consistent with the principle of proportionality', and the services case, Case C–118/96 *Safir* v. *Skattemyndigheten*

requirements' in the field of goods. In all cases the Court recognizes that there exists a non-exhaustive list of national interests worthy of protection[122] (such as consumer protection, worker protection, cultural policy[123]) which are compatible with the objectives of the EU,[124] and which should take precedence over the free movement provisions, provided that the steps taken are proportionate and, where appropriate, compatible with fundamental human rights. These public-interest requirements are examined in more detail in Chapter 12.

3.4 Non-Discriminatory Measures

(a) Pure non-discrimination

Since measures which discriminate on grounds of nationality (either directly or indirectly) breach the Treaty, it should follow that measures which do not discriminate do not breach the Treaty. This was the approach taken by the Court in the *Clinical Biology Laboratories* case.[125] Belgian law provided that for a laboratory to qualify for reimbursement from a sickness insurance scheme, all of its members, partners, and directors had to be doctors or pharmacists. The Court found that since the legislation applied without distinction to Belgian nationals and those from other Member States, it did not breach Article 49 TFEU (see fig. 7.3).

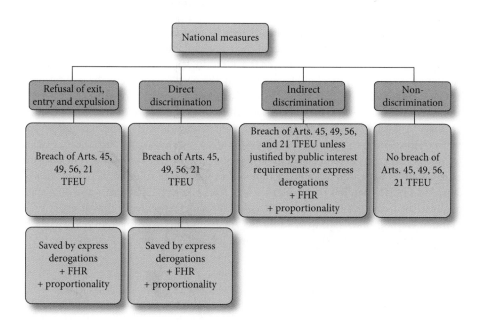

Fig. 7.3 The non-discrimination model

i *Dalarnas Län* [1998] ECR I–1897, para. 22: Art. 56 TFEU 'precludes the application of any national legislation which, without *objective justification*, impedes a provider of services from actually exercising the freedom to provide them' (emphasis added).

122 See Tesauro AG in Case C–118/96 *Safir* [1998] ECR I–1897, para. 29.
123 Case C–288/89 *Gouda* [1991] ECR I–4007.
124 Case C–464/02 *Commission v. Denmark (company vehicles)* [2005] ECR I–7929, para. 53.
125 Case 221/85 *Commission v. Belgium* [1987] ECR 719.

(b) Non-discriminatory measures which prevent or hinder market access

However, a number of cases decided in the mid 1990s concerned measures which were not discriminatory (i.e., no discrimination either in law or in fact) but still hindered access to the market. Should these rules be caught by the Treaty? It will be recalled that the Court said in *Keck*[126] that non-discriminatory certain selling arrangements did not breach Article 34 TFEU. This prompted various Member States to argue in the workers case, *Bosman*,[127] considered in Case Study 8.1, and in the services case, *Alpine Investments*,[128] that the *Keck* principle should be extended to the free movement of persons.

Alpine Investments concerned a Dutch law prohibiting cold-calling to sell financial services both within and outside the Netherlands. The Court said that the Dutch law was 'general and non-discriminatory and neither its object nor effect [was] to put the national market at an advantage over providers of services from other Member States'.[129] The British and Dutch governments therefore argued that since this case was analogous to a non-discriminatory measure governing selling arrangements the principles of *Keck* should apply, with the result that the rule should not breach Article 56 TFEU.

The Court disagreed. It emphasized that the Dutch law deprived operators of a 'rapid and direct technique for marketing and for contacting potential clients in other Member States'.[130] For this reason the Dutch law was not analogous to the selling arrangements in *Keck*:[131] while *Keck* concerned a situation where there was *no* hindrance of trade between Member States (i.e., access to the market was not affected), the prohibition on cold-calling in *Alpine* did '*directly affect access to the markets in services* in the other Member States and [was] thus capable of hindering intra-[Union] trade in services'.[132] Having established a breach (see fig. 7.4), due to the fact that the rule, while non-discriminatory, did affect market access, the Court then considered the question of justification. It accepted that the prohibition on cold-calling could be justified by the need to safeguard the reputation of the Dutch financial markets[133] and that the measures taken were proportionate.

Does *Alpine* mean then that the *Keck* ruling does not apply to free movement of persons?[134] The answer may well be no.[135] If *Keck* is removed from its specific 'goods' context (certain selling arrangements, a non-legal category developed to curb the excesses of *Dassonville*) and considered instead in terms of its purpose (the removal of non-discriminatory matters which do not substantially affect inter-state trade from the purview of Article 34 TFEU), then it is possible to see how *Keck*-like principles can—and do—apply equally to the free movement of persons. *Graf*[136] provides a pointer in that direction.

Graf, a German national, worked for his Austrian employer for four years when he terminated his contract in order to take up a job in Germany. Under Austrian law, a

---

[126] Joined Cases C–267 and 268/91 *Keck and Mithouard* [1993] ECR I–6097, considered in Ch. 5.

[127] Case C–415/93 *Union Royale Belge de Société de Football Association v. Bosman* [1995] ECR I–4921.

[128] Case C–384/93 *Alpine Investments BV v. Minister van Financiën* [1995] ECR I–1141. See also Case C–275/92 *Customs and Excise v. Schindler* [1994] ECR I–1039.

[129] Para. 35.   [130] Para. 28.   [131] Para. 36.

[132] Para. 38, emphasis added. See also the *Golden Shares* cases: e.g., Case C–463/00 *Commission v. Spain* [2003] ECR I–4581 and Case C–98/01 *Commission v. UK* [2003] ECR I–4641 on the free movement of capital, considered in Ch. 14.

[133] Para. 43.

[134] See D. O'Keeffe and A. Bavasso, 'Four freedoms, one market and national competence. In search of a dividing line' in D. O'Keeffe and A. Bavasso (eds.), *Judicial Review in European Union Law: Liber Amicorum in Honour of Lord Slynn of Hadley* (The Hague: Kluwer, 2000).

[135] See to that effect, Tizzano AG's views in Case C–442/02 *Caixa-Bank v. Ministère de l'Économie, des Finances et de l'Industrie* [2004] ECR I–8961, para. 73.

[136] Case C–190/98 *Graf v. Filzmozer Maschinenbau GmbH* [2000] ECR I–493.

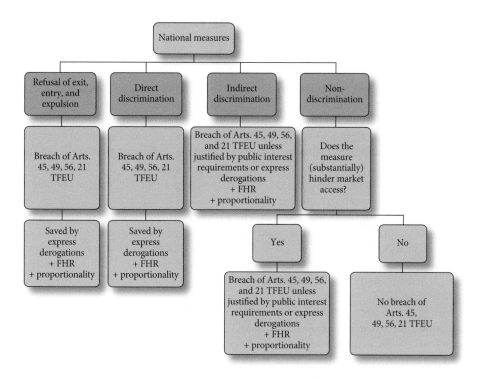

Fig. 7.4 The non-discrimination model and market access

worker employed by the same employer for more than three years was entitled to compensation on termination of his contract provided that he was dismissed (and did not just resign). Graf argued that this rule contravened Article 45 TFEU because the effect of the rule was that, by moving to another state, he lost the chance of being dismissed in Austria and, with it, the chance of claiming compensation.

The Court disagreed: the Austrian law was genuinely non-discriminatory[137] and did not preclude or deter a worker from ending his contract of employment in order to take a job with another employer.[138] The Court explained that the entitlement to compensation when the employer dismissed an employee was not dependent on the worker's choosing whether to stay with his current employer but on a future and hypothetical event, namely being dismissed.[139] The Court concluded that '[s]uch an event is *too uncertain and indirect* a possibility for legislation to be capable of being regarded as liable to hinder free movement for workers'. Thus, the dismissal was too remote to be considered liable to affect free movement.[140] Putting it another way, non-discriminatory measures which do not substantially hinder access to the (labour) market[141] or whose effect on free movement is too

---

[137] Para. 18.   [138] Para. 24. See also Case C–542/08 *Barth* [2010] ECR I–3189, para. 39.

[139] Para. 24. See also Case C–542/08 *Barth* [2010] ECR I–3189, para. 39.

[140] See also Joined Cases C–418/93 etc. *Semeraro Casa Uno Srl* [1996] ECR I–2975, para. 32 and Case C–168/91 *Konstantinidis* [1993] ECR I–1191, para. 15 concerning Art. 49 TFEU; Cf. Case C–159/90 *SPUC* v. *Grogan* [1991] ECR I–4685, para. 24, where the Court noted that the link between the student associations and abortions carried out by clinics in other Member States was 'too tenuous' for the prohibition on the distribution of information to be regarded as a restriction within the meaning of Art. 56 TFEU.

[141] Case C–518/06 *Commission* v. *Italy (motor insurance)* [2009] ECR I–3491, para. 66; Case C–565/08 *Commission* v. *Italy (maximum fees for lawyers)* [2011] ECR I–2101, para. 51. Both cases are discussed further in Ch. 11.

remote,[142] fall outside Article 45 TFEU[143] (and the other Treaty provisions—see fig. 7.4) in much the same way as non-discriminatory certain selling arrangements cases (*Punto Casa*,[144] *Boermans*[145]) which do not substantially hinder access to the market fall outside Article 34 TFEU.

Thus, it would seem that rules which merely *structure the market*[146] on which goods are sold and people carry out their economic activities do not generally breach the Treaty. They are the rules of the game, to which all of those conducting their activities in the state must comply. Some rules, like the labour laws at issue in *Graf*, or environmental or consumer laws, reflect social choices made by a democratically elected national government. Other rules actually make the market, as *Deliège*[147] demonstrates. A successful Belgian judo player complained that the Belgian judo federation's failure to select her for various international competitions breached Article 56 TFEU. The Court disagreed, saying that although selection rules inevitably had the effect of limiting the number of participants in a tournament, such a limitation was inherent in the conduct of an international high-level sports event. In other words, without any rules there would be no competition. The Court continued that such rules could not in themselves be regarded as constituting a restriction on the freedom to provide services prohibited by Article 56 TFEU.[148]

Pulling the strands of the case law together, it could be said that *Graf* and *Deliège* and, in the context of goods, *Punto Casa* and *Boermans*, all concerned non-discriminatory rules which did not substantially hinder access to the market and so did not breach the Treaty provisions.[149] These rules stand at one stage removed from the good being imported or person performing the economic activity. In the interests of subsidiarity, they are the very type of measures which should fall outside the scrutiny of EU law. Just because they reduce the 'economic attractiveness' of pursuing the activity does not mean they should be caught by the Treaty.[150] But, if the non-discriminatory measures do substantially hinder access to the market, then they do breach the Treaty provision and need to be justified (see fig. 7.4). This was the outcome in *Alpine* and *Bosman*. It was also the outcome the Court appeared to be suggesting in the goods case, *Commission* v. *Italy (trailers)*[151] (see fig. 4.2).

[142] In Case C–212/06 *Walloon Government* [2008] ECR I–1683 Sharpston AG supported this approach (paras. 55–6). See also Joined Cases C–11 and 12/06 *Morgan* [2007] ECR I–9161, para. 32. Cf. Case C–211/08 *Commission* v. *Spain (unscheduled hospital treatment)* [2010] ECR I–5267, para. 72.

[143] See also Case C–134/03 *Viacom Outdoor Srl* v. *Giotto Immobilier SARL (Viacom II)* [2005] ECR I–1167, para. 3. For a discussion of the debate about the merits of the legal test based on remoteness and the economic test based on 'substantial' hindrance of market access, see Ch. 5.

[144] Joined Cases C–69 and 258/93 *Punto Casa SpA* [1994] ECR I–2355.

[145] Joined Cases C–401 and 402/92 *Boermans* [1994] ECR I–2199.

[146] I am grateful to Michael Dougan for this phrase. See also the use of the solidarity principle in Case C–70/95 *Sodemare* [1997] ECR I–3395, para. 29, to justify excluding the application of Art. 49 TFEU to national rules which allow only non-profit-making private operators to participate in running old people's homes.

[147] Joined Cases C–51/96 and C–191/97 *Deliège* v. *Ligue Francophone de Judo et Disciplines Associés* [2000] ECR I–2549, para. 64. See *Wilander* v. *Tobin* [1997] 2 CMLR 346 for an English decision in the same vein.

[148] Para. 64.

[149] See also the views of Walker LJ, as he then was, in the Court of Appeal in *Professional Contractors' Group* v. *Commissioners of Inland Revenue* [2002] 1 CMLR 46, para. 69.

[150] Tizzano AG in Case C–442/02 *Caixa-Bank* [2004] ECR I–8961, para. 58.

[151] Case C–110/05 [2009] ECR I–519, considered in Chs. 4 and 5.

4. GOING BEYOND THE DISCRIMINATION MODEL

4.1 The Market Access Approach: Restrictions Liable to Prohibit, Impede, or Render Less Attractive Free Movement

So far we have concentrated on the fact that Articles 45, 49, 56 (and 21) TFEU prohibit discrimination on the ground of nationality. In essence the cases considered so far have adopted a three-stage analysis:

(1) identifying a comparator group (this stage is often overlooked in practice except in tax cases)

(2) classifying the measure as, e.g., directly or indirectly discriminatory and so finding a breach and

(3) examining justification and proportionality.

In cases such as *Alpine* and *Bosman* we have also seen how the Court has brought non-discriminatory national measures within the scope of the Treaty where they prevented or substantially hindered access to the market. These cases, decided in the mid 1990s, were indicative of a more general change of approach by the Court away from a three stage approach towards a two-stage analysis based on market access (see fig. 7.5):

(1) identifying a restriction and thus a breach and

(2) examining justification and proportionality.

This shift from a discrimination approach to a restriction approach can be traced back to *Säger*,[152] where the Court said that Article 56 TFEU required:

not only the elimination of all discrimination against a person providing services on the ground of his nationality *but also* the abolition of any restriction, even if it applies without

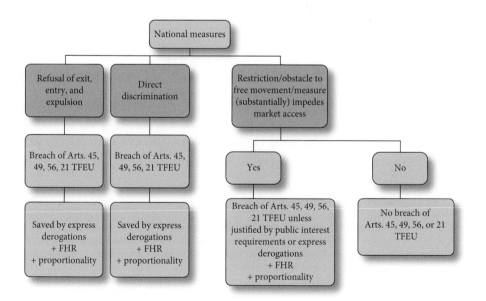

Fig. 7.5 The restrictions/market access approach

[152] Case C–76/90 [1991] ECR I–4221, para. 12, emphasis added.

distinction to national providers of services and to those of other Member States, when *it is liable to prohibit or otherwise impede* the activities of a provider of services established in another Member State where he lawfully provides similar services.

The Court continued that any such restriction could be justified by imperative reasons relating to the public interest.[153]

Säger demonstrated a greater willingness by the Court to scrutinize national rules which, even potentially ('liable to'), prohibit, impede, or restrict the individual's right to free movement. The Court is therefore making a more significant incursion into national regulatory autonomy than under its pure discrimination approach: unless Member States can justify their conduct, a national rule which is liable to prohibit or otherwise impede free movement will breach Union law, even if it does not discriminate against nationals.

The facts of *Kraus*[154] illustrate the importance of the change signalled by *Säger*. Kraus, a German student, complained that he was not allowed to use his British LLM title in Germany without prior authorization from the German authorities. If he had obtained an academic diploma from a German university, no such authorization would have been required. *Kraus* therefore concerned discrimination—not on the grounds of nationality (after all, Kraus was German)—but rather on the grounds that he had received training in another Member State which disadvantaged him when he returned to his country of origin (Germany).[155] Thus, he suffered discrimination based on the fact that he had exercised his rights of free movement and received some of his education in another Member State.[156]

Focusing on the obstacles to free movement created by the German rule rather than on any discrimination, the Court said that Articles 45 and 56 TFEU precluded any national measure governing the conditions under which an academic title obtained in another Member State could be used, where that measure, even though applicable without discrimination on grounds of nationality (i.e., non-discriminatory), was '*liable to hamper or to render less attractive* the exercise by Union nationals, including those of the Member State which enacted the measure, of *fundamental freedoms* guaranteed by the Treaty'.[157] The Court then considered whether this national rule could be justified. According to the Court it was legitimate for Germany to impose the restriction on the ground of 'the need to protect a public which will not necessarily be alerted to abuse of academic titles'.[158] It then considered the proportionality of the rule and, as with its more recent case law on goods, emphasized the need for good governance and fair procedures to be applied in making the decision whether to authorise the use of the title.[159]

The *Kraus* judgment, focusing on the question of hindrance to the exercise of one of the fundamental freedoms rather than on discrimination, was not in any way an isolated decision. Its formulation has been more or less repeated in similar terms in numerous subsequent cases.[160]

---

[153] Case C–76/90 *Säger* [1991] ECR I–4221, para. 15.

[154] Case C–19/92 [1993] ECR I–1663. See also Case C–279/00 *Commission* v. *Italy (temp agencies)* [2002] ECR I–1425.

[155] See also Case C–370/90 *Surinder Singh* [1992] ECR I–4265, para. 23.

[156] The Court is not consistent in the formula it uses. See also Case C–224/98 *D'Hoop* v. *Office national de l'emploi* [2002] ECR I–6191, para. 34, where the Court said that by linking the grant of tide-over allowances to the condition of having obtained the required diploma in Belgium, Belgian law thus '*places at a disadvantage certain of its nationals simply because they have exercised their freedom to move* in order to pursue education in another Member State' (emphasis added), considered further in Ch. 10. See Poiares Maduro AG's Opinion in Joined Cases C–158 and 159/04 *Alfa Vita* [2006] ECR I–8135, para. 46, where he thought the test that applied to all Treaty provisions was 'discrimination against the exercise of freedom of movement'.

[157] Para. 32, emphasis added.   [158] Para. 35.   [159] Para. 42. See further Ch. 12.

[160] See, e.g., Case C–55/94 *Gebhard* [1995] ECR I–4165, para. 37, considered in Ch. 8; Joined Cases C–369 and 376/96 *Arblade, Leloup and Sofrage SARL* [1999] ECR I–8453, para. 33; Case C–3/95 *Sandker* [1996] ECR I–6511, para. 25.

At a push, the measure in *Kraus* could have been considered indirectly discriminatory on the grounds of nationality: the requirement for the qualification to be authorized prior to use (*Kraus*) might have had a disparate impact on migrants.[161] The measure in *Kraus* could even have been considered directly discriminatory because only qualifications obtained in other Member States needed prior authorization.[162] Yet, in *Kraus* and the subsequent case law the Court did not go down either route. This was probably sensible since it would have required an unnecessarily broad reading of the terms direct or indirect discrimination. Instead, the Court focused on the more general question of whether the measure was liable to prevent or hinder access to the market or exercise of the freedom and, finding it was, required the measure to be justified. The Court's stance in these cases is sometimes referred to as its 'market access' approach (a phrase broad enough to include *exercise* of market freedoms, as *Kraus* shows[163]), an approach it now applies not only to free movement of services and freedom of establishment but also to the free movement of workers,[164] free movement of citizens,[165] and, as we shall see in Chapter 14, free movement of capital.[166]

Perhaps because of the cumbersome language involved and the unsuitability of applying the language of 'market access' to certain groups—such as retired migrant citizens who have moved to another state—the Court has, in more recent cases, replaced the *Säger/Kraus* 'market access' formula with the simpler wording, examining whether the national measure constitutes a 'restriction' on, or an 'obstacle' to, free movement. The language of 'restrictions' reflects the text of Articles 49[167] and 56 TFEU;[168] the language of 'obstacles' reflects the original Article 3 EEC. Both terms are synonymous with the 'market access' test.[169] As the Court put it succinctly in *Volksbank România*,[170] in the context of Article 56 TFEU, '"restriction" within the meaning of Article 56 TFEU relates to measures by which the exercise of the freedom to provide services is prohibited, impeded or rendered less attractive'.

Where the obstacle is created by the home state (state of origin) the Court sometimes uses a different formula, a formula based on disadvantages. This can be seen in *Kranemann*[171] concerning a German rule which provided that trainees who did their

---

[161] This was the approach adopted in Case C–281/98 *Angonese* [2000] ECR I–4139, paras. 40–6.

[162] However, this would have been discrimination based on the place where the service was provided and not on the nationality of the claimant: Case C–158/96 *Kohll* [1998] ECR I–1931, para. 33. See also Case C–55/98 *Skatteministeriet v. Bent Vestergaard* [1999] ECR I–7641, para. 22. These cases are considered further in Ch. 11.

[163] The Court said: 'the situation of a Union national who holds a postgraduate academic title which, obtained in another Member State, facilitates *access* to a profession or, at least, the *pursuit* of an economic activity, is governed by [Union] law' (para. 23, emphasis added).

[164] Case C–464/02 *Commission v. Denmark (company vehicles)* [2005] ECR I–7929, para. 45, emphasis added.

[165] Case C–192/05 *Tas-Hagen v. Raadskamer WUBO van de Pensioen- en Uitkeringsrad* [2006] ECR I–10451, paras. 30–1.

[166] Case C–367/98 *Commission v. Portugal* [2002] ECR I–4731, paras. 44–5.

[167] See, e.g., Case C–250/95 *Futura Particpations SA* [1997] ECR I–2471; Case C–446/03 *Marks & Spencer v. Halsey* [2005] ECR I–10837, para. 34.

[168] See, e.g., Case C–255/04 *Commission v. France (performing artists)* [2006] ECR I–5251, para. 38.

[169] See, e.g., Joined Cases C–147 and 148/06 *SECAP SpA v. Comune di Torino* [2008] ECR I–3565, para. 28: 'the automatic exclusion of abnormally low tenders to contracts of certain cross-border interest could deprive economic operators from other Member States of the opportunity of competing more effectively with operators located in the Member State in question and thereby *affect their access to the market in that State*, thus *impeding the exercise* of freedom of establishment and freedom to provide services, which constitutes a *restriction* on those freedoms'.

[170] Case C–602/10 EU:C:2012:443, para. 73.

[171] Case C–109/04 *Kranemann v. Land Nordrhein-Westfalen* [2005] ECR I–2421, para. 25. See also Case C–232/01 *Van Lent* [2003] ECR I–11525, para. 15; Case C–345/05 *Commission v. Portugal (transfer of property)* [2006] ECR I–10633, paras. 20–2; Case C–192/05 *Tas-Hagen* [2006] ECR I–10451, paras. 30–1.

practical legal training in Germany were entitled to reimbursement of all their travel expenses, whatever the distance between their home and their place of training, but those who did their training in another Member State had to pay themselves for the part of the journey outside Germany. The Court said:

> [T]he Treaty provisions relating to freedom of movement for persons ... preclude measures which might place [Union] nationals at a disadvantage when they wish to pursue an economic activity[172] in the territory of another Member State.[173]

The Court continued that the German rule therefore constituted 'an obstacle' to the free movement of workers even if applied without regard to the nationality of the workers concerned.[174] Further, the rule could not be justified: aims of a purely economic nature could not constitute pressing reasons of public interest justifying a restriction on the fundamental freedom.[175]

4.2 Problems with the Restrictions Formula

As we have seen, there is little to choose between the *Säger* formula and that based on obstacles, and in cases such as *Kraus* and *Kranemann* the Court used both.[176] Both formulas reflect the ambition in Article 3(c) EEC and Article 26 TFEU of achieving an internal market without frontiers. Both raise problems.

First, the meaning of the individual terms 'hindrance', 'obstacles', and 'restrictions'[177] is far from clear. Take, for example, the case of *Carpenter*. What was the obstacle which 'deterred' Mr Carpenter from exercising his freedom to provide cross-border services— the separation of husband and wife which would be 'detrimental to their family life',[178] the potential loss of child care,[179] or the emotional distress involved? Such cases come very close to saying the mere existence of a national rule constitutes a restriction.[180]

Secondly, the market access/restrictions approach makes no reference to the size or scale of the impediment: it is sufficient that there is an impediment or restriction or there is liable to be one.[181] While *Graf* would indicate that there needs to be more than a remote

---

[172] E. Spaventa, *Free Movement of Persons in the EU: Barriers to movement and their constitutional context* (The Hague: Kluwer, 2007), Ch. 7 argues that use of this language shows that the Court is actually developing a more general right not just to free movement but to 'exercise an economic activity in another Member State', a view supported by Case C–464/02 *Commission* v. *Denmark (company cars)* [2005] ECR I–7929, para. 34, where the Court declared that 'The provisions of the Treaty on freedom of movement for persons are intended to facilitate the pursuit by [Union] citizens of occupational activities of all kinds throughout the [Union].'

[173] *Kranemann*, n. 171, para. 25. In the context of services the rule may be phrased rather differently: Case C–17/00 *De Coster* v. *Collège des bourgmestre et échevins de Watermael-Boitsfort* [2001] ECR I–9445, para. 30: 'Article [56 TFEU] precludes the application of any national rules which have the effect of making the provision of services between Member States more difficult than the provision of services purely within one Member State.'

[174] Para. 26. For a similar approach in an establishment case, see Joined Cases C–151 and 152/04 *Nadin* [2005] ECR I–11203, para. 34.

[175] Para. 34.

[176] See, e.g., paras. 28 and 32 in Case C–19/92 *Kraus* [1993] ECR I–1663. See also Case C–118/96 *Safir* [1998] ECR I–1897, paras. 23 and 25; Case C–79/01 *Payroll Data Services* [2002] ECR I–8923, paras. 26–7.

[177] Case C–464/02 *Commission* v. *Denmark (company vehicles)* [2005] ECR I–7929, para. 52; cf. paras. 35–7, where the emphasis is on 'obstacles'.

[178] Para. 39.   [179] Para. 44.

[180] See, e.g., Case C–98/01 *Commission* v. *UK (BAA)* [2003] ECR I–4641, considered in Ch. 14.

[181] Case C–49/89 *Corsica Ferries* [1989] ECR I–4441, para. 8: 'the Articles of the [TFEU] concerning the free movement of goods, persons, services and capital are fundamental [Union] provisions and any restriction, even minor, of that freedom is prohibited', a view repeated in Case C–212/06 *Walloon Government* [2008] ECR I–1683, para. 52.

impediment to the free movement of persons to trigger an application of the Treaty, a view that appears to be enjoying support in a number of more recent cases,[182] in most cases it still takes very little to engage the Treaty. For example, in *Bosal*[183] the Court found a breach of Article 49 TFEU due to its assessment that the Dutch tax rule 'might dissuade' a parent company from carrying on its activities through the intermediary of a subsidiary established in another Member State. This decision cost the Dutch treasury millions.

Once the Court finds the Treaty applies, the defendant (usually the Member State but not always) can of course, justify their national rules. However, where the national rules concern social policy the Court is forced to make difficult—and often political—decisions about the legitimacy and proportionality of these policy choices when it lacks the institutional capacity to gather and process the relevant economic/social/cultural information. This is the third problem with the restrictions approach, a problem demonstrated by the Court's decision in *Viking*.[184]

In order to make costs savings, Viking, a Finnish company, wanted to reflag its vessel in Estonia. In response, the Finnish seamen's union (FSU) called their members out on strike. The Court found that the trade union's proposed strike action was a restriction on Viking's freedom of establishment. In its defence, the trade union argued that the strike was justified on the ground of worker protection, a position that the Court in principle accepted.[185] However, it then went on to curtail the circumstances in which that argument could be raised:

> [E]ven if that action—aimed at protecting the *jobs and conditions of employment* of the members of that union *liable to be adversely affected* by the reflagging of the *Rosella*—could reasonably be considered to fall, at first sight, within the objective of protecting workers, such a view would no longer be tenable if it were established that the jobs or conditions of employment at issue were not jeopardised or under serious threat.[186]

The Court also gave a narrow reading to the proportionality principle. When considering the necessity limb of the proportionality test, the Court said that industrial action should be the last resort; and that national courts would have to verify whether the union had exhausted all other avenues under Finnish law before the industrial action was found proportionate. In reaching this conclusion the Court, apparently unwittingly, trampled over a range of social values. For example, it ignored the fact that the strike action was protected by the Finnish constitution; it seemed unaware that the (exhaustive?) criteria it prescribed for taking strike action (jobs and conditions of employment are under serious threat) limits the possibility of taking industrial action even in the UK where national laws are already strict; the criteria rules out political strikes which are protected by various national systems; and the Court applies the proportionality principle to strike action

---

[182] See, e.g., Case C–500/06 *Corporación Dermoestética* [2008] ECR I–5785, para. 33, where the Court said that a ban on national television advertising of medical and surgical treatments constituted a 'serious obstacle' to freedom of establishment and free movement of services; and in Case C–518/06 *Commission v. Italy (motor insurance)* [2009] ECR I–3491, para. 66 the Court said that an obligation to contract constitutes a 'substantial interference in the freedom of contract'. In earlier cases the Court was more interested in the directness of the impediment rather than its significance: Case C–384/93 *Alpine Investments* [1995] ECR I–1141, para. 38 and Case C–415/93 *Bosman* [1995] ECR I–4921, para. 103. See H. Toner, 'Non-discriminatory obstacles to the exercise of Treaty rights: Articles 39, 43, 49 and 18 EC' (2004) 23 YEL 275, 285–6 who argues that there are two possible thresholds: direct *or* significant. If the obstacle is direct then its effect needs only be perceptible; if the measure is significant or substantial then the obstacle does not need to be direct.

[183] Case C–168/01 *Bosal Holding BV v. Staatssecretaris van Financiën* [2003] ECR I–9409.

[184] Case C–438/05 [2007] ECR I–10779.   [185] Case C–438/05 *Viking* [2007] ECR I–10779, para. 77.

[186] Case C–438/05 *Viking* [2007] ECR I–10779, para. 81, emphasis added. This is a reference to the fact that Viking, presumably on good advice, had given an undertaking that neither it nor companies in the same group would 'by reason of the reflagging terminate the employment of any person employed by them'.

which in some systems, notably the UK's, have never before been subject to a proportion-ality review[187] (not least because of the paradox that the more successful the strike action is from a trade union perspective, the less likely it is to be proportionate).

Yet in other cases involving cultural issues the Court has taken a sensitive—and def-erential—approach to the national rules. Consider, for example, *United Pan Europe Communications*,[188] a case decided at much the same time as *Viking*. In order to safeguard the pluralistic and cultural range of programmes on television networks, Belgium law required cable operators to broadcast certain television programmes which had 'must-carry' status transmitted by certain broadcasters in the French and Flemish communities. The Court said that a must-carry regime directly determined the conditions for access to the market for services, by requiring foreign providers to negotiate the conditions for access to the network, an obligation not imposed on the providers of services having must-carry status (primarily national providers). The legislation therefore breached Article 56 TFEU but could be justified on the grounds of cultural policy (safeguarding, in the audiovisual sector, the freedom of expression of the different social, cultural, religious, philosophical, or linguistic components which exist in that region). On the question of proportionality, the Court said that the legisla-tion was suitable (having regard to the bilingual nature of the Brussels-Capital region). On the question of necessity, the Court recognized a wide margin of discretion in the Member States but laid down certain conditions of good governance.[189] While many would laud this deference to the Member States, the Court's apparently diverging case law on justifications and proportionality generates considerable uncertainty and unpredictability.

The fourth problem with the shift away from a model focused on removing *discrimina-tory* obstacles to free movement to one based on removing any obstacles or restrictions to free movement is that it paves the way for opportunistic challenges to a whole variety of national laws never intended to interfere with free movement. Take for example, the 70 mph speed limit on British motorways. A German tourist, in defence to a prosecution for speeding, might argue that the speed limit is a restriction on his freedom to receive services (as a tourist) under Article 56 TFEU. Under the non-discrimination model such arguments would automatically fail because speed limits apply equally to nationals and migrants alike.[190] Under the market access approach, however, it is possible to see how such arguments might run and a breach of Article 56 TFEU might be found. Speed limits can of course be justified on the grounds of public and/or road safety.[191] But the problem lies with proportionality. While setting a speed limit might be a suitable means of achiev-ing the public-safety objective, it is not obvious that a 70 mph limit is no more restrictive than necessary to achieve that objective (why not 69, 68, or 71 or 72 mph?).[192]

---

[187] This is one of the main reasons why the trade union movement so objected to the Commission's so-called Monti II proposals (COM(2012) 130), which were intended to address the problems created by the *Viking* decision and to which 12 Member States (19 national parliaments) put up the 'yellow card' under the Subsidiarity Protocol introduced by the Lisbon Treaty: <http://ecrgroup.eu/?p=7038> and <http://europeangreens.eu/news/greens-welcome-commissions-withdrawal-monti-ii-proposals>.

[188] Case C–250/06 *United Pan-Europe Communications Belgium SA v. Etat belge* [2007] ECR I–11135.

[189] Namely the award of must-carry status must first of all be subject to a transparent procedure based on criteria known by broadcasters in advance, it must be based on objective criteria which are suita-ble for securing pluralism and the criteria on the basis of which must-carry status is awarded must be non-discriminatory.

[190] This point was recognized, albeit rather obliquely, in the 9th recital of the Services Dir. 2006/123, which is considered in detail in Ch. 11.

[191] Case C–55/93 *Criminal Proceedings against van Schaik* [1994] ECR I–4837; Joined Cases C–151 and 152/04 *Nadin* [2005] ECR I–11203, para. 49.

[192] Cf. Case C–110/05 *Commission v. Italy (trailers)* [2009] ECR I–519, para. 67, 'Member States cannot be denied the possibility of attaining an objective such as road safety by the introduction of general and simple rules which will be easily understood and applied by drivers and easily managed and supervised by the

In the field of taxation the problem is even more acute. An Irish entrepreneur might argue that the higher rate of corporate tax in the UK deters him from establishing himself in the UK in breach of Article 49 TFEU (even though the tax rates apply equally to the British entrepreneurs). Now the principal reason for taxation is to raise revenue for national exchequers. However, as we have already seen in Chapter 6, economic arguments, such as the loss of tax revenue[193] or the cost to the national exchequer,[194] are not accepted as justifications and so the British tax rule might be considered unlawful.[195]

Fifthly, and perhaps most fundamentally, as we noted in Chapter 1, the Treaty is based on an (ill-defined) model of competitive federalism: states are free to enact laws which respond to local choices. However, the free movement provisions of the Treaty as interpreted through the lens of the restrictions model, threatens to jeopardize these very choices. As Johnston and Syrpis put it,[196] 'the Court has yet to develop a nuanced account of the circumstances under which regulatory diversity poses an obstacle to market integration'.

The problems with the restrictions model were noted by Advocate General Tizzano in his influential opinion in *Caixa-Bank*.[197] He expressed profound misgivings about the 'rather broad concept of restriction' in the case law covering all 'national measures *liable* to hinder *or make less attractive the exercise of fundamental freedoms* guaranteed by the Treaty'.[198] He said that such a broad approach to 'restrictions' allows economic operators, both national and foreign, to abuse Article 49 TFEU in order to oppose any national measure that, solely because it regulated the conditions for pursuing an economic activity, could in the final analysis narrow profit margins and hence reduce the attractiveness of pursuing that particular economic activity.[199] Echoing the sentiments expressed by Advocate General Tesauro in his important opinion in the goods case, *Hünermund*,[200] he continued:[201]

> However, that would be tantamount to bending the Treaty to a purpose for which it was not intended: that is to say, not in order to create an internal market in which conditions are similar to those of a single market and where operators can move freely, but in order to establish a market without rules. Or rather, a market in which rules are prohibited as a matter of principle, except for those necessary and proportionate to meeting imperative requirements in the public interest.

He therefore advocated a return to a non-discrimination plus market access approach[202] (see fig. 7.4): where the principle of non-discrimination is respected, a national measure

---

competent authorities.' See also Case C–250/08 *Commission v. Belgium (immovable property)* EU:C:2011:793, para. 81, where the Court accepted without question that a limit of €12,500, as the maximum amount which could be offset against registration duties payable, was 'entirely proportionate'.

[193] Case C–464/02 *Commission v. Denmark (company vehicles)* [2005] ECR I–7929, para. 45, citing the free movement of capital decision in Case C–319/02 *Manninen* [2004] ECR I–7477, para. 49.

[194] Case C–109/04 *Kranemann* [2005] ECR I–2421.

[195] Cf. Case C–434/10 *Aladzhov* [2011] ECR I–11659, para. 38, where the Court appeared to offer a more creative solution: if the money is used as the basis of choices of economic and social policy then the measures could not be considered to have been adopted to serve exclusively economic ends.

[196] A. Johnston and P. Syrpis, 'Regulatory competition in European company law after *Cartesio*' (2009) 34 *ELRev.* 378, 379.

[197] Case C–442/02 *Caixa-Bank* [2004] ECR I–8961.

[198] Para. 39, emphasis in the original, criticizing, in particular, Case C–255/97 *Pfeiffer Großhandel* [1999] ECR I–2835.

[199] Para. 62. The Court itself acknowledged this in Case C–290/04 *FKP Scorpio* [2006] ECR I–9641, para. 46: 'the application of the host Member State's national rules to providers of services is liable to prohibit, impede or render less attractive the provision of services to the extent that it involves expense and additional administrative and economic burdens'.

[200] Case C–292/92 *Hünermund* [1993] ECR I–6787, para. 1, which influenced the ruling in *Keck*, considered further in Ch. 5.

[201] Para. 63.   [202] Para. 66.

cannot be described as a restriction on the freedom of movement of persons unless the measure 'directly affects market access'. He added that this approach makes it possible to reconcile the objective of merging the different national markets into a single common market with the continuation of Member States' general powers to regulate economic activities.[203] Such an approach also resonates with the presumptions in the certain selling arrangements case law (*Keck/De Agostini*): non-discriminatory restrictions do not breach the Treaty *unless* it can be shown they interfere with market access. As we shall see in Chapter 11 there are signs that, in the field of taxation at least, the Court may be heeding the Advocate General's advice.[204]

E. CAN THE TREATY PROVISIONS BE INVOKED AGAINST THE DEFENDANT?

1. THE QUESTION OF DIRECT EFFECT

Assuming the matter falls within the personal, material, and territorial scope of the free movement rules, the final question is whether those rules can be invoked against this particular defendant. This brings us to the vexed question of direct effect. It is clear that the free movement provisions are directly effective and have been since the expiry of the transitional period. In respect of Article 45 TFEU on workers, direct effect was first acknowledged by the Court in *French Merchant Seamen*[205] and confirmed in *Van Duyn*,[206] where the Court ruled that, despite the derogations from the principle of free movement contained in Article 45(3) TFEU, the provisions of Article 45(1) and (2) TFEU imposed a sufficiently precise obligation to confer direct effect. The Court has also ruled that Articles 49 TFEU on establishment, 56 TFEU on services, and 21(1) TFEU on citizenship are (vertically) directly effective in *Reyners*,[207] *Van Binsbergen*,[208] and *Baumbast*[209] respectively. Not only can the claimants[210] invoke their directly effective rights against the host state (the more usual situation)[211] but they can also do so against the home state,[212] provided the situation is not wholly internal.

---

[203] Case C–292/92 *Hünermund* [1993] ECR I–6787, para. 68.

[204] Case C–134/03 [2005] ECR I–1167. For further examples, see Case C–387/01 *Weigel* v. *Finanzlandes direction für Vorarlberg* [2004] ECR I–4981, considered in Ch. 8, and Joined Cases C–544 and 545/03 *Mobistar SA* v. *Commune de Fleron* [2005] ECR I–7723, considered in Ch. 11. See also Case C–453/04 *Innoventif* [2006] ECR I–4929, considered in Ch. 11, in respect of other charges.

[205] Case 167/73 *Commission* v. *France* [1974] ECR 359, para. 41.

[206] Case 41/74 [1974] ECR 1337, para. 8.   [207] Case 2/74 [1974] ECR 631, para. 32.

[208] Case 33/74 *van Binsbergen* v. *Bestuur van de Bedrijfsvereniging voor de Metaalnijverheid* [1974] ECR 1299, para. 27.

[209] Case C–413/99 *Baumbast* [2002] ECR I–7091.

[210] The applicants can be the workers, self-employed, or service providers themselves or employers applying on their behalf: Case C–350/96 *Clean Car* [1998] ECR I–2521, para. 24. See also Case C–232/01 *van Lent* [2003] ECR I–11525, para. 20. Recruitment agencies can also benefit from the rights laid down by Art. 45 TFEU: Case C–208/05 *ITC Innovative Technology Center GmbH* v. *Bundesagentur für Arbeit* [2007] ECR I–181, para. 25.

[211] E.g., Case 41/74 *Van Duyn* [1974] ECR 1337.

[212] This arises in cases concerning impediments to the 'export' of the worker, self-employed person, or company and service: e.g., Case C–384/93 *Alpine Investments* [1995] ECR I–1141, para. 30; Case C–107/94 *Asscher* [1996] ECR I–3089, para. 32; Case C–18/95 *Terhoeve* [1999] ECR I–345, para. 39; and to cases about returners: e.g., Case C–19/92 *Kraus* [1993] ECR I–1663, para. 15.

For many years it was not clear whether the provisions of the Treaty on free movement of persons had both vertical and horizontal direct effect[213] or only vertical direct effect. In *Walrave and Koch*[214] the Court suggested that the Treaty provisions had both: it said 'the rule on non-discrimination applies in judging *all legal relationships* in so far as these relationships, by reason either of the place they are entered into or the place where they take effect, can be located within the territory of the [Union]'. The Court also said that in addition to public authorities, the ban on discrimination 'extends likewise to rules of any other nature aimed at collectively regulating gainful employment and services'.[215] Yet subsequent cases concerned action taken by public authorities[216] or professional regulatory bodies (e.g., the Bar Council,[217] the Italian Football Association,[218] and the International Cycling Union[219]). This suggested an extended form of vertical direct effect only, not because the state is controlling the actions of these bodies but rather because the effect of decisions made by professional regulatory bodies was equivalent to state intervention. Some describe this as *private* governance.

However, in *Clean Car*[220] the Court provided a strong hint that the free movement of *workers* provision might have both vertical and horizontal direct effect, and this was subsequently confirmed in *Angonese*.[221] Applicants applying for jobs in a private bank had to produce a certificate of bilingualism issued by the local authority.[222] The Court noted that since working conditions were governed not only by laws but also by agreements and other acts adopted by private persons, there would be inequality in the application of Article 45 TFEU if it applied only to acts of a public authority.[223] Drawing on the long-established case law interpreting Article 157 TFEU on equal pay,[224] the Court then ruled that the prohibition of discrimination in Article 45 TFEU applied both to agreements intended to regulate paid labour collectively and to contracts between individuals.[225]

Therefore, Article 45 TFEU has horizontal direct effect, at least where the fundamental principle of non-discrimination is breached,[226] but it is not clear whether this ruling will also apply to Articles 21(1) TFEU on citizenship, 49 TFEU on establishment, and 56 TFEU on services. In *Viking*,[227] Advocate General Poiares Maduro argued that these provisions should have horizontal direct effect when the private action was capable of effectively restricting others from exercising their right to freedom of movement.[228] However, the Court did not appear to go that far. It said that Article 49 TFEU could be 'relied on by a

---

[213] Cf. Case 43/75 *Defrenne* v. *Sabena* [1976] ECR 455 concerning Art. 157 TFEU on equal pay.

[214] Case 36/74 [1974] ECR 1405, dispositif, emphasis added.   [215] Para. 17.

[216] See, e.g., the Home Office in Case 41/74 *Van Duyn* [1974] ECR 1337 and local authorities in Case 197/84 *Steinhauser* v. *Ville de Biarritz* [1985] ECR 1819 and Case C–168/91 *Konstantinidis* v. *Stadt Altensteig-Standesamt* [1993] ECR I–1191.

[217] Case 71/76 *Thieffry* v. *Conseil de l'ordre des avocats à la cour de Paris* [1977] ECR 765; Case C–309/99 *Wouters* [2002] ECR I–1577, para. 120.

[218] Case 13/76 *Donà* [1976] ECR 1333.   [219] Case 36/74 *Walrave and Koch* [1974] ECR 1405.

[220] Case C–350/96 [1998] ECR I–2521, itself confirming the hint in Case C–415/93 *Bosman* [1995] ECR I–4921, para. 86.

[221] Case C–281/98 [2000] ECR I–4139.   [222] Paras. 6–7.   [223] Para. 33.

[224] Esp. Case 43/75 *Defrenne* v. *Sabena* [1976] ECR 455.   [225] Para. 34.

[226] Para. 36. See also Case C–94/07 *Raccanelli* v. *Max-Planck Gesellschaft (MPG)* [2008] ECR I–5939, para. 46, where the Court held that 'the prohibition of discrimination based on nationality laid down by Article 45 TFEU applies equally to private-law associations such as MPG'.

[227] Case C–438/05 *Viking* [2007] ECR I–10779, para. 43.

[228] In Case C–58/08 *Vodafone* v. *Secretary of State for Business, Enterprise and Regulatory Reform* [2010] ECR I–4999, paras. 21–4, he argued that the Court should apply its case law on the horizontal application of the free movement rules to its analysis of the internal market legal basis, Art. 114 TFEU.

private undertaking against a trade union or an association of trade unions'.[229] It added that in 'exercising their autonomous power to negotiate pay and conditions of employment with employers, trade unions participate in the drawing up of agreements seeking to regulate paid work *collectively*'.[230] This tends to suggest the Court is equating the role of trade unions with that of professional regulatory bodies.[231] On the other hand, the Court does say (obiter?) that 'the fact that certain provisions of the Treaty are formally addressed to the Member States does not prevent rights from being conferred at the same time on any individual who has an interest in compliance with the obligations laid down [citing the equal pay case *Defrenne (No. 2)*] … Such considerations must also apply to Article [49 TFEU] which lays down a fundamental freedom'.[232] The question of full horizontal direct effect thus remains open.

2. REMEDIES

A corollary to the principle of direct effect is the remedy available to the claimant. As we shall see in Chapter 11, *Factortame III*[233] makes clear that an action for damages is, in principle, available to an individual (in that case where there was a breach of Article 49 TFEU) provided three conditions are satisfied:

- the rule of law is intended to confer rights on individuals
- the breach of Union law is sufficiently serious
- there is a direct causal link between the breach of the obligation by the state and the damage sustained by the injured parties.

In *Factortame III* the defendant was the state. The decision leaves open the question of whether a Union remedy in damages might also be available against a trade union[234] or, in the context of Article 45 TFEU, other private parties. There is support from the competition field that Union law requires such a remedy to exist.[235] The Court alluded to the point briefly in *Raccanelli*[236] concerning alleged discrimination against a foreign doctoral student by the Max Planck Institute (MPI), one of the foremost research

---

[229] Case C–438/05 *Viking* [2007] ECR I–10779, para. 61. See also Case C–341/05 *Laval* [2007] ECR I–11767 in respect of Art. 56 TFEU. These rulings create problems for trade unions which have now been placed in the same position as states, with the same responsibilities, albeit that unlike states, trade unions have one principal objective, protecting the interests of their members. Further, while trade unions are subject to the same obligations as states, it is difficult for them ever to be able to invoke any of the defences in Art. 52 TFEU, such as public policy, which were drafted with states in mind.

[230] Para. 65, emphasis added. See A. Dashwood, '*Viking* and *Laval*: Issues of horizontal direct effect' (2007–8) 10 *CYELS* 525.

[231] This lack of clarity is exacerbated by the fact that the Court somewhat surprisingly cited the decision in Case C–265/95 *Commission v. France (strawberries)* [1997] ECR I–6959, a case on *omissions* by the state, not *acts*. This case is considered further in Ch. 4.

[232] Paras. 58–9.

[233] Joined Cases C–46 and 48/93 *Brasserie du Pêcheur SA v. Federal Republic of Germany* and *R. v. Secretary of State for Transport, ex p. Factortame (Factortame III)* [1996] ECR I–1029. Principles of national procedural autonomy, effectiveness, and equivalence apply to any claims to enforce the free movement of persons: see, e.g., Case C–429/12 *Pohl v. ÖBB-Infrastruktur* EU:C:2014:12.

[234] When the case of *Laval* returned to the Swedish court, exemplary damages were awarded to Laval of about €60,000 and the trade unions had to pay Laval's costs of about €230,000: U. Bernitz and N. Reich (2011) 48 *CMLRev.* 603.

[235] See, e.g., Case C–453/99 *Courage v. Creehan* [2001] ECR I–6297, discussed by A. Albors-Llorens, '*Courage v. Creehan*: Judicial activism or consistent approach?' (2002) 61 *CLJ* 38.

[236] Case C–94/07 *Raccanelli* [2008] ECR I–5939.

institutes in Europe. MPI is established under German private law in the form of an as-sociation operating in the public interest. The Court said that neither Article 45 TFEU nor Regulation 492/11 prescribed 'a specific measure to be taken by the Member States or associations such as [MPI] in the event of a breach of the prohibition of discrimin-ation, but leaves them free to choose between the different solutions suitable for achiev-ing the objective of those respective provisions, depending on the different situations which may arise'.[237] It continued that 'it is for the referring court to assess, in the light of the national legislation applicable in relation to non-contractual liability, the nature of the compensation which the applicant in the main proceedings would be entitled to claim'.[238]

F. CONCLUSIONS

The case law on free movement of persons ranges from the personal (as in *Carpenter*, where deportation risked breaking up the family unit) to the commercial (provision of TV signals by large companies). While common principles apply across this spectrum, the Court has adapted the principles to take account of the subject matter. In particular, the Court has in recent years used the principle of citizenship of the Union to shape the case law relating to these 'personal' cases, often prioritizing the protection of fundamen-tal human rights.

The most important development in the case law is the shift from the discrimination model towards one based on market access. From the perspective of market integration, this is clearly an important development. However, by focusing on market access through the restrictions/obstacles approach, the Court has made an important policy shift away from respecting the autonomy of the Member States and the integrity of their rules (the effect of the non-discrimination model) towards greater Union intervention (the market access model). The result may well be deregulatory if a national rule is found to obstruct trade and no Union norm is put in its place. To avoid this outcome and to protect some state autonomy, the Court needs to be willing to interpret and apply the public-interest requirements broadly. This has not always been the case.

In Chapters 8–13 we will consider the detailed rules in respect of workers, establish-ment, services, citizenship, and TCNs. We begin by examining the rules on workers.

FURTHER READING

On reverse discrimination

E. SPAVENTA, 'Seeing the wood despite the trees? On the scope of Union citizenship and its constitutional effects' (2008) 45 *CMLRev.* 13.

A. TRYFONIDOU, 'Reverse discrimination in purely internal situations: An incongruity in a citizens' Europe' (2008) 35 *LIEI* 43, 63–4.

On the discrimination approach

L. DANIELE, 'Non-discriminatory restrictions on the free movement of persons' (1997) 22 *ELRev.* 191.

---

[237] Para. 50.   [238] Para. 51.

G. Davies, *Nationality Discrimination in the European Internal Market* (The Hague: Kluwer, 2003).

E. Spaventa, *Free Movement of Persons in the EU: Barriers to movement and their constitutional context* (Hague: Kluwer, 2007).

On direct effect

E. Lohse, 'Fundamental freedoms and private actors: Towards an "indirect horizontal effect"' (2007) 13 *European Public Law* 159.

D. Wyatt, 'Horizontal effect of fundamental freedoms and the right to equality after *Viking* and *Mangold*, and the implications for Community competence' (2008) 4 *Croatian Yearbook of European Law and Policy* 1.

On the question of convergence across the freedoms

K. Mortelmans, 'Towards convergence in the application of the rules on free movement and on competition?' (2001) 38 *CMLRev.* 613.

N. Nic Shuibhne, *The Coherence of EU Free Movement Law: Constitutional Responsibility and the Court of Justice* (Oxford: OUP, 2013).

O. Odudu, 'Economic activity as a limit to Union law' in C. Barnard and O. Odudu (eds.), *The Outer Limits of European Union Law* (Oxford: Hart Publishing, 2009).

S. O'Leary, 'Free movement of persons and services' in P. Craig and G. de Búrca (eds.) *The Evolution of EU Law*, 2nd edn (Oxford: OUP, 2011).

M. Poiares Maduro, 'Harmony and dissonance in free movement' and H. Jarass, 'A unified approach to the fundamental freedoms' in M. Andenas and W.-H. Roth (eds.), *Services and Free Movement in EU Law* (Oxford: OUP, 2002).

8

FREE MOVEMENT OF WORKERS AND THE SELF-EMPLOYED

A. INTRODUCTION

Article 45 TFEU, an 'integral part of the internal market',[1] gives workers the right to move freely across the EU to seek and take up employment in another Member State on the same terms as nationals. Article 49 TFEU extends the same rights to the self-employed. The original idea behind Articles 45 and 49 TFEU—and an idea still relevant in times of economic crisis—was to enable workers/the self-employed from states with high levels of unemployment to move to other states with high levels of employment. In the host state the migrant worker[2] could find a job, probably benefit from higher wages than in the home

---

[1] UK New Settlement Decision, 18–19 Feb. 2016.

[2] The use of the term 'migrant worker' is controversial. The argument goes that since both migrant and non-migrant workers are citizens of the Union, why focus on their migrant status? This book will, however,

state, and provide the skills needed by the host state. Furthermore, the EU rules on free-dom of movement meant that employers had a larger potential pool of workers from which to draw, and the principle of non-discrimination meant that employers selected candidates based on merit, not nationality. At least, this was the theory. In practice workers and the self-employed—at least those from the original Member States—often preferred to stay (unemployed) in a state they were familiar with, in the company of family and friends.

The Union responded to this problem by adopting a series of measures giving rights not only to workers (and subsequently the self-employed) but also their families in an attempt to encourage them to move. Most notable in this respect was Regulation 1612/68 (now Regulation 492/2011).[3] The legislature's approach was reinforced by judicial intervention. The Court has been instrumental in helping to secure the free movement of workers and the self-employed, by removing obstacles which impeded free movement and then by find-ing ways to ensure that migrant workers, the self-employed, and their families became integrated into the host state. And with these developments came a change in perspec-tive. Workers, in particular, were no longer simply viewed as factors of production needed to fulfil the objectives of the common market. Now they were seen as EU citizens with rights enforceable against the host state. Ultimately, this led to the adoption of the Citizens' Rights Directive (CRD) 2004/38, which gave rights not only to migrant workers and the self-employed but also to a range of other migrant citizens. This directive is discussed in detail in Chapter 10. The controversial Services Directive 2006/123[4] also applies to the self-employed. This will be considered in Chapter 11. In this chapter we focus on the rights given to workers, principally by the Treaty but also by Regulation 492/11 and the Enforcement Directive 2014/54,[5] and to the self-employed, mainly by the Treaty and the CRD. Underpinning both Regulation 492/11 and the CRD is the principle of equal treatment: that the migrant worker/self-employed person should be treated in the same way as their domestic equivalent unless there are proportionate justifiable reasons why not. In other words, workers moving under Article 45 TFEU and the self-employed moving under Article 49 TFEU are in a different situation to those moving temporarily under Article 56 TFEU: the former group are subject to host state control; the latter to home state control.

While levels of migration between the original Member States (the EU-15) was low, this was not the case with workers from the EU-10[6]—the states which joined the EU in 2004—particularly those from the EU-8 states (i.e., the eastern European countries) who were keen to take advantage of free movement rights. The Accession Treaty made provision for transitional arrangements which allowed the 'old' Member States (EU-15) to decide whether they would permit free movement of workers based on the '2+3+2' formula. This scheme obliged the Member States to declare in 2006, and again three years later in May 2009, whether they would open up their labour markets for workers from the Accession States. Any remaining restrictions ended on 30 April 2011.[7] All the Member States, except Ireland, Sweden, and the UK, ini-tially imposed labour-market restrictions on those coming from the EU-8 in 2004,[8]

---

use the term 'migrant workers' to distinguish those coming from other countries from those workers who have not migrated (i.e., national workers).

[3] [2011] OJ L141/1   [4] [2006] OJ L376/36.   [5] [2014] OJ L128/8.

[6] Poland, Lithuania, Latvia, Estonia, the Czech Republic, Slovakia, Hungary, and Slovenia (EU-8)—the former Eastern bloc countries—plus Cyprus and Malta.

[7] A similar '2+3+2' scheme is in place in respect of workers from Romania and Bulgaria, which joined the EU on 1 January 2007. For these workers the restrictions ended on 31 December 2013.

[8] For a summary, see Commission, 'The impact of free movement of workers in the context of EU enlarge-ment', COM(2008) 765, 5.

largely out of fear that an influx of 'cheap' Eastern European labour would displace local labour and drive down wages. The result was that the lion's share of migration from the EU-8 came to the UK (and Ireland). The fear that the UK had 'lost control of its borders' and that many migrants were claiming social welfare benefits, including those who were working, eventually contributed to creating the conditions that led the British Prime Minister, David Cameron, to hold an in-out referendum on Britain's continued membership of the EU in June 2016. Prior to the referendum he negotiated the New Settlement Agreement for the UK in the EU. Some of the most important aspects of this agreement (in fact a Decision between the heads of state or government binding under international law) concern social benefits for migrant workers. These will be discussed later in this chapter. However, we begin by examining the fundamental question: who is a worker and who is a self-employed person?

B. THE PERSONAL SCOPE OF THE TREATY PROVISIONS

1. WORKERS

Article 45(1) TFEU provides 'Freedom of movement for workers shall be secured within the Union.' Although there is no definition of the term 'worker' in the Treaty, the Court has insisted that it be given a broad Union meaning, based on objective criteria to ensure uniform interpretation across the Member States.[9] In essence, where Union nationals are in a relationship of subordination—i.e., they are under the control of the employer—they are workers. As the Court put it in *Lawrie-Blum*,[10] the essential feature of an employment relationship is that 'for a certain period of time a person performs services for and under the direction of another person in return for which he receives remuneration'. The national court must decide whether a relationship of subordination exists.[11] The sphere of employment,[12] the nature of the legal relationship between employer and employee (whether or not it involves public law status or a private law contract),[13] and the fact that the individual lives in one state and works in another (frontier workers)[14]—are all immaterial. On the facts of *Lawrie-Blum* the Court found that a trainee teacher was a worker for the purpose of Article 45(1) TFEU.

---

[9] See Case 75/63 *Unger v. Bestuur der Bedrijfsvereniging voor Detail handel en Ambachten* [1964] ECR 1977; Case 53/81 *Levin v. Staatssecretaris van Justitie* [1982] ECR 1035, paras. 11–12; Case 139/85 *Kempf v. Staatssecretaris van Justitie* [1986] ECR 1741, para. 15; Case 66/85 *Lawrie-Blum v. Land Baden-Württemberg* [1986] ECR 2121, para. 16.

[10] Case 66/85 [1986] ECR 2121, paras. 16–17.

[11] Case C–337/97 *Meeusen v. Hoofddirectie van de Informatie Beheer Groep* [1999] ECR I–3289, para. 15. In Case C–94/07 *Raccanelli v. Max-Planck Gesellschaft (MPG)* [2008] ECR I–5939, para. 37 the Court of Justice left it up to the national court to decide whether a researcher preparing a doctoral thesis on the basis of a grant contract concluded with the MPG satisfied the test of subordination and remuneration. Cf. Case C–107/94 *Asscher v. Staatssecretaris van Financiën* [1996] ECR I–3089, para. 26, where the Court said that a director and sole shareholder of a company was not a worker because company directors are not subordinate.

[12] Case 36/74 *Walrave and Koch* [1974] ECR 1405, para. 21.

[13] Case 152/73 *Sotgiu v. Deutsche Bundespost* [1974] ECR 153, para. 5. See also Case C–270/13 *Haralambidis v. Calogero Casilli* EU:C:2014:2185, para. 38 (the president of port authority could be a 'worker'); Case C–232/09 *Danosa v. LKB Līzings SIA* [2010] ECR I–11405, para. 51 (board members providing services to a company were workers).

[14] Case C–379/11 *Caves Krier Frères Sarl v. Directeur de l'administration de l'emploi* EU:C:2012:798, para. 27.

The worker must also be engaged in a 'genuine and effective' economic activity within the meaning of Article 2 EC (repealed by the Lisbon Treaty but much of the substance is repeated in Article 3 TEU). While most activities satisfy this requirement[15]— including playing professional football,[16] doing an apprenticeship,[17] and other types of training[18]—this may not always be the case. For example, work as part of a community-based religion might not constitute an economic activity. This was at issue in *Steymann*,[19] where a plumber worked for a Bhagwan community as part of its commercial activities. On the facts, the Court considered that since the community looked after his material needs and paid him pocket money this might constitute an indirect *quid pro quo* for genuine and effective work, and so Steymann could be considered a worker.

On the other hand, in *Bettray*[20] the Court found that paid activity provided by the state as part of a drug rehabilitation programme did not represent a genuine and effective economic activity, since the work, which was designed for those who could not take up work under 'normal' conditions, was tailored to an individual's needs and was intended to reintegrate them into the employment market. By contrast, in *Trojani*[21] the Court of Justice left it to the national court to decide whether Trojani's work, performed for and under the direction of a Salvation Army hostel for about 30 hours a week as part of a programme reintegrating individuals to the labour market, was 'real and genuine' paid activity, taking into account the status and practices of the hostel, the content of the social reintegration programme, and the nature and details of performance of the services.[22]

The economic activity must also not be on 'such a small scale as to be purely marginal and ancillary'.[23] Although this hurdle might raise particular difficulties for part-time workers, the Court has generally found that they are still workers. For example, in *Levin*[24] the Court found that a British woman working part-time as a chambermaid in the Netherlands could be a worker, even though she earned less than a subsistence wage, because, according to the Court, part-time work constituted an effective means of improving an individual's living conditions.[25] In *Kempf*[26] the Court also found that the work of a part-time music teacher was not on 'such a small scale as to be purely marginal and ancillary', even though his income was supplemented by social security benefits.[27] The Court said that once a finding of effective and genuine employment

[15] See, e.g., Case 13/76 *Donà v. Mantero* [1976] ECR 1333, para. 12.
[16] Case C–415/93 *Bosman* [1995] ECR I–4921, para. 73.
[17] Case C–188/00 *Kurz, née Yüce v. Land Baden-Württemberg* [2002] ECR I–10691, decided in the context of the EEC–Turkey Association Agreement.
[18] Case C–109/04 *Kranemann* [2005] ECR I–2421; Case C–10/05 *Mattern v. Ministre du Travail et de l'emploi* [2006] ECR I–3145, para. 21.
[19] Case 196/87 *Steymann v. Staatssecretaris van Justitie* [1988] ECR 6159, para. 14.
[20] Case 344/87 *Bettray v. Staatssecretaris van Justitie* [1989] ECR 1621, para. 17. Cf. Case C–1/97 *Birden v. Stadtgemeinde Bremen* [1998] ECR I–7747, decided in the context of the EEC–Turkey Association Agreement, where a person employed under a job-creation scheme was considered a worker. See also Case C–14/09 *Genc v. Land Berlin* [2010] ECR I–931.
[21] Case C–456/02 *Trojani v. CPAS* [2004] ECR I–7573.   [22] Para. 24.
[23] See, e.g., Case C–357/89 *Raulin v. Minister van Onderwijs en Wetenschappen* [1992] ECR I–1027, para. 10. The mere fact that the employment is of short duration cannot of itself, exclude the employment from Art. 45 TFEU: Case C–413/01 *Franca Ninni-Orasche v. Bundesminister für Wissenschaft, Verkehr und Kunst* [2003] ECR I–1187, para. 25.
[24] Case 53/81 [1982] ECR 1035, para. 17.   [25] Para. 15.
[26] Case 139/85 [1986] ECR 1741.   [27] See also Art. 14(4)(a) CRD.

had been made, it was irrelevant whether the individual subsisted on his earnings or whether his pay was used to add to other family income[28] or was supplemented by public funds.[29] However, in *Raulin*[30] the Court again emphasized the role of the national court in making the final decision as to who is a worker. It said that an '*oproep-kracht*' (an on-call worker) on a 'zero hours' contract, who was not actually guaranteed any work or obliged to take up any work offered and often worked only a very few days per week or hours per day, could be a 'worker' but that it was a matter for the national court to decide, taking into account the irregular nature and limited duration of the services provided.

The case law identifying a worker was usefully summarized in *Kurz*,[31] where the Court said:

> neither the sui generis nature of the employment relationship under national law, nor the level of productivity of the person concerned, the origin of the funds for which the remuneration is paid or the limited amount of remuneration can have any consequence in regard to whether or not the person is a worker.

This tends to suggest that the Court will find that an individual is a worker where possible, a view confirmed in *Vatsouras*.[32] The referring court had found that the 'brief minor' professional activity engaged in by Mr Vatsouras 'did not ensure him a livelihood'.[33] Nevertheless, the Court of Justice said that:

> independently of the limited amount of the remuneration and the short duration of the professional activity, it cannot be ruled out that that professional activity, following an overall assessment of the employment relationship, may be considered by the national authorities as real and genuine, thereby allowing its holder to be granted the status of 'worker' within the meaning of Article [45 TFEU].[34]

The Court has extended the definition of 'worker' to include those seeking work.[35] While the period allowed for work-seekers to remain in the host state depends on the rules of that state, they must be given at least three months to look for work,[36] although if they are dependent on social security they may be asked to leave.[37] At the time of the decision in *Antonissen*[38] migrants in the UK had six months to look for work,[39] which the Court found to be compatible with Union law. If, at the end of the six-month period, work-seekers can show that they have a genuine chance of being employed, they cannot be required to leave the host state. For this reason the Court said in *Commission v. Belgium*[40] that a Belgian law requiring a work-seeker to leave the state automatically on the expiry of the three-month period breached Article 45 TFEU. Article 14(4)(b)

---

[28] Case 53/81 *Levin* [1982] ECR 1035.   [29] Para. 14.

[30] Case C–357/89 [1992] ECR I–1027.   [31] Case C–188/00 [2002] ECR I–10691, para. 32.

[32] Joined Cases C–22 and 23/08 *Vatsouras* [2009] ECR I–4585, para. 30.

[33] Para. 25.   [34] Para. 30.

[35] Case C–85/96 *Martínez Sala* v. *Freistaat Bayern* [1998] ECR I–2691, para. 32; Case C–138/02 *Collins* v. *Secretary of State for Work and Pensions* [2003] ECR I–2703, para. 29. Cf. Art. 45(3) TFEU, which envisages that the worker has already found a job before leaving for the host state.

[36] In certain circumstances work-seekers are entitled to social security benefits for three months under Art. 64 of Reg. 883/04 from 1 Mar. 2010.

[37] Declaration of the Council accompanying Dir. 68/360 and Reg. 492/11 ([1968] OJ Spec. Ed. (I) 475).

[38] Case C–292/89 *R*. v. *IAT, ex p. Antonissen* [1991] ECR I–745, para. 21.

[39] Statement of Changes to the Immigration Rules (HC 169).

[40] Case C–344/95 *Commission* v. *Belgium* [1997] ECR I–1035, para. 18.

CRD confirms this line of case law, making clear that Union citizen work-seekers (and their family members) cannot be expelled so long as they can 'provide evidence that they are continuing to seek employment and that they have a genuine chance of being engaged'. No time limit is specified.

2. THE SELF-EMPLOYED

Article 49 TFEU provides that 'restrictions on the freedom of establishment of nationals of a Member State in the territory of another Member State shall be prohibited'. This gives nationals of one Member State the right to establish themselves as self-employed persons in another Member State.[41] The Treaty does not define 'self-employed', but in *Jany*[42] the Court explained that, unlike workers, the self-employed work outside a relationship of subordination, they bear the risk for the success or failure of their employment, and they are paid directly and in full.[43] The case concerned Czech and Polish women working as prostitutes in the Netherlands.[44] They paid rent to the owner of the premises and received a monthly income (of between FL 1,500 and 1,800), which they declared to the tax authorities. The Court considered them to be self-employed. The fact that some consider prostitution immoral did not alter the Court's conclusions: recognizing the margin of discretion allowed to the Member States in these sensitive areas, the Court said that it would not substitute its own assessment for that of the Member States where an allegedly immoral activity was practised legally.[45]

Jany suggests that Article 49 TFEU permits individuals to engage in a wide range of economic activities in other Member States and still be considered self-employed. As the Court put it in *Barkoci and Malik*,[46] a self-employed person could conduct 'activities of an industrial or commercial character, activities of craftsmen, or activities of the professions of a Member State'.[47] The breadth of Article 49 TFEU was summed up by the Court in the leading case of *Gebhard*:[48]

> the concept of establishment within the meaning of the Treaty is therefore a very broad one, allowing a [Union] national to participate, on a stable and continuous basis, in the economic life of a Member State other than his state of origin and to profit therefrom,

---

[41] But not a third country: Case C–102/05 *Skatteverket* v. *A and B* [2007] ECR I–3871; Case C–157/05 *Holböck* v. *Finanzamt Salzburg-Land* [2007] ECR I–4051, para. 28. The Treaty also envisages another type of establishment for individuals: participating in the formation of a company in another Member State (Art. 49(2) TFEU) within the meaning of Art. 54 TFEU (by, e.g., becoming a shareholder in a company (Case 182/83 *Fearon* v. *Irish Land Commission* [1985] ECR 3677, para. 9; Case C–251/98 *Baars* v. *Inspecteur der Belastingdienst Particulieren/Ondernemingen Gorinchem* [2000] ECR I–2728, para. 22; Case C–212/97 *Centros* v. *Erhvervs- og Selskabsstyrelsen* [1999] ECR I–1459, para. 19) or a director (Case C–221/89 *Factortame II* [1991] ECR I–3905).

[42] Case C–268/99 *Jany and others* v. *Staatssecretaris van Justitie* [2001] ECR I–8615. See also Joined Cases C–151 and 152/04 *Nadin* [2005] ECR I–11203, para. 31.

[43] Paras. 34 and 70–1.

[44] The case was decided under the Europe Agreements but in this regard the Court said that the principles were the same as those under Art. 49 TFEU (para. 38).

[45] Para. 56. However, the Court could not resist adding: 'Far from being prohibited in all Member States, prostitution is tolerated, even regulated, by most of those States, notably the Member State concerned in this case [the Netherlands]' (para. 57).

[46] Case C–257/99 *R.* v. *Secretary of State for the Home Department, ex p. Barkoci and Malik* [2001] ECR I–6557, para. 50. This was in the context of Art. 45(3) of the Association Agreement which has wording 'similar or identical to' Art. 49 TFEU.

[47] See also Case C–55/94 *Gebhard* [1995] ECR I–4165, para. 23, 'all types of self-employed activity'.

[48] Case C–55/94 *Gebhard* [1995] ECR I–4165, para. 25,

so contributing to social and economic penetration within the [Union] in the sphere of activities as self-employed persons.[49]

3. OTHERS DEEMED 'WORKERS' AND 'SELF-EMPLOYED'

Article 7(3) CRD makes provision for those Union citizens who are no longer workers or self-employed to retain worker or self-employed status in four situations:

(a) where the individual cannot work because s/he is temporarily incapacitated through illness or accident[50]

(b) where the individual has become *involuntarily* unemployed after having been employed for more than one year, and has registered as a job-seeker with the relevant employment office

(c) where the individual has become *involuntarily* unemployed after having completed a fixed-term contract of less than one year or after having become involuntarily unemployed during the first twelve months and after having registered as a job-seeker with the relevant employment office (in this situation the status of worker can be retained for no less than six months)

(d) where the individual embarks on vocational training (unless the individual is involuntarily unemployed, the retention of the status of worker requires the training to be related to the previous employment).[51]

The Court has added to this list through the interpretation of Article 45 TFEU. *Saint Prix* concerned a woman who gave up work and gave up seeking work due to the physical constraints of the late stages of pregnancy and the aftermath of childbirth. The Court ruled that a woman in this situation retained the status of worker provided that she returned to work or found another job within a reasonable period after the birth of her child.[52]

C. THE RIGHTS CONFERRED ON WORKERS

1. INTRODUCTION

Article 45(2) TFEU provides that free movement of workers includes the abolition of any discrimination based on nationality between workers of the Member States, as regards employment, remuneration, and other conditions of work and employment. Article 45(3) TFEU then adds that free movement comprises the right to:

- accept offers of employment actually made
- move freely within the territory of the Member States for this purpose

---

[49] Para. 25. This is the establishment equivalent of the requirement in the field of workers to be engaged in a genuine and effective economic activity which is not ancillary or purely marginal. See also Art. 4(5) of the Services Dir. 2006/123/EC ([2006] OJ L376/36), considered further in Ch. 11.

[50] Cf. Case C–43/99 *Leclere* [2001] ECR I–4265, considered at n. 195.

[51] Case 39/86 *Lair* [1988] ECR 3161.

[52] Case C–507/12 *Saint Prix* v. *Secretary of State for Work and Pensions* EU:C:2014:2007, para. 47. The Court cited Joined Cases C–482 and 493/01 *Orfanopoulos* v. *Land Baden-Württemberg* [2004] ECR I–5257, para. 50, where the Court ruled that prisoners who were employed before their imprisonment could continue to be duly registered as belonging to the labour force of the host Member State provided that they actually find another job within a reasonable time after their release.

- stay in the Member State for the purpose of the employment
- remain in the Member State after having been employed.

In addition, the Court has recognized that workers have the right, derived directly from the Treaty, to leave their state of origin,[53] to enter the territory of another Member State, and to reside and pursue an economic activity there.[54] The details of these rights were originally expanded by three secondary measures: Directive 68/360[55] on the rights of entry and residence, Regulation 1612/68 on the free movement of workers[56] (now Regulation 492/11), and Regulation 1251/70[57] on the right to remain. Directive 68/360 and Regulation 1251/70,[58] along with a number of other Union directives, as well as the family rights provisions laid down in Articles 10–11 of Regulation 1612/68, have been repealed and replaced by the CRD 2004/38. This means that workers enjoy rights under Article 45 TFEU, the CRD, and Regulation 492/11 (see fig. 7.1). Often the Court will interpret the Treaty in the light of the secondary legislation.[59] However, in the event of a conflict with the secondary legislation or where the secondary legislation does not apply, the Treaty will, of course, prevail.[60] Therefore migrant workers can start working before completing the formalities to obtain any residence certificate because the right of residence is a fundamental right derived from the Treaty and is not dependent upon the possession of a residence permit.[61] Workers' employment rights are also derived from the Treaty[62] but further detail is provided by Regulation 492/11, which applies exclusively to workers, as does Directive 2014/54, which has the same scope as Regulation 492/2011.[63] This chapter will focus on these secondary measures.

2. EMPLOYMENT RIGHTS

Regulation 492/11 was originally designed both to facilitate the free movement of workers and their families and to ensure their integration into the community of the host state. For our purposes, Regulation 492/11 falls into two parts: (1) the right of *access* to a post ('eligibility') on non-discriminatory terms (Chapter I, section I); and (2) the right to equal treatment while doing that job (i.e., while *exercising* the rights of free movement) (Chapter I,

---

[53] Case C–10/90 *Masgio* v. *Bundesknappschaft* [1991] ECR I–1119, paras. 18–19; Case C–415/93 *Bosman* [1995] ECR I–4921, para. 104; Case C–18/95 *Terhoeve* [1999] ECR I–345, paras. 37–8.

[54] Case C–363/89 *Roux* v. *Belgium* [1991] ECR I–273, para. 9; Case C–18/95 *Terhoeve* [1999] ECR I–345, para. 38.

[55] [1968] OJ Spec. Ed. (II) L485.

[56] [1968] OJ Spec. Ed. (I) 475. When enacting the regulation the Council took into account, first, the importance for the worker, from a human point of view, of having his entire family with him and, secondly, the importance, from all points of view, of the integration of the worker and his family into the host Member State without any difference in treatment in relation to nationals of that state (Case 249/86 *Commission* v. *Germany* [1989] ECR 1263, para. 11).

[57] [1970] OJ Spec. Ed. L142/24, 402.

[58] This was repealed by Commission Reg. 635/2006 ([2006] OJ L112/9).

[59] Case C–278/03 *Commission* v. *Italy (recruitment of teaching staff)* [2005] ECR I–3747, para. 15.

[60] Joined Cases C–197 and 203/11 *Libert* EU:C:2013:288, paras. 39–40.

[61] Case 118/75 *Watson and Belmann* [1976] ECR 1185, paras. 15–16.

[62] Case C–208/05 *ITC Innovative Technology Center GmbH* [2007] ECR I–181, para. 36, where the Court decided the case purely under Art. 45 TFEU, consideration of the regulation being 'unnecessary'.

[63] Art. 1(2).

section II). In addition, the basic principle of equal treatment contained in Article 24(1) CRD also applies to migrant workers.

2.1 Access to Employment

Article 1 of Regulation 492/11 reiterates the substance of Article 45 TFEU: any national of a Member State 'has the right to take up an activity as an employed person, and to pursue such activity, within the territory of another Member State', enjoying the same priority as a national. The worker may conclude and perform contracts of employment in accordance with the laws of the host state.[64] Any provisions which discriminate against foreign nationals or hinder foreign nationals from obtaining work are not permissible[65] unless justified.

(a) Direct discrimination

As we saw in Chapter 7, the prohibition against discrimination applies both to directly and indirectly discriminatory measures. Measures are directly discriminatory where the migrant worker is treated less favourably than the national worker. This was the case with the '3+2 rule' in *Bosman*,[66] considered in Case Study 8.1, and the law in *Commission* v. *Italy*[67] providing that private security work could be carried out only by Italian security firms employing Italian nationals. Further examples of directly discriminatory measures are contained in Article 3(1)(a) of Regulation 492/11, which says that provisions laid down by law, regulation, or administrative action or administrative practices of a Member State shall not apply 'where they limit application for and offers of employment, or the right of foreign nationals to take up and pursue employment or subject these to conditions not applicable in respect of their own nationals'. Such directly discriminatory measures breach Article 45 TFEU (and the Regulation and the CRD) and can be saved (probably) only by reference to one of the express derogations laid down by the Treaty or the secondary legislation (see fig. 7.2).

Regulation 492/11 also identifies and seeks to eliminate other directly discriminatory barriers to access to employment. For example, Article 4(1) provides that national provisions which restrict, by number or percentage, the employment of foreign nationals in any undertaking do not apply to nationals of the other Member States. Therefore, in *Commission* v. *France*[68] the Court said that a French rule requiring a ratio of three French seamen to one non-French seaman on a merchant ship contravened Article 4(1). Article 4(2) says that if there is a requirement that an undertaking has to employ a minimum percentage of national workers, then nationals of the other Member States count as national workers. Article 6 adds that the engagement and recruitment of a worker must not depend on medical, vocational, or other criteria which are discriminatory on the grounds of nationality. However, it does permit the employer to require the migrant worker to take a vocational test when offering employment.

---

[64] Art. 2.

[65] Art. 3(1). Some examples of prohibited practices are listed in Art. 3(2): prescribing a special recruitment procedure for foreign nationals, restricting the advertising of vacancies in the press, and imposing additional requirements on applicants from other Member States of subjecting eligibility for employment to conditions of registration with employment offices.

[66] Case C–415/93 [1995] ECR I–4921.

[67] Case C–283/99 *Commission* v. *Italy* [2001] ECR I–4363.

[68] Case 167/73 *Commission* v. *France (French merchant seamen)* [1974] ECR 359.

(b) Indirect discrimination

Indirectly discriminatory measures also breach Article 45 TFEU and the regulation unless objectively justified[69] or saved by one of the express derogations (see fig. 7.2). As we have seen, indirect discrimination focuses on the effect of a measure, a point confirmed by Article 3(1) of Regulation 492/11,[70] which 'makes explicit the principles formulated in Article [45 TFEU] with regard, specifically, to access to employment'.[71] Article 3(1)(b) says that provisions laid down by national law, regulation, or administrative action or practices will not apply where, 'though applicable irrespective of nationality, their exclusive or principal aim *or effect* is to keep nationals of other Member States away from employment offered'.[72] Common examples of indirectly discriminatory rules are those requiring either a period of service or residence in the host state before enjoying a particular benefit. Therefore, in *Scholz*,[73] the Court found the refusal by an Italian selection board to take into account a German applicant's previous employment in Germany to be unjustified indirect discrimination.[74] Similarly, a British rule in *Collins*[75] that entitlement to a job-seeker's allowance was conditional upon a requirement of being habitually resident in the UK was indirectly discriminatory. However, the Court found that the British rule could be justified; the question of proportionality of the national measure was left to the national court.[76]

Language requirements may well be indirectly discriminatory measures but can usually be justified. This is expressly recognized by the second paragraph of Article 3(1) of Regulation 492/11, which provides that the principle of equal treatment does not apply in respect of 'conditions relating to linguistic knowledge required by reason of the nature of the post to be filled'. This provision was successfully relied on by the Irish government in *Groener*.[77] The case concerned a Dutch woman who was refused a permanent post at a design college in Dublin, where she had already been teaching, because she did not speak Gaelic. Even though she did not need to use Gaelic for her work, the Court upheld the language requirement because it formed part of government policy to promote the use of the Irish language as a means of expressing national culture and identity.[78] It said that since education was important for the implementation of such a policy, the requirement for teachers to have an adequate knowledge of the Irish language was compatible with Article 3(1), provided that the level of knowledge was not disproportionate to the objective pursued.[79]

The Court did say in *Groener* that the Irish government could not require that the linguistic knowledge be acquired in Ireland.[80] This point was developed in *Angonese*.[81] The

---

[69] See, e.g., Case C–15/96 *Kalliope Schöning-Kougebetopoulou* v. *Freie und Hansestadt Hamburg* [1998] ECR I–47. See also Case C–187/96 *Commission* v. *Greece* [1998] ECR I–1095; Case C–350/96 *Clean Car* [1998] ECR I–2521.

[70] According to Case C–281/98 *Angonese* [2000] ECR I–4139, para. 22, this provision applies only to states, not to employers.

[71] Case C–278/03 *Commission* v. *Italy (recruitment of teaching staff)* [2005] ECR I–3747, para. 15.

[72] Emphasis added.

[73] Case C–419/92 *Scholz* v. *Opera Universitaria di Cagliari and Cinzia Porcedda* [1994] ECR I–505.

[74] Para. 11.

[75] Case C–138/02 *Collins* [2004] ECR I–2703, considered further later. See also Case C–346/05 *Charteignier* v. *ONEM* [2006] ECR I–10951.

[76] Subsequently the national court found the rule to be proportionate, a view that other UK courts have followed in respect of challenges to other social security benefits which impose a residence requirement (e.g., *Patmalniece* v. *Secretary of State for Work and Pensions* [2011] UKSC 11, where the Supreme Court said that the habitual residence requirement could be justified on the grounds that this discrimination was justified because the regulations were a proportionate response to the legitimate aim of protecting the public purse.

[77] Case 379/87 *Groener* v. *Minister for Education* [1989] ECR 3967.   [78] Paras. 18–19.

[79] Para. 21.   [80] Para. 23.   [81] Case C–281/98 [2000] ECR I–4139.

case concerned a requirement imposed by a bank operating in Bolzano (the Italian and German-speaking province of Italy) that admission to its recruitment competition was conditional on possession of a certificate of bilingualism. Because this certificate could be obtained only in Bolzano, Angonese, an Italian national who had studied in Austria, was not able to compete for a post in the bank on the ground that he lacked the Bolzano certificate, even though he submitted other evidence of his bilingualism. The Court found the bank's rule to be indirectly discriminatory,[82] even though the requirement affected Italian nationals resident in other parts of Italy as well as nationals from other Member States. It said that since the majority of residents of the province of Bolzano were Italian nationals, the obligation to obtain the certificate put nationals of other Member States at a disadvantage compared with residents of the province, making it difficult, if not impossible, for them to get jobs in Bolzano.[83] On the question of justification, the Court said that while the bank could justify requiring job applicants to have a certain level of linguistic knowledge, the fact that it was impossible to show proof of this knowledge by any other means—in particular by equivalent qualifications from other Member States—was disproportionate,[84] and so the bank's requirement breached Article 45 TFEU.

Sometimes a particular language requirement cannot be justified at all. *Las*[85] concerned a Flemish law requiring employment contracts concluded between a worker and an employer whose established place of business was in the Dutch-speaking region of Belgium to be drafted in Dutch; non-compliance resulted in the nullity of the contract. Las, a Dutch national, whose contract was drafted in English successfully challenged the Flemish rule as contravening Article 45 TFEU: 'the establishment of free and informed consent between the parties requires those parties to be able to draft their contract in a language other than the official language of that Member State'.[86]

(c) Non-discriminatory measures which hinder market access

Non-discriminatory national measures which (substantially) impede access to the market also breach Article 45 TFEU (and presumably Regulation 492/11 and the CRD) unless objectively justified (see fig. 7.4). We can see this in *Bosman*[87] (Case Study 8.1), where the Court found that the football transfer fee rules, albeit non-discriminatory, 'directly affect[ed] players' access to the employment market in other Member States'[88] and therefore constituted an unjustified 'obstacle to the freedom of movement of workers'.[89] If, on the other hand, the effect of the national legislation is 'too uncertain and indirect ... to be capable of being regarded as liable to hinder free movement for workers', as in *Graf*,[90] then the measure does not breach Article 45 TFEU.[91]

(d) The restrictions/obstacles approach

In the area of free movement of workers, the discrimination approach is most firmly entrenched. However, as we saw in Chapter 7, the general trend in the field of free movement of persons is to move from the non-discrimination approach to the 'restrictions'/'obstacles' test,[92] even in cases where previously the Court would have categorized the measure as

---

[82] The Court reasoned that 'in order for a measure to be treated as being discriminatory on grounds of nationality, it is not necessary for the measure to have the effect of putting at an advantage all the workers of one nationality or of putting at a disadvantage only workers who are nationals of other Member States, but not workers of the nationality in question' (para. 41).

[83] Para. 39.   [84] Para. 44.   [85] Case C–202/11 *Las* v. *PSA Antwerp* EU:C:2013:239.
[86] Para. 31.   [87] Case C–415/93 [1995] ECR I–4921.   [88] Para. 103.
[89] Para. 104.   [90] Case C–190/98 [2002] ECR I–493.   [91] Paras. 24–5. See Ch. 7.
[92] Case C–464/02 *Commission* v. *Denmark (company vehicles)* [2005] ECR I–7929, paras. 46 and 52.

being indirectly discriminatory.[93] If the Court finds there is an 'obstacle', 'barrier', 'restriction', or 'impediment' to free movement, it then examines whether the rule can be
objectively justified and whether the steps taken are proportionate. Despite the prepon-
derance of the discrimination model, free movement of workers has not been immune
from the development of the 'restrictions' approach, as *Lyyski*[94] demonstrates.

The case concerned a Swedish rule requiring an individual wanting to follow a special
teacher training course at a designated university in Sweden to be employed at a Swedish
school in order to complete the practical component of their training. The Court said that
the rule placed those, like Mr Lyyski who was employed in a Swedish-speaking school in
Finland, 'at a disadvantage'.[95] The legislation was thus 'liable to restrict the freedom of
movement of workers', which was prohibited by Article 45 TFEU. The Court continued
that the requirement to be employed in a Swedish school constituted an 'obstacle to freedom of movement'[96] which could be justified on the grounds of preserving or improving the education system (Sweden had introduced this programme because it foresaw
a shortage of qualified teachers). The Court also thought the Swedish requirement was
proportionate: the programme was temporary and the requirement to be employed in a
Swedish school assisted in the process of monitoring and assessing the practical stage of
the training.[97] However, the Court said the requirement had to be applied flexibly and on
a case-by-case basis; account had to be taken of the merits of each individual applicant
and whether the individual could be exempted from the practical part of the training.[98]

The justifications which states can raise can be broad. This point was confirmed in the
UK New Settlement Decision. Under the heading 'Interpretation of Current EU Rules',
Section D.1(a) provides:

> [I]f overriding reasons of public interest make it necessary, free movement of workers
> may be restricted by measures proportionate to the legitimate aim pursued. Encouraging
> recruitment, reducing unemployment, protecting vulnerable workers and averting the
> risk of seriously undermining the sustainability of social security systems are reasons of
> public interest recognised in the jurisprudence of the Court of Justice of the European
> Union for this purpose, based on a case by case analysis.

The significance of allowing the inclusion of potentially economic justifications is considered further in Chapter 12.

In most cases where the Court applies the restrictions approach it finds a breach of the
Treaty. However, occasionally it considers that the rule does not restrict free movement
and so there is no breach of Article 45 TFEU.[99] This can be seen in *Burbaud*,[100] where the
Court said that the requirement of passing an exam in order to take up a post in the public
service could not 'in itself be regarded as an obstacle' to free movement.[101]

---

[93] Cf. Case C–15/96 *Schöning-Kougebetopoulou* [1998] ECR I–47 (discrimination analysis of length
of service provisions) with Case C–224/01 *Köbler* v. *Republik Österreich* [2003] ECR I–10239 (restrictions
analysis of service provisions).

[94] Case C–40/05 *Lyyski* v. *Umeå universitet* [2007] ECR I–99. More recently, see Case C–379/09 *Casteels*
v. *British Airways* [2011] ECR I–1379, para. 30.

[95] Para. 37. See also Case C–202/11 *Las* EU:C:2013:239, para. 19.   [96] Para. 38.

[97] Paras. 42–3.   [98] Para. 49.

[99] Case C–33/99 *Fahmi and Cerdeiro-Pinedo Amado* v. *Bestuur van de Sociale Verzekeringsbank* [2001]
ECR I–2415, para. 43.

[100] Case C–285/01 *Isabel Burbaud* v. *Ministère de l'Emploi et de la Solidarité* [2003] ECR I–8219.

[101] Para. 96. To emphasize the point, the Court said that inasmuch as all new jobs are subject to a recruitment procedure, the requirement of passing a recruitment competition could not 'in itself be liable to dissuade candidates who have already sat a similar competition in another Member State from exercising their
right to freedom of movement as workers' (para. 97). In a similar vein, see Joined Cases C–51/96 and C–191/97
Deliège [2000] ECR I–2549, para. 64, discussed in Ch. 7.

Case Study 8.1: SPORT AND THE FREE MOVEMENT OF PERSONS

Sport, particularly the big money world of professional sport, provides an interesting case study of how the principles outlined—of non-discrimination, market access, justification, and pro-portionality—have been used to remove barriers to the mobility of sportsmen and women. However, those running professional sport have not always seen the benefits of applying Union law. They have long claimed that 'sport is special', due to its social and educational function, and so should not be subject to Union law at all. Generally, the Court disagrees.[102]

Relatively early in its case law the Court made clear that sport was subject to Union law but only insofar as it constituted an economic activity.[103] Therefore, in *Donà* v. *Mantero*[104] the Court ruled that the activities of professional or semi-professional football players who were employed or provided a service fell within the scope of Articles 45 and 56 TFEU. However, perhaps in recognition of the special nature of sport, the Court built in a de facto exception to this rule for *national* teams. Relying on the contentious justification that such national games were not commercial in nature, it said that Union law did not prevent the adoption of rules 'excluding foreign players from participation in certain matches for reasons which are not of an economic nature, which relates to the particular nature and context of such matches and are thus of sporting interest only, such as, for example, matches between national teams from different countries'.[105] The Court did add that '[t]his restriction on the scope of the provisions in question must however remain limited to its proper objective'. Therefore, in respect of the nationality of players that can be fielded, clubs (e.g., Manchester United and Chelsea) are subject to Union law, while national sides (e.g., England and France) are not.[106]

This national-team rule is not the only 'exception' carved out by the Court from the provisions on the free movement of persons. As we saw in *Deliège*,[107] the Court said that federation rules concerning the selection of athletes for international competitions did not constitute a restriction on the provision of services[108] and so fell outside Article 56 TFEU.[109] In this way the Court has ensured a considerable degree of autonomy for sporting organizations to set their own rules.

For those sporting situations which do fall within the scope of Union law, the principle of non-discrimination on the grounds of nationality applies. The early cases concerned direct discrimination. For example, in *Donà*[110] the Court said that national rules providing that only those football players who were affiliated to the Italian Football Federation could play in professional matches, affiliation being open to Italian players only, breached Union law. This ruling led to a 'gentlemen's agreement' between the Commission and the Union of European Football Associations (UEFA) under which national associations had to allow each first division team to field at least three foreign players and two 'acclimatized'[111] foreigners in

---

[102] Cf. Joined Cases C–403 and 429/08 *Murphy* v. *Media Protection Services* [2011] ECR I–9083, paras. 100–1, discussed further in Ch. 11. See generally S. Van den Bogaert and A. Vermeersch, 'Sport and the EC Treaty: A tale of uneasy bedfellows' (2006) 6 *ELRev.* 800.

[103] Case 13/76 *Donà* v. *Mantero* [1976] ECR 1333, para. 12.

[104] Case 13/76 *Donà* v. *Mantero* [1976] ECR 1333, para. 12. See also Case 36/74 *Walrave and Koch* v. *Association Union Cycliste Internationale* [1974] ECR 1405, para. 4.

[105] Para. 14.   [106] Para. 15.

[107] Joined Cases C–51/96 and C–191/97 [2000] ECR I–2549, para. 64. See S. Van den Bogaert, 'The Court of Justice on the Tatami: Ippon, Waza-Ari or Koka?' (2000) 25 *ELRev.* 554.

[108] Para. 64.

[109] The Commission's Decision in the *Mouscron* case, which anticipated the Court's ruling in *Deliège*. In *Mouscron* the Commission said that the UEFA Cup rule requiring each club to play its home match at its own ground (and not at a neighbouring ground) was a sports rule that did not fall within the scope of the Treaty competition rules ('Limits to application of Treaty competition rules to sport: Commission gives clear signal', IP/99/965).

[110] Case 13/76 [1976] ECR 1333. See also Case 36/74 *Walrave and Koch* [1974] ECR 1405.

[111] Players who have played in the country for an uninterrupted period of five years.

domestic league matches from the 1992 season—the so-called '3+2 rule'. This was one of the rules challenged in *Bosman*.[112]

Bosman was a Belgian national employed by the Belgian first division club RC Liège. When his contract expired he wanted to play for the French second division club, US Dunkerque. Because no transfer certificate had been sent to the French Football Federation, Bosman was left without a club for the following season. He did manage to sign two short contracts with French clubs before ending up at Olympic de Charleroi, a Belgian third division club. There was strong circumstantial evidence that Bosman was being boycotted by other clubs which might have employed him.[113] He argued that the 3+2 rule contravened Article 45 TFEU. The Court agreed, arguing that the principle of non-discrimination applied to clauses contained in the regulations of sporting associations which restricted the rights of nationals of other Member States to take part in football matches. It said that the nationality clause related to the essence of the activity of professional players: if Union law did not apply to this situation, then Article 45 TFEU would be 'deprived of its practical effect and the fundamental right of free access to employment which the Treaty confers individually on each worker in the [Union] rendered nugatory'.[114]

Despite losing on this point in *Bosman*, the football authorities insist that it is still necessary for some sort of national quota to be introduced because, they argue, in the absence of a quota young talent is not able to develop in the club at which they are trained because they cannot play in the first team; that the ability of tops clubs to buy up all of the talent means that competition at national level is not balanced; that national team managers see fewer nationals playing in national leagues, which gives them less choice to select players; and with players moving from club to club there is a loss of national identity of clubs.[115] FIFA, the international football federation, therefore proposed introducing a 6+5 rule, which would permit clubs to field a maximum of five players who were not eligible to play for the national team of the country of that club. Not surprisingly, the Commission said that this rule would be contrary to Union law.[116] The rule was also opposed by some football managers, like Arsenal's Arsène Wenger, who argued that spectators want to see the best football players and that the quality of English players is not enhanced by removing from them the incentive to improve their performance to win a place in the club side.[117] The proposal was later dropped.[118]

By contrast, the European football association, UEFA, has introduced a 'Homegrown player rule' which applies to games in the Champions League and the UEFA Cup.[119] Clubs competing in these competitions must include a minimum number of locally trained players in their squad (from the 2010/11 season clubs could not name more than 17 non-home-grown players over 21 in a squad of 25[120]). Clubs are not obliged to play these home-grown players in any match. UEFA defines locally trained players as those who, regardless of their nationality,

---

[112] Case C–415/93 [1995] ECR I–4921.   [113] Para. 37.

[114] Para. 129. The Court reached the same conclusion in respect of an equivalent rule applied to a Slovakian handball player employed by a German club in the context of the Association Agreement between the Communities and Slovakia: Case C–438/00 *Deutscher Handballbund eV* v. *Maros Kolpak* [2003] ECR I–4135. See also Case C–265/03 *Simutenkov* v. *Mininsterio de Educación y Cultura* [2005] ECR I–2579, where the Court (Grand Chamber) reached the same decision in respect of the Communities–Russia partnership agreement in respect of a Russian footballer playing in Spain; and Case C–152/08 *Real Sociedad de Fútbol SAD and Kahveci* v. *Consejo Superior de Deportes* EU:C:2008:450 under the EEC–Turkey Association Agreement.

[115] 'FIFA: We'll convince the Commission on national quotas', *EurActiv*, 11 Sept. 2008.

[116] 'UEFA rule on "home-grown players": Compatibility with the principle of free movement of persons', <http://www.europa.eu/rapid/pressReleasesAction.do?reference=IP/08/807>.

[117] D. Pannick QC, 'Sports minister will lose his war against foreigners', *The Times*, 27 Nov. 2007.

[118] <http://www.bbc.co.uk/sport1/hi/football/8733164.stm>.

[119] <http://www.uefa.org/protecting-the-game/protection-young-players/news/newsid=276829.html>.

[120] Further details can be found at <http://www.premierleague.com>.

have been trained by their club or by another club in the same national association for at least three years between the age of 15 and 21. UEFA sees this rule as one step towards addressing the problem created by the *Bosman* ruling that 'the richest clubs have been able to stockpile the best players, which makes it easier for them to dominate both national and European competitions'.[121] The home-grown player rule, while potentially indirectly discriminatory,[122] is more carefully tailored than the 6+5 rule. The Commission has therefore indicated that it thinks the rule can be justified. It said the objectives of the rule, namely promoting training for young players and consolidating the balance of competitions, seem 'legitimate objectives of general interest, as they are inherent to sporting activity', and proportionate.

In more recent cases the Court has gone beyond the discrimination model, focusing instead on whether the measure has restricted the sportsperson's access to the market. This can be seen in respect of the other rule at issue in *Bosman* concerning transfer fees. According to federation rules, on the expiry of a contract with Club A, a professional footballer could not play for Club B until Club A had released his registration. This was usually conditional on Club B paying a transfer fee to Club A. The Court said that these rules were not discriminatory because they applied equally to transfers between clubs belonging to different national associations within the same Member State and were similar to those governing transfers between clubs belonging to the same national association.[123] Nevertheless, the Court concluded that since the transfer rules 'directly affect players' access to the employment market in other Member States', they were capable of impeding free movement of workers and so breached Article 45 TFEU (see fig. 7.4).[124] For this reason the Court said that UEFA's rules could not be deemed comparable to those on selling arrangements for goods to which the principle in *Keck* applied.[125] The Court reached a similar conclusion in *Lehtonen*,[126] where the rules of a Belgian basketball association prohibited a basketball club from fielding players from other Member States (who had been transferred after a specific date) in national championship matches. The Court said that such rules were liable to restrict the freedom of movement of players, which was contrary to Article 45 TFEU.[127] Likewise, in *Olympique Lyonnais*[128] the Court said that a French collective agreement requiring a 'joueur espoir' (a player aged between 16 and 22 employed as a trainee by a professional club under a fixed-term contract) to sign, at the end of his training period, a professional contract with the club which trained him under pain of being sued for damages, was likely to discourage that player from exercising his right of free movement under Article 45 TFEU.

Having established a breach of Article 45 TFEU in *Bosman*, *Lehtonen*, and *Olympique Lyonnais*, the Court then turned to the question of justification. In *Lehtonen* the Court recognized that transfer periods could be justified on the ground of ensuring the regularity of sporting competitions:[129] late transfers could substantially change the sporting strength of

---

[121] R. Williams and A. Haffner, 'FIFA quotas ruled offside?' [2008] *New Law Journal* 1017.

[122] Case 222/86 [1987] ECR 4097. See also Dec. 2000/12 *1998 Football World Cup* ([2000] OJ L5/55) on the distribution of tickets for the World Cup in France, which was restricted to residents in France. The Commission said that this rule offended against 'fundamental [Union] principles' (para. 102). See also S. Weatherill, '0033149875354: Fining the organisers of the 1998 Football World Cup' [2000] *ECLR* 275.

[123] Para. 103.   [124] Para. 103.

[125] Para. 103. See also the discussion of Case C–384/93 *Alpine Investments* [1995] ECR I–1141, paras. 36–8, and Case C–275/92 *Schindler* [1994] ECR I–1039, para. 45.

[126] Case C–176/96 *Lehtonen and Castors Canada Dry Namur-Braine ASBL v. Fédération royale belge des sociétés de basket-ball ASBL (FRBSB)* [2000] ECR I–2681.

[127] Para. 49.

[128] Case C–325/08 *Olympique Lyonnais SASP v. Olivier Bernard, Newcastle United FC* [2010] ECR I–2177, para. 35.

[129] Case C–176/96 *Lehtonen* [2000] ECR I–2681, para. 53.

one or other team in the course of the championship. The Court noted that this would call into question the comparability of results between the teams taking part in that championship and consequently the proper functioning of the championship as a whole.[130] However, the Court said that such measures had to be proportionate and suggested that, on the facts, this was not the case because looser deadlines applied to players from non-European zone countries without that jeopardizing competitions.

In *Bosman* the Court also decided that the football federation rules were not proportionate on the facts. However, it began by recognizing that sport was special:[131]

> In view of the considerable social importance of sporting activities and in particular football in the [Union], the aims of maintaining a balance between the clubs by preserving a certain degree of equality and uncertainty as to results and of encouraging the recruitment and training of young players the transfer fees had to be accepted as legitimate.[132]

In other words, as Weatherill explains, unlike the widget market where producers aim to gain the largest market share, if necessary by driving their rivals off the market, sport is based on a notion of mutual interdependence. In sport, opponents are there to be beaten, but the whole point of the endeavour is destroyed if opponents are, literally, beaten out of sight;[133] and the Court recognized that steps taken to ensure this could be justified on the grounds of maintaining a competitive balance between the teams, and encouraging training programmes.

However, the Court then considered the proportionality question. It said that the transfer rules were not an adequate means of maintaining financial and competitive balance in the world of football because they neither precluded the richest clubs from securing the services of the best players nor did they prevent the availability of financial resources from being a decisive factor in competitive sport, thus considerably altering the balance between clubs.[134]

In respect of the argument that transfer fees helped cover the cost of training new talent, the Court accepted that the prospect of receiving transfer fees was likely to encourage football clubs to seek new talent and train young players.[135] However, it said that, because it was impossible to predict with any certainty the sporting future of young players (only a limited number went on to play professionally), those fees were by nature contingent and uncertain. They were also unrelated to the actual cost borne by clubs of training both future professional players and those who would never play professionally. The Court therefore concluded that the prospect

---

[130] Case C–176/96 *Lehtonen* [2000] ECR I–2681, para. 54.

[131] The social importance of sport has assumed a growing importance as the Treaty has been amended. First, Decl. 29 on Sport was annexed to the Treaty of Amsterdam, where the states emphasized the 'social significance of sport'. This was more fully articulated in the Declaration annexed to the Conclusions of the Nice European Council in Dec. 2000 which talked of 'the specific characteristics of sport and its social function in Europe'. The position was emphasized in the Lisbon Treaty. Art. 165(1) TFEU says 'The Union shall contribute to the promotion of European sporting issues, while taking account of the specific nature of sport, its structures based on voluntary activity and its social and educational function', a point recognized by the Court in Case C–325/08 *Olympique Lyonnais* [2010] ECR I–2177, para. 40. See also Commission, 'White Paper on sport', COM(2007) 391, 13: 'The case law of the European courts and decisions of the European Commission show that the specificity of sport has been recognised and taken into account' in sport 'but it cannot be construed so as to justify a general exemption from the application of EU law.' This was followed up by a further communication, 'Developing the European dimension', COM(2011) 12.

[132] Para. 106. See also Case C–325/08 *Olympique Lyonnais* [2010] ECR I–2177, para. 41.

[133] S. Weatherill, '"Fair play please": Recent developments in the application of EC law to sport' (2003) 40 *CMLRev.* 51. See also Art. 165(2) TFEU, which says that one aspect of Union action is to develop 'the European dimension in sport, by promoting fairness and openness in sporting competitions and cooperation between bodies responsible for sports, and by protecting the physical and moral integrity of sportsmen and sportswomen, especially the youngest sportsmen and sportswomen'.

[134] Para. 107.   [135] Para. 108.

of receiving such fees could be neither a decisive factor in encouraging the recruitment and training of young players nor an adequate means of financing such activities, particularly in the case of smaller clubs.

For these reasons the Court rejected the football authorities' arguments on the basis of suitability. For good measure, it also suggested that the transfer fee rules went beyond what was necessary to attain the objectives. Referring to Advocate General Lenz's Opinion, the Court accepted that the same aims could be achieved at least as efficiently by other means which did not impede freedom of movement of workers.[136] He had suggested two more proportionate possibilities: (1) to negotiate collectively specified limits for the salaries of the players; (2) to distribute the clubs' receipts among the clubs. Specifically, this meant that part of the income obtained by a club from the sale of tickets for its home matches should be distributed to other clubs. Similarly, the income received for awarding the rights to transmit matches on television could be divided up between all the clubs. The Court therefore concluded that Article 45 TFEU precluded the application of rules relating to transfer fees.

Similarly, in *Olympique Lyonnais* the Court said that a scheme providing for the payment of compensation for the costs of training where a young player (Olivier Bernard), at the end of his training, signs a professional contract with a club (Newcastle United) other than the one which trained him (Olympique Lyonnais) could, in principle, be justified by the objective of encouraging the recruitment and training of young players. However, once again, the Court found the scheme disproportionate because (1) the damages were not calculated in relation to the training costs actually incurred by Olympique Lyonnais but in relation to the total loss suffered by the club; and (2) the amount of that loss was established on the basis of criteria which were not determined in advance.

Although *Bosman* was decided on the basis of Article 45 TFEU, rumbling in the background were Articles 101 and 102 TFEU on competition which had so influenced the Advocate General.[137] It is in the arena of competition law that most of the subsequent challenges to sport rules have been thrashed out including complaints to the Commission about FIFA rules on football player agents,[138] UEFA regulations allowing national football associations to block the broadcasting of football,[139] and UEFA's rule prohibiting multiple ownership of clubs.[140] In the world of competitive swimming two professional swimmers were banned for two years for taking Nandrolone, a prohibited substance. They complained to the Commission that swimming's anti-doping rules infringed their economic freedoms under Article 56 TFEU on services and Articles 101 and 102 TFEU on competition law. The Commission rejected their complaints and the swimmers applied to the General Court for the Commission's decision to be annulled.[141] They lost before the General Court and again before the Court of Justice,[142] which, while setting aside the

---

[136] Para. 110.

[137] The Court would have been forced to consider the issue in Case C–264/98 *Balog* v. *ASBL Royal Charleroi*, removed from the register on 2 Apr. 2001. Much of the AG's unpublished Opinion in that case can be found in A. Egger and C. Stix-Hackl, 'Sports and competition law: A never-ending story?' [2002] *ECLR* 81.

[138] The case was closed with the Commission recognizing that FIFA could regulate the profession in an attempt to promote good practice as long as access remained open and non-discriminatory: IP/02/585, 18 Apr. 2002.

[139] The Commission permitted revised regulations allowing a block of two and a half hours on Saturday or Sunday (and not the weekend as a whole): IP/01/583, 20 Apr. 2001. However, the Commission's views are not always correct: see Joined Cases T–185, 299 and 300/00 *M6* v. *Commission* [2002] ECR II–3805.

[140] The Commission found that the rule which provides that no two clubs participating in a club competition could be directly or indirectly controlled by the same entity or managed by the same person could be justified by the need to guarantee the integrity of the competitions: IP/02/942, 27 Jun. 2002. See also the Commission's Communication in [1999] OJ C363/2.

[141] Case T–313/02 *Meca-Medina and Majcen* v. *Commission* [2004] ECR II–3291.

[142] Case C–519/04 P [2006] ECR I–6991. E. Szyszczak, 'Competition and sport' (2007) 32 *ELRev.* 95.

General Court's decision, also dismissed the application for the annulment of the Commission's Decision. While the General Court adopted a generous approach towards the autonomy of sport, the Court of Justice took a stricter line:[143]

> The mere fact that a rule is purely sporting in nature does not have the effect of removing from the scope of the Treaty the person engaging in the activity governed by that rule or the body which has laid it down.

This is the enduring problem for the Court(s): as Weatherill puts it, 'Sporting rules have an economic effect. But without some fundamental rules there is no sport.'[144]

The *Bosman* judgment transformed professional football, changing the composition of many teams and putting an end to transfer fees for players out of contract.[145] Clubs have responded by hiring stars on longer contracts, with money previously used for transfer fees being diverted into wage packets, making millionaires out of many European players. But for Jean-Marc Bosman the litigation did not pay. He was left heavily in debt and, with his professional career over and his marriage in tatters, he moved back in with his parents,[146] and even had a spell in prison.[147] In early 1997 some of the world's top players planned a testimonial for him in Barcelona. However, the Spanish FA and FIFA objected to the match, blaming Bosman for the large number of foreign players in the Spanish league.[148] The match did eventually go ahead but Bosman's name could not be officially connected with the event.[149] An out-of-court settlement of £312,000[150] was finally paid by the Belgian football authorities in December 1998—more than eight years after the expiry of his contract.

On a more positive note, the formula given by the Court in *Bosman* provided the framework for the football industry to negotiate new transfer rules. A breakthrough came in 2001[151] when rules were agreed by UEFA, FIFA, and the Commission which, inter alia, provided for:

- a system of training compensation to encourage and reward the training effort of clubs, in particular small clubs, for players aged under 23
- the creation of solidarity mechanisms redistributing a significant proportion of income to clubs involved in the training and education of a player, including amateur clubs
- the creation of one transfer period per season, and a further limited mid-season window, with a limit of one transfer per player per season
- minimum and maximum duration of contracts of respectively one and five years.

---

[143] Case C–519/04 P *Meca-Medina and Majcen* [2006] ECR I– 6991, para. 57.

[144] S. Weatherill, 'Anti-doping revisited: The demise of the rule of "purely sporting interest"' [2006] *ECLR* 645.

[145] The *Bosman* ruling also applied to those players from states which had trade agreements with the EU. See also Case C–264/98 *Balog* v. *ASBL Royal Charleroi*, removed from the register on 2 Apr. 2001.

[146] J. Northcroft, 'The abandoned pioneer', *Scotland on Sunday*, 15 Sept. 1996, 25; A. Dunn, 'Jean-Marc's the Boss Man: His fight for freedom was worth fortune to football stars', *The People*, 2 Jan. 2000, 54.

[147] <http://www.express.co.uk/sport/football/407361/Jean-Marc-Bosman-s-jail-ruling>.

[148] J. Webster, 'Spanish ire over Bosman fundraiser', *The European*, 20 Feb. 1997, 15; B. Oliver, 'Sport around the world: Bosman out in the cold in Spain', *Daily Telegraph*, 1 Mar. 1997, 18. See also D. Campbell, '"Foreigners killing football": UEFA chief's call for firm action against "global teams" at big clubs', *Observer*, 11 Mar. 2001, 1.

[149] B. Sutherland, 'Stars turn out for Bosman', *The Herald*, 28 Apr. 1997; J. Culley, 'Bosman reaps belated reward', *Independent*, 28 Apr. 1997.

[150] *Independent*, 23 Dec. 1998, 20, cited in S. Weatherill (2000) 25 *ELRev*. 282, 283. See also the essays on *Bosman* in M. Poiares Maduro and L. Azoulai (eds.), *The Past and Future of EU Law* (Oxford: Hart Publishing, 2010).

[151] IP/01/314, 6 Mar. 2001.

In 2002 the Commission considered this proposal to be balanced and closed its investi-gation.[152] Since then the Commission and UEFA have been working more closely together, and eventually the Commission approved UEFA's Financial Fair Play (FFP) Regulations, first agreed in 2009, intended to prevent professional football clubs spending more than they earn in the pursuit of success (i.e., they must 'live within their own means'). The Commission and UEFA issued a joint statement[153] suggesting that the FFP rules were compatible with EU state aid policy.

2.2 Exercise of the Employment

(a) Equal treatment in respect of the terms and conditions of employment

While Chapter I, Section I of Regulation 492/11 concerns initial access to employment, Section II concerns the 'exercise' of (as opposed to access to) employment, i.e., rules con-cerning terms and conditions of employment. Article 7(1) states that a migrant worker must not be treated:

> differently from national workers ... in respect of any conditions of employment and work, in particular as regards remuneration, dismissal, and, should he become unemployed, reinstatement or reemployment.[154]

Most of the case law concerns indirectly discriminatory measures. For example, in *Allué and Coonan*[155] an Italian law limited the duration of contracts of employ-ment of foreign-language assistants, without imposing the same limitation on other workers. Since only 25 per cent of foreign-language assistants were Italian nation-als, the law essentially concerned nationals of other Member States. It was indirectly discriminatory[156] and could not be justified.

As we have already seen, residence requirements are also likely to be indirectly dis-criminatory. So, in *Clean Car*[157] the Court found that an Austrian rule requiring busi-ness managers to be resident in Austria before they could work in Vienna breached Article 45 TFEU. It noted that the rule was liable to operate mainly to the detriment of nationals of other Member States since the majority of non-residents were foreigners.[158] Austria sought to justify the residence requirement on the grounds that the manager needed to be resident to be effective in the business, to be served with a notice of any fines imposed, and to have those fines enforced against him. The Court found these justifications disproportionate: the residence requirement was either inappropriate to achieve the aim pursued or went beyond what was necessary for that purpose.[159] It also noted that other, less restrictive measures were available to achieve the objective, such as serving a notice of the fines at the registered office of the company employing the manager.

---

[152] See <http://ec.europa.eu/sport>.   [153] Joint Statement issued 21 Mar. 2012.

[154] Art. 7(1) applies only to payments made by virtue of statutory or contracted obligations incumbent on the employer as a condition of employment: see Case C–315/94 *Peter de Vos* v. *Stadt Bielefeld* [1996] ECR I–1417.

[155] Case 33/88 *Allué and Coonan* v. *Università degli studi di Venezia* [1989] ECR 1591. The Court extended this ruling to nationals of a non-EU state in the context of Art. 37(1) of the Europe Agreement: Case C–162/00 *Land-Nordrhein-Westfalen* v. *Beata Pokrzeptowicz-Meyer* [2002] ECR I–1049, para. 44.

[156] Para. 12.

[157] Case C–350/96 [1998] ECR I–2521. See also Case C–461/11 *Radziejewski* v. *Kronofogdemyndigheten i Stockholm* EU:C:2012:704 (residence requirement imposed in order to receive debt relief).

[158] Para. 29.   [159] Para. 34.

Length of service requirements may also be indirectly discriminatory.[160] In *Schöning-Kougebetopoulou*,[161] the Court found that a collective agreement providing for promotion on grounds of seniority, but which took no account of service performed in another Member State, 'manifestly' worked to the detriment of migrant workers and so breached Article 45 TFEU. The Court rejected the justifications based on rewarding loyalty to the employer and motivating employees because, on the facts, service with other legally separate employers was taken into account and so the loyalty argument could not be sustained.[162]

Article 7(4) of Regulation 492/11 provides that clauses from a collective agreement or contract which discriminate against workers from other Member States, are null and void insofar as they lay down or authorize discriminatory conditions.[163] Until the parties amend the agreement to eliminate the discrimination, the migrant workers enjoy the same rules as those which apply to nationals.[164]

(b) Equal treatment in respect of tax advantages

Article 7(2) of Regulation 492/11 provides that a worker will enjoy the same social *and* tax advantages as national workers. Both limbs of Article 7(2) have caused serious problems for the Court as it struggles to reconcile its jurisprudence on free movement and the creation of a single market with two of the most sensitive areas of national competence—the welfare state and taxation; matters which traditionally have a strongly territorial dimension. We begin by considering taxation, where there has been a proliferation of cases.

(i) Differential treatment of residents and non-residents

International tax law generally envisages that residents and non-residents can and should be treated differently in terms of taxation: generally residents are taxed on their worldwide income while non-residents are taxed merely on the income they receive in that particular state. The corollary of this is that it is the state of residence which also offers the individual various tax reliefs. Yet, under EU law, as we have seen, discrimination on the grounds of residence is prima facie unlawful. The Court of Justice has tried to square the circle[165] by saying that the circumstances of residents and those of non-residents are generally not comparable and so the principle of equal treatment should not apply.[166] However, if, on the

---

[160] Case 15/69 *Württembergische Milchverwertung Südmilch AG* v. *Ugliola* [1969] ECR 363 (German law provided that a period spent performing military service in Germany—but not in other Member States—had to be taken into account by an employer when calculating periods of service for the purposes of pay or other benefits).

[161] Case C–15/96 [1998] ECR I–47. See also Case C–187/96 *Commission* v. *Greece* [1998] ECR I–1095; Case C–195/98 *Österreichischer Gewerkschaftsbund, Gewerkschaft öffentlicher Dienst* v. *Republik Österreich* [2000] ECR I–10497; Case C–27/91 *URSSAF* v. *Le Manoir* [1991] ECR I–5531 and Case C–419/92 *Scholz* [1994] ECR I–505.

[162] Para. 27.

[163] Case C–400/02 *Merida* v. *Bundesrepublik Deutschland* [2004] ECR I–8471; Case C–172/11 *Erny* v. *Daimler AG-Werk Wörth* EU:C:2012:157.

[164] Case C–15/96 *Kalliope Schöning-Kougebetopoulou* [1998] ECR I–47, para. 33, applying by analogy the Art. 157 TFEU case law on equal pay: e.g., Case C–184/89 *Nimz* v. *Freie und Hansestadt Hamburg* [1991] ECR I–297, para. 18; Case C–33/89 *Kowalska* v. *Freie und Hansestadt Hamburg* [1990] ECR I–2591, para. 20.

[165] In Case C–414/06 *Lidl Belgium GmbH & Co.KG* v. *Finanzamt Heilbronn* [2008] ECR I–3601, para. 22, the Court said that 'for the purposes of the allocation of fiscal competence, it is not unreasonable for the Member States to draw guidance from international practice and, particularly, the model conventions drawn up by the OECD'. For further discussion of how the Court has reconciled the principles of international tax law with EU law, see Ch. 11.

[166] Case C–279/93 *Schumacker* [1995] ECR I–225; Case C–376/03 *D* [2005] ECR I–5821, para. 37; Case C–336/96 *Gilly* v. *Directeur des services fiscaux du Bas-Rhin* [1998] ECR I–2793, para. 49.

facts of the case, the situations of the resident and non-resident taxpayers can be considered comparable, then it would be discriminatory to treat the two situations differently. This is particularly so in the case of frontier workers, as the *Schumacker*[167] case showed.

Mr Schumacker, a Belgian national, lived in Belgium with his family but worked in Germany. As a non-resident worker his wages were subject to German income tax but he was denied certain benefits which were available to resident taxpayers. The Court ruled that a non-resident taxpayer who received all or almost all of his income in the state of employment was objectively in the same situation as a resident in that state who did the same work there. Because the situation of residents and non-residents was comparable, the Court said that the German rules gave rise to discrimination because the non-resident taxpayer did not have his personal and family circumstances taken into account either in his state of residence (where he received no income) or in his state of employment (where he was not resident).[168] Consequently, his overall tax burden was greater than that of a resident taxpayer.[169] The German rules therefore breached Article 45 TFEU and could not be justified.

While the Court required Germany to take Schumacker's personal and family circumstances into account, *Renneberg*[170] went further by requiring the state asserting unlimited taxation to extend to non-residents, considered to be in a comparable situation to residents, all tax advantages on the same terms as residents.[171] The case concerned a Dutch citizen working in the Netherlands but living in Belgium, where he obtained more than 90 per cent of his income. Had he been a Dutch resident he would have enjoyed tax relief on his home based on the difference between the rental value of the house and the interest paid on the mortgage. Since he lived outside the Netherlands he enjoyed some tax relief on his home but at a lower rate. He argued that, following *Schumacker*, his situation was comparable to that of a resident and so he should have enjoyed the higher level tax relief. The Court agreed and found that the Dutch rules breached Article 45 TFEU.

As Vording explains, the effect of the ruling is that Mr Renneberg managed to have his cake and eat it.[172] While the Dutch tax system provided a generous subsidy for owner-occupied housing through its tax system, the Belgian system did not. In the Netherlands the tax subsidy was ultimately reflected in higher house prices, estimated at between 15 and 30 per cent, which was not the case in Belgium. Therefore, the consequence of the Court's decision was to give Mr Renneberg the benefit of the higher Dutch tax advantage while he enjoyed living in cheaper Belgian housing. This is an illustration of the problem identified already of the Court applying its single market case law to a situation which

---

[167] Case C–279/93 [1995] ECR I–225. See also Case C–383/05 *Talotta* v. *Etat belge* [2007] ECR I–2555, where the Court reached a similar conclusion in the context of Art. 49 TFEU.

[168] Para. 38. Cf. Case C–391/97 *Gschwind* v. *Finanzamt Aaachen-Außenstadt* [1999] ECR I–5451, para. 32, because the state of residence (the Netherlands) could take the personal and family circumstances of the individual into account, since 50 per cent of his income was received there, Art. 45 TFEU permitted a German rule under which resident married couples were granted favourable tax treatment while the same treatment of non-resident married couples was made subject to the condition that at least 90 per cent of their total income had to be subject to tax in Germany.

[169] Para. 28. See also Case C–152/03 *Ritter-Coulais* v. *Finanzamt Germersheim* [2006] ECR I–1711, para. 38 concerning the failure by the state of employment (Germany), when determining income tax liability in Germany, to take rental income losses incurred in France into account. This case was decided solely under Art. 45 TFEU, which was found to be breached.

[170] Case C–527/06 *Renneberg* v. *Staatssecretaris van Financiën* [2008] ECR I–7735.

[171] This is confirmed in Case C–9/14 *Staatssecretris van Financiën* v. *Kieback* EU:C:2015:406.

[172] H. Vording, '*Renneberg* v. *Staatssecretaris van Financiën*: The problem of an extended *Schumacker* rule' [2009] *British Tax Review* 67.

arises because of a disparity between national tax systems.[173] This problem is exacerbated by the application of the restrictions-based approach.

(ii) The restriction/obstacle approach

While most of the tax cases concerning Article 45 TFEU are considered under the discrimination approach, the Court started to apply the restrictions model, especially where the home state rule was under challenge. This can be seen in *Commission v. Germany (subsidy on dwellings)*,[174] which concerned a German rule granting a subsidy for owner-occupied dwellings to which individuals liable to unlimited taxation of income in Germany were entitled, provided that the dwellings built or purchased were situated in Germany. The Court found that 'Provisions preventing or deterring a national of a Member State from leaving his country of origin in order to exercise his right to freedom of movement constitute an obstacle to that freedom ... prohibited by Articles [45 TFEU] and [49 TFEU].'[175] The Court said that while the aim of encouraging the building of dwellings in its territory in order to ensure an adequate supply of housing was a justification, the German rule went beyond what was necessary to attain the objective pursued.[176]

However, as we saw in Chapter 7, the restrictions case law is open to misuse. For example, a migrant might argue that the fact that income tax rates are higher in State B than State A (a difference created by the Member States' fiscal autonomy, which includes freedom to set their own tax rates) discourages individuals from moving from State A to State B to seek work and so restricts their freedom of movement under Article 45 (or 49) TFEU. *Weigel*[177] shows that the Court is trying to put a stop to such arguments. The case concerned a German husband and wife who transferred their residence to Austria, where Mr Weigel had a job. They both brought their cars with them, which had to be re-registered in Austria for which a hefty tax was charged. The Court rejected their arguments that this tax breached Article 45(2) TFEU, noting that the Austrian rule applied 'without regard to the nationality of the worker concerned to all those who registered a car in Austria and, accordingly, it is applicable without distinction'.[178] The Court then added that 'It is true that [the tax] is likely to have a negative bearing on the decision of migrant workers to exercise their right to freedom of movement.'[179] Under the *Säger* formula, this observation would have been enough for a finding of a breach of Article 45 TFEU, which the Member State would then have to justify.[180] However, in *Weigel* the Court resorted to the pure non-discrimination approach (see fig. 7.3) and said that, provided that nationals and migrants were treated in the same way, the fact that the tax regimes of the different Member States were different was compatible with Union law.[181]

(iii) Justification

Having established that the situations are comparable and that the national rule is discriminatory (or a restriction on free movement of workers), the next question is whether the rule can be justified. The Court rejects pure economic justifications such as a reduction in

---

[173] See the Dutch government's arguments to that effect at para. 74 of *Renneberg*.
[174] Case C–152/05 [2008] ECR I–39. See also Case C–345/05 *Commission v. Portugal (exemption from capital gains tax)* [2006] ECR I–10633; Case C–104/06 *Commission v. Sweden (deferral of capital gains tax)* [2007] ECR I–671.
[175] Paras. 22 and 29.   [176] Para. 27.
[177] Case C–387/01 *Weigel v. Finanzlandes direction für Vorarlberg* [2004] ECR I–4981.
[178] Para. 52.   [179] Para. 54.
[180] See, by analogy, the Art. 56 TFEU case, Joined Cases C–430 and 431/99 *Sea-Land Service* [2002] ECR I–5235, considered in Ch. 11.
[181] Para. 55. The Court reached the same conclusion under Art. 21 TFEU in Case C–365/02 *Lindfors* [2004] ECR I–7183. See also Geelhoed AG's discussion in Case C–374/04 *ACT Group Litigation* [2006] ECR I–11673, paras. 43–7.

tax revenue[182] or the cost to the national exchequer.[183] However, in *Bachmann*[184] the Court recognized the 'need to preserve the cohesion of the tax system' as a potential justification.

Bachmann concerned a Belgian law according to which the cost of life insurance premiums could not be deducted from taxable income where the premiums were paid in other Member States. This was because Belgian tax law gave the individual the choice of either having tax deducted on the premiums and then paying tax on future benefits or not having tax deducted on the premiums and then not paying tax on future benefits. If Bachmann was able to deduct tax on premiums paid in Germany, the Belgian authorities would have no way of being able to tax future benefits also payable in Germany.[185] For this reason the Court said that the Belgian rules were justified because there was a 'direct link' between the right to deduct contributions and the taxation of sums payable by insurers under pension and life assurance contracts; and that preserving that link was necessary to safeguard the cohesion of the tax system.[186] Since *Bachmann* Member States have regularly invoked fiscal cohesion as a justification for their tax policies, but almost always without success.[187]

Another justification recognized by the Court is the effectiveness of fiscal supervision[188] but again Member States have generally had little success in actually relying on it.[189] For instance, in *Schumacker* Germany said that administrative difficulties prevented the state of employment (Germany) from determining the income received by non-residents in their state of residence (Belgium). The Court rejected this argument, reasoning that this difficulty could be overcome through the application of what is now Directive 2011/16[190] on mutual assistance in the field of taxation.[191]

By contrast in *X and Passenheim-van Schoot*,[192] the Court did uphold the fiscal supervision justification in the case of taxpayers who had deliberately hidden details of their bank accounts in other Member States. They were subject to additional assessments and were fined. The Court said that the national rules constituted a restriction of both the freedom to provide services and of the free movement of capital[193] but the measures could be justified on the grounds of the effectiveness of fiscal supervision and the prevention of tax evasion. On the question of proportionality, the Court said that where taxable items were concealed from the tax authorities of the taxing state, which meant that it could not request information from the competent authorities of the other Member State to establish correctly the amount of tax due, an extended recovery period of 12 years (as opposed to

---

[182] Case C–464/02 *Commission* v. *Denmark (company vehicles)* [2005] ECR I–7929, para. 45, citing the free movement of capital decision Case C–319/02 *Manninen* [2004] ECR I–7477, para. 49. See also C–422/01 *Försäkringsaktiebolaget Skandia (publ)* v. *Riksskatteverket* [2003] ECR I–6817, paras. 51–2, where the Court rejected arguments based on the need to preserve the tax base.

[183] Case C–109/04 *Kranemann* [2005] ECR I–2421.

[184] Case C–204/90 *Bachmann* v. *Belgian State* [1992] ECR I–249, para. 21, and Case C–300/90 *Commission* v. *Belgium* [1992] ECR I–305, para. 14.

[185] Para. 23.

[186] Paras. 21–3. In Case C–35/98 *Verkooijn* [2000] ECR I–4071, paras. 57–8 the Court insisted that there had to be a direct link in respect of one and the same taxpayer, although this limitation has since been dropped: e.g., Case C–319/02 *Manninen* [2004] ECR I–7477.

[187] See, e.g., Case C–80/94 *Wielockx* v. *Inspecteur der Directe Belastingen* [1995] ECR I–2493; Case C–107/94 *Asscher* [1996] ECR I–3089; Case C–264/96 *Imperial Chemical Industries (ICI)* v. *Colmer* [1998] ECR I–4695. Cf. Case C–157/07 *Finanzamt für Körperschaften III in Berlin* v. *Krankenheim Ruhesitz am Wannsee-Seniorenheimstatt GmbH* [2008] ECR I–8061.

[188] Case 120/78 *Cassis de Dijon* [1979] ECR 649.

[189] See, e.g., Case C–254/97 *Baxter* v. *Premier Ministre* [1999] ECR I–4809; Case C–55/98 *Skatteministeriet* v. *Bent Vestergaard* [1999] ECR I–7641.

[190] [2011] OJ L64/12   [191] Para. 45.

[192] Joined Cases C–155 and 157/08 *X and E.H.A. Passenheim-van Schoot* v. *Staatssecretaris van Financiën* [2009] ECR I–5093.

[193] Paras. 32–3.

5 years if the assets had been in the taxing state) did not go beyond what was necessary to guarantee the effectiveness of fiscal supervision and to prevent tax evasion. Nor did Union law preclude the fine imposed for concealment of the foreign assets and income from being calculated as a proportion of the amount to be recovered and over that longer period.[194]

(c) Equal treatment in respect of social advantages

(i) Definition

Not only does Article 7(2) of Regulation 492/11 require equal treatment for workers and those who have retained worker status[195] in respect of tax advantages but it also requires 'social advantages' to be provided on a non-discriminatory basis. In *Even*[196] the Court defined social advantages broadly to include all benefits:[197]

> which, whether or not linked to a contract of employment, are generally granted to national workers primarily because of their objective status as workers *or by virtue of the mere fact of their residence on the national territory* and the extension of which to workers who are nationals of other Member States therefore seems suitable to *facilitate their mobility* within the [Union].

The concept of social advantage includes benefits granted as of right[198] or on a discretionary basis,[199] and those granted after employment has terminated.[200] It also covers benefits not directly linked to employment, such as language rights,[201] grant of funding for studies,[202] death benefits,[203] and rights to be accompanied by unmarried companions.[204] These benefits do not necessarily 'facilitate mobility', as the *Even* formula requires, but do assist in integrating the migrant worker into the host state.[205]

Thus, the justification for a broad reading of the term 'social advantage' have varied over time,[206] *Hartmann*[207] offered a new perspective on the justification for extending

---

[194] Joined Cases C–155 and 157/08 *X and Passenheim-van Schoot* [2009] ECR I–5093, para. 76.

[195] Case C–43/99 *Leclere* [2001] ECR I–4265 made clear that a former worker could enjoy an invalidity pension under Art. 7(2) because it was linked with his previous employment but he could not claim *new* rights under Art. 7(2) which had no link with his former occupation.

[196] Case 207/78 *Criminal Proceedings against Even* [1979] ECR 2019.

[197] Para. 22, emphasis added.

[198] See, e.g., Case C–111/91 *Commission* v. *Luxembourg* [1993] ECR I–817; Case C–85/96 *Martínez Sala* [1998] ECR I–2691, para. 28; Case C–206/10 *Commission* v. *Germany (benefits for the blind)* EU:C:2011:283, para. 34.

[199] Case 65/81 *Reina* v. *Landeskreditbank Baden-Württemberg* [1982] ECR 33, para. 17.

[200] See, e.g., Case C–57/96 *Meints* v. *Minister van Landbouw, Natuurbeheer en Visserij* [1997] ECR I–6689, para. 36 (payment to agricultural workers whose employment contracts are terminated); Case C–35/97 *Commission* v. *France (supplementary retirement pension points)* [1998] ECR I–5325; Case C–258/04 *Office national de l'empoli* v. *Ioannidis* [2005] ECR I–8275, para. 34.

[201] Case 137/84 *Criminal Proceedings against Mutsch* [1985] ECR 2681, para. 18 (criminal proceedings in the defendant's own language).

[202] Case C–542/09 *Commission* v. *Netherlands (higher education)* EU:C:2012:34, para. 48. This includes 'assistance granted for maintenance and education': Case C–20/12 *Giersch* v. *Etat du Grand-Duché de Luxembourg* EU:C:2013:411, para. 38.

[203] Case C–237/94 *O'Flynn* [1996] ECR I–2617 (social security payments to help cover the cost of burying a family member).

[204] Case 59/85 *Netherlands* v. *Reed* [1986] ECR 1283, para. 28.

[205] E. Ellis, 'Social advantages: A new lease of life' (2003) 40 *CMLRev*. 639, 648.

[206] Case C–287/05 *Hendrix* v. *Raad van Bestuur van het Uitvoeringsinstituut Werknemersverzekeringen* [2007] ECR I–6909, para. 52. *Hendrix* mainly concerned limitations on exportability (permitted by the Social Security Reg. 883/2004) to incapacity benefit payable to young people in the Netherlands. This was considered by reference not only to the regulation but also to the equal treatment principle under Art. 45 TFEU and Reg. 492/11 (cf. Case C–523/13 *Larcher* EU:C:2014:2458, where the Court decided the case by reference to the Social Security Reg. only). In Case C–333/13 *Dano* v. *Jobcenter Leipzig* EU:C:2014:2358 the Court did not follow the *Hendrix* approach and applied only the CRD, not the Treaty.

[207] Case C–212/05 *Hartmann* v. *Freistaat Bayern* [2007] ECR I–6303.

social advantages to migrant workers, in this case frontier workers. The Court said that the Austrian wife of a German worker, both of whom resided in Austria while he continued to work in Germany, could claim a German child-raising allowance because receipt of the allowance reduced the worker's obligation to contribute to family expenses.[208]

There are, however, limits to the scope of Article 7(2), as the facts of *Even* itself demonstrate.[209] The case concerned Belgian regulations providing that a retirement pension could begin, if requested, up to five years prior to the normal pension age of 65, albeit with a reduction for early payment. This reduction was not made in the case of Belgians who had served in the Allied Forces during the Second World War and who had received an invalidity pension granted by an Allied country. Mr Even, a French national living in Belgium, received an invalidity pension from the French government, and he wished to receive the full Belgian state pension when he took early retirement. The Court said that the relevant Belgian legislation could not be considered a social advantage granted to a national worker because it benefited those who had given wartime service to their own country and 'its essential objective is to give those nationals an advantage by reason of the hardships suffered for that country'.[210] *Even* can perhaps be explained on the basis of the sensitive issues at stake: the Court did not want to face a future claim made by a migrant who was a former soldier but who had not served with the Allied Forces.

(ii) Family members

The decision in *Even*, with its reference to 'residence on the national territory', shows that Article 7(2) applies to benefits granted by the host state not just to its workers[211] but also to its residents.[212] This has been read to mean that both migrant workers *and* their families can enjoy the social advantages offered by the home state.[213] The Court justified this development on the ground that Article 7(2) was essential not only to encourage free movement of workers as well as their families,[214] but also to ensure 'the best possible conditions for the integration of the Union worker's family in the society of the host Member State'.[215] This reading is now confirmed by Article 24(1) CRD, which says that the benefit of the right to equal treatment 'shall be extended to family members who are non-nationals of a Member State and who have the right of residence or permanent residence'.

(iii) UK New Settlement Decision and its effect on social advantages

Generally, however, the Court's generous approach to social advantages has caused friction in some receiving Member States, especially the UK, which has argued that

---

[208] Para. 26.

[209] Case 207/78 [1979] ECR 2019. See also Case C–315/94 *De Vos* [1996] ECR I–1417. Cf. Case 15/69 *Ugliola* [1970] ECR 363.

[210] Para. 23. See also Case C–386/02 *Baldinger* v. *Pensionsversicherungsanstalt der Arbeiter* [2004] ECR I–8411, para. 19, where the Court said that an Austrian allowance granted to Austrian prisoners of war was also not a social advantage. It was not granted to national workers because of their status as either workers or residents.

[211] This includes those who are not resident in the territory of the providing state: Case C–57/96 *Meints* [1997] ECR I–6689, para. 50; Case C–337/97 *Meeusen* [1999] ECR I–3289, para. 21.

[212] Jacobs AG in Case C–43/99 *Leclere* [2001] ECR I–4265, para. 96.

[213] Cf. the early decision in Case 76/72 *Michel S.* v. *Fonds national de reclassement social des handicapés* [1973] ECR 457, para. 9, where the Court limited social advantages to workers.

[214] See, e.g., Case 94/84 *ONEM* v. *Deak* [1985] ECR 1873, para. 23.

[215] Case C–413/99 *Baumbast and R.* v. *Secretary of State for the Home Department* [2002] ECR I–7091, para. 50. See also Case 32/75 *Fiorini (née Christini)* v. *SNCF* [1975] ECR 1085. See also Case C–278/94 *Commission* v. *Belgium (tideover benefits)* [1996] ECR I–4307; Case C–185/96 *Commission* v. *Greece (attribution of large family status)* [1998] ECR I–6601.

40 per cent of EU migrants claim in-work (e.g. housing benefit and tax credits) or out-of-work benefits (a claim that has been subsequently criticized[216]). Securing reforms on these issues was a key component of the British Prime Minister's new settlement negotiations in Brussels on 18 and 19 February 2016. He obtained two important concessions.

First, on *in-work benefits* the New Settlement Decision provides for a so-called 'emergency brake' properly known as the 'alert and safeguard mechanism'.[217] In essence, if the situation is bad enough (i.e. there has been an inflow of workers from other Member States of exceptional magnitude over an extended period of time) in the host state, then the state can notify the Commission and Council that the situation affects 'essential aspects of its social security system, including the primary purpose of its in-work benefits system or which leads to difficulties which are serious and liable to persist in its employment market or are putting an extensive pressure on the proper function of its public services'. The Council can authorize (for up to seven years) the Member State to limit the access of *newly arriving* EU workers to non-contributory in-work benefits for a total period of up to four years from the commencement of employment.[218] The limitation is to be graduated, from an initial complete exclusion but gradually increasing access to such benefits to take account of the growing connection of the worker with the labour market of the host Member State. The European Commission has already accepted that the situation in the UK satisfies the exceptional magnitude test.[219]

Secondly, the New Settlement Decision makes concessions about the exportability of child benefit under the Social Security Regulation 883/2004.[220] It does not ban the exportability of child benefit, as the British Prime Minister had requested, but it will allow the indexation of such benefits to the conditions of the Member State where the child resides.[221] At first this applies only to new claims made by EU workers in the host Member State, but from 1 January 2020 this will also apply to existing claims.

These changes will require the amendment of secondary EU legislation (and so will be applicable to all Member States). This will be set in motion only if the UK votes to remain a member of the EU on 23 June 2016. The legislation will follow the standard ordinary legislative procedure, which means the agreement of the European Parliament and Council of Ministers is required. Any resulting amendment to the secondary legislation might be challenged before the Court of Justice as potentially contravening Article 45 TFEU since they are both directly discriminatory measures which are being applied to those who are economically active (and not the less favoured non-economically active).

---

[216] <https://www.statisticsauthority.gov.uk/wp-content/uploads/2016/03/Letter-from-Sir-Andrew-Dilnot-to-Sir-Robert-Devereux-10-March-2016.pdf>.

[217] Section D.2(b).

[218] On the difficulties associated with the phrase 'commencement of employment', see S. Peers, <http://eulawanalysis.blogspot.it/2016/02/the-final-uk-renegotiation-deal.html>. On the political economy issues, see J. Portes, <http://www.niesr.ac.uk/blog/always-crashing-same-car-emergency-brake-eu-migration#.Vu6KhOY8LX4>.

[219] Annex VI, Declaration of the Commission.

[220] See also Case C–308/14 *Commission* v. *UK* on other aspects of the UK rules on the payment of child benefit; Cruz-Villalón's AG's Opinion supported the UK's position EU:C:2015:666.

[221] Annex V, Declaration of the Commission provides that these conditions include the standard of living and the level of child benefit applicable in that Member State.

(iv) Work-seekers

If family members can enjoy social advantages on the same terms as nationals, does the same rule apply to work-seekers? Early case law suggested that work-seekers did not enjoy access to social advantages in the same way as employed workers[222] but in *Collins*[223] the Court changed its mind. Collins was an Irish work-seeker who came to the UK looking for employment. A week after his arrival he claimed Jobseeker's Allowance but was turned down on the grounds that he was not habitually resident in the UK. The Court began by stating the orthodox position that, as a work-seeker, the rights Collins enjoyed under Article 45 TFEU and Regulation 492/11 were limited to equal treatment in respect of access to employment: he did not enjoy equal treatment in respect of social (financial) advantages. However, the Court then said that 'in view of the establishment of citizenship of the Union', it was no longer possible to exclude from the scope of Article 45 TFEU benefits of a 'financial nature intended to facilitate access to employment in the labour market of a Member State'.[224] *Collins* therefore sent out a clear message: orthodox tenets of the Court's earlier case law (in particular on workers) had to be given a 'citizenship' reading, which might lead to a different result.[225]

At first sight, the Court's approach to the Treaty provisions in *Collins* sits uncomfortably with Article 24(2) CRD, which provides that Member States are not obliged to provide social assistance during the citizen's first three months of residence or longer in the case of work-seekers remaining in the host Member State under Article 14(4)(b) CRD; namely, when they provide evidence that they are continuing to seek employment and that they have a genuine chance of being engaged. The term 'social assistance' is not defined in the directive. However, in *Brey*[226] the phrase 'social assistance system' in Article 7(1)(b) CRD was defined as covering:

> all assistance introduced by public authorities, whether at national, regional or local level, that can be claimed by an individual who does not have resources sufficient to meet his own basic needs and the needs of his family and who, by reason of that fact, may become a burden on the public finances of the host Member State during his period of residence which could have consequences for the overall level of assistance which may be granted by that state.

It is likely that the phrase 'social assistance' in Article 24(2) CRD will be defined in the same way:[227] 'social assistance' looks to need and is more likely to be discretionary, requiring a decision of some authority on the suitability of the applicant for support from destitution.[228] This understanding of the function of social-assistance benefits was

---

[222] Case 316/85 *Centre public d'aide sociale de Courcelles (CPAS)* v. *Lebon* [1987] ECR 2811 and Case C–3/90 *Bernini* [1992] ECR I–1071.

[223] Case C–138/02 *Collins* [2004] ECR I–2703.

[224] See also Joined Cases C–22 and 23/08 *Vatsouras* [2009] ECR I–4585, para. 37.

[225] Cf. now Case C–333/13 *Dano* EU:C:2014:2358, which suggests a less generous approach to EU citizenship, discussed in Ch. 10.

[226] Case C–140/12 *Brey* EU:C:2013:565, para. 61.

[227] See Case C–578/08 *Chakroun* [2010] ECR I–1839, para. 45, where the Court, when interpreting the Family Reunification Dir. 2003/86, said 'social assistance' refers to assistance granted by public authorities, whether at national, regional, or local level, which can be claimed by an individual who does not have stable and regular resources sufficient to maintain himself and his family.

[228] According to R. White, *EC Social Security Law* (Harlow: Longman, 1999), 5–6, social assistance can be contrasted to 'social security', which was based on ideas of social insurance against the occurrence of risks facing those in work (sickness, unemployment, and accidents) and other 'risks' in life which were likely to occur (childbirth, retirement, and the needs of survivors on the death of the breadwinner). Having paid insurance contributions (in the UK through national insurance) the individual would become entitled to

recognized by the Court in *Alimanovic*.[229] The Court said that where the predominant function of the benefits was to cover 'the minimum subsistence costs necessary to lead a life in keeping with human dignity' the benefits were considered social assistance.

Returning to the dilemma presented by *Collins*, the Court managed to square this circle by declaring in *Vatsouras*[230] that '[b]enefits of a financial nature which, independently of their status under national law, are intended to facilitate access to the labour market cannot be regarded as constituting "social assistance" within the meaning of Article 24(2) of Directive 2004/38.' In other words, benefits aimed at labour market *integration* are considered social advantages and not social assistance and so do not fall within the derogation under Article 24(2). However, social advantages remain subject to the principle of equal treatment in Article 45(2) TFEU[231] (and Article 7(2) of Regulation 492/11), which means that Member States can justify their (indirectly discriminatory) residence requirements, in particular by reference to the requirement for there to be 'a real link between the job-seeker and the labour market' of the host state.[232] This is likely to be accepted by the Court provided the requirement is proportionate. We return to this point in the next section.

Yet this distinction between social advantages (intended to facilitate labour market integration, which work-seekers can claim on equal terms with nationals, subject to justification) and social assistance (which they cannot) has been muddied by the UK's New Settlement Decision. In the section on interpretation of current EU rules, the Decision says:

> Member States may reject claims for social assistance by EU citizens from other Member States who do not enjoy a right of residence or are entitled to reside on their territory solely because of their job-search. This includes claims by EU citizens from other Member States for benefits whose predominant function is to cover the minimum subsistence costs, even if such benefits are also intended to facilitate access to the labour market of the host Member States.

Thus, EU work-seekers can also be denied benefits which are primarily social assistance but which contain a social advantage element.

Finally, and for clarification, the discussion so far concerns work-*seekers*. Workers and those who have retained that status on the basis of, for example, Article 7(3)(c) (involuntary unemployment) who are looking for work will be entitled to social advantages and social assistance.[233] However, once the period of retained status has expired (i.e., after six months in the case of Article 7(3)(c) CRD), then Article 14(4)(b) CRD may be engaged (continuing to seek employment and genuine chance of being engaged). This was the situation in *Alimanovic*. The Court said that those residing under Article 14(4)(b) CRD are entitled to equal treatment in respect of access to social assistance but the host state can rely on the derogation under Article 24(2) CRD not to grant that social assistance.[234] No individual assessment needs to be made in this case.[235]

---

the benefit on the occurrence of the particular risk, without the application of any means test. However, the distinction between the two terms has become blurred, first, because entitlement to social assistance has tended to become a matter of right rather than discretion and, secondly, because the burden of funding social insurance has resulted in moves to require a test of means even for some insurance-based benefits.

[229] Case C–67/14 *Jobcenter Berlin Neukölln* v. *Alimanovic* EU:C:2015:597, para. 45.

[230] Joined Cases C–22 and 23/08 [2009] ECR I–4585, para. 45.

[231] This reasoning also enabled the Court to conclude that by interpreting Art. 24(2) CRD in the light of Art. 45(2) TFEU this has 'not disclosed any factor capable of affecting the validity of Article 24(2)' (para. 46).

[232] Paras. 38–40.   [233] Joined Cases C–22 and 23/08 *Vatsouras* [2009] ECR I–4585, para. 54.

[234] Case C–67/14 *Jobcenter Berlin Neukölln* v. *Alimanovic* EU:C:2015:597, para. 57.

[235] Para. 59.

(v) Real link test

As *Collins* has shown,[236] the 'real' link test (i.e., there must be a 'genuine link' between the person applying for the benefit and the state where the benefit was given[237]) has become an important safety valve for Member States to control who has access to benefits. This point was confirmed in the UK's New Settlement Decision. Under the heading 'Interpretation of current EU rules', Section D.1 provides:

> Based on objective considerations independent of the nationality of the persons con-
> cerned and proportionate to the legitimate aim pursued, conditions may be imposed in
> relation to certain benefits to ensure that there is a real and effective degree of connection
> between the person concerned and the labour market of the host Member State.

However, as the Court emphasized in *Collins*, any link—such as a residence requirement or a requirement that the person had genuinely sought work for a reasonable period in the host state[238]—had to be proportionate: it had to rest on clear criteria known in advance, judicial redress had to be available, and the period of residence could not exceed what was necessary for the national authorities to satisfy themselves that, *in casu*, the person concerned was genuinely seeking work in the employment market of the host state.[239]

Through its use of the 'real link' test, the Court has been able to help reconcile the traditionally territorial approach to the payment of social-welfare benefits with the need to facilitate free movement. Nevertheless, the EU's approach still stands in sharp contrast to that adopted by the US Supreme Court: it has consistently found unconstitutional state laws which grant social welfare benefits only to individuals who have resided in the state for a year.[240]

Finally, a note of realism should be injected here.[241] The Commission's own independent research found 'little evidence in the literature and stakeholder consultations to suggest that the main motivation of EU citizens to migrate and reside in a different Member State is benefit-related as opposed to work or family-related'.[242] It adds that this is 'underpinned by data which show that in most countries, immigrants are not more intensive users of welfare than nationals. Where they are more intensive users, they tend to use intensely only specific types of benefits linked to their socio-economic circumstances as migrants'. It concludes 'Our analysis of EU data shows that migrants are less likely to receive disability and unemployment benefits in most countries studied'.[243]

(d) Equal treatment and vocational training

(i) Access to training

Not only does Regulation 492/11 require equal treatment in respect of tax and social advantages but the principle also applies in respect of access to vocational training for workers and the children of workers.[244] Article 7(3) provides that a worker shall 'have access

---

[236] Case C–138/02 *Collins* [2004] ECR I–2703, para. 67.   [237] Para. 70.   [238] Para. 70.

[239] Para. 72. The proportionality of the measure was upheld by the national court: [2005] UKSSCSC CJSA_4065_1999 (4 Mar. 2005).

[240] See, e.g., *Shapiro* v. *Thompson* 394 US 618 (1969); *Saenz* v. *Roe* 526 US 489 (1999).

[241] See <http://www.migrationobservatory.ox.ac.uk/commentary/pulling-power-why-are-eu-citizens-migrating-uk>.

[242] <http://ec.europa.eu/employment_social/empl_portal/facebook/20131014%20GHK%20study%20web_EU%20migration.pdf>.

[243] See also <http://archive.openeurope.org.uk/Content/Documents/Open_Europe_Free_Movement_141124.pdf>.

[244] Art. 2(1)(h) of Dir. 2014/54.

to training in vocational schools and retraining centres' under the same conditions as national workers. In *Gravier*[245] the Court defined 'vocational training' broadly to include any form of education which prepares an individual for a qualification or which provides the necessary training or skills for a particular profession, trade, or employment. In *Blaizot*[246] the Court confirmed that vocational training could be received at universities, except in the case of courses intended for students 'wishing to improve their general knowledge rather than prepare themselves for a particular occupation'.[247]

Access to training is one thing; the level of fees for that training is another. In *Gravier* the Court said that since access to training was likely to promote free movement of persons by enabling them to obtain a qualification in the Member State where they intended to work,[248] the conditions of access to vocational training fell within the scope of the Treaty. Therefore, if a host state charged a registration fee to migrant students but not to its own students, there was a breach of Article 18 TFEU.[249]

The principle that migrant students must have access to higher education on the same terms as nationals and to be charged the same fees has started to pose significant problems for states, such as the UK and Ireland, which are net recipients of students. In respect of the availability of places, in the UK at least, every incoming migrant EU student will take a place which might have been occupied by a domestic student.[250] These issues were considered directly by the Court in *Commission* v. *Austria*.[251] Austrian law allowed broad access to higher education for holders of Austrian school leaving certificates but subjected those with comparable certificates from other Member States to more stringent requirements. The principal ground offered by Austria to justify its indirectly discriminatory rules[252] was to preserve the 'homogeneity of the Austrian higher or university education system'. It argued that if it did not impose some limitation, Austria, with its policy of unrestricted access to all levels of education,[253] could expect a large number of students with diplomas awarded in other states (especially Germany), who had failed to be admitted to higher education courses in those states, to try to attend higher education courses in Austria. Such a situation, it argued, would cause 'structural, staffing and financial problems'.[254]

The Court found that there was little evidence that this was in fact a problem[255] and even if it was, the justification based on preserving the homogeneity of the Austrian higher education system was not, in fact, made out by the Austrian government.[256] Even if it was a problem, the Court offered a simple solution: excessive demand for access to specific courses could be met by the adoption of specific non-discriminatory measures such as the establishment of an entry examination or the requirement of a minimum grade.[257]

---

[245] Case 293/83 *Gravier* v. *Ville de Liège* [1985] ECR 593, para. 30. For background, J. Shaw, 'From the margins to the centre: Education and training law and policy' in P. Craig and G. de Búrca (eds.), *The Evolution of EU Law* (Oxford: OUP, 1999).

[246] Case 24/86 *Blaizot* v. *Université de Liège* [1988] ECR 379.

[247] Paras. 19–20. See also Case C–40/05 *Lyyski* [2007] ECR I–10025, paras. 28–30 (teacher training course constituted vocational training).

[248] Para. 24.   [249] Para. 26.

[250] See M. Dougan, 'Fees, grants, loans and dole cheques: Who covers the costs of migrant education within the EU?' (2005) 42 *CMLRev.* 943.

[251] Case C–147/03 [2005] ECR I–5969, noted in Rieder (2006) 43 *CMLRev.* 1711. See also Case C–73/08 *Bressol* v. *Gouvernement de la Communauté française* [2010] ECR I–2735.

[252] Para. 47.

[253] According to the AG's Opinion, this policy was introduced to improve the percentage of Austrian citizens with a higher education qualification, which was one of the lowest in the EU (para. 26).

[254] Para. 50, citing the Court's case law on access to healthcare services (Case C–158/96 *Kohll* [1998] ECR I–1931, para. 41 and Case C–368/98 *Vanbraekel* [2001] ECR I–5363) by analogy.

[255] Para. 65.   [256] Para. 66.   [257] Para. 61.

It also noted that the risks alleged by the Austrian government were not exclusively an Austrian problem[258] 'but have been and are suffered by other Member States'[259] (including Belgium, which had introduced similar restrictions which were also found to breach Union law[260]).

(ii) Funding

Gravier concerned fees, not grants. Maintenance grants can constitute 'social advantages' within the meaning of Article 7(2) of Regulation 492/11.[261]

But the case law on Article 7(2) is open to exploitation by those who do short-term casual work in another Member State and then claim entitlement to social advantages in the form of a grant for further study in that state. The Court had to address this problem in *Lair*[262] and *Brown*.[263] *Lair* concerned a French woman who had moved to Germany, where she worked on a series of part-time contracts. Having decided to study for a languages degree at a German university, she unsuccessfully sought a maintenance grant from the German authorities. The Court recognized that people who had previously pursued an effective and genuine activity in the host state could still be considered workers and so could receive a maintenance grant under Article 7(2) but only on condition that there was a link between the previous occupational activity[264] and the studies,[265] unless the migrant worker became involuntarily unemployed, when no link was required before a maintenance grant was awarded.[266] The result in *Lair* has now been incorporated into Article 7(3)(d) CRD.

Brown was different. He was a student with dual French and British nationality who lived in France for many years before getting a place at a British university to read engineering. He was sponsored by Ferranti and worked for the company in the UK for eight months before starting his course. He then claimed that he was a worker and so was entitled to a grant from the British authorities under Article 7(2). The Court refused to recognize him

---

[258] See Austrian Chancellor Wolfgang Schussel's subsequent criticism of the Court of Justice for extending its competence into areas where there is 'decidedly no [Union] law such as on access of foreign students to Austrian universities'. He called for the debate on the future of the EU to focus not only on the fate of the Constitution but also on the role of the Court of Justice: *euobserver.com*, 3 Jan. 2006.

[259] Para. 62.

[260] Case C–65/03 *Commission* v. *Belgium* [2004] ECR I–6427. Nevertheless, in Mar. 2006 the Minister for Higher Education proposed capping the number of foreign students to 30 per cent in areas dominated by foreign students such as veterinary medicine, where French students count for 86 per cent of the total students studying in Belgium. The minister said that the reform could save €15 million that could be reinvested in Belgian education: *euobserver.com*, 22 Mar. 2006.

[261] Case C–3/90 *Bernini* v. *Minister van Onderwijs en Wetenschappen* [1992] ECR I–1071, para. 23, where the Court ruled that descendants of workers could rely on Art. 7(2) to obtain study finance under the same conditions as children of national workers. This also applies to non-resident children of migrant workers (Case C–337/97 *Meeusen* [1999] ECR I–3289, para. 25) but not to workers who have returned to their states of origin (Case C–33/99 *Fahmi* [2001] ECR I–2415, para. 46).

[262] Case 39/86 *Lair* v. *Universität Hannover* [1988] ECR 3161. See also Case C–357/90 *Raulin* [1992] ECR I–1027, para. 21.

[263] Case 197/86 *Brown* v. *Secretary of State for Scotland* [1988] ECR 3205.

[264] The host state cannot make the right to the same social advantages conditional upon a minimum period of prior occupational activity (Case 39/86 *Lair* [1988] ECR 3161, para. 44). In Case C–413/01 *Ninni-Orasche* [2003] ECR I–13187, para. 42, the Court added that the mere fact the individual is employed on a fixed-term contract does not mean that when the contract expires the employee is automatically to be regarded as voluntarily unemployed.

[265] If no link exists between the study and the previous occupational activities, the person does not retain the status of migrant worker (Case C–357/89 *Raulin* [1992] ECR I–1027).

[266] Para. 37.

as a worker, viewing his work for Ferranti as merely ancillary to his studies.[267] Therefore, he could not receive a maintenance grant under Article 7(2), nor could he rely on the general prohibition of discrimination in Article 18 TFEU to obtain the grant. This position has been confirmed by Article 24(2) CRD, which provides that, prior to the acquisition of permanent residence (primarily, under Article 16 CRD, after five years' residence), the host state is not obliged to grant maintenance aid for studies, including vocational training, consisting of student grants or loans to persons other than workers, the self-employed, persons who retain such status and members of their families.[268]

(e) Equal treatment and other benefits

Equality is not confined to tax and social advantages and vocational training. Article 8(1) of Regulation 492/11 provides that migrant workers must also enjoy equality of treatment with nationals in respect of trade union membership and the exercise of rights related to trade union membership, 'including the right to vote and to be eligible for the administration or management posts of a trade union'. In *ASTI I* and *ASTI II*[269] the Court ruled that Article 8 applied to the right to vote and to stand in elections held by bodies such as occupational guilds to which workers were required to belong, to which they had to pay contributions and which were responsible for defending and representing their interests. However, Article 8 does provide that workers can be excluded from taking part in the management of bodies governed by public law and from holding office governed by public law.[270] The Austrian government relied on this clause in *Commission* v. *Austria (workers' chambers)*[271] to justify its exclusion of all non-Austrians from standing for election to workers' chambers. Unsurprisingly, the Court said that, as a derogation to a fundamental freedom, the public law exception had to be interpreted narrowly.[272] Since there was little difference between the role of workers' chambers in *Commission* v. *Austria* and the role of the guilds in the *ASTI* cases, the *Austria* case fell within the scope of Article 8 of Regulation 492/11 (and Article 45 TFEU)[273] and Austria was in breach of the principle of equal treatment.

Finally, Article 9 of Regulation 492/11 provides that workers must enjoy all the rights and benefits accorded to national workers in matters of housing, including ownership, and the right to put their names on housing lists in the region where they are employed. Therefore, in *Commission* v. *Greece*[274] the Court found a rule restricting a foreigner's right to own property in Greece breached the free movement rules, since access to housing and ownership of property was the corollary of free movement.[275]

3. ENFORCEMENT OF RIGHTS

Having recognized the gap between the law on free movement of workers and its application in practice,[276] the EU adopted the Enforcement Directive 2014/54 to assist in

---

[267] Case 197/86 *Brown* [1988] ECR 3205, para. 27. Cf. Case C–542/09 *Commission* v. *Netherlands (higher education)* EU:C:2012:346 and Case C–46/12 *LN* EU:C:2013:97, which took a more generous view of intention.

[268] This is confirmed in Case C–46/12 *LN* EU:C:2013:97, para. 32.

[269] Case C–213/90 *Association de Soutien aux Travailleurs Immigrés* v. *Chambre des Employés Privés (ASTI I)* [1991] ECR I–3507 and Case C–118/92 *Commission* v. *Luxembourg (ASTI II)* [1994] ECR I–1891.

[270] Art. 8.   [271] Case C–465/01 [2004] ECR I–8291.   [272] Para. 39.

[273] The Austrian law had already been condemned in Case C–171/01 *Wählergruppe, 'Gemeinsam Zajedno/ Birlikte Alternative und Grüne Gewerkschafter Innen/UG'* [2003] ECR I–4301, which concerned Art. 10 of the EEC–Turkey Agreement, which is interpreted in the same way as Art. 8 of Reg. 492/11.

[274] Case 305/87 *Commission* v. *Greece* [1989] ECR 1461. See also Case 63/86 *Commission* v. *Italy (social housing)* [1988] ECR 29, considered in Ch. 9.

[275] Para. 18.   [276] Recital 5, Dir. 2014/54.

the 'effective exercise of the freedom of movement of workers'. The key provision of the directive is found in Article 3(1): a strong(er) obligation on states to ensure that judicial remedies are available 'to all Union workers and members of their family who consider that they have suffered or are suffering from unjustified restrictions and obstacles to their right to free movement or who consider themselves wronged by a failure to apply the principle of equal treatment to them, even after the relationship in which the restriction and obstacle or discrimination is alleged to have occurred has ended'. This is for the enforcement of obligations under Article 45 TFEU and under Articles 1–10 of Regulation (EU) No. 492/2011, but only after 'possible recourse to other competent authorities including, where they deem it to be appropriate, conciliation procedures'. Interest groups and trade unions may engage, either on behalf of, or in support of, Union workers and members of their family, with their approval, in any judicial and/or administrative procedure provided for the enforcement of the free movement rights.[277] Claimants must also be protected from victimization.[278] National rules of procedure concerning representation and defence in court proceedings and national rules on time limits apply.[279] However, consistent with the Court's case law on effective remedies, 'those national time-limits shall not render virtually impossible or excessively difficult the exercise of those rights'. Finally, as with the more general equality directives, Directive 2014/54 requires Member States to designate a body to promote equal treatment and to support Union workers and members of their family.

D. THE RIGHTS ENJOYED BY THE SELF-EMPLOYED

1. RIGHTS OF DEPARTURE, ENTRY, AND RESIDENCE

So far we have concentrated on the rights enjoyed by workers. These were originally laid down by Regulations 1612/68. The EU adopted a similar, but not identical, directive for the self-employed: Directive 73/148/EEC on the abolition of restrictions on movement and residence within the Union for nationals of Member States with regard to establishment and the provision of services.[280] This directive required Member States to abolish restrictions on the movement and residence of nationals wishing to establish themselves in another Member State as a self-employed person under Article 49 TFEU and those wishing to provide or receive services on a temporary basis as a self-employed person in another Member State under Article 56 TFEU. It also gave rights to the members of the self-employed person's family.

This directive has now been repealed and replaced by the Citizens' Rights Directive 2004/38 in respect of freedom of establishment (but not free movement of services, albeit that service providers will, in fact, fit into its provisions), the details of which are considered in Chapter 10. There is no equivalent to Regulation 492/11 for the self-employed. However, much of the content of Directive 73/148 has been read into the Treaty provision itself and it is to Article 49 TFEU we shall refer (the rights of services providers are considered separately in Chapter 9). So the Court has already recognized that Article 49 TFEU prohibits:

- a home state from hindering the establishment of one of its own nationals in another Member State[281]

---

[277] Art. 3(2).   [278] Art. 3(6).   [279] Art. 3(4) and (5).   [280] [1973] OJ L172/14.
[281] Case C–251/98 *Baars* [2000] ECR I–2787, para. 28. See also Case 81/87 *Ex p. Daily Mail* [1988] ECR 5483, para. 16.

- a requirement that a migrant be registered with the relevant authorities before obtaining the right of residence,[282] since the grant of a residence permit has merely probative value—it is not constitutive of the right of residence[283]
- a rule providing that failure to register would result in deportation breaches Article 49 TFEU, since this would negate the right of residence conferred by the Treaty.[284]

Thus Article 49 TFEU embraces rights of exit from State A, entry to State B, and residence there.

2. THE RIGHT OF ACCESS TO SELF-EMPLOYMENT IN THE HOST STATE

2.1 Introduction

What rights does an individual enjoy once in State B? According to Article 49 TFEU, freedom of establishment includes the 'right to take up *and* pursue' activities as a self-employed person 'under the conditions laid down for its own nationals by the law of the country where such establishment is effected'. Article 49 TFEU therefore distinguishes between:

(1) the right to take up an activity (access—i.e., the initial right to take up work as a self-employed person) and

(2) the right to pursue that activity once in the host state (exercise—i.e., the terms and conditions of employment and the facilities necessary to exercise that profession).

Although there is a fine line between access to self-employment and its exercise,[285] we shall use this distinction as a way of examining the case law. In this section we look at questions of access; in Section 3 we look at exercise.

2.2 Primary and Secondary Establishment

Article 49 TFEU applies to both primary and secondary establishment. With *primary* establishment, an individual leaves State A to set up a permanent establishment in State B; with *secondary* establishment, an individual maintains an establishment in State A[286] while setting up a second professional base (e.g., an office or chambers) in State B. This was the situation in *Klopp*,[287] where a German national and member of the Düsseldorf Bar wished to practise in Paris as an *avocat* while remaining a member of the Düsseldorf Bar and retaining his residence and chambers there. His application was rejected by the Paris Bar on the ground that an *avocat* could have only one set of chambers, which had to be in the region of Paris. The effect of the French rule was to allow *avocats* to have a primary, but not a secondary, establishment. For lawyers established in other Member States this meant that they could exercise their rights of establishment but only

---

[282] Case C–363/89 *Roux* [1991] ECR I–273, para. 11.

[283] Case 48/75 *Royer* [1976] ECR 497, para. 31; Case C–363/89 *Roux* [1991] ECR I–273, para. 12.

[284] Case C–363/89 *Roux* [1991] ECR I–273, para. 11.

[285] See, e.g., Case C–19/92 *Kraus* [1993] ECR I–1663, para. 23, where the Court considered the terms interchangeably.

[286] Either as an employee or a self-employed person in State A: Case 143/87 *Stanton* v. *Inasti* [1988] ECR 3877, para. 12.

[287] Case 107/83 *Ordre des Avocats au Barreau de Paris* v. *Klopp* [1984] ECR 2971, para. 19. See also Case C–53/95 *Inasti* v. *Kemmler* [1996] ECR I–703; Case C–162/99 *Commission* v. *Italy (dentists)* [2001] ECR I–541, para. 20.

by giving up their first place of establishment. The Court said that in principle the French rule breached Article 49 TFEU: Article 49 TFEU entitled individuals to maintain more than one establishment.[288] In the interests of the administration of justice, the Court said that France was justified in requiring lawyers to abide by its rules of professional ethics[289] and to practise in such a way as to maintain sufficient contact with their clients and the courts, but this could be facilitated by 'modern methods of transport and telecommunications',[290] without the need for living in the locality and giving up their primary establishment.

2.3 Equal Treatment and Beyond

(a) The discrimination approach

The principle of equal treatment laid down in Article 49 TFEU means that, in the absence of specific Union rules, each Member State is free to regulate access to a profession in its territory,[291] provided it does not directly or indirectly discriminate on the grounds of nationality (see fig. 7.2). A directly discriminatory measure (one which treats migrants less favourably than nationals) breaches Article 49 TFEU and can be saved only by reference to one of the express derogations. Therefore, in *Reyners*[292] the Court said that a Belgian rule preventing a qualified Dutch national from practising as a lawyer in Belgium on the grounds of his nationality breached Article 49 TFEU.[293]

Indirectly discriminatory measures (those which ostensibly treat the migrant and the national in the same way but in fact disadvantage the migrant) also breach Article 49 TFEU unless they can be objectively justified or saved by an express derogation. Such measures include national laws requiring professionals to hold a licence before they can practise and/or be registered with a professional body,[294] usually after having passed the relevant examinations and holding certain qualifications. These rules can be considered indistinctly applicable because they require migrants to shoulder the dual burden of having to satisfy first the home, and then the host, state authorities of their suitability to practise, while nationals have to satisfy only one authority (that of the home state). This reading holds true in the case of secondary establishment (where the requirements of the home and host states apply simultaneously) but less so in the case of primary establishment, where only one set of registration requirements applies at any given time (those of the home state followed by those of the host state).

The Court usually finds that indirectly discriminatory requirements can in principle be justified. For example, in *Gullung*[295] the Court said a French requirement for all lawyers to be registered at the Bar before practising could be justified on the ground of ensuring 'the observance of moral and ethical principles and the disciplinary control of the activity of lawyers'[296] or, as the Court put it in *Vlassopoulou*,[297] for reasons relating to the organization of the profession, qualifications, professional ethics, supervision, and liability. The steps taken must, however, be proportionate.

---

[288] Para. 19.

[289] Case C–359/09 *Ebert* v. *Budapesti ügyvédi Kamara* [2011] ECR I–269, para. 42, the reference to professional ethics could include membership of the Bar of the host state.

[290] Paras. 21–2.   [291] Case 107/83 *Klopp* [1984] ECR 2971, para. 17.

[292] Case 2/74 *Reyners* v. *Belgian State* [1974] ECR 631.

[293] See also Case 38/87 *Commission* v. *Greece* [1988] ECR 4415; Case C–252/99 *Commission* v. *Italy* [2001] ECR I–4195; Case C–161/07 *Commission* v. *Austria (certification)* [2008] ECR I–10671.

[294] E.g., Case 292/86 *Gullung* v. *Conseils de l'ordre des avocats du barreau de Colmar* [1988] ECR 111.

[295] Case 292/86 *Gullung* [1988] ECR 111.   [296] Para. 29.

[297] Case 340/89 *Vlassopoulou* v. *Ministerium für Justiz, Bundes- und Europaangelegenheiten Baden-Württemberg* [1991] ECR I–2357, para. 15.

(b) The 'restrictions' approach

In respect of non-discriminatory national rules, the Court has changed its position.[298] As we saw in Chapter 7, while in the early days the Court thought that non-discriminatory rules did not breach Article 49 TFEU,[299] subsequent case law focused more on whether the rule nevertheless hindered market access or constituted a restriction on free movement. This can be seen in *Gebhard*.[300] Gebhard, a German lawyer (*Rechtsanwalt*) with chambers in Stuttgart, established a set of chambers in Milan and called himself *avvocato*. He was eventually suspended by the Milan Bar because he had been practising under the title *avvocato* without being registered with the Milan Bar. The Court focused on the obstacles to freedom of establishment created by the Italian rules. It said:[301]

> national measures liable to *hinder or make less attractive the exercise of fundamental freedoms* guaranteed by the Treaty must fulfil four conditions: they must be applied in a non-discriminatory manner; they must be justified by imperative requirements in the general interest; they must be suitable for securing the attainment of the objective which they pursue; and they must not go beyond what is necessary in order to attain it.

The decision in *Gebhard* marked a shift to the market access approach (even in cases of '*exercise*' of '*fundamental freedoms*' (and not just Article 49 TFEU)). Since *Gebhard* the case law has talked about whether the national measure is liable 'to prohibit, impede or render less attractive'[302] access to, or exercise of, the right of establishment rather than the elimination of discrimination. So, for example, in *Haim II*[303] the Court found that a language requirement imposed on dentists wishing to practise in Germany restricted establishment under Article 49 TFEU. In *Wouters*[304] the Court assumed that a Dutch rule prohibiting multi-disciplinary partnerships between members of the Bar and accountants constituted a restriction on the right of establishment. In *Commission v. Greece (computer games)*[305] the Court said a prohibition on traders from other Member States operating electronic and computer games breached Article 49 TFEU; and in *Apothekerkammer des Saarlandes*[306] the Court said that a rule excluding non-pharmacists from operating pharmacies, 'denying other economic operators access to this self-employed activity' constituted a restriction within the meaning of Article 49 TFEU. In all four cases the focus then shifted to the question of whether the national measure could be justified and the steps taken were proportionate.

---

[298] Except, probably, in the field of public procurement: Case C–64/08 *Engelmann* [2010] ECR I–8219.

[299] Case 221/85 *Commission* v. *Belgium (clinical laboratories)* [1987] ECR 719.

[300] Case C–55/94 [1995] ECR I–4165.

[301] Para. 37, emphasis added. See also Case C–19/92 *Kraus* [1993] ECR I–1663, considered further in Ch. 7.

[302] Case C–79/01 *Payroll Data Services (Italy) Srl, ADP Europe SA and ADP GSI SA* [2002] ECR I–8923, para. 26.

[303] Case C–424/97 *Haim* v. *Kassenzahnärtzliche Vereinigung Nordrhein (Haim II)* [2000] ECR I–5123, para. 57.

[304] Case C–309/99 *J.C.J. Wouters, J.W. Savelbergh and Price Waterhouse Belastingadviseurs BV* v. *Algemene Raad van de Nederlandse Orde van Advocaten* [2002] ECR I–1577, para. 122, and Art. 25 of the Services Dir. 2006/123, considered in Ch. 11.

[305] Case C–65/05 *Commission* v. *Greece (computer games)* [2006] ECR I–10341, paras. 50–2.

[306] Joined Cases C–171 and 172/07 *Apothekerkammer des Saarlandes* v. *Saarland* [2009] ECR I–4171, paras. 23–4. See also Case C–89/09 *Commission* v. *France (bio-medical analysis)* [2010] ECR I–12941, that non-biologists could not hold more than 25 per cent shares in a bio-medical company was a restriction on freedom of establishment (para. 49) but could be justified, but a prohibition on biologists holding capital in more than two companies could not.

The Court has tended to recognize a broad range of justifications put forward by the Member State. So, for example, in *Haim II* the Court found that the German-language requirement could be justified on the ground that dentists had to be able to communicate with their patients and the relevant authorities.[307] Although it recognized that there was a need for a certain number of dentists capable of communicating in Turkish to serve the Turkish community,[308] the Court indicated that the requirement to speak German could be justified on the facts. In *Commission* v. *Greece* the Court accepted in principle the Greek government's justification for excluding foreign operators from operating computer games because computer games were easy to adapt to become games of chance and this could lead to serious social problems, as well as the loss of tax revenue. However, the Court found the rules disproportionate because Greece had not established that it had implemented 'all the technical and organisational measures likely to have achieved the objective pursued by that Member State using measures which were less restrictive of intra-[Union] trade'.

(c) Restricting the restrictions approach

While the market access/restrictions approach has proved effective in attacking a wide range of rules which impede access to the market, we also know from the discussions in Chapters 1 and 7 that it can reach too deeply into the national systems and force a whole range of national rules to be justified where their effect on inter-state trade is in fact too remote or insubstantial. There are some signs that the Court has begun to recognize this as a problem and place limits on the reach of the restrictions approach by introducing a threshold requirement. This can be seen in the Grand Chamber decision of *Commission* v. *Italy (maximum fee for lawyers).*[309]

Italian law lays down rules requiring lawyers to comply with maximum tariffs for the calculation of their fees in the absence of an agreement between lawyer and client. The Commission argued that the rules had the effect of discouraging lawyers established in other Member States from establishing themselves in Italy. The Court disagreed. It said that the Italian rules did not constitute a restriction solely because other Member States applied less strict, or more commercially favourable, rules to providers of similar services established in their territory,[310] nor did they constitute a restriction just because service providers had to accustom themselves to a new set of rules.[311] The Court then said:

51. By contrast, such a restriction exists, in particular, if those lawyers are deprived of the opportunity of gaining access to the market of the host Member State under conditions of normal and effective competition ...

52. The Commission has not, however, demonstrated that the contested provisions have such an object or effect.

The Commission therefore failed to establish a breach of EU law.

Thus, the Court said expressly that mere differences between national rules are not sufficient to constitute a restriction. However, alongside this clarification comes complication, for the Court introduced, possibly for the first time, competition law concepts ('conditions of normal and effective competition ... object and effect') in order to elucidate the market access test.[312] In the past the Court has deliberately avoided requiring

---

[307] Case C–424/97 *Haim II* [2000] ECR I–5123, para. 59.
[308] Para. 60. Cf. Case 379/87 *Groener* [1989] ECR 3967.
[309] Case C–565/08 [2011] ECR I–2101.   [310] Para. 49.   [311] Para. 50.
[312] See also Case C–602/10 *SC Volksbank România* v. *CJPC* EU:C:2012:443, para. 80: 'it is not evident that that national provision renders access to the Romanian market less attractive and, in the event of access

economic analysis in the field of free movement since the litigants have generally been individuals who lack the resources to conduct such an analysis. The fact that this case was brought by the Commission, with the ability to produce more substantial economic evidence, might help to explain the Court's change in emphasis and its insistence, in subsequent cases, that the burden on the Commission is high: in *Commission v. Germany (care insurance)*[313] the Court said it was insufficient for the Commission merely to invoke the case law on restrictions, without precision or detailed explanations, as to why a restriction contrary to EU law existed on the facts.

3. THE EXERCISE OF ACTIVITIES AS A SELF-EMPLOYED PERSON

3.1 Equal Treatment and Beyond

So far we have considered the application of both the non-discrimination principle and the *Gebhard* hindrance/obstacle approach to national rules affecting *access* to self-employment. We turn now to consider the application of these principles to measures which interfere with the *exercise* of the profession, in particular in respect of the terms and conditions under which it is performed.[314]

As we have already seen, national measures which discriminate—either directly or indirectly—on the ground of nationality in respect of access to a profession are prohibited unless justified. The same rules apply to the *exercise* of a profession. *Commission v. Italy (dentists)*[315] is a good example of a directly discriminatory rule. Italian law provided that dentists who transferred their residence to another Member State lost their registration with the Italian dental association. Since this rule did not apply to Italian nationals the Court found that it breached Article 49 TFEU. Similarly, in *Commission v. Belgium (air traffic)*[316] the Court said that a Belgian law requiring 'foreigners' (i.e., non-Belgians) to have been resident in Belgium for at least one year in order to register an aircraft breached Article 49 TFEU. The Court said the rule 'clearly constitute[s] discrimination on the grounds of nationality which impedes the exercise of the freedom of establishment of those persons'.[317] Indirect discrimination is also prohibited, as *Fearon*[318] shows. The Court said that an exemption from an Irish rule on the compulsory acquisition of land for those who had resided for more than a year within three miles of the land was indirectly discriminatory but could be justified on grounds of preserving the ownership of land for those who worked on it.

As with the cases on access to the market, increasingly the Court has abandoned the equal treatment principle in favour of the formula based on removing obstacles or restrictions to the exercise of the freedom of establishment. This can be seen in *Konstantinidis*.[319] Konstantinidis, a Greek national, worked in Germany as a self-employed masseur and assistant hydrotherapist. Although his name was entered into the marriage register as Konsta*d*inidis, he argued that the correct transcription of his name from the Greek should have been Konsta*nt*inidis. He sought to have the register

[313] Case C–562/10 *Commission v. Germany* EU:C:2012:442, para. 52.
[314] See by analogy Art. 7(1) of Reg. 492/11, considered in this chapter.
[315] Case C–162/99 [2001] ECR I–541, para. 36.
[316] Case C–203/98 *Commission v. Belgium* [1999] ECR I–4899.   [317] Para. 13.
[318] Case C–182/83 [1985] ECR I–3677, paras. 10–11.
[319] Case C–168/91 *Christos Konstantinidis* v. *Stadt Altensteig* [1993] ECR I–1191.

corrected because, he said, the distortion of his name could cause potential clients to confuse him with other masseurs, and this interfered with his business contrary to Article 49 TFEU.[320]

Having noted that the Treaty did not prevent the transcription of a Greek name into Roman characters,[321] the Court began by using the discrimination framework to determine whether the national rules on transliteration were capable of placing Konstantinidis 'at a disadvantage in law or in fact, in comparison with the way in which a national of that Member State would be treated in the same circumstances'.[322] It said that the German rules breached Article 49 TFEU only insofar as their application caused a Greek national 'such a degree of inconvenience as in fact to interfere with his freedom to exercise the right of establishment'.[323] It continued that the interference would be sufficiently substantial if, as a result of the transcription, the spelling of Konstantinidis' name led to a modification of the pronunciation with the risk that clients might confuse him with others.[324]

While Advocate General Jacobs reached much the same conclusion, his approach was inspired by fundamental human rights[325] and not market values. He said that a Union national who goes to another Member State as a worker or a self-employed person was entitled not just to pursue his trade or profession and to enjoy the same living and working conditions as nationals of the host state but also to assume that:

> wherever he goes to earn a living in the European [Union], he will be treated in accordance with a common code of fundamental values, in particular those laid down in accordance with the European Convention on Human Rights. In other words, he is entitled to say *'civis europeus sum'* [I am a European citizen] and to invoke the status in order to oppose any violation of his fundamental rights.[326]

This Opinion, delivered just as the Treaty on European Union was being concluded, contained an important recognition of the changing attitude towards migrants: they were not only factors of production but were also citizens with fundamental (civil and political) rights. This approach eventually inspired the seminal decisions such in *Martínez Sala*[327] and *Baumbast*[328] on the free movement of citizens, cases considered in detail in Chapter 10.

In *Skanavi*[329] the Court was also encouraged to decide an establishment case under the citizenship provisions, but it declined. Mrs Skanavi, a Greek national working in Germany, had failed to exchange her Greek driving licence for a German one within one year of residence, as required by Union law. As a result, she was prosecuted for driving without a licence and fined. The Court said that while Member States were competent to impose penalties for a breach of such rules, they could not impose a penalty so disproportionate to the gravity of the infringement that this became an obstacle to the free

---

[320] For a similar case in the field of citizenship, but without the emphasis on interference with business, see Jacobs AG's Opinion in Case C–148/02 *Carlos Garcia Avello* v. *Etat Belge* [2003] ECR I–11613, considered further in Ch. 10.

[321] Para. 14.   [322] Para. 13.   [323] Para. 15.   [324] Para. 16.

[325] See, e.g., para. 40: 'A person's right to his name is fundamental in every sense of the word. After all, where are we without our name? It is our name that distinguishes each of us from the rest of humanity. It is our name that gives us a sense of identity, dignity and self-esteem. To strip a person of his rightful name is the ultimate degradation, as is evidenced by the common practice of repressive penal regimes which consists in substituting a number for a prisoner's name.'

[326] Para. 46.   [327] Case C–85/96 *Martínez Sala* v. *Freistaat Bayern* [1998] ECR I–2691.

[328] Case C–413/99 *Baumbast and R.* v. *Secretary of State for the Home Department* [2002] ECR I–7091.

[329] Case C–193/94 *Criminal Proceedings against Sofia Skanavi and Konstantin Chryssanthakopoulos* [1996] ECR I–929. See also Case C–476/01 *Kapper* [2004] ECR I–5205, para. 36.

movement of persons. For this reason the Court said that it would be disproportionate to treat a person who had failed to exchange her driving licence as if she were driving without a licence[330] because a criminal conviction would damage her ability to exercise certain trades or professions which would constitute a further, lasting restriction on free movement.[331]

Finally, in *Kemmler*[332] the Court adopted a different version of the obstacles formula: the Court said that a host-state rule requiring that social security contributions be made to a national scheme when the self-employed person already contributed to benefits in his home state where he habitually resided 'inhibits the pursuit of occupational activities outside the Member State' and so breached Article 49 TFEU unless the requirement could be justified.[333]

3.2 Enjoyment of Social Advantages

The principle of equal treatment also applies in respect of the enjoyment of various general facilities necessary to pursue self-employed activity—i.e., the enjoyment of social advantages, to use the term found in Article 7(2) of the Workers' Regulation 492/2011. While the original Establishment Directive did not contain any equivalent provision to Article 7(2), the Court has used Article 49 TFEU to achieve the same result (a position now supported by Article 24(1) CRD). This can be seen in *Steinhauser*,[334] a case concerning a German artist who was not allowed to participate in a tendering process for the use of an art and craft boutique in the French city of Biarritz, on the ground that he was not French. He claimed that he had been directly discriminated against contrary to Article 49 TFEU. The defendant local authority argued that Article 49 TFEU applied only to conditions regulating *access* to a profession and so did not apply to this case. The Court disagreed, ruling that Article 49 TFEU included the right not only to take up activities as a self-employed person but also to pursue those activities in the broadest sense,[335] including renting business premises.[336]

In other words, Mr Steinhauser should have enjoyed a social advantage (a boutique for selling his wares) on the same terms as nationals. Likewise, a migrant should enjoy housing 'under the same conditions as his competitors' who are nationals.[337] Therefore, in *Commission* v. *Italy (social housing)*[338] the Court said an Italian law allowing only Italians to purchase or lease housing built with the help of public funds and to obtain a reduced-rate mortgage breached Article 49 TFEU. In a similar vein the Court found in *Commission* v. *Greece (housing)*[339] that a rule allowing Greek nationals, but not migrants, to purchase immovable property breached Article 49 TFEU.

3.3 Taxation, Equal Treatment, and Beyond

As with Article 45 TFEU and Article 7(2) of Regulation 492/11 on workers, the Court has interpreted Article 49 TFEU to require equal treatment not only in respect of social advantages but also tax advantages for the self-employed (see also Article 24(1) CRD). Many of the cases concern claims by non-residents that they are being treated differently

---

[330] Case C–193/94 *Skanavi* [1996] ECR I–929, para. 37. [331] Para. 38.
[332] Case C–53/95 *Kemmler* [1996] ECR I–703, para. 12. [333] Para. 12.
[334] Case 197/84 *Steinhauser* v. *City of Biarritz* [1985] ECR 1819.
[335] The Court referred to the General Programme for the Abolition of Restrictions on the Freedom of Establishment, which expressly excluded the imposition of conditions on the power to exercise rights normally attached to the activity of a self-employed person, including submitting of tenders (OJ Spec. Ed. 2nd Series IX, 7 Restrictions, A).
[336] Para. 16. [337] Case 63/86 *Commission* v. *Italy (social housing)* [1988] ECR 29, para. 16.
[338] Case 63/86 [1988] ECR 29, para. 14. [339] Case 305/87 [1989] ECR 1461, para. 23.

to residents. In these cases the Court looks to see if the situation of the claimant is in fact similar to the position of a resident. If the situations are not similar then the Court finds no breach of Article 49 TFEU. If the situations are similar—particularly the case with 'frontier' self-employed workers—the Court then examines the question of discrimination. For example, *Wielockx*[340] concerned a Dutch law which provided that non-residents were not allowed to set up a pension reserve qualifying for deductions under the same tax conditions as those of a resident taxpayer. Wielockx was a self-employed Belgian national residing in Belgium who received his whole income from a partnership in a physiotherapy practice in the Netherlands. For this reason he was considered to be in objectively the same situation as a resident. The Court said that excluding him from favourable pension arrangements amounted to indirect discrimination contrary to Article 49 TFEU. It also found that such discrimination could not be justified on the ground of fiscal cohesion.[341]

Asscher[342] confirms that a residence criterion can be indirectly discriminatory. Asscher was a Dutch national who worked in Belgium while residing in the Netherlands and then moved to Belgium. Although he worked in a self-employed capacity in both countries, he was treated as a non-resident in the Netherlands and taxed at a higher rate than residents. The Court noted that a residence criterion was 'liable to act mainly to the detriment of nationals of other Member States, since non-residents are most frequently non-nationals'.[343] The rule therefore breached Article 49 TFEU[344] and, once again, could not be justified on the ground of ensuring cohesion of the tax system.[345]

While in most of the tax cases concerning the self-employed (or small family businesses[346]) the Court has relied on the traditional concepts of discrimination, in some cases the Court has resorted to the *Gebhard* hindrance/restriction formula, especially in respect of those national rules which discourage individuals from leaving their home state. This can be seen in *De Lasteyrie du Saillant*.[347] Under French law, a taxpayer wishing to leave France and establish himself elsewhere became liable to tax on income which had not yet been realized; had he stayed in France there would have been no such liability until increases in value were actually realized. The Court said that such a rule was liable to hinder freedom of establishment,[348] 'even if it is of limited scope or minor importance',[349] and could not, on the facts, be justified by generalized concerns to prevent tax avoidance.[350]

[340] Case C–80/94 *Wielockx v. Inspecteur der Directe Belastingen* [1995] ECR I–2493. See also Case C–346/04 *Conijn v. Finanzamt Hamburg-Nord* [2006] ECR I–6137.
[341] The question of justifications in respect of taxation is considered further in Ch. 12.
[342] Case C–107/94 *Asscher v. Staatssecretaris van Financiën* [1996] ECR I–3089, para. 38; Case C–329/05 *Finanzamt Dinslaken v. Meindl* [2007] ECR I–1107, para. 28. Cf. Case C–104/06 *Commission v. Sweden (sale of residential property)* [2007] ECR I–671, para. 25, where the Court used the *Gebhard* language of hindrance to describe the residence criteria.
[343] Para. 38.   [344] Para. 49.
[345] Cf. Case C–302/12 *X v. Minister van Financiën* EU:C:2013:756, para. 31, where the Court found the rule to 'result only from the non-discriminatory exercise of the tax systems of both Member States concerned' and so did not breach Art. 49 TFEU.
[346] Case C–464/05 *Geurts v. Administratie van de BTW* [2007] ECR I–9325, paras. 20–2.
[347] Case C–9/02 *De Lasteyrie du Saillant v. Ministère de l'Economie, des Finances et de l'Industrie* [2004] ECR I–2409. See also Case C–314/08 *Filipiak v. Dyrektor Izby Skarbowej w Poznaniu* [2009] ECR I–11049, para. 67.
[348] Para. 48.   [349] Para. 43.
[350] The same applies to those wishing to receive services such as insurance from another Member State: Case C–150/04 *Commission v. Denmark (insurance)* [2007] ECR I–1163, para. 76.

E. QUALIFICATIONS

1. THE CONTEXT

The refusal by a host state to recognize qualifications acquired in other EU states has represented a serious practical obstacle to free movement of workers and freedom of establishment. Although Article 53 TFEU allows the Council to adopt directives for the mutual recognition of diplomas, for many years the requirement of unanimity in Council[351] slowed the process (the Directive on Architects[352] alone took 17 years to agree), and the directives were also limited in scope (e.g., the Directive on Lawyers' Services[353] applied only to services and not to establishment).[354] Nevertheless a number of so-called vertical directives were adopted, harmonizing the diverse national rules profession by profession. This led to directives on doctors, nurses, dentists, and vets,[355] as well as a number of directives concerning a range of industries such as manufacturing and processing, small craft, food and retail,[356] the activities of intermediaries, and the building industry.[357] The advantage of these directives was that once the individual had completed the minimum training specified in the directive and acquired the qualification, then recognition was automatic:[358] the host state had to accept the equivalence of the qualifications and could not require the individual to comply with requirements other than those laid down by the relevant directives.[359]

But this approach left many sectors not covered by harmonization, which left the Court with the task of reconciling (1) the host state's legitimate need for qualified people to do certain jobs with (2) the fundamental principle of freedom of movement. In the early days the Court said that if Union law had not laid down provisions to secure the objective of freedom of establishment, the Member States and legally recognized professional bodies[360] retained the jurisdiction to adopt the necessary measures,[361] provided that they complied with the obligations of cooperation laid down by Article 4(3) TEU[362] and the principle of non-discrimination.[363] This point was made in *Patrick*,[364] where a British architect applied for authorization to practise in France but his application was rejected

---

[351] Now the ordinary legislative procedure applies.

[352] Council Dir. 85/384/EEC ([1985] OJ L223/15) (now repealed and replaced by the RPQ Dir. 2005/36).

[353] Council Dir. 77/249/EEC ([1977] OJ L78/17). See Case 427/85 *Commission v. Germany (Re lawyer's services)* [1988] ECR 1123; Case C–294/89 *Commission v. France* [1991] ECR I–3591.

[354] However, see now EP and Council Dir. 98/5/EC ([1998] OJ L77/36) to facilitate practice of the profession of lawyer on a permanent basis in a Member State other than that in which the qualification was obtained. These directives are considered in Ch. 9.

[355] See, e.g., Dirs. 75/362/EEC ([1975] OJ L167/1) and 75/363/EEC ([1975] OJ L167/14) on doctors, 77/452/EEC ([1977] OJ L176/1) on nurses responsible for general care, 78/686/EEC ([1978] OJ L233/1) on dentists. These directives have now been repealed and replaced by the Recognition of Professional Qualifications (RPQ) Dir. 2005/36 ([2005] OJ L255/22).

[356] See, e.g., Dirs. 64/427/EEC ([1963–4] OJ Spec. Ed. (I) 148), 75/369/EEC ([1995] OJ L167/29), and 68/367 ([1968] OJ Spec. Ed. (I) Ch. II–513). These directives have now been repealed and replaced by the RPQ Dir.

[357] Dir. 64/224/EEC ([1963–4] OJ Spec. Ed. (I) 126). This directive has now been repealed and replaced by the RPQ Dir.

[358] Case C–154/93 *Abdullah Tawil-Albertini v. Ministre des Affaires Sociales* [1994] ECR I–451, para. 11.

[359] Case C–238/98 *Hocsman v. Ministre de l'Emploi et de la Solidarité* [2000] ECR I–6623, para. 33.

[360] Case 71/76 *Thieffry v. Conseil de l'ordre des avocats à la Cour de Paris* [1977] ECR 765.

[361] Case 292/86 *Gullung* [1988] ECR 111.

[362] Case 222/86 *UNECTEF v. Heylens* [1987] ECR 4097, para. 10.

[363] Case C–61/89 *Criminal Proceedings against Marc Gaston Bouchoucha* [1990] ECR I–3551.

[364] Case 11/77 *Patrick v. Ministre des affaires culturelles* [1977] ECR 1199.

on the ground that there was neither a diplomatic convention between the UK and France concerning the mutual recognition of certificates nor an EU directive on recognition of architectural qualifications.[365] However, the Court said that the need for directives had 'become superfluous with regard to implementing the rule on nationality since this is henceforth sanctioned by the Treaty itself with direct effect'.[366] Therefore, the French authorities could not, on the grounds of nationality, deny Patrick the right to establish himself, nor could they require him to satisfy additional conditions (such as being authorized to practise) which were not applicable to nationals.

However, the principle of non-discrimination could itself be an obstacle to free movement. If an individual has taken six years to qualify as a lawyer in State A, the principle of non-discrimination would probably allow the authorities in State B to permit the individual to practise but on the same terms as nationals (i.e., by recommencing their studies in State B, thus taking several further years to qualify). For this reason, in the seminal case of *Vlassopoulou*[367] the Court shifted the emphasis to mutual recognition. A Greek lawyer who worked in Germany advising on Greek and EU law had her application to join the local German Bar rejected on the ground that she had not pursued her university studies in Germany, had not sat the two German state exams, and had not completed the preparatory stage, although she did hold a German doctorate. The Court ruled that:[368]

> national requirements concerning qualifications may have the effect of *hindering nationals of the other Member States in the exercise* of their right of establishment guaranteed to them by Article [49 TFEU]. That could be the case if the national rules in question took no account of the knowledge and qualifications already acquired by the person concerned in another Member State.

The Court then elaborated on the principle of mutual recognition. It said that the host state had to compare a migrant's qualifications and abilities with those required by the national system to see whether the applicant had the appropriate skills to join the equivalent profession. If the comparison revealed that the holder had the knowledge and qualifications which were, if not identical, then at least equivalent to the national diploma, then the host state was obliged to recognize the diploma. If, on the other hand, the comparison revealed that the applicant only partially fulfilled the necessary qualifications, then the host Member State could require the applicant to demonstrate that she had acquired the relevant knowledge and qualifications, which then had to be taken into account.[369] The Court added that to ensure that the Member States complied with the obligations inherent in the principle of mutual recognition, the decision-making body had to give reasons for its decisions, which also had to be reviewable by the courts to verify compatibility with Union law.[370]

Vlassopoulou effectively pre-empted the 'diabolically complex and completely unnecessary'[371] Council Directive 89/48/EEC on mutual recognition of higher education

---

[365] However, see Council Dir. 85/384/EEC ([1985] OJ L223/15) on the mutual recognition of formal qualifications in architecture now repealed and replaced by the RPQ Dir.

[366] Para. 13.   [367] Case C–340/89 [1991] ECR I–2357.

[368] Para. 15, emphasis added. See also Case C–19/92 *Kraus* [1993] ECR I–1663, para. 32.

[369] Paras. 17–21. In Case C–345/08 *Krzystof Peśla* [2009] ECR I–11049 the Court said that EU law required the host state to carry out the examination of equivalence in the light of the academic and professional training and experience as a whole before requiring a candidate to take an aptitude test. The knowledge to be taken as a reference point for the purposes of assessing whether a candidate can be admitted directly to a legal traineeship, was that attested by the qualification required in the host state.

[370] C–104/91 *Colegio Oficial de Agentes de la Propriedad Inmobiliaria v. José Luis Aguirre Borrell and others* [1992] ECR I–3003, para. 16.

[371] J. Lonbay (1991) 16 *ELRev.* 507, 516.

diplomas and the complementary Directive 92/51/EEC[372] on lower level training, so-called 'horizontal' directives adopted to complement and gradually replace the existing vertical directives. Nevertheless the EU proceeded with these directives and subsequently added a third, Directive 99/42/EC,[373] extending the mutual recognition approach to the industrial and professional sectors previously covered by earlier vertical directives. As the Court put it in *Commission* v. *Greece*,[374] these so-called 'general-system' directives essentially establish 'a presumption that the qualifications of an applicant entitled to pursue a regulated profession in one Member States are sufficient for the pursuit of that profession in the other Member States'. Most significantly, the general-system directives were not intended to harmonize the conditions for taking up or pursuit of the various professions: this remained a matter for Member States' competence 'within the limits imposed by [Union] law'.[375] Although this approach avoided some of the problems associated with the negotiation of sector-specific directives, the gain came at a price. The general-system directives did not guarantee automatic recognition;[376] they merely required the host state authorities to consider the migrant's qualifications and, if the qualifications proved to be lacking in terms of duration and content, the host state could impose additional requirements.

In an attempt to reorganize, rationalize, and standardize the principles which applied across both the vertical and horizontal directives, the Parliament and Council adopted a single directive, Directive 2005/36,[377] repealing and replacing the earlier directives on the recognition of professional qualifications (RPQ Directive). It is a complicated directive, running to 120 pages including annexes. The next sections give an outline of some of the key principles underpinning the RPQ Directive. Where the directives do not apply, the host Member State remains competent to define the exercise of the particular activities,[378] including the power to impose criminal penalties on a national of another Member State for the illegal pursuit of a regulated profession,[379] provided that the host state respects Article 49 TFEU and the principles in *Vlassopoulou* in particular.[380]

2. THE RPQ DIRECTIVE

2.1 The Basic Rules

The RPQ Directive applies to all nationals of a Member State wishing to pursue a 'regulated profession' in a Member State other than that in which they obtained their professional qualifications on either a self-employed or employed basis.[381] It thus covers

[372] [1989] OJ L19/16 and [1992] OJ L209/25.   [373] [1999] OJ L201/77.
[374] Case C–274/05 *Commission* v. *Greece* [2008] ECR I–7969, para. 30.
[375] Case C–274/05 *Commission* v. *Greece* [2008] ECR I–7969, para. 38. The directives also do not concern the choice of recruitment and selection procedure for filling posts and they cannot be relied on as the basis for the right actually to be recruited: Case C–586/08 *Rubino* [2009] ECR I–12013, para. 27.
[376] Case C–39/07 *Commission* v. *Spain (hospital pharmacists)* [2008] ECR I–3435, para. 39.
[377] [2005] OJ L255/22.   [378] Case C–108/96 *Mac Quen* [2001] ECR I–837, para. 24.
[379] Case C–104/91 *Borrell* [1992] ECR I–3003, para. 19.
[380] Case C–164/94 *Georgios Aranitis* v. *Land Berlin* [1996] ECR I–135; Case C–456/05 *Commission* v. *Germany (psychotherapists)* [2007] ECR I–10517; Case C–586/08 *Rubino* v. *Ministero dell'Università e della Ricerca* [2009] ECR I–12013, para. 34; Case C–477/13 *Eintragungsausschuss bei der Bayerischen Architektenkammer* EU:C:2015:239, para. 42: 'the Member States must comply with their obligations in relation to the mutual recognition of professional qualifications pursuant to Article 49 TFEU, where the applicant cannot avail himself of the mechanism of recognition of professional qualification provided for by the relevant directive'.
[381] Art. 2(1). In Case C–39/07 *Commission* v. *Spain (hospital pharmacists)* [2008] ECR I–3435, para. 33 the Court has added that 'a profession is deemed regulated ... where access to the professional activity

those moving under Articles 45, 49, and 56 TFEU. A regulated profession involves the pursuit of a 'professional activity'[382] access to which is subject to the possession of specific professional qualifications[383] which, in turn, are defined as qualifications attested by evidence of formal qualifications, an 'attestation of competence', and/or professional experience.[384] In principle, the host state must recognize qualifications obtained in one or more states which allow their holder to pursue the same qualification there.[385] Article 4(1) adds:

> The recognition of professional qualifications by the host Member State allows the beneficiary to gain access in that Member State to the same[386] profession as that for which he is qualified in the home state and to pursue it in the host Member State under the same conditions as its nationals.

The directive then distinguishes between those providing services on a temporary basis (Title II) and those wishing to establish themselves on a permanent basis (Title III). We shall consider these two situations in turn.

2.2 Free Provision of Services

According to Article 5(1), any Member State national legally established in a Member State (State A) may provide services on a temporary and occasional basis, account being taken of the duration, frequency, regularity, and continuity of the provision of services, in another Member State (State B) under their original professional title without having to apply for recognition of their qualifications. However, if service providers relocate outside their Member State of establishment (State A) in order to provide services, they must also provide evidence of two years' professional experience if the profession in question is not regulated in State A.[387] Conversely, if the profession is regulated, then the two years' practice cannot be required.[388]

The directive lays down a number of administrative provisions, including the possibility for the host state, State B, to require the service provider to make a declaration prior to providing any services on its territory, to renew it annually, and to give details of any insurance cover or other means of personal or collective protection with regard to professional liability.[389] State B can also require that the first application be accompanied by certain documents listed in Article 7(2), such as proof of the nationality of the service provider, of their legal establishment, and of their professional qualifications. State B can also require that, where the service is provided under the professional title of the Member State of establishment or under the formal qualification of the service provider, service providers furnish the recipient of the service with certain information, particularly with regard to insurance coverage against the financial risks connected with any challenge to their professional liability.[390]

---

constituting that profession or its exercise is governed by laws, regulations or administrative provisions creating a system under which that professional activity is expressly reserved to those who fulfil certain conditions and access to it is prohibited to those who do not fulfil them'.

[382] Art. 1(c).   [383] Art. 3(1)(a).

[384] Art. 3(1)(b). In Case C–424/09 *Toki* v. *Ipourgos Ethnikis Pedias kai Thriskevmaton* [2011] ECR I–2587, para. 35 the Court said that it is sufficient for that experience to involve, 'in a framework of full-time work, the continuous and regular pursuit of a range of professional activities which characterise the profession concerned, but it need not cover all those activities'. The office of legal secretary at the Cour de cassation is not a regulated profession: Case C–298/14 *Brouillard* v. *Jury du concours de recrutement de référendaires près la Cour de cassation* EU:C:2015:652, para. 45 (and so the Treaty, not the RPQ applied (para. 53)).

[385] Art. 1.   [386] I.e., 'the activities covered are comparable': Art. 4(2).

[387] Art. 5(1)(b).   [388] Art. 5(1)(b).   [389] Art. 7(1).   [390] Art. 9.

2.3 Freedom of Establishment

The directive also makes provision for a professional to become established in another Member State in order to conduct a professional activity there on a stable basis. The directive comprises the three existing systems of recognition:

- the general system for the recognition of professional qualifications (Chapter I)
- the system of automatic recognition of qualifications attested by professional experience in certain industrial, craft, and commercial sectors (Chapter II)
- the system of automatic recognition of qualifications for specific professions (doctor, nurse, dentist, vet, midwife, pharmacist, and architect (Chapter III)).

However, as the Court has made clear in *Commission v. Spain (pharmacists)*, 'the right to recognition of diplomas is guaranteed as an expression of the fundamental right of freedom of establishment',[391] so any interpretation of the directive must be read subject to Article 49 TFEU. We shall now consider the three situations envisaged by the directive.

(a) The general system for the recognition of professional qualifications

This 'general' system applies as a fallback to all the professions not covered by specific rules of recognition (Chapters II and III considered at (b) and (c)) and to certain situations where the migrant professional does not meet the conditions set out in other recognition schemes.[392] This general system is based on the principle of mutual recognition, subject to the application of compensatory measures if there are substantial differences[393] in the levels of training between the home and host states.[394]

The basic rules are set out in Article 13, which distinguishes between two situations. The first concerns access to, or pursuit of, a 'regulated profession' (i.e., a professional activity access to which is subject to one of the five levels[395] of professional qualifications[396]) in both the home state (State A) and the host state (State B).[397] Here the competent authority in State B may not refuse, on the grounds of inadequate qualifications, to authorize a national of another Member State access to, and pursuit of, the profession under the same conditions as for nationals, provided that the applicant holds a training qualification obtained in another Member State (State A), issued by a competent authority, which attests to a level of training at least equivalent to the level immediately below[398] that required in the host Member State.[399] There are five levels of qualifications identified in Directive 2005/36, reflecting the levels in the three original general-system directives. These range from the lowest (level (a) 'attestation of competence') to the highest (levels (d) and (e) 'diplomas',[400] which require

---

[391] Case C–39/07 *Commission v. Spain (pharmacists)* [2008] ECR I–3435, para. 37.   [392] Art. 10.

[393] According to Joined Cases C–422, 425 and 426/09 *Vandorou v. Ipourgos Ethnikis Pedias kai Thriskevmaton* [2010] ECR I–12411, in setting those compensatory measures account must be taken of all practical experience which, in whole or part, covers those differences.

[394] In accordance with recital 14 in the preamble to the RPQ Dir., the recasting by that directive does not affect the mechanism of recognition established by Dirs. 89/48 and 92/51. See also Case C–586/08 *Rubino* [2009] ECR I–12013, para. 27.

[395] Art. 11.   [396] Art. 3(1)(a).   [397] Art. 13(1).

[398] This requirement, while at first sight surprising, reflects the fact that in some states acquiring a qualification takes longer than others without in any way reflecting the quality of the qualification. So in the UK it takes on average three years to obtain a degree; in other states it takes four to five years.

[399] Art. 13(1).

[400] Diplomas may be composed of a set of documents evidencing formal qualifications: Case C–286/06 *Commission v. Spain* [2008] ECR I–8025, para. 55. It is sufficient that the education and training were received 'mainly' in the Union. The education and training may have been received wholly or partly in a Member State other than the one which awarded the qualification (see also Case C–274/05 *Commission v. Greece* [2008] ECR I–7969, para. 28).

three- or four-year university degrees or equivalent plus professional training).[401] Any of the qualifications must be issued by a competent authority in a Member State, designated in accordance with the legislative, regulatory, or administrative provisions of that Member State.[402] It is up to the competent authorities of the awarding state to ensure the quality of the training and education and to verify, in the light of the rules applicable within the framework of their professional education and training system, whether the conditions necessary for their award are fulfilled.[403] This means, for example, that State B cannot refuse to recognize a diploma awarded by a competent authority in State A because the education and training in State A or B leading to the award of the diploma was provided by a body which could not have been recognized as an educational establishment in State B.[404]

The second situation identified in Article 13 of the directive is where the profession concerned is not regulated in State A[405] but it is regulated in State B and subject to the possession of specific professional qualifications. In this situation State B must grant access to and pursuit of the profession to applicants who have pursued that profession for two years full-time in State A over the preceding ten years.

In either the first or second situations, the host Member State can make recognition of qualifications subject to the applicant's completing compensatory measures,[406] namely an aptitude test[407] or an adaptation period[408] of up to three years if:[409]

- the training is one year shorter than that required by the host Member State or
- the training received covers substantially different matters to those covered by the formal training required in the host Member State or
- the profession as defined in the host Member State comprises one or more regulated professional activities which do not exist in the corresponding profession in the applicant's home Member State, and that difference consists of specific training which covers substantially different matters from those covered by the migrant.

The host Member State must, in principle, offer the applicant the choice between an adaptation period and an aptitude test[410] but it can derogate from this requirement in respect of those professions requiring a precise knowledge of national law and in respect of which the provision of advice and/or assistance concerning national law is an essential and constant aspect of the professional activity.[411] It can also derogate with the Commission's permission.[412]

---

[401] Art. 11. Therefore, a solicitor awarded the title by the Law Society, having completed a three-year university degree followed by a vocational training course (the Legal Practice Course) and who has completed a two-year training contract, holds a 'diploma' for the purpose of the directive.

[402] Art. 13(1) and (2).

[403] Case C–151/07 *Khatzithanansis* v. *OEEK* [2008] ECR I–9013, paras. 30–1.

[404] Para. 34.   [405] Art. 13(2).

[406] Art. 14. However, states must have legislated to this effect: Case C–142/04 *Aslanidou* v. *Ypourgas Ygeias & Pronoias* [2005] ECR I–7181, para. 35. See also Case C–141/04 *Peros* v. *Techniko Epimelitirio* [2005] ECR I–7163.

[407] Art. 3(1)(h).

[408] Adaptation period means a period of supervised practice in the host state under the responsibility of a qualified member of the profession, possibly accompanied by further training; the period of supervised practice is the subject of an assessment (Art. 3(1)(g)).

[409] Art. 14(1).   [410] Art. 14(2), first para.

[411] Art. 14(3). For a consideration of the meaning of this phrase, see Case C–149/05 *Price* v. *Conseil des ventes volontaires de meubles aux enchères publiques* [2006] ECR I–7691; Case C–118/09 *Koller* [2010] ECR I–13627. In Case C–197/06 *Confederatie van Immobiliën-Beroepen van België VZW* v. *Van Leuken* [2008] ECR I–2627, paras. 35–8, the Court indicated that a profession which is, in the host Member State, open to persons who have not received significant education and training in law cannot be considered to be one 'whose practice requires precise knowledge of national law' and the derogation did not apply to the profession of estate agent in Belgium. The situations listed in the derogation are exhaustive: Case C–274/05 *Commission* v. *Greece* [2008] ECR I–7969, para. 44.

[412] Art. 14(2), paras. 2–3.

In *Colegio de Ingenieros*[413] the Court noted that compensatory measures had to be restricted to those cases where they were proportionate to the objective pursued because, due to the time and effort involved, they could be a 'highly dissuasive factor for a national of a Member State exercising his right under the Directive'. For this reason the Court ruled that the directive did permit the 'partial' taking up of a regulated profession, thereby allowing the migrant professional to dispense with the requirement of having to comply with the compensatory measures and allowing him to take up his professional activities immediately. This meant that in principle an Italian engineer qualified only in hydraulics could take up the more general profession of civil engineer in Spain. Although this might lead to some confusion on the part of the consumer, the Court said this could be avoided by requiring the migrant professional to mention the names and locations of the bodies or examining board which awarded them their academic titles and/or require the professional to use their titles in the original language form as well as in translation.[414]

The 2005 directive also introduces the concept of 'common platforms', drawn up by representative professional associations, which are suitable for compensating for substantial differences which have been identified between the training requirements existing in the various Member States for a given profession.[415] If such a platform is likely to make the mutual recognition of qualifications easier, the Commission can submit it to the Member States and adopt an implementing measure.[416] In these circumstances, the host state must waive the imposition of compensatory measures on applicants who meet the platform's conditions.

(b) System of automatic recognition of qualifications attested by professional experience in certain industrial, craft, and commercial activities

As we have seen, Chapter I of the directive offers a qualified version of mutual recognition: mutual recognition applies subject to the application of compensatory measures if there are substantial differences between the training acquired by the migrant and the training required in the host Member State. Chapter II contains the second approach to mutual recognition found in the original sector-specific directives. The industrial, craft, and commercial activities listed in the directive[417] are subject to the *automatic* recognition of qualifications attested by professional experience provided that conditions concerning the duration and form of professional experience (in a self-employed or employed capacity) are satisfied.[418] Account is also taken of previous training and this may reduce the amount of professional experience required. All previous training should, however, be proven by a certificate recognized by the Member State or judged by a competent professional body to be fully valid. Thus, Chapter II of the directive offers an unqualified version of mutual recognition.

(c) System of automatic recognition of qualifications for specific professions

Chapter III deals with specific professions. As with the previous sector-specific directives, each Member State must automatically recognize certificates of training, on the basis of

---

[413] Case C–330/03 *Colegio de Ingenieros de Caminos, Canales y Puertos* v. *Adminstración del Estado* [2006] ECR I–801, para. 24. See also Case C–197/06 *Van Leuken* [2008] ECR I–2627, paras. 40–1.

[414] Para. 25.   [415] Art. 15(1).   [416] Art. 15(2).

[417] I.e., those sectors previously covered by professional activity covered by the former 'transitional' directives (Dirs. 64/222/EEC, 64/427/EEC, 68/364/EEC, 68/366/EEC, 68/368/EEC, 70/523/EEC, 75/368/EEC, 75/369/EEC, 82/470/EEC, and 82/489/EEC, already consolidated by Dir. 1999/42/EC).

[418] Arts. 17–19.

coordination of the minimum training conditions, covering the professions of doctors, nurses responsible for general care, dental practitioners, specialized dental practitioners, veterinary surgeons, midwives, pharmacists, and architects.[419] For the qualification to be recognized, the directive lays down minimum training conditions and the minimum duration of studies for each of these professions. The formal qualifications conforming to the directive issued by the Member States are listed in an annex (Annex V). Holders of these qualifications can practise their profession in any Member State. The effect of Chapter III is therefore unqualified mutual recognition combined with partial harmonization (of the training requirements).

(d) Common provisions

Chapter IV of Title III of the Directive contains the procedure for submitting a request for mutual recognition of professional qualifications.[420] It also permits migrant professionals to use the title conferred on them by the home state as well as the professional title of the corresponding host Member State.[421] If a profession is regulated in the host Member State by a private association or organization, the migrant must also be able to become a member of that organization or association and thus be able to use the corresponding title.[422]

Title IV contains detailed rules for pursuing the profession, including the possibility for the host state to require migrants to have knowledge of the relevant language necessary for practising the profession.[423] It also requires close collaboration between the competent authorities in the host Member State and the home Member State,[424] by, for example, requiring each Member State to designate a coordinator to facilitate the uniform application of the directive[425] and to designate contact points which must provide citizens with information on the recognition of professional qualifications and to assist them in enforcing their rights, particularly through contact with the competent authorities to rule on requests for recognition.[426]

(e) Abuse

States have long expressed a concern about the provisions of the directives being abused, a concern the Court acknowledged in *Commission v. Spain (engineers)*[427] but ultimately dismissed: the fact that nationals of a Member State wishing to pursue a regulated profession choose to qualify for that profession in their preferred Member State cannot of itself constitute an abuse. Therefore, Spain's refusal to recognize an engineering qualification granted by the Italian authorities on the basis of studies carried out solely in Spain but coordinated by an Italian university, and involving an exam in Italy, meant that Spain breached the directive.

The issue arose again, in a more blatant case of bootstrapping in *Consiglio degli Ingegneri*.[428] In both Italy and Spain the profession of engineer is conditional on possession of a university diploma and registration in the register of the relevant professional

---

[419] The directive also recognizes the principle of automatic recognition for medical and dental specializations common to at least two Member States under existing law but limits future additions to Dir. 2005/36 to those that are common to at least two-fifths of the Member States.

[420] Arts. 50–1.   [421] Art. 52(1).   [422] Art. 52(2).

[423] See, e.g., Case E–1/11 *Norwegian Appeal Board for Health Personnel v. Dr A* [2011] EFTA Ct. Rep. 484.

[424] Art. 56(1).

[425] Art. 56(4). This is facilitated by the use of the internal market information system (IMI): Dir. 2013/55 ([2013] OJ L354/132).

[426] Art. 57.

[427] See, e.g., Case C–286/06 *Commission v. Spain* [2008] ECR I–8025, paras. 69–72.

[428] Case C–311/06 *Consiglio degli Ingegneri v. Ministero della Giustizia, Marco Cavallera* [2009] ECR I–415.

body. In addition, the Italian, but not the Spanish, system provides for a state examination which a candidate must pass in order to be entitled to pursue the profession. Cavallera held a first degree in mechanical engineering awarded by the University of Turin (Italy) after three years' education. He then applied for, and obtained, homologation in Spain of his Italian qualification (i.e., certification that his Italian degree was equivalent to a corresponding Spanish degree); this in turn allowed him to accede to the regulated profession in Spain, because Spain did not require an additional state examination. On the basis of the certificate of homologation, Cavallera enrolled in the register of one of the 'colegios de ingenieros técnicos industriales' in Catalonia, in order to pursue the regulated profession of industrial technical engineer in Spain, specializing in mechanical engineering. However, he never worked in Spain, nor did he follow any course of study nor take any exams under the Spanish education system, nor did he take the state examination provided for under Italian legislation for the purpose of being entitled to pursue the profession of engineer. Nevertheless, he wanted to rely on the mutual recognition of diplomas directive to gain access to the profession of engineer in Italy, even though he had not sat the state examination required under Italian law.

Without relying on the abuse of law doctrine, the Court said Cavallera could not rely on the directive. It said that a 'diploma' did not include a certificate issued by a Member State (Spain) which did not attest to any education or training covered by the education system of that Member State and was not based on either an examination taken or professional experience acquired in that Member State.[429] Were the directive to apply, this would be tantamount to allowing a person who had merely obtained a qualification in the Member State in which he studied (Italy), which did not in itself provide access to that regulated profession, nonetheless to gain access to that profession, even though the homologation certificate obtained elsewhere (Spain) provided no evidence that the holder had acquired an additional qualification or professional experience.[430] That would be contrary to the principle, enshrined in the directive, that Member States reserve the option of fixing the minimum level of qualification necessary to guarantee the quality of services provided within their territory.[431]

The line between legitimate exercise of free movement, such as in the *Commission v. Spain (engineers)* case, and situations deemed to fall outside the ambit of the directive, as illustrated by *Consiglio degli Ingegneri*, is clearly a thin one. In both situations, the applicants had spent the entirety of their studies in the Member State in which they later sought to work as engineers. Similarly, in both cases, the academic qualifications as between the relevant systems (Spain and Italy) were deemed equivalent by competent authorities; the only difference being that in *Commission v. Spain (engineers)*, an Italian university certified the Spanish course as equivalent to its own before the students took up their studies, whereas in *Consiglio degli Ingegneri* the Spanish ministry of education merely certified the equivalence between Cavallera's Italian degree and the degrees awarded in the Spanish system *ex post*. The only distinction of any significance that it seems to be possible to draw between the two situations is that the students in the *Commission v. Spain (engineers)* case also went to Italy to pass the Italian state exam for engineers at the end of their studies, whereas Cavallera could not point to any qualification or experience obtained in Spain. The outcome of the *Consiglio degli Ingegneri* case would have been different if Cavallera had worked, even for a very short time, in Spain before returning to Italy.[432]

---

[429] Case C–311/06 *Consiglio degli Ingegneri* [2009] ECR I–415, para. 56.   [430] Para. 57.
[431] Para. 57.   [432] I am grateful to Carsten Zatschler for this point.

(f) Qualifications obtained in third countries

A particular problem has arisen in respect of Union nationals who, after acquiring professional qualifications in a third country, return to work in Member State A which does recognize their qualification before going to work in State B which does not. Does Union law require the authorities in State B to apply the directives or the *Vlassopoulou* principles? At first the answer seemed to be no[433] but in *Haim I*[434] the Court said that State B was required to conduct a *Vlassopoulou*-type comparison, examining whether and to what extent the *experience* already acquired in another Member State corresponded to that required by State B.[435] In *Hocsman*[436] the Court went one stage further. It required State B to take account of all of the *formal qualifications* acquired elsewhere as well as practical experience when making the *Vlassopoulou* comparison. Hocsman, an Argentinian, acquired Spanish nationality in 1986 and then became a French citizen in 1998. His Argentine medical diploma was recognized by the authorities in Spain, where he was authorized to practise as a specialist in urology in 1986. He was, however, refused permission to practise in France owing to the fact he held an Argentine diploma. Clarifying its earlier case law,[437] the Court said that the French authorities had to take into consideration:

> all the diplomas, certificates and other evidence of formal qualifications of the person concerned and his relevant experience, by comparing the specialised knowledge and abilities so certified and that experience with the knowledge and qualifications required by the national rules.[438]

Similar principles are applied to highly qualified third-country national (TCN) employees wishing to work in the EU under the blue card scheme.[439] This is considered further in Chapter 13.

F. CONCLUSIONS

In the case law on workers it is possible to detect the embryo of what later became EU citizenship. In particular, the Court's decisions on social advantages under Article 7(2) of Regulation 492/11 went far beyond what was necessary to ensure the mobility of workers. The ever-expanding rights given to the worker's family members provided the testing ground for the Court's more ambitious jurisprudence on rights for EU citizens who are not economically active.[440] And now, in cases such as *Collins*, we see how the Court has used its citizenship case law to justify removing limitations on the exercise of Union rights. It is, however, this broad and generous reading of the citizenship provisions which has created the conditions for mistrust of EU rules on free movement in some Member States, in particular the UK.

The human rights orientation which underpins much of the Court's case law on workers is less visible in respect of freedom of establishment. In this area we see a greater preoccupation with ensuring that individuals gain access to the host state's market and

---

[433] Case C–154/93 [1994] ECR I–451.   [434] Case C–319/92 [1994] ECR I–425.

[435] Para. 29. Haim then sued the German Association of Dental Practitioners of Social Security Schemes for *Factortame III* damages for the loss suffered by being denied the possibility of practising as a dentist for the scheme: Case C–424/97 *Haim II* [2000] ECR I–5123.

[436] Case C–238/98 [2000] ECR I–6623.   [437] Para. 30.   [438] Para. 35.

[439] Dir. 2009/50 ([2009] OJ L155/17). The UK, Ireland, and Denmark are not taking part.

[440] See, e.g., Case C–184/99 *Grzelczyk* [2001] ECR I–6193, considered further in Ch. 12.

do not suffer impediments once on that market. In this respect the establishment case law has more in common with the case law on services. It is to this subject that we turn in Chapter 9.

FURTHER READING

Commission Communications on free movement

Commission Communication, 'Reaffirming the free movement of workers: Rights and major developments', COM(2010) 373.

Commission Staff Working Document, *Free Movement of Workers in the public sector*, SEC(2010) 1609.

Commission Staff Working Document, *Impact Assessment on measures facilitating the exercise of rights conferred on workers in the context of free movement of workers*, SEC(2013) 149.

On the link between free movement of workers and EU citizenship

A. CASTRO OLIVEIRA, 'Workers and other persons: Step-by-step from movement to citizenship—Case law 1995–2001' (2002) 39 *CMLRev.* 77.

S. O'LEARY, 'Developing an ever closer union between the peoples of Europe? A reappraisal of the case law of the Court of Justice on the free movement of persons and EU citizenship' (2008) 27 *YEL* 167.

On the shift from the principle of equal treatment to the market access test

E. JOHNSON and D. O'KEEFFE, 'From discrimination to obstacles to free movement: Recent developments concerning the free movement of workers 1989–1994' (1994) 31 *CMLRev.* 1313.

R. WHITE, 'Free movement, equal treatment and citizenship of the union' (2005) 54 *ICLQ* 885.

On the question of benefit entitlements for workers

M. DOUGAN, 'Cross-border educational mobility and the exportation of student financial assistance' (2008) 33 *ELRev.* 723.

M. DOUGAN, 'Expanding the frontiers of Union citizenship by dismantling the territorial boundaries of the national welfare states?' in C. Barnard and O. Odudu (eds.), *The Outer Limits of European Law* (Oxford: Hart Publishing, 2009).

E. ELLIS, 'Social advantages: A new lease of life' (2003) 40 *CMLRev.* 639.

C. O'BRIEN, 'Real links, abstract rights and false alarms: The relationship between the ECJ's "real link" case law and national solidarity' (2008) 33 *ELRev.* 643.

D. O'KEEFFE, 'Equal rights for migrants: The concept of social advantages in Article 7(2), Regulation 1612/68' (1985) 5 *YEL* 92.

A comparative perspective

G. ROSBERG, 'Free movement of persons in the United States' in T. Sandalow and E. Stein (eds.), *Courts and Free Markets: Perspectives form the United States and Europe* (Oxford: Clarendon Press, 1982).

On the experience of migrant workers enforcing their rights

C. BARNARD and A. LUDLOW, 'Enforcement of employment rights by EU-8 migrant workers in employment tribunals' (2016) 45 *ILJ* 1.

On questions of taxation

F. VANISTENDAEL, 'The consequences of *Schumacker* and *Wielockx*: Two steps forward in the tax procession of Echternach' (1996) 33 *CMLRev.* 255.

9

FREEDOM FOR INDIVIDUALS
TO PROVIDE
AND RECEIVE SERVICES

A. INTRODUCTION

Articles 56–7 TFEU lay down the principle of freedom to provide services on a temporary basis by a person established in one Member State to a recipient established in another. Article 56(1) TFEU provides:

> Within the framework of the provisions set out below, restrictions on freedom to provide services within the Union shall be prohibited in respect of nationals of Member States who are established in a Member State other than that of the person for whom the services are intended.

Article 57 TFEU then gives a partial and negative definition of services:[1]

---

[1] See also Art. 58 TFEU: 'Freedom to provide services in the field of transport shall be governed by the provisions of the Title relating to transport'.

> Services shall be considered to be 'services' within the meaning of this Treaty where they are normally provided for remuneration, in so far as they are not governed by the provisions relating to freedom of movement for goods, capital and persons.
> …
> Without prejudice to the provisions of the Chapter relating to the right of establishment, the person providing a service may, in order to do so, temporarily pursue his activity in the Member State where the service is provided, under the same conditions as are imposed by that State on its own nationals.

The principle of non-discrimination emphasized in Article 57(3) TFEU is repeated in Article 61 TFEU:

> As long as restrictions on freedom to provide services have not been abolished, each Member State shall apply such restrictions without distinction on grounds of nationality or residence to all persons providing services within the meaning of the first paragraph of Article 56.

Article 57 TFEU defines services and applies the principle of equal treatment to the service provider.[2] While the structure of Articles 56–7 TFEU does not differ very much from the Treaty provisions on workers and establishment, for many years services were seen as the poor relation to the other freedoms because Article 57 TFEU suggested that the services provisions were subordinate ('*insofar as they are not governed by the provisions relating to freedom of movement for goods, capital and persons*'). However, in reality, growth in the economy has essentially been driven by services,[3] which now account for 70 per cent of GDP and employment in the majority of the Member States. This has been reflected in the case law: an increasing number of cases have been decided under Articles 56–7 TFEU in the last decade or so.[4] Perhaps reflecting this change of perspective, the Court said in *Fidium Finanz*[5] that Article 57 TFEU did not establish any order of priority between the freedom to provide services and other freedoms; the reference in Article 57 TFEU to 'insofar as they are not governed by the provisions relating to' the other freedoms merely related to the definition of 'services'. It continued: 'The notion of "services" covers services which are not governed by other freedoms, in order to ensure that all economic activity falls within the scope of the fundamental freedoms.'[6] The Court will therefore determine the centre of gravity of the particular case before deciding which Treaty provision applies.[7]

However, services pose intellectual and practical problems not experienced with the other freedoms. 'Services' cover a vast range of situations:[8] service providers can move from one state to another to provide professional services (as lawyers,

---

[2] See also General Programme for the Abolition of Restrictions of Freedom to Provide Services ([1961] OJ Spec. Ed. Second Series IX/3).

[3] Commission, 'The state of the internal market for services', COM(2002) 441, 5.

[4] Sometimes alongside other Treaty provisions such as Art. 34 TFEU (e.g., Joined Cases C–34–36/95 *De Agostini* [1997] ECR I–3843) and sometimes instead of other Treaty provisions such as Art. 63 TFEU on capital (e.g., Case C–118/96 *Safir* v. *Skattemyndigheten i Dalarnas Län* [1998] ECR I–1897, para. 35).

[5] Case C–452/04 *Fidium Finanz AG* v. *Bundesanstalt für Finanzdienstleistungsaufsicht* [2006] ECR I–9521, para. 32.

[6] Para. 32.

[7] Para. 34. Cf. the third chamber decision in Case C–384/08 *Attanasio Group Srl* v. *Comune di Carbognano* [2010] ECR I–2055, para. 39, which appears to suggest that Art. 56 TFEU applies only if Art. 49 TFEU does not.

[8] Provided the services are legal: Case C–137/09 *Josemans* v. *Burgemeester van Maastricht* [2010] ECR I–13109 (sale of narcotics through channels not controlled by the competent authorities).

accountants, or architects) or various trades (the infamous Polish plumber); service receivers might move between states in search of healthcare, tourism, or education; and, of increasing importance, neither provider nor receiver move but the service itself does (e.g., over the web, such as Internet gambling). Regulations in the states also vary: in some states it is the service itself which is regulated; in others it is the service provider. With this variety of situations and methods of regulation it is difficult to have a 'one size fits all' model for addressing restrictions on freedom to provide services. This helps to explain why adopting a single 'Services' Directive presented significant difficulties. Since the directive applies to both freedom of establishment and free movement of services and concerns largely small businesses it will be considered in detail in Chapter 11.

For the Court, the variety of services situations has also posed problems.[9] As Advocate General Jacobs pointed out in *Säger*,[10] where the provider of the service spends a substantial period of time in the host state (e.g., an architect supervising the execution of a large building project) there is a fine line between services and establishment. There is also a potential overlap with the free movement of goods, where the person providing the service transmits it in the form of a product (e.g., the provider of an educational service posts a series of books and CDs). Yet it remains important to distinguish between the relevant provisions on free movement of persons: home-state control is increasingly the guiding principle behind free movement of services whereas host-state control guides the position of migrant workers and the self-employed.

This chapter will follow the structure of the previous chapter on free movement of workers and the self-employed: it will consider who is entitled to benefit from the services provisions (Section B) and the rights they enjoy in respect of (1) initial access to the market, (2) the exercise of the freedom, and (3) the enjoyment of social advantages (Section C). The focus in this chapter is primarily on natural persons, where a number of key principles were developed. The position of freedom of legal persons to provide and receive services is considered in Chapter 11.

B. WHO CAN RELY ON ARTICLES 56 AND 57 TFEU?

1. THE THREE ASPECTS OF THE FREEDOM

1.1 The Freedom to Provide Services

The first paragraph of Article 56 TFEU provides that:

> [R]estrictions on freedom to provide services within the Union shall be prohibited in respect of nationals of Member States who are established in a State other than that of the person for whom the services are intended.[11]

Article 56 TFEU therefore envisages the situation where the service provider established in State A, holding the nationality of one of the Member States[12] (not necessarily that of

---

[9] Case C–215/01 *Schnitzer* [2003] ECR I–4847, para. 30.

[10] Case C–76/90 *Säger* [1991] ECR I–4221, paras. 25–6.

[11] Art. 56(2) TFEU allows the EP and Council, by the ordinary legislative procedure, to extend the provisions of the services chapter to nationals of a third country who provide services and are established in the EU.

[12] Both conditions need to be satisfied: Case C–290/04 *FKP Scorpio* [2006] ECR I–9461, paras. 67–8.

State A), provides services in Member State B and then returns to State A once the activity is completed.

Article 56 TFEU can be used to challenge rules laid down by both the host state (State B) and the home state (State A) which obstruct the provision of services. Most cases concern barriers raised by the host state (State B). For example, in *Van Binsbergen*[13] a Dutch national, Kortmann, living in Belgium, challenged a Dutch rule requiring legal representatives to be established in the Netherlands before they could represent a person in the Dutch courts. The Court found that, in principle, the Dutch rule breached Article 56 TFEU.

However, an increasing number of cases concern obstacles to the provision of services created by the home state. Perhaps the most remarkable decision in this line of case law is *Carpenter*,[14] where a Filipino national married to a British husband successfully challenged British immigration rules which were going to result in her deportation on the ground that this would be detrimental to their family life and, therefore, to the conditions under which Mr Carpenter exercised the freedom to provide services.[15] Mr Carpenter ran a business selling advertising space in medical and scientific journals. Although the business was established in the UK, where the publishers of the journals were based, some of his work was conducted with advertisers established in other Member States. The Court found that such services fell within Article 56 TFEU, 'both in so far as the provider travels for that purpose to the Member State of the recipient and in so far as he provides cross-border services without leaving the Member State in which he is established'.[16] The Court said, '[t]hat freedom could not be fully effective if Mr Carpenter were to be deterred from exercising it by obstacles raised in his country of origin to the entry and residence of his spouse'.[17]

1.2 The Freedom to Travel to Receive Services

The text of Articles 56–7 TFEU is confined to giving rights for service providers only. However, if service providers can travel to the state of the recipient, then logic would suggest that the recipient should also be able to travel to the state of the provider. The Council took this view in (the now repealed) Directive 73/148, where Article 1(b) required the abolition of restrictions on the movement and residence of 'nationals wishing to go to another Member State as recipients of services'. Subsequently, the Court confirmed that the Treaty applied to this situation. In *Luisi and Carbone*[18] two Italians were fined for taking more money out of Italy than the (then) currency regulations permitted in order to go to other Member States as tourists and to receive medical treatment. The Court said that the freedom to receive services from a provider established in another Member State was the 'necessary corollary' of the freedom to provide services.[19] Therefore, the Court said that tourists, individuals receiving medical treatment, and those travelling for the purpose of (private) education or business should have the right of free movement without being obstructed by restrictions, even in relation to payment.[20] This decision paved the way for various attempts at medical tourism, with a view to gaining access to treatment not

---

[13] Case 33/74 *J.H.M. van Binsbergen v. Bestuur van de Bedrijfsvereniging voor de Metaalnijverheid* [1974] ECR 1299.

[14] Case C–60/00 *Carpenter* [2002] ECR I–6279.

[15] Para. 39.   [16] Para. 29.   [17] Para. 39.

[18] Joined Cases 286/82 and 26/83 *Luisi and Carbone v. Ministero del Tesoro* [1984] ECR 377.

[19] Para. 10.   [20] Para. 16.

available in the home state[21] or, at least, gaining access more quickly than would otherwise be the case.[22]

Finally, some cases have elements of both providing and receiving services. For example, in *Commission v. France (performing artists)*[23] the Court said that French law, which presumed artists had 'salaried status' resulting in them being subject to the social security scheme for employed workers, constituted a restriction on freedom to provide services. The Court said that the French system was 'likely both to discourage the artists in question from providing their services in France and discourage French organisers of events from engaging such artists'.[24]

1.3 Neither Provider nor Recipient Travels

The Court has also said that Articles 56–7 TFEU apply where neither the provider nor the recipient of the service travels but the service itself moves (e.g., by phone, email, the Internet, or cable).[25] Two commercial cases illustrate this point: *Alpine Investments*[26] and *Bond*.[27] It will be recalled from Chapter 7 that in *Alpine Investments* the Dutch Ministry of Finance prohibited a Dutch company from telephoning individuals in the Netherlands or in other Member States to offer them various financial services (cold-calling) unless they had the prior written consent of the clients. The Court ruled that Article 56 TFEU covered services which the provider offered by telephone to potential recipients established in other Member States without moving from the Member State in which the service provider was established.[28]

Bond concerned multiple provision of services. Dutch law prohibited the distribution by cable of radio and television programmes transmitted from other Member States which contained advertising aimed at the Dutch public. The Court noted that the transmission of programmes across frontiers involved two distinct, cross-frontier services:[29] (1) the service provided by the cable companies in the receiving state (the Netherlands) to the broadcasting companies in the transmitting state (e.g., Luxembourg) by re-transmitting programmes to their subscribers; and (2) the service provided by the broadcasting companies in the transmitting state to advertisers in the receiving state (the Netherlands) in broadcasting adverts aimed at potential customers in the Netherlands. The Court also noted that both services were provided for remuneration.[30] First, the cable network

---

[21] Case C–159/90 *The Society for the Protection of Unborn Children Ireland Ltd (SPUC) v. Stephan Grogan* [1991] ECR I–4685 (abortion); Case C–157/99 *H.T.M Peerbooms v. Stichting CZ Groep Zorgverzekeringen* [2001] ECR I–5473.

[22] Case C–157/99 *B.S.M Geraets-Smits v. Stichting Ziekenfonds VGZ; H.T.M Peerbooms v. Stichting CZ Groep Zorgverzekeringen* [2001] ECR I–5473 (neuro-stimulation).

[23] Case C–255/04 *Commission v. France (performing artists)* [2006] ECR I–5251, para. 38. In Case C–154/89 *Commission v. France (tour guides)* [1991] ECR I–659 the Court clarified that the activities of a tourist guide from the home state (State A) who takes tourists on a tour from State A to a host state (State B) may be subject to two distinct sets of legal rules: (1) if a tour company from State A is established in State B and employs its own guides established in State A, then it is the tour company that provides the service; (2) if a tour company from State A hires self-employed tourist guides who are established in State B, then it is *the guide* who provides the service. Art. 56 TFEU applied to both situations (para. 10).

[24] Para. 38.

[25] See, e.g., Case 62/79 *SA Compagnie générale pour la diffusion de la télévision Coditel v. Ciné Vog Films* [1980] ECR 881; Joined Cases C–34–36/95 *De Agostini* [1997] ECR I–3843.

[26] Case C–384/93 *Alpine Investments* [1995] ECR I–1141. See also Case C–243/01 *Piergiorgio Gambelli* [2003] ECR I–13031, para. 54 (betting services provided over the Internet).

[27] Case 352/85 *Bond van Adverteerders v. Netherlands* [1988] ECR 2085.

[28] Para. 42. See also the cases on cross-border advertising, e.g., Case C–405/98 *Gourmet International Products* [2001] ECR I–1795, para. 39.

[29] Paras. 14–15.   [30] Para. 16.

operators were paid in the form of fees which they charged their subscribers for the service they provided to the broadcasters. The Court said that it was irrelevant that the broadcasters did not generally pay the cable network operators for relaying their programmes because Article 57 TFEU did not require the service to be paid for by those for whom it was performed. Secondly, the broadcasters were paid by the advertisers for the service of broadcasting the adverts.

2. PERFORMANCE OF A SERVICE FOR REMUNERATION

Bond emphasized the importance of both the provision of a service and remuneration. It is to these subjects that we now turn. Article 57 TFEU provides that services shall be considered 'services' within the meaning of the Treaty where they are 'normally provided for remuneration' and provided on a temporary basis. Article 57 TFEU therefore has three elements: (1) services, (2) remuneration, and (3) temporary. We shall look at these in turn.

2.1 What Activities Constitute 'Services'?

Article 57(1) TFEU gives examples of what constitutes a service, including activities of craftsmen and the professions, and activities of an industrial and commercial character. The case law has significantly expanded on this rather anachronistic list. From *Luisi and Carbone* we have already seen how tourism,[31] medical,[32] financial,[33] business, and educational activities all constitute services. As we shall see in Chapter 11, the transmission of a television signal[34] and a signal by cable television constitute a service.[35] In other cases the Court has said that the provision of people by an employment agency,[36] debt-collection work,[37] lotteries,[38] bank building loans,[39] insurance,[40] and sporting activities[41] are all services. Given the breadth of the subject matter included within the definition of services[42] and the scope of the Treaty provisions, it is hard to think of areas of (economic) activity excluded from the protection of the Treaty.[43]

---

[31] See also Case C–198/89 *Commission* v. *Greece* [1991] ECR I–727 (guiding by a tourist guide is a service).

[32] This applies to care provided both in and out of a hospital environment: Case C–157/99 *Geraets-Smits and Peerbooms* [2001] ECR I–5473, para. 53. See also Case C–159/90 *SPUC* v. *Grogan* [1991] ECR I–4685.

[33] Case C–384/93 *Alpine Investments BV* [1995] ECR I–1141.

[34] Case 155/73 *Sacchi* [1974] ECR 409, para. 6. However, the Court said that trade in material, sound recordings, films, apparatus, etc. used for the diffusion of television signals was subject to the rules relating to the free movement of goods.

[35] Case 52/79 *Procureur du Roi* v. *Debauve* [1981] ECR 833, para. 8; or, as the Court put it in Case 352/85 *Bond* [1988] ECR 2085 and Joined Cases C–34–36/95 *De Agostini* [1997] ECR I–3843, the service of transmitting programmes and advertisements from broadcasters in one Member State to cable networks in another. This is considered further in Ch. 11.

[36] Case 279/80 *Criminal Proceedings against Alfred John Webb* [1981] ECR 3305.

[37] Case C–3/95 *Reisebüro Broede* v. *Sandker* [1996] ECR I–6511, para. 24.

[38] Case C–275/92 *Schindler* [1994] ECR I–1039.

[39] Case C–484/93 *Svensson* v. *Ministre du Logement et d'Urbanisme* [1995] ECR I–3955 (legal persons); Case C–222/95 *Société Civile Immobilière Parodi* v. *Banque H. Albert de Bary et Cie* [1997] ECR I–3899.

[40] Case C–118/96 *Safir* [1998] ECR I–1897, para. 22.

[41] Joined Cases C–51/96 and C–191/97 *Deliège* [2000] ECR I–2549.

[42] The Court has made clear that the special nature of certain services, e.g., social security, does not remove them from the scope of the fundamental principle of freedom of movement: Case 279/80 *Webb* [1981] ECR 3305, para. 10, Case C–158/96 *Kohll* v. *Union des Caisses de Maladie* [1998] ECR I–1931 paras. 20–1.

[43] For further examples, see Art. 4(1) of the Services Dir. and 34th recital, considered in Ch. 11.

2.2 Services Are 'Normally Provided for Remuneration'

(a) The need for an economic link

Article 57(1) TFEU provides that services are 'normally provided for remuneration', i.e., 'consideration for the service in question [which] is normally agreed upon between the provider and the recipient of the service'.[44] This provision was introduced to exclude gratuitous services from the scope of the Treaty. This point was emphasized in *Jundt*,[45] which concerned a German lawyer, resident in Germany, who taught a 16-hour course at the University of Strasbourg for which he received a small honorarium (about €500). The Court said that he was a service provider under Article 56 TFEU, even though the activity was carried out on a quasi-honorary basis. It added that for the Treaty provisions to apply, 'the activity must not be provided for nothing' although there is no need 'for the person providing the service to be seeking to make a profit'.[46]

The Court has used the requirement of 'remuneration' to exclude services without a direct economic link between the provider and the recipient from the scope of the Treaty. This can be seen in *SPUC* v. *Grogan*.[47] Handbooks prepared and distributed by various Irish students' unions included information about the availability of legal abortion in the UK and the identity and location of a number of abortion clinics in the UK. The Society for the Protection of the Unborn Child (SPUC), an anti-abortion group, argued that the distribution of such information contravened the Irish ban on abortion and so sought an injunction against Grogan, the president of the students' union, to restrain the distribution of the handbooks. In his defence, Grogan argued that because he was providing information about the availability of a service the injunction constituted an obstacle to the freedom to provide services contrary to Article 56 TFEU.

Setting the moral debate about abortion to one side,[48] the Court agreed that abortion performed in accordance with the law of a particular Member State did constitute a service within the meaning of Article 57 TFEU.[49] However, it said that Union law did not apply to the provision of information about the identity and location of clinics in another Member State providing abortions[50] because the information was not distributed on behalf of an economic operator established in another Member State.[51] The Court concluded that the information constituted a 'manifestation of freedom of expression and of the freedom to impart and receive information which is independent of the economic activity carried on by clinics in another Member State'.[52] This conclusion enabled the Court to avoid deciding a case where *EU* fundamental *economic* rights (freedom to travel to receive a service) appeared to collide with a fundamental tenet of a *national* constitution (the right to life of the unborn).[53] Eventually the European Court of Human Rights and the Member States in an Intergovernmental Conference were left to resolve some of the issues arising from the case (see Case Study 9.1).

---

[44] Joined Cases C–372 and 3/09 *Peñarroja Fa* [2011] ECR I–1785, para. 40.

[45] Case C–281/06 *Jundt* v. *Finanzamt Offenburg* [2007] ECR I–12231.   [46] Paras. 32–3.

[47] Case C–159/90 [1991] ECR I–4685.   [48] Para. 20.

[49] Para. 21. This classification of abortion as a service (or by the language used) offended many: see, e.g., M. Kenny, 'The dilemma that won't go away', *The Sunday Telegraph*, 23 Feb. 1992, 13, who asked 'Is that all it is—[is abortion] like hairdressing or chiropody? Where is conscience? Where is feeling?'

[50] Para. 27.   [51] Para. 26.   [52] Para. 26.

[53] Para. 26. The Court may have feared a supremacy challenge: see the veiled threats made by Walsh J in the Supreme Court in *Grogan*: 'any answer to the reference received from the European Court of Justice will have to be considered in the light of our own constitutional provisions', considered in S. O'Leary, 'The Court of Justice as a reluctant constitutional adjudicator: An examination of the abortion information case' (1992) 17 *ELRev.* 138, 154–7.

The judgment in *SPUC* v. *Grogan* has been much criticized[54] because the Court's reasoning turned on the absence of an economic link between the information provider (Grogan) and the service provider (the abortion clinics). Had the abortion clinics paid the students' union—even a small sum—for providing the information the outcome would (and arguably, should) have been different. And even on the facts as they stood there was an indirect economic link in the relationship: although the clinics did not pay the students' union for distributing the information, the pregnant women who received the information would have paid the abortion clinics in England and Wales for the termination. According to (the admittedly more commercial case) *Bond*,[55] that might have been sufficient to bring the matter within the scope of Union law because the Court said that it was not relevant that 'some of those services are not paid for by those for whom they are performed'.[56]

With the benefit of hindsight, a better way of understanding the case might be to view it as a *Graf*-type situation,[57] where the effect on Union law of the Irish courts granting an injunction was too remote and so did not create a sufficiently substantial impediment to access to the market. The Court said as much, noting that the link between Grogan and the abortion clinics in other Member States was 'too tenuous for the prohibition on the distribution of information to be regarded as a restriction' falling within Article 56 TFEU.[58]

The Advocate General adopted a different—and more sustainable—approach. He thought that the rule developed in the goods case, *GB-INNO*[59] (where consumers' freedom to shop in another Member State was compromised if they were deprived of access to advertising in their own state), should also apply to services. He considered that the Irish ban on abortion constituted a non-discriminatory impediment to intra-Union trade in services, contrary to Article 56 TFEU, but one that could be justified under Article 52 TFEU, to which Article 62 TFEU refers, on the ground of public policy because it related to 'a policy choice of a moral and philosophical nature the assessment of which is a matter for the Member States'.[60] He also considered that the steps taken to pursue the objective of protecting the unborn life were proportionate and compatible with fundamental human rights.

Case Study 9.1: IRISH ABORTION, BRITISH IVF, AND EU LAW

The decision in *SPUC* v. *Grogan* focused international attention on the Irish ban on abortion found in Article 40.3.3 of the Constitution. It provides:

> The State acknowledges the right to life of the unborn and, with due regard to the equal right to life of the mother, guarantees in its laws to respect, and, as far as practicable, by its laws to defend and vindicate that right.[61]

---

[54] See, e.g., O'Leary, n. 53, 146.

[55] Case 352/85 [1988] ECR 2085, para. 16. See also Joined Cases C–51/96 and 191/97 *Deliège* [2000] ECR I–2549, para. 56.

[56] Para. 16.   [57] Case C–190/98 *Graf* [2000] ECR I–493. See further Ch. 7.

[58] Para. 24. See T. Hervey, 'Buy baby: The European Union and regulation of human reproduction' (1998) 18 *OJLS* 207.

[59] Case C–362/88 *GB-INNO-BM* v. *Confédération du commerce luxembourgeois* [1990] ECR I–667, para. 8.

[60] Para. 26.

[61] Ss. 58–9 of the Offences Against the Person Act 1861 make it a criminal offence unlawfully to procure or to assist in the procurement of abortion.

This provision was introduced in 1983[62] to copper-fasten the prohibition against abortion contained in the Offences Against the Person Act 1861 from any attempts by an activist judiciary to use the constitutional right to privacy[63] to legalize abortion in the manner of the US Supreme Court in *Roe* v. *Wade*.[64]

By contrast, in Great Britain abortion is legal and freely available (within the limits of the Abortion Act 1967). About 8,000 Irish women come to Britain for abortions each year,[65] often after receiving advice from welfare clinics in Ireland. These clinics were prevented from giving such information in *Attorney General (SPUC)* v. *Open Door Counselling and Dublin Well Woman Centre*,[66] where, relying on Article 40.3.3, the Irish Supreme Court granted an injunction restraining welfare clinics from assisting pregnant women travelling abroad to obtain abortions. The clinics challenged this decision before the European Court of Human Rights,[67] where the majority of the Court upheld their complaint and found a breach of Article 10 on freedom of expression.[68] While recognizing that the injunction pursued 'the legitimate aim of the protection of morals of which the protection in Ireland of the right to life of the unborn is one aspect',[69] the Court found the restriction to be over-broad and disproportionate.[70]

While *Open Door Counselling* forced the Irish government to confront the potential conflict between the application of its abortion laws and human rights, the earlier case of *Grogan* (discussed in this chapter) had obliged the Irish government to address the potential conflict between Article 56 TFEU and Article 40.3.3 of the Irish Constitution. As we have seen, the Court of Justice fudged the issue but indicated that Irish law was compatible with Article 56 TFEU. To put the matter beyond doubt, the Member States agreed at Maastricht to add the 'Abortion' Protocol protecting Article 40.3.3 from challenge under EU law. The Protocol, as originally drafted, provides:

Nothing in the Treaty on European Union, or in the Treaty establishing the European Communities, or in the Treaty or Acts modifying or supplementing those Treaty, shall affect the application in Ireland of Article 40.3.3. of the Constitution of Ireland.[71]

[62] 8th Amendment of the Constitution Act 1983. However, as the *Irish Times* noted, the turn-out in the referendum on the amendment was 53.6 per cent. Of those, 66.45 per cent voted in favour of the amendment, 35.79 per cent of eligible voters: A. Murdoch, 'The Irish myth of a blinkered society', *Independent on Sunday*, 8 Mar. 1992, 8.

[63] This concern was triggered by the Irish Supreme Court's decision in *McGee* v. *Attorney General* [1974] IR 284.

[64] 410 US 113 (1973).

[65] A. Tate, 'Day trippers: The women forced to come to England for abortions', *The Mirror*, 20 Jul. 2002, 16 and 18.

[66] [1988] IR 593.

[67] *Open Door Counselling and Dublin Well Woman* v. *Ireland*, Series A, No. 246 (1993) 15 EHRR 244 (judgment of 29 Oct. 1992).

[68] Cf. Van Gerven AG's views in Case C–159/90 *SPUC* v. *Grogan* [1991] ECR I–4685.

[69] Para. 63.   [70] Para. 74.

[71] Protocol No. 17 annexed to the EU Treaty and to the Treaty establishing the European Communities. For a summary of the debate about the meaning and scope of this Protocol (esp. the phrase 'in Ireland'), see J. Kingston and A. Whelan, with I. Bacik, *Abortion and the Law* (Dublin: Round Hall, Sweet & Maxwell, 1997), esp. 167–70. See now Protocol No. 35 of the Lisbon Treaty, which is drafted in broadly the same terms. In order to reassure the Irish people, with a view to persuading them to vote in favour of the Lisbon Treaty in Sept. 2009, the European Council adopted a Decision at its 18/19 Jun. 2009 meeting, which came into force on the same date as the TEU and TFEU, making clear that 'Nothing in the Treaty of Lisbon attributing legal status to the Charter of Fundamental Rights of the European Union, or in the provisions of that Treaty in the area of Freedom, Security and Justice affects in any way the scope and applicability of the protection of the right to life in Article 40.3.1, 40.3.2 and Article 40.3.3'. This Decision formed a Protocol to the Croatian Accession Treaty.

This Protocol was included in the Treaty 'by stealth and without reference of the issue to the Dail [Irish lower house of Parliament]'.[72] While it was intended to satisfy the pro-life lobby,[73] the Protocol caused consternation among liberals who feared that it denied Irish women access to information[74] and removed the rights of EU citizens to travel to another Member State to receive services. Moreover, the Protocol did not actually succeed in its primary purpose of putting an end to challenges based on Union law, as the X case[75] showed. X was a 14-year-old girl who became pregnant after being raped by a friend's father. Her parents brought her to London for an abortion and hoped that tissue collected from the foetus would provide the necessary forensic evidence to convict the man. When the papers were sent to the Irish Attorney General[76] he successfully sought an injunction from the High Court in Dublin preventing the girl from travelling to London for the abortion.[77] This forced the family to return to Ireland,[78] with X threatening to kill herself. The Supreme Court reversed the High Court's decision and lifted the injunction,[79] thereby allowing the girl to return to London for the abortion. The majority ruled, not on EU law, but on the basis of the wording in Article 40.3.3, that abortion was permissible if there was a 'real and substantial risk to the life as distinct from the health of the mother, which can only be avoided by the termination of her pregnancy'.[80]

In the light of the confusion generated by the X case, and given the risk that in the Irish referendum on the ratification of the Maastricht Treaty liberals would vote against the Treaty if the issue of the right to travel were not resolved,[81] the Irish government sought to have a 'ten-minute' inter-governmental conference (IGC) to amend its Maastricht Protocol.[82] Fearing that this would pave the way for other states to revisit aspects of the Treaty that they wished to change, the Heads of State refused the request but they did agree to the addition of a (non-binding) Declaration which provided:[83]

> That it was and is their intention that the Protocol shall not limit freedom to travel between Member State or, in accordance with conditions which may be laid down, in conformity with Union law, by Irish legislation, to obtain or make available in Ireland information relating to services lawfully available in Member States.[84]

The Irish people then voted in favour of the Maastricht Treaty, which was ratified by Ireland in the summer of 1992.

---

[72] F. Murphy, 'Maastricht: Implementation in Ireland' (1994) 19 *ELRev.* 94.

[73] C. O'Brien, 'A constitutional change could get Ireland out of a tight spot on abortion', *The Times*, 1 Apr. 1992, 14.

[74] *EP News*, 9–13 Mar. 1992, 4. See also the Debates of the European Parliament, No. 3–416/207–218, 12 Mar. 1992.

[75] *Attorney General* v. *X* [1992] 2 CMLR 277.

[76] Cf. E. Gorman and T. Walker, 'Law chief regrets abortion trauma', *The Times*, 10 Apr. 1992.

[77] Judgment of the High Court of Costello J [1992] 2 CMLR 277, 281.

[78] J. Langton, 'Ireland's anguish', *Sunday Telegraph*, 23 Feb. 1992, 13.

[79] [1992] 2 CMLR 277, 290.   [80] Para. 38.

[81] There was also concern that the pro-life groups would vote against the Treaty because, in their view, it paved the way for a more liberal abortion regime.

[82] T. Jackson and A. Murdoch, 'EC dashes Irish hopes of amending treaty', *Independent*, 6 Apr. 1992.

[83] Declaration of the High Contracting Parties to the TEU of 1 May 1992 ([1992] OJ C191/109).

[84] The Amendment continued: 'At the same time the High Contracting Parties solemnly declare that, in the event of a future constitutional amendment in Ireland which concerns the subject matter of Article 40.3.3 of the Constitution of Ireland and which does not conflict with the intention of the High Contracting Parties hereinbefore expressed, they will, following the entry into force of the Treaty on European Union, be favourably disposed to amending the said Protocol so as to extend its application to such constitutional amendment if Ireland so request.'

However, the Declaration did not help Mr Grogan because the Irish High Court refused to allow it to be taken into account when deciding his case on its return from Luxembourg.[85] Morris J explained that since the Maastricht Treaty had not come into force at the time of the litigation it could not be relied on.[86] The High Court therefore concluded that the Irish prohibition on third parties providing a woman with information about abortion clinics in the UK did not contravene Union law and made permanent the injunction sought by SPUC against Grogan.[87]

SPUC's success was short-lived. As part of the deal to appease the liberals to secure a 'yes' vote in the Maastricht referendum, the Irish government committed itself to holding three referenda. The first two concerned the right of Irish citizens to travel abroad and to have free access to information about abortion. These were supported by a two-to-one majority. The third referendum, on tightening up the Supreme Court's decision in X, was defeated by a two-to-one majority. As a result of these referenda, Article 40.3.3 of the Constitution was amended to read, first:

This subsection shall not limit freedom to travel between the State and another State.[88]

And, secondly, that:

This subsection shall not limit freedom to obtain or make available, in the State, subject to such conditions as may be laid down by law, information relating to services lawfully available in another State.[89]

Despite these amendments, five years later another case similar to X came to public attention, this time concerning a 13-year-old rape victim.[90] She was said to be suicidal, and eventually the High Court did allow her to travel to England for an abortion.[91] In March 2002 a further referendum was held on whether to reverse the Supreme Court's ruling in X in order to prevent abortion even if the mother threatened suicide or if there were legitimate threats to the life of the mother. The proposal was rejected by a narrow margin.[92]

Ireland has not been alone in struggling to reconcile aspects of its social policy with EU law. In the UK, Diane Blood became famous for her successful attempt to circumvent the restrictions laid down in the Human Fertilisation Embryology Act 1990 by relying on Articles 56-7 TFEU. When the Bloods were trying to conceive a child, Steven Blood contracted meningitis. While he was in a coma, Mrs Blood requested the doctors to take samples of his sperm. They did so but, since he was in a coma, they did not obtain his written consent as required by the 1990 Act. This meant that Diane Blood could not receive IVF treatment in the UK. Stephen died soon after. Subsequently Diane Blood sought IVF treatment using her husband's sperm, which

---

[85] *SPUC* v. *Grogan* [1993] 1 CMLR 197.   [86] Paras. 30–4.

[87] Para. 14. This was despite the fact that the Irish government had made a statement in Strasbourg that the right to information on abortion did exist in Irish law. See Murphy, n. 72, 104.

[88] 13th Amendment of the Constitution Act 1992. A Dutch women's group tried to push the right to travel to receive an abortion one stage further. In Jun. 2001 Women on Waves sailed the *Aurora*, a 'floating reproductive health centre', into the international waters 12 miles off the Irish coast to offer abortions to Irish women (N. Byrne, 'Anti-abortionists charter boat to confront "Aurora"', *Independent*, 15 Jun. 2001. They failed to acquire the necessary licence under Dutch law to carry out abortions and so could not provide terminations.

[89] 14th Amendment of the Constitution Act 1992.

[90] M. Sheehan and J. Burns, 'Court stops girl's abortion trip' and 'For pity's sake', *Sunday Times*, 23 Nov. 1997.

[91] J. Kierans, 'Outrage as teenage rape victim prepares to abort pregnancy; Irish girl prepares for abortion in Britain', *People*, 30 Nov. 1997.

[92] 618,485 people voted for (45 per cent) and 629,041 (50.4 per cent) voted against, with a turnout of around 45 per cent: R. Cowan, 'Irish reject tougher abortion law: Tight result in referendum fails to clear up confusion', *Guardian*, 8 Mar. 2002, 2.

she wanted to take to Belgium where the consent rule did not apply. However, the UK authority, the HFEA, refused to grant permission because the conditions laid down in the 1990 Act had not been met.

In the Court of Appeal, the Master of the Rolls recognized that the refusal of permission to export the sperm made impossible the provision of fertilization services in another Member State.[93] Nevertheless, he said that given the ethical and moral considerations raised by artificial insemination, the UK was justified[94] in taking measures to prevent abuse and undesirable practices from occurring.[95] However, he found on the facts that the HFEA had failed to take two important considerations into account: it had not given due consideration to the effect of Article 56 TFEU, nor had it recognized that this case was unique (after this judgment there would be no further cases where sperm was preserved without consent).[96] The HFEA then reversed its decision and Diane Blood travelled to Belgium for the treatment. At the end of 1998 Diane Blood gave birth to a son, Liam,[97] and, after receiving further treatment, another son, Joel, in 2002.[98]

(b) Services and the welfare state

Services provided as part of the welfare state have presented particular problems for Union law. Given that most are paid for out of the public purse but are free at the point of delivery, the absence of remuneration between the provider and the recipient suggests that they should fall outside the scope of Articles 56–7 TFEU. This is the case with state education. As the Court said in *Humbel*,[99] state education did not constitute a service because the state was not seeking to engage in gainful activity—it was merely fulfilling its duties towards its own population in the social, cultural, and educational fields, and was paid for by the public.[100] Because the same considerations do not apply to education in the private sector, the Court said in *Wirth*[101] that private education could constitute a service when it was financed essentially out of private funds, in particular by students or their parents, and where the provider sought to make an economic profit.[102]

In *Geraets-Smits and Peerbooms*[103] some of the Member States relied on *Humbel* to argue that hospital services were also 'special'[104] and so did not constitute an economic activity within the meaning of Article 57 TFEU because patients received care in a hospital without having to pay for it themselves, albeit that in an insurance-based 'Bismarck' system, such as that in the Netherlands, all or part of the cost of the treatment was paid

---

[93]   R. v. *Human Fertilisation and Embryology Authority, ex p. Diane Blood* [1997] 2 CMLR 591, para. 52. See generally D. Morgan and R. Lee, 'In the name of the father? *Ex parte Blood*: Dealing with novelty and anomaly' (1997) 60 *MLR* 840.

[94]   Citing Cases C–384/93 *Alpine Investments* [1995] ECR I–1141 and C–275/92 *Schindler* [1994] ECR I–1039.

[95]   Para. 54. Some of these issues were explored further in *U* v. *W* [1997] 2 CMLR 431.

[96]   Para. 61.   [97]   S. Oldfield, 'Liam is his Daddy to a T', *Daily Mail*, 31 Dec. 1998, 2.

[98]   'Overjoyed Diane Blood cradles her second son', *Daily Mail*, 19 Jul. 2002, 1. The Human Fertilisation and Embryology Act 1990 prohibited the father's name from being used on the children's birth certificates. Subsequently, the government admitted that this rule contravened the Human Rights Act 1998 and this has now been rectified by the Human Fertilisation and Embryology (Deceased Fathers) Act 2003.

[99]   Case 263/86 *Belgium* v. *Humbel* [1988] ECR 5365.   [100]   Paras. 17–19.

[101]   Case C–109/92 *Wirth* v. *Landeshauptstadt Hannover* [1993] ECR I–6447.   [102]   Para. 17.

[103]   Case C–157/99 [2001] ECR I–5473 considered at nn. 219–33.

[104]   Para. 54. See also the AGs' Opinions in Cases C–368/98 *Vanbraekel* v. *ANMC* [2001] ECR I–5363 and C–157/99 *Geraets-Smits and Peerbooms* [2001] ECR I–5473.

for directly by the relevant sickness scheme. The Court disagreed. It said that, despite the special nature of hospital services, EU law still applied.[105] Then, the Court said that the payments made by the sickness insurance funds under contractual arrangements between the funds and the hospitals were consideration for the hospital services, even if payable at a flat rate. For this reason they 'unquestionably represent remuneration for the hospital which receives them and which is engaged in an activity of an economic character'.[106] In *Müller-Fauré*[107] the Court went further, focusing on the fact that the treatment received abroad had been paid for by the patient. It did not refer to the relationship either between the patient and the sickness fund or the sickness fund and the healthcare provider.[108] This suggests, and *Watts*[109] confirms, that Article 56 TFEU applies equally to a benefits-in-kind, 'Beveridge' system, like the British one, where healthcare is provided to patients directly, without the medium of sickness funds, and paid for by general taxation.[110] In reaching this conclusion the Court opened up a market—healthcare—previously reserved almost exclusively to Member States.[111] This approach may spill over to other sectors, as states increasingly apply a market model to the provision of welfare services.[112]

2.3 The Temporary Nature of Services

The key factor distinguishing services from establishment is duration: while a person who stays in the host state permanently is likely to be covered by the rules relating to establishment,[113] a person staying there on a 'temporary'[114] basis is likely only to be providing services. How can the two situations be distinguished? In *Gebhard*[115] the Court said that the temporary nature of the activities has to be determined 'in the light, not only of the duration of the provision of the service but also of its regularity, periodicity or continuity'. Thus, as the Court indicated in *Schnitzer*,[116] there is no magic formula for determining whether the rules on services or those on establishment apply: it has to be decided by the national court on a case-by-case basis. However, in *Trojani*[117] the Court made clear that an activity carried out on a permanent basis, or at least without a foreseeable limit to its duration, would not fall within the services provisions. That said, service providers under Article 56 TFEU can equip themselves with some form of infrastructure in the host Member State (e.g., an office, chambers, or consulting rooms), provided it is necessary to perform the services.[118] However, a requirement by the state for a service provider to have premises would breach Article 56 TFEU since it negates the freedom to provide services.[119]

---

[105] C–157/99 *Geraets-Smits and Peerbooms* [2001] ECR I–5473, para. 54.

[106] Para. 58.

[107] Case C–385/99 *V.G. Müller-Fauré v. Onderlinge Waarborgmaatschappij oz Zorgverzekeringen UA* [2003] ECR I–4509.

[108] Para. 39.   [109] Case C–372/04 *Watts v. Bedford Primary Care Trust* [2006] ECR I–4325.

[110] E. Spaventa, 'Public services and European law: Looking for boundaries' (2003) 6 *CYELS* 271.

[111] G. Davies, 'Welfare as a service' [2002] *LIEI* 27.

[112] Davies, n. 111, 38–9.

[113] Case 2/74 *Reyners v. Belgium State* [1974] ECR 631; Case 11/77 *Patrick v. Ministre des affaires culturelles* [1977] ECR 1199.

[114] Art. 57(2) TFEU.

[115] Case C–55/94 [1995] ECR I–4165, para. 27, considered in Ch. 11. See also Case 63/86 *Commission v. Italy (social housing)* [1988] ECR 29 and Case C–298/99 *Commission v. Italy* [2002] ECR I–3129, para. 56.

[116] Case C–215/01 *Schnitzer* [2003] ECR I–4847, paras. 30–2.

[117] Case C–456/02 *Trojani v. CPAS* [2004] ECR I–7573, para. 28.   [118] Para. 27.

[119] Case C–134/05 *Commission v. Italy (extra-judicial debt recovery)* [2007] ECR I–6251, para. 43; Case C–404/05 *Commission v. Germany (inspection of organic production)* [2007] ECR I–10239, para. 34.

C. THE RIGHTS CONFERRED
ON SERVICE PROVIDERS AND RECEIVERS

1. RIGHTS OF DEPARTURE, ENTRY, AND RESIDENCE

Article 56 TFEU, together with Directive 73/148,[120] originally regulated the rights of entry and residence for those who actually move to provide or receive a service. This directive was repealed but not altogether replaced by the Citizens' Rights Directive (CRD) 2004/38.[121] Natural persons who are service providers going to another Member State for less than three months will be covered by Article 6 CRD in the same way as any other migrant (see fig. 10.2) but legal persons and those providing services for a longer period are not expressly covered by the CRD. For most purposes, this is not significant because in the field of services the Court has always placed much reliance on the Treaty provisions—and not secondary legislation—to give rights to service providers. This can be seen in *Oulane*.[122] A French service recipient was arrested in a goods tunnel closed to the public in Rotterdam Central station, with a view to his deportation on the ground that he failed to present a valid identity card or passport. The Court, having cited the relevant provisions on rights of residence contained in Directive 73/148 and noted that the conditions laid down were left unchanged by Directive 2004/38,[123] concluded that a detention order issued by the Dutch authorities constituted 'an unjustified restriction on the freedom to provide services and is therefore contrary to Article [56 TFEU]'.[124]

2. RIGHTS OF ACCESS TO THE MARKET IN SERVICES
IN OTHER MEMBER STATES

The right of entry to the host state is closely linked with questions of access to the market more generally. This section examines in more detail the nature of the obstacles that prevent or impede access to the market in services.

2.1 Discriminatory Measures

(a) Distinctly applicable measures

Article 57 TFEU provides that 'the person providing the service may ... temporarily pursue his activity in the Member State where the service is provided, under the same conditions as are imposed by that State on its own nationals'. It therefore prohibits discrimination on the ground of nationality against those wishing to provide/receive services.

The problem with applying the principle of non-discrimination is the choice of comparator. The obvious candidate is a person providing equivalent services who is established in the host state. However, establishment connotes more permanence than the

---

[120] Dir. 73/148 ([1973] OJ L172/14) on the abolition of the restrictions on movement and residence within the Union for nationals of Member States with regard to establishment and the provision of services.

[121] This directive is considered in detail in Ch. 10.

[122] Case C–215/03 *Oulane v. Minister voor Vreemdelingenzaken en Integratie* [2005] ECR I–1215, para. 38.

[123] Para. 20.   [124] Para. 44.

provision of services; and the service provider already has a place of establishment—in the home state. Recognizing this problem, the Court noted in *Säger*[125] that:

> a Member State may not make the provision of services in its territory subject to compliance with all the conditions required for establishment and thereby deprive of all practical effectiveness the provisions of the Treaty whose object is, precisely, to guarantee the freedom to provide services.

This ruling helps to explain in part the Court's decision in the controversial decision in *Laval*[126] discussed in Chapter 11: host states cannot require temporary service providers and their staff to comply with all of the host state's labour standards since they have already satisfied the standards in the home state. Applying both sets of rules imposes a double burden and this would deprive Article 56 TFEU of all practical effectiveness.[127] Nevertheless, in the early cases the Court did apply the principle of non-discrimination.

The Court spelt out the meaning of the principle of direct discrimination in *Gouda*:[128]

> Article [56 TFEU] entails, in the first place, the abolition of any discrimination against a person providing services on *the grounds of his nationality or the fact that he is established in a Member State other than the one in which the service is provided.*

Thus, Article 56 TFEU prohibits (direct) discrimination not only on the grounds of nationality as with the other Treaty provisions, but also on the grounds of the place of establishment (see fig. 9.1), a wider concept of discrimination than is found in the other freedoms. The Court continued that:[129]

> national rules which are not applicable to services without discrimination as regards their origin are compatible with [Union] law only in so far as they can be brought within an express exemption, such as that contained in Article [62 TFEU, which refers to Art. 52 TFEU].

Thus, in respect of direct discrimination on the ground of nationality, the Court reaffirmed the orthodox position that direct discrimination breaches Article 56 TFEU and can be saved only by reference to one of the express derogations and not by reference to the judicially developed public interest requirements (discussed in Chapter 12). While the Court has wavered on this point over the years, it did re-confirm the orthodoxy in *Laval*[130] and again in *Commission v. Poland (Germany/Poland agreement)*.[131]

Where discrimination is based on the fact that the service provider is established in another Member State, the Court said in *Gouda* that such discrimination could also be saved only by reference to the express derogations found in Articles 52 and 62 TFEU.[132] However, if the national rule is drafted in terms of requiring a service provider to be established and/or to have a residence[133] in the host state, the mirror image of a rule discriminating

---

[125] Case C–76/90 [1991] ECR I–4221, para. 13. See also Case 33/74 *Van Binsbergen* [1974] ECR 1299, para. 11; Case 205/84 *Commission* v. *Germany (the insurance cases)* [1986] ECR 3755, para. 26; Case C–484/93 *Svensson* [1995] ECR I–3955 (legal persons); Case C–118/96 *Safir* [1998] ECR I–1897, para. 30.

[126] Case C–341/05 *Laval* [2007] ECR I–987.

[127] See also Case C–164/99 *Portugaia Construções* [2002] ECR I–787.

[128] Case C–288/89 *Stichting Collectieve Antennevoorziening Gouda* v. *Commissariaat voor de Media* [1991] ECR I–4007, para. 10, emphasis added.

[129] Para. 11.

[130] Case C–341/05 *Laval* [2007] ECR I–987, paras. 116–17. See also Case C–490/04 *Commission* v. *Germany (posted workers)* [2007] ECR I–6095, para. 86.

[131] Case C–546/07 [2010] ECR I–439, para. 47 (although cf. paras. 43 and 51).

[132] See also Case 352/85 *Bond* [1988] ECR 2085, para. 32; Case C–260/89 *ERT* v. *DEP* [1991] ECR I–2925, para. 24. For further discussion and a proposed reconciliation of the case law, see Tesauro AG's Opinion in Case C–118/96 *Safir* [1998] ECR I–1897, para. 31.

[133] See Case 39/75 *Coenen* v. *The Sociaal-Economische Raad* [1975] ECR 1547.

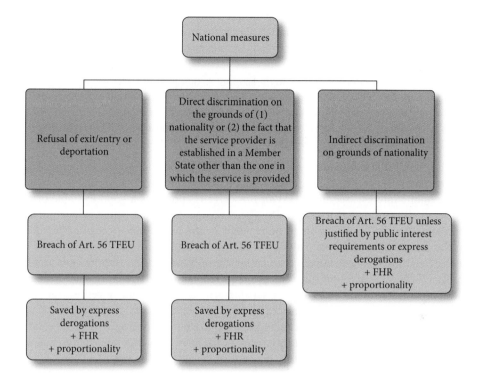

Fig. 9.1 The discrimination approach to free movement of services

against those established in another Member State, then the Court sometimes treats this version of the rule as being indirectly discriminatory on the ground of nationality.[134] Such discrimination also breaches Article 56 TFEU[135] but can be justified not only by the express derogations but also by the broader public-interest requirements.[136] However, given the serious consequences for the provision of services of a national rule requiring establishment, the Court will carefully scrutinize any justification offered.[137]

(b) Indistinctly applicable measures

In *Gouda*[138] the Court also confirmed that unjustified indistinctly applicable measures were prohibited by Article 56 TFEU. It said:

> 12. In the absence of harmonisation of the rules applicable to services, or even of a system of equivalence, restrictions on the freedom guaranteed by the Treaty in this field may

---

[134] Cf. Case C–546/07 *Commission* v. *Germany (Germany/Poland Agreement)* [2010] ECR I–439, paras. 39–40.

[135] See, e.g., Case C–294/97 *Eurowings Luftverkehrs AG* v. *Finanzamt Dortmund-Unna* [1999] ECR I–7447, para. 19. In more recent cases the Court describes such rules as having a 'dissuasive' effect on free movement of services amounting to 'a denial of that freedom': Case C–150/04 *Commission* v. *Denmark (insurance)* [2007] ECR I–1163, para. 40.

[136] For an illustration of complete conceptual and legal confusion, see Case C–484/93 *Svensson* [1995] ECR I–3955, para. 15: discrimination based on the place of establishment can 'only be justified on the *general interest* grounds referred to in Article [52(1) TFEU] to which Article [62 TFEU] refers' (emphasis added). The Court then considers general interest grounds relating to the coherence of the fiscal regime and not the derogations listed in Art. 52 TFEU (paras. 16–18).

[137] See, e.g., Case 33/74 *Van Binsbergen* [1974] ECR 1299, considered in the following section.

[138] Case C–288/89 [1991] ECR I–4007, para. 12.

arise in the second place as a result of the application of national rules which affect any person established in the national territory to persons providing services established in the territory of another Member State who already have to satisfy the requirements of that State's legislation.

13. ... [S]uch restrictions come within the scope of Article [56 TFEU] if the application of the national legislation to foreign persons providing services is not justified by overriding reasons relating to the public interest or if the requirements embodied in that legislation are already satisfied by the rules imposed on those persons in the Member State in which they are established.

In other words, those measures which impose a dual burden on foreign service providers breach Article 56 TFEU unless they can be justified by overriding reasons relating to the public interest (see fig. 9.1). *Van Binsbergen*[139] provides a good example of an indirectly discriminatory measure. The Court recognized that a Dutch rule requiring representatives before tribunals to be resident in the Netherlands could be justified on the ground of professional rules of conduct connected with the administration of justice (relating to organization, qualifications, professional ethics, supervision, and liability).[140] However, it found the residence requirement to be disproportionate because the administration of justice could be satisfactorily ensured by measures less restrictive to the freedom to provide services, such as choosing an address for service.[141] In *Navileme*[142] the Court ruled that a Portuguese requirement imposing a residence condition on EU citizens wishing to obtain a recreational boating licence breached Article 56 TFEU. The Court considered mainly the express derogations by way of a defence (and found that none were made out, not least because a residence criteria bore no relation to ensuring safety of navigation at sea).

(c) Non-discriminatory measures

The cases considered so far have all involved some form of discrimination which restricted the free movement of services. As with the early case law on establishment, there was a period when the Court said that a national measure which was genuinely non-discriminatory did not breach Article 56 TFEU. For example, in *Debauve*[143] it said that a national ban on transmitting advertisements by cable television did not breach Articles 56–7 TFEU 'if those rules are applied without distinction as regards the origin, whether national or foreign, of those advertisements, the nationality of the person providing the services, or the place where he is established'.[144]

However, as the Court's case law increasingly took market access into account,[145] it recognized that non-discriminatory measures did in principle breach Article 56 TFEU if they were liable to prevent or impede access to the market. We saw this in *Alpine Investments*,[146] considered in Chapter 7, and we can also see it in *Schindler*.[147] The Schindlers were agents of SKL, a public body responsible for organizing lotteries on behalf of four *Länder* in

---

[139] Case 33/74 [1974] ECR 1299.   [140] Para. 12.   [141] Para. 16.

[142] Case C–509/12 *IPTM* v. *Navileme-Consultadoria Nautica* EU:C:2014:54.

[143] Case 52/79 *Debauve* [1981] ECR 833.

[144] Para. 16. See also Case 15/78 *Société générale alsacienne de banque SA* v. *Koestler* [1978] ECR 1971, para. 6. For criticisms of this view, see Van Gerven AG in Case C–159/90 *SPUC* v. *Grogan* [1991] ECR I–4685, paras. 19–22.

[145] The foundations of such jurisprudence can be traced back to the early case law: see, e.g., Case 39/75 *Coenen* [1975] ECR 1547, para. 6. See, esp., Case C–76/90 *Säger* [1991] ECR I–4221, para. 12.

[146] Case C–384/93 [1995] ECR I–1141. See also Case C–118/96 *Safir* [1998] ECR I–1897, para. 30.

[147] Case C–275/92 [1994] ECR I–1039.

Germany. They sent advertisements and application forms to the UK inviting people to participate in the German lottery, and were prosecuted for breaching the (then) national law banning lotteries. The Court said that the national legislation prohibiting the holding of large lotteries was a non-discriminatory obstacle to the freedom to provide services, which contravened Article 56 TFEU because it was liable to prohibit free movement of services.[148] However, it continued that, bearing in mind the moral, religious, and cultural aspects of gambling, the restriction could be justified on the ground of preventing the lottery from becoming 'a source of private profit', as well as avoiding 'the high risk of crime or fraud' and 'the incitement to spend which may have damaging individual and social consequences'.[149]

2.2 Measures 'Liable to Prohibit or Otherwise Impede' Freedom to Provide Services

Cases such as *Alpine* and *Schindler* marked a stepping stone towards a more general reliance on the market access test. In fact, reliance on the market access test had already been signalled by the Court in the early case of *Van Binsbergen*[150] and confirmed in its seminal decision of *Säger*,[151] where it said that Article 56 TFEU requires:

> *not only* the elimination of all discrimination against a person providing services on the grounds of his nationality *but also* the abolition of any restriction even if it applies without distinction to national providers of services and to those of other Member States, when it is liable to prohibit or otherwise impede the activities of a provider of services established in another Member State where he lawfully provides similar services.[152]

Säger concerned a German law requiring those monitoring patents to have a licence. This licence was granted on condition that the individual held certain professional qualifications (e.g., as a lawyer or patent agent). Dennemayer, a British company, monitored patents on behalf of clients, particularly in Germany, and informed them when the fees for renewing the patents became due. The commission charged by Dennemayer was lower than that charged by German patent agents who complained that Dennemeyer was breaching German law by trading without a licence; Dennemayer argued that the German law itself breached Article 56 TFEU. The Court found that the German rule prevented undertakings established in other Member States from providing services to patent holders established in the national territory, and prevented patent holders from freely choosing the manner in which their patents were to be monitored.[153] The rule therefore breached Article 56 TFEU unless it could be justified (see fig. 9.2).[154]

The *Säger* formulation, often simplified to the question 'Does the national law constitute a restriction on the freedom to provide services?',[155] the test which the Court has applied in most subsequent services cases,[156] avoids the intellectual somersaults involved

---

[148] Paras. 47–8. See also Case C–36/02 *Omega* [2004] ECR I–9609, para. 25.

[149] Para. 60.   [150] Case 33/74 [1974] ECR 1299, paras. 10–11.

[151] Case C–76/90 [1991] ECR I–4221. Cf. Case 205/84 *Commission* v. *Germany (insurance cases)* [1986] ECR 3755, para. 25.

[152] Para. 12, emphasis added.   [153] Para. 14.

[154] See also Case C–255/04 *Commission* v. *France (performing artists)* [2006] ECR I–5251, para. 29.

[155] See, e.g., Case C–243/01 *Gambelli* [2003] ECR I–13031, para. 45.

[156] See, e.g., Case C–43/93 *Vander Elst* [1994] ECR I–3803, para. 14; Case C–272/94 *Guiot* [1996] ECR I–1905, para. 10; Case C–222/95 *Parodi* [1997] ECR I–3899, para. 18; Case C–58/98 *Corsten* [2000] ECR I–7919, para. 33.

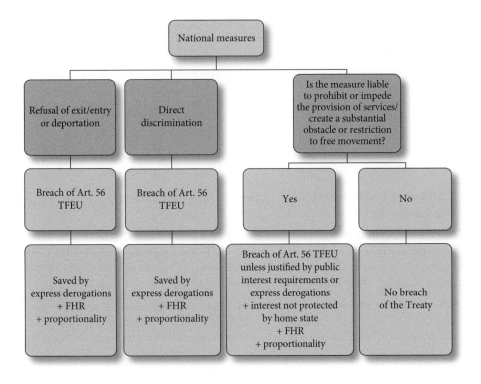

Fig. 9.2 The effect of *Säger* on free movement of services

in deciding whether particular national rules are indistinctly applicable or non-discrim-inatory but hinder market access (direct discrimination is still usually treated separately as fig. 9.2 shows).

The influence of the change wrought by *Säger* can be seen in *Commission* v. *Italy*,[157] another case about patent agents. Italian law required patent agents established in an-other Member State to be entered on the Italian register of patent agents before providing a service there. Registration was conditional on having a residence or place of business in Italy. Instead of considering—as it would have done in the past—whether registration and residence requirements discriminated in some way, due to the additional expense and administrative and economic burdens for businesses established in another Member State,[158] the Court merely observed that the Italian rules constituted 'a *restriction* within the meaning of Article [56 TFEU]'.[159] The focus then shifted to questions of justification and proportionality (see Section 2.3).

However, the more recent cases have made clear that rules of a Member State do not constitute a 'restriction' solely 'by virtue of the fact that other Member States apply less strict, or economically more favourable, rules to providers of similar services established in their territory'. The question of what constitutes a restriction was at issue in *Kostas*

---

[157] Case C–131/01 *Commission* v. *Italy* [2003] ECR I–1659. See also Case C–389/05 *Commission* v. *France (insemination of bovine semen)* [2008] ECR I–5337, para. 66; Joined Cases C–372 and 73/09 *Peñarroja Fa* [2011] ECR I–1785 (no person could be enrolled in a national register of court experts unless he had been enrolled in a register maintained by a *cour d'appel* for three consecutive years).

[158] Case C–49/98 *Finalarte* [2001] ECR I–7831, para. 70.

[159] Emphasis added, para. 27, and para. 42 on the residence requirement. See also Case C–165/98 *Mazzoleni* [2001] ECR I–2189, para. 24; Case C–215/01 *Schnitzer* [2003] ECR I–4847, para. 34; Case C–496/01 *Commission* v. *France (bio-medical analysis)* [2004] ECR I–2351, para. 64.

Konstadinides.[160] The case raised the question whether a German state law requiring doctors' fees to be reasonable and calculated on the basis of the official regulation on doctors' fees breached Article 56 TFEU. The Court ruled that the existence of a 'restriction' could not be deduced from the mere fact that doctors established in Member States other than Germany had to submit, for calculating their fees for services provided in the territory of the *Land* of Hesse, to the rules applicable in that *Land*. So the mere existence of a rule in the host state was not sufficient to trigger the restrictions jurisprudence. However, the Court added that in the absence of any flexibility of the system at issue, the application of such a system, which would be liable to have a deterrent effect on doctors from other Member States, would constitute a restriction within the meaning of the Treaty which needed to be justified and the measures had to be proportionate.

2.3 Justification and Proportionality

(a) Grounds of justification

As we have seen, indistinctly applicable measures and measures which hinder the provision of services between Member States can be justified, using the language in *Säger*,[161] by 'imperative reasons relating to the public interest and which apply to all persons or undertakings pursuing an activity in the State of destination, *in so far as that interest is not protected by the rules to which the person providing the services is subject in the Member State in which he is established*'.

In *Gouda*[162] the Court listed a number of examples of imperative reasons in the public interest,[163] including consumer protection and worker protection. We shall consider these public-interest grounds in more detail in Chapter 12. For now it is sufficient to note that given the sensitivity of the issues raised by some of the cases on services, the Court has applied these public-interest requirements with a considerable degree of flexibility. In some cases it is prepared to engage in a detailed scrutiny of the justifications advanced by the Member States and/or in the question of proportionality, as the broadcasting cases indicate (see Case Study 11.2). In other cases, particularly those touching upon sensitive socio-cultural issues, it has afforded Member States a considerable margin of appreciation.[164] *Schindler* is the prime example of this. There the Court accepted without question all the justifications advanced by the UK government about the social ills of gambling, despite the fact that the Court knew that the National Lotteries Act 1993 had gone through Parliament permitting the creation of the very type of lottery which the UK government had so forthrightly condemned in *Schindler*.[165] The Court's extreme leniency in *Schindler* has not been repeated, although, as Chapter 11 shows, gambling remains a sensitive sector.

(b) Home-state control

When considering whether the host state's action could be justified in the field of services, *Säger* added the additional criteria that the national court had to take into account the

---

[160] Case C-475/11 EU:C:2013:542.

[161] Case C-76/90 [1991] ECR I-4221, para. 15, emphasis added.

[162] Para. 13. See generally J. Fernández Martin and S. O'Leary, 'Judicial exceptions to the free provision of services' (1995) 1 *ELJ* 308 and the updated version in M. Andenas and W. H. Roth (eds.), *Services and Free Movement in EU Law* (Oxford: OUP, 2002).

[163] Also described as 'overriding reasons in the public interest', 'justified by the general good' (Case 279/80 *Webb* [1981] ECR 3305, paras. 16–17) and 'mandatory grounds in the general interest' (Case C-224/97 *Ciola* [1999] ECR I-2517, para. 15).

[164] This is the description used by the Court in Case C-67/98 *Questore di Verona* v. *Diego Zenatti* [1999] ECR I-7289, paras. 15 and 33.

[165] See, e.g., paras. 31 and 51.

action already taken by the *home* state to protect that particular interest (see fig. 9.2). This is a reflection of the principle of home-state control or country of origin. The importance of this principle can be seen in *Guiot*.[166] The Court said that a national law requiring an employer providing a service in the host Member State to pay employer's contributions to the social security fund of the host Member State, in addition to the contributions paid to the social security fund in the state in which the employer was established, placed an additional financial burden on the employer which was liable to restrict the freedom to provide services. It said that the national legislation could be justified by the public interest relating to the 'social protection of workers in the construction industry'.[167] Then, reflecting the country-of-origin principle (CoOP), the Court said that if the workers enjoyed the same protection, or essentially similar protection, by virtue of employer's contributions already paid by the employer in the Member State of establishment,[168] which was a matter for the national court to decide,[169] then the justification was not made out. In other cases, the Court has said that failure to take into account supervision which has already been carried out in the home state means the national measure fails the test of proportionality.[170]

The requirement that the host state take account of the measures put in place by the home state to protect the relevant interest is important because, in respect of services, the primary regulator is the home state and the host state can impose only supplementary controls. In this regard, the services case law follows that on goods, where, in cases such as *Biologische Producten*,[171] the Court ruled that the host state could require the product to undergo a fresh examination but had to take into account the results of tests already carried out by the state of origin. The home-state control rule does not apply to Articles 45 and 49 TFEU on the free movement of workers and establishment where the primary regulator is the host state and so the controls imposed by the home state are of little relevance. The CoOP lay at the heart of the debate about the Services Directive, which is considered in Chapter 11.

(c) Proportionality

Finally, the Court requires that the steps taken to protect the public interest must be proportionate, i.e., appropriate for securing the attainment of the objective which they pursue and must not go beyond what is necessary in order to attain it.[172] Once again it is possible to see how the intensity of the Court's review varies according to the sensitivity of the subject matter. Where national rules do not raise politically difficult issues, the Court's scrutiny tends to be quite intrusive. For example, in *Säger* itself the Court found that the licensing requirements for those monitoring patents exceeded what was necessary to protect the public interest because the services were straightforward (alerting clients when fees were due), the service provider gave no advice to the clients (who were themselves experts in the field), and there was no risk to clients if those monitoring

---

[166] Case C–272/94 *Guiot* [1996] ECR I–1905. See also Case C–496/01 *Commission* v. *France (bio-medical analysis)* [2004] ECR I–2351, para. 71.

[167] Para. 16.

[168] Para. 17. See also Joined Cases C–369 and 376/96 *Arblade* [1999] ECR I–8453, para. 80.

[169] On the facts the Court observed that the Belgian and Luxembourg contributions at issue in practice covered the same risks and had a similar, if not identical, purpose (para. 19).

[170] Case C–465/05 *Commission* v. *Italy (private security activities)* [2007] ECR I–11091, para. 63.

[171] Case 272/80 *Criminal Proceedings against Biologische Producten BV* [1981] ECR 3277, para. 14, considered further in Ch. 6.

[172] Joined Cases C–369 and 376/96 *Arblade* [1999] ECR I–8453, para. 35.

the patents failed in their task (the German patent office itself also sent out official reminders).

Similarly, in the *Tourist Guide*[173] case the Court found that while the requirement that tourist guides possess a licence could in principle be justified by 'the general interest in consumer protection and in the conservation of the national historical and artistic heritage', such a requirement was disproportionate.[174] The Court noted that the rule had the effect of reducing the number of tourist guides, leading tour operators to use local guides, with the drawback that the tourists 'do not have a guide who is familiar with their language, their interests and their specific expectations'. The Court added that the profitable operation of such group tours depended on the commercial reputation of the operator, who faced competitive pressure from other tour companies. These factors compelled companies to be selective in employing tourist guides and to exercise some control over the quality of their services.

Case Study 9.2: QUALIFICATIONS AND THE LEGAL PROFESSION

As we saw in Chapter 9, host state rules on the use of professional titles can prove to be a serious impediment for professionals wishing to work in another Member State. The recognition of legal qualifications has proved to be a particularly thorny issue given the major differences between the legal systems of the Member States. For this reason, the legal profession has been more regulated by EU law than most.[175] The first directive, 77/249 on the provision of services,[176] enabled lawyers to provide services in other Member States under the control of their home state and using their home state title, but subject to the same conditions laid down for lawyers established in the host state, with the exception of any conditions requiring residence or registration of a professional activity in that state.[177] The directive also made provision for lawyers providing services to be introduced to the presiding judge and the president of the relevant Bar and to work in conjunction with a local lawyer.[178]

The rules laid down in the directive are, of course, subject to the Treaty provisions, including Article 56 TFEU. The importance of this can be seen in *AMOK*,[179] where German law provided that the unsuccessful litigant in proceedings before a German court did not have to pay the costs of the local lawyer as well as the lawyer providing the service. The Court said that the German rule requiring the hiring of a local German lawyer had the effect of discouraging parties from having recourse to lawyers established in other Member States: 'The freedom of such lawyers to provide their services would thereby be obstructed and the harmonisation of the sector, as initiated by the Directive, adversely affected.'[180]

The influence of Article 56 TFEU can also be seen in *Cipolla*.[181] The Court said that national law setting a professional scale of charges which permitted no derogation was liable

---

[173] Case C–180/89 *Commission* v. *Italy* [1991] ECR I–709.

[174] Para. 24. See also Case C–11/95 *Commission* v. *Belgium* [1996] ECR I–4115, para. 55.

[175] See further S. Claessens, *Free Movement of Lawyers in the European Union* (Nijmegen: Wolf Legal Publishers, 2008).

[176] Dir. 77/249/EC ([1977] OJ L78/17).   [177] Art. 4(1).

[178] This ensures that the service-providing lawyer can act within the local judicial system, has the necessary support, and can comply with local procedural and ethical rules: Case 427/85 *Commission* v. *Germany* [1988] ECR 1123, but such requirements cannot be disproportionate: Case C–294/89 *Commission* v. *France* [1991] ECR I–3591.

[179] Case C–289/02 *AMOK Verlags GmbH* v. *A & R Gastronomie GmbH* [2003] ECR I–15059.

[180] Para. 39.   [181] Joined Cases C–94 and 202/04 *Cipolla* v. *Fazari* [2006] ECR I–2049.

to render access to the Italian legal services market more difficult for lawyers established in other Member States and was therefore likely to restrict the exercise of their activities providing services in breach of Article 56 TFEU. However, the Court recognized that the Italian government might be able to justify the restriction on the grounds of consumer protection and safeguarding the proper administration of justice[182] but it was for the national court to assess the proportionality of the measure, bearing in mind the specific context of the Italian legal market (an extremely large number of lawyers who might be encouraged to compete against each other on price, with the risk of deterioration of the quality of the services provided).[183]

Directive 77/249 made no provision for mutual recognition of diplomas. This was addressed by Directive 89/48/EEC—and now the RPQ Directive 2005/36, considered in Chapter 8—which requires lawyers trained in a system which differs from that of the host state either to sit an aptitude test or to complete an adaptation period in order for their diplomas of be recognized by another Member State.

The final piece in the lawyers' jigsaw was Directive 98/5/EC.[184] While Directive 77/249 concerns lawyers' *services*, Directive 98/5/EC concerns lawyers' *establishment*. It represents a new phase in the recognition of qualifications because it specifically provides that a person's *authorization* to practise in their home Member State must be taken into account by the host state. The directive gives lawyers two options. First, it enables them to practise permanently and without restriction under their *original* professional title[185] in another Member State and on the same basis as the host state's own lawyers,[186] giving advice on the laws of the home and host state as well as on EU and international law. Lawyers who are fully qualified in one Member State will simply have to register with the Bar or other competent authority in the host state on the basis of their registration in the home state,[187] without the need for either an aptitude test or an adaptation period or any language test.[188]

Secondly, the directive makes it easier to acquire the professional title of the host state. A migrant lawyer who has 'effectively and regularly' practised in the law of the host state, including Union law, for at least three years under his home state title can seek admission to the profession of lawyer in the host state (i.e., can use both the host state and the home state's title) without having to undergo an aptitude test or adaptation period.[189]

3. THE EXERCISE OF SERVICE ACTIVITY

3.1 Social Advantages

Having looked at rules which prevent or impede initial *access* to the services market in another Member State, we turn now to consider rules which impede the actual performance of, or the receipt of, a service in the host state. In the absence of provisions equivalent to Articles 7(1) and (2) of Regulation 492/11 on workers, the Court has read Article 56 TFEU so as to require equal treatment in respect of the terms and conditions on which the service is provided or received and equal treatment in respect of social and tax advantages. We begin by considering social advantages.

---

[182] Joined Cases C–94 and 202/04 *Cipolla* [2006] ECR I–2049, para. 64.   [183] Para. 67.

[184] [1998] OJ L77/36. The validity of this directive was unsuccessfully challenged in Case C–168/98 *Luxembourg* v. *European Parliament and Council* [2000] ECR I–9131.

[185] Art. 2.   [186] Arts. 6–7.   [187] Art. 3(1).

[188] Case C–506/04 *Wilson* v. *Ordre des avocats du barreau de Luxembourg* [2006] ECR I–8613.

[189] Art. 10. Concerns about whether three years' practice is enough to really qualify the individual in the law of the host state underpinned Luxembourg's unsuccessful challenge to the directive in Case C–168/98 *Luxembourg* v. *European Parliament and Council* [2000] ECR I–9131.

In *Cowan*[190] a British tourist was attacked and robbed outside a Metro station in Paris. He was refused criminal injuries compensation because he was neither a French national nor a French resident. The Court said that when Union law guarantees a person the right to go to another Member State, the corollary of the right is that the individual be protected from harm on the same basis as nationals and persons residing there. Consequently, the principle of non-discrimination applied to recipients of services, even where the compensation was financed by the treasury.[191]

For similar reasons, in *Commission* v. *Spain (museums)*[192] the Court condemned a Spanish law providing for free admission to state museums for Spanish nationals and foreigners resident in Spain but not to tourists. The Commission pointed out that since visiting museums encourages tourists, as recipients of services, to go to another Member State, there was a close link between freedom of movement and museum admission. The Court found that the Spanish rules breached both Article 18 TFEU and Article 56 TFEU.[193]

3.2 Tax Advantages

The discrimination model applies equally to taxation. In *Blanco*,[194] under Italian law winnings from casinos situated in Italy were payable free from income tax; those received from casinos in other Member States were treated as income and so were subject to income tax. According to the Court, this difference in tax treatment reduced the attractiveness of going to another Member State to play games of chance[195] and so constituted a discriminatory restriction on the freedom to provide services[196] which could not be saved under any of the express derogations provided in Articles 52 and 62 TFEU.

D. THE HEALTHCARE CASES

1. INTRODUCTION

One of the areas where Articles 56–7 TFEU have had the most profound effect is the cross-border provision of healthcare. Healthcare has traditionally been provided on a territorial basis. Patients contribute to a national system either through taxation or by paying premiums into an insurance scheme. In return, healthcare is available from a locally based provider. Yet the provision of healthcare is extremely costly and increasingly so with an ageing population and ever greater availability of expensive new technology and treatments. All Member States have therefore struggled to balance the infinite demands of their population with finite budgets. This has led to various forms of cost control measures including rationing, through, for example, waiting lists.

The only express provision made originally by Union law for treatment in other Member States was the Social Security Regulation 1408/71.[197] Article 22(1) required

[190] Case 186/87 *Cowan* v. *Le Trésor Public* [1989] ECR 195. See also Case 63/86 *Commission* v. *Italy (social housing)* [1988] ECR 29, para. 19 and Case C–484/93 *Svensson* [1995] ECR I–3955.
[191] Para. 17. In a similar vein, see Case C–164/07 *Wood* v. *Fonds de garantie des victimes des actes de terrorisme et d'autres infractions* [2008] ECR I–4143. Cf. Case C–109/92 *Wirth* [1993] ECR I–6447, considered at n. 101.
[192] Case C–45/93 [1994] ECR I–911; Case C–388/01 *Commission* v. *Italy* [2003] ECR I–721, para. 12.
[193] See also Case C–20/92 *Hubbard* v. *Hamburger* [1993] ECR I–3777, para. 14.
[194] Joined Cases C–344 and 367/13 *Blanco and Fabretti* v. *Agenzia delle Entrate* EU:C:2014:2311.
[195] Para 31.   [196] Para. 33.
[197] Consolidated version [1997] OJ L28/1.

the home state (State A) to meet bills incurred by State A patients while in the host state (State B) in two situations: first, where they needed emergency medical treatment using what was the form E111 and now the European Health Insurance Card;[198] and, secondly, where they had been expressly authorized to receive non-emergency treatment in State B using the E112 form.[199] In respect of the second situation, Article 22(2) explained that authorization could not be refused where the treatment was among the benefits provided for in State A[200] and where the patient could not be given the treatment within the time normally necessary for obtaining the treatment in State A,[201] taking into account the patient's current state of health and the probable course of the disease. If the costs of the treatment in State B were higher than those in State A, then the relevant body in State A had to meet those additional costs where authorization was granted.[202] However, Article 22(2) put the funder of the healthcare, and not the patient, in charge of the decision whether the patient could get treatment abroad and, in the past, such authorizations were relatively rare. Under Regulation 883/04,[203] which replaced Regulation 1408/71 from March 2010, emergency health treatment is provided under Article 19(1); travel for the purpose of receiving treatment is covered by Article 20, which still requires authorization.

How do Articles 56–7 TFEU fit into this framework? Their relevance first became apparent in *Luisi and Carbone*[204] and *SPUC* v. *Grogan*,[205] which showed that EU nationals could in principle travel to another Member State to receive medical treatment because medical services constituted 'services' within the meaning of Article 57 TFEU. But who pays for the treatment? If patients cannot get the treatment they want within a reasonable time at home, can they be treated in another Member State and then, under Articles 56–7 TFEU, expect their own Member State to foot the bill? If so, Union law would pose a considerable threat to careful planning for comprehensive healthcare provision at national level. The easiest way of avoiding such problems would have been for the Court to say that Union law did not apply to national healthcare provision since healthcare did not constitute an economic activity. However, as we have already seen, the Court rejected

---

[198] Art. 22(1)(a). See also 'Communication from the Commission concerning the introduction of a European health insurance card', COM(2003) 73 final, and its adoption by Commission Dec. 189/03 ([2003] OJ L276/1). There was also special provision for pensioners and members of their families when they require treatment abroad in Art. 31 of Reg. 1408/71 (Case C–326/00 *Idryma Koinonikon Asfaliseon (IKA)* v. *Vasilios Ioannidis* [2003] ECR I–1703). However, Reg. 1408/71 was then amended to bring the entitlements of the rights of other patients more closely into line with the rights of these pensioner patients (see Reg. 631/2004/EC ([2004] OJ L100/1)). So all patients are now entitled, during a stay in another Member State for a reason other than the receipt of the treatment, to treatment 'which become[s] necessary on medical grounds during a stay in the territory of another Member State/the Member State other than the State of residence, taking into account the nature of the benefits and the expected length of the stay'.

[199] Art. 22(1)(c). Where authorization has been granted, concerns about the planning and organization of hospital care cannot be invoked by the competent state: Case C–145/03 *Heirs of Annette Keller* v. *INSS* [2005] ECR I–2529, para. 62. Case C–466/04 *Acereda Herrera* v. *Servicio Cántabro de Salud* [2006] ECR I–5431 added that authorization does not entitle the patient or any accompanying person to be reimbursed for costs of travel, accommodation, and subsistence when in the host state except for the costs of accommodation and meals in hospital.

[200] This limitation was upheld in Case C–157/99 *Geraets-Smits and Peerbooms* [2001] ECR I–5473, para. 45.

[201] This requirement was interpreted in Case C–372/04 *Watts* v. *Bedford Primary Care Trust* [2006] ECR I–4325 to mean whether the hospital treatment required by the patient's medical condition could be provided in the home state within 'an acceptable time which ensures its usefulness and efficiency'.

[202] Art. 36 of Reg. 1408/71.   [203] [2004] OJ L166/1.

[204] Joined Cases 286/82 and 26/83 [1984] ECR 377.   [205] Case C–159/90 [1991] ECR I–4685.

this approach[206] and said that Articles 56–7 TFEU did apply to healthcare. Instead, it has used the public-interest requirements and the proportionality principle to reconcile the individual's right to travel in order to receive treatment in another Member State with the home state's duty to provide adequate healthcare to the population as a whole.

2. *KOHLL* AND *DECKER*: OPENING UP THE MARKET

This process of reconciliation began with *Kohll*,[207] which concerned the Luxembourg healthcare system according to which medical services were offered on a reimbursement basis. The insurance rules permitted treatment to be received in other Member States but required prior authorization from the sickness fund which was meeting the cost. No requirement for prior authorization was imposed in respect of treatment received domestically. When Mr Kohll's daughter was refused permission to receive orthodontic treatment in Germany he argued that the Luxembourg rules breached Article 56 TFEU. In principle the Court agreed, arguing that because the rules had the effect of making the provision of services between Member States more difficult than the provision of services purely within one Member State,[208] they breached Article 56 TFEU unless they could be justified.

The Luxembourg authorities put forward two justifications for the authorization requirement: first, that it constituted the only effective and least restrictive means of controlling expenditure on health and balancing the budget of the social security system. While the Court accepted this argument in principle,[209] it rejected it on the facts. Because Kohll sought reimbursement for the treatment in Germany at the same rate that applied in Luxembourg and according to the tariff laid down by the insurance scheme, there was no significant effect on the financing of healthcare or the social security scheme.[210]

Secondly, Luxembourg argued that the rule could be justified on public-health grounds in order to ensure both the quality of the medical treatment and a balanced medical and hospital service open to all. Once again, the Court accepted the argument in principle, but rejected it on the facts. It said that since the conditions for taking up and pursuing the professions of doctor and dentist had been the subject of several coordinating and harmonizing directives, Luxembourg could not raise such public-health concerns.[211] It also said that Luxembourg had failed to produce any evidence showing that the rules were indispensable for the maintenance of an essential treatment facility or medical service in Luxembourg. Since the rules could not be justified, the authorization requirement breached Articles 56–7 TFEU, despite the fact that Article 22(2) of Regulation 1408/71 expressly envisaged prior authorization.[212]

Kohll therefore suggested that Articles 56–7 TFEU were able to reshape the contours of Article 22 (now Article 20). The importance of what the Treaty provisions could achieve was again seen in *Vanbraekel*.[213] In that case prior authorization was wrongfully withheld

---

[206] Case C–157/99 *Geraets-Smits and Peerbooms* [2001] ECR I–5473, paras. 52–9.
[207] Case C–158/96 [1998] ECR I–1931. Cf. Case C–120/95 *Decker v. Caisse de maladie des employés privés* [1998] ECR I–1831 (on goods) in which no prior authorization was sought.
[208] Para. 33.   [209] Para. 41.   [210] Paras. 40 and 42.   [211] Paras. 47–9.
[212] In Case C–56/01 *Patricia Inizan v. Caisse primaire d'assurance maladie des Hauts-de-Seine* [2003] ECR I–12403, para. 26, the Court nevertheless still found Art. 22(2) to be valid.
[213] Case C–368/98 [2001] ECR I–5363. Cf. Case C–512/08 *Commission v. France (major medical equipment)* [2010] ECR I–8833.

from a patient insured in Belgium who had received treatment in France. The question raised was at what level the reimbursement should be made—according to the higher tariffs payable if the treatment had been provided in Belgium or the lower tariffs payable if the treatment was received abroad. Article 56 TFEU was used to fill the gap. The Court noted that if a patient had a lower level of cover when receiving hospital treatment in another Member State (France) than when undergoing the same treatment in the state where he was insured (Belgium), this could 'deter, or even prevent, that person from applying to providers of medical services established in other Member States and constitutes, both for insured persons and service providers, a barrier to freedom to provide services'.[214] The Court also rejected the justifications put forward by the Belgian government. It said that reimbursement of the higher amount which would have been payable had the treatment been carried out in Belgium neither jeopardized a balanced medical and hospital service open to all nor had a significant effect on the functioning of the social security scheme.[215] Article 56 TFEU therefore required reimbursement at the higher rate.

Kohll and the related case *Decker*, on goods, created 'lively' reactions in the healthcare world[216] because they suggested that in respect of non-hospital (extramural) care, a prior authorization requirement could not be justified, with the result that patients (as opposed to the healthcare service or sickness funds) could demand treatment in other Member States and be reimbursed for the costs of that treatment.[217] As Van der Mei put it, reimbursement of the costs of cross-border healthcare no longer seemed a rarely granted privilege but a judicially enforceable right.[218] However, *Decker* and *Kohll* left open two questions: first, whether the same rules applied to hospital (intramural) healthcare and, secondly, whether the principles laid down in those cases applied to a system based on benefits in kind rather than on reimbursement. These questions were considered by *Geraets-Smits and Peerbooms*[219] and *Müller-Fauré and van Riet*.[220]

3. INTRAMURAL CARE

Both cases concerned the Dutch healthcare system, which, like the Luxembourg system, is funded through a sickness insurance scheme. However, unlike the Luxembourg scheme which provides a right for the insured to be reimbursed for medical bills paid to providers (a restitution system), the Dutch scheme provides benefits in kind. This means that the sickness funds enter into agreements with (local) healthcare providers (usually hospitals in the Netherlands)[221] and the insured patient must go to one of the contracted providers for treatment. Unlike the Luxembourg system, the patient does not pay and then get reimbursed. Instead, the contracted providers are paid directly by the sickness funds.[222]

---

[214] *Vanbraekel*, n. 213, para. 45. See also Art. 7(4) of the Patients' Rights Dir. 2011/24, considered at n. 252.

[215] Paras. 51–2.

[216] W. Palm et al., *Implications of Recent Jurisprudence on the Co-ordination of Health Care Protection Systems* (Brussels: Association Internationale de la Mutualité, 2000).

[217] Case C–255/09 *Commission v. Portugal (non-hospital medical expenses)* [2011] ECR I–10547, the state's total failure to provide for reimbursement of extramural care received in another Member State breached Art. 56 TFEU. Likewise a state's refusal to provide any authorization for intramural care in another Member State is also contrary to Art. 56 TFEU and the Social Security Reg.: Case C–173/09 *Elchinov v. Natsionalna zdravnoosiguritelna kasa* [2010] ECR I–8889.

[218] A. P. van der Mei, 'Cross-border access to health care within the European Union: Some reflections on *Geraets-Smits and Peerbooms* and *Vanbraekel*' (2002) 9 *MJ* 189.

[219] Case C–157/99 [2001] ECR I–5473.   [220] Case C–385/99 *Müller-Fauré* [2003] ECR I–4509.

[221] Para. 66.   [222] See C–385/99 *Müller-Fauré* [2003] ECR I–4509, para. 105.

While the basic rule was that patients receive treatment from contracted providers, the Dutch sickness funds did authorize treatment from non-contracted providers (both at home and abroad) on two conditions: first, that the treatment was 'normal in the professional circles concerned' and, secondly, that the treatment by the non-contractual provider was necessary for the patient, having first assessed the treatment available in the Netherlands, and whether it could be obtained without undue delay. The compatibility of these conditions with Union law was considered in *Geraets-Smits and Peerbooms*, which largely concerned the question of the availability of the treatment, and *Müller-Fauré and van Riet* concerning undue delay.[223]

Mrs Geraets-Smits, a Dutch national suffering from Parkinson's disease, sought reimbursement for the costs of her medical treatment in Germany, which she claimed was better than that provided in the Netherlands. Mr Peerbooms, a Dutch national in a persistent vegetative state, was transferred to Austria for neuro-stimulation treatment. He could not have obtained this treatment in the Netherlands, where the technique was used only experimentally. In both cases reimbursement was refused on the ground that satisfactory and adequate treatment was available in the Netherlands.

The Court found that the prior-authorization rules laid down by the insurance schemes for treatment by non-contracted providers 'deter, or even prevent, insured persons from applying to providers of medical services established in another Member State and constitute, both for insured persons and service providers, a barrier to freedom to provide services'.[224] In principle the rules therefore breached Article 56 TFEU.

The Court then considered the justifications for the authorization requirement. It noted that the Dutch system was planned to ensure sufficient and permanent access to a balanced range of high-quality hospital treatments (i.e., by establishing and equipping an appropriate number of hospitals evenly distributed throughout the country),[225] while at the same time trying to control costs and prevent wastage of financial, technical, and human resources.[226] Allowing patients to go to any non-contracted hospital would jeopardize this careful planning at a stroke.[227] For these reasons the Court found that a system of prior authorization for intramural care was in principle 'both necessary and reasonable' on public-health grounds in order to guarantee a 'rationalised, stable, balanced and accessible supply of hospital services'[228] provided that the conditions under which the authorization was granted—both substantively and procedurally—could themselves be justified.[229]

Looking first at the *procedural* conditions,[230] the Court said that these could be justified provided the procedural system was easily accessible for patients; that the decision whether to grant authorization was based on objective, non-discriminatory, and predetermined criteria; that the request was dealt with objectively and impartially and

---

[223] Spaventa, n. 110.

[224] Para. 69. Cf. Case C–444/05 *Stamatelaki* v. *OAEE* [2007] ECR I–3185 (total ban on treatment abroad breached Art. 56 TFEU).

[225] Para. 76. These principles apply equally to the provision of services by pharmacies: Joined Cases C–570 and 571/07 *Blanco Perez* EU:C:2008:138.

[226] Paras. 78–9. All this at a time when the healthcare sector has to satisfy increasing needs with limited funding.

[227] Case C–385/99 *Müller-Fauré* [2003] ECR I–4509, para. 82.   [228] Paras. 80–1.

[229] As elaborated by Case C–385/99 *Müller-Fauré* [2003] ECR I–4509, para. 66.

[230] On the importance of the procedural requirements, see Case C–205/99 *Analir* [2001] ECR I–1271, paras. 37–8.

within a reasonable time; and that refusals to grant authorization were capable of being challenged in judicial or quasi-judicial proceedings.[231]

The Court then turned to the *substantive* conditions for attaining authorization, beginning with the requirement that the treatment had to be 'normal in the professional circles concerned'. It found this to be justified provided it took account of what was sufficiently tried and tested[232] by *international* science (as opposed to simply national science, which would tend to favour national treatment).[233] The Court thought that the second condition, necessity of the proposed treatment, could also be justified on grounds both of public health and of ensuring the financial stability of the sickness insurance system,[234] provided that the condition was construed as meaning that authorization to receive treatment in another Member State could be refused only if the same or equally effective treatment could be obtained without undue delay from a contracted provider in the home state.[235] The Court recognized that if contracted providers were not given priority, this would put at risk the very principle of having contractual arrangements with hospitals and so 'undermine all the planning and rationalisation carried out in this vital sector'.[236] Thus, while rejecting the territorial nature of healthcare services, the Court did recognize the value of a 'closed' system based on a number of contracted providers.

However, when considering whether the treatment could be granted without undue delay from a contracted provider, the Court said that the national authorities had to consider all the circumstances of each specific case, taking into account both the patient's medical history and condition, and the degree of pain or the nature of the patient's disability, which might make it impossible or extremely difficult for the patient to carry out a professional activity.[237] This subjective approach, based on the individual patient's state of health, meant that a state could not refuse permission for treatment abroad simply because it would mean that the patient would jump the waiting list. Therefore, in *Van Riet* the Dutch sickness fund could not refuse to pay for Mrs van Riet's treatment (an arthroscopy) in Belgium, where it was available much sooner than in the Netherlands, simply because appropriate treatment was available in the Netherlands without undue delay. In deciding whether to authorize treatment the fund had to take into account Mrs van Riet's medical condition and medical history (she had been suffering pain for eight years).

4. EXTRAMURAL CARE

The cases we have considered so far (*Geraets-Smits and Peerbooms* and *Van Riet*) concerned hospital services. We turn now to non-hospital services which were

---

[231] Case C–157/99 *Geraets-Smits* [2001] ECR I–5473, para. 90.

[232] I.e., the authorities must take into consideration all the relevant available information, e.g., existing scientific literature and studies, the authorized opinions of specialists, and whether the proposed treatment is covered by the sickness insurance system of the Member State in which the treatment is provided (para. 98).

[233] Para. 97.   [234] Paras. 105–6.

[235] Para. 104. In Case C–268/13 *Petru* v. *Casa Județeană de Asigurări de Sănătate Sibiu* EU:C:2014:2271 the Court said that in deciding whether effective treatment was available reference had to be made to all hospital establishments in the state of residence and not just the local hospital (where the claimant argued there was a lack of medication and basic medical supplies and infrastructure).

[236] Para. 106. The Court added that if the contracted provider could not provide the treatment, the sickness fund could not give priority to a non-contracted national provider (para. 107).

[237] C–385/99 *Müller-Fauré* [2003] ECR I–4509, para. 90.

considered in *Müller-Fauré*. While on holiday in Germany, Müller-Fauré underwent major dental treatment. When the Dutch sickness fund refused to reimburse her because she had not received prior authorization for the treatment, she argued that this requirement breached Article 56 TFEU. The Court agreed, but this time found no justification for the authorization rule. It said that no evidence had been produced to show that if patients were allowed to travel to another Member State for non-hospital treatment without authorization, this would seriously undermine the financial balance of the Dutch scheme.[238] As the Court noted, care is generally provided near the patient's residence, in a cultural environment familiar to the patient, and allows a relationship of trust to build up with the treating doctor.[239] For these reasons the Court anticipated that the numbers taking advantage of the possibility of (non-hospital) treatment in other Member States would be small due to the barriers of language, geography, the cost of staying abroad, and the lack of information about the care provided there.[240]

However, the Court did add an important caveat to its ruling, which it had already mentioned in *Kohll*[241] and *Decker*:[242] patients from State A travelling to State B for extramural treatment but without prior authorization could claim reimbursement of the treatment cost, but only within the limits of the cover provided by the sickness insurance scheme in State A[243] (rather than for all expenses incurred, which would have been the case under Article 22 of Regulation 1408/71). The Court also said that State A could impose other conditions on reimbursement insofar as they were neither discriminatory nor an obstacle to free movement (e.g., requiring that a GP should refer a patient to a specialist consultant).[244]

5. APPLICATION OF THESE PRINCIPLES TO THE BRITISH NHS

Do these principles also apply to the British National Health Service (NHS), a benefits-in-kind system, where care is basically free at the point of delivery but paid for out of taxation? *Watts*[245] answered yes. Watts suffered from severe arthritis of the hips but was told in October 2002 that, since her case was 'routine', there would be a one-year wait for surgery. She therefore applied to the Bedford Primary Care Trust (PCT) for authorization to undergo surgery abroad under the E112 scheme but this was refused, on the ground that treatment could be provided to the patient 'within the Government's NHS Plan targets' and so 'without undue delay'. She therefore sought judicial review of the PCT's decision. Subsequently, her health deteriorated and she was re-examined in January 2003, when she was listed for surgery within three or four months. Although Bedford PCT repeated its refusal to issue an E112, in March 2003 Mrs Watts nevertheless underwent a hip replacement operation in France for which she paid £3,900. She continued with her judicial review application, claiming in addition reimbursement of the medical fees incurred in France, but her application was dismissed on the ground that she had not had to face undue delay after the re-examination of her case in January 2003. The Court of Appeal referred the matter to the Court of Justice.

In *Watts* the Court was less concerned with the Article 56 TFEU aspect of the case than with the application of the regulation. It said that, in order to be entitled to refuse

---

[238] Para. 93.   [239] Para. 96.   [240] Para. 95.   [241] Para. 42.
[242] Para. 40.   [243] Paras. 98 and 106.   [244] Para. 106.
[245] Case C–372/04 *Watts* v. *Bedford Primary Care Trust* [2006] ECR I–4325.

authorization on the ground of waiting time, the competent institution (essentially the PCT) had to establish that:

> the waiting time, arising from objectives relating to the planning and management of the supply of hospital care … does not exceed the period which is acceptable in the light of an objective medical assessment of the clinical needs of the person concerned in the light of his medical condition and the history and probable course of his illness, the degree of pain he is in and/or the nature of his disability at the time when the authorization is sought.[246]

It adopted a similar approach under Article 56 TFEU.[247] Furthermore, it added, the setting of waiting times should be done 'flexibly and dynamically', so that the period initially notified to the person concerned could be reconsidered in the light of any deterioration in the patient's state of health occurring after the first request for authorization. For good measure it added that Article 56 TFEU required the UK to reimburse Mrs Watts' travel and accommodation costs where it would have reimbursed those costs had the travel occurred in the UK. *Watts* therefore shows that the UK practice of the blanket use of waiting lists as a way of managing limited NHS resources could not be justified if account was not taken of the individual circumstances of the applicant.

6. SUMMARY OF THE CASE LAW

So this case law tells us that medical services fall within the scope of Articles 56–7 TFEU. Prior authorization requirements in principle breach Article 56 TFEU but are likely to be justified for intramural care (where there seems to be a presumption of legality) but not for extramural care (where there seems to be a presumption of illegality). This largely institutional distinction between intra- and extramural care creates a number of difficulties. Does it turn on the physical location of the treatment (GP's surgery or hospital out-patient department) or the type of treatment (minor or major surgery)?[248] Cross-border access to *hospital* care, therefore, remains governed by Regulation 1408/71 and now Regulation 883/04, but insured persons may be entitled to authorization in a greater number of cases than the few falling within the ambit of Article 22(2) of Regulation 1408/71. For example, following *Van Riet* account should be taken not only of the patient's current state of health (as required by the regulation) but also the past medical record. And, in respect of waiting lists, account should not just be taken of 'the time normally necessary' for the treatment in State A but consideration must also be given to 'all circumstances of each specific case', which may include the circumstances of the patient[249] as well as a more objective reading of what constitutes a 'normal' waiting time.[250] Thus, the Court's approach is more patient-centred than the original model conceived under the Social Security Regulation.

7. THE PATIENTS' RIGHTS DIRECTIVE

All these developments have, however, forced the Commission to explore the implications of the Court's decisions on patient mobility and healthcare in the EU[251] to work

---

[246] Case C–372/04 *Watts* [2006] ECR I–4325, para. 68.   [247] Paras. 119–20.
[248] E. Steyger, 'National health systems under fire (but not too heavily)' (2002) 29 *LIEI* 97, 106.
[249] See G. Davies, 'Medical treatment abroad' (2003) 153 *NLJ* 938, 939.
[250] See also Case C–385/99 *Müller-Fauré* [2003] ECR I–4509, para. 92.
[251] Commission Communication, 'Follow-up to the high level reflection process on patient mobility and healthcare developments in the European Union', COM(2004) 301 final. See also Commission Communication, 'Modernising social protection for the development of high-quality, accessible and

out ways, for example, of reaching a 'common understanding on patients' rights, entitlements and duties', and working out methods of sharing spare capacity and transnational care. The Commission originally intended to include healthcare services in the Services Directive 2006/123 but this proved too controversial. Eventually a specific directive was adopted on 'the application of patients' rights to cross-border healthcare'.[252] The directive falls into three parts. First, it prescribes common principles to be embedded in all health systems including common standards on quality and safety, as well as the provision of information necessary for informed choice, complaints procedures (Chapter II). Secondly, it establishes a framework for cooperation with regard to issues such as recognition of prescriptions and E-health (Chapter IV). Thirdly, it aims to systematize the Court's healthcare case law (Chapter III). As with the case law, it distinguishes in practice between extramural care in other Member States for which authorization by the home state is not required, and intramural care which still requires authorization. However, the language of extra- and intramural care is not used: instead the directive distinguishes between treatment for which prior authorization is—and is not—required. Yet, the Court's case law is again obviously reflected in the content of the directive. For example, Article 8(2) provides:

> Healthcare that may be subject to prior authorisation shall be limited to healthcare which:
> (a) is made subject to planning requirements relating to the object of ensuring sufficient and permanent access to a balanced range of high-quality treatment in the Member State concerned or to the wish to control costs and avoid, as far as possible, any waste of financial, technical and human resources and:
>   (i) involves overnight hospital accommodation of the patient in question for at least one night; or
>   (ii) requires use of highly specialised and cost-intensive medical infrastructure or medical equipment;[253]
> (b) involves treatments presenting a particular risk for the patient or the population; or
> (c) is provided by a healthcare provider that, on a case-by-case basis, could give rise to serious and specific concerns relating to the quality or safety of the care, with the exception of healthcare which is subject to Union legislation ensuring a minimum level of safety and quality throughout the Union.

It is up to the Member States to inform the Commission of the treatments that fall into category (a). Moreover, again reflecting the Court's case law, a prior authorization requirement, including the criteria and the application of those criteria, must be restricted to what is necessary and proportionate to the objective to be achieved and may not constitute a means of arbitrary discrimination or an unjustified obstacle to free movement.[254]

With regard to requests for prior authorization, according to Article 8(3) of the directive, the Member State of affiliation must assess whether the conditions laid down under Regulation 883/2004 have been met. If so the prior authorization must be granted

---

sustainable health care and long term care: support for the national strategies using the "open method of coordination"', COM(2004) 304 final, and the Commission's consultation paper regarding 'Community action on health services', SEC(2006) 1193/4, 26 Sept. 2006.

[252] EP and Council Dir. 2011/24/EU ([2011] OJ L88/45).

[253] See also the planning limitation for the Member State of affiliation in respect of other requirements in Art. 7(7), and rules on reimbursement in Art. 7(9). The planning limitation is also available for the Member State of treatment in respect of safeguard measures in Art. 4(3).

[254] Art. 8(1).

pursuant to that regulation. Thus Article 8(3) gives priority to the Regulation 883/2004 regime unless the patient requests otherwise. If the directive does apply, then a Member State of affiliation cannot refuse authorization in cases of undue delay:[255]

> the patient is entitled to the healthcare in question in accordance with Article 7, and when this healthcare cannot be provided on its territory within a time limit which is medically justifiable, based on an objective medical assessment of the patient's medical condition, the history and probable course of the patient's illness, the degree of the patient's pain and/or the nature of the patient's disability at the time when the request for authorisation was made or renewed.

Article 9 lays down various administrative procedures including due process guarantees such as the need for a decision to be reasoned and subject to judicial review. Article 7 lays down general principles for reimbursement of costs, which again reflect the Court's case law. It therefore seems that the directive has helped to ensure that there is not a divergence between the approach under the Social Security Regulation and the approach under the directive, thereby reducing the space for invoking the Treaty in the absence of the directive. And, in so doing, helps Member States regain control over flows of patients in and out of their healthcare systems.

E. CONCLUSIONS

The case law discussed in this chapter demonstrates the problems posed by the sheer variety, nature, and duration of services. Another facet of the problem concerns the broad matrix of interests at stake: the interests of the state of establishment and those of the state where the service is provided, both of which may (or may not) want to encourage the export and import of the service; the interests of the potential providers and recipients of the service, especially when the recipient travels to receive a service (e.g., tourist and healthcare services), and the interests of those who might lose out when chasing scarce resources (e.g., those still on waiting lists). Given such a spectrum of interests, national regulation of services tends to be more detailed and complex because, unlike goods, it is not just the service itself but also the service provider, its staff, and equipment which are being regulated. This has posed a tremendous challenge to the Court in balancing the Union interest in opening up the services market with the need to preserve the often legitimate interests of the state. Because one size does not fit all, the standard model of non-discrimination on the grounds of nationality—possibly suitable in the early days of the Union when the provision of services was less complex—does not readily resolve issues raised by the different barriers to the provision and receipt of services. Increasingly the Court falls back on the *Säger* hindrance/obstacle model, finds most national measures to breach Article 56 TFEU, and then focuses on the question of justification and proportionality. As the healthcare cases demonstrate, the Court's analysis of justification can be extremely detailed, but in cases where this proves to be too politically difficult it accepts the justification raised by the Member State without question.

---

[255] Art. 8(5). See also the use of the undue delay concept in the administrative requirements in Art. 9(3).

FURTHER READING

On the services case law generally

M. ANDENAS and W. H. ROTH, *Services and Free Movement in EU Law* (Oxford: OUP, 2003).

S. ENCHELMAIER, 'Always at your service (within limits): The ECJ's case law on Article 56 TFEU (2006–11)' (2011) 36 *ELRev.* 615.

V. HATZOPOULOS, *Regulating Services in the European Union* (Oxford: OUP, 2012).

The Court's approach to healthcare and the Patients Rights Directive

S. DE LA ROSA, 'The Directive on Cross-Border Healthcare or the art of codifying complex case law' (2012) 49 *CMLRev.* 15.

L. HANCHER and W. SAUTER, 'One step beyond: From *Sodemare* to *DocMorris*: The EU's freedom of establishment case law concerning healthcare' (2010) 47 *CMLRev.* 117.

V. HATZOPOULOS, '*Killing* national health and insurance systems but *healing* patients? The European market for healthcare services after the judgments of the Court in *Vanbraekel* and *Peerbooms*' (2002) 39 *CMLRev.* 683.

V. HATZOPOULOS and T. HERVEY, 'Coming into line: The EU's Court softens on cross-border healthcare' (2012) 8 *Heath Economics Policy and Law* 1.

T. HERVEY and J. McHALE, *European Union Health Law: Themes and Implications* (Cambridge: CUP, 2016).

T. HERVEY and J. McHALE, *Health Law and the European Union* (Cambridge: CUP, 2004).

T. HERVEY and L. TRUBEK, 'Freedom to provide healthcare services in the EU: An opportunity for "hybrid governance"' (2007) 13 *Columbia Journal of European Law* 623.

C. NEWDICK, 'Citizenship, free movement and health care: Cementing individual rights by corroding social solidarity' (2006) 43 *CMLRev.* 1645.

W. ROTH, 'The European Economic Community's law on services: Harmonisation' (1988) 25 *CMLRev.* 35.

W. SAUTER, 'Harmonisation in healthcare: The EU Patients' Rights Directive', TILEC Discussion Paper, DP 2011–030.

J. W. VAN DE GRONDEN et al. (eds.), *Health Care and EU Law* (The Hague: Asser Press, 2011).

A. P. VAN DER MEI, *Cross-Border Access to Public Benefits* (Oxford: Hart Publishing, 2002).

On abortion and free movement law

D. R. PHELAN, 'The right to life of the unborn v Promotion of trade in services: The European Court of Justice and the normative shaping of the European Union' (1992) 55 *MLR* 670.

10

UNION CITIZENSHIP

A. INTRODUCTION

So far we have considered the position of those nationals who have exercised their rights of free movement as workers, the self-employed, and the providers and recipients of services. These migrants have been described as market citizens (*homo economicus* or the *bourgeois*) who participate in, and benefit from, the common market as economic actors.[1] Yet, they constitute only a small percentage of the EU's working population: prior to the 2004 enlargement, approximately 1.5 per cent of EU-15 citizens lived and worked in a different Member State from their country of origin (less than 3 million people)—a proportion that had hardly changed during the previous 30 years.[2] Post enlargement, the figure stands at about 14.1 million[3] (out of a total population of about 500 million), albeit that many more millions of EU citizens exercise their right to travel to other Member States temporarily—particularly as tourists or as students.

This means that the vast majority of Union nationals who are economically active have never exercised their rights of free movement under Articles 45, 49, and 56 TFEU (except in their capacity as tourists). Yet, Union law continues to affect many aspects

---

[1] M. Everson, 'The legacy of the market citizen' in J. Shaw and G. More (eds.), *New Legal Dynamics of the European Union* (Oxford: Clarendon Press, 1995).

[2] <http://www.ec.europa.eu/employment_social/workersmobility_2006>.

[3] COM(2013) 837, 3.

of the daily lives of those nationals who do not, or cannot, exercise their rights of free movement. Such individuals often feel at best removed, and at worst alienated, from those taking decisions in their name. This legitimacy gap has presented a major challenge for the EU: what can be done to enable all nationals to identify with, and feel loyalty to, the EU?

The concept of 'Citizenship of the Union', introduced at Maastricht, formed a key part of the Union's response, aiming to provide the glue to help bind together nationals of all the Member States. Union citizenship is both a retrospective and prospective concept: retrospective in that it contains a recognition that the EU has its own people; prospective in that it is through citizenship that communities and identities are constituted.[4] However, the concept of Union citizenship is itself subject to an important limitation: it can be enjoyed only by those holding the nationality of one of the Member States and, as we saw in Chapter 7, the decision as to who enjoys nationality of a Member State is largely a matter for national law. Union citizenship has therefore not helped the 18.5 million (and rising) third-country nationals (TCNs) who are legally resident in the EU.[5] Many contribute to the economies of the host country and so, indirectly, to the EU, but they are excluded from the rights granted to citizens.[6] This chapter will examine the concept of Union citizenship and the rights EU citizens enjoy; in Chapter 13 the position of TCNs is considered.

B. CITIZENSHIP OF THE UNION

While a desire to create a 'Europe for Citizens'[7] or a 'People's Europe'[8] dates back to the early 1970s, it was not until the Spanish pressed the issue at Maastricht[9] that the idea of Union citizenship took concrete form. A new Part Two, entitled 'Citizenship of the Union', was added to the EC Treaty by the Maastricht Treaty in 1992, establishing 'Citizenship of the Union' and listing a number of specific rights which citizens can enjoy.

The inclusion of the citizenship provisions into the Treaties started a lengthy and ongoing debate about the nature of EU citizenship, focusing on two interrelated questions. First, what model of citizenship can and should the Union adopt? The copious literature is full of suggestions, including market citizenship (focusing on the rights of economic actors), social citizenship (emphasizing the social-welfare rights of citizenship), or republican citizenship (based on active citizen participation in the decision-making process). Secondly, given that the EU is a *sui generis*, transnational polity, should EU citizenship aim to replicate citizenship of a nation state (so that European citizenship means citizenship of a European nation state), or should the

---

[4] See J. Shaw, *Citizenship of the Union: Towards post-national membership*, specialized course delivered at the Academy of European Law, Florence, Jul. 1995.

[5] Commission, 'First Annual Report on Migration and Integration', COM(2004) 508.

[6] They are sometimes described as 'denizens'. See, e.g., K. Groenendijk, 'The Long-Term Residents Directive, denizenship and integration' in A. Baldaccini, E. Guild, and H. Toner (eds.), *Whose Freedom, Security and Justice? EU immigration and asylum law and policy* (Oxford: Hart Publishing, 2007), 429.

[7] See the Tindemans Report on the European Union, which contained a chapter entitled 'Towards a Europe for citizens' (Bull. EC 8/1975 II no. 12, 1), which was drawn up at the request of the Paris summit in 1974.

[8] See the two Adonnino Reports of 1985 to the European Council on a People's Europe (Bull. EC Suppl. 7/85).

[9] See the Spanish memorandum on citizenship, 'The road to European citizenship', Co.SN 3940/90, 24 Sept. 1990.

EU aim to create a new, post-national form of citizenship based on multiple-level associations and identifications at regional, national, and European level? If the latter, to what extent, if at all, is it legitimate to draw on the literature and ideas relating to the development of citizenship of a nation state in mapping and analysing what is occurring at EU level?

In practice, many authors do take this literature as their starting point since this informs most individuals' understanding of citizenship. This chapter draws on one particular strand of the literature, examining whether the term citizenship is or should be based on ideas of inclusion or exclusion.[10] An approach to citizenship based on inclusionary ideologies casts the net of potential beneficiaries widely, including not only nationals (whether economically active or not) but also those TCNs who are lawfully resident. It envisages that these citizens enjoy a broad range of civil, political, economic, and social rights. This version of citizenship is sometimes referred to as 'social citizenship'[11] and has some resonance in the EU as the EU develops, albeit in a piecemeal fashion, a range of social policies.[12]

By contrast, the exclusionary approach to citizenship constructs the identity of the citizen through the 'Other': the TCN who needs to be excluded to make the citizen 'secure'.[13] For a while the exclusionary model seemed to be in the ascendancy in the EU. For example, at Amsterdam a new objective was introduced into (now) Article 3(2) TEU—of maintaining and developing 'an area of freedom, justice and security without internal frontiers' in which 'the free movement of persons is ensured in conjunction with appropriate measures with respect to external border controls, asylum, immigration and the prevention and combating of crime'. This idea is developed further by Title V of Part Two TFEU. Yet the reality is inevitably more complex than this and, as we shall see in Chapter 13, the need to welcome TCN migrant workers to fill jobs in areas where there are skills gaps and to help address problems created by an ageing population has forced the EU to rethink any exclusionary agenda suggested by Article 3 TEU.

We begin by examining the citizenship offered by the EU to its nationals, taking Held's understanding of citizenship as our starting point. He says:[14]

> Citizenship has meant a reciprocity of rights against, and duties towards, the community. Citizenship has entailed membership, membership of the community in which one lives one's life. And membership has invariably involved degrees of participation in the community.

Held's definition suggests that there are three interconnected strands to citizenship: (1) rights and duties, (2) membership, and (3) participation. These ideas will form the framework in which we examine EU citizenship.

---

[10] See, e.g., J. D'Oliveira, 'European citizenship: Its meaning, its potential' in R. Dehousse (ed.), *Europe after Maastricht: An ever closer union?* (Munich: Law Books in Europe, 1994), 141–6; J. Shaw, 'The many pasts and futures of citizenship in the European Union' (1997) 22 *ELRev.* 554.

[11] M. Dougan, 'Free movement: The workseeker as citizen' (2001) 4 *CYELS* 93, 103.

[12] C. Barnard, 'EU social policy: From employment law to labour market reform' in P. Craig and G. de Búrca (eds.), *The Evolution of EU Law*, 2nd edn (Oxford: OUP, 2011).

[13] Shaw, n. 10, 571. See also G. de Búrca, 'The quest for legitimacy in the European Union' (1996) 59 *MLR* 349, 356–61.

[14] D. Held, 'Between state and civil society: Citizenship' in G. Andrews (ed.), *Citizenship* (London: Lawrence and Wishart, 1991), 20, cited in Shaw, n. 10.

C. RIGHTS AND DUTIES

1. THE MAIN TREATY PROVISIONS

1.1 Part Two TFEU

As we have seen, for Held, the first limb of citizenship is a reciprocity of rights against, and duties towards, the community. Marshall, in his earlier, classic work on (British) citizenship,[15] also recognized that citizenship involved full membership of the community which has gradually been achieved through the historical development of individual rights, starting with civil rights (basic freedoms from state interference), followed by political rights (such as electoral rights), and, most recently, social rights (including rights to education, healthcare, unemployment insurance, and old-age pensions—the rudiments of a welfare state). Where does the EU stand against this yardstick? Article 20(2) TFEU provides that 'Citizens of the Union shall enjoy the rights and be subject to the duties provided for in the Treaties. They shall have, *inter alia*':[16]

- the right to move and reside freely within the territory of the Member States,[17] subject to the limitations and conditions laid down in the Treaties and by the measures adopted to give them effect
- the right to vote in local and European elections in the host state and stand as a candidate[18]
- the right to diplomatic and consular protection from the authorities of any Member State in third countries[19]
- the right to petition the European Parliament and the right to apply to the ombudsman and to address the institutions and advisory bodies of the Union in any one of the official languages of the EU.[20]

These rights are to be exercised in accordance with the conditions and limits defined by the Treaties and by the measures adopted thereunder.

This rather motley collection of rights falls far short of the full panoply envisaged by Marshall. In part this is due to the Union's lack of competence, particularly in fields connected with the welfare state, and in part due to the principle of subsidiarity—can and

---

[15] T. H. Marshall, *Citizenship and Social Class* (Cambridge: CUP, 1950), 28–9.

[16] Art. 25 TFEU requires the Commission to report every three years on the application of these provisions. On this basis, the Council, acting unanimously in accordance with the special legislative procedure and after obtaining the consent of the European Parliament, may adopt provisions to strengthen or to add to the rights listed in Art. 20(2) TFEU. These provisions will enter into force only after their approval by the Member States in accordance with their respective constitutional requirements (Art. 25, para. 2 TFEU).

[17] See also Art. 45(1) of the Charter.

[18] See also Art. 39(1) of the Charter. See also Recommendation C/2014 14/391 addressing the consequences of disenfranchisement of Union citizens exercising their rights to free movement, C(2014) 391 final, following up on EU Citizenship Report, COM(2013) 269.

[19] See also Art. 46 of the Charter. Of 166 countries outside the EU, there are only three where all 27 Member States are represented (COM(2009) 262). An estimated 8.7 per cent of EU citizens (7 million people) travelling outside the EU do so to countries where their Member State is not represented (COM(2009) 263). The Lisbon Treaty added a new Art. 23(2) TFEU giving powers to the Council to adopt directives to facilitate diplomatic and consular protection in accordance with the special legislative procedure and after consulting the European Parliament. See Dir. 2015/637 on the coordination and cooperation measures to facilitate consular protection for unrepresented citizens of the Union in third countries ([2015] OJ L106/1).

[20] See also Art. 44 of the Charter.

should the Union be attempting to replicate welfare-state provision which is already extensively and expensively provided for at national level? This demonstrates the problem of using literature written in the context of the nation state as a measure by which to assess the EU. For this reason, it might be fairer to say that the rights contained in Part Two supplement and complement rights granted at national level.[21]

It is also a mistake to look at the four substantive rights listed in Part Two in isolation. Article 20(2) TFEU makes clear that the four rights listed are merely examples ('inter alia'). The reference to the fact that '[c]itizens shall enjoy the rights … provided for in the Treaties' means that *migrant* citizens also enjoy the right to non-discrimination on the ground of nationality found in Article 18 TFEU,[22] while all citizens (not just those who have exercised their rights of free movement) can enjoy the right to equal treatment, originally on the ground of sex, now on other grounds,[23] along with other social, environmental, and consumer rights. Most importantly, now, for EU citizens is the entry into force of the Charter of Fundamental Rights of the European Union (the Charter),[24] albeit subject to the special position of the UK and Poland as laid down by the protocol.[25] The protection of human rights will be further reinforced by the EU's accession to the European Convention on Human Rights provided for by Article 6(2) TEU if (when) that happens.[26]

1.2 The Charter

The Charter has proved increasingly influential in shaping the Court's interpretation of the law. The Charter and/or fundamental rights as general principles of law are now the starting point for much of the Court's analysis.[27] The Charter has been used as a ground for striking down EU legislation,[28] for steering the interpretation of key provisions,[29] for even extending the reach of EU law,[30] and, possibly in the future, as a vehicle for striking a better balance between economic and social rights following the controversy in

---

[21] See also Art. 9 TEU: 'Citizenship of the Union shall be additional to national citizenship and shall not replace it', repeated in Art. 20(1) TFEU.

[22] See, e.g., Case C–274/96 *Bickel and Franz* [1998] ECR I–7637, considered at n. 49. For a possibility that non-migrant citizens might also enjoy some other rights, see Case C–46/12 *LN* EU:C:2013:97, paras. 28–9.

[23] See Art. 19 TFEU and the directives adopted under it: Dir. 2000/43 on race and ethnic origin ([2000] OJ L180/22) and the Framework Dir. 2000/78 ([2000] OJ L303/16) prohibiting discrimination on grounds of age, religion, belief, disability, and sexual orientation.

[24] Art. 6(1) TEU.

[25] Protocol No. 30 on the application of the Charter of Fundamental Rights of the European Union to Poland and the United Kingdom. See now Case C–411/10 *NS* v. *Secretary of State for the Home Department* [2011] ECR I–13905, para. 120, which confirms that Art. 1(1) of Protocol 30 'explains Article 51 of the Charter with regard to the scope thereof' and so does not exempt the UK and Poland.

[26] See also Commission Communication, 'An area of freedom, security and justice serving the citizen', COM(2009) 262, 7. The Fundamental Rights Agency (established by Council Reg. 168/2007 ([2007] OJ L53/1)) assists the EU institutions and Member States through research projects and data collection. Many thought human rights would have been strengthened further through the EU's accession to the ECHR. The Court of Justice, however, found the draft accession agreement to be contrary to EU law: *Opinion 2/13 (accession to the ECHR)* EU:C:2014:2454.

[27] Case C–555/07 *Kücückdeveci* v. *Swedex GmbH* [2010] ECR I–365, para. 22; Case C–571/10 *Kamberaj* v. *IPES* EU:C:2012:233, paras. 60–2; but not in cases involving the crisis, so far: see, e.g., Case C–128/12 *Sindicato dos Bancários do Norte* EU:C:2013:149. See further C. Barnard, 'The Silence of the Charter' in S. de Vries, U. Bernitz, and S. Weatherill (eds.), *The EU Charter of Fundamental Rights as a Binding Instrument: Five Years On* (Oxford: Hart Publishing, 2015).

[28] Joined Cases C–92 and 93/09 *Volker and Schecke GbR* v. *Land Hessen* [2010] ECR I–11063; Case C–236/09 *Association belge des consommateurs Test-Achats* [2011] ECR I–773.

[29] Joined Cases C–71 and 99/11 *Bundesrepublik Deutschland* v. *Y, Z* EU:C:2012:518, para. 56.

[30] Case C–256/11 *Dereci* v. *Bundesministerium für Inneres* [2011] ECR I–11315, para. 72.

Viking.[31] These developments enabled Advocate General Sharpston to conclude in *Ruiz Zambrano*[32] that:

> Fundamental rights have thus become a core element in the development of the Union as a process of economic, legal and social integration aimed at providing peace and prosperity to all its citizens.

However, the Charter's existence serves to highlight an ongoing tension that pervades the area of law concerning citizenship. Fundamental rights are seen as universal, capable of being enjoyed by all human beings. By contrast, the majority of the rights in Part Two TFEU on citizenship of the Union can be enjoyed only by EU citizens, who benefit from them by virtue of their nationality. It might also be thought that the rights outlined by Part Two TFEU and the Charter are all enforceable vertically against the body bestowing the title 'citizen', i.e., the EU. In fact, most are enforced vertically but against the state—either the citizen's own state (in the case of social, consumer, and environmental rights) or the host state (in respect of the free movement rights). Only a few rights are enforceable vertically against the EU (the right to petition the Parliament and to contact the ombudsman).[33] Therefore, one of the conundrums of EU citizenship is that rights intended to foster a commitment to the Union are actually being exercised against the Member States.

The relationship between the Union citizen and the Member States also explains another potential tension. The Union gives rights but—despite the wording of Article 20(2) TFEU—demands little by way of duties from its citizens (e.g., to pay taxes, to participate in the defence of the country, to obey the law, to vote, willingness to work).[34] These duties are owed to the Member States and thus it is the Member States which bear the burden—using national taxpayers' money—of the rights. And because the Member States hold the purse strings, and ultimately the decision-making power, they are not prepared to relinquish their sovereignty fully. Therefore, while, under international law, citizens of a state cannot be deported, no matter how bad or impecunious they might be, migrant EU citizens can still be deported from the host state.[35] In this respect EU citizenship is more partial than would first appear.

1.3 Article 21(1) TFEU

Of the rights laid down in Articles 20–5 TFEU, Article 21(1) TFEU is considered the 'primary'[36] right. It gives EU citizens the right to move *and* reside freely within the territory of the Member States, subject to the limitations and conditions laid down in the Treaties and by the measures adopted to give them effect.[37] The initial question facing

---

[31] Case C–438/05 *Viking* [2007] ECR I–10779. See, e.g., Case C–271/08 *Commission* v. *Germany (occupational pensions)* [2010] ECR I–7091, para. 44 and, in particular, Trstenjak AG's Opinion at paras. 183–93.

[32] Case C–34/09 *Ruiz-Zambrano v. ONEM* [2011] ECR I–1177, para. 154.

[33] See S. O'Leary, 'The relationship between Community citizenship and the protection of fundamental rights in Community law' (1995) 32 *CMLRev.* 519.

[34] See, e.g., C. Closa, 'Citizenship of the Union and nationality of the Member States' (1995) 29 *CMLRev.* 487, 509.

[35] This issue is considered in more detail in Ch. 12. Note, in the same spirit, that Member States can still reserve certain senior jobs in the public service to nationals only (Art. 45(4) TFEU and Arts. 51 and 62 TFEU).

[36] La Pergola AG in Case C–85/96 *Martínez Sala* v. *Freistaat Bayern* [1998] ECR I–2691, para. 18.

[37] The European Parliament and Council, acting in accordance with the ordinary legislative procedure, may 'adopt provisions with a view to facilitating the exercise of the rights referred to in paragraph 1' (Art. 21(2) TFEU) where the Treaties have not provided the necessary powers. However, in respect of

the Court was whether Article 21(1) TFEU merely codified the existing law (as the drafters appear to have intended), in which case it was largely unremarkable,[38] or whether it
went beyond the existing law and created a free-standing right to movement for *all* Union
citizens, irrespective of their economic or financial standing. If so, then Article 21 TFEU
was of considerable importance. After a certain amount of prevarication, when the Court
made passing reference to the citizenship provisions but only to reinforce its interpretation of Article 45, 49, or 56 TFEU,[39] the Court finally decided on the importance of
citizenship when it declared in paragraph 31 of *Grzelczyk*[40] that:

> Union citizenship is destined to be the fundamental status of nationals of the Member
> States, enabling those who find themselves in the same situation to enjoy the same treat-
> ment in law irrespective of their nationality, subject to such exceptions as are expressly
> provided for.[41]

This paved the way for the Court in *Baumbast*[42] to sever the link between free movement
and being economically active:

> the Treaty on European Union does not require that citizens of the Union pursue a profes-
> sional or trade activity, whether as an employed or self-employed person, in order to enjoy
> the rights provided in Part Two [TFEU], on citizenship of the Union.

This change in approach resulted in the finding in *Chen*[43] that a *baby*, with Chinese national parents, born in Northern Ireland, who, as a result had nationality of the Republic
of Ireland (i.e. Irish nationality) under Irish law, enjoyed the rights of Union citizenship.
She therefore enjoyed the right to reside in the UK under Article 21(1) TFEU, subject to
the limitations and conditions laid down by the Person of Independent Means Directive
90/364 (now Article 7(1)(b) CRD), which had to be interpreted narrowly.[44]

From the case law it is now possible to say that, subject to the limitations and conditions laid down in the Treaty and the secondary legislation, all EU citizens enjoy under
Article 21(1) TFEU:[45]

- the right to leave their home state (a prohibition on the right to leave is 'the antithesis
  of the freedom conferred by Union citizenship to move and reside within the territory of the Member States')[46]

---

social security or social protection Art. 21(3) TFEU provides that the Council must act in accordance with
the special legislative procedure.

[38] Even prior to Maastricht there were a number of decisions which can be seen with the benefit of
hindsight to have a citizenship component: e.g., Case 186/87 *Cowan* [1989] ECR 195, discussed in Ch. 9;
Case 293/83 *Gravier* v. *City of Liège* [1985] ECR 593, discussed in Ch. 8.

[39] See, e.g., Case C–193/94 *Skanavi* [1996] ECR I–929; Case C–274/96 *Bickel and Franz* [1998] ECR I–7637.

[40] Case C–184/99 [2001] ECR I–6193, echoing La Pergola AG in Case C–85/96 *Martínez Sala* [1998] ECR
I–2691, para. 18.

[41] See also La Pergola AG in Case C–85/96 *Martínez Sala* [1998] ECR I–2691, para. 20., who said the
introduction of Union citizenship created a new status for the individual, 'a new individual legal standing
in addition to that already provided for', and Art. 21 TFEU attaches to that new status the right to move and
reside freely.

[42] Case C–413/99 *Baumbast and R.* v. *Secretary of State for the Home Department* [2002] ECR I–7091,
para. 83.

[43] Case C–200/02 *Chen* v. *Secretary of State for the Home Department* [2004] ECR I–9925.

[44] This is discussed in detail in Ch. 12.

[45] A full discussion of the development of this case law can be found in Ch. 15 of the first edition of
this book.

[46] Case C–249/11 *Byankov* EU:C:2012:608, para. 79. See also Case C–434/10 *Aladhov* v. *Zamestnik director na Stolichna direktsia na vatreshnite raboti kam Ministerstvo na vatreshnite raboti* [2011] ECR I–11659.

- the initial right of entry into another Member State[47]
- a free-standing and directly effective right of residence in another Member State[48]
- the right to enjoy social advantages on equal terms with nationals[49] for those lawfully resident[50] in another Member State
- the right to have decisions taken against them regularly reviewed.[51]

The rights provided by Article 21(1) TFEU must now be viewed in the context of the Citizens' Rights Directive (CRD) 2004/38.[52] Given the significance of this directive for delivering citizens' rights and the burgeoning case law, we shall discuss its content in the light of the case law already decided under Article 21 TFEU.[53]

2. THE CITIZENS' RIGHTS DIRECTIVE (CRD) 2004/38

2.1 Introduction

The CRD sets out detailed provisions governing the rights of EU citizens to move and reside freely in another Member State. It repeals and replaces the directives facilitating the migration of the economically active: Directive 68/360[54] on the rights of entry and residence; Regulation 1251/70[55] on the right to remain; the two Union directives on establishment and services;[56] and the three 1990 Residence Directives, which gave rights to the semi-economically active[57] (students, persons of independent means (PIMs), and the retired).[58] At the heart of the CRD lies the basic idea that the rights enjoyed by the migrant citizen and their family members increase the longer a person is resident in another Member State.[59]

Case E–26/13 *The Icelandic State* v. *Gunnarsson* [2014] EFTA Ct. Rep. 254, para. 82 shows that the right to leave can be inferred in Art.7(1)(b) CRD (see C. Burke and O. Hannesson (2015) 52 *CMLRev.* 1111).

[47] Case C–357/98 *Ex p. Yiadom* [2000] ECR I–9265.

[48] Case C–413/99 *Baumbast* [2002] ECR I–7091, para. 84.

[49] Case C–274/96 *Bickel and Franz* [1998] ECR I–7637 (translation facilities), more recently confirmed in Case C–322/13 *Rüffler* EU:C:2014:189; Case C–85/96 *Martínez Sala* [1998] ECR I–2691 (child allowance); Case C–184/99 *Grzelczyk* [2001] ECR I–6193 (minimex).

[50] Case C–85/96 *Martínez Sala* [1998] ECR I–2691; Case C–456/02 *Trojani* [2004] ECR I–7573.

[51] Case C–249/11 *Byankov* EU:C:2012:608, paras. 79–81.

[52] In its Report on the Application of the Directive (COM(2008) 840/3, 3) the Commission notes that 'The overall transposition of Directive 2004/38 is rather disappointing. Not one Member State has transposed the Directive effectively and correctly in its entirety. Not one Article of the Directive has been transposed effectively and correctly by all Member States.'

[53] This interconnection of primary and secondary rules raises difficult constitutional issues but, from a pragmatic point of view, it does ensure a coherent approach: see D. Thym, 'The elusive limits of solidarity: Residence rights of and social benefits for economically inactive Union citizens' (2015) 52 *CMLRev.* 17, 24.

[54] [1968] OJ Spec. Ed. (II) L257/13/485.

[55] This was repealed by Commission Reg. 635/2006 ([2006] OJ L112/9).

[56] Dir. 73/148 ([1973] OJ L172/14) and Dir. 75/34 ([1975] OJ L14/10).

[57] The Court views these groups as non-economically active. However, this semi-economically active term will be used to describe this group, who do have sufficient resources, to distinguish them from those without any resources, who will be described as non-economically active.

[58] Council Dir. 90/364/EEC ([1990] OJ L180/26) on the rights of residence for persons of sufficient means; Council Dir. 90/365/EEC on the rights of residence for employees and self-employed who have ceased their occupational activity ([1990] OJ L180/28); and Council Dir. 93/96 on the rights of residence for students ([1993] OJ L317/59). These directives have been repealed and replaced by the Citizens' Rights Dir. 2004/38 ([2004] OJ L158/77).

[59] The cross-border element remains essential: Case C–127/08 *Metock* v. *Minister for Justice, Equality and Law Reform* [2008] ECR I–6241, para. 77. See also 3rd recital of the CRD: 'Union citizenship should be the

In *Metock*[60] the Court insisted that the CRD could not be interpreted restrictively nor could its provisions be interpreted so as to deprive them of their effectiveness. The Court also noted the continuum between the legislation pre-dating the CRD and the CRD,[61] but recognized that the CRD raised standards: it said that the CRD 'aims in particular to "strengthen the right of free movement and residence of all Union citizens", so that Union citizens cannot derive less [sic] rights from that directive than from the instruments of secondary legislation which it amends or repeals'.[62]

This positive assessment of the role and potential of EU citizenship needs to be tempered somewhat by the chill winds of change and a greater political realism heralded by *Brey*[63] and confirmed in *Dano*[64] and the subsequent case law. In *Brey* the Court said the CRD is intended to 'facilitate and strengthen the exercise of the primary and individual right' to move and reside freely but it is also intended to set out the conditions governing the exercise of the right including the requirement for the non-economically active to have sufficient resources, and the possibility for host states not to provide social assistance for the first three months.[65] That condition is based on the idea that the 'exercise of the right of residence for citizens of the Union can be subordinated to the legitimate interests of the Member States—in the present case, the protection of their public finances'.[66] In other words, while the Court still repeats the 'fundamental status' mantra from paragraph 31 of *Grzelczyk*, it is paying much more attention to the final phrase of paragraph 31: 'subject to such exceptions as are expressly provided for'.[67]

2.2 THE PERSONAL SCOPE OF THE CITIZENS' RIGHTS DIRECTIVE

(a) The Union citizen

The directive applies to Union citizens, defined, as with Article 20(1) TFEU, as 'any person having the nationality of a Member State'[68] who moves to, or resides in, a Member State other than that of which he or she is a national.[69] In fact, as we shall see, after the first three months and up to five years, it really applies only to those Union citizens who have sufficient resources, either through employment or independently, who will not become an unreasonable burden on the host state.

(b) Family members

(i) Mandatory admission

The directive also applies to family members, irrespective of nationality,[70] who 'accompany *or* join'[71] the Union citizen who 'move[s] to or reside[s] in a Member State other than

---

fundamental status of nationals of the Member States *when* they exercise their right of free movement and residence' (emphasis added).

[60] Case C–127/08 *Metock* [2008] ECR I–6241, paras. 84 and 93.   [61] Para. 59.   [62] Para. 59.
[63] Case C–140/12 *Brey* EU:C:2013:565, para. 53.   [64] Case C–333/13 *Dano* EU:C:2014:2358.
[65] Case C–140/12 *Brey* EU:C:2013:565, para. 53.   [66] Para. 55.
[67] See, e.g., Case C–333/13 *Dano* EU:C:2014:2358, paras. 58 and 60.
[68] Art. 2(1).   [69] Art. 3(1).
[70] See also the 5th recital to the directive: 'The right of all citizens to move and reside freely within the territory of the Member States should, if it is to be exercised under objective conditions of freedom and dignity, be also granted to their family members, irrespective of nationality.'
[71] Fifth recital to the directive. Emphasis added.

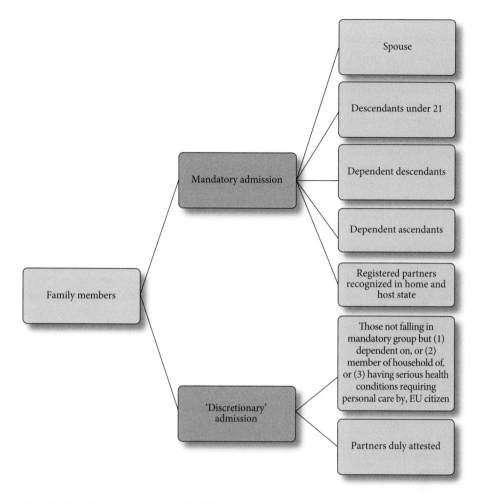

Fig. 10.1 Family members under the CRD

that which they are a national'.[72] As with the original Article 10 of Regulation 1612/68, the family members fall into two groups: (1) those who must be admitted[73] and (2) those whose entry and residence the host state must merely facilitate, in accordance with their national law[74] (see fig. 10.1). In respect of the first group, the definition of family members is drafted more broadly than in the original Regulation 1612/68. The following are covered:[75]

---

[72] Case C–34/09 *Ruiz Zambrano* [2011] ECR I–1177, para. 39; Case C–434/09 *McCarthy* [2011] ECR I–3375, paras. 36–43. In Case C–218/14 *Singh* v. *Minister for Justice and Equality* EU:C:2015:476, para. 55 the family members of a Union citizen can claim the right of residence only in the host state in which the EU citizen resides and not in another Member State.

[73] Art. 3(1).

[74] Art. 3(2). Case C–83/11 *Secretary of State for the Home Department* v. *Rahman* EU:C:2012:519, para. 24 confirms that Art. 3(2) gives Member States a wide discretion including laying down a requirement as to the nature and duration of dependence to ensure that the dependence is genuine and stable and not brought about with the sole objective of obtaining entry into and residence in the host state.

[75] Art. 2(2) CRD.

Spouse

The Court has approached the term 'spouse' in a conventional manner: it is the person to whom the EU citizen is married under the laws of the state where the marriage was entered into. In *Diatta*[76] the Court considered the situation of a couple who were married but separated. The case concerned a Senegalese woman married to a French national who lived and worked in Germany. Eventually she separated from her husband and lived in separate accommodation with the intention of divorcing. The authorities refused to renew her residence permit on the ground that she was no longer a family member of an EU national and did not live with her husband. The Court ruled that the (then) Article 10 of Regulation 1612/68 did not require members of a migrant's family to live permanently together. It reasoned that if cohabitation of spouses was a mandatory condition for a residence permit, the worker could cause his spouse to be expelled from the Member State at any moment, simply by throwing her out of the house.

Diatta therefore suggests that separated couples must be allowed to remain in the host state. However, the position under the CRD may be different. To enjoy a right of residence under Article 7(1)(d) CRD the family members must be 'accompanying or joining a Union citizen', and to acquire permanent residence under Article 16(2) CRD the family members must have 'legally resided with the Union citizen in the host state for a continuous period of five years'.[77] While this suggests a requirement of actual cohabitation, *Singh* says the right of the TCN to accompany or join the EU citizen must be 'understood as referring not to an obligation for the spouses to live together but an obligation for them both to remain in the Member State in which the Union citizen resides, and not in another Member State'.[78] However, *Onuekwere*[79] says that periods spent in prison by the TCN family member do not count towards the five-year period to gain the right of permanent residence.

A divorced spouse's position is different again. In *Diatta*[80] the Court said that a 'marital relationship cannot be regarded as dissolved so long as it has not been terminated by the competent authority'.[81] This would suggest that only on the completion of all the formal stages of divorce proceedings, including the grant of a decree absolute, will the spouse's dependent right of residence in the Member State cease. However, as we shall see, Article 13 of Directive 2004/38 does give certain legal protection to divorcees.

The term 'spouse' does not include cohabitees. This was shown in *Reed*,[82] where the Court ruled that an English woman wishing to join her cohabitee in the Netherlands could not rely on the original Article 10 of Regulation 1612/68 because she was not a spouse. However, on the facts of the case Reed was successful because under *Dutch* law foreigners in a stable relationship with a Dutch national were entitled to reside in the Netherlands. If Ms Reed were not allowed to remain in the Netherlands, this would be discriminatory, contrary to Articles 18 and 45 TFEU and Article 7(2) of Regulation 492/11. The position of cohabitees is now also covered, at least in part, by the discretionary admission provisions in Article 3(2)(b) CRD, provided the relationship is durable and duly attested.

---

[76] Case 267/83 *Diatta* v. *Land Berlin* [1985] ECR 567.
[77] Cf. the more favourable position under the Long-Term Residents Dir. 2003/109 ([2003] L16/44), adopted under Art. 63(3)(a) and (4) EC, discussed in Ch. 13. The TCN family member will enjoy a right to permanent residence and equal treatment rights in the first state without having to move to a second Member State.
[78] Case C-218/14 *Singh* v. *Minister for Justice and Equality* EU:C:2015:476, para. 55.
[79] Case C-378/12 *Onuekwere* v. *Secretary of State for the Home Department* EU:C:2014:13, para. 27.
[80] Case 267/83 [1985] ECR 567.   [81] Para. 20.   [82] Case 59/85 [1986] ECR 1283.

To date the Court has not willingly looked behind the marriage 'veil' to see whether the marriage is valid. However, Article 35 CRD provides:

> Member States may adopt the necessary measures to refuse, terminate or withdraw any right conferred by this Directive in the case of abuse of rights or fraud, such as marriages of convenience.

This provision comes with the caveat that any measure taken has to be proportionate and subject to the procedural safeguards provided in the directive.[83] In its guidance on the directive,[84] the Commission is more expansive: 'Marriages validly contracted anywhere in the world must be in principle recognized for the purpose of the application of the Directive.' It continues that:

> Forced marriages, in which one or both parties is married without his or her consent or against his or her will, are not protected by international or Union law. Forced marriages must be distinguished from arranged marriages, where both parties fully and freely consent to the marriage, although a third party takes a leading role in the choice of partner, and from marriages of convenience.[85]

Thus the host state is not obliged to admit the spouse of a forced marriage but must admit the spouse of an arranged marriage. The Commission also says that Member States are not obliged to recognize polygamous marriages, contracted lawfully in a third country, which may be in conflict with their own legal order. It adds 'This is without prejudice to the obligation to take due account of the best interests of children of such marriages.'

One further question has caused the Court difficulty: must the TCN spouse (or other family member) accompany the migrant EU citizen when moving from State A to State B, or can the TCN spouse join the EU citizen in State B directly from a third country?[86] While it had long been thought that the latter position was correct, *Akrich*[87] cast doubt on this orthodoxy and suggested that only once the TCN spouse had lawfully entered one EU state under national immigration law (the first point of entry principle) and lawfully resided there (the prior lawful residence (PLR) principle) could the TCN spouse enjoy the rights of free movement with his EU citizen wife.[88] However, in *Metock*[89] the

---

[83] Arts. 30–1 CRD, considered in detail in Ch. 12.

[84] Commission Guidance for better transposition and application of Dir. 2004/38: COM(2009) 313, 4.

[85] Marriages of convenience ('marriages contracted for the *sole* purpose of enjoying the right of free movement and residence under the Directive that someone would not have otherwise') are given special attention in the guidance in the section on abuse and fraud: COM(2009) 313, 15 (emphasis in the original). It suggests some criteria which indicate likely abuse (e.g., the couple have never met before their marriage; they are inconsistent about their respective personal details; they do not speak a language understood by both). The Commission says that these criteria are possible triggers for investigation only; they are not in any way conclusive. See also the Commission's *Handbook on addressing the issue of alleged marriages of convenience between EU citizens and non-EU nationals in the context of EU law on free movement of EU citizens*, SWD(2014) 284. See also the UK's New Settlement Decision, Section D.1(c), which, under the heading of interpretation of current law, says that Member States can 'address cases of contracting or maintaining marriages of convenience' with TCNs for the purpose of making use of free movement as a route for bypassing national immigration law. The Commission is to facilitate increased administrative cooperation to assist the fight against abuse of rights and fraud. The Commission is to provide guidance on the concept of marriage of convenience (Annex VII of the UK's New Settlement Decision).

[86] See, e.g., M. Elsmore and P. Starup, case note on *Jia* (2007) 44 *CMLRev.* 787.

[87] Case C–109/01 *Secretary of State for the Home Department v. Akrich* [2001] ECR I–9607, noted by E. Spaventa (2005) 42 *CMLRev.* 225.

[88] However, the Court added that where the marriage was genuine, the UK had to have regard to respect for Mrs Akrich's family life under Art. 8 ECHR, which suggested that the UK should admit husband and wife on human rights grounds (para. 58).

[89] Case C–127/08 *Metock* [2008] ECR I–6241, para. 58. See A. Tryfonidou, 'Family reunification rights of (migrant) Union citizens: Towards a more liberal approach' (2009) 15 *ELJ* 634.

Court expressly reversed the PLR principle. The case concerned four TCNs who arrived in Ireland and unsuccessfully applied for asylum. While still resident in Ireland they married migrant EU citizens who were also resident in Ireland. None of the marriages was a marriage of convenience. The TCN spouses were all refused a residence card by the Irish authorities on the ground that they did not satisfy the PLR principle.

The Court said that 'if Union citizens were not allowed to lead a normal family life in the host Member State, the exercise of the freedoms they are guaranteed by the Treaty would be seriously obstructed'.[90] It continued that the directive applied to all Union citizens who moved to, or resided in, a Member State other than that in which they were a national, and to their family members who accompanied *or* joined them in that Member State, regardless of whether the TCN has already been lawfully resident in another Member State.[91]

Thus, by giving a broad interpretation to the verb 'joined', the Court abandoned the PLR principle. However, the Court went further than simply reversing *Akrich* since it also gave rights not only to pre-existing couples (family reunification) but also to couples that meet in the host state (family formation).[92] The reason for this was that were the host state to refuse to grant TCN family members a right of residence this might discourage Union citizens from continuing to reside in the host state.[93] As Costello points out, in reaching this conclusion the Court rejects the usual conception of spousal dependency underpinning family reunification law, where the trailing spouse follows the worker to another Member State.[94] Instead, 'the Directive becomes an instrument for both family formation and family reunification, two modes of family migration that Member States often seek to differentiate'.

However, the UK New Settlement Decision plans to take the law back to the position in *Akrich*. If the UK votes to stay in the EU, the Commission will adopt a proposal to complement the CRD (it will thus apply to all Member States) to exclude from the scope of free movement rights (1) TCNs who had no prior lawful residence in a Member State before marrying a Union citizen (the situation in *Akrich*) and (2) TCNs who marry a Union citizen only after the Union citizen has established residence in the host Member State (reversing the family formation aspect of *Metock*). In these cases, the host Member State's immigration law will apply to the TCN.[95]

Registered partners

So far we have examined the position of spouses. We turn now to consider the position of 'partner', a new category introduced by the directive. In respect of registered partners, the CRD follows the approach adopted in *Reed*. It gives rights to 'the partner with whom the Union citizen has contracted a registered partnership, on the basis of legislation of a Member State' provided that 'the legislation of the host Member State treats registered partnerships as equivalent to marriage and in accordance with the conditions laid down in any such legislation'.[96] In other words, only if the partnership is recognized by both the home and host states will the registered partner enjoy the rights laid down by the CRD.

---

[90] Case C–127/08 *Metock* [2008] ECR I–6241, para. 62.   [91] Para. 70.

[92] Para. 99. See also Case C–551/07 *Sahin* [2008] ECR I–10453.   [93] Para. 92.

[94] C. Costello, '*Metock*: Free movement and "normal family life" in the Union' (2009) 46 *CMLRev.* 587, 601. On the Commission's response to Member State concerns about the implications of the Court's rights-based approach for their conception of discretionary migration control, see COM(2009) 313, 17–18.

[95] On the potential complications arising from the new rules, see S. Peers, <http://eulawanalysis.blogspot.it/2016/02/the-final-uk-renegotiation-deal.html>.

[96] Art. 2(2)(b).

Therefore, a British man who has entered into a civil partnership under the British Civil Partnership Act 2004 with a Brazilian man, would be able to go with his Brazilian civil partner to Sweden to reside and work there under the CRD since Swedish law recognizes registered partnerships of homosexual couples. By contrast, this couple will not be able to rely on the directive to reside and work in Greece since Greece does not recognize registered partnerships. Partners in this situation, as well as unmarried heterosexual couples whose relationship is not formally recognized by law, will have to rely on the discretionary provisions in Article 3(2)(b) in order to persuade the host state to admit the Union citizen's partner.

Descendants under 21 and dependent descendants and ascendants

Directive 2004/38 gives rights to the Union citizen's direct descendants under the age of 21 and dependent descendants, as well as to those of the spouse or registered partner.[97] It also gives rights to the dependent ascendants (e.g., parents, grandparents) of the Union citizen and the Union citizen's spouse or registered partner.[98] In *Lebon*[99] the Court made clear that dependency was a question of fact. It said that a dependant was 'a member of the family who is supported by the worker',[100] adding that there was no need to determine the reasons why the dependant required the worker's support or to enquire whether the dependants could support themselves by working.[101]

In *Jia*[102] the Court developed the definition of dependency in the context of dependent relatives in the ascending line (Chinese mother-in-law (Mrs Jia) of German self-employed migrant (Mrs Li) working in Sweden). It said that, in order to determine dependency, an individual assessment was necessary. This meant that the host state (Sweden) had to assess whether, having regard to the applicant's 'financial and social conditions', she was not in a position to support herself. The need for material support from the Union national or her spouse had to exist in Mrs Jia's state of origin (China) (or the country from which she came) when she applied to join the Union national (Mrs Li).[103] The Court said that the host state could require proof of dependency, adduced by 'appropriate means',[104] but that did not necessarily mean a document from the Chinese authorities. On the other hand, a mere undertaking from a Union national or his/her spouse to support the family member 'need not be regarded as establishing the existence of that family member's situation of real dependence'.[105]

---

[97] The children do not need to be blood relatives: Case C–275/02 *Ayaz* v. *Land Baden-Württemberg* [2004] ECR I–8765, para. 45, a case under the EEC–Turkey Association Agreement, which the Court said was to be interpreted in line with Reg. 492/11 and the CRD. The Court ruled that stepchildren are also covered. The Commission's Guidance (COM(2009) 313, 5) adds that the provision includes 'relationships or minors in custody of a permanent legal guardian. Foster children and foster parents who have temporary custody may have rights under the Directive, depending upon the strength of the ties in the particular case. There is no restriction as to the degree of relatedness.'

[98] In respect of all of these categories of family members 'documentary evidence that the conditions laid down' are met is required for those seeking a right of residence: Art. 8(5)(d) CRD.

[99] Case 316/85 [1987] ECR 2811.

[100] Para. 22. The support must be material rather than emotional: COM(2009) 313, 5.

[101] Para. 22.　　[102] Case C–1/05 *Jia* [2007] ECR I–1.

[103] Para. 37. The Commission's Guidance (COM(2009) 313, 5) adds 'The Directive does not lay down any requirement as to the minimum duration of the dependency or the amount of material support provided, as long as the dependency is genuine and structural in character.' In Case C–423/12 *Reyes* v. *Migrationsverket* EU:C:2014:16, para. 24 the Court said that the fact that an EU citizen pays a sum of money for a significant period to the descendant necessary to support the descendant in the country of origin shows that the descendant is in a real situation of dependence vis-à-vis the citizen. The descendant cannot be required to show that he tried to find work in the state of origin and/or otherwise tried to support himself.

[104] Para. 41.　　[105] Paras. 42–3.

(ii) Discretionary Admission

In respect of the second group (those whose admission must be facilitated), according to Article 3(2) two sorts of family members fall into this category:

(a) any other family members,[106] not falling under Article 2(2) who, in the country from which they have come, are dependants[107] or members of the household of the Union citizen having the primary right of residence, or where serious health grounds strictly require the personal care of the family member by the Union citizen[108]

(b) the partner with whom the Union citizen has a durable relationship, duly attested.[109] The terms 'durable' and 'duly attested' are not defined in the directive, although the Commission suggests that they could be determined by reference to a certain minimum period of being together.

While Article 3(2) requires the host state merely to 'facilitate entry and residence' of this second group, the directive provides a strong steer that the normal rule will be to permit entry. Article 3(2)(b) provides: 'The host Member State shall undertake an extensive examination of the personal circumstances and shall *justify any denial* of entry or residence to these people' (emphasis added). In *Rahman*[110] the Court said that while Article 3(2) was not directly effective, an applicant was entitled to judicial review of 'whether the national legislation and its application have remained within the limits of the discretion set by that directive'.[111]

2.3 Rights of Departure, Entry, and Return

Having considered the personal scope of the directive, we now examine the rights that migrant EU citizens and their family members enjoy, starting with the rights of departure, entry, and return, then looking at the right of residence, and finally at the right to equal treatment.

(a) *The right to depart from the home state*

National rules which preclude or deter nationals of a Member State from leaving their state of origin interfere with freedom of movement, even if they apply to all migrants.[112] Directive 2004/38 reinforces, and the case law confirms,[113] the Treaty right to depart from a Member State—not necessarily the state of origin—where Union citizens and their families currently live.[114] According to the directive, Union citizens and their family members may leave the Member State by producing a valid identity card or passport (passport only for TCN family members), which the Member State is obliged to issue or renew.[115] The passport[116] must be valid for all Member States and for any states through which the holder

---

[106] The degree of relatedness is not specified: COM(2009) 313, 5.

[107] The family members must show dependence in the country from which they have come: Case C–83/11 *Rahman* EU:C:2012:519, para. 34.

[108] The fact that these conditions are satisfied must be proved by a document issued by the relevant authority in the country of origin or country from which they are arriving in the case of those seeking residence under Art. 7: Art. 8(5)(e).

[109] By contrast, the fact that a 'durable relationship, duly attested' exists is satisfied merely by 'proof' for those seeking residence under Art. 7: Art. 8(5)(f).

[110] Case C–83/11 *Rahman* EU:C:2012:519, para. 22.   [111] Para. 25.

[112] See, e.g., the workers' cases: Case C–10/90 *Masgio v. Bundesknappschaft* [1991] ECR I–1119, paras. 18–19; Case C–415/93 *Bosman* [1995] ECR I–4921, para. 104; and Case C–232/01 *Hans van Lent* [2003] ECR I–11525, para. 21.

[113] See Case C–33/07 *Ministerul Administrației și Internelor v. Jipa* [2008] ECR I–5157, paras. 17–20; Case C–127/08 *Metock* [2008] ECR I–6241, para. 68.

[114] Art. 4(1).   [115] Art. 4(3). No exit visa or equivalent formality may be imposed.

[116] If the passport is the only document with which the person may lawfully leave the country, it must be valid for at least five years: Art. 4(4).

must pass when travelling between Member States.[117] Expiry of the identity card or passport on the basis of which the person entered the host state and was issued with a registration certificate or card is not to constitute a ground for expulsion from the host state.[118]

(b) The right to enter the host state

Host states must allow Union citizens and their families to enter their territory but, in order to find out who is on their territory,[119] host states can ask the migrant to produce an identity card or passport (passport only for TCN family members).[120] No visa or other entry formality can be demanded from Union citizens[121] but they can be demanded from a member of the worker's family who is not an EU national.[122] This is one of a number of examples of the way in which the CRD distinguishes between the treatment of EU and non-EU national family members. However, in *MRAX*[123] the Court said that a refusal to allow entry due to the non-production of valid passports/identity cards, and where necessary a visa, would be disproportionate if TCN spouses were able to prove their identity and marital ties in other ways and there was no evidence that they represented a risk to public policy, security, or health. This position is now confirmed in Article 5(4) CRD.

Although Member States are entitled to check passports/identity cards (and visas where necessary) at the frontier, the compatibility of such border formalities with the notion of a 'Europe without internal frontiers' laid down in Article 26 TFEU was questioned in two cases brought by the Commission. In the first, *Commission v. Belgium*,[124] non-Belgian EU nationals residing in Belgium were required to produce their residence or establishment permits in addition to their passports or identity cards. The Court said that such controls could constitute a barrier to free movement if carried out in a systematic, arbitrary, or unnecessarily restrictive manner.[125] In the second case, *Commission v. Netherlands*,[126] the Court ruled that national legislation requiring citizens to answer questions put by border officials regarding the purpose and duration of their journey and the financial means at their disposal was incompatible with Directive 68/360 (now the CRD). In these two cases the Court has curtailed the level of checks that can occur at an internal frontier. Nevertheless, it said in *Wijsenbeek*[127] that, despite Article 26 TFEU (on the single market)

---

[117] Art. 4(4). Having produced a passport or identity card, the Member State may not demand from the worker an exit visa or similar document: Art. 4(2).

[118] Art. 15(2).   [119] Case C–265/88 *Messner* [1989] ECR 4209.

[120] Art. 5(1). Art. 5(4) provides that where an EU citizen or a TCN family member does not have the necessary travel documents (or visas), the Member State must give them every reasonable opportunity to obtain the documents or to corroborate or prove by other means that they are covered by the right to freedom of movement and residence.

[121] Art. 5(1), 2nd para.

[122] Art. 5(2). Case 157/79 *R. v. Pieck* [1980] ECR 2171, para. 10. The list of third countries whose nationals need visas when crossing the external border of the Member States is determined by Council Reg. 539/2001 ([2001] OJ L81/1). Member States must grant TCN family members 'every facility' to obtain the necessary visas, which must be issued free of charge and on the basis of an accelerated procedure. The Commission considers that delays of more than four weeks are not reasonable: COM(2009) 313, 6. Possession of a valid residence card issued under Art. 10 CRD exempts family members from the visa requirement: see Case C–202/13 *R. (on the application of McCarthy) v. Secretary of State for the Home Department* EU:C:2014:2450.

[123] Case C–459/99 *MRAX v. Belgium* [2002] ECR I–6591, para. 61.

[124] Case 321/87 *Commission v. Belgium* [1989] ECR 997.   [125] Para. 15.

[126] Case C–68/89 *Commission v. Netherlands* [1991] ECR I–2637.

[127] Case C–378/97 *Criminal Proceedings against Florus Ariël Wijsenbeek* [1999] ECR I–6207. The facts of *Wijsenbeek* occurred in Dec. 1993 before the provisions of Title IV of Part Three of the Treaty of Amsterdam came into force (now Title V of Part Three TFEU). However, the Schengen provisions were operative at that time and these allowed for the crossing of internal borders without checks. Yet, because this freedom is subject to derogations on the grounds of public policy and national security, the Court said that until common rules were adopted checks could be made (para. 43).

and Article 21 TFEU (on the free movement of citizens), Member States could still require individuals, whether EU citizens or not, to establish their nationality on entering a Member State at an internal frontier of the EU.[128] Therefore, a Dutch MEP could be required to hand over his passport to immigration control when he arrived in the Netherlands on a flight from Strasbourg. Further, Member States could impose penalties for breach of the requirement to present an identity card or passport, provided that the penalties are comparable to those which apply to similar national infringements and are proportionate.[129]

Finally, Article 5(5) CRD permits the host Member State to require the migrant to report his/her presence to the authorities within a reasonable and non-discriminatory period of time. Failure to comply may make the migrant 'liable to proportionate and non-discriminatory sanctions'. In this regard the directive confirms the decision in *Watson and Belmann*,[130] where the Court found that an Italian law providing for migrants to be deported if they failed to register with the Italian authorities within three days of entering Italy was unlawful.[131]

(c) The right to return to the home state

The right to return to the home state is not expressly dealt with by the CRD but is covered by the Treaty, as interpreted by the Court, which has applied the CRD by analogy. The right to return was considered in *Surinder Singh*,[132] examined in Chapter 7, and arose again in *Eind*.[133] The case concerned a Dutch worker who was employed in the UK where he was joined by his 11-year-old Surinamese daughter. The UK gave her a right to reside as a family member of a worker under what is now Article 2(2) CRD. Less than two years later, father and daughter returned to the Netherlands but Mr Eind could not work because he was ill and so received social assistance. The daughter's application for a residence permit was turned down on the ground that since her father was not economically active, he was no longer covered by Union law and so neither was she.

The Court said that while Article 2(2) gave the TCN daughter a right to install herself with the worker in the UK,[134] it did not entail an autonomous right to free movement for the family member.[135] However, following references to the Treaty provisions on citizenship,[136] the Court said that the right of the migrant worker to return and reside in the Netherlands, after having been gainfully employed in the UK, was 'conferred by [Union] law, to the extent necessary to ensure the useful effect of the right to free movement for workers under Article [45 TFEU]'.[137] The Court said that Mr Eind would be deterred from exercising his right of free movement if he could not return to the Netherlands, economically active or not.[138] Likewise he would also be deterred from exercising his rights of free movement if he could not continue living together with close family members on his return to the Netherlands. So, under (unspecified) Union law, the daughter had the 'right to install herself with her father' in the Netherlands, even though her father was not economically active, provided that she was under 21 or dependent.[139] In *O and B*[140] the Court

---

[128] *Wijsenbeek*, n. 127, para. 45.   [129] Case C–215/03 *Oulane* [2005] ECR I–1215, para. 38.

[130] Case 118/75 *Watson and Belmann* [1976] ECR 1185. In Case C–357/98 *Ex p. Yiadom* [2000] ECR I–9265, para. 25 provisions protecting Union nationals who exercise the fundamental freedom of movement under Art. 21(1) TFEU had to be interpreted in their favour.

[131] See also Case C–265/88 *Messner* [1989] ECR 4209. In respect of a TCN spouse of a migrant worker, see Case C–459/99 *MRAX* [2002] ECR I–6591, para. 78.

[132] Case C–370/90 [1992] ECR I–4265.

[133] Case C–291/05 *Minister voor Vreemdelingenzaken en Integratie v. Eind* [2007] ECR I–10719.

[134] Para. 21.   [135] Para. 23.   [136] Paras. 28–32.

[137] Para. 32.   [138] Para. 35.   [139] Paras. 38–9.

[140] Case C–456/12 *O and B v. Minister voor Immigratie, Integratie en Asiel* EU:C:2014:135, para. 61.

was more specific: Article 21(1) TFEU gave rights to EU citizens to bring TCN family members back to the home state with them, applying the CRD by analogy, provided that there had been genuine residence in the host state (i.e., for a period of more than three months[141]). The UK's New Settlement Decision provides that the Commission is to issue guidelines on this point:

> Member States can address specific cases of abuse of free movement rights by Union citizens returning to their Member State of nationality with a non-EU family member where residence in the host Member State has not been sufficiently genuine to create or strengthen family life and had the purpose of evading the application of national immigration rules.

2.4 The Right of Residence in the Host State

Not only does the CRD guarantee the right to leave the home state and enter the host state, it also grants the migrant the right of residence. The directive essentially envisages three periods of residence (see fig. 10.2): (1) up to three months, (2) three months to five years, and (3) (generally) five years and beyond.

(a) Right of residence for up to three months

Those resident for up to three months enjoy a 'right of residence'. According to Article 6, provided Union citizens (whether economically active or not)[142] can produce a valid identity card or passport, and they wish to stay for up to three months only, Member States must grant them the right of residence.[143] The same applies to TCN family members, including TCNs accompanying or joining the Union citizen, on production of a valid passport.[144] However, this right of residence is not unlimited: apart from the general

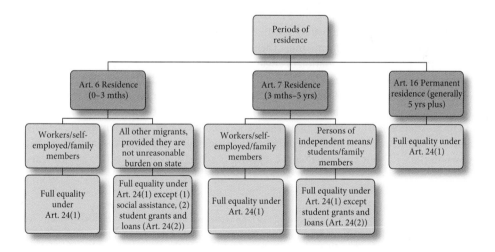

Fig. 10.2 Periods of residence and entitlement to equal treatment under the CRD

---

[141] This is discussed further in Ch. 7. In *O and B* the Court said that short periods of residence, e.g. weekends and holidays spent in the host state, even when considered together, fell within the three-month rule in Art. 6 and so did not satisfy the requirement of genuine residence (para. 59).

[142] In this respect the directive does not depart so much from the position under the case law when, following Case 186/87 *Cowan* [1989] ECR 195, all tourists were recipients of services.

[143] Art. 6(1).   [144] Art. 6(2).

derogations, it is also subject to the condition that the migrants do not become 'an unreasonable burden on the social assistance system of the host state'.[145]

(b) Right of residence for more than three months and up to five years

(i) Citizens' and family members

Those resident for more than three months but less than five years also enjoy a 'right of residence'. According to Article 7(1) CRD, all Union citizens have the right of residence on the territory of another Member State for more than three months if they are:

(a) workers or self-employed[146]

(b) persons of independent means, namely they have sufficient resources for themselves and their family members not to become a burden on the social-assistance system of the host Member State and medical insurance[147]

(c) students who are enrolled at a private or public establishment, accredited or financed by the host state with comprehensive sickness insurance cover in the host Member State and able to assure the relevant national authority, by means of a declaration or by such equivalent means as they may choose, that they have sufficient resources for themselves and their family members not to become a burden on the social-assistance system of the host Member State during their period of residence[148]

(d) family members accompanying or joining the Union citizen,[149] whether they are nationals of a Member State or not.[150]

Only where the host state has a reasonable doubt as to whether a Union citizen or his/her family members satisfies these conditions can the Member States verify whether the conditions are fulfilled. This verification cannot be carried out systematically.[151]

The host state can require Union citizens to register with the relevant authorities.[152] The deadline for registration may not be less than three months from the date of arrival.[153] A registration *certificate* must then be issued[154] on production of a valid identity card or passport,[155] a confirmation of engagement from the employer or certificate of employment or proof that they are self-employed, or proof that they satisfy the conditions of being of independent means or a student.[156] Failure to comply with the registration requirement may render the person concerned liable to 'proportionate and non-discriminatory sanctions'. The issuing of a registration certificate or equivalent gives the host state the opportunity to check not only whether the migrant satisfies the conditions laid down in the CRD but also whether the migrant is a 'desirable' person. This is confirmed

---

[145] Art. 14(1).

[146] Union citizens retain the right of residence so long as they remain workers/self-employed persons: see Art. 7(3), considered further in Ch. 8.

[147] This group includes the retired who were originally covered by their own directive, Dir. 90/365: Case E–26/13 *The Icelandic State* v. *Gunnarsson* [2014] EFTA Ct. Rep. 254, para. 78.

[148] The conditions as to sufficient resources and medical insurance are considered in more detail in Ch. 12.

[149] A more limited range of family members can enjoy the Art. 7 rights where the Union citizen is a student: Art. 7(4).

[150] Art. 7(1)(d) and (2).   [151] Art. 14(2).   [152] Art. 8(1).   [153] Art. 8(2).

[154] Art. 8(2). The issuing of these certificates or equivalent documents must be free of charge or for a charge not exceeding that imposed on nationals for the issuing of similar documents: Art. 25(2).

[155] The expiry of the identity card/passport which was the basis for entering the host state and the issuing of a registration certificate or registration card cannot constitute a ground for expulsion: Art. 15(2).

[156] Art. 8(3).

by Article 27(3) CRD, which provides the host state may request the Member State of origin and, if necessary, other Member States to provide information concerning any previous police record the migrant may have. However, this is the exception not the rule: the Article makes clear that the host state may request this information only if it considers it 'essential' and '[s]uch enquiries shall not be made as a matter of routine'.

A registration certificate is also issued to family members of Union citizens who are themselves Union citizens. The host Member State may, however, require the EU family members to produce not only a valid identity card or passport but also the Union citizen's registration certificate, together with documentary evidence that the family members fall within a relationship covered by Article 2(2).[157] By contrast, TCN family members must[158] be issued with a 'residence *card*'[159] provided they produce broadly equivalent documents to those required for EU national family members.[160] The residence card (but not the registration certificate) is valid for five years from the date of issue (or for the envisaged period of residence of the Union citizen if that is less than five years)[161] but will expire as a result of prolonged absences.[162] The renewal requirement makes it easier for the host state to monitor the activities of TCNs. In respect of both the registration certificate and the residence card, the host state can carry out checks on compliance with any requirement deriving from national legislation for non-nationals to carry these documents, provided the same requirement applies to their own nationals as regards identity cards.[163]

A migrant worker can reside and start working before completing the formalities to obtain a residence permit[164] because the right of residence is a fundamental right derived from the Treaty and is not dependent upon the possession of particular documents;[165] residence permits have only probative value,[166] as *Martínez Sala*[167] shows. A Spanish national living in Germany since 1968 held various residence permits which had expired and a series of documents saying that she had applied for an extension of her permit. She then had a baby and applied for a child allowance but her application was rejected on the grounds that she had neither German nationality, nor a residence entitlement, nor a residence permit. The Court said that it was discriminatory to require a national of another

---

[157] Art. 8(5).

[158] The obligation to issue the residence card is mandatory because EU—not national—immigration law applies.

[159] This exempts TCN family members from the visa requirement under Art. 5(2).

[160] Arts. 9–10. The list of documents to be produced is exhaustive: recital 14 and Case C–127/08 *Metock* [2008] ECR I–6241, para. 53. Member States may require that documents be translated, notarized, or legalized where the national authority concerned cannot understand the language in which the particular document is written, or have a suspicion about the authenticity of the issuing authority (COM(2009) 313, 7).

[161] Art. 11(1).

[162] The validity of the residence card is not affected by temporary absences not exceeding six months or longer absences up to 12 months for important reasons such as pregnancy and childbirth (Art. 11(2)).

[163] Art. 26. See also Case C–327/02 *Panayotova* v. *Minister voor Vreemdelingenzaken en Integratie* [2004] ECR I–11055, para. 27: the granting of residence permits must be based on a procedural system which is easily accessible and capable of ensuring that the persons concerned will have their applications dealt with objectively and within a reasonable time, and refusals to grant a permit must be capable of being challenged in judicial or quasi-judicial proceedings. According to the Commission (COM(2009) 313, 7), the residence card for a TCN must be issued within six months.

[164] Art. 25.

[165] Case 118/75 *Watson and Belmann* [1976] ECR 1185, paras. 15–16. This is now confirmed in Art. 25(1) CRD and recital 11. See also Poiares Maduro AG's Opinion in Case C–524/06 *Huber* v. *Germany* [2008] ECR I–9705, para. 19.

[166] To this effect, see Case 48/75 *Royer* [1976] ECR 497, para. 50. The same rule also applies to a TCN spouse of a migrant worker: Case C–459/99 *MRAX* [2002] ECR I–6591, para. 74.

[167] Case C–85/96 [1998] ECR I–2691.

Member State to produce a document (the residence permit) to obtain the benefit when its own nationals were not required to do the same.[168] In *Oulane* the Court added that since the right of residence was derived directly from the Treaty, it was not legitimate for the host state to require the EU migrant to produce a passport when he could prove his identity by other means.[169] Further, it said that detention and deportation based solely on the failure of the person to comply with legal formalities concerning the monitoring of aliens 'impair the very substance of the right' and were 'manifestly disproportionate to the seriousness of the infringement'.[170]

Once Union citizens have registered themselves, what use can the host-state authorities make of the information supplied? This question arose in *Huber*[171] concerning a centralized register held by the German authorities which contained certain personal data relating to foreign nationals who were resident in Germany for more than three months. The register was used for statistical purposes and by the security and police services and by the judicial authorities. Mr Huber, an Austrian national, worked in Germany as a self-employed insurance agent. He asked for his data to be deleted from the register, alleging discrimination since no similar database existed for German nationals.

The Court ruled that the use of a register of data for the purpose of providing support to the authorities responsible for applying the rules on residence was, in principle, legitimate and compatible with the prohibition of discrimination on grounds of nationality laid down by Article 18(1) TFEU.[172] However, the Court said that such a register should not contain any information other than what was 'necessary', within the meaning of Article 7(e)[173] of the Data Protection Directive 95/46.[174] The Court then distinguished between personal data contained in the documents referred to in Articles 8(3) (proof of (self-)employment) and 27(1) CRD (derogations), which it considered was 'necessary' for applying the rules on residence,[175] and personal data containing individualized personal information for statistical purposes, which was not.[176] The Court also said that, as a citizen who had moved under Article 21 TFEU, Mr Huber enjoyed the right to non-discrimination under Article 18 TFEU.[177] Because Union citizens were treated differently to nationals in respect of the systematic processing of personal data for the purposes of fighting crime, this constituted discrimination prohibited by Article 18(1) TFEU.[178]

(ii) Family members' rights on the death or departure of the Union citizen or on divorce

Articles 12–13 of the Citizens' Rights Directive 2004/38 give family members the right to retain their residence in the host state on the death or departure of the EU citizen or in the event of divorce, annulment of marriage, or termination of registered partnership. In the case of the death or departure of the Union citizen, family members who are EU nationals[179] will continue to enjoy the right of residence.[180] In the case of

---

[168] For an extension of this principle to the member of a Turkish worker's family legally residing in a Member State, see Case C–262/96 *Sürül v. Bundesanstalt für Arbeit* [1999] ECR I–2685.

[169] Case C–215/03 *Oulane* [2005] ECR I–1215, para. 25.   [170] Para. 40.

[171] Case C–524/06 *Huber v. Germany* [2008] ECR I–9705.   [172] Para. 58.

[173] 'Member States shall provide that personal data may be processed only if: ... (e) processing is necessary for the performance of a task carried out in the public interest or in the exercise of official authority vested in the controller or in a third party to whom the data are disclosed.'

[174] [1995] OJ L281/31.   [175] Para. 59.   [176] Para. 68.

[177] Para. 73.   [178] Para. 80.   [179] Art. 12(1), para. 1.

[180] From the way Art. 12(1) is drafted, it would appear that the conditions to be a worker/self-employed/otherwise self-supporting/student/family member do not apply to the right of residence under Art. 7. They apply only to the right to acquire permanent residence.

the death (but not departure) of the EU citizen, TCN family members retain the right of residence provided that they have been residing in the host state as family members for at least a year before the citizen's death.[181] In order to attain permanent residence they must be workers/self-employed/have independent means or be members of the family, already constituted in the host Member State, of a person satisfying these requirements.

In the case of divorce or equivalent, the CRD makes provision for 'legal safeguards to people whose right of residence is dependent on a family relationship by marriage and who could therefore be open to blackmail with threats of divorce'.[182] Article 13(2) therefore says that TCN family members do not lose the right of residence where:

- prior to the divorce or equivalent, the marriage or registered partnership lasted at least three years including one year in the host Member State[183] or

- by agreement between the spouses or partners or by court order, the TCN spouse or partner has custody of the Union citizen's children or

- this is warranted by particularly difficult circumstances, such as having been a victim of domestic violence while the marriage or registered partnership was subsisting or

- by agreement between the spouses or partners or by court order, the TCN spouse or partner has the right of access to a minor child, provided that the court has ruled that such access must be in the host state and for as long as is required.[184]

In addition, in order to obtain *permanent* residence the TCN family members must show that they are workers/self-employed/have independent means (but cannot be a student) or they are members of the family already constituted in the host Member State of a person satisfying these requirements. These conditions laid down in Article 13(2) do not apply to family members who are nationals of a Member State,[185] who will continue to enjoy a right of residence, no matter how short the original marriage. However, they will also need to show they are economically active or self-sufficient or a student or family member to obtain *permanent* residence.

Despite the strictness of the rules in relation to TCN family members, there is one important exception: if the EU citizen leaves the host state or dies his/her children will not lose their right of residence, nor will the parent with actual custody of the children irrespective of nationality, provided that the children reside in the host state and are enrolled at an educational establishment for the purposes of studying there, until the completion of their studies.[186]

(c) Right of permanent residence

The third 'tier' of residence rights is the right to permanent residence. There are two ways of acquiring permanent residence: (1) through five years' continuous legal residence; or (2) through a shorter period for those who were economically active either as a worker or as a self-employed person who satisfy certain conditions. In both situations the directive

---

[181] Art. 12(2), para. 1.   [182] COM(2001) 257, 15.

[183] Case C–218/14 *Singh v. Minister for Justice and Equality* EU:C:2015:476 adds a further condition. It provides that a divorced TCN, whose marriage satisfied the conditions in the CRD, could not retain a right of residence in the host Member State where the commencement of the divorce proceedings was preceded by the departure from the host state of the spouse who is an EU citizen.

[184] Art. 13(2).   [185] Art. 12(1).

[186] Art. 12(3), reflecting the decisions in Joined Cases 389 and 390/87 *Echternach and Moritz* [1989] ECR 723 and Case C–413/99 *Baumbast and R.* [2002] ECR I–7091.

considers the migrants to be so assimilated into the host state that they are regarded and treated as nationals in all but name. This is a remarkable development. We shall examine the two situations in turn.

(i) Article 16: Five years' residence

Union citizens and their family members, including TCNs,[187] who have resided legally for a continuous period of five years in the host state,[188] have the right of permanent residence there.[189] As the Court said in *Lassal*,[190] citing recital 17 of the directive, 'the right of permanent residence is a key element in promoting social cohesion and was provided for by that directive in order to strengthen the feeling of Union citizenship'.

The right is not dependent on the Union citizen being a worker/self-employed person or having sufficient resources/medical insurance,[191] albeit that the migrant EU citizen will, according to *Ziolkowski*,[192] have had to have been a worker/self-employed/student/PIM/ family member under Article 7 CRD during the previous five years in order to accrue the five-year period of residence: residence under national law will not suffice. The family members of a Union citizen to whom Article 12(2) (death/departure of the Union citizen) or Article 13(2) (divorce or equivalent) apply, who satisfy the conditions laid down in those Articles (e.g., the family members are workers/self-employed) will also acquire the right of permanent residence after residing legally for a period of five consecutive years in the host state.[193]

Continuity of residence is not affected by temporary absences not exceeding a total of six months a year, or by absences of a longer duration for compulsory military service, or by one absence of a maximum of 12 consecutive months for important reasons such as pregnancy and childbirth, serious illness, study or vocational training, or a posting in another Member State or a third country.[194] On the other hand, continuity of residence is broken by any expulsion decision duly enforced against the person concerned.[195] Once acquired, the right of permanent residence is lost only through absence from the host Member State for a period exceeding two consecutive years.[196]

(ii) Article 17: Other ways of acquiring permanent residence

While five years' residence is the usual way for acquiring a right to permanent residence, it is also possible for a migrant or their family members to acquire a right to permanent residence before they have completed a continuous period of five years' residence in the situations which were originally laid down in Regulation 1251/70[197] and Directive

---

[187] Art. 16(2).

[188] Continuous periods of residence spent in the host state before the CRD came into force (30 Apr. 2006) count towards this period: Case C–162/09 *Secretary of State for Work and Pensions* v. *Lassal* [2010] ECR I–9217, para. 40. See also Case C–325/09 *Secretary of State for Work and Pensions* v. *Dias* [2011] ECR I–2359.

[189] Art. 16(1).   [190] Case C–162/09 [2010] ECR I–9217, para. 32.

[191] Case C–162/09 [2010] ECR I–9217. In Case E–4/11 *Clauder* [2011] EFTA Ct. Rep. 216 the EFTA Court ruled that since the retention of a right to permanent residence under Art. 16 CRD is not subject to the conditions in Chapter III and the right of permanent residence confers a derived right on the beneficiary's family members, then the derived right is not subject to a condition to have sufficient resources (para. 47).

[192] Joined Cases C–424 and 425/10 *Ziolkowski* v. *Land Berlin* [2011] ECR I–14035. The Court of Appeal of England and Wales has confirmed that periods spent in prison do not count towards the five-year period: *C* v. *Secretary of State for the Home Department* [2010] EWCA Civ 1406. See also Case C–400/12 *Secretary of State for the Home Department* v. *M. G.* EU:C:2014:9, para. 38 by analogy (considered in Ch. 12).

[193] Art. 18.   [194] Art. 16(3).   [195] Art. 21.   [196] Art. 16(4).

[197] [1970] OJ Spec. Ed. L142/24, 402. Repealed by Commission Reg. 635/2006 ([2006] OJ L112/9).

75/34.[198] Article 17(1) provides that workers and the self-employed have the right to permanent residence in three situations:

(1) retirement at the pension age[199] or through early retirement, provided they have been employed in the host state for the preceding 12 months[200] and resided in the host state continuously for more than three years

(2) incapacity, provided they have resided for more than two years in the host state[201] and have ceased to work due to some permanent incapacity

(3) frontier workers, provided after three years of continuous employment and residence in the host State A, they work in an employed or self-employed capacity in State B, while retaining their residence in State A to which they return each day or at least once a week.

The conditions as to length of residence and employment in (a) and (b) do not apply if the worker/self-employed person's spouse or partner[202] is a national of the host state or has lost the nationality of the host state through marriage to the worker/self-employed person.[203]

The worker/self-employed person's family members residing with him in the host state (irrespective of nationality) are also entitled to benefit from the reduced period of residence. According to Article 17 CRD, they too can enjoy permanent residence in the host state where either (1) the worker/self-employed person is entitled to permanent residence under Article 17(1);[204] or (2) under Article 17(4) the worker/self-employed person dies during his working life but before having acquired the right to permanent residence under 17(1) and:

(a) the worker/self-employed person had resided continuously in the host state for two years at the time of death or

(b) the death resulted from an accident at work or occupational disease or

(c) the surviving spouse lost the nationality of the host state through marriage to the worker/self-employed person.

In *Givane*[205] the Court showed that it will interpret these requirements strictly. Givane, a Portuguese national, worked in the UK as a chef for three years before going to India for ten months. He then returned to the UK with his Indian wife and three children but died less than two years later. The Court upheld the British authorities' decision refusing Givane's family indefinite leave to remain on the grounds that Givane had not satisfied the requirements of what is now Article 17(4), which required him to have resided in the UK for the two years immediately preceding his death.[206] Such a literal reading of the requirement stands in stark contrast to the generous approach to the interpretation of other

---

[198] On the right of the self-employed to remain ([1975] OJ L14/10). Repealed by the CRD.

[199] If the law of the host state does not grant the right to an old-age pension to certain categories of self-employed persons, the age condition is deemed to have been met once the person has reached the age of 60.

[200] Periods of involuntary unemployment duly recorded by the relevant employment office, periods not worked for reasons not of the person's own making, and absences from work or cessation of work due to illness or accident are to be regarded as periods of employment: Art. 17(1), para. 3.

[201] If the incapacity is due to an occupational accident or disease entitling the worker to a pension for which an institution of the state is entirely or partially responsible, then no condition to length of residence is imposed.

[202] Partner as defined in Art. 2(2)(b) CRD.   [203] Art. 17(2).   [204] Art. 17(3).

[205] Case C–257/00 *Givane v. Secretary of State for the Home Department* [2003] ECR I–345.

[206] Para. 46.

provisions of Union law based on the right to family life in cases such as *Carpenter*.[207] More striking still is the fact that the Court uses the integration argument to justify *excluding* Givane's family from the UK. The Court said that the two-year requirement was intended to establish a significant connection between the Member State and the worker and his family and 'to ensure a certain level of their integration in the society of that state'.[208]

As we have seen in this chapter, in the case of those family members faced with the death or departure of the Union citizen in circumstances not covered by Article 17, and in the case of those family members faced with divorce or equivalent, they can acquire permanent residence only if they meet the requirements laid down in Article 7(1) (i.e., they must be workers/self-employed/persons of independent means/students[209]/family members[210]) and have resided legally for a period of five consecutive years in the territory of the host state.[211]

(iii) Administrative formalities

Proof of permanent residence is given by the Member State issuing, as soon as possible, a 'document certifying permanent residence', having verified the Union citizen's duration of residence.[212] Article 21 provides that continuity of residence is attested by any means of proof in use in the host Member State. In respect of the family members who are not nationals of a Member State, the host state must issue a permanent residence card, renewable automatically every ten years,[213] within six months of the submission of the application.[214] According to Article 20(3), interruption in residence not exceeding two consecutive years will not affect the validity of the permanent residence card.

2.5 The Right to Equal Treatment for EU Citizens

(a) Article 24(1) and (2) CRD: Equal treatment and the limitations

The cornerstone of the CRD is Article 24(1) laying down a general right of equal treatment (i.e., no direct or indirect discrimination, considered in subsection (b)) 'within the scope of the Treaty' for all Union citizens residing on the basis of the directive in the territory of the host state. The Article continues that the benefit of this right is to be extended to family members who are not nationals of a Member State but who have the right of residence or permanent residence.

However, Article 24(1) expressly makes the principle of equal treatment '[s]ubject to such specific provisions as are expressly provided for in the Treaty and secondary law'. Therefore, it is possible for the host state to derogate from the principle of equal treatment on the grounds, inter alia, of public policy, public security, public health, and employment in the public service.

---

[207] Case C–60/00 *Carpenter* [2002] ECR I–6279, para. 38. See also Case C–413/99 *Baumbast* [2002] ECR I–7091; Case C–459/99 *MRAX* [2002] ECR I–6591, paras. 53–61.

[208] Para. 46.

[209] This does not apply to TCN family members: Art. 12(2), para. 2 concerning death or departure; Art. 13(2), para. 2 concerning divorce or equivalent.

[210] With the added condition in the case of TCN family members that they are members of the family already constituted in the host Member State, of a person satisfying those requirements: Art. 12(2), para. 2 concerning death or departure; Art. 13(2), para. 2 concerning divorce or equivalent.

[211] Art. 18, referring to Art. 12(2) concerning death or departure; Art. 13(2) concerning divorce or equivalent.

[212] Art. 19.   [213] Details of the reapplication process are found in Art. 20(2).   [214] Art. 20(1).

Of more practical significance are the limitations in Article 24(2) CRD (see fig. 10.2). The first concerns *social assistance*:[215] the host state is not obliged to confer entitlement to it during the first three months of residence. This is not subject to any individual assessment: it is a total exclusion.[216] Advocate General Wathelet in *Garcia-Nieto*[217] explained the rationale for this, namely maintaining the financial equilibrium of the social security system of the Member States. He continued:

> Since the Member States cannot require Union citizens to have sufficient means of subsistence and personal medical cover for a three-month stay, it is legitimate not to require Member States to be responsible for them during that period.
>
> Otherwise, granting entitlement to social assistance to Union citizens who are not required to have sufficient means of subsistence could result in relocation en masse liable to create an unreasonable burden on national social security systems.

This analysis fits with the changing dynamic outlined earlier, away from promoting freedom of movement towards protecting state coffers. However, the exclusion in Article 24(2) CRD, as a 'derogation from the principle of equal treatment',[218] does not apply to workers, self-employed persons, persons who retain such status, and members of their families.[219] So they can invoke the equal treatment principle not only in respect of social advantages under the Workers' Regulation 492/11 but also in respect of social assistance during the first three months. However, as we saw in Chapter 8, Article 24(2) CRD contains a further limitation on the principle of equal treatment in respect of work-seekers. Migrant work-seekers will not enjoy social assistance for the first three months and any period beyond three months during which Union citizens can provide evidence that they are continuing to seek employment and that they have a genuine chance of being engaged.[220]

The corollary of the restriction in Article 24(2) CRD is that after three months there is no limitation on, for example, students and PIMs claiming social assistance.[221] However, this is a double-edged sword: if students and PIMs do have recourse to social assistance this suggests they do not satisfy the criteria in Article 7(1)(b) and (c) CRD (having sufficient resources for themselves and their family members not to become a burden on the social-assistance system of the host Member State) and so they risk being removed. Yet, if Union citizens do have recourse to social assistance, 'An expulsion measure shall not be the automatic consequence.'[222] Furthermore, except on the grounds of public policy, security, and health, an expulsion measure may not be adopted against Union citizens or their family members if the Union citizens are workers/self-employed/work-seekers with a genuine chance of being engaged.[223] Thus Member States must undertake a careful balancing exercise. This is considered further in Chapter 12.

The second exception to the equal treatment principle provided by Article 24(2) CRD concerns *maintenance aid* for studies, including vocational training: the host state is not obliged to give grants or student loans to Union citizens or their family members until

---

[215] See the definition in Case C–140/12 *Brey* EU:C:2013:565, para. 61, considered in Chs. 8 and 12.

[216] Case C–299/14 *Vestische Arbeit Jobcenter Kreis Recklinghausen* v. *Garcia-Nieto* EU:C:2016:114, para. 46.

[217] Paras. 70–1. This was expressly approved by the Court, EU:C:2016:114, para. 45.

[218] Joined Cases C–22 and 23/08 *Vatsouras* [2009] ECR I–4585, para. 34.

[219] Case C–299/14 *Garcia-Nieto* EU:C:2016:114, para. 44.

[220] Art. 14(4)(b). Joined Cases C–22 and 23/08 *Vatsouras* [2009] ECR I–4585, para. 35.

[221] A point recognized by the Court in *Brey*, paras. 65–6.

[222] Art. 14(3) CRD. If they are expelled, the procedural protection provided in Arts. 30 (notification) and 31 (judicial/administrative redress) CRD apply to any such decision: Art. 15(1) CRD.

[223] Art. 14(4) CRD.

they have acquired permanent residence except to those who are economically active and their family members. This exception is considered further in subsection (b).

Finally, *Dano*[224] makes clear that Union citizens can claim equal treatment with nationals under Article 24(1) CRD only if their residence in the territory of the host state complies with the conditions laid down by the directive in the first place. In other words, lawful residence under Article 6, 7, or 16 CRD must *precede* equal treatment; EU citizens cannot use the equal treatment principle to access social security benefits in order to provide them with sufficient resources to give them the right of residence under Article 7 CRD.[225] This point was confirmed in section D.1(b) of the UK's New Settlement Decision under the heading 'Interpretation of current EU rules':

> The right of economically non active persons to reside in the host Member State depends under EU law on such persons having sufficient resources for themselves and their family members not to become a burden on the social assistance system of the host Member State, and on those persons having comprehensive sickness insurance.

A summary of the limitations on the equal treatment principle to the different groups of individuals exercising their rights to free movement can be found in fig. 10.3.

What, then, is meant by the principle of equal treatment? There are many decisions under Regulation 492/11, which were discussed in Chapter 8. There are, however, a number of cases decided under Article 21(1) TFEU in respect of social advantages[226] for citizens lawfully resident in the host state, and it is these cases that we shall now consider in determining the meaning of equal treatment.

(b) Social advantages and equal treatment

(i) Direct and indirect discrimination

As we saw in the chapters on workers, establishment, and services, the principle of equal treatment extends to social advantages. In the citizenship context, the main social advantages which have been an issue have been welfare benefits and financial assistance for education and training. The welfare benefits cases tend to concern directly discriminatory rules; the cases on financial assistance for education and training indirect discrimination.

Martínez Sala[227] was the first case on equal treatment in respect of social advantages decided under Article 21(1) TFEU. As we saw earlier, she was a Spanish national who had been living in Germany since 1968, when she was 12. The German authorities refused to give her a child-raising allowance on the grounds that she was neither a German national nor did she have a residence permit. If she had been a worker she would have been entitled to the benefit as a social advantage under Article 7(2) of Regulation 492/11. Given her background, it was unlikely that she was a worker (or an employed person within the meaning of Regulation 883/04).[228] The Court therefore considered her situation under Part Two TFEU on non-discrimination and citizenship.

It said that, as a national of a Member State lawfully residing in the territory of another Member State,[229] Martínez Sala came within the personal scope of the citizenship provisions.[230] She therefore enjoyed the rights laid down by Article 20(2) TFEU, including the

---

[224] Case C–333/13 *Dano* EU:C:2014:2358, para. 69.
[225] Case C–333/13 *Dano* EU:C:2014:2358, para. 74.
[226] The meaning of the term 'social advantages' is considered in detail in Ch. 8.
[227] Case C–85/96 [1998] ECR I–2691.
[228] It was for the national court to make the final decision.
[229] This was merely probative and not constitutive of the right to residence.
[230] Para. 61. See the essays on this case in M. Poiares Maduro and L. Azoulai (eds.), *The Past and Future of EU Law* (Oxford: Hart Publishing, 2010).

	0–3 months (Art. 6 CRD)	3 mths–5 years (Art. 7 CRD)	5 years+ (Art. 16 CRD)
Workers/ self-employed/ retained the status/family members	Full equal treatment under Treaty and Art. 24(1) CRD (possibly including social assistance)	Full equal treatment under Treaty and Art. 24(1) CRD	Full equal treatment under Treaty and Art. 24(1) CRD
Work-seekers	Full equal treatment under Art. 45 TFEU and Art. 24(1) CRD except for: (1) social assistance (2) student grants and loans (Art. 24(2) CRD) Equal treatment in respect of social advantages (Art. 7(2) of Reg 492/11)	Full equal treatment under Treaty and Art. 24(1) CRD except for: (1) social assistance (Arts. 14(4)(b) and 24(2) CRD) (2) student grants and loans (Art. 24(2) CRD) Equal treatment in respect of social advantages	Not applicable
Students	Full equal treatment under Arts. 21 and 18 TFEU and Art. 24(1) CRD except for: (1) social assistance (2) student grants and loans (Art. 24(2) CRD)	Full equal treatment under Arts. 21 and 18 TFEU and Art. 24(1) CRD except for student grants and loans (Art. 24(2) CRD); need to call on social assistance indicates non-compliance with Art 7(1)(c) CRD	Full equal treatment under Arts. 21 and 18 TFEU and Art. 24(1) CRD
PIMs	Full equal treatment under Art. 21 TFEU and Art. 24(1) CRD except for: (1) social assistance (2) student grants and loans (Art. 24(2) CRD)	Full equal treatment under Art. 21 TFEU and Art. 24(1) CRD except for student grants and loans (Art. 24(2) CRD); need to call on social assistance indicates non-compliance with Art 7(1)(b) CRD	Full equal treatment under Arts. 21 and 18 TFEU and Art. 24(1) CRD
Others (non-economically active)	Full equal treatment under Art. 21 TFEU and Art. 24(1) CRD except for: (1) social assistance (2) student grants and loans (Art. 24(2) CRD)	If Art. 7(1)(b) CRD not satisfied no right to equal treatment (*Dano*)	If non-compliant with the terms of Art. 7(1)(b) CRD, no right of permanent residence

Fig. 10.3 Rights of EU citizens in other Member States

right not to suffer discrimination on grounds of nationality under Article 18 TFEU[231] in respect of all situations falling within the material scope of the Treaties.[232] This included the situation where a Member State refused to grant a benefit provided to all persons lawfully resident in the territory of that state on the ground that the claimant did not have a document (a residence permit) which nationals were not obliged to have.[233] On this basis the Court concluded that Martínez Sala was suffering from direct discrimination on the ground of nationality contrary to Article 18 TFEU[234] and, since it was direct discrimination, it could not be objectively justified (see fig.7.2).[235]

Martínez Sala's lawful residence may have derived from national, rather than EU law, and specifically from her actual presence on German territory and the fact that the German authorities had not requested her to leave.[236] In other words, because she was not *un*lawfully resident in Germany she was entitled to equal treatment under EU law. This view is supported by *Trojani*.[237] Trojani was a French national who had been living in a Salvation Army hostel in Belgium, where, in return for board and lodging and some pocket money, he did various jobs for about 30 hours a week. In respect of his rights as a citizen, the Court said that while Trojani did not derive from Article 21 TFEU the right to reside in Belgium due to his lack of resources,[238] since he was lawfully resident in Belgium, as was shown by the residence permit which the Belgian authorities had issued to him, he could benefit from the principle of equal treatment laid down in Article 18 TFEU:[239] 'a citizen of the Union who is not economically active may rely on Article [18 TFEU] where he has been lawfully resident in the host state for a certain period of time *or* possesses a residence permit'.[240]

This position now needs to be reconsidered in the light of *Dano*.[241] Shortly after her arrival in Germany, the city of Leipzig issued Ms Dano with a residence certificate of unlimited duration for EU nationals. Eighteen months later it issued her with a duplicate certificate. She was refused particular special non-contributory cash benefits, a decision upheld by the Court of Justice on the ground that she did not satisfy the requirements in Article 7(1)(b) CRD and so did not enjoy equal treatment. At no stage in its reasoning did the Court refer to the residence permit issued by the German authorities, nor to the decisions in *Martínez Sala* and *Trojani*. Nor did it engage in any of the creative gymnastics via the citizenship and equal treatment provisions to deliver equality for the *Dano* family. *Dano* provides a strong hint of a significant change in direction: there needs to be residence under EU law (specifically Article 7 CRD for non-economically active migrants), not under national law, before the principle of equal treatment is engaged.

A number of cases on student financing concern indirectly discriminatory rules. Here a distinction needs to be drawn between those cases concerning financing being provided by the host state and that provided by the sending state. In respect of host-state financing conditions, the Court has allowed Member States a considerable degree of latitude. This can be seen in *Bidar*.[242] Bidar, a French national, had lived in the UK with his

---

[231] It also includes the right to free movement under Art. 21(1) TFEU: Case C–221/07 *Zablocka-Wehrmüller* v. *Land Baden-Württemberg* [2008] ECR I–9029, para. 25.
[232] Para. 62.   [233] Para. 62.   [234] Para. 64.   [235] Para. 64.
[236] See also Art. 6(a) of the Council of Europe Convention on Social and Medical Assistance 1953, which provides that the Contracting Parties shall abstain from expelling an alien lawfully resident 'on the sole ground that he is in need of assistance'.
[237] Case C–456/02 *Trojani* [2004] ECR I–7573.   [238] Para. 36.   [239] Paras. 37 and 40.
[240] Para. 43, emphasis added.   [241] Case C–333/13 *Dano* EU:C:2014:2358.
[242] Case C–209/03 [2005] ECR I–2119.

grandmother after his mother's death. He subsequently went to university but was turned down for financial assistance to cover his maintenance costs, in the form of a student loan, on the grounds that he did not satisfy the criteria of being settled in the UK, nor did he satisfy the residence requirements laid down by British law. The Court found these conditions to be indirectly discriminatory since they risked placing nationals of other Member States at a disadvantage. However, the Court also accepted that while, in the organization and application of their social-assistance schemes, Member States had to show a degree of financial solidarity with nationals of other Member States, it was legitimate for a Member State to grant assistance only to students who had demonstrated a degree of integration into the society of that state. This integration could be shown through a period of residence. The Court suggested that a three-year residence requirement was compatible with Union law[243] but that the requirement to be 'settled' was not, since it was impossible for a student from another Member State ever to obtain settled status.[244] In *Förster*[245] the Court, drawing on the five-year rule in Article 24(2) CRD,[246] said that a condition of five years' continuous residence for entitlement to maintenance grants and loans, could not be seen as excessive in order to ensure the degree of integration of migrants in the host Member State.[247] The Court added that since the residence requirement was applied by the national authorities on the basis of clear criteria known in advance, this guaranteed 'a significant level of legal certainty and transparency' in the context of the award of maintenance grants.[248]

In respect of funding provided by home states for their own students to study abroad the Court has been much less tolerant towards restrictive national rules. This can be seen in *Morgan*.[249] Under German law the award of education and training grants for studies in another Member State was subject to a twofold obligation (the 'first-stage studies condition'): (1) to have attended an education or training course for at least one year in Germany; and (2) to continue only that same education or training in another Member State. The application of these conditions meant that Rhiannon Morgan, a German national, who moved to the UK, where she worked for a year as an au pair before commencing her studies at a British university, was refused a grant by the German authorities.

The Court found that because of the personal inconvenience, additional costs, and possible delays which it entailed, the first-stage studies condition was liable to discourage citizens of the Union from leaving Germany in order to pursue studies in another Member State.[250] It therefore constituted a restriction on freedom of movement for citizens of the Union contrary to Article 21(1) TFEU.[251] The German government put

---

[243] Cf. the five-year residence requirement in Art. 24(2) CRD, which was upheld as proportionate in Case C–158/07 *Förster* [2008] ECR I–8507, para. 53.

[244] See generally K. Hailbronner, 'Union citizenship and access to social benefits' (2005) 42 *CMLRev.* 1245.

[245] Case C–158/07 *Förster v. Hoofddirectie van de Informatie Beheer Groep* [2008] ECR I–8507, para. 52.

[246] Respecting the non-regression clause in the CRD, the UK has maintained its three-year rule.

[247] It added that Member States remained free to award maintenance grants to students from other Member States without the five-year residence requirement (para. 59).

[248] Paras. 56–7.

[249] Joined Cases C–11 and 12/06 *Morgan v. Bezirksregierung Köln* and *Iris Bucher v. Landrat des Kreises Düren* [2007] ECR I–9161.

[250] Para. 30. See also Case C–220/12 *Thiele Meneses v. Region Hannover* EU:C:2013:683 (requirement of permanent residence disproportionate).

[251] Para. 32.

forward a number of justifications for its rule, all of which were subject to a strict proportionality review. For example, it said that the condition was justified as a way of
showing integration into German society.[252] However, the Court noted the personal
situation of the applicant: she had been raised in Germany and completed her schooling there. This demonstrated her integration into German society. Therefore, the
first-stage studies condition as a proxy for showing integration was too general and exclusive and so was disproportionate.[253] In *Prinz and Seeburger*[254] the Court was equally
critical of a requirement of an uninterrupted three-year period of residence as the sole
proxy for showing 'a sufficient level of integration into German society' before an individual could receive assistance for maintenance and training. Other facts should also
be looked at, such as the fact that the claimant is a national, was educated in the home
state for a significant period, family, employment, and language skills, or the existence
of other social and economic factors.[255]

At the heart of all of these decisions involving education—and benefits—lies the seminal decision in *D'Hoop*,[256] which concerned a Belgian national who completed her secondary education in France where she obtained the *baccalauréat*.[257] She then returned
to Belgium for her university education. At the end of her university studies she applied
to the Belgian authorities for a tide-over allowance—a type of unemployment benefit
granted to young people who have just completed their studies and are seeking their first
job. Her application was rejected on the ground that she had not received her secondary
education in Belgium.

The Court said that, as a Belgian national, she fell within the personal scope of
the citizenship provisions,[258] and that as a free mover she fell within the material
scope of the Treaty provisions. The Court therefore said that she could rely on
the principle of equal treatment even against her own state after having studied
abroad.[259]

But what discrimination had she suffered?[260] It could be argued that the national
rule was indirectly discriminatory: in order to obtain a tide-over allowance individuals had to receive their secondary education in Belgium. This had a disparate
impact on non-nationals (as well as some nationals like D'Hoop) and so breached
Article 21 TFEU unless objectively justified.[261] In fact the Court adopted a different
approach: the discrimination was due to the fact she had exercised her rights of free
movement:[262]

> By linking the grant of tideover allowances to the condition of having obtained the
> required diploma in Belgium, the national legislation thus *places at a disadvantage*

---

[252] See also Case C–209/03 *Bidar* [2005] ECR I–2119, paras. 56–7.

[253] Joined Cases C–11 and 12/06 *Morgan* [2007] ECR I–9161, paras. 42–6. See also Case C–220/12 *Thiele
Meneses* EU:C:2013:683 (requirement of permanent residence disproportionate), discussed in Ch. 12.

[254] Joined Case C–523 and 585/11 EU:C:2013:524.   [255] Para. 38.

[256] Case C–224/98 *D'Hoop* v. *Office national de l'emploi* [2002] ECR I–6191.

[257] The Court said that the provisions on citizenship of the Union were applicable as soon as they entered
into force and so they applied to the present discriminatory effects of situations arising prior to the citizenship provisions coming into force (citing Case C–195/98 *Österreichischer Gewerkschaftsbund* v. *Republik
Österreich* [2000] ECR I–10497, paras. 54–5, and Case C–290/00 *Duchon* v. *Pensionsversicherungsanstalt der
Angestellten* [2002] ECR I–3567, paras. 43–4).

[258] Para. 27.   [259] Para. 31.

[260] See also A. Iliopoulou and H. Toner, 'A new approach to discrimination against free movers' (2003)
28 *ELRev.* 389.

[261] Para. 36.   [262] Para. 34, emphasis added.

certain of its nationals simply because they have exercised their freedom to move in order to pursue education in another Member State.

The Court continued that '[s]uch inequality of treatment is contrary to the principles which underpin the status of citizen of the Union'.[263] In subsequent cases, the Court said such disadvantage constituted a 'restriction' on free movement;[264] an analysis the Court has used particularly where it is the rules of the home state that create the obstacles to free movement.[265] The national rule therefore breached Article 21(1) TFEU unless it could be objectively justified.

The Court examined the question of justification in *D'Hoop* even though no evidence had been submitted to it on this point. It said that since the tide-over allowance aimed at facilitating the transition from education to the employment market, it was legitimate for the national legislature to ensure that a 'real link' existed between the applicant for that allowance and the geographic employment market concerned. However, as with the later cases of *Morgan* and *Prinz*, the Court found the single criteria—the place of secondary education—was too crude. Using the Court's language, it was 'too general and exclusive in nature' and that it unduly favoured an element which was not necessarily representative of a real and effective degree of connection between the applicant for the tide-over allowance and the geographic employment market, to the exclusion of all other representative elements. It therefore went beyond what was necessary to attain the objective pursued.[266]

(ii) Discrimination caused by similar treatment

The cases considered so far all concern discrimination caused by the different treatment of similarly situated groups. *Garcia Avello*[267] concerns the opposite: discrimination arising from the fact that differently situated groups were being treated in a similar way. Carlos Garcia Avello, a Spanish national, married Isabelle Weber, a Belgian national, and they lived together in Belgium. They had two children, dual nationals, who were given their father's surname (Garcia Avello). He then applied to the Belgian authorities to have the children's surnames changed to Garcia Weber, reflecting the Spanish pattern for surnames which comprise the first element of the father's surname (Garcia) followed by the mother's maiden name (Weber). While Belgian law did permit a change of surname when serious grounds were given, the Belgian authorities did not apply this exception to Garcia Avello because usually 'children bear their father's surname'.

---

[263] Para. 35. Case C–135/99 *Ursula Elsen v. Bundesversicherungsanstalt für Angestellte* [2000] ECR I–10409. See also Case C–28/00 *Kauer v. Pensionsversicherungsanstalt der Angestellten* [2002] ECR I–1343, para. 44; Case C–302/98 *Sehrer v. Bundesknappschaft* [2000] ECR I–4585, para. 32; Case C–522/10 *Reichel-Albert v. Deutsche Rentenversicherung Nordbayern* EU:C:2012:475, para. 39.

[264] See, e.g., Case C–499/06 *Nerkowska* [2008] ECR I–3993; Case C–221/07 *Zablocka-Wehrmüller* [2008] ECR I–9029, para. 35. The 'restriction' approach is considered later.

[265] M. Cousins, 'Citizenship, residence and social security' (2007) 32 *ELRev.* 386, 394.

[266] Para. 39. For further discussion as to what constitutes a genuine link (e.g., presence in the host state, contributions to/connections with the social security scheme) and how the requirement needs to reflect the elements of the benefit in question, see Case C–258/04 *Office national de l'empoli v. Ioannidis* [2005] ECR I–8275, paras. 30–3; Case C–503/09 *Stewart v. Secretary of State for Work and Pensions* [2011] ECR I–6497, paras. 90–3; Case C–75/11 *Commission v. Austria (reduced fares for students)* EU:C:2012:605, paras. 61–3.

[267] Case C–148/02 *Carlos Garcia Avello v. Etat Belge* [2003] ECR I–11613, noted by T. Ackermann (2007) 44 *CMLRev.* 141.

The Court confirmed that the citizenship provisions applied to this case. It noted that since Mr Garcia Avello's children held the nationality of two Member States, they enjoyed the status of citizen of the Union.[268] This meant that they enjoyed equal treatment with nationals of the host state in respect of situations falling within the material scope of the Treaties, in particular those involving the freedom to move and reside in the territory of the Member States.[269] Therefore, the children could not suffer discrimination on the ground of nationality in respect of their surname. Because the Garcia Avello children, holding both Spanish and Belgian nationality, were in a different situation from Belgian nationals holding just one (Belgian) nationality,[270] they had a 'right to be treated in a manner different to that in which persons having only Belgian nationality are treated, unless the treatment in issue can be justified on objective grounds'.[271] Since the Court rejected the justifications put forward by the Belgian government (the immutability of surnames as a founding principle of the social order and integration of nationals from other Member States), the Court concluded that Articles 18 and 20 TFEU precluded the Belgian authorities from refusing a name change to the Garcia Avello children.[272]

(iii) Restrictions approach

Although most of the landmark citizenship cases were decided under the non-discrimination/equal treatment model, the more general shift to a restrictions/market access approach seen elsewhere in the free movement case law can also be seen in the field of citizenship.[273] It was first seriously raised by Advocate General Jacobs in *Pusa*[274] and confirmed by the Court in *Tas-Hagen*.[275] The case concerned a Dutch law that made payment of a benefit to civilian war victims conditional on the applicants being resident in the Netherlands at the time that they made their application. This law, said the Court, was liable to dissuade Dutch nationals such as Mrs Tas-Hagen from exercising her freedom to move and reside outside the Netherlands.[276] It therefore constituted a 'restriction on the freedoms conferred by Article [21(1) TFEU] on every citizen of the Union'.[277] The Court recognized that the Dutch law could be justified on the grounds of solidarity with the population of the Netherlands both before and after the war but thought the requirement of residence to be disproportionate. While acknowledging that, in respect of benefits not covered by Union law, Member States enjoyed a wide margin of appreciation in deciding what criteria were to be used in assessing connection to society,[278] a residence criterion was not a satisfactory indicator of the degree of connection of civilian war victims to the Netherlands when it was liable to lead to different results for individuals resident abroad whose integration into Dutch society was in all respects comparable.[279]

---

[268] *Garcia Avello*, n. 267, para. 21.   [269] Para. 24.   [270] Paras. 34 and 37.   [271] Para. 34.

[272] Para. 44. The Court may now apply the 'restrictions' approach to such cases: see, e.g., Case C–353/06 *Grunkin-Paul* [2008] ECR I–7639, see n. 280.

[273] See Editorial Comments, 'Two-speed European citizenship? Can the Lisbon Treaty help close the gap?' (2008) 45 *CMLRev.* 1, 2.

[274] Case C–224/02 *Pusa* v. *Osuuspankkien Keskinäinen Vakuutusyhtiö* [2004] ECR I–5763, para. 18.

[275] Case C–192/05 *Tas-Hagen* v. *Raadskamer WUBO van de Pensioen- en Uitkeringsrad* [2006] ECR I–10451, paras. 30–1. See also Case C–345/05 *Commission* v. *Portugal (transfer of property)* [2006] ECR I–10633, para. 24.

[276] Para. 32.   [277] Para. 31.   [278] Para. 36.

[279] Para. 38. Cf. Case C–103/08 *Gottwald* v. *Bezirkshautmannschaft Bregenz* [2009] ECR I–9117, para. 36. See further G. Davies, '"Any place I hang my hat?" or: Residence is the new nationality' (2005) 11 *ELJ* 43,

For the Court, the advantage of the restrictions approach is that it is an effective tool to strike down state rules that deter departure from the state; traditional discrimination analysis can be difficult to apply in this context, as we saw in *D'Hoop*. Yet the risk is that the restrictions model can be all-embracing and used as a basis for challenging any national rule which proved inconvenient to the migrant citizen. The Court therefore added a threshold requirement: in *Grunkin-Paul*,[280] another case involving the migrant parents' desire to use one form of surname (double-barrelling the two parents' surnames), which had been prohibited by the host state, the Court said that a discrepancy in surnames was likely to result in 'serious inconvenience'[281] in the child's day-to-day life as he moved between Denmark and Germany.

Where, as is the general situation, the Court finds a presumptive breach of Article 21 TFEU, the Court turns to the question of justification (see further Chapter 12) and, most importantly, proportionality. The striking feature of a number of the citizenship cases is the Court's requirement that the personal circumstances of each individual be taken into account, despite the administrative burden this might entail.[282] *Nerkowska*[283] provides a good example. It concerned a claim for a disability pension granted by Poland to civilian victims of war and repression which had been rejected on the ground that the claimant was resident in another Member State. She was born in 1946 in the territory of present-day Belarus. Her parents were deported to Siberia, where they died. She was then deported in 1951 to the former USSR, where she lived under 'difficult conditions'. She returned to Poland in 1957 and lived there until 1985, when she moved to Germany. The Court said that the Polish rule on residence constituted a restriction on free movement of citizens[284] but could be justified on the grounds of (1) ensuring that there was a connection between Poland and the recipient of a benefit, and (2) the necessity of verifying that the recipient continued to satisfy the conditions for grant of that benefit.[285]

However, the Court found the Polish rule requiring residence throughout the period of payment of the benefit was disproportionate: the fact that a person was a national of the Member State granting the benefit and had lived in Poland for more than 20 years was sufficient to establish a connection between that State and the recipient of the benefit. Furthermore, the objective of verifying that the recipient of a disability pension continued to satisfy the conditions for its grant could be achieved by other means which, although less restrictive, were just as effective.[286]

There is, however, a risk attendant on such an individualized approach. As the healthcare cases considered in Chapter 9 show, the emphasis on protecting the individual over

---

who laments challenges to a residence requirement for the damage it does to a community's ability to offer benefits to local residents.

[280] Case C–353/06 *Grunkin-Paul* [2008] ECR I–7639.

[281] Paras. 23 and 29. See also Case C–391/09 *Malgožata Runevič-Vardyn and Łukasz Paweł Wardyn v. Vilniaus miesto savivaldybės administracija* [2011] ECR I–3787, para. 76. In Case C–208/09 *Sayn-Wittgenstein* v. *Landeshauptmann von Mann* [2010] ECR I–13693, para. 71 the refusal by the Austrian authorities to allow an Austrian national adopted by a German father to use the German nobility title 'von' in her name was a restriction on free movement under Art. 21 TFEU (but one that could be justified).

[282] Cf. the Art. 110 TFEU case, Case C–74/06 *Commission* v. *Greece (registration tax on imported cars)* [2007] ECR I–7585, para. 29.

[283] Case C–499/06 *Nerkowska Zakład Ubezpieczeń Społecznych Oddział w Koszalinie* [2008] ECR I–3993.

[284] Para. 34.   [285] Paras. 37–9.

[286] Para. 46. See also Case C–221/07 *Zablocka-Wehrmüller* [2008] ECR I–9029, para. 41. Cf. Case C–103/08 *Gottwald* [2009] ECR I–9117, para. 32, where the Court found that a residence criterion could be justified as a condition for the granting of a free annual road toll disc for people with disabilities in Austria, and was proportionate since there was no minimum period of residence required, the term residence was interpreted broadly, and the disc was also provided to non-residents who regularly travelled in Austria.

the interests of the community reflects what Newdick terms an 'institutional "asymme-try" within the EU, in which the Court of Justice favours private "economic" interests over the public "welfare" policies identified by national governments'.[287] He argues that this market citizenship is consistent with inequality because individual choice, rather than government policy, is the dominant influence.

(iv) Quantitative and qualitative approach to equal treatment

The Article 21(1) TFEU cases might suggest that migrant citizens who are not economi-cally active now have the right to claim all benefits available in the host state (whether classified as social assistance or social advantages) on the same terms as nationals, unless the benefits are expressly excluded by Union law or there are objectively justified reasons why not. If this analysis is correct, then the creation of citizenship of the Union leads to what Iliopoulou and Toner describe as the 'perfect assimilation' approach, where the treatment of Union migrants is placed on an equal footing with that of nationals of the host Member State unless Union law specifically provides otherwise.[288] But, when looked at carefully, the Article 21 TFEU cases, now read in the light of the more recent cases interpreting Article 24(2) CRD, do not support the full assimilationist approach and ac-tually suggest an incremental approach to residence and equality—the longer migrants lawfully reside (and, following *Dano*, under EU law) in the Member State, the greater the number of benefits they receive on equal terms with nationals. But the acquisition of ever more rights is not just quantitative but qualitative, as the Court put it in *Onuekwere*, a case concerning periods of imprisonment of TCN family members:

> Such integration, which is a precondition of the acquisition of the right of permanent residence laid down in Article 16(1) of Directive 2004/38 is based not only on territorial and temporal factors but also on qualitative elements, relating to the level of integration in the host Member State … to such an extent that the undermining of the link of inte-gration between the person concerned and the host Member State justifies the loss of the right of permanent residence even outside the circumstances mentioned in Article 16(4) of Directive 2004/38.

In other words, where the individual is subject to a custodial sentence that is 'an indica-tion that the person concerned has not respected the values of the society of the host Member State'[289] and so interrupts the process of integration.

But on what basis are non-economically active migrants entitled to (financially expen-sive) maintenance on equal terms with nationals? Unlike migrant workers, it cannot be argued that they have contributed to the economy of the host state[290] through taxation.[291] Instead, the answer appears to lie in the degree to which the EU citizen is integrated into the community of the host state, combined with a notion of social solidarity between members of that community.[292] At national level, welfare states are legitimized at least in

---

[287] C. Newdick, 'The European Court of Justice, trans-national health care, and social citizen-ship: Accidental death of a concept' (2008) 26 *Wisconsin International Law Journal* 844, 864.

[288] A. Iliopoulou and H. Toner (2002) 39 *CMLRev.* 609, 616. This is what Léger AG had in mind in Case C–214/94 *Boukhalfa v. Bundesrepublik Deutschland* [1996] ECR I–2253, para. 63.

[289] Case C–400/12 *MG* EU:C:2014:9, para 31.

[290] Although the Court's case law on the definition workers, to include migrants who received only limited wages and worked a small number of hours (e.g., Case 139/85 *Kempf* [1986] ECR 1741 and Case C–357/89 *Raulin* [1992] ECR I–1027), rather undermines the substance of this rationale.

[291] For a criticism of such arguments see Geelhoed AG's Opinion in Case C–209/03 *Bidar* [2005] ECR I–2119, para. 65.

[292] In his opinion in Case C– 70/95 *Sodemare SA* [1997] ECR I–3395, para. 29, Fennelly AG defined soli-darity as the 'inherently uncommercial act of involuntary subsidization of one social group by another'.

part by a diffuse sense of solidarity: national taxpayers pay their taxes to help look after their fellow citizens in need. This solidarity is founded on some sense of shared interests, which in turn is based on a shared nationality[293] and/or a shared identity. Thus *national* citizenship leads to the evolution of a sense of *national* solidarity. The striking feature of both *Grzelczyk* and *Bidar* is that the Court has taken the concept of *European Union* citizenship, the 'fundamental status of nationals of the Member States',[294] to justify the creation of a sense of *transnational* solidarity between (taxpaying) nationals of a host Member State and (impoverished migrant) nationals of other Member States, with the result that the migrant needs to be treated in the same way as nationals in respect of access to certain social advantages.

However, this sense of transnational solidarity seems to be increasingly attenuated, at least in the case of non-economically active migrant citizens. Benefit tourists have become the new reviled figures of Europe (despite the absence of hard evidence that they actually exist[295]). Section D.1(b) of the UK's New Settlement Decision confirms that:

> Member States have the possibility of refusing to grant social benefits to persons who exercise their right to freedom of movement solely in order to obtain Member States' social assistance although they do not have sufficient resources to claim a right of residence.

A *qualitative* approach to integration can also be found in the directive, albeit not in the context of establishing rights to equal treatment in respect of length of residence but in respect of an expulsion decision. Under Article 28 CRD the host state must take account of considerations such as 'how long the individual concerned has resided on its territory, his/her age, state of health, family and economic situation, social and cultural integration into the host Member State and the extent of his/her links with the country of origin'[296] when deciding whether to expel an individual.

(c) Tax advantages

It was only in the mid 2000s that cases began to arise concerning EU citizens alleging that tax rules, often those of the state of origin, constituted an impediment to/restriction on their rights of free movement. These arguments coincided with a more general shift by the Court from the discrimination model towards the restrictions approach in the field of taxation, a move documented in detail in Chapters 8 and 11. This can be seen in *Pusa*,[297] concerning a Finnish pensioner living in Spain who owed money in Finland. An attachment order was made against his pension for the purpose of recovering the debt. Had he resided in Finland, the income tax he owed would have been deducted first in order to calculate what was left of his monthly pension to which an attachment order could have been

The meaning of solidarity in the EU context is considered further in C. Barnard, 'Solidarity as a tool of new governance' in G. de Búrca and J. Scott (eds.), *New Governance and Constitutionalism in Europe and the US* (Oxford: Hart Publishing, 2006).

[293] See D. Miller, 'In defence of nationality' in D. Miller, *Citizenship and National Identity* (Cambridge: Polity Press, 2000), cited in N. Barber, 'Citizenship, nationalism and the European Union' (2002) 27 *ELRev.* 241, 250, who notes that nationality is the principal source of solidarity.

[294] Case C–184/99 *Grzelczyk* [2001] ECR I–6193, paras. 30–1; Case C–148/02 *Garcia Avello* [2003] ECR I–11613, paras. 22–3; and Case C–209/03 *Bidar* [2005] ECR I–2119, para. 31.

[295] See, e.g., ICF et al., *Study for the Commission: Impact of mobile EU citizens on national social security systems* (2013), <http://ec.europa.eu/social/main.jsp?langId=en&catId=89&newsId=1980&furtherNews=yes>.

[296] See also Joined Cases C–482 and 493/01 *Orfanopoulos v. Land Baden-Württemberg* [2004] ECR I–5257, para. 99.

[297] Case C–224/02 *Pusa* [2004] ECR I–5763, see n. 274.

made. However, since he resided in Spain, no such initial deduction was made. The Court ruled that the difference in treatment unjustifiably resulted in Mr Pusa being 'placed at a disadvantage by virtue of exercising his right to move and reside freely'[298] contrary to Article 21(1) TFEU. Similar reasoning was used in *Schwarz*,[299] a case concerning tax relief. The Schwarz children, who were German, attended a school for the exceptionally gifted and talented in Scotland. Their parents did not get tax relief on the schooling; had the children been educated in Germany, the parents would have received the tax relief. The Court said that the German rule disadvantaged the children of nationals merely by reason of the fact that they had exercised their freedom of movement and this obstacle could not be justified.

Pusa and *Schwarz* concerned challenges by nationals who had exercised their rights of free movement against the home state; *Rüffler*[300] concerned a challenge by a migrant citizen to host state tax laws. It concerned a German claimant who retired to Poland, where he lived on his German pension. Under Polish law only contributions paid to a Polish health insurance body were tax deductible. Because Mr Rüffler paid his contributions to a German body he did not benefit from the tax advantage. The Court found that the situation of a retired (German) taxpayer resident in Poland and receiving pension benefits paid under the compulsory health insurance scheme of another Member State, and that of a Polish retired person also resident in Poland but receiving his pension under a Polish health insurance scheme, were comparable since both were subject to an unlimited liability to tax in Poland. The Court then found that because the Polish rules disadvantaged taxpayers, like Mr Rüffler, who had exercised their freedom of movement to take up residence in Poland,[301] they therefore constituted 'a restriction on the freedoms conferred by Article [21(1) TFEU] on every citizen of the Union'[302] which could not be justified.

While the restrictions approach is an effective way of subjecting national tax rules which hinder free movement to review under Union law, this model sits uncomfortably with the international tax law principles of fiscal sovereignty and territoriality. As we have seen, the Court has more recently developed its understanding of the implications of these principles for its analysis,[303] with the result that it has tended to revert to the discrimination approach. The citizenship tax cases are no exception, as *Lindfors*[304] and *Schempp*[305] made clear. In these cases the Court said that mere difference between the tax regime of one Member State and another was not sufficient to trigger Article 21(1) TFEU: migrant citizens had to show that they had suffered disadvantage in comparison with nationals. *Schempp* also emphasized that the claimant and the comparator had to be similarly situated. On the facts the Court ruled that the situation of Mr Schempp, a German national, who made maintenance payments to his former spouse, now resident in Austria, which were not tax deductible, was not comparable with the situation of a German national who made equivalent payments to a former spouse resident in Germany which were tax deductible. There was therefore no breach of the principle of non-discrimination.

---

[298] Case C–224/02 *Pusa* [2004] ECR I–5763, para. 31. See also Case C–520/04 *Turpeinen* [2006] ECR I–10685; Case C–152/05 *Commission v. Germany (subsidy on dwellings)* [2008] ECR I–39, para. 30.
[299] Case C–76/05 *Schwarz and Gootjes-Schwarz v. Finanzamt Bergisch Gladbach* [2007] ECR I–6849. See also Case C–318/05 *Commission v. Germany (school fees)* [2007] ECR I–6957.
[300] Case C–544/07 *Rüffler v. Dyrektor Izby Skarbowej we Wrocławiu Ośrodek Zamiejscowy w Wałbrzychu* [2009] ECR I–3389.
[301] Para. 72.   [302] Para. 73.   [303] See further Chs. 9 and 10.
[304] Case C–365/02 *Lindfors* [2004] ECR I–7183, para. 34.
[305] Case C–403/33 *Schempp v. Finanzamt München* [2005] ECR I–6421, para. 45.

2.6 Specific Rights for Family Members

So far we have concentrated on the meaning of equal treatment in the general context of Article 24 CRD and under Articles 18 and 21(1) TFEU. The CRD lays down specific rights for families. Not only will they enjoy the right to equal treatment in respect of social advantages and social assistance, as we have already seen, but also in respect of the right to work, schooling, and housing.

(a) Equal treatment and the right to work

Article 23 CRD permits the Union citizen's family members who have the right of residence or the right of permanent residence to take up employment or self-employment in the host state (but not in any other state[306]), irrespective of the nationality of the family member.[307] These family members will enjoy equal treatment in respect of their terms and conditions of employment, as well as in respect of dismissal rights under Article 24(1) CRD.

(b) Equal treatment and schooling

With a view to encouraging the integration of migrant children into the society of the host state,[308] Article 10 of Regulation 492/11 requires the children of an EU national who is, or has been, employed in another Member State, to be admitted to that state's general educational, apprenticeship, or vocational training courses.[309] This provision remains in Regulation 492/11 and has not been replicated in the CRD 2004/38. Strictly speaking, the right therefore extends only to the children of *workers*.

Member States are obliged to encourage these children to attend such courses and, if necessary, make special efforts to ensure that the children can take advantage of educational and training facilities on an equal footing with nationals.[310] The reference to 'children' includes not only school-age children but also those over the age of 21 who are no longer dependent on the working parent. In *Gaal*[311] the Court refused to make a link between the limitations imposed in the original Article 10 of Regulation 1612/68 (identification of family members) and the rights contained in Article 12 of Regulation 16/2/68, now Article 10 of Regulation 492/11. It said that the principle of equal treatment required that the children of migrant workers should be able to continue their studies in order to be able to complete their education successfully.

Article 10 says that admission for migrant workers' children to education and training must be on the same conditions as for nationals. The reference to 'same conditions' is broadly construed. In the early case of *Casagrande*[312] the Court ruled that the term 'conditions' extended to 'general measures intended to facilitate educational attendance', including a grant for maintenance and training. Therefore, it was unlawful for the German

---

[306] Case C–10/05 *Mattern* v. *Ministre du travail et de l'Emploi* [2006] ECR I–3145, para. 27.

[307] Case 131/85 *Gül* v. *Regierungspräsident Düsseldorf* [1986] ECR 1573.

[308] Case 9/74 *Casagrande* v. *Landeshauptstadt München* [1974] ECR 773, para. 7.

[309] These are to be read disjunctively: Joined Cases 389 and 390/87 *Echternach and Moritz* [1989] ECR 723. See further Ch. 7.

[310] Case 9/74 *Casagrande* [1974] ECR 773, para. 8. Council Dir. 77/486/EEC ([1977] OJ L199/139) on the education of migrant workers' children requires that free tuition is available, including the teaching of the official language of the host state (Art. 2) and that the host state must promote the teaching of the children's mother tongue and culture (Art. 3). This applies equally to children with a disability: Case 76/72 *Michel S.* [1973] ECR 457, paras. 15–16.

[311] Case C–7/94 *Landesamt für Ausbildungsforderung Nordrhein-Westfalen* v. *Gaal* [1995] ECR I–1031.

[312] Case 9/74 [1974] ECR 773.

authorities to refuse a monthly maintenance grant payable to school-age children to the daughter of an Italian working in Germany. The right to a maintenance grant applies even where the children decide to receive their education in their state of origin. For this reason the Court ruled in *Di Leo*[313] that the German authorities could not refuse a grant to the daughter of an Italian migrant worker employed in Germany for 25 years on the grounds that she wished to study medicine in her state of origin (Italy).[314]

The importance of the right to education was emphasized in *Baumbast*,[315] which concerned a German national who had been working in the UK. Relying on his rights under Regulation 492/11 he had brought his Colombian wife and children with him to the UK. However, when he ceased working the British authorities refused to renew his residence permit or those of his family with the result that the children could not complete their education in the UK. The Court found that the UK's decision breached Article 45 TFEU because, as the Court explained, to prevent a child of an EU citizen from continuing his education in the host state might 'dissuade that citizen from exercising the rights to freedom of movement laid down in Article [45 TFEU] and would therefore create an obstacle to the effective exercise of the freedom thus guaranteed by the [EU Treaties]'.[316] For much the same reason, in *R*[317] the children of an American woman and her French husband who worked in the UK were entitled to carry on their education in the UK, even though the parents were divorced and the children were living with their mother (a non-EU national).[318]

If the children of migrants can continue receiving their education in the host state, then in order to be able to enjoy that right they need someone to look after them. This was also confirmed in *Baumbast and R*. Reading Article 10 of Regulation 492/11 in the light of the requirement of respect for family life under Article 8 ECHR, the Court said the right conferred by Article 10 'necessarily implies' that the child has the right to be accompanied by the person who is his primary carer and who is entitled to reside with the child during his studies,[319] notwithstanding that the carers might not have had independent rights under EU law[320] because they are TCNs.[321] This case law has now been codified by Article 12(3) CRD.

In *Ibrahim*[322] the Court put together *Gaal* and *Baumbast* to conclude that the children of a national of a Member State (Denmark), who works or has worked in the host Member State (the UK), and the TCN parent who is their primary carer can claim a right of residence in the UK on the sole basis of Article 10 of Regulation 492/11, without such a right being conditional on their having sufficient resources and comprehensive sickness insurance cover in that state. In *Teixeira*[323] the Court added that the right of residence in the host Member State of the parent who was the primary carer for a child of a migrant worker, where that child was in education in that state, was not conditional on one of the child's parents having worked as a migrant worker on the date on which the child started in education. It also said that the right of residence in the host Member State of the parent who was the primary carer for a child of a migrant worker, where that child was in education, ended when the child reached the age of majority, unless the child continued to need the presence and care of that parent in order to be able to pursue and complete his or her

---

[313] Case C–308/89 *Di Leo* v. *Land Berlin* [1990] ECR I–4185.   [314] Para. 12.
[315] Case C–413/99 [2002] ECR I–7091.   [316] Para. 50.
[317] Case C–413/99 [2002] ECR I–7091.   [318] Paras. 60–2.   [319] Para. 73.   [320] Para. 71.
[321] See also Case C–200/02 *Chen* v. *Secretary of State for the Home Department* [2004] ECR I–9925.
[322] Case C–310/08 *London Borough of Harrow* v. *Ibrahim* [2010] ECR I–1065.
[323] Case C–480/08 *Teixeira* v. *London Borough of Lambeth* [2010] ECR I–1107. See also Case C–45/12 *ONAFTS* v. *Ahmed* EU:C:2013:390, paras. 44–7.

education. In *Alarape*[324] the Court said, in determining whether an adult child does need the presence and care of his parent, account needs to be taken of, inter alia, the age of the child, whether the child is residing in the family home, or whether the child needs financial or emotional support from the parent in order to be able to continue and to complete his education. *Alarape* also added that periods of residence in a host state completed by TCN family members on the basis of looking after a child in education cannot be taken into consideration for the purposes of acquisition by those family members of a right of permanent residence.[325]

(c) Equal treatment and housing

Originally, Article 10(3) of Regulation 1612/68 provided that workers were obliged to have available for their families 'housing considered as normal' for national workers in the region where they are employed. According to *Diatta*,[326] the purpose of Article 10(3) was both to implement public policy and to protect public security by preventing immigrants from living in precarious conditions.[327] In *Commission* v. *Germany*[328] German law required family members of EU migrant workers to have appropriate housing not only upon their arrival but also for the duration of their residence. The Court said that the German law went too far and that Article 10(3) applied solely when the worker and his family were first reunited.[329] Once the family had been brought together the position of the migrant worker was no different from that of a national. Article 10(3) was deleted by the CRD and not replaced.

D. MEMBERSHIP

1. INTRODUCTION

So far we have concentrated on the first strand of David Held's citizenship matrix, rights (and duties). The rights for migrants are extensive. It is, however, surprising, how little reference is made to duties for those migrants unless the more recent citizenship case law can be read as saying that there is a duty to be economically active or self-supporting in order to enjoy the rights of free movement and residence. We turn now to the second strand in Held's definition, membership. As far as membership is concerned, it has a legal and psychological dimension. The formal, legal indicator of membership is nationality.

2. NATIONALITY

Nationality demarcates the national from the alien; it is the manifestation of citizenship to the outside world and the juridical tie between the individual and the community.[330] Two consequences flow from nationality: the state assumes certain responsibilities for the individual holding its nationality and the individual is subject to the government of that particular state.

Nationality is also the principal indicator of membership for the EU. According to Article 20(1) TFEU, '[e]very person holding the nationality of a Member State shall be

---

[324] Case C–529/11 *Alarape* v. *Secretary of State for the Home Department* EU:C:2013:290, para. 30.
[325] Para. 48.   [326] Case 267/83 [1985] ECR 567.
[327] Para. 10.   [328] Case 249/86 [1989] ECR 1263.
[329] Confirmed in Case C–244/13 *Ogieriakhi* EU:C:2014:2068, para. 46.
[330] C. Closa, 'Citizenship of the Union and nationality of Member States' (1995) 32 *CMLRev*. 487.

a citizen of the Union'. From this it is clear that it is the Member States, and not the EU, which are the gatekeepers to EU citizenship.[331] This was confirmed in *Kaur*,[332] where the Court said 'under international law, it is for each Member State, having due regard to [Union] law, to lay down the conditions for the acquisition and loss of nationality'.[333] Furthermore, the host Member State is not in a position to criticize another Member State's attribution of nationality.[334]

In *Kaur* the Court also said that, when exercising their powers in the sphere of nationality, the Member States must have due regard to EU law. The significance of this observation can be seen in *Rottman*.[335] An Austrian national was accused of serious fraud in Austria. He moved to Germany and applied for naturalization, without mentioning the proceedings against him in Austria. He was granted German nationality and, as a result, he lost his Austrian nationality under Austrian law. However, when the German authorities learned that he was the subject of judicial investigation in Austria, they sought to withdraw his naturalization with retroactive effect.

The Court of Justice recognized that a decision withdrawing naturalization because of deception corresponded to a reason relating to the public interest and that it was 'legitimate for a Member State to wish to protect the special relationship of solidarity and good faith between it and its nationals and also the reciprocity of rights and duties, which form the bedrock of the bond of nationality'.[336] However, the Court also recognized at paragraph 42 that the decision by the German authorities risked rendering him stateless, as well as depriving him of 'the status conferred by Article [20 TFEU] and the rights attaching thereto'. For this reason the matter—insofar as it concerned the consequences for an individual in the light of EU law—did fall within the ambit of EU law and so was subject to EU law principles including proportionality.[337] The Court added that the principle of proportionality might include giving Rottman a reasonable period of time to try to recover Austrian nationality.[338]

For some, *Rottman* marked a decisive turning point in the Court's approach to EU citizenship: it was no longer just about facilitating free movement but about giving substance to the status.[339] Certainly the decision, and particularly the Court's remarks in paragraph 42, paved the way for the momentous and highly controversial decision in *Ruiz Zambrano*.[340] Mr Ruiz Zambrano was a failed asylum seeker from Columbia living in Belgium, benefiting from *non-refoulement* protection stating that he should not be sent back to Colombia in view of the civil war in that country. Although he did not have a work permit he did have a job and paid social security contributions. He and his Columbian

---

[331] This is confirmed by the Declaration on Nationality of a Member State appended to the TEU. In the case of a person with dual nationality, the Court ruled in Case C–369/90 *Micheletti* v. *Delagación del Gobierno en Cantabria* [1992] ECR I–4239, para. 10 that if a person was able to produce one of the documents referred to in Council Dir. 73/148/EEC ([1973] OJ L172/14) (now CRD) to prove they were a national of one Member State, other Member States were not entitled to dispute that status on the ground that the person concerned was also a national of a non-Member State, the nationality of which took precedence under the host state's law.

[332] Case C–192/99 *R.* v. *Secretary of State for the Home Department, ex p. Kaur* [2001] ECR I–1237 noted by H. Toner (2002) 39 *CMLRev.* 881.

[333] Para. 19. The conditions might include a period of residence, birth, and family ties.

[334] Case C–200/02 *Chen* [2004] ECR I–9925.

[335] Case C–135/08 *Rottman* v. *Freistaat Bayern* [2010] ECR I–1449.   [336] Para. 51.

[337] Para. 55. For criticism (obiter), see *Pham* v. *Secretary of State for the Home Department* [2015] UKSC 19.

[338] Paras. 55–9.

[339] D. Kochenov and R. Plender, 'EU citizenship: From an incipient form to an incipient substance? The discovery of the Treaty text' (2012) 37 *ELRev.* 369.

[340] Case C–34/09 *Ruiz Zambrano* v. *ONEM* [2011] ECR I–1177.

wife had two children in Belgium who, under Belgian law as it then stood, had Belgian nationality. When the authorities discovered his lack of a work permit they stopped him working. They also denied him unemployment benefits and refused to let him regularize his situation in terms of obtaining a residence permit. The Court assumed that the effects of these decisions would 'lead to a situation where those children, citizens of the Union, would have to leave the territory of the Union in order to accompany their parents'.[341] The problem for Mr Ruiz Zambrano, a TCN, was that the case concerned a wholly internal situation: none of the family had moved from Belgium to another Member State. This did not deter the Court. It decided the case not under Article 21 TFEU on the rights of free movement but as with *Rottman*, under Article 20 TFEU. It said:[342]

> Article 20 TFEU precludes national measures which have the effect of depriving citizens of the Union of the *genuine enjoyment of the substance of the rights* conferred by virtue of their status as citizens of the Union.
>
> A refusal to grant a right of residence to a third country national with dependent minor children in the Member State where those children are nationals and reside, and also a refusal to grant such a person a work permit, has such an effect.

The Court continued that a refusal to grant a right of residence would lead to a situation where the children, citizens of the Union, would have to leave the territory of the Union in order to accompany their parents. Moreover, the Court added that if a work permit was not granted to Mr Ruiz Zambrano, he would risk not having sufficient resources to provide for himself and his family, which would also result in the children having to leave the territory of the Union. In those circumstances, the Court concluded that the children—citizens of the Union—would, in fact, be unable to exercise the substance of the rights conferred on them by virtue of their status as citizens of the Union.[343] The Court therefore concluded that Article 20 TFEU required Mr Ruiz Zambrano to be given both a residence and work permit.[344]

The decision was greeted with delight from human rights lawyers (even though the decision, unlike the Advocate General's Opinion, contained no reference to human rights) but serious protest from interior ministries of the Member States who saw it as a means of 'driving a coach and horses' through their immigration (and social security) rules.[345] Subsequent case law suggests that *Ruiz Zambrano* has been confined to the specific facts of the case: a genuine family unit where vulnerable EU national young children risked being removed with their TCN parents from the safe territory of the EU to a (dangerous?) third country. For example in *McCarthy*[346] the claimant was not able to rely on the principle in *Ruiz Zambrano* to bring her Jamaican husband to the UK. She was a dual UK/Irish national, who had lived her entire life in the UK. She was not a worker or a self-employed person. The Court said that the decision by the UK authorities not to grant Mr McCarthy a residence permit did not have the effect of depriving Mrs McCarthy of the genuine enjoyment of the substance of the rights associated with her status as a Union citizen, nor of impeding the exercise of her right to move and reside freely within the territory of the Member States, in accordance with Article 21 TFEU.[347] The Court also said that, by

---

[341] Para. 44.   [342] Paras. 42–3.   [343] Para. 44.

[344] If the TCN 'Zambrano' carer cannot work are they entitled to benefits? The Court of Appeal of England and Wales ruled in *Sanneh* v. *Secretary of State for Work and Pensions* [2015] EWCA Civ 49 that the UK was entitled to pay benefits on a different and less generous basis than those paid to EU citizens.

[345] I. Solanke, 'Using the citizen to bring the refugee in' (2012) 75 *MLR* 101, 108–10.

[346] Case C–434/09 *McCarthy* v. *Secretary of State for the Home Department* [2011] ECR I–3375. Although cf. Szpunar AG's Opinion in Case C–165/14 *Rendón Marín* EU:C:2016:75.

[347] Para. 49.

contrast with the case of *Ruiz Zambrano*, the national measure did not have the effect of obliging Mrs McCarthy, an EU national, to leave the territory of the European Union.[348]

Two further cases reinforce the narrow reading of *Ruiz Zambrano*. In *Iida*[349] a TCN husband married a German national, and had a child with her. The wife and child then moved to Austria. Since he neither accompanied nor joined his wife in Austria, he could not claim a right of residence in Germany derived from his relationship with a Union citizen. In *O and S*[350] a TCN mother with permanent residence rights in Finland, where she trained and worked, had a baby with a Finnish husband. The baby had Finnish nationality. The husband and wife subsequently divorced and she married a TCN with whom she had a further baby who was also a TCN. The question was whether the TCN father could rely on his stepson's EU citizenship to argue that he, the stepfather, was entitled to a right of residence. While the Court left it to the national court to have a final say, the Court did say that the principles laid down in *Ruiz Zambrano* applied only in 'exceptional circumstances' and that since the stepchild was not economically dependent on the stepfather but on the mother, the principle in *Ruiz Zambrano* did not apply. Nevertheless, in *Alokpa*[351] the Court did concede that if Article 21 TFEU did not apply to the EU citizen children of a TCN the national court should determine whether a right of residence may be granted to the TCN 'exceptionally—if the effectiveness of the Union citizenship that her children enjoy is not to be undermined'.

3. BELONGING AND IDENTITY

So far we have concentrated on the legal indicators of membership. The psychological dimension of membership is harder to articulate, but at its core lies a sense of belonging and identity. To a certain extent legal links can help foster a sense of 'common identity and shared destiny',[352] particularly in the EU where law has been so central to the integration process.[353] The EU has been proactive in taking other steps to develop a sense of belonging—the EU flag, EU day (9 May), EU motto (United in diversity), and EU anthem ('Ode to Joy' from Beethoven's Ninth Symphony),[354] the red passport, the pink driving licence, town-twinning, and student mobility programmes (Erasmus/Socrates). Some commentators are dismissive of these top-down attempts to create a true European citizenship, arguing that they cannot overcome the historical legacy of market citizenship, which is essentially premised on self-interest.[355] Others are concerned that the continued emphasis on market citizenship excludes those who do not conform[356] and so, for many, citizenship undermines, rather than creates, a sense of identity at EU level. And for those who do not hold the nationality of one of the Member States exclusion may be total.

---

[348] *McCarthy*, n. 346, para. 50. See also Case C–256/11 *Dereci* [2011] ECR I–11315. These families have the right to live somewhere together but not somewhere in particular: N. Nic Shuibhne (2012) 49 *CMLRev.* 349, 373.

[349] Case C–40/11 *Iida* v. *Stadt Ulm* EU:C:2012:691. See also Case C–87/12 *Ymeraga* v. *Ministre du travail, de l'emploi et de l'immigration* EU:C:2013:291.

[350] Joined Cases C–356 and 357/11 *O and S* v. *Maahanmuuttovirasto* EU:C:2012:776.

[351] Case C–86/12 *Alokpa* v. *Ministre du travail, de l'emploi et de l'immigration* EU:C:2013:645, para. 33.

[352] Jacobs AG in Joined Cases C–92 and 326/92 *Phil Collins* [1993] ECR I–5145, para. 11.

[353] See M. Cappelletti, M. Seccombe, and J. H. H. Weiler (eds.), *Integration through Law* (Berlin: De Gruyter, 1985).

[354] These were listed in Art. I-8 of the Constitutional Treaty under the heading 'The symbols of the Union'. Many thought that the EU had gone too far with these trappings of statehood and the symbols were dropped from the Lisbon Treaty.

[355] S. Douglas-Scott, *Constitutional Law of the European Union* (Harlow: Longman, 2002), 492.

[356] Everson, n. 1.

A further criticism of the creation of EU citizenship is that it comes at the expense of national or regional identity. The EU is at least aware of these concerns. Article 4(2) TEU requires the Union to respect 'the national identities of the Member States, inherent in their fundamental structures, political and constitutional, inclusive of regional and local self-government',[357] while Article 167 TFEU requires the Union to contribute to the 'flowering of the cultures of the Member States, while respecting their national and regional diversity'.[358] Advocate General Jacobs picked up on the diversity theme in *Garcia Avello*,[359] noting that the intention of Article 21 TFEU was to allow free, and possibly repeated or even continuous, movement within a single 'area of freedom, security and justice' (AFSJ), in which 'both cultural diversity and freedom from discrimination' are ensured. The Court reached similar conclusions in the same case, reasoning that the Belgian practice of refusing to change a child's surname to reflect the Spanish pattern was 'neither necessary nor even appropriate for promoting the integration within Belgium of the nationals of other Member States'.[360]

The AFSJ introduced at Amsterdam, to which Advocate General Jacobs referred, is part of the EU's response to concerns about exclusion, especially of TCNs, and failure to recognize the diversity of states in the EU. According to Article 67(1) TFEU:

> The Union shall constitute an area of freedom, security and justice with respect for fundamental rights and the different legal systems and traditions of the Member States.

The subsequent paragraphs of Article 67 TFEU then consider freedom, security and justice in turn. Article 67(2) TFEU concerns *freedom*. It provides that the Union shall 'ensure the absence of internal border controls for persons and shall frame a common policy on asylum, immigration and external border control, based on solidarity between Member States, which is fair towards third-country nationals'.[361] Thus 'freedom' means free movement of EU nationals as well as 'fair' Union-based migration policies for TCNs. These policies have now been elaborated by the European agenda on migration,[362] which recognizes the EU's long-term economic and demographic challenges (an ageing population and a demand for skilled labour).

Article 67(3) TFEU concerns *security*:

> The Union shall endeavour to ensure a high level of security through measures to prevent and combat crime, racism and xenophobia, and through measures for coordination and cooperation between police and judicial authorities and other competent authorities, as

---

[357] A principle recognized in Case C–391/09 *Malgožata Runevič-Vardyn* [2011] ECR I–3787, para. 86, where the Court said the protection of the national identity includes the protection of the official language, reiterated in Case C–202/11 *Las* EU:C:2013:239, para. 26 and by Bot AG in Case C–399/11 *Melloni* EU:C:2013:107, para. 139. See also the Union's approach to subsidiarity as laid down in Art. 5(3) TEU and Protocol (No. 2) on the application of the principles of subsidiarity and proportionality, and Protocol (No. 3) on the role of national parliaments in the European Union. See further Ch. 15.

[358] See also Art. 3(3) TEU: The Union shall 'respect its rich cultural and linguistic diversity, and shall ensure that Europe's cultural heritage is safeguarded and enhanced'. In Case C–161/06 *Skoma-Lux* [2007] ECR I–10841, the Court said that obligations contained in EU legislation which had not been published in the Official Journal in the (official) language of a new Member State could not be imposed on individuals in that state. In Case C–288/89 *Gouda* [1991] ECR I–4007, para. 13 the Court took the 'social, cultural, religious and philosophical' diversity of the Netherlands into account (see Case Study 11.2). See also Case 379/87 *Groener* [1989] ECR 3967, considered in Ch. 8.

[359] Case C–148/02 *Garcia Avello* [2003] ECR I–11613, para. 72.   [360] Para. 43.

[361] The reference to the need to be fair to TCNs is also new. The para. continues that 'For the purpose of this Title, stateless persons shall be treated as third-country nationals.'

[362] COM(2015) 240.

well as through the mutual recognition of judgments in criminal matters and, if necessary, through the approximation of criminal laws.

The Hague Programme 2004–9 prioritized the security agenda and is used to justify
keeping out TCNs who might pose a threat to the security of EU insiders. This exclusionary policy risked undermining the more integrationist stance envisaged by Article 67(2)
TFEU. Finally, Article 67(4) TFEU concerns *justice*. Article 67(4) TFEU says: 'The Union
shall facilitate access to justice, in particular through the principle of mutual recognition
of judicial and extra-judicial decisions in civil matters.'[363] In its AFSJ Communication,[364]
the Commission says that priority must be given to mechanisms that facilitate people's
access to the courts so that they can enforce their rights, especially their contractual
rights, throughout the Union.[365]

Attempts have been made to locate the citizen more firmly at the heart of the AFSJ.
For example, in its Communication, 'An Area of freedom, security and justice serving
the citizen',[366] it said 'All action taken in future should be centred on the citizen', focusing on, for example, 'promoting citizens rights', emphasizing the role of fundamental
rights, especially respect for the 'human person and human dignity', and for the other
rights enshrined in the Charter. Data protection is particularly emphasized. Secondly,
the Commission talks of a 'Europe of justice'. This is considered later. Thirdly, the priority
of 'a Europe that protects' emphasizes the need for a domestic security strategy. This can
now be found in the European Agenda on Security:[367]

> The European Union aims to ensure that people live in an area of freedom, security and
> justice, without internal frontiers. Europeans need to feel confident that, wherever they
> move within Europe, their freedom and their security are well protected, in full compli-
> ance with the Union's values, including the rule of law and fundamental rights.

Thus, 'membership' for EU citizens is in large part about ensuring their safety.

E. PARTICIPATION

An important way of fostering a sense of belonging comes through participation in the
life of the community. This is the third strand in Held's matrix of citizenship. In the Greek
city state (polis) all citizens (for which read free men with property) actively participated
in the legislative process. This is the fullest, richest, and most active kind of citizenship,
underpinned by ideas of equality (at least among those allowed to participate). Viewed in
this light, citizenship is a status, different from nationality, which requires active involvement by the citizen in shaping the polity. In the modern state the concept of democracy
has evolved from participative democracy in the republican style (with all men participating), to representative democracy (where the people elect their representatives). Now

---

[363] See, e.g., Council Reg. 743/2002 establishing a general Community framework of activities to facilitate the implementation of judicial cooperation in civil matters ([2002] OJ L115/1); Council Dir. 2003/8/
EC ([2003] OJ L26/41) on improving access to justice in cross-border disputes by establishing minimum
common rules relating to legal aid for such disputes.

[364] COM(2009) 262, 2.

[365] See, e.g., Reg. (EC) No. 861/2007 establishing a European Small Claims Procedure ([2007] OJ L199/1);
Reg. 1896/2006 creating a European order for payment procedure ([2006] OJ L399/1); Reg (EC) No. 593/2008
([2008] OJ L177/6) on the law applicable to contractual obligations (Rome I); Reg (EC) No. 1393/2007 ([2007]
OJ L324/79) on the service in the Member States of judicial and extrajudicial documents; Dir. 2008/52/EC
([2008] OJ L136/3) on certain aspects of mediation in civil and commercial matters.

[366] COM(2009) 262.   [367] COM(2015) 185, 2

the only active participation expected of citizens is to vote and possibly to stand as a candidate in elections.

1. REPRESENTATIVE DEMOCRACY

1.1 Introduction

One of the distinguishing features of the Constitutional Treaty was its expressed commitment to democracy. This has survived in the Lisbon Treaty. The title on democratic principles begins, in Article 9 TEU, with a statement of commitment to the principle of democratic equality:

> In all its activities, the Union shall observe the principle of the equality of its citizens, who shall receive equal attention from its institutions, bodies, offices and agencies.

Article 10(3) TEU adds 'Every citizen shall have the right to participate in the democratic life of the Union.' The centrality of the representative model in the EU is recognized in Article 10(1) TEU: 'The functioning of the Union shall be founded on representative democracy.' Article 10(2) TEU then identifies the two routes by which the citizen's voice is heard at EU level: (1) directly, through their MEPs ('Citizens are directly represented at Union level in the European Parliament'); and (2) indirectly via Member State participation ('Member States are represented in the European Council by their Heads of State or Government and in the Council by their governments, themselves democratically accountable either to their national parliaments,[368] or to their citizens').

   Article 10(2) TEU thus emphasizes the multi-faceted nature of representative democracy in the EU: while recognizing that the EU gains some legitimacy through direct elections to the European Parliament, the Article makes express the parallel legitimacy derived from elections to national parliaments which hold government ministers representing Member State interests in the EU to account. This indirect route to legitimacy is important since the turnout in elections to the European Parliament is so low. One response to this might be the creation of pan-European political parties. This is envisaged by Article 10(4) TEU, which says 'Political parties at European level contribute to forming European political awareness and to expressing the will of citizens of the Union.'

1.2 Elections to the European Parliament

The only democratically elected body in the EU is the European Parliament.[369] Article 8 of the Act concerning the election of the representatives of the European Parliament by direct universal suffrage[370] provides that 'the electoral procedure shall be governed in each Member State by its national provisions'. Further, the 1976 Act does not 'expressly and precisely'[371] define who is entitled to vote and to stand as a candidate in elections to the European Parliament—questions which go to the core of 'the principles of democracy

---

[368] National parliaments, too, have a greater role, especially in respect of ensuring compliance with the principle of subsidiarity: see Arts. 5(3) and 12 TEU and Protocol (No. 1) on the Role of National Parliaments in the European Union and the first use of the yellow card procedure in respect of the Monti II proposal (COM(2012) 130).

[369] Art. 223 TFEU.

[370] Annexed to Council Dec. 76/787/ECSC, EEC, Euratom ([1976] OJ L278/1) as amended by Council Dec. 2002/772/EC, Euratom ([2002] OJ L283/1). See also Art. 14(3) TEU: 'The members of the European Parliament shall be elected for a term of five years by direct universal suffrage in a free and secret ballot.'

[371] Case C–650/13 Delvigne v. Commune de Lesparre-Médoc EU:C:2015:648, para. 31.

on which the Union is based'.[372] This suggests that these issues are a matter for national law. However, three cases suggest that EU law principles will apply to Member State decisions. The first two cases, *Spain* v. *UK* and *Eman*,[373] raised issues as to the entitlement to vote by those living in overseas territories. *Spain* v. *UK* raised the question whether a Member State (the UK) was entitled to extend the right to vote in elections to the European Parliament to nationals of non-member countries resident in Europe (Gibraltar, a British Crown Colony which does not form part of the UK and to which only parts of Union law apply). The European Court of Human Rights had condemned the UK for failing to hold elections to the European Parliament in Gibraltar contrary to Article 3 of Protocol No. 1 of the Convention.[374] In response, the UK established a new electoral region which combined Gibraltar with an existing region in England (the South West) and created a special electoral register. Spain argued that the extension of the right to vote in elections to the European Parliament to people who were not citizens of the Union breached Union law. The Court of Justice disagreed. It said that the definition of those entitled to vote and stand as a candidate in elections to the European Parliament fell within the competence of each Member State and that EU law did not preclude a Member State from granting those rights to individuals who had close links to it, as well as to their own nationals or citizens of the Union resident in their territory.[375]

While *Spain* v. *UK* concerned a state extending the right to vote to non-nationals, *Eman* concerned the opposite situation: a state (the Netherlands) excluding certain categories of its own nationals resident in an overseas territory associated to the Union (OCT),[376] in this case Aruba, from the right to vote and to stand as a candidate in European elections. The Court said that individuals who held the nationality of a Member State and who lived or resided in a territory which was one of the OCTs could rely on the rights conferred on citizens of the Union.[377] However, the Court said that Article 22(2) TFEU on voting rights of *migrants* (see below) did not apply to a national residing in an OCT who wished to exercise his right to vote in the Member State of which he was a national.[378] Nevertheless, the Court said that the Dutch authorities were in breach of the principle of equal treatment because Dutch nationals resident in a non-Member State did have the right to vote in European elections but Dutch nationals resident in the Netherlands Antilles or Aruba did not,[379] and that the Dutch had failed to offer an objective justification for such difference in treatment.[380] For good measure, the Court also suggested that a remedy in damages should be available as a result of the breach of Union law.[381]

The third case, *Delvigne*,[382] concerned the right to vote by prisoners. Under French law as it stood when Delvigne was convicted of a serious criminal offence the conviction also

---

[372] Tizzano AG in his Joined Opinion in Cases C–145 and 300/04 *Kingdom of Spain* v. *United Kingdom of Great Britain and Northern Ireland; M.G. Eman and O.B. Sevinger* v. *College van burgemeester en wethouders van Den Haag* [2006] ECR I–7917.

[373] Cases C–145/04 *Spain* v. *UK* [2006] ECR I–7961; C–300/04 *Eman and Sevinger* [2006] ECR I–8055 (noted by L. Besselink (2008) 45 *CMLRev.* 787).

[374] *Matthews* v. *UK*, no. 24833/94 [1999] ECHR 12.

[375] Para. 78. See also Case C–535/08 *Pignataro* [2009] ECR I–50: the provisions on Union citizenship permit a national rule requiring a candidate for election to a regional assembly to reside in that region at the time of nomination.

[376] Art. 355 TFEU.		[377] Paras. 27–9.

[378] The Court justified this decision by reference to the case law of the European Court of Human Rights, which had ruled that the criterion linked to residence was acceptable to determine who were entitled to the right to vote and to stand as a candidate in elections: *Melnychenko* v. *Ukraine*, no. 17707/02 [2004] ECHR 528, paras. 56–7.

[379] Para. 58.		[380] Para. 60.		[381] Para. 70.

[382] Case C–650/13 *Delvigne* EU:C:2015:648.

entailed being deprived of the right to vote. The Court said in exercising its competence to decide who was entitled to vote in elections to the European Parliament, France was implementing EU law within the meaning of Article 51(1) of the Charter and that the deprivation of the right to vote was a limitation on the exercise of the right guaranteed in Article 39(2) of the Charter. However, the Court found that the restriction could be justified: it was laid down by law, it respected the essence of the right (only specific people under specific conditions were excluded on account of their conduct), and the limitation was proportionate since it took into account the nature and gravity of the criminal offence committed.[383]

So far we have concentrated on the rights of *nationals* to vote and stand as a candidate in elections.[384] Article 22 TFEU permits *migrant* EU citizens to vote and stand as a candidate in elections for local[385] and European elections,[386] subject to 'derogations where warranted by problems specific to a Member State'. Two directives have been adopted to implement these rights which provide for equal treatment: migrant EU citizens have the right to vote and stand as a candidate in municipal or European elections provided they satisfy the same conditions as the host state imposes on its own nationals.[387] The flip side of the coin is that migrant citizens cannot participate in the most important elections—those for the national parliaments.[388] This is a further example of the partial nature of EU citizenship.

1.3 Deliberative or Participatory Democracy

Many argue that, with turnout for European Parliament elections being so low, the EU still suffers from a serious democratic deficit. As part of its response, the Commission[389] issued a White Paper on Governance identifying five principles underpinning good governance: openness, participation, accountability, effectiveness, and coherence.[390] The White Paper also placed much emphasis on citizen participation as a way of supplementing representative democracy.[391] In the absence of an identifiable public space

---

[383] Paras. 47–9.

[384] Case C-145/04 *Kingdom of Spain* v. *United Kingdom of Great Britain and Northern Ireland* [2006] ECR I-7961, para. 76.

[385] See also Art. 40 of the Charter; Dir. 94/80/EC ([1994] OJ L368/38), as amended by Dir. 96/30/EC ([1996] OJ L122/14), laying down detailed arrangements for the exercise of the right to vote and to stand as a candidate in municipal elections by citizens of the Union residing in a Member State of which they are not nationals.

[386] See also Art. 40 of the Charter; Dir. 93/109/EC ([1993] OJ L329/34) on the right to vote and stand as a candidate in elections to the European Parliament for citizens of the Union residing in a Member State of which they are not nationals. This directive provides that entitlement to vote and to stand as a candidate in the Member State of residence is conferred on people who are citizens of the Union but who are not nationals of the Member State where they reside and who satisfy the conditions applicable to nationals of that state in respect of the right to vote and to stand as a candidate, and are not deprived of those rights in their home Member State.

[387] In practice, few take advantage of this possibility: only 11.9 per cent of EU citizens resident in another Member State voted in the 2004 elections to the European Parliament: MEMO/06/484, Brussels, 13 Dec. 2006.

[388] See A. O'Neill, Evidence to the Scottish Parliament, Dec. 2015.

[389] Partly to lay to rest its own ghosts: see, e.g., Committee of Independent Experts, *First Report on Allegations Regarding Fraud, Mismanagement and Nepotism in the EC*, presented to the EP, 15 Mar. 1999.

[390] COM(2001) 428. For a detailed discussion of this document, see C. Joerges, Y. Mény, and J. H. H. Weiler (eds.), *Mountain or Molehill? A critical appraisal of the Commission White Paper on Governance*, Jean Monnet Working Paper No. 6/01 and the special edition of the *European Law Journal* (2002) vol. 8(1).

[391] Commission Discussion Paper, 'Commission and non-governmental organisations: Building a stronger partnership', COM(2000) 11: 'The decision-making process in the EU is first and foremost legitimized by the elected representatives of the European people. However, NGOs can make a contribution in fostering a more participatory democracy both within the European Union and beyond.'

and a common language the chances of this happening are slim. More realistic is the possibility of citizen participation through alternative intermediaries, primarily 'civil society'.[392] According to the White Paper, it is civil society that 'plays an important role in giving voice to the concerns of citizens' and delivers 'services that meet people's needs'.[393] The value of the involvement of civil society is now acknowledged by Article 11 TEU. Article 11(1) TEU provides that 'The institutions shall, by appropriate means, give citizens and representative associations the opportunity to make known and publicly exchange their views in all areas of Union action.' Article 11(2) TEU adds that the institutions must maintain an 'open, transparent, and regular dialogue with representative associations and civil society',[394] now facilitated by the Commission's Communication on minimum standards for consultation of interested parties.[395] This is reinforced by Article 11(3) TEU, which requires the Commission to carry out broad consultations with parties concerned in order to ensure that the Union's actions are coherent and transparent.[396]

In some sectors dialogue with representative associations has already been formalized. For example, in the field of employment law and labour market regulation, the social partners (management and labour) are the interlocutors.[397] Their involvement was constitutionalized by Articles 154–5 TFEU[398] requiring the Commission to consult management and labour about whether there should be any legislation in the field and, if so, its content. Social partners can also negotiate collective agreements, which can be given legislative effect by a Council 'decision'.[399] The European Parliament has no formal role in this process except to be 'informed'.[400] A number of directives have been adopted using this 'collective' route to legislation, including directives on parental leave, part-time work, and fixed-term work.[401] When the validity of the Parental Leave Directive 96/34 was challenged in *UEAPME*[402] by an organization representing small and medium-sized enterprises, which had been excluded from the negotiation process, the General Court endorsed this alternative 'collective' approach to lawmaking.

But this broadening of the consultation and legislative process raises further problems of representativity (and accountability) of the interlocutors. To what extent do they really represent the views of their members and to what extent are these views more generally representative? This issue lay at the heart of UEAPME's challenge to the Parental Leave

---

[392] According to the Governance White Paper, COM(2001) 428, 14, civil society includes the following: trade unions and employers' organizations ('social partners'); non-governmental organizations; professional associations; charities; grass-roots organizations; organizations that involve citizens in local and municipal life, with a particular contribution from churches and religious communities.

[393] COM(2001) 428, 14.

[394] Churches and non-confessional organizations are singled out in Art. 17(3) TFEU.

[395] Commission Communication, 'Towards a reinforced culture of consultation and dialogue: General principles and minimum standards for consultation of interested parties by the Commission', COM(2002) 704.

[396] See also Art. 15 TFEU: 'In order to promote good governance and ensure the participation of civil society, the Union institutions, bodies, offices and agencies shall conduct their work as openly as possible.'

[397] C. Barnard, 'Governance and the social partners' (2002) 8 *ELJ* 80.

[398] See also Art. 152 TFEU.

[399] Art. 155(2) TFEU. The term 'decision' is used in Art. 155(2) TFEU but has been interpreted to mean any legally binding act, in particular, directives.

[400] Art. 155(2) TFEU.

[401] Council Dir. 96/34/EC on Parental Leave ([1996] OJ L145/4) repealed and replaced by Council Dir. 2010/18/EU ([2010] OJ L68/13); Council Dir. 97/81/EC on Part-time Work ([1998] OJ L14/9); and Council Dir. 99/70/EC on Fixed-Term Work ([1999] OJ L175/43). See further C. Barnard, *EC Employment Law* (Oxford: OUP, 2012), Ch. 2.

[402] Case T–135/96 *Union Européenne de l'artisanat et des petites et moyennes entreprises (UEAPME) v. Council* [1998] ECR II–2335.

Directive.[403] The agreement on parental leave had been negotiated by the intersectoral social partners—UNICE (the European employers' association, now called BUSINESS-EUROPE), CEEP (the public sector employers' association), and ETUC (the European trades union confederation). UEAPME argued that since the interests of small and medium-sized undertakings differed from those represented by UNICE, UEAPME should also have been at the negotiating table. The General Court disagreed. It said that it was for the Commission to examine the representativity of the signatories to collective agreements and the Council had to verify whether the Commission had fulfilled this task, and on the facts it was appropriate that in the case of an intersectoral directive, the intersectoral social partners should negotiate. However, in the light of the problems in *UEAPME* the Commission said in its Governance White Paper that civil society organizations had to 'tighten up their internal structures, furnish guarantees of openness and representativity, and prove their capacity to relay information or lead debates in the Member States'.[404]

1.4 Direct Participation

Perhaps the most striking example of direct citizen participation is the introduction by the Lisbon Treaty of Article 11(4) TEU which provides that:

> Not less than one million citizens who are nationals of a significant number of Member States may take the initiative of inviting the Commission, within the framework of its powers, to submit any appropriate proposal on matters where citizens consider that a legal act of the Union is required for the purpose of implementing the Treaties.[405]

Inserted as a last-minute addition to the text, this 'European Citizens Initiative' (ECI) envisages active and direct participation of EU citizens in a way never before experienced in the EU.[406] However, this provision itself poses a challenge to representative democracy given those million make up a very small percentage of the EU's total population,[407] and a risk that the process be captured by interest groups who have the organizational capacity to bring people together. Will this provision in fact expose the legislative system to unnecessary and undesirable influence?[408]

1.5 Conclusions

Despite the various attempts to make the EU more explicitly democratic many EU citizens were not convinced. The rejection of the Constitutional Treaty by the voters of France and the Netherlands in 2005 caused profound shock waves to reverberate across the EU. The voters of these two countries—founding members of the European project—sent out a strong message of their discontent. It is difficult to say for sure why the voters turned against a text whose aims were, according to the Laeken declaration,[409] to respond to citizens' calls for a 'clear,

---

[403] See G. Britz and M. Schmidt, 'The institutionalised participation of management and labour in the legislative activities of the European Community: A challenge to the principle of democracy under Community law' (2000) 6 *ELJ* 45, esp. 66–7.

[404] COM(2001) 428, 17.

[405] The operational detail of this Article, including the minimum number of Member States involved, is to be fleshed out in accordance with the first para. of Art. 24 TFEU.

[406] For details, see EP and Council Reg. (EU) No. 211/2011 ([2011] OJ L65/1) and Implementing Reg. (EU) No. 1179/2011 ([2011] OJ L301/3).

[407] Editorial Comments, 'Direct democracy and the European Union … is that a threat or a promise' (2008) 45 *CMLRev.* 929. M. Dougan, 'What are we to make of the Citizens' Initiative?' (2011) 48 *CMLRev.* 1807. For the first ECI to reach a million signatures, see <http://ec.europa.eu/citizens-initiative/> on the right to water.

[408] The Commission sought views on some of these thorny questions in its Green Paper on a European Citizens' Initiative: COM(2009) 622.

[409] <http://www.consilium.europa.eu/ueDocs/cms_Data/docs/pressData/en/ec/68827.pdf>.

open, effective, democratically controlled [Union] approach' and to bring citizens closer to the 'European design'. Nevertheless, surveys have indicated that for those voting on the European issues (as opposed to those giving a bloody nose to the incumbent national government), their concerns ranged from specific fears generated by reading the text, in particular its perceived excessive market liberalism (i.e., it was 'too British'[410]), to more general concerns about the EU's expansion, both geographically and in terms of competence.

The whole saga does not reflect well on the Union's own democratic structures, despite various attempts by the Commission to engage with EU citizens, through, for example, its 'Plan D for democracy, dialogue and debate'.[411] A decision has been adopted, now entitled 'Europe for citizens'[412] (replacing the original title 'Citizens for Europe',[413] a shift deemed psychologically significant in the light of the ratification crisis), establishing a programme promoting active European citizenship. However, many citizens remain to be convinced, a problem exacerbated by the financial crisis and a perception that the EU's response is not helping.

2. ACCESS TO JUSTICE

2.1 Access to Information

(a) Regulation 1049/2001

There is a further dimension to the right to participate: the need for citizens to have access to courts and other bodies to challenge decisions taken by the lawmakers.[414] First, however, they need to know what is going on. The right for citizens to gain access to information was given a Treaty basis at Amsterdam.[415] Article 15 TFEU provides that any citizen of the Union *and* any natural or legal person residing or having a registered office in a Member State has a right of access to the documents of the Union institutions, bodies, offices, and agencies, whatever their medium,[416] subject to the principles laid down in Regulation 1049/2001,[417] which are supplemented by rules of procedure for each institution.[418]

---

[410] T. Garton-Ash, 'What is to be done: Blairism is the answer to Europe's ills but we need someone else to deliver it', *The Guardian*, 2 Jun. 2005, describing the French perception of the Constitutional Treaty as 'too much enlarged to include new countries, too Anglophone, and too enamoured of liberal-free market economics'.

[411] COM(2005) 494.

[412] COM(2006) 542; EP and Council Dec. 1904/2006 establishing for the period 2007 to 2013 the programme 'Europe for Citizens' to promote active European citizenship ([2006] OJ L378/32), as amended.

[413] COM(2005) 116.

[414] For the importance of this dimension, see A. Wiener and V. della Sala, 'Constitution-making and citizenship practice: Bridging the democracy gap in the EU?' (1997) 35 *JCMS* 595, 602–3.

[415] See also the Final Act of the Treaty on European Union signed at Maastricht on 7 Feb. 1992, where the Member States incorporated Decl. 17 on the right of access to information: 'The Conference considers that transparency of the decision-making process strengthens the democratic nature of the institutions and the public's confidence in the administration.' In Case C–58/94 *Netherlands* v. *Council* [1996] ECR I–2169, para. 35 the Court noted that Decl. 17 links the public's right of access to documents to the 'democratic nature of the institutions'.

[416] See also Art. 1(1) TEU; Art. 42 of the Charter. This issue is considered further in D. Curtin, 'Citizens' fundamental right of access to EU information: An evolving digital *passepartout*' (2000) 37 *CMLRev.* 7.

[417] [2001] OJ L145/43. The regulation concerns access to *documents*, not to information more generally: Case T–264/04 *WWF European Policy Programme* v. *Council* [2007] ECR II–911, para. 76. A proposal for a revised measure can be found at COM(2008) 229.

[418] In addition, the EU has given effect to the Århus Convention to Union institutions and bodies (Reg. (EC) No. 1367/2006 ([2006] OJ L264/13)), which guarantees the public the right of access to environmental

In *Svenska Journalistförbundet*[419] the Court said that the objective of Regulation 1049/2001 was to give effect to the 'principle of the largest possible access for citizens to information with a view to strengthening the democratic character of the institutions and the trust of the public in the administration'.[420] This point was emphasized in *Sweden* v. *Council*[421] concerning the refusal by the Council to give access to an opinion of its legal service on a proposal for a directive laying down minimum standards for the reception of applicants for asylum. The General Court upheld the Council's decision; the Court of Justice set aside the General Court's judgment. In so doing, it noted the need for the Council to balance the particular interest to be protected by non-disclosure of the document against the public interest in the document being made accessible in the light of the advantages stemming 'from increased openness, in that this enables citizens to participate more closely in the decision-making process'[422] and confers 'greater legitimacy on the institutions in the eyes of European citizens'.[423] It said those considerations are clearly of particular relevance where the Council is acting in its legislative capacity, as is apparent from recital 6 of the preamble to Regulation 1049/2001, according to which wider access must be granted to documents in precisely such cases.

(b) The principle of good administration

Article 9 TEU says that citizens shall 'receive equal attention from its institution, bodies, offices and agencies'. Article 10(3) TEU adds that the decision-making process needs to be based on the principles of transparency and subsidiarity. This is operationalized in Article 15(2) TFEU, which says that 'The European Parliament shall meet in public, as shall the Council when considering and voting on a draft legislative act.'[424] The Council has put this into practice by amending its rules of procedure.

Article 41 of the Charter of Fundamental Rights, entitled 'Right to good administration',[425] is more explicit. Article 41(1) contains the general principle that 'Every person [not just an EU citizen] has the right to have his or her affairs handled impartially, fairly and within a reasonable time by the institutions, bodies, offices and agencies of the Union.' Article 41(2) spells out more precisely what the right includes:

- the right of every person to be heard before any individual measure which would affect him or her adversely is to be taken
- the right of every person to have access to his or her file, while respecting the legitimate interests of confidentiality and of professional and business secrecy
- the obligation of the administration to give reasons for its decisions.

---

information held by the Union institutions and bodies. These must also make environmental information available to the public in easily accessible electronic databases.

[419] Case T–174/95 *Svenska Journalistförbundet* v. *Council of the European Union* [1998] ECR II–2289.

[420] Para. 66. The europa website (<http://europa.eu/index_en.htm>) provides free access to information about the EU and its policies; <http://eur-lex.europa.eu/en/index.htm> provides free access to all legislation, consultation documents, and the judgments of the Court of Justice.

[421] Joined Cases C–39 and 52/05 *Sweden* v. *Council* [2008] ECR I–4723.   [422] Para. 45.

[423] Para. 59. See also Case C–64/05 P *Sweden* v. *Commission* [2007] ECR I–11389, para. 54.

[424] See also Art. 16(8) TEU: 'The Council shall meet in public when it deliberates and votes on a draft legislative act'. By implication, the same transparency does not apply to non-legislative acts.

[425] See also Joined Cases C–154 and 155/04 *R.* v. *Secretary of State for Health, ex p. Alliance* [2005] ECR I–8419, para. 82.

When things go wrong, Article 41(3) provides that every person has the right to have the Union make good any damage caused by the institutions or servants in the performance of their duties, in accordance with the general principles common to the laws of the Member States.

2.2 Non-Judicial Avenues

In practice, there are few cases where the Court has, in fact, been prepared to award compensation. This makes the non-judicial routes more important. EU citizens—together with natural or legal persons residing or having their registered office in a Member State—have the right under Article 24 TFEU both to petition the European Parliament in accordance with Article 227 TFEU[426] and to apply to the ombudsman in accordance with Article 228 TFEU.[427] They can write in any one of the Union languages and receive a reply in that language.[428] As with a complaint based on good administration under Article 41 of the Charter, a petition to the European Parliament is confined to matters affecting the complainant directly. There is no such limitation in respect of applications to the European ombudsman (nor in respect of access to information), which allows public-spirited citizens to raise matters of more general concern via this route. This range of rights and remedies is available in respect of breaches committed by *Union* institutions. The Treaty appears to offer no specific protection to citizens when faced with maladministration by *national* authorities exercising Union law powers.

2.3 Judicial Avenues

In respect of the courts, the EU envisages access at two levels: at European level to enable citizens to challenge decisions of the Union institutions and at domestic level to challenge decisions of the national authorities which interfere with Union law rights or to challenge the decisions of the EU institutions indirectly. In respect of remedies against national authorities, the Court has been active in guaranteeing Union rights, by developing the principles of direct effect and supremacy of Union law,[429] and the principles of effective judicial protection.[430] These proceedings complement the power to bring Article 258 TFEU enforcement proceedings initiated by the Commission but often as a result of complaints by individuals about (in)action by Member States.[431] The Commission has made the complaints process more user-friendly.[432]

However, the Court of Justice has been far more reticent about ensuring such full access to the Court by citizens when seeking to challenge the acts of the Union institutions directly. In its now (in)famous line of cases on *locus standi* for non-privileged applicants

---

[426] See also Art. 44 of the Charter. The Charter applies to residents as well as citizens.

[427] See also Art. 43 of the Charter.   [428] Art. 24(4) TFEU. See also Art. 41(4) of the Charter.

[429] Case 26/62 *NV Algemene Transport-en Expeditie Onderneming Van Gend en Loos* v. *Nederlands Administratie de Belastingen* [1963] ECR 1; Case 6/64 *Costa* v. *ENEL* [1964] ECR 585. See also Decl. 17 concerning primacy added by the Lisbon Treaty.

[430] See, e.g., Joined Cases C–6 and 9/90 *Francovich and Bonifaci* v. *Italy* [1991] ECR I–5357; Case 222/84 *Johnston* v. *RUC* [1986] ECR 1651; Joined Cases C–46 and 48/93 *Brasserie du Pêcheur and Factortame* [1996] ECR I–1029; Case C–432/05 *Unibet* v. *Justitiekanslern* [2007] ECR I–2271; Case C–279/09 *DEB* v. *Bundesrepublik Deutschland* [2010] ECR I–13849.

[431] See, the SOLVIT mechanism. SOLVIT helps EU citizens and businesses find fast and pragmatic solutions to problems arising from the incorrect application of EU law by national administrations, within a deadline of ten weeks: <http://ec.europa.eu/solvit/index_en.htm>.

[432] A notice containing a standard form for complaints to be submitted to the Commission ([1999] OJ C119/5) and a consolidated version of the internal procedural rules applicable to its relations with the complainant in the context of the infringement proceedings (COM(2002) 141) have been published by the Commission.

wishing to challenge legislative acts under Article 263 TFEU, the Court has ensured that only in the most exceptional circumstances will an individual be granted standing.[433] Interest groups, acting as intermediaries, have fared little better.[434] While the Court has emphasized that proceedings can be started in the national court and then a preliminary reference sought under Article 267 TFEU, as Advocate General Jacobs explained in *UPA*,[435] in certain circumstances this possibility is not available, leaving individuals without a remedy.

F. CONCLUSIONS

As Preuss put it, Union citizenship began as a terminological pooling of the few rights which the individual enjoyed in other Member States. It neither generated an inner bond between the Union and the individual nor did it presuppose such an inner connection as a precondition for acquiring it.[436] The developments in the mid-2000s, both legislative and judicial, suggested that the time might have come to reconsider this initial assessment. While it cannot be said that the developments have generated a 'European citizenry' which could 'pave the way for the transition to a European Federal State', they have certainly enriched the status of citizenship, by creating some bonds between individuals and the Union different to (but not stronger than) those which exist between individuals and their own Member States.[437] The principle of solidarity was particularly influential in fostering that nascent relationship. And here a process of boot-strapping took place— citizenship (imposed from above) was used to justify taking limited steps in the name of solidarity and solidarity was being used from the bottom up to foster a growing sense of citizenship. With the benefit of hindsight this period might come to be seen as the golden age of EU citizenship.

However, even in this period the Court showed some awareness of the sensitivities of the issue, in particular concerns about 'benefit tourism'.[438] As a result, it allowed Member States to insist on a demonstrable link with the host state's territory before an individual became entitled to benefits or student finance, whether it was through a period of residence as in *Bidar*, or a genuine link with the employment market of the host state as in *Collins*. If it were otherwise then any enforced equality would have the potential to generate such hostility and anti-migrant feeling among host state nationals that, far from fostering a sense of Union citizenship, it could do the reverse. In the UK concerns about the levels of immigration from elsewhere in the EU and the perceived deleterious effect this was having on already stretched public services eventually led to an in-out referendum on EU membership. This changing political context, not just in the UK but also in France and Germany, may have prompted the Court to revisit its citizenship case law and, in

---

[433] Case C–50/00P *UPA* v. *Council* [2002] ECR I–6677. Cf. the strong Opinion of Jacobs AG to the contrary and the decision of the General Court in Case T–177/01 *Jégo Quéré & Cie SA* v. *Commission* [2002] ECR II–2365.

[434] Case C–312/95 P *Stichting Greenpeace Council (Greenpeace International)* v. *Commission* [1998] ECR I–1651.

[435] Case C–50/00P *UPA* v. *Council* [2002] ECR I–6677. See also Case C–131/03 P *R.J. Reynolds Tobacco Holdings Inc.* v. *Commission* [2006] ECR I–7795, paras. 81–2.

[436] U. Preuss, 'Problems of a concept of European citizenship' (1995) 1 *ELJ* 267.

[437] Preuss, n. 436, 268.

[438] That is 'moving to a Member State with a more congenial social security environment': Case C–456/02 *Trojani* [2004] ECR I–7573, Geelhoed AG's Opinion, para. 13 (and see para. 18). See also his Opinion in *Bidar* in para. 66.

decisions such as *Dano* and *Alimanovic*, insisted on strict compliance with the provisions of the CRD and no more. As Anderson puts it, 'Across Europe, citizenship is increasingly cast as being deserved by hard working, self-reliant individuals prepared to take responsibility for themselves.'[439] The recent decisions of the Court of Justice increasingly conform to this standard. Weiler put the point succinctly: 'as the [Union] has grown in size, in scope, in reach and despite a high rhetoric including the very creation of "European citizenship" there has been a distinct disempowerment of the individual European citizen, the specific gravity of whom continues to decline as the Union grows'.[440]

Is there a way forward? Weiler advocates that EU citizenship should be understood as a supranational construct grounded in belonging simultaneously to two different *demoi* based on different subjective factors of identification.[441] At one and the same time, he argues, individuals can, say, be British nationals, based on a strong sense of cultural identification and belonging, and also European citizens, based on, first, an acceptance of the legitimacy and authority of decisions made by fellow European citizens (underpinned by the 'social contract' of the common Treaties) and, secondly, shared values which transcend ethno-national diversity. These shared values include a commitment to principles of solidarity expressed through the welfare state, the European social model, and human rights as embodied in the ECHR and now the Charter. Yet his suggestions have themselves been criticized for being too assimilationist, excluding those who do not share these values.[442]

Others have argued that the EU should aim at decoupling the concepts of state, nation, national identity, and nationality in favour of a form of post-national membership radically different from a (nation) statist concept of citizenship.[443] Underpinning this idea is active participation, as well as the more traditional passive conferral of rights, and it is here that the EU is engaged in some of its most elaborate citizenship-building. The advantage of such an understanding of citizenship is that nationality becomes increasingly unimportant. In this interpretation of citizenship there should be a place for legally resident TCNs. The legal position of TCNs is the subject of Chapter 13. In Chapter 12, we shall consider the limits to the rights of free movement, which, as we shall see, have been influenced by the case law on citizenship.

FURTHER READING

Commission guidance

Commission Communication, 'Helping national authorities fight abuses of the right to free movement: Handbook on addressing the issue of alleged marriages of convenience between EU and non-EU nationals in the context of EU law on free movement of EU citizens', COM(2014) 604.

Commission Communication, 'On guidance for better transposition and application of Directive 2004/38/EC on the right of citizens of the Union and their family members to move and reside freely within the territory of the Member States', COM(2009) 313.

'EU Citizenship Report 2013', COM(2013) 269.

---

[439] B. Anderson, '"Heads I win, tails you lose". Migration and the worker citizen' (2015) 68 *CLP* 179, 195.
[440] J. H. H. Weiler, 'The European Union belongs to its citizens: Three immodest proposals' (1997) 22 *ELRev.* 150.
[441] J. H. H. Weiler, 'To be a European citizen—Eros and civilization' (1997) 4 *JEPP* 495.
[442] N. Barber, 'Citizenship, nationalism and the European Union' (2002) 27 *ELRev.* 241.
[443] Shaw, n. 4, 47.

The CRD

E. Guild, S. Peers, and J. Tomkin, *The EU Citizenship Directive: A commentary* (Oxford, OUP, 2014).

The development of the EU citizenship case law

C. Calliess, 'The dynamics of European citizenship: From bourgeois to citoyen' in A. Rosas, E. Levits, and Y. Bot (eds.), *The Court of Justice and the Construction of Europe: Analyses and perspectives on sixty years of case law* (The Hague: Asser Press, 2012).

M. Dawson and E. Muir, 'Individual, institutional and collective vigilance in protecting fundamental rights in the EU: Lessons from the Roma' (2011) 48 *CMLRev.* 751.

M. Dougan, N. Nic Shuibhne, and E. Spaventa, *Empowerment and Disempowerment of the European Citizenship* (Oxford: Hart Publishing, 2012).

M. Everson, 'The legacy of the market citizen' in J. Shaw and G. More (eds.), *New Legal Dynamics of the European Union* (Oxford: Clarendon Press, 1995).

D. Kochenov and R. Plender, 'EU citizenship: From an incipient form to an incipient substance? The discovery of the Treaty text' (2012) 37 *ELRev.* 369.

D. Kostakopoulou, 'Ideas, norms and European citizenship: Explaining institutional change' (2005) 68 *MLR* 233.

B. Kunoy, 'A union of national citizens: The origins of the court's lack of *avant-gardisme* in the *Chen* case' (2006) 43 *CMLRev.* 179.

N. Nic Shuibhne, 'Limits rising, duties ascending: The changing legal shape of Union citizenship' (2015) 52 *CMLRev* 889.

N. Nic Shuibhne, 'The outer limits of EU citizenship: Displacing economic free movement rights?' in C. Barnard and O. Odudu (eds.), *The Outer Limits of European Union Law* (Oxford: Hart Publishing, 2009).

N. Nic Shuibhne, 'The resilience of EU market citizenship' (2010) 47 *CMLRev.* 1597.

S. O'Leary, *The Evolving Concept of Community Citizenship* (The Hague: Kluwer, 1996).

N. Reich, 'Union citizenship: Metaphor or source of rights?' (2001) 7 *ELJ* 4.

J. Shaw, 'Citizenship and enlargement: The outer limits of EU political citizenship' in C. Barnard and O. Odudu (eds.), *The Outer Limits of European Union Law* (Oxford: Hart Publishing, 2009).

J. Shaw, 'Citizenship: Contrasting dynamics at the interface of integration and constitutionalism' in P. Craig and G. de Búrca (eds.), *The Evolution of EU Law* (Oxford: OUP, 2011).

A. Somek, 'Solidarity decomposed: Being and time in European citizenship' (2007) 32 *ELRev.* 787.

E. Spaventa, 'Seeing the wood despite the trees? On the scope of Union citizenship and its constitutional effects' (2008) 45 *CMLRev.* 13.

F. Wollenschläger, 'A new fundamental freedom beyond market integration: Union citizenship and its dynamics for shifting the economic paradigm of European integration' (2011) 17 *ELJ* 1.

See also the special issue of the *German Law Journal*, 'EU Citizenship: Twenty Years On' (2014) 15 *GLJ* 735.

On specific cases and challenges to the Court's approach

C. Costello, '*Metock*: Free movement and "normal family life" in the Union' (2009) 46 *CMLRev.* 587.

G. Davies, 'Legislative control of the European Court of Justice' (2014) 51 *CMLRev.* 1579.

N. Nic Shuibhne, '(Some of) the kids are alright' (2012) 49 *CMLRev.* 349.

A. Tryfonidou, 'Redefining the outer boundaries of EU law: The *Zambrano, McCarthy* and *Dereci* trilogy' (2012) 18 *EPL* 493.

The benefit cases

C. O'Brien, 'Real links, abstract rights and false alarms: The relationship between the ECJ's "real link" case law and national solidarity' (2008) 33 *ELRev.* 643.

D. Thym, 'The elusive limits of solidarity: Residence rights of and social benefits for economically inactive Union citizens' (2015) 52 *CMLRev.* 17.

H. Verscheuren, 'Preventing "benefit tourism" in the EU: A narrow or broad interpretation of the possibilities offered by the ECJ in *Dano*?' (2015) 52 CMLRev. 363.

Electoral rights

H. Lardy, 'The political rights of Union citizenship' (1996) 2 *EPL* 611.

P. Oliver, 'Electoral rights under Article 8b of the Treaty of Rome' (1996) 33 *CMLRev.* 473.

J. Shaw, *The Transformation of Citizenship in the European Union: Electoral rights and the restructuring of political space* (Cambridge: CUP, 2007).

11

FREEDOM OF ESTABLISHMENT AND FREEDOM TO PROVIDE SERVICES: LEGAL PERSONS

A. INTRODUCTION

In Chapters 8 and 9 we considered freedom of establishment and free movement of services from the perspective of natural persons. In this chapter we focus on these Treaty provisions from the perspective of legal persons (companies, branches, agencies, and subsidiaries). In particular, we consider how the Court has addressed restrictions on both access to, and exercise of, freedom of establishment (Section B) and then freedom to provide services (Section C), building on the principles established in Chapters 8 and 9. However, as we shall see, it is not always easy to extend principles developed in the context of natural persons to the corporate form and the Court has had to make some relevant adaptions, particularly given the diversity of approaches under national law to the recognition of a company (i.e., registered office only (for those states applying the incorporation theory) or registered office and real seat (for those states applying the *siège réel* theory)). Further, while the citizenship case law has played a key role in shaping the development of free movement of natural persons, this has not been the case with legal persons.

The chapter concludes with an examination of the controversial Services Directive 2006/123,[1] which in part codifies and in part develops the Court's approach to both freedom of establishment and free movement of services (Section D).

B. THE FREEDOM OF ESTABLISHMENT

1. INTRODUCTION

Article 49 TFEU concerns the establishment of natural persons and companies, branches, and agencies in other Member States on a permanent or semi-permanent basis. It provides:

> Within the framework of the provisions set out below, restrictions on the freedom of establishment of nationals of a Member State in the territory of another Member State shall be prohibited. Such prohibition shall also apply to restrictions on the setting-up of agencies, branches or subsidiaries by nationals of any Member State established in the territory of any Member State.
>
> Freedom of establishment shall include the right to take up and pursue activities as self-employed persons and to set up and manage undertakings, in particular companies or firms within the meaning of the second paragraph of Article 54, under the conditions laid down for its own nationals by the law of the country where such establishment is effected, subject to the provisions of the Chapter relating to capital.

Article 54 TFEU talks specifically about companies:

> Companies or firms formed in accordance with the law of a Member State and having their registered office, central administration or principal place of business within the Union shall, for the purposes of this Chapter, be treated in the same way as natural persons who are nationals of Member States.
>
> 'Companies or firms' means companies or firms constituted under civil or commercial law, including cooperative societies, and other legal persons governed by public or private law, save for those which are non-profit-making.

Article 55 TFEU adds:

> Member States shall accord nationals of the other Member States the same treatment as their own nationals as regards participation in the capital of companies or firms within the meaning of Article 54, without prejudice to the application of the other provisions of the Treaties.

In respect of companies, the Treaty thus contemplates two forms of establishment:

- the right to set up and manage undertakings, in particular, companies or firms within the meaning of the second paragraph of Article 54 TFEU in another Member State (primary establishment)

---

[1] [2006] OJ L376/36.

- the right to set up agencies, branches, or subsidiaries by nationals of any Member State established in the territory of any Member State (secondary establishment);[2] provided there is a permanent establishment, the establishment does not need to have separate legal personality.[3]

As the Court emphasized in *Cadbury Schweppes*,[4] in both situations Article 49 TFEU presupposes (1) actual establishment of the company or branch, etc. in the host state (i.e., permanent presence) and (2) the pursuit of a genuine economic activity there. Both conditions must be fulfilled for Article 49 TFEU to apply. This can be seen in *Stauffer*.[5] An Italian charitable foundation had commercial premises in Germany which it rented out, the letting being managed by a German property agent. The Court said that Article 49 TFEU did not apply because, while holding immovable property indicated permanent presence, there was no genuine economic activity because the property was not actively managed. The Court said that Article 63 TFEU on free movement of capital applied instead.

Stauffer shows the close proximity between Article 49 TFEU and Article 63 TFEU. The Court has struggled to distinguish between them but the more recent case law suggests that the provisions on establishment, not capital, will apply where:

- national provisions apply to existing holdings[6]—or the acquisition of holdings[7]—by nationals of State A in the capital of a company established in State B, giving them a definite influence on the company's decisions and allowing them to determine its activities
- national rules which affect relations within a group of companies.[8]

We turn now to consider the rights enjoyed by legal persons under Article 49 TFEU.

2. THE RIGHTS CONFERRED ON LEGAL PERSONS

2.1 The Right of Departure

(a) Daily Mail and Cartesio

The problem of extending the case law on individuals to companies was highlighted by one of the earliest decisions in this field, *Daily Mail*.[9] We have already seen how Article 49 TFEU and the original Directive 73/148 (now the CRD) grant individuals the right to leave their home state without restriction in order to take up self-employment in another state. However, in *Daily Mail* the Court said that the same rule did not apply to companies. Daily Mail, an investment company incorporated under English law with its registered office in London, wanted to avoid paying UK tax when selling a significant part of its assets. It therefore decided to transfer its central management

---

[2] Art. 49 TFEU, para. 1.
[3] Case C–414/06 *Lidl Belgium GmbH & Co. KG v. Finanzamt Heilbronn* [2008] ECR I–3601, para. 15.
[4] Case C–196/04 *Cadbury Schweppes v. Commissioners of the Inland Revenue* [2006] ECR I–7995, para. 54.
[5] Case C–386/04 *Centro di Musicologia Walter Stauffer* [2006] ECR I–8203, para. 19. See also Case C–451/05 *ELISA v. Directeur general des impost* [2007] ECR I–8251, paras. 65–7.
[6] Case C–231/05 *Oy AA* [2007] ECR I–6373, para. 20.
[7] Case C–251/98 *Baars* [2000] ECR I–2787, paras. 21–2, and Case C–208/00 *Überseering* [2002] ECR I–9919, para. 77.
[8] Case C–446/04 *FII Group Litigation* [2006] ECR I–11753, para. 118; Case C–231/05 *Oy AA* [2007] ECR I–6373, para. 23.
[9] Case 81/87 *Ex p. Daily Mail* [1988] ECR 5483.

and control to the Netherlands prior to the sale of the shares, while maintaining its legal personality and status as a UK company.[10] Before it could change residence, the UK Treasury needed to give its approval but, although Daily Mail had applied for permission to relocate, it moved its office to the Netherlands without waiting for the Treasury's response.

Daily Mail subsequently sought a declaration that the requirement to obtain consent was unnecessary under Articles 49 and 54 TFEU. The Court disagreed. Having pointed to the wide variety of national laws on the factors providing a connection to the national territory and the absence of coordination directives, it concluded that neither Article 49 TFEU nor Article 54 TFEU conferred on companies incorporated in State A the right to transfer—without any restriction or impediment from State A—their central management, control, and administration to State B while at the same time retaining their status as companies in State A.[11] This judgment does not mean that companies cannot move their residence but that—at the present stage of development of Union law—restrictions can be imposed on emigrating companies by the home state.

Some commentators saw the case as a prompt either to the Union legislature to make use of its powers under Article 50(2) TFEU to coordinate and/or harmonize company law[12] or to the Member States to enter into agreements under Article 293 EC (repealed by the Lisbon Treaty) on the mutual recognition of companies or firms and the retention of legal personality in the event of transferring their seat from one state to another.[13] Others questioned the compatibility of this ruling with the more recent case law on free movement of capital and services where the Treaty provisions cover both exit (emigration) and entry (immigration).[14]

The Court had an opportunity to reconsider its decision in *Daily Mail* in *Cartesio*.[15] The case concerned a limited partnership seeking to transfer its operational headquarters from Hungary to Italy while remaining registered in Hungary, so that its legal status could continue to be governed by Hungarian law.[16] The Hungarian commercial court refused to enter the new address in the local register on the ground that the transfer was not possible under Hungarian law. It held that a firm (partnership or company) that wished to transfer its operational headquarters to another Member State first had to be wound up in Hungary and then reconstituted under the law of the new Member State (Italy). However, the Advocate General said 'Articles [49 TFEU] and [54 TFEU] preclude national rules which make it impossible for a company constituted under national law to transfer its operational headquarters to another Member State.' He also thought the rules could not be justified.

---

[10] For this reason, under the incorporation theory the case did not concern the transfer of the company's seat, merely its fiscal residence.

[11] Case 81/87 *Ex p. Daily Mail* [1988] ECR 5483, para. 24.

[12] Cf. Case C–212/97 *Centros* [1999] ECR I–1459, para. 28: 'the fact that company law is not completely harmonised in the [Union] is of little consequence. Moreover, it is always open to the Council, on the basis of the powers conferred upon it by Article [50(2)(g) TFEU], to achieve complete harmonisation.' For details on EU company law legislation, see J. Wouters, 'European Community law: Quo vadis?' (2000) 37 *CMLRev.* 257 and C. Barnard with J. Snell, 'Free movement of legal persons and the provision of services' in C. Barnard and S. Peers (eds.), *European Union Law* (Oxford: OUP, 2014) (parts of the present chapter draw on this chapter).

[13] J. Lever (1989) 26 *CMLRev.* 327, 331.

[14] See, e.g., E. Wymeersch, 'The transfer of the company's seat in European company law' (2003) 40 *CMLRev.* 661, 677.

[15] Case C–210/06 *Cartesio Oktató és Szolgáltató bt* [2008] ECR I–9641.

[16] Hungarian company law is based on the real seat theory.

The Court offered a more nuanced perspective. It distinguished between two situations: (1) where the seat of a company incorporated under the law of one Member State was transferred to another Member State with *no* change as regards the law which governs that company (the situation in *Daily Mail* and *Cartesio*); and (2) where a company governed by the law of one Member State moves to another Member State with an attendant change as regards the national law applicable (reincorporation).[17]

In respect of the first situation, the Court said the matter fell outside the scope of Union law because the company no longer satisfied the preconditions of being a company formed under national law. In the absence of harmonization, it was for *national law* to define the connecting factor (i.e., registered office only (for those states applying the incorporation theory) or registered office and real seat (for those states applying the *siège réel* theory)) required for a company to be regarded as incorporated under the law of that Member State (thereby mirroring the situation with natural persons where national law decides whether the individual holds the nationality of the Member State).[18] National law also determined the conditions required for the company to maintain its status as a company incorporated under the law of that Member State. This included the possibility for that Member State not to permit a company governed by its law to retain that status if the company intended to reorganize itself in another Member State by moving its seat to the territory of the latter, thereby breaking the connecting factor required under the national law of the Member State of incorporation.[19]

If a company reorganized itself in this way then it was no longer a company formed and existing under (Hungarian) law and so fell outside the scope of Article 54 TFEU and so Union law did not apply.[20] This meant that in the circumstances of Cartesio, Hungarian law could insist on the Hungarian company being wound up prior to being reconstituted in Italy without this constituting a restriction on freedom of establishment.[21]

By contrast, in the second situation the Court said that the company was *converted* into a form of company which was governed by the law of the Member State to which it had moved (Italy). The Court said that the power of Member States to determine the connecting factor could not justify the Member State of incorporation (Hungary) preventing that company from converting itself into a company governed by the law of the new Member State (Italy) to the extent that it was permitted by that (Italian) law to do so, by requiring the company's winding-up or liquidation. The Court said that such a barrier (the winding-up or liquidation) to the actual conversion of a company 'constitutes a restriction on the freedom of establishment of the company concerned which, unless it serves overriding requirements in the public interest, is prohibited under Article [49 TFEU]'.[22]

(b) The right to establish a branch or agency

Although the applicants were not successful in *Daily Mail* or *Cartesio*, it seems likely that, had they wanted to establish only a branch, agency, or subsidiary in the host state, they could have relied on Article 49 TFEU against the home state to enable them to exercise their freedom of establishment in another Member State. This was confirmed in *X AB and Y AB*,[23] where the Court said Article 49 TFEU prohibited the state of origin

---

[17] Para. 111.   [18] Para. 109.   [19] Para. 110.

[20] For criticisms, see M. Szydło (2009) 46 *CMLRev.* 703, 714–19.

[21] Cf. Case C–371/10 *National Grid Indus BV* [2011] ECR I–2273 where a company transferred its effective management from the Netherlands to the UK. This did not affect its status as a company incorporated under Dutch law (which applies the incorporation theory to companies). Nevertheless the Court said the company could rely on Art. 49 TFEU to challenge the lawfulness of exit tax rules applied by the Dutch authorities.

[22] Para. 113.   [23] Case C–200/98 *X AB and Y AB* v. *Riksskatteverket* [1999] ECR I–8261.

'from hindering the establishment in another Member State of ... a company incorporated under its legislation which comes within the definition contained in Article [54
TFEU]'.[24] Therefore, a Swedish law preventing Swedish companies with subsidiaries in
other Member States from receiving certain types of tax concessions breached Article 49
TFEU unless justified.

2.2 Access to the Market of the Host State

(a) Primary and secondary establishment

As we have seen, Articles 49 and 54 TFEU contemplate both primary and secondary establishment. In respect of primary establishment, a company (or an individual) can exercise its right of establishment by taking part in the incorporation of a company in another
Member State (see also Case Study 11.1). In that regard, Article 55 TFEU ensures that the
out-of-state company will enjoy the same treatment as nationals of that Member State as
regards participation in the capital of the new company.[25] Primary establishment can also
occur where a company transfers its seat from one state to another. In practice, this is rare,
and some states actually forbid it.[26]

 More common is the situation where companies create a *secondary* establishment in
the host state by setting up branches, agencies, or subsidiaries. The Treaty does not define
these terms but in *Somafer*,[27] a case on the interpretation of similar terms in the then
Brussels Convention, the Court ruled:

> the concept of branch, agency or other establishment implies a place of business
> which has the appearance of permanency, such as the extension of a parent body, has
> a management and is materially equipped to negotiate business with third parties
> so that the latter, although knowing that there will if necessary be a legal link with
> the parent body, the head office of which is abroad, do not have to deal directly with
> such parent body but may transact business at the place of business constituting the
> extension.

It does not even matter if the establishment cannot be formally classed as a branch or
agency, Article 49 will still apply to the entity.[28]

 The Court has been particularly keen to ensure that secondary establishment is effective. In particular, it has prevented host states from insisting that business can be conducted only through a primary establishment (with a registered office, headquarters, and
principal place of business in the host state) since this would negate the very right of
secondary establishment. This can be seen in *Commission v. Italy (foreign securities dealing)*.[29] In order to set up as a securities dealer in Italy, Italian law required the dealer to
be constituted in the form of a limited company with its registered office in Italy. The
Commission successfully argued that this requirement prevented dealers from other
Member States from making use of other forms of establishment, especially branches or
agencies, and discriminated against them by obliging them to bear the expense of setting up a new company. The Court said that Article 49 TFEU expressly left traders free to
choose the appropriate legal form in which to pursue their activities in another Member
State. In seeking to justify the breach, the Italian authorities argued that the requirement

---

[24] Case C–200/98 *X AB and Y AB* [1999] ECR I–8261, para. 26.
[25] Case 81/87 *Ex p. Daily Mail* [1988] ECR 5483, para. 17.
[26] E.g., Germany and Austria: Wymeersch, n. 14, 668.
[27] Case 33/78 *Somafer SA v. Saar-Ferngas AG* [1978] ECR 2183.
[28] Case 205/84 *Commission v. Germany (insurance)* [1986] ECR 3755.
[29] Case C–101/94 *Commission v. Italy (Re restrictions on foreign securities dealing)* [1996] ECR I–2691.

was necessary for supervising and effectively sanctioning the dealer in question. The Court disagreed, reasoning that Italy had failed to show that this was the 'only means' of achieving the objective.

The Court's wish to make the provisions on secondary establishment effective has been extended to the case of discrimination against *employees* on the ground that the company has its registered office in another Member State. Therefore, in *Segers*[30] the Court ruled that Articles 49 and 54 TFEU prohibited a Member State from excluding the director of a company from a national sickness insurance scheme on the ground that the company had its registered office in another Member State, even though it did not conduct any business there. The Court said that discrimination against employees in connection with social security protection 'indirectly restricts the freedom of companies of another Member State to establish themselves through an agency, branch or subsidiary in the Member State concerned'.[31]

Finally, the Court has generally stopped states from giving preferential treatment through its tax law to companies established in a state over those with only a branch or agency in the state. This can be seen in *Commission* v. *France (tax credits)*.[32] In order to avoid double taxation (which will occur where income is taxed once as corporation tax in the hands of the distributing company and again in the hands of the shareholder when distributed as dividends), France granted tax credits to recipients of dividends distributed by French companies. However, these tax credits were granted only where the recipient had a registered office in France. Therefore, in the case of a foreign parent, only a subsidiary—but not a branch or agency—could receive the tax credit. The Court said that Article 49 TFEU expressly left traders free to choose the appropriate legal form in which to pursue their activities in another Member State and that freedom of choice could not be limited by discriminatory tax provisions.[33] The rule therefore breached Article 49 TFEU and could not be justified on the facts. The Court reached the same conclusion in *Royal Bank of Scotland (RBS)*,[34] where it found that a Greek law taxing company profits at a higher rate if its seat was in another Member State than if its seat was in Greece breached Article 49 TFEU.

However, there is an important difference between *Commission* v. *France* and *RBS*. In *RBS* the Court considered the rule to be directly discriminatory since the discrimination was based on the location of the company's seat and the seat gives a company its nationality.[35] Since the case concerned direct discrimination on the ground of nationality the Court looked only at the express derogations found in Article 52 TFEU and, because the Greek government had not relied on any of the grounds listed in Article 52 TFEU, it could not justify its legislation.[36] By contrast, in *Commission* v. *France* the Court considered a rule based on the location of a company's registered office (and thus its seat under the real seat doctrine) to be indirectly discriminatory. If the rule is considered indirectly

---

[30] Case 79/85 *Segers* v. *Bedrijfsvereniging voor Bank- en Verzekeringswegen, Groothandel en Vrije Beroepen* [1986] ECR 2375.

[31] Para. 15.

[32] Case 270/83 [1986] ECR 273. See also Case C–170/05 *Denkavit International BV* v. *Ministre de l'Economie, des Finances et de l'Industrie* [2006] ECR I–11949, para. 29.

[33] Para. 22.

[34] Case C–311/97 *Royal Bank of Scotland plc* v. *Elliniko Dimosio (RBS)* [1999] ECR I–2651.

[35] See also Case C–1/93 *Halliburton Services BV* v. *Staatssecretaris van Financiën* [1994] ECR I–1137, esp. para. 20.

[36] Cf. Case C–105/07 *NV Lammers & Van Cleeff* v. *Belgische Staat* [2008] ECR I–173, para. 19, where the Court considered that discrimination on the basis of a company's seat could be justified (para. 25).

discriminatory then it can be saved by both objective justifications and the express derogations (see fig. 7.2).

(b) Going beyond the primary and secondary establishment dichotomy

In more recent cases the Court has not focused so much on whether there is an interference in primary and secondary establishment. Rather, it has merely examined the question whether there had been an interference with freedom of establishment. *SEVIC*[37]
provides a good example. It concerned an inbound merger (i.e., the acquisition of a foreign company by a domestic company) by acquisition (the absorption of a Luxembourg
company (SVC) by a German company (SEVIC)). However, German law on company
transformations allowed for mergers only between companies established in Germany.
While the Advocate General worked hard to show how an inbound merger could actually
be viewed, from the German company's point of view, as the equivalent to setting up a
secondary establishment in Luxembourg,[38] the Court did not bother with such reasoning. Instead, it made the general observation:[39]

> the right of establishment covers all measures which permit or even merely facilitate
> access to another Member State and the pursuit of an economic activity in that State by al-
> lowing the persons concerned to participate in the economic life of the country effectively
> and under the same conditions as national operators.

The Court therefore said that cross-border mergers (making no express distinction
between inbound and outbound mergers) constituted an exercise of the freedom of
establishment. Since such mergers could not be registered in the German commercial
register, this was likely to deter the exercise of freedom of establishment.[40] The Court
recognized that while the national rules could be justified on the grounds of protecting
the interests of creditors, minority shareholders, and employees, as well as protecting
the effectiveness of fiscal supervision and the fairness of commercial transactions, the
German law was nevertheless disproportionate because it involved a general refusal to
register a merger between an in-state and out-of-state company, even where the protection of public interests, such as shareholder protection, was not threatened.[41]

A similar disregard as to how precisely Article 49 TFEU was engaged can be seen
in *Viking*.[42] A Finnish company wanted to reflag its vessel as Estonian. This decision
precipitated threats of strike action to be taken by members of the Finnish Seamen's
Union. In one short paragraph the Court found the proposed strike action to be a
'restriction' on freedom of establishment and so in principle contrary to Article
49 TFEU.

Viking and *SEVIC* are therefore good illustrations of how the Court has used Article
49 TFEU to stop national rules interfering with corporate decisions to restructure in the
way that they see fit to meet market conditions. As it said in *SEVIC*:

> Cross-border merger operations, like other company transformation operations,
> respond to the needs for cooperation and consolidation between companies estab-
> lished in different Member States. They constitute particular methods of exercise
> of the freedom of establishment, important for the proper functioning of the inter-
> nal market, and are therefore amongst those economic activities in respect of which

---

[37] Case C–411/03 *SEVIC Systems* [2005] ECR I–10805.   [38] Tizzano AG, paras. 35–7.
[39] Para. 18.   [40] Para. 22.   [41] Para. 30.
[42] Case C–438/05 *International Transport Workers' Federation and Finnish Seamen's Union* v. *Viking Line
ABP and OÜ Viking Line Eesti* [2007] ECR I–10779.

Member States are required to comply with the freedom of establishment laid down by Article [49] TFEU.

Case Study 11.1: THE *FACTORTAME* LITIGATION

The Court's desire to ensure both primary and secondary establishment of companies is central to an understanding of its ruling in *Factortame II*. In order to understand this litigation it has to be placed in context.

At the heart of the problem lay the Common Fisheries Policy (CFP),[43] which divided up fishing quotas on national lines,[44] and the Act of Accession of Spain to the EU, which restricted the number of Spanish vessels allowed to fish in the EU. In order to circumvent these restrictions Spanish fishing companies started 'quota-hopping', i.e., registering their boats as British and then fishing under the British quota, even though they lacked any genuine link with the UK.[45] The British government tried to prevent this by imposing nationality and residence requirements on the owners and crew of fishing vessels to ensure that there was a real economic link between the ship and the country of registration. For example, in 1983 the UK required 75 per cent of the crew of a British fishing boat to be EU nationals (Spain was not then a member of the EU). The Irish government replicated these British rules, fearing that the Spanish quota-hoppers might turn their attention to Ireland once the restrictive British rules were in place. Equivalent Irish legislation was found compatible with EU law in *Pesca Valentia*.[46]

In 1986 the UK imposed new licence conditions for vessels fishing under the UK quota, relating first to the crew of the vessel (75 per cent EU nationals, 75 per cent resident in the UK, and all contributing to the UK social security scheme) and, secondly, to the operation of the vessel (e.g., at least 50 per cent of the catch had to be landed and sold in the UK). In *Ex p. Agegate*[47] the Court upheld the nationality and social security conditions but found that the residence condition could not be justified. In *Jaderow*[48] the Court said that Member States could require vessels to operate from national ports,[49] provided the vessels were not required to depart from a national port on all their fishing trips.

Despite these various steps, quota-hopping continued, and following a further wave of Spanish registrations in 1986-7,[50] the Merchant Shipping Act 1988 was passed, together with the Merchant Shipping (Registration of Fishing Vessels) Regulations 1988.[51] The 1988 Act created a new register for all British fishing vessels, including those already registered under the

---

[43] For full details, see R. Churchill, 'The EEC's fisheries management system: A review of the first five years of its operation' (1988) 25 *CMLRev.* 369, C. Noirfalisse, 'The Community system of fisheries management and the *Factortame* case' (1992) 12 *YEL* 325, and R. Churchill, 'Quota hopping: The common fisheries policy wrongfooted?' (1990) 27 *CMLRev.* 209.

[44] The CFP was based on total allowable catches (TACs), prescribing the amount of fish which could be caught from a particular stock over a particular period, and quotas allocated among the Member States dividing up the TACs. The CFP also envisaged various long-term conservation measures, including closed seasons, closed areas, and minimum fish sizes.

[45] Noirfalisse, n. 43, 334–5.

[46] Case 223/86 *Pesca Valentia Ltd* v. *Minister for Fisheries and Forestry, Ireland and the Attorney General* [1988] ECR 83.

[47] Case C–3/87 *The Queen* v. *Minister of Agriculture, Fisheries and Food, ex p. Agegate Ltd* [1989] ECR 4459.

[48] Case C–316/87 *The Queen* v. *Minister of Agriculture, Fisheries and Food, ex p. Jaderow Ltd* [1989] ECR 4509. See also the enforcement proceedings brought by the Commission: Case C–279/89 *Commission* v. *UK* [1992] ECR I–5785.

[49] Evidenced by the landing of a proportion of its catches or the vessel's periodic presence in the national port.

[50] Noirfalisse, n. 43, 337.   [51] SI 1988/1926.

Merchant Shipping Act 1894. According to section 14(1) of the 1988 Act, a fishing vessel could be registered in the new register only if all the following applied:

(1) the vessel was British-owned[52]

(2) the vessel was managed, and its operations directed and controlled, from within the UK

(3) any charterer, manager, or operator of the vessel was a qualified (British) person or company.[53]

Despite its obviously discriminatory nature, the UK was advised that:

> any discrimination that arises out of the proposed measures [what became the 1988 Act] is a natural consequence of the [common fisheries policy] itself which divides quotas along national lines ... We consider that rules on nationality of fishing vessels are the most appropriate way of establishing a genuine link between the Member States and the vessel intending to fish for the Member State's quota.[54]

Nevertheless, the 1988 Act precipitated challenges at both Union and national levels. At Union level, the Commission brought enforcement proceedings against the UK under Article 258 TFEU for a declaration that section 14 of the 1988 Act breached Article 49 TFEU.[55] It also successfully applied for an interim order under Article 278 TFEU requiring the UK to suspend the application of the nationality requirements laid down in section 14.[56] The UK complied with effect from November 1989.

At national level, judicial review proceedings were brought by the owners or operators of 95 fishing vessels which had been registered as British under the Merchant Shipping Act 1894[57] but could not satisfy one or more of the conditions laid down in the 1988 Act and so were deprived of the right to fish from April 1989.[58] The Divisional Court made an Article 267 TFEU reference on the substantive issues of Union law raised in the proceedings (the case which became *Factortame II*). The Divisional Court also ordered that, by way of interim relief, the application of the 1988 Act[59] and the 1988 Regulations had to be suspended. In *Factortame I*[60] the Court of Justice said that *Union* law required the granting of interim relief to secure effective interim protection of directly effective rights. For this reason the national rule (no injunction against the Crown) had to be set aside; the House of Lords obliged and granted interim relief on the facts.[61]

---

[52] According to s. 14(2), a fishing vessel was deemed to be British-owned if the legal title to the vessel was vested wholly in one or more qualified persons or companies and if the vessel was beneficially owned by one or more qualified companies or, as to not less than 75 per cent, by one or more qualified persons.

[53] According to s. 14(7) 'qualified person' meant a person who was a British citizen resident and domiciled in the UK and 'qualified company' meant a company incorporated in the UK and having its principal place of business there, at least 75 per cent of its shares being owned by one or more qualified persons or companies and at least 75 per cent of its directors being qualified persons.

[54] Quoted by Lord Slynn in *Factortame (No. 5)* [2000] 1 AC 524, 543E.

[55] Case C–246/89 *Commission* v. *UK* [1991] ECR I–4585.

[56] Case C–246/89 R *Commission* v. *UK* [1989] ECR 3125, Order of the President of the Court.

[57] These facts are set out in detail in Case C–213/89 R. v. *Secretary of State for Transport, ex p. Factortame Ltd (Factortame I)* [1990] ECR I–2433, paras. 3–13.

[58] Some fishing vessels had originally been registered in Spain but were subsequently registered in the UK; others had always been registered in the UK but had been purchased by the complainant companies. For a fuller exposition of the parties, see N. Green, 'Proportionality and the supremacy of Parliament in the UK' in E. Ellis (ed.), *The Principle of Proportionality in the Laws of Europe* (Oxford: Hart Publishing, 1999), 159.

[59] In particular Part II laying down the registration conditions.

[60] Case C–213/89 [1990] ECR I–2433.

[61] R. v. *Secretary of State for Transport, ex p. Factortame Ltd* [1991] 1 AC 603.

On the issue of substance, the Court of Justice ruled in *Factortame II*,[62] and again in the enforcement proceedings brought by the Commission,[63] that the conditions laid down for the registration of vessels should not form an obstacle to freedom of establishment within the meaning of Article 49 TFEU.[64] Beginning by defining the conditions for the grant of 'nationality' to a ship, the Court said that each Member State had to comply with the prohibition on discrimination against nationals of other Member States on grounds of their nationality. Therefore, the Court ruled that the nationality condition on the owners or charterers of a vessel, or the shareholders and directors of a company, was contrary to Article 49 TFEU.[65] The Court added that such a condition was also contrary to Article 55 TFEU, under which Member States had to accord nationals of the other Member States the same treatment as their own nationals as regards participation in the capital of companies or firms.

The Court then turned to the requirements that the owners, charterers, managers, and operators of the vessel or, in the case of a company, the shareholders and directors, be resident and domiciled in the UK. It found these requirements to be unjustifiably indirectly discriminatory: while the majority of UK nationals satisfied these requirements automatically as they were resident and domiciled in the UK, nationals of other Member States would in most cases have to move their residence and domicile to the UK in order to comply with them.[66] The requirements therefore breached Article 49 TFEU.

By contrast, the Court found that the rule that a vessel had to be managed and its operations directed and controlled from within the UK was compatible with Union law since it 'essentially coincides with the actual concept of establishment' within the meaning of Article 49 TFEU 'which implies a fixed establishment'.[67] On the other hand the Court said that such a requirement would not be compatible with Article 49 TFEU if it precluded registration of a secondary establishment.

To summarize, the Court accepted the Commission's argument that the conditions laid down by the 1988 Act breached Article 49 TFEU in two ways:[68]

- by preventing *nationals* of other Member States from setting up and acting as directors of companies in the sea fisheries sector in the UK (i.e., by interfering with primary establishment)[69]

- by restricting the possibility for *companies* of other Member States to pursue sea-fishing activities from the UK through agencies, branches, or subsidiaries (i.e., by interfering with secondary establishment).

However, in reaching its conclusions, Noirfalisse[70] suggests that the Court blurred the distinction between the grant of nationality and the freedom of establishment. She argues that the

---

[62] Case C–221/89 [1991] ECR I–3905.

[63] Case C–246/89 *Commission* v. *UK* [1991] ECR I–4585. Other states also attempted to address the problems of quota-hopping. Their measures were equally unsuccessful: e.g., Case C–93/89 *Commission* v. *Ireland* [1991] ECR I–4569, para. 15: 'by requiring nationals of other Member States to set up an Irish company before obtaining a licence to fish at sea, Ireland has failed to fulfil its obligations under Article [49 TFEU]'; Case C–151/96 *Commission* v. *Ireland* [1997] ECR I–3327 (nationality requirement for owner); Case C–334/94 *Commission* v. *France* [1996] ECR I–1307 (nationality requirement for owner and crew).

[64] Para. 23.   [65] Para. 30.   [66] Para. 32.   [67] Para. 34.

[68] Case C–246/89 *Commission* v. *UK* [1991] ECR I–4585, para. 19, and Mischo AG's Opinion, paras. 29–33. See also Art. 14(1) of the Services Dir., considered in Section D.

[69] Cf. Case C–299/02 *Commission* v. *Netherlands (registration of ships)* [2004] ECR I–9761, paras. 20–1, where the Court ruled that national measures requiring as a condition for being able to register a ship in the Netherlands that the shareholders, directors, and natural persons responsible for day-to-day management of the Union company owning the ship have Union or EEA nationality constituted an obstacle to freedom of establishment and was not a proportionate means of attaining the goal of exercising effective control and jurisdiction over ships flying the Dutch flag.

[70] Noirfalisse, n. 43, 344–6.

prohibition of discrimination on the ground of nationality in Articles 18 and 49 TFEU presupposes the existence of the concept of nationality; a national of a Member State cannot invoke Article 49 TFEU to *obtain* the nationality of another Member State where he wishes to establish. Under international law each state can fix the conditions for granting its nationality to its ships: there must exist a genuine link between the state and the ship.[71] She therefore argues that the 1988 Act was merely the expression of the exclusive power of a Member State to define its own ships. It did not concern the exercise of the right to establishment at all.

When *Factortame II* returned to the UK, the Divisional Court made an order giving effect to the Court's judgment and also directed the claimants to give particulars of their claims for damages, covering expenses and losses incurred between 1 April 1989 (when the 1988 Act came into force) and 2 November 1989 (when it was repealed). It then made a further reference to the Court of Justice on the question of state liability. In *Factortame III*[72] the Court said that the principle of state liability was inherent in the system of the Treaty, whatever organ of the state was responsible for the breach.[73] In an area such as the registration of vessels and fisheries, which conferred a wide discretion on the legislature, the Court said that Union law conferred a right to reparation where three conditions were met:[74] (1) the rule of law was intended to confer rights on individuals (this condition was 'manifestly satisfied'[75]); (2) the breach of Union law was sufficiently serious (the Court gave a strong hint that it considered the UK's breach to be sufficiently serious, in particular because the nationality condition constituted 'direct discrimination manifestly contrary to [Union] law'); and (3) there was a direct causal link between the breach of the obligation by the state and the damage sustained by the injured parties (this was a matter for the national courts to decide).

The Divisional Court, the Court of Appeal, and the House of Lords[76] all found that the breaches of Union law resulting from the 1988 Act were in principle sufficiently serious to give rise to liability for any damage that might have been caused to the applicants.[77] Following its comprehensive defeat in the *Factortame* litigation, the UK sought to have a protocol added to the EC Treaty at Amsterdam allowing Member States to impose requirements ensuring that vessels had a real economic link with the populations dependent on fisheries and related industries in that state.[78] The UK was unsuccessful.

---

[71] See Art. 5(1) of the Convention of the High Seas of 1958, referred to by the Court.

[72] Joined Cases C–46 and 48/93 *Brasserie du Pêcheur SA* v. *Federal Republic of Germany and R. v. Secretary of State for Transport, ex p. Factortame (Factortame III)* [1996] ECR I–1029.

[73] Para. 32.　　　　[74] Para. 51, considered further in Ch. 6.

[75] 'The essence of Article [49 TFEU] is to confer rights on individuals' (Case 2/74 *Reyners* [1974] ECR 631, para. 25).

[76] [1997] EuLR 475, [1998] EuLR 456, and [2000] 1 AC 524 respectively.

[77] The rulings on damages precipitated a further outcry in the British press, with significantly varying estimates as to how much the claims would cost the British taxpayer. These ranged from £55 million to £100 million: see, e.g., G. Wilson, 'The final humiliation: Britain must pay Spanish fishermen "up to £100 million"', *Daily Mail*, 29 Oct. 1999. The case rumbled on: see, e.g., *R. v. Secretary of State, ex p. Factortame (No. 7)* [2001] 1 CMLR 47 (QBD (T&CC)) on the legal nature of the claim, the applicable limitation periods, and the nature of the damages that could be awarded; *R. (on the application of Factortame Ltd)* v. *Secretary of State for Transport, Local Government and the Regions (No. 8)* [2002] EWCA Civ 932, concerning the question whether an agreement made in July 1998 under which the claimants, Factortame Ltd, now in a 'parlous financial state', agreed to pay accountants, Grant Thornton, 8 per cent of the damages awarded for services ancillary to the conduct of the litigation was champertous and therefore unenforceable. According to the ICC Directory of UK Companies, Factortame itself seems to have ceased trading and is now lying dormant on the register of companies (its last annual return was submitted on 9 May 2001).

[78] Draft Protocol to the EC Treaty: Quota Hopping Memo by the UK, IGC, Jul. 1996.

(c) Regulatory competition

(i) Centros

Given the Court's enthusiasm to encourage secondary establishment, could those wishing to form a company take advantage of EU rules by incorporating a company in State A which has lenient incorporation rules and then, relying on Articles 49 and 54 TFEU, set up a branch or agency in State B, thereby avoiding State B's more onerous rules of incorporation? Early cases on services suggested that this tactic would fail since it is a well-established principle that EU law cannot be relied on for abusive or fraudulent ends.[79] In *Centros*,[80] however, the Court appeared to reach the opposite conclusion.

Centros Ltd was a private company incorporated in the UK by two Danish citizens, Mr and Mrs Bryde, who were its sole shareholders. With a view to trading in Denmark, they applied to have a branch of the company registered in Denmark. At the time of the registration request, Centros had never traded in the UK, and for this reason the Danish registrar of companies refused to register the branch. He considered that the company was actually seeking to register its principal business establishment in Denmark and not just a branch, and that the Brydes were seeking to evade Danish law on minimum capital requirements. In Denmark, companies had to have at least DKr 200,000 (approximately £20,000)[81] when they were formed; this was not the case in the UK.

The Court ruled that the registrar's refusal to grant the registration request constituted an obstacle to the freedom of establishment,[82] saying that it was 'immaterial' that the company was formed in the UK only for the purpose of establishing itself in Denmark, where its main or entire business was to be conducted.[83] It also said that this was not a case of abuse because the national rules which the Brydes were trying to avoid were rules governing the formation of companies and not rules concerning the pursuit of certain trades, professions, or businesses.[84] In other words, they were not fraudulently taking advantage of the provisions of Union law[85] because they were doing what the Treaty expressly permits, namely incorporating in one Member State and setting up a secondary establishment in another.[86]

The Danish government sought to justify the refusal to register on the ground of the need to maintain its rules on minimum capital requirements. First, it said that the rules reinforced the financial soundness of companies in order to protect public creditors against the risk of seeing the debts owed to them become irrecoverable. The Court said this justification was inadequate because it was inconsistent—the vital factor in the registrar's refusal to grant the registration request was the failure of the company to trade in the UK. This was immaterial to the protection of creditors since they would have been no better off had the company previously traded in the UK and been able to register its branch in Denmark.[87] Furthermore, EU company information disclosure directives put

---

[79] See, e.g., Case 33/74 *Van Binsbergen* v. *Bedrijfsvereniging Metaalnijverheid* [1974] ECR 1299, para. 13; Case C–23/93 *TV10* v. *Commissariaat voor de Media* [1994] ECR I–4795, para. 21, considered in Section C, 1.5.

[80] Case C–212/97 [1999] ECR I–1459.

[81] See M. Siems, 'Convergence, competition, *Centros* and conflicts of law: European company law in the 21st century' (2002) 27 *ELRev.* 47, 49. Minimum capital requirements themselves may be a restriction on freedom of establishment: see Joined Cases C–357–359/10 *Duomo Gpa* v. *Comune di Baranzate* EU:C:2012:283.

[82] Paras. 29–30.   [83] Para. 17, citing Case 79/85 *Segers* [1986] ECR 2375.

[84] Para. 26.   [85] Para. 24.

[86] Para. 27. See also Case C–196/04 *Cadbury Schweppes* v. *Commissioners of the Inland Revenue* [2006] ECR I–7995, para. 36.

[87] Para. 35.

Danish creditors on notice that Centros Ltd was not a company governed by Danish law. The refusal to register was not only unjustifiable, it was also disproportionate. The Court said that the Danish authorities could have adopted less-restrictive measures by, for example, making it possible in law for public creditors to obtain the necessary guarantees.

The Danish government also argued that its law aimed at protecting all creditors from the risk of fraudulent bankruptcy due to the insolvency of companies whose initial capitalization was inadequate. The Court was more sympathetic towards this argument. It said Denmark could adopt measures preventing or penalizing fraud. However, the Court added that combating fraud did not justify a practice of refusing to register a branch of a company which had its registered office in another Member State[88]—but did not suggest what steps states could take to combat fraud which would be compatible with Union law.

In *Inspire Art*[89] the Court repeated its ruling in *Centros*, this time in respect of Dutch rules on minimum capital requirements and directors' liability which applied to companies deliberately established in another Member State (the UK) to avoid the Dutch rules but carrying on their activities exclusively or almost exclusively in the Netherlands through a branch.[90] The Court said that the Dutch rules had the effect of unjustifiably impeding the exercise by companies of freedom of establishment.[91] It added that the reasons why a company was formed in the UK and the fact that it carried on its activities exclusively in the Netherlands did not deprive the company of the right to invoke the freedom of establishment guaranteed by the Treaty, save where abuse was established on a case-by-case basis.[92]

(ii) The Delaware effect?

For some, the decision in *Centros* gave the green light to a Delaware-style race to the bottom coming to the EU in the field of company law.[93] These commentators argue that companies were now free to incorporate in the state with the most lax incorporation standards and then, using branches or agencies, carry on the bulk of their operations in other states which apply 'higher' standards for incorporation. One brake on this race to the bottom—the use of the public-interest requirements—was not applied on the facts in *Centros*.

In company law there is another potential brake on any such race to the bottom, the *siège réel* ('real seat') doctrine, which applies in countries such as France, Germany, and Italy. According to this doctrine, the national courts will view the reality of the situation rather than the legal form, and so will regard the applicable law as that of the Member State in which the company has its main centre of operations (head office or principal place of business) rather than that of the state of incorporation. The effect of this doctrine is to prevent companies from doing what Centros did—that is, the doctrine limits freedom of incorporation.

By contrast, the UK, Ireland, the Netherlands, and, to a certain extent, Denmark operate a 'state of incorporation' rule,[94] according to which the applicable law is that of the state in which the company is incorporated or registered, irrespective of whether it has a physical presence there. Therefore, as the facts of *Centros* demonstrate, English law permits companies to be incorporated in the UK but with their residence or main operations in another Member State. This outcome would not be permitted by Member States which operate the *siège réel* doctrine.

---

[88] Case C–212/97 *Centros* [1999] ECR I–1459, para. 38.

[89] Case C–167/01 *Kamer van Koophandel en Fabrieken voor Amsterdam* v. *Inspire Art Ltd* [2003] ECR I–10155.

[90] Para. 100.   [91] Para. 101.   [92] Para. 105.   [93] See further Ch. 1.

[94] Danish law was essentially applying the incorporation theory for corporate capacity and the real seat theory for recognition of foreign companies, based on the perceived abuse of Danish rules on minimum capital requirements: J. Hansen, 'A new look at *Centros*: From a Danish point of view' (2002) 13 *EBLRev.* 85.

Centros called into question the status of the *siège réel* doctrine under Union law. Although the judgment is far from clear on this point, it could be argued that the Court was suggesting that the validity of an incorporation in one Member State (the UK) could not be called into question in another (Denmark) on the grounds that the principal business presence or central administration of the company concerned was not located in the state of incorporation. However, since the *siège réel* doctrine was not clearly before the Court, this interpretation cannot be relied on with any certainty. Nevertheless, it is arguable that, after *Centros*, the *siège réel* doctrine does pose an obstacle to freedom of establishment which needs justification.

These questions were confronted more directly by the Court in *Überseering*.[95] Überseering, a Dutch company, sued a German company, NCC, for defective work carried out by NCC on Überseering's behalf in Germany. Prior to bringing the proceedings, all the shares in Überseering were acquired by two German nationals. The German court found that, since Überseering had transferred its centre of administration to Germany, as a company incorporated under Dutch law it did not have legal capacity in Germany because it had not been formed according to German law[96] and so could not bring proceedings.[97] German law thus refused to recognize the legal personality which Überseering enjoyed under Dutch law (and continued to enjoy under Dutch law even after its centre of administration had been moved),[98] with the result that the German courts effectively denied the company access to justice in Germany.

The Court said that because Überseering was a company validly incorporated under the law of the Netherlands, where its registered office was established, it had no alternative under German law but to reincorporate in Germany if it wished to enforce its rights under a contract before a German court.[99] This contravened Articles 49 and 54 TFEU because '[t]he requirement of reincorporation of the same company in Germany is therefore tantamount to outright negation of freedom of establishment'.[100] Further, since this concerned an outright *negation* of freedom of establishment the German rules could not be justified.[101]

The effect of *Überseering* may be to erode the *siège réel* doctrine still further. It requires German courts to recognize companies validly formed under Dutch law, even though they would not be recognized under German law. Indeed, a company with its 'registered office, central administration or principal place of business within the [Union]' cannot be denied access to any other Member State.[102] This does not necessarily mean that the Court is privileging the incorporation theory; rather that it is paying more attention to the state in which the company has been incorporated.[103]

(d) From equal treatment to the restrictions approach

So far we have focused on the right to leave a Member State and the right to enter another state through primary and secondary establishment. We turn now to the other main right provided by the Treaty—the principal of equal treatment laid down in the first paragraph of Article 54 TFEU. In other words, there must be no discrimination based on a company's nationality or, rather its 'seat',[104] which, as the Court ruled in *Commission* v. *France*

---

[95] Case C–208/00 *Überseering BV* v. *Nordic Construction Co. Baumanagement GmbH (NCC)* [2002] ECR I–9919.

[96] For a full explanation, see Wymeersch, n. 14, 674.   [97] Para. 9.

[98] Paras. 63 and 71.   [99] Para. 79.   [100] Paras. 80–1.   [101] Paras. 92–3.

[102] Wymeersch, n. 14, 680.   [103] Wymeersch, n. 14, 689.

[104] Case C–330/91 *R.* v. *Inland Revenue Commissioners, ex p. Commerzbank AG* [1993] ECR I–4017, para. 13, correcting the translation error found in Case 270/83 *Commission* v. *France (tax credits)* [1986] ECR 273.

(tax credits)[105] serves as the connecting factor with the legal system of a particular state. A company's seat is the state in which the company or firm, formed in accordance with the law of a Member State, has its registered office, central administration, or principal place of business.[106] Therefore, direct discrimination is discrimination on the ground of the company's seat; indirect discrimination involves the use of criteria which, 'by the application of other criteria of differentiation, lead in fact to the same result'.[107]

Case Study 11.1 on the *Factortame* litigation provides some good examples of discriminatory situations. However, as with other areas of free movement, the Court is increasingly moving towards the restrictions/market access approach, as was seen in *Centros*[108] (discussed earlier).

The restrictions approach has been followed in a number of subsequent cases. For example, in *Commission v. Italy (trade fairs)*[109] the Court said that a national rule requiring the authorities to give their approval before a trade fair could take place constituted a restriction on the freedom of establishment. Likewise, in *EFTA Surveillance Authority v. Norway*[110] the EFTA Court said that Norway's decision to introduce an exclusive right for one state-owned company to run all games of chance and gambling, thereby excluding private operators from the market, constituted:

> a restriction on the freedom of establishment and the freedom to provide services, as it completely removes them from the market and insofar denies them access to that market ... The restrictions are of a non-discriminatory nature, since the contested legislation applies without distinction to domestic and foreign operators of gaming machines.[111]

However, on the facts, the Court found the Norwegian rules justified and proportionate.

Finally, in *Commission v. Italy (motor insurance)*[112] the Court found that an Italian obligation to contract imposed on all insurance companies operating in the field of third party liability motor insurance and in relation to all vehicle owners constituted a restriction on freedom of establishment (and freedom to provide services). In this case the Court emphasized the significance of the restriction. It said the imposition by a Member State of an obligation to contract 'constitutes a *substantial* interference in the freedom to contract which economic operators, in principle, enjoy'.[113] It continued that in a sector like insurance, 'such a measure affects the relevant operators' access to the market, in particular where it subjects insurance undertakings not only to an obligation to cover any risks which are proposed to them, but also to requirements to moderate premium rates'.[114] It concluded that 'Inasmuch as it obliges insurance undertakings which enter the Italian market to accept every potential customer, that obligation to contract is likely to lead, in terms of organisation and investment, to significant additional costs for such undertakings.'[115] The rules therefore beached the Treaty but could be justified on the grounds of social protection for victims of road traffic accidents. The Court also said the rules were proportionate.

---

[105] Case 270/83 *Commission v. France (tax credits)* [1986] ECR 273, para. 18.
[106] See V. Edwards, 'The secondary establishment of companies: The case law of the Court of Justice' (1998) 18 *YEL* 221, 225–6.
[107] Case C–330/91 *Ex p. Commerzbank AG* [1993] ECR I–4017, para. 14.
[108] Case C–212/97 [1999] ECR I–1459, para. 34. See also Case C–221/89 *Factortame II* [1991] ECR I–3905.
[109] Case C–439/99 *Commission v. Italy* [2002] ECR I–305, para. 39. See also Case C–169/07 *Hartlauer Handelsgesellschaft mbH v. Wiener Landesregierung* [2009] ECR I–1721. See also Arts. 9–13 of the Services Dir. considered in Section D.
[110] Case E–1/06 [2007] EFTA Ct. Rep. 8.   [111] Para. 27.
[112] Case C–518/06 *Commission v. Italy (motor insurance)* [2009] ECR I–3491.
[113] Para. 66, emphasis added.   [114] Para. 67.   [115] Para. 68.

(e) Modifying the restrictions approach

The reference to the need to show a *substantial* restriction on freedom of establishment in *Commission* v. *Italy (motor insurance)* suggests that the Court may be trying to modify the full force of the restrictions approach by introducing a threshold requirement. A similar suggestion can be found in the goods case *Commission* v. *Italy (trailers)*[116]—decided at about the same time as *Motor Insurance*—where the Court talked about the rules having a 'considerable influence' on consumer behaviour.[117] The introduction of an economic threshold requirement was confirmed by the Grand Chamber in *Commission* v. *Italy (maximum fees for lawyers)*.[118] But inevitably there is a lack of consistency: in *X*,[119] decided only a year after *Commission* v. *Italy (maximum fees for lawyers)*, the Court said:

> suffice it to point out that a restriction on a fundamental freedom is prohibited by the TFEU, even if it is of limited scope or minor importance.

Despite the *X* case, *Commission* v. *Italy (maximum fees for lawyers)* seems to have presaged a greater wariness by the Court about finding restrictions on free movement and possibly something of a shift back to a discrimination analysis. This can be seen in *DHL*,[120] a case which concerned national rules imposed on providers of postal services, who were not subject to the universal service obligation, a mandatory external procedure for dealing with complaints from users of those services. The Court found that such a rule was not a restriction on freedom of establishment because:

> First, that measure is applied, without discrimination on grounds of nationality, to all providers established in Belgium of postal services which are outside the scope of the universal service. Secondly, ... operators cannot expect Member States not to have structures in place which afford legal protection for the interests of their customers and provide out-of-court procedures for settling disputes. Lastly, nearly all Member States have extended the external complaints schemes to providers of postal services which are outside the scope of the universal service.

These cases are the latest attempts by the Court to try to rein in the use of the restrictions formula in inappropriate cases. Some have suggested that it is necessary to carve a *Keck*-style certain selling arrangements (CSAs) exception out of Article 56 TFEU.[121] However, in *Omega*[122] Advocate General Stix-Hackl counselled against any such development, arguing that the transposition of the distinction made in *Keck* to freedom to provide services was unpersuasive because:

> where there are sufficient international implications, a rule on arrangements for the provision of any service—irrespective of location—must constitute a restriction of relevance to

---

[116] Case C–110/05 *Commission* v. *Italy (trailers)* [2009] ECR I–519, considered further in Ch. 5.

[117] Para. 56. Cf. Case C–602/10 *SC Volksbank România* v. *CJPC* EU:C:2012:443, para. 81, where the Court uses the tortious remoteness test to find that the effect of a national rule prohibiting credit institutions from levying certain bank charges was too indirect and uncertain to be regarded as liable to hinder intra-Union trade. See also Case C–483/12 *Pelckmans Turnhout NV* EU:C:2014:304, para. 25 (effect of Sunday trading rules on freedom to provide services too uncertain and indirect).

[118] Case C–565/08 [2011] ECR I–2101.

[119] Case C–498/10 *X NV* v. *Staatssecretaris van Financiën* EU:C:2012:635, para. 30.

[120] Case C–148/10 *DHL International NV* v. *Belgisch Instituut voor Postdiensten en Telecommunicatie* [2011] ECR I–9543.

[121] See, e.g., the Member States' submissions in Case C–384/93 *Alpine Investments* [1995] ECR I–1141.

[122] Case C–36/02 *Omega* [2004] ECR I–9609, para. 36. See also Case C–356/08 *Commission* v. *Austria* [2009] ECR I–108, where the Court avoided the Austrian government's arguments that the requirement to open a bank account with a bank in the region concerned a method of use to which *Keck* applied.

[Union] law simply because of the incorporeal nature of services, without any distinction at all being permissible in this respect between rules relating to arrangements for the provision of services and rules that relate directly to the services themselves.[123]

In other words, while in the field of free movement of goods it is possible to draw a distinction between rules regulating the good itself (product requirement rules which are in principle caught by Article 34 TFEU) and rules which apply to those selling the good (certain selling arrangements, which are in principle not caught), it is not so easy to make a distinction between rules regulating the service and those regulating the service provider. In *Pelckmans*[124] the Court used the 'too uncertain and indirect' test to deliver the same result as in *Keck* to find that restrictions on Sunday trading were not capable of hindering freedom to provide services.

2.3 The Exercise of the Right of Establishment

Once the company has established itself or a branch in the host state then it must enjoy the same terms and conditions and other benefits available to national companies. Therefore, in *Commission v. Italy (data processing)*[125] the Court said that an Italian law, providing that only companies in which all or a majority of shares were directly or indirectly in public or state ownership could conclude agreements for data-processing systems for public authorities, 'essentially favour[ed] Italian companies'[126] and so breached Article 49 TFEU. It could not be justified on the facts.

Rules restricting the freedom of establishment are also prohibited. This can be seen in *Pfeiffer*.[127] Pfeiffer operated a large supermarket in Austria under the name Plus KAUF PARK. It obtained a court order restraining Löwa, a rival German discount store operating in Austria, from using the trade name 'Plus'. The Court of Justice ruled that such an order was 'liable to constitute an impediment' to Löwa's aim of realizing a uniform advertising concept across the EU, contrary to Article 49 TFEU.[128] However, the Court said that because the primary aim of the national law was to safeguard trade names against the risk of confusion[129] it could be justified by overriding requirements in the general interest relating to the protection of industrial and commercial property interests, and the court's order was proportionate since there was a risk of confusion between the two trade names.

By contrast, in *Neri*[130] the Court found the steps taken by the Italian government to protect educational standards to be disproportionate. A British company, ESE, set up 12 branches in Italy where, for a fee, it provided courses which were validated by Nottingham Trent University (NTU), which also awarded a BA degree at the end of the course. Neri

---

[123] Case C–287/03 *Commission v. Belgium (loyalty bonus)* [2005] ECR I–3761 lends support to the AG's view that the concept of CSA should not be applied to services. Belgian law prevented vendors from making a 'linked offer', through its customer-loyalty programme, of products and services dissimilar to those principally sold. While the Court dismissed the Art. 258 TFEU application on the grounds that the Commission had failed to establish a breach of Art. 56 TFEU, at no stage did the Court suggest that Art. 56 TFEU would not apply because the national rule affected selling arrangements. Cf. now the UCPD 2005/29, considered in Ch. 5 and Joined Cases C–261 and 299/07 *VTB-VAB* [2009] ECR I–2949.

[124] Case C–483/12 *Pelckmans Turnhout NV* EU:C:2014:304, para. 25.

[125] Case 3/88 [1989] ECR 4035. See also Case C–272/91 *Commission v. Italy* [1994] ECR I–1409.

[126] Para. 9.

[127] Case C–255/97 *Pfeiffer Großhandel GmbH v. Löwa Warenhandel GmbH* [1999] ECR I–2835.

[128] Para. 20.

[129] This corresponded to the specific subject matter of the trade name: Case C–317/91 *Deutsche Renault* [1993] ECR I–6227, para. 37.

[130] Case C–153/02 *Valentina Neri v. European School of Economics (ESE Insight World Education System Ltd)* [2003] ECR I–13555.

enrolled on one such course and then discovered that the Italian authorities had a practice of not recognizing the degree awarded on this course even though it was legally recognized in the UK. The Court noted that this Italian practice was 'likely to deter students from attending these courses and thus seriously hinder the pursuit by ESE of its economic activity' in Italy.[131] While the Court recognized that the professed aim of the Italian measure—to ensure high standards of university education—was legitimate, the steps taken were not proportionate because Italian law permitted similar arrangements to those between NTU and ESE, and the Italian practice meant that the authorities refused to recognize any foreign degree.[132]

2.4 Taxation

(a) Introduction

An increasingly large number of cases in the area of freedom of establishment (and capital) concern the question of whether national tax law interferes with free movement. Enterprising lawyers began to argue that because, say, the corporation tax rate was higher in the UK than in Ireland this constituted an 'impediment' or 'restriction' on an Irish company's ability to establish a subsidiary in the UK.[133] Such arguments forced states, like the UK, to justify their higher rate and show that it was proportionate. The problem is that the justification for levying tax is essentially economic—taxation is the principal source of revenue for all states, which they then use to provide a range of public and other services—and the Court will not generally accept pure economic justifications.

The application of the restrictions approach to tax cases led to substantial losses to national treasuries,[134] which increasingly began to express serious concerns about the Court's interference in this sensitive area.[135] Part of the problem was that the principles of international tax law operate rather differently to those of the single market. In the next section we shall look at the key principles of tax law as they relate to free movement. We shall then consider how the Court has reconciled international principles of tax law with Article 49 TFEU.

(b) Principles of tax law in cross-border situations

Direct taxation remains one of 'the fundamental sacrosanct bastions of national sovereignty'.[136] Member States remain free to identify:

- the tax unit (those over whom they wish to assert legislative fiscal jurisdiction, usually those resident in the state and the profits which arise in that state)
- the tax base (i.e., the nature and quantum of the receipts it wishes to tax and the identification of the entitlement to and nature of tax reliefs[137])

---

[131] Para. 43.   [132] Paras. 47–9.

[133] See, e.g., Case C–196/04 *Cadbury Schweppes* [2006] ECR I–7995.

[134] E.g., when the Court struck down the national rule in Case C–168/01 *Bosal Holding BV* [2003] ECR I–9409 it was estimated that the direct costs of the case amounted to €1.2 billion between 2003 and 2010. Even after changing its legislation it is estimated that the cost to the Netherlands was €0.55 billion a year to comply with the judgment: S. Kingston, 'The boundaries of sovereignty: The Court's controversial role applying the internal market rules to taxation' (2006–7) 9 *CYELS* 287.

[135] This was recognized by Commissioner Kovács: <http://ec.europa.eu/taxation_customs/resources/documents/common/about/speeches/51201tdi.pdf>. See also the introduction of Art. 65(4) TFEU by the Lisbon Treaty (considered in Ch. 14), which was seen as a direct rebuff to the Court.

[136] Kingston, n. 134.

[137] See the attempts at a Union 'common consolidated corporate tax base': <http://www.ec.europa.eu/taxation_customs/taxation/company_tax/common_tax_base/index_en.htm>.

- the tax rate
- how they wish to administer, assess, collect, and recover tax.[138]

In other words, states enjoy fiscal autonomy,[139] which means, as the Court has now recognized, that Member States are 'not obliged therefore to adapt their own tax systems to the different systems of tax of the other Member States' in order to eliminate difficulties for claimants arising from 'the exercise in parallel by those Member States of their fiscal sovereignty'.[140]

Thus, the *existence* of tax law is a matter for Member State competence. However, how the Member State decides to *exercise* that competence remains subject to Union law[141] and in particular the principle of equal treatment. The application of Union law to national systems of tax is problematic. Where the taxation is directly discriminatory, the Court can deal with the situation in the usual way (breach of Article 49 TFEU, express derogations available: see fig. 7.2).[142] However, in the field of freedom of establishment a number of the cases concern the situation where national rules treat resident companies differently to non-residents. As we have already seen, it is classic single-market case law that residence is a suspect ground of differential treatment and usually constitutes unlawful indirect discrimination.[143]

However, under international (and thus national) tax law residence is *the* legitimate ground of differentiation. Under international tax law, *residents* of a taxing state are taxed on their worldwide profits ('unlimited taxation'), while *non-residents* are taxed on profits arising from sources located in that taxing state ('limited taxation').[144] This distinction is referred to as the principle of territoriality;[145] national rules respecting that principle should not breach EU law. This point was recognized by the Court in *Futura Participations*.[146] The case concerned a Luxembourg rule that while all income earned by *resident* taxpayers was taxable, irrespective of where it was earned, for *non-resident* taxpayers only profits and losses arising from Luxembourg activities were taken into account when calculating tax payable in Luxembourg. The Court found that this rule was compatible with Article 49 TFEU because it conformed to the fiscal principle of territoriality.

The corollary of the distinction between residents and non-residents is that generally the state of residence grants taxpayers all the tax advantages (relating to, in the case of individuals, their personal and family circumstances because their personal and financial interests are centred there and so the state of residence can best assess the taxpayers' ability to pay tax).[147] The same will not apply to non-residents.

---

[138] J. Ghosh, *Principles of the Internal Market and Direct Taxation* (Oxford: Key Haven, 2007), 1–14. See also Case C–374/04 *Test Claimants in Class IV of the ACT Group Litigation* v. *Commissioners of Inland Revenue* [2006] ECR I–11673, para. 50: 'It is for each Member State to organise, in compliance with Union law, its system of taxation of distributed profits and, in that context, to define the tax base as well at the tax rates which apply to the company making the distribution and/or the shareholder to whom the dividends are paid, in so far as they are liable to tax in that State.'

[139] Case C–298/05 *Columbus Container Services BVBA & Co.* v. *Finanzamt Bielefeld-Innenstadt* [2007] ECR I–10451, para. 53. See also the discussion of the principle in respect of Art. 110 TFEU in Ch. 3.

[140] Case C–67/08 *Block* v. *Finanzamt Kaufbeuren* [2009] ECR I–883, para. 31.

[141] See, e.g., Case C–246/89 *Commission* v. *UK* [1991] ECR I–4585.

[142] Case C–155/09 *Commission* v. *Greece (transfer tax)* [2011] ECR I–65.

[143] Case C–175/88 *Biehl* v. *Administration des contributions du grand-duché de Luxembourg* [1990] ECR I–1779, para. 14.

[144] See further Ghosh, n. 138, 4.   [145] Ghosh, n. 138.

[146] Case C–250/95 *Futura Participations SA and Singer* v. *Administration des Contributions* [1997] ECR I–2471, para. 22.

[147] Case C–279/93 *Finanzamt Köln-Altstadt* v. *Schumacker* [1995] ECR I–225, para. 32, considered further in Ch. 8.

The problem for those resident in State A but receiving profits in State B is that they risk being taxed twice: once by the source state (State B) and then again in the home state (State A), where they are taxed on worldwide profits. To avoid this problem, a vast network of bilateral Double Taxation Conventions (DTCs) has been drawn up between states agreeing on which state enjoys priority in cross-border situations.[148] International tax law lays down the general rule that priority of taxation lies with the source state, meaning that it is up to the home state (State A) to alleviate the double taxation. However, as we have seen, given the principle of fiscal sovereignty, the home state is not obliged to alleviate the double taxation, nor is it required to do so under Union law.[149] If the home state decides not to alleviate the double taxation, this is certainly 'liable to hinder' free movement but each of these restrictions is simply 'an inevitable result of Member States' tax sovereignty and the co-existence of 28 tax systems, which can be eliminated only by (at present unforthcoming) legislation'.[150]

However, for a while the Court viewed these and other hindrances as unlawful restrictions on free movement, and so applied its restrictions jurisprudence with full vigour. In an influential opinion in *ACT Group Litigation*[151] Advocate General Geelhoed distinguished between 'quasi-restrictions' (restrictions resulting inevitably from the coexistence of national tax systems), which should not be caught by Article 49 TFEU, and true restrictions, which should. In respect of the latter group, he said that because the criteria determining direct tax jurisdiction are residence- or source-based, this essentially means that 'all "truly" restrictive national direct tax measures will also, in practice, qualify as directly or indirectly discriminatory measures'. In other words, in the context of tax, true restrictions can and should be analysed (only) under the discrimination approach. Therefore, if the rule is truly non-discriminatory it will not breach the Treaty.

The Court's response to the criticisms levelled at its tax jurisprudence took two forms. First, in decisions such as *Marks & Spencer*,[152] the Court maintained its restrictions case law but developed a more nuanced, state-friendly approach to justifications and proportionality. Secondly, in cases such as *FII*[153] the Court appeared to follow the advice of Advocate General Geelhoed and moved towards the adoption of a more discrimination-based analysis.

(c) Marks & Spencer

Marks & Spencer (M&S)[154] concerned a British company which had subsidiaries in the UK and in a number of Member States. In 2001 it ceased trading in continental Europe owing to record losses in the 1990s. M&S then claimed group relief from the UK tax authorities for the losses incurred by its Belgian, German, and French subsidiaries. However, under British law, the resident companies in a group (i.e., UK-based subsidiaries) could

---

[148] S. Kingston, 'A light in the darkness: Recent developments in the ECJ's direct tax jurisprudence' (2007) 44 *CMLRev.* 1321, 1331.

[149] Case C–194/06 *Orange European Smallcap Fund* [2008] ECR I–3747, paras. 37–41. In this respect the Court's case law on double *taxation* stands in stark contrast to its approach to double *regulation* in cases such as *Cassis de Dijon* (Case 120/78 [1979] ECR 649).

[150] Kingston, n. 148, 1331.   [151] Case C–374/04 *ACT Group Litigation* [2007] ECR I–11673.

[152] Case C–446/03 *Marks & Spencer plc v. Halsey (Her Majesty's Inspector of Taxes)* [2005] ECR I–10837. This case had the potential to cost national treasuries billions if the decision went against them: A. Cordewener and I. Dörr (2006) 43 *CMLRev.* 855, with the German government alone forecasting possible losses of €30 billion if the Court had found the rules incompatible with Union law.

[153] Case C–446/04 *Test Claimants in the FII Group Litigation (No. 1) v. Commissioner of Inland Revenue* [2006] ECR I–11753.

[154] Case C–446/03 [2005] ECR I–10837.

set off their profits and losses among themselves but were not allowed do so where the losses were incurred by subsidiaries which had no establishment in the UK and did not trade there.

The Court said that the British rules on group relief breached Article 49 TFEU because they discouraged undertakings from setting up subsidiaries in other Member States[155] and so constituted a restriction on freedom of establishment.[156] To this extent it followed the advice of its Advocate General Poiares Maduro, who rejected a discrimination-based approach on the grounds that it was 'not sufficient to safeguard all the objectives comprised in the establishment of the internal market'[157] and argued in favour of applying the restriction-based approach: taxation should not be seen as distinct but should be subject to 'the same concept of restriction on freedom of establishment which is applicable to [non-tax] areas.'[158]

Yet in applying the restrictions approach, the Court appeared to confuse the distinction between the existence of a taxing jurisdiction (a matter for national law) and its exercise (a matter for Union law).[159] Following the well-recognized distinction in treatment between residents and non-residents, the UK did not tax the non-resident subsidiaries on their profits because the non-UK subsidiaries did not fall in the scope of the UK's tax jurisdiction. The corollary of this is that the UK should not have been obliged to take into account the non-UK subsidiaries' losses and so the Court should have said that the UK group relief provisions did not breach Article 49 TFEU at all.[160] However, under the restrictions approach, the Court required the UK to take the non-resident subsidiaries' losses into account,[161] thereby extending the scope of the UK's tax jurisdiction.

Having gone down the route of finding a breach of EU law the Court did, however, recognize the necessary asymmetry between the treatment of profits and losses at the justification stage. The UK offered—and the Court accepted[162]—three justifications:[163]

- protecting a balanced allocation of the power to impose taxation between the various Member States concerned, so that profits and losses are treated symmetrically in the same tax system[164]

- avoiding the risk of the double use of losses which would exist if the losses were taken into account in the Member State of the parent company (the UK) and in the Member States of the subsidiaries (Belgium, France, Germany)

- avoiding the risk of tax avoidance which would exist if the losses were not taken into account in the subsidiaries' Member States. In other words, preventing the situation that might occur within a group of companies, where losses might be transferred to the companies established in the Member States which apply the highest rates of taxation and in which the tax value of the losses is therefore the highest.[165]

This deference to Member State interest—and the implicit recognition that states need the revenue from taxation—is one of the striking and novel features of the case.

---

[155] Case C–446/03 *Marks & Spencer* [2005] ECR I–10837, para. 31.
[156] Para. 34.   [157] Para. 34.   [158] Para. 35.
[159] See Case C–385/00 *de Groot* v. *Staatssecretaris van Financiën* [2002] ECR I–11819, para. 94, which expressly recognizes this distinction.
[160] Ghosh, n. 138, 82–3.
[161] A matter the Court speedily dismissed at para. 40.   [162] Para. 51.   [163] Para. 43.
[164] See also Case C–182/08 *Glaxo Wellcome* [2009] ECR I–8591, para. 88, where the justification was upheld on the facts in the context of an Art. 63 TFEU case.
[165] The provisions are not cumulative despite suggestions to the contrary in *M&S*: Case C–414/06 *Lidl Belgium GmbH & Co. KG* v. *Finanzamt Heilbronn* [2008] ECR I–3601, para. 40.

However, while the Court generally accepted the proportionality of the UK's rules it said that the measures were not proportionate where:[166]

- the non-resident subsidiary had exhausted the possibilities available in its state of residence of having the losses taken into account in its state of residence for the accounting period concerned by the claim for relief and also for previous accounting periods and

- there was no possibility for the foreign subsidiary's losses to be taken into account in its state of residence for future periods either by the subsidiary itself or by a third party, in particular where the subsidiary has been sold to that third party.

Consequently, where the resident parent company demonstrated to the tax authorities that these conditions were fulfilled, it was contrary to freedom of establishment to prevent the parent from deducting from its taxable profits in that Member State (the UK) the losses incurred by its non-resident subsidiaries.[167] However, this exception was narrowly drawn and the *M&S* judgment by and large endorsed the legality of the UK's group relief scheme.

The facts of *Oy AA*[168] were broadly similar to those in *M&S*, albeit that this time it was the profits of a Finnish subsidiary being transferred to an out-of-state parent rather than the losses. The Court repeated its approach in *M&S* but this time found the Finnish group-relief rules proportionate, but without clearly distinguishing between *Oy AA* and *M&S*. *Oy AA* did, however, indicate the more general shift to upholding the validity of national taxation schemes.

(d) A shift to the discrimination approach

While *M&S* and *Oy AA* demonstrated a more generous construction of the justifications in favour of upholding national tax laws deemed to be a restriction on freedom of establishment, in other cases the Court appeared to reject altogether a pure restrictions approach in favour of a model more sensitive to the well-recognized distinction between residents and non-residents. This model has discrimination at its core. In the field of establishment, this change was first identified in *Innoventif*,[169] a case concerning not a tax but a charge. The Court said that a German law, making registration of a branch of a limited company established in another Member State subject to the payment of an advance on the anticipated cost of the publication of the objects of the company, was 'not liable to place companies from other Member States in a less favourable factual or legal situation than companies from the Member States of establishment'.[170] The payment of an advance therefore did not 'constitute an obstacle to the pursuit of the company's activities'.

Confirmation of a more general move towards a discrimination-based approach can be seen in two Grand Chamber decisions delivered on the same day: *FII Group Litigation (No. 1)*[171] and *ACT Group Litigation*.[172] *ACT* concerned 'outgoing' dividends, i.e., dividends paid by a UK subsidiary to a non-UK parent. Consistent with the principles of international tax law already outlined, the non-UK parent was not liable for UK tax on

---

[166] Para. 55.   [167] Para. 55.

[168] Case C–231/05 *Oy AA* [2007] ECR I–6373. See also Case C–337/08 *X Holding Bv* v. *Staatssecretaris van Franciën* [2010] ECR I–1215 and Case C–311/08 *SGI* v. *Belgium* [2010] ECR I–487.

[169] Case C–453/04 *Innoventif* [2006] ECR I–4929.   [170] Para. 39.

[171] Case C–446/04 *Test Claimants in the FII Group Litigation (No. 1)* v. *Commissioner of Inland Revenue* [2006] ECR I–11753.

[172] Case C–374/04 *Test Claimants in Class IV of the ACT Group Litigation* [2006] ECR I–11673. The discussion that follows draws extensively on Kingston, n. 148.

the dividends but nor was it entitled to a UK tax credit on those dividends. By contrast, UK parents receiving 'upstream' dividends from UK subsidiaries would have received a tax credit for the ACT paid by the UK subsidiary.

FII (No. 1) concerned the reverse situation—'incoming' dividends payable by a non-UK subsidiary to a UK parent. As Kingston succinctly puts it, in *FII (No. 1)* the UK parent company was liable to UK corporation tax on the incoming dividends. It was granted tax relief for any foreign tax which the non-UK subsidiary had paid on the dividends abroad but was not otherwise entitled to a UK tax credit on them. By contrast, a UK parent receiving dividends from a UK subsidiary would not be liable to corporation tax on the dividends and would have received a tax credit for the ACT which the UK subsidiary had paid. In both *ACT* and *FII (No. 1)* the claimants argued that the UK rules breached Article 49 TFEU.

In *ACT* the Court found that the UK rules were compatible with Article 49 TFEU. The Court said that the situation of a UK parent and a non-UK parent was not comparable because the non-UK parent was not subject to the tax charge while the UK parent was subject to the charge.[173] Therefore, the UK rules did 'not constitute discrimination prohibited by Article [49 TFEU]'.[174] By contrast, in *FII (No. 1)*, the Court found that the rules did breach Article 49 TFEU because they were discriminatory. As the Court put it:[175]

> Article [49 TFEU] precludes a national measure which allows a resident company which has received dividends from another resident company to deduct the amount of ACT paid by the latter company from the amount of ACT for which the former company is liable, whereas a resident company which has received dividends from a non-resident company is not entitled to make such a deduction in respect of the corporation tax which the last-mentioned company is obliged to pay in the State in which it is resident.

Putting it another way, because the UK had chosen to exercise tax jurisdiction over a resident parent company with or without a resident subsidiary, the discrimination arose because in one case (where the subsidiary was resident) a tax credit was given, in the other case (where the subsidiary was non-resident) it was not.[176] The Court concluded:

> Such a difference in treatment has the effect of discouraging United Kingdom-resident companies from investing their capital in a company established in another Member State and also has a restrictive effect as regards companies established in other Member States in that it constitutes an obstacle on their part to the raising of capital in the United Kingdom.[177]

A parent company which has been obliged to pay tax unlawfully can bring an action for repayment of that unlawfully levied tax.[178]

---

[173] Case C–374/04 *ACT Group Litigation* [2006] ECR I–11673, para. 58. For a further example, see Case C–282/07 *Etat belge—SPF Finances* v. *Truck Center SA* [2008] ECR I–10767, para. 49.

[174] Para. 72.

[175] Para. 94. For a further example of discrimination between nationally sourced dividends and foreign sourced dividends, this time in the method used for calculating the tax, see Case C–35/11 *Test Claimants in the FII Group Litigation (No. 2)* EU:C:2012:707, para. 65.

[176] See also Case C–418/07 *Société Papillon* v. *Ministère du Budget, des comptes publics et de law function publique* [2008] ECR I–8947.

[177] Para. 97. For further examples of cases involving the taxation of residents where the Court requires foreign and domestically sourced income to be treated equally, see Case C–347/04 *Rewe Zentralfinanz eG* v. *Finanzamt Köln-Mitte* [2007] ECR I–2647; Case C–201/05 *Test Claimants in the CFC and Dividend Group Litigation* v. *Commissioners of Inland Revenue* [2008] ECR I–2875, Order of 23 Apr. 2008, para. 42.

[178] Case C–35/11 *Test Claimants in the FII Group Litigation (No. 2)* EU:C:2012:707, para. 87.

Subsequently, in *FII (No. 2)*[179] the Court expressly confirmed the discrimination approach and clearly stated the principle of fiscal autonomy:

> It should be noted in this regard that, since European Union law, as it currently stands, does not lay down any general criteria for the attribution of areas of competence between the Member States in relation to the elimination of double taxation within the European Union ..., each Member State remains free to organise its system for taxing distributed profits, provided, however, that the system in question does not entail discrimination prohibited by the FEU Treaty.

(e) Prevention of abuse of law: Wholly artificial arrangements

We have already examined a number of justifications which, following *M&S*, have been successfully raised by states to save their tax regimes. One justification which has started to assume considerable significance in the field of taxation[180] in recent years is prevention of abuse of law. This can be seen in *Cadbury Schweppes*.[181]

In order to try to prevent companies setting up subsidiaries in states with more favourable tax regimes, the UK introduced the controlled foreign company (CFC) rules. Consistent with the principle of territoriality, UK parent companies were not taxed on non-resident subsidiaries' profits. However, there was an exception to this rule concerning CFCs, i.e., non-resident subsidiary companies in which a UK parent owned a holding of more than 50 per cent. The profits of the CFC were subjected to tax in the UK when the corporation tax in the country of the subsidiary's residence was less than three-quarters of the rate applicable in the UK. The resident parent did receive a tax credit for the tax paid by the CFC but the system was designed to make the resident company pay the difference between the tax paid in the foreign country and the tax which would have been paid had the company been resident in the UK. Unless their situation fell within one of a number of exceptions to the legislation, parent companies wishing to avoid the CFC regime had to show that neither the main purpose of the transactions which gave rise to the profits of the CFC nor the main reason for the CFC's existence was to achieve a reduction in UK tax by means of the diversion of profits (the so-called motive test).

The UK applied its CFC rules to Cadbury Schweppes, which had established a subsidiary in Ireland where the tax rate was 10 per cent. It therefore charged Cadbury Schweppes corporation tax of nearly £9 million. Cadbury's challenged this decision as being incompatible with Article 49 TFEU. Reiterating the principles established in *Centros*,[182] the Court said the fact that a company was established in a Member State for the purpose of benefiting from more favourable legislation did not in itself suffice to constitute an abuse of the freedom of establishment.[183] It therefore said that because the CFC legislation involved a difference in the treatment of resident companies on the basis of the level of taxation imposed on the company in which they had a controlling holding, it constituted a restriction on freedom of establishment.[184]

---

[179] Para. 40.

[180] See also Commission Communication, 'The application of anti-abuse measures in the area of direct taxation—within the EU and in relation to third countries', COM(2007) 785.

[181] Case C–196/04 *Cadbury Schweppes* v. *Commissioners of the Inland Revenue* [2006] ECR I–7995. For the EFTA Court's decision on Norwegian CFC rules, see Joined Cases E–3 and 20/13 *Olsen* v. *Norwegian State* [2014] EFTA Ct. Rep. 400.

[182] Case C–212/97 [1999] ECR I–1459.   [183] Para. 37.

[184] Para. 46. See also Case C–471/04 *Finanzamt Offenbach am Main-Land* v. *Keller Holding GmbH* [2006] ECR I–2107.

On justification the Court said that the national measure restricting freedom of establishment could be justified on the ground of preventing abusive practices, i.e., 'the specific objective of such a restriction must be to prevent conduct involving the creation of *wholly* artificial arrangements which do not reflect economic reality, with a view to escaping the tax normally due on the profits generated by activities carried out on national territory'.[185] The question was whether the rules were disproportionate. Relying on its seminal decisions on abuse in *Emsland-Stärke*[186] and *Halifax*,[187] the Court continued:[188]

> In order to find that there is such an [artificial] arrangement there must be, in addition to a subjective element consisting in the intention to obtain a tax advantage, objective circumstances showing that, despite formal observance of the conditions laid down by Union law, the objective pursued by freedom of establishment ... has not been achieved.

In other words, to be compatible with the Treaty, the tax legislation had to give parent companies the opportunity of showing that, despite the existence of tax motives, the incorporation of a CFC reflected economic reality, i.e., that there was an actual establishment intended to carry on genuine economic activities in the host Member State. This finding had to be based on 'objective factors which were ascertainable by third parties with regard, in particular, to the extent to which the CFC physically exists in terms of premises, staff and equipment' and not as a 'letter box' or 'front' subsidiary.[189]

Despite the cautious terms in which the abuse doctrine is drafted, some, including Advocate General Poiares Maduro in *Cartesio*,[190] think that the Court's ruling allowing Member States to be 'wary' of 'letter box' companies 'represents a significant qualification of the rulings in *Centros* and *Inspire Art*'. Nevertheless, the Court continued its *Cadbury Schweppes* approach in the *Thin Cap* case.[191] This concerned a UK law targeting the practice of thin capitalization (whereby a group of companies seeks to reduce the taxation of profits made by one of its subsidiaries by electing to fund that subsidiary by way of loan—rather than equity—capital, thereby allowing that subsidiary to transfer profits to a parent company in the form of interest which is deductible in the calculation of its taxable profits, and not in the form of (non-deductible) dividends). Where the parent company is resident in a state in which the rate of tax is lower than that which applies in the state in which its subsidiary is resident, the tax liability may thus be transferred to a state which has a lower tax rate. By providing that the interest was to be treated as a distribution, the UK legislation was able to prevent practices the sole purpose of which was to avoid the tax that would normally be payable on profits generated by activities undertaken in its territory.[192]

Once again, the question was whether the UK rules were disproportionate. The Court said they were, unless two conditions were satisfied. First, the legislation had to provide for a consideration of objective and verifiable elements which made it possible to identify the existence of a purely artificial arrangement, entered into for tax reasons alone, and allowed taxpayers to produce, if appropriate and without being subject to undue administrative constraints, evidence as to the commercial justification for the transaction in

---

[185] Case C–196/04 *Cadbury Schweppes* [2006] ECR I–7995, para. 55, emphasis added.
[186] Case C–110/99 *Emsland-Stärke* [2000] ECR I–11569, paras. 52–3.
[187] Case C–255/02 *Halifax* [2006] ECR I–1609, paras. 74–5.   [188] Para. 64.
[189] Paras. 65–8.   [190] Case C–210/06 [2008] ECR I–9641, para. 29.
[191] Case C–524/04 *Test Claimants in the Thin Cap Group Litigation* v. *Commissioners of Inland Revenue* [2007] ECR I–2107.
[192] Paras. 76–7.

question. Secondly, if it was established that such an arrangement existed, that legislation had to treat that interest as a distribution only insofar as it exceeded what would have been agreed upon at arm's length.

More generally, the Court has made clear that national legislation cannot operate a 'general presumption of abusive practices'[193] and that it is usually more proportionate for a state to rely on Directive 2011/16/EU on administrative cooperation in the field of tax to obtain from the competent authorities of another Member State[194] any information which is necessary to enable it to effect a correct assessment of the taxes covered by the directive.[195]

(f) Remedies

If the Court finds that the national taxation is discriminatory or constitutes an obstacle to the freedom of establishment, then the applicants need to have an effective remedy. The Court emphasized this point in *Metallgesellschaft*[196] concerning a British rule permitting subsidiaries resident in the UK to pay dividends to their parent company without having to pay advance corporation tax (ACT) on condition that the parent company was also resident in the UK. The subsidiaries still had to pay mainstream corporation tax (MCT) but they did this at the end of a particular period. However, if the parent company had its seat in another Member State the subsidiaries had to pay the ACT up front, although it could subsequently be set off against any liability to MCT. Subsidiaries with a parent company resident in the UK therefore had a cashflow advantage over those where the parent was not resident in the UK. The Court said that this rule constituted an unjustifiable breach of Article 49 TFEU.

It then considered whether subsidiaries with a parent not resident in the UK could claim for the payment of interest covering the loss of the use of the sums paid by way of the ACT. It said:

> In such circumstances, where the breach of [Union] law arises, not from the payment of the tax itself but from its being levied prematurely, the award of interest represents the 'reimbursement' of that which was improperly paid and would appear to be essential in restoring the equal treatment guaranteed by Article [49 TFEU].[197]

Following *Factortame I*, the Court dismissed the argument that under English law a claim in *restitution* might not be available. That rule had to be set aside because such a claim was essential to rectify the breach of Article 49 TFEU.[198] However, the 'ancillary questions' relating to such a claim, such as the payment of interest, including the rate of interest and the date from which it must be calculated[199] were a matter for the Member States.

The Court then considered the situation if the claimants' claims were treated as claims for *compensation* for damage caused by breach of Union law. It said that breach of Article 49 TFEU entitled the taxpayer to payment of damages in a sum equal to the interest accrued on the tax which they had paid from the date of premature payment until the date on which it properly fell due. Citing *Factortame III*, the Court said that where national

---

[193] Case C–105/07 *NV Lammers & Van Cleeff* [2008] ECR I–173, para. 27.

[194] OJ [2011] L64/1. This obligation does not apply to information from third countries: Case C–446/04 *FII (No. 1)* [2006] ECR I–11753, para. 170.

[195] Case C–451/05 *ELISA* v. *Directeur général des impôts* [2007] ECR I–8251, para. 92. For an equivalent case in the field of services, see Case C–433/04 *Commission* v. *Belgium (tax fraud)* [2006] ECR I–10653, paras. 39–40. However, the same will not be true where third countries are involved: Case C–101/05 *Skatteverket* v. *A* [2007] ECR I–11531, paras. 61–3.

[196] Joined Cases C–397 and 410/98 *Metallgesellschaft Ltd and Hoechst* v. *Commissioners of Inland Revenue* [2001] ECR I–1727.

[197] Para. 87.   [198] Paras. 88–9.   [199] Case C–470/04 *N* [2006] ECR I–7409.

law excluded loss of profit as a head of damage this breached Union law because it made reparation of damage practically impossible—especially in the context of economic or commercial litigation.[200]

The key criteria for state liability claims is, as we saw in Case study 11.1, that the damage has to be sufficiently serious. In *FII*[201] the Court suggested that given the rapid evolution of the Court's case law in the field of taxation it was unlikely that any breach could be considered sufficiently serious[202] and so Member States would not be liable. For this reason, claimants prefer to argue that their remedy should be in restitution, not state liability, although the Court has refused to be drawn on this debate: 'it is not for the Court to assign a legal classification to the actions brought before the national court by the claimants in the main proceedings.'

Finally, *Thin Cap*[203] placed an additional hurdle in the way of claimants: 'the national court may, in order to establish the recoverable losses, determine whether the injured parties have shown reasonable diligence in order to avoid those losses or to limit their extent and whether, in particular, they availed themselves in time of all legal remedies available to them'.

Box 1: SUMMARY OF THE PRINCIPLES FROM THE TAX CASES

Read together, the tax cases are authority for the following propositions:[204]

- *Basic rule*: different treatment of resident and non-resident taxpayers is compatible with Union law (*Futura Participations*). If, however, the situations of the two are deemed comparable (e.g., where the non-resident earns 90 per cent or more of their income in the source state[205]), the source state must take their personal and family circumstances into account (*Schumacker*).

- *Residents and incoming income*: in the case of *resident* taxpayers, home-state legislation which treats income or related losses coming from, for example, subsidiaries in another Member State differently and usually less favourably than those coming from the home state breach Articles 49 and 54 TFEU unless justified (*M&S, FII*).[206] However, where the non-resident subsidiary has the possibility of having its losses taken into account in its state of residence, then these can be ignored by the parent's home state (*M&S*). Where there is no difference in treatment the national legislation is lawful.[207]

- *Residents and outgoing income*: in the case of *resident* taxpayers, home-state legislation which treats income going to another Member State differently and usually less favourably than if the income had stayed in the home state breaches Articles 49 and 54 TFEU unless justified (*De Lasteyrie du Saillant*).

- *Non-residents and expenditure*: while the source state is not generally obliged to treat non-residents in the same way as residents (unless non-residents receive 90 per cent of their

---

[200] Joined Cases C–397 and 410/98 *Metallgesellschaft* [2001] ECR I–1727, para. 91.
[201] Case C–446/04 *FII (No. 1)* [2006] ECR I–11753, para. 215.   [202] Para. 201.
[203] Case C–524/04 *Thin Cap Group Litigation* [2007] ECR I–2107, para. 124.
[204] This analysis develops some of the ideas in Kingston, see n. 148, 1331–4.
[205] E.g., Case C–279/93 *Schumacker* [1995] ECR I–225.
[206] Case C–105/07 *NV Lammers & Van Cleeff* [2008] ECR I–173, paras. 20–4. In the field of free movement of capital, see, e.g., Case C–35/98 *Staatssecretaris van Financiën* v. *Verkooijen* [2000] ECR I–40711; Case C–319/02 *Manninen* [2004] ECR I–7477.
[207] Case C–298/05 *Columbus Container Services BVBA & Co.* v. *Finanzamt Bielefeld-Innenstadt* [2007] ECR I–10451, para. 40.

income in the host state[208]), the source state must allow the non-resident to deduct business expenses (e.g., tax advice[209]) which have a 'direct economic connection' to the income received from the business activity in the source state[210] and the same tax rate should be applied.[211]

- *Non-residents and outgoing resources*: while in the earlier cases differential treatment by the home state of money payable by a subsidiary to a non-resident parent than to a resident parent constituted a restriction on freedom of establishment,[212] the more recent case law considers the situation of the resident and non-resident parent as not being comparable and so the matter falls outside Article 49 TFEU (*ACT*).

C. FREEDOM TO PROVIDE AND RECEIVE SERVICES

As we saw in Chapter 9, Articles 56–7 TFEU allow natural and legal persons to provide or receive services in another Member State in return for remuneration. In this section we shall consider the specific issues which have arisen in respect of legal persons wishing to provide services temporarily in another Member State.

1. THE RIGHTS CONFERRED ON SERVICE PROVIDERS AND RECEIVERS

1.1 The Rights of Access to the Host State's Market on Equal Terms with Nationals

Service providers from other Member States enjoy equal treatment with nationals both in respect of initial access to the host state's market and also once they are on that market. So, as before, the principle of equal treatment means no direct or indirect discrimination on the grounds of nationality/origin. *FDC* provides an example of direct discrimination.[213] Under Spanish law, film distributors would be granted a licence to dub foreign (mainly US) films on condition that they also distributed a Spanish film at the same time. The Court said that this rule breached Article 56 TFEU because it gave preferential treatment to the producers of Spanish films over producers established in other Member States, since only Spanish producers had a guarantee that their films would be distributed. The Spanish government tried to justify the rule for reasons of cultural policy, but this was rejected by the Court on the ground that cultural policy was not one of the exhaustive list of derogations in Article 52 TFEU.

Direct discrimination also covers less favourable treatment on the basis of establishment (see fig. 9.2). This was confirmed by the Court in *Svensson and Gustafsson*,[214] which

---

[208] Case C–346/04 *Conijn* v. *Finanzamt Hamburg-Nord* [2006] ECR I–6137, para. 18.
[209] Case C–346/04 *Conijn* [2006] ECR I–6137, para. 21.
[210] Case C–345/04 *Centro Equestre da Lezíria Grande* v. *Bundesamt für Finanzen* [2007] ECR I–1425, para. 38. See also Case C–290/04 *FKP Scorpio* [2006] ECR I–9461, para. 49.
[211] This principle is derived from the recent movement of services case, Case C–234/01 *Gerritse* v. *Finanzamt Neukölln-Nord* [2003] ECR I–5933, paras. 53–4.
[212] Case C–324/00 *Lankhorst-Hohorst GmbH* v. *Finanzamt Steinfurt* [2002] ECR I–11779, para. 32. See also Case C–168/01 *Bosal Holding* [2003] ECR I–9409, para. 27: 'a parent company *might be* dissuaded from carrying on its activities' through a subsidiary established in another state (emphasis added).
[213] Case C–17/92 *Federación de Distribuidores Cinematográficos* v. *Estado Español et Unión de Productores de Cine y Televisión* [1993] ECR I–2239, para. 15. See also Joined Cases C–447 and 448/08 *Sjöberg* [2010] ECR I–6921 (stricter penalties for promotion of gambling organized in another Member State than on the national territory).
[214] Case C–484/93 *Svensson and Gustafsson* [1995] ECR I–3955.

concerned Swedish nationals resident in Luxembourg (at a time when Sweden was not yet an EU member) who were refused an interest rate subsidy on a building loan because they had borrowed the money from a (Belgian) institution which did not satisfy the requirement of being established in Luxembourg. The Court said:

> the rule in question entails *discrimination based on the place of establishment*. Such discrimination can only be justified on the general interest grounds referred to in Article [52 TFEU], to which Article [62 TFEU] refers, and which do not include economic aims.

Commission v. *Germany (insurance cases)*[215] provides a good example of an indistinctly applicable rule. The Court found that German rules requiring insurance companies wishing to provide insurance in Germany to be both established and authorized in Germany breached Articles 56–7 TFEU because the rules increased costs for those providing services in Germany, especially when the insurer conducted business there only occasionally.[216] These requirements therefore constituted 'the very negation of the fundamental freedom to provide services'.[217] On the question of justification,[218] the Court noted the sensitivity of the insurance sector,[219] given the number of policyholders affected, the difficulty facing anyone taking out insurance to judge the financial viability of an insurance company, and the fact that insurance was based on future and often unpredictable events.[220] For these reasons the Court considered that the German restrictions on the freedom to provide services could be justified on the ground of consumer protection and that those interests were not adequately protected in the state of establishment. However, while it found that the authorization requirement was proportionate, it said the residence requirement was not.

As we have seen elsewhere, the Court swiftly moved beyond a pure equal treatment model towards a model based on removing non-discriminatory restrictions to market access. One of the earliest cases which showed this shift was *Alpine Investments*.[221] It will be recalled from Chapter 9 that the case concerned a Dutch rule prohibiting cold-calling by the Dutch financial services industry both within and outside the Netherlands. It was argued that since this rule was non-discriminatory, EU law would not apply, following the principles laid down in *Keck*.[222] The Court disagreed: it said the Dutch rule breached Article 56 TFEU since although non-discriminatory,[223] it 'directly affects access to the markets in services in the other Member States and is thus capable of hindering intra-Union trade in services'.[224]

1.2 The Right of Access to the Host State's Market Without Restrictions

In fact, the change towards the restrictions approach had already been signalled in the earlier case of *Säger*,[225] where the Court said that Article 56 TFEU required:

> *not only* the elimination of all discrimination against a person providing services on the ground of his nationality *but also* the abolition of any *restriction*, even if it applies

---

[215] Case 205/84 *Commission* v. *Germany (the insurance cases)* [1986] ECR 3755.   [216] Para. 28.
[217] Para. 19. See also Case C–279/02 *Commission* v. *Italy (temp agencies)* [2002] ECR I–1425, para. 18.
[218] Para. 27. See further Commission Interpretative Communication, 'Freedom to Provide Services and the General Good in the Insurance Sector', C(1999) 5046.
[219] Case 205/84 *Commission* v. *Germany (insurance cases)* [1986] ECR 3755, now Dir. 2009/138/EC on the taking-up and pursuit of the business of Insurance and Re-insurance ([2009] OJ L335/1): Case C–191/99 *Kvaerner* v. *Staatssecretaris van Financiën* [2001] ECR I–4447, para. 38.
[220] Paras. 30–1.   [221] Case C–384/93 *Alpine Investments* [1995] ECR I–1141.
[222] Joined Cases C–267 and 268/91 *Keck and Mithouard* [1993] ECR 1–6097.   [223] Para. 35.
[224] Para. 38.   [225] Case C–76/90 *Säger* [1991] ECR I–4221, para 12, emphasis added.

without distinction to national providers of services and to those of other Member States, when *it is liable to prohibit or otherwise impede* the activities of a provider of services established in another Member State where he lawfully provides similar services.

We turn now to consider some examples of national rules which have been considered to constitute restrictions on free movement.

(a) Examples of restrictions

The Court has considered a wide variety of national rules to be restrictions on freedom to provide services. For example, it has said that authorization requirements of, for example, private security firms, detective agencies, and their managers were restrictions contrary to Article 56 TFEU.[226] Where the authorization or licensing requirements are subject to a territorial limitation, the Court is particularly suspicious,[227] especially when used to prevent an 'excessive number of foreign undertakings from establishing themselves' in that area.[228]

Translation requirements are also restrictions due to the 'additional expense and the administrative and financial burden for undertakings established in another Member State'.[229] An obligation to swear an oath of allegiance to the state where the service is provided is an 'impediment to' the pursuit of an out-of-state operator's activities in the host state which 'impairs its access to the market',[230] as are conditions relating to maximum/minimum staffing levels,[231] and obligations to lodge guarantees with the relevant authorities.[232] Legislation defining the conditions of access to the activity of professional assistance in tax matters, which did not take into account qualifications of the company and the natural person providing the services, constituted a restriction on the freedom to provide services by a tax consultancy company.[233] Similarly, legislation setting compulsory minimum fees, or at least permitting control by the relevant authorities of the fees charged, have also been considered restrictions on freedom to provide services.[234]

Broadcasting restrictions can also breach Article 56 TFEU. This can be seen in the complex case of *Murphy*.[235] England's Football Association Premier League (FAPL) granted exclusive licences to the highest bidder (BSkyB in the UK) in respect of broadcasting rights for live transmission of Premiership games on a territorial basis and for three-year terms. Successful bidders each undertook to prevent the public from receiving their broadcasts outside the area for which they held a licence, in particular by encrypting the broadcasts and ensuring that decoding devices were not sold for use outside the territory for which they held a licence. Given the high prices that BSkyB charged for the commercial showing of Premiership matches in the UK, a number of pubs and restaurants, including one run

---

[226] Case C–189/03 *Commission v. Netherlands (private security firms)* [2004] ECR I–9289, para. 17. See also Case C–43/93 *Vander Elst* [1994] ECR I–3803, para. 15; Case C–451/99 *Cura Anlagen GmbH v. Auto Service Leasing GmbH (ASL)* [2002] ECR I–3193, para. 37; Case C–205/99 *Analir v. Administración General del Estado* [2001] ECR I–1271, para. 22; Case C–410/96 *Criminal Proceedings against André Ambry* [1998] ECR I–7875, para. 30; Case C–288/02 *Commission v. Greece* [2004] ECR I–10071, para. 30.

[227] Case C–134/05 *Commission v. Italy (extra-judicial debt recovery)* [2007] ECR I–6251, para. 64; Case C–465/05 *Commission v. Italy (private security activities)* [2007] ECR I–11091, para. 58.

[228] Case C–465/05 *Commission v. Italy (private security activities)* [2007] ECR I–11091, para. 78.

[229] Case C–490/04 *Commission v. Germany (posted workers)* [2007] ECR I–6095, para. 69.

[230] Case C–465/05 *Commission v. Italy (private security activities)* [2007] ECR I–11091, para. 46.

[231] Case C–465/05 *Commission v. Italy (private security activities)* [2007] ECR I–11091, para. 105.

[232] Case C–465/05 *Commission v. Italy (private security activities)* [2007] ECR I–11091, para. 109.

[233] Case C–342/14 *X-Steurberatungsgesellschaft v. Finanzamt Hannover-Nord* EU:C:2015:827.

[234] Case C–465/05 *Commission v. Italy (private security activities)* [2007] ECR I–11091, para. 127.

[235] Joined Cases C–403 and 429/08 *Murphy* [2011] ECR I–9083.

by Mrs Murphy, began to use foreign decoding devices to access satellite broadcasts of the Premiership games from another Member State, particularly Greece, despite the territorial condition imposed on the use of those decoders.

The Court found that UK law which gave legal protection to the territorial restriction clauses in the contracts between the broadcasters and the FAPL and between the broadcasters and their customers was a restriction on free movement of services. The Court said that while the protection of intellectual property rights was a potential justification, FAPL could not claim copyright in the Premiership matches themselves as they could not be classified as 'works' requiring intellectual creation. However, given the special nature of sport, the Court recognized that Member States could protect sporting events, where appropriate, by virtue of protection of intellectual property by putting in place specific legislation, or protecting agreements between the right holders and the broadcasters, and this would be a justifiable limit on the freedom to provide services. However, in conducting its proportionality review, the Court said that the Member State could only protect the 'specific subject matter' of the right, i.e., the 'right to exploit commercially the marketing or making available of the protected subject matter, by the grant of licences in return for payment of remuneration'. This did not, however, guarantee the right holders 'the opportunity to demand the highest possible remuneration'; the remuneration could only be 'reasonable in relation to the economic value of the service provided'. This was not the case on the facts. The premium paid to FAPL guaranteed absolute territorial exclusivity resulting in artificial price differences between the partitioned national markets: 'Such partitioning and such an artificial price difference to which it gives rise are irreconcilable with the fundamental aim of the Treaty, which is completion of the internal market.'

Finally, advertising restrictions also breach Article 56 TFEU. So, in *Gourmet*[236] the Court said that a prohibition on advertising had a particular effect on the cross-border supply of advertising, given the international nature of the advertising market. It therefore constituted a restriction on the freedom to provide services. Similarly, in *Bacardi*[237] the Court found the French 'loi Evin' prohibiting direct and indirect television advertising of certain alcoholic drinks breached Article 56 TFEU because (1) the owners of the advertising hoardings had to refuse any advertising for alcoholic beverages if the sporting event was likely to be retransmitted in France; (2) the French rules impeded the provision of broadcasting services for television programmes because French broadcasters had to refuse all retransmission of sporting events in which hoardings bearing advertising for alcoholic beverages marketed in France might be visible; and (3) the organizers of sporting events taking place outside France could not sell the retransmission rights to French broadcasters if the transmission of the television programmes of such events was likely to contain indirect television advertising for those alcoholic beverages. The Court said that such restrictions could, however, be justified on the grounds of public health and that the steps taken were proportionate.[238]

Restrictions on advertising of gambling have proved particularly sensitive. In *HIT hoteli*[239] the Court said that a ban on advertising, in State B, of gambling lawfully provided in State A was a restriction on free movement of services but could be justified.

---

[236] Case C–405/98 [2001] ECR I–1795, para. 39. See also now the effect of the UCPD 2005/29 ([2005] OJ L149/22), considered in Ch. 5.

[237] Case C–429/02 *Bacardi* v. *Télévision Française 1 SA* [2004] ECR I–6613. See also Case C–262/02 *Commission* v. *France* [2004] ECR I–6569.

[238] Paras. 37–41.

[239] Case C–176/11 *HIT hoteli* v. *Bundesministerium für Finanzen* EU:C:2012:454, para. 17.

(b) Gambling cases

Gambling has long been subject to detailed regulation in all Member States, given the social and public-policy risks associated with it and the revenue opportunities it creates for operators and the state alike. Unsurprisingly the Court has found these national rules to be restrictions on freedom to provide services and/or establishment. Some of the rules relate to limiting the locations where gambling can occur. For example, in *Anomar*[240] the Court said that Portuguese rules restricting the right to operate games of chance or gambling solely to casinos in permanent or temporary gaming areas breached Article 56 TFEU, as did a Greek prohibition on the installation of computer games in venues other than casinos in *Commission* v. *Greece*.[241] Other states confine those entitled to run gambling activities to public and private monopolies. The Court has said such rules breach Article 56 TFEU,[242] as do rules confining off-course betting to a single company which was closely controlled by the state.[243] In other states the providers of gambling services must be licensed (and the national rules specify the circumstances in which the licence is to be withdrawn). These rules also constitute restrictions.[244] In *Placanica*[245] the Court said that an Italian rule prohibiting—on pain of criminal penalties—the pursuit of activities in the betting or gaming sector without a licence or police authorization constituted a restriction on the freedom to provide services, as did a rule prohibiting Italian intermediaries from facilitating the provision of betting services on behalf of a British supplier.[246] The effect of a number of these national rules has been to prohibit Internet gambling and, unsurprisingly, the Court has found that these rules constitute a restriction on freedom to provide services.[247] Finally, in *Berlington Hungary*[248] the Court suggested that a fivefold increase in the flat rate tax to be paid in slot machines to be operated in amusement arcades could be a restriction on free movement of services.

In nearly all of the cases discussed, the Court found the rules to be justified on various of the grounds first laid down in *Schindler*,[249] namely preventing gambling and avoiding the lottery from becoming the source of private profit; avoiding the risk of crime or fraud; and avoiding the risk of incitement to spend, with damaging individual and social consequences. The real balancing was done through the proportionality review.

In *Schindler* (discussed in Chapter 9) the Court did not consider proportionality at all when upholding the national rule banning lotteries. This approach did not last. In *Läärä*[250] the Court did examine proportionality but its approach was remarkably

---

[240] Case C–6/01 *Anomar* v. *Estado português* [2003] ECR I–8621, para. 66.

[241] Case C–65/05 *Commission* v. *Greece* [2006] ECR I–10341, para. 56.

[242] Case C–46/08 *Carmen Media Group* v. *Land Schleswig-Holstein* [2010] ECR I–8149 and Case C–258/08 *Ladbrokes Betting & Gaming* v. *Stichting de Nationale Sporttotalisator* [2010] ECR I–4757, respectively.

[243] Case C–212/08 *Zerturf Ltd* v. *Premier Ministre* [2011] ECR I–5633. Rules prescribing the legal form and amount of share capital or the holder of a company may also constitute restrictions: Case C–347/09 *Dickinger* [2011] ECR I–8185; Case C–64/08 *Engelmann* [2011] ECR I–8219.

[244] Case C–463/13 *Stanley International Betting Ltd* v. *Ministero dell'Economia e delle Finanze* EU:C:2015:25, para. 46. See further 'Green Paper on on-line gambling in the Internal Market', COM(2011) 128.

[245] Joined Cases C–338, 359 and 360/04 *Placanica* [2007] ECR I–1891, paras. 42 and 44. See also Case C–433/04 *Commission* v. *Belgium (tax fraud)* [2006] ECR I–10653, para. 32.

[246] See also Joined Cases C–316 and 358–360/07 *Stoß* v. *Wetteraukreis* [2010] ECR I–8069.

[247] Case C–46/08 *Carmen Media Group* [2010] ECR I–8149; Case C–212/08 *Zerturf* [2011] ECR I–5633. See further the Commission's 'Green Paper on on-line gambling in the Internal Market', COM(2011) 128.

[248] Case C–98/14 *Berlington Hungary* v. *Hungarian State* EU:C:2015:386, para. 42.

[249] Case C–275/92 [1994] ECR I–1039.

[250] Case C–124/97 [1999] ECR I–6067. See also Case C–6/01 *Anomar* v. *Estado português* [2003] ECR I–8621.

hands-off.[251] The case concerned a Finnish law granting exclusive rights to run the operation of slot machines to a public body, with the revenue raised going into the public purse. This rule had the effect of preventing a British company from operating its slot machines in Finland. The Court said that while such legislation constituted an impediment to freedom to provide services because it directly or indirectly prevented operators in other Member States from making slot machines available to the public,[252] it could be justified on the grounds laid down in *Schindler*,[253] and the steps taken were proportionate.[254] The Court said that it was for the Member States to decide whether to prohibit the operation of such machines or only to restrict their use.[255]

This judicial deference towards the Member States may partly be explained by the fact that, in these cases involving an activity which is legal in one state but illegal in another, the Court is wary of imposing the values of the majority of the states (where lotteries are lawful, albeit highly regulated) on the minority (where lotteries are unlawful).[256] In this respect, the Court's approach stands in stark contrast to the majoritarian approach detected by Poiares Maduro in respect of product requirements under Article 34 TFEU.[257] However, the Court has increasingly insisted that Member States be consistent in their policy. So, where a Member State justifies the restriction on free movement by reference to the need to prevent incitement to squander money on gambling and to combat gambling addiction, while at the same time encouraging the development of other games of chance which pose higher risks of addiction with a view to maximizing revenue, the Court has said that the national court may legitimately conclude that the restriction is not suitable for attaining the objective in 'a consistent and systematic manner'.[258] Further, in *Berlington Hungary*[259] the Court said that any state policy, especially if it is a new policy, must meet the requirements of legal certainty and the protection of legitimate expectations, which might include giving existing traders time to adapt to the new situation.[260]

Another explanation why the Court tends to be more deferential to the Member States in respect of national regimes regulating gambling is that these cases concern the situation of a service which moves but the provider and recipient do not.[261] In these cases traditional frontier controls imposed on migrants to protect the interests of the state do not function, and for this reason the Court may be more willing to allow Member States greater scope to protect their own interests. Only if the value judgments of the Member State appear manifestly unfounded will the national rule breach EU law.[262] This might

---

[251] See also Case C–36/02 *Omega* [2004] ECR I–9609, discussed in Ch. 12 and Joined Cases C–94 and 202/04 *Cipolla v. Fazari* [2006] ECR I–2049; Case C–250/06 *United Pan Europe Communications v. Belgium* [2007] ECR I–11135.

[252] Para. 29.   [253] Para. 33.

[254] Para. 42. See also Case C–42/07 *Liga Portuguesa de Futebol Profissional (CA/LPFP) v. Departamento de Jogos da Santa Casa da Misericórdia de Lisboa* [2009] ECR I–7633, where the Court found the Portuguese ban on operators established in other Member States from offering gambling over the Internet was also proportionate to the objective of the fight against crime.

[255] Fundamental rights also apply but the Court will not consider the application of Arts. 15–17 of the Charter separately from the claims made under Art. 56 TFEU: Case C–390/12 *Pfleger* EU:C:2014:281.

[256] See, e.g., Case C–275/92 *Schindler* [1994] ECR I–1039, para. 32.

[257] M. Poiares Maduro, *We the Court: The European Court of Justice and the European economic constitution* (Oxford: Hart Publishing, 1998), 68, 72ff., citing cases such as Case 178/84 *Commission v. Germany (beer purity)* [1987] ECR 1227 and Case 407/85 *3 Glocken* [1988] ECR 4233, considered in Ch. 6.

[258] Case C–46/08 *Carmen* [2010] ECR I–8149, para. 71; Joined Cases C–186 and 209/11 *Stanley Bet Ypourgos Oikonomias kai Oikonomikon* EU:C:2013:550. However, controlled expansion may be consistent: Case C–212/08 *Zerturf* [2011] ECR I–5633.

[259] Case C–98/14 *Berlington Hungary v. Hungarian State* EU:C:2015:386, para. 92.

[260] Para. 87.   [261] See also Case C–384/93 *Alpine Investments* [1995] ECR I–1141.

[262] See G. Straetmans (2000) 37 *CMLRev.* 991, 1001.

help to explain why, in *Gambelli*,[263] the Court indicated that an Italian law imposing criminal penalties, including imprisonment, on private individuals in Italy who collaborated over the web with a British bookmaker to collect bets—an activity normally reserved to the Italian state monopoly CONI—was disproportionate; although the Court said it was ultimately for the national court to decide bearing in mind that betting was encouraged in the context of games organized by licensed *national* bodies[264] and that the British supplier was already regulated in the UK.[265]

In other cases the Court looks at the coherence of the outcome and the means. For example, in *Lindman*[266] the Court found that a Finnish law, which taxed lottery wins when the lottery took place in another Member State but not when they occurred in Finland, was not appropriate to achieve the objective of preventing wrongdoing and fraud, the reduction of social damage caused by gaming, the financing of activities in the public interest, and ensuring legal certainty. The Court said that the file disclosed no evidence demonstrating 'the existence of a particular causal relationship between such risks and participation by nationals ... in lotteries organised in other Member States'.[267]

More recently, the Member States have started to argue that restrictions on gambling are necessary in order to ensure state control over the profits which are then used for social purposes. The Court is suspicious, as *Zenatti*[268] shows. The case concerned an Italian law prohibiting the taking of bets on sporting competitions except through specially appointed bodies which then used the funds to promote sporting activities, especially in deprived areas. The Court said that such a limitation on who could take bets was acceptable only if, from the outset, it reflected a concern to bring about a genuine diminution in gambling opportunities and if the financing of social activities constituted only an incidental beneficial consequence[269] and not the real justification for the restrictive policy. If the real aim of the limitation was to fund social activities, that motive could not in itself be regarded as an objective justification for restrictions on the freedom to provide services.

These lottery cases demonstrate a further noteworthy feature: even where the national law was apparently directly discriminatory, the Court allowed the Member States to justify the discrimination by reference to the broad public-interest requirements laid down in *Schindler*, not just the express derogations, as the orthodox jurisprudence might suggest.[270] However, the Court's case law is not consistent on this point. In the more recent decision, *Commission* v. *Spain (lottery winnings)*[271] the Court was adamant that the discriminatory Spanish rule (lottery winnings from lotteries organized in Spain were tax exempt while those from lotteries in other Member States were not) could not be saved by overriding reasons in the public interest but only express derogations 'namely public policy, public security or public health'.[272] Tantalizingly, the Court left open the question

---

[263] Case C–243/01 *Gambelli* [2003] ECR I–13031. See also Joined Cases C–338, 359 and 360/04 *Placanica* [2007] ECR I–1891, para. 58. Cf. Case E–1/06 *EFTA Surveillance Authority* v. *Norway* [2007] EFTA Ct. Rep. 8, para. 51.

[264] Para. 72.   [265] Para. 73.

[266] Case C–42/02 *Lindman* [2003] ECR I–13519.   [267] Para. 26.

[268] Case C–67/98 [1999] ECR I–7289, para. 36. See also Joined Cases C–338 and 360/04 *Placanica* [2007] ECR I–1891, paras. 53–4.

[269] See also Case E–3/06 *Ladbrokes Ltd* v. *Government of Norway* [2007] EFTA Ct. Rep. 86, para. 48; Case E–1/06 *EFTA Surveillance Authority* v. *Norway* [2007] EFTA Ct. Rep. 8, para. 39.

[270] Cf. this merging of the public-interest requirements with the express derogations can also be seen in the 40th recital of the preamble to the Services Dir., considered in Section D, and the briefer definition in Art. 4(8).

[271] Case C–153/08 [2009] ECR I–9735.

[272] Para. 37. See also Case C–347/09 *Dickinger* [2011] ECR I–8185, para. 79.

whether the objective of preventing money laundering and combating tax evasion could fall within the definition of public policy.[273]

(c) Country-of-origin principle

As we saw in Chapter 9, the host state cannot, in normal commercial situations, impose the full range of requirements on temporary service providers as it can on those establishing themselves.[274] However, in sensitive sectors the Court may disregard this principle. This can be seen in *Jyske Gibraltar*,[275] which concerned a Spanish rule requiring credit institutions providing services in its territory, without being established there, to forward directly to the Spanish financial intelligence unit (FIU) its reports on suspicious operations and any other information requested by the FIU. The Court found this rule was a restriction on the free movement of services. However, the Court said the breach could be justified, inter alia, on the grounds of combating money laundering and terrorist financing,[276] and that the steps taken were proportionate. They were *suitable* because, since the Spanish authorities had exclusive jurisdiction with regard to the criminalization, detection, and eradication of offences committed on its territory, it was justified that information concerning suspicious transactions carried out in Spain be forwarded to the Spanish FIU.

The rules were also *no more restrictive than necessary* because, although there was provision in EU secondary law for the credit institution to provide information to the FIU of its home state which could then be shared with the FIU in the host state, there were deficiencies in the procedure. In particular, because disclosure relating to suspicious transactions was carried out to the home state FIU there was no obligation under the EU legislation for that information to be forwarded automatically to the host state FIU (Spain). This meant that the Spanish FIU might not have information corroborating the suspicions necessary so as to send a request for information to the FIU of the Member State of origin. Therefore, the Court said that even though disclosure to the Spanish FIU gave rise to additional expenses and administrative burdens on the part of service providers, those burdens were relatively limited given that the credit institutions already had to establish infrastructure necessary for information to be forwarded to the home state's FIU.

(d) Restrictions created by the home state

An increasing number of cases concern obstacles to the provision of services created by the home state, State A. For example, in *Ciola*[277] the Court said that an Austrian company which provided moorings for boats on Lake Constance to boat owners resident in other Member States could rely on Article 56 TFEU against the Austrian authorities when the authorities limited the number of moorings available for boat owners resident abroad. In *Gourmet*[278] the Court went further and said that a national rule preventing undertakings established in State A from offering advertising space in their publications to *potential* advertisers established in other Member States could be challenged in State A as contrary to Article 56 TFEU.[279]

---

[273] Case C–153/08 *Commission v. Spain (lottery winnings)* [2009] ECR I–9735, para. 39.
[274] Case C–272/94 *Guiot* [1996] ECR I–1905. See also Case C–496/01 *Commission v. France (bio-medical analysis)* [2004] ECR I–2351, para. 71.
[275] Case C–212/11 *Jyske Bank Gibraltar Ltd* v. *Administración del Estado* EU:C:2013:270.
[276] Para. 62.   [277] Case C–224/97 *Ciola* v. *Land Vorarlberg* [1999] ECR I–2517, paras. 11–12.
[278] Case C–405/98 *Gourmet International Products (GIP)* [2001] ECR I–1795, para. 35.
[279] See also Case C–384/93 *Alpine Investments BV* [1995] ECR I–1141, para. 19: prior existence of an identifiable recipient was not a condition for the application of the provisions on the freedom to provide services.

Sometimes the Court uses somewhat different language to capture the breach. This can be seen in *Skandia*[280] concerning Swedish rules which treated an occupational pension insurance policy taken out by a Swedish company with an out-of-state insurer less favourably than if the policy had been taken out with a Swedish company. The Court said:

> In the perspective of a single market and in order to permit the attainment of the objectives thereof, Article [56 TFEU] precludes the application of any national legislation which has the effect of making the provision of services between Member States more difficult than the provision of services purely within one Member State.[281]

In other words, the Court now looks at a particular rule from the perspective of the migrant service provider/company: is there a rule in the home or host state which is liable to interfere with its access to the market? The fact that the rule treats national service providers in just the same way is irrelevant: the question is the impact the rule has on the out-of-state provider.

Case Study 11.2: BROADCASTING, ADVERTISING, AND THE FREEDOM TO PROVIDE SERVICES

The application of the EU rules on justification and proportionality can be seen in the case law on the compatibility with Article 56 TFEU of restrictive (primarily Dutch and Belgian) national laws regulating broadcasting, retransmission of programmes, and advertising. For example, in *Bond*[282] the Court found that a Dutch law, the *Kabelregeling*, banning advertising intended especially for the Dutch public, breached Article 56 TFEU. Even if it could be justified on the ground of maintaining 'the non-commercial and thereby pluralistic nature' of the Dutch broadcasting system, the Court found that the ban was not proportionate because there were less restrictive ways of achieving the objective by, for example, prohibiting the advertising of certain products or on certain days and limiting the duration and frequency of advertisements.

The successor regulations to the *Kabelregeling*, the *Mediawet*, were also condemned by the Court in *Gouda*.[283] Under the *Mediawet*, only those broadcasters having a non-commercial structure could advertise. The law also imposed the limits on advertising which the Court had indicated in *Bond* would be legitimate (i.e., limits concerning quantity, placement, and timing). The requirement relating to the non-commercial structure of broadcasters was justified by the Dutch government on the ground of cultural policy. This argument was rejected by the Court because it thought that there was no connection between cultural policy and the structure of foreign broadcasting bodies. By contrast, the Court thought that the condition relating to advertising could in principle be justified on the grounds of consumer protection and cultural policy. However, it found on the facts that the rules did operate to limit competition in advertising and so breached Article 56 TFEU.

The *Mediawet* also required national broadcasters to use the technical resources of the Dutch public studio to make 75 per cent of their programmes. In *Commission* v. *Netherlands*[284] the Court found that because this rule prevented or limited national broadcasters from using the services of undertakings established in other Member States it breached Article 56 TFEU. Once again the Dutch government relied on a justification based on cultural policy, and again

---

[280] C–422/01 *Skandia* [2003] ECR I–6817.   [281] Para. 26.
[282] Case 352/85 [1988] ECR 2085.   [283] Case C–288/89 [1991] ECR I–4007.
[284] Case C–353/89 [1991] ECR I–4069, para. 23.

the Court rejected it on the ground of proportionality: the measure was not suitable to achieve the objective.

The result of these cases was to favour the right of the broadcaster in the transmitting state to provide services. In this respect the case law on broadcasting fits within the general principle laid down in *Säger* of home-state control: the home state primarily regulates the activities of the broadcaster transmitting from its territory. The host (receiving) state can impose controls on broadcasters from other Member States but such controls are supplementary. And, as *Bond*, *Gouda*, and *Commission* v. *Netherlands* demonstrate, in practice the Court is unwilling to accept any interference with the broadcaster's freedom to provide services by the host state.

The Court's approach is reflected in Directive 2010/13/EU, originally called the Television without Frontiers (TWF) Directive 89/552[285] and now, since 2007, the Audiovisual Media Services (AVMS) Directive. The original version of the directive was intended to secure the freedom to provide television services.[286] The 2007 amendments distinguish between linear (TV transmissions) and non-linear services (e.g., web clips). While there are certain common rules—and this is reflected in changes to the language (e.g., references to 'television broadcasts' are replaced by 'audiovisual media services'[287] and 'broadcasters' have become 'media service providers')—non-linear services are subject to greater self-regulation. We shall focus primarily on linear services.

The directive is based on the 'transmitting-state' principle,[288] which means, according to *De Agostini*,[289] that the transmitting state has the primary responsibility for ensuring that 'media service providers' (broadcasters[290]) established in that state comply with national rules coordinated by the directive on the 'organisation and financing of broadcasts and the content of programmes'.[291]

The corollary of the transmitting-state principle is that the receiving state must allow programmes received from the transmitting state to be shown in its territory without restriction.[292]

---

[285] [1989] OJ L298/23. The TWF Dir. was overhauled by EP and Council Dir. 2007/65 ([2007] OJ L332/27) and renamed the Audiovisual Media Services Dir. The codified version, Dir. 2010/13/EU ([2010] OJ L 95/1), repeals the earlier directives. An amended text has recently been proposed: COM(2016) 287.

[286] Case C–412/93 *Leclerc-Siplec* [1995] ECR I–179, para. 28.

[287] Explained in Art. 1(a)(i) as 'a service as defined by Articles 56 and 57 [TFEU] which is under the editorial responsibility of a media service provider and the principal purpose of which is the provision of programmes in order to inform, entertain or educate, to the general public by electronic communications networks within the meaning of [Article 2(a)] of Directive 2002/21/EC. Such an audiovisual media service is either a television broadcast ... or an on-demand audiovisual media service ... A "television broadcast" (i.e. a linear audiovisual media service) means an audiovisual media service provided by a media service provider for simultaneous viewing of programmes on the basis of a programme schedule. An "on-demand audiovisual media service" (i.e. a non-linear audiovisual media service) means an audiovisual media service provided by a media service provider for the viewing of programmes at the moment chosen by the user and at his individual request on the basis of a catalogue of programmes selected by the media service provider.'

[288] Art. 2(1) provides that 'Each Member State shall ensure that all audiovisual media services transmitted by media service providers under its jurisdiction comply with the rules of the system of law applicable to audiovisual media services intended for the public in that Member State.' See also Case C–11/95 *Commission* v. *Belgium* [1996] ECR I–4115, para. 42; Case C–14/96 *Criminal Proceedings against Paul Denuit* [1997] ECR I–2785, para. 32. In addition Art. 4(6) makes the transmitting state responsible for ensuring that the media service provider complies with the provisions of the directive.

[289] Joined Cases C–34–36/95 [1997] ECR I–3843, para. 28.

[290] See Case C–89/04 *Mediakabel BV* v. *Commissariaat voor de media* [2005] ECR I–4891 on the meaning of television broadcasting services.

[291] Art. 2(2)–(5) lays down the rules to determine which media service providers are under the jurisdiction of a Member State.

[292] Art. 3(1) provides that 'Member States shall ensure freedom of reception and shall not restrict retransmissions on their territory of audiovisual media services from other Member States for reasons which fall within the fields co-ordinated by this Directive.'

Therefore, the principle of mutual recognition underlies Directive 2010/13: a television programme legitimately broadcast in one Member State can be rebroadcast in another without restriction.[293] Even if the receiving Member State considers that the transmitting state is not exercising proper control, the receiving state cannot unilaterally adopt corrective or protective measures but must bring infringement proceedings under Article 259 TFEU or request the Commission to take action under Article 258 TFEU.[294]

Article 3(2) lists the circumstances in which the receiving state can derogate from the rule of home-state control. It provides that if a television broadcast[295] comes from another Member State which 'manifestly, seriously and gravely' infringes Article 27 concerning programmes which might seriously impair the physical, mental, or moral development of minors[296] and/or Article 6 concerning audiovisual media services containing 'incitement to hatred based on race, sex, religion or nationality' and the broadcaster has infringed Article 27 and/or Article 6 on at least two occasions in the previous 12 months, then the Member State must notify the broadcaster and the Commission. If attempts at seeking an amicable settlement fail then the receiving state can provisionally suspend retransmission until the Commission determines whether the suspension is compatible with Union law.

The UK has made more use of this provision than any other Member State.[297] In particular, it banned reception of the Red Hot Dutch channel, broadcast initially via satellite from the Netherlands and then from Denmark.[298] The UK also relied on it to suspend the transmission of Eurotica Rendez-Vous by a Danish satellite television company. The Commission upheld the UK's decision as being compatible with the directive.[299]

Having concentrated on cases concerning broadcasting, we turn now to advertising[300] or 'audiovisual commercial communication'[301] as it is now called by the AVMS Directive. Although the basic rules are the same (i.e., the transmitting-state principle still applies), the advertising provisions of Directive 2010/13 are more prescriptive than those on broadcasting. So while

[293] C. Jones, 'Television without frontiers' (1999/2000) 19 *YEL* 299, 308.

[294] Case C–11/95 *Commission* v. *Belgium* [1996] ECR I–4115, paras. 36–7, referring to Case C–5/94 *Hedley Lomas* [1996] ECR I–2553, para. 20, considered in Ch. 6.

[295] Member States can derogate from on-demand audiovisual media services on the grounds of public policy, public health, public security, and the protection of consumers (Art. 3(4)).

[296] See also Rec. 2006/952/EC on the protection of minors and human dignity and on the right of reply in relation to the competitiveness of the European audiovisual and on-line services industry ([2006] OJ L378/72).

[297] Information in this section comes from Jones, n. 293, 318–19.

[298] *R.* v. *Secretary of State for National Heritage, ex p. Continental Television* [1993] 3 CMLR 387 and referred to the Court in Case 327/93 *Red Hot Television*. The reference was removed from the register on 29 Mar. 1996 because Red Hot Dutch went bankrupt.

[299] The Commission's decision was unsuccessfully challenged under Art. 263 TFEU in Case T–69/99 *Danish Satellite TV (DSTV)* v. *Commission* [2001] ECR II–4039. The Court found that DSTV did not have *locus standi* since it was not directly concerned by the act and was therefore not entitled to seek its annulment.

[300] The indirect advertising rules at issue in Case C–429/02 *Bacardi* v. *Télévision Française 1 SA* [2004] ECR I–6613 did not fall under the AVMS Dir. so were considered solely by reference to Art. 56 TFEU.

[301] Art. 1(h) says ' "audiovisual commercial communication" means images with or without sound which are designed to promote, directly or indirectly, the goods, services or image of a natural or legal entity pursuing an economic activity. Such images accompany or are included in a programme in return for payment or for similar consideration or for self-promotional purposes. Forms of audiovisual commercial communication include, inter alia, television advertising, sponsorship, teleshopping and product placement.' One of the more controversial features of the revised directive is that it allows for 'product placement' in television programmes (but not news, documentaries, or children's programmes), i.e., 'any form of audiovisual commercial communication consisting of the inclusion of or reference to a product, a service or the trade mark thereof so that it is featured within a programme, in return for payment or for similar consideration'. The details are set out in Art. 11.

the broadcasting provisions say little about content or quality (leaving that for the Member State where the broadcaster is established), the directive does lay down a number of more detailed rules concerning the content of television advertising,[302] prescribing the conditions under which advertisements can be broadcast, prohibiting the use of certain techniques, and limiting the amount of broadcast time which can be devoted to advertising.[303]

The provisions concerning both advertising and broadcasting are minimum requirements,[304] which, according to Article 4(1), means that *transmitting* states can 'require media service providers under their jurisdiction to comply with more detailed or stricter rules' in the areas covered by the directive. This is, however, subject to the free movement clause[305] contained in Article 3(1), which provides that Member States must not 'restrict retransmissions on their territory of audiovisual media services from other Member States for reasons which fall within the fields coordinated by this Directive'. Therefore, in *Leclerc-Siplec*[306] a French government ban on advertising in the distribution sector was compatible with Article 4(1) of the directive,[307] since it was applied by the *transmitting* state to broadcasters under its jurisdiction and did not affect the freedom of broadcasters established in other Member States, which met the minimum requirements laid down by the directive, from providing services.[308] Although a ban seems inconsistent with the directive's express aim of facilitating the provision of services, France could legitimately impose such a rule because the directive lays down only minimum standards.

Apart from the free movement clause, the only ceiling constraining Member States when enacting the stricter requirements is compatibility with the Treaty provisions, in particular Articles 34 and 56 TFEU. On the facts, the Court found that the French rules did not breach Article 34 TFEU because they were classified as certain selling arrangements and so, following the decision in *Keck*,[309] fell outside Article 34 TFEU.[310]

The relationship between Directive 2010/13 and the Treaty provisions was explored further in *De Agostini*,[311] this time concerning the rights of the *receiving* state to limit the activities of an advertiser. De Agostini, a Swedish company belonging to an Italian group, advertised a children's magazine about dinosaurs on TV3 (broadcast to Scandinavia by satellite from the UK) and on TV4 (a Swedish television station). This magazine was printed in Italy in a number of languages and it formed part of a series. With each issue came one part of a model dinosaur: children buying the whole series would have collected all parts of the model. The consumer ombudsman argued that this campaign contravened the Swedish ban on advertising aimed at children. The case was joined with *TV Shop*. TV Shop, which specialized in teleshopping, broadcast

---

[302] E.g., Art. 9(c) requires that audiovisual commercial communications should not prejudice respect for human dignity, be discriminatory, encourage behaviour prejudicial to health and safety or the environment; Art. 9(d) prohibits the advertising of cigarettes and other tobacco products. Art. 9(e) concerns advertisements directed at minors and Art. 9(g) provides that audiovisual commercial communications must not cause moral or physical detriment to minors by, e.g., exploiting children's inexperience, credulity, or pester power.

[303] E.g., Art. 9(1)(a) and (b) requires that TV advertising and teleshopping be readily recognizable and should not use subliminal techniques (see Case C–195/06 *KommAustria* v. *ORF* [2007] ECR I–8817 on the meaning of teleshopping in the context of prize games). Art. 23 concerns the quantity of advertising permitted, and Art. 24 gives details of when advertising and teleshopping spots can be used.

[304] Minimum standards directives are considered further in Ch. 15.

[305] Free movement clauses are considered further in Ch. 15.

[306] Case C–412/93 [1995] ECR I–179.   [307] Para. 44.   [308] Para. 41.

[309] Joined Cases C–267 and 268/91 [1993] ECR I–6097, para. 16.

[310] See also Case C–6/98 *ARD* v. *PRO Sieben Media* [1999] ECR I–7599, paras. 45–8 and Joined Cases C–320, 328, 329, 337, 338 and 339/94 *RTI* v. *Ministero delle Poste e Telecomunicazioni* [1996] ECR I–6471.

[311] Joined Cases C–34–36/95 [1997] ECR I–3843. See also now the effect of the UCPD 2005/29 ([2005] OJ L149/22), discussed in Ch. 5.

'infomercials' for Body de Lite skincare products and the detergent Astonish on TV3 and on a Swedish home-shopping channel. This time the consumer ombudsman sought to restrain misleading advertising for these products.

The logic of Directive 2010/13 suggests that, with the exception of the derogations laid down in the directive, the receiving state (Sweden) could not limit the advertisements broadcast by an out-of-state service provider. The Court disagreed. It noted that the directive, while coordinating national provisions on television advertising and sponsorship, did so only partially.[312] It continued that while the directive provided that Member States were to ensure freedom of reception and were not to impede retransmission on grounds relating to television advertising and sponsorship (the areas which had been harmonized), 'it does not have the effect of excluding completely and automatically the application of rules other than those specifically concerning the broadcasting and distribution of programmes'[313] (the area which had not been harmonized). Therefore, the receiving state could apply its general rules on misleading advertising to television advertisements broadcast from other Member States in order to ensure the overriding interest of consumer protection.[314] They could do this provided that those national rules did not involve secondary control of television broadcasts (i.e., control additional to that which the broadcasting Member State had to carry out)[315] and did not prevent retransmission of television broadcasts coming from other Member States.[316] In response to arguments from the Commission and De Agostini that this ruling would undermine the transmitting-state principle, the Court pointed to Directive 2006/114,[317] which would be 'robbed of its substance in the field of television advertising if the receiving Member State were deprived of all possibility of adopting measures against an advertiser'.[318]

The Court then considered whether the Swedish rules breached Article 34 TFEU. As we saw in Chapter 5, the Court adopted a more sophisticated analysis to its own *Keck* jurisprudence than it had done in *Leclerc-Siplec*. While recognizing that a prohibition on television advertising aimed at children constituted a certain selling arrangement,[319] it found that an outright ban might have a greater impact on products from other Member States (see fig. 5.2).[320] The ban therefore breached Article 34 TFEU and needed to be justified under either a *Cassis* mandatory requirement or an Article 36 TFEU derogation.[321] The Court reached a similar conclusion in respect of Article 56 TFEU but by a different route. There was no mention of certain selling arrangements. Instead, by applying *Bond* and *Gouda*, it found that the national rules prohibiting advertising constituted a restriction on the freedom to provide services, but that a receiving state (Sweden) could take measures against an advertiser in relation to television advertising, provided that those provisions were necessary for meeting overriding requirements of general public importance or one of the Article 52/62 TFEU derogations, and that the steps taken were proportionate. The Court then returned to the directive and its application to the ban on advertising aimed at children. It said that, given the provisions specifically devoted to the protection of minors, Sweden could no longer apply rules specifically designed to control the *content* of advertising with regard to minors. In this field, at least, harmonization is total and the principle of transmitting-state control reasserted.[322]

---

[312] Para. 32.   [313] Para. 33.   [314] Para. 28.
[315] Paras. 34–5.   [316] Para. 38.   [317] [2006] OJ L376/21.
[318] Para. 37. However, cf. Case C–99/01 *Linhart* v. *Hans Biffl* [2002] ECR I–9375, para. 24.
[319] Para. 39.
[320] Para. 42. See the more assertive statement to that effect in Case C–405/98 *Gourmet International Products (GIP)* [2001] ECR I–1795, para. 21.
[321] Paras. 45–6.
[322] A. Criscuolo, 'The "TV without frontiers" Directive and the legal regulation of publicity in the European Community' (1998) 23 *ELRev.* 357, 362.

Leaving aside the ruling on the compatibility with the directive of a ban on advertising aimed at children, *De Agostini* produces a paradoxical result: the application of two harmonization directives and two fundamental Treaty provisions gives the green light to the Member States to *hinder* free movement in advertising.[323] Any such restrictions on advertising may infringe the freedom of expression under Article 10(1) ECHR but, as the Court pointed out in *RTL Television*[324] (a case on the interpretation of the (then) TWF Directive), the restrictions could be justified under Article 10(2). The restrictions pursued a legitimate aim involving the protection of consumers as television viewers (citing *Gouda*), as well as their interest in having access to quality programmes, and the steps taken were proportionate.

It seems that the case law before and after the TWF/AVMS directive is less different than would at first appear. This is perhaps not so surprising: as the Court made clear in *UTECA*,[325] the directive does not completely harmonize the rules relating to the areas which it covers. Nevertheless, the Member States still have to satisfy the fundamental freedoms. *UTECA* concerned a Spanish rule requiring television operators to earmark 5 per cent of their operating revenue for the pre-funding of European cinematographic films and films made for television and, more specifically, to reserve 60 per cent of that 5 per cent for the production of works of which the original language is one of the official languages of that Member State. While the Court considered that the 5 per cent earmarking was not a restriction, the 60 per cent rule was, but could be justified on the grounds of defending and promoting Spanish multilingualism[326] and the rule was proportionate.

1.3 The Position of the Provider's Workforce

So far we have concentrated on the right of the company to gain access to the market of the host Member States. Early on it became clear that the right of market access included the company's right to bring its workforce with it, irrespective of nationality. In *Rush Portuguesa*[327] a Portuguese company used its own third-country national (TCN) workforce[328] to carry out a contract building a railway line in France. Rush's use of its own TCN workforce contravened French rules which provided that only the French Office d'Immigration could recruit TCNs (i.e., non-EU) workers. However, the Court ruled that Articles 56–7 TFEU 'preclude a Member State from prohibiting a person providing services established in another Member State from moving freely on its territory *with all his staff*'.[329] The Court continued that Member States also could not make the movement of staff subject to restrictions such as a condition as to engagement *in situ* or an obligation to obtain a work permit because such conditions discriminated against guest service providers in relation to their competitors established in the host country who were able to use their own staff without restrictions.

---

[323] Criscuolo, n. 322, 363. Cf. UCPD 2005/29, considered in Ch. 5.

[324] Case C–245/01 *RTL Television GmbH* v. *Niedersächsische Landesmedienanstalt für proviaten Rundfunk* [2003] ECR I–12489, paras. 68–74.

[325] Case C–222/07 *UTECA* v. *Administración General del Estado* [2009] ECR I–1407, para. 19.

[326] Paras. 26–7. For a similarly benign approach to Member State rules, see Case C–250/06 *United Pan-Europe Communications Belgium SA* v. *Etat belge* [2007] ECR I–11135.

[327] Case C–113/89 *Rush Portuguesa* v. *Office national d'immigration* [1990] ECR I–1417.

[328] The workforce was actually Portuguese, but at the time the transitional arrangements for Portuguese accession to the EU were in place and Portuguese workers did not enjoy the rights of free movement. For our purposes the Portuguese workers constitute third-country nationals (see para. 4 of the judgment).

[329] Para. 12, emphasis added. See also Case C–43/93 *Vander Elst* v. *Office des Migrations Internationales* [1994] ECR I–3803.

The result of *Rush Portuguesa* is that Article 56 TFEU allows companies from State A (e.g., Portugal) to 'post' (i.e., send) their own workforce to provide a service in State B (e.g., France), even where the workforce includes TCNs, provided that the TCN workers do not seek access to the labour market in the host state and that they return to their country of origin or residence once the contract is finished.[330] While this decision was good news for companies supplying services, it raised the spectre of what some term 'social dumping', i.e., service providers taking advantage of cheaper labour (and inferior labour standards) in their own state (Portugal) to win a contract in the host state (France).[331] The Court sought to address these concerns in *Rush Portuguesa* by ruling at paragraph 18 that the host state *can* apply all of its labour laws to the provider's workforce, thereby removing the competitive advantage enjoyed by the service provider, namely its cheaper labour.

The position taken by the Court in *Rush Portuguesa* was apparently reinforced by the enactment of Directive 96/71 on Posted Workers.[332] The directive no longer gives the host Member State the discretion as to whether to apply its labour standards to posted workers; instead it *requires* the host state to apply to posted workers a 'nucleus of mandatory rules'[333] listed in Article 3(1), in particular relating to wages (but only minimum rates of pay), working time, and equal treatment, as laid down either by law or, in the case of the construction industry, collective agreements which satisfy certain conditions laid out in Article 3(8). At least initially, trade union lawyers, particularly from the wealthier northern European states, welcomed the directive as a way of protecting labour standards in those states from being undermined by posted workers from southern and eastern states. However, employers involved in posting staff argued that because the directive had the effect of requiring the out-of-state service provider to adapt its terms and conditions of employment each time it posted workers to another Member State, the directive interfered with, rather than promoted, the provision of services.[334]

It was against this backcloth that the *Laval*[335] dispute arose. The case concerned a Latvian company which won a contract to refurbish a school in Sweden using its own Latvian workers, who earned about 40 per cent less than comparable Swedish workers. The Swedish construction union wanted Laval to apply the Swedish collective agreement to its Latvian staff but Laval refused, in part because the collective agreement was unclear as to how much Laval would have to pay its workers, and in part because it imposed various additional obligations on Laval such as paying a 'special building supplement' to an insurance company to finance group life insurance contracts. There followed a union picket at the school site, a blockade by construction workers, and sympathy industrial action by the electricians unions. Although this industrial action was permissible under Swedish law, Laval brought proceedings in the Swedish labour court, claiming that this action was contrary to *Union* law (in particular Article 56 TFEU) and the Posted Workers Directive 96/71.

The Court required a narrow reading of the directive: the host state could insist on applying its labour law rules to posted workers *but*, contrary to paragraph 18 of *Rush Portuguesa*, only in respect of those matters exhaustively[336] listed in Article 3(1) of the

---

[330] Case C–43/93 *Vander Elst* [1994] ECR I–3803, para. 21.

[331] Germany was particularly exercised by this problem. See W. Streeck, 'Neo-voluntarism: A new social policy regime' (1995) 1 *ELJ* 31, 42.

[332] Dir. 96/71/EC ([1996] OJ L18/1). A revised directive has been proposed: COM(2016) 128. An enforcement Directive 2014/67 ([2014] OJ L159/11) has also been adopted.

[333] 13th recital of the directive.

[334] See, e.g., P. Davies, 'The Posted Workers Directive and the EC Treaty' (2002) 31 *ILJ* 298, 300.

[335] Case C–341/05 *Laval* [2007] ECR I–987.

[336] Case C–341/05 *Laval* [2007] ECR I–987, para. 71. This is more clearly expressed in Case C–319/06 *Commission* v. *Luxembourg* [2008] ECR I–4323, para. 26. For a full discussion, see C. Barnard, 'The UK and

directive. Because Article 3(1) did not cover matters such as the 'special building supplement' and the other insurance premiums, these could not be applied to the Latvian posted workers.[337] The Court also said that the requirement to pay Latvian workers Swedish rates of pay was not compatible with the directive. This was because Sweden had failed to comply with the precise terms of Article 3(1) and (8) of the directive by neither enacting minimum wage legislation nor expressly taking advantage of the complex provisions in Article 3(8) which allowed minimum wage rates to be set by collective agreements.[338] More generally, because the trade unions' demands fell outside the scope of the directive,[339] industrial action taken to enforce the terms of the Swedish collective agreement was incompatible with Article 56 TFEU.[340]

Laval shows that the Posted Workers Directive is primarily a measure to facilitate free movement of services and not a measure to realize social-policy objectives; a point confirmed by its legal basis (Articles 53(2) and 62 TFEU). This view is reinforced by the Court's observations that the directive is 'first' intended to 'ensure a climate of fair competition between national undertakings and undertakings which provide services transnationally',[341] and that the mandatory rules for minimum protection in Article 3(1) prevent a situation from arising where the out-of-state provider competes unfairly against the host state.[342] Only 'secondly' does the Court refer to the worker protection element of the directive.[343] It could, therefore, be argued that the Court has reached a careful compromise in these cases: posted workers will enjoy the better terms and conditions of employment in the host state but only if the host state has complied with the provisions of the directive to the letter. If it has not, then any attempt to apply the host-state rules will breach both the directive and Article 56 TFEU. According to this analysis, the directive and Article 56 TFEU are mutually reinforcing: the restrictive interpretation of the directive is derived from Article 56 TFEU and the substance of Article 56 TFEU is derived from the directive.[344]

The key to understanding the Court's approach in *Laval* is essentially the country-of-origin principle, also known as home-state control. The basic rule is that since the Latvian workers are employed in Latvia and only work temporarily in Sweden, it is Latvian law that applies. An equal treatment approach requiring the Latvian employer to apply all of Swedish law to posted Latvian workers undermines Article 56. The selected rules which Article 3(1) of the directive requires the host state (Sweden) to apply to the Latvian workers are justified in the name of worker protection. The rules in Article 3(1) of the directive are, however, viewed by the Court as an exception to the Treaty provision on free movement services and so are narrowly construed.

1.4 Tax Advantages

In one sense, it could be argued that, by analogy with the Court's case law on natural persons, a company's right to bring its workforce with it is a social advantage (like the

---

posted workers: The effect of *Commission* v. *Luxembourg* on the territorial application of British labour law' (2009) 38 *Industrial Law Journal* 122.

 [337] Case C–341/05 *Laval* [2007] ECR I–987, para. 83. [338] Para. 67.

 [339] *Laval* suggests that failure to comply with the terms of the directive means that a breach of Art. 56 TFEU cannot be justified (paras. 108–11). By contrast, Case C–346/06 *Dirk Rüffert* v. *Land Niedersachsen* [2008] ECR I–1989, para. 36 suggests non-compliance with the directive amounts to a breach of Art. 56 TFEU.

 [340] By implication, in these situations the preambular para. in Dir. 96/71, to the effect that 'this Directive is without prejudice to the law of the Member States concerning collective action to defend the interests of trades and professions', becomes irrelevant.

 [341] *Laval*, n. 335, para. 74. [342] Para. 75. [343] Para. 76.

 [344] See esp. *Rüffert*, n. 339, para. 36.

natural person's right to bring his or her partner[345]). Likewise, legal persons enjoy the same tax advantages as nationals.

(a) The provision of services

Initially, the Court applied the equal treatment model to taxation. This can be seen in *De Coster*,[346] where a Belgian tax on satellite dishes encouraged subscribers to receive their programmes by cable instead (no tax was levied on cable). Because Belgian distributors had unlimited access to cable distribution,[347] the Court found that this rule had a particular impact on broadcasters established in other Member States whose programmes could be received only by satellite.[348] The tax therefore breached Article 56 TFEU and could not be justified.[349]

Subsequently, the Court applied the restrictions approach. For example, in *Sea-Land Service*[350] the Dutch authorities levied a tariff to cover the cost of navigation services charged on sea-going vessels but not on inland waterway vessels. Sea-Land argued that the tariff was indirectly discriminatory because the majority of those operating inland waterway vessels were Dutch. The Court found that while there was no discrimination because the two means of transport were not comparable, the tariff imposed on sea-going vessels was liable to 'impede or render less attractive' the provision of those services and so breached Article 56 TFEU.[351] However, it ruled that the tariff could be justified on the ground of public security provided there was a correlation between the amount of the tariff and the cost of the service from which the sea-going vessels benefit.

The facts of this case highlight the problem of applying the restrictions model to taxation. What is the impediment to out-of-state actors? It is the actual payment of the tax. There is no particular impediment for the out-of-state vessel since there is no discrimination. The Court appears to have seen the force of this argument in *Viacom II*[352] and *Mobistar*.[353] In *Mobistar* the Court found that a municipal tax on transmission pylons, masts, and antennae for GSM (global system mobile) communications, which applied 'without distinction to national providers of services and to those of other Member States and affects in the same way the provision of services within one Member State and the provision of services between Member States', did not breach Article 56 TFEU where the only effect was to create additional costs in respect of the service in question.[354] In *Viacom II*[355] the Court found that a municipal tax on outdoor advertising, applied on a non-discriminatory basis and fixed at a level considered 'modest in relation to the value of the services provided', did not breach Article 56 TFEU since 'the levying of such a

---

[345] See Case 59/85 *Netherlands* v. *Reed* [1986] ECR 1283.
[346] Case C–17/00 *De Coster* v. *Collège des bourgmestre et échevins de Watermael-Boitsfort* [2001] ECR I–9445.
[347] Para. 31.   [348] Para. 35.
[349] See also Case C–169/08 *Presidente del Consiglio dei Ministri* v. *Regione Sardegna* [2009] ECR I–10821.
[350] Joined Cases C–430 and 431/99 *Inspecteur van de Belastingdienst Douane, district Rotterdam* v. *Sea-Land Service Inc. and Nedlloyd Lijnen BV* [2002] ECR I–5235, para. 32.
[351] Para. 32. See also Case C–345/04 *Centro Equestre da Lezíria Grande* v. *Bundesamt für Finanzen* [2007] ECR I–1425, para. 29.
[352] Case C–134/03 [2005] ECR I–1167. See also Case C–222/07 *UTECA* v. *Administración General del Estado* [2009] ECR I–1407, para. 22.
[353] Joined Cases C–544 and 545/03 *Mobistar* v. *Commue de Fléron* [2005] ECR I–7723. Cf. Case C–17/00 *De Coster* [2001] ECR I–9445.
[354] Para. 35. See also Case C–98/14 *Berlington Hungary* v. *Hungarian State* EU:C:2015:386, paras. 36–40.
[355] Case C–134/03 [2005] ECR I–1167.

tax is not on any view liable to prohibit, impede or otherwise make less attractive the provision of advertising services to be carried out in the territory of the municipalities concerned'.[356]

(b) Receipt of services

The cases considered so far concern national rules which are intended to discourage service *providers* from other Member States exercising their rights in the host state. Yet, there is also a group of cases concerning national rules intended to discourage potential national service *recipients* from receiving that service in another state. When considering the validity of these rules the Court often uses the language of discrimination. For example, in *Bent Vestergaard*[357] Danish tax law distinguished between professional training courses held at tourist resorts in other Member States and those taking place in Denmark. While Danish law presumed that courses held abroad were an excuse for a holiday, with the result that the costs were not tax-deductible, it did not apply the same presumption to courses held in Denmark. The Court found that such a rule involved an unjustifiable difference in treatment based on the place where the service was provided and therefore breached Article 56 TFEU.[358] Similarly, in *Laboratoires Fournier*[359] the Court said that French law restricting the benefit of a tax credit only to research carried out in France, differentiated according to the place where the services were provided, contrary to Article 56 TFEU. In other cases the Court says that national rules making the provision of services between Member States more difficult than the provision of services within just one Member State[360] also breach Article 56 TFEU.[361]

While the language used in all these cases carries overtones of direct discrimination, the Court in fact seems to regard such rules as impeding, deterring,[362] or constituting a restriction on[363] the exercise of the freedom to receive services[364] which can then be justified not only by the express derogations laid down in the Treaty but also by the broader public-interest requirements.

1.5 Abuse

Although the Court has done much to encourage the provision of services, it is wary of the services rules being abused by individuals who deliberately establish themselves in State A in order to provide services to customers in State B, thereby avoiding State B's

---

[356] Case C–134/03 *Viacom II* [2005] ECR I–1167, paras. 37–8.

[357] Case C–55/98 *Skatteministeriet v. Bent Vestergaard* [1999] ECR I–7641.   [358] Para. 22.

[359] Case C–39/04 *Laboratoires Fournier SA v. Direction des vérifications nationales et internationales* [2005] ECR I–2057, para. 15. See also Case C–150/04 *Commission v. Denmark (insurance)* [2007] ECR I–1163, para. 42, where the Court used the language of dissuasion.

[360] Case C–158/96 *Kohll* [1998] ECR I–1931, para. 33. See also Case C–381/93 *Commission v. France (maritime services)* [1994] ECR I–5154, para. 17; Case C–136/00 *Danner* [2002] ECR I–8147, para. 29; Case C–118/96 *Safir* [1998] ECR I–1897, para. 23; Case C–17/00 *De Coster* [2001] ECR I–9445, para. 30; Case C–422/01 *Försäkringsaktiebolaget Skandia (publ), Ola Ramstedt v. Riksskatteverket* [2003] ECR I–6817, para. 26.

[361] However, where the rules do not have the effect of making the provision of services more difficult between states than those offered purely within one Member State there is no breach of Art. 56 TFEU: Case C–8/02 *Leichtle v. Bundesanstalt für Arbeit* [2004] ECR I–2641, para. 37; Case C–281/06 *Jundt* [2007] ECR I–12231, para. 52.

[362] Case C–76/05 *Schwarz and Gootjes-Schwarz v. Finanzamt Bergisch Gladbach* [2007] ECR I–6849, para. 66.

[363] Case C–281/06 *Jundt* [2007] ECR I–12231, para. 55.

[364] See Case C–118/96 *Safir* [1998] ECR I–1897, paras. 25 and 30; Case C–290/04 *Scorpio* [2006] ECR I–9461, para. 33. See also the discussion of Case C–109/04 *Kranemann* [2005] ECR I–2421 in Ch. 7.

more restrictive rules. It therefore said in *Commission* v. *Germany (insurance cases)*[365] that a host state (State B) was allowed to take measures to prevent a person from directing his activity entirely or principally towards his territory, but doing so by services rather than establishment simply to avoid the professional rules of conduct which would be applicable to him had he been established in State B. The Court said that such a situation would be subject to judicial control under the provisions on establishment rather than on services.

As we saw in Case Study 11.2, the Netherlands, with its restrictive broadcasting laws, has been particularly affected by attempts to avoid its rules, with Dutch companies setting up commercial stations in Luxembourg and, relying on the services provisions, using the Luxembourg station to broadcast programmes back to the Netherlands. The Dutch government passed a law prohibiting broadcasting organizations established in the Netherlands from investing in a broadcasting company established in another Member State which provided services directed towards the Netherlands. In *Veronica*[366] the Court said that such a rule did not breach Article 56 TFEU where it had the specific effect of ensuring that those organizations could not improperly evade the obligations deriving from the national legislation concerning the pluralistic and non-commercial content of those programmes.[367] It reached a similar conclusion in *TV10*,[368] where it said that a Member State (the Netherlands) could regard as a domestic broadcaster a radio and television organization which established itself in another Member State (Luxembourg) in order to provide services which were intended for Dutch territory. The Court said that the aim of the measure was to prevent organizations which established themselves in another Member State from being able, by exercising the freedoms guaranteed by the Treaty, wrongfully to avoid obligations under national law, in this case those designed to ensure the pluralist and non-commercial content of programmes. However, the *TV10* approach did differ in one respect from that in *Veronica* because the Court seemed to have classified the principle of abuse as a ground for justifying restrictions on the freedom to provide services, and no longer as a ground for precluding the Treaty's application.

However, in *VT4*[369] the Court appeared to backtrack. VT4, a broadcaster established in the UK, made programmes aimed at the Flemish public and transmitted the signals from the UK to Belgium. The Belgian authorities thought VT4 had been established in the UK merely to circumvent the application of Flemish law. The Court said that just because all the broadcasts and advertisements were aimed at the Flemish public did not mean that VT4 could not be regarded as being established in the UK. Without referring to either *Veronica* or *TV10*, it continued that the Treaty did not 'prohibit an undertaking from exercising the freedom to provide services if it does not offer services in the Member State in which it is established'.[370] Therefore, the pendulum seems to have swung back towards the Court's original stance supporting those wishing to provide services; a change which coincided with the adoption of the TWF/AVMS Directive, which laid down criteria for determining in which state a broadcaster was established.[371] As *Centros*[372] subsequently

---

[365] Case 205/84 [1986] ECR 3755, para. 22, reaffirming Case 33/74 *Van Binsbergen* [1974] ECR 1299, para. 13.

[366] Case C–148/91 *Vereniging Veronica Omroep Organisatie* v. *Commissariaat voor de Media* [1993] ECR I–487.

[367] Para. 13.

[368] Case C–23/93 *TV10 SA* v. *Commissariaat voor de Media* [1994] ECR I–4795 and the note by P. Wattel (1995) 32 *CMLRev.* 1257.

[369] Case C–56/96 *VT4 Ltd* v. *Vlaamse Gemeenschap* [1997] ECR I–3143.

[370] Para. 22.   [371] See Art. 2 of Dir. 2010/13.

[372] Case C–212/97 *Centros* [1999] ECR I–1459.

confirmed, there is nothing abusive about simply taking advantage of the Treaty provisions on free movement.

D. THE SERVICES DIRECTIVE 2006/123

So far we have concentrated on the application of the Treaty provisions on establishment and services. We turn now to consider the Services Directive 2006/123[373] whose aim, like that of the Treaty, was to open up the market in services. The Directive distinguishes between the freedom of establishment (Section 3) and the freedom to provide services (Section 4). First, however, we shall look at the scope of the directive (Sections 1 and 2).

1. SCOPE

1.1 The Meaning of Services

According to Article 2(1), the directive applies to 'services supplied by providers established in a Member State'. Services are defined in accordance with the GATS definition: ' "Service" means any self-employed economic activity, normally provided for remuneration, as referred to in Article [57 TFEU]'.[374] The list of services found in Article 57 TFEU has been updated by the directive to include:

- business services such as management consultancy, certification,[375] and testing; facilities management, including office maintenance; advertising; recruitment services; and the services of commercial agents

- services provided both to businesses and to consumers, such as legal or fiscal advice; real estate services such as estate agencies; construction, including the services of architects; distributive trades; the organization of trade fairs; car rental; and travel agencies

- consumer services such as those in the field of tourism, including tour guides; leisure services, sports centres, and amusement parks; and, to the extent that they are not excluded from the scope of application of the directive, household support services, such as help for the elderly.[376]

The striking feature about this list is that the services identified are relatively uncontroversial and are often provided by small operators (SMEs).

1.2 Requirements, Restrictions, and Barriers

Assuming the activity is a service within the meaning of the directive then the directive can be used to challenge 'requirements which affect access to or the exercise of a service activity'.[377] The word 'requirement' is broadly construed by Article 4(7) of the directive:

any obligation, prohibition, condition or limit provided for in the laws, regulations or administrative provisions of the Member States or in consequence of case-law,

---

[373] [2006] OJ L376/36. The following draws on the more extensive discussion in C. Barnard, 'Unravelling the Services Directive' (2008) 45 *CMLRev.* 323, which also explains some of the background to the directive.
[374] Art. 4(1).
[375] Case C–593/13 *Presidenza del Consiglio dei Ministri* v. *Rina Services* EU:C:2015:399, para. 24.
[376] 33rd recital. The limited scope of the directive has already been reorganized by the Court: Case C–577/10 *Commission* v. *Belgium (self-employed)* EU:C:2012:814, para. 50.
[377] 9th recital.

administrative practice, the rules of professional bodies, or the collective rules of professional associations or other professional organisations, adopted in the exercise of their legal autonomy.

While the broad definition of 'requirement' is intended to give the Services Directive the widest possible reach, for the overzealous, it will catch rules never intended to be covered by Union law. The 9th recital was included in the preamble to provide some sort of get-out clause. The recital distinguishes between two situations. The first sentence provides that where requirements affect the access to, or the exercise of,[378] a service activity, the directive will apply. This recital suggests that courts should adopt a market access, rather than a discrimination, reading of the directive.

However, the second sentence of the 9th recital says that the directive does not apply:

> to requirements, such as road traffic rules, rules concerning the development or use of land, town and country planning, building standards as well as administrative penalties imposed for non-compliance with such rules which do not specifically regulate or specifically affect the service activity but have to be respected by providers in the course of carrying out their economic activity in the same way as by individuals acting in their private capacity.[379]

Thus, certain non-discriminatory 'rules of the game', using the language of *Deliège*,[380] are presumptively lawful. This view is reinforced by the unusual phrase 'in the same way as by individuals acting in their private capacity'. So, if the rules apply to all individuals, irrespective of their nationality or the status in which they are acting, they are lawful. However, if the service provider can show that the rules do 'specifically regulate or specifically affect the service activity' then they may be unlawful and need to be justified. Therefore, because the Belgian requirement of driving on the right is non-discriminatory and applies to all Belgians including those acting in their private capacity, it is presumptively compatible with the directive.

2. EXCLUSIONS, LIMITATIONS, AND DEROGATIONS

2.1 Exclusions and limitations

We have already seen that the directive does not cover non-economic activity, matters which are not considered as services (such as goods), and non-discriminatory rules of the game. The directive also contains more specific exclusions, limitations, and derogations. The principal *exclusions* can be found in Article 2(2)–(3). These provisions list those service sectors to which the directive 'does not apply'. The list is long and broad,[381] including services of general interest,[382] financial services,[383] electronic communication services and networks,[384] services in the field of transport,[385] temporary work agencies,[386]

---

[378] Case 197/84 *Steinhauser* v. *City of Biarritz* [1985] ECR 1819 had already established that Art. 49 TFEU covered both access to and exercise of the freedom of establishment.

[379] This recital is referred to in Joined Cases C–197 and 203/11 *Libert* EU:C:2013:288, para. 104. The Court therefore does not answer questions about the Services Dir. (but does consider the application of Art. 56 TFEU (para. 48)).

[380] Joined Cases C–51/96 and C–191/97 *Deliège* v. *Ligue Francophone de Judo et Disciplines Associés* [2000] ECR I–2549.

[381] Cf. the Commission's original proposal, which listed only three excluded services (financial services, electronic communications, and transport).

[382] Art. 2(2)(a).   [383] Art. 2(2)(b).   [384] Art. 2(2)(c).

[385] Art. 2(2)(d). This includes transport by inland waterway and urban transport services but not pleasure boats: Joined Cases C–340 and 341/14 *Trijber and Hamsen* EU:C:2015:641, paras. 48, 50, and 56.

[386] Art. 2(2)(e).

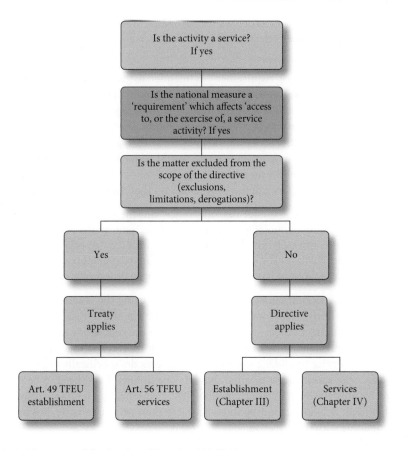

Fig. 11.1 The scope of the Services Directive 2006/123

and private security services.[387] Most importantly, from the perspective of this chapter and Chapter 9, healthcare services;[388] audiovisual services;[389] and gambling activities,[390] including lotteries, gambling in casinos, and betting transactions, are excluded from the scope of the directive. In addition, Article 2(3) adds that 'This Directive shall not apply to the field of taxation.' The Treaty provisions on services will continue to apply to these areas (see fig. 11.1).[391]

Article 1(2)–(7) of the directive spells out a further group of *limitations*. Of perhaps most interest is Article 1(6)–(7). Introduced to provide reassurance to the trade union

---

[387] Art. 2(2)(k).

[388] Art. 2(2)(f). This is to be interpreted broadly: Case C–57/12 *Femarbel* v. *Commision comunautaire commune de Bruxelles-Capitale* EU:C:2013:517, para. 35 (it may include care activities in day care and night care centres where there is some medical provision 'to maintain or restore the state of health of patients, where that activity is carried out by healthcare professionals'). The phrase includes optician services: Case C–539/11 *Ottica New Line di Accardi Vincenzo* v. *Comune di Campobello di Mazara* EU:C:2013:591. Note the reference to the (broader) recital to expand the scope of the exclusion (para. 18).

[389] Art. 2(2)(g).   [390] Art. 2(2)(h). See also the 25th recital of the preamble.

[391] See Case C–342/14 *X-Steurberatungsgesellschaft* v. *Finanzamt Hannover-Nord* EU:C:2015:827, para. 41; Case C–539/11 *Ottica New Line di Accardi Vincenzo* EU:C:2013:591, para. 23.

movement, which saw the Services Directive as a potential threat to labour standards in the light of the disputes in *Viking*[392] and *Laval*,[393] Article 1(6) makes clear that the directive *does not affect* labour law and social security legislation of the Member States[394] and Article 1(7) adds that the directive *does not affect* the exercise of fundamental rights as recognized in the Member States and by Union law, including the right to negotiate, conclude, and enforce collective agreements and to take industrial action.

2.2 Other derogations

There are other derogations which apply to specific parts of the directive, most importantly Article 17, entitled 'additional derogations', and Article 18, 'case-by-case derogations', both of which derogate from Chapter IV on the free movement of services. In addition, some of the requirements in Chapter III on establishment are subject to the full range of public-interest requirements (ORRPI) developed by the Court of Justice ('broad justifications'), while some of the requirements in Chapter IV are subject to the express derogations provided in the Treaty plus environmental protection ('narrow justifications'). These are considered in Section 4.

3. CHAPTER III ESTABLISHMENT

3.1 Introduction

The directive tries to codify the extensive case law on freedom of establishment of service providers in Chapter III. Article 4(5), drawing on the decision in *Gebhard*,[395] defines establishment as 'the actual pursuit of an economic activity, as referred to in Article [49] of the Treaty, by the provider for an indefinite period and through a stable infrastructure from where the business of providing services is actually carried out'.[396] The directive therefore covers the situation where providers of services wish to establish themselves in the state and provide services there either as a new business (primary establishment) or where an existing business wishes to set up a new establishment, such as a branch or agency (secondary establishment).

3.2 Wholly Internal Situations

There is a debate as to whether Chapter III applies not only to out-of-state providers wishing to establish themselves in the host state (cross-border service provision) but also to in-state providers wishing to establish themselves, either through primary or secondary establishment, in their own state (wholly internal situations).[397] Some support for a broad reading of Chapter III comes from the preamble, which says that the concept of the provider should 'not be limited solely to cross-border service provision ... but should also cover cases in which an operator establishes itself in *a* Member State in order to develop its service activities there'.[398] Further, Chapter III on establishment, unlike

---

[392] Case C–438/05 *International Transport Workers' Federation* v. *Viking Line ABP* [2007] ECR I–10779.

[393] Case C–341/05 *Laval* [2007] ECR I–987.

[394] See also the 15th recital, which expressly refers to the Charter and the accompanying explanations.

[395] Case C–55/94 *Gebhard* [1995] ECR I–4165, para. 25.

[396] Fuller details are provided in the 37th recital.

[397] Commission Handbook on the Services Dir., OPEC, 2007 ('Handbook') also available at <http://ec.europa.eu/internal_market/services/docs/services-dir/guides/handbook_en.pdf>, 31. The handbook has been cited by the Court as an aid to interpretation: Case C–57/12 *Femarbel* v. *Commission comunautaire commune de Bruxelles-Capitale* EU:C:2013:517, paras. 37 and 46.

[398] 36th recital, emphasis added.

Chapter IV on Services, makes no reference to the need to be established in *another* Member State.[399]

The issue was actually discussed during the negotiations: an amendment proposing that the directive should be confined to inter-state situations was rejected by the IMCO Committee of the European Parliament. This tends to suggest that the directive does apply to wholly internal, as well as inter-state, situations. However, there are two arguments against this position. First, the Court, albeit somewhat uncertainly, is holding the line that Union law on free movement of persons does not apply to wholly internal situations.[400] The counter argument to this is that the Services Directive achieves for establishment what harmonization directives do for goods: product standard directives cover all manufactured or marketed goods even though Article 34 TFEU applies only to cross-border situations. Secondly, while the legal bases of the directive (Articles 53 and 62 TFEU) make no reference to transnational situations, Article 53 is in the same chapter as Article 49 TFEU, which refers to cross-border situations only. In *Trijber*[401] the Court was presented with an opportunity to consider this point but avoided it by finding that the recipients of the service could be nationals from another Member State.

Whatever the scope of the directive, the establishment chapter specifically deals with two groups of rules: (1) authorization schemes, and (2) requirements which are prohibited or subject to evaluation (see fig. 11.2). We shall consider these in turn.

3.3 Authorization Schemes

(a) The rules

Article 9(1) provides that authorization schemes, broadly defined as obligations on a service provider to be in some way authorized, accredited, licensed, or registered before it can operate in a particular country,[402] are not permitted.[403] In fact, this prohibition is subject to an 'unless' clause broadly replicating the Court of Justice's case law on justifications:[404] authorization schemes are permitted provided that:

- they do not discriminate (either directly or indirectly) against the provider in question
- the scheme is justified by an overriding reason relating to the public interest (ORRPI)
- the objective pursued cannot be attained by means of a less restrictive measure (e.g., monitoring the activities of the service provider or making a simple declaration).

This is the classic formulation found in cases such as *Gebhard*: non-discriminatory authorization schemes can be justified by public-interest requirements (ORRPI), provided the steps taken are proportionate. So what are the ORRPI?

---

[399] See also Art. 2(1), on scope, which does not refer to an inter-state element. It merely provides: 'This Directive shall apply to services supplied by providers established in *a* Member State' (emphasis added). The same language is used in the 16th recital. Cf. 5th recital: 'Since the barriers in the internal market for services affect operators who wish to become established in *other* Member States as well as those which provide a service in another Member State without being established there' (emphasis added).

[400] Case C–212/06 *Walloon Government* [2008] ECR I–1683, considered in Ch. 7.

[401] Joined Cases C–340 and 341/14 *Trijber and Hamsen* EU:C:2015:641, para. 42.

[402] BERR Consultation Paper 2007, 65.

[403] This is subject to the caveat in Art. 9(3) that 'This section shall not apply to those aspects of authorisation schemes which are governed directly or indirectly by other [Union] instruments'; cf. Art. 3(1).

[404] Case C–55/94 *Gebhard* [1995] ECR I–4165.

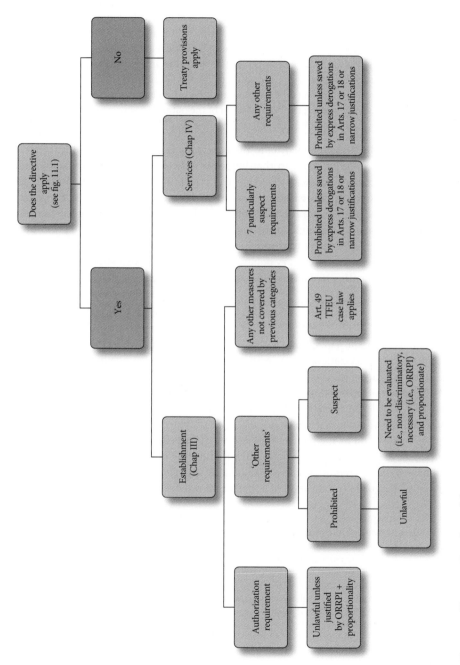

Fig. 11.2 Chapters III and IV of the Services Directive

(b) ORRPI

The directive, following the lead given by the Court, adopts a broad and non-exhaustive approach to 'overriding reasons relating to the public interest'. According to Article 4(8), the phrase means:

> reasons recognised as such in the case law of the Court of Justice, including the following grounds: public policy (which includes issues relating to human dignity, the protection of minors and vulnerable adults and animal welfare);[405] public security; public safety; public health; preserving the financial equilibrium of the social security system; the protection of consumers, recipients of services and workers; fairness of trade transactions; combating fraud; the protection of the environment and the urban environment; the health of animals; intellectual property; the conservation of the national historic and artistic heritage; social policy objectives and cultural policy objectives.[406]

The list of overriding reasons relating to the public interest found in the 40th recital of the preamble[407] is even longer than that found in Article 4(8). Some of the additional headings do reflect the case law of the Court (e.g., the prevention of unfair competition, safeguarding the sound administration of justice) but some are new or have not appeared in this form before (e.g., 'cultural policy objectives, including safeguarding the freedom of expression of various elements, in particular social, cultural, religious and philosophical values of society; the need to ensure a high level of education, ... the promotion of the national language; ... and veterinary policy'.) With such extensive justifications available to the host state, the directive has not in fact adjusted 'the scope of host state regulatory competence'.[408]

(c) The criteria for granting authorization

Not only must the requirement to be authorized be justified but so must the criteria applied in granting the authorization. Once again, the criteria used must be non-discriminatory, justified by overriding reasons in the public interest, and proportionate.[409]

The question of proportionality of authorization criteria was at issue in *Trijber and Hamsen*.[410] In order to operate a window prostitution business in the Netherlands, it was a condition of the authorization that the service provider be able to communicate in a language understood by the recipients of a service (the prostitutes). The Court found the requirement to be suitable to strengthen the monitoring of criminal activities and proportionate: it did not require the use of an official language of the Member State (Dutch) but merely a language and the level of language knowledge demanded was not that high.

---

[405] See the 41st recital: 'The concept of "public policy", as interpreted by the Court of Justice, covers the protection against a genuine and sufficiently serious threat affecting one of the fundamental interests of society and may include, in particular, issues relating to human dignity, the protection of minors and vulnerable adults and animal welfare. Similarly, the concept of public security includes issues of public safety.'

[406] In Joined Cases C–340 and 341/14 *Trijber and Hamsen* EU:C:2015:641, para. 68 the Court ruled that ORRPI covers public order, specifically preventing criminal offences being committed against prostitutes, in particular human trafficking, forced prostitution, and child prostitution.

[407] Cf. the 56th recital, which appears to offer an alternative, shorter, and exhaustive list of overriding reasons relating to the public interest.

[408] S. Weatherill, 'Promoting the consumer interest in an integrated services market', Mitchell Working Paper Series, 1/2007, 7.

[409] The definition of proportionality is not provided here. Cf. Art. 10(3)(c) where a strict proportionality test is applied. For a thorough discussion of the proportionality test in the UK context, see *R. (on the application of Lumsdon) v. Legal Services Board* [2015] UKSC 1276.

[410] Joined Cases C–340 and 341/14 *Trijber and Hamsen* EU:C:2015:641, paras. 73–5.

Not only must the criteria be non-discriminatory, justifiable, and proportionate, they must also be:

- clear and unambiguous
- objective
- made public in advance
- transparent and accessible.[411]

These conditions for essentially good governance, especially transparency, had already begun to surface in the Court's case law interpreting the Treaty.[412]

The influence of the Court's case law, in particular mutual recognition, can also be felt elsewhere: for example, conditions for granting authorization for a new establishment must not duplicate requirements and controls which are equivalent or essentially comparable to those already conducted in another Member State or in the same Member State.[413] Again, following the Court's case law, the directive provides that the authorization must enable the provider to have access to the service activity, or to exercise that activity, throughout the national territory unless there are good reasons why not (e.g., where separate planning permission is required for the opening of each shop).[414] In practical terms, the effect of the directive is that authorizations granted by one local authority bind other local authorities unless there are good reasons otherwise.[415]

(d) Procedural protection

The directive guarantees a certain level of procedural protection. It provides that decisions relating to authorization (e.g., refusing or withdrawing authorization but not its granting), have to be fully reasoned and subject to review by the courts;[416] that the authorization should not be for a limited period, subject to certain public-interest justifications;[417] and that authorization procedures have to be clear, made public in advance,[418] not unduly complicated,[419] and dealt with expeditiously.[420] Likewise, where the number of authorizations is limited, due to scarcity of available natural resources or technical capacity, any selection procedure must also comply with principles of fairness.[421]

---

[411] Art. 10(2).

[412] See, e.g., Case C–95/01 *Greenham and Abel* [2004] ECR I–1333, considered in Ch. 6; Case C–157/99 *Geraets-Smits and Peerbooms* [2001] ECR I–5473, considered in Ch. 9; Case C–54/99 *Association Eglise de Scientologie de Paris* v. *The Prime Minister* [2000] ECR I–1335, considered in Ch. 14. These cases continue to be applied in areas not covered by the directive: Case C–470/11 *Garkalns SIA* EU:C:2012:505, para. 42.

[413] Art. 10(3) and the 61st recital of the preamble. See, by analogy, the goods case, Case C–292/94 *Criminal Proceedings against Brandsma* [1996] ECR I–2159.

[414] Art. 10(4) and the 59th recital. See also Case C–134/05 *Commission* v. *Italy* [2007] ECR I–6251.

[415] Handbook, 36.   [416] Art. 10(6). See, by analogy, Case 222/86 *Heylens* [1987] ECR 4097.

[417] Art. 11(1). In Joined Cases C–340 and 341/14 *Trijber and Hamsen* EU:C:2015:641, para. 66 authorizations to operators of pleasure boat tours could be limited in time for the protection of the environment and public safety.

[418] Art. 13(1). See, by analogy, Case C–503/99 *Commission* v. *Belgium* [2002] ECR I–4809.

[419] Art. 13(2).

[420] Art. 13(3). If no response is given within the set time, the authorization is deemed to have been granted: Art. 13(4) and 63rd recital.

[421] Art. 12(1). See also 62nd recital. In establishing the rules for the selection procedure Member States can take into account various public-interest requirements including social-policy objectives, health and safety of employees and the self-employed, and preservation of the environment as well as 'overriding reasons relating to the public interest': Art. 12(3). Any authorization must be granted for a limited period: Art. 12(2).

3.4 'Other Requirements'

The directive concerns not only authorization schemes but also 'other requirements'. In respect of these 'other requirements',[422] the directive distinguishes between (1) those which are prohibited, and (2) those which are 'suspect' and need to be evaluated.

(a) Prohibited requirements

Article 14 lists eight requirements which are *prohibited*. This means that there are no overriding reasons in the public interest (ORRPI) justifications or derogations provided by the directive available to Member States.[423] Further, as the Court confirmed in *Rina Services*, primary law cannot be used to justify one of the prohibited requirements, despite the wording of Article 3(3) of the directive (Member States are to apply its provisions 'in compliance with the provisions on the rules of the Treaty'), because this would ultimately undermine the 'ad hoc harmonisation' intended by the directive.[424] The Court continued that to concede that the prohibited requirements could be justified under primary law would be 'tantamount to reintroducing such case-by-case examination, under the FEU Treaty, for all the restrictions on freedom of establishment'.[425] In other words, the Court considers that prohibited requirements under Article 14, rules requiring 'systematic and swift removal',[426] is an area of exhaustive harmonization to which only the directive and not the Treaty applies.

The prohibited requirements draw extensively on the Court's case law. The first group concerns those rules which are discriminatory, either directly or indirectly. These include nationality requirements for the provider, its staff, individuals holding the share capital, or members of the provider's management or supervisory bodies;[427] or a requirement that these individuals be resident in the territory.[428] In the case of companies it also includes requirements about the location of the registered office.[429]

The directive also rules out requirements forbidding a provider from having an establishment in more than one Member State,[430] or on being entered in the registers or enrolled with professional bodies in more than one Member State.[431] In addition, it prohibits restrictions on the freedom of a provider to choose between a principal or a secondary establishment,[432] as well as the case-by-case application of an economic test making the granting of an authorization subject to proof of the existence of an economic

---

[422] Defined by Art. 1(7) to mean 'any obligation, prohibition, condition or limit provided for in the laws, regulations or administrative provisions of the Member States or in consequence of case-law, administrative practice, the rules of professional bodies, or the collective rules of professional associations or other professional organisations, adopted in the exercise of their legal autonomy; rules laid down in collective agreements negotiated by the social partners shall not as such be seen as requirements within the meaning of this Directive'.

[423] A point confirmed by Case C–593/13 *Presidenza del Consiglio dei Ministri* v. *Rina Services* EU:C:2015:399, para. 22.

[424] Para. 37.   [425] Para. 38.   [426] Para. 39.

[427] Case C–221/89 *Factortame II* [1991] ECR I–3905.

[428] Case C–350/96 *Clean Car* [1998] ECR I–2521.

[429] See also Art. 14(3) 'restrictions on the freedom of a provider to choose between a principal or a secondary establishment, in particular an obligation on the provider to have its principal establishment in their territory, or restrictions on the freedom to choose between establishment in the form of an agency, branch or subsidiary': considered in Case C–593/13 *Rina Services* EU:C:2015:399, para. 25.

[430] Case 96/85 *Commission* v. *France* [1986] ECR 1475.

[431] See also Case 107/83 *Klopp* [1984] ECR 2971.

[432] Case C–212/97 *Centros* [1999] ECR I–1459.

need or market demand.[433] The directive also prohibits competing operators from being involved in the decisions of competent authorities in the granting of individual authorizations; it prevents states from obliging operators to obtain financial guarantees or insurance from operators established in that state;[434] and it prohibits states from obliging providers to have been previously registered or to have previously exercised the activity for a given period in that state.[435] The importance of Article 14 was emphasized in *Rina Services*:[436] these prohibited requirements had to be 'removed, systematically and as a matter of priority'.

(b) Suspect requirements

Article 15(2) identifies a further eight requirements, a number of which have already been considered 'restrictions' on freedom of establishment in the case law, which are 'suspect' or subject to evaluation. These include quantitative or territorial restrictions (e.g., a rule limiting the number of operators providing a service in a particular area or limiting the number of operators per head of population or setting a minimum distance between operators[437]); an obligation on a provider to take a specific legal form (e.g., a requirement that only legal persons can provide a particular service, thereby excluding natural persons from the market);[438] or a requirement that non-profit-making bodies only can provide a service[439]); a ban on having more than one establishment in the territory of the same state;[440] and requirements fixing a minimum number of employees[441] or fixing minimum or maximum tariffs with which the provider must comply (thereby depriving service providers the right to compete on price or quality).[442]

Unlike the prohibited requirements, the directive requires Member States to evaluate whether these suspect requirements are compatible with the conditions laid down in Article 15(3),[443] namely checking whether they are (1) non-discriminatory (i.e., neither directly nor indirectly discriminatory on the grounds of nationality/location of registered office); (2) necessary[444] (i.e., the requirements must be justified 'by an overriding reason relating to the public interest'); and (3) proportionate (this is the strict proportionality test: 'requirements must be suitable for securing the attainment of the objective

---

[433] This provision does not apply to territorial planning requirements which do not pursue economic aims but serve overriding reasons relating to the public interest (Art. 14(5)).

[434] See also 67th recital.

[435] See also 68th recital and Case C–203/98 *Commission* v. *Belgium (aerial photography)* [1999] ECR I–4899.

[436] Case C–593/13 *Rina Services* EU:C:2015:399, para. 26.

[437] Case 140/03 *Commission* v. *Greece (opticians)* [2005] ECR I–3177; Joined Cases C–570 and 571/07 *Pérez and Gómez* [2010] ECR I–4629; Case C–89/09 *Commission* v. *France (bio-medical analysis)* [2010] ECR I–12941; Case C–400/08 *Commission* v. *Spain (hypermarkets)* [2011] ECR I–1915; Case C–84/11 *Susisalo* EU:C:2012:374.

[438] Case C–171/02 *Commission* v. *Portugal* [2004] ECR I–5645.

[439] Case C–439/99 *Commission* v. *Italy (trade fairs)* [2002] ECR I–305.

[440] Cf. Art. 14(2) prohibiting national rules preventing service providers from having an establishment in *more* than one state.

[441] See Case C–514/03 *Commission* v. *Spain (security services)* [2006] ECR I–963.

[442] See also Joined Cases C–94 and 202/04 *Cipolla* [2006] ECR I–11421. The other requirements listed in Art. 15 are rules relating to shareholding of capital (e.g., requirements on companies to hold a minimum amount of capital); requirements reserving the right to provide certain services to particular providers; an obligation on the provider to supply other specific services jointly with the principal service. Cf. Case C–565/08 *Commission* v. *Italy (maximum tariffs)* [2011] ECR I–2101.

[443] Confirmed in Case C–593/13 *Rina Services* EU:C:2015:399, para. 32.

[444] Confusingly so-called when what is actually meant is objective justification, the language used in, e.g., Art. 10(2)(b).

pursued; they must not go beyond what is necessary to attain that objective and it must not be possible to replace those requirements with other, less restrictive measures which attain the same result'[445]). The Commission's handbook places much emphasis on the need to apply the proportionality principle in respect of these suspect requirements. For example, in respect of the ban on having more than one establishment on the territory, the Commission argues that 'in many cases Member States will be able to ensure the objective of high quality of services by other less restrictive means, such as a requirement to have qualified staff providing the service'.[446]

It is likely that requirements which are not listed as prohibited or suspect and which are not considered as authorizations under Articles 9–10 will continue to be subject to the traditional review under Article 49 TFEU as interpreted by the Court in cases such as *Gebhard*.[447] Since the Services Directive broadly endorses the Court of Justice's case law on public-interest requirements, it is likely that the outcomes under the directive and the Treaty will not be very different, albeit that any case decided under Article 49 TFEU will certainly require a transnational element.

3.5 Reporting, Mutual Evaluation, and the Standstill Provision

Chapter III of the directive contains reporting provisions: Article 9(2) requires Member States to identify their authorization schemes and give reasons to show why they are justified and proportionate.[448] A similar provision applies to suspect requirements needing to be evaluated.[449] These reports feed into the process of mutual evaluation.[450]

Article 15(6) introduces a partial standstill clause. This provides that Member States cannot introduce any new 'suspect' requirement of the kind listed in Article 15(2), from 28 December 2006, unless justified by an ORRPI under Article 15(3). Further, Article 15(7) applies a simplified notification procedure to such requirements: the Member State must notify the rules to the Commission, which must inform the other Member States. However, unlike the procedure under the Information Directive 2015/1535,[451] there is no standstill clause: the notifying state is free to adopt the requirement prior to any Commission decision.[452] The Commission then has three months to examine the compatibility of any new requirement with Union law and, where appropriate, adopt a decision requesting the notifying state to refrain from adopting the requirement or to abolish the requirement.[453] This is a significant innovation aimed at controlling *ex ante* the introduction of barriers to establishment but nevertheless less effective than the Information Directive 2015/1535[454] procedure where, following cases such as *Unilever*,[455] the standstill provisions have legal consequences. The Information Directive, discussed in Chapter 4, does apply to draft technical regulations, which includes rules on information society services; that is, any service normally provided for remuneration, at a distance, by electronic means,

---

[445] Cf. Art. 10(2)(c), where no such detail is provided.

[446] Handbook, 47.   [447] COM(2004) 2, 23.

[448] The reporting obligation does not apply to the criteria and conditions for the granting of an authorization: 58th recital.

[449] Art. 15(5). In this report the states need to specify (1) the requirements they intend to maintain and the reason why they consider that those requirements comply with Art. 15(3), (2) the requirements which have been abolished, and (3) the requirements which have been made less stringent.

[450] Art. 39(5).   [451] [2015] OJ L241/1.

[452] It is therefore unlikely that Case C-194/94 *CIA* [1996] ECR I-2201 will apply to Art. 15(7).

[453] Notification made under Dir. 98/34 is deemed to fulfil the obligation of notification provided for in the Services Dir.

[454] [2015] OJ L241/1.   [455] Case C-443/98 *Unilever* [2000] ECR I-7535.

and at the request of the recipient of services. There are some key exceptions, including financial services and radio and TV broadcasting.

4. CHAPTER IV FREEDOM TO PROVIDE SERVICES

Following its radical overhaul by the McCreevy draft, Chapter IV on free movement of services, especially section 1, contains some of the most opaque provisions of the directive. This problem is exacerbated by the awkward mismatch between the original draft (Country-of-origin principle (CoOP) + derogations) and the final version (no CoOP + derogations), and between the directive and the case law under the Treaty.[456] We start by considering the most controversial provision of the whole directive, Article 16.

4.1 Article 16(1): Freedom to Provide Services v. The CoOP

The first and second paragraphs of Article 16(1) contain the general statements that:

> Member States shall respect the right of providers to provide services in a Member State other than that in which they are established.
> The Member State in which the service is provided shall ensure free access to and free exercise of a service activity within its territory.

The third paragraph of Article 16(1) adds that 'Member States shall not make access to or exercise of a service activity in their territory subject to compliance with any requirements' which do not satisfy the principle of non-discrimination, a narrow range of justifications, and proportionality.

The three parts of Article 16(1), based essentially on the Treaty language of freedom to provide services, replaced the controversial CoOP found in the original Article 16(1) of the, so-called Bolkestein draft. This said:

> Member States shall ensure that providers are subject only to the national provisions of their Member State of origin which fall within the coordinated field.

It continued that Article 16(1) covered national provisions relating to access to and the exercise of a service activity, in particular those requirements governing the behaviour of the provider, the quality or content of the service, advertising contracts, and the provider's liability. The original Article 16(2) then made clear that the Member State of origin was to be responsible for supervising the provider and the services provided by him, including services provided by him in another Member State. Article 16 was then subject to the three express derogations (general, transitional, and case-by-case derogations laid down in Articles 17–19).

For the Commission, the use of the country-of-origin principle in the Bolkestein version of the Services Directive was a logical extension of, for example, the TWF (now AVMS) Directive 2010/13 (considered in Case Study 11.2),[457] and the E-commerce Directive 2000/31,[458] both of which had the country-of-origin principle at their core.[459] However, the Services Directive was considerably more ambitious than its sectoral forebears, since its horizontal approach meant that it covered all the sectors in its scope[460]

---

[456] Art. 3(3) expressly provides that 'Member States shall apply the provisions of this Directive in compliance with the rules of the Treaty on the right of establishment and the free movement of services.'

[457] [1989] OJ L298/23.   [458] [2000] OJ L178/1.

[459] For a discussion on the three generations of the CoOP in the legislative practice of the EU: V. Hatzopoulos, 'Legal aspects in establishing the internal market for services', College of Europe Research Paper in Law 6/2007, 27–9.

[460] See, e.g., COM(2004) 2, 8.

not just specific sectors. Further, while the TWF/AVMS Directive 2010/13 contained a mix of deregulation (country-of-origin principle) and re-regulation through minimum harmonization (e.g., rules on protection of minors, prohibition of racism), the Bolkestein proposal concerned deregulation (country-of-origin principle) and only very limited re-regulation. Given the broad and unidentified nature of services covered, more extensive re-regulation was not possible.

For this reason, among others, a large number of states lined up against the CoOP and the original Article 16 was doomed to fail in its pure CoOP form. The European Parliament's intervention secured the removal of the CoOP wording and replaced it with something apparently more anodyne now found in the current Article 16(1). But how great, in fact, is the difference between the CoOP and the freedom to provide services? Under the country-of-origin principle, the principal regulator would have been the home state, reinforced by the presumption that the host state could not impose any additional requirements unless there were very good reasons (listed in the derogations in the original Articles 17–19). On one view, the present Article 16 comes close to a country-of-origin principle: while the original version of Article 16 defined the law which could be applied (the home-state law), the current version defines the law that cannot be applied (the host-state law).[461] Another reading is that the current approach appears to reverse the country-of-origin principle:[462] it accepts that the host state can impose its own restrictions on the service provider, where there are good reasons for so doing, account being taken of the protection already provided in the home state.[463] This latter reading broadly reflects the case law of the Court where the CoOP is not as firmly embedded in respect of services as it is in free movement of goods. As we have seen,[464] the CoOP does exist, but not in terms of establishing the breach (as is the case for goods), but in terms of justifying the breach where the Court requires the host state to take into account requirements already imposed by the home state.

In practice, the difference between the original and current versions of Article 16 may well be one of emphasis rather than substance: the country-of-origin principle raises a strong presumption of illegality of the host-state measure; the current approach may raise a weaker presumption of illegality. This may mean that service providers will continue having to investigate the rules (justified under Article 16(1), third sentence and Article 16(3)) in each state in which they provide services, although their task will be made easier by the establishment of PSCs to provide recipients, in their state of residence, clear, easily accessible information, including by electronic means, about requirements applicable to service activities.[465]

4.2 Article 16(2): Particularly Suspect Requirements

In its original version, Article 16 contained a list of *prohibited* requirements which could not be saved by any general justifications but to which the express derogations in Articles 17–19 applied. This approach was changed in the final version of the directive. Article 16(2) identifies seven requirements (including an obligation on the provider to

---

[461] This reading is supported by looking at the three sentences of Art. 16(1) together.

[462] However, despite the change of wording in Art. 16(1), elements of the country-of-origin principle remain elsewhere in the directive, provisions which came almost unamended from the Bolkestein draft. See, e.g., Art. 29, which requires the authorities in the state of *establishment* to provide information to the host state about the legitimacy of the service provider. If the host state has reason to think that the service provider does not comply with the laws of the home state, the state of *establishment* must carry out checks, inspections, or investigations.

[463] This reading is supported by Art. 16(1), third sentence.

[464] See, e.g., Case C–76/90 *Säger* [1991] ECR I–4221, para. 15.   [465] Art. 21.

have an establishment in the territory of the host state[466] or to obtain an authorization from the host state's competent authorities, including an entry in a register;[467] and
a ban on the provider setting up a certain form or type of infrastructure, including
an office or chambers[468]) which can be saved not only by the express derogations in
Article 17 and the case-by-case derogations in Article 18, but also by a narrow list of
public-interest requirements provided for by the directive. In practice, it is likely that
states will find the seven requirements hard to justify. Therefore, we might term these
requirements 'particularly suspect'.

The narrow list of public-interest requirements can be used to justify not only the seven
requirements listed in Article 16(2) but also, according to Article 16(1), third paragraph,
'any [other] requirements' which affect access to or exercise of a service activity in another
Member State, such as a rule requiring the use of a particular language in the host state
(see fig. 11.2).

4.3 (Narrow) Justifications

The narrow justifications are listed in Article 16(1), third paragraph, and largely repeated
in Article 16(3).[469] According to Article 16(1), third paragraph, Member States shall not,
'make access to or exercise of a service activity in their territory subject to compliance
with any requirements' which do not respect the principles of (a) non-discrimination,
(b) necessity, and (c) proportionality.

Article 16(1) explains 'non-discrimination' in the following terms: 'the requirement
may be neither directly nor indirectly discriminatory with regard to nationality or, in the
case of legal persons, with regard to the Member State in which they are established'. This
is fairly standard fare, although no reference is made to discrimination on the grounds of
establishment which, as we have seen, is a well-established prohibited ground of discrimination in the Court's case law on services.[470]

The language of 'necessity' is misleading.[471] It does not in fact refer to the first limb
of a proportionality test but rather to justifications: 'the requirement must be justified for reasons of public policy, public security, public health or the protection of the
environment'. In fact, even the language of justifications is misleading because the list
contained in heading (b) is actually an expanded list of express derogations found in
the Treaty; environment has been added. No reference is made to the judicially developed overriding reasons relating to the public interest (ORRPI) used in Chapter III
on establishment. It must therefore be assumed that the drafters of the directive deliberately decided not to apply the full gamut of ORRPI to the seven requirements
listed in Article 16(2) of the directive and 'any [other] requirements'.[472] In this way the
directive reflects the long-established idea that the host state has more right to intervene in respect of establishment (hence the broad ORRPI justifications) than it does in
respect of services, where the principal regulator is the home state (hence the narrow
justifications).

---

[466] Case 33/74 *van Binsbergen* [1974] ECR 1299. In Case C–397/10 *Commission* v. *Belgium* [2011] ECR
I–95, para. 21 the Court said that the obligation for an undertaking to have a particular form or legal status
was an important restriction on free movement of services.

[467] Case C–390/99 *Canal Satélite* [2003] ECR I–607.

[468] Case C–55/94 *Gebhard* [1995] ECR I–4165.

[469] The McCreevy draft (COM(2006) 160) did not dare address this overlap: the version of Art. 16 that
got through the European Parliament was treated as almost sacred: J. Flower, 'Negotiating the Services
Directive' (2006–7) 9 *CYELS* 217, 229.

[470] Case 33/74 *van Binsbergen* [1974] ECR 1299.   [471] See also Art. 15(3)(b).

[472] See BERR (now BIS) Consultation Paper 2007, 68: 'No other justifications will be sufficient.'

Heading (c), proportionality, is more straightforward. Here the directive adopts the traditional two-pronged approach—the requirement must be suitable for attaining the objective pursued, and must not go beyond what is necessary to attain that objective. Integral to the proportionality review in the case law is a requirement on the host state to take account of the levels of protection provided to secure that interest in the home state.[473] This is not referred to in Article 16(1) but is implicit in the provisions on mutual assistance in Chapter VI.

4.4 Derogations

As we have seen, in the original version of the directive, the country-of-origin principle was flanked by general derogations, transitional derogations, and case-by-case derogations. This basic structure has remained largely intact in the final version of the directive, despite the (apparent) removal of the country-of-origin principle, but it is now supplemented by the justifications considered in Section 3.3. The derogations are now divided into two: the 'additional derogations' found in Article 17 and the case-by-case derogations found in Article 18.

The 'additional derogations' in Article 17 concern matters such as services of general economic interest in the utility sector and judicial recovery of debts[474] as well as matters covered by specific Union measures, including the Posted Workers Directive 96/71,[475] the Lawyers Directive 77/249,[476] Title II of the Professional Qualifications Directive 2005/36,[477] and the Citizens' Rights Directive 2004/38.[478] Article 16 will not apply to these areas.

The 'case-by-case' derogations found in Article 18 apply 'in exceptional circumstances only'.[479] Article 18(1) permits Member States to 'take measures relating to the safety of services' in respect of a particular provider established in another Member State. Article 18(2) adds two further caveats. First, a derogation can be made only after the mutual assistance procedure laid down in Article 35 has been complied with. The second caveat is that before the host state can take measures relating to the safety of a particular service, it must ensure (1) that there has been no harmonization in the field, (2) that the measures provide for a higher level of protection of the recipient than would be the case in a measure taken by the home state, (3) that the home state has not taken any measures or has taken measures which are insufficient as compared with those referred to in Article 35(2), and (4) that the measures are proportionate.[480]

Given this elaborate procedure, it is hard to imagine a Member State ever making use of Article 18 when they can invoke the (narrow) justifications in Article 16(1).

4.5 The Reporting Provisions

Buried in Article 45(5), and not in the Chapter on Services, are the reporting provisions: the Member States had to present a report to the Commission, by 28 December 2009, on the national requirements whose application can be justified, giving reasons.[481] By implication, all Member States had to first screen their national legislation. After the 2009 deadline, Member States must inform the Commission of any changes in their

---

[473] Case C–76/90 *Säger* [1991] ECR I–4221, para. 15.   [474] See also 85th recital.
[475] This is probably unnecessary given the exclusion in Art. 3(1)(a). See also the 86th and 87th recitals.
[476] [1977] OJ L78/17.   [477] [2005] OJ L255/22.
[478] [2004] OJ L158/77.   [479] See also 91st recital.
[480] Finally, Art. 18(3) makes clear that the case-by-case derogations under Art. 18 do not affect other Union instruments in which the freedom to provide services is guaranteed and where case-by-case derogations are provided, notably the E-commerce Dir.
[481] This is possibly a narrower reporting obligation than that under, e.g., Art. 9(2).

requirements or any new requirements, together with the reasons for them (presumably based on Article 16(1) and (3), although this is not stated). The Commission must inform the other Member States but the Member States remain free to adopt the provisions in question. The Commission is then to provide annual 'analyses and orientations on the application of these provisions in the context of this Directive'.

These screening provisions were introduced in the 2006 draft of the directive, possibly to offset some of the consequences of removing the CoOP. At first blush these provisions appear to mirror the procedure for evaluating suspect requirements under Article 15 on establishment. There are, however, some significant differences. In particular, the services provisions are not subject to the full mutual evaluation procedure (despite the fact that the Commission says that the two procedures are in fact similar[482]); neither are they subject to either the same quasi-standstill provision found in Article 15(6) of the directive, nor to the equivalent of the procedure in the Technical Standards Directive 98/34.

5. RIGHTS OF RECIPIENTS OF SERVICES

Recipients of services also enjoy rights under the directive. Article 19 says that *home* states cannot impose requirements on recipients which restrict their use of a service supplied by a provider established in the host state. It then offers two examples of such restrictions:

- an obligation on the recipient to obtain authorization from, or to make a declaration to, the competent authorities of the home state (however, non-discriminatory authorization schemes are permitted[483])

- discriminatory limits on the grant of financial assistance by reason of the fact that the provider is established in another Member State or by reason of the location of the place at which the service is provided.[484]

The striking feature of these examples is that they are firmly rooted in the discrimination model while, as we have seen, the case law under Article 56 TFEU has moved beyond that.[485]

Article 20 is directed at the *host* state. Article 20(1) contains the general prohibition against discrimination (not restrictions/obstacles): 'Member States shall ensure that the recipient is not made subject to discriminatory requirements based on his nationality or place of residence.' This sentiment is amplified in Article 20(2), which says that 'Member States shall ensure that the general conditions of access to a service, which are made available to the public at large by the provider, do not contain discriminatory provisions relating to the nationality or place of residence of the recipient.' However, the obligations in Article 20(2) go beyond the state: all providers are under an obligation not to discriminate. This is a far-reaching provision which shows how the regulation of the provision of services can penetrate deep into the private sphere.

Article 20(2) contains the intriguing caveat that the principle of non-discrimination does not preclude 'the possibility of providing for differences in the conditions of access where those differences are directly justified by objective criteria'. This might mean that providers can impose different prices for postage and packaging depending on the location of the client.[486] However, it is not clear whether Article 20(2) means that all discrimination,

---

[482] Handbook, 79.   [483] 92nd recital.

[484] See Case C–55/98 *Bent Vestergaard* [1999] ECR I–7641 (see n. 357).

[485] See, e.g., Case C–158/96 *Kohll* [1998] ECR I–1931, para. 33. See also Case C–381/93 *Commission v. France (maritime services)* [1994] ECR I–5154, para. 17; Case C–136/00 *Danner* [2002] ECR I–8147, para. 29; Case C–118/96 *Safir* [1998] ECR I–1897, para. 23.

[486] BERR Consultation Paper 2007, 61.

direct or indirect, can be objectively justified, contrary to well-established case law, or whether it means that, in order to establish discrimination, the two situations have to be comparable and if there are objective differences between the situation of the service recipient and the migrant then no prima facie case of discrimination can be established.

Finally, Article 21 is intended to encourage potential recipients of a service to use services provided in other Member States by imposing requirements on the *home* state to provide information about consumer protection, the availability of dispute settlement in the providing state, and contact details of consumer bodies which can provide practical assistance.[487]

6. QUALITY OF SERVICES

It might be thought that a chapter on the quality of services would be the core of any directive on services and that it would contain detailed rules on how quality might be achieved. This is not, in fact, the case with the Services Directive, not least because this would not be feasible in a horizontal directive spanning over 80 sectors. Instead, much of Chapter V is actually devoted to the requirement of providing clear, timely information with a view to creating transparency in the transnational services market and building confidence.[488] For example, Article 22(1) lists 'indispensable' information which must be provided by the provider,[489] including information about the provider (e.g., name, legal status, form, contact details) and about the service (e.g., the price of the service, and insurance guarantees).[490] Article 24 imposes a general obligation on Member States to remove all total prohibitions on commercial communications; special provisions apply to the regulated professions.[491]

Further, albeit voluntary, confidence-building measures can be found in Article 23. Article 23(1) provides that Member States 'may' ensure[492] that providers established in their territory, whose services present a direct and particular risk to the health and safety of the recipient/third party/financial security of the recipient,[493] subscribe to professional liability insurance appropriate to the nature and the extent of the risk, or provide a guarantee or similar.[494]

Only in Article 26 does the chapter turn to the real question of quality of services and this is on a non-mandatory basis: 'Member States shall, in cooperation with the Commission, take accompanying measures to encourage providers to take action on a *voluntary basis* in order to ensure the quality of service provision'[495] in particular through

---

[487] Art. 21(2).

[488] See the equivalent provisions in Art. 5 of the E-commerce Dir. 2000/31 discussed by A. Lopez-Tarruella, 'A European Community regulatory framework for electronic commerce' (2001) 38 *CMLRev.* 1337.

[489] Art. 22(2) explains how this can be done. See also the 96th recital.

[490] See also the overlap in Art. 27(1).

[491] In Case C–119/09 *Société fiduciaire nationale d'expertise comptable* v. *Ministre du Budget, des Comptes publics et de la Fonction publique* [2011] ECR I–2551 the Court ruled that Art. 24 precluded national legislation which totally prohibited the members of a regulated profession, such as the profession of qualified accountant, from engaging in canvassing.

[492] In the 2004 version of the directive, the obligation was mandatory. Note the more mandatory language in the 98th and 99th recitals but the important caveat in the 99th recital: 'there should be no obligation for insurance companies to provide insurance cover'.

[493] These terms are all defined in Art. 23(5).

[494] This provision does not affect professional insurance or guarantee arrangements provided for in other Union instruments: Art. 23(4). The Commission has powers to flesh out the details of this provision, under the comitology procedures: Art. 23(4).

[495] Emphasis added.

certification or assessment of their activities by independent or accredited bodies; and drawing up their own quality charter or participation in quality charters or labels (e.g., the star classification system for hotels[496]) by professional bodies at Union level. This is the softest of the provisions in Chapter V.

7. THE ROLE OF THE STATE

One of the distinctive features of the Services Directive concerns the onerous obligations it places on the states. These are found primarily in Chapter II concerning administrative simplification (which require states to get their own houses in order) and Chapter VI on administrative cooperation (which require states to cooperate with each other).

7.1 Administrative Simplification

In respect of administrative simplification, Article 5(1) requires Member States to 'examine the procedures and formalities' applicable to the access to, and exercise of, a service activity (e.g., submission of documents and filing a declaration or registration to the relevant authorities) and simplify them where they are not sufficiently simple.[497] These few words, especially when read in conjunction with the specific screening obligations resulting from Chapters III and IV, impose a dramatic and onerous requirement not only on the Member States but also on the professional bodies, organizations, and associations[498] to verify that all national laws and other professional rules are compatible with the directive. If carried out thoroughly, and in the spirit of cooperation required by Article 4(3) TEU, the directive requires states and professional bodies to trawl through the many thousands of pages of their rulebooks to check whether the rules fall within the scope of the directive and, if they do, which rules may constitute barriers to the provision of services or the establishment of service providers. States must then either remove these barriers or justify them where appropriate and/or simplify the procedures, and then report back to the Commission on what they have done.[499] This legislative spring clean fits well with the Better Regulation agenda advocated by the Barroso Commission.[500]

Of more practical importance to service providers is the obligation on the Member States to establish a—real or virtual—point of single contact (PSC) through which it is possible to *complete*[501] all procedures and formalities (e.g., authorizations, declarations, notifications, the allocation of a company registration number[502]), whether imposed at central, regional, or local level.[503] These PSCs must, according to Article 7, provide providers and recipients of services with certain key information in a variety of Union languages.[504]

---

[496] According to Art. 26(3) information on the significance of certain labels and the criteria for applying labels and other quality marks relating to services must be easily accessed by providers and recipients. See also 102nd recital with the additional powers to the Commission to issue a mandate for the drawing up of specific European standards under Dir. 98/34 ([1998] OJ L204/37).

[497] This reflects the Union's own expressed intention to simplify its legislation: the Institutional Agreement on Better Law Making ([2003] OJ C321/1), para. 35.

[498] Art. 4(7) and Handbook, 77.   [499] Art. 39(1) and (5).

[500] See, e.g., Commission Communication, 'Strategic review of better regulation in the European Union', COM(2006) 689; 'A single market review', COM(2007) 60, 6. This is considered further in Ch. 15.

[501] Cf. Art. 57 of Recognition of Professional Qualifications Dir. 2005/36 ([2005] OJ L255/22), where the contact point merely provides information and assistance about having professional qualifications recognized. The PSC will allow individuals to have their qualifications actually recognized.

[502] Handbook, 26.   [503] This is largely repeated in Art. 8(1).   [504] Art. 7(5).

Chapter II does not 'draw any distinction between domestic and foreign providers'.[505] Therefore, its provisions apply in the same way to service providers established in another Member State and to service providers established (or wishing to establish) in the territory of their own Member State.[506] The thinking behind this is pragmatic. In the same way that domestic providers will benefit from any programme of legislative/administrative simplification which will also assist out-of-state providers, so should domestic providers also benefit from administrative support through use of PSCs.

7.2 Administrative Cooperation

Chapter VI on administrative cooperation returns to a theme familiar from free movement of goods: mutual assistance 'in order to ensure the supervision of providers and the services they provide'.[507] This is the corollary of the mutual recognition provisions found in the directive. Article 5(3) is one of the relatively few examples of mutual recognition provisions. It requires host states to accept documents from other Member States which serve equivalent purposes. Mutual recognition thus has the potential to avoid a proliferation of rules applicable to service providers, but it only works if there is confidence between states and a willingness on the part of the host state to engage proactively with the home state and to cooperate. Mutual assistance is therefore intended to foster trust in the legal framework and supervision in other Member States.

To persuade states to cooperate, the directive designates which state is responsible in particular situations.[508] This is supported by a 'clear, legally binding obligation for Member States to cooperate effectively'.[509] In this way the Services Directive builds on Regulation 2006/2004 on the cooperation between consumer protection authorities.[510] In practical terms, Member States have to designate one or more liaison points[511] as well as facilitating both operational cooperation and the provision of information by providers established in the home state to the competent authorities in other Member States.[512]

The success of the directive will, of course, depend on Member States' enthusiasm to comply with their screening obligations. The initial signs were not that encouraging. There was no fanfare on 28 December 2009, the date for the implementation of the directive, because, according to press reports, only 11 Member States had completed the steps necessary to put the directive onto their national statute books, still fewer had completed all the necessary operational steps in time.[513]

E. CONCLUSIONS

In this chapter we have seen the strong parallels being developed in the case law on the freedom of establishment of companies and free movement of services. For many years the principle of non-discrimination on the ground of nationality underpinned this jurisprudence. However, since *Gebhard*, the Court has shifted its focus from equal

---

[505] Handbook, 20–1.   [506] Handbook, 20–1.
[507] Art. 28(1). See also 108th recital. See also similar provisions in the Patients' Rights Dir. 2011/24/ EU in Chapter IV.
[508] Arts. 29–35.   [509] Arts. 29–35.   [510] [2004] OJ L364/1, referred to in 104th recital.
[511] Art. 28(2).   [512] Art. 28(3)–(7).
[513] 'Services law needs robust application', *European Voice*, 7 Jan. 2010. For an up-to-date assessment, see <http://ec.europa.eu/internal_market/services/docs/services-dir/implementation/report/SWD_2012_148_en.pdf>. Wide-ranging information on implementation can be found at <http://ec.europa.eu/internal_market/services/services-dir/implementation_en.htm>.

treatment to the removal of obstacles to access to the host state's market, and the exercise of the freedom—although in the field of taxation there is a move back to applying the discrimination approach. In all cases the possibility of derogating from the free movement provisions remains crucial to the Member States, either using the express derogation or the public-interest justifications and it is to this subject that we turn in Chapter 12.

FURTHER READING

Primary and secondary establishment

V. EDWARDS, 'The secondary establishment of companies: The case law of the Court of Justice' (1998) 18 *YEL* 221.

Regulatory competition

C. BARNARD and S. DEAKIN, 'Market access and regulatory competition' in C. Barnard and J. Scott (eds.), *The Law of the Single European Market: Unpacking the premises* (Oxford: Hart Publishing, 2002).

P. CABRAL and P. CUNHA, '"Presumed innocent": Companies and the exercise of the right of establishment under Community law' (2000) 25 *ELRev.* 157.

S. DEAKIN, 'Legal diversity and regulatory competition: Which model for Europe?' (2006) 12 *ELJ* 440.

S. DEAKIN, 'Two types of regulatory competition: Competitive federalism versus reflexive harmonisation. A law and economics perspective on *Centros*' (1999) 2 *CYELS* 231.

R. DRURY, 'Migrating companies' (1999) 24 *ELRev.* 354.

W. SCHÖN, 'Playing different games? Regulatory competition in tax and company law compared' (2005) 42 *CMLRev.* 331.

M. SIEMS, 'Convergence, competition, *Centros* and conflicts of law: European company law in the 21st century' (2002) 27 *ELRev.* 47.

K. SØRENSEN, 'Prospects for European company law after the judgment of the European Court of Justice in *Centros Ltd*' (1999) 2 *CYELS* 203.

EU company law

V. EDWARDS, *EC Company Law* (Oxford: OUP, 1999).

E. WYMEERSCH, 'The transfer of the company's seat in European company law' (2003) 40 *CMLRev.* 661.

EU tax law

J. GHOSH, *Principles of the Internal Market and Direct Taxation* (Oxford: Key Haven Publications, 2007), 82–3.

M. GRAETZ and A. WARREN, 'Dividend taxation in Europe: When the ECJ makes tax policy' (2007) 44 *CMLRev.* 1577.

S. KINGSTON, 'The boundaries of sovereignty: The ECJ's controversial role applying the internal market rules to taxation' (2006–7) 9 *CYELS* 287.

J. SNELL, 'Non-discriminatory tax obstacles in Community law' (2007) 56 *ICLQ* 339.

Abuse of law

R. DE LA FERIA and S. VOGENAUER (eds.), *Prohibition of Abuse of Law: A new general principle of EU Law* (Oxford: Hart Publishing, 2011).

P. SCHAMMO, 'Arbitrage and abuse of rights in the EC legal system' (2008) 14 *ELJ* 351.

Gambling cases

J. ANDERSON and D. DOUKAS, 'Commercial gambling without frontiers: When the ECJ throws, the dice is loaded' (2008) 27 *Yearbook of European Law* 237.

Services Directive

C. BARNARD, 'Unravelling the Services Directive' (2008) 45 *CMLRev.* 323.

Commission Communication, 'On the Implementation of the Services Directive: A Partnership for new growth in services', COM(2012) 261 final, and the accompanying Staff Working Document, SWD(2012) 148.

Audiovisual Media Services Directive

M. BURRI-NENOVA, 'The New Audiovisual Media Services Directive: Television without frontiers, television without cultural diversity' (2007) 44 *CMLRev.* 1689.

The *Viking* and *Laval* litigation

A. C. L. DAVIES, 'One step forward, two steps back? The *Viking* and *Laval* cases in the ECJ' (2008) 37 *ILJ* 126.

M FREEDLAND and J. PRASSL (eds.), *Viking, Laval and Beyond* (Oxford: Hart Publishing, 2015).

I. LIANOS and O. ODUDU, *Regulating Trade in Services in the EU and the WTO: Trust, distrust and economic integration* (Cambridge: CUP, 2012).

Posted workers

C. BARNARD, 'More posting' (2014) 43 *ILJ* 194.

P. DAVIES, 'Posted workers: Single market or protection of national labour law systems' (1997) 34 *CMLRev.* 571.

12

DEROGATIONS, LIMITATIONS, AND JUSTIFICATIONS

A. INTRODUCTION

Chapters 8–11 concerned the specific rights enjoyed by migrant workers, the self-employed, providers/receivers of services, and citizens in the host state. We turn now to examine the express powers given to the Member States by Union law to prevent or restrict migrants from enjoying those rights in full. The express derogations laid down by the Treaty fall into two categories: general derogations (public policy, public security, and public health) and specific derogations (employment in the public service). In principle, the *general* derogations are used to justify a decision to refuse a person entry or to expel them, as well as justifying any discriminatory measure or other conduct which prevents or impedes access to the market or exercise of the freedom (see fig. 7.2). In practice, however, because the general derogations are used as a means of controlling migration they are invoked more commonly by states than other actors. The *specific* derogation applies only to the initial refusal of access to employment in the public sector.

In addition to these express derogations the three directives on the rights of residence adopted in the 1990s contained limitations.[1] In particular, they required those seeking residence (students, persons of independent means, and the retired) to have sufficient resources and medical cover. With the repeal of the three directives, the limitations have been incorporated into the Citizens' Rights Directive 2004/38 (CRD). As a result of the case law on citizenship, the limitations laid down by these directives were subject to an increasingly strict proportionality review before becoming a precondition to enjoying the right of residence.

Supplementing the express derogations are the 'public interest' requirements developed by the Court. Initially, these public-interest requirements could be invoked by the Member States to justify indirectly discriminatory and non-discriminatory national rules, together with those rules which prevent or impede market access. In more recent cases there are signs that these justifications can also be invoked to defend directly discriminatory measures too, although the case law is not consistent. In this chapter we shall examine the express derogations laid down by the Treaty (Sections B and C), the limitations laid down by the CRD (Section D), and the public-interest justifications developed by the Court (Section E). We begin by considering the express derogations.

B. PUBLIC POLICY, PUBLIC SECURITY, AND PUBLIC HEALTH

1. INTRODUCTION

Article 45(3) TFEU allows Member States to derogate from the principle of free movement of workers on the grounds of public policy, public security, and public health. Articles 52 and 62 TFEU contain the same derogations for establishment and services. The burden of proof is on the defendant state to show that one of the derogations justifies its rule.[2] States have to put forward 'precise evidence' capable of establishing the existence of a derogation; general assertions of the public-policy interest at stake are not sufficient.[3]

Member States use express derogations to preserve their sovereign rights to control who enters their territory and who resides there. However, as we saw in Chapter 6, derogations to fundamental freedoms are interpreted strictly so that their scope cannot be determined unilaterally by a Member State without being subject to control by the Court.[4] In *Orfanopoulos*[5] the Court went so far as to say that 'a particularly restrictive' interpretation

---

[1] Council Dir. 90/364/EEC ([1990] OJ L180/26) on the rights of residence for persons of sufficient means; Council Dir. 90/365/EEC on the rights of residence for employees and self-employed persons who have ceased their occupational activity ([1990] OJ L180/28); and Council Dir. 93/96 on the rights of residence for students ([1993] OJ L317/59). These directives have been repealed and replaced by the Citizens' Rights Dir. 2004/38 ([2004] OJ L158/77).

[2] See, e.g., Case C–260/04 *Commission* v. *Italy (horse race betting licences)* [2007] ECR I–7083, para. 33.

[3] Case C–161/07 *Commission* v. *Austria (certification)* [2008] ECR I–10671, para. 37.

[4] See, e.g., Case 41/74 *Van Duyn* v. *Home Office* [1974] ECR 1337, para. 18; Case C–348/96 *Calfa* [1999] ECR I–11, para. 23; Case C–114/97 *Commission* v. *Spain* [1998] ECR I–6717, para. 34. Case C–441/02 *Commission* v. *Germany* [2006] ECR I–3449, paras. 32–5 contains a useful summary of the rules applicable to the express derogations.

[5] Joined Cases C–482 and 493/01 *Orfanopoulos* v. *Land Baden-Württemberg* [2004] ECR I–5257, para. 53.

of the derogations is required in the case of citizens of the Union. The case law on derogations makes clear that:

- the derogations are read subject to the general principles of law, in particular
  proportionality[6] and fundamental human rights[7]
- the list of derogations is exhaustive[8]
- the derogations will not apply where Union directives provide for exhaustive harmonization of the field[9]
- derogations cannot be used to serve economic purposes.[10] Therefore, a Member State
  cannot rely on a derogation to justify excluding foreign nationals from its labour
  market simply because unemployment is high in the state and there is a political need
  to preserve jobs for nationals.[11]

The bare bones of the general derogations were originally fleshed out by the provisions
of Directive 64/221,[12] which regulated the state's response to the conduct by *individuals*.[13]
Directive 64/221 was repealed and replaced by the CRD.[14] Article 27(1) CRD makes clear
that Member States may restrict the freedom of movement and residence of Union citizens (i.e., any person having the nationality of a Member State, not just workers and the
self-employed) and their family members (irrespective of nationality), on grounds of
public policy, public security, or public health. However, while apparently reiterating the
provisions of the Treaty, in fact the directive has actually limited the circumstances in
which the host state can invoke the derogations because the CRD is premised on the
idea that the longer individuals reside in the host state, the harder it is for that state

---

[6] Case C–100/01 *Ministre de l'Intérieur* v. *Olazabal* [2002] ECR I–10981, para. 43; Case C–108/96 *Mac Queen* [2001] ECR I–837, para. 31; Case C–3/88 *Commission* v. *Italy* [1989] ECR I–4035, para. 15; Case C–348/96 *Calfa* [1999] ECR I–11, para. 23.

[7] See Case C–260/89 *ERT* v. *DEP* [1991] ECR I–2925, para. 43, where the Court said that the application of the derogations in Arts. 52 and 62 TFEU had to be appraised in the light of the general principle of freedom of expression in Art. 10 ECHR.

[8] Case C–17/92 *Federación de Distribuidores Cinematográficos* v. *Estado Español et Unión de Productores de Cine y Televisión* [1993] ECR I–2239, para. 20 (cultural policy is not one of the derogations set out in Art. 52 TFEU); Case C–388/01 *Commission* v. *Italy* [2003] ECR I–721, para. 20 (cohesion of the tax system not one of the derogations under Art. 52 TFEU).

[9] Case C–421/98 *Commission* v. *Spain (architects)* [2000] ECR I–10375, paras. 41–2.

[10] See, e.g., Case 352/85 *Bond* v. *Netherlands* [1988] ECR 2085, para. 34; Case C–384/08 *Attanasio Group* [2010] ECR I–2055, para. 55; and Art. 27(1) CRD.

[11] Cf. the transitional limitations on free movement of workers contained in the Accession Agreements.

[12] [1963–64] OJ Spec. Ed. (I), 117.

[13] According to Art. 2, Dir. 64/221 applied to all measures (legislative measures and individual decisions taken in applying the legislation (Case 36/75 *Rutili* [1975] ECR 1219, para. 21) as well as to judicial
decisions (Case 30/77 *R.* v. *Bouchereau* [1977] ECR 1999) concerning entry into the territory, issue or
renewal of residence permits, and expulsion from the territory). This suggests that the *directive* did
not apply to restrictions on access to employment or the general regulation of employment relations.
By contrast, it was thought that the *Treaty* derogations applied both to exclusion/expulsion *and* to
discrimination in respect of access to employment and discrimination in respect of the terms and conditions on which employment is granted or exercised (see, e.g., Case C–350/96 *Clean Car Autoservice*
v. *Landeshauptmann von Wien* [1998] ECR I–2521, para. 24, referring to Case C–415/93 *Bosman*
[1995] ECR I–4921, paras. 84–6). Although cf. Case C–114/97 *Commission* v. *Spain* [1998] ECR I–6717,
para. 42; Case C–355/98 *Commission* v. *Belgium* [2000] ECR I–1221, para. 29, which suggested that
the Treaty derogations applied to exclusion/expulsion decisions only and not to decisions concerning
wider employment matters.

[14] [2004] OJ L158/77.

to deport them (see fig. 12.2). Because the provisions of the CRD draw on Articles of Directive 64/221, as interpreted by the Court, this chapter examines the CRD with reference to the position under Directive 64/221.

2. PUBLIC POLICY AND PUBLIC SECURITY

2.1 Introduction

Despite the fact that the Treaty suggests that public policy and public security are separate derogations, the Court's case law has largely subsumed public security under the heading of public policy. The Court has given Member States a certain margin of discretion to determine what constitutes public policy in the light of their national needs.[15] For example, in *Van Duyn*[16] the Court said that the particular circumstances in which a Member State could rely on the concept of public policy might 'vary from one country to another and from one period to another'. It was therefore 'necessary to allow the competent national authorities an area of discretion within the limits imposed by the Treaty'. Similarly, in *Jany*[17] the Court said that '[Union] law does not impose on Member States a uniform scale of values as regard the assessment of conduct which may be considered to be contrary to public policy'.[18] Yet, in respect of individuals this margin of discretion is limited by the provisions of what is now the CRD.

2.2 Public Policy and the Individual

(a) Personal conduct

The starting point for determining what constitutes public policy and public security in respect of the individual was Article 3(1) of Directive 64/221,[19] now Article 27(2) CRD, first paragraph, which says that measures taken on the grounds of public policy must be 'based exclusively on the *personal conduct* of the individual concerned'.[20] The corollary of this is, as the Court pointed out in *Bonsignore*,[21] that extraneous matters unrelated to the individual may not be taken into account. Bonsignore was convicted of a firearms offence and of causing the death of his brother by negligence when handling a pistol for which he had no licence. A deportation order was made against him for reasons of a 'general preventive nature': faced with a resurgence of violence among immigrant communities,[22] the national court wanted to make an example of Bonsignore to deter others. The Court of Justice said that deportation in these circumstances would contravene the directive; deportation could be ordered, but only in the case of breaches of the peace and public security actually caused by the individual defendant himself.[23]

---

[15] Joined Cases 115 and 116/81 *Adoui and Cornuaille* v. *Belgian State* [1982] ECR 1665, para. 8.

[16] Case 41/74 *Van Duyn* [1974] ECR 1337, para. 18.

[17] Case C–268/99 [2001] ECR I–8615, para. 60.

[18] See also Case C–36/02 *Omega* [2004] ECR I–9609, para. 31.

[19] This provision is directly effective: Case 41/74 *Van Duyn* [1974] ECR 1337, para. 15.

[20] Emphasis added. While the category of public policy and public security is usually considered from the perspective of personal conduct, the annex to Dir. 64/221 listed diseases and disabilities which might threaten public security or public policy. It identified drug addiction, profound mental disturbance, and manifest conditions of psychotic disturbance with agitation, delirium, hallucinations, or confusion as falling within this category. This list does not appear in the CRD.

[21] Case 67/74 *Bonsignore* v. *Oberstadtdirektor of the City of Cologne* [1975] ECR 297, confirmed in Case C–441/02 *Commission* v. *Germany (Italian migrants)* [2006] ECR I–3449, para. 93.

[22] Mayras AG doubted the basis for such an order. He expressed himself to be 'rather sceptical' of the deterrent effect of a deportation order. He feared it masked xenophobia ([1975] ECR 297, 315).

[23] Paras. 6–7.

The question of what constitutes personal conduct was considered in detail in *Van Duyn*.[24] Mrs Van Duyn was refused entry into the UK to work as a secretary for the Church of Scientology. Although membership of this church was not prohibited by the British authorities, the church's activities were considered to be 'socially harmful'.[25] The Court said that the personal conduct did not need to be unlawful before a Member State could invoke the public-policy exception. It was sufficient that the conduct be deemed 'socially harmful' and that the state had taken administrative measures to counteract these particular activities.[26] In *Wahl*[27] the EFTA Court reached a similar conclusion about the Hell's Angels, a motorcycle organization 'associated with organized crime'.[28] The Court said that Iceland was not obliged to declare the organization unlawful before it could deny a member of the Hell's Angels leave to enter (an outright prohibition might have the effect of driving the organization underground) but the authorities 'must have clearly defined their standpoint as regards the activities of the organization' and must have taken 'administrative measures to counteract those activities'.

The Court was also asked to decide in *Van Duyn* whether membership of a particular organization could constitute personal conduct. It ruled that a person's past association could not, in general, justify a decision refusing him the right to move freely; but a person's present association with an organization could constitute personal conduct, because present association reflected a voluntary participation in the activities of an organization, as well as an identification with its aims and designs.[29]

More controversially, the Court also suggested in *Van Duyn* that the host state could refuse a national of another Member State the benefit of the rules on the free movement of persons, even though the state did not place a similar restriction on its own nationals.[30] Therefore, the UK could refuse to allow a Dutch national to enter the UK to work for the Church of Scientology on public-policy grounds while permitting, albeit with disapproval, a British national to do the very same job. The Court justified this decision by reference to the principle of international law[31] that Member States have no authority to refuse entry or to expel their own nationals from the territory of their own state.[32]

However, this aspect of the ruling in *Van Duyn* sits uncomfortably with the general principle of non-discrimination on the ground of nationality and subsequent case law has implicitly reversed this aspect of the judgment. It is now clear that Member States must apply the doctrine of non-discrimination insofar as it is consistent with the principles of international law. Therefore, if equivalent conduct on the part of the state's own nationals is not subject to 'repressive measures or other genuine and effective measures intended to combat such conduct',[33] it cannot be a cause for expelling migrants. This can be seen in

---

[24] Case 41/74 [1974] ECR 1337.

[25] On 25 Jul. 1968 the Minister of Health said in the House of Commons that 'Scientology is a pseudo-philosophical cult ... [It] is socially harmful. It alienates members of families from each other and attributes squalid and disgraceful motives to all who oppose it ... There is no power under existing law to prohibit the practice of Scientology; but the government have concluded that it is so objectionable that it would be right to take all steps within their power to curb its growth.' These steps included preventing foreign nationals from entering to study or work there. As Mayras AG noted, the UK's lack of power to take measures against the Church is 'one consequence of a particularly liberal form of government'.

[26] Para. 19.   [27] Case E–15/12 *Wahl v. Iceland* [2013] EFTA Ct. Rep. 534, paras. 100–1.

[28] Para. 89.   [29] Para. 17.   [30] Para. 21.   [31] Para. 22.

[32] See further Case C–171/96 *Pereira Roque v. Governor of Jersey* [1998] ECR I–4607, paras. 49–50; Case C–348/96 *Calfa* [1999] ECR I–11, para. 20. This principle is reinforced by Art. 27(4) CRD: the Member State which issued the migrant's passport or identity card (usually the state of origin) must allow the migrant who has been expelled on the grounds of an express derogation to re-enter its territory without any formality, even if the document is no longer valid or the nationality of its holder is in dispute.

[33] Joined Cases 115 and 116/81 *Adoui and Cornuaille* [1982] ECR 1665, para. 8; confirmed in Case E–15/12 *Wahl* [2013] EFTA Ct. Rep. 534, paras. 104–5.

Adoui and Cornuaille,[34] where two French prostitutes[35] were refused permission to reside in Belgium on public-policy grounds, despite the fact that prostitution was not prohibited by Belgian legislation.[36] The Court said that Member States were not entitled to base the exercise of their discretion on 'assessments of certain conduct which would have the effect of applying an arbitrary distinction to the detriment of nationals of other Member States'.[37] Therefore, Member States must be consistent in their conduct towards nationals and migrants. As the Court put it succinctly in *Jany*,[38] conduct by migrants (prostitution) which a Member State (the Netherlands) accepts on the part of its own nationals could not be regarded as constituting a genuine threat to public order.

The concept of personal conduct adopted in *Van Duyn* was further narrowed in *Bouchereau*.[39] The Court said that the public-policy exception could be invoked to justify restrictions on the free movement of workers only if 'there was a genuine and sufficiently serious threat affecting one of the fundamental interests of society'.[40] Therefore, a simple infringement of the social order by breaching the law (possessing drugs) would not be enough to justify steps taken on public-policy grounds. For similar reasons, in *Adoui*[41] the Court said that being a prostitute did not constitute sufficiently serious personal conduct to justify applying the derogations. Likewise, in *Jipa*[42] the Court said that the mere fact that a national of a Member State (Romania) had been deported from another state (Belgium) on the grounds of being an illegal resident there did not constitute sufficiently serious personal conduct to justify restricting his right to travel.

The Court has since repeatedly emphasized just how strictly it applies the 'genuine and sufficiently serious threat' test. In *Commission v. Germany (Italian migrants)*[43] Germany was condemned for expelling EU migrants on 'serious' public-policy grounds, a lower standard than the EU test of '*genuine and sufficiently* serious threat affecting a fundamental interest of society'. This tough line can also be seen in *Commission v. Spain (SIS)*.[44] Two Algerians married to EU citizens were refused entry into Spain because of a Schengen 'alert' which had been issued against them.[45] The Schengen Contracting States had agreed that they would issue an 'alert' concerning a third-country national (TCN) spouse on grounds of public policy and public security, terms which were more loosely defined than their equivalents in the EU directive. The Court said that the existence of an alert against a TCN was evidence that there were reasons for refusing entry to the TCN but such evidence had to be corroborated by information enabling the host state to verify whether the individual constituted a present and sufficiently serious threat affecting the fundamental

---

[34] Joined Cases 115 and 116/81 *Adoui and Cornuaille* [1982] ECR 1665.

[35] Or, as the Court delicately put it, they worked at a bar that was 'suspect from the point of view of morals'.

[36] Para. 6, although certain incidental activities, such as the exploitation of prostitution by third parties and various forms of incitement to debauchery, were unlawful.

[37] Para. 7.

[38] Case C–268/99 *Jany* [2001] ECR I–8615, para. 61. This case concerned the Association Agreements with Poland and the Czech Republic.

[39] Case 30/77 [1977] ECR 1999.

[40] Para. 35. This test has also been applied in the context of the EEC–Turkey Association Council Dec. (considered further in Ch. 13): Case C–340/97 *Nazli* [2000] ECR I–957, paras. 56–61.

[41] Joined Cases 115 and 116/81 [1982] ECR 1665.

[42] See also Case C–33/07 *Ministerul Administrației și Internelor* v. *Jipa* [2008] ECR I–5157, para. 25.

[43] Case C–441/02 *Commission* v. *Germany (Italian migrants)* [2006] ECR I–3449. See also Case C–249/11 *Byankov* EU:C:2012:608, paras. 40–2.

[44] Case C–503/03 *Commission* v. *Spain* [2006] ECR I–1097.

[45] Further details about Schengen can be found at <http://ec.europa.eu/dgs/home-affairs/what-we-do/policies/borders-and-visas/index_en.htm>.

interests of society. Because the Spanish authorities had failed to verify whether the two Algerians did satisfy the *Bouchereau* test, Spain was in breach of Union law. This case therefore shows that, in the case of conflict between Schengen rules and the Treaty/CRD, the rules of the Treaty/CRD will take precedence.

Article 3(2) of Directive 64/221 and now Article 27(2) CRD provides that previous criminal convictions will not themselves constitute reasons for taking measures on the ground of public policy.[46] This issue was considered in *Bouchereau*,[47] where a French national working in England was convicted of unlawful possession of drugs. Six months earlier he had pleaded guilty to a similar offence and had been given a 12-month conditional discharge. The magistrate now wished to deport him on the ground of public policy. The Court decided that the existence of a criminal conviction could be taken into account only insofar as the circumstances which led to that conviction were evidence of 'personal conduct constituting a *present threat* to the requirements of public policy' by showing a propensity to commit the similar acts again.[48] This was a matter for the national court to decide.

The importance of showing that the individual constitutes a present threat to public policy was emphasized in *Calfa*.[49] Greece had expelled Calfa for life on the ground that she had been convicted of obtaining and being in possession of drugs for personal use. The Court ruled that Calfa could be expelled for having committed a criminal offence provided that her personal conduct created a genuine and sufficiently serious threat affecting one of the fundamental interests of society.[50] Under Greek law foreign nationals convicted under the drugs law were automatically expelled for life.[51] The Court said that because no account was taken of the personal conduct of the offender or of the danger which she represented to the requirements of public policy, Greek law breached the directive.[52] This case therefore makes clear that states can only take measures against individuals who have committed a criminal offence if, *in addition*, they constitute a present, genuine, and sufficiently serious threat to one of the fundamental interests of society.[53] In *Orfanopoulos*[54] the Court added that Member States also had to take into account factual matters which occurred after the final decision of the competent authorities which might point to the cessation or the substantial diminution of the present threat that the individual posed to public policy.[55]

This case law on personal conduct, starting with *Van Duyn*, has been incorporated into Article 27(2) CRD (figure 12.1 illustrates how Article 27(2) shapes the host state's decision-making process). It provides:

> Measures taken on grounds of public policy or public security shall comply with the principle of proportionality and shall be based exclusively on the personal conduct of the individual concerned.
>
> Previous criminal convictions shall not in themselves constitute grounds for taking such measures.

---

[46] Pending prosecutions are irrelevant: see *GW (EEA reg 21: fundamental interests) Netherlands* [2009] UKAIT 50 on the UK's refusal to allow Geert Wilders, a Dutch MP and leader of the right-wing Freedom Party, entry to the UK to show his controversial film 'Fitna' in the House of Lords: <http://cmr.jur.ru.nl/cmr/docs/wilders.AIT.pdf>.

[47] Case 30/77 [1977] ECR 1999.   [48] Paras. 28–9.

[49] Case C–348/96 [1999] ECR I–11.   [50] Para. 25.

[51] See also Joined Cases C–482 and 493/01 *Orfanopoulos* [2004] ECR I–5257, para. 53.

[52] Para. 27. See also Case C–50/06 *Commission v. The Netherlands (criminal convictions)* [2007] ECR I–4383, para. 46; Case C–434/10 *Aladzhov* [2011] ECR I–11659, para. 43.

[53] Case C–441/02 *Commission v. Germany (Italian migrants)* [2006] ECR I–3449, para. 35.

[54] Joined Cases C–482 and 493/01 *Orfanopoulos* [2004] ECR I–5257, para. 82.

[55] See also Case C–467/02 *Cetinkaya v. Land Baden-Württemberg* [2004] ECR I–10895, para. 47 concerning the EEC–Turkey Association Agreement, considered further in Ch. 13.

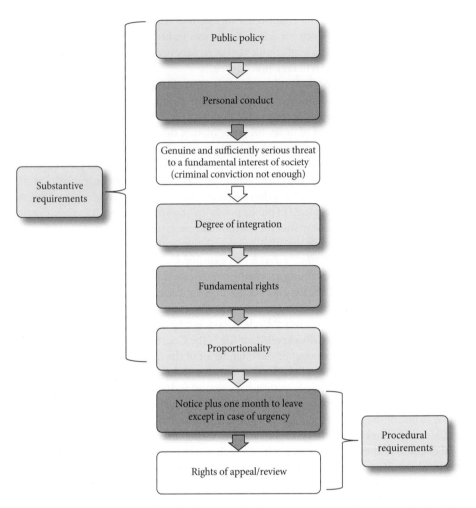

Fig. 12.1 Factors to be considered before an individual can be deported on grounds of public policy or public security

Article 27(2) CRD continues:

> The personal conduct of the individual concerned must represent a genuine, present and sufficiently serious threat affecting one of the fundamental interests of society. Justifications that are isolated from the particulars of the case or that rely on considerations of general prevention shall not be accepted.

According to the EFTA Court in *Wahl*,[56] it is for the national court to determine, in accordance with the principles of equivalence and effectiveness, whether the personal conduct satisfies the genuine, present, and sufficiently serious threat test.

The issue of public policy was also addressed by the UK's New Settlement deal. The Decision of the Heads of State or Government says:

> Host Member States may also take the necessary restrictive measures to protect themselves against individuals whose personal conduct is likely to represent a genuine and serious threat to public policy or security. In determining whether the conduct of an

---

[56] Case E–15/12 *Wahl* v. *Iceland* [2013] EFTA Ct. Rep. 534, paras. 128–30.

individual poses a present threat to public policy or security, Member States may take into account past conduct of the individual concerned and the threat may not always need to be imminent. Even in the absence of a previous criminal conviction, Member States may act on preventative grounds, so long as they are specific to the individual concerned.

The changes proposed to the derogations subtly alter the balance of power between individual and state, making it easier for countries like the UK to deport individuals. First, the Decision allows host Member States to take the necessary restrictive measures to protect themselves against individuals whose personal conduct is 'likely' (as opposed to 'does') represent a genuine and serious threat to public policy or security. Secondly, the Decision takes the emphasis away from the current focus on present conduct by individuals to look more closely at their past conduct. Thirdly, the UK Decision adds for the first time that 'the threat may not always need to be imminent' and that Member States, even in the absence of a previous criminal conviction, can act on preventative grounds, so long as they are specific to the individual concerned.

A Declaration added to the Decision commits the Commission to clarifying:

- that Member States may take into account past conduct of an individual in the determination of whether a Union citizen's conduct poses a 'present' threat to public policy or security;
- that the Member States may act on grounds of public policy or public security even in the absence of a previous criminal conviction on preventative grounds but specific to the individual concerned;
- the notions of 'serious grounds of public policy or public security' and 'imperative grounds of public security' (the terms used at the five-year and ten-year stage (see fig. 12.2)). Moreover, when the CRD is next amended the Commission will examine the thresholds to which these notions are connected.

These changes, which will come into force only if the UK votes to remain, did not deliver on the Prime Minister's demands for 'tougher and longer' re-entry bans for foreign rough sleepers, beggars, and fraudsters but did satisfy his demands for stronger measures to allow EU criminals to be deported.[57]

(b) Measures which can be taken against a person exercising free movement rights

(i) Exclusion or expulsion

Neither the Treaty nor Directive 2004/38 specify what measures can be taken against a migrant EU citizen by the state on the grounds of public policy or public security. The most extreme measures taken by states are exclusion (the refusal to allow an individual to enter the country), as in *Van Duyn*, or expulsion/deportation (the removal of an individual who has already entered the state), as in *Calfa*.[58] However, as the Court said in *Watson and Belmann*,[59] deportation 'negates the very right conferred and guaranteed by the Treaty'.[60] For this reason Directive 2004/38 introduces additional protection against

---

[57] <http://www.telegraph.co.uk/news/uknews/immigration/11259473/David-Cameron-Im-ready-to-lead-Britain-out-of-Europe-if-migrant-reforms-fail.html>.

[58] If expulsion/deportation is ordered, the state which issued the identity card or passport must allow the holder to re-enter its territory, even if the document is no longer valid or the nationality of its holder is in dispute (Art. 27(4) CRD). See also Case C–459/99 *MRAX* [2002] ECR I–6591 on the position of TCNs.

[59] Case 118/75 [1976] ECR 1185; Case 157/79 *R. v. Pieck* [1980] ECR 2171, paras. 18–19; Case C–265/88 *Criminal Proceedings against Messner* [1989] ECR 4209, paras. 14–15. See also Case C–329/97 *Ergat* [2000] ECR I–1487 in respect of Turkish workers.

[60] Case 118/75 *Watson and Belmann* [1976] ECR 1185, para. 20.

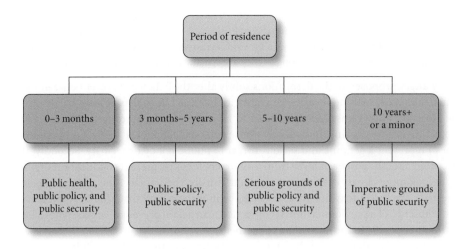

Fig. 12.2 When the different derogations can be invoked

expulsion. Article 28(1) provides that when deciding whether to deport an individual on the grounds of public policy or public security, the host state must take into account length of residence, age, health, family and economic situation, social and cultural integration into the host state, and enduring ties with the individual's country of origin.[61] Furthermore, citizens and their family members who have permanent residence (i.e., more than five years) cannot be deported, according to Article 28(2), save on serious grounds of public policy or public security. Minors[62] and citizens who have resided in the host state for the previous ten years[63] cannot be deported at all, according to Article 28(3), except if the decision is based on 'imperative grounds of public security' (not public policy), as defined by Member States 'in accordance with their national needs, which can vary from one Member State to another and from one era to another'[64] (see fig. 12.2). This strict approach to derogations for those with permanent residence status means that the migrant EU citizen is treated (almost) like a national in all but name. Under international law, states cannot deport their own nationals; under the CRD the same is almost true for EU permanent residents.

However, the new gradations found in Article 28(2)–(3) CRD introduce distinctions which are hard to apply in practice. It is difficult to distinguish between, on the one

---

[61] See also Joined Cases C–482 and 493/01 *Orfanopoulos* [2004] ECR I–5257, para. 99, couching this right in terms of the right to family life under Art. 8 ECHR, which had to be weighed in the balance.

[62] Except if the expulsion is necessary for the best interests of the child as provided for in the UN Convention on the Rights of the Child 1989.

[63] According to Case C–145/09 *Land Baden-Württemberg* v. *Tsakouridis* [2010] ECR I–11979, para. 38, it is for the national court to decide whether a Union citizen has resided in the host Member State for the ten years preceding the expulsion decision. All the relevant factors must be taken into account in each individual case, in particular the duration of each period of absence from the host Member State, the cumulative duration and the frequency of those absences, and the reasons why the person concerned left the host Member State, reasons which may establish whether those absences involve the transfer to another state of the centre of the personal, family, or occupational interests of the person concerned. In Case C–400/12 *Secretary of State for the Home Department* v. *M. G.* EU:C:2014:9, para. 38 the Court said a period of imprisonment is, in principle, capable both of interrupting the continuity of the period of residence for the purposes of Art. 28(3)(a) CRD and of affecting the decision regarding the grant of the enhanced protection, even where the person concerned resided in the host Member State for the ten years prior to imprisonment.

[64] Case C–348/09 *PI* v. *Oberbürgermeisterin der Stadt Remscheid* EU:C:2012:300, para. 23.

hand, deportation for 'ordinary' public-policy reasons, which applies to individuals with less than five years' residence who represent a 'genuine, present and *sufficiently serious* threat affecting one of the fundamental interests of society' (Article 27(2)) and, on the other hand, deportation for '*serious* grounds of public policy or public security', which applies to those migrants with permanent residence (Article 28(2)).

Even the phrase 'imperative grounds of public security' in Article 28(3),[65] for those with more than ten years residence, is not so clear. In *Tsakouridis*[66] the Court emphasized that Article 28(3) 'considerably strengthens' the protection against expulsion enjoyed by individuals[67] and that the criteria in Article 28(3) are 'considerably stricter' than 'serious grounds' within the meaning of Article 28(2).[68] It concluded that '[t]he concept of "imperative grounds of public security" presupposes not only the existence of a threat to public security,[69] but also that such a threat is of a particularly high degree of seriousness, as is reflected by the use of the words "imperative reasons".'[70] Yet, on the facts, the Court concluded that 'the fight against crime in connection with dealing in narcotics as part of an organised group' was capable of being covered by the concept of 'imperative grounds of public security'.[71]

In reaching the conclusion the Court referred to Framework Decision 2004/757/JHA,[72] which says that 'illicit drug trafficking poses a threat to health, safety and the quality of life of citizens of the Union, and to the legal economy, stability and security of the Member States'. In *PI*[73] the Court referred to the criminal offences listed in Article 83(1) TFEU, including sexual exploitation of children, to help identify offences which might 'pose a direct threat to the calm and physical security of the population' and thus be covered by the concept of 'imperative grounds of public security'.[74] However, the Court added three caveats. First, the manner in which such offences were committed had to disclose particularly serious characteristics. This was a matter for the referring court to determine on the basis of an individual examination of the specific case. Secondly, the issue of any expulsion measure was conditional on the requirement that the personal conduct of the individual concerned had to represent a genuine, present threat affecting one of the fundamental interests of society or of the host Member State, which implied, in general, the existence in the individual concerned of a propensity to act in the same way in the future. Thirdly, the host Member State had to take account of considerations such as how long the individual had resided on its territory, his/her age, state of health, family and economic situation, social and cultural integration into that state, and the extent of his/her links with the country of origin.

Whether deportation (as opposed to some lesser restriction) can be justified turns largely on the question of proportionality.[75] Deportation cannot be automatic,[76] nor can there be a presumption that the migrant should be expelled.[77] Deportation for 'technical' infringements of the host state's law is also not permissible, as *Watson and Belmann* demonstrates. The Court said that the deportation of a migrant for failing to have reported to the police the place where she was staying within three days of entering the country was 'so disproportionate to the gravity of the infringement that it becomes an obstacle to the

---

[65] Recital 24 talks of 'exceptional circumstances'.
[66] Case C–145/09 *Tsakouridis* [2010] ECR I–11979, para. 28.   [67] Para. 28.   [68] Para. 40.
[69] The Court referred to its good case law to define public security, i.e., that it covers both a Member State's internal and external security, that a threat to the functioning of the institutions and essential public services and the survival of the population, as well as the risk of a serious disturbance to foreign relations or to peaceful coexistence of nations, or a risk to military interests, may affect public security (paras. 43–4).
[70] Para. 41.   [71] Para. 56.   [72] [2004] OJ L335/8.
[73] Case C–348/09 *PI* EU:C:2012:300.   [74] Para. 33.   [75] Art. 27(2).
[76] Case C–408/03 *Commission* v. *Belgium* [2005] ECR I–2647.
[77] Joined Cases C–482 and 493/01 *Orfanopoulos* [2004] ECR I–5257, para. 92.

free movement of persons'.[78] In much the same vein, Article 15(2) of Directive 2004/38 provides that the expiry of an identity card or passport is not sufficient to justify deportation. The Court has also emphasized that such decisions must be subject to an effective remedy. This can be seen in *Byankov*,[79] which concerned the unusual situation of a state refusing to allow one of its nationals to leave the country until he had settled a debt. The Court objected to the absolute nature of the prohibition and the fact that it was not coupled with 'any exceptions, temporal limitation or possibility of regular review of the factual and legal circumstances underpinning it'.

Article 33 adds that expulsion orders cannot be issued by the host Member State as a penalty or legal consequence of a custodial penalty unless they comply with the general principles concerning sufficiently serious threat laid down in Article 27, protection against expulsion under Article 28, and the rules concerning public health under Article 29.[80] Furthermore, if an expulsion order is enforced more than two years after it was issued, the Member State must check whether the individual is currently and genuinely a threat to public policy or public security and must assess whether there has been any material change in the circumstances since the expulsion order was issued.[81]

(ii) Other measures

The national system can, of course, impose other, less severe, sanctions for breaches of national law than expulsion. For example, in *Pieck*[82] the Court said the host state could fine or imprison a migrant for breaching national laws on immigration formalities, provided that the penalties were comparable to those for equivalent offences committed by nationals. In *Rutili*[83] the Court said that restricting a person's right of residence to a limited area in the country was also possible under Article 18 TFEU[84] (not under Article 45(3) TFEU[85]), provided that the Member State could impose similar restrictions on its own nationals.[86] Therefore, the French minister could prohibit Rutili, an Italian national who had spent all his life in France, from living in certain regions of France due to his political and trade union activities if the minister could do the same to a national.

The approach based on non-discrimination in *Rutili* was confirmed in Article 22 CRD:

> The right of residence and the right of permanent residence shall cover the whole territory of the Member State. Member States may impose territorial restrictions on the right of residence and the right of permanent residence only where the same restrictions apply to their own nationals.

Nevertheless, the Court diluted the non-discrimination approach in *Olazabal*,[87] where it upheld legislation allowing for movement restrictions, the very rules it had found unlawful in *Rutili*. Olazabal, a Spanish national of Basque origin, was a member of ETA, 'an armed and organised group whose activity constitute[d] a threat to public order'.[88] As a result of his involvement in the kidnapping of a Spanish industrialist he was sentenced to 18 months' imprisonment in France followed by a four-year ban on residing in the vicinity of the Spanish border. He argued that the residence ban was discriminatory since nationals could not be subject to any such limitation. The Court rejected his arguments.

---

[78] Case 118/75 *Watson & Belmann* [1976] ECR 1185, para. 21. See also Case C–215/03 *Oulane* [2005] ECR I–1215, paras. 38 and 40.
[79] Case C–249/11 *Byankov* EU:C:2012:608, para. 44.   [80] Art. 33(1).   [81] Art. 33(2).
[82] Case 157/79 *R. v. Pieck* [1980] ECR 2171, paras. 18–19.   [83] Case 36/75 [1975] ECR 1219.
[84] Para. 49.
[85] The Court made clear that Art. 45(3) TFEU applied to prohibitions on residence only in respect of the whole territory and not by reference to its internal subdivisions (paras. 46–8).
[86] Para. 50.   [87] Case C–100/01 *Olazabal* [2002] ECR I–10981, para. 45.   [88] Para. 35.

It said that because Union law allowed migrants to be subject to the ultimate sanction (deportation) they could therefore be subject to less severe measures—such as facing restrictions on their right of residence—without it being necessary for identical measures to be applied to nationals.[89]

Thus, by examining the facts of *Olazabal* through the lens of proportionality, rather than non-discrimination, the Court reached an entirely different conclusion to the one in *Rutili*. It distinguished the two cases on factual grounds: Rutili was, to all intents and purposes, French; Olazabal was a migrant worker. Furthermore, there was some suspicion in *Rutili* that the action taken against him was on the ground of his trade union activities, which itself would have contravened Article 8 of Regulation 492/11. By contrast Olazabal was a terrorist and could have been deported for that reason.[90]

The Court also clarified the criteria laid down in *Rutili*. It said that a Member State could—under Article 45(3) TFEU—limit a worker's right of residence to a part of the national territory provided that:[91]

- such action was justified by reasons of public order or public security based on his individual conduct

- those reasons were so serious that otherwise he would have been prohibited from residing in, or banished from, the whole of the national territory

- the conduct which the Member State concerned wished to prevent gave rise, in the case of its own nationals, to punitive measures or other genuine and effective measures.

This case highlights one of the (many) questions raised as to the compatibility of the CRD with the Treaty: *Olazabal* concerned the interpretation of the Treaty while Article 22 CRD on territorial scope is a provision in the (hierarchically inferior) directive.

(iii) Fundamental human rights

When taking the decision whether to deport a migrant, the host state must take into account not only the principle of proportionality but also fundamental human rights; a fact that the Court has emphasized in a number of cases, notably *Carpenter*[92] and *Orfanopoulos*.[93] It will be recalled from Chapter 9 that *Carpenter* concerned a decision by the UK to deport Mrs Carpenter, a Filipino national, who, having overstayed her entry permit to the UK, married a British national. Faced with the threat of deportation, Mrs Carpenter argued, and the Court accepted, that this would restrict her husband's ability to carry on business as a service provider in other Member States since she looked after his children while he was away.[94] However, the Court said that a Member State could 'invoke reasons of public interest to justify a national measure which is likely to obstruct the exercise of the freedom to provide services only if that measure is compatible with the fundamental rights whose observance the Court ensures'.[95] On the question of fundamental rights, the Court said that the decision to deport Mrs Carpenter constituted:

an interference with the exercise by Mr Carpenter of his right to respect for his family life within the meaning of Article 8 of the [ECHR] ... which is among the fundamental rights

---

[89] Para. 41.   [90] Paras. 34–6.   [91] Para. 45.

[92] Case C–60/00 *Carpenter* [2002] ECR I–6279, paras. 40–1, considered further in Chs. 7 and 9.

[93] Joined Cases C–482 and 493/01 *Orfanopoulos* [2004] ECR I–5257, confirmed in Case C–441/02 *Commission* v. *Germany (Italian migrants)* [2006] ECR I–3449, paras. 108–9.

[94] Para. 17.

[95] Para. 40, citing Case C–260/89 *ERT* [1991] ECR I–2925, para. 43, and Case C–368/95 *Familiapress* [1997] ECR I–3689, para. 24. Cf. Art 51(1) of the Charter, which applies to the Member States 'only when they are implementing Union law'. No reference is made to derogations.

which, according to the Court's settled case-law, restated by the Preamble to the Single European Act and by Article 6(2) EU, are protected in [Union] law.[96]

Drawing on the case law of the European Court of Human Rights, the Court then said that even though no right of an alien to enter or to reside in a particular country was guaranteed by the Convention, 'the removal of a person from a country where close members of his family are living may amount to an infringement of the right to respect for family life as guaranteed by Article 8(1) of the Convention'. It continued that such an interference would infringe the Convention if it did not meet the requirements of Article 8(2) ECHR, namely that the deportation had to be in accordance with the law, motivated by one or more of the legitimate aims under Article 8(2) and 'necessary in a democratic society' (justified by a pressing social need and proportionate).[97] The Court concluded that the decision to deport Mrs Carpenter did not 'strike a fair balance' between the competing interests of the right of *Mr* Carpenter to respect for his family life on the one hand and the maintenance of public order and public safety, on the other.[98] Even though Mrs Carpenter had infringed UK immigration laws by overstaying her visa she did not constitute a danger to public order and safety. Therefore, the decision to deport her was not proportionate (see fig. 7.5).

In *Orfanopoulos*[99] the Court also emphasized that the state needed to take into account fundamental human rights in deciding whether to deport a migrant, in this case a Greek national convicted of drugs and violence offences but who had lived most of his life in Germany where he had a wife and children. The Court said that the assessment had to be made by the national authorities, on a case-by-case basis, to decide where a fair balance lay between the legitimate interests in complying with the general principles of Union law and the protection of fundamental rights such as the right to family life.[100]

(c) The right to reapply

In *Adoui*[101] the Court made clear that excluded or expelled individuals had to have the chance to reapply to return to the state from which they had been expelled. This point was more recently confirmed in *Shingara*,[102] where the Court said that, because a decision excluding migrants from entering a Member State was a derogation from the fundamental principle of freedom of movement, it could not be of unlimited duration.[103] Therefore, a Union national expelled from a Member State could apply for a fresh residence permit.[104] If that application was made after a reasonable time, the competent administrative authority in the host state had to consider whether there had now been a material change in the circumstances which had justified the first decision ordering expulsion.[105]

---

[96] Case C–60/00 *Carpenter* [2002] ECR I–6279, para. 41. See also Case C–63/99 *R. v. Secretary of State for the Home Department, ex p. Gloszczuk* [2001] ECR I–6369, para. 85; Case C–235/99 *R. v. Secretary of State for the Home Department, ex p. Kondova* [2001] ECR I–6427, para. 90; Case C–413/99 *Baumbast* [2002] ECR I–7091, para. 72; Case C–109/01 *Akrich* [2003] ECR I–9607, paras. 58–9.

[97] Para. 42, citing *Boultif* v. *Switzerland*, no. 54273/00 [2001] ECHR 497, paras. 39, 41, and 46.

[98] Para. 43.   [99] Joined Cases C–482 and 493/01 *Orfanopoulos* [2004] ECR I–5257.

[100] Para. 100. Fundamental rights and proportionality are not the only general principles of law that the Court has to take into account. It will also look at, e.g., legitimate expectations and legal certainty: Case C–97/05 *Gattoussi* v. *Stadt Rüsselsheim* [2006] ECR I–11917, para. 42.

[101] Joined Cases 115 and 116/81 [1982] ECR 1665, para. 12; Case C–348/96 *Calfa* [1999] ECR I–11, para. 27.

[102] Joined Cases C–65 and 111/95 *R. v. Secretary of State for the Home Department, ex p. Mann Singh Shingara and ex p. Abbas Radiom* [1997] ECR I–3343.

[103] Para. 40. See also Case C–235/99 *Ex p. Kondova* [2001] ECR I–6427, para. 90; Case C–63/99 *Ex p. Gloszczuk* [2001] ECR I–6369, para. 85.

[104] Para. 39.   [105] Para. 39.

Article 32(1) CRD confirms that a Member State cannot issue orders excluding individuals from their territory for life. Individuals must be able to submit an application to lift an exclusion order after a reasonable period and, in any event, after three years, establishing a material change in their circumstances from those which justified the decision ordering their exclusion in the first place. Member States then have six months to reach a decision, during which time the applicant remains excluded.[106]

2.3 Public Policy and Legal Persons

Until *Omega*[107] there had been little case law where states invoked the public-policy derogation to restrict the activities of corporate bodies. In *Centros*[108] the Danish government tried to justify its rules on minimum capitalization on the public-policy ground of protecting creditors from the risk of fraudulent bankruptcy due to the insolvency of companies whose initial capitalization was inadequate. The Court simply said 'that the reasons put forward do not fall within the ambit of Article [52 TFEU]'. However, in *Segers*[109] the Court recognized that the need to combat fraud might fall within the express derogations, although on the facts it found that the refusal to accord sickness benefit to a director of a company formed in accordance with the law of another Member State could not be justified.

In subsequent cases, the Court has drawn on the rules developed in the context of natural persons to other situations in which public policy is invoked. For example, in *Commission v. UK (open skies)*[110] the Court referred to the *Bouchereau* formula in its definition of public policy when deciding whether to refuse operating authorizations to an airline.[111] The *Open Skies* decision also confirmed the approach taken in the free movement of capital case, *Église de Scientologie*,[112] where the Court said that any person affected by a restrictive measure based on a public-policy derogation had to have access to legal redress.

However, it was only in *Omega*[113] that the Court really got to grips with the public-policy derogation in the context of corporate conduct. The case concerned a decision by the Bonn Police Authority to ban Omega, a German company using British equipment, from running a laserdrome where, through the use of laser guns fired at fixed sensory tags attached to players' jackets, it was possible to 'play at killing'. The decision was taken on public-policy grounds: 'the commercial exploitation of games involving the simulated killing of human beings infringed a fundamental value enshrined in the national [German] constitution, namely human dignity'.[114] The Court appeared to recognize that the protection of fundamental rights, including the protection of human dignity, actually constituted the public-policy derogation.[115] Therefore, a fundamental principle of particular resonance in Germany[116] was successfully invoked by the German government to

---

[106] Art. 32(2).   [107] Case C–36/02 [2004] ECR I–9609.

[108] Case C–212/97 *Centros* [1999] ECR I–1459, para. 34. See also Case C–260/89 *ERT v. DEP* [1991] ECR I–2925, para. 25.

[109] Case 79/85 *Segers* [1986] ECR 2375, para. 17.

[110] Case C–466/98 *Commission* v. *UK* [2002] ECR I–9427.

[111] Para. 57. See also Case C–168/04 *Commission* v. *Austria* [2006] ECR I–9041, para. 64; Case C–465/05 *Commission* v. *Italy (private security activities)* [2007] ECR I–11091, para. 50.

[112] Case C–54/99 *Association Eglise de Scientologie de Paris* v. *The Prime Minister* [2000] ECR I–1335, paras. 17–18.

[113] Case C–36/02 [2004] ECR I–9609. See also Case C–319/06 *Commission* v. *Luxembourg* [2008] ECR I–4323.

[114] Para. 32.

[115] Paras. 33–4, 36, and 41, as well as Stix-Hackl AG's Opinion, although cf. para. 35, where the Court appears to be discussing human rights in terms of the public-interest justification.

[116] Although it had been recognized by the Court in Case C–377/98 *Netherlands* v. *Parliament and Council* [2001] ECR I–7079.

limit the free movement of services. Furthermore, the Court found the German rule to be proportionate because it prohibited only the variant of the laser game which fired on human targets—i.e., playing at killing people.[117] This conclusion is unsurprising given the strong emphasis generally placed by the Court on margin of discretion given to Member States.[118]

3. PUBLIC HEALTH

3.1 Public Health and the Individual

The annex to Directive 64/221 provided an exhaustive list of diseases or disabilities which could trigger action against an individual on public-health grounds: those subject to quarantine listed in International Health Regulation No. 2 of the World Health Organization of 25 May 1951, tuberculosis (TB), syphilis, and other infectious or contagious diseases or contagious parasitic diseases if they are subject to provisions for protection of nationals of the host country. Migrants who were HIV positive or who suffered from AIDS found themselves in a particularly invidious position.[119] Some Member States tried to deny them admission[120] although there was no express provision for this in the directive.[121] However, in its 1999 Communication the Commission rejected the use of any measures which could lead to 'social exclusion, discrimination or stigmatisation of persons with HIV/AIDS'.[122] More generally, the Commission observed that the public-health grounds were 'somewhat outdated'. It concluded that 'restrictions of free movement can no longer be considered a necessary and effective means of solving public health problems'.

The public-health derogation contained in Directive 64/221 was updated by Article 29(1) CRD, which now refers to diseases with epidemic potential, as defined by the relevant instruments of the World Health Organization, and other infectious diseases or contagious parasitic diseases but with the additional condition that they must be the subject of protection provisions applying to nationals of the host state.

Unlike the public-policy and public-security derogations, which can be invoked in respect of the migrant's initial entry to the territory or at any time during the first five years of the migrant's stay, the public-health derogation can be invoked only to justify the initial refusal of entry or the refusal to issue a first residence certificate or card (i.e., diseases occurring after a three-month period from the date of arrival cannot constitute grounds for expulsion from the territory)[123] (see fig. 12.2). Thus, once recognized, the right of residence cannot be contested on health grounds. In exceptional cases (i.e., only in cases where 'there are serious indications that it is necessary') the host state can require those entitled to the right of residence to undergo a (free) medical examination, within three months of the date of arrival.[124]

---

[117] Case C–36/02 *Omega* [2004] ECR I–9609, para. 39.   [118] Para. 31.

[119] See W. Van Overbeek, 'AIDS/HIV infection and the free movement of persons within the Community' (1990) 27 *CMLRev.* 791.

[120] Guild notes that in Bavaria there was an attempt to use HIV/AIDS as a public-health ground for expulsion but it was quickly stopped as illegal under the directive: E. Guild, 'Security of residence and expulsion of foreigners: European Community law' in E. Guild and P. Minderhoud (eds.), *Security of Residence and Expulsion: Protection of aliens in Europe* (The Hague: Kluwer, 2000) 64.

[121] The Union's treatment of its own staff or job applicants with HIV is instructive. The Court has ruled that the requirement that every person undergo a medical examination did not infringe Art. 8 ECHR provided that the individual consented: Case C–404/92P *X* v. *Commission* [1994] ECR I–4737, para. 17.

[122] 'Special measures concerning the movement and residence of citizens of the Union which are justified on the grounds of public policy, public security, or public health', COM(99) 372, 12.

[123] Art. 29(2).   [124] Art. 29(3).

3.2 Public Health and Welfare Policies

When a Member State tries to justify its welfare policies on public-health grounds, the Court has not referred to Directive 64/221 or the CRD. Instead, it applies principles similar to those developed in the context of Article 36 TFEU,[125] including scrutinizing carefully whether the public-health derogation invoked by the state is supported by the facts. This can be seen in *Corporación Dermoestética*,[126] where the Italian government relied on public-health grounds to justify its ban on advertising medical and surgical treatments on national television by private healthcare clinics. However, because clinics could advertise on local television the Court said that the rules exhibit 'an inconsistency … and cannot therefore properly attain the public health objective which they seek to pursue'.

Generally, however, the Court takes a sympathetic view of a state's freedom to organize its own healthcare system, as *Kohll*,[127] *Geraets-Smits*,[128] and *Müller-Fauré*[129] show. As discussed in Chapter 9, in all three cases national law required individuals to obtain prior authorization before they could receive non-emergency medical treatment in other Member States. In each case the Court ruled that this requirement breached Article 56 TFEU[130] and the question was then whether the 'exporting' state (usually the state where the patient was insured, the state of origin) could justify the restriction. In each case the exporting state argued that the authorization requirement was necessary in order to maintain a high-quality, balanced medical hospital service open to all.[131]

The Court recognized that such an objective, 'even if intrinsically linked to the method of financing the social security system', could fall within the derogations on grounds of public health under Article 52 TFEU insofar as it contributed to the attainment of a high level of health protection.[132] The Court also held that Article 52 TFEU permitted Member States 'to restrict the freedom to provide medical and hospital services in so far as the maintenance of treatment capacity or medical competence on national territory is essential for the public health, and even the survival of, the population'.[133] Disregarding, or at least modifying,[134] the well-established principle that derogations cannot be used to serve economic objectives,[135] the Court said in *Geraets-Smits*[136] that the authorization requirement helped to meet 'a desire to control costs and to prevent, as far as possible, any wastage of financial, technical and human resources'. It added that such wastage was all the more damaging because 'it is generally recognised that the hospital care sector generates considerable costs and must satisfy increasing needs, while the financial resources which may be made available for health care are not unlimited, whatever the mode of funding applied'. The Court therefore concluded that in principle a system of prior authorization

---

[125] E.g., in Joined Cases C–171 and 172/07 *Apothekerkammer des Saarlandes* v. *Saarland* [2009] ECR I–4171, para. 30 the Court cited Case C–170/04 *Rosengren* [2007] ECR I–4071, para. 49. See Ch. 6. See also Case C–73/08 *Bressol* v. *Gouvernement de la communauté française* [2010] ECR I–2735, paras. 62–74.

[126] Case C–500/06 *Corporación Dermoestética* [2008] ECR I–5785, para. 39.

[127] Case C–158/96 *Kohll* [1998] ECR I–1931. For the parallel case on goods, see Case C–120/95 *Decker* [1998] ECR I–1831.

[128] Case C–157/99 *Geraets Smits and Peerbooms* [2001] ECR I–5473.

[129] Case C–385/99 *Müller-Fauré and van Riet* [2003] ECR I–4509.

[130] This issue is considered in detail in Ch. 9.

[131] *Kohll*, n. 127, para. 50; *Geraets-Smits*, n. 128, para. 73; *Müller-Fauré*, n. 129, para. 67.

[132] *Kohll*, n. 127, para. 50; *Geraets-Smits*, n. 128, para. 73.

[133] *Kohll*, n. 127, para. 51; *Geraets-Smits*, n. 128, para. 74.

[134] A point recognized in the goods case, Case C–141/07 *Commission* v. *Germany (pharmacies for hospitals)* [2008] ECR I–6935, para. 60 and Case C–512/08 *Commission* v. *France (major medical equipment)* [2010] ECR I–8833, paras. 39–40. See further Section E, 2.

[135] A principle that the Court expressly refers to in *Kohll*, n. 127, para. 41.   [136] Para. 79.

was both 'necessary and reasonable' on public-health grounds to guarantee a 'rationalised, stable, balanced and accessible supply of hospital services'.[137]

However, in *Müller-Fauré* the Court made clear that a refusal to grant prior authorization based, not out of fear of wastage resulting from hospital overcapacity, but solely on the ground that there were waiting lists for the hospital treatment concerned, could not amount to a properly justified restriction on freedom to provide services.[138] The Court could not see how waiting times were necessary to safeguard the protection of public health—quite the contrary. If the only reason related to 'considerations of a purely economic nature' they could not 'as such justify a restriction on the fundamental principle of freedom to provide services'.[139]

The general deference to a Member State's assessment of its own health policy seen in the 'healthcare tourism' cases can also be found in *Mac Queen*.[140] Belgian law provided that only ophthalmologists could perform eye examinations, excluding opticians who were not qualified medical doctors. Noting the importance of protecting public health,[141] the Court said that reserving the right to carry out eye tests to ophthalmologists could be regarded as an appropriate means of ensuring a high level of health protection. The restriction was therefore lawful provided that the national court considered the steps proportionate. However, the Court did add that while the Belgian authorities might be justified in concluding that at present there might be a risk to public health if opticians were authorized to carry out certain eyesight examinations, 'an assessment of this kind is liable to change with the passage of time, particularly as a result of technical and scientific progress'.[142]

In a similar vein the Court upheld a rule excluding non-pharmacists from running pharmacies on public-health grounds in *Apothekerkammer des Saarlandes*.[143] Referring to the precautionary principle,[144] the Court said that a Member State could take the measures that reduce, as far as possible, a public-health risk including, more specifically, a risk to the reliability and quality of the provision of medicinal products to the public, products whose therapeutic effects distinguish them substantially from other goods due to the serious harm they can cause to patients if they are consumed unnecessarily or incorrectly.[145] The Court concluded that given the power accorded to the Member States to determine the level of protection of public health, Member States could require that medicinal products be supplied by pharmacists enjoying genuine professional independence.

---

[137] In *Kohll* this approach underpinned the Court's reasoning in respect of the overriding requirement of excluding the risk of seriously undermining the financial balance of the social security system and not the public-health derogation.

[138] Case C–157/99 *Geraets Smits* [2001] ECR I–5473, para. 92.

[139] *Müller-Fauré*, n. 129, para. 92. See also Case C–372/04 *Watts* [2006] ECR I–4325, considered further in Ch. 9, and Case C–115/08 *Land Oberösterreich* v. ČEZ [2009] ECR I–10265, para. 109.

[140] Case C–108/96 *Mac Queen* [2001] ECR I–837, paras. 28–30. This position is reinforced by Art. 168(1) TFEU and Art. 35 of the Charter under which 'a high level of protection for human health is to be ensured in the definition and implementation of all policies and activities of the European Union' (both of which were referred to in Case C–84/11 *Susisalo* EU:C:2012:374, para. 37).

[141] Art. 3(1)(p).   [142] Para. 36.

[143] Joined Cases C–171 and 172/07 *Apothekerkammer des Saarlandes* [2009] ECR I–4171, 140–1. See also Joined Cases C–159–161/12 *Venturini* v. *ASL Varese* EU:C:2013:791 (para-pharmacists). Cf. Case C–539/11 *Ottica New Line di Accardi Vincenzo* EU:C:2013:591, where the Court hinted that the need for rapid access to opticians services was less than for medical services and so the interest in having a shop close by was less acute; Case C–367/12 *Sokoll-Seebacher* v. *Hemetsberger* EU:C:2014:68, where the Court rejected a rigid rule on determining the need for the establishment of a new pharmacy based on 'people remaining to be served'.

[144] See further Ch. 6.   [145] Paras. 30–2.

4. PROCEDURAL REQUIREMENTS

4.1 General Provisions

Directive 64/221 laid down minimum procedural requirements to protect migrants faced with a decision refusing renewal of a residence permit or ordering expulsion on the grounds of public policy, public security, and public health. These requirements were much criticized because they were minimal but complex and consequently generated a large volume of case law. Directive 2004/38 has improved upon and simplified the procedural protection. It requires that migrants facing any decision taken against them on the grounds of public policy, public security, and public health must be informed in writing in such a way that they are able to comprehend its content and the implications for them.[146] They must also be told 'precisely and in full' of the grounds on which the decision in their case is based (unless this is contrary to the interests of the security of the state)[147] in order to enable the migrant to prepare an effective defence.[148] Further, the notification must specify the court or administrative authority with which the person concerned may lodge an appeal, the time limit for the appeal and, where applicable, the time allowed for the person to leave the territory. Except in 'duly substantiated' cases of urgency, the period provided for leaving the country must not be less than one month from the date of notification (see fig. 12.1).[149]

4.2 Remedies

(a) The new rules

The CRD provides for the availability of certain remedies. In the original Directive 64/221, Article 8 required the individual to have the same legal remedies as nationals. Where no legal remedies were available (or the remedies were inadequate in some way), then Article 9 said that individuals had to be able to exercise their right of defence before a 'competent authority' which could not be the same as that which adopted the measure restricting their freedom.[150] While the original drafts of the CRD broadly followed the distinction between the Article 8 and 9 remedies, the final version of the CRD abandoned this approach. Instead, Article 31(1) CRD provides that:[151]

> The persons concerned shall have access to judicial and, where appropriate, administrative redress procedures in the host Member State to appeal against or seek review of any decision taken against them on the grounds of public policy, public security or public health.

[146] Art. 30(1) CRD. See also Joined Cases 115 and 116/81 *Adoui and Cornuaille* [1982] ECR 1665, para. 13.

[147] Art. 30(2). In Case C–300/11 *ZZ* v. *Secretary of State for the Home Department* EU:C:2013:363 the Court read Art. 30(2) CRD in the light of Art. 47 of the Charter, in the context of a decision refusing ZZ, an EU national, entry into the UK on the grounds that he had been involved in terrorist activities as part of the Armed Islamic Group network. His appeal had been heard by the Special Immigration Appeals Commission (SIAC) in an open and closed judgment where in the open judgment SIAC said little of the case against ZZ had been revealed to him. The CJEU said Art. 30(2), as an exception had to be interpreted restrictively, but that where reasons of state security are at stake, national courts had to have techniques and rules of procedure to accommodate both the state's security concerns and the individual's procedural rights.

[148] Case 36/75 *Rutili* [1975] ECR 1219, para. 39; Joined Cases 115 and 116/81 *Adoui and Cornuaille* [1982] ECR 1665, para. 13. See also Case C–277/11 *MM* v. *Minister of Justice, Equality and Law Reform* EU:C:2012:744 decided in the context of the Asylum Dir. 2004/83, which draws heavily on the Charter to support the right to be heard.

[149] Art. 30(3).

[150] Case 36/75 *Rutili* [1975] ECR 1219, para. 35.

[151] The importance of this provision and its implication for the more general right to effective judicial protection was noted by the General Court in Case T–228/02 *OMPI* v. *Council* [2006] ECR II–4665. Case C–249/11 *Byankov* EU:C:2012:608, para. 54 made clear that the procedural safeguards required by Art. 31 CRD apply at the time when the measures restricting those rights are adopted. See also Case C–430/10 *Gaydarov* [2011] ECR I–11637.

In addition, Article 31(3) CRD provides that the 'redress procedures shall allow for an examination of the legality of the decision, as well as of the facts and circumstances on which the proposed measure is based. They shall ensure that the decision is not disproportionate, particularly in view of the requirements laid down in Article 28 CRD [concerning protection against expulsion].'

Despite the fact that the content of Article 31 CRD differs from that of Articles 8 and 9 of Directive 64/221, it is likely that the Court will draw on its pre-existing case law to interpret the provision.[152] For this reason, we shall now examine the salient features of the Court's jurisprudence under Directive 64/221.

(b) Access to judicial redress: Appeal and review

While Article 31(1) CRD talks of 'access to judicial ... procedures in the host Member State to appeal against or seek review of any decision', Article 8 of Directive 64/221 gave the migrant the same legal remedies as nationals in respect of acts of the administration when the migrant was faced by a decision concerning entry, or the refusal to issue or renew a residence permit, or a decision ordering expulsion from the territory. Consistent with the principle of national procedural autonomy, the Court said that Article 8 did not govern the ways in which remedies were to be made available (for instance by stipulating the courts from which such remedies could be sought)[153] and this is likely to be extended to Article 31. However, the Court said in *Ex p. Shingara*[154] that Member States could not execute a decision ordering expulsion before the migrant was able to avail himself of the Article 8 remedy.

In *Ex p. Shingara* the Court was also asked whether the requirement on Member States to provide 'the same legal remedies' referred to (1) specific remedies available in respect of decisions concerning entry by *nationals* of the state concerned (*in casu* an appeal to an immigration adjudicator), or (2) only to remedies available in respect of acts of the administration generally (*in casu* an application for judicial review, a less substantial remedy than an appeal). The Court said that no account could be taken of the remedies available to *nationals* concerning the right of entry because the two situations were not comparable. As we have already seen, with nationals the right of entry is a consequence of the status of being a national; by contrast, with migrants Member States have the discretion whether to invoke the public-policy derogation. Therefore, since an appeal to an immigration adjudicator was ruled out, migrants were left with the same remedies as those available against acts of the administration generally and the Court said that this satisfied the obligation under Article 8. Given that Article 31 CRD expressly provides for appeal or review in the alternative, it is likely that *Shingara* will continue to apply.

In *Pecastaing*[155] the Court said that the 'same remedies' would include suspension of the acts challenged, if this remedy was available to nationals. However, it added that Article 8 did not oblige the host state to allow the migrant to remain in its territory throughout the

---

[152] While the protection given to individuals was greater under Art. 9 than under Art. 8 of Dir. 64/221, Art. 8 had the broader scope. It applied to decisions concerning entry, refusal to issue or renew a residence permit, or ordering expulsion from the territory; Art. 9 applied only to decisions refusing to issue or renew a residence permit or ordering expulsion. Therefore, Art. 9 did not lay down any requirements in relation to decisions refusing *entry* to the territory (Case C–357/98 *Ex p. Yiadom* [2000] ECR I–9265, para. 33) on the ground that individuals refused entry are usually not physically present in the territory and so cannot submit a defence in person before the competent authority. For this reason individuals refused entry were confined to the protection given by Art. 8.

[153] Case 48/75 *Royer* [1976] ECR 497, para. 60.

[154] Joined Cases C–65 and 111/95 [1997] ECR I–3343, para. 24.

[155] Case 98/79 *Pecastaing* v. *Belgium* [1980] ECR 691, para. 12.

entire proceedings, so long as he was able to obtain a fair hearing and to present his defence in full.[156] This is now confirmed in Article 31(4), which allows Member States to exclude the individual from their territory pending the redress procedure but adds that 'Member States may not prevent the individual from submitting his/her defence in person, except where his/her appearance may cause serious troubles to public policy or public security or when the appeal or judicial review concerns a denial of entry or residence.'

(c) Administrative redress

Article 31 CRD envisages that administrative redress must be available where appropriate *in addition* to judicial redress. This is a marked change from Article 9 of Directive 64/221, which allowed access to a competent authority,[157] which differed from the decision-maker, only where there were no legal remedies or where the legal remedies were inadequate in some way (i.e., there was no right of appeal to a court of law, or the appeal was only in respect of the legal validity of the decision, or the appeal did not have suspensory effect).

The authority making the final decision (refusing renewal of a residence permit or ordering expulsion of the holder of a residence permit) could not, save in cases of urgency, take a decision until a 'competent authority' had given its view,[158] based on an exhaustive examination of all the facts and circumstances of the case, including the expediency of the proposed measure.[159]

Some of the more general rules developed by the Court in the context of its case law under Article 9(1) are likely to be applied equally to administrative redress under Article 31 CRD, including the requirement that while Member States can decide on the procedure by which a person appears before the competent authority, the individual must enjoy 'the same rights of defence and assistance or representation as the domestic law of that country provides for',[160] and must be informed of the authority's decision.[161]

4.3 Assessment

Even with the changes introduced by the CRD, it is not at all clear how much attention is actually paid in practice to the (limited) procedural safeguards laid down by the directive. For example, in Euro 2000 when large numbers of English football fans (EU citizens and recipients of services) were deported from Belgium, it seems they were given none of the basic protection provided by the then directive.[162] By contrast, in the British case of *Gough*

---

[156] Case 98/79 [1980] ECR 691, para. 13; Case C–357/98 *Ex p. Yiadom* [2000] ECR I–9265, para. 35. On interim orders, see Art. 31(2) CRD.

[157] Art. 9 did not define the term 'competent authority'. In Case 131/79 *Ex p. Santillo* [1980] ECR 1585 the Court recognized that a recommendation for deportation made by a criminal court at the time of conviction could constitute an opinion given by a competent authority, provided that the court has taken account of Art. 3(2) of Dir. 64/221, now Art. 27(2) CRD (that the mere existence of criminal convictions did not automatically constitute grounds for deportation). However, the Court has made clear that the competent authority does not have to be judicial in nature: all that Art. 9 requires is for the authority to perform its duties in absolute independence; that it is not directly or indirectly subject to any control by the administrative body empowered to take the measures provided for in the directive; and that the authority follow a procedure which enables the person concerned, on the terms laid down by the directive, effectively to present his defence and that all the factors to be taken into account by the administration are placed before it.

[158] Art. 9(1). See also Case 48/75 *Royer* [1976] ECR 497, para. 61.

[159] Joined Cases 115 and 116/81 *Adoui and Cornuaille* [1982] ECR 1665, para. 15.

[160] Art. 9(1); Joined Cases C–297/88 and C–197/89 *Dzodzi v. Belgium* [1990] ECR I–3763, para. 62.

[161] Joined Cases C–297/88 and 197/89 *Dzodzi* [1990] ECR I–3763; Case C–175/94 *Gallagher* [1995] ECR I–4253.

[162] V. Chaudhary and A. Osborn, 'England's glory night marred by fans' riots', *The Observer*, 18 Jun. 2000. Addressing the problems of football hooliganism has been left to soft law measures (see, e.g., Res. on hooliganism and the free movement of football supporters ([1996] OJ C166/40); Council Res. concerning

and Smith,[163] where the appellants unsuccessfully challenged banning orders preventing them from attending certain football matches both in the UK and abroad, the Divisional Court[164] and the Court of Appeal did give careful consideration to the appellants' rights under both the Treaty and Directive 64/221.

C. PUBLIC-SERVICE EXCEPTION

1. INTRODUCTION

It has been traditional for Member States, as part of the exercise of their sovereignty,[165] to reserve certain public-service jobs to their own nationals.[166] Article 45(4) TFEU provides that the principles of free movement of workers and non-discrimination on the ground of nationality do not apply to 'employment in the public service'. Articles 51 and 62 TFEU contain an equivalent provision in respect of establishment and services, albeit drafted in rather different terms. Article 51 TFEU says that '[t]he provisions of this chapter shall not apply ... to activities which in that State are connected, even occasionally, with the exercise of official authority'. The justification for this derogation is that particular posts presume a 'special relationship of allegiance to the State' and a 'reciprocity of rights and duties which form the foundation of the bond of nationality'.[167]

Because Articles 45(4), 51, and 62 TFEU represent further exceptions to fundamental freedoms they must also be narrowly construed,[168] with their scope limited to what is 'strictly necessary for safeguarding the interests of the State which that provision allows the Member States to protect'.[169] Therefore, in *Sotgiu*[170] the Court said that Article 45(4) TFEU applied only to conditions of access to employment; it did not authorize discriminatory conditions of employment once access had been granted. This meant that the German postal service could not rely on Article 45(4) TFEU to justify its refusal to pay Sotgiu, an Italian national, a separation allowance granted to German workers, on the ground that he was employed in the public service. The Court said that the fact that Sotgiu had been admitted to the service denied the existence of those interests which justified the derogation.

2. ARTICLE 45(4) TFEU: 'EMPLOYMENT IN THE PUBLIC SERVICE'

The Court has insisted on a Union definition of the phrase 'employment in the public service'.[171] In *Commission v. Belgium*[172] it explained that the jobs envisaged by Article 45(4)

---

a handbook with recommendations for international police cooperation and measures to prevent and control violence and disturbances in connection with football matches with an international dimension, in which at least one Member State is involved ([2002] OJ C22/1, updated [2006] OJ C322/1 and again in [2010] OJ C165/1).

[163] *Gough and Smith v. Chief Constable of Derbyshire* [2002] 2 CMLR 11.

[164] *Gough and Smith*, n. 163, Laws LJ.

[165] See Mancini AG in Case 307/84 *Commission v. France* [1986] ECR 1725, para. 2.

[166] Art. 45(4) TFEU cannot be used to justify excluding nationals who have exercised their rights of free movement from jobs in the public service: Case C–298/14 *Brouillard v. Jury du concours de recrutement de référendaires près la Cour de cassation* EU:C:2015:652.

[167] Case 149/79 *Commission v. Belgium* [1980] ECR 3881, para. 10.

[168] Case 152/73 *Sotgiu v. Deutsche Bundespost* [1979] ECR 153, para. 4.

[169] Case 225/85 *Commission v. Italy* [1987] ECR 2625.   [170] Case 152/73 [1979] ECR 153, para. 4.

[171] See, e.g., Case C–473/93 *Commission v. Luxembourg* [1996] ECR I–3207, para. 26.

[172] Case 149/79 [1982] ECR 1845, para. 7.

'involve direct or indirect participation in the exercise of powers conferred by public law and duties designed to safeguard the interests of the State or of other public authorities'. The Court continued that these jobs are 'characteristic of specific activities of public service insofar as [they are] invested with the exercise of public power *and* the responsibility for safeguarding the general interests of the State'.[173] It is not clear whether these requirements are to be read cumulatively or disjunctively. A cumulative reading is consistent with the view that Article 45(4) TFEU must be interpreted restrictively; but support can be found in *Commission v. Italy*[174] for the argument that the requirements are to be read disjunctively.

The other question facing the Court is whether the phrase 'public service' requires an institutional or a functional approach. The *institutional* or organic approach, which is supported by the wording of Article 45(4) TFEU, views the institution and its personnel as a whole, regardless of the specific functions carried out by individuals within the organization. This approach would allow a Member State to reserve all jobs in a particular organization, such as the civil service, to nationals even where some of those jobs are of a purely administrative or technical nature and involve no tasks designed to safeguard the interests of the state. This interpretation has been favoured by states keen to reserve as many posts as possible for their own nationals.[175] By contrast, the *functional* approach looks at the work required of a particular post to see if it involves direct or indirect participation in the exercise of powers conferred by public law and duties designed to safeguard the interests of the state. The functional approach would allow Member States to reserve only certain posts to nationals.

Consistent with the view that derogations are narrowly construed, the Court actually adopts the functional approach.[176] On a case-by-case basis, it examines the tasks and responsibilities inherent in the post[177] to see if they fulfil 'the very strict conditions'[178] of Article 45(4) TFEU rather than considering the nature of the legal relationship between the employee and the employing administration or the individual's job description.[179] This approach has led the Court to find that most jobs do not benefit from the Article 45(4) TFEU derogation. It has said that none of the following jobs constitute employment in the public service:

- a teacher in a state school[180]
- a state nurse[181]
- a foreign-language assistant in a university[182]
- various posts on the state railways[183]
- a local government employee[184]

---

[173] Emphasis added.   [174] Case 225/85 [1987] ECR 2625, paras. 9–10.

[175] See the Belgian government's arguments in Case 149/79 *Commission* v. *Belgium* [1980] ECR 3881.

[176] Case C–473/93 *Commission* v. *Luxembourg* [1996] ECR I–3207, para. 27.

[177] Case 149/79 *Commission* v. *Belgium* [1982] ECR 1845, para. 8; Case C–473/93 *Commission* v. *Luxembourg* [1996] ECR I–3207, para. 27.

[178] Case C–473/93 *Commission* v. *Luxembourg* [1996] ECR I–3207, para. 33.

[179] Case 152/73 *Sotgiu* [1974] ECR 153.

[180] Case 66/85 *Lawrie-Blum* [1986] ECR 2121; Case C–4/91 *Bleis* v. *Ministère de l'education nationale* [1991] ECR I–5627.

[181] Case 307/84 *Commission* v. *France* [1986] ECR 1725.

[182] Case 33/88 *Allué and Coonan* [1989] ECR 1591.

[183] Case 149/79 *Commission* v. *Belgium* [1982] ECR 1845.

[184] Case 149/79 *Commission* v. *Belgium* [1980] ECR 3881 and [1982] ECR 1845 (plumbers, carpenters, electricians, gardeners).

- a trainee lawyer[185]
- a seaman[186]
- a job in research not involving sensitive research work[187] and
- a post in the lower echelons of the civil service.

On the other hand, in the rather odd case of *Commission* v. *Belgium*[188] the Court found that local authority posts for architects, supervisors,[189] and night watchmen did fall within the Article 45(4) TFEU exception. Less controversially, it said in *Commission* v. *Italy*[190] that those involved in advising the state on scientific and technical questions were employed in the 'public service'.

While it is difficult to draw any clear principles from the case law, it seems that senior government jobs can be confined to nationals only, even though this may mean that Article 45(4) TFEU represents a barrier to promotion for non-nationals.[191] However, where the exercise of public-law powers is purely marginal and ancillary to the principal function of the posts, then such jobs generally fall outside Article 45(4) TFEU. This is the view taken by the Commission in its Communication designed to eliminate restrictions in areas of the public sector,[192] where it listed jobs in the public sector to which, in normal circumstances, Article 45(4) TFEU did not apply. These included public healthcare services; employment in state educational institutions; research for non-military purposes in public establishments; and public bodies responsible for administering public commercial services, including public transport, gas or electricity distribution, air or maritime navigation, post and telecommunications, and broadcasting.

The Commission followed up its Communication on public-sector posts with enforcement proceedings against defaulting Member States. For example, Greece was condemned for maintaining for its own nationals posts in education, healthcare, the utilities, public transport, post and telecommunications, radio and television broadcasting, the Athens opera, and municipal and local orchestras;[193] and Luxembourg was condemned for restricting posts in the public sectors of research, education, health, inland transport, post, telecommunications, and the utilities to its own nationals.[194] In the field of education, the Luxembourg government argued that teachers had to be Luxembourg nationals in order to 'transmit traditional values' and that, in view of the size of the country and its specific demographic situation, the nationality requirement was an essential condition for preserving Luxembourg's national identity. While recognizing that the preservation of national identities was a legitimate aim, the Court said that the Luxembourg government's response was disproportionate. It argued that Luxembourg's interest could be effectively safeguarded otherwise than by a general exclusion of nationals from other Member States, in particular by imposing conditions relating to training, experience, and knowledge of the language.[195]

---

[185] Case C–109/04 *Kranemann* v. *Land Nordrhein-Westfalen* [2005] ECR I–2421, para. 19, where the Court made clear that the concept of employment in the public service did not encompass employment by a private natural or legal person, whatever the duties of the employee.
[186] Case C–37/93 *Commission* v. *Belgium* [1993] ECR I–6295.
[187] Case 225/85 *Commission* v. *Italy* [1987] ECR 2625.
[188] Case 149/79 *Commission* v. *Belgium* [1982] ECR 1845, para. 8.
[189] Namely head technical office supervisor, principal supervisor, works supervisor, and stock controller.
[190] Case 225/85 *Commission* v. *Italy* [1987] ECR 2625, para. 9.
[191] Para. 10.   [192] 88/C 72/02.
[193] Case C–290/94 *Commission* v. *Greece* [1996] ECR I–3285.
[194] Case C–473/93 *Commission* v. *Luxembourg* [1996] ECR I–3207. See also Case C–173/94 *Commission* v. *Belgium* [1996] ECR I–3265.
[195] Case C–473/93 *Commission* v. *Luxembourg* [1996] ECR I–3263, paras. 32–5.

The Commission has, however, suggested that Article 45(4) TFEU would apply to the police and other forces of order, the armed forces, the judiciary, tax authorities, and the diplomatic service.[196] This approach was reflected in the Court's decisions in *Anker*[197] and the *Spanish Merchant Navy* case,[198] albeit subject to a proportionality review. In *Anker* the Court upheld in principle a German law requiring the post of master of a fishing vessel flying the German flag to be held by a German national. Because the job entailed duties connected to the maintenance of safety and to the exercise of police powers, particularly in the case of danger on board, together with powers of investigation, coercion, and punishment, the Court said that the post entailed direct participation in the exercise of powers conferred by public law for the purposes of safeguarding the general interest of the state.[199] It added that even though masters were employed by private bodies, this did not take the matter outside the scope of Article 45(4) TFEU because they were acting as 'representatives of public authority in the service of the general interests of the State'.[200]

However, the Court emphasized that, to benefit from the Article 45(4) TFEU derogation, the powers had to be exercised on a regular basis and could not represent only a 'very minor part of their activities'.[201] It therefore found that the post of master of small-scale deep-sea fishing vessels, which involved skippering small boats with a small crew and participating in fishing and processing fish products did not benefit from the Article 45(4) TFEU derogation.[202] In the *Spanish Merchant Navy* case[203] the Court followed *Anker*, and found that the posts of master and chief mate in the Spanish merchant navy were also posts in which exercise of the duty of representing the flag state was in practice only occasional and so again did not benefit from the Article 45(4) TFEU derogation.[204]

3. THE EXERCISE OF 'OFFICIAL AUTHORITY'

In respect of freedom of establishment, Article 51 TFEU contains an equivalent derogation to that in Article 45(4) TFEU; Article 62 TFEU extends this to services. Article 51 TFEU talks of the 'exercise of official authority', which more clearly suggests a functional approach than the Article 45(4) TFEU equivalent 'employment in the public service'.[205] Since the Court applied the functional test to Article 45(4) TFEU and since the objectives of Article 51 TFEU are similar to those of Article 45(4) TFEU, it is likely that the case law on Article 45(4) TFEU will apply equally to Article 51 TFEU.[206]

[196] [1988] OJ C72/2; P. Watson, 'Free movement of workers: Recent cases' (1989) 14 *ELRev.* 415. And even in respect of these sectors, the Commission has since tightened up its approach: COM(2002) 694, 19.
[197] Case C–47/02 *Albert Anker, Klaas Ras, Albertus Snoek* v. *Bundesrepublik Deutschland* [2003] ECR I–10447.
[198] Case C–405/01 *Colegio de Oficiales de la Marina Mercante Española* v. *Administración del Estado* [2003] ECR I–10391.
[199] Para. 61.   [200] Para. 62.   [201] Para. 63.
[202] Para. 64. See also Case C–270/13 *Haralambidis* EU:C:2014:2185, where the Court found that the post of president of a port authority did not fall into the Art. 45(4) derogation.
[203] Case C–405/01 *Colegio de Oficiales de la Marina Mercante Española* [2003] ECR I–10391.
[204] Para. 45. See also Case C–89/07 *Commission* v. *France* [2008] ECR I–45: requirement of French nationality for access to the posts of master (captain) and officer (chief mate) on all vessels flying the French flag could not be justified under Art. 45(4) TFEU. See also Case C–447/07 *Commission* v. *Italy* [2008] ECR I–125; Case C–94/08 *Commission* v. *Spain* [2008] ECR I–160.
[205] Case C–151/14 *Commission* v. *Latvia* EU:C:2015:577, para. 73: 'it is by reference to the nature of the relevant activities themselves, not by reference to that status as such', that it must be ascertained whether those activities fall within the exercise of official authority exception.
[206] Cf. Case C–283/99 *Commission* v. *Italy* [2001] ECR I–4363, para. 25.

The nature of what constitutes official authority was at issue in *Reyners*,[207] where the Court examined whether the profession of *avocat* could be confined to nationals on the ground that *avocats* were connected with the public service of administration of justice. The Court said that Article 51 TFEU had to be narrowly construed: it applied only to those activities which had a 'direct and specific connection with official authority'.[208] It continued that Article 51 TFEU would justify the exclusion of a whole profession only where those activities were linked to that profession in such a way that freedom of establishment would require the host Member State to allow the exercise by non-nationals, even occasionally, of functions related to official authority.[209] This would not be the case with the legal profession, where contact with the courts, although regular and organic, did not constitute the exercise of official authority because it was possible to separate tasks involving the exercise of official authority from the professional activity taken as a whole.[210]

In subsequent cases the Court has also rejected arguments based on Article 51 TFEU. It has found that none of the following jobs involve the exercise of official authority:

- road traffic accident expert, whose reports were not binding on the courts[211]
- the technical job of designing, programming, and operating data-processing systems[212]
- transport consultant[213]
- vehicle inspector[214]
- court translators[215]
- notaries[216]
- certification activities carried out by companies classified as certification bodies.[217]

In *Commission v. Belgium (security guards)*[218] the Court said that the activities of private security firms, security systems firms, and internal security services were not normally directly and specifically connected with the exercise of official authority. As the Court said in *Commission v. Spain*,[219] merely making a contribution to the maintenance of public security, which any individual could be called upon to do, did not constitute exercise of official authority. Similarly, in *Thijssen*[220] the Court held that the office of an approved Commissioner responsible for the monitoring of insurance companies did not constitute the exercise of official authority, although the Court did recognize that the

[207] Case 2/74 [1974] ECR 631.   [208] Para. 45.   [209] Para. 46.   [210] Para. 51.
[211] Case C–306/89 *Commission v. Greece* [1991] ECR I–5863, para. 7.
[212] Case C–3/88 *Commission v. Italy* [1989] ECR I–4035, para. 13.
[213] Case C–263/99 *Commission v. Italy* [2001] ECR I–4195.
[214] Case C–438/08 *Commission v. Portugal (road safety)* [2009] ECR I–10219. In Case C–160/08 *Commission v. Germany (ambulance service)* [2010] ECR I–3713.
[215] Joined Cases C–372 and 73/09 *Peñarroja Fa* [2011] ECR I–1785, para. 45.
[216] See, e.g., Case C–47/08 *Commission v. Belgium (notaries)* [2011] ECR I–4105; Case C–151/14 *Commission v. Latvia* EU:C:2015:577, para. 74, where the Court emphasized that notaries practise their profession in conditions of competition, which is not characteristic of the exercise of official authority.
[217] Case C–593/13 *Presidenza del Consiglio dei Ministri v. Rina Services* EU:C:2015:399, para. 22.
[218] Case C–355/98 *Commission v. Belgium* [2000] ECR I–1221, para. 26. See also Case C–283/99 *Commission v. Italy* [2001] ECR I–4363, para. 20; Case C–465/05 *Commission v. Italy* [2007] ECR I–11091, para.40.
[219] Case C–114/97 *Commission v. Spain* [1998] ECR I–6717, para. 37.
[220] Case C–42/92 *Thijssen v. Controldienst voor de verzekeringen* [1993] ECR I–4047.

Insurance Inspectorate itself, which had the task of both supervising the application of the law and making new regulations, did exercise official authority because its supervisory function served to protect insured parties and the public interest.[221] These cases therefore suggest that derogations under Articles 51 and 62 TFEU must be restricted to activities which, in themselves, are directly and specifically connected with the exercise of official authority; functions that are merely auxiliary and preparatory, especially when carried out by a private body, which are supervised by an entity which effectively exercises official authority by taking the final decision, are excluded from the definition of the exercise of official authority.[222]

D. OTHER LIMITATIONS

1. INTRODUCTION

So far we have concentrated on the express derogations laid down by the Treaty (public policy, public security, public health, and employment in the public service). In respect of migrant workers, the self-employed, and service providers/receivers these express derogations are the only grounds on which they can be refused entry or deported. For those who do not fall within one of these classifications, the position is different. Prior to the CRD, refusal of entry/deportation could occur without the host state showing one of the express derogations and without the individual benefiting from the procedural protection laid down in Directive 64/221. For example, states could deport work-seekers who had not found a job in the host state after three months (unless they could show that they had genuine chances of being employed[223]) without any rights to notice or to be heard. The CRD has changed this. Article 15(1) CRD extends the procedures laid down in Articles 30 CRD (notification of decisions) and Article 31 CRD (procedural safeguards) to 'all decisions restricting free movement of Union citizens and their family members on grounds other than public policy, public security or public health'. Article 15(1) CRD now also applies to those given the rights of free movement under the original 1990 Residence Directives[224] (students, the retired, and persons of independent means)—directives which were repealed and replaced by the CRD—who are refused entry or deported for not satisfying the criteria provided by the directive concerning adequate financial resources and sickness insurance.[225]

2. THE LIMITATIONS: FINANCIAL RESOURCES AND SICKNESS INSURANCE

The original three 1990 Residence Directives, while all driven by the desire to allow those who were self-supporting to move to another Member State, in fact differed in their detail.

---

[221] Para. 11.

[222] Case C–404/05 *Commission* v. *Germany (inspection of organic production)* [2007] ECR I–10239, para. 38; Case C–438/08 *Commission* v. *Portugal (vehicle inspection)* [2009] ECR I–10219, para. 37.

[223] See now Art. 14(4)(b) CRD, considered further in Ch. 8.

[224] See n. 1.

[225] Case C–364/10 *Hungary* v. *Slovak Republic* EU:C:2012:630, para. 52 added a further—very specific—exception: where a Union citizen performs the duties of a head of state then, under international law, this justifies an exception to the rights of free movement under Art. 21 TFEU and the CRD. Slovakia therefore did not have to guarantee the President of Hungary access to its territory.

Persons of independent means (PIMs) and their family members, originally covered by the so-called 'Playboy' Directive 90/364 and now by Article 7(1)(b) CRD,[226] have the right of residence on the territory of another Member State for a period longer than three months if they:

> have sufficient resources for themselves and their family members not to become a burden on the social assistance system of the host Member State during their period of residence and have comprehensive sickness insurance cover in the host Member State.[227]

The meaning of the phrase 'social assistance system' of the host state was considered in *Brey*,[228] where the Court said it covered:

> all assistance introduced by public authorities, whether at national, regional or local level, that can be claimed by an individual who does not have resources sufficient to meet his own basic needs and the needs of his family and who, by reason of that fact, may become a burden on the public finances of the host Member State during his period of residence which could have consequences for the overall level of assistance which may be granted by that state.

The Court said that a non-contributory pension supplement funded by the state fell within this definition.

According to Article 8(4) CRD, broadly replicating the equivalent provision of Directive 90/364, Member States may not lay down a fixed amount which they regard as 'sufficient resources' but they must take into account the personal situation of the person concerned. In all cases this amount must not be higher than the threshold below which nationals of the host Member State become eligible for social assistance, or, where this criterion is not applicable, higher than the minimum social security pension paid by the host Member State.[229] In *Commission* v. *Belgium (Portuguese migrants)*[230] the Court made clear that the authorities of the host Member State were entitled to undertake the necessary checks to ensure the 'existence, amount and availability' of those resources.

As far as sickness insurance is concerned, the Commission's guidance[231] provides that any insurance cover, private or public, contracted in the host Member State or elsewhere, is acceptable in principle, so long as it provides comprehensive coverage[232] and does not create a burden on the public finances of the host Member State. The guidance also says that pensioners fulfil the condition of comprehensive sickness insurance cover if they are entitled to health treatment on behalf of the Member State which pays their pension.

The Retired Persons Directive 90/365 was drafted in similar terms to Directive 90/364, but it specified that the individual had to be in receipt of an invalidity or early retirement pension, or old age benefits or a pension in respect of an industrial accident or disease 'of an amount sufficient to avoid becoming a burden on the social security system of the Member State'. These requirements have now been wrapped up into the persons of independent means provisions (Article 7(1)(b) CRD).

---

[226] See Art. 7(1)(d) and (2) in respect of the rights of residence of family members.

[227] Case C–209/03 *Bidar* [2005] ECR I–2119, para. 36 suggests that the burden of proof is on the state to show that the individual does not have sufficient resources or sickness insurance prior to removing the individual from the state rather than on the EU citizen to show that he has sufficient resources/medical insurance to entitle him to stay.

[228] Case C–140/12 *Brey* EU:C:2013:565, para. 61. See further Chs. 8 and 10.

[229] Art. 8(4) CRD. See also COM(2009) 313, 8.

[230] Case C–408/03 *Commission* v. *Belgium (Portuguese migrants)* [2006] ECR I–2647, para. 44.

[231] COM(2009) 313, 9–10.   [232] Cf. Case C–413/99 *Baumbast* [2002] ECR I–7091.

The Students Directive 93/96 differed somewhat from the other two Residence Directives and these differences have been reproduced in Article 7(1)(c) CRD. It provides that Union citizen students and their (reduced group of[233]) family members have the right of residence on the territory of another Member State for a period longer than three months if the students:

- are enrolled in a recognized educational establishment[234] for the principal purpose of following a course of study, including vocational training
- have comprehensive sickness insurance cover in the host state
- can assure the relevant national authority (but not prove), 'by means of a declaration or by such equivalent means as they may choose' that they have sufficient resources for themselves and their family members 'not to become a burden on the social assistance system of the host Member State during their period of residence'.

Because a student's financial position might change with the passage of time for reasons beyond his control, the Court said in *Grzelczyk*[235] that the truthfulness of his declaration was to be assessed only at the time when it was made. Article 8(3) CRD adds that, for the purpose of getting a registration certificate, Member States cannot require the declaration to refer to any specific amount of resources. Unlike the other two Residence Directives, no minimum level of resource was specified in the original Students Directive but Article 8(4) CRD on assessing sufficient resources appears to apply to students as well as to persons of independent means.

In *Commission* v. *Italy*[236] the Commission gave two reasons for the difference between the financial provisions concerning students and those applying to persons of independent means (and retired persons). The first related to the planned length of stay—the student's stay in the host state was only temporary (since it was limited to the duration of the studies), whereas the stay of the other two groups was potentially indefinite. The second concerned the fact that students were more likely to find work to supplement their income than the other two groups. Therefore, the risk of students becoming a burden on social assistance was less than in the case of persons of independent means. Furthermore, under Article 2 of the Students Directive (but not under the CRD), the validity of student residence permits could be limited to one year, renewable annually. Therefore, the Court said, the national authorities could intervene more rapidly where a student became a burden on national social assistance.

Finally, Article 3 of the original Students Directive 93/96 made clear that the host state was not obliged to pay maintenance grants to migrant students. The essence of this provision was replicated in Article 24(2) CRD, which says there is no right to equal treatment in respect of 'maintenance aid for studies ... consisting in student grants or student loans' for those not having the right of *permanent* residence (i.e., usually after five years) or who are not engaged in an economic activity (workers, the

---

[233] According to Art. 7(4)(d) CRD only the spouse, the registered partner recognized by the law of both the home and host state, and dependent children have the right of residence as family members. Discretionary admission under Art. 3(2) CRD applies to his/her dependent relatives in the ascending line and those of his/her spouse or registered partner.

[234] I.e., a private or public establishment, accredited or financed by the host Member State on the basis of its legislation or administrative practice.

[235] Case C–184/99 *Grzelczyk* [2001] ECR I–6193, para. 45.

[236] Case C–424/98 [2000] ECR I–4001, paras. 40 and 45.

self-employed), persons who retain their worker/self-employed status, and members of their families.[237] In other words, only those who are economically active/retain that status or who have permanent residence (usually after five years' residence) will enjoy maintenance aid for studies.

3. THE LIMITS TO THE LIMITATIONS

3.1 (Sufficiently) Sufficient Resources

The limitations laid down by the original Residence Directives and now the CRD indicate that while Member States were willing to admit the economically active and their families, they would not admit others unless they were able to support themselves. This prompted one commentator to observe that the EU had not yet reached the stage where the peoples of the Member States were considered as just one community, mutually extending solidarity, where revenues and financial charges are shared irrespective of national boundaries.[238] However, this perspective was put to the test in *Grzelczyk*.[239] Grzelczyk was a French student studying at university in Belgium. Having supported himself during the first three years of his course, largely by working part-time, he applied to the Belgian authorities for the minimex (a non-contributory social security benefit paid to nationals in need) to help fund him during his final year of study. He was refused the benefit on the ground that he was neither a Belgian national nor a migrant worker and so he suffered (direct) discrimination contrary to Article 18 TFEU,[240] which the Court said he could rely on because, as a citizen of the Union, he was lawfully resident in Belgium having exercised his fundamental rights under Article 21(1) TFEU.[241] Further, while recognizing that Article 3 of the original Students Directive 93/96 (now Article 24(2) CRD) did not establish any right to payment of a maintenance grant, it noted that the directive did not preclude students from receiving other social security benefits.[242]

But the very fact that Grzelczyk had applied for the minimex raised a further dilemma:[243] was this an indication to the host state authorities that he no longer satisfied the requirements in the Students Directive 93/96 (now Article 7(1)(c) CRD) of having sufficient resources? This view was confirmed in *Brey* in the context of Article 7(1)(b) CRD: the fact that a migrant who is not economically active may be eligible in the light of his low pension to receive a benefit classed as social assistance[244] could be an indication that he does not have sufficient resources to avoid becoming an unreasonable burden on the social-assistance scheme of the host state.[245]

In *Grzelczyk* the Court said that while a Member State could withdraw or not renew a residence permit of a student who had recourse to social assistance,[246] such measures could not be the *automatic* consequence of a migrant student having recourse to the host state's social-assistance system.[247] Further, the Court said that the Belgian authorities had to provide some temporary support to migrant EU citizens, as they would

---

[237] See further Ch. 9.   [238] C. Tomuschat (2000) 37 *CMLRev*. 449, 454.

[239] Case C–184/99 [2001] ECR I–6193.   [240] Para. 30.

[241] Para. 33, citing Case C–274/96 *Bickel and Franz* [1998] ECR I–7637.   [242] Para. 39.

[243] M. Dougan and E. Spaventa, 'Educating Rudy and the (non-)English patient: A double bill on residency rights under Article 18 EC' (2003) 28 *ELRev*. 697.

[244] See further Ch. 10.   [245] Case C–140/12 *Brey* EU:C:2013:565, para. 63.   [246] Para. 42.

[247] Para. 43. See also Case C–408/03 *Commission* v. *Belgium (Portuguese migrants)* [2006] ECR I–2647, para. 68.

to nationals, given that there existed 'a certain degree of financial solidarity' between nationals of a host Member State and nationals of other Member States,[248] but only for so long as the EU citizens did not become an unreasonable burden on public finances, particularly if the difficulties which a beneficiary of the right of residence encountered were temporary.[249]

Grzelczyk therefore suggests that a state cannot withdraw a student's residence permit or refuse to renew it simply because he has become a temporary burden on public funds. It is only when the burden becomes unreasonable that this can occur. This is now confirmed in Article 14(3) CRD:

> An expulsion measure shall not be the automatic consequence of a Union citizen's or his or her family member's recourse to the social assistance system of the host Member State.[250]

But when does a migrant become an unreasonable burden? In its guidance,[251] the Commission says that the authorities must carry out a proportionality test. To this end, it says that Member States may develop a points-based scheme as an indicator based on three sets of criteria:[252]

(1) duration
- For how long is the benefit being granted?
- Outlook: is it likely that the EU citizen will get out of the safety net soon?
- How long has the residence lasted in the host Member State?

(2) personal situation
- What is the level of connection of the EU citizen and his/her family members with the society of the host Member State?
- Are there any considerations pertaining to age, state of health, family, and economic situation that need to be taken into account?

(3) amount
- What is the total amount of aid granted?
- Does the EU citizen have a history of relying heavily on social assistance?
- Does the EU citizen have a history of contributing to the financing of social assistance in the host Member State?

This case-by-case assessment was confirmed in *Brey*: in assessing the burden placed by the individual on the national social-assistance scheme as a whole, the national authorities must carry out an overall assessment by reference to the personal circumstances characterizing the individual situation of the person.[253] This does, however, duck the question; given the vast social security budgets in all Member States, it is most unlikely that any single individual can ever become an unreasonable burden on it. However, a large number of indigent migrants could do so. This seems to be the view taken in *Dano*, which is considered in Section 3.5.

---

[248] Para. 44.   [249] Para. 44. See now recital 10 CRD.
[250] If Union citizens/their family members are expelled on these grounds, the procedural protection provided in Arts. 30 (notification) and 31 CRD (judicial/administrative redress) apply to any such decision: Art. 15(1) CRD. The host Member State cannot impose a ban on entry in the context of such an expulsion decision: Art. 15(3) CRD.
[251] COM(2009) 313, 8–9.   [252] See also recital 16 CRD.   [253] *Brey*, n. 228, para. 64.

3.2 (Sufficiently) Sufficient Medical Insurance

While the Court in *Grzelczyk* imposed limits on the requirement to have sufficient resources, in *Baumbast*[254] the Court imposed limits on the requirement to have medical insurance, this time in the context of the original Persons of Independent Means
Directive 90/364 (now Article 7(1)(b) CRD). Baumbast, a German national, brought
his family to the UK. They lived off private income and did not rely on financial assistance from the state. They also had comprehensive medical insurance in Germany and
they travelled there when necessary for treatment. However, they did not have medical
insurance providing emergency cover should they need it in the UK. For this reason,
the Secretary of State refused to renew Mr Baumbast's residence permit and the residence documents of his Columbian wife and children. The question for the Court was
whether the UK was entitled to insist upon Baumbast complying fully with the requirements of Directive 90/364. The Court said that the directive's limitations were subject
to the principle of proportionality.[255] Because Mr Baumbast basically satisfied all the
limitations laid down in Directive 90/364,[256] it would amount to a disproportionate interference with the exercise of the right of residence if he were denied residence simply
on the ground that his sickness insurance did not cover the emergency treatment given
in the host Member State.[257]

3.3 The Follow-Up to *Grzelczyk* and *Baumbast*

Baumbast paved the way for the controversial decision in *Chen*.[258] Chen's parents, who were
Chinese, wished to have a second child but this was forbidden in China due to its then single-
child policy. With the benefit of good legal advice, Mrs Chen entered the UK when she was
six months pregnant and moved to Belfast to give birth. Under the Irish Constitution as it
then stood, the *ius soli* (law of the soil) was the sole criterion for the acquisition of Irish nationality so that any child born anywhere on the island of Ireland acquired Irish nationality,
irrespective of any family connections with Ireland. So the baby, Catherine, was Irish. With
her Irish passport, Catherine and her mother moved to Wales.[259]

The Court said that Catherine, even though only eight months old, enjoyed the
rights of Union citizenship. She could therefore enjoy the right to reside under Article
21(1) TFEU, subject to the limitations laid down by the Person of Independent Means
Directive 90/364 (Article 7(1)(b) CRD). These she satisfied: she had both sickness insurance and sufficient resources, so that she did not become a burden on the British
state. The fact that these resources came from her mother was irrelevant: the Court
noted that the directive laid down no condition as to the origin of the resources, merely

[254] Case C–413/99 *Baumbast and R.* [2002] ECR I–7091. For a fuller discussion of these judgments see
COM(2003) 101.
[255] Para. 91.   [256] Para. 92.   [257] Para. 93.
[258] Case C–200/02 *Chen v. Secretary of State for the Home Department* [2004] ECR I–9925.
[259] In an attempt to put an end to such 'citizenship' or 'passport tourism', the Irish Constitution was
amended (79 per cent of those voting were in favour, 21 per cent against), removing citizenship as a constitutional right and restoring to the *Oireachtas* (Irish Parliament) the power to legislate in relation to the
acquisition of Irish nationality and citizenship. This led to the Irish Nationality and Citizenship Act 2004
granting citizenship now on the basis of a combination of not only *ius soli* but also *ius sanguinis* (in the case
of non-national parents, one of the child's parents must have had a substantial connection with Ireland by
being legally resident there for a number of years): A. Tryfonidou, 'Case C–200/02 *Chen*: Further cracks in
the "great wall" of the European Union' (2005) 11 *EPL* 527, 531. According to press reports, the Chen family
'fled their luxury apartment in Wales' and returned to China: 'Voters' right to scrap this rule', *News of the
World*, 13 Jun. 2004.

that they be sufficient.[260] In a similar vein, the Court said in *Commission* v. *Belgium (Portuguese migrants)*[261] that the provider of those 'sufficient resources' did not need to have a 'legal link' with the beneficiary (such as the link between parent and child in *Chen*).[262] Therefore, it was enough, for the purposes of the directive, for a Portuguese national living in Belgium with her daughters to be financially supported by her long-standing Belgian partner even though he was not legally obliged to provide for her: she 'had' sufficient resources.

3.4 Assessment

The careful articulation of the proportionality principle in *Baumbast* and again in *Chen* and *Commission* v. *Belgium*, limiting the Member State's right to rely on the limitations laid down in the Residence Directives, helps to explain *Grzelczyk*: Grzelczyk could not be refused a minimex because he had been lawfully residing in Belgium for three years, during which time he had had sufficient resources (and medical insurance). Now that he was suffering 'temporary difficulties' it would be disproportionate to deny him the minimex; and paying him the minimex temporarily was certainly more proportionate than withdrawing his right of residence before the end of the course.

In all four cases the Court placed much emphasis on the fact that the individuals were citizens of the Union and, in the words of *Grzelczyk*, could benefit from 'a certain degree of financial solidarity'[263] with nationals of a host Member State in 'emergency' situations (pressing financial or medical need). In this way the Court has used the citizenship principle to limit the limitations to the directives: all that is now required is sufficiently sufficient resources and health insurance.[264] Whatever the original intentions of the EU legislator, EU citizenship has helped to foster, at least to a limited extent, solidarity among citizens of the Union, a solidarity nurtured by the Court.

3.5 The Decision in *Dano*

However, this creative view of the role of EU citizenship needs to be reconsidered in the light of *Dano*. As we saw in Chapter 10, Ms Dano, a Romanian national with limited education, moved to Germany with her son. She did not work but was supported by her sister. They unsuccessfully applied for special non-contributory benefits. The Court of Justice upheld this decision, relying on a literal reading of the CRD, unadorned by any reference to the Treaty provisions on citizenship. Having resided in Germany for more than three months but less than five years but without having engaged in economic activity, the Danos could rely only on the person of independent measures provision, Article 7(1)(b)

---

[260] Para. 33. See also Case C–86/12 *Alokpa* v. *Ministre du travail, de l'emploi et de l'immigration* EU:C:2013:645, para. 30; Case C–218/14 *Singh* EU:C:2015:476 (resources coming from the TCN spouse count towards sufficient resources). In *W (China) and X (China)* v. *Secretary of State for the Home Department* [2006] EWCA Civ 1494, the British Court of Appeal ruled that both Chinese parents of an EU citizen child, together with the (four-year-old) child herself, had to satisfy the two conditions of possession of sickness insurance and sufficient resources in order to enjoy the right of free movement. In *Liu* v. *Secretary of State for the Home Department* [2007] EWCA Civ 1275 the Court of Appeal said there was no obligation on states to adjust their laws to enable TCN parents of an EU citizen child to be able to work so as to provide sufficient resources for the child.

[261] Case C–408/03 [2006] ECR I–2647.   [262] Para. 46.

[263] Case C–184/99 *Grzelczyk* [2001] ECR I–6193, para. 44.

[264] Dougan and Spaventa, n. 243.

CRD. However, since they did not have sufficient resources they could not claim a right of residence in Germany under the CRD. Therefore, they could not invoke the principle of non-discrimination in Article 24(1) of the directive.[265]

As the Court said, Article 7(1)(b) CRD seeks to prevent economically inactive Union citizens from using the host Member State's welfare system to fund their means of subsistence. The fact that this results in unequal treatment between Union citizens who have made use of their freedom of movement rights and nationals of the host Member State with regard to the grant of social benefits is an inevitable consequence of Article 7(1)(b) CRD. *Dano* thus sends the message that the model of EU citizenship is no longer one based purely on integration (EU migrants should be entitled to benefits to help them integrate into the host Member State). Rather, it is one based on earning rights through length of residence, which satisfies the detailed requirements of the CRD. Lawful residence, which in the case of PIMs requires having sufficient resources, has become a precondition to enjoying the right to equal treatment. Article 21 TFEU will be used ever less for softening the edges of those requirements.

E. PUBLIC-INTEREST JUSTIFICATIONS

1. INTRODUCTION

The (general) express derogations are available in respect of any breach of Union law (refusal of entry as well as directly, indirectly, and non-discriminatory measures and other restrictions on free movement). However, as we saw in Chapter 7, indirectly discriminatory and non-discriminatory measures which hinder free movement (see fig. 7.4), together with measures which prevent or impede market access (see fig. 7.5) and possibly, occasionally, even directly discriminatory measures, can be saved by a broader category of objective justifications/public-interest requirements.[266] In *O'Flynn* we saw that the language of objective justification was used in the context of free movement of workers. In respect of establishment and services, the Court tends to talk about justifications in the 'public' or 'general interest' or 'imperative requirements'[267] but it seems likely that these terms are the functional equivalent of 'objective justifications',[268] which in turn are the free movement of persons' equivalent to mandatory requirements in the field of goods. In all cases the Court recognizes that there exist certain national interests which are worthy of protection[269] and should take precedence over the free movement provisions. However, the burden is on the defendant state to prove the existence of any such justification[270] and explain the link between the justification put forward and the

---

[265] See also Case C–299/14 *Vestische Arbeit Jobcenter Kreis Recklinghausen* v. *Garcia-Nieto* EU:C:2016:114, para. 51.

[266] Joined Cases C–344 and 367/13 *Blanco and Fabretti* v. *Agenzia delle Entrate* EU:C:2014:2311, para. 38, which contains a clear statement of the orthodoxy. Cf. Section D.1(a) of the UK's New Settlement deal also suggested that it is unnecessary to distinguish between direct and indirect discrimination, although it is not clear on this point.

[267] Case C–76/90 *Säger* [1991] ECR I–4221, para. 15; Case C–55/94 *Gebhard* [1996] ECR I–4165, para. 37.

[268] This view is supported by the workers case, Case C–195/98 *Österreicher Gewerkschaftsbund* [2000] ECR I–10497, para. 45, where the Court reported that the Austrian government contended that the restrictions on free movement were 'justified by overriding reasons of public interest and are consistent with the principle of proportionality', and the services case, Case C–118/96 *Safir* [1998] ECR I–1897, para. 22: 'Article [56 TFEU] precludes the application of any national legislation which, without objective justification, impedes a provider of services from actually exercising the freedom to provide them.'

[269] See Tesauro AG in Case C–118/96 *Safir* [1998] ECR I–1897, para. 29.

[270] See, e.g., Case C–260/04 *Commission* v. *Italy (horse race betting licences)* [2007] ECR I–7083, para. 33.

measures taken to achieve it.[271] In other words, the justification must be actually made out; it is not sufficient for a state to invoke it without supporting evidence.[272]

In *Gebhard*,[273] a case on establishment, the Court elaborated on the requirements necessary for the national rule to satisfy the test of justification. It said that national measures liable to hinder or make less attractive the *exercise of fundamental freedoms* (note how the Court has generalized its approach beyond the specifics of the case) guaranteed by the Treaty had to fulfil four conditions in order not to breach the Treaty. They had to:

- be applied in a non-discriminatory manner
- be justified by imperative requirements in the general interest
- be suitable for securing the attainment of the objective which they pursued
- not go beyond what was necessary to attain it.[274]

2. THE JUSTIFICATIONS RECOGNIZED BY THE COURT

So what are the justifications recognized by the Court so far? In the services case, *Gouda*,[275] the Court listed the public-interest grounds which it had already recognized:

- professional rules intended to protect the recipients of a service[276]
- protection of intellectual property[277]
- protection of workers[278]
- consumer protection[279]
- conservation of the national historic and artistic heritage[280]

---

[271] Joined Cases C–151 and 152/04 *Nadin* [2005] ECR I–11203, para. 52; Case C–243/01 *Gambelli* [2003] ECR I–13031, para. 63. The Court may well scrutinize the stated objectives rigorously as in Case C–169/07 *Hartlauer Handelsgesellschaft mbH* v. *Wiener Landesregierung and others* [2009] ECR I–1721.

[272] See, e.g., Case C–389/05 *Commission* v. *France (insemination of bovine semen)* [2008] ECR I–5337, para. 103, where the Court rejected the French government's justification based on town and country planning because its arguments were not 'substantiated by any statistical information or data'.

[273] Case C–55/94 [1995] ECR I–4165.   [274] Para. 37.

[275] Case C–288/89 [1991] ECR I–4007.

[276] Joined Cases 110 and 111/78 *Ministère public* v. *Willy van Wesemael* [1979] ECR 35, para. 28. In Case C–3/95 *Sandker* [1996] ECR I–6511, para. 38, the Court spelled out this justification more fully: 'the application of professional rules to lawyers, in particular those relating to organization, qualifications, professional ethics, supervision and liability, ensures that the ultimate consumers of legal services and the sound administration of justice are provided with the necessary guarantees in relation to integrity and experience'.

[277] Case 62/79 *Coditel* [1980] ECR 881; Joined Cases C–403 and 429/08 *Murphy* v. *Media Protection Services* [2011] ECR I–9083, para. 94.

[278] Case 279/80 *Criminal Proceedings against Webb* [1981] ECR 3305, para. 19; Joined Cases 62 and 63/81 *Seco* v. *EVI* [1982] ECR 223, para. 14. Subsequently in Case C–272/94 *Criminal Proceedings against Guiot* [1996] ECR I–1905, para. 16, the Court stressed the importance of the social protection of workers in the construction industry. However, this did not permit strike action to enforce terms and conditions of employment which exceed the exhaustive list in Art. 3(1) of the Posted Workers Dir. 96/71: Case C–341/05 *Laval* [2007] ECR I–987, para. 110.

[279] Case 220/83 *Commission* v. *France (co-insurance)* [1986] ECR 3663, para. 20; Case 252/83 *Commission* v. *Denmark (co-insurance)* [1986] ECR 3713, para. 20; Case 205/84 *Commission* v. *Germany (insurance)* [1986] ECR 3755, para. 30; Case 206/84 *Commission* v. *Ireland (co-insurance)* [1986] ECR 3817, para. 20; Case C–180/89 *Commission* v. *Italy (tourist guides)* [1991] ECR I–709, para. 20.

[280] Case C–180/89 *Commission* v. *Italy* [1991] ECR I–709, para. 20.

- turning to account the archaeological, historical, and artistic heritage of a country and the widest possible dissemination of knowledge of the artistic and cultural heritage of a country[281]
- cultural policy.[282]

As with *Cassis*, the list in *Gouda* is not exhaustive. The Court has also recognized a number of other public-interest grounds. Chalmers loosely divides the justifications into four groups. The first group concerns market externalities (where a transaction fails to take account of somebody's interests and that person is not deemed to have a choice in the matter).[283] This heading includes justifications such as:

- guaranteeing the quality of skilled trade work and protecting those who have commissioned such work[284]
- the protection of the interests of creditors, minority shareholders, and employees[285]
- protection of the environment[286]
- promotion of tourism[287]
- promoting sustainable settlement in a designated area (essentially a regional policy goal) where there has been a decline in population due to harsh climate, vast distances, and sparse population[288]
- road,[289] port,[290] and maritime safety[291]
- the need to safeguard the reputation of the Dutch financial markets (and to protect the investing public).[292]

A second group concerns civil liberties (i.e., ensuring that the economic freedoms do not compromise the political values which are central to protecting human dignity, autonomy, and equality) such as the protection of human dignity,[293] equal treatment between citizens,[294] or freedom of expression and assembly.[295]

---

[281] Case C–154/89 *Commission* v. *France* [1991] ECR I–659, para. 17; Case C–198/89 *Commission* v. *Greece* [1991] ECR I–727, para. 21.

[282] Case C–288/89 *Gouda* [1991] ECR I–4007, paras. 22–3; Case C–353/89 *Commission* v. *Netherlands* [1991] ECR I–4069; and Case C–23/93 *TV10* [1994] ECR I–4795.

[283] D. Chalmers et al., *EU Law* (Cambridge: CUP, 2006), 833–4.

[284] Case C–58/98 *Josef Corsten* [2000] ECR I–7919, para. 38.

[285] Case C–208/00 *Überseering* [2002] ECR I–9919, para. 92.

[286] Case C–17/00 *De Coster* v. *Collège des bourgmestre et échevins de Watermael-Boitsfort* [2001] ECR I–9445, paras. 36–7; Joined Cases C–151 and 152/04 *Nadin* [2005] ECR I–11203, para. 52; Case C–338/09 *Yellow Cab* [2010] ECR I–13927, para. 50.

[287] Case C–338/09 *Yellow Cab* [2010] ECR I–1392, para. 50.

[288] Case E–3/05 *EFTA Surveillance Authority* v. *Norway* [2006] EFTA Ct. Rep. 102 para. 57.

[289] Case C–55/93 *Criminal Proceedings against van Schaik* [1994] ECR I–4837; Joined Cases C–151 and 152/04 *Nadin* [2005] ECR I–11203, para. 49.

[290] Joined Cases C–128 and 129/10 *Navtiliaki Etairia Thasou AE* [2012] ECR I–1885, para. 45.

[291] Case C–509/12 *IPTM* v. *Navileme-Consultadoria Nautica* EU:C:2014:54, para. 23.

[292] Case C–384/93 *Alpine Investments* [1995] ECR I–1141, para. 44. See also Case C–222/95 *Parodi* v. *Banque H. Albert de Bary* [1997] ECR I–3899, para. 22, where the Court noted that the banking sector was a particularly sensitive area from the perspective of consumer protection.

[293] Case C–36/02 *Omega* [2004] ECR I–9609.

[294] Case C–208/09 *Sayn-Wittgenstein* [2010] ECR I–13693, para. 89.

[295] See the goods case, Case C–112/00 *Schmidberger* [2003] ECR I–5659, discussed in Ch. 6. The Court tentatively also recognized the right to accommodation in Case C–345/05 *Commission* v. *Portugal (transfer of property)* [2006] ECR I–10663, para. 31.

A third group concerns what Chalmers describes as protecting certain 'socio-cultural' practices (i.e., protecting local institutions which 'enable local or national markets to function, while securing reliability, trust and credibility'):

- ensuring the balance between sports clubs[296]
- prevention of social dumping[297] or unfair competition[298]
- prevention of abuse of free movement of services[299] or Union law more generally[300]
- avoiding disturbances on the labour market[301]
- ensuring the survival of small and medium-sized undertakings and the maintenance of employment[302]
- ensuring social protection of workers in respect of, for example, social security provision[303] and employment rights[304]
- combating fraud, particularly social security fraud,[305] illegal employment[306] and bogus self-employment,[307] combating undeclared work,[308] and ensuring the efficacy of controls and supervision by, for example, the labour inspectorate[309]
- ensuring the adequacy of regular maritime services to, from, and between islands[310]
- preserving or improving the education system,[311] including higher education,[312] and encouraging student mobility[313]
- protecting the official national language[314] (by imposing rules on the spelling of that language)[315]
- the promotion of mobility and integration of disabled people and the wish to ensure that there is a connection between the society of the Member State concerned and the recipient of the benefit[316]
- addressing the housing needs of the less affluent population (social housing policy).[317]

---

[296] Case C–415/93 *Bosman* [1995] ECR I–4921, para. 106; Case C–176/96 *Lehtonen v. FRSB* [2000] ECR I–2681, para. 54.
[297] Case C–244/04 *Commission v. Germany* [2006] ECR I–885, para. 61; Case C–341/05 *Laval* [2007] ECR I–987, para. 103.
[298] Case C–60/03 *Wolff & Müller v. Pereira Félix* [2004] ECR I–9553, para. 41.
[299] Case C–244/04 *Commission v. Germany* [2006] ECR I–885, para. 38.
[300] Case C–147/03 *Commission v. Austria (higher education)* [2005] ECR I–5969, para. 70. See further the discussion of the tax cases in Ch. 11.
[301] Case C–445/03 *Commission v. Luxembourg* [2004] ECR I–10191, para. 38.
[302] Case C–464/05 *Geurts v. Administratie van de BTW* [2007] ECR I–9325, para. 26.
[303] Case C–255/04 *Commission v. France* [2006] ECR I–5251, para. 47.
[304] Case C–202/11 *Las* EU:C:2013:239, para. 28.
[305] Case C–577/10 *Commission v. Belgium (self-employed)* EU:C:2012:814, para. 45.
[306] Case C–255/04 *Commission v. France* [2006] ECR I–5251, para. 52.
[307] Case C–577/10 *Commission v. Belgium (self-employed)* EU:C:2012:814, para. 45.
[308] Case C–577/10 *Commission v. Belgium (self-employed)* EU:C:2012:814, para. 45.
[309] Case C–202/11 *Las* EU:C:2013:239, para. 28.
[310] Case C–205/99 *Analir* [2001] ECR I–1271, para. 27.
[311] Case C–40/05 *Lyyski* [2007] ECR I–99, para. 39. See also Case C–281/06 *Jundt* [2007] ECR I–12231, para. 58: 'promoting teaching, research and development'.
[312] Case C–20/12 *Giersch v. Etat du Grand-Duché de Luxembourg* EU:C:2013:411, para. 53.
[313] Case C–220/12 *Thiele Meneses* EU:C:2013:683, para. 49.
[314] Case C–202/11 *Las* EU:C:2013:239, para. 24.
[315] Case C–391/09 *Malgožata Runevič-Vardyn* [2011] ECR I–3787, para. 87.
[316] Case C–103/08 *Gottwald* [2009] ECR I–9117, para. 32.
[317] Joined Cases C–197 and 203/11 *Libert* EU:C:2013:288, para. 52.

A fourth group of justifications relates to the 'preservation of public order',[318] i.e. 'to supply services that are necessary for the government of its territory'. Here the Court is concerned with protecting certain values or interests as well as safeguarding the machinery of government that enables such protection. The list therefore includes the public interests recognized in *Schindler*[319] to justify a ban on lotteries (e.g., preventing gambling and avoiding the lottery from becoming the source of private profit; avoiding the risk of crime or fraud; avoiding the risk of incitement to spend, with damaging individual and social consequences), as elaborated in the subsequent gambling cases to include 'moral, religious and cultural factors'.[320] In these sorts of cases the Court offers states a wide scope for discretion in areas deemed sensitive ideologically or associated with particular risks[321] or where the Internet is involved.[322] The 'machinery of government' justifications include:

- protecting litigants[323] and preserving the systems of administration of justice[324]

- the coherence of a scheme of taxation[325]

- protecting a balanced allocation of the power to impose taxation between the various Member States concerned, so that profits and losses are treated symmetrically in the same tax system[326]

- the effectiveness of fiscal supervision[327] and debt relief measures[328] but not pure administrative convenience[329]

- the balanced allocation of the power to impose taxes between the Member States[330]

- the need to ensure the effective collection of income tax,[331] and preventing wholly artificial arrangements aimed solely at escaping national tax normally due[332]

---

[318] This heading is expressly recognized in Case C–465/05 *Commission* v. *Italy (private security activities)* [2007] ECR I–11091, para. 74. In that case the Italian government justified its requirement to limit licences for security guards to a particular territory on the grounds of the protection of public order and security, to ensure that private security activities were carried out safe from infiltration by local criminal organizations. The justification failed on the ground that it was not proportionate.

[319] Case C–275/92 [1994] ECR I–1039.

[320] Case C–243/01 *Gambelli* [2003] ECR I–13031, para. 63. These cases are discussed further in Ch. 11.

[321] Van Gerven AG in Case C–145/88 *Torfaen Borough Council* v. *B & Q plc* [1989] ECR 3851, para. 102.

[322] Case C–46/08 *Carmen Media Group* [2010] ECR I–8149, paras. 100–4.

[323] Joined Cases C–372 and 73/09 *Peñarroja Fa* [2011] ECR I–1785, para. 55.

[324] Case C–3/95 *Sandker* [1996] ECR I–611. In a similar vein, in Joined Cases C–147 and 148/06 *SECAP SpA* v. *Comune di Torino* [2008] ECR I–3565, para. 32 the Court endorsed a justification based on ensuring that the local administration can function without having its capacity so overwhelmed that it might jeopardize the attainment of a project.

[325] Case C–204/90 *Bachmann* [1992] ECR I–249. This is considered further in Ch. 8. See also, e.g., Case C–300/90 *Commission* v. *Belgium* [1992] ECR I–305; Case C–294/97 *Eurowings Luftverkehrs AG* [1999] ECR I–7447, para. 19.

[326] Case C–182/08 *Glaxo Wellcome* [2009] ECR I–8591, para. 88. For the justification relating to national schemes of taxation, see Ch. 11.

[327] Case C–55/98 *Bent Vestergaard* [1999] ECR I–7641, para. 23. However, a general presumption of tax avoidance or tax fraud is not sufficient to justify a fiscal measure which compromises the objectives of the Treaty: Case C–433/04 *Commission* v. *Belgium* [2006] ECR I–10653, para. 35.

[328] Case C–461/11 *Radziejewski* EU:C:2012:704, para. 36.

[329] Case C–212/08 *Zerturf* [2011] ECR I–5633, para. 48.

[330] Case C–446/03 *Marks & Spencer plc* v. *Halsey* [2005] ECR I–10837, para. 51. This is considered further in Ch. 11. See also Case C–330/07 *Jobra Vermögensverwaltungs-Gesellschaft mbH* v. *Finanzamt Amstetten Melk Scheibbs* [2008] ECR I–9099, para. 32.

[331] Case C–290/04 *Scorpio* [2006] ECR I–9461, para. 35.

[332] Case C–196/04 *Cadbury Schweppes* [2006] ECR I–7995, para. 51. This is considered further in Ch. 11.

- preserving the financial balance of a social security scheme[333]
- preventing fraud on the social security system[334]
- combating drug tourism,[335] money laundering, and terrorist financing[336]
- controlling costs, and preventing wastage of financial, technical, and human resources[337]
- the obligation of solidarity, which is 'characterised, in particular, by funding through contributions the amount of which is not strictly proportionate to the risks insured and by the granting of benefits the amount of which is not strictly proportionate to contributions'[338]
- the need for legal certainty.[339]

However, as with its case law under Article 258 TFEU enforcement proceedings, Member States cannot plead 'provisions, practices or situations prevailing in its domestic legal order, including those resulting from the constitutional organization of that State, to justify the failure to observe obligations arising under [Union] law'.[340] Therefore, in the *Walloon* case the Flemish government could not plead the requirements inherent in the division of powers within the Belgian federal structure and, particularly, the fact that the Flemish community could exercise no competence in relation to care insurance in respect of those residing in the territory of other linguistic communities, to justify excluding those French-speaking non-residents who worked in the Flemish part from access to the care insurance scheme.

Some of the justifications recognized in the third and fourth category come close to the very type of economic justifications which the Court has rejected in other cases.[341] For example, in *SETTG*[342] the Court said that a Greek law requiring all tourist guides to have a particular employment relationship with their employer (which effectively prevented self-employed tourist guides from other Member States from providing services in Greece) could not be justified on the ground of 'maintaining industrial peace as a means of bringing a collective dispute to an end and thereby preventing any adverse effects on an economic sector and consequently on the economy of the State'.[343] The Court said that such a justification had to be regarded as an 'economic aim'[344]

---

[333] Case C–158/96 *Kohll* [1998] ECR I–1931, para. 41. This is considered further in Ch. 11.

[334] Case C–406/04 *De Cuyper* [2006] ECR I–6947, para. 41.

[335] Case C–137/09 *Josemans* v. *Burgemeester van Maastricht* [2010] ECR I–13019, para. 65.

[336] Case C–212/11 *Jyske Bank Gibraltar Ltd* v. *Administración del Estado* EU:C:2013:270.

[337] Case C–157/99 *Geraets-Smits and Peerbooms* [2001] ECR I–5473, paras. 78–9.

[338] Case C–350/07 *Kattner Stahlbau GmbH* v. *Maschinenbau- und Metall- Berufsgenossenschaft* [2009] ECR I–1513, para. 87. See also Case C–192/05 *Tas-Hagen* [2006] ECR I–10451, paras. 34–5.

[339] Case C–347/06 *ASM Brescia SpA* v. *Comune di Rodengo Saiano* [2008] ECR I– 5641, para. 64; Joined Cases C–660/11 and C–8/12 *Biasci* EU:C:2013:550.

[340] Case C–212/06 *Walloon Government* [2008] ECR I–1683, para. 58.

[341] Even outside the economic justifications the Court has not been prepared to extend the list indefinitely: e.g., Case C–18/95 *Terhoeve* [1999] ECR I–345, para. 45, where the Court held that considerations of a purely administrative nature could not make lawful a restriction on the free movement of persons.

[342] Case C–398/95 *SETTG* v. *Ypourgos Ergasias* [1997] ECR I–3091.

[343] Para. 25. See also Joined Cases C–49, 50, 52–54 and 68–71/98 *Finalarte* [2001] ECR I–7831, paras. 38–9 and Case C–164/99 *Portugaia Construções Lda* [2002] ECR I–787, paras. 25–6, where the Court rejected the justification for the imposition of national social legislation on posted workers of protecting the domestic construction industry and reducing unemployment to avoid social tensions.

[344] See also Case C–137/04 *Rockler* v. *Försäkringskassan* [2006] ECR I–1141, para. 24. The Court will look to see if the expressed aim is genuinely economic or whether, viewed objectively, the rules actually

which could not constitute a reason relating to the general interest that justified a restriction on the freedom of establishment.[345] For similar reasons the Court has rejected arguments based on a reduction in tax revenue as an overriding reason in the public interest,[346] the cost to the national exchequer,[347] or the need to maximize revenue.[348] Hatzopoulos explains the different treatment between public-order justifications which have been accepted by the Court and other cases where the aim is considered economic on the ground that the former serve a 'structural' purpose (see, e.g., the healthcare cases such as *Kohll*,[349] *Geraets-Smits*,[350] and *Müller-Fauré*[351] considered earlier) and so are regarded more leniently than those which do not.[352] Arrowsmith develops this argument by suggesting that the bald statement that the EU interest in free movement always trumps state economic interests is now too simplistic, not least because for the Eurozone states the EU has an interest in Member States' fiscal stability.[353] She argues that in fact the evolution of the case law shows that the Court draws a distinction between those economic objectives which have a protectionist aim (e.g., saving the state money in the crudest sense) and those which do not. Where the justification is not protectionist the Court does and should adopt a case-by-case approach, balancing the variety of economic interests at stake, as it did in the health-care cases.[354] This view has received some support in the UK's New Settlement deal. It provides that in addition to the express derogations, overriding reasons of the public interest can be invoked by Member States, provided that the national measures are proportionate. Section D.1(a) continues:

> Encouraging recruitment, reducing unemployment, protecting vulnerable workers and averting the risk of seriously undermining the sustainability of social security systems are reasons of public interest recognised in the jurisprudence of the Court of Justice of the European Union for this purpose, based on a case by case analysis.

---

serve another, legitimate objective. This approach can be seen in Joined Cases C–49/98 etc *Finalarte* [2001] ECR I–7831.

[345] Case C–398/95 *SETTG* [1997] ECR I–3091, para. 23. Cf. Jacobs AG's suggestion in Case C–147/03 *Commission v. Austria (students)* [2005] ECR I–5969 that if the Court said that migrant students were entitled to maintenance grants 'the financial burden of the free movement of students on state resources would become significant', and this would be a good reason for states to be allowed to invoke economic grounds, albeit narrowly tailored, to justify certain restrictions on their availability to migrants.

[346] Case C–464/02 *Commission v. Denmark (company vehicles)* [2005] ECR I–7929, para. 45, citing the free movement of capital decision in Case C–319/02 *Manninen* [2004] ECR I–7477, para. 49. See also C–422/01 *Skandia* [2003] ECR I–6817, paras. 51–2, where the Court rejected arguments based on the need to preserve the tax base.

[347] Case C–109/04 *Kranemann* [2005] ECR I–2421.

[348] Case C–347/09 *Dickinger* [2011] ECR I–8185.

[349] Case C–158/96 *Kohll* [1998] ECR I–1931. For the parallel case on goods, see Case C–120/95 *Decker* [1998] ECR I–1831.

[350] Case C–157/99 *Geraets Smits and Peerbooms* [2001] ECR I–5473.

[351] Case C–385/99 *Müller-Fauré and van Riet* [2003] ECR I–4509.

[352] V. Hatzopoulos, 'Recent developments of the case law of the ECJ in the field of services' (2000) 37 *CMLRev.* 43, 79.

[353] S. Arrowsmith, 'Rethinking the approach to economic justifications under the EU's free movement rules' (2015) 68 *CLP* 307.

[354] See also the student financing cases considered later. In Case C–220/12 *Thiele Meneses* EU:C:2013:683, para. 43 the Court said 'while budgetary considerations may underlie a Member State's choice of social policy and influence the nature or scope of the social protection measure which it wishes to adopt, they do not in themselves constitute an aim pursued by that policy'.

F. PROPORTIONALITY

1. SUITABILITY AND NECESSITY

Once the Member State has identified an express derogation or a public-interest require-ment which the Court has accepted, a court (theoretically the national court but often the Court of Justice) will determine whether the steps taken by the Member State to realize that objective are, where appropriate, compatible with fundamental human rights[355] and proportionate. The burden of proof is on the defending state.[356] The Court offers various formulations of the proportionality test[357] but, as we saw in Chapter 6, the proportionality issue essentially raises two questions: first, whether the measures are suitable for securing the attainment of the objective and, secondly, whether they go beyond what is neces-sary in order to attain it.[358] As Straetmans observes,[359] the first question requires only a marginal control of the aptitude or suitability of the national legislation to obtain the aim pursued. By contrast, the second question requires courts to determine whether the interest pursued cannot be satisfied by other, less restrictive means.

The application of this two-stage approach can be seen in *De Coster*[360] concerning a decision by the Belgian authorities to tax satellite dishes. This had the effect of imposing a charge on the reception of television programmes by satellite while no equivalent charge was payable on those received by cable. The tax was found to interfere with the provision of services because broadcasters from other states were not allowed the unlimited access to cable distribution which Belgian broadcasters enjoyed. However, the Belgian author-ities argued that the tax could be justified on the ground of preventing 'the uncontrolled proliferation of satellite dishes in the municipality and thereby [preserving] the quality of the environment'. While the Court doubted whether the measure was *suitable* to attain that objective,[361] it was convinced that the tax exceeded what was *necessary* to achieve the objective of protecting the urban environment. It suggested that alternative, less-restrictive methods existed for achieving this objective,[362] such as laying down rules about the size of the dishes, their position, and the way in which they were fixed to a build-ing, or requiring the use of communal dishes.[363]

By contrast, the Court thought that the proportionality test had been satisfied in *Alpine Investments*. It agreed that the national law banning cold-calling was suitable, noting that the consumer was generally caught unawares by a cold call and so was in no position either to ascertain the risks inherent in the type of transactions or to compare the quality

---

[355] See Case C–60/00 *Carpenter* [2002] ECR I–6279, paras. 40–1, considered earlier.

[356] See, e.g., Case C–465/05 *Commission v. Italy (private security activities)* [2007] ECR I–11091, para. 76.

[357] See, e.g., Case C–288/89 *Gouda* [1991] ECR I–4007, para. 15: 'the application of national provisions to providers of services established in other Member States must be such as to *guarantee* the achievement of the intended aim and must not go beyond that which is necessary in order to achieve that objective. In other words, it must not be possible to obtain the same result by less restrictive rules' (emphasis added); Case C–157/99 *Geraets-Smits and Peerbooms* [2001] ECR I–5473, para. 75: 'to make sure that the measures do not exceed what is objectively necessary for that purpose and that the same result cannot be achieved by less restrictive rules'.

[358] See, e.g., Case C–67/98 *Zenatti* [1999] ECR I–7289, para. 29.

[359] G. Straetmans (2000) 37 *CMLRev.* 991, 1002.   [360] Case C–17/00 [2001] ECR I–9445.

[361] Para. 37. See also Case C–79/01 *Payroll Data Services* [2002] ECR I–8923, paras. 32–7.

[362] Para. 37.

[363] For another good example of the Court applying the 'necessity' limb of the proportionality test, see Case 352/85 *Bond* [1988] ECR 2085, para. 37.

and price of the caller's services with competitors' offers. On the question of necessity, the Court found that the rules were no more restrictive than necessary: although cold-calling was prohibited, other techniques for making contact with clients were still permitted. It also noted that the rules applied only to potential clients but not to existing clients and that the prohibition was limited to the sector in which abuses had been found (the commodities futures market).[364] The Court added that just because other Member States imposed less strict requirements to achieve the same objectives[365] did not mean that the Dutch rules were disproportionate.[366]

Likewise, in *Josemans*[367] the Court found that a Dutch rule limiting to residents only access to 'coffee shops' (where the sale of cannabis is tolerated) could be justified on the grounds of maintenance of public order and was proportionate: it was a *suitable* measure to 'deal with a large influx of residents from other Member States' wishing to buy cannabis. The rule was also *not more restrictive than necessary* since other policies had been applied and proved insufficient and ineffective. The Court specifically rejected the possibility of granting non-residents access to coffee shops while refusing to sell cannabis to them, as an alternative, on the grounds that (1) it would not be easy to control and monitor with accuracy that cannabis was not being served to, or consumed by, non-residents; and (2) there was a danger that such an approach would encourage the illegal trade in, or the resale of, cannabis by residents to non-residents inside coffee-shops. As with *Commission v. Italy (trailers)*,[368] in 'public order' situations the Court tends towards a pro-state, pragmatic approach to proportionality upholding 'general rules which are easily managed and supervised by the national authorities'[369] and allowing them the discretion to decide whether, in the gambling cases, to prohibit, wholly or in part, betting or 'only to restrict them and, to that end, to lay down more or less strict supervisory rules'.[370]

By contrast, is the increasing number of cases where Member States argue that the requirement imposed is justified by the need for a sufficient link of integration with the society of the state. One such requirement is residence, an indirectly discriminatory rule. The Court is suspicious of residence being used as a proxy for showing integration, not least because it particularly disadvantages frontier workers. It often expresses its concerns, as it did in *Giersch*,[371] in the language of proportionality: 'a condition of residence may be disproportionate if it is too exclusive in nature because it favours an element which is not necessarily representative of the real and effective degree of connection and excludes all other representative elements' such as employment in the host state, including by the parent, for a period of time or, as the Court said in *Thiele Meneses*,[372] the existence of other indicators such as language skills, or other social and economic factors.

Giersch concerned a Luxembourg rule making grant of financial aid for higher education studies conditional on residence by the student in Luxembourg. This was justified on the ground of encouraging students to work in Luxembourg 'in order to contribute to its economic development'. The Court itself suggested alternative requirements which might be a more proportionate way of achieving the objective than a residence requirement, including a system of financing which made the grant of the loan, or repayment of the

---

[364] Case C–384/93 *Alpine Investments* [1995] ECR I–1141, para. 54.

[365] E.g., in the UK broking firms were required to tape-record unsolicited phone calls (para. 50).

[366] Paras. 50–7.   [367] Case C–137/09 *Josemans* [2010] ECR I–13109.

[368] Case C–110/05 *Commission* v. *Italy (trailers)* [2009] ECR I–519, para. 67, discussed in Ch. 4.

[369] Case C–137/09 *Josemans* [2010] ECR I–13109, para. 82.

[370] Case C–463/13 *Stanley International Betting Ltd* v. *Ministero dell'Economia e delle Finanze* EU:C:2015:25, para. 52.

[371] Case C–20/12 *Giersch* v. *Etat du Grand-Duché de Luxembourg* EU:C:2013:411, para 72.

[372] Case C–220/12 *Thiele Meneses* EU:C:2013:683 (requirement of permanent residence disproportionate).

outstanding balance, or its non-reimbursement, conditional on the student who receives it working or residing in Luxembourg.

2. GOOD GOVERNANCE

As *De Coster* shows, the Court is prepared to offer guidance as to what measures it considers proportionate. Often this means, ensuring that the authorities comply with requirements of good governance and in particular the need for access to a review process. This can be seen in the healthcare cases discussed in Chapter 9; we can see it again in *Kraus*.[373] It will be recalled that the German authorities said that a migrant had to be authorized before he could use his LLM title awarded by a non-German university. The Court said it was legitimate for Germany to impose the restriction on the ground of 'the need to protect a public which will not necessarily be alerted to abuse of academic titles'[374] but required Germany to show that:

- the authorization procedure was intended solely to verify whether the postgraduate academic title was properly awarded
- the procedure was easily accessible and was not excessively expensive
- reasons were given for any refusal of authorization
- the refusal could be the subject of judicial procedures
- any penalty for non-compliance with the authorization procedure was not disproportionate to the gravity of the offence.[375]

This case highlights a point we have seen elsewhere that the Court requires Member States to show flexibility in the application of its rules[376] and must take into account the individual circumstances of the migrant's case.[377]

More generally, rules restricting free movement must be consistent with the objective pursued,[378] transparent,[379] and sufficiently legally certain, i.e., the rules of law must be clear, precise, and predictable as regards their legal effects. Where they fail these tests, then the rules cannot be 'considered proportionate to the objectives pursued'.[380]

G. CONCLUSIONS

Questions have been raised about the compatibility of the Treaty derogations with the objectives of the internal market, and more specifically with the notion of Union citizenship laid down by Articles 20–1 TFEU. In particular, Articles 45(4) and 51 TFEU represent a continued respect for national sovereignty at a time when efforts are being made to promote a European consciousness through Union citizenship, and when employers are being encouraged to appoint on merit and not nationality. However, no attempt has been made to amend these derogations and Directive 64/221 continues—only slightly

---

[373] Case C–19/92 [1993] ECR I–1663. See also Case C–279/00 *Commission v. Italy (temp agencies)* [2002] ECR I–1425.

[374] Para. 35.   [375] Para. 42.   [376] Case C–213/05 *Geven* [2007] ECR I–6347.

[377] Case C–40/05 *Lyyski* [2007] ECR I–99, para. 49.

[378] Case C–275/12 *Elrick v. Bezirksregierung Köln* EU:C:2013: 684, para. 33.

[379] Joined Cases C–25 and 26/14 *UNIS v. Ministre du Traail, de l'emploi et de la Formation professionnelle et du dialogue social* EU:C:2015:821, para. 38.

[380] Case C–318/10 *SIAT v. Etat Belge* EU:C:2012:415, paras. 58–9; Case C–342/14 *X-Steurberatungsgesellschaft v. Finanzamt Hannover-Nord* EU:C:2015:827, para. 59.

modified—in the CRD 2004/38. Yet, as we saw in *Grzelczyk* and *Baumbast* the concept of citizenship has begun to impinge on the interpretation of the general derogations and the limitations laid down in what were the 1990 Residence Directives, an approach imbued with a strong fundamental rights orientation. In the early 2000s the notion of EU citizenship also began to cast a different light on the derogations; the decision in *Dano* may mark something of a U-turn in this trajectory. Meanwhile the number and range of the justifications recognized by the Court are becoming ever broader. Often the Court finds that the states have not made out the justification on the facts or that, even if the justification is made out, the steps taken to achieve the particular goal are not proportionate. However, in its use of the justifications, the Court has found the necessary flexibility to help it reconcile market integration with the need to protect national interests.

FURTHER READING

Commission Communications

A. BARAV, 'Court recommendation to deport and the free movement of workers in EEC law' (1981) 6 *ELRev.* 139.

Commission Communication, 'On the Special Measures concerning the movement and residence of citizens of the Union which are justified on the grounds of public policy, public security, or public health 1999', COM(99) 372.

Commission Communication, 'On guidance for better transposition and application of Directive 2004/38/EC on the right of citizens of the Union and their family members to move and reside freely within the territory of the Member States', COM(2009) 313.

The approach to the express derogations

N. NIC SHUIBHNE, 'Derogating from the free movement of persons: When can EU citizens be deported?' (2005–6) 8 *CYELS* 187.

N. NIC SHUIBHNE, 'The outer limits of EU citizenship: Displacing EU free movement rights' in C. Barnard and O. Odudu (eds.), *The Outer Limits of European Union Law* (Oxford: Hart Publishing, 2009).

F. WOOLDRIDGE, 'Free movement of EEC nationals: The limitation based on public policy and public security' (1977) 2 *ELRev.* 190.

Employment in the public service

J. HANDOLL, 'Article 48(4) and non-national access to public employment' (1988) 13 *ELRev.* 223.

C. LENZ, 'The public service in Article 48(4) EEC with special reference to the law in England and in the Federal Republic of Germany' [1989] 15 *LIEI* 75.

G. MORRIS, S. FREDMAN, and J. HAYES, 'Free movement and the public sector' (1990) 19 *ILJ* 20.

The approach to the limitations

M. DOUGAN, 'The constitutional dimension to the case law on Union citizenship' (2006) 31 *ELRev.* 613.

M. DOUGAN and E. SPAVENTA, 'Educating Rudy and the (non-)English patient: A double-bill on residency rights under Article 18 EC' (2003) 28 *ELRev.* 699.

M. Dougan and E. Spaventa '"Wish you weren't here …" New models of social solidarity in the European Union' in M. Dougan and E. Spaventa (eds.), *Social Welfare and EU Law: Essays in European law* (Oxford: Hart Publishing, 2005).

S. Giubboni, 'Free movement of persons and European solidarity' (2007) 13 *ELJ* 360.

A. P. Van Der Mei, 'EU law and education: Promotion of student mobility versus protection of education systems' in M. Dougan and E. Spaventa (eds.), *Social Welfare and EU Law: Essays in European law* (Oxford: Hart Publishing, 2005).

The role of fundamental human rights

E. Deards, 'Human rights for football hooligans?' (2002) 27 *ELRev.* 206.

S. de Vries, U. Bernitz, and S. Weatherill (eds.), *The Protection of Fundamental Rights in the EU after Lisbon* (Oxford: Hart Publishing, 2013).

13

LEGALLY RESIDENT THIRD-COUNTRY NATIONALS AND THE EU

A. INTRODUCTION

According to Article 3 TEU, the Union shall 'offer its citizens an area of freedom, security, and justice without internal frontiers, in which free movement of persons is ensured in conjunction with appropriate measures with respect to external border controls, asylum, immigration and the prevention and combating of crime'. Thus, in an area of freedom, security, and justice (AFSJ) citizens have the right to move freely; but they also have a right to security. This is achieved principally at the external borders of the EU where there is greater emphasis on keeping out 'undesirable' third-country nationals (TCNs)[1] and managing the immigration that is permitted. The relationship

---

[1] Commission Communication, 'Towards integrated management of the external borders of the Member States of the European Union', COM(2002) 233, 4. For an example of the Court putting up external frontiers, see Case C–109/01 *Akrich* [2003] ECR I–9607.

between EU law and national law is complex. It used to be said that while *Union* law gives EU citizens the right to move freely, *national* immigration law determines the conditions under which TCNs can enter a Member State (either directly from the third country or from another Member State), have access to the labour market, be joined by their families, and become naturalized. However, as we shall see, increasingly EU law is occupying the traditional domain of national law, albeit subject to complicated derogations for certain Member States.

Yet, even with the increasing presence of EU law in the area of rights of TCNs, there remain key differences between Union citizens and TCNs: unlike EU citizens, TCNs generally do not enjoy free movement between Member States (secondary movement), subject to some notable exceptions (students, researchers, blue-card holders), and this causes fragmentation in the single market. Furthermore, for EU citizens the state's ability to exclude or expel is interpreted restrictively; for TCNs the relationship between the individual and the state is reversed. Because TCNs do not, as a rule, have a right of admission or protection from expulsion as a matter of EU law, the rights of the state to ensure security take precedence over the rights of the individual.[2]

Migration, particularly of TCNs, is also a highly emotive, politically sensitive subject,[3] as the migrant crisis has shown. Mass migration is both a threat and an opportunity. It is an opportunity because TCNs can bring much-needed skills and youth to reinvigorate an ageing population. It is a threat because an influx of the 'other' poses a significant challenge economically (to jobs for nationals and to the welfare state), culturally (different religions, different values), and socially (how to integrate the TCNs into existing communities). More recently, any discussion about migration is inevitably overlaid by concerns about security, especially in the wake of the terrorist attacks of 9/11, the London and Madrid bombings,[4] and the attacks in Paris and Brussels, together with more general concern about organized crime. Depending on the economic and security situation of the time, the political discourse ebbs and flows: from encouraging migration (see, e.g., the EEC–Turkey Association agreement discussed in Section D) to discouraging migration (see, e.g., the central thrust of the Hague programme governing policy in the field of freedom, security, and justice for the years 2005–10, followed by the Stockholm programme 2010–14).

This basic tension between the opportunities and threats posed by TCN migration gives rise to a number of questions: should there be limits on the numbers of TCNs admitted to a Member State? Once admitted, what rights should they enjoy: the right to work, to equal treatment with nationals, to move to another Member State? Should TCNs be encouraged (or even required) to integrate? This chapter will look at the Union's answer to some of these questions by focusing on the EU's legislation concerning legal migration by TCNs to the EU and the rights of TCNs residing lawfully in the EU. This is intended to provide a point of comparison with the rights of migrant EU workers. The chapter will therefore not consider the position of asylum seekers. The chapter will also not look at the vexed, tortuous development of EU competence in this field, nor the

---

[2] E. Guild, 'Security of residence and expulsion of foreigners: European Community law' in E. Guild and P. Minderhoud (eds.), *Security of Residence and Expulsion: Protection of aliens in Europe* (The Hague: Kluwer, 2000), 63.

[3] COM(2000) 757, 5: 'The social conditions which migrants face, the attitudes of the host population and the presentation by political leaders of the benefits of diversity and of pluralistic societies are all vital to the success of immigration policies.'

[4] Albeit that the London bombers were actually British-born. EU Council, 'European Union plan of action on combating terrorism', Council Doc. 10010/3/04, 11 Jun. 2004. The Commission says that in 2007 almost 600 failed, foiled, or successfully executed terrorist attacks were carried out in 11 Member States (COM(2009) 263).

position in respect of external border controls and visas.[5] The reader is, however, alerted to the fact that certain Member States are not bound by all legislation in this field but they do have the right to opt in.

B. MEASURES CONCERNING THOSE ALREADY LAWFULLY RESIDENT IN THE EU

1. FAMILY REUNIFICATION

For the past twenty years, family reunification has been one of the main sources of immigration to the EU.[6] The Family Reunification Directive 2003/86[7] was the first of two measures put forward by the Commission aimed at integrating TCNs into the community of the host state and ensuring fair treatment of TCNs. The directive provides that a TCN ('the sponsor')[8] residing lawfully in the territory of a Member State, holding a residence permit issued by a Member State valid for a year or more, with reasonable prospects of obtaining the right of permanent residence, can apply for family reunification[9] (usually while the TCN family members are outside the territory).[10] As with Article 3(1) of the Citizens' Rights Directive (CRD) 2004/38, the Family Reunification Directive makes a distinction between those family members who must be admitted (spouse and minor children[11]) and those whom the Member State has a discretion whether to admit (first-degree relatives in the direct ascending line, where they are dependent on the TCN or his or her spouse and do not enjoy proper family support in the country of origin, adult unmarried children where they cannot support themselves, and an unmarried partner (in a duly attested long-term relationship or registered partnership)).[12] The list of family members entitled to join the TCN is shorter than in the case of migrant workers under the CRD. In the case of spouses, Article 4(5) of the directive permits Member States to fix a minimum age, which must not be greater than 21 years, that must be attained by the sponsor[13] and his or her spouse prior to the latter being permitted to join the sponsor for reunification. This was introduced to 'ensure better integration and to prevent forced marriages'.[14]

The right to reunification is also dependent on evidence of the existence of 'normal' accommodation for a comparable family in the same region, sickness insurance for the

---

[5] A summary can be found in the fourth edition of this book.   [6] COM(2008) 610, 3.

[7] [2003] OJ L251/12. The UK, Ireland, and Denmark are not taking part in this measure. See also the Commission's report on the application of the directive: COM(2008) 610 and the Green Paper on the right to family reunification of TCNs living in the EU, COM(2011) 735.

[8] The directive therefore does not apply to non-migrant nationals wanting to be joined by TCN family members (e.g., a German living in Germany wanting to be joined by his Chinese wife). This situation is covered by national law.

[9] Art. 1. Under Art. 8 Member States may require the sponsor to have stayed lawfully in their territory for a period not exceeding two years. This provision was unsuccessfully challenged in Case C–540/03 *EP* v. *Council (Family Reunification Directive)* [2006] ECR I–5769.

[10] Art. 5(3).

[11] Art. 4(1), 2nd para., contains a derogation for a child over 12 who arrives independently from the rest of his or her family.

[12] Art. 4(2).

[13] States may prescribe that spouses and registered partners must have reached the age of 21 by the date when the application seeking to be considered family members entitled to reunification is lodged: Case C–338/13 *Moorzi* v. *Bundesministerin für Inneres* EU:C:2014:2092, para. 19.

[14] Case C–338/13 *Moorzi* EU:C:2014:2092, para. 12.

TCN and the family members, and that the sponsor has stable and regular resources which are higher than or equal to the level of resources which are sufficient to maintain the sponsor and the family members.[15] This is a derogation to the basic right and so must be interpreted restrictively and in the light of fundamental rights, taking particular account of the interests of the child.[16] Therefore, in *Chakroun*[17] the Court ruled that it was contrary to the directive for the Member State to adopt rules resulting in family reunification being refused to a sponsor who has proved that he has stable and regular resources sufficient to maintain himself and his family but who, given the level of his resources, will nevertheless be entitled to claim special assistance to meet exceptional, individually determined, essential living costs and tax refunds granted by local authorities on the basis of his income or income-support measures in the context of local authority minimum-income policies.

If these conditions are not satisfied then the family may not be reunified with the paradoxical result that a so-called 'Family Reunification' Directive actually has the opposite effect. Yet, in the Parliament's challenge to the validity of the directive in *EP v. EU Council (Family Reunification Directive)*,[18] the Court upheld the validity of the directive, approving the margin of discretion given to the Member States. The European Parliament had argued that the directive's provisions enabling Member States to restrict family reunification (e.g., where children are aged over 12 years and arrive independently from the rest of their family, the Member State may, before authorizing entry and residence, verify whether they meet an integration condition provided for by its existing legislation on the date of implementation of the directive) were contrary to fundamental rights, in particular the right to respect for family life under Article 8 ECHR and the right to non-discrimination under the EU Charter. The Court dismissed the action but did stress that fundamental human rights were binding on Member States when they implemented Union rules and that they had to apply the directive's rules in a manner consistent with the requirements governing human rights protection, especially regarding family life and the principle of protecting the best interests of the child.[19]

In order to ensure the integration of the family members, the directive allows Member States to require the TCN family members to comply with integration measures, such as attending language courses.[20] In *K*[21] the Court considered what measures the state can impose to facilitate the integration of the sponsor's family members. It said:[22]

> It cannot be disputed that the acquisition of knowledge of the language and society of the host Member State greatly facilitates communication between third country nationals and nationals of the Member State concerned and, moreover, encourages interaction and the development of social relations between them. Nor can it be contested that the acquisition of knowledge of the language of the host Member State makes it less difficult for third country nationals to access the labour market and vocational training.

While the Court accepted that the requirement to pass a civic integration examination at a basic level was capable of ensuring that the nationals of third countries acquired knowledge which was 'undeniably useful for establishing connections with the host Member State',[23] the principle of proportionality required that specific individual circumstances, such as the age, illiteracy, level of education, economic situation, or health of a sponsor's

---

[15] Art. 7(1)(c).   [16] Joined Cases C–356 and 357/11 *O and S* EU:C:2012:776, paras. 77–81.
[17] Case C–578/08 *Chakroun* [2010] ECR I–1839, para. 52.
[18] Case C–540/03 [2006] ECR I–5769.   [19] Paras. 104–5.   [20] Art. 7(2).
[21] Case C–153/14 *K* v. *Minister van Buitenlandse Zaken* EU:C:2015:453.
[22] Para. 53.   [23] Para. 54

relevant family members had to be taken into consideration in order to dispense those family members from the requirement to pass an examination when, due to those circumstances, they were unable to take or pass that examination.[24] Further, the Court said that the fees for taking the exam (here the cost of the examination preparation pack, charged as a single payment, was €110 and the course fees were €350, with family members of the sponsor incurring the course fees every time that they took the examination) were capable of making family reunification impossible or extremely difficult.[25]

The directive also provides for family members to enjoy access to employment and self-employment,[26] education, and vocational training,[27] but not social security or social assistance. After five years the spouse and children who have reached majority have the right to an autonomous residence permit independent of that of the sponsor.[28]

2. RIGHTS OF LONG-TERM RESIDENTS

The Long-Term Residents Directive 2003/109[29] was the second measure proposed by the Commission aimed at integrating TCNs into the community of the host state and ensuring their fair treatment.[30] The aim of this directive is to establish a common status of long-term resident for those TCNs who have resided 'legally and continuously' for five years in the territory of the Member State concerned.[31] A long-term residence permit, valid for at least five years,[32] will be granted where the TCN has adequate resources and sickness insurance.[33] It is automatically renewable on expiry.[34] However, Member States can require TCNs to comply with (unspecified) 'integration conditions',[35] before becoming long-term residents, tests which are usually reserved to granting an individual citizenship of a state, not merely long-term residence status. These integration conditions can include passing a civic integration exam,[36] provided that the objectives of the

---

[24] Case C–153/14 *K* EU:C:2015:453, para. 58.   [25] Para. 69.
[26] Art. 14(2) allows Member States to delay the exercise of employment/self-employment rights for up to 12 months.
[27] Art. 14(1).   [28] Art. 15(1).
[29] [2003] OJ L16/44, adopted under Art. 63(3)(a) and (4) EC. The directive does not apply to the UK, Ireland, and Denmark.
[30] COM(2001) 127.
[31] Art. 4(1). The Court has insisted that the five-year period be respected: Case C–469/13 *Tahir* v. *Ministero dell'Interno and Questura di Verona* EU:C:2014:2094. There is a long list of lawful residence in Art. 3(2) which will not entitle the TCN to long-term residence status: e.g., students, refugees, au pairs.
[32] Art. 8(2). In Case C–508/10 *Commission* v. *The Netherlands* EU:C:2012:243, the Dutch government charged a fee of €201 for this permit and up to €830 for other permits. The Court ruled that while states can charge for issuing a residence permit that charge must be proportionate and not deprive the directive of its effectiveness. The Court found the Dutch rules to be '*per se disproportionate* and liable to create an obstacle to the exercise of the rights conferred by that Directive' (para. 78, emphasis added).
[33] Cf. the CRD 2004/38, which does not impose the same obligations on EU citizens who have permanent residence.
[34] Art. 9 makes provision for the loss of long-term resident status including in the case of fraudulent acquisition of the status or absence from the territory for more than 12 consecutive months.
[35] Art. 5(2). See the 4th recital: 'The integration of third-country nationals who are long-term residents in the Member States is a key element in promoting economic and social cohesion, a fundamental objective of the [Union] stated in the Treaty.' Yet, K. Groenendijk suggests ('The Long-Term Residents Directive, denizenship and integration' in A. Baldaccini, E. Guild, and H. Toner (eds.), *Whose Freedom, Security and Justice? EU immigration and asylum law and policy* (Oxford: Hart Publishing, 2007), 448) that some Member States have taken advantage of this possibility to create a new barrier to acquiring secure status for TCNs.
[36] Case C–579/13 *P, S* v. *Commissie Sociale Zekerheid Breda* EU:C:2015:369.

directive are not undermined, bearing in mind the level of knowledge required to pass the civic integration examination, the accessibility of the courses and material necessary to prepare for that examination, the amount of fees applicable to TCNs as registration fees to sit that examination, and the specific individual circumstances, such as age, illiteracy, or level of education.[37]

Long-term residents enjoy not only a secure residence but also equal treatment with nationals as regards a number of matters, including access to employment (but not in respect of activities which entail even occasional involvement in the exercise of public authority or activities that are reserved to nationals under laws in force on 25 November 2003), education and training (including study grants),[38] recognition of diplomas, social protection and social assistance (including social security),[39] and access to goods and services. As *Kamberaj*[40] makes clear, these provisions must be interpreted in the light of the Charter, to which the Preamble of the directive expressly refers, and bearing in mind the integration objective of the directive. The individual can be expelled only on the grounds of personal conduct but not, apparently, lack of resources.[41] In addition, the long-term resident 'with reasonable prospects of obtaining the right of permanent residence' will also enjoy the right to family reunion under Directive 2003/86.[42] Both the Family Reunification Directive and the Long-Term Residents Directive are subject to derogations on the grounds of public policy, security, and health.[43]

Long-term residents with a long-term resident permit (and their families) will also enjoy the rights of free movement to other Member States (i.e., secondary mobility). The directive provides that long-term residents (and their families) can *reside* in (but makes no provision on entry into[44]) the territory of another Member State for more than three months[45] if they are exercising an economic activity as an employed or self-employed person or studying there and have adequate resources and sickness insurance, or simply have adequate resources and sickness insurance.[46] This directive demonstrates the increasing parallelism between the rights of legally resident TCNs and those of nationals of the Member States who are citizens of the Union.[47] The logical conclusion of this process of approximating the position of long-term legally resident TCNs to that of Member State nationals is the opportunity to obtain the nationality of the Member State in which they reside. This was endorsed by the European Council[48] and the Commission.[49]

---

[37] Para. 49. In the *P* case the Court considered the €1,000 fine each time an individual failed the exam was 'relatively high' (para. 51).

[38] Subject to limits in Art. 11(3).

[39] The rights in Art. 11(1) can be limited: Art. 11(4), albeit, as a derogation, it must be interpreted strictly: Case C–571/10 *Kamberaj* v. *IPES* EU:C:2012:233, para. 86.

[40] Case C–571/10 *Kamberaj* EU:C:2012:233, paras. 80 and 81.   [41] Art. 6.   [42] Art. 3(1).

[43] The 14th preambular para. of Dir. 2003/86 provides that the notion of public policy and public security covers cases in which a TCN belongs to an association which supports terrorism, supports such an association, or has extremist aspirations.

[44] S. Bolaert-Souminen, 'Non-EU nationals and Council Directive 2003/109/EC on the status of third-country nationals who are long-term residents: Five paces forward and possibly three paces back' (2005) 42 *CMLRev.* 1011, 1030.

[45] This goes beyond the rights already provided in the Schengen *acquis*, which merely gives rights to move for up to three months.

[46] For criticism of these provisions, see A. Kocharov, 'What intra-Community mobility for third-country workers' (2008) 33 *ELRev.* 913, 919.

[47] COM(2001) 74, para. 1.7.

[48] However, access to nationality is a matter reserved solely for national powers: COM(2001) 127, para. 5.5.

[49] COM(2003) 323, 22.

C. THE 'FIRST ADMISSIONS' DIRECTIVES

1. INTRODUCTION

The two directives considered so far—on Family Reunification and Long-Term Residents—focused on the integration of TCNs who had already been admitted to a Member State under *national* law. The Commission's other proposals have been concerned with managing legal migration flows and in particular giving certain groups a right of entry—under *Union* law—to the Member States. The first proposal, a directive on the conditions of entry and residence of TCNs for the purpose of paid employment and self-employed economic activities,[50] was seen as the 'cornerstone of immigration policy' and central to addressing the 'shortage of skilled labour in certain sectors of the labour market'.[51] It provided for the grant of a renewable 'residence permit-worker' to a TCN, subject to certain formalities, valid for three years, where a job vacancy could not be filled by an EU citizen or other TCNs already legally resident in the EU (the 'economic needs test' or 'Union preference' test). Such a permit would have allowed the TCN to enter into, and reside in, the territory of the issuing state, exercise the activities authorized by the permit, and enjoy equal treatment with nationals in a number of areas, including working conditions, recognition of qualifications, social security including healthcare, and access to goods and services.

Given that this proposal was merely a 'first step' in achieving a Union policy, it did not affect Member States' responsibility for deciding whether to admit economic migrants, taking into account the needs of their labour markets and their overall capacity to integrate them (a point now enshrined in Article 79(5) TFEU[52]). Nevertheless, despite the professed importance of this directive, it could not be agreed upon and the proposal was withdrawn.[53]

The Commission therefore focused instead on sectoral-specific measures as part of its approach to managing legal economic migration.[54] This led to the adoption of directives on students and volunteers, scientific researchers, as well as highly skilled workers (the Blue Card Directive). We shall consider each in turn.

2. STUDENTS AND VOLUNTEERS DIRECTIVE 2004/114

The first sectoral directive was Directive 2004/114, on the conditions of entry and residence for TCNs for the purpose of studies, pupil exchange, vocational training, or voluntary service.[55] This measure is less market-oriented than the unsuccessful proposed directive on the conditions of entry and residence of TCNs for the purpose of paid employment and self-employment because the stay of migrants covered by Directive 2004/114 is temporary and viewed as a form of 'mutual enrichment for the migrants who benefit directly from it, both for their country of origin and for the host country, while helping mutual familiarity

---

[50] COM(2001) 386.   [51] Preambular paras. (3) and (6).

[52] 'This Article shall not affect the right of the Member States to determine volumes of admission of third-country nationals coming from third countries to their territory in order to seek work, whether employed or self-employed.'

[53] COM(2005) 462.   [54] See, e.g., the Commission's Green Paper COM(2004) 811.

[55] Council Dir. 2004/114/EC ([2004] OJ L375/12) adopted on the basis of Art. 63(3)(a) and (4) EC. The UK, Ireland, and Denmark are not taking part in the directive. In Case C–15/11 *Sommer* v. *Landesgeschäftsstelle des Arbeitsmarktservice Wien* EU:C:2012:371 the Court said the EU citizens (*in casu* Bulgarian nationals) could not be treated less favourably than TCNs benefiting from their rights under Dir. 2004/114.

between cultures',[56] with the mobility of students being intended to promote Europe as a world centre of excellence for studies and vocational training.[57] Despite these worthy words, the directive does have a labour-market dimension since, as the Commission notes, many Member States provide certain TCNs with the opportunity to remain after their training 'so as to remedy shortages of skilled manpower'.[58] This directive requires those covered to have adequate resources and medical insurance.[59] Students and unremunerated trainees can also have limited access to the employment market. The directive also provides for derogations on public-policy, security, and health grounds.

3. THE DIRECTIVE ON SCIENTIFIC RESEARCH

Directive 2004/114 was followed by Directive 2005/71 on a specific procedure for admitting third-country nationals for the purposes of scientific research.[60] TCN researchers working with an approved research organization in the Member States are to be given a residence permit for a period of at least a year provided they have the relevant documentation and can show sufficient resources and medical insurance. Their family members can accompany them. The directive does allow the researchers to teach for a certain number of hours and to enjoy equal treatment with Member State nationals in respect of terms and conditions of employment, dismissal, and social security.

The directive also gives TCNs the right to carry out part of their research in another Member State. By allowing secondary mobility, these first admissions directives mark a new stage in the evolution of policy in respect of TCNs. The rationale for this is competition rather than principle: the EU was losing out to the US in attracting the brightest and the best from third countries. Secondary mobility rights are seen as a pull factor to make the EU more attractive as a destination.[61]

4. THE BLUE CARD DIRECTIVE

The third and perhaps most important of the first admissions directive is Directive 2009/50[62] on highly qualified workers (the so-called 'Blue Card' Directive). A TCN with a job offer for 'highly qualified' work (i.e., work requiring higher education qualifications or, where permitted by national law, five years' equivalent professional experience) in an EU Member State, who has sickness insurance and is not considered a threat to public policy, security, or health, must be issued with an EU blue card.[63] Member States do not, however, need to issue a blue card where, for example, the vacancy could be filled by a member of

---

[56] COM(2002) 548, 2.   [57] Case C–15/11 *Sommer* EU:C:2012:371, para. 39.

[58] COM(2002) 548, 3.

[59] The detailed criteria are laid down in Arts. 6 and 7 of the directive, which is considered an exhaustive list: Case C–491/13 *Ali ben Alaya* v. *Bundesrepublik Deutschland* EU:C:2014:2187, para. 36.

[60] [2005] OJ L289/15 adopted under Art. 63(3)(a) and (4) EC. Ireland has notified its wish to participate in this measure; the UK and Denmark are not participating. This directive was supplemented by two recommendations, the first on facilitating admission, the second on short-term visas.

[61] Kocharov, n. 46, 915 says that the US attracts 55 per cent of all skilled migrants worldwide, the EU attracts only 1/11th of that number.

[62] [2009] OJ L155/17 adopted under Art. 63(3)(a) and (4) EC. The UK, Ireland, and Denmark are not taking part. A public consultation was launched on the Blue Card Dir. and the EU's labour migration policies: <http://ec.europa.eu/dgs/home-affairs/what-is-new/public-consultation/2015/consulting_0029_en.htm>.

[63] Arts. 5 and 7.

the national or Union workforce, where the Member State deems the volume of admission of TCNs is too high, or where the job is in a sector suffering from a lack of qualified workers in the country of origin (e.g., healthcare).[64] Once in possession of a blue card, the TCNs must do the work they came for during the first two years; after that, Member States *may* grant the persons concerned equal treatment with nationals as regards access to highly qualified employment.[65] Blue-card workers also enjoy equality in respect of other matters including working conditions, freedom of association, social security, and goods and services.[66] The Family Reunification Directive 2003/86 gives rights to the family members of the TCN blue-card holder. Finally, the directive allows for secondary mobility. It prescribes the right of residence (but not entry) in the second Member State for the TCN blue-card holder and their family members[67] after 18 months of legal residence in the first Member State in order to undertake highly qualified employment.

5. THE HORIZONTAL DIRECTIVE

Complementing these three sectoral directives is the horizontal directive, Council directive 2011/98/EU,[68] on a single application procedure for a permit for TCNs to reside and work in the territory of a Member State and on a common set of rights for TCNs legally residing in a Member State. There are two limbs to this measure. The first, concerns those seeking to come to the EU to work. It provides for a single application procedure, resulting in a single permit to work and stay. No additional permits (e.g., work permits) can then be required. Member States decide who can be admitted; no criteria are laid down by the directive. The second limb of the directive concerns those who are already legally residing in an EU Member State. Those legally working but not yet holding long-term resident status are to enjoy equal treatment in respect of employment related matters.

6. SEASONAL WORKERS AND INTRA-CORPORATE TRANSFEREES

More recently, the directives have been adopted concerning seasonal workers and intra-corporate transferees. The former are seen as particularly vulnerable on the labour market, facing exploitation and poor working conditions. Directive 2014/36/EU on seasonal workers[69] applies to those entering an EU state to work temporarily in the EU to 'carry out an activity dependent on the passing of the seasons', pursuant to a fixed-term contract concluded directly with an employer established in a Member State. The concept of a seasonal activity is in turn defined as an 'activity that is tied to a certain time of the year by a recurring event or pattern of events linked to seasonal conditions during which required labour levels are significantly above those necessary for usually ongoing operations'. For those entering for less than three months the EU's borders and visas legislation continues to apply, and makes a number of cross-references to those measures. A maximum period of stay for seasonal workers cannot be for less than five months and not more than nine months in any 12-month period. After the expiry of that period, the TCN must leave the

---

[64] Arts. 6 and 8.   [65] Art. 12.   [66] Art. 15.   [67] Arts. 18–19.

[68] [2011] OJ L343/1. This was adopted under Art. 79(2) TFEU. The UK, Ireland, and Denmark are not taking part. There are some notable exceptions to this directive, e.g., family members covered by the CRD, posted workers, and those covered by the Long-Term Residents Dir.

[69] [2014] OJ L94/375. The UK, Ireland, and Denmark have opted out of this directive.

territory of the Member State unless the Member State has issued a residence permit under national or Union law for purposes other than seasonal work.[70]

The criteria for admission are strict: a valid work contract specifying pay and hours of work and other conditions as well as accommodation.[71] The individual must also have sickness insurance and sufficient resources so as not to be a burden on the social-assistance scheme. In addition, they must not be a threat to public policy, security, or health. Once in the EU, workers are entitled to extend their work contract or change employer, provided they meet the entry conditions and no grounds for refusal apply.[72]

Seasonal workers have the right to equal treatment with nationals of the host country as regards terms of employment, such as the minimum working age, working conditions (such as pay and dismissal, working hours, leave, and holidays), and health and safety regulations.[73] This equal treatment also applies to branches of social security (benefits linked to sickness, invalidity, and old age), training, advice on seasonal work offered by employment offices, and other public services, except for public housing. However, EU countries do not have to apply equal treatment with regard to unemployment and family benefits and can limit equal treatment on tax benefits, education, and vocational training.

Finally, in recognition of the vulnerability of this group of workers, EU countries must introduce measures to prevent possible abuses and sanctions where abuses arise.[74] They must also set in place mechanisms to monitor working conditions,[75] and systems to deal with complaints against employers.[76]

Different issues are addressed by the intra-corporate transfer (ICT) Directive 2014/66/EU[77] on skilled workers transferring for a maximum of three years.[78] As the Commission succinctly puts it,[79] companies outside the EU now have a common set of rules and requirements and EU companies now have better and faster access to global talent to meet staffing needs for managers, specialists, and graduate trainees. In addition to the fast-track entry procedure and the single application for a combined work and residence permit, the directive includes more attractive residence conditions for the families[80] and enhanced mobility within the EU.[81] ICTs will also benefit from the same working conditions as posted workers whose employer is established within EU territory.[82] ICTs therefore stand in a stronger position than seasonal workers with rights for family members as well as for themselves.

D. THE RIGHTS OF TURKISH WORKERS AND THEIR FAMILIES IN THE EU

1. INTRODUCTION

The EEC–Turkey Association Agreement of 1963 gives the most extensive rights to TCNs legally residing in the EU, other than to EEA and Swiss nationals. While it does not affect the Member State's right to decide whether to admit a Turkish national,[83] nor the conditions under which they may take up their first employment, (subject to the application of the legislation outlined, in particular the Family Reunion Directive and the Long-Term Residents

---

[70] Art. 14.　　[71] Arts. 5 and 6.　　[72] Art. 15.　　[73] Art. 23.　　[74] Art. 17.
[75] Art. 24.　　[76] Art. 25.　　[77] [2014] OJ L157/1.　　[78] Art. 12.
[79] <http://ec.europa.eu/dgs/home-affairs/what-we-do/policies/legal-migration/work/index_en.htm#2>.
[80] Art. 19.　　[81] Arts. 20–2.　　[82] Art. 18.
[83] Case C–237/91 *Kus* v. *Landeshauptstadt Wiesbaden* [1992] ECR I–6781, para. 25; Case C–434/93 *Ahmet Bozkurt* v. *Staatssecretaris van Justitie* [1995] ECR I–1475, para. 21.

Directive)[84] it does give Turkish workers an increasing number of rights the longer they are employed in the host state. The Agreement also does not give Turkish nationals the right to move between one EU state and another[85] but, unlike any other Union agreement (apart from the EEA and the EU/Swiss Treaty on free movement of persons), Article 12 of the Turkey Association Agreement envisages eventual free movement of persons between the Union and Turkey, guided by the principles laid down in Articles 45–7 TFEU.[86] This objective has influenced the Court's interpretation of the Agreement and the secondary legislation,[87] particularly Decision 1/80 of the Association Council on the development of the Association. This prompted the Court to observe in *Kurz*[88] that the aim and broad logic of Decision 1/80 is to 'seek to promote the integration of Turkish workers in the host Member State'. In this chapter we shall focus on the most litigated of the rules: those concerning the right to work for Turkish workers and their family members. We shall focus on these rules by way of comparison to the rights enjoyed by EU workers under Article 45 TFEU and the CRD 2004/38. It will be seen, as the Court made clear in *Ziebell*,[89] that the position of EU citizens is far more favourable. The Court said that the CRD, 'far from pursuing a purely economic objective, aims to facilitate the exercise of the primary and individual right to move and reside freely within the territory of the Member States that is conferred directly on Union citizens by the Treaty, and it aims in particular to strengthen that right'.[90] By contrast, the EEC–Turkey Association Agreement pursues solely an economic objective and is restricted to the gradual achievement of the free movement of workers.[91] For long-term Turkish residents, the Court may use the Long-Term Residents Directive 2003/109 as a framework for analysing their position instead.[92]

2. EMPLOYMENT RIGHTS

2.1 Introduction

For the purposes of this chapter the relevant secondary legislation is Decision 1/80;[93] fleshing out the rights of Turkish workers already legally resident and employed in the EU. Article 6(1) provides that a Turkish worker, duly registered as belonging to the labour force of a Member State, is entitled to:

- the renewal of his permit to work for the same employer, if a job is available, after *one year's* legal employment

---

[84] Cf. the EU legislation outlined in Section C, which increasingly gives the EU competence over these matters. For discussion, see S. Peers, 'EC immigration law and EC association agreements: Fragmentation or integration?' (2009) 34 *ELRev*. 628, discussing Case C–228/06 *Soysal* [2009] ECR I–1031.

[85] Case C–171/95 *Tetik* v. *Land Berlin* [1997] ECR I–329, para. 29; Case C–325/05 *Derin* v. *Landkreis Darmstadt-Dieburg* [2007] ECR I–6495, para. 66.

[86] Art. 12 is not directly effective since it sets out a programme, and its provisions are not sufficiently precise and unconditional: Case 12/86 *Demirel* v. *Stadt Schwäbisch Gmünd* [1987] ECR 3719, paras. 23 and 25. Art. 36 of the additional protocol annexed to the Association Agreement lays down the timetable for the progressive attainment of freedom of movement of workers. This is also not directly effective: Case 12/86 *Demirel* [1987] ECR 3719, paras. 23 and 25.

[87] See, e.g., Case C–1/97 *Birden* v. *Stadtgemeinde Bremen* [1998] ECR I–7747. See also Case C–416/96 *El-Yassini* v. *Secretary of State for the Home Department* [1999] ECR I–1209, where the Court found that its interpretation of the EEC–Turkey Association Agreement did not apply to the EEC–Morocco Agreement because the Morocco Agreement did not provide for consideration of Morocco's accession to the EU, nor was it aimed at progressively securing freedom of movement for workers.

[88] Case C–188/00 [2002] ECR I–10691, para. 45.

[89] Case C–371/08 *Ziebell* v. *Land Bad-Württemberg* [2011] ECR I–12735.

[90] Para. 69.   [91] Para. 72.   [92] Para. 79.

[93] This is directly effective: Case C–192/89 *Sevince* v. *Staatssecretaris van Justitie* [1990] ECR I–3461, para. 26. For a statement of the supremacy of Dec. 1/80, see Case C–188/00 *Kurz* [2002] ECR I–10691, para. 68.

- respond to another offer of employment, with an employer of his choice, made under normal conditions and registered with the employment services of that state, for the same occupation, after *three years* of legal employment and subject to the priority to be given to workers of the Member States of the Union

- free access in that Member State to any paid employment of his choice, after *four years* of legal employment.

This shows that while Member States retain the competence to regulate both the entry to their territory and the conditions under which Turkish nationals take up their first employment,[94] Article 6(1) of Decision 1/80 applies after the first year's employment.[95] The basic premise under Article 6(1) is that the longer Turkish workers are employed, the more integrated they are considered in the host state and so the greater the rights they enjoy. This means that after four years' employment the individual is no longer dependent on the continuing existence of the conditions for access to the rights laid down in the three indents. This means he or she enjoys much greater freedom, including temporarily interrupting the employment relationship.[96] By contrast, those still building up the four years must be engaged in legal employment for one, three, or four years, without any interruption, except for that provided in Article 6(2). This provides that annual holidays and absences for reasons of maternity or an accident at work or short periods of sickness are treated as periods of legal employment. By contrast, periods of involuntary unemployment duly certified by the relevant authorities and long absences on account of sickness are not to be treated as periods of legal employment, but are not to affect rights acquired as the result of the preceding period of employment.[97]

2.2 The Criteria under Article 6(1)

The rights laid down in Article 6(1) are conditional on (1) being a worker, (2) being 'duly registered as belonging to the labour force of a Member State', and (3) on a period of 'legal employment'. The Court enforces these specific requirements of Article 6(1) with some rigour so as not to 'undermine the coherence of the system set up by the Association Council with a view to gradually consolidating the position of Turkish workers in the host Member State'.[98]

The first condition, being a worker, is interpreted consistently with the equivalent term in Article 45 TFEU[99] and so we shall not discuss it further here. The second condition,

---

[94] Case C–294/06 R. (ex p. Payir) v. Secretary of State for the Home Department [2008] ECR I–203.

[95] Case C–237/91 Kus [1992] ECR I–6781, para. 25; Case C–434/93 Bozkurt [1995] ECR I–1475, para. 21.

[96] Case C–230/03 Sedef v. Freie und Hansestadt Hamburg [2006] ECR I–157, para. 46.

[97] Case C–4/05 Güzeli v. Oberbürgermeister der Stadt Aachen [2006] ECR I–10279 confirms that if one of these situations occurs (i.e., involuntary unemployment or long-term sickness), this does not affect the rights that the Turkish worker has already acquired owing to preceding periods of employment. Note in Case C–230/03 Sedef [2006] ECR I–157 the lenient and practical approach the Court took to the phrase 'involuntary unemployment duly certified by the relevant authorities' in the case of a Turkish seaman employed in Germany for 15 years.

[98] Case C–230/03 Sedef [2006] ECR I–157, para. 37. See also Case C–268/11 Gülbahce v. Freie und Hansestadt Hamburg EU:C:2012:695 (precluding national authorities from withdrawing the residence permit of a Turkish worker with retroactive effect from the point in time at which there was no longer compliance with the ground on the basis of which his residence permit had been issued under national law if there is no question of fraudulent conduct on the part of that worker and that withdrawal occurs after the completion of the period of one year of legal employment provided for in the first indent of Art. 6(1) of Dec. 1/80).

[99] See Ch. 8: Case C–1/97 Birden [1998] ECR I–7747, para. 23; Case C–188/00 Kurz [2002] ECR I–10691, para. 30; Case C–294/06 Ex p. Payir [2008] ECR I–203; Case C–14/09 Genc v. Land Berlin [2010] ECR I–931, para. 27.

'duly registered as belonging to the labour force of a Member State', requires the national courts to consider whether the legal relationship of employment can be located within the territory of a Member State, or retains a sufficiently close link with that territory, taking account of the place where the person was hired, the territory on or from which the paid employment was pursued, and the applicable national legislation in the field of employment and social security law.[100]

In *Altun*[101] the Court elaborated further. It said the concept of being 'duly registered' as belonging to the labour force embraced all workers who have met the conditions laid down by law or regulation in the host Member State and who were thus entitled to pursue an occupation in its territory. It said that notwithstanding a temporary interruption of the employment relationship, a Turkish worker continued to be duly registered as belonging to the labour force in the host Member State during a period reasonably necessary for him to find other paid employment, regardless of the cause of the absence of the individual from the labour force, provided that that absence is temporary. Therefore, workers and apprentices are considered duly registered as belonging to the labour force[102] as is an individual, like Mr Altun, who is involuntary unemployed following the declaration of insolvency of the undertaking in which he was working. A Turkish worker is excluded from the labour force only if he no longer has any chance of rejoining the labour force or has exceeded a reasonable time limit for finding new employment after the end of the period of inactivity.

In respect of the third condition, 'legal employment', the Court has said that the phrase 'presupposes a stable and secure situation as a member of the labour force'[103] and the existence of an undisputed right of residence.[104] The Court has so far found that there was no legal employment in two situations: first, in *Sevince*,[105] where a Turkish worker was able to continue in employment only by reason of the suspensory effect deriving from his appeal against deportation and, secondly, in *Kol*,[106] where a Turkish national was employed under a residence permit issued to him as a result of fraudulent conduct (he had entered a marriage of convenience with a German national), for which he was subsequently convicted.

The Court has also strictly enforced the periods of time laid down in the three indents of Article 6(1). This can be seen in *Eroglu*.[107] A Turkish worker worked lawfully for employer A for one year. She then worked for employer B. Subsequently, she sought an extension of her work permit in order to work for employer A again. The Court said that she was not entitled to do this under Article 6(1) because this would allow the worker to

---

[100] Case C–98/96 *Ertanir* [1997] ECR I–5179, para. 39; Case C–4/05 *Güzeli* [2006] ECR I–10279, para. 37.

[101] Case C–337/07 *Altun v. Stadt Böblingen* [2008] ECR I–10323, paras. 23–6.

[102] Case C–188/00 *Kurz* [2002] ECR I–10691, para. 45.   [103] *Kurz*, n. 102, para. 30.

[104] *Kurz*, n. 102, para. 48. This even includes short periods during which the Turkish worker did not hold a valid residence or work permit: Case C–98/96 *Ertanir* [1997] ECR I–5179, para. 69.

[105] Case C–192/89 *Sevince* [1990] ECR I–3461, para. 32. In a similar vein, see also Case C–237/91 *Kus* [1992] ECR I–6781, para. 18, where the Court ruled that a worker did not fulfil the requirement of 'legal employment' where a right of residence was conferred on him only by the operation of national legislation permitting residence in the host country pending completion of the procedure for the grant of the residence permit, on the ground that he had been given the right to remain and work in that country pending a final decision on his right of residence.

[106] Case C–285/95 *Kol v. Land Berlin* [1997] ECR I–3069, para. 25. See in a similar vein Case C–37/98 *R. v. Secretary of State for the Home Department, ex p. Savas* [2000] ECR I–2927, para. 67 concerning a Turkish national unlawfully present in the host Member State.

[107] Case C–355/93 *Eroglu v. Land Baden-Württemberg* [1994] ECR I–5113, para. 14. See also Case C–386/95 *Eker v. Land Baden-Württemberg* [1997] ECR I–2697, where the Court ruled that if the worker left employer A before the expiry of one year to work for employer B, the worker had to work for a full year for employer B before he was entitled to the renewal of work and residence permits.

change employers under the first indent before the expiry of the three years prescribed in the second indent.[108]

The third indent of Article 6(1) concerns those Turkish workers who are duly integrated into the labour market. They have the right to give up one job to seek any other job.[109] The key feature here is that the worker must be deemed still to be a member of the labour force during any periods of absence from work. Therefore, in *Bozkurt*[110] the Court ruled that a Turkish national was not entitled to remain in the host state if he had reached retirement age or had suffered an industrial accident which left him totally and permanently unfit for further employment, since he was considered to have left the workforce for good. However, where the incapacity was only temporary and did not affect his fitness to continue exercising his right to employment he could still enjoy the right to join the labour force. In *Nazli*[111] the Court took this one stage further and said that a temporary break caused by detainment pending trial did not cause the Turkish worker to forfeit his rights under the third indent of Article 6(1), provided that he found a new job within a reasonable period after his release. In *Dogan*[112] the Court extended the ruling in *Nazli* to a Turkish worker imprisoned for four years. The Court said that the effectiveness of the rights to employment and residence conferred on Turkish workers by the third indent applied regardless of the cause of absence from the labour force, provided that the absence was temporary.[113]

The decision in *Bozkurt* highlights the unfavourable position in which Turkish nationals find themselves in the absence of express legislation, equivalent to what was Regulation 1251/70 on the right to remain for EU nationals (now the Citizens' Rights Directive), which protects their position. While the Long-Term Residents Directive 2003/109 may now cover some Turkish workers in this position, the rights of residence under the Turkey Association Agreement, while among the most extensive of all the Union agreements, are still firmly tied to the exercise of economic activity (actual employment) and are far from matching the general rights of residence available to Union citizens.[114]

Although the Court has been strict in the application of the criteria laid down in Article 6(1) to Turkish workers, it has also required the Member States to satisfy their side of the agreement. So, Member States cannot deprive Turkish workers of the rights laid down by Article 6(1) nor 'impede the exercise' of such rights.[115] Therefore, in *Ertanir*[116] the Court said that a German rule permitting specialist chefs to reside in Germany for no more than three years was incompatible with Article 6(1).[117] In *Sevince*[118] the Court said that the employment rights of Turkish workers laid down by Article 6(1) necessarily implied a right of residence because, in the absence of such a right, access to the labour market and the right to work would be deprived of all legal effect.[119]

---

[108] See also Case C–4/05 *Güzeli* [2006] ECR I–10279, para. 45, where the Court said that eight months' employment was insufficient under the first indent.

[109] Case C–340/97 *Nazli* v. *Stadt Nürnberg* [2000] ECR I–957, para. 35.

[110] Case C–434/93 *Bozkurt* [1995] ECR I–1475, paras. 39–40.

[111] Case C–340/97 *Nazli* [2000] ECR I–957, para. 41.

[112] Case C–383/03 *Dogan* v. *Sicherheitsdirektion für das Bundesland Vorarlberg* [2005] ECR I–6237.

[113] Para. 20.   [114] Considered in Ch. 10.

[115] Case C–188/00 *Kurz* [2002] ECR I–10691, para. 67. Case C–268/11 *Gülbahce* v. *Freie und Hansestadt Hamburg* EU:C:2012:695, para. 49 (Member States cannot add additional restrictions). The rights in Art. 6(1) are also directly effective: Case C–188/00 *Kurz* [2002] ECR I–10691, para. 26.

[116] Case C–98/96 *Ertanir* [1997] ECR I–5179, para. 34: despite the wording of Art. 6(3): 'The procedures for applying paragraphs 1 and 2 shall be those established under national rules.'

[117] See also Case C–36/96 *Günaydin* v. *Freistaat Bayern* [1997] ECR I–5143, paras. 36–8.

[118] *Günaydin*, n. 117, para. 29.

[119] See also Case C–237/91 *Kus* [1992] ECR I–6781, para. 23.

2.3 Other Rights

Once they are duly registered as belonging to the labour market of the host state, Turkish workers do enjoy equal treatment with Union workers in respect of remuneration and other conditions of work under Article 10 of Decision 1/80.[120] In *Wählergruppe Gemeinsam Zajedno*[121] the Court interpreted the phrase 'other conditions of work' to include the right for Turkish workers to stand as candidates in elections to bodies representing the legal interests of workers. Therefore, Austrian rules restricting eligibility for election to a body such as a chamber of workers to Austrians only breached Article 10.

Worker representation is one of three areas where Turkish workers have more rights than those TCNs covered by the Long-Term Residents Directive 2003/109 (see Section B, 2). The other two areas are protection from expulsion and access to employment. However, in respect of access to social assistance and equal treatment, Directive 2003/109 offers more favourable rights than Decision 1/80. As Groenendijk points out,[122] the Long-Term Residents Directive grants Turkish citizens and other TCNs the right to look for work, to live, and to work in other Member States and the Family Reunification Directive gives them the right to family reunion. In this way the directives complement and supplement the provisions under Decision 1/80.

3. FAMILY RIGHTS

3.1 The Right to Employment

The first paragraph of Article 7 of Decision 1/80 provides that the members of the family of a Turkish worker who is 'duly registered as belonging to the labour force of a Member State'[123] (with no reference this time to the concept of 'legal employment' which appears in Article 6(1) of Decision 1/80) and who have been 'authorized to join him' are, subject to the priority to be given to workers of Member States of the Union, entitled to:[124]

- respond to any offer of employment after they have been legally resident for at least three years in that Member State
- enjoy free access to any paid employment of their choice provided that they have been legally resident there for at least five years.[125]

These rights are directly effective and can be invoked by the TCN spouse of a Turkish worker, provided the conditions laid down in Article 7 are satisfied.[126]

---

[120] This provision is directly effective: Case C–171/01 *Wählergruppe Gemeinsam Zajedno/Birklikte Alternative und Grüne GewerkschafterInnen/UG* [2003] ECR I–4301, para. 57.

[121] Case C–171/01 *Wählergruppe Gemeinsam Zajedno/Birklikte Alternative und Grüne GewerkschafterInnen/ UG* [2003] ECR I–4301.

[122] Groenendijk, n. 35, 442.

[123] This is interpreted in the same way as the equivalent phrase in Art. 6(1): Case C–337/07 *Altun* [2008] ECR I–10323, para. 28.

[124] The first para. of Art. 7 is directly effective: Case C–351/95 *Kadiman* v. *Freistaat Bayern* [1997] ECR I–2133, para. 28. These rights apply equally to family members of Turkish workers who have acquired the nationality of the host state (while also retaining Turkish nationality): Joined Cases C–7 and 9/10 *Staatssecretaris van Justitie* v. *Kahveci* EU:C:2012:180.

[125] Case C–373/03 *Aydinili* v. *Land Baden-Württemberg* [2005] ECR I–6181: a Turkish national who has resided for five years did not forfeit rights under this provision due to prolonged absence from the labour market due to imprisonment.

[126] Case C–451/11 *Dülger* v. *Wetteraukreis* EU:C:2012:504.

According to *Kadiman*,[127] the purpose of this first paragraph is to 'create conditions conducive to family unity', first by enabling family members to be with a migrant worker and then by consolidating their position by granting them the right to obtain employment in the host state (and a concomitant right of residence[128]). Therefore, the host state could require actual cohabitation by the Turkish workers[129] and their family members during the first three years, even where there were accusations of domestic violence, subject to absences for a reasonable period and for legitimate reasons in order to take holidays or visit family in Turkey.[130] The Court said that the cohabitation requirement was intended to prevent Turkish nationals from evading the stricter requirements laid down in Article 6 by entering sham marriages and then taking advantage of the generous requirements of Article 7.[131]

However, the Court has made clear that cohabitation does not necessarily mean marriage (unlike the approach adopted under Articles 2–3 CRD). In *Eyüp*[132] a Turkish couple living in Austria divorced but continued to live together. During this period of cohabitation they had a further four children. He was a worker and she looked after the children. They then remarried and continued to cohabit. Since they constantly maintained a common legal residence within the meaning of Article 7 the Court said that the period of cohabitation counted towards calculating the periods of legal residence. In *Ayaz*[133] the Court drew on the definition of family members under Regulation 1612/68 (now the CRD) to help determine the meaning of the equivalent term in Decision 1/80. It ruled that the phrase did not require a blood relationship: stepchildren were also covered.

However, Article 7 does not affect the power of the Member State to authorize family members to join the Turkish worker,[134] to regulate their stay until they become entitled to respond to any offer of employment, and, if necessary, to allow them to take up employment before the expiry of the initial period of three years,[135] always subject to the provisions of the European Convention on Human Rights.[136] Union law requires only that during the three-year period members of the worker's family must be granted a right of residence.[137] Once those three years have expired, Member States can no longer attach conditions to the residence of a member of a Turkish worker's family.[138] Once five years have expired, the person derives 'an individual employment right directly from Decision 1/80' and 'a concomitant right of residence'.[139]

[127] Case C–351/95 *Kadiman* [1997] ECR I–2133, para. 33.

[128] Case C–325/05 *Derin* [2007] ECR I–6495, para. 47.

[129] The Turkish workers themselves had to be duly registered as belonging to the labour force of that state: Case C–337/07 *Altun* [2008] ECR I–10323, para. 32.

[130] *Altun*, n. 129, para. 48.   [131] *Altun*, n. 129, para. 38.

[132] Case C–65/98 *Safet Eyüp* v. *Landesgeschäftsstelle des Arbeitsmarktservice Vorarlberg* [2000] ECR I–4747.

[133] Case C–275/02 *Ayaz* v. *Land Baden-Württemberg* [2004] ECR I–8765, para. 45.

[134] Case C–467/02 *Cetinkaya* v. *Land Baden-Württemberg* [2004] ECR I–10895, para. 26: Art. 7 also applies to family members actually born in the host state. The position of a Turkish worker's family members is therefore less favourable than an EU worker's family members, who enjoy an unconditional right to install themselves with the migrant Union workers under *Union* law, not national law: Case C–325/05 *Derin* [2007] ECR I–6495, paras. 61–3. However, the Family Reunification Dir. 2003/86 may now affect the Member State's powers.

[135] Case C–351/95 *Kadiman* [1997] ECR I–2133, para. 32.

[136] Case C–325/05 *Derin* [2007] ECR I–6495, para. 64.   [137] *Derin*, n. 136, para. 29.

[138] Case C–329/97 *Ergat* v. *Stadt Ulm* [2000] ECR I–1487.

[139] *Ergat*, n. 138, para. 40. Once those rights have been obtained, they cannot be lost as a result of divorce: Case C–303/08 *Bozkurt* [2010] ECR I–13445. See also Case C–467/02 *Cetinkaya* [2004] ECR I–10895,

3.2 The Position of a Turkish Worker's Children

The second paragraph of Article 7,[140] which is more favourable than the first paragraph,[141] provides that children of Turkish workers who have completed a course of vocational training[142] in the host country may respond to any offer of employment there, irrespective of the length of time they have been resident in that Member State, provided that one of their parents has been legally employed in the Member State for at least three years. Since this paragraph is not intended to create conditions conducive to family unity, the Court said in *Akman*[143] that the child's right to respond to any offer of employment was not conditional on the Turkish worker parent residing in the host Member State at the time when the child wished to take up employment following vocational training. In *Eroglu*[144] the Court extended its rulings in *Sevince* and *Kus* to the second paragraph of Article 7, saying that 'any offer of employment necessarily implies the recognition of a right of residence for that person'.[145]

Finally, in *Derin*[146] the Court considered how the rights under Article 7 could be lost. One way would be because the individual constitutes, on account of his own conduct, a 'genuine and sufficiently serious threat to public policy, public security or public health', in accordance with Article 14(1). The second way is that the individual has left the territory of the host state for a significant length of time without legitimate reason. The Court has emphasized that these are the only ways that individuals can lose their rights under Article 7. Therefore, a Turkish national cannot be deprived of his rights either because he was unemployed on account of being sentenced to a term of imprisonment, even one of several years' duration, or because he never acquired rights relating to employment and residence pursuant to Article 6(1) of that decision, or because he was 'not active on the labour market for several years' (i.e., he attended various training course but never completed them).[147]

4. DEROGATIONS

Article 14(1) allows states to derogate from the rights provided on the grounds of public policy, public security, and public health.[148] The Court interprets these provisions consistently with those under the EU Treaties (e.g., Article 45(3) TFEU),[149] as far as possible,[150]

---

paras. 32–3. Failure to obtain a residence permit in time can be punished, but only by penalties which are proportionate and comparable to those for minor offences committed by nationals but, as with Union nationals, this does not include deportation, which would deny the very right of residence (Case C–467/02 *Cetinkaya* [2004] ECR I–10895, paras. 56–7). Therefore, administrative documents such as a residence permit are only 'declaratory of the existence of those rights and cannot constitute a condition for their existence' (Case C–434/93 *Bozkurt* [1995] ECR I–1475, para. 30).

[140] The 2nd para. of Art. 7 is directly effective: Case C–355/93 *Eroglu* [1994] ECR I–5113, para. 17.

[141] Case C–325/05 *Derin* [2007] ECR I–6495, para. 42.

[142] See also Art. 9, which gives Turkish children residing legally in a Member State access to education and training courses on the same terms as nationals as well as possible access to 'benefit from advantages provided for under the national legislation in that area'. According to Case C–374/03 *Gürol* v. *Bezirksregierung Köln* [2005] ECR I–6199, Art. 9 is directly effective and the 'advantages' include grants.

[143] Case C–210/97 *Akman* v. *Oberkreisdirektor des Rheinisch-Bergischen-Kreises* [1998] ECR I–7519, paras. 43–4. See also Case C–462/08 *Bekleyen* [2010] ECR I–563.

[144] Case C–355/93 *Eroglu* [1994] ECR I–5113.   [145] Para. 20.

[146] Case C–325/05 *Derin* [2007] ECR I–6495, para. 54.

[147] Case C–453/07 *Er* v. *Wetteraukreis* [2008] ECR I–7299, para. 31.

[148] Art. 14(1). This is an exhaustive list: Case C–502/04 *Torun* v. *Stadt Augsburg* [2006] ECR I–1563.

[149] See further Ch. 12.

[150] Case C–467/02 *Cetinkaya* [2004] ECR I–10895, para. 39, which also confirms that the case law on derogations under Dir. 64/221 (now CRD) also applies to Dec. 1/80. See also Case C–136/03 *Dörr*

and in the light of the original directive 64/221 on derogations but not in the light of the superior protection against expulsion provided in the CRD.[151] In *Derin*[152] the Court set out the framework according to which the national authorities could act: they are 'obliged to assess the personal conduct of the offender and whether it constitutes a present, genuine and sufficiently serious threat to public policy and security, and in addition they must observe the principle of proportionality'. In particular, a measure ordering expulsion based on Article 14(1) may be taken only if the personal conduct of the person concerned indicates a specific risk of new and serious prejudice to the requirements of public policy. Consequently, such a measure cannot be ordered automatically following a criminal conviction and with the aim of general deterrence. In the case of *Ziebell*[153] concerning a Turkish national resident for more than ten years the Court added further conditions:[154]

- the long-term resident concerned can be expelled solely where he/she constitutes a genuine and sufficiently serious threat to public policy or public security and the expulsion decision is 'indispensable to safeguard that interest'[155]

- the expulsion decision cannot be founded on economic considerations

- before adopting such a decision, the competent authorities of the host Member State are required to take account of the duration of residence in their territory, the age of the person concerned, the consequences of expulsion for the person concerned and family members, links with the country of residence, or the absence of links with the country of origin.

E. CONCLUSIONS

This chapter started with the basic dichotomy of insiders versus outsiders, with insiders—nationals of one of the Member States—being in a favoured position. However, on closer examination the rules on EU citizens and those on TCNs show that this picture is less accurate than would at first appear. EU nationals who do not migrate or who are not economically active may find themselves marginalized by the application of rules which prioritize those who exercise their (economic) freedom of movement, while TCNs now may find that, as a result of developments under Title V of Part Three TFEU, they begin to enjoy something of a quasi- or civic citizenship.[156] Of course, this characterization is also not complete. Decisions of the Court of Justice, in particular in *Grzelczyk*[157] and *Baumbast*,[158] have done much to give rights to migrant citizens who are not economically active; although *Dano*[159] shows that the Court's attitude to non-economically active migrant citizens might be changing, while the advent of the Charter and developments in the field of social, consumer, and environmental policy have benefited citizens who do not migrate. Meanwhile, the measures which have the most inclusive effect on TCNs still fall far short of Held's three-stranded definition of citizenship (considered in detail

---

v. *Sicherheitsdirektion für das Bundesland Kärnten* [2005] ECR I–4759; Case C–349/06 *Polat* v. *Rüsselsheim* [2007] ECR I–8167, para. 29; Case C–97/05 *Gattoussi* v. *Stadt Rüsselsheim* [2006] ECR I–11917, para. 41 (in the context of the Euro–Mediterranean Agreement).

[151] Case C–371/08 *Ziebell* v. *Land Baden-Württemberg* [2011] ECR I–12735, para. 74.
[152] Case C–325/05 *Derin* [2007] ECR I–6495, para. 74.
[153] Case C–371/08 *Ziebell* [2011] ECR I–12735.   [154] Para. 80.   [155] Para. 84.
[156] COM(2003) 336, 30 and N. Reich, 'Union citizenship: Metaphor or source of rights?' (2001) 4 *ELJ* 4, 18.
[157] Case C–184/99 [2001] ECR I–6193.   [158] Case C–413/99 *Baumbast and R.* [2002] ECR I–7091.
[159] Case C–333/13 *Dano* EU:C:2014:2358.

in Chapter 10): while legally resident TCNs have some rights, owing to the absence of any clear Union competence they have no ability to participate in the political process in the host state; nor do they have a strong sense of membership. As we have seen, it has already proved difficult for the EU to foster a sense of membership among EU nationals; this task may prove harder in respect of TCNs who come from extraordinarily diverse backgrounds.[160]

However, it is striking that two principles have been used to combat the sense of exclusion experienced by both EU nationals and TCNs: integration and, to a limited extent, solidarity. The language of integration underpinned the Court of Justice's justification for broadening the rights enjoyed by EU migrant workers and their families. It is the same language which has been used by the heads of state at Tampere, by the Commission in its two Communications,[161] and now by the Lisbon Treaty in the concept of 'fair treatment' in respect of TCNs. However, when considering the position of TCNs the Commission makes clear that integration entails bilateral commitments:[162]

> integration should be understood as a two way process based on mutual rights and corresponding obligations of legally resident third country nationals and the host society which provides for full participation of the immigrant.

It continued that this implies, on the one hand, that it is the responsibility of the host society to ensure that the formal rights of immigrants are in place so that the individual can participate in economic, social, cultural, and civil life but, on the other, 'that immigrants respect the fundamental norms and values of the host society and participate actively in the integration process, without having to relinquish their own identity'. In this respect the Union is expecting more of TCNs than it does of migrant EU citizens.[163]

Solidarity has also been used to justify giving rights to both migrant citizens and TCNs.[164] The language of solidarity was used by the Court in *Grzelczyk* to justify giving limited social advantages to a migrant student. It is also used in the Commission's Communication on illegal immigration[165] to justify operational cooperation, and thus financial cooperation, between the Member States to keep illegal immigrants out of the EU or to return them to their Member States, language which is repeated in the strongest terms in the Lisbon Treaty.[166] In this way solidarity is being used to attain both inclusionary and exclusionary results.

FURTHER READING

Commission documents

Commission, 'A European Agenda on Migration', COM(2015) 240.

Migration of TCNs

S. Iglesias Sánchez, 'Free movement of third country nationals in the European Union? Main features, deficiencies and challenges of the new mobility rights in the area of freedom, security and justice' (2009) 15 *ELJ* 791.

---

[160] For a critique, see N. Barber, 'Citizenship, nationalism and the European Union' (2002) 27 *ELRev.* 241.
[161] COM(2000) 757 and COM(2003) 336.   [162] COM(2003) 336, 17–18.
[163] See also EU Council, *The Hague Programme: Strengthening freedom, security and justice in the European Union*, Council Doc. 16054/04, 11.
[164] Council Doc. 16054/04, 4.   [165] COM(2003) 323, 17.   [166] Art. 80 TFEU.

S. Peers, 'Towards equality: Actual and potential rights of third country nationals in the European Union' (1996) 33 *CMLRev.* 7.

The Long-Term Residents Directive

S. Peers, *EU Justice and Home Affairs Law*, 3rd edn (Oxford: OUP, 2011).

S. Peers, 'Implementing equality? The directive on long-term resident third-country nationals' (2004) 29 *ELRev.* 437.

Family rights

G. Barratt, 'Family matters: European Community Law and third-country family members' (2003) 40 *CMLRev.* 369.

S. Peers, 'Family reunion and Community law' in N. Walker (ed.), *Europe's Area of Freedom, Security and Justice* (Oxford: OUP, 2004).

The Charter

S. Peers, J. Kenner, T. Hervey, and A. Ward, *Commentary on the EU Charter of Fundamental Rights* (Oxford: Hart Publishing, 2014).

Comprehensive analysis of the AFSJ

S. Peers, *EU Justice and Home Affairs Law*, Vols I and II, 4th edn (Oxford: OUP, 2016).

The field as a whole

S. Peers, *EU Justice and Home Affairs Law*, 3rd edn (Oxford: OUP, 2012).

PART IV

FREE MOVEMENT
OF CAPITAL

14

FREE MOVEMENT OF CAPITAL AND ECONOMIC AND MONETARY UNION

A. INTRODUCTION

Free movement of capital, the fourth fundamental freedom,[1] concerns investment,[2] rather than, as with establishment and services, entrepreneurial activity. The idea underpinning what is now Article 63 TFEU was that restrictions—or controls—on capital should be removed so that capital could flow to where it could be optimally invested. However, the movement of capital was not liberalized at the same rate as the other freedoms because of concerns about capital flight—from less-developed areas of the EU to more developed, and from areas where tax on that capital was high to areas of lower rates of taxation. The Court therefore ruled that the original Treaty provision, Article 67 EEC, was not directly effective and so Member States could restrict capital movements in a number of ways.

The advent of the single market gave some muscle to this area of law. It was only then that capital movements were finally liberalized. The free movement of capital was given renewed impetus by the establishment of economic and monetary union (EMU): the achievement of free capital movements was a condition for entry into the first stage of monetary union. This demonstrates the interconnection between monetary policy and free movement of capital, especially in respect of exchange rates. And since, in practice, free movement of capital and fixed exchange rates cannot be achieved in an economic area in which diverging economic and monetary policies are applied, economic *and* monetary union is the natural complement to the common market.

This chapter begins by examining why free movement of capital is considered an important part of any trading area before briefly examining the evolution of the right in the EU. The chapter then analyses the detail of the Treaty provisions on capital.

B. THE NEED FOR FREE MOVEMENT OF CAPITAL

According to Molle, capital can be considered free if entrepreneurs can satisfy their need for capital and investors can offer their disposable capital in the country where conditions are most favourable to them.[3] He summarizes the advantages of the integration of capital markets in the following terms:[4]

- it diminishes the risk of disturbances which tend to occur in small markets
- it increases the supply of capital, because better investing prospects mobilize additional savings
- it enables those who are in need of capital to raise larger amounts in forms better tailored to their needs
- it makes for equal production conditions and thus fewer disturbances of competition in the common market.

He also lists the reasons why a Member State may wish to impede the export of capital:[5] the fear of capital drain-offs, reinforcing the economies of other states to the detriment

---

[1] Case C–483/99 *Commission v. France* [2002] ECR I–4781, para. 45; Case C–463/00 *Commission v. Spain* [2003] ECR I–4581, para. 68; Case C–302/97 *Klaus Konle v. Republik Österreich* [1999] ECR I–3099, para. 38.

[2] Case C–47/12 *Kronos International v. Finanzamt Leverkusen* EU:C:2014:2200.

[3] W. Molle, *The Economics of European Integration: Theory, practice, policy*, 5th edn (Aldershot: Ashgate, 2006).

[4] Molle, n. 3, 218.   [5] Molle, n. 3.

of its own; the loss of currency reserves which may jeopardize its ability to meet its other international obligations; the need to maintain equilibria in the economy, both internally (a large outflow of capital may compel a high rate of interest when the state actually needs a low rate of interest) and externally (capital outflow may lead to devaluation of the currency, making imports more expensive, thereby importing inflation); and loss of confidence of the international markets in policy measures. Member States may also wish to impede the import of capital, again for reasons of internal and external disequilibria (avoiding an unnecessarily low rate of interest or an upward adaptation of the exchange rate), and also because capital is power, therefore capital in foreign hands means that the state loses some authority over its own economy.

In the EU the basic rule, contained in what is now Article 63(1) TFEU, is free movement of capital. However, the interests of the Member States in impeding free movement are recognized by the express derogations found in Article 65 TFEU, which are more numerous than for the other freedoms. As this chapter shows, it took the EU some time to achieve complete free movement of capital but the pace of change has been fast and the case law on capital reflects developments in respect of the other freedoms.

C. THE DEVELOPMENT OF FREE MOVEMENT OF CAPITAL AND PAYMENTS

1. CAPITAL

Because capital movements were closely linked to the stability of economic and monetary policy of the Member States, liberalization took longer for capital than for persons, services, and goods.[6] This was recognized in the original Treaty provisions on capital, which were drafted in more cautious, less 'imperative' terms[7] than the other three freedoms. The basic provision, Article 67(1) EEC, provided that:

> During the transitional period and to the extent necessary to ensure the proper functioning of the common market, Member States shall progressively abolish between themselves all restrictions on the movement of capital belonging to persons resident in Member States and any discrimination based on the nationality or on the place of residence of the parties or on the place where such capital is invested.

Article 68 EEC urged Member States to be 'as liberal as possible' in granting exchange authorizations. Article 69 EEC gave the Council powers to issue directives while Article 70 EEC required the Commission to propose to the Council measures for the progressive coordination of the exchange rate policies of the Member States.

Since Article 67(1) EEC did not abolish restrictions on the movement of capital by the end of the transitional period, their abolition was left to the Council adopting directives on the basis of Article 69 EEC.[8] The first such directive was adopted in 1960,[9] followed by a second in 1963.[10] According to these directives, all movements of capital were divided into four lists (A, B, C, and D) annexed to the directives. In respect of the movements covered

---

[6] L. Flynn, 'Coming of age: The free movement of capital case law 1993–2002' (2002) 39 *CMLRev.* 773.

[7] Case 203/80 *Casati* [1981] ECR 2595, para. 19.

[8] Case 203/80 *Casati* [1981] ECR 2595, paras. 8–13; Case C–484/93 *Svensson and Gustavsson* v. *Ministre du Logement et de l'Urbanisme* [1995] ECR I–3955, para. 5; Case C–222/95 *Société civile immobilière Parodi* v. *Banque H. Albert de Bary et Cie* [1997] ECR I–3899, paras. 11–12.

[9] First Dir. for the implementation of Art. 67 of the Treaty ([1959–62] OJ Spec. Ed. 49).

[10] Second Council Dir. 63/21/EEC ([1963–4] OJ Spec. Ed. 5).

by lists A and B, the directives prescribed unconditional liberalization; for movements covered by list C, Member States could maintain or reimpose exchange restrictions if free movement of capital was capable of forming an obstacle to the achievement of its economic policy objectives. In the case of the movements referred to in list D (e.g., the physical importation and exportation of financial assets, including bank notes), the directives did not require the Member States to adopt any liberalizing measures.

Against this backcloth, the Court concluded in *Casati*[11] in 1981 (some years after its seminal judgments in *Dassonville*[12] and *Cassis de Dijon*[13]) that complete freedom of movement of capital could undermine the economic policy of one of the Member States or create an imbalance in its balance of payments.[14] It therefore said that Article 67(1) EEC differed from the provisions on goods, persons, and services in the sense that there was an obligation to liberalize capital movements only 'to the extent necessary to ensure the proper functioning of the common market'.[15] For this reason Article 67 EEC was not directly effective.[16] Thus, as Snell points out,[17] with the other freedoms a determined Court and an enlightened Commission provided leadership for the reluctant Member States. By contrast, with free movement of capital the Member States were very much in the driving seat in the early period, with the 'Court silent and the Commission at times even an outright opponent of liberalization'. He concludes that from the perspective of the theoretical accounts of European integration (considered in Chapter 1), the free movement of capital displays features of liberal intergovernmentalism, which is not the framework the four freedoms have traditionally been associated with.

The most important measure adopted by the Council in this early period was Directive 88/361,[18] which did bring about 'the full liberalization of capital movements'.[19] Article 1(1) of the directive provided that 'Member States shall abolish restrictions on movements of capital taking place between persons resident in Member States.' The directive contained a (non-exhaustive)[20] nomenclature of capital movements in the annex, but this was to facilitate the application of the directive and not to introduce distinctions in treatment.

The coming into force of Directive 88/361 on 1 July 1990 marked the first stage of monetary union. The Maastricht Treaty provided that the second stage was to begin on 1 January 1994.[21] By that time, *all* Member States had to comply with, inter alia, the provisions of Article 63 TFEU on free movement of capital and put in place multiannual programmes to ensure the lasting convergence necessary to achieve EMU.[22] During the second stage Member States also had to avoid excessive government deficits[23] and had to start the process leading to the independence from government control of their central banks.[24] The European Monetary Institute (EMI), the precursor to the European Central Bank (ECB), was also established at the start of the second stage.[25] This was all a precursor

---

[11] Case 203/80 *Casati* [1981] ECR 2595, paras. 9–10.   [12] Case 8/74 [1974] ECR 837.
[13] Case 120/78 [1979] ECR 649.   [14] *Casati*, n. 11, para. 9.   [15] *Casati*, n. 11, para. 10.
[16] Case 203/80 *Casati* [1981] ECR 2595.
[17] J. Snell, 'Free movement of capital: Evolution as a non-linear process' in P. Craig and G. de Búrca (eds.), *The Evolution of EU Law* (Oxford: OUP, 2011).
[18] [1988] OJ L178/5.
[19] Joined Cases C–358 and 416/93 *Criminal Proceedings against Aldo Bordessa* [1995] ECR I–361, para. 17.
[20] Case C–222/97 *Manfred Trummer and Peter Mayer* [1999] ECR I–1661, para. 21.
[21] Art. 116(1) EC (now repealed by the Lisbon Treaty).
[22] Art. 116(2) EC (now repealed by the Lisbon Treaty).
[23] Art. 116(4) EC (now repealed by the Lisbon Treaty).
[24] Art. 116(5) EC (now repealed by the Lisbon Treaty).
[25] Art. 117 EC. The Statute of the EMI was laid down in a separate protocol.

to the start of the third stage, on 1 January 1999,[26] when for the Eurozone states the national currencies were replaced by a single currency. From 1 January 2002 euro coins and notes were put into circulation and on 28 February 2002 the national 'legacy' currencies were finally withdrawn.

2. PAYMENTS

The provisions on capital were complemented by those on payments. Article 106(1) EEC, first paragraph, originally provided that:

> Each Member State undertakes to authorise, in the currency of the Member State in which the creditor or beneficiary resides, any payments connected with the movement of goods, services or capital, and any transfers of capital and earnings, to the extent that the movement of goods, services, capital and persons between Member States has been liberalised pursuant to this Treaty.

This required Member States to authorize means of payment as consideration for trade in goods, persons, services, or capital,[27] and for this reason the Court suggested that it was perhaps the most important provision in the (then) EEC Treaty for the purposes of attaining a common market.[28] As the Court put it in *ED Srl*,[29] the provision on payments was intended 'to enable a person liable to pay a sum of money in the context of a supply of goods or services to discharge that contractual obligation voluntarily without undue restriction and to enable the creditor freely to receive such a payment'. In *Luisi and Carbone*[30] the Court found Article 106(1) EEC to be directly effective.

Despite (or maybe because of) the importance of Article 106(1) EEC, the Court has traditionally adopted a rather cautious approach to its interpretation, as shown by the early case of *Lambert*.[31] Lambert, a cattle dealer, was a Luxembourg national who accepted payment in cash for sales of cattle in other Member States contrary to Luxembourg laws requiring payment in foreign currency to be received only in the form of a bank transfer or a cheque (not cash) paid through a bank. The Court accepted that the requirements laid down by the Luxembourg law were legitimate[32] because they dealt solely with the *way* in which the exporter had to receive payment;[33] they did not impede either the importer making the payment in Luxembourg francs or the cattle dealer receiving that payment, and so were not a barrier to the liberalization of payments.

Lambert also clarified the distinction between Article 106 EEC and Article 67 EEC. It said that while Article 106 EEC covered current payments, i.e., the transfers of foreign exchange which constitute the consideration within the context of an underlying transaction (of goods, persons, services, or capital), Article 67 EEC covered movements of capital, i.e., financial operations essentially concerned with the investment of funds, rather than remuneration for a service. The significance of this distinction was reduced

---

[26] Art. 121(4) EC (now repealed by the Lisbon Treaty). See also the Declaration by the Council (Ecofin) and the ministers meeting in that Council issued on 1 May 1998 ([1998] OJ L139/28); Council Reg. 974/98 ([1998] OJ L139/1).

[27] Case 308/86 *Ministère public* v. *Lambert* [1988] ECR 4369, para. 10; Joined Cases C–163, 165 and 250/94 *Criminal Proceedings against Sanz de Lera* [1995] ECR I–4830, para. 17.

[28] Case 7/78 *R.* v. *Thompson* [1978] ECR 2247, para. 22. Therefore, means of payment are not goods within the meaning of Art. 34 TFEU.

[29] Case C–412/97 *ED Srl* v. *Italo Fenocchio* [1999] ECR I–3845, para. 17.

[30] Joined Cases 286/82 and 26/83 *Luisi and Carbone* [1984] ECR 377.

[31] Case 308/86 *Ministère public* v. *Lambert* [1988] ECR 4369, para. 10.

[32] Case 308/86 *Lambert* [1988] ECR 4369, para. 16.   [33] Para. 16.

by the Maastricht Treaty, which radically overhauled the provisions on capital and payments to coincide with the adoption of the new rules on the single currency. In a single Chapter, the Treaty on European Union brought together both the provisions on capital, which were amended largely to reproduce the contents of Directive 88/361,[34] and those on payments. Article 73b(1) EC (the Maastricht Treaty number), renumbered at Amsterdam as Article 56(1) EC and at Lisbon as Article 63(1) TFEU, provides that 'all restrictions on the movement of capital between Member States and Member States and third countries shall be prohibited'. Article 63(2) TFEU, replacing Article 106 EEC, prohibits 'all restrictions on payments'. This chapter shall focus on capital, the provision which has proved more important in practice.

D. THE SCOPE OF THE PROVISIONS ON CAPITAL

1. THE DEFINITION OF 'CAPITAL'

While the Treaty does not define the term 'movements of capital' (or indeed 'payments' under Article 63(2) TFEU) in fact the Court often looks to the annex of Directive 88/361 for guidance as to what constitutes capital. As it noted in *Trummer and Mayer*,[35] inasmuch as Article 63(1) TFEU 'substantially reproduces' the contents of Article 1 of Directive 88/361, the nomenclature in respect of movements of capital annexed to Directive 88/361 still has 'the same indicative value', for the purposes of defining the notion of capital movements, as it did before the entry into force of Article 63 *et seq*.[36] On the facts of *Trummer and Mayer* the Court found that mortgages, which 'represent the classic method of securing a loan linked to a sale of real property' were transactions covered by the nomenclature[37] and so were 'inextricably linked to a capital movement'.[38] The Court has also recognized that investments in real property,[39] its administration,[40] and its sale[41] constituted a movement of capital.

'Direct investment' in a company by means of a shareholding with the view to effectively participating in the management and control of a company[42] constitutes a capital movement, as does acquiring shares on the capital market solely with the intention of making a financial investment (a 'portfolio' investment[43]), and the resale of shares

---

[34] Case C–222/97 *Manfred Trummer and Peter Mayer* [1999] ECR I–1661, para. 21.

[35] Case C–222/97 *Manfred Trummer* [1999] ECR I–1661.

[36] See Colomer AG's criticism of this interpretative approach in, e.g., Case C–98/01 *Commission v. UK* [2003] ECR I–4641, para. 39.

[37] Case C–222/97 *Manfred Trummer* [1999] ECR I–1661, para. 23. Mortgages constitute an 'other guarantee' within the meaning of point IX of the nomenclature, headed 'Sureties, other guarantees and rights of pledge'.

[38] Case C–222/97 *Manfred Trummer* [1999] ECR I–1661, para. 24.

[39] Case C–98/01 *Commission v. UK* [2003] ECR I–4641, para. 22; Case C–302/97 *Konle* [1999] ECR I–3099, para. 22; Case C–423/98 *Alfredo Albore* [2000] ECR I–5965, para. 14; Joined Cases C–515 and 527–540/99 *Hans Reisch* v. *Bürgermeister der Landeshauptstadt Salzburg* [2002] ECR I–2157, para. 30; Case C–364/01 *The Heirs of H. Barbier* v. *Inspecteur van de Belastingdienst Particulieren* [2003] ECR I–15013, para. 58; Case C–512/03 *Blanckaert* v. *Inspecteur van de Belastingdienst* [2005] ECR I–7685, para. 35; Case C–376/03 *D.* v. *Inspecteur van de Belastingdienst/Particulieren/Ondernemiingen buitenland te Heerlen* [2005] ECR I–5821, para. 24. See point II of Annex I of the nomenclature.

[40] Case C–386/04 *Centro di Musicologia Walter Stauffer* [2006] ECR I–8203, para. 24.

[41] Case C–443/06 *Hollmann* v. *Fazenda Pública* [2007] ECR I–8491, para. 31.

[42] Case C–367/98 *Commission v. Portugal (Golden Share)* [2002] ECR I–4731, para. 38.

[43] Joined Cases C–282 and 283/04 *Commission v. Netherlands* [2006] ECR I–9141, para. 19.

to the issuing company.[44] In addition, inheritances,[45] banknotes and coins,[46] gifts in money or in kind,[47] granting credit on a commercial basis,[48] and guarantees granted by non-residents to residents or by residents to non-residents[49] all constitute movements of capital.

Even where the transaction is not listed in the annex, it can still constitute a capital movement within the meaning of Article 63(1) TFEU. Therefore, in *Verkooijen*[50] the Court found that the receipt of dividends from a foreign company, although not listed in the annex, fell within the scope of the Treaty because it was linked to some of the measures in the annex.[51] On the other hand, in *Sanz de Lera*[52] the Court made clear that where individuals filled their car with money and tried to take it out of the country, this did not constitute a capital movement in the legal sense of the term.

One striking feature of the discussion so far is that, unlike the case law on free movement of persons, it is only very rarely that the Court has added the requirement that the capital movement be an 'economic activity':[53] it seems the Court assumes that a movement of capital within Article 63 TFEU, like a movement of goods under Article 34 TFEU, to be economic. Similarly, as with goods, the focus is mainly on the capital and less on the (natural or legal) person holding or owning the capital. There is no specification as to the nationality of the holder.

2. THE TERRITORIAL SCOPE

2.1 Inter-State Movement

For Article 63(1) TFEU to apply, there must be a movement of capital between Member States. In most cases this is self-evident. However, in *Block*[54] the Court briefly considered the issue where a person resident in Germany at the date of death left to another person, also resident in Germany, capital claims against a financial institution in Spain on which inheritance tax was levied both in Germany and in Spain. The Court said that this was not a situation purely internal to a Member State and so Article 63(1) TFEU applied.

---

[44] Case C–265/04 *Bouanich* v. *Skatteverket* [2006] ECR I–923, para. 29.

[45] Case C–513/03 *Heirs of M.E.A. van Hilten-van der Heijden* v. *Inspecteur van de Belastingdienst/Particulieren/Ondernemingen buitenland te Heerlen* [2006] ECR I–1957, paras. 41–2: 'An inheritance consists of the transfer to one or more persons of the estate left by a deceased person or, in other words, a transfer to the deceased's heirs of the ownership of the various assets, rights, etc., of which that estate is composed.'

[46] Joined Cases C–358 and 416/93 *Criminal Proceedings against Aldo Bordessa* [1995] ECR I–361, para. 13.

[47] Case C–318/07 *Hein Persche* v. *Finanzamt Lüdenscheid* [2009] ECR I–359, para. 27.

[48] Case C–452/04 *Fidium Finanz AG* v. *Bundesanstalt für Finanzdienstleistungsaufsicht* [2006] ECR I–9521, para. 43.

[49] Case C–279/00 *Commission* v. *Italy* [2002] ECR I–1425, para. 36.

[50] Case C–35/98 *Staatssecretaris van Financiën* v. *Verkooijen* [2000] ECR I–4071. See also Case C–319/02 *Manninen* [2004] ECR I–7477.

[51] Paras. 28–9.

[52] Joined Cases C–163, 165 and 250/94 *Criminal Proceedings against Sanz de Lera* [1995] ECR I–4830.

[53] Cf. Case C–326/07 *Commission* v. *Italy* [2009] ECR I–2291, para. 35: 'Direct investments, that is to say, investments of any kind made by natural or legal persons which serve to establish or maintain lasting and direct links between the persons providing the capital and the undertakings to which that capital is made available in order to carry out an economic activity fall within the ambit of Article [63 TFEU].'

[54] Case C–67/08 *Block* v. *Finanzamt Kaufbeuren* [2009] ECR I–883, para. 21.

2.2 Movement Between an EU Member State and a Third Country

(a) The reasons for the broad reach

The striking feature that distinguishes Article 63 TFEU from the other fundamental free-doms is that it expressly applies not only to the abolition of all restrictions on capital and payments between Member States but also those between Member States and third countries.[55] Snell offers three reasons for the extension of territorial scope:[56] first, the free movement of capital between Member States would undermine capital controls towards third countries as investors would enter or exit the EU via the most liberal jurisdiction to access the target state. Secondly, the credibility of the single currency is bolstered by the liberalization. Thirdly, the extension contributes to the principle of an open market economy expressed in Article 119 TFEU.

(b) The limitations on the broad reach

However, the remaining provisions of Chapter 4 TFEU on free movement of capital make clear that the movement of capital and payments between Member States and third coun-tries is actually more limited than the provisions of Article 63 TFEU would at first suggest. This is because, in addition to the derogations laid down in Article 65 TFEU (considered in Section F), free movement of capital and payments to third countries are subject to four further potential restrictions. Peers describes these in the following terms.[57]

The first, and in practice the most important, is historic: Article 64(1) TFEU grand-fathers any restrictions existing at 31 December 1993[58] on four types of free movement of capital (but not payments) pursuant to EU or national law.[59] The second is potential: ac-cording to Article 64(2) TFEU, the European Parliament and Council may adopt meas-ures concerning the same four types of capital moving to and from third countries. In addition, Article 64(3) TFEU allows the Council, acting unanimously in accordance with

---

[55] The Court confirmed this point in Case C–101/05 *Skatteverket* v. *A* [2007] ECR I–11531. Cf. Case C–102/05 *Skatteverket* v. *A and B* [2007] ECR I–3871, para. 29, which confirms that the scope of Art. 49 TFEU does not extend to situations concerning the establishment of a company of a Member State in a non-Member State. See also Case C–157/05 *Holböck* v. *Finanzamt Salzburg-Land* [2007] ECR I–4051, para. 28; Case C–524/04 *Thin Cap* [2007] ECR I–2107, para. 100. In addition, Case C–452/04 *Fidium Finanz AG* [2006] ECR I–9521, para. 25 confirms that Art. 56 TFEU cannot be relied on by a company established in a third country.

[56] See n. 17.

[57] S. Peers, 'Free movement of capital: Learning lessons or slipping on spilt milk?' in C. Barnard and J. Scott (eds.), *The Law of the Single European Market: Unpacking the premises* (Oxford: Hart Publishing, 2002), 335–6. See also Case C–524/04 *Thin Cap Litigation* [2007] ECR I–2107, para. 171, where the Court of Justice suggested that additional justifications may be acceptable in the case of third-country restrictions.

[58] For a discussion about how to determine whether the national legislation 'existed' on a particular date, see Case C–101/05 *A* [2007] ECR I–11531, paras. 47–9; Case C–157/05 *Holböck* [2007] ECR I–4051, paras. 41–2; Case C–541/08 *Fokus Invest AG* v. *FIAG* [2010] ECR I–1025, para. 42; Case C–384/09 *Prunus SARL* v. *Directeur des services fiscaux* [2011] ECR I–3319, paras. 34–7; Joined Cases C–436 and 437/08 *Haribo Lakritzen Hans Riegel BetriebsgmbH* v. *Finanzamt Linz* [2011] ECR I–305, paras. 134–7.

[59] I.e., direct investment, establishment, the provision of financial services, or the admission of secur-ities to capital markets. The phrase 'direct investment' concerns 'investments of any kind undertaken by natural or legal persons and which serve to establish or maintain lasting and direct links between the per-sons providing the capital and the undertakings to which that capital is made available in order to carry out an economic activity' and which allow the shareholder to participate effectively in the management of the company or its control: Case C–157/05 *Holböck* [2007] ECR I–4051, paras. 34–7 (which also made clear that tax legislation could fall in Art. 64(1) TFEU). See also Case C–194/06 *Orange European Smallcap Fund* [2008] ECR I–3747, para. 102; Case C–181/12 *Welte* v. *Finanzamt Velbert* EU:C:2013:62, para. 35 (derogation must be narrowly construed and does not apply to the house of the parents of the deceased made for private purposes unconnected with the carrying out of an economic activity).

the special legislative procedure and after consulting the European Parliament, to adopt measures which 'constitute a step backwards in Union law as regards the liberalization of the movement of capital to or from third countries'. The Lisbon Treaty added a further significant provision in Article 65(4) TFEU. This allows the Commission or the Council, on an application from a Member State, to adopt a decision stating that 'restrictive tax measures adopted by a Member State concerning one or more third countries are to be considered compatible with the Treaty insofar as they are justified by one of the objectives of the Union and compatible with the proper functioning of the internal market'. This unusual provision allows the Council—not the Court—to rule on the legality of national measures.[60] It is seen as a rebuff to the Court that its 'restrictions' case law (see Section E) has been going too far.[61]

The third restriction concerns balance of payments: Article 66 TFEU allows the Council to take safeguard measures for up to six months '[w]here, in exceptional circumstances, movements of capital to or from third countries cause, or threaten to cause, serious difficulties for the operation of economic and monetary union'.

The final provision is political: Article 75 TFEU, as redrafted by the Lisbon Treaty and moved to Title V TFEU on the area of freedom, security, and justice, allows the European Parliament and Council to define a framework for administrative measures concerning capital or payments, such as freezing of funds, financial assets, or economic gains 'belonging to, or owned by or held by, natural or legal persons, groups or non-state entities'[62] in order to prevent and combat terrorism or related activities.[63]

3. THE DIRECT EFFECT OF ARTICLE 63 TFEU

So far we have considered the definition of capital and its territorial scope. The next question is whether it has direct effect. As we have seen, the Court ruled that Article 67 EEC was not directly effective,[64] due to insufficient liberalization of the rules on capital at the time. However, in *Sanz de Lera* the Court ruled that Article 73b(1) EC, now Article 63(1) TFEU was directly effective.[65] In *A*[66] the Court said that Article 63(1) TFEU 'lays down a clear and unconditional prohibition for which no implementing measure is needed and which confers rights on individuals which they can rely on before the courts'. Article 63

---

[60] Cf. Art. 108(2), para. 3 TFEU on state aids.   [61] Snell, n. 17.

[62] This particular drafting, and that of Art. 215 TFEU, overcomes the problem of Arts. 60(1) and 301 EC, identified in Joined Cases C–402 and 415/05 P *Kadi* v. *Council* [2008] ECR I–6351, para. 216, which provided the (then) EC with no competence to impose measures on addressees in no way linked to the governing regime of a third country. See also Decl. 25 on Arts. 75 and 215 TFEU on the rights of the individual or entities concerned by such measures. The Court of Justice has jurisdiction to hear judicial review actions brought by natural or legal persons against the Common Foreign and Security Policy (CFSP) measure identifying the individual/company and the implementing regulation imposing the restrictions: Art. 275(2) TFEU.

[63] See Art. 9 of Protocol 21 for the position of Ireland in respect of this provision and Decl. 65 for the position of the UK. Art. 60(2) EC empowered Member States to take unilateral action against a third country with regard to capital movements and payments 'for serious political reasons and on grounds of urgency', provided that the Council has not acted. The Council could subsequently override these restrictions. This was repealed by the Lisbon Treaty but Art. 215 TFEU allows for the imposition of economic and financial sanctions. Cf. Case C–124/95 *R.* v. *HM Treasury and Bank of England* [1997] ECR I–81 concerning the relationship between sanctions legislation limiting payment to third countries and the CCP.

[64] Case 203/80 *Casati* [1981] ECR 2595.

[65] Joined Cases C–163, 165 and 250/94 *Criminal Proceedings against Sanz de Lera* [1995] ECR I–4830, para. 41; Joined Cases C–358 and 416/93 *Criminal Proceedings against Aldo Bordessa* [1995] ECR I–361, para. 33 regarding Art. 1 of Dir. 88/361.

[66] Case C–101/05 *Skatteverket* v. *A* [2007] ECR I–11531, para. 21.

TFEU is also directly effective in respect of the movement of capital between Member States and third countries. As the Court put it in *A*, Article 63(1) TFEU, in conjunction with Articles 64–5 TFEU, 'may be relied on before national courts and may render national rules that are inconsistent with it inapplicable, irrespective of the category of capital movement in question'.[67]

Article 63 TFEU is certainly vertically directly effective; and since the majority of cases concern challenges to national legislation on, for example, taxation—a quintessentially vertical subject matter—the difficult questions as to the potential horizontal application of Article 63 TFEU have not be broached. However, given that the Court has not yet expressly ruled that Article 49 TFEU on freedom of establishment and Article 56 TFEU on free movement of services have full horizontal direct effect,[68] it seems unlikely that Article 63 TFEU, a later developing freedom, will do so either. This view receives some support from *Commission v. Germany (Volkswagen)*.[69] Germany argued that its Volkswagen law was not a measure within the meaning of the Court's case law because the law was based on a private agreement which was entered into in 1959 between workers and trade unions. In return for relinquishing their claim to a right of ownership over the company, the workers and the trade unions secured the assurance of protection against any large shareholder which might gain control of the company. If the Court had thought that Article 63 TFEU had horizontal direct effect, it could have dismissed Germany's argument on this basis. Instead, it said that the fact that the agreement had become the subject of a law, this sufficed for it to be considered as a national measure for the purposes of the free movement of capital.[70] It added: 'The exercise of legislative power by the national authorities duly authorised to that end is a manifestation *par excellence* of State power.'[71]

4. THE RELATIONSHIP BETWEEN THE PROVISIONS ON CAPITAL AND THE OTHER FREEDOMS

4.1 Freedom of Establishment v. Free Movement of Capital

The cases considered so far have already indicated the potential overlap between free movement of capital and the other freedoms, a point recognized by the Court in *Casati*:[72]

> freedom to move certain types of capital is, in practice, a precondition for the effective exercise of other freedoms guaranteed by the Treaty, in particular the right of establishment.

The close connection between the different Treaty provisions is also recognized in Article 65(2) TFEU, which says that 'The provisions of this chapter [on capital and payments] shall be without prejudice to the applicability of restrictions on the right of establishment which are compatible with the Treaty.' In addition, Article 50 TFEU, the legal basis for measures to attain freedom of establishment, expressly provides in paragraph (2)(e) that the European Parliament, Council, and the Commission are to carry out the duties devolved on them by enabling 'a national of one Member State to acquire and use land and buildings situated in the territory of another Member State', traditionally seen as an area covered by the free movement of capital.

---

[67] *Skatteverket*, n. 66, para. 27.   [68] This issue is discussed further in Ch. 7.
[69] Case C–112/05 [2007] ECR I–8995. See also Case C–478/98 *Commission v. Belgium (Eurobond)* [2000] ECR I–7587, where the Belgian government tried to avoid liability by arguing that it was acting in its capacity as a private contractor (para. 20). The Court disputed this on the facts (paras. 22–5).
[70] Para. 26. Cf. the effect of the decision in Case C–438/05 *Viking* [2007] ECR I–10779.
[71] Para. 27.   [72] Case 203/80 *Criminal Proceedings against Guerrino Casati* [1981] ECR 2595.

The Court's case law on which Treaty provision it wishes to apply is somewhat unclear. In a number of cases in the late 1990s/early 2000s, the Court showed a preference for using Article 49 TFEU where possible.[73] This was followed by a period when it applied the capital provisions together with the rules on establishment.[74] This was not altogether surprising—with the liberalization of the capital provisions and a convergence of the tests to be applied to determine whether a restriction exists, the practical importance of the interaction between the different Treaty provisions became less significant. However, in the most recent cases the Court has attempted to identify the principal purpose of the rules—establishment or capital—and then apply the appropriate Treaty provision.

In certain cases the Court has expressed a preference for applying Article 49 TFEU. For example, Article 49 TFEU applies to national rules which affect relations within a group of companies.[75] Further, in cases where the shareholding gives the holder a 'definite influence' over the company's decisions the provisions on freedom of establishment apply to any national restrictions.[76] However, if the shareholdings are acquired solely to make a financial investment, without any intention to influence the management and control of the company, Article 63 TFEU only applies.[77] This reflects the distinction between entrepreneurial activity (Article 49 TFEU) and investment (Article 63 TFEU) which we drew at the outset of this chapter. However, in cases where the legislation is 'not intended to apply only to stakes which enable the holder to have definite influence on a company's decisions and to determine the company's activities'—or where the Court is not sure that all the claimants satisfy the definite influence test—the Court examines the legislation in relation to both Articles 49 and 63 TFEU.[78] If, however, the national rules relating to the tax treatment of dividends from a third country, which do not apply exclusively to situations in which the parent company exercises decisive influence over the company paying the dividends, this will be assessed in the light of Article 63 TFEU only.[79]

4.2 Free Movement of Services v. Free Movement of Capital

A similar ebb and flow of the case law emerges in respect of freedom to provide services. The link between capital and services is recognized in Article 58(2) TFEU, which provides that the liberalization of banking and insurance services connected with movement of capital is to be effected in step with the liberalization of movement of capital. At first the Court was reluctant to apply the capital provisions,[80] but subsequently it applied the

---

[73] See, e.g., Case C–200/98 *X and Y* [1999] ECR I–8261, para. 30; Joined Cases C–397 and 401/98 *Metallgesellschaft* [2001] ECR I–1727, para. 75; Case C–251/98 *Baars* [2000] ECR I–2787. But see also Case C–414/06 *Lidl Belgium GmbH & Co. KG v. Finanzamt Heilbronn* [2008] ECR I–3601, para. 16.

[74] Case C–503/99 *Commission* v. *Belgium* [2002] ECR I–4809, para. 59. See also Case C–374/04 *ACT Group* [2006] ECR I–11673, paras. 37–8; and Case C–446/04 *FII Group Litigation* [2006] ECR I–11753. Cf. Case C–150/04 *Commission* v. *Denmark* [2007] ECR I–1163, para. 76, the Court, having applied Arts. 45, 49, and 56 TFEU, said there was no need to look at Art. 63 TFEU.

[75] Case C–446/04 *FII Group Litigation* [2006] ECR I–11753, para. 118; Case C–231/05 *Oy AA* [2007] ECR I–6373, para. 23.

[76] Case C–231/05 *Oy AA* [2007] ECR I–6373, para. 20. See also, e.g., Case C–251/98 *Baars* [2000] ECR I–2787, paras. 21–2; Case C–436/00 *X, Y* v. *Riksskatteverket* [2002] ECR I–10829, para. 67.

[77] Case C–35/11 *Test Claimants in the FII Group Litigation* EU:C:2012:707, para. 92. In Case C–47/12 *Kronos International* v. *Finanzamt Leverkusen* EU:C:2014:2200, the Court said that a 10 per cent shareholding does not necessarily constitute a controlling stake and so Art. 63 TFEU applied.

[78] Case C–531/06 *Commission* v. *Italy (pharmacists)* [2009] ECR I–4103, para. 40. See also Case C–374/04 *ACT* [2006] ECR I–11673, para. 37; Case C–164/12 *DMC Beteiligungsgesellschaft mbH* v. *Finanzamt Hamburg Mitte* EU:C:2014:20, para. 31.

[79] Case C–35/11 *FII (No. 2)* EU:C:2012:707, para. 99.

[80] Case C–410/96 *Criminal Proceedings against André Ambry* [1998] ECR I–7875, para. 40; Case C–118/96 *Safir* [1998] ECR I–1897, para. 35.

Treaty provisions on services together with those on capital.[81] However, most recently it has shown a greater willingness to examine the centre of gravity of the national rules and then applies either the Treaty provisions on services or those on capital, as appropriate.[82]

This change of approach—both in respect of establishment and services—can perhaps be explained by the fact that only Article 63 TFEU applies to transactions involving third countries. By keeping the Treaty provisions distinct, the Court avoided indirectly extending the territorial scope of the other freedoms. The Court made this clear in *Fidium Finanz*,[83] where it said that if the 'predominant consideration' of the national legislation was freedom to provide services then a third-country company could not rely on Article 56 TFEU. Therefore, German rules which made companies granting credit on a commercial basis subject to prior authorization, which in turn depended on the company having its central administration or branch in Germany, had as their predominant purpose access to the financial market. So this was a case concerning the entrepreneurial activity of provision of financial services and thus fell under Article 56 TFEU, which could not be relied on by a Swiss company. By contrast, in *Wagner-Raith*[84] the case concerned holdings in investment funds held in the Cayman Islands. Since this was about investments in a product (rather than the entrepreneurial activity of offering the investments for sale) and the resulting taxation on the proceeds of that investment, the 'purpose' of the national rule related 'at least principally to capital movements'.[85]

4.3 Areas in Which Free Movement of Capital Only Applies

There has now been sufficient case law on Article 63 TFEU to identify five areas of national rules where the Court tends to apply the capital provisions alone:

- property purchase and investment,[86] building, and land subdivision[87]
- currency and other financial transactions[88]
- loans[89]
- investments in companies, especially where the national rule affects those who do not have a dominant interest in the company[90]
- the *Golden Share* cases[91]—i.e., cases involving newly privatized companies in sensitive sectors such as energy, where the state's golden share enables it to retain a degree of influence over the activities of the company.

---

[81] Case C–148/91 *Vereniging Veronica Omroep Organisatie v. Commissariaat voor de Media* [1993] ECR I–487, para. 15; Case C–279/00 *Commission v. Italy (temporary labour)* [2002] ECR I–1425, para. 41; Case C–334/02 *Commission v. France (tax on investment income)* [2004] ECR I–2229, para. 25; Joined Cases C–155 and 157/08 *X and E.H.A. Passenheim-van Schoot v. Staatssecretaris van Financiën* [2009] ECR I–5093, para. 76.

[82] Case C–452/04 *Fidium Finanz* [2006] ECR I–9521, para. 34; Case C–42/07 *Liga Portuguesa* [2009] ECR I–7633, para. 47.

[83] Case C–452/04 [2006] ECR I–9521.

[84] Case C–560/13 *Finanzamt-Ulm v. Wagner-Raith* EU:C:2015:347.   [85] Para. 34.

[86] Case C–302/97 *Konle* [1999] ECR I–3099, para. 39; Joined Cases C–515 and 527–540/99 *Reisch* [2002] ECR I–2157, para. 32, the *Golden Share* cases, e.g., Case C–483/99 *Commission v. France* [2002] ECR I–4781, para. 38, and Case C–364/01 *Barbier* [2003] ECR I–15013, para. 63.

[87] Joined Cases C–197 and 203/11 *Libert* EU:C:2013:288, para. 62.

[88] Joined Cases C–358 and 416/93 *Bordessa* [1995] ECR I–361.

[89] *Commission v. Belgium*, n. 69.   [90] *Commission v. Italy*, n. 78, paras. 47–8.

[91] Case C–367/98 *Commission v. Portugal* [2002] ECR I–4731; Case C–483/99 *Commission v. France* [2002] ECR I–4781, para. 41. Cf. Case C–326/07 *Commission v. Italy* [2009] ECR I–2291, where the Court considered the case under Arts. 49 and 63 TFEU.

In addition, the Court has applied Article 63 TFEU to the tax treatment of certain capital movements, especially in connection with property purchase, investment, inheritance, and charitable gifts.

E. WHAT IS PROHIBITED UNDER ARTICLE 63(1) TFEU?

1. INTRODUCTION

Having established whether Article 63 TFEU applies, we turn now to consider what national measures are prohibited under Article 63 TFEU. The original provision, Article 67 EEC, talked of the abolition of 'all restrictions on the movement of capital' *and* 'any discrimination based on the nationality or on the place of residence of the parties or on the place where such capital is invested'. The Maastricht amendments to Article 67 EEC dropped the reference to discrimination and referred only to 'restrictions'. Yet, the Court has used both the discrimination model and the restrictions model to eliminate measures which interfere with the free movement of capital, even in respect of decisions based on the post-Maastricht version of Article 63(1) TFEU.

2. THE DISCRIMINATION APPROACH

2.1 Direct and Indirect Discrimination

Article 67 EEC prohibited discrimination on three grounds:

- nationality
- the place of residence of the parties
- the place where capital was invested.

In this way Article 67 EEC anticipated subsequent developments in the field of services, where the Court has now prohibited discrimination on all three grounds. Although Article 63(1) TFEU makes no reference to the language of discrimination, it seems likely that, following the model of the other three freedoms, Article 63(1) TFEU prohibits national measures which are both directly and indirectly discriminatory as well as non-discriminatory measures which (substantially) hinder access to the market.

In fact, most of the case law has concerned direct discrimination. Sometimes the national governments concede the discrimination issue. For example, in *Commission v. Portugal*,[92] one of the so-called *Golden Share* cases, it was 'common ground' that national rules precluding investors from other Member States from acquiring more than a given number of shares in certain newly privatized Portuguese companies in sensitive sectors involved 'unequal treatment of nationals of other Member States and restricts the free movement of capital'.

In other cases the Court examines the discrimination issue for itself. For example, in *Konle*[93] the Court said that an Austrian rule from 1993 which exempted Austrian—but not foreign—nationals from having to obtain authorization before acquiring a plot of land which was built on, and thus from having to demonstrate that the planned purchase

---

[92] Case C–367/98 [2002] ECR I–4731, para. 40.
[93] Case C–302/97 *Konle v. Republik Österreich* [1999] ECR I–3099.

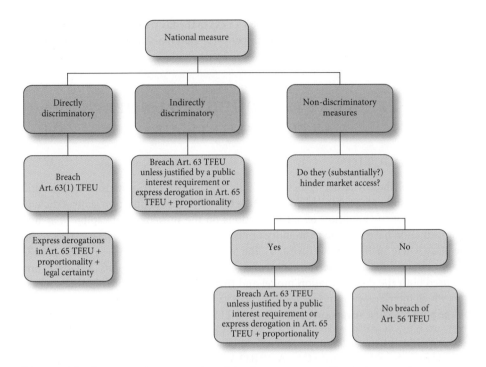

Fig. 14.1 The discrimination approach and the free movement of capital

would not be used to establish a secondary residence, created a 'discriminatory restriction against nationals of other Member States in respect of capital movements between Member States'.[94] Similarly, in *Albore*[95] an Italian law exempting Italians—but not foreign nationals—from the requirement of obtaining authorization before buying a property in areas designated as being of military importance was found to be discriminatory. In both *Konle* and *Albore* the Court then applied the orthodox rule that direct discrimination could be saved only by reference to the express derogations (see fig. 14.1).[96]

Case law on indirect discrimination is harder to find but most of it arises in the field of tax rules which have a disparate impact on non-residents. This can be seen in *Hollman*.[97] Under Portuguese law, non-residents were subject to a higher rate of capital gains tax than residents. This was found to be an unjustified breach of Article 63(1) TFEU.

Outside the field of taxation, the EFTA Court found indirectly discriminatory a rule in *EFTA Surveillance Authority* v. *Norway*[98] which granted to private undertakings a time-limited concession for the acquisition of waterfalls for energy production, with an obligation to surrender all installations to the Norwegian state without compensation at the expiry of the concession period, while allowing Norwegian public undertakings to benefit from concessions for an unlimited period of time.[99] The EFTA Court said that 'The differentiation is liable to operate to a particular disadvantage for foreign investors, since the rules in fact exclude them from benefiting from the more favourable provisions

---

[94] *Konle*, n. 93, para. 23. The Court of Justice made this finding in respect of the pre-Accession law.
[95] Case C–423/98 *Alfredo Albore* [2000] ECR I–5965, para. 16.
[96] Case C–302/97 *Konle* [1999] ECR I–3099, para. 24; Case C–423/98 *Albore* [2000] ECR I–5965, para. 17.
[97] Case C–443/06 *Hollmann* v. *Fazenda Pública* [2007] ECR I–8491, para. 36.
[98] Case E–2/06 [2007] EFTA Ct. Rep. 164.   [99] Para. 66.

applying to Norwegian public owners.'[100] The rules therefore breached the provisions on the free movement of capital (and establishment), could be justified on the grounds of environmental protection and the security of the energy supply but were not proportionate.

So far we have talked about discrimination on the grounds of nationality, place of residence of the parties, or the place where capital was invested. Section A.1 of the UK's New Settlement deal adds an additional ground of prohibited discrimination:

> Discrimination between natural or legal persons based on the official currency of the Member State, or, as the case may be, the currency that has legal tender in the Member State, where they are established is prohibited. Any difference of treatment must be based on objective reasons.

While this may well in fact reflect the general principle of non-discrimination under EU law it provides a useful clarification and confirmation of the principle.

2.2 Non-Discriminatory National Rules

So far we have considered direct and indirectly discriminatory rules. In the *Golden Share* cases of 2003[101] the Court appeared to follow *Alpine Investments*[102] and found that non-discriminatory measures which hindered access to the market breached Article 63(1) TFEU unless they could be objectively justified. For example, in *Commission v. UK*,[103] concerning the golden share in British Airports Authority (BAA), the Court said that although national rules limiting the acquisition of shareholdings over a certain level[104] applied without distinction to both residents and non-residents, 'it must nonetheless be held that they affect the position of a person acquiring a shareholding as such and are thus liable to deter investors from other Member States from making such investments and, consequently, affect access to the market'. This formulation comes close to the restrictions model used in the other *Golden Share* cases (see Section 3).

The UK had argued in this case that the principle in *Keck*[105] applied, suggesting that rules requiring prior authorization from the national authorities before major structural changes occurred in newly privatized companies or before more than a certain number of shares in those companies were acquired, did not restrict access to the market and so did not affect the free movement of capital. The Court disagreed, arguing that '[t]he measures at issue do not have comparable effects to those of the rules which the judgment in *Keck and Mithouard* regarded as not falling within the scope of Article [34 TFEU]'.[106] It continued that the restrictions 'affect the position of persons acquiring a shareholding as such and are thus liable to deter investors from other Member States from making such investments and, consequently, affect access to the market'.[107]

As with *Alpine Investments*,[108] the Court does not appear to be ruling out the possibility that *Keck*-style principles can apply to free movement of capital; rather it seems to be suggesting that in a case where prior authorization is at stake—a situation which the Court has ruled on numerous previous occasions constitutes a restriction on the movement of capital[109]—there is a hindrance of market access and so there is a breach of Article 63(1) TFEU. If, however, the breach is not substantial or is too remote from affecting

---

[100] Para. 65. It could even be argued that the rules were directly discriminatory. The Court also used the language of 'restrictions' (para. 64).

[101] See, e.g., Case C–463/00 *Commission v. Spain* [2003] ECR I–4581 and Case C–98/01 *Commission v. UK* [2003] ECR I–4641.

[102] Case C–384/93 *Alpine Investments* [1995] ECR I–1141.

[103] Case C–98/01 [2003] ECR I–4641.

[104] Para. 47. See also Case C–463/00 *Commission v. Spain* [2003] ECR I–4581, para. 61.

[105] Joined Cases C–267 and 268/91 [1993] ECR I–6097, considered in Ch. 5.   [106] Para. 59.

[107] Para. 61.   [108] Case C–384/93 [1995] ECR I–1141.   [109] See further Ch. 11.

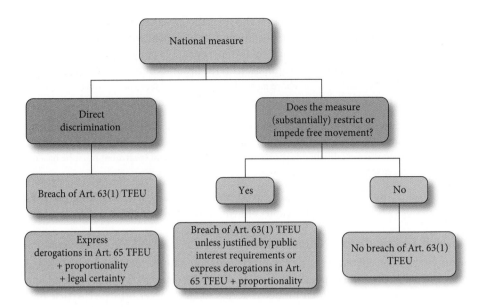

Fig. 14.2 The restrictions/obstacles-based approach

inter-state capital movements, then the Court might argue that, following the case law on goods and persons, principles similar to those laid down in *Keck*, or in *Graf*[110] (the too-uncertain and indirect rule),[111] would apply and there would be no breach of Article 63(1) TFEU (see fig. 14.2).

3. NATIONAL RULES WHICH RESTRICT OR CREATE AN OBSTACLE TO THE FREE MOVEMENT OF CAPITAL

3.1 Establishing a Breach

In most cases, a discrimination model is difficult to apply to capital movement: with the advent of the single currency it is not logical to assimilate foreign currencies with foreign nationals. It may be for this reason—together with a desire for convergence with the other freedoms—that the Court has increasingly used a restrictions-based approach to free movement of capital. This change in direction was most clearly signalled by the *Golden Share* cases decided in 2002, where the Court fully embraced the *Säger*[112] formulation developed in the context of services. For example, in *Commission* v. *Portugal*[113] the Court confirmed that the prohibition found in Article 63(1) TFEU 'goes beyond the mere elimination of unequal treatment, on grounds of nationality, as between operators on the financial markets'.[114] It continued:[115]

> Even though the rules in issue may not give rise to unequal treatment, they are liable to impede the acquisition of shares in the undertakings concerned and to dissuade investors

---

[110] Case C–190/98 *Graf* v. *Filzmozer Maschinenbau GmbH* [2000] ECR I–493, considered in Ch. 7.

[111] Case C–412/97 *ED Srl* v. *Italo Fenocchio* [1999] ECR I–3845, para. 11. For further discussion on this point, see Chs. 5 and 7.

[112] Case C–76/90 [1991] ECR I–4221, considered in Chs. 7 and 11.

[113] Case C–367/98 [2002] ECR I–4731; Case C–483/99 *Commission* v. *France* [2002] ECR I–4781, para. 41.

[114] Para. 44.   [115] Para. 45.

in other Member States from investing in the capital of those undertakings. They are therefore liable, as a result, to render the free movement of capital illusory.

Therefore, a Portuguese rule requiring potential shareholders to seek prior authorization from the Portuguese authorities to hold more than a specified number of shares in certain Portuguese companies constituted a restriction on the movement of capital,[116] even though it did not involve any discriminatory or particularly restrictive treatment of nationals of other Member States.[117] This shift reflects the language of Article 63(1) TFEU, which prohibits 'all *restrictions* on the movement of capital'. However, in some cases the language of 'obstacles' is used[118]; in others, especially those involving a challenge to a home state rule, the Court continues to refer to measures which are liable to, for example, 'dissuade [home state] residents from obtaining loans or making investments in other Member States'.[119]

In other cases, the Court mixes language based on restrictions and obstacles with that based on discrimination. For example, in *Lenz*[120] the Court noted that the Austrian legislation produced 'a restrictive effect in relation to companies established in other Member States, inasmuch as it constitutes an obstacle to their raising capital in Austria'. The Court continued, 'To the extent that revenue from capital originating in another Member State receives less favourable tax treatment than revenue from capital of Austrian origin, the shares of companies established in other Member States are, for investors living in Austria, less attractive than the shares of companies established in that Member State.' Whichever formula is used, the Court usually finds that there is, in principle, a breach of Article 63(1) TFEU. It then considers whether the national law can be justified either under the judicially developed public-interest requirements or, more commonly, under the broad express derogations, and whether the steps taken are proportionate (Section F).

3.2 A Threshold Requirement?

The question of whether there should be a threshold requirement before the national rule is considered a restriction—which has concerned the Court in respect of the other freedoms[121]—has not yet troubled the Court in respect of capital. There is, however, one possible exception. In *STEKO*[122] the Court said 'It is insignificant . . . that the difference in treatment existed only for a limited period of time . . . That fact alone does not preclude the difference in treatment from having *significant* effects . . . or, therefore, from giving rise to a *genuine* restriction on the free movement of capital' (emphasis added). This leaves the door open for a threshold requirement to apply, should the Court so choose.

---

[116] Para. 46. See also Joined Cases C–282 and 283/04 *Commission* v. *Netherlands* [2006] ECR I–9141, para. 24.

[117] Para. 43.

[118] This term was used in Joined Cases C–282 and 283/04 *Commission* v. *Netherlands* [2006] ECR I–9141, para. 20. In para. 27 the Court said that a possible refusal by the Dutch government to approve an important decision 'would be capable of depressing the value of the shares of that company and thus reduces the attractiveness of an investment in such shares'. As Snell points out (n. 17), 'Taken at face value, this [test] would open most national rules to challenge under the free movement of capital, as any interference with economic freedom is likely to depress the share prices in some companies.'

[119] Case C–478/98 *Commission* v. *Belgium (Eurobond)* [2000] ECR I–7587, para. 18. Case C–484/93 *Svensson and Gustavsson* [1995] ECR I–3955, para. 5.

[120] Case C–315/02 *Lenz* v. *Finanzlandesdirektion für Tirol* [2004] ECR I–7063, para. 21.

[121] See Chs. 4 and 7.

[122] Case C–377/07 *Finanzamt Speyer-Germersheim* v. *STEKO Industriemontage* [2009] ECR I–299, para. 29. See also Case C–318/07 *Persche* [2009] ECR I–359, para. 38.

3.3 Examples of Restrictions on the Free Movement of Capital

Despite the problems with the restrictions model, which we have already discussed in Chapters 1 and 7, it is now the norm for the free movement of capital. Therefore, we turn to examine what sort of measures the Court has said constitute a restriction on the free movement of capital. Looking at the five areas identified earlier (Section D, 4.3) where Article 63(1) TFEU typically applies, we shall consider the types of measure which have been considered restrictions in respect of each.

The first area where Article 63(1) applies is property purchase and investment. Here, authorization rules are one of the most common requirements imposed by Member States and are always considered restrictions. This can be seen in *Konle*,[123] where the Court said an Austrian rule of 1996 requiring prior authorization for the acquisition of land 'entails, by its very purpose, a restriction on the free movement of capital'. It could be regarded as compatible with Article 63(1) TFEU only if justified.

Residence requirements connected with the purchase of property, often seen as indirectly discriminatory, are also more often now described as 'restrictions'. Thus in *Festersen*[124] the Court said that a Danish rule making it a condition for acquiring agricultural property that the acquirer took up his fixed residence on that property, 'while not discriminat[ing] between Danish nationals and nationals of other Member States... [nevertheless] restricts the free movement of capital'.

Cross-border currency and other financial transactions is the second area where the Treaty provisions on capital tend to apply. These currency transactions may take the form of physical movement of cash as in *Bordessa*,[125] where the Court said that a rule requiring the export of coins, banknotes, or bearer cheques conditional upon an administrative authorization would cause 'the exercise of the free movement of capital to be subject to the discretion of the administrative authorities and thus be such as to render that freedom illusory'. It continued that the authorization requirement 'might have the effect of impeding capital movements carried out in accordance with [Union] law'.

Alternatively, the movement may be electronic, as in *Trummer and Mayer*.[126] There the Court said that a national rule prohibiting the registration of a mortgage in the currency of another Member State weakened the link between the debt to be secured, payable in the currency of another Member State, and the mortgage, whose value could, as a result of subsequent currency exchange fluctuations, end up being lower than that of the debt to be secured, thereby reducing the effectiveness of the security, and thus its attractiveness. The Court therefore said that the national rule was 'liable to dissuade the parties concerned from denominating a debt in the currency of another Member State, and may thus deprive them of a right which constitutes a component element of the free movement of capital and payments'.[127] It added that the rules might also cause the parties to incur

---

[123] Case C–302/97 *Klaus Konle* [1999] ECR I–3099, para. 39; Joined Cases C–515 and 527–540/99 *Reisch* [2002] ECR I–2157, para. 32; Case C–567/07 *Minister voor Wonen, Wijken en Integratie* v. *Woningstichting Sint Servatius* [2009] ECR I–9021, para. 22.

[124] Case C–370/05 [2007] ECR I–1129, para. 25.

[125] Joined Cases C–358 and 416/93 *Bordessa* [1995] ECR I–361, para. 25. Cf. Case 157/85 *Luigi Brugnoni and Roberto Ruffinengo* v. *Cassa di risparmio di Genova e Imperia* [1986] ECR I–2013, para. 22 for an early example of an authorization rule and the Court's more qualified approach.

[126] Case C–222/97 *Manfred Trummer and Peter Mayer* [1999] ECR I–1661, confirmed in Case C–464/98 *Westdeutsche Landesbank Girozentrale* v. *Friedrich Stefan and Republik Österreich* [2001] ECR I–173, para. 19.

[127] Para. 26.

additional costs by requiring them, purely for the purpose of the registration, to value the debt in the national currency and formally register that currency conversion.[128]

In a different context, the Court ruled in *Commission v. Italy (temporary labour)*[129] that an Italian requirement that an out-of-state undertaking engaged in the provision of temporary labour in Italy had to establish a guarantee of 700 million lire with a credit institution having its registered office or a branch office in Italy before it could provide services was a restriction on capital movement.

Loans is the third area where Article 63(1) TFEU tends to apply. In *Svensson and Gustafsson*[130] the Court ruled that Luxembourg law requiring a bank to be established in Luxembourg for recipients of loans residing in its territory to obtain an interest rate subsidy from the State was 'liable to dissuade those concerned from approaching banks established in another Member State and therefore constitute[d] an obstacle to movements of capital such as bank loans' and could not be justified. In *Commission v. Belgium (Eurobond)*[131] the Belgian rule went even further because it prevented Belgian residents from subscribing to a loan issued in German marks on the Eurobond market. The Court said this rule went 'well beyond a measure which is intended to dissuade residents of a Member State from subscribing to a loan issued abroad' and thus 'all the more' constituted a restriction on the free movement of capital within the meaning of Article 63(1) TFEU.[132]

Investments in companies and shares is the fourth area where Article 63(1) TFEU applies.[133] Once again, authorization requirements are considered to be restrictions. So, in *Church of Scientology*[134] the Court said that 'A provision of national law which makes a foreign investment subject to prior authorization constitutes a restriction on the movement of capital'. *Commission v. Italy (pharmacists)*[135] concerned a different type of measure: the national legislation provided that members of companies and firms operating pharmacies had to be qualified pharmacists. The Court said that this 'prevents investors from other Member States who are not pharmacists from acquiring stakes in companies and firms of that kind'. The national legislation therefore imposed restrictions within the meaning of Articles 49 and 63(1) TFEU.

The *Golden Share* cases are the fifth area where Article 63(1) TFEU applies. Obligations imposed by the 'golden share' holder, usually the state acting as regulator albeit in the guise of a market participant, are considered restrictions on free movement of capital. So, as we saw in *Commission v. Portugal*,[136] the obligation to seek authorization from the state prior to holding more than a certain number of shares constituted a restriction on free movement of capital.[137] In *Federconsumatori*[138] a rule which gave public shareholders the right to participate in the board of directors in a more significant way than their status as shareholders would normally allow also constituted a restriction on the free movement

---

[128] Para. 27. Cf. Case C–168/01 *Bosal* [2003] ECR I–9409, para. 27 for even more relaxed language.

[129] Case C–279/00 [2002] ECR I–1425, para. 37.   [130] Case C–484/93 [1995] ECR I–3955, para. 10.

[131] Case C–478/98 [2000] ECR I–7587.   [132] Para. 19.

[133] Case C–531/06 *Commission v. Italy (pharmacists)* [2009] ECR I–4103, para. 40.

[134] Case C–54/99 *Association Eglise de Scientologie de Paris v. The Prime Minister* [2000] ECR I–1335, para. 14.

[135] Case C–531/06 [2009] ECR I–4103, paras. 47–8.

[136] Case C–367/98 [2002] ECR I–4731; Case C–483/99 *Commission v. France* [2002] ECR I–4781, para. 41.

[137] This was one of the three major obstacles to the free movement of capital identified by the Commission in its Communication on Certain Legal Aspects concerning intra-EU investment ([1997] OJ C220/15).

[138] Joined Cases C–463 and 464/04 *Federconsumatori v. Comune di Milano* [2007] ECR I–10419, paras. 23–4.

of capital. Likewise, a golden shareholder's power to oppose the acquisition of certain shareholdings or the conclusion of certain agreements by shareholders representing at least 5 per cent of voting rights, as in *Commission* v. *Italy*,[139] was considered a restriction on the free movement of capital. In *Commission* v. *Germany*[140] the Court said that a law capping voting rights of every shareholder in Volkswagen at 20 per cent, introducing a blocking minority at 20 per cent for important company decisions,[141] and allowing the federal government and the state of Lower Saxony to appoint two members each of the supervisory board,[142] thus enabling them to participate in a more significant manner in the activities of the supervisory board than their status as shareholders would normally allow, also breached Article 63(1) TFEU.

Essent[143] concerned the opposite of golden shares: the prohibition of privatization. Dutch law prohibited, inter alia, the sale to private investors of shares held in the electricity and gas distribution system operators active in the Netherlands. While the Court noted that the Treaty did not preclude either the nationalization[144] of undertakings or their privatization, any such decision had to comply with the Treaty. The Court said that the prohibition of privatization meant that no private investor could acquire shares in the capital of an electricity or gas distribution system operator active in the Netherlands and so was a restriction on free movement under Article 63.[145]

4. TAXATION

4.1 Restriction v. Discrimination Approach

While authorization and other similar requirements are classic examples of 'restrictions' on the free movement of capital, an increasing number of cases concern taxation of capital—or the holders of capital—which, the taxpayer argues, interferes with free movement. In some of the cases there are direct parallels with the tax advantage jurisprudence considered in Chapters 8, 10, and 11. The Court's changing approach to the classification of taxation issues seen under Article 49 TFEU is repeated in respect of Article 63 TFEU: up until the mid-2000s the cases focused on the question of whether the taxation rule constituted a restriction on free movement; later cases suggested a retreat to a discrimination-based analysis. However, the Court tends to paper over the cracks by describing any such discriminatory treatment as 'a restriction on the free movement of capital which is, in principle, prohibited by Article [63(1) TFEU]'.[146]

Sandoz[147] is a good example of the Court applying a restriction-based approach towards tax rules. It concerned stamp duty payable under Austrian law on a loan taken out

---

[139] Case C–326/07 [2009] ECR I–2291, para. 40. See also the Commission's Communication on Certain Legal Aspects concerning intra-EU investment ([1997] OJ C220/15). In the EEA context, see Case E–9/11 *EFTA Surveillance Authority* v. *Norway* [2012] EFTA Ct. Rep. 442.

[140] Case C–112/05 *Commission* v. *Germany (Volkswagen)* [2007] ECR I–8995, paras. 56 and 68.

[141] Lower Saxony held 20 per cent of the shares. It therefore enjoyed an indirect veto on all major decisions of the company. After the Court's decision in *Volkswagen I*, all other restrictions on free movement were repealed except the blocking minority rule. In Case C–95/12 *Commission* v. *Germany* EU:C:2013:676 the Court upheld the German reforms as compatible with Art. 63 TFEU.

[142] The supervisory board is not a decision-making body but a monitoring body.

[143] Joined Cases C–105–107/12 *Staat der Nederlanden* v. *Essent NV* EU:C:2013:677.

[144] The Court noted 'Such a prohibition falls within the scope of Article 345 TFEU.'

[145] Para. 47.

[146] Case C–157/05 *Holböck* v. *Finanzamt Salzburg-Land* [2007] ECR I–4051, para. 30.

[147] Case C–439/97 *Sandoz GmbH* [1999] ECR I–7041. For another example, see Case C–35/98 *Verkooijen* [2000] ECR I–4071.

by an Austrian company from a Belgian company. No tax was payable under Belgian law. The Court said that since the Austrian law deprived Austrian residents of the possibility of taking out a tax-free loan with a non-resident company 'such a measure is likely to deter such residents from obtaining loans from persons established in other Member States'.[148] It continued that 'such legislation constitutes an obstacle to the movement of capital' within the meaning of Article 63(1) TFEU.[149] Thus, the mere imposition of tax was enough to constitute a restriction which had to be justified.

The approach adopted in this case now needs to be read in the light of the velvet revolution of late 2006/early 2007 in cases such as *FII Group Litigation*[150] and *ACT Group Litigation*,[151] considered in Chapter 11, where the Court was forced to re-examine its 'restrictions' jurisprudence and largely replace it with a discrimination analysis. It will be recalled that 'It is for each Member State to organise, in compliance with European Union law, its system for taxing income from investment capital and, in that context, to define the basis of assessment and the tax rate which apply to the shareholder receiving them'.[152] Further, under the principles of international tax law, *residents* of a taxing state are taxed on their worldwide profits ('unlimited taxation'), while *non-residents* are taxed on profits arising from sources located in that taxing state ('limited taxation').

4.2 Examples of Cases Where the State's Taxation Policy Breaches Article 63 TFEU

We shall now consider the application of Article 63(1) TFEU in the four main areas where national tax rules have been challenged: inheritances, property ownership, transactions involving shares, and charitable gifts.

(a) Inheritances

In respect of inheritances, the problem has been that when taxing income received by natural or legal persons from, for example, inheritances in other Member States, State A taxes an inheritance received in State B differently, and usually less favourably, than would be the case if the receipts had come from inheritances received in State A. This can be seen in *Jäger*,[153] where an inheritance consisting of agricultural land and forestry situated in France was subject, in Germany, to inheritance tax higher than that which would have been payable had the assets inherited been situated exclusively within Germany. The Court said that the German rule had the effect of restricting the movement of capital by reducing the value of an inheritance situated outside Germany. The rule therefore breached Article 63(1) TFEU and could not be saved by the Article 65(1)(a) TFEU derogation (which expressly allows discrimination between residents and non-residents (considered further in Section F)).

---

[148] Para. 19. Cf. Case E–1/00 *State Debt Management Agency* v. *Íslandsbanki–FBA hf.* [2000] EFTA Ct. Rep. 8, where the EFTA Court did not consider the imposition of a heavier burden on foreign transactions as being automatically a restriction, although it did on the facts (para. 26).

[149] Para. 20. See also Case C–484/93 *Svensson and Gustavsson* [1995] ECR I–3955, para. 8.

[150] Case C–446/04 *FII* [2006] ECR I–11753.   [151] Case C–374/04 *ACT* [2006] ECR I–11673.

[152] Case C–157/10 *Banco Bilbao Vizcaya Argentaria SA* v. *Administración General del Estado* [2011] ECR I–13023, para. 29.

[153] Case C–256/06 *Jäger* [2008] ECR I–123, para. 32. Case C–132/10 *Halley* v. *Belgische Staat* [2011] ECR I–8353 (different limitation periods for the valuation of shares in resident and non-resident companies in connection with inheritance tax). See also Case C–67/08 *Block* [2009] ECR I–883, para. 24 (although no discrimination was found on the facts).

While *Jäger* concerned discrimination based on the location of the inherited property, *Eckelkamp*[154] concerned discrimination based on the residence of the deceased. Under Belgian law, an inheritance consisting of immoveable property situated in Belgium was subject to transfer duties higher than inheritance duties that would have been payable had the deceased been residing in Belgium at the time of her death (she had been living in Germany). The Court said that the Belgian rule restricted the movement of capital in breach of Article 63 TFEU by reducing the value of an inheritance.[155] Once again, the Court said that the restriction could not be saved under Article 65(1)(a) TFEU.

Where there is no discrimination, the national law is lawful (see fig. 14.1), as *Van Hilten-van der Heijden*[156] shows. Dutch law provided that the estate of a national of a Member State who died within ten years of ceasing to reside in the Netherlands was to be taxed as if that national had continued to reside in the Netherlands, while providing for relief in respect of the taxes levied in the state to which the deceased had transferred her residence. The Court found that this law did not constitute a restriction on the movement of capital.[157] It reasoned that by enacting identical taxation provisions for the estates of nationals who transferred their residence abroad and for those who remained in the Netherlands, Dutch law did not discourage nationals who transferred their residence abroad from making investments in the Netherlands, nor those who remained in the Netherlands from investing in another Member State, nor did it diminish the value of the estate of nationals who had transferred their residence abroad.[158]

(b) Property

Two main issues have arisen in respect of property. The first concerns the location of the property: where, as in *ELISA*,[159] a resident of State A receives income from property in State B which is taxed at a higher rate (or does not benefit from an exemption) than had the property been situated in State A. As with the cases on inheritance, the Court usually finds that State A's scheme breaches Article 63(1) TFEU.

The second issue, which arose in *Blanckaert*,[160] concerned differential treatment of the property owner depending on resident or non-resident status. The case concerned a Belgian resident who had invested in property in the Netherlands. Dutch law provided that non-resident taxpayers, who received income in the Netherlands from savings and investments but who were not insured under the Dutch social security scheme, were not entitled to tax credits in respect of national insurance. By contrast, resident taxpayers, who were insured under the Dutch social security scheme but otherwise in the same situation as non-residents, were entitled to those credits. Had the case been decided under Article 45 or 49 TFEU the Court may well have said that the situations of the resident and non-resident were not comparable and so there was no breach of Union law. However, since this case concerned free movement of capital, the Court said that 'Less favourable tax treatment for non-residents only might deter the latter from investing in property in the Netherlands. The legislation was therefore capable of hindering the free movement of capital.' However, the Court did take account the differences between the

---

[154] Case C–11/07 *Eckelkamp* v. *Belgische Staat* [2008] ECR I–6845, para. 44. See also Case C–181/12 *Welte* v. *Finanzamt Velbert* EU:C:2013:662, para. 25.

[155] Para. 46. See also Case C–43/07 *Arens-Sikken* [2008] ECR I–6887, para. 40, decided the same day as *Eckelkamp*.

[156] Case C–513/03 *van Hilten-van der Heijden* [2006] ECR I–1957.

[157] Para. 45.   [158] Para. 46.

[159] Case C–451/05 *ELISA* v. *Directeur general des impôts* [2007] ECR I–8251.

[160] Case C–512/03 *Blanckaert* v. *Inspecteur van de Belastingdienst* [2005] ECR I–7685, para. 39.

situation of residents and non-residents at the derogation stage and, considering that their situations were not comparable, found that the Dutch law could be justified under Article 65(1)(a) TFEU.

(c) Shares, dividends, and deductions

As with the property and inheritance cases, it is in principle contrary to Article 63(1) TFEU for the home state to apply differential tax treatment to shares, dividends, or deductions depending on the place where the capital was invested. This can be seen in *STEKO Industriemontage*,[161] where a resident company could not deduct from its taxable revenue reductions in profit resulting from the partial write-down of holdings in non-resident companies. By contrast, a resident company could deduct such reductions in profit from its taxable revenue where they related to holdings in resident companies. So, resident companies holding depreciated shares in non-resident companies were in a less favourable situation than those holding shares in resident companies. The national rule therefore constituted an 'obstacle' to free movement contrary to Article 63 TFEU.[162]

While *STEKO* concerned treatment of residents' incoming income and losses, *Amurta SGPS*[163] concerned outgoing dividends. Dutch law applied a withholding tax on dividends distributed by a company in the Netherlands to a company established in another Member State (Portugal) while exempting from that tax the dividends paid to a company liable to corporation tax in the Netherlands. The Court said that treating dividends paid to companies established in another Member State less favourably than dividends paid to companies established in the Netherlands was liable to deter companies established in another Member State from investing in the Netherlands and thus constituted a restriction on the free movement of capital prohibited by Article 63(1) TFEU[164] which could not be justified.

Finally, *Manninen*[165] concerned incoming dividends. Mr Manninen was fully taxable in Finland. He held shares in a Swedish company. The profits distributed by the Swedish company in the form of dividends to Mr Manninen had already borne corporation tax in Sweden. He was then subject to income tax on those profits in Finland. Had the dividends been paid by a Finnish company there would have been a tax credit for the corporation tax already paid. The Court said that the Finnish tax legislation had the effect of deterring fully taxable persons in Finland from investing their capital in companies established in Sweden. It also constituted an obstacle to companies raising capital in Finland because revenue from capital of non-Finnish origin received less favourable tax treatment than dividends distributed by companies established in Finland. The Court also found the Finnish rule could not be justified (see Section F, 2).

Where there is no discrimination then the national law is compatible with Article 63(1) TFEU. This can be seen in *Kerckhaert-Morres*,[166] where Belgian legislation did not make any distinction between dividends from companies established in Belgium and dividends from companies established in another Member State (France)—both dividends were taxed at the same rate and so there was no breach of Article 63(1) TFEU.[167] The Court added that any adverse consequences arising from the Belgian system (the dividends had already been taxed in France, leading to 'juridical' double taxation—the taxation of the

---

[161] Case C–377/07 *Finanzamt Speyer-Germersheim* v. *STEKO Industriemontage* [2009] ECR I–299.
[162] Paras. 25–7.
[163] Case C–379/05 *Amurta SGPS* v. *Inspecteur van de Belastingdienst* [2007] ECR I–9569.
[164] Para. 28.   [165] Case C–319/02 *Manninen* [2004] ECR I–7477.
[166] Case C–513/04 *Kerckhaert-Morres* v. *Belgium* [2006] ECR I–10967, paras. 17–18.
[167] See also Case C–298/05 *Columbus Container Services* [2007] ECR I–10451, para. 40.

same income twice in the hands of the same person) were the result of the exercise in parallel by two Member States of their fiscal sovereignty.[168] In reaching this conclusion the Court acknowledged the point made by Advocate General Geelhoed in *ACT Group Litigation*[169] that 'quasi-restrictions' brought about by the coexistence of two systems of taxation should fall outside the Treaty.

(d) Charitable gifts

The principle of equal treatment applies equally to tax relief on charitable donations, as *Persche*[170] shows. A German national claimed a tax deduction in respect of gifts (bed linen, towels, zimmer frames, and toys), valued at about €18,000, to a retirement home and a children's home in Portugal. He was refused the deduction on the basis of German law which allowed for the deduction for tax purposes of gifts to charitable bodies in Germany but excluded that tax advantage for gifts to bodies established and recognized as charitable in another Member State.

The Court said that since the possibility of obtaining a tax deduction could have 'a significant influence on the donor's attitude, the inability in Germany to deduct gifts to bodies recognised as charitable if they are established in other Member States is likely to affect the willingness of German taxpayers to make gifts for their benefit'.[171] The German legislation therefore constituted a restriction on the free movement of capital contrary to Article 63(1) TFEU which could not be justified.

4.3 Cases Involving Movement of Capital Between a Member State and a Third Country

The discussion so far shows that, in the context of free movement of capital, Article 63(1) TFEU is less about the movement of capital itself than about facilitating other cross-border transactions requiring capital. As we have seen, the Court finds relatively easily that any obstacle to such transactions is a restriction contrary to Article 63(1) TFEU which needs to be justified. Does this case law apply equally to movements of capital between Member States and third countries? In *A*,[172] Germany and the Netherlands argued forcibly that it should not. Drawing on arguments which the Court itself has used to find that provisions of the WTO Agreements should not have direct effect,[173] the states said that by extending the 'restrictions' case law to relations with third countries 'the [Union] would unilaterally open up the [Union] market to third countries without retaining the means of negotiation necessary to achieve liberalisation on the part of those countries'. The Court disagreed[174] and applied its 'restrictions' case law.

A concerned a Swedish law which granted taxpayers living in Sweden an exemption from tax in respect of dividends distributed in the form of shares in a subsidiary by a limited liability company established in Sweden or in another state within the EEA but refused to grant them that exemption where such a distribution was made by a company established in a third country outside the EEA, unless that country had concluded a convention providing for the exchange of information with Sweden. The Court said that the effect of such legislation was to discourage taxpayers residing in Sweden from investing their capital in companies established outside the EEA.[175] The Swedish law 'therefore entails a restriction of the movement of capital between Member States and third countries

---

[168] *Kerckhaert-Morres*, n. 166, para. 21.

[169] Case C–374/04 [2007] ECR I–11673, considered in Ch. 11.

[170] Case C–318/07 *Persche* [2009] ECR I–359. See also Case C–10/10 *Commission* v. *Austria* (gifts to teaching and research institutions) [2011] ECR I–5389.

[171] Para. 38.   [172] Case C–101/05 *Skatteverket* v. *A* [2007] ECR I–11531, para. 38.

[173] See further Ch. 2.   [174] Para. 38.   [175] Para. 42.

which, in principle, is prohibited by Article [63(1) TFEU]'.[176] However, the Court found that the Swedish rule could be justified on the grounds of fiscal supervision, particularly because the framework of cooperation between the competent authorities of the Member States established by Directive 2011/16/EU did not exist in respect of relations with authorities of non-Member States. This might suggest that while the Court is prepared to cast the Article 63(1) TFEU net widely to catch restrictions on the movement of capital with third countries so that it can scrutinize them, it might be more lenient in respect of accepting the justifications proposed by the Member States, a point made explicit in *FII*:[177]

> it may be that a Member State will be able to demonstrate that a restriction on capital movements to or from non-member countries is justified for a particular reason in circumstances where that reason would not constitute a valid justification for a restriction on capital movements between Member States.

5. PUBLIC-INTEREST REQUIREMENTS AND PROPORTIONALITY

5.1 Public-Interest Requirements

As the previous discussion indicated, where there is a breach of Article 63(1) TFEU, the Court will consider whether the national rule can be justified. In *Commission* v. *Portugal*[178] the Court followed the approach adopted in *Gebhard*[179] in respect of justifications. It said:

> The free movement of capital, as a fundamental principle of the Treaty, may be restricted only by national rules which are justified by reasons referred to in Article [65(1) TFEU] or by overriding requirements of the general interest and which are applicable to all persons and undertakings pursuing an activity in the territory of the host Member State. Furthermore, in order to be so justified, the national legislation must be suitable for securing the objective which it pursues and must not go beyond what is necessary in order to attain it, so as to accord with the principle of proportionality.[180]

As with the other freedoms, the list of justifications is open-ended[181] and wide ranging. The list does, however, preclude justifications of a purely economic nature. So in *Manninen*[182] the Court rejected 'reduction in tax revenue' as an overriding reason in the public interest[183] and in *Verkooijn*[184] the Court rejected as an argument for a more favourable tax regime for companies established in the Netherlands 'the intention to promote the economy of the country by encouraging investment by individuals in companies with their seat in the Netherlands'.[185] That said, the Court has accepted that national legislation

---

[176] Para. 43.   [177] Case C–446/04 *FII (No. 1)* [2006] ECR I–11753, para. 121.

[178] Case C–367/98 *Commission* v. *Portugal* [2002] ECR I–4731.

[179] Case C–55/94 [1995] ECR I–4165, considered further in Ch. 8.

[180] See also Joined Cases C–515 and 527–540/99 *Reisch* [2002] ECR I–2157, para. 33: 'The national rules pursue, in a non-discriminatory way, an objective in the public interest and if they observe the principle of proportionality, that is if the same result could not be achieved by other less restrictive measures.'

[181] See further the discussion of the list of justifications in Ch. 12.

[182] Case C–319/02 *Manninen* [2004] ECR I–7477, para. 49.

[183] See also Case C–367/98 *Commission* v. *Portugal* [2002] ECR I–4731, para. 52, where the justification based on the 'need to safeguard the financial interest of the Portuguese republic' was also rejected. The Court also rejected the argument based on the need to preserve the Portuguese system of property ownership.

[184] Case C–35/98 *Verkooijn* [2000] ECR I–4071, paras. 47–8.

[185] Cf. Case C–194/06 *Orange European Smallcap Fund* [2008] ECR I–3747, para. 93, for hints to the contrary.

may constitute a justified restriction 'when it is dictated by reasons of an economic nature in the pursuit of an objective in the public interest'.[186]

The justifications can be roughly divided into three. One group concern public order, as broadly construed. For example, in *Commission v. Italy (Golden Share)*[187] the Court recognized that certain restrictions on the free movement of capital could be justified by the need for 'the minimum supply of energy resources and goods essential to the public as a whole, the continuity of public service, national defence, the protection of public policy and public security and health emergencies'. In *A*[188] the Court recognized the justification of the need to guarantee the effectiveness of fiscal supervision;[189] in *DMC*[190] the preservation of the balanced allocation of the power to impose taxes between Member States; in *Miljoen*[191] the application of double taxation conventions; and in *STEKO*[192] the need for a seamless transition from an earlier system to its replacement.

A second group of justifications relate to the protection of the values of the state, again as broadly construed. So in *Commission v. Austria (gifts for teaching and research institutions)*[193] the Court recognized that the promotion of research and development could constitute a public interest requirement. A number of cases have concerned justifications connected with rules on the use of land. For example, in *Konle*[194] the Court said that a Member State could justify its prior-authorization requirement for the acquisition of land by relying on a 'town and country planning objective such as maintaining, in the general interest, a permanent population and an economic activity independent of the tourist sector in certain regions'. In *Reisch*[195] the Court added that that finding could 'only be strengthened by other concerns which might underlie those same measures such as the protection of the environment'.[196] By analogy, in *Sint Servatius*[197] the Court recognized requirements relating to public-housing policy and to the financing of that policy could constitute overriding reasons in the general interest. And in *Ospelt*[198] the Court recognized that a prior-authorization requirement before purchasing agricultural land could be justified on the grounds of:

> preserving agricultural communities, maintaining a distribution of land ownership which allows the development of viable farms and sympathetic management of green spaces and the countryside as well as encouraging a reasonable use of the available land by resisting pressure on land, and preventing natural disasters.[199]

---

[186] Joined Cases C–105–107/12 *Essent NV* EU:C:2013:677, paras. 51–2.

[187] Case C–326/07 [2009] ECR I–2291, para. 45.   [188] Case C–101/05 *A* [2007] ECR I–11531.

[189] See also Art. 65(1)(b) TFEU.

[190] Case C–164/12 *DMC Beteiligungsgeschaft mbH* EU:C:2014:20, para. 46.

[191] Joined Cases C–10, 14 and 17/14 *Miljoen v. Staatssecretaris van Financiën* EU:C:2015:608, para. 76.

[192] Case C–377/07 *STEKO* [2009] ECR I–299, para. 50.

[193] Case C–10/10 [2011] ECR I–5389, para. 37.

[194] Case C–302/97 *Konle* [1999] ECR I–3099. This part of the judgment concerned the post-Accession law.

[195] Joined Cases C–515 and 527–540/99 *Reisch* [2002] ECR I–2157.   [196] Para. 34.

[197] Case C–567/07 *Sint Servatius* [2009] ECR I–9021, para. 30. See also Joined Cases C–197 and 203/11 *Libert* EU:C:2013:288, para. 67.

[198] Case C–452/01 *Ospelt v. Schlössle Weissenberg Familienstiftung* [2003] ECR I–9743.

[199] Para. 39. In a similar vein see also Case C–370/05 *Festersen* [2007] ECR I–1129, para. 27, where the Court accepted the Danish government's arguments based on the need 'first, to preserve the farming of agricultural land by means of owner-occupancy, which constitutes one of the traditional forms of farming in Denmark, and to ensure that agricultural property be occupied and farmed predominantly by the owners, second, as a town and country planning measure, to preserve a permanent agricultural community and, third, to encourage a reasonable use of the available land by resisting pressure on land'. However, the Court found the residence requirement disproportionate.

In *Essent*,[200] the case concerning the Dutch rule keeping the supply of gas and electricity in public hands, the Court recognized a range of justifications for the Dutch rule including the need for concerted action in order to guarantee fair competition, the ultimate aim of that action being to protect consumers and the objective of guaranteeing adequate investment in the electricity and gas distribution systems in order to ensure security of energy supply. The question of proportionality of the Dutch rule was for the national court to decide.

A third group of public interest requirements concern the protection of interests of third parties. So, for example, in *VBV*,[201] the Court recognized 'the need to guarantee the stability and security of the assets administered by an undertaking for collective investment created by a severance fund, in particular by the adoption of prudential rules' as a public interest requirement.

In practice, justifications are often not made out on the facts.[202] For example, in *Trummer and Mayer*[203] the Court said that while a Member State was in principle entitled to take the necessary measures to ensure that a mortgage system clearly and transparently prescribed the respective rights of mortgagees *inter se*, as well as the rights of mortgagees as a whole vis-à-vis other creditors,[204] the need to achieve this had not been shown.

5.2 Proportionality

Even if the justification is made out, the Court often finds that the national measure is not proportionate. This is particularly the case with a prior-authorization requirement. For example, in *Konle* the Court said that given the risk of discrimination inherent in a system of prior authorization for the acquisition of land and the other possibilities available to Austria for ensuring compliance with its town and country planning guidelines, the authorization procedure constituted a restriction on capital movements which was not essential to prevent infringements of the national legislation on secondary residences. It also added that the state could be liable in damages to individuals who had suffered a sufficiently serious breach of Union law.[205]

The Court did, however, say in *Konle* that a requirement of a *declaration* prior to the purchase of building plots, coupled with penalties for breach of the declaration,[206] would comply with Union law.[207] In *Reisch* the Court added that the requirement of prior notification provided the acquirer of the title with an element of legal certainty and was better suited to preventing certain damage which was reparable only with difficulty, caused by hastily completed building projects.[208] For this reason, a declaration/notification requirement was compatible with Union law.

The question of authorization versus declaration has had a long history. It was first raised, not in respect of the acquisition of immovable property, but concerning national rules making currency exports conditional on prior authorization. For example, in

---

[200] Joined Cases C–105–107/12 *Staat der Nederlanden* v. *Essent NV* EU:C:2013:677.

[201] Case C–39/11 *VBV—Vorsorgekasse* v. *FMA* EU:C:2012:327, para. 31.

[202] Cf. Case C–101/05 *A* [2007] ECR I–11531, where the justification was made out but in a third-country context where different rules may well apply in the absence of a framework of mutual cooperation between EU Member States and third countries. See also Case C–446/04 *FII* [2006] ECR I–11753, para. 121, considered at n. 74.

[203] Case C–222/97 *Trummer and Mayer* [1999] ECR I–1661.   [204] Para. 30.   [205] Paras. 58–9.

[206] Any penalties must themselves be proportionate: in Case C–213/04 *Burtscher* v. *Stauderer* [2005] ECR I–10309 the penalty provided was the retroactive invalidity of the property transaction and this was found incompatible with Art. 63 TFEU.

[207] Paras. 44–8.   [208] Para. 36.

Bordessa[209] an Italian leaving Spain by car was stopped at the French border and found to be carrying banknotes worth 50 million pesetas. Since he did not have the prior authorization required by Spanish law for the export of such a sum, he was arrested and the money confiscated. The Court said that because authorization had the effect of suspending currency exports and making them conditional on the consent of the administrative authorities, this might make the free movement of capital illusory.[210] For this reason, the Court usually finds that a prior declaration, giving 'useful information as to the nature of the planned operation and the actual identity of the declarant',[211] was more proportionate. Therefore, in *Bordessa* the Court said that a prior declaration might be one of the requisite measures which Member States were permitted to take since, unlike prior authorization, it did not entail suspension of the transaction but did still allow the national authorities to exercise effective supervision[212] to uphold public policy and effective supervision to prevent infringements of national law and regulations.[213]

However, the Court has recognized that in some circumstances there may still be a role for prior authorization. For example, in *Commission* v. *Portugal*, one of the *Golden Share* cases, the Court acknowledged that[214] 'certain concerns'[215] could justify 'the retention by Member States of a degree of influence within undertakings that were initially public and subsequently privatised, where those undertakings are active in fields involving the provision of services in the public interest or strategic services' (variously in the banking, insurance, energy, and transport sectors).[216] Therefore, the Court suggested that a prior-authorization requirement could be justified provided it was proportionate, and satisfied good governance requirements, namely the awarding of authorization, had to be based on objective, non-discriminatory criteria which were known in advance to the undertakings concerned, and all persons affected by a restrictive measure had to have a legal remedy available to them.[217] Since this was not made out on the facts, the Portuguese law breached Article 63(1) TFEU.

In *Commission* v. *Spain*,[218] another of the *Golden Share* cases, the Spanish government attempted to justify its prior-authorization requirement on the grounds of 'overriding requirements of the general interest linked to strategic imperatives and the need to ensure continuity in public services'. The Court rejected this on the ground that the companies concerned (a group of banks and a company producing tobacco) had no public-service objectives.

The *Golden Share* cases also provide a good example of the rigorous way the Court has applied the proportionality principle to requirements other than those relating to authorization.[219] For example, in *Commission* v. *Germany (Volkswagen)*[220] the Court

---

[209] Joined Cases C–358 and 416/93 *Bordessa* [1995] ECR I–361.   [210] Paras. 24–5.

[211] Joined Cases C–163, 165 and 250/94 *Sanz de Lera* [1995] ECR I–4830, para. 38. Ongoing provision of information of solvency is also more proportionate than an authorization requirement: Case C–39/11 *VBV* EU:C:2012:327, para. 33.

[212] Para. 27.   [213] Para. 28.

[214] Citing the Commission's Communication on certain legal aspects concerning intra-EU investment, 97/C 220/6 ([1997] OJ C220/15).

[215] But not those concerning systems of property ownership, referred to in Art. 345 TFEU (para. 48).

[216] Case C–367/98 *Commission* v. *Portugal* [2002] ECR I–4731, para. 47; Case C–483/99 *Commission* v. *France* [2002] ECR I–4781, para. 43; and Case C–503/99 *Commission* v. *Belgium* [2002] ECR I–4809, para. 43.

[217] Case C–205/99 *Analir* [2001] ECR I–1271, paras. 35 and 38; Case C–567/07 *Sint Servatius* [2009] ECR I–9021, para. 35.

[218] Case C–463/00 [2003] ECR I–4581.

[219] Cf Joined Cases C–105–107/12 *Staat der Nederlanden* v. *Essent NV* EU:C:2013:677, considered earlier, where the Court adopts a strongly pro-state line and provides no discussion on proportionality.

[220] Case C–112/05 [2007] ECR I–8995.

recognized protection of workers and minority shareholders as potential justifications but said that Germany had been unable to explain why, in order to meet these object- ives, it was appropriate and necessary for the Federal and state authorities to maintain a strengthened and irremovable position in the capital of that company.[221]

Proportionality also defeated the Dutch government's claim that its golden share in the privatized post office was necessary in *Commission v. Netherlands*.[222] The Court recognized that the guarantee of a service of general interest, such as a universal postal service, could constitute an overriding reason in the general interest justifying an obstacle to the free movement of capital.[223] However, the Court found that the special share went beyond what was necessary to safeguard the solvency and continuity of the provider of the universal postal service: the special rights were not limited to the company's activities as provider of a universal postal service. The Court added that the exercise of those special rights was not based on any precise criterion and did not have to be backed up by any statement of reasons, thereby making effective judicial review impossible.[224]

More generally, the Court has insisted that the state had to identify the public interest at stake and formulate in a specific and precise manner the connection between the criteria and the specific powers to which they relate.[225] This can be seen in *Cibrian Fernandez*.[226] German law operated a taxation scheme intended to encourage the building of rental property in Germany (but not outside Germany). The Court found that the scheme was not appropriate: instead of targeting places where the shortage of housing was particu- larly acute, the taxation scheme applied to all categories of rental property 'from the most basic to the most luxurious'. That being the case, the Court said it could not be assumed that 'private investors, who are motivated in particular by financial considerations, will meet the allegedly socio-political objective' of the German tax law.[227]

F. EXPRESS DEROGATIONS

1. INTRODUCTION

One explanation why there is less extensive case law on justifications in the field of cap- ital than in respect of the other freedoms is because of the breadth of the express dero- gations and the fact that the derogations embrace some aspects of the public-interest requirements found elsewhere. Article 65(1) TFEU contains two express derogations, one specific and one general. The specific one relates to tax. Article 65(1)(a) TFEU states that the provisions of Article 63 TFEU are without prejudice to the right of the Member States:

> to apply the relevant provisions of their tax law which distinguish between taxpayers who are not in the same situation with regard to their place of residence or with regard to the place where their capital is invested.

---

[221] Para. 74.

[222] Joined Cases C–282 and 283/04 *Commission v. Netherlands* [2006] ECR I–9141, para. 19.

[223] Para. 38.   [224] Para. 40.

[225] See also Case C–326/07 *Commission v. Italy (Golden Share)* [2009] ECR I–2291, para. 52.

[226] Case C–35/08 *Grundstücksgemeinschaft Busley and Cibrian Fernandez* v. *Finanzamt Stuttgart-Körperschaften* [2009] ECR I–9807.

[227] Para. 32.

Article 65(1)(b) TFEU, replicating Article 4 of Directive 88/361,[228] contains the general derogation. It provides that the provisions of Article 63 TFEU shall be without prejudice to the right of Member States:

> to take all requisite measures to prevent infringements of national law and regulations, in particular in the field of taxation and the prudential supervision of financial institutions, or to lay down procedures for the declaration of capital movements for purposes of administrative or statistical information, or to take measures which are justified on grounds of public policy or public security.

Thus, the express derogations contained in Article 65(1)(b) TFEU are a mixture of the standard public-policy/public-security derogations found elsewhere in the Treaty together with special provisions concerning taxation which reflect the mandatory requirements on the effectiveness of fiscal supervision.[229] Article 65(3) TFEU then adds:

> The measures and procedures referred to in paragraphs 1 and 2 shall not constitute a means of arbitrary discrimination or a disguised restriction on the free movement of capital and payments as defined in Article 63.

This is the equivalent to the second sentence of Article 36 TFEU on goods.[230]

Given the similarities and overlaps between the Article 65 TFEU derogations and the derogations found elsewhere in the Treaty, it is not surprising that the Court draws on its jurisprudence in respect of the other freedoms when interpreting the Article 65 TFEU derogations. For example, in *Casati*[231] the Court said that:

> The administrative measures or penalties [imposed by Member States for breach of national rules] must not go beyond what is strictly necessary, the control procedures must not be conceived in such a way as to restrict the freedom required by the Treaty and they must not be accompanied by a penalty which is so disproportionate to the gravity of the infringement that it becomes an obstacle to the exercise of that freedom.

The Court offered a more detailed list of limitations on the use of the derogations in the *Church of Scientology*[232] case. It said that:

- derogations from the fundamental principle of free movement of capital had to be interpreted strictly, so that their scope could not be determined unilaterally by each Member State without any control by the Union institutions[233]

- derogations could not be misapplied so as, in fact, to serve purely economic ends[234]

- any person affected by a restrictive measure based on such a derogation had to have access to legal redress[235]

- derogations were subject to the principle of proportionality.

The Court then added that restrictions on free movement of capital also had to be subject to the principle of legal certainty. It said that individuals had to be 'apprised of the extent of their rights and obligations deriving from Article [63 TFEU]'.[236] Although legal

---

[228] Joined Cases C–358 and 416/93 *Bordessa* [1995] ECR I–361, para. 22.
[229] Case C–478/98 *Commission v. Belgium (Eurobond)* [2000] ECR I–7587.
[230] See further Ch. 6.   [231] Case 203/80 *Casati* [1981] ECR 2595, para. 27.
[232] Case C–54/99 *Eglise de Scientologie* [2000] ECR I–1335, paras. 17–18.
[233] Citing Case 36/75 *Rutili* [1975] ECR 1219, paras. 26–7.   [234] *Rutili*, para. 30.
[235] Case 222/86 *Unectef v. Heylens* [1987] ECR 4097, paras. 14–15.
[236] Para. 22. See also Case E–3/11 *Pálmi Sigmarsson v. Central Bank of Iceland* [2011] EFTA Ct. Rep. 430.

certainty is a general principle of law, only in respect of free movement of capital is the requirement so clearly stated.

The limited nature of the Article 65 TFEU derogations was emphasized by the Court in *Commission* v. *Portugal,*[237] where Portugal tried to justify its golden share rules on the ground of the need to safeguard Portuguese financial interests. The Court said that unless such reasons fell within the scope of Article 65(1) TFEU (e.g., relating to tax law), 'the general financial interests of a Member State cannot constitute adequate justification'[238] because 'economic grounds can never serve as justification for obstacles prohibited by the Treaty'.[239] Therefore, the Court refused to accept 'the economic policy objectives' raised by the Portuguese government in justification, namely choosing a strategic partner, strengthening the competitive structure of the market, or modernizing and increasing the efficiency of means of production.

Having examined the general rules relating to the express derogations we shall now consider the derogations in turn, starting with the specific provision on tax.

2. ARTICLE 65(1)(a) TFEU: TAX PROVISIONS DISTINGUISHING BETWEEN RESIDENT AND NON-RESIDENT TAXPAYERS OR THE PLACE WHERE THEIR CAPITAL IS INVESTED

Under Article 65(1)(a) TFEU, national laws can continue to distinguish between taxpayers according to their place of residence[240] or the place where their capital is invested.[241] However, as the Court emphasized in *Lenz,*[242] this provision has to be interpreted strictly and does not mean that any tax legislation making a distinction between taxpayers on the listed grounds is automatically compatible with the Treaty. This specific tax derogation is confined to tax laws which were already in existence at the end of 1993.[243]

The Court considered Article 65(1)(a) TFEU in the leading cases of *Verkooijen*[244] and *Manninen.*[245] These cases establish that under this provision[246] the national court must consider:

(1) *the comparability of the situations.* If the situations are not objectively comparable, then the measure is lawful

(2) if, on the other hand, the situations are comparable then the court has to consider whether the different treatment can be *justified by overriding reasons in the general*

---

[237] Case C–367/98 [2002] ECR I–4731.   [238] Para. 52.

[239] Para. 52, citing Case C–265/95 *Commission* v. *France* [1997] ECR I–6959, para. 62 (as regards the free movement of goods) and Case C–398/95 *SETTG* [1997] ECR I–3091, para. 23 (in relation to freedom to provide services).

[240] Case C–512/03 *Blanckaert* [2005] ECR I–7685, para. 41.

[241] Case C–315/02 *Lenz* v. *Finanzlandesdirektion für Tirol* [2004] ECR I–7063, para. 24.

[242] Case C–315/02 *Lenz* [2004] ECR I–7063, para. 26.

[243] 'The Conference affirms that the right of Member States to apply the relevant provisions of their tax law as referred to in Article 73d(1)(a) of this Treaty will apply only with respect to the relevant provisions which exist at the end of 1993. However, this Declaration shall apply only to capital movements between Member States and to payments effected between Member States' (Decl. 7 on Art. 73d EC (now Art. 65 TFEU) annexed to the Final Act of the TEU). The Court does not often mention this limitation or dismisses reference to it: see, e.g., Case C–256/06 *Jäger* v. *Finanzamt Kusel-Landstuhl* [2008] ECR I–123, para. 39.

[244] Case C–35/98 *Verkooijen* [2000] ECR I–4071.

[245] Case C–319/02 *Manninen* [2004] ECR I–7477, para. 29.

[246] Or under the judicially developed public-interest requirements: Case C–377/07 *STEKO* [2009] ECR I–299, para. 30.

interest and whether the steps taken are proportionate. If the differential treatment cannot be justified then the national measure is considered to be arbitrarily discriminatory contrary to Article 65(3) TFEU.

Article 65(1)(a) TFEU therefore effectively codifies[247] the Court's decisions in *Schumacker*[248] (that national provisions which distinguish on the grounds of residence of taxpayers were compatible with Union law provided that they applied to situations which were not objectively comparable) and *Bachmann*[249] (that national tax law could be justified by overriding reasons in the general interest, in particular in relation to the cohesion of the tax system).[250] However, there is one major difference: in *Schumacker*, a case decided under the free movement of workers, the Court considered the question of comparability at the stage of establishing whether there was a breach of Article 45 TFEU. Generally, in the free movement of capital case law, this question is considered at the defence stage, i.e., after it has been established that there is a breach of Article 63 TFEU.[251]

In respect of the first question, comparability, the Court will look carefully to see whether the situations of the different taxpayers are objectively comparable. Its approach can be seen in *Blanckaert*,[252] concerning a Dutch law which appeared to favour resident over non-resident taxpayers in terms of tax credits. In fact the Court found that the distinction was not between residents and non-residents but between those who were insured under the Dutch social security scheme and those who were not (with only the former potentially benefiting from a tax credit where their deductions exceeded their contributions). The Court found that the situation of the two groups of taxpayers was not comparable and so the national rules fell within the scope of the derogation.[253]

More usually, however, the Court does find that the two situations are comparable. For example, in *Persche*[254] the Court said that the Portuguese charity and German charities were in a comparable situation in terms of their tax treatment, as was the situation in *Hollman*,[255] where the Court said that non-residents selling property in Portugal were in a comparable situation to a resident selling property. Likewise, in *Bouanich*[256] the Court said there was no objective difference between the situation of residents and non-residents as to justify different treatment where Swedish law provided that in respect of a share repurchase by a company, payments made to resident shareholders were taxed as

---

[247] A point the Court itself noted in *Verkooijn*. It thus rejected the arguments of the intervening governments that it was a new invention.

[248] Case C–279/93 [1995] ECR I–225, considered further in Ch. 8.

[249] Case C–204/90 *Bachmann* [1992] ECR I–249.

[250] Cases such as Case C–118/96 *Safir* [1998] ECR I–1897 and Case C–136/00 *Danner* [2002] ECR I–8147 (considered in Ch. 11), which might have benefited from the provision, were decided under the services provisions.

[251] Although cf. Case C–376/03 *D* v. *Inspecteur van de Belastingdienst/Particulieren/Ondernemingen buitenland te Heerlen* [2005] ECR I–5821, paras. 34–8, where, following *Schumacker*, the question of comparability went to determining whether there had been a breach of Art. 63 TFEU in the first place. Since the Court considered the situations of the resident and the non-resident taxpayer not to be comparable there was no breach of Art. 63 TFEU.

[252] Case C–512/03 *Blanckaert* [2005] ECR I–7685, para. 39.

[253] See also Case C–194/06 *Orange European Smallcap Fund* [2008] ECR I–3747, para. 65.

[254] Case C–318/07 *Hein Persche* [2009] ECR I–359, para. 50.

[255] Case C–443/06 *Hollmann* v. *Fazenda Pública* [2007] ECR I–8491, para. 53. See also Case C–562/07 *Commission* v. *Spain (taxation of capital gains)* [2009] ECR I–9553, para. 59; Joined Cases C–338–347/11 *Santander Asset Management SGIIC SA* v. *Directeur des residents à l'étranger et des services généraux* EU:C:2014:286, para. 44; Case C–489/13 *Verest* v. *Belgian State* EU:C:2014:2210, para. 32.

[256] Case C–265/04 *Bouanich* v. *Skatteverket* [2006] ECR I–923, para. 41.

a capital gain with a right to deduct the cost of acquisition, while equivalent payments to non-residents were taxed as a dividend without there being a right to deduct the cost of acquisition.[257]

If the Court has found that the situations of the two groups of taxpayers are comparable, it then looks at the second question, namely whether the restriction can be justified by an overriding reason in the general interest.[258] The most common justification invoked is the threat to the cohesion of the national tax system. In *Weidert*[259] the Court repeated the *Bachmann*[260] principle that there needed to be a direct link between the tax advantage (the tax relief granted to the taxpayer resident in the home state) for the acquisition of shares in companies established in that Member State and an offsetting fiscal levy. As the Court pointed out, on the facts the tax advantage on the acquisition of shares was not offset by the taxation of the dividends which those companies subsequently paid, not least because there was no guarantee that the companies in which the investment was made would pay dividends.[261] There was therefore no direct link between the tax advantage and the offsetting fiscal levy and so the Article 65(1)(a) TFEU derogation could not be relied on.[262]

Another justification recognized by the Court is the effectiveness of fiscal supervision.[263] In *Stauffer* the Court said that a host Member State was entitled to ascertain in a clear and precise manner whether the body (in this case a charitable foundation) met the conditions imposed by national law to be entitled to the tax exemption available to equivalent national foundations and to monitor its effective management by, for example, requiring the submission of annual accounts and an activity report. However, while such checks might prove difficult in the case of foundations established in other Member States, disadvantages of a purely administrative nature were not sufficient to justify a refusal by the home state to grant tax exemptions to the out-of-state charitable foundation.

There are, however, a number of justifications which the Court has rejected.[264] For example, in *Lenz*[265] the Court said that a reduction in tax receipts could not be regarded as an overriding reason in the public interest; and in *Commission v. France*[266] the Court said that a general presumption of tax avoidance or fraud was not sufficient to 'justify a fiscal measure which compromises the objectives of the Treaty'. These cases show that the Court adopts a fairly strict approach to justification and, even where it recognizes the public interest, usually finds it is not justified on the facts.

Having considered the specific tax derogation we turn now to examine the general derogations.

---

[257] Paras. 40–1. See also Case C–377/07 *STEKO* [2009] ECR I–299, para. 33; Case C–540/07 *Commission v. Italy* [2009] ECR I–10983, paras. 51–4; Case C–182/08 *Glaxo Wellcome* [2009] ECR I–8591, paras. 69–74; Joined Cases C–10, 14 and 17/14 *Miljoen v. Staatssecretaris van Finaciën* EU:C:2015:608, paras. 65–74.

[258] Case C–256/06 *Jäger* [2008] ECR I–123, para. 52.

[259] Case C–242/03 *Ministre des Finances* v. *Weidert and Paulus* [2004] ECR I–7379.

[260] Case C–204/90 *Bachmann* [1992] ECR I–249, considered in Ch. 8.   [261] Para. 23.

[262] Cf. Case C–250/08 *Commission* v. *Belgium* [2011] ECR I–12341 and Case C–322/11 *K* EU:C:2013:716 (where cohesion justification was made out and the national rules were found proportionate).

[263] Case C–386/04 *Walter Stauffer* [2006] ECR I–8203, para. 47.

[264] See also the more detailed discussion on these justifications in Ch. 11, especially in respect of the justification concerning the fight against tax evasion (unsuccessfully raised in Case C–540/07 *Commission v. Italy* [2009] ECR I–10983, paras. 58–9 in respect of intra-EU movement but successfully raised in respect of movements of capital between Italy and EEA countries).

[265] Case C–315/02 *Lenz* [2004] ECR I–7063, para. 40.

[266] Case C–334/02 *Commission v. France* [2004] ECR I–2229, para. 27.

3. ARTICLE 65(1)(b) TFEU: GENERAL DEROGATIONS

3.1 'All requisite measures to prevent infringements of national law and regulations, in particular in the field of taxation and the prudential supervision of financial institutions'

One of the (non-exhaustive) list of named areas in which Member States can take 'requisite measures' to prevent infringements of national law is the 'field of taxation'. As with Article 65(1)(a) TFEU, this includes measures intended to ensure effective fiscal supervision and to combat illegal activities such as tax evasion.[267] This derogation was successfully relied on by the Austrian government in *Sandoz*.[268] It will be recalled that the case concerned stamp duty payable under Austrian law on a loan taken out by an Austrian company from a Belgian company. No tax was payable under Belgian law. The Court said that the main objective of the Austrian law was to ensure equal treatment for those natural or legal persons resident in Austria entering into a contract for a loan. The Court continued that since the effect of the measure was to compel individuals to pay the duty, 'it prevents taxable persons from evading the requirements of domestic tax legislation through the exercise of freedom of movement of capital'.[269] The Court added that since the Austrian rule applied to all borrowers resident in Austria without distinction as to nationality or the place where the loan was contracted, the Austrian legislation did not constitute a means of arbitrary discrimination. The Austrian rule was therefore lawful.

Sandoz can be compared with the *Eurobond* case,[270] where the Court said that 'a general presumption of tax evasion or tax fraud cannot justify a fiscal measure' especially where the measure consists in 'an outright prohibition on the exercise of a fundamental freedom' guaranteed by Article 63 TFEU.[271] Therefore, by prohibiting the acquisition by Belgian residents of securities of a loan issued abroad, Belgium breached Article 63 TFEU.

While taxation and the prudential supervision of financial institutions are expressly listed as the grounds on which Member States can take all requisite measures to prevent infringements of national law and regulations, the non-exhaustive nature of the list in Article 65(1)(b) was emphasized in *Bordessa*,[272] where the Court said that other measures were also permitted insofar as they were designed to prevent 'illegal activities of comparable seriousness, such as money laundering, drug trafficking or terrorism'.[273]

3.2 To lay down procedures for the declaration of capital movements for the purposes of administrative or statistical information

There has been no case law on this provision giving guidance on how it is to be construed. However, it is remarkable for its breadth and for the fact that there is no equivalent provision in respect of the other freedoms.

3.3 Public Policy and Public Security

The Court has drawn on the case law from the other freedoms to give meaning to the terms public policy and public security. For example, in *Church of Scientology*[274] the Court relied on the persons case law[275] to establish that while Member States were still, in

---

[267] Case C–478/98 *Commission v. Belgium (Eurobond)* [2000] ECR I–7587, para. 38.

[268] Case C–439/97 *Sandoz* [1999] ECR I–7041.

[269] Para. 24. See also Joined Cases C–155 and 157/08 *Passenheim-van Schoot* [2009] ECR I–5093.

[270] Case C–478/98 *Commission v. Belgium (Eurobond)* [2000] ECR I–7587.   [271] Para. 45.

[272] Joined Cases C–358 and 416/93 *Bordessa* [1995] ECR I–361.   [273] Para. 21.

[274] Case C–54/99 *Association Eglise de Scientologie* [2000] ECR I–1335, para. 17.

[275] See further Ch. 12.

principle, 'free to determine the requirements of public policy and public security in the light of their national needs', these grounds had to be interpreted strictly, which meant that public policy and public security could be relied on only if there was 'a genuine and sufficiently serious threat to a fundamental interest of society';[276] that the steps taken were necessary only for the protection of the interests which they were intended to guarantee; and that those objectives could not be attained by less restrictive measures.[277] It is this provision which was relied on by the Cypriot government in 2013 to justify imposing strict limits on capital movements following the savers' 'bail-in' as a condition for the troika 'bail-out'.

The *Church of Scientology* case concerned a French rule making direct foreign investment subject to prior authorization. As we have seen, the Court often finds that systems of prior authorization are not necessary, favouring instead a system based on declarations.[278] However, where a genuine and sufficiently serious threat to public policy or public security is at stake, a system of prior declaration might prove inadequate to counter the threat.[279] The Court said that given the difficulty, in the case of direct foreign investments, of identifying and blocking capital once it has entered another Member State, this might make it necessary to prevent transactions which would adversely affect public policy or public security by using a system of prior authorization. However, because, on the facts, prior authorization was required for every direct foreign investment thought to represent a threat to public policy and public security, without any more detailed definition,[280] and investors were given no indication as to the specific circumstances in which prior authorization was required, the Court found the French system to contravene the principle of legal certainty and so breached Article 63(1) TFEU.[281]

In *Albore*[282] the Court drew on its goods case law to define public security in the context of an Italian rule requiring foreigners to have authorization prior to living in certain areas of military importance. Having noted that public security included the external security of a Member State,[283] the Court said that a mere reference to the requirements of defence of the national territory was not sufficient to justify discrimination on grounds of nationality.[284] It continued that the position would be different only if it were demonstrated, for each area to which the restriction applied, that non-discriminatory treatment of the nationals of all the Member States would expose Italian military interests to real, specific, and serious risks which could not be countered by less-restrictive procedures.[285]

The goods case law also inspired the Court in *Commission* v. *Belgium*.[286] The case concerning the Belgian government's golden shares in two energy companies.[287] These shares entitled it to oppose any transfer, use as security, or change in the intended destination of lines and conduits or of certain other strategic assets and certain management decisions regarded as contrary to the guidelines for the country's energy policy. The Belgian government justified its golden shares on the public-security ground of safeguarding energy supplies in the event of a crisis, which, following the goods case *Campus Oil*,[288]

---

[276] Citing Case 36/75 *Rutili* [1975] ECR 1219, para. 28, and Case C–348/96 *Calfa* [1999] ECR I–11, para. 21.

[277] Case C–54/99 *Eglise de Scientologie* [2000] ECR I–1335, para. 18.   [278] Para. 19.

[279] Para. 20. Cf. Case C–567/07 *Sint Servatius* [2009] ECR I–9021, para. 28, where the Court found that the need to promote social housing did not satisfy the public-policy derogation.

[280] Para. 21.   [281] Para. 22.   [282] Case C–423/98 [2000] ECR I–5965.

[283] Citing Case C–367/89 *Richardt* [1991] ECR I–4621, para. 22, considered in Ch. 6.

[284] Case C–423/98 [2000] ECR I–5965, para. 21.   [285] Para. 22.

[286] Case C–503/99 *Commission* v. *Belgium* [2002] ECR I–4809.

[287] For a more detailed discussion on the background to the *Golden Share* cases, see D. Wyatt and A. Dashwood, *European Union Law*, 5th edn (London: Sweet & Maxwell, 2006), 854–63.

[288] Case 72/83 *Campus Oil* [1984] ECR 2727.

the Court had accepted as a legitimate public interest,[289] provided that the legislation enabled Belgium to ensure a minimum level of energy supplies in the event of a genuine and sufficiently serious threat,[290] and that the steps taken were proportionate.

On the facts, the Court found the Belgian rules to be justified and proportionate because the scheme was based, not on a prior authorization, but on *ex post facto* opposition. This procedure generally gave the energy companies a free hand in decision-making unless and until the government decided to intervene. Where the government did intervene—and the area for intervention was limited to cases in which the objectives of energy policy were jeopardized—the legislation provided that the government had to adhere to strict time limits, give reasons for intervention, and be subject to effective review by the courts.[291] Therefore, the Court said, the Belgian scheme made it possible to guarantee, on the basis of objective criteria which were subject to judicial review, the effective availability of the lines and conduits providing the main infrastructure for the domestic conveyance of energy products. This enabled Belgium to intervene with a view to ensuring compliance with the public-service obligations incumbent on the energy companies while at the same time observing the requirements of legal certainty.

This conclusion can be contrasted with the Court's decision in another *Golden Share* case, *Commission v. France (Elf-Aquitane)*,[292] which concerned a French rule requiring prior authorization of any direct or indirect shareholding in Elf-Aquitane over and above certain limits. The Court said that because the investors were given no indication as to the specific, objective circumstances in which prior authorization would be granted or refused, the system was contrary to the principle of legal certainty.[293] It added that such a wide discretionary power constituted 'a serious interference with the free movement of capital, and may have the effect of excluding it altogether'.[294] Consequently, the Court found the French system disproportionate.

G. CONCLUSIONS

With the advent of EMU, free movement of capital is no longer the poor relation. It is starting to attract the judicial and academic attention that might be expected of a provision so central to the creation of the internal market. Since 1992 the number of cases decided under Article 63(1) TFEU has increased significantly. The striking feature of this case law is the Court's willingness to apply principles developed in respect of the other freedoms, notably the freedom to provide services, to shape its jurisprudence on capital.

Free movement of capital is the fourth and final 'freedom'. However, negative integration can only go so far. A single market needs positive integration to ensure that it works effectively. Chapter 15 examines the problems facing the Union in deciding whether to regulate, what form that regulation might take, and how best to deliver on particular policy goals.

---

[289] *Campus Oil*, n. 288, para. 46. [290] Para. 48.
[291] Paras. 49–51. Cf. Case C–463/00 *Commission v. Spain* [2003] ECR I–4581, paras. 78–80 and Case C–244/11 *Commission v. Greece* EU:C:2012:694, paras. 83–6, where these conditions were not satisfied.
[292] Case C–483/99 [2002] ECR I–4781.
[293] Para. 50. See also Case C–463/00 *Commission v. Spain* [2003] ECR I–4581, paras. 76–7.
[294] Para. 51.

FURTHER READING

The context

J. SNELL, 'The varieties of capitalism and the limits of European integration' (2012) 13 *Cambridge Yearbook of European Legal Studies* 415.

Free movement of capital

L. FLYNN, 'Coming of age: The free movement of capital case law 1993–2002' (2002) 39 *CMLRev.* 773.

HM Government, *The Single Market: Financial Services and the Free Movement of Capital, Balance of Competence Review* (2014).

P. OLIVER and J.-P. BACHÉ, 'Free movement of capital between the Member States: Recent developments' (1989) 26 *CMLRev.* 61.

S. PEERS, 'Free movement of capital: Learning lessons or slipping on spilt milk?' in C. Barnard and J. Scott (eds.), *The Law of the Single European Market: Unpacking the premises* (Oxford: Hart Publishing, 2002).

J. SNELL, 'Free movement of capital: Evolution as a non-linear process' in P. Craig and G. de Búrca (eds.), *The Evolution of EU Law* (Oxford: OUP, 2011).

J. USHER, 'Capital movements and the Treaty on European Union' (1992) 12 *YEL* 35.

J. USHER, 'The evolution of the free movement of capital' (2008) 31 *Fordham Intl. LJ* 1533.

J. USHER, *The Law of Money and Financial Services in the European Community* (Oxford: Clarendon Press, 2000).

Golden Share cases

C. GERNER-BEUERLE, 'Shareholders between the market and the state: The VW law and other interventions in the market economy' (2012) 49 *CMLRev.* 97.

Capital and taxation

Commission Communication, 'Removing cross-border tax obstacles for EU citizens', COM(2010) 769.

B. J. M. TERRA and P. J. WATTEL, *European Tax Law*, 5th edn (Alphen aan den Rijn: Kluwer Law International, 2008).

Free movement of capital and freedom of establishment

W. SCHÖN, 'Free movement of capital and freedom of establishment', Max Planck Institute for Tax Law and Public Finance Working Paper 2015-03.

PART V
COMPLETING
THE SINGLE MARKET

15
REGULATING
THE INTERNAL MARKET

A. INTRODUCTION

In 1957 the European Economic Community set itself the task of creating a common market with the attainment of the four freedoms at its core. This book has concentrated on the Treaty provisions intended to achieve this objective and their interpretation by the Court of Justice. While in theory these Treaty provisions should have been sufficient to allow for successful regulatory competition—where states compete to attract products and factors of production—in practice regulatory competition has not produced the result anticipated, owing to the absence of the necessary conditions for such competition to function as the textbooks would predict. This market failure, together with the derogations provided by the Treaty and the mandatory/public interest requirements developed by the Court, meant that there would always be a need for harmonization legislation enacted by the Union institutions. Such harmonization would help the market to function properly while at the same time protecting vital public interests such as consumer protection and public health. Harmonization was always envisaged, even by the original Treaty: the Treaty of Rome gave wide-ranging powers to the (then) Community to enact secondary legislation.

By setting harmonized standards, EU law enables goods, persons, services, and capital to move freely. When viewed from this perspective, harmonization is the complement of the four freedoms. However, it remains a sensitive matter both legally and politically. For example, to what extent should a single harmonized standard set by the EU replace diverse national standards? And at what level should that standard be set—at the standard of the lowest state in the EU, at the highest, or somewhere in between? The aim of this chapter is to examine the power to harmonize (i.e., the power to adopt legislative acts and the possibility to supplement them by non-legislative acts), the different approaches to harmonization adopted by the Union, and the problem of implementation and enforcement of Union standards.

B. THE POWER TO HARMONIZE

1. INTRODUCTION

The 1985 Single Market White Paper proposed the adoption of about 300 measures to eliminate the three principal barriers to trade (physical, technical, and fiscal) identified in the White Paper.[1] The problem facing the EU was how to realize these measures within a relatively short time frame when the principal legal bases provided by the EEC Treaty (Article 100 EEC (now Article 115 TFEU) and Article 235 EEC (now Article 352 TFEU)) required unanimous voting. The Single European Act 1986 provided an answer. It introduced a new legal basis, Article 100a EEC (now Article 114 TFEU), with qualified-majority voting (QMV). Given the importance of Article 114 TFEU to the attainment of the single market, it is this legal basis that we shall focus on.[2]

2. ARTICLE 114 TFEU

2.1 The Conditions to be Satisfied under Article 114 TFEU

Article 114(1) TFEU provides 'Save where otherwise provided in the Treaty' the European Parliament and Council, acting in accordance with the ordinary legislative procedure, are to adopt 'measures' (not just directives[3]) 'for the approximation of the provisions laid down by law, regulation, or administrative action in Member States which have as their

---

[1] See further Ch. 1.

[2] The internal market is identified as an area of 'shared' competence by Art 4(2) TFEU. According to Art. 2(2) TFEU, 'When the Treaties confer on the Union a competence shared with the Member States in a specific area, the Union and the Member States may legislate and adopt legally binding acts in that area. The Member States shall exercise their competence to the extent that the Union has not exercised its competence. The Member States shall again exercise their competence to the extent that the Union has decided to cease exercising its competence.' See also Decl. 18.

[3] Although a Declaration annexed to the SEA requires the Commission to give precedence to the use of directives, in practice this is not always the case (see, e.g., the regulation at issue in Case C–66/04 *UK v. EP and Council (smoke flavourings)* [2005] ECR I–10553). Cf. Art. 115 TFEU, which allows for the use of directives only.

object the establishment and functioning of the internal market'.[4] There are therefore two limits to the use of Article 114 TFEU. First, resort to Article 114 TFEU can be made where no other specific legal basis applies.[5] In other words Article 114 TFEU, a general provision, is a residual legal basis (although at times this seems to be honoured more in the breach than the observance). The importance of this limitation was, however, emphasized in *Commission* v. *Council (VAT)*,[6] where the Court said that if the Treaty contained a more specific provision that was capable of constituting the legal basis for the measure, the measure had to be founded on that provision. Therefore, on the facts, the Court ruled that two Union measures intended to consolidate and strengthen administrative cooperation in the field of VAT should not have been adopted under Article 114(1) TFEU but under the (more specific) tax legal bases, Article 113 TFEU.

The second limit on the use of Article 114 TFEU is that the measures adopted under Article 114 TFEU must be for approximation of laws (also known as harmonization).[7] Therefore, measures which do not harmonize cannot be adopted under Article 114 TFEU. This can be seen in *ECS*,[8] where the Parliament and the Commission argued that a regulation establishing a European Cooperative Society should have been adopted on the basis of Article 114 TFEU and not Article 352 TFEU. The Court disagreed, reasoning that because the national laws remain unchanged by the regulation (the aim of the measure was to create a new form of cooperative society in addition to national forms) the regulation did not lead to 'approximation' of national laws and so Article 114 TFEU could not be used.

In its original version, the procedure laid down by Article 114(1) TFEU was a QMV and cooperation with the European Parliament; since Maastricht the co-decision procedure has applied, now called the ordinary legislative procedure. However, Article 114(2) TFEU expressly provides that Article 114(1) TFEU cannot be used to adopt fiscal measures,[9] nor measures relating to the free movement of persons, nor measures relating to the rights and interests of employed persons—areas considered to be too sensitive to be the subject of QMV.[10]

The Union has adopted a large number of directives under Article 114 TFEU ranging from rules on the financial markets to directives on illegal logging, technical standards, and imports of seal products. Case Study 15.1 shows how Article 114 TFEU has been used to regulate tobacco production and advertising and the problems this has generated.

---

[4] See also Art. 26(3) TFEU giving the Council the power, on a proposal from the Commission, to determine the guidelines and conditions necessary to ensure balanced progress in all the sectors concerned, and the Commission's duty in Art. 27 TFEU to take into account the extent of the effort that certain economies showing differences in development will have to sustain for the establishment of the internal market. It may propose appropriate provisions. If these provisions take the form of derogations, they must be of a temporary nature and must cause the least possible disturbance to the functioning of the internal market.

[5] The Lisbon Treaty removed the reference in Art. 95 EC (ex Art. 100a EEC) to 'By way of derogation from Article 94 (ex Article 100)'. The reordering of Arts. 94–5 EC (Art. 95 EC has become Art. 114 TFEU and Art. 94 EC has become Art. 115 TFEU) reflected what happened in practice: Art. 114 TFEU had become the principal legal basis of the two.

[6] Case C–533/03 *Commission* v. *Council (VAT)* [2006] ECR I–1025, para. 45.

[7] The Court appears to use the two terms interchangeably: see, e.g., Case C–217/04 *UK* v. *EP and Council (European Network and Information Security Agency (ENISA))* [2006] ECR I–3771, para. 43.

[8] See, e.g., Case C–436/03 *EP and Commission* v. *Council (ECS)* [2006] ECR I–3733.

[9] In Case C–533/03 *Commission* v. *Council (VAT)* [2006] ECR I–1025, para. 47 the Court said that the words 'fiscal measures' covered not only all areas of taxation, without drawing any distinction between the types and duties or taxes concerned, but also all aspects of taxation, whether material rules or procedural rules.

[10] Pre-Lisbon, measures adopted in these fields were assumed to be subject to unanimous vote under Art. 94 EC due to the reference in Art. 95(1) EC to the phrase 'By way of derogation from Article 94'. However, it may well be that the expansion of Union competence into the areas listed in Art. 114(2) TFEU means that specific legal bases should be applied instead.

Case Study 15.1: REGULATING TOBACCO PRODUCTION AND ADVERTISING

The health risks associated with smoking have long been a matter of concern for the Member States. Even before the EU was given express powers over public health by the Maastricht Treaty, the Council, and the Representatives of the Governments of the Member States issued a resolution on a programme of action against cancer in 1986.[11] This led to the adoption of Directives 89/622/EEC on tobacco labelling[12] and 90/239/EEC on the maximum tar yield of cigarettes,[13] both based on Article 114 TFEU and supported by references to the Council resolution. According to the preambles to the directives, Article 114 TFEU was used because the differences between the laws, regulations, and administrative provisions were likely 'to constitute barriers to trade and to impede the establishment and operation of the internal market'.[14]

Directive 89/622 on tobacco labelling required the health warning 'Tobacco seriously damages health' to be displayed on all packets of tobacco products. This warning had to cover at least 4 per cent of each large surface of the packet. Directive 90/239 on tar yield provided that the tar yield could not be greater than 15 mg per cigarette as from 31 December 1992 and 12 mg from 31 September 1997, with Greece being given a special exemption until 31 December 2006. Since both directives laid down minimum standards, Member States could require a physically larger warning or lower levels of tar for domestically produced cigarettes. However, if a Member State did impose stricter standards on its own producers, the 'free movement' clause[15] required the state to allow cigarettes produced in other Member States which complied only with the minimum standards laid down in the directive to be sold in its country.

Directives 89/622/EEC and 90/239/EEC were amended a number of times and were eventually repealed, recast, and amended by Directive 2001/37/EC[16] on the manufacture, presentation, and sale of tobacco products (the Tobacco Control Directive), which was based on both Article 114 TFEU and Article 207 TFEU on the common commercial policy. This directive reduced maximum tar yields still further (to 10 mg), for the first time set maximum nicotine and carbon monoxide levels,[17] and imposed stricter labelling requirements, including an increase in size of the health warning: the general warning (e.g., 'Smoking kills/Smoking can kill') now had to cover at least 30 per cent of the surface area of the packet,[18] and an additional warning (e.g., 'Smokers die younger') had to cover at least 40 per cent of the surface area.[19] Like its predecessors, Directive 2001/37 also contained a free movement clause.[20] As we shall see, the validity of this directive, or at least parts of it, was unsuccessfully challenged in *Ex p. BAT*,[21] *Swedish Match*,[22] and *Arnold André*.[23]

Directive 2014/40 on the manufacture, presentation, and sale of tobacco and related products (such as e-cigarettes), also adopted under the single market legal bases including Article 114 TFEU, repealed Directive 2001/37 in May 2016.[24] The size of the warning and picture

---

[11] [1986] OJ C184/19.   [12] [1989] OJ L158/30.   [13] [1990] OJ L137/36.

[14] See preamble to Dir. 89/622 ([1989] OJ L158/30).

[15] Considered further in Case C–11/92 *R. v. Secretary of State for Health, ex p. Gallaher Ltd* [1993] ECR I–3545.

[16] [2001] OJ L194/26. See also Commission Dec. 2003/641/EC on the use of colour photographs or other illustrations as health warnings on tobacco packages ([2003] OJ L226/24).

[17] Art. 3(1)–(2).   [18] Art. 5(2)(a) and (5).   [19] Art. 5(2)(b) and (5).   [20] Art. 13.

[21] Case C–491/01 *The Queen v. Secretary of State for Health, ex p. British American Tobacco (Investments) Ltd and Imperial Tobacco Ltd (BAT)* [2002] ECR I–114 TFEU. See also Case T–311/00 *British American Tobacco (Investments) Ltd v. Commission* [2002] ECR II–2181 on access to the Commission's documents on which it based its proposal.

[22] Case C–210/03 *R. v. Secretary of State for Health, ex p. Swedish Match* [2004] ECR I–11893.

[23] Case C–434/02 *Arnold André GmbH & Co. KG v. Landrat des Kreises Herford* [2004] ECR I–11825.

[24] [2014] OJ L127/1.

has increased still further: it must cover 65 per cent of the front and back of the packet. It also bans flavoured cigarettes, such as fruit and menthol, and slim, lipstick-style packaging intended to encourage young women to smoke. Health warnings will be mandatory on e-cigarette packages. The choice of legal basis was challenged in *Philip Morris*.[25] In *Poland v. Parliament and Council*[26] the Polish government challenged the use of Article 114 TFEU as a legal basis for banning menthol cigarettes, and argued that the ban on marketing menthol cigarettes breaches the principles of subsidiarity and proportionality. *Pillbox 38*[27] challenged the obligations on e-cigarette manufacturers and/or retailers for breaches of the Charter, and the principles of subsidiarity and proportionality. A yellow card (see Section 4) had been raised by a number of Member States' parliaments but insufficient to trigger the yellow card procedure. The same Advocate General heard all three cases and rejected all the claims, as did the Court of Justice.[28]

At much the same time as the original tobacco labelling and tar yield directives were adopted, the 'Television without Frontiers' (TWF) Directive 89/552/EEC was also enacted[29] (now called the Audiovisual Media Services Directive (AVMS) 2010/13/EU), which, according to Article 9(1)(d), prohibited 'all forms of audiovisual commercial communications for cigarettes and other tobacco products'.[30] With the TWF/AVMS Directive in place, campaigners called for a ban on other forms of cigarette and tobacco advertising that took place away from the point of sale (e.g., on the radio, posters, billboards, and in newspapers and magazines) as well as a ban on sponsorship by tobacco companies (especially sports sponsorship). This was the essence of Directive 98/43/EC on Tobacco Advertising.[31] The directive, which was adopted by a majority of Member States (Austria and Germany voted against, Denmark and Spain abstained), set a (high) minimum standard,[32] banning all forms of advertising and sponsorship of tobacco products.[33] However, unlike Directive 89/622 on tobacco labelling and Directive 90/289 on tar yield, Directive 98/43 did not contain a free movement clause for products which met its provisions. The directive was due to have been implemented by 30 July 2001 but it made provision for delayed implementation for specific sectors: one year for the press, two years for sponsorship, and, 'in exceptional circumstances' existing tobacco sponsorship of events or activities organized at world level (primarily formula one racing) would have continued until 2006.[34]

[25] Case C–547/14 *Philip Morris* v. *Secretary of State* EU:C:2016:325. Kokott AG's Opinion was delivered on 23 Dec. 2015 (EU:C:2015:853).

[26] Case C–358/14 *Poland* v. *Parliament and Council* EU:C:2016:323.

[27] Case C–477/14 *Pillbox 38 (UK) Ltd, trading as 'Totally Wicked'* v. *Secretary of State for Health* EU:C:2016:324. Kokott AG's Opinion was delivered on 23 Dec. 2015 (EU:C:2015:854).

[28] The Court's decisions were handed down on 4 May 2016.

[29] [1989] OJ L298/23 repeated and replaced by Dir. 2010/13/EU ([2010] OJ L95/1). See Case Study 11.2 for further details about this directive. The directive was based on Art. 53(1) TFEU on the free movement of persons and Art. 62 TFEU. The ban on radio advertising of tobacco was introduced by Dir. 2003/33 ([2003] OJ L152/16), to mirror the television ban and this was an influential factor in persuading the Court to uphold the validity of Dir. 2003/33 in Case C–380/03 *Germany* v. *European Parliament and Council (Tobacco Advertising II)* [2006] ECR I–11573, paras. 64 and 70.

[30] As a result of changes introduced by Dir. 2007/65 to Dir. 89/552, audiovisual media services or programmes are not to be sponsored by undertakings whose principal activity is the manufacture or sale of cigarettes and other tobacco products (Art. 10(2) of Dir. 2010/13/EU). In addition, Art. 11(4) provides that where states allow product placement in programmes, these are not to contain product placement of tobacco products or cigarettes or product placement from undertakings whose principal activity is the manufacture or sale of cigarettes and other tobacco products.

[31] [1998] OJ L213/9.

[32] Art. 5. Minimum standards directives are considered in more detail at nn. 244–56.

[33] Art. 5(1).   [34] Art. 6(3).

Although Directive 98/43 was adopted under the internal-market legal bases Articles 53(1), 62, and 114 TFEU, it was widely thought to be a public-health measure. Article 168 TFEU had been introduced by the Maastricht Treaty to provide the Union with express competence in the field of public health. The competence was, however, specifically limited by Article 168(5) TFEU, which provided that the Council can adopt 'incentive measures designed to protect and improve human health,... excluding any harmonisation of the laws and regulations of the Member States'.

The Union's competence to act in this sensitive area and its choice of legal basis lay at the heart of Germany's successful challenge to Directive 98/43 in *Tobacco Advertising I*,[35] where the Court said that Article 168(5) TFEU did not mean that harmonizing measures adopted on the basis of other provisions of the Treaty could not have any impact on the protection of human health.[36] Some support for this view can be found in Article 114(3) TFEU,[37] which provides that the Commission, when making proposals, must 'take as a base a high level of protection, taking account in particular of any new development based on scientific facts'.[38] In subsequent cases, the Court went further, saying that the Union legislature could not be prevented from relying on Article 114 TFEU 'on the ground that public health protection is a *decisive* factor in the choices to be made'.[39] However, the Court added in *Tobacco Advertising I* that other Articles of the Treaty could not be used 'as a legal basis in order to circumvent the express exclusion of harmonization laid down in Article [165 TFEU]'.[40]

Having implied that the directive might have been a disguised health measure,[41] the Court made no further reference to the public-health provision.[42] Instead, it focused on the question of the circumstances in which Article 114 TFEU could be used to adopt EU legislation.[43] It said that where the Union measure was genuinely[44] intended to improve the conditions for the establishment and functioning of the internal market,[45] and actually had that effect,[46] then Article 114(1) TFEU could be used in two, alternative,[47] situations:

- where the legislation contributes to the elimination of likely obstacles to the exercise of fundamental freedoms

---

[35] Case C–376/98 *Germany* v. *European Parliament and Council* [2000] ECR I–8419. See also Case C–74/99 *R.* v. *Secretary of State for Health, ex p. Imperial Tobacco* [2000] ECR I–8599.

[36] Para. 78.

[37] On the legal effects of Art. 114(3) TFEU: Case C–350/03 *Schulte* v. *Deutsche Bausparkasse Badenia AG* [2005] ECR I–9215, para. 61.

[38] Though this does not necessarily have to be the highest standard that is technically possible. Case C–284/95 *Safety HI-Tech* v. *S & T Srl* [1998] ECR I–4301, para. 49. See also Art. 9 TFEU, which requires the Union to take a range of values into account, including public health and Art. 168(1) TFEU, which says that a high level of human health shall be ensured in the definition and implementation of all Union policies and activities.

[39] See, e.g., Case C–380/03 *Germany* v. *European Parliament and Council (Tobacco Advertising II)* [2006] ECR I–11573, para. 39 (emphasis added) and paras. 92–8; Case C–58/08 *R. (on the application of Vodafone Ltd)* v. *Secretary of State for Business, Enterprise and Regulatory Reform* [2010] ECR I–4999, para. 36 (consumer protection).

[40] Case C–376/98 *Tobacco Advertising I* [2000] ECR I–8419, para. 79.

[41] For a discussion on why the Member States agreed to a measure which apparently exceeded the limits they had chosen to lay down in Art. 168(5) TFEU, see G. de Búrca, 'The tobacco judgment: Political will versus constitutional limits' in *The ECJ's Tobacco Advertising Judgment*, CELS Occasional Paper No. 5, 2000, 13–15.

[42] Case C–380/03 *Tobacco Advertising II* [2006] ECR I–11573.

[43] Case C–376/98 *Tobacco Advertising I* [2000] ECR I–8419, paras. 83–4 and 95.

[44] Para. 84.   [45] Para. 83.

[46] Although not very clearly stated in *Tobacco Advertising I*, it can be seen in paras. 84, 102, 104, and 107–8.

[47] Case C–380/03 *Tobacco Advertising II* [2006] ECR I–11573, para. 67.

• where the legislation contributes to the removal of appreciable distortions of competition which are likely to arise from the diverse national rules.[48]

We examine in more detail the circumstances in which Article 114 TFEU can be used in Section 2.2. On the facts of *Tobacco Advertising I* the Court found that a number of the provisions in Directive 98/43 could not be adopted under Article 114 TFEU and, because these measures were so interconnected with the directive as a whole, the Court annulled the whole directive rather than simply severing the offending Articles. The Council and the EP subsequently readopted the directive with the offending parts removed[49] and this directive was again challenged by Germany in *Tobacco Advertising II*.[50] This time Germany was unsuccessful.

2.2 The Circumstances in Which Article 114 TFEU Can Be Used

(a) Elimination of obstacles to the exercise of fundamental freedoms

As we have seen from Case Study 15.1, in *Tobacco Advertising I* the Court said that Article 114(1) TFEU could be used to adopt EU measures in two situations. The first is where those measures contribute to the elimination of obstacles to the exercise of fundamental freedoms. The following example illustrates this point. State B has stricter rules than State A on the quantity of additives that can be used in a product. State B's rules, although justified on public-health grounds, create an obstacle to the free movement of goods because State A's goods need to be adapted before they can be imported into State B. The solution to this problem would be to enact a common standard under Article 114 TFEU to eliminate these obstacles to trade.[51]

In *Tobacco Advertising I* the Court made clear that not only could Article 114(1) TFEU be used to adopt measures dealing with actual obstacles to trade (see the additives example just given), but it could also be used to address future obstacles to trade which might emerge due to the 'multifarious development of national laws'.[52] In this case, the emergence of such obstacles had to be 'likely' and the measure in question had to be 'designed to prevent them'.[53] Therefore, in *Tobacco Advertising I*[54] the Court said that Directive 98/43's ban on advertising of tobacco products in (the confusingly named) 'non-static advertising media' (periodicals, magazines, and newspapers) could be adopted on the basis of Article 114(1) TFEU, since this would help to ensure the free movement of press products. The Court said that, even though the obstacles to trade were potential rather than actual, it was 'probable' that the obstacles would arise in the future.[55] In *Inuit II*[56] the Court added that the preamble to the measure need only indicate the general situation which led to its

---

[48] See Poiares Maduro AG's view in Case C–58/08 *Vodafone* [2010] ECR I–4999, that a proper reading of Art. 114 TFEU had to distinguish between what triggers Union harmonization (the risk of obstacles to free movement or distortions of competition) and the scope and content of that harmonization. In respect of scope and content, he argued that the Union should be able to pursue a variety of policy goals, not limited to market integration, policy goals usually pursued by national measures which are to be replaced by Union harmonization (para. 8).

[49] EP and Council Dir. 2003/33 on the approximation of laws relating to advertising and sponsorship of tobacco products ([2003] OJ L152/16).

[50] Case C–380/03 *Germany v. European Parliament and Council* [2006] ECR I–11573.

[51] Case C–491/01 *Ex p. BAT* [2002] ECR I–11453, paras. 64–5.

[52] This language is actually taken from Case C–491/01 *Ex p. BAT* [2002] ECR I–11453, para. 61.

[53] Case C–491/01 *Ex p. BAT* [2002] ECR I–11453.

[54] Case C–376/98 *Tobacco Advertising I* [2000] ECR I–8419, para. 98.   [55] Para. 97.

[56] Case C–398/13 P *Inuit Tapiriit Kanatami v. Commission* EU:C:2015:535, para. 29.

adoption and the general objectives it was intended to achieve; there was no need to identify the number and identity of the Member States whose national rules were the source of the measure.

The obstacles to free movement also have to be appreciable. For this reason, the Court found in *Tobacco Advertising I* that Article 114(1) TFEU could not be used to ban advertising in 'static advertising media' (e.g., posters, parasols, ashtrays, and other articles used in hotels, restaurants, and cafés). This was because the effect on free movement of goods was too uncertain and indirect:[57] the prohibition on advertising could not be justified by the need to eliminate obstacles to the free movement of advertising media or the freedom to provide services in the field of advertising.[58] This view was reinforced by the fact that the directive did not contain a free movement clause.[59] By contrast, Directive 2001/37 on tobacco control did contain such a clause, and for this reason the Court said in *Ex p. BAT* that because Member States could not prevent the import, sale, or use of tobacco products which did comply with the directive, the directive did improve the conditions for the functioning of the internal market.[60] Therefore, Directive 2001/37 was correctly adopted under Article 114(1) TFEU.

(b) Removal of appreciable distortions of competition

According to *Tobacco Advertising I*, the second situation in which Article 114(1) TFEU can be used is where the Union adopts measures to remove distortions of competition arising from the diverse national rules. To a certain extent this second ground overlaps with the first: any obstacle to trade is also likely to distort competition. However, this second ground is broader, covering situations where, owing to the absence of regulation in State A, the producers or service providers established there enjoy a competitive advantage in terms of production costs over their competitors in State B who face substantial regulation. A harmonization directive would iron out these cost differences.[61]

Once again, Article 114(1) TFEU can be used to address actual, as well as potential, distortions of competition. The Court made this clear in *Titanium Dioxide*, where it said that the Union could also legislate where the distortions were 'likely' to arise from the diverse national rules.[62] Moreover, the distortions had to be 'appreciable'.[63] In *Tobacco Advertising I* the Court explained that it was not sufficient for the EU legislature to rely on single market legal bases 'with a view to eliminating the smallest distortions of competition',[64] i.e., where the effects on competition were 'remote and indirect'.[65] It explained that in the absence of such a requirement 'the powers of the [Union] legislature would be practically unlimited',[66] and that would be incompatible with the principle embodied in Article 5(2) TEU that the powers of the Union are limited to those specifically conferred on it.[67] For this reason the Court said that the adoption of Directive 98/43 under

---

[57] It is, however, rather puzzling why posters, ashtrays, and parasols were classified as static rather than non-static since the arguments made about non-static media seem equally applicable to these so-called static media.

[58] Case C–376/98 *Tobacco Advertising I* [2000] ECR I–8419, para. 99.

[59] *Tobacco Advertising I*, n. 58, para. 101.   [60] *Tobacco Advertising I*, n. 58, para. 74.

[61] For arguments to this effect, see Case C–300/89 *Commission* v. *Council (titanium dioxide)* [1991] ECR I–2867.

[62] *Commission* v. *Council (titanium dioxide)*, n. 61, para. 15.

[63] Case C–376/98 *Tobacco Advertising I* [2000] ECR I–8419, para. 106.

[64] Para. 107. See also para. 84: 'If a mere finding of disparities between national rules and of the abstract risk of obstacles to the exercise of fundamental freedoms or of distortions of competition liable to result therefrom were sufficient to justify the choice of Article [114 TFEU] as a legal basis, judicial review of compliance with the proper legal basis might be rendered nugatory.'

[65] Para. 109. Cf. Case C–190/98 *Graf* [2000] ECR I–493, para. 25, considered in Ch. 7.

[66] *Tobacco Advertising I*, n. 63, para. 107.   [67] Para. 83.

Article 114(1) TFEU could not be justified on the ground of the distortion of competition caused to the advertising industry. It recognized that while advertising agencies and producers of advertising media established in Member States which imposed fewer restrictions on tobacco advertising were at an advantage in terms of economies of scale and increase in profits, the effects of such advantages on competition were 'remote and indirect' and did not 'constitute distortions which could be described as appreciable'.[68]

The Court also rejected the justification based on the distortions of competition in the marketing of tobacco products. The Commission had argued that, in Member States where advertising was restricted, producers and sellers of tobacco products had to resort to price competition to influence their market share. The Court dismissed these arguments, saying that in these states the national laws constituted a '*restriction* of forms of competition which applied to all economic operators in those Member States'[69] and not a distortion. Because the national laws merely *restricted* competition rather than distorted it, no harmonization was possible under Article 114(1) TFEU.[70] To some commentators, this distinction between *distortions* of competition (which justify Union measures under Article 114(1) TFEU) and *restrictions* (which do not) reflects the distinction drawn in *Keck*[71] between product requirements (to which Article 34 TFEU applies) and non-discriminatory measures such as selling arrangements (to which Article 34 does not apply);[72] although with the increasing use of the 'restrictions' analysis in the case law on negative integration, this distinction seems increasingly less tenable.

Finally, the Court considered whether Article 114(1) TFEU could be used to harmonize national rules concerning sports sponsorship by tobacco companies. It noted that prohibiting sponsorship in some Member States and authorizing it in others caused certain sports events to be moved, affecting the conditions of competition for undertakings associated with such events.[73] Since this gave rise to an appreciable distortion on competition, it did justify an EU measure adopted under Article 114 TFEU but not an outright ban on advertising of the kind proposed by the directive.[74]

2.3 The Follow-Up to *Tobacco Advertising I*

Given that the Court could not separate those parts of the directive which had been validly adopted and those which had not, it annulled the directive in its entirety.[75] The Council and Parliament then adopted a new, more tailored measure, Directive 2003/33[76] on advertising and sponsorship of tobacco products, covering those areas of Directive 98/43 which the Court had said could be validly adopted under the internal-market legal bases.[77] Article 3 of Directive 2003/33 bans advertising in the press and other printed publications ('non-static' advertising media), except for publications intended exclusively for professionals in the tobacco trade and for publications not intended for the Union

---

[68] Para. 109.   [69] Para. 113, emphasis added.

[70] See also Case C–412/93 *Leclerc–Siplec* [1995] ECR I–179, considered in Ch. 5, where restrictions on advertising applied equally to all traders operating in the state and did not make a distinction, in law or in fact, between domestic and imported goods. These were certain selling arrangements which did not breach Art. 34 TFEU.

[71] Joined Cases C–267 and 268/91 *Keck and Mithouard* [1993] ECR I–6097.

[72] See also Geelhoed AG's Opinion in Case C–434/02 *Arnold André* [2004] ECR I–11825, para. 65. See also the direct links between the Art. 34 TFEU case law (e.g., Case C–405/98 *Gourmet International Products* [2001] ECR I–1795) and the Art. 114 TFEU case law made in Case C–380/03 *Tobacco Advertising II* [2006] ECR I–11573, para. 42. Cf. G. Davies, 'Can selling arrangements be harmonised?' (2005) 30 *ELRev*. 371 and Poiares Maduro AG's views on parallelism in Case C–58/08 *Vodafone* [2010] ECR I–4999, paras. 21–4.

[73] *Tobacco Advertising I*, n. 63, para. 110.   [74] Para. 111.   [75] Para. 117.

[76] [2003] OJ L152/16.

[77] EP and Council Dir. 2003/33 on the approximation of laws relating to advertising and sponsorship of tobacco products ([2003] OJ L152/16).

market. According to the preamble, this ban was justified by the need to overcome 'an appreciable risk of obstacles to free movement' created by diverse national laws.[78] Article 4 prohibits all forms of radio advertising for tobacco products as well as tobacco sponsorship of radio programmes. Article 5 prohibits tobacco sponsorship of events taking place in more than one Member State. This was justified by the need to address national rules giving rise to 'an appreciable risk of distortion of the conditions of competition'.[79] The directive also contains a free movement clause.[80]

In *Tobacco Advertising II*[81] the Court upheld the validity of Articles 3–4 of the directive. Having analysed the existing national law on tobacco advertising and the risks of new barriers arising as a result of the accession of the new Member States, the Court said the barriers and risks of distortions of competition warranted intervention by the Union legislature on the basis of Article 114 TFEU,[82] and that Articles 3–4 were in fact designed to eliminate or prevent obstacles to the free movement of goods/services or to remove distortions of competition, not least because of the existence of the free movement clause.[83]

In the light of the decisions in *Tobacco Advertising I* and *Ex p. BAT* it is clear that the Union does not have the power to intervene in all cases where the market does not function optimally, since this would be tantamount to providing the Union with a general legislative power.[84] However, the Union can legislate to overcome the geographic fragmentation of the EU market. As Bernard puts it, the Union does not have the power under Article 114(1) TFEU to ensure the functioning of the common *market* (i.e., the market in general) but does have the power to regulate matters to ensure the functioning of the *common* market (i.e., the creation of a single, unified market).[85]

2.4 The Case Law after *Tobacco Advertising I*

(a) Departing from Tobacco Advertising I

Although the Court sent out a strong message in *Tobacco Advertising I* that there were limits to the use of Article 114 TFEU and that it could not be used to regulate all aspects of economic life,[86] subsequent cases suggest that the Court might be relaxing its tough stance, upholding a number of uses of Article 114 TFEU which might not apparently satisfy either the detail or the spirit of the *Tobacco Advertising I* ruling.[87] For example,

---

[78] Fourth recital.   [79] Fifth recital.

[80] According to Art. 8, 'Member States shall not prohibit or restrict the free movement of products which comply with this Directive.'

[81] Case C–380/03 *Germany v. European Parliament and Council (Tobacco Advertising II)* [2006] ECR I–11573.

[82] Para. 68.   [83] Para. 73.

[84] Cf. M. Ludwig's note on *Tobacco Advertising II*, (2007) 44 *CMLRev.* 1159, 1176.

[85] N. Bernard, 'The future of European economic law in the light of the principle of subsidiarity' (1996) 33 *CMLRev.* 633, 640–1.

[86] See also the politically important decision in Joined Cases C–317 and 318/04 *Parliament v. Council (passenger name records)* [2006] ECR I–4721, where the Court ruled that Art. 114 TFEU, read in conjunction with Art. 25 of Dir. 95/46/EC on the protection of individuals with regard to the processing of personal data and on the free movement of such data, could not justify (then) Community competence to conclude an agreement between the EC and the USA on the processing and transfer of passenger name record (PNR) data by air carriers to the US Department of Homeland Security. Because the agreement related to data-processing operations which were excluded from the scope of the directive, the decision implementing the agreement could not be adopted under Art. 114 TFEU. Any internal market objective was purely incidental; the real objectives of the agreement (prevention of terrorism, organized crime, and protection of privacy) were objectives of the then EU, not EC, Treaty.

[87] See S. Weatherill, 'Competence and legitimacy' in C. Barnard and O. Odudu (eds.), *The Outer Limits of European Union Law* (Oxford: Hart Publishing, 2009), 19–20, who argues that the Court's approach is now 'competence-enhancing and not competence-restricting'. He also argues that the result of Case C–176/03

the Court has since made clear that the phrase 'measures for the approximation' in Article 114 TFEU conferred on the legislature a broad discretion as regard the method most appropriate for achieving the desired result, in particular in areas characterized by complexity.[88] Measures adopted can consist of requiring all Member States to authorize the marketing of products, subjecting any such authorization to certain conditions, or even *prohibiting* the marketing of products.[89] Therefore, in *Swedish Match* and *Arnold André*[90] the Court said that a total ban on the marketing of oral tobacco products such as snuff (finely ground tobacco consumed by placing it between the gum and the lip) in the Tobacco Control Directive 2001/37 could be adopted under Article 114 TFEU,[91] even though a *ban* might appear to fly in the face of a single market in goods.[92] And in *Österreichischer Rundfunk*[93] the Court said that the Data Protection Directive could be adopted under Article 114 TFEU even though it applied to a wholly internal situation. The Court said that 'recourse to Article [114 TFEU] as a legal basis does not presuppose the existence of an actual link with free movement between Member States in every situation referred to by the measure founded on that basis'.[94] It was sufficient that the measure adopted under Article 114 TFEU was actually intended to improve the conditions for the establishment and functioning of the internal market.[95]

(b) Indirect harmonization

Subsequent cases raised other difficulties for the Court. For example, can Article 114 TFEU be used to create legal forms which help the internal market to run smoothly but are not about harmonization per se? Two Advocates General thought not[96] but the Court disagreed. In *UK* v. *EP and Council (European Network and Information Security Agency (ENISA))*[97] the Court said that Article 114 TFEU could be used to establish a Union body responsible for contributing to the implementation of a process of harmonization where, for example, the Union body provided services to national authorities and/or operators which affected the homogenous implementation of harmonizing instruments and was likely to facilitate their application.[98] The Court added that the tasks conferred on such a body did, however, have to be closely linked to the subject matter of the harmonization legislation.[99] Therefore, ENISA[100] could be established on the basis of Article 114 TFEU since its aim was to assist the Commission and the Member States with

---

Commission v. *Council (criminal penalties)* [2005] ECR I–7879 hints at the use of Art. 114 TFEU to make a harmonized criminal law.

[88] Case C–380/03 *Tobacco Advertising II* [2006] ECR I–11573, para. 42.

[89] *Tobacco Advertising II*, n. 88, para. 43.

[90] Case C–210/03 *Swedish Match* [2004] ECR I–11893; Case C–434/02 *Arnold André* [2004] ECR I–11825.

[91] *Arnold André*, n. 90, para. 35. See also the discussion of the proportionality of the ban in para. 54.

[92] See also Reg. (EC) No. 1007/2009 ([2009] OJ L286/36) on trade in seal products, which essentially banned the import of seal products.

[93] Case C–465/00 [2003] ECR I–4989, para. 41. Case C–101/01 *Lindqvist* [2003] ECR I–12971, paras. 40–1.

[94] See also Case C–398/13 P *Inuit II* EU:C:2015:535, para. 40, where the Court said that there was no requirement that measures taken on the basis of Art. 114 TFEU were limited solely to markets for products in which trade was relatively sizeable.

[95] Case C–380/03 *Tobacco Advertising II* [2006] ECR I–11573, para. 80.

[96] Stix-Hackl AG in Case C–436/03 *ECS* [2006] ECR I–3733; Kokott AG in Case C–217/04 *UK* v. *EP and Council (ENISA)* [2006] ECR I–3771.

[97] Case C–217/04 *ENISA* [2006] ECR I–3771.   [98] Paras. 44–5.

[99] Para. 45.

[100] ENISA is an example of the relatively recent phenomenon of establishing an agency to facilitate decision-making by ensuring independence and expertise.

meeting the requirements of network and information security, as part of a wider package of measures,[101] thereby ensuring the smooth functioning of electronic communications services.

In *Smoke Flavourings*[102] the Court also upheld the use of Article 114 TFEU as a legal basis for a regulation which did not harmonize laws but established procedures (then the regulatory procedure laid down by the Comitology decision[103] now delegated acts under Article 290 TFEU) for the approval of lists of authorized products which could be used in 'smoked' foods. The UK had argued that Article 114 TFEU could be used only to harmonize national laws—i.e., Article 114 TFEU could be used to achieve at Union level what Member States could have achieved at national level on their own (direct harmonization); it could not be used to establish Union bodies, confer tasks on these bodies or establish authorization procedures such as those in *Smoke Flavourings* (indirect harmonization). However, Advocate General Kokott said that Article 114 TFEU could be used to approximate laws both directly *and* indirectly in a 'multi-stage model with intermediate steps'[104] and the Court appeared to accept her view. It said that Article 114 TFEU could be used to adopt a measure which merely defines the basic provisions essential for achieving the objective which then confers power on the Commission to adopt the harmonization measures needed for the implementation of the legislative act in question.[105] In other words, Article 114 TFEU could be used to establish a parent measure which delegates implementing power to the Commission.

The Court also said that where the Union legislature provided for harmonization which comprised several stages, for instance the fixing of a number of essential criteria set out in a basic (parent) regulation followed by scientific evaluation of the substances concerned and the adoption of a positive list of substances authorized throughout the Union (the subordinate measure), two conditions had to be satisfied:

- the Union legislature had to determine in the basic act the essential elements of the harmonizing measure in question

- the mechanism for implementing those elements had to be designed in such a way that it led to a harmonization within the meaning of Article [114 TFEU].

In particular, the Court said the parent measure had to establish detailed rules for making decisions at each stage of an authorization procedure, and determine and circumscribe precisely the powers of the Commission as the body which had to take the final decision. That applied in particular where the harmonization in question consisted of drawing up a list of products authorized throughout the Union to the exclusion of all other products.[106]

Given the emphasis in *Smoke Flavourings* on the need for the parent measure to prescribe carefully and in detail the relevant procedure for adopting subordinate measures, the Court's decision in the earlier case of *Alliance for Natural Health*[107] came as something of a surprise. *Alliance for Natural Health* concerned the Food Supplements Directive 2002/46,[108] a classic single-market measure in the sense that it had been introduced to harmonize the rules on food supplements, such as vitamins and minerals, which had been the subject of much (diverse) national legislation which in turn had been challenged by traders under Article 34 TFEU. States invariably, and often successfully, invoked Article 36 TFEU to defend their rules,[109] and in so doing created (legitimate) obstacles to

---

[101] *ENISA*, n. 97, para. 60.

[102] Case C–66/04 *UK v. EP and Council (smoke flavourings)* [2005] ECR I–10553.

[103] Considered in Section C.   [104] Para. 33.   [105] Para. 50.   [106] Paras. 47–9.

[107] Joined Cases C–154 and 155/04 *Alliance for Natural Health* [2005] ECR I–6451.

[108] [2002] OJ L183/51.

[109] E.g., Case C–192/01 *Commission v. Denmark* [2003] ECR I–9693; Case C–24/00 *Commission v. France (nutrients)* [2004] ECR I–1277; Case C–95/01 *Greenham and Abel* [2004] ECR I–1333. See further Ch. 6.

trade. Directive 2002/46 was intended to address these obstacles by creating an EU-wide regime. It envisaged a two-stage approach to the harmonization of the rules in this area. By 1 August 2003 Member States had to permit trade in foods containing vitamins and minerals which had been 'positive listed' (i.e., approved). This obligation was ensured through a free movement clause. By 1 August 2005 Member States had to prohibit trade in products that did not comply with the requirements of the directive.

While Advocate General Geelhoed and the Court recognized that the directive had an internal-market dimension and so was correctly adopted on the basis of Article 114 TFEU, the Advocate General was much concerned about the proportionality of the measure.[110] He said that the legal instruments which put the positive list system into effect had to be designed with care since they had a far-reaching impact on the freedom of market operators: they impeded the continuation of activities previously regarded as lawful and subjected new developments to a prior assessment by the Commission before they could be positive-listed.[111] He argued that the directive failed in three respects:[112]

- the directive, in delegating power to the Commission and the comitology committee, provided no substantive norm for the decision-makers to follow as a guiding principle to decide whether a product should appear on the positive list[113]

- the directive did not make clear whether private parties themselves could submit substances for evaluation[114]

- if they could, then the directive failed to provide a clear procedure to provide minimum guarantees for protecting the parties' interests.

He concluded, 'this procedure, in so far as it may exist and in so far as it may deserve this title, has the transparency of a black box'.[115] He therefore considered the directive invalid.

The Court agreed that it would have been 'desirable' for the directive to have contained provisions which ensured that the application process be completed transparently and within a reasonable time[116] but, unlike the Advocate General, the Court thought that this was not sufficient to jeopardize the validity of the directive because of the Commission's general duty, under the principle of sound administration, to act transparently and within a reasonable time. It therefore upheld the validity of the directive.

The cases considered so far concern delegation. The *Vodafone*[117] case raised a further difficult question for the Court: can Article 114 TFEU be used as a legal basis for a measure affecting the conduct of private parties, *in casu* a regulation establishing Union-wide maximum prices for roaming on public mobile phone networks? The Advocate General thought it could. While he doubted that the EU had shown that the risk of possible future differences in national price controls created obstacles to trade justifying regulation under Article 114 TFEU,[118] he did think that the EU legislator could regulate roaming prices under Article 114 TFEU to remove 'restrictions to free movement arising from the behaviour of private parties which disfavours cross-border economic activity'.[119] In so

---

[110] *Alliance for Natural Health*, n. 107, para. 38.   [111] Para. 66.   [112] Para. 68.

[113] This, he emphasized, was particularly serious: para. 69. The Court disagreed: it said that the procedure for modifying the positive list was linked to recitals in the directive which made clear that the Commission had to use public health as the yardstick for modification.

[114] There was an internal conflict in the directive between the preamble, which said that private operators could do so, and the body of the directive, which said that it was for the Member States.

[115] Para. 85.   [116] Para. 81.

[117] Case C–58/08 R. *(on the application of Vodafone Ltd)* v. *Secretary of State for Business, Enterprise and Regulatory Reform* [2010] ECR I–4999.

[118] Para. 18.   [119] Para. 19.

doing, he asked the Court to apply 'the logical consequences of its case-law on the horizontal application of free movement rules to its analysis of Article [114 TFEU]'.[120]

The Court took a different line. It said that the high level of retail charges had been regarded as a persistent problem by national regulatory authorities (NRAs), public authorities, and consumer protection associations throughout the EU and that attempts to solve the problem using the existing EU legal framework had not had the effect of lowering charges. The Court also said that there was pressure on the Member States to use their residual competence in the field to address the problem. EU legislation was therefore necessary to forestall action by the Member States which would have been 'liable to cause significant distortions of competition and to disrupt the orderly functioning of the [Union]-wide roaming market'.[121] The Regulation was therefore correctly adopted on the basis of Article 114 TFEU.

Finally, in *Short Selling*[122] the Court had to consider what sort of measures could be adopted under Article 114 TFEU. The UK argued that Article 114 TFEU could be used only for measures of general application. Therefore, it could not be used as a legal basis for the European Securities and Markets Authority (ESMA) to take individual measures directed at natural or legal persons engaged in short-selling. The Court disagreed. It said Article 114 TFEU gave the legislature discretion as to the most appropriate form of harmonization and that discretion was particularly important where 'highly technical and specialist analyses' had to be made and the body (ESMA) had to respond 'swiftly and appropriately'.[123] Further, ESMA's intervention was necessary to improve the functioning of the financial markets.

3. CHOICE OF LEGAL BASIS

So far we have focused on the question of whether the Union has the competence at all to adopt measures under Article 114 TFEU (see fig. 15.1). We turn now to the question of where a secondary measure could have been adopted on one of a number of legal bases. In addition to the general legal bases (Articles 114–15 TFEU and 352 TFEU), there are various specific legal bases which could be used for measures which might have implications for the internal market, in particular Article 43 TFEU (agriculture), Article 50 TFEU (freedom of establishment), Article 62 TFEU (freedom to provide services), Article 173 TFEU (industrial policy), and Article 192 TFEU (environment). This can lead to the situation where the proposed measure appears to raise single-market issues as well as issues covered by another legal basis. What rules should apply? As we have seen, Article 114(1) TFEU is supposed to be a residual legal basis, only to be used where there is no other suitable provision. Yet, in *Titanium Dioxide*[124] the Court favoured the use of Article 114 TFEU over (the more specific) Article 192 TFEU on the environment as the choice of legal basis for adopting a directive on disposing of waste by the titanium dioxide industry.[125] The Court said that, since environmental and health measures were a burden on undertakings, competition could be appreciably distorted in the absence of harmonization; thus Article 114(1) TFEU applied. If this logic were accepted, then *Titanium Dioxide* would have had the effect of marginalizing all other legal bases since nearly all Union measures have some cost implication.

---

[120] *Vodafone*, n. 117, para. 21.   [121] Para. 47.

[122] Case C–270/12 *UK v. European Parliament and Council* EU:C:2014:18.

[123] Paras. 103 and 105.   [124] Case C–300/89 [1991] ECR I–2867.

[125] Dir. 89/428/EEC ([1989] OJ L201/56).

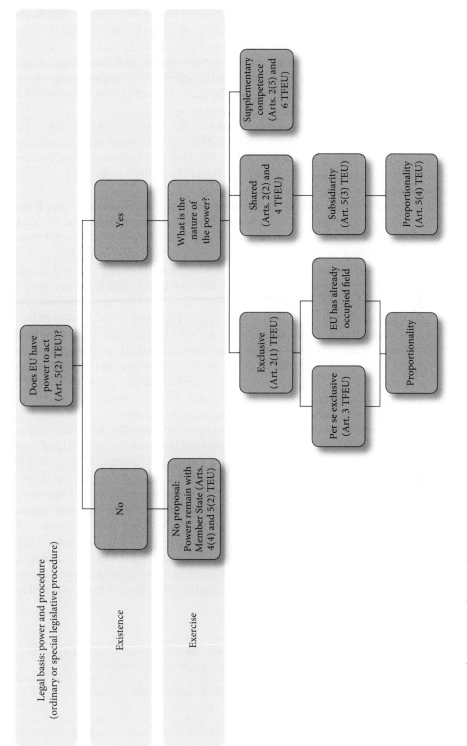

Fig. 15.1 Considerations in the EU's legislative process

In reality, the Court's judgment may have disguised a policy preference for Article 114 TFEU at a time when Article 114 TFEU required the more democratic cooperation procedure,[126] allowing for a greater involvement of the European Parliament, while other Treaty provisions, like the environmental basis (Article 130s EEC as it then was), required only simple consultation. However, such reasoning was much criticized because it allowed procedural rules to determine the choice of legal basis rather than the substantive content of the measure, and significant doubt has now been cast on elements of *Titanium Dioxide*. In the *Waste Directive*[127] case the Court said that recourse to Article 114 TFEU was not justified where the measure to be adopted had 'only the incidental effect of harmonizing market conditions within the [Union]'[128] and in *Beef Labelling*[129] the Court refused to countenance an argument that Article 114 TFEU should be used due to its more democratic procedures.

Therefore, it can now be said that if an examination of a Union act shows that it has a twofold purpose, one of which is identifiable as main or predominant and the other merely incidental or 'ancillary', the act must be founded on the sole, predominant, legal basis.[130] Exceptionally, the Court will accept a dual basis. As the Court said in *Ex p. BAT*,[131] if it is established that the act simultaneously pursues a number of objectives, indissociably linked, without one being secondary and indirect in relation to the other, such an act may be founded on the various corresponding legal bases.[132] On the facts of the case, the Court said that because the directive had been properly adopted on the basis of Article 114 TFEU it could not simultaneously have Articles 114 TFEU and 207 TFEU for a legal basis: the provisions affecting tobacco products exported to non-EU states were secondary to the aim and content of the directive as a whole, which was primarily designed to improve the conditions for the functioning of the internal market.[133] However, since the reference to Article 207 TFEU was a formal defect only, it did not invalidate the directive because the procedures under the two bases were essentially similar.[134]

With a greater use of the ordinary legislative procedure following the Lisbon Treaty, these Treaty-base disputes should become less common. However, the residual legal basis in Article 352 TFEU is not subject to the ordinary legislative procedure. In its revised form it provides that if action by the Union should prove necessary, within the framework of the policies defined in the Treaty, to attain one of the objectives set out in the Treaty (thereby broadening the scope of the original Article 308 EC, which was limited to action necessary to attain the common market),[135] and the Treaty has not provided the necessary powers, the Council, acting unanimously on a proposal from the Commission and after obtaining the consent of the European Parliament, must adopt the appropriate measures. Those measures may be legislative in character, in which case they are deemed to have been adopted by the special legislative procedure. Perhaps in a nod to

---

[126] *Titanium Dioxide*, n. 124, para. 20.

[127] Case C–155/91 *Commission v. Council (Waste Directive)* [1993] ECR I–939.   [128] Para. 19.

[129] Case C–269/97 *Commission and Parliament v. Council (beef labelling)* [2000] ECR I–2257.

[130] Case C–491/01 *Ex p. BAT* [2002] ECR I–11453, para. 94. For an example in the field of the internal market, see Case C–137/12 *Commission v. Council (conditional access)* EU:C:2013:675, para. 76.

[131] Case C–491/01 *Ex p. BAT* [2002] ECR I–11453, para. 94.

[132] *Opinion 2/00* [2001] ECR I–9713, para. 23.   [133] Paras. 95–6.

[134] Cf. Case C–211/01 *Commission v. Council (carriage of goods by road and combined transport)* [2003] ECR I–8913, para. 52.

[135] Note the additional safeguard in Art. 352(2) TFEU: 'Using the procedure for monitoring the subsidiarity principle referred to in Article 5(3) of the Treaty on European Union, the Commission shall draw national Parliaments' attention to proposals based on this Article.' Some national parliaments (e.g., the UK's parliament) have added additional requirements when a measure is being proposed under Art. 352 TFEU.

the problems generated by *Tobacco Advertising I* and the Court's cavalier approach to the non-harmonization provision in Article 168(5) TFEU, Article 352(3) provides 'Measures based on this Article shall not entail harmonisation of Member States' laws or regulations in cases where the Treaties exclude such harmonisation.'[136]

One of the most controversial uses of Article 352 TFEU was the proposal for the adoption of the so-called Monti II Regulation[137] intended to address the problems arising from the Court's decision in *Viking*,[138] which trade unionists saw as limiting their right to strike. This proposal was intended to strike a better balance between principles of free movement and the right to strike while introducing an alert mechanism which required Member States to notify the Commission of 'serious acts or circumstances affecting the effective exercise of the freedom of establishment or the freedom to provide services which could cause grave disruption to the proper functioning of the internal market and/or which may cause serious damage to its industrial relations system or create serious social unrest in its territory or in the territory of other Member States'. A number of Member States objected to the use of Article 352 TFEU as the legal basis and argued that the Commission was deliberately using Article 352 TFEU to circumvent the limits in Article 153(5) TFEU, which provides that the provisions of Article 153(5) TFEU will not apply to 'pay, the right of association, the right to strike or the right to impose lock-outs'. The Yellow Card Procedure under the Subsidiarity Protocol (see Section 4) was invoked for the first time and the Commission withdrew the proposal.

4. THE APPLICATION OF THE PRINCIPLES OF SUBSIDIARITY AND PROPORTIONALITY TO MEASURES ADOPTED UNDER ARTICLE 114 TFEU

In areas, such as the internal market, where the Union's competence is not exclusive,[139] measures adopted must respect the principle of subsidiarity[140] (i.e., they should be taken at the lowest appropriate level[141]) (see fig. 15.1). If an application of the subsidiarity principle reveals that the Union should act, any measure adopted must also be proportionate (no more extensive than necessary to achieve the objective).[142] For many years the Court has been reluctant to engage in a detailed examination of the compatibility of a Union act with the principles of subsidiarity and proportionality because, as it explained in *Ex p. BAT*,[143] 'the [Union] legislature must be allowed a broad discretion in an area such as that involved in the present case, which entails political, economic, and social choices on its part, and in which it is called upon to undertake complex assessments'. Consequently, the legality of a measure adopted can be affected 'only if the measure is

---

[136] See also the limit in Art. 352(4): 'This Article cannot serve as a basis for attaining objectives pertaining to the common foreign and security policy and any acts adopted pursuant to this Article shall respect the limits set out in Article 40, second paragraph, of the Treaty on European Union.' See also Decls. 41–2 annexed to the final act.

[137] COM(2012) 130.   [138] Case C–438/05 *Viking Line* [2007] ECR I–10779.

[139] Art. 5(3) TEU. See also Case C–491/01 *Ex p. BAT* [2002] ECR I–11453, para. 179.

[140] As Case C–491/01 *Ex p. BAT* [2002] ECR I–11453 indicates, subsidiarity will also apply to situations where the Union has already exercised its shared competence, with at least some pre-emptive effects, and replaces that legislation with revised rules (the Tobacco Control Dir.).

[141] This is reflected in the revised language (in italics) of Art. 5(3) TEU, which provides that the 'Union shall act only if and in so far as the objectives of the proposed action cannot be sufficiently achieved by the Member States, either at *central level or at regional and local level*'.

[142] Art. 5(4) TEU.   [143] Case C–491/01 [2002] ECR I–11453, para. 123.

manifestly inappropriate having regard to the objective which the competent institution is seeking to pursue'.[144]

Subsidiarity has proved a particularly sensitive issue. In the past, the Court has been reluctant to review the merits of complaints alleging breach of subsidiarity, viewing subsidiarity more as a political than as a legal principle. In particular, it has refused to examine whether the criteria laid down in Article 5(3) TEU (i.e., whether the action can be sufficiently achieved by the Member States or, whether by reason of the scale or effects of the proposed action, it could be better achieved by the Union) have been met.[145] Instead, the Court has been content to focus on the procedural aspects of the subsidiarity principle, checking to see whether the Union institutions have actually considered the implications for the principle of subsidiarity of the proposed measure;[146] it has not been prepared to look behind those reasons to see whether they were justified. For example, in *Working Time*[147] the Court simply observed that if harmonization was at issue this 'necessarily' presupposed Union-wide action,[148] without examining the prior question of whether there was a need for harmonization in this area. Similarly, in *Biotechnological Inventions*[149] the Court argued that the objective pursued by the directive, to ensure the smooth operation of the internal market by preventing or eliminating differences between the legislation and practice of the various Member States, could not be achieved by action taken by the Member States alone. As the scope of the protection of biotechnological inventions had immediate effects on trade and on intra-Union trade, it was clear that 'given the scale and the effects of the proposed action, the objective in question could be better achieved by the [Union]'.[150]

However, in *Ex p. BAT*[151] the Court showed itself a little more willing to consider the merits of the subsidiarity principle in deciding whether the EU should have adopted the Tobacco Control Directive 2001/37. It began by considering 'whether the objective of the proposed action could be better achieved at [Union] level'.[152] It said that since the directive's objective was to eliminate the barriers raised by the differences which still existed between the laws of the Member States on the manufacture, presentation, and sale of tobacco products, 'such an objective cannot be sufficiently achieved by the Member States individually and calls for action at [Union] level, as demonstrated by the multifarious development of national laws in this case'. It therefore considered that the objective of the directive could be better achieved at Union level.[153] In effect this is a clearer articulation of the point made in *Working Time* and *Biotechnological Inventions* that harmonization requires EU action. Rather curiously, the Court then appeared to merge the tests of subsidiarity and proportionality. It said that:

> the intensity of the action undertaken by the [Union] in this instance was also in keeping with the requirements of the principle of subsidiarity in that . . . it did not go beyond what was necessary to achieve the objective pursued.[154]

---

[144] *Ex p. BAT*, n. 143, para. 123.

[145] N. Bernard, 'The future of European economic law in the light of the principle of subsidiarity' (1996) 33 *CMLRev.* 633, 653.

[146] Case C–233/94 *Germany* v. *Parliament and Council (deposit guarantee schemes)* [1997] ECR I–2405.

[147] Case C–84/94 *UK* v. *Council* [1996] ECR I–5755.   [148] Para. 47.

[149] Case C–377/98 *Netherlands* v. *Parliament and Council* [2001] ECR I–7079.   [150] Para. 32.

[151] Case C–491/01 [2002] ECR I–11453. See also Joined Cases C–154 and 155/04 *Alliance for Natural Health* [2005] ECR I–6451, paras. 105–6. See also Case C–58/08 *Vodafone* [2010] ECR I–4999, para. 78 and Case C–508/13 *Estonia* v. *Parliament and Council* EU:C:2015:403, paras. 49–55. See also the AG's Opinion in Case C–358/14 *Poland* v. *Parliament and Council* EU:C:2015:848 for a somewhat more searching review.

[152] *Ex p. BAT*, n. 143, para. 180.

[153] Paras. 181–3. See also Case C–103/01 *Commission* v. *Germany (PPE)* [2003] ECR I–5369, para. 47.

[154] Para. 187.

The Court also found the Tobacco Control Directive's provisions proportionate. For example, when considering the obligation to give information on the tar, nicotine, and carbon monoxide levels and to print health warnings on the packets, it noted that these were appropriate measures for attaining a high level of health protection when the barriers raised by national laws on labelling were removed.[155] The Court continued that although the directive required more of the surface area of the packaging to be used for warnings, it also allowed for sufficient space to be left for the manufacturers to affix other material, in particular trade marks. For this reason, the Court concluded, 'the [Union] legislature has not overstepped the bounds of the discretion which it enjoys in this area'.[156]

Similarly, in *Tobacco Advertising II*[157] the Court made clear that a tailored ban on tobacco advertising (the ban did not apply to publications intended for professionals in the tobacco trade or published in third countries) was proportionate.[158] It was also compatible with Article 10 ECHR on the freedom of expression. As the Court said, the discretion enjoyed by the competent authorities in determining the balance to be struck between freedom of expression in Article 10(1) and objectives in the public interest referred to in Article 10(2) varies for each of the goals justifying restrictions on that freedom and depends on the nature of the activities in question. When a certain amount of discretion is available, 'review is limited to an examination of the reasonableness and proportionality of the interference. This holds true for the commercial use of freedom of expression in a field as complex and fluctuating as advertising.'[159]

Amendments introduced by the Lisbon Treaty are intended to improve the monitoring and enforcement of the subsidiarity principle through *ex ante* control by national parliaments, the bodies that stand to lose most by Union action, rather than by *ex post* review by the Court.[160] Article 5(3) TEU says that the Union's institutions must apply the principle of subsidiarity in accordance with Protocol No. 2 on the principles of subsidiarity and proportionality. National parliaments are to ensure compliance with the principle of subsidiarity in accordance with Protocol No. 1 on the role of national parliaments in the European Union.[161] Protocol No. 2 introduces the so-called 'yellow card' procedure (discussed in Section 3 earlier in respect of the Monti II proposal), under which any national parliament or chamber can object to a proposed EU measure, on the grounds that it does not comply with the principle of subsidiarity, by issuing a reasoned opinion. Where one-third of the national parliaments object, the proposal must be formally reviewed by the EU institutions.[162] Heightened scrutiny applies to a proposal under the ordinary legislative procedure, which is objected to by a simple majority of votes allocated to national parliaments.

The UK's New Settlement deal makes provision for the introduction of the so-called red card procedure. Section C.2 of the Decision of the Heads of State or Government provides that 'Where reasoned opinions on non-compliance of a draft Union legislative act

---

[155] Para. 131.   [156] Para. 132.

[157] Case C–380/03 *Germany* v. *European Parliament and Council* [2006] ECR I–11573, para. 148.

[158] See also the AG's Opinion in Case C–358/14 *Poland* v. *Parliament and Council* EU:C:2015:848.

[159] Para. 155, citing the controversial decision in Case C–71/02 *Karner* [2004] ECR I–3025, para. 51.

[160] Although Art. 8 of Protocol No. 2 on the principles of subsidiarity and proportionality confirms that 'The Court of Justice of the European Union shall have jurisdiction in actions on grounds of infringement of the principle of subsidiarity by a legislative act', brought in accordance with the rules laid down in Art. 263 TFEU by 'Member States, or notified by them in accordance with their legal order on behalf of their national Parliament or a chamber thereof'.

[161] See also Art. 12(a)–(b) TEU.

[162] For a full explanation of the procedure, see M. Dougan, 'The Treaty of Lisbon 2007: Winning minds, not hearts' (2008) 45 *CMLRev.* 617, 657–61.

with the principle of subsidiarity, sent within 12 weeks from the transmission of a draft, represent more than 55% of the vote allocated to the national parliaments, the Council Presidency will include the item on the agenda of the Council' for a comprehensive discussion. Following such discussion the representatives of the Member States will 'discontinue the consideration' of the draft, unless the draft is amended to accommodate the concerns. In other words, despite the language of red card, this is not in fact a blocking measure and the voting in Council configurations in Council could already achieve this outcome. Perhaps of more significance in practice is the clear statement that 'The choice of the right level of action therefore depends, inter alia, on whether the issue under consideration has *transnational* aspects which cannot be satisfactorily regulated by action by Member States and on whether action at Union level would produce clear benefits by reason of its scale or effects compared with actions at the level of Member States.'

5. DEROGATIONS FROM MEASURES ADOPTED UNDER ARTICLE 114(1) TFEU

Perhaps the most striking and controversial feature of Article 114 TFEU is that Article 114(4)–(5) TFEU makes express provision for Member States to derogate from a measure adopted under Article 114(1) TFEU.[163] This was the price for the introduction of QMV into Article 114(1) TFEU.[164] Originally the possibility of opting out of Article 114(1) TFEU measures was confined, by Article 114(4) TFEU, to national measures existing at the time when the harmonization measure was adopted (i.e., pre-existing national measures).[165] Article 114(4) TFEU says:

> If, after the adoption of a harmonisation measure by the European Parliament and the Council, by the Council or by the Commission, a Member State deems it necessary to *maintain* national provisions on grounds of major needs referred to in *Article 36*, or relating to the protection of the environment or the working environment, it shall notify the Commission of these provisions as well as the grounds for maintaining them.[166]

The Amsterdam Treaty extended the possibility of derogating from measures adopted under Article 114(1) TFEU to national rules adopted *after* the enactment of the harmonization measure. So Article 114(5) TFEU allows a Member State 'to *introduce* national provisions based on new scientific evidence…on grounds of a problem specific to that Member State arising *after* the adoption of the harmonisation measure'.[167] This scientific

---

[163] This is the only way that derogation can occur: Joined Cases C–281 and 282/03 *Cindu Chemicals v. College voor de Toelating van bestrijdingsmiddelen* [2005] ECR I–8069, para. 47. See also Commission Communication, 'Article 95 (paragraphs 4, 5 and 6) of the Treaty Establishing the European Community', COM(2002) 760 final.
[164] The opt-out applies only to measures adopted under Art. 114(1) TFEU and not to those adopted under any other legal basis: Case C–183/00 *González Sánchez v. Medicina Asturiana SA* [2002] ECR I–3901, para. 23.
[165] E.g., Sweden applied for a derogation under Art. 114(4) TFEU from Dir. 94/36 ([1994] OJ L237/4) to maintain its prohibition on the use of E124 (cochineal red) in foodstuffs. The Commission then failed to respond to the notification. However, in Case C–319/97 *Criminal Proceedings against Kortas* [1999] ECR I–3143 the Court ruled that Sweden could not apply its national rules until authorized to do so by the Commission (para. 28). Cf. Case C–194/94 *CIA* [1996] ECR I–2201, considered in Ch. 4.
[166] Emphasis added.
[167] Emphasis added. On the need to produce new scientific evidence, see Commission Dec. 2003/1/EC relating to 'national provisions on limiting the importation and placement on the market of certain NK fertilizers of high nitrogen content and containing chlorine notified by France pursuant to Art. [114(5) TFEU]' ([2003] OJ L1/72).

evidence—which must be both new and raising a problem specific to the applicant Member State—can relate only to the protection of the environment or the working environment. Thus, unlike Article 114(4) TFEU, the grounds listed in Article 36 TFEU cannot be invoked to justify a national derogation under Article 114(5) TFEU.[168] This is because, as the Court explained in *Commission v. Denmark*[169] in respect of Article 114(4) TFEU, the EU institutions already know of the national provisions but choose not to take them into account, while the adoption of new national legislation under Article 114(5) TFEU is more likely to jeopardize harmonization. For this reason the grounds under which Article 114(5) TFEU can be invoked are more limited.

The Amsterdam Treaty also elaborated on the procedure to be followed once a Member State has notified either an existing or a new national measure. On receipt of a notification, Article 114(6) TFEU provides that the Commission has six months (or 12 in the case of complexity) to approve or reject the national provisions 'after having verified whether or not they are a means of arbitrary discrimination or a disguised restriction on trade between Member States and whether or not they shall constitute an obstacle to the functioning of the internal market'.[170] If the Commission does not respond within the six-month period the national provisions are deemed to have been approved.[171] If the Commission does respond and authorizes a Member State to maintain or introduce national provisions derogating from a harmonization measure, the Commission can examine whether to propose an adaptation of the harmonization measure,[172] especially when the national provisions approved by the Commission offer a level of protection which is higher than the harmonization measure.[173] Article 114(9) TFEU then provides an expedited procedure, by way of derogation from Articles 258–9 TFEU, to bring a Member State directly before the Court of Justice if the Commission or another Member State considers that a Member State is making improper use of the derogation procedure.

Despite the initial fears of some commentators,[174] Article 114(4)–(5) TFEU has not been much invoked by Member States,[175] except in the area of GMOs. The most notorious case was a derogation obtained by Germany from Directive 91/173 on dangerous substances[176] enabling it to maintain stricter standards for PCPs (pentachlorophenol) than those provided in the directive.[177] But the case's notoriety arose not from Germany's abuse of

---

[168] This distinction was recognized by the Court in Case C–512/99 *Germany v. Commission* [2003] ECR I–845, paras. 40–1, and again in Case C–3/00 *Denmark* v. *Commission* [2003] ECR I–2643, paras. 57–8.

[169] Case C–3/00 *Commission* v. *Denmark* [2003] ECR I–2643, para. 57.

[170] For an example of this process see the Dutch notification on maintaining national provisions concerning the use of short-chain chlorinated paraffins (SCCP) (2003/C 100/07).

[171] This will prevent the problem that arose in Case C–319/97 *Kortas* [1999] ECR I–3143, see n. 165, from recurring. See also Case C–439/05 P *Land Oberösterreich* v. *Commission* [2007] ECR I–7141, para. 41, where the Court of Justice emphasized that the authors of the Treaty intended, in the interests of both the notifying Member State and the proper functioning of the internal market, that the procedure laid down in Art. 114 TFEU should be swiftly concluded. It added that this objective would be difficult to reconcile with a requirement for prolonged exchanges of information and observations. Therefore, there was no right to a hearing. See generally N. De Sadeleer, 'Procedures for derogations from the principle of approximation of laws under Article 95' (2003) 40 *CMLRev.* 889.

[172] Art. 114(7) TFEU. Art. 114(8) TFEU makes specific provision regarding Member State difficulties in the public-health field where that area has already been the subject of harmonization.

[173] Case C–3/00 *Commission* v. *Denmark* [2003] ECR I–2643, para. 65.

[174] P. Pescatore, 'Some critical remarks on the "Single European Act"' (1987) 24 *CMLRev.* 9, 12.

[175] Hitherto the Commission's decisions have concerned PCP, creosote, mineral wool, food colourings, sulphates and nitrites, and nitrates used in foodstuffs.

[176] [1991] OJ L85/34.

[177] This directive had been the result of a German notification in 1987 under what is now Dir. 2015/1535 of a draft regulation restricting PCP concentration in wood-treatment preparations.

the procedure but from the Commission's procedural failings in respect of the decision granting the derogation to Germany.[178] As the Court said in *France* v. *Commission*,[179] the Commission had merely described in general terms the content and aim of the German rules and then stated that those rules were compatible with Article 114(4) TFEU 'without explaining the reasons of fact and law on account of which the Commission considered that all the conditions contained in Article [114(4) TFEU] were to be regarded as fulfilled in the case in point'.[180] In particular, the Court said, the Commission should have checked whether the German provisions were justified on the grounds of the major needs mentioned in Article 114(4) TFEU and were not a means of arbitrary discrimination or a disguised restriction on trade.[181]

The Court has also been prepared to take a tough line under Article 114(5) TFEU, requiring Member States to show that they have satisfied the conditions prescribed. This can be seen in the Austrian GMO case. The provincial government of Upper Austria wanted to ban GMOs, on the basis of a scientific report, in order (1) to safeguard organic and traditional farming which is characteristic of the region, and (2) to protect natural biodiversity, particularly in sensitive ecological areas, as well as genetic resources, from 'contamination' by GMOs. Since this ban would contravene the controversial Directive 2001/18 on the deliberate release of GMOs into the environment,[182] the Austrian government notified the Commission of its draft legislation, in accordance with Article 114(5) TFEU. The Commission referred the matter to the European Food Safety Authority,[183] which found that (1) there was no new scientific evidence, in terms of risk to human health and the environment, to justify the prohibition;[184] (2) there were no new data that would change the environmental risk assessment conducted on GMOs that currently held marketing consent in the EU; and (3) there was no scientific evidence to indicate that Upper Austria had unusual or unique ecosystems that required separate risk assessments from those carried out for Austria as a whole.[185] The Commission therefore rejected the Austrian application.[186]

The Land of Upper Austria unsuccessfully sought judicial review of the Commission's decision.[187] The General Court emphasized that, in order to avoid prejudicing the

---

[178] Dec. of 2 Dec. 1992, not published in the OJ but summarized in a Communication ([1992] OJ C334/8).

[179] Case C–41/93 *France* v. *Commission* [1994] ECR I–1829.   [180] Para. 36.

[181] Para. 27. The Commission remade the decision authorizing the German government to maintain its stricter rules. The Danish government was also authorized to maintain stricter rules on PCPs after having notified its draft national laws under Art. 114(4) TFEU (Dec. 96/211 ([1996] OJ L68/32)). At first it had argued that Dir. 91/173 represented minimum rather than complete harmonization. The Commission disagreed. Eventually Denmark was persuaded to make an application under Art. 114(4) TFEU to maintain the stricter national rules, and the measure was considered under the Dir. 2015/1535 procedure.

[182] [2001] OJ L106/1.

[183] <http://www.efsa.europa.eu/en.html>. The reference was made in accordance with Reg. 178/2002 ([2002] OJ L31/1).

[184] If the Commission itself does not properly analyse the relevant scientific evidence this is 'apt to vitiate not only its determination as to whether there was a specific problem but the entirety of its determination of the conditions for applying Articles [114(5)–(6) TFEU], and, particularly, that of the proportionality of the measure notified': Case C–405/07 P *The Netherlands* v. *Commission* [2008] ECR I–8301, para. 77.

[185] Opinion of the Scientific Panel on Genetically Modified Organisms on a question from the Commission related to the Austrian notification of national legislation governing GMOs under [Art. 114(5) TFEU] (2003) 1 *The EFSA Journal* 1.

[186] Commission Dec. 2003/653 ([2003] OJ L230/34). See also Commission Dec. 2008/62/EC ([2008] OJ L16/17), where the Commission rejected a similar request from Poland on the grounds of the absence of any new scientific evidence relating to the protection of the environment or the working environment.

[187] Joined Cases T–366/03 and 235/04 *Land Oberösterreich* v. *Commission* [2005] ECR II–4005.

binding nature and uniform application of Union law, the procedures laid down in Article 114(4)–(5) TFEU were both intended to ensure that no Member State applied national rules derogating from the harmonized legislation without obtaining prior approval from the Commission. In that respect, the rules applicable to national measures notified under Article 114(4) TFEU did not differ significantly from those which applied to national measures still in draft form notified under Article 114(5) TFEU.[188] In respect of Austria's application under Article 114(5) TFEU, the Court noted that Austria had failed to satisfy the burden of proof that there existed specific problems faced by Upper Austria[189] and, since one of the cumulative conditions laid down in Article 114(5) TFEU had not been satisfied, Austria could not derogate from Directive 2001/18.[190] The Court of Justice upheld the General Court's decision.[191] However, Austria's protests were not in vain: Directive 2015/412 was adopted allowing Member States the possibility of restricting or prohibiting the cultivation of GMOs in their territory.[192]

6. NON-LEGISLATIVE ACTS

The legislative acts can be supplemented by 'non-legislative acts'. For our purposes, these non-legislative acts take two forms. The first is Article 290 TFEU *delegated acts*. These can be regulations, directives, or decisions adopted by the Commission which supplement or amend certain non-essential elements of the legislative acts. Drawing on the Court's decisions in cases like *Smoke Flavourings*, the Treaty now provides that the parent legislative act must lay down the objectives, content, scope, and duration of the delegation. It also specifies the conditions to which the delegation is subject (i.e., the EP or the Council may decide to revoke the delegation (a more exceptional measure of control), or the delegated act may enter into force only if no objection has been expressed by the EP or Council within the period expressed by the legislative act).

The second type of non-legislative acts are Article 291 TFEU *implementing acts*. These can be regulations, directives, or decisions which are adopted by the Commission to ensure uniform conditions for implementing legislative acts. The parent 'legislative act' will confer implementing powers on the Commission. The procedure by which the Commission acts (the advisory procedure for less politically controversial matters or the examination procedure for more controversial matters, e.g., programmes with substantial implications, taxation, health and safety) is also specified in the parent measure. The detail of those procedures is spelled out in Regulation 182/2011.[193] In summary, where the advisory procedure is used the Commission must take the 'utmost account' of the opinion of the relevant 'comitology' committee, composed of representatives of the Member States and chaired by the Commission, but is not obliged to follow it. By contrast, under the examination procedure if the relevant comitology procedure votes against the implementing measure the Commission cannot adopt it but the Commission can submit the draft to the appeal committee for further deliberation.

The use of these two types of non-legislative acts can be seen in the context of illegal logging. EP and Council Regulation 995/2010, adopted under Article 114 TFEU, lays down the obligations of operators who place timber and timber products on the market.[194] It prohibits the placing of illegally harvested timber on the EU market and sets

---

[188] Para. 44.   [189] Paras. 64–5.   [190] Para. 69.

[191] Case C–439/05 P *Land Oberösterreich* v. *Commission* [2007] ECR I–7141.

[192] [2015] OJ L68/1, considered by M. Lee, 'GMOs in the internal market: New legislation on national flexibility' (2016) 79 *MLR* 317.

[193] [2011] OJ L55/13.   [194] OJ [2010] L295/23.

up a system of due diligence for operators when placing timber on the market to min-imize the risk of placing illegally harvested timber on the market. The bare bones of the due diligence system are contained in Article 6(1) of the Regulation. Article 6(2) of the Regulation provides that detailed rules necessary to ensure the uniform implementation of paragraph 1 must be adopted in accordance with the examination procedure.[195] These rules were adopted by Commission Implementing Regulation 607/2012.[196]

Regulation 995/2010 also made provision for the establishment of monitoring organ-izations, which must maintain and evaluate the due diligence system and take action against an operator not using the due diligence system. It identifies the criteria for rec-ognizing and withdrawing recognition from the monitoring organizations. Article 8(7) provides that 'In order to supplement and amend the procedural rules with regard to the recognition and withdrawal of recognition of monitoring organisations and, if experi-ence so requires, to amend them, the Commission may adopt delegated acts in accord-ance with Article 290 TFEU'. The Commission duly adopted Delegated Regulation 363/2012 on the procedural rules for the recognition and withdrawal of recognition of moni-toring organizations as provided for in Regulation 995/2010.[197]

It is, in fact, often difficult in any particular case to determine whether the measure is classified as an implementing act or a delegated one. However, in *Biocidal Products* the Court indicated that its review of the choice would be light-touch.[198] It said:

> It must be noted that the EU legislature has discretion when it decides to confer a dele-gated power on the Commission pursuant to Article 290(1) TFEU or an implementing power pursuant to Article 291(2) TFEU. Consequently, judicial review is limited to mani-fest errors of assessment as to whether the EU legislature could reasonably have taken the view…that the system require uniform conditions for implementation.

C. DIFFERENT APPROACHES TO HARMONIZATION

1. INTRODUCTION

Having examined the Union's power to harmonize national rules, we turn now to con-sider the different approaches adopted by the Union to harmonization. In essence, har-monization involves replacing the multiple and divergent national rules on a particular subject with a single EU rule. This rule is intended to protect certain beneficial interests, which would otherwise be protected by national law and justified on the ground of one of the express derogations or a public-interest requirement (e.g., consumer protection and public health), while at the same time advancing free trade and market integration. The Union has long faced the problem of how to realize a harmonized, uniform standard and thus a level playing field upon which firms can compete, while at the same time respect-ing (even fostering) the diversity of the national systems. The EU has experimented with different types of harmonization measure—exhaustive, optional, partial, minimum, reflexive—which we shall examine in turn. However, we begin by examining the situ-ation where no harmonization is necessary at all: mutual recognition.

---

[195] This was formerly the regulatory procedure (Art. 5 of Council Dec. 1999/468 ([1999] OJ L184/23)): Art. 13(1)(c) of Reg. 182/2011.
[196] [2012] OJ L177/16.   [197] [2012] OJ L115/12.
[198] Case C–427/12 *Commission v. Parliament and Council* EU:C:2014:170.

2. MUTUAL RECOGNITION

The principle of mutual recognition means that products/services lawfully put on the market in one Member State can and should be allowed access to the markets in other Member States because they have already satisfied home-state controls. This principle—found in the Treaty[199] and confirmed by *Cassis de Dijon*[200]—lies at the heart of the single market, where standard-setting and enforcement are decentralized, thus removing the need for harmonization. The result of this approach is to put the national systems of regulation into competition.[201]

Mutual recognition goes beyond the simple requirement that the host state must not discriminate on the ground of nationality. As Armstrong puts it, it requires host states to be 'other-regarding' in the sense that they must recognize and give meaning to information about the regulatory history of a product, service, or worker coming from another Member State.[202] Host state *administrators* need to be open to the regulatory systems of other Member States and active in their assessment of equivalence. The duty to be 'other-regarding' also applies to *legislators*. National legislation must not foreclose the possibility of accepting products complying with equivalent standards made in other Member States. Therefore, in *Foie Gras*[203] France was condemned by the Court for adopting a law on the use of the term '*foie gras*' without including a mutual recognition clause in its legislation. Such a clause would permit *foie gras* produced to equivalent standards in other Member States to be sold in France. The Commission now requires mutual recognition clauses to be included in all technical regulations to alert economic operators to the existence of the principle,[204] although *Commission* v. *France (nutrients)*[205] cast doubt on the validity of this requirement, especially in legislation which is not susceptible to having such a clause imposed (e.g., legislation requiring authorization such as that at issue in the *Nutrients* case).[206]

However, despite the promise offered by the principle of mutual recognition as a vehicle for ensuring both market access and national regulatory diversity, its full potential has been limited by administrators who are reluctant to recognize the equivalence of foreign products.[207] As we saw in Chapters 4 and 6, the Mutual Recognition Regulation 764/2008, laying down procedures relating to the application of certain national technical rules to products lawfully marketed in another Member State, attempts to overcome this problem. The effect of this regulation is to make clear that the burden of proof is on the host state as to why it is denying market access rather than on the trader as to why its goods should be admitted.

---

[199] Art. 53 TFEU on the mutual recognition of diplomas and Art. 293 EC (repealed by Treaty of Lisbon) on the mutual recognition of companies and legal persons.

[200] Case 120/78 [1979] ECR 649.   [201] This is considered further in Chs. 1 and 4.

[202] K. Armstrong, 'Mutual recognition' in C. Barnard and J. Scott (eds.), *The Law of the Single European Market: Unpacking the premises* (Oxford: Hart Publishing, 2002), 231.

[203] Case C–184/96 *Commission* v. *France* [1998] ECR I–6197.

[204] The *Foie Gras* case came to the Commission's attention as a result of France's notification of its draft legislation under the Technical Standards Dir. 2015/1535. This directive is seen by the Commission as an important instrument to promote mutual recognition because the Member States can have their own rules recognized when the draft national legislation is sent to other Member States: Commission Communication, 'Management of the mutual recognition of national rules after 1992' (93/C 353/04), para. 36.

[205] Case C–24/00 *Commission* v. *France (nutrients)* [2004] ECR I–1277, para. 28.

[206] For more detailed discussion, see M. Jarvis (2004) 41 *CMLRev.* 1395, 1401–5.

[207] Commission Communication, 'Mutual recognition in the context of the follow-up to the action plan for the single market' (Jun. 1999), 5, and Council Res. of 28 Oct. 1999 on mutual recognition (2000/C 141/02), para. 12. See also Commission Communication, 'Internal market strategy. Priorities 2003–2006', COM(2003) 238, 7, on ways to improve the effectiveness of the operation of the mutual recognition principle.

The role of mutual recognition has also been limited by the Court, first by the introduction of mandatory requirements which can rebut the presumption of mutual recognition,[208] and, secondly, by the development of the principle of functional equivalence,[209] which requires those making an assessment of equivalence to take into account not only the foreign standards but also the broader context in which the goods/services are to be used. This can be seen in *Commission v. France (woodworking)*[210] concerning woodworking machines manufactured in Germany according to standards which took account of the fact that those (Germans) operating them would have a high level of training. However, in France, standards were premised on the fact that (French) users of the machines had to be protected from their own mistakes and so presupposed a low (or non-existent) level of training. Given these differences between the systems, the Court allowed France to apply its own standards to the imported German goods.

While the principle of mutual recognition is attractive and continues to be a key pillar of the single-market programme, the serious limits on its use have meant that it is not a miracle solution and that there is still a need for harmonization legislation to ensure free movement.[211] This can take a number of forms: exhaustive, optional, minimum, and reflexive. We start by examining exhaustive harmonization.

3. EXHAUSTIVE HARMONIZATION

3.1 What Is It?

As the name suggests, exhaustive (or full) harmonization concerns situations where diverse national rules are replaced by a single EU rule, leaving no room for Member State action. A number of such directives have been adopted in the field of goods and all impose a twofold obligation on the Member States:

- to permit the goods complying with the directive to be freely imported and marketed (the free movement clause)
- to prohibit the sale of goods not complying with the directive, even when manufacture and sale take place wholly inside one Member State (the exclusivity clause).

Directive 76/768,[212] concerning the content of cosmetics together with their packaging and labelling, provides a good example of exhaustive harmonization in the field of goods. Article 7(1) of Directive 76/768 contains the free movement clause:

> Member States may not, for reasons related to the requirements laid down in this Directive and the Annexes thereto, refuse, prohibit or restrict the marketing of any cosmetic products which comply with the requirements of this Directive and the Annexes thereto.

---

[208] See further Ch. 6.

[209] J. H. H. Weiler, 'The constitution of the common market place: Text and context in the evolution of the free movement of goods' in P. Craig and G. de Búrca (eds.), *The Evolution of EU Law* (Oxford: OUP, 1999), 366–7.

[210] Case 188/84 *Commission v. France* [1986] ECR 419. Cf. Case 124/81 *Commission v. UK (UHT milk)* [1983] ECR 203, where the Court obliged Member States to recognize regulations and controls which provided equivalent guarantees to their own.

[211] Commission, 'Second biennial report on the application of the principle of mutual recognition in the single market', COM(2002) 419, para. 3.

[212] [1976] OJ L262/169, as amended on numerous occasions. The directive has now been repealed and replaced by Reg. (EC) No. 1223/2009 ([2009] OJ L342/59) with effect from 1 Dec. 2010. The original directive is used, by way of illustration here, since its terminology is more straightforward.

Article 3 of Directive 76/768 contains the exclusivity clause:

> Member States shall take all necessary measures to ensure that only cosmetic products which conform to the provisions of this Directive and its Annexes may be put on the market.

Once the Union has adopted an exhaustively harmonized standard[213] Member States cannot unilaterally impose stricter standards because their action is *pre-empted*. For example, Article 6(1) of the Cosmetics Directive 76/768 and its annexes list the information which must appear on the packaging of cosmetics. Because this list is 'exhaustive', the Court said in *Provide*[214] that Germany could not require further information concerning the quantity and quality of a particular product.[215]

The UK also discovered the full effects of pre-emption in *Dim-dip Headlights*.[216] The annex to Directive 76/756/EEC[217] contained a list of all the lighting and light-signalling devices that were permitted on motor vehicles. This list did not include the dim-dip device which, for safety reasons, British law required vehicles to have. The Court said that because the annex contained an exhaustive list of all the lighting devices considered necessary or acceptable for motor vehicles,[218] the UK could not unilaterally require manufacturers who had satisfied the harmonized technical rules set out in Directive 76/756/EEC to comply with this additional British requirement. Thus, in the name of free movement, the UK was deprived of the possibility of imposing additional safety standards. If the area had not been harmonized and the matter had been dealt with by the Court solely under Articles 34 and 36 TFEU, such additional requirements might well have been justified. However, as the Court said in *Van Bennekom*,[219] when EU directives made provision for the full harmonization of all the measures needed to ensure, inter alia, the protection of human and animal health and life, then recourse to Article 36 TFEU ceased to be justified.

Given the pre-emptive effects of exhaustive harmonization, the Court will check to see whether the directive does in fact fully harmonize the field. This can be seen in *Crespelle*,[220] a case concerning the unlikely subject of trade in deep-frozen bovine semen. Directive 88/407[221] on health requirements of bovine semen made provision for the collection and processing of semen in the Member State of dispatch and transport to the state of destination. It did not, however, address the question of the storage or use of semen in the state of destination. The Court therefore said that since health conditions in intra-Union trade in bovine semen had not yet been fully harmonized at EU level, the state of destination (France) could take unilateral action and, relying on the health grounds in Article 36 TFEU, require importers of bovine semen to store it in an authorized insemination and production centre.[222]

---

[213] As with Dir. 2001/37, which imposed stricter standards concerning maximum tar yields of cigarettes: Case C–491/01 *Ex p. BAT* [2002] ECR I–11453, paras. 77–8.

[214] Case 150/88 *Parfümerie-Fabrik* v. *Provide* [1989] ECR 3891, para. 28.   [215] See n. 214.

[216] Case 60/86 *Commission* v. *UK* [1988] ECR 3921. In the environmental field, see Case C–2/90 *Commission* v. *Belgium (Walloon waste)* [1992] ECR I–4431, paras. 20–1.

[217] [1976] OJ L262/1. The directive has been repealed and replaced by Reg. (EC) No. 661/2009 ([2009] OJ L200/1).

[218] *Commission* v. *UK*, n. 216, paras. 9 and 11.

[219] Case 227/82 *Criminal Proceedings against Leendert van Bennekom* [1983] ECR 3883, para. 35. See also the discussion of the Unfair Commercial Practices Directive 2005/29 ([2005] OJ L149/22) in Ch. 5.

[220] Case C–323/93 *Société Civile Agricole du Centre d'Insémination de la Crespelle* v. *Coopérative d'Elevage et d'Insémination Artificielle du Département de la Mayenne* [1994] ECR I–5077.

[221] [1988] OJ L194/10, now repealed and replaced by Reg. 2016/429 ([2016] OJ L84/1).

[222] Paras. 34–5.

3.2 The Problem with Exhaustive Harmonization

Exhaustively harmonized rules have their attractions for producers: by developing a clear set of rules which manufacturers can apply, they create a level playing field for competition, thereby reducing transactions costs. However, negotiating the content of those rules can take years[223] because, given the pre-emptive effects of any Union rule, Member States are determined to ensure that their own national interests are protected (see Case Study 4.1: Jam and Chocolate) and, where the legal basis requires unanimous voting in Council, any unpopular proposal can be blocked almost indefinitely. And, once adopted, the same obstacles make such legislation difficult to amend to take account of innovation or other unforeseen circumstances, making harmonization conservative and inflexible. Furthermore, by its very nature, exhaustive harmonization eliminates the chance for diversity and experimentation at national level and so raises the spectre of creating Euro-products (sausages, beer, cheese); fears exacerbated by certain parts of the (British) press vigilant for a good Euro-scandal. This has resulted in scare stories about the demise of the prawn-cocktail crisp,[224] and tales of European bans on matters as diverse as homemade jam, round cheese, the sale of plants at church fetes, donkeys from beaches, and darts from pubs.[225] Yet this is a caricature of exhaustive harmonization: as Case Study 15.1 demonstrates, harmonization legislation has helped accommodate national differences through derogations,[226] opt-outs, and phased implementation. In areas such as consumer law, the Commission has returned to the use of exhaustive harmonization, reasoning that the benefits outweigh the disadvantages.[227] The Consumer Rights Directive 2011/83[228] provides an example. Article 4 says:

> Member States shall not maintain or introduce, in their national law, provisions diverging from those laid down in this Directive, including more or less stringent provisions to ensure a different level of consumer protection, unless otherwise provided for in this Directive.

3.3 Subordinate Legislation

Further flexibility is introduced into exhaustive harmonization measures by provisions allowing for adaptation to technical progress through subordinate legislation—either delegated acts, where the Commission's activities are overseen by both the Parliament and the Council, or implementing acts, where the Commission's activities are overseen by

---

[223] E.g., the Architects Dir. took 17 years to agree and the Pharmacists Dir. 16 years: Lord Cockfield, *The European Union: Creating the single market* (Chichester: Wiley Chancery, 1994), 79.

[224] According to the *Daily Telegraph* (1 May 1991, 19), 'Herr Martin Bangemann, the corpulent crisp-hating German who has apparently been the architect of European attempts to scupper the slightly kinky-flavoured crisps we British so enjoy, has been an easy target. On Tuesday he was pursued around Luxembourg by journalists inviting him to try a prawn cocktail crisp or tomato ketchup or Worcestershire sauce.' In fact this scare was caused by an oversight—the crisps had been left off a catalogue of permissible foods containing artificial sweeteners.

[225] Taken from, inter alia, 'Hurd highlights myths and lunacies of Brussels', *Herald*, 7 Nov. 1992, 7; P. Kingsnorth, 'Yes, we have no rules about abnormally bent bananas', *Independent*, 3 Jul. 1995, 4.

[226] See, in particular, the use of Art. 114(4)–(5) TFEU, as the Court pointed out in Joined Case C–281 and 282/03 *Cindu Chemicals BV v. College voor de toelating van bestrijdingsmiddelen* [2005] ECR I–8069, para. 47, or derogations expressly provided for in the directive itself, as the Court recognized in Case C–439/06 *Citiworks* v. *Flughafen Leipzig* [2008] ECR I–3913, para. 63.

[227] See, e.g., COM(2002) 208, 7; COM(2007) 99, 7. For criticism, see S. Weatherill, 'Maximum or minimum harmonisation: What kind of "Europe" do we want' in K. Boele-Woelki and W. Grosheide (eds.), *The Future of European Contract Law: Essays in honour of Ewoud Hondius* (Utrecht: Kluwer, 2007).

[228] [2011] OJ L304/64.

various comitology committees. In *Alliance for Natural Health*[229] the Court recognized the value of the comitology procedure:[230]

> [It] is intended to reconcile, on the one hand the requirement for effectiveness and flexibility arising from the need regularly to amend and update aspects of [Union] legislation in the light of developments in scientific understanding in the area of protection of human health and safety and, on the other, the need to take account of the respective powers of the [Union] institutions.

An example of the application of the comitology procedures can be found in Article 10 of the original Cosmetics Directive 76/768. This provided that the Standing Committee on Cosmetic Products (comprising representatives of the Member States) would assist the Commission[231] under the regulatory committee procedure (now the examination procedure) in amending the lists of substances which cannot be used in cosmetics. Scientific expertise is provided by the Scientific Committee on Consumer Safety (SCCS).[232] The role of the SCCS was emphasized in *Angelopharm*,[233] where the Court said that since the purpose of consulting the Scientific Committee was to ensure that measures adopted at EU level were necessary and adapted to the objective pursued by the Cosmetics Directive of protecting human health, 'consultation of the Committee must be mandatory in all cases'.[234]

Extensive use is also made of subordinate legislation in the Lamfalussy process, which is considered at Section 7.3.

3.4 Conclusions

Despite the various techniques to ensure flexibility, hostility to exhaustive European regulation was acute. In the UK, the so-called 'Metric Martyrs' case, *Thoburn*,[235] demonstrated this most clearly. According to Directive 80/181/EC[236] as amended, metric measures had to be the primary indicators for goods sold loose from 31 December 2000. Imperial measures could be used until January 2010 but only as secondary indicators.[237] Steve Thoburn, a British greengrocer, was successfully prosecuted for using scales calibrated only in imperial measures. He and four others appealed to the Divisional Court, unsuccessfully invoking the doctrine of implied repeal to challenge the validity of the UK's implementation of the EU directives.[238] They were bitter in defeat and used their new-found celebrity to challenge the legitimacy of EU lawmaking.[239] Against this backcloth of hostility it is not surprising that the EU increasingly looked to other types of harmonization.

---

[229] Joined Cases C–154 and 155/04 [2005] ECR I–6451.   [230] Para. 78. See Section B earlier.
[231] Art. 10. This is still the case under Art. 32 of the Cosmetics Reg. 1223/2009.   [232] Art. 8(2).
[233] Case C–212/91 *Angelopharm GmbH* v. *Freie Hansestadt Hamburg* [1994] ECR I–171.
[234] Para. 38.   [235] *Thoburn* v. *Sunderland City Council* [2003] QB 151.
[236] [1980] OJ L39/40.
[237] After public consultation, the Commission agreed to lift the sunset clause for the UK and Ireland and to permit the use of supplementary indications indefinitely: Commission, 'Pints and miles will not disappear due to Commission proposal', IP/07/1297, now Dir. 2009/3/EC ([2009] OJ L114/10).
[238] *Thoburn* [2002] EWHC 195 (Admin), [2002] 1 WLR 247. Had the Metric Martyrs tried to challenge the validity of the directive instead of raising points of UK constitutional law, they might have enjoyed more success, since it could be argued that a directive regulating loose, over-the-counter sales could not be justified on the grounds of removing obstacles to intra-Union trade under Art. 114 TFEU; nor was such a measure compatible with the principles of subsidiarity and proportionality.
[239] Neil Herron of the Metric Martyrs Defence Fund expressed his disgust at the ruling: 'It shows our laws can be overturned by a gathering of unelected bureaucrats over which we have no democratic control.' P. Crosbie and M. Davill, 'Death of pounds and ounces', *Sun*, 19 Feb. 2002, 8. The front-page story is headed 'SURRENDER. Pound of bananas banned as our judges cave in to Europe. So who's running Britain now? BRUSSELS'.

4. OPTIONAL HARMONIZATION

One such alternative is optional harmonization, where directives provide a harmonized standard which manufacturers can *choose* whether to follow. Such directives therefore have a free movement clause but not an exclusivity clause. This means that if manufacturers wish to trade goods across frontiers, then the harmonized standard must be applied; if they wish to operate on a local market only, they can decide whether to apply the harmonized standard or continue to apply national rules. Directive 71/316 on measuring instruments[240] provides an example of such harmonization. The preamble makes it clear that initially EU standards would complement national standards and later, after the required conditions develop, national standards would be replaced by Union standards.

While optional harmonization offers some advantages, by avoiding the disruption to existing markets and preventing technical progress from being stifled, it does raise problems in respect of trade in non-conforming products and difficulties with Articles 34–6 TFEU. It has therefore been little used.

5. MINIMUM HARMONIZATION

5.1 What Is It?

Minimum harmonization is one of the most common forms of approximation used today. As the name suggests, the Union sets minimum standards but Member States are free to impose higher standards on their own goods and services. This partly explains the popularity of minimum standards directives: they help to reconcile the need for a level playing field for competition (the minimum standards) with space to accommodate national diversity (above those minima). This is particularly important in more welfare-orientated areas such as social and consumer policy that merely interface with, rather than serve, the economic demands of the single market.

Although minimum harmonization directives have been around since the early days of the EU,[241] their use was constitutionalized by the Single European Act 1986, when certain new legal bases expressly provided that the Union should adopt directives laying down 'minimum requirements'[242] and that these directives did not 'prevent any Member State from maintaining or introducing more stringent protective measures compatible with the Treaty'.[243] Even though Articles 114–15 TFEU do not contain an express minimum standards clause, minimum harmonization directives have also been adopted under these bases,[244] as the Tobacco Labelling Directive 89/622 and the Tobacco Control Directive 2001/37 (considered in Case Study 15.1) both show.

---

[240] Council Dir. 71/316/EEC of 26 Jul. 1971 on the approximation of the laws of the Member States relating to common provisions for both measuring instruments and methods of metrological control ([1971] OJ L202/1), repealed by Dir. 2009/34 ([2009] OJ L106/7).

[241] For an early example, see Art. 11 of Council Dir. 69/466/EEC and the discussion in Case 4/75 *Rewe-Zentralfinanz GmbH* v. *Landwirtschaftskammer* [1975] ECR 843. See also Case C–44/01 *Pippig Augenoptik GmbH & Co. KG* v. *Hartlauer Handelsgesellschaft mbH* [2003] ECR I–3095, para. 40.

[242] E.g., Art. 153(2)(b) TFEU.

[243] Art. 153(4) TFEU. Similar provisions appear in Art. 193 TFEU on environmental protection, also introduced by the SEA 1986, and in Art. 169(4) TFEU on consumer protection, introduced by the Maastricht Treaty.

[244] Under Art. 115 TFEU: e.g., Art. 5 of Council Dir. 98/59/EC ([1998] OJ L225/16) on collective redundancies. Under Art. 114 TFEU: e.g., Art. 8 of Dir. 93/13 on unfair terms in consumer contracts ([1993] OJ L95/29). See also the Edinburgh European Council's conclusions in 1992 that where it is necessary to set standards at Union level, 'consideration should be given to setting minimum standards, with freedom for the Member States to set higher standards, not only in the areas where the Treaty so requires...but also in other areas where this would not conflict with the objectives of the proposed measure or with the Treaty.'

Minimum harmonization directives therefore provide the floor below which national legislation cannot fall. This floor is exhaustively harmonized and may be set at a relatively high level. As the Court explained in the *Working Time* case, minimum standards do not mean minimal standards: the term minimum requirements 'does not limit [Union] action to the lowest common denominator, or even the lowest level of protection established by the Member States'.[245] Over and above the floor, Member States are free to choose whether to adopt more stringent measures than those resulting from EU law.[246] The only constraints on that freedom are the provisions of the EU Treaties.[247]

Buet,[248] concerning doorstep selling, provides a good example of how the Treaty set the ceiling beyond which national legislation cannot go. Doorstep selling was regulated by Directive 85/577/EEC on the protection of the consumer in respect of contracts negotiated away from business premises.[249] The directive did not prohibit doorstep selling; rather it aimed to protect the consumer from the surprise element associated with such contracts by giving the consumer a right of cancellation.[250] However, Article 8 of the directive allowed Member States to adopt or maintain more favourable provisions to protect the consumers,[251] which, according to the preamble, might include 'a total or partial prohibition on the conclusion of contracts away from business premises'.[252] This was the approach adopted by French law. The question in *Buet* was whether the French provisions were compatible with Article 34 TFEU. The Court acknowledged that the French law constituted an obstacle to imports and breached Article 34 TFEU but found that it could be justified on the grounds of protecting consumers, especially those who were particularly vulnerable, against the risk of ill-considered purchases. Thus, the French prohibition on door-to-door selling, which gave consumers more protection than that laid down by the floor in the directive, was also compatible with the ceiling provided by the Treaty provisions (Articles 34–6 TFEU).

5.2 Reverse Discrimination

Laws protecting consumers are territorial in nature. Not only do they apply to all companies established in the state which sets standards above the directive's minima (e.g., France) but

[245] Case C–84/94 *UK* v. *Council* [1996] ECR I–5755, para. 56.
[246] See also *Opinion 2/91* [1993] ECR I–1061, para. 16, and Case C–2/97 *Società Italiana Petroli SpA* v. *Borsana* [1998] ECR I–8597.
[247] Case C–1/96 *Ex p. Compassion in World Farming* [1998] ECR I–1251, para. 63, considered later and Case C–169/89 *Criminal Proceedings against Gourmetterie van den Burg* [1990] ECR I–2143, para. 9. As to whether fundamental rights might also constitute a 'ceiling', see F. De Cecco, 'Room to move minimum harmonisation and fundamental human rights' (2006) 43 *CMLRev.* 9.
[248] Case 382/87 *Buet* v. *Ministère public* [1989] ECR 1235, para. 8, also considered in Ch. 6. In the field of services, see, e.g., Joined Cases C–34–36/95 *De Agostini* [1997] ECR I–3843 concerning the AVMS Dir. 2010/13 ([2010] OJ L 95/1), considered in Case Study 11.2, where the Court found that the national rule could in principle be justified and so did not breach Art. 56 TFEU, although ultimately this was a matter for the national court to decide. Cf. Case C–410/96 *André Ambry* [1998] ECR I–7875, where the Court found that the national rule did breach the Art. 56 TFEU ceiling.
[249] [1985] OJ L372/31. This directive has now been repealed and replaced by the Consumer Rights Dir. 2011/83 ([2011] OJ L304/64), which is an exhaustive harmonization measure (see Art. 4).
[250] Preamble to the directive.
[251] Cf. the Product Liability Dir. 85/374/EEC ([1985] OJ L210/29), which does not contain the equivalent clause and so is an exhaustive harmonization directive: Case C–183/00 *González Sánchez* [2002] ECR I–3901.
[252] Cf. Case C–376/98 *Tobacco Advertising I* [2000] ECR I–8419, paras. 101–5, where the presence in a directive of a clause permitting Member States to introduce stricter rules that impede imports complying with the requirements of the harmonization directive may be relevant in determining whether the use of Art. 114 TFEU is valid.

they also apply to those companies wishing to trade in France but established in another Member State where only the minimum standards laid down by the directive have been implemented. So, if a company wishes to leave France in order to avoid the ban on doorstep selling and set up in Belgium, where it can engage in doorstep selling, it will nevertheless have to respect France's standards when trading in France. Therefore, in respect of *consumer protection* rules, when a Member State sets higher standards than the directive's minima its businesses do not suffer a competitive disadvantage and consumers benefit.

The situation may be different in respect of minimum standards directives which regulate *products*. For example, if French law requires goods manufactured in France to be produced according to standards above the directive's minima, the French manufacturer may be placed at a competitive disadvantage when exporting its goods to Belgium, where the manufacturer has to comply only with the minimum standards laid down by the directive. This disadvantage also extends to sales within France. If, due to the free movement clause, the directive requires that France admits Belgian goods manufactured according to the minimum requirements laid down by the directive, while French goods have to be manufactured according to the higher French standards, French producers may suffer a competitive disadvantage when faced with competition from their Belgian rivals. The disadvantage experienced by national producers forced to comply with 'superior' national laws is known as 'reverse discrimination'.

The compatibility of reverse discrimination with Union law was considered by the Court in *Gallaher*,[253] a case concerning the UK's implementation of Directive 89/622[254] on tobacco labelling (see Case Study 15.1). The directive required that indications of tar and nicotine levels and health warnings should cover 'at least 4%' of the surface area of the packet. Although the UK voted against the directive, arguing that it represented an undue incursion into national competence,[255] the British implementing rules actually exceeded the minimum requirements laid down by the directive since they required that the warnings cover 'at least 6%' of the surface of the packet.[256] However, in accordance with the free movement clause in Article 8 of the directive,[257] the UK regulations provided that an importer of cigarettes from another Member State was to be regarded as complying with the requirements of UK law if the packets carried the warnings in English and those warnings complied with the rules of the state of origin (normally 4 per cent).[258] Various tobacco companies argued that this different treatment led to reverse discrimination and inequalities in conditions of competition[259] but the Court rejected their argument, saying that the reverse discrimination was the consequence of 'the degree of harmonization sought by the provisions in question, which lay down minimum requirements'.[260]

[253] Case C–11/92 [1993] ECR I–3545.   [254] Now Dir. 2001/37.

[255] S. Weatherill, 'Regulating the internal market: Result orientation in the Court of Justice' (1994) 19 *ELRev.* 55, 57.

[256] Even though the directive did not state explicitly that any of its provisions set minimum standards only, the Court accepted that the expression 'at least' gave the Member States the liberty to decide that the indications and warnings were to cover a greater surface area in view of the level of public awareness of the health risks associated with tobacco consumption.

[257] Art. 8(1) provides: 'Member States may not, for reasons of labelling, prohibit or restrict the sale of products which comply with this Directive.'

[258] *Gallaher*, n. 253, para. 20.   [259] Para. 22.

[260] Para. 22. See also Case C–128/94 *Hans Hönig* v. *Stadt Stockach* [1995] ECR I–3389, para. 17; Case C–14/00 *Commission* v. *Italy (chocolate)* [2003] ECR I–513, paras. 72–3. However, in Case C–222/91 *Ministero delle Finanze and Ministero della Sanità* v. *Philip Morris Belgium SA* [1993] ECR I–3469 the Court recognized that not all of the provisions of the directive laid down minimum standards: e.g., Art. 4(2) of the directive provided for the use of only a single specific health warning. Since this provision did not lay down a minimum requirement the Member State could not require more than one warning (para. 28).

The same rule about reverse discrimination applies equally to exports, as *Compassion in World Farming (CWF)* demonstrates.[261] Directive 91/629/EEC[262] laid down minimum standards for the protection of fattening calves, including minimum provisions on housing space and diet. Article 11(2) provided that 'Member States may, in compliance with the general rules of the Treaty, maintain or apply *within their territories* stricter provisions for the protection of calves than those laid down in this Directive'.[263] Stricter standards were applied in the UK. The Court confirmed that the UK could not, as CWF had advocated, ban exports of calves for rearing in veal crates to countries which had implemented the directive but which did not have the same high standards as the UK. Such a result would have given extraterritorial effect to UK law and undermined the harmonization achieved by the directive. The Court said that:

> the fact that the Member States are authorised to adopt within their own territory protective measures stricter than those laid down in a directive does not mean that the Directive has not exhaustively regulated the powers of the Member States in the area of the protection of veal calves.[264]

In other words, the floor laid down by the directive was exhaustively harmonized regarding imported/exported goods. The UK was free to insist upon higher standards, but only in respect of British calves.

The effect of these rulings might be to prompt a company to move to a Member State which requires only the (cheaper) minimum standards laid down by the directive and then, relying on the directive's free movement clause, import products into the UK, thereby circumventing the higher British standards.[265] Faced with the prospect of an exodus of companies (and thus the loss of British employment), the UK might decide to drop its higher standards and require only the directive's minima. In this way a minimum rule risks becoming a maximum rule. If this is the case then the level at which that minimum is set becomes an important issue for the purpose of consumer protection.

However, some commentators can see commercial advantages for producers manufacturing in states which do insist on higher standards. For example, Scharpf argues that national regulations setting standards above the minima may serve as a certificate of superior quality.[266] Where this is the case, high levels of regulation imposed by France or the UK may create a competitive advantage for the companies subjected to them, and thus exert a competitive pressure on other governments to raise their own level of regulation. These national product regulations may then induce a race to the top, particularly if the French or British market is considered attractive and big enough, with governments of other Member States being persuaded to regulate at French/British levels (or at least their producers voluntarily manufacturing according to French/British standards) so that they do not lose out competitively. This is sometimes referred to as the 'California effect',[267]

---

[261] Case C–1/96 [1998] ECR I–1251.

[262] [1991] OJ L340/28. This directive has now been repealed and replaced by Dir. 2008/119/EC ([2009] OJ L10/7).

[263] Emphasis added.   [264] Case C–1/96 *CWF* [1998] ECR I–1251, para. 63.

[265] These problems could be avoided if there was no free movement clause, although following *Tobacco Advertising I* the legality of such directives adopted under Art. 114 TFEU is uncertain because they do not assist in the process of market integration: manufacturers still have to comply with the different standards of the Member States.

[266] F. Scharpf, 'Introduction: The problem-solving capacity of multi-level governance' (1997) 2 *JEPP* 520.

[267] D. Vogel, 'Trading up and governing across: Transnational governance and environmental protection' (1997) 4 *JEPP* 556, 571.

where states in the USA copied the stricter environmental standards of California in order to enable their producers to trade on the Californian market.

Minimum harmonization is inevitably a compromise between market integration and ensuring sufficient flexibility for Member States. In terms of market integration, the free movement clause has the advantage of ensuring that out-of-state traders will have to comply with only one set of rules across the EU, even if producers in a state which requires higher standards may suffer a competitive disadvantage. From the perspective of diversity and regulatory autonomy, minimum harmonization also has merits because Member States are free to experiment above the minima, if they so choose. Member States must inform the Commission of the steps they have taken to implement the directive,[268] which gives the Commission a large database of comparative national practice to inform any proposed amendments to the directive.[269]

6. THE NEW APPROACH TO TECHNICAL HARMONIZATION AND STANDARDIZATION

6.1 Introduction

The old vertical approach to harmonization was based on common, detailed, technical rules applying to individual sectors. However, the 1980s witnessed a renaissance of a simpler method of regulation known as the 'new approach', which formed a key pillar in the Commission's White Paper on completing the internal market.[270] These new-approach directives are horizontal,[271] applying throughout an industry as a whole rather than to specific groups within that industry. Given their broad field of application, these directives set out general principles rather than detailed rules, leaving wide latitude for interpretation,[272] and rely on private bodies to set voluntary standards. In fact, this 'new' approach is hardly new. It was first tried in the Low Voltage Directive 73/23/EEC[273] and the experience gained formed the basis of a Commission Communication,[274] approved by the Council in a 'Resolution on a new approach to technical harmonisation and standards', which contained a 'model' new-approach directive.[275] This was followed up by a Commission Communication and a Council Resolution 'Enhancing the implementation of the new approach directives'. More significant revisions have occurred with the Requirements

---

[268] Directives now contain a fairly standard clause requiring Member States to 'communicate to the Commission the texts of the provisions of national law which they adopt in the field governed by the Directive': e.g., Art. 10 of Dir. 93/13 on unfair terms in consumer contracts.

[269] S. Weatherill, 'Pre-emption, harmonisation and the distribution of competence to regulate the internal market' in Barnard and Scott, n. 581, cites an example from the environmental field: a four-year concession made on accession allowing Austria, Finland, and Sweden to apply stricter environmental and health standards generated a review that led to the adoption of higher EU-wide standards in a number of relevant areas (COM(98) 745).

[270] COM(85) 310 final, 19–20.

[271] See Case C–359/92 *Germany* v. *Council (product liability)* [1994] ECR I–3681, paras. 23–4.

[272] N. Burrows and H. Hiram, 'Legal articulation of policy in the EC' in T. Daintith (ed.), *Implementing EC Law in the UK: Structures for indirect rule* (Chichester: Wiley, 1995), 45.

[273] Council Dir. 73/23/EEC on the harmonization of the laws of Member States relating to electrical equipment designed for use within certain voltage limits ([1973] OJ L77/29), now repealed and replaced by Dir. 2006/95 ([2006] OJ L374/10). For a full discussion of the 1973 directive see T. Hartley, 'Consumer safety and the harmonisation of technical standards: The Low Voltage Directive' (1982) 7 *ELRev.* 55.

[274] COM(85) 19.

[275] 85/C 136/01. Commission, 'Enhancing the Implementation of New Approach Directives', COM(2003) 240, 5, and Council Res. of 10 Nov. 2003. For details, see <http://www.newapproach.org>.

for Accreditation and Market Surveillance (RAMS) Regulation 765/2008,[276] which has laid down general principles on the accreditation of conformity assessment bodies, on CE marking, and on market surveillance; and Decision 768/2008/EC[277] on a common framework for the marketing of products, which provides common principles and reference provisions for the purposes of legislation based on the new-approach principles. Both of these measures, which formed part of the Commission's 2007 Goods Package,[278] apply to all the new-approach directives which were revised to take account of the changes they introduce.

6.2 The Fundamental Principles

The Commission summarizes the new approach in the following terms: it ensures free movement of goods on condition that a manufacturer guarantees that they are safe. The legislation sets out the level of protection to be achieved but does not prejudge the choice of technical solution to achieve the levels.[279] The new approach is based on five fundamental principles.[280] First, legislative harmonization is limited to the adoption of essential safety standards with which products placed on the market must conform. Once goods conform to those standards and a CE marking is placed on the goods, they must enjoy free movement throughout the Union without the need for verification.[281] Secondly, the task of drawing up the technical specifications which satisfy the essential requirements is entrusted to specialist standardization organizations, CEN,[282] CENELEC,[283] and ETSI,[284] acting by QMV,[285] on a mandate from the Commission.[286] Thirdly, these technical standards are voluntary, and the producer has the choice of either manufacturing in accordance with the standards set by the voluntary bodies or manufacturing according to other standards and then proving that they conform with the essential requirements of the directive through a system of tests and certificates.[287] Fourthly, products manufactured in conformity with harmonized standards are presumed to conform to

---

[276] [2008] OJ L218/30. See L. Gorywoda, 'The new European legislative framework for the marketing of goods' (2009–10) 16 *Columbia Journal of European Law* 161.

[277] [2008] OJ L218/82. It covers the general obligations of economic operators, the presumption of conformity, formal objections against harmonized standards, rules for the CE marking, requirements for conformity assessment bodies and notification procedures, and the provisions concerning procedures dealing with products presenting a risk which should be aligned to that decision.

[278] This was considered in Ch. 4.

[279] Commission, 'Package on internal market for goods', MEMO/07/54.

[280] 'Guidelines for a new approach to technical harmonisation and standards' in Annex II of Council Res. 85/C 136/01; and Commission, 'Enhancing the implementation of the new approach directives', COM(2003) 240, 5.

[281] See also Case 123/76 *Commission* v. *Italy* [1977] ECR 1449, para. 13.

[282] *Comité Européen de Normalisation.*   [283] *Comité Européen de Normalisation Electronique.*

[284] European Telecommunications Standards Institute.

[285] The use of QMV was challenged in Case 123/76 *Commission* v. *Italy* [1977] ECR 1449. Although the Court did not discuss the point, Warner AG said that national standards organizations could decide 'by common agreement' to be bound by QMV.

[286] See General Guidelines for the Cooperation between CEN, CENELEC, and ETSI and the European Commission and EFTA ([2003] OJ C91/7), supplementing the General Guidelines for Cooperation adopted in 1984 (CEN/CENELEC Memo. 4), which confer a monopoly of standard setting on CEN, CENELEC, and now ETSI.

[287] This was facilitated by the Global Approach to Testing and Certification aimed at coordinating the different practices and procedures across Europe: COM(89) 209. See further M. Egan, *Constructing a European Market* (Oxford: OUP, 2001), 126–9; and Commission, *Guide to the Implementation of Directives Based on the New Approach and the Global Approach* (Luxembourg: OPEC, 2000). There is now a dedicated website to the new approach: <http://www.newapproach.org/>.

the essential requirements established by the directive.[288] Finally, Member States must take all appropriate enforcement measures, including market surveillance, to ensure that non-conforming products are withdrawn from the market.

6.3 The Toy Safety Directive

The paradigm example of a new-approach directive is the Toy Safety Directive 2009/48.[289] This updates and replaces the original Toy Safety Directive 88/378,[290] which itself was considered a key test for the new approach to harmonization[291] because it unblocked proposals for a directive on toy safety based on the old approach which had dragged on since the mid 1970s. A proposed directive put forward in 1979 contained over 80 pages of technical annexes.[292] By contrast, the new-approach proposal (what became Directive 88/378) took less than two years to adopt, had 15 Articles and four relatively short annexes covering seven pages. Directive 2009/48 is somewhat longer (57 Articles and five annexes) but is based on broadly similar principles, albeit revised to take account of the RAMS Regulation and Decision 768/2008 on marketing of products.

According to the directive, any toy, defined as a product designed or intended for use in play by children under 14 years old,[293] may be placed on the market, but only if it meets essential safety requirements. These safety requirements are both general, as set out in Article 10(2) ('Toys, including the chemicals they contain, shall not jeopardise the safety or health of users or third parties when they are used as intended or in a foreseeable way, bearing in mind the behaviour of children'), and particular, as set out in Annex II to the directive. The onus is on the Member States to ensure that toys cannot be placed on the market unless they meet these essential safety requirements.[294] The annex identifies six specific risks: physical and mechanical, flammability, chemical, electrical, hygiene, and radioactivity. In some cases the requirements are drafted in general terms, setting objectives to be achieved rather than specifying detailed technical rules. For example, the annex provides '[t]oys, and their parts must not present a risk of strangulation'. Other requirements are more technical and prescriptive, including the requirement that 'Toys shall not be powered by electricity of a nominal voltage exceeding 24 volts direct current (DC) or the equivalent alternating current (AC) voltage, and their accessible parts shall not exceed 24 volts DC or the equivalent AC voltage.'

A manufacturer has two ways to ensure that toys satisfy these essential safety requirements. The first is to manufacture the toy according to harmonized standards produced by CEN and CENELEC[295] in accordance with Directive 2015/1535.[296] Conformity with harmonized standards[297] provides a presumption of conformity with the essential safety requirements of the directive.[298] The manufacturer is then entitled to affix the CE mark (the French acronym for 'European Conformity' (EC)) confirming that the toys comply with the essential safety requirements laid down by the directive.[299] This process of

---

[288] Case 815/79 *Criminal Proceedings against Gaetano Cremonini and Maria Luisa Vrankovich* [1980] ECR 3583, para. 13.

[289] [2009] OJ L170/1.   [290] [1988] OJ L187/1.

[291] M. Egan, *Constructing a European Market* (Oxford: OUP, 2001), 169.   [292] Egan, n. 291, 171.

[293] Art. 2(1). Certain exceptions to this definition are listed in Annex I, which broadly covers products not intended for children, such as scale models for adult collectors and those requiring supervision such as fireworks. Further exceptions (e.g., playground equipment for public use) can be found in Art. 1(2).

[294] Art. 10(1).

[295] CEN/CENELEC's role is referred to in the preamble only.   [296] [2015] OJ L241/1.

[297] In addition, the manufacturer must use the internal production control procedure set out in Module A of Annex II to Dec. 768/2008/EC (Art. 19(2) of Dir. 2009/48).

[298] Art. 13. See also Case C–14/02 *ATRAL* [2003] ECR I–4431, para. 51.

[299] Art. 8(1). The manufacturer must also keep certain specified information available.

self-certification is a central feature of the directive. Contrary to popular belief,[300] the CE mark does not represent a guarantee of quality, nor does it indicate prior approval of the toy. It merely shows that the manufacturer declares that it has applied all relevant EU directives.[301] The Commission has recognized that the function of CE marking is misunderstood but has not made significant changes. Article 30 of the RAMS Regulation 765/2008 merely reiterates that 'The CE marking shall be the only marking which attests the conformity of the product with the applicable requirements of the relevant [Union] harmonisation legislation providing for its affixing.' The Commission also intends to run an information campaign explaining the true meaning of the CE marking.[302] It also makes provision for Member States to take action against improper use of the CE marking.

The second method of ensuring compliance with essential safety standards is to manufacture the toy in accordance with a model which has been 'EC-type examined' by an approved, conformity assessment body (referred to as a notified body) in the state of manufacture.[303] In essence, the notified body will test a sample of the toy to see whether it satisfies the essential safety requirements laid down by the directive. The testing body then issues an 'EC-type examination certificate',[304] which means that the manufacturer can attach the CE mark to each production toy as a self-declaration that the toy has been manufactured in accordance with the sample which has been the subject of an EC-type examination certificate. This second route for compliance was introduced to encourage innovation in new toys where the existing standards are inadequate to establish compliance with the essential safety requirements.[305]

Once the toy complies with the directive and bears the CE mark, it enjoys free movement. The host Member State must assume compliance with the essential safety requirements and cannot impede the toy from being placed on its market[306] (unless the state's market surveillance authorities consider that it presents a risk to health and safety[307]). The host state certainly cannot require products with the CE marking from other Member States to undergo a prior-authorization procedure or any other procedure designed to multiply the number of people required to affix the conformity marking.[308] From this perspective the directive is a total harmonization measure:[309] once the manufacturer[310] complies with the essential requirements its goods will have free access to the markets of all the Member States, with the CE mark acting as a kind of passport. The Member States certainly cannot invoke any Treaty provisions (e.g., Article 36 TFEU) to justify any national measures which derogate from the provisions of the directive.[311] However,

---

[300] Commission Communication, 'Enhancing the implementation of the new approach directives', COM(2003) 240.

[301] COM(2007) 35, 9.   [302] MEMO/07/54.

[303] An application for 'EC–type' examination, performance of that examination, and issue of the 'EC–type' examination certificate are to be carried out in accordance with the procedures set out in Module B of Annex II to Dec. No. 768/2008/EC. 'EC–type' examination shall be carried out in the manner specified in the 2nd indent of point 2 of that Module: Art. 20(1).

[304] Art. 20.

[305] In a similar vein, in the context of Art. 34 TFEU, see Joined Cases C–388 and 429/00 *Radiosistemi* [2002] ECR I–5845 and Case C–13/01 *Safalero Srl* v. *Prefetto di Genova* [2003] ECR I–8679.

[306] Art. 12.   [307] Art. 42.

[308] Case C–132/08 *Lidl Magyarország Kereskedelmi bt* v. *Nemzeti Hírközlési Hatóság Tanácsa* [2009] ECR I–3841, para. 28.

[309] See Annex II, B, II.1 of Council Res. 85/C 136/01 and Case C–288/08 *Kemikalieinspektionen* v. *Nordiska Dental AB* [2009] ECR I–11031, para. 44; Case C–132/08 *Lidl Magyarország Kereskedelmi bt* [2009] ECR I–3841, para. 43.

[310] The directive also imposes obligations on other economic operators, such as importers and distributors: Arts. 4–9.

[311] Case C–132/08 *Lidl Magyarország Kereskedelmi bt* [2009] ECR I–3841, para. 42.

the principle of mutual recognition also plays a role: the host state must assume that, for example, the certificates issued by the notified body in the state of origin after testing the toy, are equivalent to the host state's standards or tests. The accreditation rules introduced by the RAMS Regulation are intended to enhance confidence in the genuine equivalence of conformity assessment testing by the 1,800 or so testing bodies in the Member States.

Finally, Member States must organize and perform surveillance of toys placed on the market in accordance with the provisions of the RAMS Regulation. This includes performing physical checks on samples of the toy.[312] Where they consider that the product presents a serious risk requiring rapid intervention, they can order the recall of the product.[313] The RAPEX mechanism (considered in Section D) is used for exchanging information with other Member States.

6.4 Assessment

While some commentators have expressed concerns that the new approach may actually reduce protection given to consumers due to the absence of specific detailed standards,[314] Pelkmans believes that the new approach is 'qualitatively an enormous improvement over the traditional approach'.[315] He argues that it is a serious attempt to achieve coherence by 'combining *total harmonization* of the objectives at issue (safety etc.) with a flexible approach of the means (standardization)'.[316] At the heart of the new approach lie the harmonized standards adopted by CEN, CENELEC, and ETSI. Some have questioned whether this constitutes an impermissible delegation of power by the Commission.[317] But the Commission argues that no delegation is involved because the standards (as opposed to the essential safety requirements) are voluntary codes and therefore independent of EU law.[318] Others have questioned the legitimacy and accountability of CEN, CENELEC, and ETSI. For example, Burrows expresses concerns that decision-making can be slow[319] and lacks transparency, prompting concerns of capture by the industry to be regulated and thus the risk of dilution of the pre-existing national standards and the exclusion of the consumer's voice. These standards bodies are also not bound by Treaty obligations such as the duty to give reasons in Article 296 TFEU or other principles of good government,[320] nor have they been subject to review by the Court of Justice.[321]

---

[312] Art. 19 RAMS Reg.   [313] Art. 20 RAMS Reg.

[314] Cf. the discussion in Ch. 6 about the effects of the judgment in Case 120/78 *Cassis de Dijon* [1979] ECR 649.

[315] J. Pelkmans, 'The new approach to technical harmonization and standardization' (1987) 25 *JCMS* 249, 259.

[316] Pelkmans, n. 315, 257.

[317] E. Previdi, 'The organisation of public and private responsibilities in European risk regulation: An institutional gap between them' in C. Joerges, K.-H. Ladeur, and E. Vos (eds.), *Integrating Scientific Expertise into Regulatory Decision-Making: National traditions and European innovations* (Baden-Baden: Nomos Verlagsgesellschaft, 1997).

[318] Burrows and Hiram, n. 272, 44, and L. Gormley, 'Some reflections on the internal market and free movement of goods' [1989/1] *LIEI* 9, 13. Cf. R. H. Lauwaars, 'The "model" directive on technical harmonisation' in R. Bieber et al. (eds.), *One European Market? A critical analysis of the Commission's internal market strategy* (Baden-Baden: Nomos Verlagsgesellschaft, 1988), 165–7.

[319] See, e.g., Council Res. of 28 Oct. 1999 (2000/C 141/02), para. 29; Council Conclusions of 1 Mar. 2002 on Standardization (2002/C 66/01). This is caused in part by lack of resources: Pelkmans, n. 315, 263.

[320] R. Dehousse, '1992 and beyond: The institutional dimension of the internal market programme' [1989/1] *LIEI* 109, 126.

[321] Although the Court may have an ancillary role in ensuring that these committees are involved in the standardization process: cf. Case C–212/91 *Angelopharm* [1994] ECR I–171. Cf. the Lisbon revisions to Art. 263(1): the Court of Justice shall review 'the legality of acts of bodies, offices or agencies of the Union intended to produce legal effects vis-à-vis third parties'.

There is some recognition of these problems by the EU institutions,[322] but, in the context of the wider debate about the quality of governance in the EU,[323] reforming the standard-setting process is not a priority.[324] This may be because the process actually works. As de Búrca puts it, one of the possible explanations for the acceptance of such 'non-democratic' bodies and networks in the EU is that elite or technocratic modes of governance have always been central to the European integration project, and the EU has never been more than a weakly democratic polity whose legitimacy has been based on factors such as the success of the single market project.[325]

7. 'NEW GOVERNANCE' APPROACHES

7.1 Introduction

Of the approaches to harmonization considered so far, the law has been used to 'perfect' the market in the sense of reproducing the outcome which the parties would have arrived at in the absence of transaction costs. Such a substantive approach to regulation presupposes that there is 'optimal' legislation which can be identified by legislators. In practice the information problems facing legislators are such that it is very difficult to identify an 'optimal' solution. For this reason there was a growing interest, dating back to the 1990s, to a more procedural approach to regulation whereby the law does not seek to achieve its ends by direct prescription (e.g., an exhaustive harmonization directive) but instead empowers local actors to promote diverse local-level approaches to regulatory problems. This has been described as 'reflexive harmonization',[326] by analogy to the idea of reflexive law,[327] where the law seeks to devolve or confer rule-making powers to self-regulatory processes.

7.2 Reflexive Harmonization and the Open Method of Coordination

This reflexive quality can be seen in minimum standards directives, which allow Member States or other actors to exceed the minimum standards, taking into account national interests. The European Works Councils (EWC) Directive[328] provides a good example. It requires the creation of an EWC or a similar information and consultation procedure in transnational companies over a certain size. Management and labour, the so-called social partners, are encouraged to set up their own EWCs or equivalent and to negotiate the terms and conditions under which they operate. If they fail to do so, the default rules found in the annex apply. These default rules induce the more powerfully placed party (the employer) to enter into a bargaining process when it otherwise would lack an incentive to do so.[329] The success of this model has been extended to the worker participation

---

[322] See, e.g., Commission, 'Efficiency and accountability in European standardisation under the new approach', COM(98) 291; Council Res. 2000/C141/01, which 'Confirms that standardisation is a voluntary, consensus-driven activity, carried out by and for the interested parties themselves, based on openness and transparency'; Parliament Res. ([1999] OJ C150/624) and the follow up Commission Report, COM(2001) 527.

[323] See the European Governance White Paper, COM(2001) 428.

[324] See COM(2001) 527, para. 4.1.

[325] G. de Búrca, 'Institutional development of the EU' in Craig and de Búrca, n. 209, 79.

[326] See, e.g., S. Deakin, 'Two types of regulatory competition: Competitive federalism versus reflexive harmonisation. A law and economics perspective on Centros' (1999) 2 CYELS 231.

[327] See generally G. Teubner, Law as an Autopoietic System (Oxford: Blackwell, 1993); R. Rogowski and T. Wilthagen (eds.), Reflexive Labour Law (Deventer: Kluwer, 1994).

[328] Dir. 2009/38/EC ([2009] OJ L122/28).

[329] I. Ayres and R. Gertner, 'Filling gaps in incomplete contracts: A theory of default rules' (1989) 99 Yale LJ 87.

provisions in a European company (Societas Europea (SE)).[330] The standard rules contained in the annex, as laid down by the legislation of the Member State in which the registered office of the SE is to be situated, apply from the date of the registration of the SE, where either the parties so agree or no agreement has been concluded at the end of the six-month deadline.

The open method of coordination (OMC) provides another, softer example of reflexive harmonization. OMC involves:

> fixing guidelines for the Union, establishing quantitative and qualitative indicators and benchmarks as a means of comparing best practice, translating these European guidelines into national and regional policies by setting specific targets, and periodic monitoring, evaluation and peer review organised as 'mutual learning processes'.[331]

The OMC process is explicitly about experimentation and learning. Most commentators agree that it should, at least in theory, increase democracy in the EU through the enhanced role for deliberation among policymakers and participation of a broad range of actors at different levels.[332]

OMC was first tried and tested in the policies supporting EMU. It then spilled over into the employment strategy, found in Title IX TFEU on employment, where guidelines are set which are then reflected in national reform programmes.[333] OMC also peppered the (now infamous) Lisbon strategy 2000 (which set the over-ambitious target of making the European economy the most competitive in the world by 2010). For example, in the context of modernizing the European social model, targets were set (e.g., raising the employment rate from an average of 61 per cent in 2000 to as close as possible to 70 per cent by 2010[334]), and comparing best practice was encouraged (e.g., Member States were to exchange experiences and best practices on improving social protection and to gain a better understanding of social exclusion[335]). The failure of the Lisbon strategy and the spectacular failure of the OMC mechanisms, used in EMU to predict and then deal with the economic crisis, has brought OMC somewhat into disrepute. Nevertheless, the follow-on programme to the Lisbon strategy, Europe 2020,[336] still relies on OMC techniques, albeit with fewer targets.[337]

Advocates of OMC argue that it offers a 'third way' for European policy between regulatory competition (with the risk of a race to the bottom) and harmonization (with the risk of ill-suited uniformity). According to the Commission,[338] OMC has greater

---

[330] See Council Reg. No. 2157/2001 on the Statute for a European Company ([2001] OJ L294/1) supplemented by Council Dir. 2001/86 with regard to the involvement of employees ([2002] OJ L294/22). For a further example of reflexive law, see EP and Council Dir. 2002/14 on the general framework for informing and consulting employees in the European company ([2002] OJ L80/29).

[331] Presidency Conclusions, Lisbon European Council, 23 and 24 Mar. 2000, para. 37.

[332] Although, for a sceptical view based on a case study taken from the Occupational Health and Safety sector, see S. Smismans, 'New modes of governance and the participatory myth', European Governance Papers (EUROGOV), No. N–06–01.

[333] Discussed further in C. Barnard, *EU Employment Law* (Oxford: OUP, 2012), Ch. 3; and D. Ashiagbor, *The European Employment Strategy: Labour market regulation and new governance* (Oxford: OUP, 2005).

[334] Presidency Conclusions, Lisbon European Council, 23 and 24 Mar. 2000, para. 30. It also envisages that the number of women in employment will increase from an average of 51 per cent today to more than 60 per cent by 2010.

[335] Presidency Conclusions, Lisbon European Council, 23 and 24 Mar. 2000, paras. 31 and 33.

[336] European Council Presidency Conclusions, 25 and 26 Mar. 2010.

[337] For suggestions as to how OMC might apply in the context of the single market: Commission Communication on an open method of coordination for the Community immigration policy, COM(2001) 387 final.

[338] <http://eur-lex.europa.eu/legal-content/EN/TXT/?uri=CELEX%3A52001DC0565>.

visibility, encourages a strategic and integrated approach, puts a particular issue in the mainstream, mobilizes all relevant actors, and encourages mutual learning. It can also be used in areas which are not so easily susceptible to regulation either because of the subject matter (e.g., employment policy) or because of a lack of clear Union competence (e.g., education). It can sit alongside a legislative approach, in areas such as employment and social policy, or it can stand alone, adding 'value' at a European level where there is little scope for legislative solutions (e.g., work at a European level defining future objectives for national education systems).[339]

Detractors of OMC say that it allows the EU to encroach into policy areas largely reserved for the Member States, that it is more opaque and unaccountable[340] than the 'classic Community method',[341] and that its success is still dependent on Member State action. If—or when—states do not fulfil their commitments, the credibility of the process is undermined.

Even if OMC worked perfectly, it is clear that there would still be a role for hard-law harmonization. As Schmitt von Sydow bluntly observes, it will be possible to buy an electrical appliance in any part of the EU and to take it across the border without restriction, but at home it may still prove impossible to plug it into the wall socket.[342]

7.3 The Lamfalussy Process

Another example of these 'new governance' techniques with a 'harder' edge than OMC is the Lamfalussy process. A committee of 'wise men', under the chairmanship of Baron Lamfalussy, identified the problems associated with the traditional approach to regulation, especially in the field of financial services.[343] It noted that blockages occur at four levels:[344]

- in the Commission itself—over-stretched, sometimes slow off the mark
- most notably in the Council of Ministers, where there is far too often a tendency to add unnecessary levels of complexity to straightforward Commission proposals (often in an attempt to try to fit (the then) 15 sets of national legislation into one Union framework)
- in the European Parliament, although less than in the past
- in the Member States, where transposition and implementation were often late and frequently incomplete.

The Lamfalussy report therefore concluded that the current regulatory system was too slow (e.g., the European Company Statute took more than 30 years to agree), too rigid (every change, however small or technical, required a full-blown Commission proposal to be negotiated by co-decision), and produced too much ambiguity both in the substance

---

[339] Governance White Paper, COM(2001) 428, 22.

[340] C. de la Porte and P. Nanz, 'The OMC: A deliberative-democratic mode of governance? The cases of employment and pensions' (2004) 11 *JEPP* 267. As Hepple puts it in *Rights at Work* (London: Sweet & Maxwell, 2005), 32, the employment guidelines are phrased in 'the mumbo-jumbo of modern management speak'.

[341] Cf. the principles of good governance set out in the Commission's White Paper on Governance, COM(2001) 428.

[342] See H. Schmitt von Sydow, 'The basic strategies of the Commission's White Paper' in Bieber et al., n. 318.

[343] Final Report of the Committee of Wise Men on the Regulation of European Securities Markets (Brussels, 2001).

[344] p. 14.

of the directive and the way the texts were implemented.[345] It also complained that the system failed to distinguish between core, enduring, essential framework principles and practical, day-to-day, implementing rules with the result that directives were too detailed and could not be adjusted expeditiously at a time when the pace of change in financial markets, global and Europe-wide, was accelerating. Lamfalussy therefore proposed a four-level approach to regulation designed to overcome the defects it had identified. It was piloted in the securities field and has since been extended to banking, insurance, and pensions.

Even with the major changes to regulation in the field of financial services since the crisis, this four-level approach remains, albeit with amendments taking into account the new regulatory architecture of the EU and the Lisbon reforms.[346] What follows is a summary of the post-Lisbon Lamfalussy framework:

- Level 1 (legislative acts): *Framework principles*—the core political principles—to be decided by normal EU legislative procedures (generally the ordinary legislative procedure). The Level 1 measure specifies the powers given to the Commission under Article 290 TFEU (for delegated acts)[347] or Article 291 TFEU (implementing acts) or whether, in the case of non-legislative acts that are binding technical standards (BTS), the relevant European Supervisory Authority (ESA) must submit draft legislation to the Commission.

- Level 2 (non-legislative acts): *Detailed technical measures*—two types of measures can be adopted at Level 2:

  (1) Binding technical standards (BTS): these are drafted by the ESA and can be adopted by the Commission as delegated or implementing regulations or decisions under Articles 290–1 TFEU. These are known as *regulatory technical standards* and *implementing technical standards* respectively. The regulatory technical standards 'shall not imply strategic decisions or policy choices and their content shall be delimited by the legislative acts on which they are based'.[348]

  (2) Other non-legislative acts adopted as either delegating measures under Article 290 TFEU or implementing measures under Article 291 TFEU. In respect of implementing measures there are three relevant comitology committees: the EU Securities Committee (ESC), the European Banking Committee (EBC), the European Insurance and Occupational Pensions Committee (EIOPC).

- Level 3: *Enhanced cooperation and networking*—the ESAs (European Securities and Markets Authority (ESMA), the European Insurance and Occupational Pensions Authority (EIOPA), and the European Banking Authority (EBA)), acting in coordination with national supervisors (who sit on the board of supervisors of the ESA),[349] and the European Systemic Risk Board are to ensure consistent and equivalent transposition of Level 1 and 2 legislation. The ESAs can issue guidelines and recommendations[350] and conduct regular peer reviews of national supervisory authorities to improve the consistency of supervision.

---

[345] Final Report of the Committee of Wise Men, n. 343, p. 15.   [346] p. 19.

[347] Although there is no comitology any more under Art. 290 TFEU, advisory committees consisting of national experts continue to exist in the area of financial services (Decl. No. 39).

[348] See, e.g., Art. 10 of the ESMA Reg. 1095/2010 ([2010] OJ L331/84).

[349] See, e.g., Art. 31 of the ESMA Reg.

[350] The BTS and the guidelines and recommendations constitute the 'common European rule book'.

- Level 4: *Strengthened enforcement*—notably with more vigorous action by the European Commission, and now the ESAs, to enforce Union law.[351] The procedure with the ESA ultimately leads to a fast-track quasi-enforcement procedure initiated by the Commission.

As this brief description of the Lamfalussy process shows, this process recognizes two layers: (1) legislative and (2) implementation/enforcement. The legislative layer is sub-divided into two: basic political choices that are translated into broad but sufficiently precise framework norms (Level 1)[352] and then operationalized through more detailed technical measures (Level 2) which are to be adopted on a faster track. The implementation/enforcement layer is also subdivided into two: Level 3 concerns practical implementation, with greater consistency in implementation using the ESAs to achieve this, and more robust enforcement (Level 4).

In assessing the effects of the Lamfalussy process pre-Lisbon, Hadjiemmanuil wrote that the Level 1 directives had indeed all included significant comitology mandates, asking the Commission to clarify and adapt certain basic definitions found in the main instrument.[353] He also noted that the detailed character of the Level 2 instruments signals a drastic departure from the minimum harmonization principle. More controversially, he identified the practice of preparing Level 2 measures while the content of the Level 1 measure has not been finalized, thereby risking pre-empting the political decisions at Level 1. He concluded that while the Lamfalussy process is complex and not as quick as originally envisaged, it has streamlined rule-making and strengthened cooperation between regulators and the coherent and equivalent application of norms by the Member States,[354] with the result that the Lamfalussy process has now been extended to banking, insurance, and pensions.

8. ENHANCED COOPERATION

The Treaties do 'enable and encourage a group of Member States to cooperate inside rather than outside the Union, where it is established that the objectives pursued by that cooperation cannot be achieved by the Union as a whole'.[355] The use of enhanced co-operation is strictly limited by the framework for enhanced cooperation between Member States found in Title IV of the TEU and Title III (Article 20 TEU) of Part Six of the TFEU (Articles 326–34 TFEU). In particular enhanced cooperation must involve at least nine Member States and must be authorized by the Council, which must give its authorization only as a last resort.[356] Further, the measure adopted:

- must be aimed at furthering the objectives of the Union, at protecting its interests, and at reinforcing its integration process[357]

- must comply with the Treaties and Union law[358]

---

[351] See, e.g., Art. 17 of the ESMA Reg.

[352] See Reg. 596/2014 on Market Abuse ([2014] OJ L173/1); the Prospectus Dir. 2003/71 ([2003] OJ L345/64); the Markets in Financial Instruments Dir. 2014/65 ([2014] OJ L173/349); the Transparency Dir. 2004/109/EC ([2004] OJ L390/38) for examples of Level 1 measures.

[353] See D. Chalmers et al., *European Union Law* (Cambridge: CUP, 2006), 815–17.

[354] This broadly favourable view is repeated in the Commission's own review of the Lamfalussy process: COM(2007) 727. A number of the reforms proposed then have now been adopted.

[355] Opinion of Bot AG in Joined Cases C–274 and 295/11 *Spain and Italy* v. *Council* EU:C:2013:240, para. 82.

[356] Art. 20(2) TEU.   [357] Art. 20(1), second subpara. TEU.   [358] Art. 326, first para. TFEU.

- must not undermine the internal market or economic, social, and territorial cohesion
- must not constitute a barrier to, or discrimination in, trade between Member States, and must not distort competition between them[359]
- must also respect the competences, rights, and obligations of those Member States that do not participate in it. Those Member States, in turn, must not impede its implementation by the participating Member States.[360]

The *Unitary Patent* case[361] suggests that enhanced cooperation has the Court's blessing. By definition, of course, any measures adopted will not bind all Member States and so will lead to further fragmentation. However, it does break a deadlock. As the story of the Unitary Patent shows, some Member States had been trying to adopt this measure for decades; Spain and Italy held out over the language rules. The Council approved the measure to go ahead under enhanced cooperation. Spain and Italy objected but to no avail.

D. COMPLETING THE INTERNAL MARKET

1. POST-1992

Most of the Commission's 282 proposals put forward in the Single Market White Paper of 1985 were adopted by the end of 1992[362] (although crucial elements such as utilities, taxation, and corporate law were still missing). The question then was where to go next. There have been numerous strategy documents and reviews.[363]

The Monti Review of May 2010 recognized 'integration fatigue', eroding the appetite among citizens for a *single* market and 'market fatigue', with a reduced confidence in the role of the market. The Report was therefore followed up with another relaunch of the single market in Spring 2011, grandly named the Single Market Act (SMA) I. This identified 'Twelve Levers to boost growth and strengthen confidence',[364] accompanied by 50 complementary actions. These levers included: Lever 2, 'citizens mobility', modernizing the rules for the recognition of professional qualifications and improving the portability of pensions; and Lever 5, 'services', revising legislation on European standardization and ensuring the implementation of the services directive. Lever 10, 'social cohesion', specified that legislation on the enforcement of the Posted Workers Directive would be introduced (now Directive 2014/67) together with legislation 'clarifying the exercise of freedom of establishment and the freedom to provide services alongside fundamental social rights'. This led to the so-called Monti II proposal, which rose and sank amid the fury of trade unions.

Despite all the fanfare surrounding the launch of SMA I, within 18 months the Commission felt obliged to issue the Single Market Act II[365] in order to inject some fresh impetus into the programme. As the Commission noted, 11 of the 12 key action proposals

---

[359] Art. 326, second para. TFEU.   [360] Art. 327 TFEU.
[361] Joined Cases C–274 and 295/11 *Spain and Italy* v. *Council* EU:C:2013:240.
[362] The Commission noted in 1992 that 32 out of the 282 measures proposed still awaited adoption, of which nine were of low priority: COM(92) 383.
[363] Commission Communication, 'The strategy for Europe's internal market', COM(99) 624. This followed on from the Single Market Action Plan, CSE(97) 1 final, which followed on from the Commission's Communication, 'The impact and effectiveness of the single market', COM(96) 520. See also COM(2003) 238; COM(2007) 724. See further I. Govaere, 'The future direction of the EU internal market: On vested values and fashionable modernism' (2009–10) 16 *Columbia Journal of European Law* 67.
[364] COM(2011) 206.   [365] COM(2012) 573.

had not yet been agreed by the European Parliament and Council. SMA II largely reiterates the content of SMA I but it returns to a familiar theme: 'The success of this endeavour will depend on whether Single Market rules are applied on the ground efficiently, in a predictable and reliable manner. To this end, the transposition and day-to-day implementation of Single Market rules by authorities in Member States is of paramount importance. The Commission will devote all its attention to this challenge.'[366]

This idea of a 'coordinated and cooperative approach' between the Commission and the Member States with a 'common objective of improved transposition, application and enforcement of single market rules',[367] is further emphasized by the Commission in its Recommendation 2009/524/EC[368] on measures to improve the functioning of the single market. It is this aspect of the post-1992 internal-market strategy—described by Weatherill as 'market management'[369]—that we shall focus on, looking first at simplification/improving the quality of legislation, secondly, the implementation of that legislation, and thirdly, enforcement.

2. MARKET MANAGEMENT

2.1 Simplification/Improving Quality of Legislation

According to the Commission, €50 billion could be saved by better-quality legislation. This emphasis on better lawmaking has been a preoccupation for the EU since the late 1990s. The 'Better Lawmaking' programme[370] was replaced by the Better Regulation for Growth and Jobs Agenda.[371] This had three strands. First, *pending* legislative proposals have been screened to ensure their consistency with the objectives of the revised Lisbon strategy to check they meet with the better regulation standards and to ensure they are not outdated. As a result, 73 proposals were withdrawn in 2015 and 400 since 2006. Proposals withdrawn in 2015 included Investor Compensation schemes, the Statute for a European Foundation, and European Tourism Quality Principles.[372]

Secondly, *existing* legislation is to be simplified. This strand builds on the earlier 'SLIM' (Simpler Legislation for the Internal Market) initiatives and is now referred to as 'REFIT', the Regulatory Fitness and Performance programme. Action is taken 'to make EU law simpler and to reduce regulatory costs, thus contributing to a clear, stable and predictable regulatory framework supporting growth and jobs'.[373] The case for simplification is a strong one.[374] For example, there were 38 directives on agricultural tractors, 13 on dangerous substances, and 11 on fertilizers.[375] The Commission launched a series of actions to simplify the content of the *acquis*,[376] update it, and reduce its volume

---

[366] See also 'Better governance for the single market', COM(2012) 259.

[367] COM(2007) 724.   [368] [2009] OJ L176/17.

[369] S. Weatherill, 'New strategies for managing the EC's internal market' (2000) 53 *CLP* 595, 598.

[370] COM(96) 559. See also the Commission's Action Plan, 'Simplifying and improving the regulatory environment', COM(2002) 278, followed up by the Commission's Communication, 'Updating and simplifying the Community *acquis*', COM(2003) 71. See also the Interinstitutional Agreement on Better Law-Making ([2003] OJ L321/1), 4.

[371] Commission Communication, 'Better regulation for growth and jobs in the European Union', COM(2005) 97.

[372] <http://ec.europa.eu/smart-regulation/refit/index_en.htm>.

[373] <http://ec.europa.eu/smart-regulation/refit/index_en.htm>.

[374] Council Res. of 8 Jul. 1996 on legislative and administrative simplification in the field of the internal market ([1996] OJ C224/5).

[375] Sutherland Report, *The Internal Market after 1992: Meeting the challenge*, Report to the EEC Commission by the High Level Group on the Operation of Internal Market 1992, 10.

[376] COM(2003) 71.

(through consolidation, codification, and removal of obsolete legislation), as well as improving its organization and presentation. This has reduced the volume of legislation: the Commission aims to reduce the *acquis* by almost 10 per cent—about 1,300 legal acts and 7,800 pages of the Official Journal.[377] More than 6,100 legal acts have been repealed since 2005.[378]

The third strand of the Commission's Better Regulation Agenda concers better quality of *new* Commission proposals, in particular through the systematic use of impact assessment[379] and public consultation[380] in the development of proposals. The details of how these are to be carried out have been laid down in the Better Regulation Guidelines.[381] The Regulatory Scrutiny Board, set up in July 2015, provides a central quality control and support function for Commission impact assessment and evaluation work.[382] It examines and issues opinions on all the Commission's draft impact assessments and of major evaluations and 'fitness checks' of existing legislation. In principle, a positive opinion is needed from the Board for an initiative accompanied by an impact assessment to be tabled for adoption by the Commission.

The approach in the Better Regulation Agenda has been confirmed and developed in the 2015 Better Regulation Package.[383] As the Commission notes,[384] better regulation is not necessarily about deregulation. It is, as we have seen throughout this book, about protecting non-market values:

> Better regulation is not about 'more' or 'less' EU legislation; nor is it about deregulating or deprioritising certain policy areas or compromising the values that we hold dear: social and environmental protection, and fundamental rights including health—to name just a few examples. Better regulation is about making sure we actually deliver on the ambitious policy goals we have set ourselves.

There is now an Interinstitutional Agreement (IIA) on Better Law-Making[385] with the European Parliament and Council to improve the quality and the results of European legislation. The agreement will enter into force once approved by all three institutions. It will bring changes across the full policy-making cycle, from consultations and impact assessment to adoption, implementation, and evaluation of EU legislation.

The need for better regulation became one of David Cameron's 'baskets' in his negotiation of the New Settlement deal. The section on competitiveness commits the relevant EU institutions and the Member States to take concrete steps towards better regulation, which is a key driver to deliver the internal market ('an essential objective' of the Union). This means 'lowering administrative burdens and compliance costs on economic operators, especially small and medium enterprises, and repealing unnecessary legislation as foreseen in the Declaration of the Commission on a subsidiarity implementation

---

[377] COM(2003) 71.   [378] <http://ec.europa.eu/smart-regulation/refit/index_en.htm>.

[379] See the Commission's *Impact Assessment Guidelines* (SEC(2005) 791) and now the 2015 Guidelines SWD(2015) 111 (<http://ec.europa.eu/smart-regulation/guidelines/docs/swd_br_guidelines_en.pdf>).

[380] Commission, 'Towards a reinforced culture of consultation and dialogue—General principles and minimum standards for consultation of interested parties by the Commission', COM(2002) 704. See now the 2015 Guidelines.

[381] <http://ec.europa.eu/smart-regulation/guidelines/toc_guide_en.htm> and the toolbox (<http://ec.europa.eu/smart-regulation/guidelines/toc_tool_en.htm>).

[382] <http://ec.europa.eu/smart-regulation/impact/iab/iab_en.htm>.   [383] COM(2015) 215.

[384] <http://ec.europa.eu/smart-regulation/better_regulation/documents/com_2015_215_en.pdf>.

[385] <http://ec.europa.eu/smart-regulation/better_regulation/documents/20151215_iia_on_better_law_making_en.pdf>.

mechanism and a burden reduction implementation mechanism, while continuing to ensure high standards of consumer, employee, health and environmental protection.'[386]

Despite all these initiatives, the problem remains that legislation, like the Services Directive,[387] adopted under the ordinary legislative procedure is the result of a large-scale political compromise, which inevitably means that there are provisions, inserted in the middle of the night to accommodate a particular interest, whose meaning is not clear or certain. As we saw in *Alliance for Natural Health*,[388] the Court has tried to use general principles of law to paper over some of the cracks.

2.2 Implementation

Even with better-quality legislation, the question is whether the Member States will actually implement it. As we have seen, the Lamfalussy report identified this as a major issue. In order to assist states with the task of implementation, the Commission issued a recommendation on the transposition of directives affecting the internal market.[389] This contains practical advice to Member States on how to address transposition problems, in particular through the appointment of a senior member of the government to take responsibility for monitoring transposition. The Commission has also set up an Internal Market scoreboard documenting the levels of implementation of directives by each Member State.[390] This has shown that implementation has been steadily improving. During the last six months for which data was available[391] the average transposition deficit—the percentage of single-market directives that have not been transposed into national law in time—remained unchanged at 0.7 per cent (down from 6.3 per cent in 1997). Croatia scored best with only 0.1 per cent while Italy the worst (1.6 per cent) by halving its previous deficit. However, while these league tables have had some success in naming and shaming, they do not reveal the quality of implementation, the level of actual compliance with the national laws, or the means of enforcement. This is something that the EU is trying to address through its annual reports monitoring the application of EU law.[392]

2.3 Enforcement

Enforcement has proved to be the greatest challenge. It has two elements: (1) the enforcement of EU rules by Member States against their own nationals, and (2) the enforcement of EU rules by nationals and the Commission against Member States. Both types of enforcement are essential to ensure continued confidence in the single market. The first element requires states to enforce national laws implementing EU law. If the EU measure is premised on the idea of home-state control (e.g., the Toy Safety Directive) this leads to the intriguing result that the home state is enforcing legislation largely for the benefit of the host state's consumers.[393] This raises the paradox of why home states would act against the interests (and votes) of home-state producers to protect largely out-of-state

---

[386] Section B.   [387] Dir. 2006/123 ([2006] OJ L376/36), discussed in Ch. 11.

[388] Joined Cases C–154 and 155/04 *Alliance for Natural Health* [2005] ECR I–6451, see n. 107.

[389] Commission Rec. 2005/309/EC ([2005] OJ L98/47). See also Commission Communication, 'Better governance for the single market', COM(2012) 259.

[390] <http://ec.europa.eu/internal_market/score/docs/score25_en.pdf>.

[391] <http://ec.europa.eu/internal_market/scoreboard/performance_by_governance_tool/transposition/index_en.htm>.

[392] See, e.g., COM(2012) 714.

[393] S. Weatherill, 'Pre-emption, harmonisation and the distribution of competence to regulate the internal market' in Barnard and Scott, n. 581, 66–9.

consumers. For domestic political reasons the home state might have the incentive not to enforce the law, raising the spectre of a race to the bottom—not in terms of *setting* rules at national level but in respect of enforcing EU rules.

However, in *Muñoz*[394] the Court made clear that individuals as well as states have the power to enforce Union standards. The case concerned a trader wishing to bring civil proceedings against a competitor to enforce Union rules on quality standards laid down in two regulations. The Court recognized that the possibility of bringing proceedings 'strengthens the practical working of the [Union] rules on quality standards'. It continued that as a 'supplement' to the action of the Member States' authorities, proceedings brought by competitors 'helps to discourage practices, often difficult to detect, which distort competition'.[395]

The second type of enforcement—of EU rules by individuals and the Commission against Member States—is more familiar territory. Individuals enforce Union law by relying on their directly effective rights,[396] and the Court has required conflicting national laws to be set aside.[397] The Commission can bring enforcement proceedings under Article 258 TFEU against a defaulting state.[398] The weakness of this type of enforcement is that it is lengthy[399] and depends on the Commission's discretion. In its Communication, 'A Europe of results: Applying [Union] law',[400] the Commission commits itself to improving the current situation, in particular by involving better integration of implementation issues throughout the policy cycle—from design of laws through the adoption process to evaluation of results—so as to reduce the need for enforcement actions. Where such proceedings are necessary, the Commission aims to streamline its processes, giving priority to cases which have the greatest impact on citizens and businesses.

3. MARKET SURVEILLANCE

Once EU legislation has been transposed into national law and importers and producers are making use of its provisions, Member States must fulfil their obligations to ensure that only compliant goods are allowed onto the market ('market surveillance'). Certain specific directives, such as the General Product Safety Directive 2001/95,[401] make provision for coordination between the Member States to remove dangerous products from the market. Most successful has been RAPEX,[402] the EU's rapid alert system for dangerous consumer products (but not food, pharmaceuticals, and medical devices, which are covered by other mechanisms). It facilitates the rapid exchange of information between Member States and the Commission on measures taken to prevent or restrict the marketing or use of products posing a serious risk to the health and safety of consumers. The importance of such procedures can be seen in Case Study 15.2. The RAMS Regulation 765/2008 extends the RAPEX system to all products which present a serious risk. In addition,

[394] Case C–253/00 *Antonio Muñoz y Cia SA v. Frumar Ltd* [2002] ECR I–7289.   [395] Para. 31.
[396] Case 26/62 *Van Gend en Loos* [1963] ECR 1.
[397] Case C–213/89 *Factortame (No. 1)* [1990] ECR I–2433.
[398] See also Commission Communication, 'Better monitoring of Community law', COM(2002) 725. See also the SOLVIT initiative, complementary to infringement proceedings, which is an attempt through administrative cooperation to make it easier to obtain redress where internal market rules are misapplied in practice: COM(2001) 702, Commission Rec. ([2001] OJ L331/79).
[399] COM(2007) 502.   [400] COM(2007) 502.   [401] [2002] OJ L11/4.
[402] For full details, see <http://ec.europa.eu/consumers/dyna/rapex/rapex_archives_en.cfm>. Commission Dec. 2010/15/EU ([2010] OJ L22/1) lays down guidelines on the management of RAPEX.

it improves the traceability of products and clarifies the obligations for economic operators.[403] It also makes provision for border controls on products from non-EU sources, which, if they do not comply with Union harmonization legislation or if the product poses a serious risk, will not be authorized for release for free circulation.[404]

Case Study 15.2: PRODUCT SAFETY, TOY SAFETY, AND BABIES' DUMMIES

Babies chew things. Teething babies chew more and are often given teething rings, dummies, and rattles to chew on. These are made out of PVC, which, in the past, was softened by the addition of plasticizers (phthalates) which have been linked to damage to the kidneys, liver, and testicles. During the 1990s, a high-profile campaign was run by certain consumer groups, such as Greenpeace,[405] arguing that phthalates can leach from products and this has a particularly serious effect on children who chew and suck over prolonged periods. This chewing can break down the plastic, which accelerates the release of the phthalates into the saliva.[406]

On 23 April 1997 the Danish authorities notified the Commission of an 'emergency situation', in accordance with Article 12 of the General Product Safety (GPS) Directive 2001/95[407] (and Article 42 of the Toy Safety Directive[408]), concerning phthalates in teething rings made in China for the Italian company Chicco. Their concerns were based on a study produced for the Danish Environmental Protection Agency which found that a baby who chewed a Chicco Softy Vinyl Sweets ring for three hours would ingest 2,219 micrograms of phthalates per kilogram of body weight—44 times the maximum amount permitted in food under EU law.[409] Although Chicco argued that the rings did not constitute any risk and conformed with the Toy Safety Directive,[410] it nevertheless withdrew the products from the market pending the results of its own tests.

In 1998 the Spanish government notified the Commission under Article 8 of the GPS Directive of the steps it was taking against phthalates. A number of other states also took steps against the phthalates, most of which were notified to the Commission under Directive 2015/1535 on the provision of information in the field of technical standards and regulations.[411] The Commission referred the matter to the relevant scientific committee on Toxicity,

---

[403] MEMO/07/54. [404] On the meaning of free circulation, see further Ch. 2.

[405] <http://www.greenpeace.org.uk/files/pdfs/migrated/MultimediaFiles/Live/FullReport/930.PDF>. Greenpeace's research was strongly contested by manufacturers in the industry: see, e.g., <http://www.ecpi.org/>. See also B. Durodié, 'Plastic panic', *Wall Street Journal Europe*, 6 Sept. 1999 and 'Calculating the cost of caution', *Chemistry and Industry*, 6 Mar. 2000, 170.

[406] Opinion of ECOSOC ([2000] OJ C117/59), para. 2.2.

[407] [2002] OJ L11/4, originally Dir. 92/59 ([1992] OJ L228/24). This directive requires producers to place only safe products on the market (Art. 3). As with the Toy Safety Dir., the GPS Dir. lists only general safety requirements (Art. 2(b)). Goods manufactured according to 'voluntary national standards transposing European standards' are 'presumed safe' (Art. 3(2), para. 2 of Dir. 2001/95). This directive also lays down procedures for dealing with dangerous products. Art. 8 concerns emergency situations. For further details, see G. Argiros, 'The EEC Directive on General Product Safety' (1994) 21 *LIEI* 125.

[408] The GPS Dir. was invoked on 'childcare articles' ('any product designed to facilitate sleep, relaxation, the feeding of children or sucking on the part of children'); the Toy Safety Dir. covered 'toys' (any product designed or clearly intended for use in play by children).

[409] D. MacKenzie, 'Alarm sounds over toxic teething rings', *New Scientist*, 14 Jun. 1997, 10.

[410] C. Joerges, 'Law, science and the management of risks to health at the national, European and international level: Stories on baby dummies, mad cows and hormones in beef' (2001) 7 *Columbia Journal of European Law* 1, 4.

[411] See further Ch. 4.

Ecotoxicity, and the Environment (CSTEE),[412] which confirmed that a precautionary approach[413] was justified. This enabled the Commission to take preventive action where evidence was 'insufficient, inconclusive or uncertain' but where failure to act would result in excessive risk to public health or the environment. This was only the third time that the principle had been invoked.[414] As an interim measure, the Commission issued a recommendation[415] that Member States had to adopt the measures required to ensure a high level of child health protection in regard to phthalate-containing soft PVC childcare articles and toys intended to be placed in the mouth.

When scientific evidence showed that this approach was not sufficient to ensure consistent,[416] high-level protection, the Commission issued a decision under Article 13 of the GPS Directive,[417] banning the use of certain phthalates in toys altogether.[418] This, the Commission argued, was a proportionate response: merely setting limits on the migration of these phthalates was not possible because there were no reliable means of testing their migration. This decision, as amended, remained in operation until amendments to the Dangerous Substances Directive 76/769 were adopted.[419] Based on the precautionary principle, these amendments distinguished, in the name of proportionality, between two groups of phthalates: (1) DEHP, DBP, BBP and (2) DINP, DIDP, and DNOP. The first group is banned altogether in toys and childcare articles; the second is banned but only in respect of 'toys and childcare articles, which can be placed in the mouth by children' (e.g., dummies and teething rings). No age limitation is specified in the directive.[420]

---

[412] <http://www.ec.europa.eu/health/scientific_committees/environmental_risks/opinions/sctee/index_en.htm>.

[413] <http://www.ec.europa.eu/health/scientific_committees/environmental_risks/opinions/sctee/index_en.htm>.

[414] Opinion of ECOSOC ([2000] OJ C117/59), para. 1.2.5.1.

[415] Commission Rec. 98/485/EC on childcare articles and toys made of soft PVC containing certain phthalates intended to be placed in the mouths of children under three years of age ([1998] OJ L217/35). The then Commissioner Emma Bonino had wanted the phthalates to be banned. Some reports of her intervention continued to reflect the theme of 'mad Brussels bureaucrats' interfering where they are not wanted: see, e.g., T. Harrison and J. Palmer, 'Eurocrats plan to ban baby dummies: But Britain says there is no risk', *Mirror*, 15 May 1998, 13; 'Rubber ducks win Euro reprieve', *The Times*, 15 May 1998. See also Commission Rec. 2006/283 on risk reduction measures for the phthalates ([2006] OJ L104/45).

[416] Cf. B. Durodié, 'Plastic panics European risk regulation in the aftermath of BSE' in J. Morris (ed.), *Rethinking Risk and the Precautionary Principle* (Leicester: Perpetuity Press, 2000), who contests much of the scientific evidence.

[417] This provision had been unsuccessfully challenged in Case C–359/92 *Germany v. Council* [1994] ECR I–3681.

[418] Commission Dec. 1999/815/EC adopting measures prohibiting the placing on the market of toys and childcare articles intended to be placed in the mouths of children under three years of age made of soft PVC containing one or more of the substances diisononyl phthalate (DINP), di(2-ethylhexyl) phthalate (DEHP), dibutyl phthalate (DBP), diisodecyl phthalate (DIDP), di-n-octyl phthalate (DNOP), and butylbenzyl phthalate (BBP) (notified under Doc. No. C(1999)4436) ([1999] OJ L315/46), as amended.

[419] Dir. 2005/84/EC ([2005] OJ L344/40). See also Guideline on the interpretation of the concept 'which can be placed in the mouth' as laid down in entry 52 of Annex XVII to REACH Reg. 1907/2006, which repealed and replaced Dir. 76/769 (<https://echa.europa.eu/documents/10162/13645/guideline_interpretation_concept_mouth_en.pdf>). This was adopted in the light of the addendum to Dir. 2005/84.

[420] This case study draws on Joerges, n. 410.

E. CONCLUSIONS

The discussion in this chapter suggests that, far from the Union being a 'market without a state',[421] in Joerges' words, the EU market is increasingly heavily regulated by the central authorities. However, this is not a case of straightforward re-regulation, with a shift of regulation from the national level to the EU, but rather a blending of the national and the Union—this is multilevel governance.[422] Modern regulatory techniques which aim to combine the benefits of centralization together with local autonomy—minimum harmonization, the new-approach directives, reflexive harmonization, and OMC—rely on a mix of centralized and decentralized regulation together with the involvement of a wide range of actors, both public and private. For this reason it may be more appropriate to talk about co-regulation or self-regulation than re-regulation.[423] This approach to regulation represents a seismic shift away from the caricature of exhaustive harmonization and the basic philosophy of 'if it moves (or even if it doesn't) harmonize it' and a far greater sensitivity to the values of diversity and local autonomy. Given the limits of the EU's powers, as *Tobacco Advertising I* makes so clear, together with the political unacceptability of doing more, such meshing of decision-making is the only viable option for the EU as it expands to 28 states and possibly beyond.

The reliance on national and sub-national actors is particularly true in the case of enforcement. The absence of an effective range of enforcement mechanisms at EU level means that the EU is dependent on enforcement at national level, and it is here that the Court of Justice has been instrumental in strengthening the hand of one of the most important defenders of the Union's interests, the individual. And so we come full circle—the four freedoms are intended to benefit the individual and it is ultimately up to the individual to ensure that they work. As the Commission itself puts it:[424]

> The Single Market is one of Europe's great achievements. In the past 50 years, it has generated new opportunities and economies of scale for European companies that have strengthened industrial competitiveness, it has created jobs and offered greater choice at lower prices for consumers and it has enabled people to live, study and work where they want. It has contributed to better integrating EU firms into international value chains and strengthening the global competitiveness of European companies.

FURTHER READING

On issues of governance and competence

K. ARMSTRONG, 'Governance and the single European market' in P. Craig and G. de Búrca (eds.), *The Evolution of EU Law* (Oxford: OUP, 1999).

D. CHALMERS, 'The democratic ambiguity of EU law making and its enemies' in A. Arnull and D. Chalmers (eds.), *The Oxford Handbook of European Union Law* (Oxford: OUP, 2015).

---

[421] C. Joerges, 'European economic law, the nation state and the Treaty of Maastricht' in R. Dehousse (ed.), *Europe After Maastricht: An ever closer union* (Munich: Law Books in Europe, 1994).

[422] L. Hooghe and G. Marks, *Multi-Level Governance and European Integration* (Lanham, Md: Rowman & Littlefield, 2001).

[423] COM(2003) 238, 26.   [424] COM(2015) 550.

A. DASHWOOD, 'Article 308 EC as the outer limit of expressly conferred Community competence' in C. Barnard and O. Odudu (eds.), *The Outer Limits of European Union Law* (Oxford: Hart Publishing, 2009).

G. DAVIES, 'Subsidiarity: The wrong idea, in the wrong place, at the wrong time' (2006) 43 *CMLRev.* 63.

N. EMILIOU, 'Subsidiarity: An effective barrier against "the enterprises of ambition"' (1992) 17 *ELRev.* 383.

J. SCOTT and D. TRUBECK, 'Mind the gap: Law and new approaches to governance in the European Union' (2002) 8 *ELJ* 1.

A. TOTH, 'The principle of subsidiarity in the Maastricht Treaty' (1992) 29 *CMLRev.* 1079.

S. WEATHERILL, 'Competence creep and competence control' (2004) 23 *YEL* 1.

S. WEATHERILL, 'The limits of legislative harmonization ten years after *Tobacco Advertising*: How the Court's case law has become a drafting guide' (2011) 12 *German Law Journal* 827.

On the different approaches to harmonization

J. CURRALL, 'Some aspects of the relation between Articles 30–36 and Article 100 of the EEC Treaty, with a closer look at optional harmonisation' (1984) 4 *YEL* 169, 179–80.

G. DE BÚRCA, 'Differentiation within the core: The case of the common market' in G. de Búrca and J. Scott (eds.), *Constitutional Change in the EU: From uniformity to flexibility* (Oxford: Hart Publishing, 2000).

M. DOUGAN, 'Minimum harmonisation and the internal market' (2000) 37 *CMLRev.* 853.

A. McGEE and S. WEATHERILL, 'The evolution of the single market: Harmonisation or liberalisation' (1990) 53 *MLR* 578, 585.

P. ROTT, 'Minimum harmonisation for the completion of the internal market? The example of consumer sales law' (2003) 40 *CMLRev.* 1107.

Single European Act 1996

C. D. EHLERMANN, 'The internal market following the Single European Act' (1987) 24 *CMLRev.* 361, 389–98.

J. FLYNN, 'How will Article 100A(4) work? A comparison with Article 93' (1987) 24 *CMLRev.* 689.

On the fate of Monti II

The Adoptive Parents, 'The life of a death foretold: The proposal for a Monti II Regulation' in M. Freedland and J. Prassl, *Viking, Laval and Beyond* (Oxford, Hart Publishing, 2015).

F. FABBRINI and K GRANAT, '"Yellow card, but no foul": The role of the national parliaments under the subsidiarity protocol and the Commission proposal for an EU regulation on the right to strike' (2013) 50 *CMLRev.* 115.

On the tobacco advertising saga

S. CROSBY, 'The new Tobacco Control Directive: An illiberal and illegal disdain for the law' (2002) 27 *ELRev.* 177.

F. DUINA and P. KURZER, 'Smoke in your eyes: The struggle over tobacco control in the European Union' (2004) 11 *JEPP* 57.

T. HERVEY, 'Up in smoke? Community (anti)-tobacco law and policy' (2001) 26 *ELRev.* 101.

D. KHANNA, 'The defeat of the European Tobacco Advertising Directive: A blow for health' (2001) 20 *YEL* 113, 115.

M. KUMM, 'Constitutionalising subsidiarity in integrated markets: The case of tobacco regulation in the European Union' (2006) 12 *ELJ* 503.

D. WYATT, 'Constitutional significance of the tobacco advertising judgment of the European Court of Justice' in *The ECJ's Tobacco Advertising Judgment*, CELS Occasional Paper No. 5, 2000.

On the debates around completing the single market

J. PELKMANS and A. CORREIA DE BRITO, *Enforcement in the EU Single Market* (Brussels: CEPS, 2012).

A. YOUNG, 'The single market: Deregulation, re-regulation and integration' in H. Wallace, M. Pollack, and A. Young (eds.), *Policy-Making in the European Union*, 6th edn (Oxford: OUP, 2010).

Assessment

HM Government, Balance of Competences Review, *The Single Market* (2013), <https://www.gov.uk/government/uploads/system/uploads/attachment_data/file/227069/2901084_SingleMarket_acc.pdf>.

INDEX

Map of the European Union

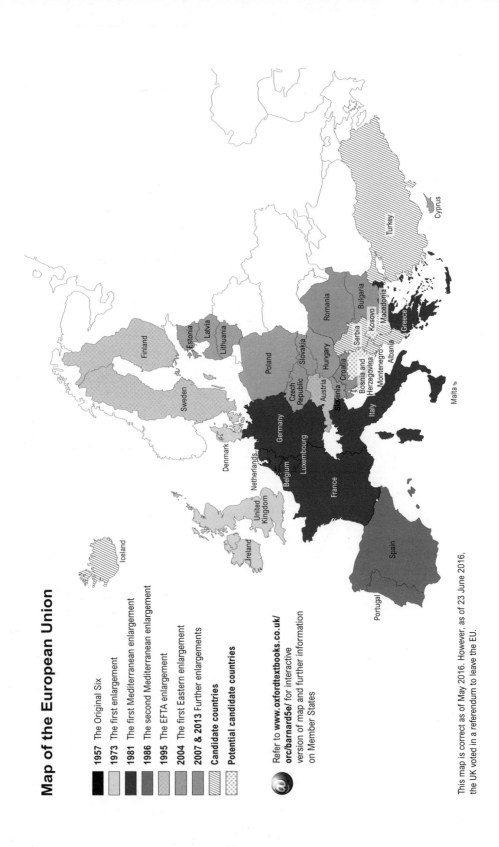

1957 The Original Six
1973 The first enlargement
1981 The first Mediterranean enlargement
1986 The second Mediterranean enlargement
1995 The EFTA enlargement
2004 The first Eastern enlargement
2007 & 2013 Further enlargements
Candidate countries
Potential candidate countries

Refer to **www.oxfordtextbooks.co.uk/ orc/barnard5e/** for interactive version of map and further information on Member States

This map is correct as of May 2016. However, as of 23 June 2016, the UK voted in a referendum to leave the EU.

Iceland

United Kingdom

Ireland

Netherlands
Denmark
Belgium
Luxembourg
Germany
France
Spain
Portugal

Finland
Sweden
Estonia
Latvia
Lithuania
Poland
Czech Republic
Austria
Slovakia
Hungary
Slovenia
Croatia
Italy
Bosnia and Herzegovina
Montenegro
Serbia
Kosovo
Albania
Macedonia
Romania
Bulgaria
Greece
Turkey
Cyprus
Malta